Law, Business, and Society

Tony McAdams

Professor and Head, Management Department, University of Northern Iowa
B. A. (History), University of Northern Iowa
J. D., University of Iowa, M.B.A., Columbia University

Contributing Authors
Amy Gershenfeld Donnella

Staff Attorney, Federal Trade Commission
B.A. (Liberal Arts), State University of New York, Stony Brook
J.D., Harvard Law School
Ms. Gershenfeld Donnella contributed Chapter 12, Labor Law (1st edition)

James Freeman

Associate Professor, Department of Management, University of Kentucky
B.S. (Economics), Wharton School, University of Pennsylvania
J.D., M.A. (Economics), University of South Carolina
L.L.M., Harvard Law School
Mr. Freeman contributed Chapter 8, Business Organizations and
Securities Regulation

Nancy Neslund

Practicing Attorney, Salem, Oregon
B.S. (Economics), Willamette University
J.D., Columbia University
L.L.M. candidate, New York University
Ms. Neslund revised Chapters 4, Introduction to Law; 5, Constitutional Law and the
Bill of Rights; 11, Labor Law and General Employment Law; and 15, Environmental
Law, for the Second edition

Law, Business, and Society

Second Edition 1989

Homewood, IL 60430
Boston, MA 02116

Sponsoring editor: Frank S. Burrows, Jr.
Project editor: Susan Trentacosti
Production manager: Carma W. Fazio
Compositor: Carlisle Communications, Ltd.
Typeface: 10/12 Times Roman
Printer: R. R. Donnelley & Sons Company

LIBRARY OF CONGRESS
Library of Congress Cataloging-in-Publication Data

McAdams, Tony.
    Law, business, and society / Tony McAdams; contributing authors,
Amy Gershenfeld Donnella, James Freeman, and Nancy Neslund. — 2nd
ed.
    p.   cm.
    Includes index
    ISBN 0–256–07374–0
    1. Business enterprises—United States. 2. Trade regulation-
-United States. 3. Business ethics—United States. 4. Industry-
-Social aspects—United States. I. Title.
    KF1355.M28 1989
    346.73'065—dc19
    [347.30665]   88–24206
                                                              CIP

Printed in the United States of America

4 5 6 7 8 9 0 DO 6 5 4 3 2 1

To our families

Preface

OVERVIEW

This text is directed to courses at both the upper-division undergraduate and masters levels in the legal environment of business and government and business, as well as business and society. To date, authors of textbooks in these areas have rather uniformly relied on a single discipline (for example, law, economics, management) as the foundation for their efforts. In this text we take an interdisciplinary approach utilizing elements of law, political economy, international business, ethics, social responsibility, and management. This large task necessarily requires certain trade-offs, but we hope the product will more accurately embrace the fullness of the business environment.

We want to emphasize at the outset that our primary goal is to produce an interesting reading experience. Naturally, accuracy and reasonable comprehensiveness cannot be sacrificed. However, our feeling is that a law text can be both intellectually and emotionally engaging without sacrificing substantive ends. To meet our objective we have given extensive attention to readings, provocative quotes, and factual details (surveys, data, anecdotes) that add flesh to the bones of legal theory.

The book is divided into five parts as follows:

Part I—Business and Society. We do not begin with the law. Rather, in chapters on Capitalism and Collectivism, Ethics, and Social Responsibility we hope to establish the influences that determine the character of our legal system.

Part I should meet these goals: *(a)* enhance student awareness of the many societal influences on business, *(b)* establish the business context from which government regulation arose, and *(c)* explore the roles of the free market, government intervention, and individual and corporate ethics in controlling business behavior.

The student must understand not merely the law, but the law in context. What forces have provoked government intervention in business? What alternatives to our current "mixed economy" might prove healthy? These considerations help the students respond to one of the critical questions of the day: To what extent, if any, *should* we regulate business?

Part II—Introduction to Law. Chapter 4 (The American Legal System) and Chapter 5 (Constitutional Law and the Bill of Rights) survey the foundations of our legal system. Here we set out the "nuts and bolts" of law, combining cases, readings, and narrative.

Part III—Trade Regulation and Antitrust. Chapter 6 (Government Regulation of Business: An Introduction) is a bit of a departure from the approach of many texts in that significant attention is directed to state and local regulation. Chapters 7 through 10 survey the heart of government regulation of business (administrative law, business organizations and securities regulation, and antitrust).

Part IV—Employer–Employee Relations. Chapters on Labor and General Employment Law and Employment Discrimination are intended not only to survey the law in those areas, but also to introduce some of the sensitive and provocative social issues that have led to today's extensive government intervention in the employment relationship.

Part V—Business and Selected Social Problems. The book closes with three chapters (Consumer Protection, Products Liability, and Environmental Protection) that emphasize the dramatic expansion in the past two decades of the public's demands on the business community.

ACCREDITATION

Our text proposal closely conforms to current AACSB curriculum accreditation standards. The relevant standard reads:

> a background of the economic and legal environment as it pertains to profit and/or nonprofit organizations along with ethical considerations and social and political influences as they affect such organizations.

An interdisciplinary thrust and emphasis on ethics is evident. At the same time, law and economics clearly must remain central ingredients in meeting our goal of establishing the business context from which government regulation arose.

Furthermore, as required by the rapidly changing nature of commerce and as recommended by the AACSB, the text devotes considerable attention to issues arising from international business. No single chapter addresses the area, but various topics throughout the text (for example, comparative economic systems, the Foreign Corrupt Practices Act, and consumer protection in international markets) afford the student a sense of the worldwide implications of American government–business regulations.

PHILOSOPHY

As noted, our primary goal is to provoke student thought. To that end, heavy emphasis is placed on analysis. Accordingly, retention of rules of law per se is not of paramount concern. The questions asked are considered more important than the answers. The student is acquainted with existing policy in the various areas not merely for the purposes of understanding and retention, but also to provoke inquiry as to the desirability of those policies. Then, where appropriate, an effort is made to explore with the student the appropriate managerial role in shaping and responding to governmental policy.

Our book represents a departure from a "pure" legal environment of business text. Part I of the text is, as explained, a necessary foundation on which the student can build a logical understanding of the regulatory process. But the business and society themes don't stop there. In virtually every chapter we look beyond the law itself to other environmental forces. For example, in the antitrust chapter economic philosophy is of great importance. Antitrust is explored as a matter of national social policy; that is, we argue that antitrust has a good deal to do with the direction of American life generally. Law is at the heart of the fair employment practices section, but materials from management, sociology, economics, and the like are used to treat fair employment as an issue of social policy rather than as a series of narrower technical legal disputes. Those kinds of approaches characterize most chapters as we attempt to examine the various problems in the whole and, to some degree, from a managerial viewpoint. Having said all this, it should be understood that the law remains the bulky core of the book.

KEY FEATURES/DEPARTURES

Extensive use of readings (for example, from *The Wall Street Journal* and the *Harvard Business Review*) seeks to give the book a stimulating, "real world" quality.

Ethics and social responsibility are at the heart of the text rather than an afterthought to meet accreditation standards.

International issues receive extensive attention.

Law cases are of a length sufficient to clearly express the essence of the decision while challenging the reader's intellect.

The law is studied in the economic, social, and political context from which it springs.

Attention is given to critics of business values and the American legal system.

Perhaps the key pedagogical tactic in the book is the emphasis on questions rather than on answers.

INSTRUCTOR'S MANUAL

A complete package of supplementary materials is included in the instructor's manual. Those materials include *(a)* general advice regarding the goals and purposes of the chapters, *(b)* summaries of the law cases, *(c)* answers for the questions raised in the text, and *(d)* a test bank.

ACKNOWLEDGMENTS

Completion of the second edition of this book depended, in significant part, on the hard work of others. The authors are pleased to acknowledge the contributions of those good people. Jill Minehart, secretary of the Management Department at the University of Northern Iowa, assisted in the clerical production of the book and patiently corrected the authors' errors. Tracy Timson, MBA student, heroically devoted the first year of her graduate assistantship to the tedious tasks of researching, editing, securing permissions, and so on that go into the production of a text. Ms. Timson and Luann McAdams, charming spouse, all contributed to the lengthy and tiring proofreading process.

The authors also thank the following professors who reviewed portions of the manuscript and otherwise provided valuable guidance:

First edition—David Chadwick-Brown, San Diego State University; John Collins, Syracuse University; Wayne Evenson, University of Northern Iowa; Nancy Hauserman, University of Iowa; Harold Hotelling, Oakland University; Carey Kirk, University of Northern Iowa; Eric Richards, Indiana University; and Arthur D. Wolfe, Michigan State University.

Second edition—Wayne Evenson, University of Northern Iowa; Harold Hotelling, Oakland University; Michael Howard, University of Iowa; Janet Richmond, University of Northern Iowa; Linda Samuels, George Mason University; Richard Trotter, University of Baltimore; Jeff Vermeer, Eastern Oregon State College.

SUGGESTIONS

The authors welcome comments and criticisms from all readers.

Tony McAdams

Contents

PART II Introduction to Law *165*

4 The American Legal System *167*

5 Constitutional Law and the Bill of Rights *222*

PART III Trade Regulation and Antitrust *259*

6 Government Regulation of Business: An Introduction *261*

PART V Business and Selected Social Problems *669*

13 Consumer Protection *671*

14 Products Liability *724*

15 Environmental Protection *776*

Law, Business, and Society

Business and Society

Chapter 1

Capitalism and Collectivism

Part One—Introduction

In the United States, we certainly cannot understand our system of laws without a firm appreciation for the principles of capitalism from which those laws spring, in pertinent part. We chose a capitalist, democratic approach to life. Other cultures have placed less faith in the market and more in government planning. The legal systems in those countries reflect a preference for greater central authority. This chapter is designed to remind the reader of some of the fundamentals of the capitalist-socialist debate in order to provide a foundation for one of the critical questions to which this book is addressed: How much government regulation of business is desirable in America? By looking at the approaches in other nations, by exploring the various political/economic possibilities, we are better prepared to think constructively about the roles of law and business in our lives. More directly, the reader should contemplate the following question: Should competitive, capitalist business values in the United States be retarded in favor of the more cooperative, communitarian approach of the collectivist states?

In this chapter we will explore the full range of the economic spectrum, moving from a laissez-faire, free market approach on the extreme right, to a command economy on the far left, and concluding with a left-center, communitarian program that might be labeled social democracy or market socialism.

The free market approach assumes that we can operate our business structure and our society at large, free of all but the most basic legal mechanisms such as contract and criminal law. The wisdom of the market—that is, our individual judgments, in combination with our individual consciences—would serve to "regulate" American life. Government regulatory agencies, occupational licensure, zoning restrictions, antitrust law, and all but the most basic government services (perhaps limited to the police, the courts, and the army) would be unnecessary.

On the other hand, the collectivist alternatives (communism, socialism, and their variations) pose the notion that the business community and society at large require more expansive government intervention than that characterizing the U.S. system. Individual judgment would be supplemented with or largely supplanted by the collective will. Ranging from a largely equalitarian, welfare state to a completely planned economy, the collectivist alternative reflects various degrees of faith in central authority and skepticism regarding independent action.

This chapter seeks to offer a genuine intellectual adventure. Students should suspend, to the degree possible, the biases, the lessons of cultural conditioning, that so effectively shape us all. Then the student will be free to objectively evaluate the economic systems we may call into our service. One's pride in being an American should not prevent the serious contemplation of alternative economic strategies that have proven successful elsewhere. One is not communist, fascist, or totalitarian in spirit merely for openly exploring and even advocating political economies other than our mixture of capitalism and state intervention. On balance, the United States may well be following the path best suited to our needs, but if so, a spirited exploration of the alternatives will only serve to illuminate that path.

Finally, this chapter should be read as a foundation of sorts for the study of law that follows. Once a society settles on some broad political and economic principles, it typically pours a thin veneer or many heavy coats (depending on the system chosen) of social control on that foundation to implement the goals of the larger system. The law serves as a primary method of social control. So, to understand the law we need to understand its roots.

Part Two—Capitalism

FOUNDATIONS

We begin with a brief reminder of the ideological foundation of American capitalism. As noted, the law develops, in part, as a response to the governing economic system. That system is a product of society's values and philosophies. We need, therefore, to assess those values and philosophies to determine which economic system is most suitable to contemporary American society.

Although many intellectual forces have played a role in shaping American capitalism, this discussion will be limited to four themes of particular historical significance.

1. John Locke's Natural Right of Property.   Locke, the brilliant English philosopher, provided in his *Two Treatises of Government* (1690) much of the intellectual underpinning of the Declaration of Independence and, thus, the course of American life. Locke argued that the rights of life, liberty, and property were natural to all humans. Those rights predated any notion of an organized society. Hence society's only control over those rights was to protect them. Locke's viewpoint was a powerful intellectual and moral argument for the establishment of industrial capitalism in which private ownership of property and freedom from government restraint were vital.

2. Adam Smith and Laissez-Faire.   Smith's *An Inquiry into the Nature and Cause of the Wealth of Nations* (1776) offered profound theoretical support to free market principles. Smith argued that the invisible hand of supply and demand would determine the price of goods. Competition would ensure the greatest good for the greatest number. Thus government should not interfere in the market system. Rather, government should fulfill only those public services (defense, justice, public works, and the like) in which business cannot practically engage. He believed government interference would only disturb the natural genius of the market.

3. Herbert Spencer and Social Darwinism.   Charles Darwin's explorations of the origins of the species led him to the theory that all of life evolved through a process of natural selection, so that the strongest and the most fit survived. Spencer applied Darwin's survival of the fittest to the development of society. He argued that the more capable individuals would inevitably rise to influential positions. Government interference would only inhibit the natural selection process. Thus, Social Darwinism provided the late-19th-century leaders of industry an ideal rationale for their positions of extreme wealth and power.

4. Max Weber and the Protestant Ethic.   In his book *The Protestant Ethic and the Spirit of Capitalism,* Weber argued that Protestants, particularly Calvinists, were moved by a religious philosophy that demanded a lifetime of disciplined effort in pursuit of good work. Salvation demanded productivity. The accumulation of worldly goods was material evidence of that productivity, but one's success was not to be squandered. Rather, it was to be reinvested to enhance the value of goods placed in human hands via God's grace. Thus hard work and thrift were moral responsibilities, and in turn, the accumulation and multiplication of worldly goods to be used for the benefit of all people served to measure one's success in meeting God's expectations. The Protestant ethic was a powerful spur to and justification for capitalist enterprise.

So, capitalism in America arose from rather noble, if debatable, intellectual premises, but capitalism also moved to the fore on the strength of promises to the people not afforded by any previous economic system. Professor and conservative commentator Irving Kristol summarized the hope offered by capitalism:

> What did capitalism promise? First of all, it promised continued improvement in the material conditions of all its citizens, a promise without precedent in human history. Secondly, it promised an equally unprecedented measure of individual freedom for all of these same citizens. And lastly, it held out the promise that, amidst this prosperity and liberty, the individual could satisfy his instinct for self-perfection—for leading a virtuous life that satisfied the demands of his spirit (or, as one used to say, his soul)—and that the free exercise of such individual virtue would aggregate into a just society.[1]

Capitalism in Theory—Ayn Rand

Capitalism was built on a sound intellectual footing and was stimulated by the promise of unprecedented general welfare. These forces, in combination with America's natural resources and an astonishingly courageous and hardy population, led to the development of a powerful economic machine. But that machine, in the view of many Americans, ran out of control for a time. The era of the Robber Barons and abuses associated with them brought widespread popular sentiment for governmental restraints on capitalism. Thus, as is discussed in subsequent chapters, America's substantially free market economy was, in increasing increments, placed under government regulation. Today ours is commonly labeled a *mixed economy.* And despite the striking rhetoric and significant deregulation strides of the Reagan free market era, America remains a nation of big government.

Our purpose now is to reconsider the merits of a purer form of capitalism. Did we turn too hastily from the market? Should we further shed our governmental role in economic affairs and restore our faith in the Invisible Hand? Or, even if the market in a substantially pure form cannot practically be achieved and relied on, may we not profit from a reminder of the nature of that system? Are at least some strides in that direction demanded? Can we, in large measure, do without regulation by law? Will a genuinely unfettered market better serve our needs than our current amalgam of business restrained by government? To answer these questions we need a firm understanding of capitalism in a pure form that has almost entirely slipped from view. The controversial philosopher and novelist Ayn Rand was an uncompromising advocate of free market principles. For example, she believed the necessary categories of government were only three in number: the police, the armed services, and the law courts. Via her philosophy of Objectivism, Rand argued that the practice of free market principles is necessary to the pursuit of a rational, moral life. Rand's viewpoint has been the subject of vigorous criticism. Its merits are for the reader to assess, but it is fair to say that she was among America's most ardent and articulate apostles of a genuine free market.

MAN'S RIGHTS

Ayn Rand

If one wishes to advocate a free society—that is, capitalism—one must realize that its indispensable foundation is the principle of individual rights. If one wishes to uphold individual rights, one must realize that capitalism is the only system that can uphold and protect them. And if one wishes to gauge the relationship of freedom to the goals of today's intellectuals, one may gauge it by the fact that the concept of individual rights is evaded, distorted, perverted, and seldom discussed, most conspicuously seldom by the so-called "conservatives."

"Rights" are a moral concept—the concept that provides a logical transition from the principles guiding an individual's actions to the principles guiding his relationship with others—the concept that preserves and protects individual morality in a social context—the link between the moral code of a man and the legal code of a society, between ethics and politics. *Individual rights are the means of subordinating society to moral law.*

Every political system is based on some code of ethics. The dominant ethics of mankind's history were variants of the altruist-collectivist doctrine which subordinated the individual to some higher authority, either mystical or social. Consequently, most political systems were variants of the same statist tyranny, differing only in degree, not in basic principle, limited only by the accidents of tradition, of chaos, of bloody strife and periodic collapse. Under all such systems, morality was a code applicable to the individual, but not to society. Society was placed *outside* the moral law, as its embodiment or source or exclusive interpreter—and the inculcation of self-sacrificial devotion to social duty was regarded as the main purpose of ethics in man's earthly existence.

Since there is no such entity as "society," since society is only a number of individual men, this meant, in practice, that the rulers of society were exempt from moral law; subject only to traditional rituals, they held total power and exacted blind obedience—on the implicit principle of: "The good is that which is good for society (or for the tribe, the race, the nation), and the ruler's edicts are its voice on earth."

This was true of all statist systems, under all variants of the altruist-collectivist ethics, mystical or social. "The Divine Right of Kings" summarizes the political theory of the first— *"Vox populi, vox dei"* of the second. As witness: the theocracy of Egypt, with the Pharaoh as an embodied god—the unlimited majority rule or *democracy* of Athens—the welfare state run by the Emperors of Rome—the Inquisition of the late Middle Ages—the absolute monarchy of France—the welfare state of Bismarck's Prussia—the gas chambers of Nazi Germany—the slaughterhouse of the Soviet Union.

All these political systems were expressions of the altruist-collectivist ethics—and their common characteristic is the fact that society stood above the moral law, as an omnipotent, sovereign whim worshiper. Thus, politically, all these systems were variants of an *amoral* society.

The most profoundly revolutionary achievement of the United States of America was *the subordination of society to moral law.*

The principle of man's individual rights represented the extension of morality into the social system—as a limitation on the power of the state, as man's protection against the brute force of the collective, as the subordination of *might* to *right*. The United States was the first *moral* society in history.

All previous systems had regarded man as a sacrificial means to the ends of others, and society as an end in itself. The United States regarded man as an end in himself, and society as a means to the peaceful, orderly, *voluntary* coexistence of individuals. All previous systems had held that man's life belongs to society, that society can dispose of him in any way it pleases, and that any freedom he enjoys is his only by favor, by the *permission* of society, which may be revoked at any time. The United States held that man's life is his by *right* (which means: by moral principle and by his nature), that a right is the property of an individual, that society as such has no rights, and that the only moral purpose of a government is the protection of individual rights.

A "right" is a moral principle defining and sanctioning a man's freedom of action in a social context. There is only *one* fundamental right (all the others are its consequences or corollaries): a man's right to his own life. Life is a process of self-sustaining and self-generated action; the right to life means the right to engage in self-sustaining and self-generated action—which means: the freedom to take all the actions required by the nature of a rational being for the support, the furtherance, the fulfillment, and the enjoyment of his own life. . . .

America's inner contradiction was the altruist-collectivist ethics. Altruism is incompatible with freedom, with capitalism, and with indi-

vidual rights. One cannot combine the pursuit of happiness with the moral status of a sacrificial animal.

It was the concept of individual rights that had given birth to a free society. It was with the destruction of individual rights that the destruction of freedom had to begin.

A collectivist tyranny dare not enslave a country by an outright confiscation of its values, material or moral. It has to be done by a process of internal corruption. Just as in the material realm the plundering of a country's wealth is accomplished by inflating the currency—so today one may witness the process of inflation being applied to the realm of rights. The process entails such a growth of newly promulgated "rights" that people do not notice the fact that the meaning of the concept is being reversed. Just as bad money drives out good money, so these "printing-press rights" negate authentic rights.

Consider the curious fact that never has there been such a proliferation, all over the world, of two contradictory phenomena: of alleged new "rights" and of slave-labor camps.

The "gimmick" was the switch of the concept of rights from the political to the economic realm.

The Democratic Party platform of 1960 summarizes the switch boldly and explicitly. It declares that a democratic administration "will reaffirm the economic bill of rights which Franklin Roosevelt wrote into our national conscience 16 years ago."

Bear clearly in mind the meaning of the concept of *"rights"* when you read the list which that platform offers:

"1. The right to a useful and remunerative job in the industries or shops or farms or mines of the nation.

"2. The right to earn enough to provide adequate food and clothing and recreation.

"3. The right of every farmer to raise and sell his products at a return which will give him and his family a decent living.

"4. The right of every businessman, large and small, to trade in an atmosphere of freedom from unfair competition and domination by monopolies at home and abroad.

"5. The right of every family to a decent home.

"6. The right to adequate medical care and the opportunity to achieve and enjoy good health.

"7. The right to adequate protection from the economic fears of old age, sickness, accidents and unemployment.

"8. The right to a good education."

A single question added to each of the above eight clauses would make the issue clear: *At whose expense?*

Jobs, food, clothing, recreation (!), homes, medical care, education, etc., do not grow in nature. These are man-made values—goods and services produced by men. *Who* is to provide them?

If some men are entitled *by right* to the products of the work of others, it means that those others are deprived of rights and condemned to slave labor.

Any alleged "right" of one man, which necessitates the violation of the rights of another, is not and cannot be a right.

No man can have a right to impose an unchosen obligation, an unrewarded duty, or an involuntary servitude on another man. There can be no such thing as *"the right to enslave."*

A right does not include the material implementation of that right by other men; it includes only the freedom to earn that implementation by one's own effort.

Observe, in this context, the intellectual precision of the Founding Fathers: they spoke of the right to *the pursuit* of happiness—*not* of the right to happiness. It means that a man has the right to take the actions he deems necessary to achieve his happiness; it does *not* mean that others must make him happy. . . .

Property rights and the right of free trade are man's only "economic rights" (they are, in fact, *political* rights)—and there can be no such thing as "an *economic* bill of rights." But observe that the advocates of the latter have all but destroyed the former. . . .

And while people are clamoring about "economic rights," the concept of political rights is vanishing. It is forgotten that the right of free speech means the freedom to advocate one's views and to bear the possible consequences, including disagreement with others, opposition, unpopularity, and lack of support. The political function of "the right of free speech" is to protect dissenters and unpopular minorities from forcible suppression—*not* to guarantee them the support, advantages, and rewards of a popularity they have not gained. . . .

Such is the state of one of today's most crucial issues: *political* rights versus *"economic* rights." It's either-or. One destroys the other. But there are, in fact, no "economic rights," no "collective rights," no "public-interest rights." The term *individual rights* is a redundancy: there is no other kind of rights and no one else to possess them.

Those who advocate laissez-faire capitalism are the only advocates of man's rights.

Source: From *The Virtue of Selfishness* by Ayn Rand. Copyright © 1961, 1964 by Ayn Rand. Copyright © 1962, 1963, 1964 by The Objectivist Newsletter, Inc. Reprinted by arrangement with New American Library, New York, New York, and with permission of the Estate of Ayn Rand.

Capitalism in Practice—Hong Kong

A free market society of the purity advocated by Ayn Rand does not now exist and perhaps never did, but history does reveal many instances of successful societies much more thoroughly capitalistic than contemporary

America (e.g., the Greek island of Delos, 169–166 B.C.; Gibraltar, 1704–1978; Singapore, 1819–1957; Great Britain and the United States, the 19th century; and colonial New South Wales, Australia, 1870–1900).[2] Perhaps one outpost of capitalism remains. Hong Kong, a small British Crown Colony on the southeast coast of China, has enjoyed remarkable growth and prosperity in a free market environment. Taxes are at a modest level, and government does play an important role in social services, but nonintervention is clearly at the heart of economic policy.

Hong Kong is unique. Its history, its geographical circumstances, and the nature of its people all contribute to Hong Kong's special affection for private enterprise. Its virtual absence of natural resources and consequent dependence on foreign trade strictly limit the government's intervention options. As the following article suggests, Hong Kong is not without problems, but the colony represents impressive evidence that capitalism mixed with very limited government can work. (Hong Kong's future as a capitalist enclave is in doubt. Great Britain and China have reached agreement on the terms for Hong Kong's passage from the British Empire to a new role as part of mainland China. The change will take effect in 1997. China has promised to allow Hong Kong to maintain its capitalist system, its own government, and personal freedom for its citizens for at least 50 years thereafter. However, recent developments cause some observers to fear that democracy for Hong Kong is doomed.)[3]

HONG KONG—A STUDY IN ECONOMIC FREEDOM

Alvin Rabushka

I submit that Hong Kong, among the world's more than 130 countries, most closely resembles the textbook model of a competitive market economy, encumbered only with the barest overlay of government. It is in this context that we should meet the pure form of *homo economicus*. His given name is *homo Hongkongus*.

Hong Kong man's first and most telling characteristic is his single-minded pursuit of making money. A companion characteristic is his emphasis on the material things in life. Hong Kong's free port, free trade economy offers for sale the latest in fashions, furnishings, foodstuffs, appliances, motor cars, gadgets, stereos—portable stereos, built-in stereos, automobile stereos, any and every conceivable brand and model of stereo at tax-free prices. If there is a new breakthrough in stereo goods to sell, some Hong Kong entrepreneur will be selling it that night. Tomorrow would mean forgone profits.

Material consumption and making money, or making money and worldly goods is what life in Hong Kong is all about. The desire to acquire and accumulate as much money as possible in the shortest period of time: in Hong

Kong, taxes do not discourage hard work. It so happens that I spent 29 August 1976, a pleasant enough Sunday, wandering about a very quiet London. What a sharp contrast it was to 5 December 1976, the Sunday I spent fighting the masses of Hong Kong for a space in the restaurants and stores. London was literally deserted and its citizens were clearly neither making nor spending money. Not so in Hong Kong. *Homo Hongkongus* works a 12- to 16-hour day, 7 days a week, almost 365 days a year—only Chinese New Year interrupts an otherwise single-minded obsession for making money. And Hong Kong's prosperous residents and overseas visitors have plenty of money to spend. I reckon there are more jewelry stores, good restaurants, and fashionable shops in Hong Kong's crowded streets than in any other city in the world—and why not, when the tax-free prices are taken into account. If economic man symbolizes competitive capitalism, he is alive, prosperous, and delightfully happy in Hong Kong. A quick glance across the border finds more than 800 million of his countrymen who ostensibly labor for love of ideology, not money or materialism.

Surely all is not well in Hong Kong. Would not a carefully designed survey of public opinion cast grave doubts on the soul of Hong Kong man? It would, of course, if we only interviewed the intellectuals, being absolutely careful not to talk with the ordinary working men and women. You see, apart from a few jobs in the universities and higher institutions of art and culture, the services of the literati are not in high demand. Indeed, the amount of high culture that Hong Kong's 4.5 million people demand is patently suboptimal; that is, it is less than most Western middle-class intellectuals, who are used to having their cultural tastes subsidized, would like. Higher education in Hong Kong is, for the most part, a path to self-improvement; if it civilizes in the process, well, OK.

Hong Kong offers a limited cultural menu of art, music, and drama. Its critics call it a cultural desert and accuse it, correctly, of being an oversized bazaar. Hong Kong offers, in truth, exactly what the market will bear. When intellectuals complain about the lack of finer things in Hong Kong they are complaining, it seems to me, of three things: first, a limited demand for their services with corresponding low incomes; second, a failure of their fellow men (who are certainly less sophisticated and therefore need cultural tutelage) to share their tastes; and third, the government's unwillingness to subsidize their tastes at community expense, perhaps the gravest failing of the capitalist economy.

Dare I reveal my boorishness by saying that I find Hong Kong's economic hustle and bustle more interesting, entertaining, and liberating than its lack of high opera, music, and drama? East has indeed met West in the market economy. Chinese and Europeans in Hong Kong have no time for racial quarrels, which would only interfere with making money. The prospect of individual gain in the marketplace makes group activity for political gain unnecessary— the market economy is truly color blind. Even harmony among ideological enemies lives in Hong Kong. The Hong Kong Hilton stands right across the street from the Bank of China.

There is simply no more exciting city on the face of the earth than Hong Kong—in large measure because it is the most robust bastion of free-wheeling capitalism. It may be, as is true of all human institutions, imperfect. I have previously criticized the Hong Kong government for its tendencies to increase spending on social programs, but can you name any other country which in 1976 enjoyed 18 percent real growth and only 3.4 percent inflation?

Source: *Hong Kong—A Study in Economic Freedom* (Chicago: University of Chicago Press, 1979), pp. 83–86. Reprinted with permission of the copyright holder, Alvin Rabushka.

Capitalism in Practice—"Privatization" in America and Abroad

Critics argue that capitalism forms a tight, rational argument on paper, but in practice the theory breaks down. Examples like Hong Kong are written off as anomalies born of special circumstances, such as Hong Kong's limited geographic dimensions. But around the globe from the Soviet Union and China to France and the United Kingdom, renewed faith in the free market is the singular economic message of the 1980s. The basic point to recognize is the free market argument that virtually all services now performed by the government may be more efficiently and more equitably "managed" by the impersonal forces of the market.

A recent survey of 1,100 cities and counties by Touche Ross & Co. found 80 percent of the respondents using or planning to use private companies to provide needed public services.[4] For example, Fargo, North Dakota, and Moorhead, Minnesota, arranged for private-sector development and operation of a bridge linking the two cities.[5] In Newton, Massachusetts, a private ambulance firm has replaced the city's service at no cost to the city. The community benefits from better service (three rescue units versus two, better trained employees, and 24-hour care), and savings to the city in the first year approached $500,000.[6] In Grants Pass, Oregon, two private companies provide fire protection:

> Bertha Miller's Grants Pass Rural Fire Department, founded about 25 years ago, is battling Phil Turnbull's Valley Fire Service. "This gives people freedom of choice," says Turnbull, 26, a self-proclaimed champion of free enterprise who raised $100,000 to start the company in 1979 and grossed $400,000 last year. Both businesses rely on paid subscribers: Miller charges a flat $40 per home or business; Turnbull, $2.15 per $1,000 of market value. Both companies will not only put out fires for subscribers but also rescue their cats from trees. And both will put out fires at nonsubscribers' homes, then send a bill ($150 per fire engine hour and $10 per fire fighter hour). Miller won't talk about earnings, but Valley Fire has done well enough to be planning its fourth fire station. Most everyone in town except Miller says competition has improved service substantially—and better service means lower rates for fire insurance.[7]

The privatization movement appears to be gaining strength in the United States. In early 1988 a bipartisan presidential commission called for the transfer of major elements of government programs and services to the private sector. The commission's major findings:

Privatization Recommendations[8]

- The Postal Service's monopoly on delivering letters should be ended over time, with private companies allowed to compete for the business.
- A system of educational "vouchers" should be established to give parents greater freedom of choice in selecting elementary or secondary schools for their children.

- The government should expand its voucher system for low-cost public housing instead of building new projects, while selling existing public housing to residents where possible.
- The management of military commissaries and federal, state, and local prisons should be contracted out.
- Airport control towers should be privately run, although the government should "continue to regulate the national airspace."

On the other hand, some studies indicate that the free market may not always provide either the best or the least expensive services. For example, a three-year study conducted by the Institute of Medicine, an arm of the congressionally chartered National Academy of Sciences, found for-profit hospitals more expensive and less cost-effective than their nonprofit equivalents. The report called for a close watch over all portions of the increasingly market-driven health care industry.[9] Professor Jonathan Goodrich reports the following primary arguments against privatization:[10]

- Unemployment of government workers because of privatization.
- Lower quality of service.
- Government loss of control and accountability.
- The government paying too much for the services done by a private company.
- The possibility of corruption and scandal.

The article that follows offers a case study of an effective privatization effort in Hong Kong.

HONG KONG'S (PRIVATE) FAST TRACK

Peter Young

Hong Kong—The inherent unprofitability of mass transit is one of the laws of nature, or so most politicians would have us believe. The budget of the U.S. Urban Mass Transit Administration is more than $4 billion, for example, the bulk of which is totally wasted according to its administrator, Ralph Stanley. . . .

But Hong Kong demonstrates that mass transit, even subways, can turn a good profit. All its transport sectors are profitable, and most are private. The bus, streetcar and ferry services are owned by private companies and receive no subsidies, although the government does build bus terminals and ferry piers for use by all companies, as well as regulating some bus routes and fares.

In addition to private buses on fixed routes, there are about 4,500 flexible-route minibuses, most individually owned. These fully deregulated minibus services have proved especially successful at serving sparsely populated districts without subsidy and acting as feeder services for the subway. All Hong Kong transport services are efficient and cheap. . . .

* * * * *

More surprising, still, is that Hong Kong's subway makes an operating profit ($25 million in the first half of 1986), although the government has had to pay some of the initial finance and interest charges. Called the Mass Transit Railway, it consists of 22.94 miles of routes with 37 stations, and moves 1.45 million passengers per weekday. The Mass Transit Railway Corp. is established as a government-owned corporation with a mission to operate along commercial lines. "Although our shareholder is the government, I regard myself as a private citizen, running a private company," stresses Eric Black, MTR's managing director.

The forceful entrepreneurial behavior characteristic of MTR would probably provoke heart attacks in most U.S. transit bureaucrats. It has launched various joint ventures with private firms to develop real estate at its stations and depots. It has, for example, roofed over its main depot and built a town for 30,000 people on top of it. "This also helped by creating more customers on the doorstep of the subway," says Mr. Leeds. Some 10 percent of the capital cost of the subway has already been raised through real estate development.

On top of this is the imaginative approach it takes to station use. Franchise operations have been opened in subway stations—you can buy a pair of jeans, get your shoes repaired or deposit your laundry in most stations—and even the operation of the ticket machines has been contracted out to the local Heng Seng Bank, which in return is allowed to operate cash machines inside the stations. The bank pays MTR about $750,000 for the privilege of issuing tickets and providing banking services. MTR no longer has the expense of issuing tickets, and also gains about $5 million a year from the float of subway fares as a direct deposit into the MTR account.

Nor are the employees allowed to run the subway for their own benefit. When a strike was launched soon after the MTR started operating, all workers were fired the next day and only some were later rehired. Despite very heavy usage the trains are clean and free of graffiti. Some might argue that it is because of Hong Kong's heavy population density that the subway is able to turn a profit. True, Hong Kong is very densely populated—but so is New York. The New York subway once made a profit when in private hands and might do so again, were it run along Hong Kong lines. Obviously, it makes no sense to build subways in areas with low population density and little prospect of high ridership. It would be cheaper in many instances to give a free limousine to every inner-city resident than to build a mass transit system. The private sector should be given the freedom to decide which services are profitable, and which are not.

The Hong Kong experience, especially with deregulated high-frequency minibuses, has been influential in persuading Britain to deregulate and privatize transit. After British bus services were fully deregulated last October, competing bus companies have been hustling for passengers on city streets and ridership is sharply up. When have you ever seen a public-sector bus actually looking for customers? You aren't likely to, which is precisely why the government should get out of the transportation business.

Source: *The Wall Street Journal,* February 19, 1987, p. 26. Reprinted by permission of *The Wall Street Journal,* © Dow Jones & Company, Inc. 1987. ALL RIGHTS RESERVED.

Questions

1. Capitalism's philosophical roots lie largely in the views of Locke, Smith, Spencer, and Weber.
   a. Do those views continue to explain our reliance on capitalism? Explain.
   b. If so, does our drift away from the free market suggest a flaw in that philosophical foundation? Explain.
   c. If not, can you suggest other doctrines or ethics that better explain our contemporary economic philosophy?

2. From the capitalist viewpoint, why is the private ownership of property necessary to the preservation of freedom?

3. Ayn Rand argued: "Altruism is incompatible with freedom, with capitalism, and with individual rights."
   a. Define altruism.
   b. Explain why Miss Rand rejected altruism.

4. In describing life in Hong Kong, Alvin Rabushka praises the "single-minded pursuit of making money" and the "emphasis on the material things in life." Rabushka admits to finding "Hong Kong's economic hustle and bustle more interesting, entertaining, and liberating than its lack of high opera, music, and drama."
   a. Although it is often criticized in America, is materialism the most certain and most interesting path to personal happiness? Explain.
   b. Would "sophisticated" culture (such as opera and drama) substantially disappear in America without government support? Explain.
   c. If so, how may we justify that support? If not, how may we justify that support?

5. Assume the federal government removed itself from the purchase and maintenance of its parks.
   a. Left to the private sector, what sorts of parks would develop under the profit incentive?
   b. Would Yellowstone, for example, survive in substantially its present state? Explain.
   c. How can it be argued that the federal parks are an unethical, undemocratic expropriation of private resources?

6. Assume the abolition of the federal Food and Drug Administration. How would the free market protect the citizenry from dangerous food and drug products?

7. Should education be returned to the free market? Explain. How would the poor finance a private-sector education?

8. Scholar Amitai Etzioni argues that America must choose between rededication to economic growth and emphasis on a quality-of-life society (slower growth, emphasis on ecology, concern for safety, harmony with oneself and others). He argues that the monetary costs and the social-psychic strains of pursuing these two divergent courses exceed America's resources, both physical and emotional.
   a. Do you agree with Etzioni? Explain.
   b. Which path would you choose? Explain.
   c. Will the market support the quality-of-life approach? Explain.

9. Puritan leaders felt concern over the morality of merchants selling goods for "more than their worth." That concern was particularly grave when the goods were scarce or in great demand.
    a. Should our society develop an ethic wherein goods are to be sold only "for what they are worth"? Explain.
    b. Can a seller make an accurate determination of worth? Explain.
    c. Does a product's worth differ from the price that product will bring in the marketplace? Explain.
    d. Personalize the inquiry: Assume you seek to sell your Ford auto for $5,000. Assume you know of several identical Fords in a similar state of repair that can be purchased for $4,500. Assume you find a buyer at $5,000. Will you unilaterally lower your price or direct the purchaser to the other autos? Explain.
    e. If not, have you acted justly? Explain.
10. Critics of our capitalist system contend that ability and effort often are less responsible for one's success than "unearned" factors such as family background, social class, luck, and willingness to cheat. Do you agree? Explain.
11. Commentator Irving Kristol asked whether it was "just" for Ray Kroc (now deceased, formerly of McDonald's) to have made so much money by merely figuring out a new way to sell hamburgers. He concluded that capitalism says it is just because he sold a good product; people want it; it is fair.
    a. Do you agree with Kristol? Explain.
    b. Does contemporary American capitalism offer excessive rewards to those clever enough to build near-term paper profits (lawyers, accountants, financial analysts) through mergers, tax write-offs, and the like while diverting scarce resources from long-term productive ventures (such as new product development or more efficient production processes)? Explain.
    c. If so, is capitalism fatally flawed? Explain.
12. Professor Robert E. Lane argued that the person who is motivated by needs for affiliation, rather than by needs for achievement, does less well in the market. Such a person is not rewarded so well as autonomous, achievement-oriented people.
    a. Is Lane correct? Explain.
    b. Is capitalism, in the long term, destructive of societal welfare in that achievement is better rewarded than affiliation? Explain.
13. Is capitalism compatible with social justice? Irving Kristol, a firm defender of capitalism, says the answer is no. Why would an ardent defender of the free market take that position?
14. Explore the argument that the federal highway program, although well-intentioned, was merely one in a series of federal interventions that distorted the market, leading, in this instance, to the long-term decline of inner cities.
15. How would the poor be cared for in a free market society?

Part Three—Collectivism

The term *collectivism* embraces various economic philosophies on the left of the political-economic spectrum; principally, communism and socialism. Capitalism is characterized by economic individualism. On the other hand, communism and the various styles of socialism are characterized by economic cooperation.

COLLECTIVIST GOALS

A critical distinction between collectivists and capitalists is that the former believe a society's broad directions should be carefully planned rather than left to what some take to be the whimsy of the market. Collectivists look on planning and government intervention as positive forces necessary to the shaping of a higher life for all. We can identify a series of goals that characterize the general agenda of collectivism whether communist, socialist, or some variant:

1. Human Liberty.   To the capitalist, collectivism appears to harshly restrain individual freedom. To the collectivist, the freedoms of capitalism are largely an illusion, accessible only to the prosperous and powerful. Collectivists lament wage slavery and exploitation of workers by owners. Work is not an act of free will sought for fulfillment, but rather forced labor required for survival in a competitive, capitalist society designed for the welfare of the few. To the collectivist, one can hardly enjoy the meaningful, higher-order freedoms of self-fulfillment, community, and love when restrained by the necessity to sustain oneself for the primary benefit of another.

2. Economic Development.   Collectivists feel that the economy must be directed toward the general interest rather than left free to multiply the welfare of successful capitalists. The market is regarded as wasteful, unfair, and based on accidents of luck and heritage. Thus, collectivists argue for central planning or controls to achieve growth, more equitable distribution of goods, and more socially useful production.

3. General Welfare.   Collectivist states seek to ensure adequate health, education, and general human services for all citizens. Free education, free health care, generous sick pay, family planning, and alcoholism programs are illustrative of the cradle-to-grave care characterizing most collectivist states.

Similarly, strenuous efforts are employed to modify the alienation said to be characteristic of capitalist economies. Marx argued that capitalist industrialism alienated (separated) workers from their work, the things produced, their employers, their co-workers, and themselves. He contended that capitalist workers were mere commodities laboring for the profit of others. Marx extended the analysis by contending that money converts love, friendship, and the entire course of human caring into a monetary relationship. In general, Marx took a profoundly humanist posture in pursuing self-actualization through a cooperative, loving society. Marx himself later appears to have abandoned these directions, but their preeminence in collectivist thought is clear.

4. Equality. Class distinctions are anathema to the collectivist. Equalitarianism is elevated to the level of a moral precept. Marx expressed the economics of equalitarianism in the powerful aphorism "from each according to his ability, to each according to his needs." All humans are equally meritorious, and distinctions among them are inherently unjust. But collectivists do not close their eyes to the reality of differentials in natural gifts. Some obviously will contribute more than others, but so far as is possible, distinctions based on individual achievement are to be muted. Thus, invidious divisions born of capitalism's competitive excesses are to be extinguished.

COMMUNISM

The Marxist-Leninist doctrine generally referred to as *communism* is, in theory, the purest form of collectivism. Like the genuine free market model discussed previously, no unadulterated collectivist economy (with the possible exception of Albania) is currently operative. Still, the Soviet Union, China, and many Eastern European nations take a predominantly collectivist approach to economics and adhere to the primary tenets of communist political ideology. However, as explained below, both the Soviets and the Chinese, in recent years, have taken the altogether remarkable direction of integrating substantial capitalist ingredients into their heretofore rigidly centralized economies.

Karl Marx took an economic view of history. He saw the production and exchange of goods and services as the foundation for all social processes, on which culture, law, and government are built. Thus, ownership of the means of production is the key to the entire character of the society. Marx found capitalism immoral, unjust, and humanly degrading. Workers, he argued, receive only subsistence wages and are debased in that the market converts their labor into a commodity. Marx believed that all value stems from labor, and, therefore, only labor should receive income. Thus, Marx was enraged by what he took to be capitalist oppression of the masses. To him the wealthy were literally a ruling class. In *The Communist Manifesto,* Marx took the position that violent revolution is the only feasible means of changing the social order. The owners of the means of production (the bourgeoisie) will not freely give up their control over a system they sincerely believe to be best. Thus the class war is seen as the only way out of oppression.

Marx felt that capitalism was doomed by an inherent developmental imbalance. He argued that the "forces of production" (technology, science, know-how) grow more rapidly than the "relations of production" (social institutions: law, monetary systems, private property arrangements). Thus, existing capitalist institutions would block the full, creative growth of the forces of production. His solution was public ownership of the means of production. Then productivity would not be limited by the faulty mechanisms of private ownership and profit.[11] This notion should be intriguing to us today, because our technological capacity (such as nuclear weapons) has run substantially in advance of our facility in dealing with those innovations. Was Marx correct and yet incorrect? Or is the full picture yet to emerge?

Communism, of course, calls for a planned economy. Theoretically, private ownership of the means of production is abolished. The state is to own the land and resources, provide for the needs of all citizens, and control prices and supplies. The market mechanism is replaced with central decisions regarding production levels, distribution, and so on. The ultimate aim of the system is a classless society controlled by all of the people. In practice, vestiges—in some instances, large segments—of free enterprise remain in all the communist states.

As noted, capitalism is enjoying a remarkable regeneration in the communist world.

THE COMMAND ECONOMY

Collectivism in its pure and most extreme form, a complete command economy unleavened by free market forces, does not exist. But many economies, including those of the Soviet Union, China, and some of the Eastern European communist nations, already fall preponderantly in the command economy mode. Of course, in recent years the Chinese have made a rather dramatic shift toward free market practices.

In a command economy, those basic economic decisions that America leaves to the market are resolved by the government. Production targets, growth rates, distribution of income, and allocation of resources are all established by central planners. The state owns the means of production and most of the property. Salaries of all producers are established by the state. All of this is accomplished via an intricately organized, multitiered bureaucracy capable of developing the plans and ensuring their implementation.

Since its revolution in 1917, the Soviet Union has been the most successful and most durable contemporary command economy. The totalitarian nature of Soviet policies, the continuing Cold War, and our visceral disapproval of communism retards Americans' ability to objectively evaluate the strengths and weaknesses of the Soviet command economy. Scholarly study suggests that the Soviet economic record, while mixed, reveals some significant strengths in the central planning approach. But, as explained in the article that follows, both the Soviets and the Chinese have tacitly conceded, at least for now, that command economics was not fulfilling their expectations.

SOVIETS NOW HAIL CHINA AS A SOURCE OF IDEAS FOR REVIVING SOCIALISM

Mark D'Anastasio

Moscow—When Deng Xiaoping first began opening up China's distressed, ideology-bound economy to market forces, the orthodox theorists of the Soviet Union sneered at the effort as "Maoism without Mao." There was certainly nothing to be learned, they added, from policies that undermined such sacred Marxist notions as egalitarianism.

That was eight years ago, and before Mikhail Gorbachev's accession. By now it is clear that Mr. Deng's moves toward free enterprise and away from central planning, though not uniformly successful, have invigorated China's economy and improved the lives of millions, especially peasants. And suddenly Moscow is sounding a different theme.

For the first time, a broad spectrum of Soviet China-watchers are saying openly that the economic path taken by the Chinese plays a role— in fact a central role—in determining the policies of Mr. Gorbachev as he strives to stir his own nation from its economic torpor.

* * * * *

Many Contrasts

Yet major differences exist in the Chinese and Soviet economic situations, differences that call into question the transferability of Mr. Deng's methods. China remains a poor, backward developing country, while the Soviet Union long ago entered the ranks of industrialized nations. The Soviet economy isn't on the verge of collapse, as China's was when Mr. Deng began his reforms. China is freer to experiment, not seeing itself as the repository of Marxist orthodoxy and the model for other socialist nations. And there are differences in attitudes and economic traditions.

In his two-year effort to revitalize the Soviet economy, Mr. Gorbachev has taken such steps as letting the state pay more for higher-quality goods, permitting a construction company in Leningrad to go bankrupt, and opening doors to foreign joint ventures. This spring and summer his controversial program has culminated in several formal laws and decrees.

A law on individual activity legalizes small-scale businesses in 29 fields, including plumbing, carpentry, dressmaking, auto repair, tutoring, and toy making, though the businesses can't hire workers. Second, a new law governing the 48,000 state enterprises aims to give local managers certain authority as of next January to make their own production plans, choose suppliers, and even set prices. Third, a set of 11 decrees diminishes, accordingly, the extensive authority of central planners. The way is cleared for such new practices as wholesale trade and letting enterprises borrow money instead of relying on state grants.

Not There Yet

Heated debate has accompanied these moves, and the resistance by bureaucrats who would lose power is far from over. Many industrial workers may be expected to resist another move, which would link wages more closely with performance.

China's liberalization is far more advanced. Its most notable success has been in agriculture, where Mr. Deng, in effect, abolished the collectives and returned to a family-farm system. Food production and farmers' incomes have soared, though there have been complaints of farmers neglecting important crops such as grain for more lucrative ones like vegetables.

Though socialism still predominates in China, its cities now teem with private food stands, restaurants, repair stalls, and many other tiny businesses. Factories, rather than pitch all their earnings into a common pot, may retain a percentage of profits, from which factory managers can raise salaries or invest in plant modernization as they see fit. . . .

What gave the Chinese reforms their impetus was the sorry situation when Mr. Deng came to power in 1978. There was a sense of urgency for change, created by Mao's disastrous Great Leap Forward of 1958–1960, his traumatic Cultural Revolution, other abrupt shifts, periodic famines, and decades of stagnant farm and industrial production. . . .

In the Soviet Union, where Communism has ruled twice as long as in China, the bureaucracy could still torpedo Mr. Gorbachev's plans. It is estimated to number an astounding 18 million people, a privileged elite whose power and perks depend on the status quo.

* * * * *

Another complication for the Soviets is ideology. Mr. Deng openly concedes that some of what Marx and Lenin said has become outdated, but Mr. Gorbachev, mindful of the Soviet role as mentor to the world's communists, must carefully justify every move by citing the founders, blaming failures on misapplication of their precepts.

* * * * *

Guns for Butter

Besides its role as ideological touchstone, the Soviet Union's superpower military status rules out some of Mr. Deng's tactics. He could unilaterally demobilize a million Chinese soldiers and slash military spending to 4.3 percent of gross national product (by Western estimates), converting much of the armaments industry to building trucks, TV sets, and washing machines.

The Soviet Union, with far greater military commitments around the world, can do no such thing. Western experts estimate it may spend as much as 14 percent of its GNP on defense, or about the percentage China was spending under Mao.

Mr. Deng's changes in agriculture provide the greatest inspiration for the Soviets. This is an area in which Mr. Gorbachev has so far achieved few changes, though he did manage to cut the farm bureaucracy by merging ministries, and collective farms now get fewer orders from absent managers on what to plant and where and when.

Like their Chinese counterparts, Soviet state and collective farmers now can sell above-plan harvests, up to 30 percent of production, in city markets and cooperative stores at free market (that is, higher) prices. But such changes don't come anywhere near China's wholesale dismantling of collectivization.

Soviet experts interviewed now support wide application of some form of family farming. Some U.S. observers, though, say it may not work so well for them. "The extended family in China is an enduring and powerful force," Mr. Goldman writes in his book *Gorbachev's Challenge*. But in Russia, feudal estates and, later, collective and state farms "have been virtually the only form of land tenure."

* * * * *

Consumer Goods

* * * * *

Mr. Deng has gone so far as to authorize a vast return of free enterprise and private ownership of the means of production in small trade, manufacturing, and service industries. A few Chinese companies have even issued shares, and there are sleepy stock markets to trade them, though this obviously capitalist trend has been strictly limited in China.

The Soviets aren't about to try stock ownership. And even the most liberal Soviet economists can't rationalize private ownership of the means of production.

* * * * *

Free enterprise exists in the Soviet Union in the form of individual labor and cooperative enterprises. Recent legislation let individuals open shops, service businesses, and restaurants.

But Western officials estimate the new laws have added no more than 200,000 people to the 100,000 already involved in small-scale enterprise under earlier legislation. . . .

Legacy of Feudalism

There are other reasons for the Russians' slow start. One is that the Soviet Union doesn't have a Hong Kong on its border to serve as an example, nor a huge community of entrepreneurial countrymen abroad wanting to invest. Hong Kong is also a source of Chinese-speaking management, technical, and marketing skill.

A less tangible factor is attitude. Far fewer Russians than Chinese have a taste for the risks of business, Soviet analysts say. "In Russia the entrepreneurial spirit was never developed," [Soviet journalist Fyodor] Burlatsky says. "Just last century we were still a nation

of serfs, and then the new system [Soviet Communism] was set up in a way that smothered all individual initiative."

* * * * *

Those who do feel entrepreneurial often face another obstacle. Says Mr. Burlatsky: "The main problem is social jealousy on the part of bureaucrats. Local officials can't bear the idea of people making several times their salaries."

* * * * *

Special Economic Zones

In heavier industries, the Chinese, as they move toward less reliance on state planning and more on market forces and initiative, simply do what seems to work. For the Soviets, every change in industrial policy is an enormous strain, carried out only against recalcitrant opposition. The Russians are astounded that Chinese factories were permitted to switch over to new forms of self-directed management quickly without a carefully elaborated blueprint from higher authorities.

In joint ventures with capitalist countries, the Chinese, while managing to frustrate plenty of foreigners with their rules on taxation, supply of local workers, and other matters, nevertheless have gone much further than the Soviets. The Russians don't plan anything like China's special economic zones and 14 coastal cities where thousands of joint ventures with foreign capitalists are under way.

* * * * *

While Mr. Gorbachev pushed through legislation permitting joint ventures, Western analysts say the idea still faces powerful opposition. "It isn't just the xenophobia; the Chinese are also xenophobic," says one West German banker with long experience here. "The image of thousands of capitalist businessmen crawling around Russia is strongly distasteful to them. Superpowers don't beg their political competitors to show them the way to modernization. They're very proud of their industry even if it's a mess.''

Source: *The Wall Street Journal,* September 18, 1987, pp. 1, 7. Reprinted by permission of *The Wall Street Journal,* © Dow Jones & Company, Inc. 1987. ALL RIGHTS RESERVED.

SOCIALISM

The distinctions between communism and socialism are not entirely clear. To some socialism is the public ownership of the sources of production (such as land, minerals, and factories), while communism is the public ownership of virtually the totality of the wealth. To others socialism and communism have similar economic roots but differ as to political direction. Historically, socialism has been associated with democratic governments and peaceful change, while communism has been characterized by totalitarianism and violent revolution. The meaning of socialism has been further obscured by those who apply the socialist label to almost every government intervention in the private sector, even though those interventions involve no element of public ownership of the means of production.[12]

Socialism in its many forms aims to retain the benefits of industrialism while abolishing the social costs often accompanying the free market. In the contemporary Western world, Norway, Denmark, Sweden, France (early in the Mitterrand era), and Great Britain (prior to Prime Minister Thatcher) are nations where socialist principles have assumed a significant presence. Nationalization is limited to only the most vital industries, such as steel, coal mining, power generation, and transportation. While nationalization may be relatively uncommon, the government is likely to be directly involved in regulating growth, inflation, and unemployment. But the biggest story in contemporary socialism is the capitalist tide that swept the world in the 1980s.

A NEW AGE OF CAPITALISM

John Greenwald

From the time of the ancient Greeks, philosophers, politicians, and just plain folk have debated the best form of society and the proper role of the state in the lives of its people. For more than a century, advocates of collective ownership and strong government control of the economy have marched under the banner of socialism. Those who champion private property, individual initiative, and the pursuit of profit are in the capitalist camp.

A decade ago, socialism seemed to be on the ascendancy, despite some severe cracks in its facade. In Bombay and Bangkok, in Lima and Lusaka, governments were nationalizing industries and imposing ever growing and restrictive regulations on private companies. The rising tide of socialism threatened to become a tidal wave. Among superpowers, the communist Soviet Union appeared to be gaining in international prestige and influence, while the capitalist United States seemed to be declining. Racked by oil crises, recession, and an inflationary fever that soared to double digits, the free enterprise system faced a doubtful, some said downright perilous, future.

All that has dramatically changed in the 1980s, as capitalism has become the spirit of the age. More and more countries are turning to free enterprise as the last, best hope for faster economic and social development. . . .

In the Third World, even socialist countries like India have increasingly turned to private enterprise in the search for more production and jobs. In Latin America, debt-plagued Argentina, which owes $51 billion to foreign creditors, is striving to dismantle some of the stifling legacy of state enterprise created by former dictator Juan Perón. Communist nations are making efforts too. In Eastern Europe, small but thriving outposts of free enterprise continue to exist amid the suffocating state presence. Half the wurst and baked goods in East Berlin come from the private sector.

* * * * *

[T]he state's share of the economy in 19 West European countries has begun falling for the first time since World War II. Public outlays accounted for 50.6 percent of gross domestic product in 1984, versus 51.1 percent the year before. Even Scandinavia, where the welfare state achieved its fullest flowering, has caught the spirit. Says Nils Lundgren, chief economist of PK Banken, Sweden's largest bank: "Deregulation, market solutions, and free enterprise are the order of the day."

Republican Congressman Jack Kemp happily says, "Capitalism is not a dirty word anymore." Actually, that is not quite right. In much of the world, the term still conjures up images of 19th-century sweatshops and colonialism. In fact, socialism's elusive promise of economic equality retains a powerful appeal in many parts of the world, and its current malaise does not mean that it could not make a comeback.

* * * * *

The resurgence of capitalism is rewriting the world's political lexicons. Social Democratic leaders across Western Europe are increasingly pro-business. Says Herbert Giersch, director of the Institute of World Economics at the University of Kiel, West Germany: "The European Commission, even under a socialist president, is pushing toward a decontrol of the capital market, a breakdown of the airline cartel, and reform of agriculture policy."

The shift toward free enterprise could have an impact on global politics. India and other countries, especially in the developing world, once considered the Soviet Union as a model for economic modernization. But now they are looking west to the United States or east to Japan, Hong Kong, and South Korea.

The reason that private enterprise is on the rise is clear. While capitalist nations, including the United States and the emerging countries of Asia, have been highly successful at creating wealth, socialism has largely proved an economic drag. Says Peter Berger, a sociologist at Boston University: "Socialist societies have been dramatically outperformed by any number of successful capitalist countries, especially in Asia."

* * * * *

Western Europe's heavily state-influenced economies provide perhaps the clearest example among industrialized countries that more government control does not promote faster development. "Europe has been growing desperately slowly," says Jean-Claude Trichet, chief of staff of France's Ministry of Economy, Finance, and Privatization. The Continent has been slow to adapt or innovate as economic events moved rapidly, a condition that was dubbed Eurosclerosis. Its experience with high-technology projects, like the Anglo-French Concorde supersonic jet and the national French computer program, have been costly disappointments.

In the decade after the 1973 oil shock, the United States created 16 million new jobs and Japan added 6 million. Yet Western Europe had practically no growth in its work force. Unemployment, which as recently as 1971 averaged 3 percent in European Community countries, is around 12 percent. The area's economies expanded just 5.6 percent between 1979 and 1984, versus 10.4 percent for the United States and 21.7 percent for Japan.

In the Third World, the failure of socialism and state ownership is evidenced by years of recession, rampant inflation, and an abundance of horror stories about grossly mismanaged government industries. In Argentina, residents may have to wait 20 years for the state communications monopoly to install their phones, and the charge for such "service" can reach $2,000. . . .

Given the obvious shortcomings of socialist ownership and planning, why did so many countries rush to adopt socialism? The answer in many ways lies in the history of early capitalism. As the Industrial Revolution gathered force in the early 19th century, employees were treated as harshly as machines and made to work under wretched and frequently dangerous conditions. In the United States, eight-year-old children could be pressed into factory service for 14-hour days. But this cruelty failed

to insulate capitalism from sudden business slumps. Between 1873 and 1929, a series of economic panics, crashes, and depressions showed the system's flaws. Notes author Peter Drucker: "In the Panic of 1873, the modern welfare state was born. A hundred years later it had run its course."

* * * * *

It was the Great Depression and World War II, though, that set the stage for the advance of socialism. More and more people demanded reforms to curb capitalism's worst abuses and remove the vicissitudes of unbridled economic life. Antitrust laws were used to break up cartels, and statutes regulating working conditions were written in the books of almost every country. Unions grew strong and won numerous benefits for their members. In the United States, the New Deal created a plethora of programs as varied as public works projects and the Social Security system. In Europe, governments after World War II went even further. They created free medical care, protected workers from being fired, and set up so many other programs that the term cradle-to-grave security was coined.

* * * * *

The Third World's turn to socialism arose in large part as a reaction to colonial rule. Even today capitalism is considered part of a hated past. "Capitalism is regarded as an ideological word and is not acceptable," says a Western diplomat stationed in Africa. When newly independent countries adopted socialism in the 1960s, they were in effect rebelling against what they saw as the economic system of departing colonial masters.

* * * * *

By the late 1970s, however, all the varied roads to socialism were converging on dead ends. "Most governments were seeking to reduce the public, and expand the market, sectors of their economies,'' writes historian Paul Johnson in his chronicle, *Modern Times.* The retreat was foretold by a swing in intellectual fashion. It began with the 1970 publication of Jean-Francois Revel's *Without Marx or Jesus,* which praised U.S. society as open and pragmatic and rejected socialism as a dogma that had failed.

In Paris, members of the New Philosophers movement were powerfully impressed by Alexander Solzhenitsyn's voluminous account, published in the mid-1970s, of the appalling Soviet gulag camps for political prisoners. The period brought the spectacle of Communist leader Pol Pot's genocide of perhaps 3 million Cambodians. Writer Bernard-Henri Lévy blamed Marxism for communist atrocities, and the charge resonated among French thinkers. Although their disillusionment was intellectual, it helped set the stage for Europe's economic shift half a decade later.

At about this same time, the once promising welfare state began running into trouble on two fronts. The first was simply cost. Programs established when economies were growing rapidly in the 50s and 60s were difficult to pay for when business hit several years of slumps in the 70s and 80s. In addition, it soon became clear that the welfare state was having a serious effect on worker incentive and individual initiative. If high taxes and generous social benefits meant that a person got just about the same rewards whether he worked hard or did little, there was less reason to do more. . . .

Much of the world's interest in capitalism is due to the recent success of the American economy in creating jobs. . . . While a large part of the world outside Asia has been stuck in a swamp of stagnation, the United States has seemed dynamic and growing. . . .

To be sure, countries are making greater use of capitalism in their own ways. When it comes to selling state-owned companies, Britain has led the way. ''The British example is important for the world,'' says John Redwood, a former

Thatcher aide. Since 1979, the Conservative government has raised $11.25 billion by unloading all or part of 18 nationalized firms.

* * * * *

France is loosening its system of *dirigisme,* or state direction of business, which goes back to the 17th century and Jean Baptiste Colbert, the minister to Louis XIV. Socialist President Francois Mitterrand nationalized 39 banks and five major industries soon after taking office in 1981. He changed course later, but not before the political damage had been done. Last March a right-wing coalition that promised to denationalize companies and promote business won control of the National Assembly.

* * * * *

Outside Europe, India has made the most dramatic shift of any non-communist nation. Since the country's independence in 1947, socialism has been an accepted part of India's political and economic system. Now the subcontinent has begun to embrace free enterprise too. The change is largely the work of Prime Minister Rajiv Gandhi, who took office in 1984 after the assassination of his mother, Indira Gandhi. Rajiv has presided over a liberalization program that has slashed taxes and produced more than 80 decrees loosening or abolishing business restrictions.

* * * * *

Gandhi's moves have put the Indian business community in an upbeat and feisty mood. The Tata Group, a sprawling giant whose operations include steel mills, power plants, and truck manufacturing, spent some $85 million a year on new plant and equipment during the regulation-choked 1970s. Now Tata invests nearly $300 million annually.

Many poverty-torn African nations are slowly turning to free enterprise in hopes of spurring growth. In an extraordinary plea for help last May before the United Nations, the

Organization of African Unity acknowledged that the "positive role of the private sector is to be encouraged." That is just a beginning. In Nigeria, President Ibrahim Babangida plans to sell the government's stake in more than 160 companies, including hotels, breweries, and appliance makers. In Kenya, ailing state-owned monopolies are finally being permitted to fail so that their operations can be taken over by private firms. Uplands Bacon, the longtime king of Kenya's pork-processing industry, went bankrupt after a new private company began devouring its business. The Ivory Coast has liquidated its national trading company along with unprofitable rice and hotel operations.

* * * * *

The foundation of private enterprise is already firmly established in the countries along the Pacific Rim, which has been the world's fastest-growing region in the past 10 years. Their prosperity is based on a unique mixture of planning and enterprise sometimes called Confucian capitalism. Says Edward Chen, director of the Center of Asian Studies at the University of Hong Kong, about newly industrialized Taiwan, South Korea, and Singapore: "The government always leaves some room for the private sector to excel and to compete and to get a reasonable rate of profit." Stressing education, hard work, and social harmony, state and business sectors have cooperated to produce the exports that fuel development.

* * * * *

Any faltering of the world economy could encourage nations to turn once again to socialism, which always has a strong idealistic appeal. People have been attracted to the concept of an egalitarian society at least since Plato, who held that "it would be well that every man should come to the colony having all things equal." In practice, of course, socialism falls far short of the promise. Privileged classes always grow up, and some people—bureaucrats or party officials—invariably do better than the rest.

* * * * *

The most productive figure in history is the individual trying to improve his status. Whether he is an Asian peasant tilling his land or an American businessman building a company, the profit incentive is a powerful force. Capitalism is not a neat, orderly system. The street vendors of Lima or Peking or New York City, some basic examples of capitalism, are more chaotic than the orderly but often empty stores in so many socialist states. Capitalism's unruliness means that it will always be subject to swings of boom and bust. The system, however, presents the constant opportunity for profit and for improvement of the individual's lot. Countries that want to develop quickly or stay abreast in a rapidly changing economic world are finding themselves drawn to free enterprise, which lets people loose so that they can lose their economic shackles.

THE MIDDLE GROUND

As tacitly acknowledged by the Chinese and the Soviets, the restraints and inefficiencies of central planning are so onerous and, in many instances, arbitrary that the utility and ideological appeal of collectivism are compromised. Thus scholars and societal leaders have sought to develop a viable middle position that embraces the communitarian virtues of socialism and the efficiencies of the marketplace. *Social democracy,* as that middle ground is often labeled, has been a powerful political force in, for example, Austria, Belgium, and the Scandinavian nations. Social democrats accept multiparty politics and believe in the gradual, democratic adoption of socialist goals. They seek to reduce the hardships of capitalism rather than to reorder society in accord with a collectivist model. Sweden and Norway are probably the most notable and most controversial examples of the successful application of socialist principles on a capitalist foundation. In the main, business still resides in private hands. Thus, an attempt is made to preserve the independence and efficiency of individual initiative. However, the state plays a powerful role by erecting a complete safety net guaranteeing cradle-to-grave care to any citizen requiring assistance to meet life's necessities. The articles that follow describe both the nature of life in the Scandinavian welfare states and the business climate in economies that seek to combine the best of both capitalism and collectivism. Note that the first article was published in 1978, while the second appeared in 1987. Read consecutively, the two articles reveal both the continuing Scandinavian preference for the welfare state and newly emergent frustrations with the financing of that cradle-to-grave care.

NORWAY: THE COST OF SAFETY

On late summer afternoons, fleets of private boats jam the Oslofjord; in winter, thousands of Norwegians spend their weekends on the country's ski slopes or on quick trips to resorts in balmy Spain. About 75 percent of all Norwegian families own their homes and close to half also have vacation retreats—a cottage on the coast or a cabin in the mountains. The humble Volkswagen has been dethroned as king of the road, replaced as Norway's best-selling car by the more luxurious Volvo.

. . . Norway has one of the world's highest living standards. Whether such bounty results mostly from the drive of 4 million people inured to hard work in a cold, rugged land or primarily from the social-democratic policies pursued by the ruling Labor Party . . . is unclear even to Norwegians. Confesses Sverre Badendyck, a retired sea captain now employed as a shipping inspector: "We *think* we live in a capitalist country. Or at least in one with a mixed economy, with a socialist government trying to make it more socialist. But we honestly don't know what we have."

Norway tolerates a considerable amount of free enterprise. All but 9 percent of industry remains in private hands, although the fledgling North Sea oil industry is state owned. Nonetheless, one of the world's most comprehensive welfare states has been fashioned by the Labor Party, in power for 36 of the past 43 years.

The *folketrygden* (people's security) law grants everyone disability, old-age, and survivors' benefits, rehabilitation assistance, and unemployment payments. Other measures provide free hospitalization, surgery, and medicines. Youngsters through the ninth grade receive dental care at their schools at no cost. Every worker is guaranteed at least four weeks of paid vacation.

Taxation rather than nationalization has been Labor's method of building Norway's socialism, which the party defines as "equality among all individuals and groups." Steeply progressive personal taxes (50 percent for a couple earning $30,000) have helped to level incomes. Says Christian Erlandsen, managing director of an Oslo auto parts firm: "After taxes the difference between me and the lowest-paid guy at this company is not very great. You can't look at just income; you must look at other values. We have our cabins, our spare time. What may be most important to me is my feeling of safety. I'm not thinking of crime as much as of health and retirement benefits. If I were to die now, for example, my wife and 15-month-old son would get 80 percent of my present income for some time. That's safety."

Business earnings are also heavily taxed: 30 percent by the national government and 20 percent by municipalities. . . .

The Labor Party tries to regulate what it does not tax. Although farmland remains in private hands, most farmers have been put under legal and financial pressure to join state-dominated cooperative marketing groups.

The government's most ambitious attempt to restructure the economy while permitting private ownership has been to give workers a voice in corporate management. A 1972 scheme for "industrial democracy" requires all firms with more than 200 employees to give worker representatives one third of the votes in the new "corporate assemblies" that replaced the traditional shareholders' meeting. . . .

There are signs that Norwegians worry about too much socialism. . . .

Although Norwegians have no intention of dismantling their social net, they are becoming increasingly irritated at its red tape. Says Ragnhild Braathen, a Telemark housewife: "The regular citizen struggles against a wall of bureaucracy." . . .

Norwegian economists fear that the state's generosity may be adversely affecting the country's economy. Norway's production costs are already the globe's highest. . . .

. . . High taxes discourage overtime work, while generous sick pay spurs absenteeism, which has doubled in recent years. On the average, 10 percent of the work force now stay away from the job daily, and in some plants the figure reaches 20 percent.

Surveying the costs of the welfare state, a businessman confesses: "I'm a little bit scared of the future." Still, Norway's variant of socialism stands a good chance of thriving—if only because of potential benefits of North Sea oil.

DOMINANT SOCIALISM OF
NORDIC REGION SHIFTS A BIT AS
PUBLIC DISAFFECTION GROWS

Marcus W. Brauchli

Malmoe, Sweden—Agneta Gandiaga runs a tight kindergarten. Her uniformed charges help prepare their own meals, learn manners, and pray each morning beside an altar.

"There is a need for old-fashioned values in children," says Ms. Gandiaga, a 39-year-old former nurse's aide. Parents in this port city seem to agree. They have signed up more than 100 toddlers on a waiting list for 24 spots at the private kindergarten. "I could easily open five more schools like this tomorrow," she says.

What is preventing her? "The socialists," Ms. Gandiaga says. She blames Sweden's ruling Social Democratic Party for trying to block private-sector alternatives to the country's social welfare system. "They think they always know what is best and don't want me to continue," Ms. Gandiaga says. "But we will show them there is more than one way."

Ms. Gandiaga's resentment isn't about to unravel Sweden's monolithic welfare state. But it reflects a growing public dissatisfaction with the socialism that has dominated life in the Nordic region for most of this century.

The shift in attitudes is by no means an ideological revolution. Socialism remains the prevalent political force in the four big Nordic countries—Sweden, Norway, Denmark, and Finland. High taxes and a cradle-to-grave welfare state still characterize life for the nearly 22 million people in this sparsely populated region. But while a voter revolt is unlikely, a growing number of critics argue that the Nordic welfare state has become a bureaucratic leviathan and must be reined in. Indeed, analysts blame a dearth of new ideas for large-scale

defections from some of the region's socialist parties.

* * * * *

Hoping to contain their losses, some socialists have adopted decidedly unsocialist-sounding themes. Here is a look at some important trends in [Sweden and Norway:]

Sweden

In many of Sweden's 284 municipalities, private groups or individuals have taken up responsibility for running social services that once were the exclusive domain of local government. Officially, the ruling Social Democratic Party opposes the idea. But even some socialist communities are allowing private-sector contractors to take over services that they can provide more cheaply. One reason: The Social Democratic government wants to simplify the country's notoriously burdensome tax structure, and savings in expenditures will make that task easier.

Hewing to their ideological roots, the Social Democrats have laid out one firm restriction on private alternatives: Nobody should profit by providing essential services like health or geriatric care.

* * * * *

Norway

Norway's socialist Labor Party, which for decades built up state involvement in industries such as electricity, oil, aluminum, and railroads, has moved away from that strategy. This year, a minority Labor government actually shut down a heavily indebted, loss-making state concern, Kongsberg Vaapenfabrikk AS.

The Labor Party, which is now 100 years old, is willing to experiment with alternatives—including some private-sector social services—because of concerns that collectivism is outdated. "We are constantly trying to change," says Einar Foerde, the Labor Party's parliamentary leader.

The country's strong economy, driven by an oil boom over the past decade, has made changing easier. Shutting Kongsberg meant no increase in unemployment, simply a shift in employers for some workers. But analysts say it nevertheless was a sign of the times.

* * * * *

Source: *The Wall Street Journal,* December 28, 1987, p. 10. Reprinted by permission of *The Wall Street Journal,* © Dow Jones & Company, Inc. 1987. ALL RIGHTS RESERVED.

Questions

1. As Marx argued, scientific knowledge in the capitalist community grows more rapidly than the social institutions designed to organize and cope with that knowledge. How do you account for that imbalance?

2. Marx felt that the flawed social institutions of capitalism would unduly restrain the bountiful forces of production. Has that been the case for the global economy? Explain.

3. Marx proposes placing the means of production in public hands. Were we to do so, would a desirable balance result so that technology and the wisdom to deal with the effects of technology would achieve a reasonable equilibrium? Explain.

4. Socialism's historical roots may be traced to early Christianity.
   a. Are socialist values more in keeping with Christian theology than are capitalist values? Explain.
   b. If your response is yes, do you believe that a committed Christian must renounce capitalism? Explain.

5. You have read that both China and the Soviet Union are adopting elements of capitalism in an effort to improve their economies. In your opinion, is capitalism a useful lever for achieving understanding and peace between the communist states and the United States? Explain.

6. Contrast Russian history with that of the United States to explain how the entrepreneurial spirit flourished in the latter but is only slowly emerging in the former. See "Soviets Now Hail China as a Source of Ideas for Reviving Socialism."

7. Reconsider the *Time* magazine article, "A New Age of Capitalism."
   a. The authors argue that the socialist ideal of a society of equality is impossible: "Privileged classes always grow up." Do you agree that equality is impossible? Explain.
   b. The authors remind us of the effectiveness of the profit motive as a stimulus for productivity. In your opinion, can forces such as love of country, concern for one's fellow being, and a strong preference for economic equality replace the role of profit as an incentive for hard work? Explain.

    c. Is socialism doomed as a meaningful economic force in the world of the 21st century? Explain.

8. The Scandinavian "middle way" seems to have produced an idyllic lifestyle: cradle-to-grave care, very productive economies, little internal strife, material abundance, and so on.

    a. Build a list of objections to the Scandinavian approach.

    b. What conditions of history, culture, and resources render the Scandinavian nations more suitable than the United States to the socialist approach?

9. *a.* Why do the Social Democrats in Sweden take the position that "nobody should profit by providing essential services like health or geriatric care"?

    b. Should we take that position in America? Explain.

10. Correspondent R. W. Apple of *The New York Times* reported that Sweden has willfully pursued a policy of economic leveling:

> As a result almost every family living near the sea has a boat, but almost all are small boats. A large percentage of families have summer houses, but none of them rivals the villas of the Riviera or the stately manor houses of Britain. Virtually no one has servants.
>
> Even among the handful of people who might be able to afford it, conspicuous consumption is frowned upon. There are fewer than 25 Rolls Royces in Sweden.[13]

    a. Is the Swedish approach preferable to the extreme conspicuous consumption permitted—and even encouraged— in this country? Explain.

    b. Is the opportunity to garner luxuries necessary to the successful operation of the American system? Explain.

    c. Does our system generate guilt among those who enjoy its fruits in quantities well beyond the norm? Explain.

11. Should an American citizen's primary duty be to herself or himself or to all other members of society? Should all humans be regarded as of equal value and thus equally worthy of our individual support? Can social harmony be achieved in a nation whose citizens fail to regard the state as a "superfamily"? Explain.

12. Distinguished professor and Pulitzer prize winner, Arthur Schlesinger, Jr., commented in *The Wall Street Journal* on the emergence of "capitalistic communism" in China:

> Mr. Deng's economic policies have brought about a considerable increase in production (especially in agriculture), in wealth, in inequality, and in corruption. White-collar crime is growing. At the end of June, the State Council promulgated a new code setting punishments for fraud, profiteering, tax evasion, unauthorized bonuses, and other "economic crimes." The State Auditing Administration has uncovered financial irregularities covering almost 2 percent of the total amount audited.
>
> The number of lawyers is increasing; in Liaoning Province alone, 2,300 lawyers have opened 122 offices. The divorce rate is also rising. Beggars and vagrants are seen more often in the streets. The de-collectivization of agriculture has elevated short-term profit over long-term considerations of land use and conservation; weakened the traditional system of irrigation,

canals, and dikes; and has exposed the countryside to new threats of soil exhaustion, erosion, pollution, and flooding.[14]

    a. Is an increase in economic crimes an inevitable by-product of the transformation from socialist/communist principles to capitalism? Explain.

    b. Schlesinger notes a general increase in social problems in China. Are social problems more pronounced in capitalist states than in those with a socialist bent? If not, why would any rational person opt for a socialist government? If so, why would any rational person opt for a capitalist government?

13. In Sweden the spanking of children is a violation of the law.
    a. What reasoning supports that legislation?
    b. Would such legislation help reduce violence in America? Explain.

14. Collectivists believe that if the means of production reside in private hands, workers will be exploited.
    a. Does American history support that contention?
    b. Is worker exploitation necessary to the success of capitalism? Explain.

15. The Eskimos, among other cultures, regarded all natural resources as free or common goods to be used but never possessed by any individual or group. What arguments may be raised to justify our notion of private ownership of natural resources?

16. Deduce the meaning of "pension fund socialism." How is it different from "corporate socialism"?

17. Swedish legislation and the policies of many companies, such as Volvo, provide for worker participation in management decisions. American firms have begun to take that direction. Would this "socialist" goal be desirable for America? Explain.

Part Four—America's Economic Future—Where Are We?

We have inspected the entire economic continuum. The issue that remains is which direction America should take.

Each philosophy possesses compelling features. Not surprisingly, the available empirical evidence is mixed. One study ranked the United States first among the nations of the world in a quality-of-life index based on five components—social, economic, energy and environment, health and education, and national vitality and security. Using only objective indicators capable of quantitative measurement, scholar Ben-Chieh Liu found the United States substantially ahead of second- and third-place Australia and Canada, respectively, even though the United States led only one of the individual categories (social—fulfilling basic human needs and providing material comfort). Sweden and Norway ranked fourth and fifth according to Liu's study.[15] On the other hand, if one looks specifically at public welfare based on literacy, life expectancy, and infant mortality, Iceland, Japan, the Netherlands, and Sweden rank 1st through 4th in the world, while the United States ranks 11th.[16] Indeed, the infant mortality data are particularly disquieting evidence that the U.S. system is not without its weaknesses. According to a report by Metropolitan Life Insurance Co., the United States ranked 16th out of 21 industrial nations with an infant mortality rate of 10.4 infant deaths per 1,000 live births in 1986.[17] Sweden, Finland, and Japan earned the best records with 6 deaths for each 1,000 live births. Furthermore, infant mortality for American black babies is nearly twice that for whites. The Children's Defense Fund reports that "a black infant born within five miles of the White House is more likely to die in the first year of life than an infant born in Trinidad and Tobago or Costa Rica."[18] Nonetheless, the problem cannot merely be consigned to the black community because the infant mortality rate for white American infants exceeds that of almost all of the nations of western Europe. These figures are all the more dispiriting in light of the fact that the United States spends more money on health care (11.2 percent of the GNP) than any other industrial nation. On the other hand, the United States ranked second in the world in per capita economic productivity in 1985. The per capita GNP of the United Arab Emirates ($19,120) ranked first in the world. The United States ($16,400) finished second, followed by Switzerland ($16,380), Kuwait ($14,270), and Norway ($13,890). Japan ranked eighth at $11,330.[19]

As economist Lester Thurow explains, the conservative solution to America's economic slippage is to "liberate free enterprise" and generally reduce the role of government.

> In thinking about this solution it is well to remember that none of our competitors became successful by following this route. Government absorbs slightly over 30 percent of the GNP in the United States, but over 50 percent of the GNP in West Germany. Fifteen other countries collect a larger fraction of their GNP in taxes.[20]

Thurow goes on to add more evidence to his doubts regarding the "conservative solution":

> Nor have our competitors unleashed work effort and savings by increasing income differentials. Indeed, they have done exactly the opposite. If you look at the earnings gap between the top and bottom 10 percent of the population, the West Germans work hard with 36 percent less inequality than we, and the Japanese work even harder with 50 percent less inequality. If income differentials encourage individual initiative, we should be full of initiative, since among industrialized countries, only the French surpass us in terms of inequality.
>
> Moreover, our own history shows that our economic performance since the New Deal and the onset of government "interference" has been better than it was prior to the New Deal. Our best economic decades were the 1940s (real per capita GNP grew 30 percent), when we had all that growth in social welfare programs. Real per capita growth since the advent of government intervention

has been more than twice as high as it was in the days when governments did not intervene or have social welfare programs.[21]

FREEDOM

Evidence and opinions are helpful in illuminating the proper direction for America, but the primary determinant of that direction presumably remains the issue of personal freedom. A decade ago the editors of *Commentary* asked 26 of the nation's leading intellectuals to assess the relationship between capitalism, socialism, and democracy.

> The idea that there may be an inescapable connection between capitalism and democracy has recently begun to seem plausible to a number of intellectuals who would once have regarded such a view not only as wrong but even as politically dangerous. So too with the idea that there may be something intrinsic to socialism which exposes it ineluctably to the "totalitarian temptation." Thus far, the growing influence of these ideas has been especially marked in Europe—for example, among the so-called "new philosophers" in France and in the work of Paul Johnson and others in England—but they seem to be receiving more and more sympathetic attention in the United States as well.
>
> How significant do you judge this development to be? Do you yourself share in it, either fully or even to the extent of feeling impelled to rethink your own ideas about capitalism and socialism and the relation of each to democracy?[22]

One of the respondents, Professor Eugene Genovese, concedes that the left must "solve the problem of democracy," but he argues that, in any case, it is only in the collectivist movements that the future, democratic or not, will be worth living.

> A real question does exist here. Can a regime that socializes the economy avoid the total centralization of political power? How, under such political centralization, do you provide a material basis for a free press, trade unions, churches, and other institutions? And without autonomous institutions, how can the freedom of the individual be protected? For that matter, how can it even be defined? Freedom cannot be absolute: every society must define its notion of the proper balance between the claims of the individual and those of the community as a whole. Thus, a free society is one that places the burden of proof on those who would restrict the individual. It remains to be proven that a socialist society can be a free society. But then, it remains to be proven, notwithstanding the experience of the United States and precious few European countries, that democracy can sustain a meaningful freedom for more than the elite.
>
> * * * * *
>
> Capitalism did not need democracy to provide freedom, for it was concerned with the freedom of the few. Only lately and largely outside the United States did it come to accept democracy as a necessity, and then only under hard blows

from the Left. Socialism must solve the problem of democracy or lose freedom as well. But where outside the socialist and communist movements are these questions being fought out in a manner that promises a future worth having?[23]

CONCLUSION

In an insightful and, in its own way, touching evaluation of the capitalism-socialism debate, international law professor Richard Falk argues that the ultimate answer humans seek is not to be found in either ideology. Perhaps Falk's words will help inspire us to push beyond the comfortable confines of conventional political economy to a vision of life that embraces and surpasses the limits of economics and politics.

The traditional capitalism/socialism debate is a sham, quite irrelevant to our prospects as a civilization, mere words. The real challenge is whether we can summon the courage and imagination to find ways to reorganize our society around a sustainable economic, ecological, and political ethic that brings people in diverse national societies credible hope for "life, liberty, and the pursuit of happiness." A beginning, and yet no more or less than that, is to nourish feelings, thoughts, and actions around the central idea of being a citizen of the planet, as well as a citizen of a country, a member of a family, race, and religion. Some sense of global identity is, I believe, the only basis on which to achieve enough detachment from the destructive forces of the modern world to form a judgment about what needs to be done within the political arena.

This may sound sentimental and apolitical; yet at this historical moment it seems critical for some of us to make the effort to stand sufficiently aside to understand what is happening. . . . Both capitalism and socialism are fundamentally methods for organizing production to maximize efficiency of output and, thereby, to assure social benefit. To go on as if the comparative merits of these two secular ideologies are what matters most ignores the dramatic, urgent reality that neither ideology has led to societies which offer much human promise for the future. We need an ideology that probes beneath the debate about productive efficiency and asks, "What for?" Ours is a time to dream and work for a world that our grandchildren might enjoy and feel secure in; that is, a world that is stable, equitable, and hopeful. Such a quest requires a commitment to a process of change that extends beyond our lifetimes. Hence it is more a religious than a political enterprise, although it partakes of both.[24]

CHAPTER QUESTIONS

1. Critics accuse capitalist nations of fascism, imperialism, and slave trading.
   a. Cite a historical example of each in a capitalist state.
   b. Are those practices symptomatic of a flaw in capitalism or simply a flaw in human nature? Explain.

      c. Is socialism a more likely vehicle for avoiding the abuses of fascism, imperialism, and racial subjugation? Explain.

2. Many commentators point to capitalism's lack of a compelling philosophy, theology, or creed. Why has capitalism failed to develop the compelling ideological fervor and loyalty that has clearly been the case with collectivism?

3. It is often argued that many intellectuals (and, in particular, many college professors) actively criticize capitalism and support collectivism.

      a. Has that been your experience? Explain.

      b. If that assessment is accurate, how do you account for leftist inclinations among intellectuals?

4. As you noted in the readings, privatization is enjoying immense popularity.

      a. Make the arguments for and against turning our prisons and jails over to private enterprise.

      b. Would you favor a penal system operated for profit? Explain.

5. If we are fundamentally selfish, must we embrace capitalism as the most accurate and, therefore, most efficient expression of human nature? Explain.

6. Economist and jurist Richard Posner has suggested a free market in babies. Given that "production costs" are relatively low and the value of babies to childless people is high, Posner observed the possibilities for mutually beneficial transactions.

      a. Explain some of the advantages and disadvantages of a market in babies.

      b. Would you favor the legalization of the sale of babies? Explain.

7. Is capitalism a necessary condition for successful democracy? Or, put another way, in a democracy will increasing state control necessarily result in the destruction of that democracy? Explain.

8. Richard Falk argues for "some sense of global identity." Does capitalism enhance or impede the development of a world community? Explain.

9. Is the absence of the necessity of work as a means of survival "the kingdom of freedom" as Marx argued? If it were in our power, should we seek to abolish work born of necessity? Explain.

10. Explain the nature of a life free of nonvoluntary work. What purpose would replace necessity as the motivating force in our lives?

11. Socialist Michael Harrington argues for life "freed of the curse of money":

> [A]s long as access to goods and pleasures is rationed according to the possession of money, there is a pervasive venality, an invitation to miserliness and hostility to one's neighbor.[25]

Should we strive to make more and more goods and services "free"? Raise the competing arguments.

12. The great intellect Adolph Berle once said: "A day may come when national glory and prestige, perhaps even national safety, are best established by a country's being the most beautiful, the best socially organized, or culturally the most advanced in the world."[26]
    a. Is collectivism necessary to achieving Berle's goal? Explain.
    b. If faced with a choice, would most Americans opt for Berle's model or for a nation preeminent in consumer goods, sports, and general comfort? Explain.

13. The 1970s were often referred to as the "Me Decade," a period of self-absorption. Pollster Daniel Yankelovich predicted this selfishness would be replaced in the 1980s with an ethic of commitment:

    > The core idea of commitment is to make people less absorbed with self and to break through the iron age of self-centeredness. The new ethic of commitment is emerging in two chief forms of expression: a hunger for deeper personal relations and a yearning to belong to a community where people share many bonds in common. At the heart of the ethic of commitment is the moral intuition that the meaning of life lies in finding a commitment outside one's self.[27]

    a. We are at the end of the '80s. Evaluate the accuracy of Yankelovich's views.
    b. If Yankelovich is correct in his contention that we seek a greater sense of community and a commitment beyond self-interest, should we opt for capitalism or socialism? Explain.
    c. Why is selfishness often considered an evil?

14. In Sweden, poverty is effectively nonexistent. In America in 1987, 13.5 percent of the population had incomes below the government poverty line of $11,611 for a family of four. That is, approximately 32.5 million Americans, the equivalent of, for example, the combined populations of Minnesota, Iowa, Wisconsin, Illinois, and Michigan, led deprived economic lives.
    a. Is that condition alone sufficient justification for American adoption of the Swedish approach? Explain.
    b. It is generally assumed that giving citizens money to combat poverty reduces those citizens' incentive to work. Do you agree? Explain.
    c. As you leave college, if you were given only enough money to lift you above the poverty line, would your incentive to work be significantly reduced? Explain.
    d. Regardless of your personal viewpoint, make the argument that welfare does not materially reduce the incentive to work.

15. Distinguished economist Robert Lekachman, among others, has argued that a "moderate" level of unemployment is beneficial to the prosperous leaders of capitalism. He contends that a significant political/economic shift to the left is necessary if all Americans are to be employed and prosperous.

    a. Build Lekachman's argument.

    b. What are the strengths and weaknesses of his case?

16. It is often argued that collectivism would require a uniformity, a "sameness" that would destroy the individuality Americans prize.

    a. Are Americans notably independent and individualistic? Explain.

    b. Explore the argument that collectivism would actually enhance meaningful individualism.

17. A visitor to China during the Maoist period observed that the Chinese children appeared "more cooperative than competitive, more altruistic than selfish." Maoist training taught children to "share toys, love and help each other, and, of course, venerate Mao."

    a. Must we similarly curb our emphasis on competition? Explain.

    b. If so, what would spur us to greater achievements?

    c. Are we taught to "love and help each other"? Explain.

    d. Wouldn't a tie be the optimal result in all games? Explain.

18. Hilda Scott wrote a book to which she affixed the provocative title, *Does Socialism Liberate Women?*

    a. Answer her question. Explain.

    b. Are minority oppression and oppression of women inevitable by-products of capitalism? Explain.

19. In Wisconsin, members of the Old Order Amish religion declined to formally educate their children beyond the eighth grade. The U.S. Supreme Court held that their First Amendment right to freedom of religion was violated by the Wisconsin compulsory education statute, which required school attendance until the age of 16. Chief Justice Burger explained:

> They object to the high school, and higher education generally, because the values they teach are in marked variance with Amish values and the Amish way of life; they view secondary school education as an impermissible exposure of their children to a "worldly" influence in conflict with their beliefs. The high school tends to emphasize intellectual and scientific accomplishments, self-distinction, competitiveness, worldly success, and social life with other students. Amish society emphasizes informal learning-through-doing; a life of "goodness," rather than a life of intellect; wisdom, rather than technical knowledge; community welfare, rather than competition; and separation from, rather than integration with, contemporary worldly society.[28]

    a. Have the Amish taken the course we should all follow? Explain.

    b. Could we do so? Explain.

20. Irving Kristol built the argument that American society has given rise to a "new class"—scientists, teachers, bureaucrats—who are actively opposed to business and the capitalist approach. The new class consists of:

> [S]cientists, teachers and educational administrators, journalists and others in the communications industries, psychologists, social workers, those law-

yers and doctors who make their careers in the expanding public sector, city planners, the staffs of the larger foundations, the upper levels of the government bureaucracy. . . . It is basically suspicious of, and hostile to, the market precisely because the market is so vulgarly democratic—one dollar, one vote. . . . The "new class"—intelligent, educated, energetic— has little respect for such a commonplace civilization. It wishes to see its "ideals" more effectual than the market is likely to permit them to be.[29]

    a. Is Kristol's argument sound?

    b. Have you had experience with people in this new class? Explain.

21. In 1975, *Business Week* analyzed the then robust movement for egalitarianism (equality). It focused on John Rawls, author of *A Theory of Justice,* who argued that society seeks fairness, "and fairness means equality." Equality of opportunity is a delusion unless it produces equality of results. Hence, "to produce genuine equality of opportunity, society must give more attention to those with fewer native assets and to those born into less favorable social positions."[30]

    a. Complete economic equality would be a very expensive proposition and thus politically—and perhaps economically—unacceptable. What steps might be taken to increase economic equality without serious economic dislocations?

    b. Even if equality were practicable, would you support such a goal? Explain.

22. Distinguished economist Gary Becker argues for a free market approach to America's immigration difficulties:

> In a market economy, the way to deal with excess demand for a product or service is to raise the price. This reduces the demand and stimulates the supply. I suggest that the United States adopt a similar approach to help solve its immigration problems. Under my proposal, anyone willing to pay a specified price could enter the United States immediately.[31]

Comment.

23. At Memorial Junior High in San Diego, students received 25 cents for each day of perfect attendance. The money (actually paper credits) was spent only for school-related goods dispensed in the school store. Initially the absentee rate dropped dramatically (6 percent to 2.8 percent), but in 38 subsequent months the improvement was modest (7 percent to 6.2 percent).[32]

    a. Evaluate the approach.

    b. Is the profit motive the key to improving the public sector generally? Explain.

24. Brandeis University professor of social policy David Gil has argued that capitalism has created a population dependent on wages and that the American family is a training ground to prepare the young to be "mindless wage slaves." Families must be sexist and authoritarian to prepare children to submit to command without question.[33] On the

other hand, John Hospers contends that we have all become wage slaves to the government.[34]

   a. Which view is more accurate? Why?

   b. Which is more ominous? Explain.

25. The Swedes, noted for their extreme tolerance of pornography, banned the movie *The Empire Strikes Back* (a sequel to *Star Wars*) for children under 15 years of age on the grounds that the movie was too violent and too frightening.

   a. Is this a false comparison? Explain.

   b. If not, do the divergent choices Sweden and America have made about the treatment of pornography and violence bear any relation to the economic systems adopted by the two societies? Explain.

   c. If you possessed the power to ban both pornography and *The Empire Strikes Back,* what would you do? Explain.

26. Cincinnati Reds manager Pete Rose was himself a great baseball star. His autograph is in demand among collectors. Many of those collectors treat baseball autographs as investment vehicles. Rose charges $8 per autograph when he attends baseball-card shows and other commercial ventures, but he says he never charges for his autograph if a fan simply catches him at a restaurant.

> "Why should I let somebody use me to make money and not make money myself?" asked Rose, who was featured at the baseball-card show at the Kentucky Fair and Exposition Center.
>
>   * * * * *
>
>   "If I thought everyone here was just a little kid who wanted my autograph, I wouldn't charge," Rose said as he signed another baseball. "But this is such a big business."[35]

In your opinion, is Rose's position an example of capitalist excess, or is he quite proper in charging for his autograph? Explain.

27. At this writing in 1988, the price of a first-class stamp has reached 25 cents. Since 1968, first-class rates have quadrupled. Had rates been tied to inflation, a first-class stamp in 1988 would have been priced at about 18 cents.[36] As you read, President Reagan's Commission on Privatization advocated a gradual end to the present Postal Service monopoly.

   a. Who might be harmed by such a change?

   b. Would you favor that change? Explain.

28. George C. Lodge and Ezra Vogel recently edited a book entitled *Ideology and National Competitiveness: An Analysis of Nine Countries,* in which they compared the industrial policies of those nine nations.[37] Lodge and Vogel argue that the success of Japan and several Southeast Asian nations in the international market is at least partially attributable to those nations' communitarian approaches to life. On the

other hand, they argue that the emphasis on individualism in the United States has harmed our ability to be internationally competitive. Do you agree with Lodge and Vogel? Explain. See Professor Jeffrey A. Hart's review of the book (*Business Horizons* 30, no. 6, November/ December 1987, p. 83).

NOTES

1. Irving Kristol, "When Virtue Loses All Her Loveliness—Some Reflections on Capitalism and 'The Free Society,'" in *Capitalism Today,* ed. Daniel Bell and Irving Kristol (New York: New American Library, 1971), p. 15.

2. Alvin Rabushka, *Hong Kong—A Study in Economic Freedom* (Chicago: University of Chicago Press, 1979), pp. 102–3.

3. See, for example, George Hicks, "The Selling Out of Hong Kong," *The Wall Street Journal,* June 15, 1987, p. 23.

4. "Private Business Finds a Growing Niche Providing Government Services," *The Wall Street Journal,* August 27, 1987, p. 1.

5. Ibid.

6. "Want to Buy a Fire Dept.?" *Newsweek,* April 25, 1983, p. 55.

7. Ibid., p. 56.

8. Associated Press, "Going Private," *Waterloo Courier,* March 18, 1988, p. A2.

9. "For-Profit U.S. Hospitals Are Found to Be More Costly," *Des Moines Register,* June 5, 1986, p. 4A.

10. Jonathan N. Goodrich, "Privatization in America," *Business Horizons* 31, no. 1 (January/February 1988), pp. 11, 16.

11. The Marxist interpretation given here relies heavily on William Ebenstein and Edwin Fogelman, *Today's Isms,* 8th ed. (Englewood Cliffs, N.J.: Prentice-Hall, 1980), p. 7.

12. The materials in this paragraph are drawn from Clair Wilcox, Willis Weatherford, Holland Hunter, and Morton Baratz, *Economies of the World Today,* 3rd ed. (New York: Harcourt Brace Jovanovich, 1976), p. 2.

13. R. W. Apple, Jr., "Swedes Feel They're Lumped Together in 'National Blandness,'" reprinted from *The New York Times* in *Lexington Leader,* July 26, 1978, p. A-15.

14. Arthur Schlesinger, Jr., "At Last: Capitalistic Communism," *The Wall Street Journal,* August 4, 1987, p. 32. Reprinted by permission of *The Wall Street Journal,* © Dow Jones & Company, Inc. 1987. ALL RIGHTS RESERVED.

15. Ben-Chieh Liu, "Economic Growth and Quality of Life," *American Journal of Economics and Sociology* 39, no. 1 (January 1980), p. 1.

16. *The New Book of World Rankings* (New York: Facts on File, 1984), p. 331.

17. Gene Koretz, "Infant Mortality Is Surprisingly High in the U.S.," *Business Week,* June 20, 1988, p. 32.

18. Associated Press, "U.S. Infant Mortality Rate High," *Waterloo Courier,* February 3, 1987, p. A-3.

19. *World Bank Atlas* (Washington, D.C.: International Bank for Reconstruction and Development/The World Bank, 1987), pp. 6–11.

20. Lester Thurow, *The Zero-Sum Society* (New York: Penguin Books, 1981), p. 7. Copyright © 1980, Basic Books, Inc.

21. Ibid, pp. 7–8.
22. "Capitalism, Socialism, and Democracy—A Symposium," *Commentary* 65, no. 4 (April 1978), p. 29.
23. Ibid., pp. 41–42.
24. Richard Falk, "A Sham Debate," in "Is Capitalism on the Way Out?" ed. Leonard Orr, *Business and Society Review* 28 (Winter 1978–79), pp. 4–6.
25. Michael Harrington, "Why We Need Socialism in America," *Dissent,* May–June 1970, pp. 240, 286.
26. Adolph Berle, *Power* (New York: Harcourt Brace Jovanovich, 1969), pp. 258–59.
27. Daniel Yankelovich, "Are You Taking Risks with Your Life?" *Parade,* May 24, 1981, pp. 4, 5.
28. *Wisconsin* v. *Yoder,* 406 U.S. 205 (1972).
29. Irving Kristol, "Business and the 'New Class,' " *The Wall Street Journal,* May 19, 1975, p. 8.
30. "Egalitarianism: Threat to a Free Market," *Business Week,* December 1, 1975, pp. 62, 64.
31. Gary Becker, "Why Not Let Immigrants Pay for Speedy Entry?" *Business Week,* March 2, 1987, p. 20.
32. "In California: Pay-As-You-Go Pedagogy," *Time,* May 11, 1981, p. 8.
33. "Capitalism Is Seen as Villain Turning Work into a Chore," The State University of Iowa *Spectator,* March 1980, p. 4.
34. John Hospers, "Free Enterprise as the Embodiment of Justice," in *Ethics, Free Enterprise and Public Policy,* ed. Richard DeGeorge and Joseph Pichler (New York: Oxford University Press, 1978), pp. 70, 84.
35. "Sports Stars Charge Money for Signing Their Autographs," (University of) *Kentucky Kernel,* April 4, 1988, p. 7.
36. "Partial Post," *The Wall Street Journal,* March 16, 1988, p. 30.
37. George C. Lodge and Ezra Vogel, *Ideology and National Competitiveness: An Analysis of Nine Countries* (Boston: Harvard Business School, 1987).

Ethics

Vice is a monster of so frightful mien,
As, to be hated, needs but to be seen;
Yet seen too oft, familiar with her face,
We first endure, then pity, then embrace.

Alexander Pope

Part One—Foundations of Ethical Theory

Chapter 1 explored the capitalism-collectivism economic continuum to remind the reader of the fundamentals of political economy and to encourage some judgment about the degree of government intervention necessary to achieve a desirable relationship between business and the balance of society. That is, might we rely on the market alone to "regulate" the course of business, or must we interpose some degree of government regulation?

Chapter 2 introduces self-regulation as a technique for achieving a more desirable role for business in society. To what extent can we rely on the ethical quality, the morality, of the businessperson and the business organization to govern the path of commerce? If we felt full faith in the free market and the ethical quality of individuals and companies, regulation by law would be reduced at least to those minimums suggested in Chapter 1 by Ayn Rand.

No effort will be made to *teach ethics;* that is, the purpose here is not to improve the reader's "ethical quotient." Rather, the goal is to sensitize the reader to the ethical component of business life. Some sense of the ethical climate of business, some glimpse of the specific ethical problems facing the businessperson should be useful in assessing the role of ethics in the business decision-making equation and in evaluating the utility of ethics as a "regulator" of business behavior. The Edelman, McDonald's, and "Bubba" Smith cases that follow are apt illustrations of the complexities of ethics.

INTRODUCTION TO ETHICS:
1. ASHER EDELMAN AND THE "REAL WORLD"

Asher Edelman built a fortune and a heavy weight reputation by skillfully "raiding" corporations such as Burlington Industries. Edelman agreed to take his skills and insight as a takeover artist to the classroom—the classroom in the M.B.A. program at Columbia University in New York City. During the fall term, 1987, Edelman taught a course entitled "Corporate Raiding: The Art of War." Edelman's goal was to encourage students to take an entrepreneurial, "real world" view of business. The final exam in the course was a requirement to find a likely takeover target for Edelman's company. As is his customary practice in the business community, Edelman offered a $100,000 finder's fee to any student who suggested a company that Edelman then elected to buy. All was well until some weeks into the term, when a student not enrolled in the course complained. Dean John Burton of the Columbia Business School disapproved of the monetary incentive. Edelman explained that he had discussed the fee with the head of the finance department before commencing the course. Edelman proposed to extend the offer to all graduate business students and to deliver an additional $100,000 to the business school if he used a student idea. Burton maintained his opposition, and Edelman withdrew his offer. In a poll conducted by Edelman after Burton explained the decision to the class, only 1 of 14 students agreed with the dean's position. On the other hand, Alison Craiglow, publisher of the campus newspaper, the *Daily Spectator,* sided with Burton: "Business school profes-sors should teach students how to be ethical and how to be good managers, not how to be millionaires."[1] For his part, Burton was particularly disturbed by the size of the incentive. "The essence of academic study is the examination of ideas and concepts," Burton explained. "With a huge cash reward, the economic incentive becomes paramount."[2] Richard West, dean of the New York University graduate business school, agreed with Burton: "It's crucial that schools do their best to teach students not to think about just making money. It may be that some students in our schools may want to sell their souls to the devil. But we should not have the devil standing at the front of the classroom."[3]

Assume the position of Dean John Burton. How would you respond to such a situation? Would you regard the problem as one of ethics or merely a matter of academic judgment? Does a cash incentive violate the pursuit of ideas? Is such a fee more acceptable in a business school than in a divinity school? Are business schools failing their ethical duties to society if they merely teach about making money?

In general, how do we determine when economic rewards are acceptable incentives and when they are not? For example, would a parent act unethically in rewarding his/her grade school child with a quarter for each A earned in school? Put perhaps more vividly, is paying for a sexual relationship an unethical act if done in those locales where such arrangements are not unlawful?

INTRODUCTION TO ETHICS:
2. McDONALD'S AND PROTESTERS

On May 4, 1970, four students were shot to death and a number of individuals were injured when a unit of the Ohio National Guard fired into a group of demonstrators on the Kent State University campus in northeastern Ohio. The students were protesting the Nixon administration's Vietnam War policy, and particularly the so-called incursion of American troops in great numbers into Cambodia. Following the Kent State episode, college campuses around America were the scene of large, often violent, demonstrations against both the war and the student deaths. Buildings were burned on a number of campuses. At many institutions emotions were so strong that instruction was halted for the balance of the term. In that volatile climate, angry students at Southern Illinois University (SIU) in Carbondale briefly drew one of America's most successful enterprises, the McDonald's fast-food chain, into the controversy. On the day following the deaths at Kent State, some SIU demonstrators demanded that the American flag at the local McDonald's be lowered to half staff. The manager did so, but a passerby who happened to be acquainted with McDonald's chairman, Ray Kroc, noted the flag and phoned Kroc. Kroc immediately ordered the flag back to full mast, at which point the demonstrators returned and threatened to burn the building unless the flag was again lowered. The manager then phoned Fred Turner, president of McDonald's.[4]

Assume Turner's role. What advice would you give to the McDonald's manager? Is this decision one of ethics? What is the morally principled course of action? Or is the decision one of pragmatics? How can the building and student goodwill be preserved while meeting Kroc's express company policy? Are the ethical decision and the pragmatic decision one and the same in this instance?

INTRODUCTION TO ETHICS:
3. "BUBBA" SMITH AND ADVERTISING

Charles "Bubba" Smith, a massive and very successful football lineman for Michigan State University and three professional teams, worked for several years after his football career in commercials for a brewing company. The clever commercials were successful in capitalizing on Smith's reputation for particularly vigorous play by showing Smith, for example, tearing the tops off beer cans with his bare hands. As explained in the article that follows, Smith came to have doubts about the ethics of his role in advertising alcohol.

Filled-Up Bubba Smith Loses Taste for Lite Beer

Bubba Smith has sworn off booze. Not drinking it, but selling it.

Bubba never did drink, but he sold a ton of beer by making cute television ads. Not anymore. Bubba has kicked the habit.

Bubba Smith may be the first athlete ever, maybe the first person ever, to give up a very lucrative, stupendously easy and really amusing job making beer commercials, just because he decided it was wrong.

Here's how it happened.

"I went back to Michigan State for the homecoming parade last year," Bubba said. "I was the grand marshal and I was riding in the back seat of this car. The people were yelling, but they weren't saying, 'Go, State, go!' One side of the street was yelling, 'Tastes great!' and the other side was yelling 'Less filling!'

"Then we go to the stadium. The older folks are yelling 'Kill, Bubba, kill!' But the students are yelling 'Tastes great! Less filling!' Everyone in the stands is drunk. It was like I was contributing to alcohol, and I don't drink. It made me realize I was doing something I didn't want to do.

"I loved doing the commercials, but I didn't like the effect it was having on a lot of little people. I'm talking about people in school. Kids would come up to me on the street and recite lines from my commercials, verbatim. They knew the lines better than I did. It was scary. Kids start to listen to things you say, you want to tell 'em something that is the truth.

"Doing those commercials, it's like me telling everyone in school, 'Hey, it's cool to have a Lite beer.' I'd go to places like Daytona Beach and Fort Lauderdale on spring breaks, and it was scary to see how drunk those kids were. It was fun talking to the fans, until you see people lying on the beach because they can't make it back to their room, or tearing up a city."

The obvious question is, why would a nondrinker like Bubba spend eight years making beer ads?

"Making those commercials, that was a joy to me," Bubba said. "I told myself I couldn't be doing nothing wrong. It seemed so innocent. You don't see things sometimes until you step back from it. Making those commercials, we were a team. It was like football, without the pain. That was an important part of my life, especially the [annual] reunion commercials. It would be five days of sheer laughter—at the shoot, after the shoot, every night."

When Bubba quit, the brewery went out and hired L. C. Greenwood, another huge, intimidating, black former football player who wears eyeglasses and a mustache. Bubba ripped the tops off beer cans. L. C. rips trees out of the ground.

"[The ad people] don't miss a beat," Bubba said.[5]

Were you in his position, would you do as Bubba Smith did in removing himself from the lucrative alcohol-advertising business? Is alcohol advertising unethical? Is such advertising unethical if directed exclusively to adults? Would you decline to work in or own a bar because of the harm that your product might do to others? What measure should we use to determine the degree of our personal responsibility for the conduct of others?

ETHICAL THEORY

Volumes of literature are devoted in general terms to the question of defining ethics. We cannot hope to advance that discussion here. Ethics, of course, involves judgments as to good and bad, right and wrong, and what ought to be. We seek to use reason in discovering how individuals ought to act. Business ethics refers to the measurement of business behavior based on standards of right and wrong, rather than relying entirely on principles of accounting and management. (In this discussion, morals will be treated as synonymous with ethics. Distinctions certainly are drawn between the two, but those distinctions are not vital for our purposes.)

Society has, in recent years, imposed dramatically expanded expectations on the business community. Meeting society's economic needs was once generally thought to be sufficient. Today, business is expected to contribute significantly to the solution of fundamental societal problems, such as pollution, discrimination, and poverty. For the firm, those demands have a clear moral component—business is to do what is "right" and "good." Of course, the individual businessperson feels the same ethical demands. Not only must the individual comply with the law, but he or she feels increasing pressure to seek out the "good" and the "right" in order to fulfill an honorable role in life. Finding and following the "right" course is not easy for any of us, but the difficulty may be particularly acute for the businessperson. He or she may feel compelled to use rather different standards on the job than in personal life. Indeed, it is often argued that personal ethics must be laid aside in favor of the organization's values. Intense scrutiny of business ethics is a recent phenomenon that has left the businessperson a bit at sea in an era of changing expectations. Although the law provides useful guideposts for minimum comportment, no firm moral theme has emerged. Therefore, when the businessperson is faced with a difficult decision, a common tactic is simply to do what he or she takes to be correct at any given moment. Indeed, in one survey of ethical views in business, 50 percent of the respondents indicated that the word *ethical* meant "what my feelings tell me is right."[6] That view strikes at ethical absolutes and argues that all moral principles are relative depending on the environmental circumstances. However, such a philosophy, without careful contemplation of the competing considerations, seems an elusive and shifting foundation on which to build an ethical perspective. Thus, a brief survey of some of the primary systems of ethical analysis may be helpful. A sense of the history of ethics will emerge, and the reader will be afforded an introductory sense of the analytical tools that would assist in reaching a reasoned ethical posture.[7]

Fletcher's Moral Continuum

As scholar Joseph Fletcher expressed it, there are three broad routes to moral decision making.[8] They represent the two extremes and the midpoint on an "ethical continuum": (*a*) the legalistic—one extreme, (*b*) the antinomian—the opposite extreme, and (*c*) the situational—the middle ground.

Legalism. Here the absolute letter of the law controls. Rules abound. And those rules are not mere guidelines; rather, they are directives to be followed. All the principal Western religions have operated on a foundation of specified legalisms, including, for example, the Ten Commandments. Imposed on that foundation are layers of statutes and codes designed to specify with particularity the "right" course of conduct.

Antinomianism. This philosophy rejects all reliance on rules, laws, maxims, credos, and the like. Every situation is unique. One must call on the elements of the situation itself to reach an ethical decision. Thus all such decisions are reached on an ad hoc, impromptu basis.

The philosophy of *existentialism,* propounded most notably by Jean-Paul Sartre, is perhaps the most powerful expression of antinomianist principles. Existentialists believe standards of conduct cannot be rationally justified, and no actions are inherently right or wrong. Thus each person may reach his or her own choice about ethical principles. That view finds its roots in the notion that humans are only what we will ourselves to be. If God does not exist, there can be no human nature, because there is no one to conceive that nature.

In Sartre's famous interpretation, existence precedes essence. First humans exist, then we individually define what we are—our essence. Therefore, each of us is free, with no rules to turn to for guidance. Just as we all choose our own natures, so must we choose our own ethical precepts. Moral responsibility belongs to each of us individually.

Situationalism. Fletcher argues for a middle ground built on maximizing Christian love or *agape* (AH-gah-pay). An ethical decision is one that produces the greatest quantity of love. Thus, the emphasis is on leading a life of loving care as exemplified by Jesus. To the situationist, reason is the route to ethical judgment, but rules are not ignored:

> The situationist enters into every decision-making situation fully armed with the ethical maxims of his community and its heritage, and he treats them with respect as illuminators of his problems. Just the same he is prepared in any situation to compromise them or set them aside *in the situation* if love seems better served by doing so.[9]

Thus rules and reason play a role in discovering the decision most in keeping with Christian love.

Teleology or Deontology—An Overview

Space constraints dictate the omission of a variety of contending formulations; namely, ethical relativism, hedonism, and pragmatism. Fletcher's moral continuum operates, for our purposes, as a broad system of classification. An alternative classification is that of teleological and deontological ethics. *Teleological ethical systems* emphasize the end, the product, the consequences of a decision. That is, the morality of a decision is determined by measuring the probable outcome. A morally correct decision is one that produces the greatest good. The teleological approach calls for reaching moral decisions by weighing the nonmoral consequences of an action. To repeat, for the teleologist the end is primary.

To the deontologist, principle is primary and consequence is secondary or even irrelevant. Maximizing right rather than good is the deontological standard. The deontologist might well refuse to lie even if doing so would maximize good. *Deontology,* derived from the Greek word meaning *duty,* is directed toward what ought to be, toward what is right. Relationships among people are important because they give rise to duties. A father may be morally committed to saving his son from a burning building, rather than saving another person who might well do more total good for society. Similarly, deontology considers motives. For example, why a crime was committed may be more important than the actual consequences of the crime.

The distinction here is critical. Are we to guide our behavior in terms of rational evaluations of the consequences of our acts, or are we to shape our conduct in terms of duty and principle—that which ought to be? To clarify these differences, we will look briefly at three ethical philosophies that illustrate the nature of the teleological-deontological debate.

Teleology

Egoism.   Egoists make the universal claim that all humans act to maximize their self-interest. Every act is selfish. Concern for the self always exceeds concern for others. Even when an act (e.g., charity) appears to have been undertaken for the primary benefit of another, that act is necessarily an effort toward the maximization of self-interest. Thus, ethical conduct is measured by the degree to which the moral decision advances the self-interest of the decision maker. It is important to note that the egoist is not merely a self-indulgent hedonist, immediately embracing short-term pleasure. Rather the egoist thesis calls for the discipline to do what ought to be done; that is, to achieve the degree of self-discipline necessary to maximize one's long-term self-interest.

Utilitarianism.   In reaching an ethical decision, good is to be weighed against evil. A decision that maximizes the ratio of good over evil for all those concerned is the ethical course. Jeremy Bentham (1748–1832) and John Stuart Mill (1806–1873) were the chief intellectual forces in the development of utilitarianism. Their views and those of other utilitarian philosophers were not entirely consistent. As a result at least two branches of utilitarianism have developed. According to *act-utilitarianism,* one's goal is to identify the consequences of a particular act to determine whether it is right or wrong. *Rule-utilitarianism* requires one to adhere to all the rules of conduct by which society reaps the greatest value. Thus the rule-utilitarian may be forced to shun a particular act that would result in greater immediate good (punishing a guilty person whose constitutional rights have been violated) in favor of upholding a broader rule that results in the greater total good over time (maintaining constitutional principles by freeing the guilty person). In sum, the principle to be followed for the utilitarian is the greatest good for the greatest number.

Deontology

Formalism. The German philosopher Immanuel Kant (1724–1804) developed perhaps the most persuasive and fully articulated vision of ethics as measured not by consequence (teleological) but by the rightness of rules. In this formalistic view of ethics, the rightness of an act depends little (or, in Kant's view, not at all) on the results of the act. Kant believed in the key moral concept of "the good will." The moral person is a person of good will, and that person renders ethical decisions based on what is right, regardless of the consequences of the decision. Moral worth springs from one's decision to discharge one's duty. Thus, the student who refuses to cheat on exams is morally worthy if his or her decision springs from duty, but morally unworthy if the decision is merely one born of self-interest, such as fear of being caught.

How does the person of good will know what is right? Here Kant propounded the *categorical imperative,* the notion that every person should act on only those principles that he or she, as a rational person, would prescribe as universal laws to be applied to the whole of humankind. A moral rule is "categorical" rather than "hypothetical" in that its prescriptive force is independent of its consequences. The rule guides us independent of the ends we seek. Kant believed that every rational creature can act according to his or her categorical imperative, because all such persons have "autonomous, self-legislating wills" that permit them to formulate and act on their own systems of rules. To Kant, what is right for one is right for all, and each of us can discover that "right" by exercising our rational faculties.

At this point it would not be surprising for the reader to be muttering a not-so-polite "So what?" As always, theory must face the test of reality. The bulk of that testing will be left to the reader. Consider again the position of the president of McDonald's receiving a call for immediate advice from the Carbondale manager threatened by mob violence. Or reflect further on Asher Edelman's $100,000 offer to his Columbia students. Or Bubba Smith's disassociation with beer advertising. Apply each philosophy articulated here to those situations. The conclusions will be strikingly dissimilar. The choices, of course, remain those of the decision maker, but a foundation in ethical theory clarifies the alternatives. For example, how would a formalist adhering to Kantian views respond to the contemporary debate (discussed later in this chapter) regarding the morality of American businesspersons paying bribes and kickbacks to secure contracts abroad? Remember the test is that of the categorical imperative: Is the moral rule one that the businessperson would prescribe as a universal law to be applied to all humans? If one accepts Kant's views, that brief exercise substantially clarifies the ethics of bribery regardless of the customs of the host country.

Questions

1. Some commentators decry what they take to be a growing sense of moral uncertainty in America. *U.S. News & World Report* explains:

   > Perhaps more important, heterogeneous 20th-century America has grown cautious about making value judgments. "[There is] a growing degree of cynicism and sophistication in our society," says Jody Powell, former press secretary to Jimmy Carter, "a sense that all things are relative and that nothing is absolutely right or wrong." When a New York City student last year turned in a purse she had found—complete with $1,000 in cash—not a single school official would congratulate her on her virtue. As her teacher explained, "If I come from a position of what is right and wrong, then I am not their counselor." The apparent translation: We no longer believe in black and white, only shades of gray.[10]

   a. Is moral relativism a threat to the nation's moral health? Explain.
   b. Is lying always wrong? Explain.

2. After years of investigation based on interviews with adults and children, psychologist Lawrence Kohlberg developed a theory of moral development holding that humans proceed through six stages before reaching moral maturity. Kohlberg built his theory from the interviewees' responses to a series of moral dilemmas. For example (stated briefly), should you steal drugs if doing so is the only way to save your spouse's life? Kohlberg's six stages proceed as follows:

   > (1) Punishment and obedience. Avoid punishment. Accept the dictates of those in authority. (2) Self-gratification. Promote one's self-interest. (3) Morality based on securing the approval of others—peer pressure. (4) Law and order. Rule orientation; accepting external authority. (5) Social contract. Agreement between the individual and the state. More personal responsibility; less reliance on authority. (6) Moral autonomy. The adult chooses universal moral standards based on justice and fairness. Logic and consistency and internal decision making have replaced reliance on rules and external authority.
   >
   > Not all people reach level 6. Indeed, Kohlberg believed many people remain fixed at stages 3 and 4. In his view, much less than a majority reach stage 5.[11]

   a. Is Kohlberg's theory consistent with your own view of moral development? Explain.
   b. Rank your moral development using Kohlberg's scale.
   c. Another psychologist, Carol Gilligan, has argued that men and women have differing moral languages. Gilligan suggests women make moral decisions based on responsibility and caring, whereas moral decision making for males is founded in rules and justice. Comment.

Part Two—Foundations of Business Ethics

Suddenly the subject of ethics has become a hot topic, not merely for academics but for the whole of American society. In recent years the major news magazines have devoted their cover stories to ethical concerns. The headlines fairly scream for attention to the issue of fundamental flaws in the American character: "A Nation of Liars?"[12] "The Decline and Fall of Business Ethics,"[13] "What's Wrong—Hypocrisy, Betrayal, and Greed Unsettle the Nation's Soul."[14] The business community is searching its collective soul over allegations of rampant greed and proof of surprisingly commonplace criminal behavior, including a remarkable series of insider-trading scandals. In turn, the academic community is wondering where we went wrong and what we must do now to help ensure grace for the several hundred thousand business school graduates produced each year. As Professor David Vogel of the University of California, Berkeley, asked rather sardonically, "Could an Ethics Course Have Kept Ivan (Boesky) from Going Bad?"[15] Apparently, John Shad, ex-chair of the Securities and Exchange Commission, thinks so, because his recent large gift to the Harvard Business School will be the financial cornerstone of a $30 million program on ethics and leadership.[16] Shad expressed his continuing faith in both the securities industry and the wisdom of honesty:

> "At the S.E.C., we've necessarily focused on the negative side of things—on frauds and abuses," Mr. Shad said in a statement. "But every analysis still indicates that we have by far the best securities markets the world has ever known—the broadest, most active, and the fairest. They're certainly not perfect, and they should be improved. But these are truly extraordinary markets—a national asset. Over $50 billion of corporate and government securities change hands daily over the phone."
>
> . . . "This is a staggering volume, and it is conducted on the basis of mutual confidence and ethical conduct," he said. "The markets work *because* of integrity. They work *despite* the abuses."
>
> "I believe ethics pays, that it's smart to be ethical," added Mr. Shad. "I think that those who go for edges, like high rollers in Las Vegas, are ultimately wiped out."[17]

As expressed previously, ethics involves the quest, via reason, for that which is good and right, that which ought to be. For the businessperson the quest has become, in recent years, particularly trying. Public cynicism is substantial. One recent poll asked:[18]

How Would You Rate the Honesty and Ethical Standards of People in These Different Fields?		
	Very High or High	*Average*	*Low or Very Low*
Clergy	67%	26%	4%
Pharmacists	65%	30%	3%
Medical doctors	58%	33%	8%
College teachers	54%	35%	5%
Bankers	37%	51%	9%
Lawyers	27%	40%	30%
Business executives	23%	54%	18%
Congressmen	20%	49%	27%
Advertising practitioners	12%	42%	39%
Car salesmen	5%	32%	59%

Source: Reprinted with permission of the copyright holder, *The Gallup Poll.*

Let's begin to clarify this volatile picture by looking at a pair of scholarly analyses that address the ethical character of the American business community, generally.

Steiner and Steiner—The Roots of Business Ethics

Scholars George and John Steiner clarify the picture by identifying six primary sources of the business ethics construct.[19]

Genetic Inheritance.   Although the view remains theoretical, sociobiologists have in recent years amassed persuasive evidence and arguments suggesting that the evolutionary forces of natural selection influence the development of traits such as cooperation and altruism that lie at the core of our ethical systems. That is, those qualities of goodness often associated with ethical conduct may, in some measure, be a product of genetic traits strengthened over time by the evolutionary process.

Religion.   Via a rule orientation exemplified by the Golden Rule (or its variations in many religions) and the Ten Commandments, religious morality is clearly a primary force in shaping our societal ethics. The question here concerns the applicability of religious ethics to the business community. Could the Golden Rule serve as a universal, practical, helpful standard for the businessperson's conduct?

Philosophical Systems.   To the Epicureans the quantity of pleasure to be derived from an act was the essential measure of its goodness. The Stoics, like the Puritans and many contemporary Americans, advocated a disciplined, hard-working, thrifty lifestyle. These philosophies and others, like those cited earlier, have been instrumental in our society's moral development.

Cultural Experience.   Here the Steiners refer to the rules, customs, and standards transmitted from generation to generation as guidelines for appropriate conduct. Individual values are shaped in large measure by the norms of the society.

The Legal System.   Laws represent a rough approximation of society's ethical standards. Thus, the law serves to educate us about the ethical course in life. The law does not and, most would agree, should not be treated as a vehicle for expressing all of society's ethical preferences. Rather, the law is an ever-changing approximation of current perceptions of right and wrong.

Codes of Conduct.   Steiner and Steiner identify three primary categories of such codes. Company codes, ordinarily brief and highly generalized, express broad expectations about fit conduct. Second, company operating policies often contain an ethical dimension. Express policy as to gifts, customer complaints, hiring policy, and the like serves as a guide to conduct and a shield by which the employee can avoid unethical advances from those outside the company. Third, many professional and industry associations have developed codes of ethics, such as the Affirmative Ethical Principles of the American Institute of Certified Public Accountants. In sum, codes of conduct seem to be a growing expression of the business community's sincere concern about ethics. However, the utility of such codes remains unsettled (see pp. 61–62).

Maccoby—Managerial Character

In his acclaimed study, *The Gamesman,* psychoanalyst Michael Maccoby identified four character types, which in his view accurately summarize the nature of those who operate America's major corporations.[20] Maccoby secured his information via interviews, dream analysis, and Rorschach tests involving 250 managers at 12 major companies. The first character type, the *craftsman,* is committed to the intrinsic satisfaction of his or her work and to the maintenance of his or her often traditional lifestyle. Though widely admired, the craftsman is unlikely to assume a commanding managerial role.

The *jungle fighter* is a competitor whose main goal is power. He or she is aggressive and may appear to be a productive leader, but he or she shuns teamwork and foments hostility, resulting in the eventual weakening of the organization.

The *company man* is the well-known stereotype of the individual beset with insecurity and relying for a sense of identity on his or her association with a powerful company.

The key figure in Maccoby's analysis is the *gamesman*. Gamesman characteristics, often in combination with others, were increasingly common as Maccoby reached higher into the corporate hierarchy. The gamesman seeks to influence change and is fascinated by risk. He or she views human relations, projects, and almost all other aspects of work as games to be mastered. He or she is fair and tough. Winning is the gamesman's primary goal.

In the jungle fighter and the company man, we recognize familiar threats to the business community's ethical integrity: the one rapacious in pursuit of power, the other fearful of maintaining individual principles in the face of organizational pressure. According to Maccoby, the emergence of the gamesman as the preeminently successful managerial model may pose the most serious, but subtle, ethical threat. The problem, expressed by Maccoby in a lyrical aphorism, is that the gamesman's work "develops his head but not his heart." The gamesman does not find satisfaction in ideology or ethical practice. Qualities of the "heart"—compassion, humor, friendliness, and loyalty—are not fulfilled by the gamesman's working experience. The gamesman is of the sort who sells that which sells best, regardless of the consequences. However, the gamesman is fair, unbigoted, and without hostility.

Maccoby's investigation is difficult to interpret in other than a pessimistic light. His analysis clearly does not depict a managerial class for which ethical principle is the dominant concern. Has Maccoby revealed a representative picture of corporate America? The question is not readily answered, but a number of studies do offer some empirical insight into the ethical climate of American business.

MANAGERIAL ETHICAL CONDUCT

Perhaps the most alarming evidence emerging from the various ethical inquiries is that a very high percentage of today's businesspeople are experiencing conflict between their personal standards and organizational demands. One survey of 1,498 managers across the nation found that 46 percent of the supervisors, 29 percent of the middle managers, and 21 percent of the executives had "sometimes" compromised their personal principles to meet an organizational demand.[21] Therefore, based on the experience of those managers, the odds are approximately one in two that the entry-level manager will feel compelled to violate his or her personal moral code in order to meet company goals. Professors Steven Brenner and Earl Molander in a 1977 study of *Harvard Business Review* subscribers found that 57 percent of the managers experienced a conflict between company interests and personal ethics.[22] On the other hand, the Brenner and Molander survey might be considered grounds for optimism in that the 57 percent figure is a substantial decline from the 75 percent affirmative response to a similar inquiry in a 1961 survey.[23]

Brenner and Molander found that the personal ethics–company interest conflict was most pronounced as to "honesty in communication" (22.3 percent reporting such a conflict) as well as "gifts, entertainment, and kickbacks" (12.3 percent). Interestingly, only 2.3 percent of the 1976 respondents reported conflicts as to "price collusion and pricing practice," while 12.5 percent of the 1961 sample reported such conflicts.[24]

Businesspeople are quite cynical about the ethical quality of the business community:

> Nearly a quarter of the 671 managers surveyed by McFeely Wackerle Jett, a search firm, contend ethics can impede a successful career; they think more than half the executives they know would bend the rules to get ahead. "I know of unethical acts at all levels of management," says one 50-year-old executive quoted in the study. "I have to do it in order to survive."
>
> Older executives generally think they are more principled than their younger counterparts. "Young M.B.A.s and lawyers are taught opportunism, cleverness, and cunning," says a 59-year-old vice president at a Midwest company. "Fairness and equity aren't given equal time or importance."
>
> *When confronted with an ethical decision, 44 percent of the executives consult themselves; 3 percent turn to God.*[25]

But perhaps these condemnations of managerial ethics merely reflect, if anything, some general weakness in the American character. For example, a recent survey of 245 scientists revealed that 1 in 3 suspected a colleague of falsifying scientific data.[26] More than 29 percent of the college students responding to a recent survey admitted to having cheated on a test during the previous year, and more than 51 percent admitted to having copied homework from another student.[27] And cheating in one form or another appears commonplace for employees whether at the managerial rank or not. Of special interest to college students are the responses of 18- to 29-year-old respondents among a Roper Poll of 1,000 Americans: 25 percent admitted to "lying to their boss or to colleagues," 28 percent admitted to "padding an expense account," and 46 percent admitted to "calling in sick when not."[28]

WHY DO SOME MANAGERS CHEAT?

We may begin by examining the value structures of those who manage. The German philosopher Edward Spranger identified six fundamental value orientations for all humans.[29] Based on Spranger's classifications, William Guth and Renato Tagiuri surveyed a group of top-level executives and arrived at the following ranking of average value scores:[30]

Value	Score
Economic	45
Theoretical	44
Political	44
Religious	39
Aesthetic	35
Social	33

Thus, managers appear to value more strongly the features of the pragmatic person than the sensitivities often associated with the lower three items. By contrast, ministers, for example, ranked the values in the following order: religious, social, aesthetic, political, theoretical, and economic.[31] In the same vein, Professor George England of the University of Minnesota found that 91 percent of 1,072 managers he surveyed believed trust to be important, but only 12 percent felt trust would help them in their careers. On the other hand, 75 percent of the managers thought ambition was important, and 73 percent thought it would help them become successful.[32]

As is the case with all of us, the businessperson brings to the job and develops on the job a set of values that is critical in determining his or her ethical course. Brenner and Molander asked their sample respondents what factors they considered influential in reaching unethical decisions. From the strongest to the weakest, the primary influences cited were (*a*) behavior of superiors, (*b*) formal policy or lack thereof, (*c*) industry ethical climate, (*d*) behavior of one's equals in the company, (*e*) society's moral climate, and (*f*) one's personal financial needs.[33] How striking that the first five of these factors all refer to forces external to the self. Are we so malleable and so wanting in personal conviction that we must find our moral truths in the view and behavior of others?

Brenner and Molander also inquired whether ethical standards had improved or declined in the previous 15 years. Then each respondent was asked to cite the one standard believed most responsible for the change. Among those who believed ethics to be in decline, the largest number (34 percent) cited declining societal standards, permissiveness, hedonism, and the like.

What are we left with? Why do some managers cheat? Why does anyone cheat? We see that many factors are at work, and that in itself is an important lesson. We are often inclined to attribute cheating merely to the desire for personal advancement. But that force, important though it is, does not fully explain cheating. Most of us wish to advance, but some of us are not willing to cheat. If you have behaved unethically at some point in your life, reflect now on the reasons. Perhaps we are all genetically predisposed to cheat in order to survive. Perhaps we are actually taught to cheat. Perhaps we simply have not fully understood the fundamental moral truths. Perhaps we all too willingly submit to the unethical example and wishes of others. Perhaps, as Karl Menninger has suggested, we have lost our sense of sin.[34]

THE CORPORATION AS A MORAL PERSON?

We have given a good deal of attention to the moral dilemma of the individual manager. At this point, an alternative conception should be considered. Many philosophers and commentators have now embraced the notion of the corporation as a person in the fullest sense of the word. Of course, the corporation has long been treated as a person of sorts in the eyes of the law. We can legitimately hold the corporation legally blameworthy for employee wrongs. But can we attribute moral responsibility to the corporation? Ordinarily we consider an individual morally responsible for act or event X only (1) if the person did X or caused X to occur and (2) if the person's conduct was intentional. Does a corporation ever do or cause any event, or are all so-called corporate acts really the decisions of an individual or individuals? And even if a corporation could act, could it do so intentionally? In a sense, can a corporation think?

How might a corporation be thought of as a fully functioning moral being? Philosopher Peter French is perhaps the leading proponent of the corporate moral personhood notion.[35] For our purposes, the theory begins with what French calls the Corporate Internal Decision Structure (CID Structure), by which he means (1) an organizational system of decision making—the organizational chart and (2) a set of procedural and policy rules. Via the CID Structure, the judgments and actions of the individual managers, officers, and directors are "processed," and those actions and judgments become the will of the corporation. Thus the corporate action process parallels that of humans. To French, the corporation displays the characteristics necessary for intentional conduct, hence his view of the corporation as a moral person. (French's argument goes on in a much more detailed and sophisticated fashion, but this glimpse will suffice here.) Many philosophers support French's position. Many differ. The critics' arguments are multiple, but at bottom the corporation, to them, does not appear to be a person. That is, even though a corporation may be *analogous* to a person, it is not necessarily *identical* to a person. For example, do corporations possess all of the rights of a person (e.g., the right to life)?[36]

Even if a corporation can be treated as a moral person, should we want to do so? We might answer yes because, in the event of wrongdoing, we could avoid the nearly impossible task of finding the guilty party within the corporate maze. Assigning individual responsibility for actions springing from the corporate decision-making structure frequently defies our principles of legal liability. Why not simply place the blame on the organization? But if we were to do so, would we somehow depreciate perhaps the central moral precept in our society; that is, the notion that each of us must accept responsibility for our actions? Would individual morality shrink if we accepted the theory of corporate moral personhood? Or is the argument moot in the sense that we already regard corporations as persons? When Ford builds a faulty auto, do we assign blame to the organization?

Questions

1. Does a corporation have a conscience? Explain. See Kenneth Goodpaster and John B. Matthews, Jr., "Can a Corporation Have a Conscience?" *Harvard Business Review,* January–February 1982, p. 136.
2. Saul Gellerman, dean of the University of Dallas Graduate School of Management, speculated about why managers who are normally good, decent people would occasionally engage in unethical conduct. Gellerman attributes the problem in part to four rationalizations. For example, he believes managers often "rationalize" their wrongdoing by convincing themselves that they will not be caught. Identify other rationalizations that permit good managers to do bad deeds. See Saul Gellerman, "Why 'Good' Managers Make Bad Ethical Choices," *Harvard Business Review,* July–August 1986, p. 85.
3. Business schools are giving increasing attention to ethics. Will that attention make a difference in the ethical quality of actual business practice? Professor David Vogel put the issue this way in the aforementioned *Wall Street Journal* commentary entitled "Could an Ethics Course Have Kept Ivan [inside trader Ivan Boesky] from Going Bad?":

> Before we set about reforming the nation's businesses through its business schools, we might want to reflect more carefully on the relationship between these two institutions. Does anyone believe that if Mr. Levine or Mr. Siegel [inside traders] had been exposed to a few lectures, or even a course, on business ethics they would have been better able to resist the temptation to benefit financially from insider information?[37]

What value, if any, is likely to be derived from the study of ethics in business schools?

Part Three—Business Ethics in Practice

PRESSURE TO CHEAT

Having established a general ethical foundation theoretically and practically, it is fitting now to turn to the pragmatics of dealing with specific ethical quandaries. The organization committed to ethical quality may be able to implement some structures and procedures to encourage decency. Corporate codes of conduct are probably the most commonly employed tool. Three out of four respondents to a survey of American corporations indicated the use of an employee code of conduct. Almost all large corporations have such a code, while the percentage declines substantially for mid-sized (75 percent) and smaller (40 percent) firms.[38] Another survey ranked the "14 most frequently prohibited employee behaviors." The most commonly prohibited behaviors were extortion, gifts, and kickbacks, which were included in 67 percent of the codes. Others cited conflicts of interest (65 percent), illegal political payments (59 percent), moonlighting (25 percent), and fraud and deception (11 percent).[39]

However, recent evidence suggests the codes may actually contribute to ethical problems. Professor William Frederick of the University of Pittsburg argues that the "culprit is not personal values but corporate culture."[40] Professor Frederick points to studies demonstrating that corporations with codes of ethics are actually cited by federal agencies more frequently than those without such codes. And Frederick argues that the codes themselves characteristically emphasize conduct that strengthens the company's profit picture. As exhibited in the table, company codes

---

What Company Codes of Conduct Stress

A study of 202 corporate codes of conduct found these subjects included at least 75 percent of the time and, similarly, found these subjects not mentioned at least 75 percent of the time.

Included	Frequency	Not Included	Frequency
Relations with U.S. government	86.6%	Personal character matters	93.6%
Customer/supplier relations	86.1	Product safety	91.0
Political contributions	84.7	Environmental affairs	87.1
Conflicts of interest	75.3	Product quality	78.7
Honest books or records	75.3	Civic and community affairs	75.2

Sources: William Frederick and James Weber, University of Pittsburgh; Marilynn Cash Mathews, Washington State University.

normally ignore the firm's role in a variety of pressing social issues.[41] In sum, Frederick's important, data-based study lends scientific support to the view that company goals often have the effect of submerging personal values, with the result that otherwise upright employees engage in wrongful conduct to meet the needs of the company.

The case that follows exposes the competing, real-life forces that sometimes cloud seemingly clear-cut issues of right and wrong. As you read, consider whether a code of conduct would have effectively combated the misdeeds recounted here.

THE B. F. GOODRICH CASE[42]

On June 18, 1967, the Ling-Temco-Vought (LTV) Aerospace Corporation placed an order with B. F. Goodrich for 202 brake assemblies for a new Air Force light attack plane, the A–7D. The contract offered B. F. Goodrich an opportunity to get back in the good graces of LTV after 10 years of some unease. For Kermit Vandivier, as technical writer, the contract marked the beginning of an incident that would eventually end his career at Goodrich. The new brake for the A–7D was special because it contained only four disks (or rotors) and weighed only 106 pounds. Aircraft weight is of primary concern because the lighter the plane, the more payload it can carry. The brake was designed by John Warren, a project engineer at Goodrich for seven years. His assistant and the man whose job it was to test the brake was 26-year-old Searle Lawson, one year out of college and six months with Goodrich. Kermit Vandivier, age 42, a high school graduate with seven children, was the technical writer who was to assist Lawson in the preparation of the data for the final report on the brake.[43]

What follows is actual testimony taken from the hearing before the Subcommittee on Economy in Government of the Joint Economic Committee of the 91st Congress on August 13, 1969. The hearing was called to investigate the charges made by Vandivier and Lawson that they falsified and altered data in the A–7D qualification report on orders from their superiors at the B. F. Goodrich plant in Troy, Ohio. The committee chairman was Senator William Proxmire of Wisconsin.

[The testimony that follows has been edited—Author.]

1. Testimony of Kermit Vandivier

In the early part of 1967, the B. F. Goodrich Wheel & Brake Plant at Troy, Ohio, received an order from the Ling-Temco-Vought Co. of Dallas, Texas, to supply wheels and brakes for the A–7D aircraft, built by LTV for the Air Force.

The tests on the wheels and brakes were to be conducted in accordance with the requirements of military specification[s.]

The wheels were successfully tested to the specified requirements, but the brake, manufactured by Goodrich, was unable to meet the required tests.

During the first few attempts to qualify the brake to the dynamic tests, the brake ran out of lining material after a few stops had been completed, and the tests were terminated. Attempts were made to secure a lining material that would hold up during the grueling 51-stop test, but to no avail.

On the morning of April 11, Richard Gloor, who was the test engineer assigned to the A–7D project, came to me and told me he had discovered that some time during the previous 24 hours, instrumentation used to record brake pressure had *deliberately* been miscalibrated.

Mr. Gloor further told me he had questioned instrumentation personnel about the miscalibration and had been told they were asked to do so by Searle Lawson, a design engineer on the A–7D.

I subsequently questioned Lawson, who admitted he had ordered the instruments miscalibrated at the direction of a superior.

Upon examining the log sheets kept by laboratory personnel, I found that other violations of the test specifications had occurred.

For example, after some of the overload stops, the brake had been disassembled and the three stators or stationary members of the brake had been taken to the plant toolroom for rework, and, during an earlier part of the test, the position of elements within the brake had been reversed in order to more evenly distribute the lining wear.

Additionally, instead of braking the dynamometer to a complete stop as required by military specifications, pressure was released when the wheel and brake speed had decelerated to 10 miles per hour.

The reason for this, I was later told, was that the brakes were experiencing severe vibrations near the end of the stops, causing excessive lining wear and general deterioration of the brake.

All of these incidents were in clear violation of military specifications and general industry practice.

I reported these violations to the test lab supervisor, Mr. Ralph Gretzinger, who reprimanded instrumentation personnel and stated that under no circumstances would intentional miscalibration of instruments be tolerated.

As for the other discrepancies noted in test procedures, he said he was aware they were happening but that as far as he was concerned the tests could not, in view of the way they were being conducted, be classified as qualification tests.

Later that same day, the worn-brake, maximum energy stop was conducted on the brake. The brake was landed at a speed of 161 MPH and the pressure was applied. The dynamometer rolled a distance of 16,800 *feet* before coming to rest. The elapsed stopping *time was 141 seconds*. By computation, this stop time shows the aircraft would have traveled over 3 miles before stopping.

Within a few days, a typewritten copy of the test logs of test T–1867 was sent to LTV in order to assure LTV that a qualified brake was almost ready for delivery.

Virtually every entry in this so-called copy of the test logs was drastically altered. As an example, the stop time for the worn-brake, maximum energy stop was changed from 141 seconds to a mere 46.8 seconds.

On May 2, 1968, the 14th attempt to qualify the brakes was begun, and Mr. Lawson told me that he had been informed by both Mr. Robert Sink, project manager at Goodrich, and Mr. Russel Van Horn, projects manager at Goodrich, that "Regardless of what the brake does on test, we're going to qualify it."

During this latest and final attempt to qualify the four-rotor brake, the same illegal procedures were used as had been used on attempt no. 13. Again, after 30 stops had been completed, the positions of the friction members of the brake were reversed in order to more evenly distribute wear.

After each stop, the wheel was removed from the brake and the accumulated dust was blown out.

During each stop, pressure was released when the deceleration had reached 10 miles per hour.

By these and other irregular procedures the brake was nursed along until the 45 normal energy stops had been completed, but by this time the friction surfaces of the brakes were almost bare; that is, there was virtually no lining left on the brake.

While these tests were being conducted, I was asked by Mr. Lawson to begin writing a qualification report for the brake. I flatly refused and told Mr. Gretzinger, the lab supervisor, who was my superior, that I could not write such a report because the brake had not been qualified.

He agreed and he said that no one in the laboratory was going to issue such a report unless a brake was actually qualified in accordance with the specification and using standard operating procedures.

He said that he would speak to his own supervisor, the manager of the technical services section, Mr. Russell Line, and get the matter settled at once.

He consulted Mr. Line and assured me that both had concurred in the decision not to write a qualification report.

I explained to Lawson that I had been told not to write the report, and that the only way such a report could be written was to falsify test data.

Mr. Lawson said he was well aware of what was required, but that he had been ordered to get a report written, regardless of how or what had to be done.

He stated if I would not write the report he would have to, and he asked if I would help him gather the test data and draw up the various engineering curves and graphic displays which are normally included in a report.

I asked Mr. Gretzinger, my superior, if this was all right, and he agreed, as long as I was only assisting in the preparation of the data.

Both Lawson and I worked on the elaborate curves and logs in the report for nearly a month. During this time we both frankly discussed the moral aspects of what we were doing, and we agreed that our actions were unethical and probably illegal.

Several times during that month I discussed the A–7D testing with Mr. Line, and asked him to consult his superiors in Akron, in order to prevent a false qualification report from being issued.

Mr. Line declined to do so and advised me that it would be wise to just do my work and keep quiet.

I told him of the extensive irregularities during testing and suggested that the brake was actually dangerous and, if allowed to be installed on an aircraft, might cause an accident.

I asked Mr. Line if his conscience would hurt him if such a thing caused the death of a pilot, and this is when he replied I was worrying about too many things that did not concern me and advised me to "do what you're told."

About the first of June 1968, Mr. Gretzinger asked if I were finished with the graphic data and said he had been advised by the chief engineer, Mr. H. C. Sunderman, that when the data was finished it was to be delivered to him—Sunderman—and he would instruct someone in the engineering department to actually write the report.

Accordingly, when I had finished with the data, I gave it to Mr. Gretzinger, who immediately took it from the room. Within a few minutes, he was back and was obviously angry.

He said that Mr. Sunderman had told him no one in the engineering department had time to write the report and that we would have to do it ourselves.

At this point Mr. Line came into the room, demanding to know "What the hell is going on." Mr. Gretzinger explained the situation again and said he would not allow such a report to be issued by the lab.

Mr. Line then turned to me and said he was "sick of hearing about this damned report. Write the ——— thing and shut up about it."

When he had left, Mr. Gretzinger and I discussed the position we were in, and Mr. Gretzinger said that we both should have resigned a long time ago. He added that there was little to do now except write the report.

Accordingly, I wrote the report, but in the conclusion, I stated that the brake had "not" met either the intent or the requirements of the specifications and was therefore "not" qualified.

When the final report was typewritten and ready for publication, the two "nots" in the conclusion had been eliminated, thereby changing the entire meaning of the conclusion.

As for the report itself, more than 80 false entries were made in the body of the report and in the logs.

Many, many of the elaborate engineering curves attached to the report were complete and total fabrications, based not on what had actually occurred, but on information which would fool both LTV and the Air Force.

The report was finally issued on June 5, 1968, and almost immediately, flights tests on the brake were begun at Edwards Air Force Base in California.

Mr. Lawson was sent by Goodrich to witness these tests, and when he returned, he described various mishaps which had occurred during the flight tests, and he expressed the opinion to me that the brake was dangerous.

That same afternoon, I contacted my attorney and after describing the situation to him, asked for his advice.

He advised me that, while I was technically not guilty of committing a fraud, I was certainly part of a conspiracy to defraud.

He further suggested a meeting with U.S. Attorney Roger Makely in Dayton, Ohio.

I agreed to this, and my attorney said he would arrange an appointment with the federal attorney.

I discussed my attorney's appraisal of our situation with Mr. Lawson, but I did not, at this time, tell him of the forthcoming visit with Mr. Makely.

Mr. Lawson said he would like to consult with my attorney, and I agreed to arrange this.

Shortly thereafter, Mr. Lawson went to the Dallas offices of LTV and, while he was gone, my attorney called and said that, upon advice of the U.S. attorney, he had arranged an interview with the Dayton office of the FBI.

I related the details of the A–7D qualification to Mr. Joseph Hathaway, of the FBI.

He asked if I could get Mr. Lawson to confirm my story, and I replied that I felt Mr. Lawson would surely do this.

Upon Mr. Lawson's return from Dallas, I asked him if he still wished to consult my attorney, and he answered, "I most certainly do."

Mr. Lawson and I went to the attorney's office, and Mr. Lawson was persuaded to speak to the FBI.

I wish to emphasize that at no time prior to Mr. Lawson's decision to speak to the FBI was he aware that I had already done so. His decision and mine were both the result of our individual actions.

Mr. Lawson related his own story to Mr. Hathaway, who advised us to keep our jobs and to tell no one that we had been to see him.

I might add here that he advised us that an investigation would be made.

About this time the Air Force demanded that Goodrich produce its raw data from the tests.

This Goodrich refused to do, claiming that the raw data was proprietary information.

Goodrich management decided that, since pressure was being applied by the Air Force, a conference should be arranged with LTV management and engineering staff.

A preconference meeting was set for Goodrich personnel in order to go over the questionable points in the report.

On Saturday, July 27, 1968, Mr. Robert Sink, Mr. Lawson, Mr. John Warren—A–7D project engineer—and I met and went over the discrepant items contained in the qualification report.

Each point was discussed at great length, and a list of approximately 40 separate discrepancies was compiled.

These, we were told by Mr. Sink, would be revealed to LTV personnel the following week.

However, by the time of the meeting with LTV, only a few days later, the list of discrepancies had been cut by Mr. Sink from 43 items to a mere 3.

Mr. Chairman, during this meeting Mr. Lawson took from the blackboard at the Goodrich conference room word for word listing of all these discrepancies.

The following two-month period was one of a constant running battle with LTV and the Air

Force, during which time the Air Force refused final approval of the qualification report and demanded a confrontation with Goodrich about supplying raw data.

On October 8, another meeting was held, again with Mr. Sink, Mr. Lawson, Mr. Warren, and myself present.

This was only one day prior to a meeting with Air Force personnel, and Mr. Sink said he had called the meeting "so that we are all coordinated and tell the same story."

He added that the Air Force had wanted to meet at the Goodrich plant, but that we—Goodrich—couldn't risk having them that close to the raw data.

"We don't want those guys in the plant," Mr. Sink said.

What happened at the meeting with the Air Force, I do not know. I did not attend.

On October 18, I submitted my resignation to Goodrich effective November 1.

[When asked what would motivate Goodrich to pass on an unqualified brake, Mr. Vandivier replied:]

I feel in the beginning stages of this program someone made a mistake, and refused to admit that mistake, and in order to hide his stupidity, or his ignorance, or his pride, or whatever it was, he simply covered up, you know, with more false statements, false information, and at the time it came time to deliver this brake, Goodrich was so far down the road there was nothing else to do.

They had no time to start over. I think it was a matter not of company policy but of company politics. I think that probably three of four persons within the Goodrich organization at Troy were responsible for this. I do not believe for a moment that the corporate officials in Akron knew that this was going on.

2. Testimony of Searle Lawson

Chairman Proxmire

When did you first become aware that there was a basic design fault in the four-rotor braking?

Mr. Lawson

I believe I became aware of it after the—I would say two or three qualification attempts, which would be in December of 1967 in that area.

Chairman Proxmire

What was this basic fault?

Mr. Lawson

The brake would not make the required number of stops as far as life of the brake. It just would not make it.

Chairman Proxmire

Did you inform your superiors of this fault?

Mr. Lawson

Yes, I did.

Chairman Proxmire

What was their response?

Mr. Lawson

Well, I was told—I wanted to change the design. That was my original request to them, to put more weight into the brake, and I was flatly refused by Mr. Warren. He said we would not put more weight in the brake.

Chairman Proxmire

Did either Mr. Sink or Mr. Van Horn ever tell you prior to the final qualification tests now what Mr. Vandivier told us "Regardless of what the brake does on the test we are going to qualify it."?

Mr. Lawson

Yes, sir.

Chairman Proxmire

What was your reaction to that statement?

Mr. Lawson

I don't know. I guess I was just dumbfounded. I did not say anything except OK.

Chairman Proxmire

Didn't it shock you that after all he is telling you that even if the brake does not meet the tests we are going to say it does, isn't that correct?

Mr. Lawson

That is correct. I don't know. I guess I had no recourse. I just accepted it.

Chairman Proxmire

Your recourse was to resign immediately?

Mr. Lawson

Yes.

Chairman Proxmire

Or take it to a higher authority. Could you have taken it to somebody else above Mr. Van Horn?

Mr. Lawson

I really didn't feel there was anybody above him that I could take it to.

Chairman Proxmire

Did you assist in the preparation of Q–6031— the Goodrich report under discussion here today—and did that report contain numerous false statements?

Mr. Lawson

There were numerous erroneous statements in there. I would not use the word false. I do not know under what test they were telling me to do this, I do not know what motivations they had, but there are changed statements in that qualifications report.

Chairman Proxmire

Changed statements you say?

Mr. Lawson

Yes.

Chairman Proxmire

How do you know they were changed?

Mr. Lawson

Because I changed them.

Chairman Proxmire

You changed them. And you did this on the basis of being told to qualify the brake?

Mr. Lawson

That is correct, sir.

Chairman Proxmire

Regardless of the situation. In order to do that you thought you had to change those statements?

Mr. Lawson

Well, I did not think I had to change them. I was told to change them.

Chairman Proxmire

How did the brake perform when the brakes were used?

Mr. Lawson

I don't know the exact number of occasions, but the lining surfaces of the brake did stick together, and the airplane slid to a stop on occasions, and the brakes had to be pried apart with a screwdriver to get it to roll again.

Chairman Proxmire

Describe as accurately as you can exactly what the brake did when the plane came in and the brakes were used.

Mr. Lawson

It would be landing under normal return from flight, and the pilot would touch down. They were doing brake tests, and he would apply the brakes at a certain velocity that was prescribed in the manuals, and they would be doing a normal braking roll and the brakes would lock up.

Chairman Proxmire

The plane would skid?

Mr. Lawson

Yes, and it would just slide.

3. Statement by R. G. Jeter

Mr. Jeter

Mr. Chairman, members of the committee, my name is R. G. Jeter and I am vice president, general counsel, and secretary of the B. F. Goodrich Company.

I have with me on my left Mr. Robert Sink, who is a senior wheel and brake design engineer and projects manager.

In listening to the testimony of the two first witnesses, I just wanted to suggest that to me it seemed incredible that more than 30 engineers, professional men who work at this plant, our Troy plant, would continue to work for a company which would countenance any, any of the conduct described by Mr. Vandivier and Mr. Lawson. It appears that everybody at our Troy plant is out of step, or were out of step, except these two men. That is the substance of their testimony.

Now the chairman has raised the question, what did the company stand to gain by this? Why would the company do this? Why would we deliberately falsify records? Why would we produce a defective brake? There is not any reason under God's creation why we would do it. The fact of the matter is we contracted with LTV to manufacture satisfactory, workable, efficient brakes for an aircraft.

Now why go and produce a brake and go through all the agony and tests and everything else of producing a defective brake so that we could set about then and manufacture another brake, to design a new brake and manufacture another brake which would work?

* * * * *

Between May 1968 and January 1969, LTV pilots made, as reported by the General Accounting Office, 229 test flights using the four-rotor brake.

In all of these 229 test flights the four-rotor brakes performed the braking function. No one has said anything to the contrary here. They brought the plane to a stop, as a matter of fact, in less than the required distance, and these are the records.

However, in these 229 flights, as noted by the GAO report, page 11, the pilot reported 12 flights and I would like to emphasize this now if I may, out of the 229 flights they reported 12 flights during which there were, and I quote "potential" problems with the brake system.

It should be understood at this point—and I am not sure that it is understood—that a brake system on an airplane consists of three principal components, one of which we manufactured, namely, the brake, the other an antiskid mechanism, and the third, the brake hydraulic system.

Now of the 12 potential problems, only 2, in only 2 of the flights in which the brake system problem was noted was there a problem related to the four-rotor brake—in 2 flights out of these 229.

This problem was that the brake linings— and our engineers have described this—knitted or fused slightly at low speeds, and this was mentioned a moment ago in connection with safety. This problem occurred at low speeds.

As I say, it has never been determined whether the knitting problem resulted from the brake design, or was because of an incompatibility between the brake and its associated parts of the braking system.

During September 1968, we started testing a new five-rotor brake. This is a month before Mr. Vandivier left our company, but he apparently did not know anything about this.

We did determine from this test, we concluded at least from this test that a brake lining change would probably not solve the problem, whereas a five-rotor brake design probably would be satisfactory.

In conclusion I want to say that on the record it has been established that B. F. Goodrich at a reasonable cost, and without any delay in the Air Force schedule, produced a brake for the A–7D, the performance of which exceeded the aircraft requirements. Throughout the entire program there were no safety incidents related to either the four- or five-rotor brake.

Further, the GAO after an intensive examination, and we think it was intensive, has found no evidence of any change or falsification of any data.

4. Testimony of Mr. Jeter and Mr. Sink

Chairman Proxmire

The GAO made an investigation. You and I differ very much on what the GAO said. Let me just start with that.

You say in your statement that, "The GAO report does not even suggest that test reports were falsified." Well, falsified is a word of intent which I am sure the GAO and everybody else is very careful about using.

We did have testimony by the GAO engineer this morning, and he told us that data did not show an honest picture.

Now let me ask you this. Professional engineer opinion has been unanimous, designer Searle Lawson, your employee, Air Force engineer expert Bruce Tremblay, and GAO engineer Guy Best have all testified this morning that the engineering practices at B. F. Goodrich in qualifying the four-rotor A–7D brake was unacceptable. In fact, each of these gentlemen has testified this morning that Goodrich is still making questionable statements about the A–7D four-rotor brake, this morning, for example, from your statement. You say, "It has never been determined whether the knitting problem resulted from brake design or was because of incompatibility between the brake and associated parts of the braking system."

As I recall, Mr. Best said that he was not sure on the basis of the data he had that he could make an assertion on that. The other two men were emphatic in saying that the knitting problem did result from the brake design.

Mr. Jeter

Yes, sir.

Chairman Proxmire

Mr. Vandivier has testified before this committee that there are more than 80 falsifications of data in the Report 26031. He and others that are or were employed by B. F. Goodrich wheel and brake plant in Troy contend that they were coerced by their superiors into writing a distorted qualification report. Would you agree that there is misinformation in this report?

Mr. Sink

I would say that the information that is in the report presents a fair analysis of the performance of the four-rotor brake during the qualification testing. There have been changes made in the data as we have noted before, but only to make them more consistent with the overall picture of the data that is available.

Chairman Proxmire

You stand alone in making that assertion. No other witness has indicated that.

* * * * *

Chairman Proxmire

Why do you believe that Mr. Vandivier and Mr. Lawson have come before this committee to tell us their part in the inclusion of this information in the qualification reports? I believe there are some inexplicable aspects of this thing; the one we all agree that Goodrich has nothing to gain by this, and I am sure that your motives, Mr. Jeter, and the motives of the other officials have been good.

On the other hand, the only logical explanation that I have heard of this whole incident was given by Mr. Vandivier when he said that pride or an attempt to hide a mistake or to save face seems to be the answer, and I can understand that.

On the other hand, I can throw right back at you why would these men come before us to make this testimony? Certainly Mr. Lawson has not anything to gain by this. He is in the industry now. He can be blackballed. He can be hurt badly.

Mr. Jeter

Well, I am not going to question their motives either, but I will answer your question, and not question their motives.

I do not know either man. I saw them here for the first time in my life so far as I know, so I guess I must assume that they sincerely believe what they say.

I think that Mr. Vandivier is talking about some subjects and writing an opinion about a qualification which he was not at all qualified to do.

Chairman Proxmire

He was your technical writer. He worked for you for three years as a technical writer. He had written over 100 reports.

Mr. Jeter

It is one thing to write down and record a lot of data results which you can read. I mean I can read temperatures myself. I am not an engineer, and this and that. And it is something else to arrive at conclusions as to which data is most significant and which is not. Where two tests are made simultaneously and they are at variance, it is an engineering judgment matter as to which one should be accepted.

Chairman Proxmire

Yes, but you see, Mr. Jeter, we do not have a problem of a man who is just unqualified; an engineer who is inexperienced making some mistakes. We have men who have come before this committee and testified that they falsified, that they manufactured this data, that it was not true and they were told to qualify the brake and shut up about it, and so they followed those instructions. That was their testimony.

Mr. Jeter

Well, they in fact were not so instructed. At least we have not been able to find—I can assure you that a very thorough investigation was made of this entire subject long before, I am sure, you heard of it, and we have yet to find man one who supports that statement which they make.

Conclusion

The four-hour hearing adjourned without reaching any definitive conclusions. The A–7D went into service with a five-disk brake made by Goodrich. Searle Lawson went to work as an engineer for LTV and was assigned to the A–7D project. Russell Line was promoted to production superintendent, and Robert Sink moved up to Line's old job. In the wake of this episode, the Defense Department made sweeping changes in its inspection and testing procedures. Kermit Vandivier went to work for the *Daily News* in Troy, Ohio, as a newspaper reporter. He now holds the position of copy editor and columnist. In 1986 Vandivier was interviewed by a reporter for the *The New York Times:*

Over a desultory dinner at the local Holiday Inn, Mr. Vandivier talked about his rebirth. He's a pleasant, fresh-faced man of 60, who wears a bushy mustache. He had on his knock-around clothes.

"The transition worked out great," he said. "A man doesn't often get a chance at age 43 to

change to a more exciting career without having to pay a penalty along the way. This thing gave me the push to take the plunge I probably never would have taken otherwise."

Oddly enough, even though he blew the whistle in a small town, and on that town's third-largest employer, he has not found a chilly reception among his neighbors. Part of the reason, he suspects, is that there were no consequences to anyone's job. "If I'd closed down the plant," he said, "I'd probably have been run out of town."

Mrs. Vandivier passed through a heavily stressful period during which she worried all the time, but the aftereffects have been mild for her, as well. "It might have mattered if I was one of these women who run about," she said. "I went out of the house once a week to get my hair done, period."

For the most part, now that the children are gone, the couple pass time with each other. "We're ordinary, dull people," she says.

Mr. Vandivier these days thinks well of Goodrich. He has always felt that the brake incident was not symptomatic of Goodrich's corporate morality.

"This was such a stupid thing," he said. "It was so unnecessary. It was like a comedy of errors. You're looking at people who were bullheaded. They're not criminals. They were incredibly dumb."

The next day, at his desk at the *Troy Daily News,* he said, "There were some emotional penalties. For instance, my immediate supervisor, who's now dead, couldn't afford to financially walk away from the job, even though he was with me all the way. I feared that the implication was that why didn't he speak out, too. People wouldn't understand that he wasn't dishonest."

What did he think of the climate for whistle blowers today?

"I think the atmosphere is great on things like space shuttle toilets and Navy screwdrivers," he said. "Those are great for editorial writers, but I'm not sure if those things are worth blowing the whistle on. For the real whistle blower, it's getting worse. People have become callous to scandal. It's like all the things that people eat that can cause cancer. I think Ralph Nader is less effective. I hate to say it, but whistle blowing has maybe become too popular.''[44]

Questions

1. After reading these excerpts from the congressional testimony, do you believe Vandivier's allegations? Explain.
2. Defend B. F. Goodrich.
3. What forces provoked the alleged wrongdoing in the case?
4. In essence, what decision faced both Gretzinger (the test lab supervisor) and Vandivier?
5. What policies might be developed to protect those in Gretzinger's situation?
6. When faced with a choice between material success and honesty, as Gretzinger and Vandivier were, why is honesty not always the chosen course?
7. Had you been Gretzinger or Vandivier, what action would you have taken? Explain.
8. Had someone died as a consequence of the faulty brakes, could Goodrich and the individuals responsible properly have been charged with manslaughter?
9. Is wrongdoing of this nature less likely in a smaller company? Explain.
10. Can you suggest some steps that a company might take to avoid a situation like that of Goodrich?
11. Allow your mind free rein. Assume each of the principal characters possessed the values hierarchy attributed earlier in this chapter to ministers.
    a. Would the results have been different? Explain.
    b. If so, should Goodrich accept as management-level personnel only those with "ministerial values"? Explain.
    c. If not, are managers essentially powerless pawns before the weight and immortality of the corporate structure? Explain.

BUSINESS CRIME—MANAGERIAL LIABILITY

The relationship between law and ethics is not easily defined. Certainly the law is an approximate reflection of society's collective ethical standards, but the law could not practically embrace and codify the fullness of our ethical code. In a free society, maximum reliance on personal beliefs, customs, values, and ethics is prized. The law is helpful in powerfully specifying some specific codes of conduct and thus offering broad guidelines for honorable behavior. But the law must be regarded only as a minimum standard, a floor on which the individual is expected to erect a more refined and detailed structure.

Criminal law as applied to business provides an apt illustration of the necessary tension between law and ethics. Society reaches various conclusions as to what is wrongful (unethical or unlawful), who is responsible, and whether that wrong is of a nature and magnitude sufficient to require formal legal intervention to buttress the weight of the individual conscience. The ambiguities in the law-ethics relationship are well represented in an executive's ironic response to allegations of a price-fixing conspiracy. When asked if he realized that his meetings with his co-conspirators were illegal, he replied:

> Illegal? Yes, but not criminal. I didn't find out until I read the indictment. . . . I assumed that criminal action meant damaging someone, and we did not do that.[45]

Extraordinary hurdles are arrayed against the effort to curb white-collar crime. Governmental investigations are hampered by a lack of funds. Mounds of documentary evidence, sometimes totaling hundreds of thousands of pages, are commonplace in white-collar prosecutions. Defendants are often able to hire America's best attorneys, while the government frequently must rely on bright but inexperienced counsel. Most damaging to the white-collar crime pursuit is probably public apathy. The outrage generated by street crime simply is not visited on the clever, less violent "crimes of the suites." In recent years, changing values and frustration with the legal system's success in pursuing business crime have led to an emphasis on holding executives personally liable for wrongdoing within the organization.

The two cases that follow offer striking evidence of a new prosecutorial zeal for pursuing criminal actions against managers.

1. THE FILM RECOVERY SYSTEMS CASE

On February 10, 1983, Stefan Golab, a 61-year-old Polish immigrant, died of acute cyanide poisoning while on the job at Film Recovery Systems (FRS), an Elk Grove Village, Illinois, corporation that extracted silver from used photographic and X-ray film. The company's work force, primarily consisting of Mexican and Polish immigrants who were working illegally and did not speak or read English, followed a unique two-step process to extract the silver. Workers first leached the film by placing it in a large vat containing a strong cyanide solution, then dumped the remnants into a second, electroplating vat, which separated the silver. It was a relatively small but lucrative operation. Riding the crest of a booming silver market, FRS's revenues during its peak years were estimated at $13 million to $20 million.[46]

In 1985 three of the chief officers of FRS were found guilty of murder and reckless conduct under a state statute that forbids knowingly committing the acts that "create a strong probability of death or great bodily harm." The firm's president, plant supervisor, and plant manager were sentenced to 25 years in prison and fined $10,000. The judge found that Golub and the other employees were the victims of both a poor ventilation system for the 140 vats at FRS and a near absence of the safety equipment required under law. And, despite regular employee complaints about dizziness, nausea, etc., the judge found that the defendants had willfully deceived the employees regarding the danger of working with cyanide. The businessmen claimed they did not know that the plant was dangerous. Apparently the murder conviction was the first of its kind in U.S. history.

2. THE SABINE CONSOLIDATED, INC., CASE

In the Sabine case, two workers, Benjamin Eaton, 40, and Juan Rodriguez, 32, were working at the bottom of a 27-foot trench on September 10, 1985, when the walls buckled, trapping them beneath tons of earth. Both men smothered. The state alleged that the soil was unstable and that the trench should have been shored up by proper safety devices or its walls sloped less sharply to prevent a cave-in.[47]

The president of Sabine entered a no-contest plea to charges of criminally negligent homicide. He was sentenced to six months in jail, but his "clean" record resulted in probation with no jail time. The Sabine case marks a new direction in managerial criminal liability for employee deaths in that the decision was built on a negligence claim. The prosecutor did not argue that the Sabine president intentionally killed his employees but that he acted with criminal negligence in failing to maintain proper safety standards. By not deferring to the traditional route of civil suits to pursue managers who violate health and safety standards, the Sabine case may prove to be the first step in opening a broad door for prosecutors to pursue criminal claims in such cases.

At this writing, both the Film Recovery Systems and Sabine decisions are on appeal. The future of criminal prosecutions for cases of this kind is uncertain. One primary area of contention is that the federal Occupational Safety and Health Act (OSHA) preempts state criminal action in workplace accidents. The argument is that OSHA authority is so broadly drawn that, absent federal permission, states simply do not have the power to prosecute for injuries on the job. To date, the few decisions in the area have been split.

Of course, most managerial crime does not result in death. Theft in one form or another is the prototypical white-collar crime. For example, FBI data reveal that bank fraud in 1986 totaled more than $1.1 billion in losses, a 30 percent increase over 1985. In explaining the "epidemic of scams and embezzlements," *The Wall Street Journal* points to greed; deregulation, which has opened new doors for the fast-buck artist; new technologies, which facilitate moving and hiding money; a volatile economy; and a tendency for banks to go easy on wrongdoers.[48] In response to these problems, the Auditing Standards Board of the American Institute of Certified Public Accountants now, for the first time, specifically requires auditors to design audits in a manner that reasonably ensures discovery of fraud. Irregularities would then be reported to the audited company's board. And the forensic accountant, a new subset of the profession, has sprung up in recent years with the specific purpose of uncovering fraud. These accountants act as detectives of a sort, burrowing much more deeply and thoroughly into the business operations of the firm than the normal audit. These changes are, at least in part, the product of recent criticism of the failure of accountants to uncover corporate fraud.

In the article that follows we receive a glimpse of how a successful professional, a managing partner at a major accounting firm, helped perpetuate a $320 million fraud.

AUDITOR'S DOWNFALL SHOWS A MAN CAUGHT IN TRAP OF HIS OWN MAKING

Martha Brannigan

Miami—Jose L. Gomez, a former managing partner of the Grant Thornton accounting firm, surrenders today to begin a 12-year prison term.

The 39-year-old Mr. Gomez pleaded guilty last year to charges, in two federal courts and an Ohio state court, involving his role in the fraud at ESM Government Securities, Inc., the once-obscure Fort Lauderdale, Florida, firm that collapsed two years ago today and triggered one of the biggest financial scandals of the decade. As ESM's auditor, Mr. Gomez knowingly approved the firm's false financial statements for five years, thus allowing the massive fraud to continue. He must serve at least four years.

In these days when white-collar crime is rocking Wall Street, Mr. Gomez's story is a particularly telling one. In some regards, he was almost a cliché: an ambitious young man who rose too far too fast and wound up in the worst sort of trouble. He says he crossed the line into criminality without even realizing it.

When Mr. Gomez's activities came to light, many people were stunned, for he had seemed the model of success. He was one of the youngest people ever to be made partner at his Chicago-based firm, which then was called Alexander Grant & Co. He was active in community affairs.

But he was also a fraud. Investors initially lost some $320 million in the scheme Mr. Gomez helped perpetrate, and the scandal was even blamed for a brief decline in the dollar on international markets.

In a recent interview, Mr. Gomez talked of his rise and fall. He says he never intended to do anything wrong. But in August 1979, just days after being told of his promotion to partner at Grant, two officers of ESM told him of a crude accounting ruse that was hiding millions of dollars in losses; they had to bring Mr. Gomez in on the scheme to keep it from unraveling.

Mr. Gomez says he had missed the ruse in two previous annual audits, signing off on bogus financial statements showing ESM to be in robust condition. He says one of the ESM officers used that error to draw him into the fraud.

Gomez

> He must had said it four or five times: "How's it going to look. It's going to look terrible for you, and you just got promoted to partner. Just give us a chance. It just takes time. We're not going to have those losses."

WSJ

> Do you think he was trying to intimidate you?

Gomez

> No question about it. And it worked. I was 31 years old. I felt I had a terrific career path in front of me and a lot of ambition. . . . And I agreed just to think about it. And a day or two later, I felt I already had gone too far. I also didn't want to face it. I didn't want to face walking in [to his superiors at Alexander Grant] and saying this is what happened.

In Chicago, Burt K. Fischer, executive partner of Grant Thornton, says Mr. Gomez's fears about his blunder were misplaced. "I can't think of a partner who made an honest mistake who has been hung out to dry," he says. The firm also contends that Mr. Gomez learned of the fraud before 1979.

Convincing Himself

Mr. Gomez says he decided to go along with the scheme at ESM, convinced that the firm's managers could make up the losses.

Gomez

> I really wanted to believe they could do it. So I just made up my mind, OK, I'm going to let them do it. At this point in time I was looking at maybe $10 million (in losses) as being the problem, in a business that you can make $10 million very easily.
>
> I never evaluated at that point, or later either, a criminal side to what I was doing. If I had, it might have been a deterrent.

WSJ

> What did you think of it as?

Gomez

> It was a professional decision, a judgment decision that I was making that I felt would eventually work itself out. I had a terrific argument with myself. It just came out that way. If I had sought some counsel from someone that I had some respect for, if I had even talked to my wife.

WSJ

> Did you go home and tell your wife?

Gomez

> No. It's interesting. We've been married 17 years now. And it's the only item I never discussed with her or shared with her in any way.

"I Was Trapped"

ESM's losses continued to mount, and Mr. Gomez continued to approve phony financial statements.

Gomez

> When I looked at this thing again in 1980 . . . the accumulated deficit is close to $100 million, and now it's a really big number no matter

how you look at it. And I was trapped. I just totally felt that I'd lost control of it.

In late 1980, ESM officers began arranging loans for Mr. Gomez, who was having personal financial problems. The loans, which weren't repaid, totaled $200,000.

Gomez

> I don't know how all these things relate to my own inability to handle my personal finances. For an accountant, it's tough to fathom—but not only would there not be a budget, there would be spending without thinking of such things as monthly payments. I had been spending on credit cards and borrowing from banks to pay the credit cards for some time. I was also looking to put a pool in my house. There were a lot of things added together. No discipline whatsoever.

WSJ

> Did you view ESM loans as a quid pro quo?

Gomez

> No. I never—and it's hard for people to accept this—I never related my actions to the money. I didn't do it for money. I did it because I didn't want to have to face up that I had made a mistake, that I had missed it originally.

WSJ

> Did you have to do special things to prevent your staff from coming upon the accounting fraud?

Gomez

> I never did.

* * * * *

WSJ

> What do you think the flaws were in the structure of the review process that allowed this thing to go on?

Gomez

> It's very easy for other professionals to look down their noses at this and say, "My God, this was so obvious." But I think the ones who are really honest are going to look at this and say, "My God, that could have happened here."

In 1977, it became apparent to me that those being promoted early were the business producers. Not necessarily that they were weak technically, but they were the ones that were able to produce new clients, who had extensive contacts. The salesmen. It became apparent to me . . . that my own promotion depended on my becoming more productive. That's when I began turning more sales oriented.

I think I would have been able to be more objective about my client relationships if I weren't so concerned about selling. And ESM was a very strong selling point for me. [The ESM account] had produced other clients, and I looked at them as being a productive vehicle.

WSJ

So you think you would have caught the fraud if it weren't for the sales pressure?

Gomez

If I had not had the sales pressure, I would perhaps have caught it before it happened.

He also thinks, in hindsight, that he was too inexperienced to be heading an audit—which he was doing at age 31 even before he was named partner in 1979.

"No Substitute for Experience"

Gomez

It's interesting for me to say this now, because if you had asked me then, I would have said, "No, you're crazy; I know more than these guys." I used to hate the term, "There's no substitute for experience," and now I realize how wise it was.

Grant Thornton's Mr. Fischer acknowledges that there has been a greater emphasis on marketing in the auditing field since the 1960s. "But it's not in lieu of the auditing function," he says. "It's in addition to auditing, which is our bread and butter. With respect to Mr. Gomez's contention that he was too young to have so much responsibility, Mr. Fischer says, "I don't buy it. That's no excuse. I was promoted to partner at a younger age than he was, and I didn't steal."

In March 1985, ESM collapsed. Mr. Gomez retained a lawyer, who told him he faced serious criminal liability. Mr. Gomez says he fell into "deep depression, and I am not a depressed individual." He was jolted out of it by the suicide in July of Stephen W. Arky, a 42-year-old Miami lawyer who had represented ESM before its collapse. Fearing that his own depression could lead to a similar end, Mr. Gomez began cooperating with the authorities. He was the first EMS figure to do so.

* * * * *

WSJ

How old are your children?

Gomez

Thirteen and 11.

WSJ

Can they understand it?

Gomez

They understand that there was something that happened to a company. They understand that Daddy was in a position to do something and he didn't do it right. And they understand that he's faced up to it and he's got to pay for it. And they also, I hope, understand that in their own life they're going to have to face things when they happen and they can't just try to get by. I've tried to use this as a lesson for them.

WSJ

How about preparing for prison?

Gomez

I don't know. I'm in limbo. I'd like to be able to find out what can I do, what can I bring. I'd like to be able to know whether I can have access to a typewriter or a minicomputer. You have to do something with your day. I imagine you can't just lie around doing nothing. I'd like to at least be able to maintain my technical profession by reading and working on things. Who knows?

Questions

1. In 1972 two young men were killed by cyanide poisoning while at work with a Pennsylvania plating company. One was assigned to pour some dry material into an unmarked tub containing a solution, while the other was working nearby. Warning labels had been removed from the tub. The employee did as instructed, and the resulting cyanide gas killed him and the nearby worker.

    a. Had you been the local prosecutor at the time, would you have sought manslaughter charges against the appropriate company officials? Explain.

    b. What additional facts would you need to know?

2. In the "Auditor's Downfall" article, Gomez asserts that "I never evaluated at that point, or later either, a criminal side to what I was doing."

    a. In your judgment, how might one fail to consider the criminal character of obviously wrongful behavior?

    b. Gomez argues that what he did was spurred in part by his firm's emphasis on attracting new business. Have accounting firms betrayed their public trust by giving excessive attention to selling? Explain.

    c. Are accountants properly educated as to their legal and ethical duties? Explain.

3. Dr. Donald Cressey, a leading expert on white-collar crime, said: "Restraints of trade, price fixing, and other major white-collar crimes are much more threatening to the national welfare than are burglaries, and robberies and other so-called street crimes."[49]

    a. Do you agree? Explain.

    b. Why might white-collar criminals receive more gentle treatment?

    c. What punishments would be most effective against white-collar criminals?

4. It is often argued that increased personal liability will substantially discourage qualified individuals from assuming top-level executive positions. Do you agree? What are your reasons?

WHISTLE BLOWING

Whistle blowers, such as Kermit Vandivier in the B. F. Goodrich/A–7D brake case, are manifestations of the power of conscience in human conduct. In 1968 A. Ernest Fitzgerald was earning $31,000 annually as a civilian cost-cutting management expert for the Air Force. Under questioning before a congressional committee Fitzgerald testified that cost overruns on the C5A cargo plane might total $2 billion. Fitzgerald lost his job. After a series of court struggles he won an order compelling his reinstatement. In 1973 he was back in an office, but he was given only trivial work assignments. Then, in 1981, a federal district court ordered Fitzgerald reinstated in his old job or an equivalent position. Ultimately his litigation against the Air Force was settled out of court. Fitzgerald received a promotion and $200,000 to assist in meeting his legal fees.[50]

As noted in the article below, Fitzgerald is the most famous of a burgeoning group of whistle blowers in both the public and private sectors. Today employees seem increasingly inclined to follow the dictates of conscience in speaking out—publicly, if necessary—against wrongdoing by their employers. Historically, complaints were taken to management and resolved there. "Going public" was considered an act of disloyalty. Americans continue to maintain a strong tradition against "squealing." Indeed, management has good reason to discourage irresponsible, precipitous whistle blowing that might disclose legitimate trade secrets, cause unnecessary conflict among employees, unfairly tarnish the company image, and so on.

THE WHISTLE BLOWERS' MORNING AFTER

N. R. Kleinfield

Charles and Jeanne Atchison live near the Cowboy City dance bar on a gravel street in a peeling white-and-gold mobile home. Weeds sway in the breeze out front. It's a street with a melancholy down-on-one's-luck feel about it. The town is Azle, Texas, a tiny speck on the periphery of Fort Worth.

A few years ago, the picture was a far prettier one. Charles (Chuck) Atchison was all set. He made good money—more than $1,000 a week—enough to pay for a cozy house, new cars, fanciful trips. But all that is gone. He's six months behind on rent for his land, and don't even ask about the legal bills.

"It's sort of like I was barreling along and I suddenly shifted into reverse," Mr. Atchison said with a rueful smile. "Well, welcome to whistle-blower country."

Chuck Atchison is 44, with a stony face and a sparse mustache. Four years ago, he stood up before regulators and exposed numerous safety infractions at the Comanche Peak nuclear plant in Glen Rose, Texas. He was a quality control inspector for Brown & Root, the construction company building the plant for the Texas Utilities Electric Company, but he says he couldn't get anyone to fix the problems. His dissidence, as well as those of others, delayed the utility from obtaining a license and prompted still-ongoing repair work.

Mr. Atchison wound up out of a job and spinning in debt. He's working again, in another industry, slowly trying to patch the leaks in his life. Though proud of his stance, he often feels psychic scars. "The whistle blower today is probably the most discriminated against individual in the country," he said. "By individuals and industry and the U.S. government that is supposedly protecting him. He gets a brand put on him and it just seems like you can't get it off with anything."

* * * * *

Whistle blowers have been much in the news of late. Bill Bush, a retired NASA worker who had been demoted, he says, for complaining that the agency needlessly channeled out work, keeps a computer file on whistle blowers that has swollen to 8,500 entries. "In the last 10 years," he says, "my sense is there's been a dramatic increase in whistle blowing."

Plenty has been written about the courage of the likes of A. Ernest Fitzgerald, the jaunty Air Force cost analyst who testified in 1969 about huge cost overruns on a Lockheed cargo plane. And, of course, everyone knows of Karen Silkwood, the late nuclear plant worker whose case charging flawed safety procedures at the Kerr-McGee plant became a heralded movie and resulted in Kerr-McGee paying her estate $1.38 million to settle charges that Miss Silkwood and her home were contaminated by company negligence.

Rarely, though, has anyone looked at what comes of whistle blowers long after the events that rocked their lives. Whistle blowers almost inevitably pay a heavy price. With few exceptions, they are driven out of not just their jobs but their professions, too. But that doesn't mean they always are reduced to dire poverty and icy isolation. Often, they are reincarnated in some new position.

That's among the conclusions of Myron Peretz Glazer, a sociology professor at Smith College, and his wife, Penina Migdal Glazer, a professor of history at Hampshire College, who talked with some 55 whistle blowers for a book they are preparing.

"Of the people we interviewed," Mr. Glazer said recently, "I would say that if you follow them over a period of time, most of them do re-create both their careers and their emotional lives. But mostly you find they had to move into other kinds of work that normally hasn't paid them as much as their former life. So while we can say blowing the whistle doesn't have to mean the end to your career, it will mean major adjustments."

Despite the proliferation of whistle blowers and public applause for them, industry and government remain intolerant of them. When Allan McDonald and Roger Boisjoly, engineers at Morton Thiokol, testified about serious problems with the space shuttle Challenger, company management transferred the two men to menial jobs. In the face of a storm of adverse publicity, they hastily reinstated them. Mr. Boisjoly, however, took a sick leave last month due to an unspecified illness he said was linked to the Challenger episode and plans to quit the company.

* * * * *

Some court actions, especially in California, have ruled in favor of unjustly dismissed corporate whistle blowers. Mr. Fitzgerald and others would like to see legislation that makes government officials personally liable for illegal acts. There is interest among certain legislators in a "bounty hunter" measure that would pay anyone who is able to prove that a contractor is bilking the government.

At bottom, though, the prognosis for whistle blowing seems ominous. "They break the unwritten law of social relationships," Mr. Glazer said. "They break a norm—the norm of loyalty."

* * * * *

Source: *The New York Times,* November 9, 1986, section 3, pp. 1, 10. Copyright © 1986 by The New York Times Company. Reprinted by permission.

Postscript

Congress and the state legislatures are increasingly providing protection for whistle blowers. For example, the 1982 Surface Transportation Assistance Act provides that interstate truckers may not fire employees in retaliation for filing a complaint about the company's failure to comply with federal and state safety regulations or for refusing to operate an unsafe truck (see *Brock* v. *Roadway Express, Inc., 55 Law Week* 4530, 1986).

Questions

1. Why is the role of "squealer" or whistle blower so repugnant to many Americans?

2. How would you feel about a classmate who blew the whistle on you for cheating on an examination? Would you report cheating by a classmate if it came to your attention? Explain.

3. Assume an employee of an American corporation speaks out to warn the public against a danger in one of the employer's products. The employee is fired.

   a. Can the employee successfully argue that the First Amendment guarantee of freedom of speech protects him or her from dismissal? Explain.

   b. Would it make a difference if the firm operated a nuclear reactor for generating electricity? Explain. (You can refer to Chapter 5 for more discussion of this issue.)

4. James Roche, former chairman of the board of General Motors Corporation, said:

   > Some critics are now busy eroding another support of free enterprise—the loyalty of a management team, with its unifying values of cooperative work. Some of the enemies of business now encourage an employee to be disloyal to the enterprise. They want to create suspicion and disharmony and pry into the proprietary interests of the business. However this is labeled — industrial espionage, whistle blowing, or professional responsibility—it is another tactic for spreading disunity and creating conflict.[51]

   Evaluate Mr. Roche's argument.

5. Other than avoiding wrongdoing, what steps might the organization take to render whistle blowing unnecessary? (You might refer to Kenneth D. Walters, "Your Employees' Right to Blow the Whistle," *Harvard Business Review,* July–August 1975, pp. 26, 31.)

6. Carl Kaufmann, an executive assistant in public affairs at Du Pont, outlined a dilemma that arose in a giant chemicals firm:

   > For years, your corporation manufactures a dye intermediate called Beta-naphthylamine without any questions of risk. Then alarming evidence begins turning up—an unusual number of tumors among workers in a plant, malignant tumors. Beta is identified by company scientists as a potent carcinogen—but hundreds of your workers were already exposed.
   >
   > Would you blow the whistle on yourself or try to do a cleanup quickly to prevent future injuries?[52]

   Answer Kaufmann's question.

BRIBERY ABROAD

Multinational business firms face a special and complex ethical dilemma. In many cultures the payment of bribes, *baksheesh* (Middle East), *mordita* (South America), or *dash* (Africa), is accepted as necessary and, in some cases, lawful ways of doing business. American firms and officers wishing to succeed abroad have faced great pressure to engage in practices that are, of course, illegal and unethical in the American culture. In recent years some 370 firms, including such respected names as Gulf Oil, Lockheed, Exxon, and 3M, have confessed to questionable payments abroad totaling perhaps $745 million. For example, Lockheed expended $12.6 million in Japan alone in seeking aircraft sales. Disclosure of widespread bribery by American firms, including government officials at the highest levels, led to the 1977 enactment of the Foreign Corrupt Practices Act (FCPA).

The act makes it a crime for American corporations to offer or provide bribes to foreign government officials to obtain or retain business. New accounting requirements make concealment of such payments difficult. Penalties include fines of up to $1 million for companies, while individuals may be fined $10,000 and imprisoned for as long as five years if they either participate in a violation or know of the violation. The act does not forbid "grease" payments to lower-level functionaries who require under-the-table compensation merely to carry out routine duties, such as securing permits and placing transatlantic calls. A *Business Week* survey suggests American businesses have now become scrupulously—even excessively—careful in avoiding improprieties.[53] For example, many companies adopted policies forbidding all payments, rather than run the risk of an employee misunderstanding the distinction between forbidden payoffs and permissible "grease."

The FCPA has placed American firms at a competitive disadvantage in that few other nations have assumed our ethical stance. For example, France has no law governing this practice, and Italy passed legislation in 1980 explicitly approving payments to foreign officials for the purpose of securing business. The FCPA has been vigorously criticized. A major problem, of course, is simply that of distinguishing between a bribe and an honest payment in return for legitimate services rendered. Professor Jeffrey Fadiman—with 22 years' experience in Afro-Asia, 7 years in the African tourist industry—offered his own experience as an example of the complexities of applying American ethics to a foreign culture.

A TRAVELER'S GUIDE TO GIFTS AND BRIBES

Jeffrey A. Fadiman

My own first experience with Third World bribery may illustrate the inner conflict Americans can feel when asked to break the rules. It occurred in East Africa and began with this request: "Oh, and Bwana, I would like 1,000 shillings as Zawadi, my gift. And, as we are now friends, for Chai, my tea, an eight-band radio, to bring to my home when you visit.''

Both *Chai* and *Zawadi* can be Swahili terms for ''bribe.'' He delivered these requests in respectful tones. They came almost as an afterthought, at the conclusion of negotiations in which we had settled the details of a projected business venture.

* * * * *

The amount he suggested, although insignificant by modern standards, seemed large at the time. Nonetheless, it was the radio that got to me. Somehow it added insult to injury. Outwardly, I kept smiling. Inside, my stomach boiled. My own world view equates bribery with sin. . . . My reaction took only moments to formulate. ''I'm American,'' I declared. ''I don't pay bribes.'' Then I walked away. That walk was not the longest in my life. It was, however, one of the least commercially productive.

As it turned out, I had misunderstood him—in more ways than one. By misinterpreting both his language and his culture, I lost an opportunity for a business deal and a personal relationship that would have paid enormous dividends without violating either the law or my own sense of ethics.

Go back through the episode—but view it this time with an East African perspective. First, my colleague's language should have given me an important clue as to how he saw our transaction. Although his limited command of English caused him to frame his request as a command—a phrasing I instinctively found offensive—his tone was courteous. Moreover, if I had listened more carefully, I would have noted that he had addressed me as a superior: he used the honorific *Bwana,* meaning ''sir,'' rather than *Rafiki* [or friend), used between equals. From his perspective, the language was appropriate; it reflected the differences in our personal wealth and in the power of the institutions we each represented.

Having assigned me the role of the superior figure in the economic transaction, he then suggested how I should use my position in accord with his culture's traditions—logically assuming that I would benefit by his prompting. In this case, he suggested that money and a radio would be appropriate gifts. What he did not tell me was that his culture's traditions required him to use the money to provide a feast—in my honor—to which he would invite everyone in his social and commercial circle whom he felt I should meet. The radio would simply create a festive atmosphere at the party. This was to mark the beginning of an ongoing relationship with reciprocal benefits.

He told me none of this. Since I was willing to do business in local fashion, I was supposed to know. In fact, I had not merely been invited to a dwelling but through a gateway into the maze of gifts and formal visiting that linked him to his kin. He hoped that I would respond in local fashion. Instead, I responded according to my cultural norms and walked out both on the chance to do business and on the opportunity to make friends.

* * * * *

Source: Reprinted by permission of the *Harvard Business Review.* An excerpt from ''A Traveler's Guide to Gifts and Bribes'' by Jeffrey A. Fadiman (July/August 1986). Copyright © 1986 by the President and Fellows of Harvard College; all rights reserved.

Question

Carl Kaufmann of Du Pont raised the following bribery issue: As the head of a multinational corporation, you learn that one of your plant managers has been arrested in a distant republic. His alleged crime is that goods found in your warehouse lack the proper customs stamp and papers.

But the truth is more complicated. For years, "grease" has been a way of life in this country's bureaucracy, and your plant manager has been paying gratuities to the customs officers. But he knows it is against home office policy, and so he stops. Their inspection follows. The price for dropping all charges: $18,000.

a. Would you pay up? Or let your man be put in jail? Explain.

b. Which alternative is more ethical?[54] Explain.

A DISSENT

To this point the chapter has been directed, rather conventionally, to the notion that the cause of decency in the corporate community will be enhanced if we achieve a sufficient understanding of ethical dilemmas and the decision systems necessary to deal with them. Therefore, it is fitting to look at an aggressively cynical viewpoint that rejects ideals in favor of a pragmatism often considered more in keeping with today's business reality.

NOTHING SUCCEEDS LIKE AN S.O.B.

R. H. Morrison

The real key to all success is perseverance. The willingness to hang in there, take the lumps that come, and get up off the floor more than once, is the attribute that you must have.

You will also have to become a dedicated, single-minded S.O.B. You have to change your thinking, your attitude toward reality, and develop what could be described as a Machiavellian outlook on the world.

1. First, you cannot be overconcerned with morality in the conventional sense. You must become convinced there is nothing essentially wrong with exploiting people and situations. The game of business is like the game of football. If the quarterback on the offensive team discovers that a defensive halfback simply cannot cover one of his pass receivers,

he will use that weakness to his maximum advantage. The defender may wind up losing his job, but this is of no concern to the quarterback. The name of the game is winning, and exploiting situations and people is part of that game.

2. You have to learn to become cool and detached in dealing with other people. You never get emotionally involved with people or situations. Essentially you view everything in terms of objects and situations. You do not suffer with intellectual analysis of the results of your actions.

3. You actually enjoy the game. You enjoy the exploitation, you derive the satisfaction from using people, things, and situations to achieve your goal. You do not do this for amusement or self-aggrandizement, but simply to get that which you are after.

4. Above all you have a rational view of society as it exists. You are neither impressed nor bothered by philosophical viewpoints that stress that the greatest goals in life are serving your fellow man.

5. In short you are not a nice guy, you are an S.O.B., dedicated to success, and having convinced yourself you need that success, it will be achieved. As for money, that's the way you keep score.

If this attitude puts some strain on your psyche, and you feel it is overly cynical or outright debasing, I would like to engage in a brief, philosophical dissertation concerning the reality of such things as truth and morals.

In point of fact, *there is no such thing as real truth in human affairs*. Let's examine the most often quoted rule of behavior, the so-called golden rule: "Do unto others as you would have others do unto you." This sounds as though it is the perfect philosophical solution to human action. However, all humans are not the same, and there are aberrations in the human psyche. If, for example, a masochist were to apply the golden rule to everybody he came in contact with, there would be many unhappy people in the vicinity.

So even the most likely sounding philosophy has holes in it. The plain truth is, that truth is a point of view.

For example, let's take a common happening that affects everybody in the vicinity. Rain! Rain falls universally on everybody in an area. The farmer says the rain is good because it makes his crops grow, and this is the truth. The roadbuilder, the owner of the baseball team, and the people going on a picnic say the rain is bad because it stops them from doing what they need to do. And that, too, is the truth. So we have several people with exactly opposing opinions about an event, and all are telling the truth. So, in fact, the truth is little more than a point of view, and it depends on whose moccasins you are standing in as to whether good or bad.

The problem with things of this nature is that people tend to take extreme viewpoints. Thus, the farmer who demands that it always rains is advocating flood. The roadbuilder who advocates that it never rains is advocating drought. The truth has to be a reasonable compromise between these points of view. And so it is with all affairs of mankind—there has to be a compromise from the extremes in order to arrive at a livable situation. But those moralists who set down rules carved in stone and hand them down as the great truth from above are little more than con men attempting to force people to live in a society that advocates a single truth or a single point of view. It very seldom works.

Morals are nothing more than social customs. They change with time, generations, and societies. For example, a cannibal is moral in a cannibalistic society. He is obviously immoral in a noncannibalistic society.

In this country we have had great changes in moral attitudes over the years, and they change every day. In the Old West, horse stealing was a hanging offense. Today it is a misdemeanor. In the early days of this country, political corruption, prostitution, slavery, and other moral outrages were common coin. Yet we had a higher percentage of people going to church in those days than we do today. . . .

Such is the continuous hold of morality on a society. Therefore, the small businessman who is stepping out into the business world can be little concerned with the changing fads of human morals, or philosophical opinions about what is or is not truth.

* * * * *

When you have made it up the mountain, reached the pinnacle, you can then do what the rest of those successful entrepreneurs have done before you. You can write a code of ethics, make speeches about morality to business and civic groups, and look down with a cold smile on all the scrambling, scratching little bastards below, trying to find their path to the top. You can even do what some of the rest of them have done—roll rocks down on them just for the hell of it, and make the road a little tougher.

I like to think of the small businessman as an eagle. A high-flying loner, whose only morality is to get that which he deems is his right. He flies alone, finds what he needs himself, and lives where and as he chooses.

I think of corporations, government bureaucracies, and others as vultures. Vultures operate in groups, picking the bones of the dead and defenseless, and are simply put here to demonstrate Machiavelli's rule that only the fittest survive. Start now!

Source: *Business and Society Review* 28 (Winter 1978–79), pp. 69–70. Reprinted by permission from the *Business and Society Review.* Copyright 1978, Warren, Gorham & Lamont Inc., 210 South Street, Boston, Mass. All rights reserved.

Questions

1. What is meant by a "Machiavellian outlook on the world"?
2. Is truth merely a point of view? Evaluate the author's argument.
3. Are morals merely relative or situational, changing according to time, place, and circumstance? Explain.
4. Assume a businessperson's goal is success and that issues of morality are of insignificant concern. Is Morrison's formula the best route to success? Explain.
5. In some eras and cultures, spiritual success has been preferable to material success. Is that the case in contemporary America? Explain.

CHAPTER QUESTIONS

1. Can the realistic businessperson expect to be both ethical and successful? Explain.
2. Resolve these ethical dilemmas posed by Carl Kaufmann of Du Pont:[55]
   a. Your corporation has developed a prescription drug that helps prevent flu or cure it. It has other potential uses too. But the Food and Drug Administration won't grant clearance. More testing, please. Your company experts think the U.S. regulators are dragging their feet beyond reason. Other governments, with high standards for judging safety and efficacy, have approved the drug for sale in their countries. Should we go ahead and market the drug overseas? Or wait for U.S. approval?
   b. Assume that federal health investigators are pursuing a report that one of your manufacturing plants has a higher-than-average incidence of cancer among its employees. The plant happens to keep excellent medical records on all its employees, stretching back for decades, which might help identify the source of the problem. The government demands the files. But if the company turns them over, it might be accused of violating the privacy of all those workers who had submitted to private medical exams. The company offers an abstract of the records, but the government

insists on the complete files, with employee names. Then the company tries to obtain releases from all the workers, but some of them refuse. If you give the records to the feds, the company has broken its commitment of confidentiality. What would you do?

3. Among your classmates, would you expect to find a difference between males and females in the rate of cheating? Explain.

4. *a.* In her book *Lying,* Sissela Bok argues that lying by professionals is commonplace. For example, she takes the position that prescribing placebos for experimental purposes is a lie and immoral. Do you agree with her position? Why or why not?

   b. Is the use of an unmarked police car an immoral deception? Explain.

   c. One study estimates that Americans average 200 lies per day if one includes "white lies" and inaccurate excuses. On balance, do you believe Americans approve of lying? Explain.

5. Professor Howard Raiffa's Competitive Decision Making course at the Harvard Business School received nationwide attention when *The Wall Street Journal* ran a front-page story explaining how Raiffa's course involved, in part, "strategic misrepresentation."[56] Students were involved in negotiating sessions, with one third of the course grade resting on their success. Hiding facts, bluffing, and lying were permissible and often resulted in a better deal. Raiffa argued that, rather than encouraging lying, he was merely trying to acquaint his students with the possibility that they might be lied to. (While the facts appear not to have been in dispute, the Harvard Business School dean, Lawrence Fouraker, felt that the *Journal* article distorted the goals of the course.) Comment on the ethics of Professor Raiffa's approach.

6. Some excerpts from an "Ethical Aptitude Test":

   As with other goods and services, the medical care available to the rich is superior to that available to the poor. The difference is most conspicuous in the application of new and expensive lifesaving techniques.[57]

   a. Is ability to pay an acceptable way to allocate such services? Explain.

   b. If not, how should such services be apportioned?

   c. Many lifesaving drugs can be tested effectively only on human beings. But often, subjects are exposed to such dangers that only those who feel they have nothing to lose willingly participate. Are there any circumstances in which it would be right to conduct such tests without ensuring that the persons tested clearly understood the risks they were taking? Explain.

   d. How much in dollars is the average human life worth?"

7. Aaron Burr said, "All things are moral to great men." Regardless of your personal point of view, defend Burr's position.

8. A pharmacist in Lexington, Kentucky, refused to stock over-the-counter weight reducers. His reasons were (1) the active ingredient

is the same as that in nasal decongestants; (2) he feared their side effects, such as high blood pressure; and (3) he felt weight reduction should be achieved via self-discipline.[58] Assume the pharmacist manages the store for a group of owners who have given him complete authority about the products stocked. Was his decision ethical? Explain.

9. When *Business and Society Review* surveyed the presidents of 500 large U.S. companies, 51 responded with their reactions to hypothetical moral dilemmas. One question was:

> Assume that you are president of a firm which provides a substantial portion of the market of one of your suppliers. You find out that this supplier discriminates illegally against minorities, although no legal action has been taken. Assume further that this supplier gives you the best price for the material you require, but that the field is competitive.
>
> Do you feel that it is proper to use your economic power over this supplier to make him stop discriminating?[59]

Give your own response to this question.

10. Paul R. Dew, executive vice president of Shamrock Foods Company, pleaded no contest in 1974 to a charge of violating antitrust laws. Dew was never sentenced or placed on probation. Rather, sentencing was delayed on the condition that Dew contribute $35,000 to St. Mary's Food Bank and that he work 45 days for the Food Bank. Those terms completed, the judge then freed Dew at the delayed sentencing hearing.

Dew later addressed an antitrust law symposium:

> I am convinced that this pattern, carefully followed with proper checks and balances, can be more effective toward serving justice, changing attitudes, and improving society than incarceration could ever accomplish in the best or poorest of prisons.[60]

Do you agree? Explain.

11. We are in the midst of a period of unprecedented concern regarding the ethical quality of the nation. However, to many observers our problems are no more serious now than has always been the case. Robert Bartley, editor of *The Wall Street Journal,* comments:

> No, we do not live in an age of moral collapse. We more nearly live in an age of moral zealotry. We are applying to ourselves, or at least to our public and private leaders, standards of ethics never before expected of ordinary mortals.[61]

Are we asking too much of ourselves? Explain.

12. In general, does the American value system favor "cheaters" who win in life's various competitions over virtuous individuals who "lose" with regularity? Explain.

13. Why is "virtue its own reward," while tangible productivity is ordinarily accorded material compensation?

14. Louis Romberg, a Toronto behavioral scientist, hooked up devices in six of a department store chain's East Coast stores to play a subliminal, continuous message behind the stores' Muzak. Just below the threshold of conscious audibility, the devices broadcast such phrases as: "I am honest. I won't steal. Stealing is dishonest." Store employees and shoppers allegedly received the message in their subconscious. After nine months, theft losses in the six stores declined 37.5 percent ($600,000).[62]

    a. Subliminal messages may or may not be persuasive. The evidence is limited and mixed. But in any case, is the practice described here for reducing crime ethically permissible? Explain.

    b. Would it be ethical to use subliminal messages to sell products? Explain.

    c. Would it be ethical to use subliminal messages to promote political candidates? How would this use differ from the others, if at all?

    d. Review your answers to (*a*) through (*c*). Is your ethical approach teleological or deontological? Explain.

15. *a.* Rank the following occupations as to your perception of their ethical quality: businesspersons, lawyers, doctors, teachers, farmers, engineers, carpenters, librarians, scientists, professional athletes, letter carriers, secretaries, journalists.

    b. In general, do you find educated professionals to be more ethical than skilled, but generally less-educated, laborers? Explain.

    c. Can you justify accepting an occupation that is not at or near the top of your ethical ranking? Explain how your ranking affects your career choices.

16. Can businesspeople successfully guide their conduct by the Golden Rule?

17. Comment on the following quotes from Albert Z. Carr:

    > [M]ost bluffing in business might be regarded simply as game strategy—much like bluffing in poker, which does not reflect on the morality of the bluffer.
    >
    > I quoted Henry Taylor, the British statesman who pointed out that "falsehood ceases to be falsehood when it is understood on all sides that the truth is not expected to be spoken"—an exact description of bluffing in poker, diplomacy, and business.

    * * * * *

    > [T]he ethics of business are game ethics, different from the ethics of religion.

    * * * * *

    > An executive's family life can easily be dislocated if he fails to make a sharp distinction between the ethical systems of the home and the office—or if his wife does not grasp that distinction.[63]

18. Anthropology professor Lionel Tiger has argued for the creation of "moral quality circles" to help improve business conduct. Tiger notes that:

> [O]ur species evolved in small groups of perhaps 25 to 200 hunters and gatherers, groups in which there was no place to hide. Over 200,000 generations or so we evolved great face-to-face sensitivity and a lively skill for "whites-of-their-eyes" assessments of others.

* * * * *

> These ancient but still-lively emotions can be tied into the nature of organizational life to help overcome the all-too-evident capacity of large groups to yield to "if you want to get along, go along." My hunch is that moral laxity emerges when members of such groups receive little or no dignified opportunity to define their moral views on practical matters without the risk of endangering their occupational health.[64]

Our moral systems sprang from that small-group context; but today, with complex industry replacing hunter/gatherers, those moral systems no longer correspond to contemporary needs. Tiger goes on to argue that we have a kind of "gene for morality" and that most of us have a rather clear sense of right and wrong. Given these conditions, he proposes the moral quality circle, in which workers would discuss the ethical implications of their duties and of the company's conduct in much the same manner that quality circles are now used to improve productivity and reliability.

Do you see any value in Tiger's proposal? Explain.

NOTES

1. Barbara Kantrowitz, "A $100,000 Question Stirs Up Columbia," *Newsweek,* October 26, 1987, p. 76.
2. Nancy J. Perry, "Edelman's Art of Reward," *Fortune,* November 9, 1987, p. 159.
3. Associated Press, "Columbia Lauded for Nixing Edelman Prize," *Waterloo Courier,* October 15, 1987, p. C6.
4. This episode was reported in J. Anthony Lucas, "As American as a McDonald's Hamburger on the Fourth of July," *The New York Times Magazine,* July 4, 1971, p. 4.
5. Scott Ostler, "That Little Voice Just Kept Chanting: 'Stop, Bubba, Stop'." Copyright, 1986, *Los Angeles Times.* Reprinted by permission. Reprinted in *Des Moines Sunday Register,* September 14, 1986, p. 12D.
6. Raymond Baumhart, *Ethics in Business* (New York: Holt, Rinehart & Winston, 1968), p. 10.
7. The author's remarks in this paragraph owe a great debt to Vincent Barry, *Moral Issues in Business* (Belmont, Calif.: Wadsworth Publishing, 1979), pp. 7–11.

8. Joseph Fletcher, *Situation Ethics—The New Morality* (Philadelphia: Westminister Press, 1966), p. 17.

9. Ibid., p. 26.

10. Merrill McLoughlin, Jeffrey L. Sheler, and Gordon Witkin, "A Nation of Liars?" *U.S. News & World Report,* February 23, 1987, pp. 54–55. Copyright, 1987, *U.S. News & World Report.*

11. The materials in this paragraph owe a great debt to Vincent Barry, *Moral Issues in Business,* 3rd ed. (Belmont, Calif.: Wadsworth Publishing, 1986), pp. 18–21.

12. McLoughlin et al., "Nation of Liars?" p. 54.

13. Myron Magnet, "The Decline and Fall of Business Ethics," *Fortune,* December 8, 1986, p. 65.

14. Walter Shapiro, "What's Wrong," *Time,* May 25, 1987, p. 14.

15. David Vogel, "Could an Ethics Course Have Kept Ivan from Going Bad?" *The Wall Street Journal,* April 27, 1987, p. 18.

16. Paul Desruisseaux, "Harvard Will Seek $30 Million for Program on Business Ethics," *The Chronicle of Higher Education,* April 8, 1987, p. 27. Copyright 1987, *The Chronicle of Higher Education.* Reprinted with permission.

17. Ibid., p. 29.

18. Gallup Poll, *Public Opinion 1985* (Wilmington, Del.: Scholarly Resources, 1986), pp. 191–93.

19. George Steiner and John Steiner, *Business, Government, and Society: A Managerial Perspective* (New York: Random House, 1979), pp. 370–76.

20. Michael Maccoby, *The Gamesman* (New York: Simon & Schuster, 1976; Bantam, 1978).

21. Barry Z. Posner and Warren H. Schmidt, "Ethics in American Companies: A Managerial Perspective," *Journal of Business Ethics* 6 (July 1987), p. 383.

22. Steven N. Brenner and Earl A. Molander, "Is the Ethics of Business Changing?" *Harvard Business Review* 55, no. 1 (January–February 1977), p. 57.

23. Raymond C. Baumhart, "How Ethical Are Businessmen?" *Harvard Business Review* 39, no. 4 (July–August 1961), p. 6.

24. Brenner and Molander, "Ethics of Business," p. 60.

25. "Ethics Are Nice, but They Can Be a Handicap, Some Executives Declare," *Labor Letter, The Wall Street Journal,* September 8, 1987, p. 1. Reprinted by permission of *The Wall Street Journal,* © Dow Jones & Company, Inc. 1987. ALL RIGHTS RESERVED.

26. Associated Press, "One in Three Scientists Suspects Colleagues Falsify Data," *Waterloo Courier,* August 30, 1987, p. A6.

27. Higher Education Research Institute, University of California–Los Angeles, as reported in "Getting an Education," *The Wall Street Journal,* April 22, 1988, p. 19.

28. "Morality," *U.S. News & World Report,* December 9, 1985, p. 52.

29. *Types of Men,* trans. P. Pigors (Halle, Germany: Niemeyer, 1928).

30. William D. Guth and Renato Tagiuri, "Personal Values and Corporate Strategy," *Harvard Business Review* 43, no. 5 (September–October 1965), p. 123.

31. Adapted from G. W. Allport, P. E. Vernon, and G. Lindzey, *Manual for the Study of Values* (Boston: Houghton Mifflin, 1960), p. 14, as reported in Archie B. Carroll, *Business and Society* (Boston: Little, Brown, 1981), p. 70.

32. Reported in Rick Wartzman, "Nature or Nurture? Study Blames Ethical Lapses on Corporate Goals," *The Wall Street Journal,* October 9, 1987, p. 21.

33. Brenner and Molander, "Ethics of Business," p. 66.

34. Karl Menninger, *Whatever Became of Sin?* (New York: Hawthorn Books, 1973).

35. For an overview, see Peter French, "The Corporation as a Moral Person," *American Philosophical Quarterly* 16, no. 3 (July 1979), pp. 297–317.

36. For one critic's view, see John Ladd, "Persons and Responsibility: Ethical Concepts and Impertinent Analogies," in *Shame, Responsibility and the Corporation,* ed. Hugh Curtler (New York: Haven Publishing, 1986), p. 77.

37. Vogel, "Ethics Course," p. 18.

38. Bernard White and B. Ruth Montgomery, "Corporate Codes of Conduct," *California Management Review* 23, no. 2 (Winter 1980), p. 80.

39. Robert Chatov, "What Corporate Ethics Statements Say," *California Management Review* 22, no. 4 (Summer 1980), p. 20.

40. Wartzman, "Nature or Nuture?" p. 21.

41. Ibid.

42. Goodrich case materials were prepared by Ms. Tracy Timson, M.B.A. student and graduate assistant, University of Northern Iowa.

43. These remarks were drawn, in part, from Kermit Vandivier, "Why Should My Conscience Bother Me?" in *In the Name of Profit,* ed. Robert L. Heilbroner (Garden City, N.Y.: Doubleday, 1972).

44. N. R. Kleinfield, "The Whistle Blowers' Morning After," *The New York Times,* November 9, 1986, section 3, pp. 1, 10.

45. Cited in Gilbert Geis, "White-Collar Crime: The Heavy Electrical Equipment Antitrust Cases of 1961," in *Criminal Behavior Systems: A Typology,* ed. Marshall B. Clinard and Richard Quinney (New York: Holt, Rinehart & Winston, 1967), p. 144.

46. William J. Maakestad, "States' Attorneys Stalk Corporate Murderers," *Business and Society Review,* no. 56 (Winter 1986), p. 21.

47. Jonathan Tasini, "A Death at Work Can Put the Boss in Jail," *Business Week,* March 2, 1987, pp. 31, 38.

48. Charles McCoy, "Financial Fraud: Theories behind Nationwide Surge in Bank Swindles," *The Wall Street Journal,* October 2, 1987, p. 15.

49. Alluded to in congressional testimony, "White-Collar Crime," Subcommittee on Crime of the Committee on the Judiciary, U.S. House of Representatives, 95th Congress, second session on white-collar crime, no. 69 (Washington, D.C.: U.S. Government Printing Office, 1979).

50. "U.S. Agrees to Promote Employee to Settle Suit against the Air Force," *The Wall Street Journal,* June 16, 1982, p. 38.

51. James M. Roche, "The Competitive System, to Work, to Preserve, and to Protect," *Vital Speeches of the Day,* May 1, 1971, p. 445, as reported in Kenneth D. Walters, "Your Employees' Right to Blow the Whistle," *Harvard Business Review,* July–August 1975, p. 26.

52. Carl Kaufmann, "A Five-Part Quiz on Corporate Ethics," *Washington Post,* July 1, 1979, p. C-1.

53. "Misinterpreting the Antibribery Law," *Business Week,* September 3, 1979, p. 150.

54. Kaufmann, "Five-Part Quiz, p. C-4.

55. Ibid.

56. William Bulkeley, "To Some at Harvard, Telling Lies Becomes a Matter of Course," *The Wall Street Journal,* January 15, 1979, p. 1.

57. Leonard C. Lewin, "Ethical Aptitude Test," *Harper's,* October 1976, p. 21.

58. Reported on WKYT TV, channel 27, "Evening News," Lexington, Kentucky, May 12, 1980.

59. "Business Executives and Moral Dilemmas," *Business and Society Review,* no. 13 (Spring 1975), p. 51.

60. Paul R. Dew, "Views from a Sentenced Executive," *Antitrust Law Journal* 47, no. 2 (1978–79), p. 729.

61. Robert Bartley, "Business Ethics and the Ethics Business," *The Wall Street Journal,* May 18, 1987, p. 18.

62. Robert Runde, "Mind Benders," *Money,* September 1978, p. 24.

63. Albert A. Carr, "Is Business Bluffing Ethical?" *Harvard Business Review* 46, no. 1 (January–February 1968), pp. 143–52.

64. Lionel Tiger, "Stone Age Provides Model for Instilling Business Ethics," *The Wall Street Journal,* January 11, 1988, p. 22.

Chapter 3

The Corporation in Society: Social Responsibility?

Part One—Corporate Power and Corporate Critics

INTRODUCTION

Before turning to the law per se it is essential to remind the reader of the context—the environment—in which the law developed. Therefore, a major purpose of this chapter is to raise some critical issues regarding the business community's relationship to the larger society. Should we "free" business from government intervention to achieve greater productivity and profit? Should business play a larger role in politics, education, and other public-sector activities? Should business assume greater responsibilities in correcting societal ills? The reader is expected to use this chapter to make a tentative assessment of the very large question: What is the proper role of business in society? Only after acquiring some preliminary grasp of that issue can one logically and fruitfully turn to various "control devices" (such as law) as a means of enforcing that proper role.

The second major goal of this chapter is that of alerting the reader to some of the primary criticisms raised against the corporate community. The successful businessperson and the good citizen must understand and intelligently evaluate the objections of those who criticize the role of the corporation in contemporary life. Of course, government regulation is, in part, a response to those criticisms. (A detailed investigation of the forces generating government intervention is offered in Chapter 6.)

The materials in this chapter necessarily cast some elements of business practice in an unfavorable light, but even the most ardent defender of American business should welcome the opportunity to understand and evaluate the critics' viewpoints. Having done so, the student will be better prepared to understand and assess—allow me to say it again—the proper role of business in society and the use of the law in regulating that role.

Public Opinion

The data suggest the American people in the 1980s both admire and mistrust big business. A 1985 Roper poll found 71 percent of the respondents holding a "highly favorable" or "moderately favorable" perception of "most large businesses." In 1978, 62 percent of the respondents held favorable opinions of big business. On the other hand, 25 percent of the 1985 respondents held "not too favorable" or "rather unfavorable" views, as compared with 32 percent in 1978.[1] Roper partially attributes the public's substantially favorable attitude toward business to our general faith in the free enterprise system as well as the economic prosperity of the mid 80s. Roper reports:

> Today, 58 percent of the public agree that "what's good for business is good for the average person." This proportion has remained virtually unchanged since we first asked the question in 1981. And probably the most notable feature of this result is that essentially similar majorities of all Americans—young and old, white collar and blue collar, liberal and conservative—concur with the proposition. The only true dissenters are black Americans, with 22 percent disagreeing and another 31 percent having mixed feelings about the coincidence of interests between business and the average person.[2]

But Roper also points to evidence of a continuing popular suspicion regarding the trustworthiness of the business community. Recent, well-publicized cases of corporate and white-collar crime have particularly unsettled the public trust. For example, among those polled who were knowledgeable about the episodes, 45 percent believed investment firm E. F. Hutton was treated too leniently when fined $2 million following a fraud conviction. Only 3 percent felt the punishment was too harsh. Indeed, executives and professionals as a class felt Hutton was treated too gently. And a 1986 *New York Times* poll found 35 percent siding with the "often maligned" federal government and 24 percent choosing big business when asked where ethical standards are higher.[3] Furthermore, Roper's polling data display overwhelming public sentiment for a government role in "keeping an eye" on business. For example, 85 percent of those polled approved of a government role in pollution cleanup. (See Chapter 7 for more government regulation data.) Roper summarized the public's attitude and warned of the possibility of increased business insensitivity:

> Consciously or subconsciously, people look at any two legs of the business–labor–government tripod to balance—to hold in check—the potential excesses of the other .... People don't want government to run much of anything, but

they do want government to "monitor" private enterprise. In a word, our system of checks and balances applies not only to the political sphere but equally to the economic one.

At the moment, Americans see business as a lesser economic danger than government or labor—which helps explain why their attitudes toward business are so favorable. Yet the danger is that business might overinterpret its current mandate from the people—that it will assume it has an unqualified license to do exactly what it wants. It may imagine that if some public policy is not good for business, it automatically is not good for America. These are the dangers of growing arrogance and insensitivity on the part of business as it enjoys its comfortable environment—the kind of arrogance that both labor and government developed after the public embraced them in the 1930s and 1940s to combat the excesses of business.[4]

Of special interest for our purposes are findings in a number of surveys indicating that women have substantially greater misgivings about big business than do men. *The New York Times* reports the results of one of its surveys of American adults:

Throughout the survey, women seemed more critical than men on questions ranging from product quality to corporate honesty. And the women were less optimistic about the prospects for financial success in modern America. Fifty-eight percent of the men still believed in the Horatio Alger dream [that one may begin poor, work hard, and become rich], compared to 44 percent of the women—and, surprisingly, only 41 percent of the working women.[5]

Think about the significance of this difference in attitudes.

Concentration of Resources

In both the public's perceptions and in fact, corporate America's very bigness is both a strength and a weakness. Size produces economics of scale and enhanced competitiveness in an increasingly demanding international market. Of course, that some American corporations are of Goliath proportions is hardly news, but a reminder of the specifics may be useful.

For example, the 1987 *Fortune* Industrial 500 shows General Motors at the top of the sales pyramid, with 1986 revenues of more than $100 billion.[6] Exxon ranked second, with more than $69 billion in sales. GM's assets in 1986 exceeded $72 billion, and, with nearly 880,000 employees, GM was America's leading industrial employer.[7] That employment is roughly equal to the population of Nashville, Orlando, Honolulu, or Birmingham. These figures assume more meaning when compared with the gross national products of the nations of the world. Based on World Bank and *Fortune* data, General Motors' 1986 sales of $102.8 billion ranked 16th among the world's economic units. Exxon ranked 23rd on that list, with sales of $69.8 billion. Thus GM placed behind Switzerland (GNP, $105.2

billion) and just ahead of Saudi Arabia ($102.1 billion). Exxon's $69.8 billion in sales exceeded the GNPs of such nations as Austria ($69.1 billion) and South Africa ($65.3 billion).[8] At the same time, we must note that the world's largest company, Nippon Telephone and Telegraph $263.5 billion in assets), is Japanese, as are 8 of the top 10 companies.[9]

Size is, of course, suggestive of power, but much more frightening to business critics is the concentration of resources that characterizes the business structure. The accompanying table offers a glimpse of industrial concentration over recent decades among the approximately 350,000 American manufacturing firms.

Largest Manufacturing Corporations—Percent Share of Assets Held: 1965 to 1984

| | Corporation rank group | |
	100 largest	200 largest
1965	46.5%	56.7
1970	48.5%	60.4
1973	44.7%	56.9
1974	44.4%	56.7
1975	45.0%	57.5
1976	45.4%	58.0
1977	45.9%	58.5
1978	45.5%	58.3
1979	46.1%	59.0
1980	46.7%	59.7
1981	46.8%	60.0
1982	47.7%	60.8
1983	48.3%	60.8
1984	48.9%	60.7

Note: Prior to 1970, excludes newspapers. Data prior to 1974 not strictly comparable with later years.

Source: Through 1981, U.S. Federal Trade Commission; thereafter, U.S. Bureau of the Census, unpublished data. As reprinted in the *Statistical Abstract of the U.S.,* 1986.

THE CORPORATE STATE

While it is beyond credible dispute that a small number of firms control a disproportionate quantity of commercial resources, vigorous debate rages over the actual concentration levels and trends in recent years. Of course, the controversy regarding corporate power would be meaningless but for the view that corporate power has resulted in harm to the public. Although scholarly opinion on the issue varies, a number of studies show a positive relationship between concentration and corporate profits.[10] Consequently, critics contend that consumers are paying the bill for "excess" profits. However, many scholars suggest stronger profits in concentrated industries are the product of efficiency rather than the abuse of monopoly power.[11] But the list of complaints ranges well beyond pure economics. From pollution, discrimination, white-collar crime, invasion of privacy, and undue political influence, to misleading advertising, and on across the spectrum of social problems, the critics lay much of the blame on the corporate community.

Many of those issues are addressed in subsequent chapters of this book. But to make the position of the corporate critics clearer, we must now look more closely at a few of the major complaints. The critics contend the power of the business community has become so encompassing that virtually all dimensions of American life have absorbed elements of the business ethic. Values commonly associated with businesspersons (competition, profit seeking, reliance on technology, faith in growth) have overwhelmed traditional humanist values (cooperation, individual dignity, human rights, meaningful service to society). In the name of efficiency and productivity, it is argued that the warmth, decency, and value of life have been debased. We engage in meaningless work in an artificial culture. Objects dominate our existence. We operate as replaceable cogs in a vast, bureaucratic machine. Our national environment is shredded in the gleeful pursuit of progress. Indeed, we lose ourselves, the critics argue. Charles Reich, former Yale University law professor, addressed the loss of self in his influential book of the Vietnam War era, *The Greening of America:*

> Of all of the forms of impoverishment that can be seen or felt in America, loss of self, or death in life, is surely the most devastating. . . . Beginning with school, if not before, an individual is systematically stripped of his imagination, his creativity, his heritage, his dreams, and his personal uniqueness, in order to style him into a productive unit for a mass, technological society. Instinct, feeling, and spontaneity are repressed by overwhelming forces. As the individual is drawn into the meritocracy, his working life is split from his home life, and both suffer from a lack of wholeness. Eventually, people virtually become their professions, roles, or occupations, and are henceforth strangers to themselves. Blacks long ago felt their deprivation of identity and potential for life. But white "soul" and blues are just beginning. Only a segment of youth is articulately aware that they too suffer an enforced loss of self—they too are losing the lives that could be theirs.[12]

Reich seems to be suggesting that the *meaning* in life, the "spiritual" tones that afford flavor and quality, are being stripped from our existence. The residue, the critics argue, is a society of hollow men and women—long on dollars, occupiers of prestigious posts, possessors of power, but bereft of the central core of goodness and purpose that affords us worth beyond worldly achievement. In the piece that follows we are reminded of one of our losses—a small, but doubtless important, part of a much larger whole.

WHERE DID YOUR GARDEN GO?

Michael Silverman

The A train ties Rockaway to the mainland of New York City. When I was a kid, this was our main access to New York, or, to put it more precisely, to the old Madison Square Garden.

The Garden was a place where the world seemed to come alive. It is difficult for me to talk about it with an adult perspective. When we are young, we feel with a certain immediacy; things are rich; we react to life. Now, when you think about it, this is not exactly a bad way to live. So, for the moment, I won't worry about adult perspective. I'll just tell you about the old Garden back in the early 60s.

When you climbed out of the subway, Eighth Avenue was alive, people jammed under the old marquee, the bars packed three deep, and all the cigar-store phones taken by guys putting in late bets with their books. When you walked in the Eighth Avenue end of the Garden the ice was right there in front of you, not stashed away at the end of a maze of concrete tunnels. Seventy-five cents got you a seat up in the side balcony and when the players skated out on the ice you could see their faces.

Now Missing: The Human Element

You had access to the players. All it took was a good shout from up there and the inimitable Lou Fontinato would be aware of your presence in the building. The Garden and the people in it were real entities, with peeling paint and human faces. When the crowd roared on some nights, you could feel the place shake under your feet.

You could connect in that place. There were human connections. You went, you felt, and you made your own connections.

That connection is dying today. People sit in airless concrete ovals. Through the convenience of a network of escalators and tunnels, you can reach your seat in the loge and never once feel a sense of place. You are just another component in a concrete oval.

There are excellent sight lines, but of what? The players have been reduced to colorful digits. From most seats in the Garden the view is the equivalent of what you get on an eight-inch TV screen.

Everything is hyped through the media. All aspects of sport are scrutinized, explained, magnified, and eventually mystified. The game becomes something we dissect and study at a distance. And, little by little, it loses its life; it becomes an artificial object. In the end, we become objective, but only at the expense of our humanity. The real connections wither away.

Your Life to Live

And this does not have to be. We, in the end, still have the ability to determine the course of our lives. But only if we recognize it as our responsibility and not let it be co-opted by those who have lost their vision. And this responsibility is there at every moment. It's there when you buy a ticket to a place like the Garden. It's there when you buy a rotten piece of fruit and accept it as the way things are.

Questions

1. *a.* Do you agree that "what's good for business is good for the average person"? Explain.

   b. Would your opinion change if the word *big* were inserted in front of business? Explain.

2. *Washington Post* columnist David Broder reflects on his satisfaction in attending a Chicago Cubs baseball game at Wrigley Field:

   > Much—perhaps too much—has been written about Wrigley Field's fidelity to baseball's past: the real grass surface, the ivy on the outfield walls, the refusal to install lights or play night games. . . . The ballpark has no electronic scoreboards, fancy frills, or other distractions to get in the way of the spectator's experience of the game of baseball. . . . Wrigley Field go [es] on, essentially unchanged. And that is something to celebrate in this over-gimmicked, overcomplicated world.[13] [In 1988, lights were installed and occasional night games were included in the Cubs' schedule—Author.]

   Silverman and Broder both lament what they take to be an increasing impersonality and technological distance in life.

   a. Is American life "over-gimmicked and overcomplicated"? Explain.

   b. Silverman says we "still have the ability to determine the course of our lives." Are you in control of your life? Explain.

Public Policy

So Michael Silverman reminds us that the progress of recent years may, in some respects, be more apparent than real. But he also argues that if some elements of the quality of life are in decline, the blame lies with us rather than the "villians" in the business community. However, we can elaborate on the case of the corporate critics by directing our attention to some areas of special concern. We will begin with politics, where critics charge that superior resources enable the business community to unfairly slant the electoral and law-making processes in favor of corporate interests.

In recent years the corporate community has taken a more direct and vigorous role in the political process. As a result, corporate critics are increasingly concerned that the financial weight of big business will prove so influential that our pluralist, democratic approach to governance may be significantly distorted. Today money is central to the task of acquiring elective office. And following election, dollars to finance lobbying on Capitol Hill can be critical in shaping congressional opinion.

Of course, corporate funds cannot lawfully be expended for federal campaign contributions. But corporations—via political action committees (PACs)—can lawfully facilitate the establishment of arrangements by which individual employees may make contributions. PACs are not limited to corporations. Labor unions, professional groups, or any group of interested persons can collect money and make political contributions under the rules of the Federal Election Commission.

The PACs have become central to the federal electoral process. According to Common Cause, PAC contributions nearly quadrupled (to $84.6 million) over an eight-year period ending in 1987, while individual donations doubled (to $142.4 million). And Common Cause noted that many members of the House have become heavily reliant on PAC funds: "In the 1986 congressional campaigns, 194 members— 44 percent of the House—raised at least half of their campaign funds from PACs."[14] As has been the case for a number of years, Congress is considering, at this writing in 1988, a bill to dampen PAC influence.

> Bills to reform campaign financing have languished in Congress in previous sessions, but . . . 44 senators—all but 2 of them Democrats—have endorsed a bill this year that would provide public financing for candidates who agree to limit their campaign spending.
>
> The bill, called the Senatorial Election Campaign Act, would limit the total amount any candidate can receive from PACs. It also would reduce the ceiling on individual PAC contributions from $5,000 per candidate for a given race to $3,000.
>
> * * * * *
>
> The bill would be financed with a $2 checkoff on individual income tax returns.[15]

As explained in the following article, campaign contributions through PACs as well as "personal appearance" fees can be very effective in capturing the attention of members of Congress.

CHICAGO FUTURES INDUSTRY, TO FEND OFF ATTACK, RALLIES LAWMAKERS WHO RECEIVED PAC FUNDS

Brooks Jackson and Bruce Ingersoll

Washington—Representative Jim Leach quietly introduced a bill . . . aimed at reducing speculation in financial futures. Barely 24 hours later, the Iowa Republican learned that Chicago commodity traders were gunning to kill his proposal.

Representative Leach said one Illinois lawmaker told him the bill was shaping up as a classic *fetcher bill,* a term used in that state's legislature to describe a measure likely to "fetch" campaign contributions for its opponents. Sure enough, one of the first to defend the traders was Democratic Representative Cardiss Collins of Illinois, recipient of $24,500 from futures-industry political action committees. She called on colleagues in the Illinois delegation to beat back the Leach bill and watch out for similar legislation.

The freewheeling Chicago futures markets are under attack in Congress as never before. Their tremendously profitable traffic in stock index futures is being blamed by Representative Leach and others for contributing to [October 1987's] stock market crash.

But the traders have spread money around Washington liberally in the past few years. Now, in their hour of need, they are finding no shortage of defenders.

The PACs of the Chicago Mercantile Exchange, the Chicago Board of Trade, and the Futures Industry Association have given a combined total of nearly $1.6 million in campaign donations to current Senate and House members since the start of 1983. During the same period, the two exchanges also have handed out more than $330,000 in personal appearance fees to scores of House and Senate members who have toured the trading pits. Furthermore, prosperous traders have poured personal gifts into the political war chests of Washington's mighty.

Representative Leach is one of the few in Congress who refuse to accept PAC donations. His bill would empower the Federal Reserve Board to require purchasers of "equity-like derivatives," including stock index futures and options, to put up as much as 50 percent in cash. Currently, the Fed sets margin requirements for stocks, while the futures exchanges set their own margin requirements. Before the October 19 stock market crash, buyers of stock futures had to put up as little as 10 cents on the dollar, or even less. The Fed requires stock buyers to pay at least half in cash.

"Speculative activity has been very high" in the futures markets, Representative Leach says. "It is certainly not the major cause of the market meltdown, but it is a contributing cause."

* * * * *

To head off tighter margin rules and other regulatory changes, the heads of the Chicago exchanges last week held what was by all accounts a council of war with the Illinois congressional delegation. Democratic Senator Alan Dixon and Democratic Representative Dan Rostenkowski arranged a luncheon in the private dining room of House Republican Leader Robert Michel. One participant says the Chicago Merc's chairman, Leo Melamed, could barely suppress his belligerence. "He was pounding on the table," this lawmaker says. "He was mad . . . . He made a forceful presentation: New York is out to get the Chicago exchanges." Mr. Melamed wasn't available for comment.

The New York versus Chicago line was later echoed by Senator Dixon, who received $38,000 from the commodity PACs. He calls "outrageous" even the suggestion that stock index futures trading was to blame for Black Monday. He contends the Big Board is mounting "a very carefully planned effort to steal the Chicago futures market."

The Chicago Merc and Board of Trade are "big business in my state, my friend," Senator Dixon says. "This is like talking about Caterpillar or United Airlines. They are important to us."

* * * * *

Meanwhile, the Chicago traders are getting support from lawmakers far from Lake Michigan's shores. Democratic Representative Ed Jones of Tennessee, chairman of the House Agriculture Committee's credit panel, convened a hurry-up hearing last week and devoted it to defending stock index futures and the CFTC's [Commodity Futures Trading Commission] supervision of the futures markets. He got $21,250 from the traders' PACs.

At the session, Democratic Representative E (Kika) de la Garza of Texas, the Agriculture Committee chairman, told lawmakers who would rein in futures trading to "cool it" until regulators finish their post-mortems on the October 19 crash. "You can't legislate against" gambling in the markets, said Representative de la Garza, who got $33,500 from the traders' PACs.

Representative de la Garza also received last year a $1,000 personal appearance fee from the Chicago Board of Trade, and accepted a two-day trip to Boca Raton, Florida, from the Chicago Merc. Representative Jones received $1,000 in fees from the two exchanges.

Those honoraria were part of a total of $57,000 in fees that the two exchanges paid to current Senate and House members last year to entice lawmakers to spend time with them. The going rate is $1,000 for a House member, $2,000 for a senator. Every year dozens of lawmakers flock to Chicago to collect.

A Dissent

Notwithstanding the concerns of Common Cause and others, one can build a powerful argument that PACs do not represent a threat to the democratic process and that campaign reform legislation will restrict free speech while adding more bureaucratic rules and rendering encumbents even tougher to beat. Robert Samuelson, commenting in *Newsweek,* explains that money is very often not the determining factor in congressional elections and about one half of the much-criticized expansion in campaign spending since 1978 is attributable to inflation. In Samuelson's view, special interest efforts are merely an expression of democracy, and he argues that those efforts do not dominate the political process in any case:

> PACs remain a minority of all contributions. In 1986 they were 21 percent for the Senate (up from 17 percent in 1984) and 34 percent for the House (level with 1984).
>
> The diversity of the 4,157 PACs dilutes their power. There are business PACs, labor PACs, pro-abortion PACs, anti-abortion PACs, importer PACs, and protectionist PACs. Contributions are fairly evenly split between Democrats ($74.6 million in 1986) and Republicans ($57.5 million.)
>
> PACs give heavily to senior, powerful congressmen, who are politically secure and not easily intimidated. According to Common Cause, Democratic Representative Augustus Hawkins of California is the most dependent on PAC contributions (92 percent). First elected in 1962, he won last year with 85 percent of the vote.
>
> Of course special interests mob Congress. That's democracy. One person's special interest is another's crusade or livelihood. To be influential, people organize. As government's powers have grown, so has lobbying by affected groups: old people, farmers, doctors, teachers. The list runs on. But PACs are only a minor influence on voting. Political scientist Frank Sorauf of the University of Minnesota reports that in 1984, the average PAC contribution to House incumbents was less than one third of 1 percent of the average congressman's total receipts.[16]

Lobbying

Those who criticize corporate influence on the legislative process are not concerned with PACs alone. Highly sophisticated and expensive lobbying is a staple of the business community's efforts to implement its legislative agenda. Of course, lobbying is defended as an efficient method of better acquainting busy politicians with the subtleties of the diverse issues they must address, and lobbying is not confined to the "big spenders" of the business community—witness the many consumer lobbies. An estimated 20,000 lobbyists annually spend perhaps $1.5 billion attempting to influence official Washington.[17] But the business community senses a decline in its Washington clout. Recently, *The Wall Street Journal* summarized the changing lobbying picture:

> The nature of business lobbying has changed markedly over the past decade. Throughout much of the postwar period, powerful business leaders could affect legislation by cutting back-room deals with a few top legislators. More recently, power has been dispersed throughout Congress, and business lobbyists have had to learn to sell their policy proposals to a bigger group of legislators and to the public at large. "The old-boy network just doesn't work that well anymore," says Raymond Hoewing, a vice president of the Public Affairs Council, a corporate-financed research group in Washington.[18]

Notwithstanding an arguable decline in the power of big business on Capitol Hill, the following article illustrates the continuing vitality of practices labeled "influence peddling" by some and "democracy at work" by others.

LOBBYING BY BUSINESSMAN FOR NEW CHINA TRADE SHOWS HOW MONEY, CONNECTIONS CAN SHAPE LAW

Monica Langley

Washington—Edward Furia, a middleman for high-dollar transactions, is looking to Congress for help with a potentially lucrative business opportunity and is willing to spend as much as $1 million to get it.

"I want to make money trading with China," says the Seattle businessman, who gets a commission on every transaction he arranges between Chinese and American businesses. "My legislative proposal would help me do that."

In no-nonsense fashion, Mr. Furia drafted a proposed measure that would increase U.S. trade with China and then hired some of Washington's top lobbyists to get the proposal into the comprehensive trade bill now moving in Congress. Lobbying for favorable legislation happens all the time, but Mr. Furia's effort exemplifies the way laws sometimes are shaped through aggressive self-interest, money, and connections.

The 45-year-old Mr. Furia calls his lobbying activities here "an investment." He likens his activities to "entrepreneurship, because I am devoting time and money to an idea that may or may not pay off."

To help see that his investment does pay off, Mr. Furia has retained lobbying pro Charles Walker, a former Treasury official, to assemble several corporations into a Committee for Fair Trade with China. "Charlie can call half of Fortune 100 CEOs," Mr. Furia boasts. Since Mr. Walker signed on, Bechtel, Inc., and United Technologies Corporation have endorsed Mr. Furia's legislative proposal.

Introduction of Amendment

Elliot Richardson, former defense secretary and attorney general, is also lobbying for Mr. Furia's proposed measure. It was Mr. Richardson's contacts that proved critical in getting a China trade proposal—though a more modest one than Mr. Furia sought—included in the trade bill recently approved by the House Ways and Means Committee.

"It was out of my respect for Elliot that I met with Mr. Furia and listened to his idea," acknowledges Representative Thomas Downey. The New York Democrat subsequently introduced an amendment to the trade bill to require an administration study of increased trade with China.

After Representative Downey got the trade subcommittee to accept the amendment, Mr. Furia began lobbying the members of the full Ways and Means Committee for a stronger

measure. A rotund, vociferous operator, Mr. Furia relentlessly stalked lawmakers and their staffs to beseech their help.

Buying New Business

His hard-nosed approach quickly drew criticism among congressional aides as a blatant attempt to buy new business through legislation. They nicknamed Mr. Furia "Ed Furious," and vowed among themselves not to let a businessman use money and contacts to buy his way into the trade bill.

"Nobody likes us for what they called my aggressive tactics," Mr. Furia concedes. "We got a lot of opposition from the staff . . . and a scolding from administration officials."

Mr. Furia's campaign began after a conversation with his neighbor, former administration official William Ruckelshaus. He told Mr. Ruckelshaus, with whom he shares a boat dock and tennis court, about his idea to increase trade with China through legislation.

Anti-Dumping Issue

Mr. Ruckelshaus put Mr. Furia in touch with Mr. Walker, who heads one of the city's top lobbying firms. Mr. Furia asked Mr. Richardson to work with him for the Furia proposal, and also hired a public relations consultant who promoted Mr. Furia's efforts to all the major media outlets here. Within a few days, Mr. Furia was charging ahead to win congressional approval of his proposal.

* * * * *

"We are having a difficult time getting our arcane complicated issues considered," Mr. Furia laments, but he says he remains hopeful.

Source: *The Wall Street Journal*, April 9, 1987, p. 56. Reprinted by permission of The Wall Street Journal, © Dow Jones & Company, Inc. 1987. ALL RIGHTS RESERVED.

Questions

1. The corporate community possesses vast resources. Noted economist John Kenneth Galbraith, among others, has argued that consumer ''wants'' can be created by skillful persuasion. Does the application of corporate resources and skills to the shaping of public and political opinion constitute a threat to democracy? Explain.

2. Anne Wexler, aide to former president Jimmy Carter, is a Washington lobbyist. She says, ''There's a need here. Government officials are not comfortable making these complicated decisions by themselves.''[19]

   a. Are lobbyists necessary for the effective operation of government? Explain.

   b. If we wanted to curb lobbying, how should we do so?

3. Richard Goodwin, assistant special counsel to President John F. Kennedy, speaks out on PACs:

   > Morally the system is bribery. It is not criminal only because those who make the laws are themselves accomplices. Government is for sale. But the bids are sealed, and the prices are very high.
   >
   > There is an easy way out: Eliminate PACs. We should place a rigorous ceiling on all congressional campaigns, allocate public funds to finance campaigns, and require television stations—the most costly component of modern political campaigns—to give a specified amount of air time to candidates.[20]

   a. Should we forbid PACs? Explain.

   b. Would such action be constitutionally permissible? Explain.

4. Edward Furia's ability to influence the political process via his money and contacts is dramatically superior to that of most Americans. As you see it, does that condition constitute an injustice to those not so well placed as Furia? Explain.

Business Values

The corporation is arguably the central institution in contemporary America. In every dimension of American life, business values are increasingly pervasive. To those who criticize the corporation, that near-blanket adoption of the business ethic signals a dangerous distortion of the nation's priorities. Judge for yourself as we take a quick glimpse at several areas of concern.

1. Schools.   Let us begin with our schools. No distinctive perception is needed to recognize the advance of business and technological training and the decline of the liberal arts. From kindergarten through graduate school, the ''business mentality'' is pervasive. Given the competitiveness of the job market, it is argued that students and their parents willingly allow and, indeed, call for a ''quick fix'' of skills (such as accounting, management, and marketing) as a replacement for occupationally ambiguous disciplines, such as history, literature, and philosophy. The bargain has been struck. The student leaves his or her formal education and proceeds into the financial security of the Corporate State, but did that person buy a good life or an empty existence? Charles Reich offers his opinion:

> The process by which man is deprived of his self begins with his institutionalized training in public school for a place in the machinery of the State. The object of the training is not merely to teach him how to perform some specific function; it is to make him become that function, to see and judge himself and others in terms of functions, and to abandon any aspect of self, thinking, questioning, feeling, loving, that has no utility for either production or consumption in the Corporate State. The training for the role of consumer is just as important as the training for a job, and at least equally significant for loss of self.

* * * * *

> Consumer training in school consists of preventing the formation of individual consciousness, taste, aesthetic standards, self-knowledge, and the ability to create one's own satisfactions. Solitude, separateness, undirected time, and silence, which are necessary for consciousness, are not permitted. Groups are encouraged to set values, inhibiting the growth of self-knowledge.[21]

2. Churches.   The recent scandal surrounding television evangelist Jim Bakker, his wife Tammy, and their stewardship of the PTL Club has focused a great deal of unfavorable attention on the various "TV ministries." Allegations of misconduct aside, that those ministries have taken on the appearance and practices of the business community has caused critics to lament the selling of religion as a commodity. For example, presidential candidate and TV minister/executive Pat Robertson devoted a chapter of his book, *Beyond Reason,* to "God's Marvelous System of Money Management." Robertson's ministry reportedly earns about $233 million annually.[22] According to newspaper columnist Jim Jones:

> Critics contend that prosperity preachers cater to greed in believers; exploit people by saying that donating to the ministries will multiply their money; give the impression that those who give will be rewarded with costly items, such as cars or houses; and change the true meaning of Bible verses to back up their teaching.[23]

3. Culture.   Professor Debora Silverman's recent book, *Selling Culture,* argues that America's great art museums are becoming mere tools of "advertising, public relations, and sales campaigns."[24] In a review of the book, columnist Jonathon Yardley explains Silverman's thesis:

> Silverman notes the coincidence between French and Chinese exhibits at the Met and sales promotions for French and Chinese goods at Bloomingdale's. She argues that such museum exhibits are staged not for the edification of the

public, but for the glorification and profit of those in what the trade calls "high-end" commerce . . . . we no longer possess a genuinely artistic culture, only a marketplace in which artist and collector, curator and director, pursue instant riches and renown.[25]

4. Sports. To the critics, the "commercialization" of sports is simply an accomplished fact. From football to bicycling, the allure of money has become so compelling that the historical purity of amateur athletics as a venue for fun and character building has been obliterated. *Business Week* devoted a recent cover story, "Nothing Sells Like Sports," to the theme of sports marketing:

These days, everything from sled-dog racing to professional beach volleyball is likely to find corporate backing.[26]

We are now the beneficiaries of corporate-sponsored college football games (e.g., the Mazda Gator Bowl and the USF&G Sugar Bowl) and corporate-sponsored arenas [e.g., the ARCO (Atlantic-Richfield) Arena, where the Sacramento Kings play NBA basketball]. College basketball and football coaches have become a booming new class of entrepreneurs, with summer camps, the lecture circuit, and contracts with shoe manufacturers (for ensuring their players take the field wearing only the designated brand).

5. Children. These complaints of commercial values magnified throughout American life are summarized in the following article.

CHILDREN'S SEARCH FOR VALUES
LEADING TO SHOPPING MALLS

Jeffrey Zaslow

St. Louis—With an almost Orwellian eeriness, giant photos of teen-age boys and girls peer out over Crestwood Plaza . . . , where shoppers hurry in and out of fashion boutiques and stores piled high with trendy merchandise.

To Jennifer Hunt, the atmosphere in malls like this is intoxicating. "I see something. I fall in love with it. I have to have it," the 15-year-old says. "My mother says I'm—what's the word? Insatiable."

To sociologists and educators, however, such scenes are a sign that the focus for children's values has shifted away from the family. With parents taking a less active role in raising their children, middle-class teens are looking outside the family to a greater degree than ever before to define their social values. "More and more kids today are looking for some form of structure in their lives," says one family psychologist. "The malls are a place they find it."

For many teens, the result is a muddling of traditional middle-class values. In the places where they hang out, it's not hard to find evidence of why many specialists are now saying that today's teens are more materialistic, less realistic, and harder to motivate than any generation before them.

If only indirectly, teens themselves often seem well aware of the differences. "The goals have changed," says Mike Jostes, 18. "When a guy's refrigerator dispenses water and ice cubes, people think he's got it made. He doesn't need kids. He's got everything."

All You Ever Wanted

* * * * *

Surrounded by the 43 apparel stores, 27 restaurants, and 19 shoe stores at nearby Chesterfield Mall, it's not hard for teenagers to feel as if the world's goods are already theirs. "You come here and see all the stuff you ever wanted," says Kelli McGuinness.

The malls are only too happy to satisfy teenagers' wants, particularly when parents are inclined to waive control. ("My parents say I'm lucky to have this mall," says 12-year-old Robby Powers as he relaxes on a bench reading a book of cartoons called "Garfield Sits around the House.") The fresh-faced teens pictured in Crestwood's courtyards are members of the mall's "student advisory board," says Lee Wagman, the mall's owner. The youths, some of whom are models, help other teens to feel "it's their mall," he explains. "We encourage a sense of proprietorship. It makes for loyalty."

Recognizing that today's parents make fewer buying decisions for their children, merchants are stepping up their marketing to youngsters. At Chesterfield, sales at Contempo Casuals rise about 10 percent after the store sponsors a fashion show at local high schools. The Wild Pair puts its Ciao booties, Zodiac boots, and other teen-oriented shoes toward the front of its store, because kids, who often roam the mall for hours, do more window shopping than adults.

Molding Buying Habits

Stores also try to mold buying habits. At Crestwood, jewelers create rings with inexpensive diamond chips to encourage kids to make diamonds "a part of their style," says Mr. Wagman.

No wonder Mike Redmond, 14, says, "Success is money mostly. I want to get the money first, then go for the happiness."

Some teens predict that technology will guarantee their happiness. "They're inventing all this stuff and everything, so you won't have to work that hard, or cook dinner, or do housework," says Brian Jacobson, 15. Already, he has some nice gadgets. "I've got a lot of extra stuff I don't need: a waterbed, a ceiling fan, a $400 bike." He earns $15 a week for vacuuming his house, and figures he drops $10 of that on video games at the mall.

But despite some optimism about the future, many youths wonder if they will be able to make family life work; they have seen failures throughout their neighborhoods. "By the time I get married, it might only last a few years, then I'll get divorced, then married again," says John Brouster, whose parents are divorced.

Teens sense their parents' confusion, too. "They thought they would live happily ever after and didn't," says John. Adds Mike Redmond: "The way things are changing, parents aren't sure what success ought to be."

Source: *The Wall Street Journal*, March 21, 1987, p. 21. Reprinted by permission of *The Wall Street Journal*, © Dow Jones & Company, Inc. 1987. ALL RIGHTS RESERVED.

THE BUSINESS RESPONSE

For many years the business community has been compelled to respond to criticism like that just elaborated. That response takes numerous forms. In America, seeking a profit within the rules certainly should not be a source of shame. And if Americans actually disapprove of the corporate community, surely adjustments would be required. And why should we criticize the business community for holding and practicing values that are simply a reflection of the preferences of the larger society? And so on.

In essence, the argument is one of power. To the critics, the corporate community exerts authority to a degree that jeopardizes societal welfare. But as noted management theorist Peter Drucker explains, one may argue that the American business community has seldom enjoyed less power than is the case today:

> No businessman anywhere these days has even a fraction of the power held 80 years ago by a J. P. Morgan, a John D. Rockefeller, an Alfried Krupp, or by the 10 or 12 private bankers who together constituted the nearly omnipotent "Court" of the Bank of England before World War I. The gainers in power have been institutions that are either hostile toward or highly critical of business: the labor union, the government bureaucracy, and the greatest gainer of them all—the university. A mere ornament of society 80 years ago, it now holds in every developed country what no earlier society ever granted an institution: the power to grant or to deny access to livelihood and careers through its unregulated monopoly of the all-important university degree.
>
> Neither in absolute nor in relative terms does business wealth today even remotely compare with that of 1900. The wealth of the richest billionaire of today, if adjusted for taxes and inflation, looks puny next to the fortunes of 80 years ago. And for the economy, the "rich" have actually become irrelevant.
>
> Eighty years ago any one of the "tycoons," whether in the United States, in Imperial Germany, in Edwardian England, or in the France of the Third Republic, could—and did—by himself supply the entire capital needed by a major industry. Today the wealth of America's 1,000 richest people, taken together, would barely cover one week of the country's capital needs. The only true "capitalists" in developed countries today are the wage earners through their pension funds and mutual funds.[27]

Questions

1. *a.* Has your education been designed primarily to prepare you for a utilitarian role as a producer and/or consumer in the Corporate State? Explain.
   b. Have you been encouraged, as Charles Reich claims, to abandon "thinking, questioning, feeling, loving"? Explain.
2. Professor Silverman bemoans the decline of a "genuinely artistic culture." Is culture, as she means it, largely irrelevant to contemporary life? Explain.

3. Pop artist Andy Warhol produced a painting of 200 $1 bills. The painting sold for $385,000. Warhol once said that ''Being good in business is the most fascinating kind of art.''

   a. What did Warhol mean?

   b. Is business America's dominant art form? Explain.

4. Big-time sports is now a big business. Has the quality of the sports experience been depreciated? Explain.

5. *a.* Are shopping malls replacing the family in American life? Explain.

   b. In your view, are mall owners and storeowners engaging in unethical conduct when they encourage teens to feel that ''it's their mall'' or when they seek to ''mold buying habits''? Explain.

   c. Do teens need protection of some sort from excessive commercial influences? Explain.

   d. If such protection is needed, what form should it take?

6. According to *The Wall Street Journal*, ''[S]hopping can be all things to all people. It can alleviate loneliness and dispel boredom; it can be a sport and can be imbued with the thrill of the hunt; it can provide escape, fulfill fantasies, relieve depression.''[28]

   a. Is shopping an American addiction that requires treatment in the manner of alcoholism, for example? Explain.

   b. Does shopping fill a void of some sort in our lives? If so, how was that void created? Or was it always there?

   c. If you reduced shopping in your life to that which is required to meet only the necessities, how would you use the time that would then be available to you?

   d. Even if shopping has assumed excessive importance in our lives, is the business community in any way to blame for that condition? Explain.

Afterword

You have now read that life is becoming increasingly arid in the Corporate State. Do you agree? If so, is the business community to blame? If we have committed ourselves too thoroughly to business values, are we to blame, or are we pawns before an over-powerful corporate community? A great American, Robert Frost, perhaps had the answer.

A Time to Talk

When a friend calls to me from the road
And slows his horse to a meaning walk,
I don't stand still and look around
On all the hills I haven't hoed
And shout from where I am, 'What is it?'
No, not as there is a time to talk.
I thrust my hoe in the mellow ground,
Blade-end up and five-feet tall,
And plod: I go up the stone wall
For a friendly visit.[29]

QUESTIONS—PART ONE

1. Thinker and futurist Herman Kahn was asked to comment on the prospects for space colonization. Kahn speculated that colonies of significance would develop in the early 21st century. But he cited two obstacles. One was that the rate at which colonization could be achieved would be instrumental in determining the excitement it would generate. The other:

   > And in the United States, we can't turn people on unless it's economic. This culture, almost alone among all cultures, will not get turned on unless it makes a profit, or is scientific or military. When NASA decided to co-operate with the Russians, the average guy said, "Down with space." He thought that the objective was to get the high ground over the Russians.[30]

   Generation of profits is a primary and necessary corporate value.
   a. Was Kahn correct in believing that our culture is more committed to profit seeking than most other cultures? Explain.
   b. Has the supremacy of profit seeking depreciated the quality of our lives? Explain.

2. *Fortune* magazine conducted a study of 82 25-year-olds who have "shown promise of becoming high-level managers or entrepreneurs." Thomas Griffith summarized the results of the study:

   > They are, *Fortune* says, bright, disciplined, hardworking, motivated: "They put their jobs ahead of most other diversions and commitments—including marriage, which many are in no hurry for, and children, which some claim they'll never want . . . . Single-mindedly chasing their objectives, they ignore what doesn't blend or harmonize with their purposefully limited landscape. They view work and life as a series of 'trade-offs' rather than compromises; for each opportunity surrendered, they demand an equal benefit in return." They pride themselves on the honesty with which they proclaim their ambitions.
   >
   >   To [former president] Ronald Reagan, these young people may embody the self-reliant American way in its purest form, but Gwen Kinkead, the writer of the *Fortune* article, can't resist a parenthetical comment: "To a stranger from another generation, they sometimes seem a grabby bunch."
   >
   >   The missing note in *Fortune's* young is idealism. They are not drones; they like the good life, the ski trips, the visits to Europe or Tahiti. If they tune out on causes, if they feel no obligation to help others, the explanation is not only that they have no time for these matters, but that they have no heart for them. They are a platoon of Tin Woodmen.[31]

   a. Does business demand Tin Woodmen? Explain.
   b. Are you a Tin Woodman? Explain.

3. David Gil, professor of social policy at Brandeis University, has "called for the dismantling of corporations that have destroyed 'self-directed work' and for the return of resources to the people for their own

direction 'in human-sized communities where people can come together and jointly determine their economic way of life.' ''[32]

a. Does our economic way of life reflect the will of the people? Explain.

b. Is the corporate form destructive of the quality of the work experience? Explain.

c. Is Gil's proposal workable? Explain.

4. Peter McCabe, managing editor of *Harper's,* reflecting on changes in his Manhattan neighborhood and life generally:

> In place of Art's Hardware Store now stands The Sensuous Bean. Where formerly there was a reasonably priced beauty salon, now one finds Better Nature (azaleas for $8.95). Sal's Cigar Store . . . has made way for Pandemonium . . . . No matter what kind of knick-knacks they carry . . . they have one thing in common . . . . —the assembling of the superfluous.
>
> To live in America today is to be constantly impressed by the ability of the superfluous to displace the useful, and by the ease with which the gratuitous can triumph over the imperative.[33]

a. McCabe's picture of contemporary commerce leaves us as consumers looking a bit artificial and foolish. Are his observations correct? Explain.

b. If so, is there cause for alarm in what he says? Explain.

c. Who is responsible for the growth of our arguably empty pop culture? Explain.

5. Should we lament the passing of the Roxbury Russet? The Russet was an American apple that, due largely to its mottled, leathery skin, did not make the commercial grade in contemporary America. Today apple growers are further from their markets and must focus on growing those varieties of apple that are most prolific and best able to withstand shipment. The surviving apples, in general, are sweet and red in color.[34] Similarly, we've seen the passing of juicy, flavorful tomatoes in favor of the more easily harvested and transported "rubber" tomato.

a. Are these examples of a trade-off of quality in favor of efficiency and productivity?

b. If so, is that trade-off necessary?

c. Who is responsible for the trade-off? Explain.

6. a. What does Reich mean by "loss of self"? Explain.

b. Do you sense any such loss in yourself? Explain.

7. As the editors of *Business Week* remarked in 1987, "A lot of people are badmouthing greed these days."[35] But the line between profit as a legitimate motivator and profit as an expression of greed is not easily drawn.

a. How do you define the point at which one passes from legitimate pursuit of profit to greed?

b. Is that point irrelevant? Explain.

8. In your judgment, which of the following quotes more accurately expresses the current American attitude toward the accumulation of money? Explain.

   Myron Magnet of *Fortune*:

   Money, money, money is the incantation of today. Bewitched by an epidemic of money enchantment, Americans in the 80s wriggle in a St. Vitus' dance of materialism unseen since the Gilded Age or the Roaring 20s. Under the blazing sun of money, all other values shine palely. And the M&A decade acclaims but one breed of hero: He's the honcho with the condo and the limo and the Miró and lots and lots of dough.[36]

   Michael Novak of the American Enterprise Institute:

   The vast majority of Americans choose what they want to do, and they don't choose merely to seek wealth. Most of the people I know seek the work that satisfies them most completely. Of course a sliver of people want money, money, money, but I think they're only a small number.[37]

9. According to *Business Week:*

   To their credit, most B-schools are now taking steps to prepare their graduates better for the practical demands of business. Many have introduced courses on the increased use of computers as management tools, the growing internationalization of American business, and other relatively new trends.[38]

   Journalist Ronnie Dugger says:

   American universities in recent years have gradually become more and more like big businesses and the students in them like units to be fitted into the evolving corporation-dominated civilization. This transformation . . . might be compared to a butterfly changing back into a grub.

   Optimistic observers welcome the change as fine—a good and necessary extension of American values and the American way. Those of us who do not agree see the universities ceasing to be free and stimulating places of learning conducted for the students' culture and development and becoming instead new adjuncts of the corporate and governmental bureaucracies.[39]

   a. To which view do you subscribe? Explain.
   b. Will education of the future be conducted primarily by corporations? Explain.

10. Ted Peters is associate professor of systematic theology at the Pacific Lutheran Seminary and the Graduate Theological Union. He asks:

    How will the advancing postindustrial culture influence the course of religion? It is my forecast that religion will become increasingly treated as a consumer item.

    Because our economy produces so much wealth, we are free to consume and consume beyond the point of satiation. There is a limit to what we can consume in the way of material goods—new homes, new cars, new electronic gadgets, new brands of beer, new restaurants, and so on. So we go beyond material wants to consume new personal experiences—such as broader travel, exotic vacations, continuing education, exciting conventions, psychotherapy, and sky diving.

What will come next and is already on the horizon is the consumption of spiritual experiences—personal growth cults, drug-induced ecstasy, world-traveling gurus, training in mystical meditation to make you feel better, etc. Once aware of this trend, religious entrepreneurs and mainline denominations alike will take to pandering their wares, advertising how much spiritual realities "can do to you." It will be subtle, and it will be cloaked in the noble language of personal growth, but nevertheless the pressure will be on between now and the year 2000 to treat religious experience as a commodity for consumption.[40]

    a. Is marketing necessary to the survival and growth of religion? Explain.

    b. Is marketing a threat to the legitimacy and value of religion? Explain.

11. Barry Commoner, the distinguished environmentalist and 1980 Citizen's Party presidential candidate, said in his campaign that the biggest problem in America today is corporate control of the country.

> There's no doubt the U.S. corporations helped build the economy, he [Commoner] says, but now they've run out of steam.
>
> Decisions by the big corporations such as General Motors are always made in the interest of maximizing their profits and do not take into account what happens to the community and the country.[41]

Is ours a Corporate State, as Commoner, Reich, and others suggest? Explain.

12. It is argued that the media—particularly television—merely parrot upper-class values and thus fail to direct adequate attention to those who criticize corporate values.

    a. Does the television industry serve as a meaningful voice in questioning "dominant corporate values"? Explain.

    b. Should it do so? Explain.

13. Much is made of corporate bigness, of how our giant institutions seem to dwarf us. Those concerns have given rise to the *Small Is Beautiful* movement, as articulated in E. F. Schumacher's book of the same name. But Samuel Florman objects:

> Perhaps what lies at the heart of the worship of smallness is an increasing revulsion against the ugliness of much of industrial America. Dams, highways, and electric transmission lines, once the symbol of a somewhat naive commercial boosterism, are now depicted as vulgar. But this association of bigness with lack of taste is not warranted. The colossal works of man are no more inherently vulgar than the small works are inherently petty. We prize robustness in life as well as delicacy.[42]

a. Is corporate America preoccupied with growth and bigness? Explain.

b. Is corporate America guilty of corrupting our visual landscape? Explain.

c. If so, is that a significant loss? Explain.

d. Is smallness an answer to problems associated with bigness? Explain.

14. Are we as individual citizens effectively helpless in the face of corporate power? Explain.

15. What forces currently operate to restrain corporate power? Do you envision any new forces developing in the future to counteract corporate power? Explain.

16. Should government go into business itself (as with oil and gas exploration) to afford competition and thus blunt corporate power? Explain.

17. Do you think allegiance to the company will become more important than allegiance to the state? Is that a desirable direction? Raise the arguments on both sides of the latter question.

18. *Business Week* stated, "Increasingly, the corporation will take over the role of the mother, supplying day-care facilities where children can be tended around the clock."[43] How do you feel about the corporation as mother? Explain.

Part Two—The Social Responsibility of Business

INTRODUCTION

As illustrated in Chapter 2 and in Part One of this chapter, the business community has been the subject of intense criticism even as the influence of business values in American life seems to have grown more dominant. That increasing business influence in conjunction with the perception of serious business misdeeds has led in recent decades to the development of the notion of a "social responsibility" for business. The issue is as follows:

Must business decision making include consideration not merely of the welfare of the firm but of society as well? For most contemporary readers, the answer is self-evident—of course business bears a social responsibility. Business has enjoyed a central and favored role in American life. As such, it must assume a measure of the burden for the welfare of the total society. Problems like discrimination, pollution, and poverty require the full strength of the nation, including the vast resources of business. Professors Brenner and Molander's survey of *Harvard Business Review* readers revealed that:

> Most respondents have overcome the traditional ideological barriers to the concept of social responsibility and have embraced its practice as a legitimate and achievable goal for business.[44]

Only 28 percent of the respondents endorsed the free market view, popularly associated with Milton Friedman, that "the social responsibility of business is to 'stick to business,' " and 69 percent agreed with the idea that " 'profit' is really a somewhat ineffective measure of business' social effectiveness." Indeed, the respondents seemed to hold a rather optimistic, activist view of business' role in society. Of those responding, 77 percent disagreed with the position that "every business is in effect 'trapped' in the business system it helped create, and can do remarkably little about the social problems of our times.[45]

The ascendance of the social responsibility concept represents one of the most striking ideological shifts in American history. From the settling of the nation until roughly 1950, business was expected to concentrate on one goal; that is, the production and distribution of the best products at the lowest possible prices. Of course, social responsibility arguments were raised, but business was largely exempt from any affirmative duty for the resolution of social problems. Rendered practical perhaps by increasing prosperity, the public, led by business scholars and critics, began in the 50s to consider a larger role for corporate America. In just three decades the role of business in society has been radically altered. Profit seeking remains central and essential, but for most businesspersons the new and rather unwieldy ingredient of social responsibility must be added to the equation. Given the business community's substantial acceptance of social responsibility, it is not surprising that the general public heartily endorses the notion:

> According to *ORC Public Opinion Index* 7 out of 10 Americans "believe that business has an obligation to help society, even if it means making less profit," with that proportion having grown significantly since 1967. Even among stockholder households, public attitude holds that "corporate social responsibility should take precedence over maximization of profits."[46]

On the other hand, public enthusiasm for business intervention in at least some social issues appears quite muted. *The New York Times* polled a sample of American adults about a variety of business questions, including the following:

> "Which of these statements comes closer to what you think: Big corporations should make special efforts to hire and promote women, or, it's up to women to get ahead on their own." Only 40 percent wanted corporations to make a special effort, while 50 percent said women should make it on their own. Women, especially working women, were no more likely to favor special efforts than were men. When the question was asked about blacks, 36 percent favored corporate special efforts while 53 percent said blacks should make it on their own.[47]

WHAT IS SOCIAL RESPONSIBILITY?

One major impediment to broad acceptance of the social responsibility concept has been that of comprehension. What is social responsibility? Many definitions have been offered, and a broad consensus seems to have emerged, but no single expression has successfully embraced the full spectrum of views. For example, Davis and Blomstrom articulated the following: "The idea of social responsibility is that decision makers are obligated to take actions which protect and improve the welfare of society as a whole along with their own interests."[48]

Kenneth Andrews suggests the same tone but offers some additional dimensions:

> By "social responsibility" we mean the intelligent and objective concern for the welfare of society that restrains individual and corporate behavior from ultimately destructive activities, no matter how immediately profitable, and leads in the direction of positive contributions to human betterment, variously as the latter may be defined.[49]

While social responsibility, framed in terms of business' duty to society, appears broadly accepted in business and among the general public, recall that a significant body of sentiment adheres to the free market view alluded to previously and perhaps best expressed by Milton Friedman:

> [In a free economy] there is one and only one social responsibility of business—to use its resources and engage in activities designed to increase its profits, so long as it stays within the rules of the game, which is to say, engages in open and free competition, without deception or fraud.[50]

Friedman believes the firm, maximizing its profits, is necessarily maximizing its contribution to society. He believes social responsibility is both unworkable and unjust. He asks how selected private individuals can know what the public interest is. He also argues that any dilution of the profit-maximizing mode—such as charitable contributions—is a misuse of the stockholders' resources. The individual stockholder, he contends, should dispose of assets according to her or his own wishes.

The Social Responsibility Debate

As indicated, social responsibility seems an increasingly accepted element of business ideology and practice, but serious reservations remain about the intellectual rigor and economic wisdom of the movement. Furthermore, the economic malaise of the late 1970s and early 80s and the Reagan administration's emphasis on free market principles seem to have somewhat dampened the ardor for imposing further duties on the business community. In that connection it will be helpful to summarize the perceptive insights of Professor Keith Davis, who built a list of the arguments for and against social responsibility.[51]

Arguments for Social Responsibility

Long-Run Self-Interest.   To the extent business improves the society of which it is a part, business will profit in the long run. By meeting the community's needs, business will have a better environment in which to operate. For example, if business contributes to community welfare, the incidence of crime should decline, which means business will pay less for protection of property, insurance, and taxes to support the police. In the long run, low-cost production requires the accomplishment of social goods.

Public Image.   Closely aligned with the long-run self-interest argument is the notion that business will profit from a better public image. The public appears to favor a social contribution on the part of business. Therefore, making that contribution should enhance the corporate image and improve business in the long run.

Viability of Business.   Business as an institution will be threatened with declining power if it fails to meet the public's expectations. Business was chartered by society, and that charter could be amended or revoked if society's demands are not met. Other groups would step in to meet the responsibilities that business failed to fulfill.

Avoidance of Government Regulation.   Business seeks the freedom to maximize its own interests. Presumably, the degree to which business voluntarily fulfills society's expectations will be matched by a commensurate decline in demands for government intervention.

Sociocultural Norms.   The businessperson is guided by society's cultural constraints. As society's norms more thoroughly embrace social responsibility, business is firmly, if subtly, moved in that direction in order to achieve acceptance by society.

Stockholder Interest.   Of course, the stockholder benefits via improved image, and so on, but beyond that, economist Henry Wallich has demonstrated that social responsibility is of direct economic benefit to the diversified portfolio holder.[52] A stockholder in a single firm might not benefit directly from overall corporate responsibility, but the multifirm stockholder can encourage socially responsible behavior, such as training the hardcore unemployed. Even if the trainee leaves the firm and moves to another, the diversified stockholder profits from the general improvement in business' labor quality.

Let Business Try. Other institutions have failed to solve America's persistent problems. Why not give business an opportunity?

Business Has the Resources. Among American institutions, business may be foremost in terms of total management talent, functional expertise, and capital resources. By applying these strengths, as well as business' innovative approaches and productivity orientation, the corporate community might achieve advances not otherwise possible.

Problems Can Become Profits. Solutions to problems may prove profitable. For example, chemical wastes can often be reclaimed at a profit.

Prevention Is Better than Curing. Social problems are nagging, persistent afflictions. Because they must be dealt with eventually, it is more economically sound to voluntarily address them now.

Arguments against Social Responsibility

Profit Maximization. Here, Professor Davis makes the free market argument of Milton Friedman and others that business' sole responsibility is lawful profit maximization.

Costs of Social Involvement. Meeting social goals is often not profitable. Business resources are limited. Particularly for small firms, burdens like meeting pollution control requirements may actually drive them out of business.

Lack of Social Skills. The expertise of businesspeople lies in the economic realm. Do we want such people reaching decisions that call for much broader social skills? Are other institutions better equipped to address social issues?

Dilution of Business' Primary Purpose. Business might be weakened in the marketplace if its leaders divide their energies and vision. Economic goals would go unattained, and social goals, also receiving only partial attention, would likewise not be met.

Weakened International Balance of Payments. Social programs add to business costs. Ordinarily those costs are recovered through increased prices. Similarly, social programs reduce productivity, which in turn ordinarily leads to higher product costs. If foreign firms operating in international markets are not similarly committed to social causes, American firms are at a competitive disadvantage. The result is fewer international sales and a weakened international balance of payments for the United States.

Business Has Enough Power.   Business influence is already felt throughout society. Combining social activities with business' traditional economic role would result in a dangerous concentration of power that would threaten our pluralist balance.

Lack of Accountability.   Accountability should always accompany responsibility. As it is, society has no clear lines of control over business' social endeavors. Business might, in a well-meaning fashion, become "benevolent, paternalistic rulers."

Lack of Broad Support.   Davis argues that opinion regarding social responsibility is severely divided. An effort by business to operate in a hostile environment would have potentially disastrous consequences. As noted, social responsibility seems to have achieved a high degree of acceptance in recent years, but some of the division Davis alludes to certainly remains and, indeed, may intensify during trying economic times.

Davis conceptualized the arguments in a clear, balanced manner. In recent years scholars have begun to intensify the empirical analysis of the virtues and liabilities of social responsibility. We are beginning to receive some "hard data" to assist in resolving the very important social responsibility debate. The next section summarizes some of those findings.

SOCIAL RESPONSIBILITY RESEARCH

Professor Lyman Ostlund surveyed a random sample of 458 top managers and 557 operating managers from Fortune 500 firms to assess their attitudes toward the arguments for and against social responsibility.[53] In general, he found the arguments against social responsibility were considered less important than the arguments favoring such involvement. Opinions of top management differed little from those of operating managers. One result seemed particularly significant. The profit maximization argument ("Society is better advised to ask only that corporations maximize their efficiency and profits") was not considered particularly important. That result is noteworthy, because it is a measure of the sentiment for the free market approach championed by Friedman and others. Having offered a favorable assessment of managers' attitudes toward social responsibilities in the abstract, it is important to consider how social responsibility fares when weighed against traditional business goals. Professors Kamal Abouzeid and Charles N. Weaver surveyed 220 executives from among the largest Texas-based corporations.[54] Respondents selected the four goals that their company took to be most important from a list of possibilities including social responsibility. Of the respondents, 21.5 percent selected social responsibility, ranking that concept seventh among eight major goals. Financial goals, growth and expansion, efficient utilization of resources, and company stability were the four goals most frequently selected.

In summary, there seems little doubt that corporate leaders have an increased sensitivity to social problems. Probably that sensitivity is not as highly developed as many in the general population would prefer. Managers seem to have adopted the rather sensible stance that traditional financial goals must be honored to maintain the viability of the firm, but that priority certainly does not exclude serious attention to social problems.

Although many dimensions of the social responsibility question have been subjected to empirical evaluation, the key inquiry beyond those addressed above is that of economic performance. Are socially responsible companies more or less profitable than others? Professors Frederick Sturdivant and James Ginter studied 67 companies identified as "exhibiting exceptional social responsiveness or lack thereof."[55] They discovered that the "best" and "honorable mention" firms substantially outperformed the "worst" firms, as measured by growth rate in earnings per share from 1964 to 1974.

> While the findings certainly will not support the argument that socially responsive companies will always out perform less responsive firms in the long run, there is evidence that, in general, the responsively managed firms will enjoy better economic performances. It would be simpleminded, at best, to argue a one-on-one cause-effect relationship. However, it would appear that a case can be made for an association between responsiveness to social issues and the ability to respond effectively to traditional business challenges.[56]

At least nine studies have found similar results,[57] but others differ.[58] For example, Gordon Alexander and Rogene Buchholz, in studying the stock market performance of 47 firms over several years, concluded that "The degree of social responsibility as measured by the rankings of businessmen and students bears no significant relationship to stock market performance."[59]

Some interesting, new evidence approaches this social responsibility/economic performance debate from a slightly different angle. Professors Alfred Marcus, Philip Bromiley, and Robert Goodman have investigated the question of whether corporate crises (e.g., product defects leading to consumer injury and death) are reflected in declining stock market prices such that companies are deterred from engaging in dangerous and wrongful (i.e., socially irresponsible) conduct. If those crises were to lead to economic "punishment" in the stock market, then we could have greater faith in the notion that the free market will protect the consumer from corporate wrong. However, the evidence from this study does not support that faith in the market. The investigators summarized their results as follows:

> The classic theory of the firm is based on the idea that managers are agents for the owners, so increasing shareholder wealth, according to this theory, is the appropriate norm for judging managerial behavior. Negative stock market returns, therefore, should discourage managers from engaging in activities that lead to corporate crises. Our paper calculates the stock market reactions to two

kinds of crises—automobile safety recalls and the toxic chemical release in Bhopal. [See Bhopal readings later in the chapter—Author.] In the auto safety case, shareholder losses are limited largely to a few days around the event (to one company, Chrysler, for two time periods, 1973–74 and 1976–77). In the Bhopal case, while Union Carbide stock suffers a steep decline in the period after the accident, within 90 trading days it begins to rebound largely because the company is undervalued and is an attractive takeover target. These results raise questions as to whether the stock market dependably discourages managers from engaging in actions that lead to corporate crises.[60]

The results are mixed. Over the years the data will reveal firmer conclusions.

SOCIAL RESPONSIBILITY IN PRACTICE

Is the actual performance of business in conformity with the principles of social responsibility? As scholar S. Prakash Sethi has expressed it, has business moved beyond mere "obligation" and "responsibility" to an active "social responsiveness" role?[61] Social responsiveness is not merely a matter of meeting social pressure. Rather business, it is argued, should take an "anticipatory" and "preventive" role in the interests of total societal welfare.

That is, the firm should develop internal processes for discovering and managing social issues. Recently, scholar Edward Epstein has upped the social responsibility ante a bit by calling for an integrated "corporate social responsibility process." Professor Epstein's approach to the corporate role in societal problems combines business ethics, corporate social responsibility, and corporate social responsiveness to enable business-people to "institutionalize value considerations into ongoing organizational decision-making processes."[62] Epstein summarized his notion of the corporate social policy process:

Corporate Social Policy Process

Institutionalization within the corporation of processes facilitating value-based individual and organizational reflection and choice regarding the moral significance of personal and corporate action. Individual and collective examination of the likely overall consequences of such actions, thereby enabling the firm's leaders both individually and collectively within the organizational setting to anticipate, respond to, and manage dynamically evolving claims and expectations of internal and external stakeholders concerning the products (specific issues of problem-related consequences) of organizational policies and behavior.[63]

The apartheid and Ford Pinto readings that follow offer examples of behavior falling at various points on the social responsibility scale. Here one acquires a sense of the difficulty of implementing socially responsible action in the face of severe economic and organizational constraints. To business critics, the apartheid and Pinto episodes suggest that some firms have failed to meet even fundamental legal responsibilities. Yet, as the readings demonstrate, many firms assume a fully socially responsive role that meets all reasonable economic, legal, ethical, and discretionary responsibilities.

Apartheid

The white minority that governs South Africa has for decades practiced a policy of racial separation and subjugation of the majority nonwhite population, as vividly expressed by Kenneth Carstens, executive director of the International Defense and Aid Fund for South Africa:

> Racism [in South Africa] is entrenched in law. . . .the majority African group, 73 percent of the population, have been assigned 13 percent of the land; they have no vote, no freedom of movement, they suffer in a rich country in which the white minority, 15 percent of the population, enjoys one of the highest standards of living in the world.[64]

That apartheid policy has been the subject of continuing, violent protest in South Africa. And in recent years, American and worldwide action against apartheid has escalated. A primary strategy in America has been the call for disinvestment. Americans have pressured U.S. corporations to leave South Africa as a means of both expressing moral outrage and applying pressure against the South African government. In the higher-education community, a highly visible manifestation of the disinvestment campaign has been the decision by a number of American universities to sell all of their investment holdings in firms having ties with South Africa. American corporations doing business in South Africa have been torn between their disapproval of apartheid and their desire to remain in South Africa to earn a profit while helping improve the quality of life for blacks. Over 50 percent of the American corporations doing business in South Africa adopted the Sullivan principles (named after their author, Reverend Leon Sullivan of Philadelphia). Since 1977 those companies sought to practice equal opportunity employment, eliminate segregated workplaces, provide equal pay and improved training for nonwhites, and generally improve the living condition of nonwhites through expenditures on housing, education, and so on. In 1987, after a decade of effort, Reverend Sullivan, in effect, conceded that the principles approach had failed when he called for all U.S. companies to leave South Africa. Sullivan also argued for trade sanctions against South Korea, trade sanctions against any nations seeking to replace the U.S. presence in South Africa, a cutoff of all U.S. imports from South Africa, and an end to diplomatic relations with the South African government until the end of apartheid. Meanwhile a number of American companies, citing the "deteriorating political and economic situation in South Africa," have decided to withdraw. The article and *The Wall Street Journal* commentary that follow outline the competing considerations in this most difficult social responsibility dilemma: Should American firms continue to do business in South Africa?

BITTER LEGACY: LEAVING SOUTH AFRICA, U.S. COMPANIES ANGER AND DISAPPOINT BLACKS

Roger Thurow

Johannesburg, South Africa—Kenneth Mason, a spokesman for the American Chamber of Commerce here, gingerly unfurls an American flag that speaks volumes about the U.S. corporations in South Africa.

The flag, frayed and soiled, was burned last September by radical students at Pace Commercial College, an elite, ultramodern secondary school situated incongruously amid the filth and poverty of the black township of Soweto. The school was the pride and joy of some 200 U.S. corporations, which spent nearly $10 million building and administering it, and Mr. Mason, speaking at a school assembly, was telling the students that the Americans were equally proud of them. "The American firms," he was saying, "are interested in your progress."

Just then, several students put a match to the flag, and it—and the Americans' pride and interest—went up in smoke. Mr. Mason was driven off the campus, with the flag draped over his shoulder. Shortly afterward, the corporate financing stopped, and the doors of the school—physically one of the best in all southern Africa—closed.

Vivid Illustration

Now, safe in his office in the comfortable northern suburbs of Johannesburg, Mr. Mason produces the flag to make clear a growing sentiment among black South Africans. "Ugly American," he says.

It is a sad epitaph to the expensive, high-profile social development efforts of U.S. corporations operating in South Africa. Pace was designed to be corporate America's shining contribution to the antiapartheid struggle—full of promise and hope and goodwill. But, instead, it is a discredited coffin of good intentions gone bad, full of frustration and disillusionment and covered by a tattered flag.

That, for the most part, is the legacy American corporations are leaving behind as they withdraw from South Africa to escape disinvestment hassles back home. During the past decade, U.S. companies, following the social conscience guidelines known as the Sullivan Code, have spent several hundred million dollars—an estimated $150 million in the past three years alone—trying to ease the pain of people oppressed by apartheid. They believed that they could make a difference in South Africa, and they encouraged the country's downtrodden blacks to believe it, too.

Basically Unrealistic

But much of this idealism was unrealistic. Corporate America never wanted to directly fight the white government here any more than it wants to confront any other governments. Corporations like to cooperate with the authorities, to be good citizens—and normally, no one expects them to do more and would be outraged if they attempted more.

Now that the American companies are leaving, many blacks inevitably feel disappointed and bitter that many of the big-money projects—such as Pace and other educational and building programs—have barely made a dent in the apartheid system. They blame the Sullivan Code for encouraging companies to take a scattergun, shortsighted approach to social development rather than concentrate their firepower on long-range structural change. Many blacks who supported U.S. disinvestment in the vain hope that it would pressure the white government to ease apartheid now feel frustrated because the companies are leaving with their dollars and social programs while the white government obstinately remains unchanged. Thus, black and mixed-race communities feel betrayed by Americans who, the communities say, raised expectations of overturning apartheid and then let them down.

* * * * *

Now in Disrepute

The lasting legacy of all this is that capitalism and free enterprise have fallen into disrepute among many black South Africans. The inability of corporate America to fundamentally change things here—coupled with the failure of the Reagan administration's policy of constructive engagement toward South Africa—is convincing many blacks that capitalism isn't to be trusted and that socialism is the only way to go in post-apartheid South Africa. By the time the school closed, for instance, Pace, which stands for Project for the Advancement of Community Education, was being called Soweto Socialist School by many black students.

"The sting of all this," says Eric Mafuna, who runs a black consulting firm based in Jo-

hannesburg, "is that it confirms suspicions already in black minds: that the West wasn't to be relied upon, that capitalism means only ruthless exploitation of the indigenous people, that free enterprise isn't to be a part of the future South Africa."

* * * * *

Although the companies have long felt caught up in a damned-if-you-do and damned-if-you-don't dilemma, this no-win feeling is being heightened by the current disinvestment drive, which kicked into high gear earlier this year when General Motors, International Business Machines, Coca-Cola, and Kodak, among others, announced their departures. People who want the companies to stay are chastising them for pulling the rug out from under the social development programs and for giving up the fight against apartheid. On the other hand, those who have been hounding the companies to leave are now blaming them for the way they are leaving—like thieves in the night, they say. General Motors, for instance, is being ridiculed for leaving after 60 years here without having any black managers ready to take over.

* * * * *

Adds T. W. Kambule, who for two decades headed Soweto's Orlando High School, the country's largest black school: "We figured the big corporations, owned by Americans, can do things for us. If you have the money, rather than fixing an old house, you tear it down and build a new one. The Americans tried to patch up things, rather than tear them down. And this system [apartheid] can't be patched up."

Undoubtedly, the patch-up jobs have significantly improved the lives of many black and mixed-race South Africans. The companies contributed thousands of university scholarships, raised pay levels in their industries, housed many families, and supplemented a woefully inadequate black educational system.

* * * * *

Such projects have given a warm feeling to the companies and to the people benefited. But, because such projects have had little effect on the big picture here, they have also left a lot of people cold.

* * * * *

"What's needed is a cooperative exercise of the corporations," says Jan Steyn, the executive chairman of the Urban Foundation, a privately financed organization striving to reform the apartheid system. "Until you get into the structural area, the capacity to force change is limited. It's undramatic and unromantic and terribly messy, but you have to do it."

This message is gradually sinking in among the 200 or so American companies still operating here. The big corporate social-spending programs announced recently—the IBM Projects Fund ($15 million over five years), the Mobil Foundation (about $20 million), and the Equal Opportunity Fund of Coca-Cola ($10 million)—are trying to pack the management boards with black leaders and to focus their efforts on projects recommended by the black community. (Both Coke and IBM say they will honor their commitments despite their recent disinvestment moves. Mobil is continuing to operate in the country.)

The companies hope that these efforts will restore some of the lost credibility and put them in touch with projects more attuned to the needs of the people they are trying to help. In the past, a score of housing projects have created more hard feelings than gratitude because they were aimed at the black middle class rather than the poorer masses living in shacks.

"The cheapest houses are still too expensive for normal workers," says a shop steward at Samcor Ltd., an auto maker 42 percent-owned by Ford Motor Company. "People are still dying for housing."

* * * * *

Source: *The Wall Street Journal,* December 23, 1986, pp.1,14. Reprinted by permission of *The Wall Street Journal,* © Dow Jones & Company, Inc. 1986. ALL RIGHTS RESERVED.

AFRICAN FAREWELL (EDITORIAL)

The morning of GM's announcement [to withdraw from South Africa], the front page of the *Washington Post* carried an interview with John T. Walker, as Washington's Episcopal bishop one of the most prestigious black clergymen in the nation. He elaborated his strong stand against disinvestment, which places him in opposition to the official Episcopal position. He urged that American companies stay in South Africa and help improve training and working conditions for blacks. There are many black leaders in the United States and South Africa who agree, but their voices have been largely drowned out by the cacophony of militance.

Black workers at American-owned businesses in South Africa have indeed been among the best-trained, best-paid, and best-housed workers in Africa. By one count, 29 American companies now have pulled out of South Africa or announced plans to this year. The departure of GM and IBM will most likely hasten the trend. Not only is business bad in South

Africa, but U.S. companies operating there face increasing pressure on their main operations in the United States. Some 30 U.S. cities have in the past year barred awards of contracts to companies doing business in South Africa. It's difficult to blame GM or IBM for decisions that may indeed serve their shareholders' best interest.

In forcing American companies to withdraw, though, American militants are destroying yet one more moderating force in South Africa. Business necessity, if nothing else, will dictate that the new owners of the plants try to maintain labor harmony. But their operations prob-

ably will be less well financed than before, and less able to exert leadership. The departures of GM, IBM, and other American corporations make it more likely that the South African economy will continue sluggish, radicalization will mount in South Africa's black communities, the government will shed what remains of its concern for Western opinion, and the livelihood and lives of all South Africans will grow more precarious.

Source: *The Wall Street Journal,* October 22, 1986, p.22. Reprinted by permission of *The Wall Street Journal,* © Dow Jones & Company, Inc. 1986. ALL RIGHTS RESERVED.

Questions

1. Based on these readings and your general knowledge, what errors in strategy can you identify in the American corporate community's approach to the apartheid problem?
2. Does the apparent failure of American corporate efforts in South Africa suggest that those companies should reject the notion of a corporate responsibility for such social problems as racism? Explain.
3. In your opinion, does socialism offer greater hope than capitalism for South African blacks? Explain.
4. Should American corporations disengage from South Africa? Explain.

Ford Pinto

THE FORD PINTO

Background

The Ford Pinto two-door sedan was introduced on September 11, 1970, as a 1971 model year vehicle. A three-door runabout version was introduced in February 1971, and the Pinto station wagon model was brought out on March 17, 1972. The design and location of the fuel tank in the Ford Pinto, and identically designed

Mercury Bobcat, were unchanged until the 1977 model year, when revision was required to meet new federal safety standards for rear-impact collisions. By that time over 1.5 million two- and three-door Pinto sedans and nearly 35,000 Bobcat sedans had been sold. Because of the different configuration of the station wagon model, the fuel tank was mounted differently and, consequently, was less susceptible to damage from rear-end collisions.

The 1971–1976 Pinto fuel tank is constructed of sheet metal and is attached to the undercarriage of the vehicle by two metal straps with mounting brackets. The tank is located behind the rear axle. Crash tests at moderate speeds have shown that, on rear-impact collisions, the fuel tank is displaced forward until it impacts the differential housing on the rear axle and/or its mounting bolts or some other underbody structure.

The Cause for Concern

Public awareness and concern over the Pinto gas tank design grew rapidly following the 1977 publication of an article by Mark Dowie in *Mother Jones,* a West Coast magazine. This article was widely publicized in the press and reprinted in full in *Business and Society Review.* The article, based on interviews with a former Ford engineer, alleged that Ford Motor Company had rushed the Pinto into production in much less than the usual time in order to gain a competitive edge. According to the article, this meant that tooling began while the car was still in the product design stage. When early Ford crash tests allegedly revealed a serious design problem in the gas tank, the tooling was well underway. Rather than disrupt this process, at a loss of time and money, to incorporate more crashworthy designs which Ford allegedly had tested, the article stated that the decision was made to market the car as it was then designed.

The Dowie article further included calculations reportedly contained within an internal company memorandum showing that the costs of making the fuel tank safety improvement ($11 per car) were not equal to the savings in lives and injuries from the estimated proportion of crashes that would otherwise be expected to result in fires. These "benefits" were converted into dollar figures based on a value or cost of $200,000 per death and $67,000 per injury, figures which were obtained from [the National Highway Traffic Safety Administration] (NHTSA). In addition the article stated that Ford had lobbied for eight years to delay the federal standard for fuel tank safety that came into force with the 1977 model year. The article alleged that Ford's opposition to Federal Motor Vehicle Safety Standard 301 was stimulated by the costly retooling that would have been required when the Pinto was first scheduled for production. In response, a Ford official characterized the allegations made in the Dowie article as distorted and containing half-truths.

The NHTSA Investigation

Based on allegations that the design and location of the fuel tank in the Ford Pinto made it highly susceptible to damage on rear impact at low to moderate closing speeds, . . . NHTSA initiated a formal defect investigation on September 13, 1977. In response to the NHTSA's requests, Ford provided information concerning the number and nature of known incidents in which rear impact of a Pinto reportedly caused fuel tank damage, fuel system leakage, or fire. Based on this information and its own data sources, in May 1978 NHTSA reported that, in total, it was aware of 38 cases in which rear-end collisions of Pinto vehicles had resulted in fuel tank damage, fuel system leakage, and/or ensuing fire. These cases had resulted in a total of 27 fatalities sustained by Pinto occupants, of which one is reported to have resulted from impact injuries. In addition, 24 occupants of these Pinto vehicles had sustained nonfatal burn injuries.

In addition, the NHTSA Investigation Report stated that prior to initial introduction of the Pinto for sale Ford had performed four rear-impact barrier crash tests. However, as Ford reported, "none of the tested vehicles employed structure or fuel system designs representative of structures and fuel systems incorporated in the Pinto as introduced in September 1970." These tests were conducted from May through November 1969.

Following initial introduction of the Pinto for sale, Ford continued a program of rear-impact tests on Pintos which included assessment of post-impact conditions of the fuel tank and/or filler pipe. Reports of 55 such tests were provided to NHTSA, including tests of Mercury Bobcats. Three items developed a history of consistent results of concern at impact speeds at low as 21.5 miles per hour with a fixed barrier: (1) the fuel tank was punctured by contact with the differential housing or some other underbody structure; (2) the fuel filler neck was pulled out of the tank; and (3) structural and/or sheet metal damage was sufficient to jam one, or both, of the passenger doors closed. Review of the test reports in question suggested to the NHTSA investigators that Ford had studied several alternative solutions to the numerous instances in which fuel tank deformation, damage, or leakage occurred during or after impact.

The NHTSA investigation concluded that the fuel tank and filler pipe assembly installed in the 1971–1976 Ford Pinto is subject to damage which results in fuel spillage and fire potential in rear-impact collisions by other vehicles at moderate closing speeds. Further, examination by NHTSA of the product liability actions filed against Ford and other codefendants involving rear impact of Pintos with fuel tank damage/fuel leakage/fire occurrences, showed that at that time nine cases had been completed. Of these, the plaintiffs had been compensated in eight cases, either by jury awards or out-of-court settlements.

Following this initial determination that a defect existed and less than a week before a scheduled NHTSA public hearing on the Pinto fuel tank problem, Ford agreed to a voluntary recall.

Criminal Charges

On September 12, 1978, following an accident involving the burning and death of three young

---

THE COST OF DYING IN A PINTO

Printed below are figures from a Ford Motor Company internal memorandum on the benefits and costs of an $11 safety improvement which would have made the Pinto less likely to burn. The memorandum purports to "prove" that the improvement is not cost effective:

Benefits
   Savings: 180 burn deaths, 180 serious burn injuries, 2,100 burned vehicles.
   Unit cost: $200,000 per death; $67,000 per injury; $700 per vehicle.
   Total benefit: 180 × ($200,000) + 180 × ($67,000) + 2,100 × ($700) = **$49.5 million.**

Costs
   Sales: 11 million cars, 1.5 million light trucks.
   Unit cost: $11 per car, $11 per truck.
   Total cost: 11,000,000 × ($11) + 1,500,000 × ($11) = **$137 million.**

Source: Mark Dowie, "How Ford Put Two Million Firetraps on Wheels," *Business and Society Review* (23), Fall 1977, pp. 46, 51. © Mark Dowie. Originally published in *Mother Jones* magazine. Reprinted with permission.

---

women in a Pinto, a county grand jury in Indiana indicted Ford Motor Company on three counts of reckless homicide and one count of criminal recklessness. The charge of reckless homicide was brought under a 1977 revision of the Indiana Penal Code that allows a corporation to be treated as a person for the purposes of bringing criminal charges. On March 13, 1980, more than two months after the trial began, the jury found Ford not guilty.

Source: Library of Congress Congressional Research Service. Background material for hearings on H. R. 7040, Subcommittee on Crime of the Committee on the Judiciary, House of Representatives, 96th Congress, 2nd session, May 1980.

Was Ford Liable under Civil Law?

Note that Ford has argued throughout the Pinto episode that, based on government data, the Pinto was less susceptible to fires from rear-end collisions than the average car on the road. The Pinto conformed to all federal safety standards at the time. Fuel tank standards for rear-end collisions were not established until 1977.

The many civil suits arising from Pinto fires have resulted in a number of large judgments and settlements against Ford. For example, the families of two Pennsylvania children killed in a Pinto fire received, according to the families' attorney, more than $2 million in an out-of-court settlement. But the most striking such trial was that of Richard Grimshaw, who received a jury verdict of $127.8 million. Grimshaw was subjected to more than 60 operations. Among other injuries he sustained the loss of his nose, left ear, and four fingers. The California Fourth Circuit Court of Appeals upheld the Grimshaw decision against Ford with a reduced damages total of $6.3 million.

Was Ford Liable under Criminal Law?

Of course, the most publicized and, in terms of legal and social policy, far-reaching Pinto trial was the Indiana criminal prosecution mentioned in the Library of Congress study. A loss in the Indiana case presumably would have opened Ford to tens of millions of dollars in punitive damage claims in the many undecided Pinto civil suits. Despite Ford's victory, some observers think the case is demonstrative of an appropriate new zeal for holding corporations and their executives criminally accountable for their behaviors. An excerpt from an editorial appearing in *The Nation* reflects that sentiment.

> Ford got off this time—perhaps as a result of the judge's controversial decision to exclude on technical grounds evidence in the form of Ford internal documents.
>
> Despite a sympathetic judge and a defense war chest of a reported $3 million (the budget of the small-town prosecutor in Winamac, Indiana, was $20,000), Ford very nearly lost the case. The jury deliberated for four days before reaching a decision.
>
> But more important then the verdict in this particular case is the principle that has been reestablished—the importance of holding corporate criminals accountable.[65]

But to Professor Richard Epstein the Indiana Pinto episode simply should not have been tried as a criminal case.

> The consequences that flow from the prosecution's theory of criminal liability only confirm what should now be evident: the Pinto case should not have been brought within the traditional modes of criminal responsibility. Such is not to rule out all possibility for public control over the production and sale of au-

tomobiles. There is nothing, for example, to prevent federal or state governments from bringing suit for *civil* fines in the event that automobile manufacturers do not conform to applicable safety standards. Such civil actions spare the government the need to prove explosive allegations of "reckless disregard and criminal intention" and give it the benefit of the lower standard of proof normally involved in civil cases. Of equal importance, they prevent any corporate defendant from being subjected to the deep moral taint that is associated in the public mind with charges of criminal wrongdoing. It is true that many of the hazards associated with criminal prosecution might be avoided by circumspection in invoking the criminal sactions. Yet in the current climate of opinion it seems almost fanciful to rely upon notions of prosecutorial self-restraint. Such self-restraint will deny to some what is, after all, the joyous opportunity of both making and seeing the mighty fall.[66]

See Chapter 2, Ethics, for a more detailed discussion of managers' criminal liability.

Questions

1. Ford's internal memoranda suggest the company had completed cost-benefit analyses balancing the cost of alterations versus the cost of deaths and injuries. Defend Ford's use of such a calculus.
2. What organizational characteristics contribute to the occurrence of arguably regrettable decisions like those associated with the Pinto?
3. Would an episode like that of the Pinto be less likely to transpire in a socialist state? Explain.
4. If the various allegations against Ford proved to be true, would you decline to work for the organization? Put another way, what dollar sum would be required for you to accept employment with Ford in a job commensurate with your interests and skills? Explain.
5. Is criminal prosecution a sensible, desirable approach to the Pinto case? Explain.
6. If the choice were yours, would you award Grimshaw the original $127.8 million, the appeals court decision of $6.3 million, or some lesser amount? Explain.
7. Are large civil penalties effective in discouraging future errors of wrongdoing? Explain.
8. Professor Terrence Kiely argues for personal, criminal liability for executives involved in cases like the Pinto: "The only way we're going to get quality products as consumers is to make corporate executives feel personally responsible for their decisions. The aim is to get them to worry and think about more than just the bottom line."[67] Comment.
9. Ford had argued that attempting to apply the criminal law in cases like the Pinto "would wipe out the basic distinction between civil wrongs and criminal offenses."[68] What did Ford mean?

CORPORATIONS AS CRIMINALS?

The Ford prosecution, in itself an innovative and much-disputed new direction in potential criminal liability, raises the larger issue of corporate crime generally. Although corporate criminal behavior is not the norm, neither is it uncommon. Of course, the business community may merely reflect the values of the larger society.

The disturbing series of insider-trading violations in recent years (see Chapter 8), highlighted by Wall Street arbitrager Ivan Boesky's $100 million civil settlement and guilty plea to one felony count of making a false statement to the Securities and Exchange Commission, is merely the latest and best-publicized evidence of serious malfeasance at the heart of business practice in America. (Boesky, who could have been sentenced to five years in prison and a $250,000 fine, received a sentence of three years' imprisonment on the grounds that he had paid a very large civil penalty and that his postarrest behavior was that of a man who sincerely regretted his conduct and sought to reform himself.) *The Nation* highlighted the most sensational recent white-collar crimes in this fashion:

> Corporate illegality usually escapes major media attention—until its tawdry existence is rediscovered in a spate of shocked headlines, as though it were a new form of Legionnaires' disease. Such was the case in the past month [May 1985], when an apparent corporate crime wave dominated the front pages. Some prominent examples:
>
> Paul Thayer, former chair of LTV, is sentenced to four years in jail for perjuring himself to a federal commission over insider-trading activities. E. F. Hutton confesses to engaging in a multibillion-dollar check-kiting scheme. General Electric admits it has defrauded the Pentagon by passing on bogus costs. The First National Bank of Boston owns up to violating the Bank Secrecy Act because it failed to report $1.22 billion in large cash transactions, some of which, according to the Justice Department, involved laundering drug money.[69]

Business crime is imposing a very heavy financial burden on society, a burden substantially exceeding that of the conventional crimes of robbery, burglary, larceny, and auto theft, the direct costs of which were estimated at perhaps $3 billion to $4 billion per year in the 1970s.[70] In 1986 Deputy Attorney General D. Lowell Jensen told a Senate committee that white-collar offenses (not limited merely to corporate crime) cost the United States an estimated $200 billion per year in both direct and indirect costs. (Indirect cost includes such things as a bank failure as a result of fraud.)[71] And the problem appears to be on the rise. For example, bank fraud in 1986 totaled more than $1.1 billion, which represented a 35 percent increase over 1985.[72] The FBI estimates fraud losses for the entire decade of the 1970s totaled less than $1.5 billion.[73] A significant measure of the present instability in our financial institutions appears attributable to fraud. According to a congressional study of banking failures in the early 80s, "Roughly one half of the bank failures and one quarter of the savings and loan collapses had as a major contributing factor criminal activities by insiders."[74]

Of course, the cost of business crime and, more generally, white-collar crime is not limited to direct financial loss. Physical injury or death and corruption of the political process are some of the regrettable by-products.

Such conduct erodes public confidence in the commercial world, exacerbates resentment against the upper economic classes, and, by example, encourages wrongdoing in the general population. One presidential study labeled white-collar crimes "the most threatening of all—not just because they are so expensive, but because of their corrosive effect on the moral standards by which American business is conducted."[75]

Further, it is important to recall that business is often the victim of crime:

> An analysis by Price Waterhouse & Co. in 1984 attributes half of the shrinkage of retailing inventory to employee theft (the rest goes to shoplifting and poor paperwork).[76]

A *Fortune* study of the decade 1970–80 reveals the alarming frequency of corporate crime. The *Fortune* study was limited to five crimes (domestic bribery, criminal fraud, illegal political contributions, tax evasions, and criminal antitrust violations) where the prosecution resulted in conviction or in a consent decree.

> Of the 1,043 major corporations in the study, 117, or 11 percent, have been involved in at least one major delinquency in the period covered. . . .Some companies have been multiple offenders. In all, 188 citations are listed covering 163 separate offenses—98 antitrust violations; 28 cases of kickbacks, bribery, or illegal rebates; 21 instances of illegal political contributions; 11 cases of fraud; and 5 cases of tax evasion.[77]

A 1982 survey reported in *U.S. News & World Report* supported the *Fortune* findings: "Of America's 500 largest corporations, 115 have been convicted in the last decade of at least one major crime or have paid civil penalties for serious misbehavior. Among the 25 biggest firms. . .the rate of documented misbehavior has been even higher."[78]

Postscript

To many, Ivan Boesky's arguably light criminal sentence is further evidence of a frustrating prosecutorial and judicial leniency with white-collar criminals. However, a recent study of white-collar crime in eight populous states concluded that "the criminal justice agencies in the jurisdictions studied do not appear to have treated the 28,012 white-collar crimes differently than they did other types of crimes.[79] Nonetheless, the study revealed that, while 60 percent of the white-collar criminals received prison terms, only 18 percent were sentenced to more than 12 months in jail.[80] By contrast, "violent offenders received prison terms of more than one year 39 percent of the time" [and] "property-crime offenders received prison terms of longer than 12 months in 26 percent of the cases."[81]

Do you believe our criminal justice system is too lenient with white-collar criminals? If so, why might that be the case? If not, do you favor harsher penalties for "street crimes" than for white-collar crimes?"

Questions

1. The *Fortune* and *U.S. News & World Report* studies suggest corporate crime is not uncommon. In your judgment, is the business community more tolerant of crime than is American society generally? Explain.
2. The *Fortune* study suggests crime may be particularly common in smaller firms: "The bribing of purchasing agents by small manufacturers and the skimming of receipts by cash-laden small retail businesses are a commonplace of commercial life." Assuming *Fortune* is correct, what forces led to that corruption?
3. It is argued that corporate crime is, in significant measure, attributable to excessive government intervention in business practice (e.g., antitrust law and safety standards). Do you agree? Explain.
4. What steps would you suggest to curb corporate crime?

A SOCIAL RESPONSIBILITY FOR THE WORLD?

On December 3, 1984, a poison gas leak from a Union Carbide India Ltd. pesticide plant in Bhopal, India, resulted in at least 2,500 deaths and perhaps 200,000 injuries.[82] Long-term effects are unknown, but partial blindness and lung and liver damage to many victims are not unlikely. In the first two months following the tragedy nearly 25 percent of the babies born to mothers affected by the leak died soon after birth, and Indian studies suggest another 1,700 people will probably die in the future. Union Carbide disputes those figures.

The Indian government filed suit against the parent, Union Carbide Corporation, alleging negligence and misrepresentation of the safety of the plant. However, Carbide claims the safety technology at Bhopal was fully equal to that in the United States and equal to that in the industry throughout the world. (Three gas leaks struck Union Carbide's West Virginia works in August 1985. No serious injuries were reported.)

In March 1985, Union Carbide released its own investigative report. The report blames the tragedy on "a unique combination of unusual events." The principal contributing factors, based on the Carbide report, included the following:

1. Five weeks prior to the accident the methyl isocyanate refining unit at the plant had run for several days at undesirably high temperatures.
2. Those high temperatures caused an undesirably high quantity of choloroform to remain in the holding tank from which the gas ultimately leaked.
3. At least 120 gallons of water were intentionally or inadvertently introduced to the tank. The chloroform and water precipitated a chemical reaction, driving the temperature in the tank to 200°C. and pushing the internal pressure up dramatically. A valve then released, and the poison gas escaped.
4. The tank's cooling system was, at the time, "nonoperational."

5. An alarm to signal high temperatures failed to operate.
6. A "scrubber," installed for the purpose of rendering harmless any escaping gas, failed to operate.
7. An employee on duty failed to check the scrubber even though a meter revealed that it was not operating.

At this writing in mid-1988, the vast machineries of the American and Indian legal systems are attempting to resolved the tragedy and compensate the victims. India is suing Union Carbide for $3.3 billion.

Experts assume a settlement will eventually be reached. If not, the legal issues to be resolved are numbingly difficult. For example: Will punitive damages be awarded? (Punitive awards are handed down in about 1 percent of all litigations.) Will Carbide contractors and suppliers bear part of the loss? (The outcome of that issue will depend in part on whether design defects are discovered in the Bhopal plant.) Finally, will Carbide and/or its executives bear criminal responsibility should wrongdoing be established? (In December 1987 the Indian government filed homicide charges against Carbide, its retired chairman, eight other Carbide officials, and two Carbide affiliates.[83] Close observers have speculated that the criminal charges may largely be designed as a lever to encourage Carbide's greater cooperation in reaching a settlement of the civil claims.)

The implications of the Bhopal case are likely to reach far beyond India and Union Carbide. As retired Carbide chairman Warren Anderson put it: "Maybe some benefits will come out of this—in terms of how people do things in other parts of the world.[84] Clearly America is firmly immersed in a world market. The implications for the social responsibility doctrine are profound and complex. The articles that follow summarize the Bhopal story up to mid-1988.[85]

THEORY OF BHOPAL SABOTAGE
IS OFFERED

Steven R. Weisman with Sanjoy Hazarika

New Delhi—Union Carbide Corporation investigators, nearing the end of a 16-month inquiry, say they have found new witnesses, documents, and scientific evidence proving that the 1984 Bhopal toxic gas disaster was caused by sabotage by a company employee.

* * * * *

Indian Government Disagrees

Indian officials and former Indian employees of Carbide's Bhopal plant vehemently dispute the company's assertions of sabotage. These officials and former workers say the company has failed to offer any proof of its charges and is maligning the people on whom it once relied to run the plant.

Talk of sabotage has figured in talk about the Bhopal disaster almost from the moment it started. Legal experts have been highly skeptical about Carbide's claim because the company's legal strategy has been to try to avoid paying hundred of millions of dollars in damages by proving that the gas leak was caused deliberately.

* * * * *

[India charges] that the plant was badly designed and that its managers were negligent. The plant was run by the company's Indian subsidiary, Union Carbide India Ltd., 50.9 percent of which is owned by the American corporation.

Question of Liability

Union Carbide says that the subsidiary is solely liable for damages, that its plant was well designed and managed, but that no plant can be protected against employee sabotage.

* * * * *

The company also maintains that 10 to 15 employees, including 3 to 5 supervisors in the Indian subsidiary, are conspiring to cover up details of the case in cooperation with Indian government investigators. Most of these employees have left Carbide and are working for the state government of Madhya, of which Bhopal is the capital.

As for who might have sabotaged the plant, Union Carbide respresentatives say they think they know but are not prepared to identify him yet. A source said suspicions rested on a plant operator on duty that night who was unhappy with a transfer to a separate part of the plant.

* * * * *

India denies all of the Carbide charges, including any suggestion that it is helping to cover up details of the investigation.

"The whole talk of sabotage is impossible," said an Indian official involved in the case, adding that specific company findings were suspicious because they [had] been raised only recently."

* * * * *

India maintains that even if the disaster was caused deliberately, Union Carbide would still be liable for damages. Indian officials say sabotage is enough of a "foreseeable" act that the corporation must still be held responsible.

India also insists that the plant's safety mechanisms were either poorly designed or not working the night of the gas leak, turning what could have been a minor accident into a catastrophe. In fact, India is hoping to win its damage claim without even proving how the gas leak occurred.

* * * * *

India has rejected Union Carbide's offer to settle out of court for $300 million to $350 million. Meanwhile, with the government suit taking precedence, lawyers representing individuals are still pressing for their right to sue.

The only assumption on which Union Carbide and the Indian government agree is that the disaster happened when a half ton to a ton of water got into one of three tanks containing. . .methyl isocyanate, a chemical used to make a pesticide known as carbaryl, marketed under the brand name Sevin.

* * * * *

Indian government analysts have concluded that the disaster started when workers were washing some equipment 350 feet away from the tank, and that the water leaked through one or two feeder lines into the tank. Most independent investigations, including one by

The New York Times in 1985, reached the same conclusion.

In making a case for sabotage, the Carbide experts are trying to prove that this could not have been the cause.

* * * * *

"A Theory It Can't Prove"

"There are only two theories, and the government is wedded to a theory it can't prove," said a person close to the Carbide investigation. "We can disprove the water-washing theory seven different ways from Sunday."

The company maintains, for example, that when Indian investigators opened the feeder lines to the tank, they were "bone dry."

* * * * *

BHOPAL RULING TESTS NOVEL LEGAL THEORY

Stephen J. Adler

If you happen to have a copy of Judge S. K. Seth's . . . opinion in the Bhopal litigation, hang onto it. It may become a hot item.

Even Union Carbide Corporation had to borrow the decision from the Indian appeals court judge, make a nearly illegible photocopy on a rickety machine in Jabalpur, India, and then retype it back home.

With lawyers in the Bhopal case slogging through the deep procedural mud of the Indian legal system, the $3 billion suit against Union Carbide involving the 1984 poison gas leak has attracted little notice lately. The remoteness of the Jabalpur courthouse—and the limited communications facilities available there—hasn't helped.

Yet the few U.S. lawyers who have studied Judge Seth's opinion recognize it as one of the most extraordinary developments in the field of mass-disaster law in years.

What the Decision Says

In essence, the judge ruled that a defendant in a personal injury suit can be required to pay damages to accident victims even *before* the defendant has been found liable at a trial. Based on that ruling, he ordered defendant Carbide to pay $190 million as an "advance" on an eventual damage award.

The innovative ruling isn't the final word; it must survive appeals in India and then be found enforceable by a U.S. court. The process could take several years.

But Judge Seth's decision—which appears to be without precedent–is likely to have an impact far beyond Bhopal. At the least, it gets lawyers and professors debating a radical new direction in personal injury law. That, in turn, might spur judges elsewhere to experiment with similar interim compensation awards. And it certainly will be cited—and embraced—by plaintiffs' lawyers in future cases.

* * * * *

In the beginning, U.S. personal injury lawyers and the Indian government contrived to try the case against Union Carbide in U.S. courts, where they expected quicker justice than in India—and a much larger verdict. But federal judge John Keenan of New York dismissed the case in May of 1986 on the ground that Bhopal was the more convenient forum. Since then a succession of Bhopal judges have failed to move the case to trial.

The fourth—and current—judge, M. W. Deo, stirred things up last December, however, when he ordered Union Carbide to pay about $270 million as interim compensation to the victims.

Enter Judge Seth of the Indian High Court in Jabalpur, where Carbide appealed the ruling. It is Judge Seth's opinion upholding the order for interim relief—for reasons different than those cited by Judge Deo—that is causing such a stir among lawyers.

The Thought That Counts

The amount Judge Seth required Carbide to pay—he reduced the original figure to $190 million—is hardly considered steep. The government of India, as representative of the victims, has been seeking $3 billion in the suit. And Carbide has itself offered at least $350 million during earlier settlement talks.

The shocker was that the judge had ordered a huge damage payment before Carbide's liability for damages, if any, had been established at a trial. At first glance, at least, the decision seems to violate any defendant's fundamental right to present evidence and to cross-examine witnesses against it. A Carbide spokesman has decried the ruling as "a judgment and decree without trial."

Yet Judge Seth's 103-page opinion is not without its logic. Typically in court cases, factual disputes are decided by a jury or, as in India, by a trial judge, based on testimony and cross-examination. But decisions about which rules of law govern the case can be made by a judge who has not heard testimony about the facts.

Applying this principle, Judge Seth ruled first that, under Indian law, a company that engages in a hazardous activity—such as operating a chemical plant—is "absolutely liable" for damages from an accident. This is true, he said, even if the company had not been negligent in the way it ran the plant.

Second, he ruled, Union Carbide had sufficient control over Union Carbide India Ltd.—which ran the plant—that the multinational would be held responsible for the accident. As a consequence, the court could dip into the company's worldwide assets to satisfy a damage judgment.

Given these rulings, it seemed highly likely that Carbide would be assessed substantial damages once the case went to trial. Why, Judge Seth asked, shouldn't the victims get some of that money now instead of waiting for the trial and multiple appeals to run their lengthy course?

* * * * *

He concluded that such an order was necessary because the Indian government's relief payments to victims amounted to "a pittance" and that "any further delay in extending appropriate relief by way of interim payment of damages. . .would have grave and tragic consequences."

Judge Seth then ordered Judge Deo to proceed with the trial. He made it clear that if the trial judge determined that the $190 million payment was unwarranted, the government of India, as the victims' representative, would have to return some or all of the advance.

Union Carbide has long argued that it isn't responsible for the accident. It has been preparing evidence that Union Carbide India Ltd.

BHOPAL: A LEGAL CHRONOLOGY

December 3, 1984: MIC gas leaks from Union Carbide pesticide plant in Bhopal, India, killing more than 2,500 people and seriously injuring many thousands more.

December 7, 1984: The first of more than 100 suits brought by American lawyers against Union Carbide is filed in a U.S. court.

January 2, 1985: All federal cases are consolidated in federal district court in New York.

April 8, 1985: The Indian government sues on behalf of the victims in New York federal court.

May 12, 1986: Federal district judge John Keenan dismisses the U.S. cases on the grounds that India is the more appropriate forum for a trial.

September 9, 1986: The Indian government, seeking $3 billion, sues on behalf of the victims in Bhopal district court.

January 4, 1987: A federal appeals court upholds the dismissal of the U.S. cases.

December 17, 1987: Bhopal district judge M. W. Deo orders Union Carbide to pay the victims about $270 million in interim relief before trial.

April 4, 1988: Indian High Court judge S. K. Seth upholds the interim relief order, but reduces the amount to $190 million.

---

is beyond the control of the multinational and thus that the multinational can't be held liable. Carbide also has maintained that sabotage—not negligence—caused the disaster.

But it is unclear how far Carbide can get with arguments that Judge Seth has now appeared to dismiss out of hand.

Has Union Carbide lost the case? Not necessarily. First, the company can appeal the decision in the Indian courts. It has already sought reconsideration by the High Court in Jabalpur and has the option of petitioning for a hearing before the Indian Supreme Court.

If Carbide loses in India, it has further recourse: It can refuse to pay. It's clear that Carbide doesn't have sufficient assets in India to satisfy the $190 million judgment. And if the company refuses to pay, the Indian government will have to ask a U.S. court to order Carbide to comply. But if the Indian judgment is sufficiently outrageous, a U.S. court might refuse to enforce it.

For Carbide, then, it may turn out that the worse the opinion, the better the outcome.

Under the Uniform Foreign Money-Judgments Recognition Act, U.S. courts are required to enforce a foreign judgment when the foreign court has jurisdiction and the judgment is not repugnant to public policy. Underlying the law is the requirement that the defendant be granted a fair proceeding in the foreign country—in other words, due process.

"Serious Doubts"

Says Harvard law professor Arthur Miller: "I have serious doubts that [Judge Seth's opinion] is enforceable. . . .Absent the classic day in court, there's an American due process issue at stake." (Mr. Miller consulted briefly for the U.S. plaintiffs' lawyers who had represented victims in U.S. courts.)

Arthur von Mehren, another Harvard law professor and a specialist on enforcement of foreign judgments, agrees that Carbide appears to have a fundamental right to defend itself. And this right, he says, includes trying to prove in court that some of the individual victims' claims were not valid. The company has alleged from the start that many of the people claiming injury from the accident became sick due to other causes. Says Mr. von Mehren: "I would think there is a very strong chance that such an opinion would not be enforced."

Yet Carbide does face one serious obstacle of its own making. The company is in the embarrassing position of having fought to get the case moved out of the U.S. courts and into the Indian system. In the process, it became a champion of the Indian judiciary, arguing that the system was sophisticated enough to do justice in a case of this magnitude.

Will Carbide be held to that view if it challenges the ruling in the United States? "Union Carbide worked very hard to get the case removed from New York to India," says Andreas Lowenfeld, a law professor at New York University. "I can't see how they could refuse to satisfy the judgment."

Previous Experiments

Professor Lowenfeld also points out that U.S. courts have begun to experiment with interim payments in mass-disaster cases when liability is established and the only question in dispute is the amount of damages and the division of responsibility among co-defendants. Such cases could bolster the Indian government's argument that Judge Seth's opinion stretches the limits of American jurisprudence only a little.

Professor Lowenfeld says he sees no problem with interim relief unless "there is a genuine possibility that there is no liability." He adds: "If Union Carbide can prove sabotage over which they had no control, then I see a problem," with the judge's order.

* * * * *

Questions

1. According to the "Sabotage" article, India is taking the position that Carbide is liable for damages at Bhopal even if the disaster were caused deliberately. India argues that sabotage is a foreseeable act. If you were the judge, how would you respond to that argument?
2. *a.* Are lives "worth" more in the United States than in India? Explain.
   b. Is such a question unconscionable? Explain.
3. Does the Indian government bear at least partial responsibility for Bhopal because the government failed to prevent the growth of "squatters communities" near the Union Carbide plant? Explain.
4. Was the Bhopal accident "less a political or moral event than a fact of industrial life"? Explain. See Fergus Bordewich, "The Lessons of Bhopal," *The Altantic,* 259, no. 3, (March 1987), pp. 30, 32.
5. *a.* Karim Ahmed, research director of the National Resources Defense Council, said

   Corporate standards on health and safety should be uniform worldwide and should not be based only on standards and norms of national governments. Such a policy states that regardless of government regulations—or, more often, lack of regulation—governing the field of industrial safety, the corporate body operating a domestic or overseas facility will adhere to the same standards.[86]

Should multinational companies employ the ethical "norms" of their host company (in this case, India), or their home country (in this case, the United States), or should they establish their own standards? Explain.

b. Now let's take Ahmed's thoughts a step further. If the multinational's own standards in an area like environmental safety are higher than those of the host country, does the multinational have a responsibility to try to persuade the host country to raise its expectations? Would that responsibility extend to withdrawing from the host country if that country failed to meet ethical standards that the multinational took to be central to an honorable order? Explain.

6. Laird Townsend, a writer commenting on Bhopal, argues that the only reliable protection for communities like Bhopal is the fear of very high damages for wrongdoers. He notes that "The company has survived the disaster, and the Indian government, too, won its election."[87] He goes on to argue: "In real life, corporations and governments will respond sufficiently only to damage threats generated by effectively tailored means such as boycotts."[88] Is the threat of very heavy damages the only realistic way of preventing future Bhopals? Explain.

7. *Dumping* is the label *Mother Jones* magazine applied to the practice of exporting products that are either banned or considered hazardous in the exporting nation. Companies in the United States and other developed nations clearly have engaged in dumping as here defined. For example, *Mother Jones* reports that millions of children's garments treated with a carcinogenic fire retardant named Tris were shipped abroad after those products were forced from the American market by the Consumer Product Safety Commission.[89]

a. Is dumping unethical if the product is not banned in the importing nation?

b. Dumping has led to charges of racism on the part of some American corporate officials and bureaucrats. Explain that charge. Do you agree? Explain.

ON THE POSITIVE SIDE OF SOCIAL RESPONSIBILITY

We have looked at several categories of suspect corporate conduct. Certainly the Pinto episode and Bhopal have been the subject of unusually hearty complaint from corporate critics. At the same time, the reader should receive a balanced picture reflecting the many virtues (in addition to providing the best products and services at the lowest prices) that the socially responsible firm can visit on society. For example, we know that "more than 500 companies have organized programs to encourage worker involvement in community service."[90] Levi Strauss supports 75 employee "community involvement teams," which use work hours to devise charitable fund-raising ventures.[91] Coca-Cola, while selling its assets in South Africa, recently placed $10 million into a group of foundations designed to improve housing, business opportunities, and education for blacks in that nation.[92] And McDonald's has been cited for its minority employment practices. Over 30 percent of McDonald's Chicago headquarters' staff are minority citizens, "and in the ranks of managers and officials, blacks hold 18.3 percent of the slots; Hispanics, 7.4 percent; and women, 40.2 percent.[93]

The following article illustrates one organization's attempt to rate companies on their approaches to social responsibility. The ratings reflect not merely criticisms but also the desirable practices of many corporations.

NEW BOOK RATES CONSUMER FIRMS ON SOCIAL ISSUES

Alan Murray

Ever worry that the Rice Krispies you eat every morning are made by a company that invests in South Africa?

Do you wonder whether the manufacturer of your toilet paper makes contributions to charity?

Did you know that Progresso spaghetti sauce is produced by a major defense contractor? That Speed Queen washers are from a conglomerate involved in nuclear weaponry? Or that the Wisk that gets collars white is made by a corporation with no black directors or officers?

Well, worry no more. The Council on Economic Priorities has just issued what it calls the first comprehensive shopping guide for the socially conscious consumer: *Rating America's Corporate Conscience.*

* * * * *

The book is filled with charts that list various products by brand name, tells what company produces each product, and then ranks the company on key social concerns. The principal criteria include:

- Does the company invest in South Africa, and, if so, has it complied with the Sullivan principles on fair labor practices?
- How much of its annual earnings does the company contribute to charity?
- Does the company have women or minorities on its board of directors or among its officers?
- Does the company have contracts related to conventional or nuclear weapons?
- Is the company willing to provide facts and figures on its social programs?

Political Action Committees

In addition, the book lists which companies make large contributions through political action committees to political candidates.

The guide provides new ways to make tough choices among brand products. Consider, for instance, cocoa mixes. The average supermarket may carry Hershey's, Swiss Miss, and Nestle's Quick. How to choose? If buyers want to support a company that contributes heavily to charity they will go for the Swiss Miss. It's made by Beatrice Companies, which donates more than 1 percent of its net pre-tax earnings to charity, according to the book. If they want, instead, to patronize a company that has stayed out of South Africa, they can buy Hershey's.

And what about peanut butter? Forget which is nuttier. For those who want to promote a company with female officers and directors, Peter Pan, also by Beatrice, comes out on top. For those more concerned about the promotion of blacks, Jif, by Procter & Gamble Co., is preferred.

* * * * *

Among hotels, the Sheraton chain, owned by ITT, scores high on contributions to charity, and also counts women and minorities among its directors and officers. Nevertheless, some travelers may have trouble sleeping there if they worry about the firm's sizable defense contracts and its involvement in South Africa.

Hilton and Hyatt are free of any role in defense or South Africa, but they are also free of high-ranking women and blacks, according to the book.

Questions

1. Has Levi Strauss deprived its stockholders of a share of their rightful earnings by encouraging employees to use company time in charitable pursuits? Explain.
2. Are you a "socially conscious consumer" (see "New Book Rates Consumer Firms on Social Issues") in the sense that your buying habits are influenced by your perception of a firm's stance on social issues? Should you be? Explain.
3. If we were able to successfully rate firms according to some social responsibility index and if most or all Americans were guided in their buying, investing, and employment decisions by that index, would ours be a better society? Explain.

BEYOND SOCIAL RESPONSIBILITY

We have reviewed social responsibility as an awkward, ill-defined concept suiting neither its detractors nor its adherents. Trying to do what's "right" is a treacherous course for every human and certainly for businesses not previously expected to look much beyond the commands of the market and the law. These difficulties have led to alternatives and supplements to the social responsibility notion. For example, some scholars have argued for a "public policy" approach that would, in their view, avoid the infirmities of social responsibility while correcting some of the deficiencies of the market. Essentially, business, government, and public interest groups would identify and resolve those problems for which the market is inadequate (e.g., negative externalities such as pollution). Thus, with each body representing its interests, decisions based on consensus would emerge. Business would function in both the marketplace and the public policy process. Business would not choose between profits and social responsibility. The demands of the market might be met, but at the same time the firm would be subject to the demands of society if its course strayed from what the citizenry expects.

Business critics place little faith in the public policy process. They fear the business voice will overwhelm the others straining to be heard. Furthermore, social responsibility, dependent as it is on corporate self-regulation and voluntarism, is regarded by the critics as only a part of the package necessary to produce a corporate community fully responsive to society's legitimate expectations. Perhaps the leading reform proposal of the late 1970s was the Corporate Democracy Act as espoused by the Nader organization and some members of Congress. During the Reagan administration, that proposal was at least temporarily at rest, but the issues raised are fundamental to the definition of business' proper role in society. Nader, his colleagues, and other corporate critics seek a fundamental realignment of the relationship between business and society. They are concerned about how the giant corporations are governed and how, in their minds, those corporations govern us. They call for a "democratic" approach to corporate governance in which, for example, employees would be afforded constitutional rights within the employment relationship; corporate decision makers would include, among others, representatives of the employees and the communities where the corporations are located; and new corporate disclosure requirements would better acquaint workers, customers, and others with company practices affecting environmental concerns, job safety, local employment levels, and so on. In sum:

> For decades the abuses of the American economy have been addressed by remedial regulation affecting the *external* relationships of the corporation; that is, don't pollute, don't price fix, don't advertise deceptively. The Corporate Democracy Act of 1980 seeks to reform the *internal* governance structure of our largest corporations so that, consistent with a market economy, companies exercise their power and discretion in more democratic and accountable ways.[94]

ADDITIONAL CASES FOR DISCUSSION

WHAT LED BEECH–NUT DOWN
THE ROAD TO DISGRACE

Chris Welles

On August 5, 1981, Jerome J. LiCari sent off a memorandum that would significantly change his life and that of his company. The memo would help bring about one of the most serious admissions of criminal wrongdoing by a major corporation—"a classic case of big corporate greed and irresponsibility," according to assistant U.S. Attorney Thomas H. Roche. It is also a case of how even the most reputable of companies, through poor judgment, can suffer an ethical breakdown.

LiCari was director of research and development for Beech–Nut Nutrition Corporation, the second-largest U.S. baby food manufacturer and a subsidiary of Swiss food giant Nestlé. For several years he had worried that Beech–Nut's apple juice products, its best-selling line, were adulterated. The juice was labeled "100 % fruit juice." But while lab tests were not conclusive, LiCari suspected that the apple concentrate Beech–Nut was buying to make its juice and other products was a blend of synthetic ingredients—a "100% fraudulent chemical cocktail," an associate later testified.

"Smoking Gun"

By 1981, LiCari, a soft-spoken, intense food scientist at Beech–Nut's main plant in Canajoharie, N.Y. was convinced. In the memo, sent to senior executives, he said that the "tremendous amount of circumstantial evidence" constituted a "grave case" against the concentrate's supplier. Yet his superiors took no action, and LiCari resigned a few months later.

The "smoking gun" memo, as prosecutors later termed it, was key evidence in a federal grand jury investigation that led to a 470-count indictment of Beech–Nut and its two top executives in November 1986. Last November Beech–Nut pleaded guilty to 215 felony counts and admitted to willful violations of the food and drug laws by selling adulterated apple products from 1981 to 1983.

Beech–Nut's president, Neils L. Hoyvald, and its operations head, John F. Lavery, pleaded not guilty and are currently on trial in New York. While Beech–Nut's guilty plea was based on the "collective knowledge" of its employees that its juice was impure, Hoyvald insisted he had no personal knowledge of the adulteration. Lavery's attorney said that while Lavery was aware of evidence the juice might be impure, he had no proof. LiCari, the government's star witness, testified that he had warned not only Hoyvald and Lavery but also senior Nestlé scientists, including Richard C. Theuer, who has replaced Hoyvald. Theuer and the Nestlé scientists denied that LiCari talked to them about the problem.

Beech–Nut's admission that it had sold millions of jars of apple juice it knew were phony shocked industry executives and company employees who were unaware of what was going on. Ever since Beech–Nut began smoking ham and bacon over beechwood fires in 1891, purity, high quality, and natural ingredients had been its trademarks—the focus of its marketing programs as well as the foundation of its corporate culture. Frank C. Nicholas, its president in 1977, when evidence shows the adulteration began, was known as "Mr. Natural." Why had Beech–Nut so egregiously strayed from its reputation and its heritage?

Self-Delusion

The answer, derived from trial testimony and numerous interviews and documents, is complex. It sheds light on the motives behind the sort of seemingly prosaic law breaking that rarely makes headlines but undermines many companies. The Beech–Nut employees involved were not hardened miscreants perpetrating a brazen swindle. They were honest and well respected. Their lapse into illicit conduct required a strong catalyst: Beech–Nut was under great financial pressure, and using cheap, phony concentrate saved millions of dollars. But it also required a pernicious climate of rationalization, self-delusion, and denial. Beech–Nut executives apparently convinced themselves that what they were doing was just a little innocuous cheating.

What they did, though, is costing Beech–Nut dearly: an estimated $25 million in fines, legal costs, and slumping sales. Mainly because of negative publicity, its juice market share has fallen about 20 percent over the past year, and sources say the company racked up near-record losses in 1987. Richard Theuer is stressing quality—internally and in a new TV ad campaign in March. "Feeding babies is a sacred trust," he says. "It's so easy to destroy a reputation and so difficult to rebuild it."

Like many business blunders, Beech–Nut's began with a deal that was too good to be true: an agreement in 1977 to buy apple concentrate from Interjuice Trading Corp., a wholesaler whose prices were about 20 percent below market.

With rumors of apple juice adulteration already widespread in the industry, the low price raised suspicions among chemists in Beech–Nut's R&D department. At the time, though, there was no official, sure adulteration test—a fact defense lawyers for Hoyvald and Lavery have stressed repeatedly. But there were several procedures that could provide strong evidence of fake ingredients such as corn sugar. The chemists concluded that the Interjuice product was probably extensively adulterated and perhaps even wholly ersatz.

In 1978 two Beech–Nut employees were sent to inspect Interjuice's concentrate source, a plant in Queens, N.Y., that was ostensibly importing from Israel. The staff members were shown a storage area but denied access to the concentrate processing facility.

Biggest Customer

That made some at Beech–Nut even more suspicious. Years later they would learn that the Queens plant was only part of a huge bogus concentrate complex, a coast-to-coast network including wholesalers, brokers, shippers, and ingredient manufacturers. At its peak, it probably grossed tens of millions of dollars annually. Beech–Nut was by far its biggest and most prominent customer, accounting for some 60 percent of its business.

Presiding over the operation was Zeev Kaplansky, who ran its distribution arm—Interjuice & Universal Juice Co., an affiliated company that later became Beech–Nut's supplier. His chief partner was Raymond H. Wells, who owned Food Complex Co., the Queens facility that manufactured the fake concentrate. Its chemists had learned how to replicate

precisely apple juice's numerous components with less costly substitutes.

Several Beech–Nut scientists, especially LiCari, said the company should stop buying from Universal Juice. But senior people at Beech–Nut, notably operations chief Lavery, 56, a 34-year Beech–Nut veteran, disagreed—mainly, extensive evidence suggests, because Beech–Nut was almost insolvent.

Still a proud brand name, Beech–Nut over the years had been stripped of its profitable divisions, such as chewing gum, and reduced to a single product, baby food, which had almost never turned a profit. Frank Nicholas, a Pennsylvania lawyer and head of a group that bought the baby foods division from Squibb Corp. in 1973, was a charismatic promoter with red hair, bushy sideburns, and lots of good ideas. He promoted naturalness and nutrition.

Shoestring

Unfortunately, the Nicholas group had acquired Beech–Nut almost entirely with borrowed money and ran it on a shoestring. They neglected the 80-year-old Canajoharie plant. And with a 15 percent market share, they couldn't begin to match the marketing outlays of Gerber Products Co., which had 70 percent. Losses mounted. By 1978, Beech–Nut owed millions to suppliers. Products containing apple concentrate accounted for 30 percent of Beech–Nut's sales, and the savings from the cheap concentrate were helping to keep the company alive. Other than saying he "didn't know a damn thing about adulteration," Nicholas refuses to comment.

After a desperate search for a buyer, Nicholas sold out to Nestlé in 1979 for $35 million. Nestlé invested an additional $60 million, hiked marketing budgets, and boosted sales. But the red ink and cost pressures persisted.

In early 1981, LiCari decided to mount a major drive to improve adulteration testing. Continuing to deal with Universal, LiCari believed, could jeopardize a major product-line restructuring that Beech–Nut was planning. The line, featuring foods designed for different ages, would emphasize nutritional values and the absence of artificial ingredients.

LiCari knew that persuading his superiors to get rid of Universal would not be easy. Other juicemakers, such as Gerber, often cut off suppliers of suspicious materials who couldn't demonstrate that their product was genuine. But Lavery, who sometimes referred to LiCari as "Chicken Little," had turned the burden of proof around. Lavery said that if LiCari wanted to switch to a more expensive supplier, he would have to prove that Universal's concentrate was adulterated.

Fresh Evidence

By August, armed with fresh evidence, LiCari felt he had an all-but-irrefutable case against Universal. Other R&D scientists agreed. His memo said that despite the "tremendous cost penalty" that switching suppliers would bring, a high-level meeting should be called to discuss the new evidence. When he got no response, he went to see Lavery, who had been sent a copy of the memo. Lavery, LiCari testified, complained that LiCari wasn't a team player and threatened to fire him.

LiCari drove down to Beech–Nut headquarters, near Philadelphia, to meet with Hoyvald. That meeting is critical to the prosecution's charges that Hoyvald knew of the adulteration problem but did nothing to remedy it.

An austere native of Denmark with hawklike features, Hoyvald had joined Beech–Nut in 1980 and replaced Nicholas in April 1981. He was recommended by Ernest W. Saunders, then the senior Nestlé executive overseeing Beech–Nut. Last year Saunders was fired as chairman of Britain's scandal-plagued Guinness PLC.

LiCari testified that he laid out his case against Universal to Hoyvald and got the impression he would look into the matter. But later Hoyvald indicated to LiCari that nothing would be done. Hoyvald testified that he didn't remember either conversation.

At a budget meeting with Hoyvald that fall, says a former employee, Lavery suggested getting a new apple concentrate supplier even though that would add costs. Lavery warned of the risk that Universal's concentrate was bogus. Hoyvald refused. He told Lavery the new budget was already too high.

At the time, Beech–Nut's losses were continuing—$2.5 million on sales of $62 million in the latest fiscal year. Hoyvald had promised Nestlé that Beech–Nut would be profitable in 1982. "The pressure was on," Hoyvald testified.

Why had Beech–Nut for years resorted to law breaking to ease that pressure? It seems certain some Beech–Nut employees should have known Universal's concentrate was adulterated. "When it comes in at that price," says a Gerber executive, "you shouldn't have to test it. You know it's fake."

Evidence suggests that Beech–Nut employees used two main arguments to justify their conduct and ease their consciences. First, they believed that many other companies were selling fake juice. What, then, was so bad about Beech–Nut doing the same thing to remain competitive? Second, they were convinced that their apple juice, even if it was adulterated, was perfectly safe. "So suppose the stuff was all water and flavor and sugar," says an executive then at Beech–Nut. "Why get so upset about it? Who were we hurting?"

Those rationalizations were badly flawed. Most companies were not selling fake apple juice. Only 5 percent of the apple juice then being sold, say industry sources, was adulterated. And while there is no evidence the fake juice was a health hazard, there is no assurance that it was not. "We just don't know the long-range effects of the synthetic ingredients," says Maurice Guerrette, a food inspection official with the New York State Agriculture & Markets Dept.

Other Beech–Nut employees, ignoring the many R&D studies offering evidence of adulteration, took refuge in the lack of a conclusive test. "They let their doubts color their judgment," says Jack Hartog, a food broker who repeatedly warned the company about Universal.

Still others took a head-in-the-sand attitude. Says a longtime Beech–Nut employee: "It was something you just hoped would go away." Nobody seriously challenged or asked for elaboration of LiCari's adverse findings. But nobody ever confronted Universal. Nobody ordered another inspection of the Queens plant. Outside the R&D department there was an almost total absence of inquiry.

Everything changed one day in June 1982, when a private investigator named Andrew Rosenzweig showed up at Canajoharie. He had been hired to look into apple juice adulteration by Processed Apples Institute, Inc., whose members made products from fresh apples. He told Beech–Nut officials that a new adulteration test, along with documents retrieved from a dumpster near the Queens plant, established that Universal's concentrate was bogus. He asked them to join other juicemakers in a lawsuit against the Universal operation.

"Stonewalling"

Beech–Nut then committed a grave tactical error. Says an attorney close to the case, whose view is shared by government officials: "They could have nipped this in the bud, owned up, paid a fine, and it would have been a pimple for them. But they stonewalled, and the stonewalling became the issue, and the case changed from civil to criminal, and it became a nightmare."

Beech–Nut immediately canceled its apple concentrate contracts. But its response to Rosenzweig's offer, a Processed Apples Institute official said later, was "hostile and uncooperative." It refused to join the PAI suit, which put the adulterators out of business a month

later. And it kept selling products made from the phony concentrate. It did not issue a national apple juice recall until October, despite warnings during the summer from the Food & Drug Administration and the New York State Agriculture Dept. that samples of its apple juice had been found to be adulterated.

Federal and state officials later charged that Beech–Nut's strategy—executed very effectively—was to avoid publicity and stall their investigations until it could unload its $3.5 million inventory of tainted apple juice products. "They played a cat-and-mouse game with us," says one investigator. When the FDA would identify a specific apple juice lot as tainted, Beech–Nut would quickly destroy it before the FDA could seize it, an act that could have created negative publicity. One day in August a New York State official notified the company that a juice sample had "little, if any, apple juice." Beech–Nut executives worried that the state might seize its entire inventory. That night, they engaged nine trucks to move the inventory out of state to a New Jersey warehouse.

Some Beech–Nut employees wanted the entire inventory destroyed or relabeled. But Hoyvald ordered it distributed "fast, fast, fast" at deep discounts, a Beech–Nut executive testified. A lot of it was exported to the Caribbean. But a sizable portion was sent to Puerto Rico, a major Beech–Nut market—and one covered by U.S. food and drug laws. An official with its local distributor testified that Beech–Nut never told him regulators had questioned the juice's authenticity. Had he known, he said, he would have refused the shipments.

Beech–Nut continued to sell mixed juices made from the bogus concentrate until March 1983—months after its recall of straight apple juice and its own lawsuit against the Universal operation in December alleging that the company's concentrate was phony.

Hoyvald insisted he still lacked "proof positive" the concentrate was bogus. And he said he acted on the advice of outside counsel, mainly Nestlé lawyer Thomas J. Ward. A confidant of Ernest Saunders, Ward in 1981 had helped Nestlé orchestrate its response to a boycott of Nestlé products stemming from its infant formula exports to the Third World. More recently, Ward has been under federal investigation for his role in the Guinness scandal.

FDA investigators initially considered Beech–Nut an innocent victim of unscrupulous suppliers. But the company's stalling tactics angered them. After an investigation, they recommended to the Justice Dept. that Beech–Nut be prosecuted for knowingly shipping adulterated goods after June 1982. A federal grand jury found incriminating evidence, including LiCari's 1981 memorandum, of Beech–Nut's knowledge before that date. The 1986 indictment also named Kaplansky and Wells. Both later pleaded guilty and are awaiting sentencing.

Shifting the Blame

Nestlé is financing a vigorous defense of John Lavery and particularly Neils Hoyvald, who is being represented by Brendan Sullivan, Oliver North's lawyer. James M. Biggar, chairman of Nestlé Enterprises, Inc., which oversees Nestlé's U.S. operations, says that acquittal of Hoyvald and Lavery would remove some of the onus of the corporate guilty plea and properly place the blame on lower-level employees. "They were the only ones who knew what was going on," he says.

District Court Judge Thomas C. Platt, Jr., instructed the jury that the government must prove beyond a reasonable doubt that the defendants were aware of a "high probability" the juice was impure and that they intentionally violated the law. He said the jury should consider the notion of "conscious avoidance," when someone has a duty to seek the truth but avoids doing so.

The verdict may turn on the jury's view of Jerome LiCari, whom prosecutor Roche called "the conscience of Beech–Nut." Defense lawyers pointed out that LiCari admitted initially lying to investigators about an anonymous letter signed "Johnny Appleseed" that he sent to the FDA in 1983 about Beech–Nut's early knowledge of adulteration.

But the most revealing evaluation of LiCari—and his relationship with Beech–Nut—was his 1981 performance report, written by John Lavery. It lauded his loyalty and technical ability but said his judgment was "colored by naivete and impractical ideals." LiCari was asked by Justice Dept. lawyer John R. Fleder in early January if he had been naive. "I guess I was," he replied. "I thought apple juice should be made from apples."

Whatever the jury decides about Neils Hoyvald and John Lavery, it is clear that too few people at Beech–Nut shared Jerome LiCari's ideals.

[Nestlé paid a $2 million fine plus $140,000 in governmental investigative expenses. And a civil class action was settled for $7.5 million. Hoyvald and Lavery were found guilty of numerous criminal charges.[95] They were each sentenced to one year and one day in prison, fined $100,000, and ordered to pay court costs expected to total tens of thousands of dollars.[96]—Author.]

Source: Reprinted from February 22, 1988 issue of *Business Week* by special permission, copyright © 1988 by McGraw-Hill, Inc.

Questions

1. The title of the article suggests Beech–Nut has been disgraced. *Disgraced,* of course, means being dishonored or shamed. Are corporations capable of suffering dishonor or shame? Explain.

2. Had Beech–Nut not been suffering financial difficulties, do you suppose this episode would have happened? Explain.
3. Important evidence in the Beech–Nut case came from a private investigator's search of a dumpster near Universal's plant. Is such a search lawful? Explain.

BUFFALO CREEK

Background

Buffalo Creek, West Virginia, is a mountain hollow some 17 miles in length. Three small forks come together at the top of the hollow to form the creek itself. In early 1972, approximately 5,000 people lived in this area, in what amounted to a continuous string of 16 villages.

Middle Fork served for several years as the site of an enormous pile of mine waste, known as a "dam" to local residents and an "impoundment" to the Buffalo Mining Company. The impoundment was there because it solved two important disposal problems for the company:

1. Each time four tons of coal are removed from the ground, one ton of slag—a wide assortment of waste materials—is also removed and must be disposed of.
2. Additionally, more than 500,000 gallons of water are required to prepare four tons of coal for shipment, and this, too, must be disposed of.

The Buffalo Mining Company began to deposit its slag in Middle Fork as early as 1957 and by 1972 was dumping approximately 1,000 tons per day. Traditionally, the company had deposited its solid waste into Middle Fork and its liquid effluent into nearby streams. However, by the 1960s coal operators were under a great deal of pressure to retain this water until some of the impurities had settled out of it. The companies were also beginning to see

the utility in having a regular supply of processing water on hand. Buffalo Mining Company responded to this by dumping new slag on top of old, in such a way as to form barriers behind which waste water could be stored and reused.

Middle Fork was described as an immense black trough of slag, silt, and water, a waste sink arranged in such a way as to create small reservoirs behind the first two impoundments and a large lake behind the third.

The Episode

According to subsequent accounts, during the night of February 25, 1972, Buffalo Mining Company officials continually monitored the Middle Fork waste site. They were reportedly uneasy because the lake water seemed to be rising dangerously close to the dam crest. The past few days had been wet ones, but such seasonal precipitation was not considered unusual. Toward dawn, company officials were concerned enough to have a spillway cut across the surface of the barrier in an effort to relieve pressure. The level continued to rise, but the company issued no public warnings. Testimony disclosed that the senior official on the site met with two deputy sheriffs who arrived on the scene to aid in an evacuation in the event of trouble. The official contended at the time that everything was under control, and the deputies left.

Just before 8 A.M., February 26, a heavy-equipment operator inspected the surface of the dam and found that not only was the water within inches of the crest—which he already knew—but that the structure had softened dramatically since the last inspection.

Within minutes the dam had collapsed. The 132 million gallons of waste water and solids roared through the breach. The wave reportedly set off a series of explosions, raising mushroom-shaped clouds into the air, and picking up "everything in its path." One million tons of solid waste were said to be caught in the flow.

Impact

A 20- to 30-foot tidal wave traveling up to 30 miles per hour devastated Buffalo Creek's 16 small communities. More than 125 people per-ished, and hundreds of others were injured. Over 4,000 survived, but their 1,000 homes, as well as most of their possessions, were destroyed.

A few hundred of the 4,000 survivors decided not to accept the settlement for real property damage offered by the coal company as reimbursement. Instead, they brought suit against the Pittston Corporation [which owned Buffalo Mining].

On Wednesday, June 26, 1974, two and a half years after the incident, the 600 or so Buffalo Creek plaintiffs were awarded $13.5 million by the Pittston Corporation in an out-of-court settlement.

Source: Library of Congress Congressional Research Service. Background material for hearings on H.R. 7040. Subcommittee on Crime of the Committee on the Judiciary, House of Representatives, 96th Congress, 2nd session, May 1980.

Questions

1. What arguments might Buffalo Mining and Pittston raise in their defense?
2. Argue on Pittston's behalf that it should not be a party to any lawsuits arising from the dam break.
3. *a.* Assume you own a fleet of taxicabs and wish to minimize your potential loss in the event of an accident. What corporate structure would you utilize to accomplish your goal? Explain.
   b. Will you succeed in minimizing your losses? Explain.
4. In your judgment, were Buffalo Mining and Pittston guilty of criminal behavior? Explain.
5. According to a 1973 account in *The Nation:*

   Three different government agencies laid the responsibility for the flood squarely on the shoulders of Buffalo Mining and Pittston. Buffalo Mining drew a $25 fine for breaking a U.S. Bureau of Mines regulation, and a mild scolding from the U.S. Department of the Interior. (Thruston Morton, who sits on the Pittston board of directors, is the brother of Rogers C. B. Morton, Secretary of the Interior.) Several Buffalo Mining officials were required to answer questions before a Logan County grand jury, but emerged unscathed.[97]

   How do you explain the mild public-sector response?
6. Was the settlement figure of $13.5 million (of which almost $3 million went to the plaintiff's lawyers) a just sum? Is that sum sufficient to discourage such conduct in the future? Was the nearly $3 million legal fee fair in light of the firm's more than 40,000 hours of labor? Explain.

FIRESTONE 500

Background

Firestone's involvement in the manufacture of steel-belted radial tires began in the early 1970s when U.S. automobile designers sought from the domestic tire industry a product that would help achieve better gasoline mileage (reduced rolling resistance) and provide a better ride. Radial tires meet these criteria and, in addition, when they are properly made and used, they last longer through improved tread wear and greater resistance to road hazards. With the domestic automobile manufacturers moving toward steel-belted radials, Firestone moved aggressively into the steel-belted radial "original equipment" market. Largely by speedy adaptation of existing equipment, Firestone became the first domestic tire manufacturer to place these tires in the original equipment market in large quantities. . . .

Firestone began marketing its first generation of steel-belted radials in 1971 and introduced the Firestone 500, also considered a first-generation steel-belted tire, in 1972.

The Cause for Concern

In 1976 the Center for Auto Safety, a private nonprofit consumer interest organization, began to notice that they were receiving a disproportionately large number of complaints on Firestone steel-belted radials. When the complaints on Firestone steel-belted radials continued into 1977, the center conducted a review of all its consumer reports on all tire failures for a selected period of time to compare Firestone tires with those of other companies. The data showed that at that time 50 percent of all tire complaint letters received by the Center for Auto Safety were on Firestone tires and that the vast majority of those were on steel-belted radials. Throughout this time the center also forwarded copies of the Firestone steel-belted radial complaints to the National Highway Traffic Safety Administration (NHTSA) and requested a defect investigation. However, the center apparently did not investigate the complaints, but simply accepted them all at face value (although in some cases there evidently were mitigating circumstances).

Alarmed by the performance of Firestone tires, the Center for Auto Safety, on November 28, 1977, wrote directly to Mario DiFederico, president of the Firestone Tire and Rubber Company, and pointed out that the complaint rate on Firestone tires was three times the average of their market share and that nearly all complaints concerned steel-belted radials. The center further provided Firestone with copies of the complaints included in its study, based on tires manufactured both by Firestone and by other companies. The center also suggested that Firestone should shift half of its advertising budget into quality control. Firestone did not respond to the center regarding this information.

On December 22, 1977, NHTSA first asked, then ordered Firestone to provide defect information on Firestone steel-belted radial tires, including lists of accidents, injuries, and deaths reported to have been caused by defective tires. On April 26, 1978, Firestone submitted a list of 213 accidents. By this time the Firestone 500 was in the final stages of being phased out of production on a size-by-size basis, a process which was completed in May of 1978.

Congressional Findings: A Serious Safety Hazard

Congressional inquiry into the safety of Firestone steel-belted radial tires commenced with preparation for hearings by the Subcommittee on Oversight and Investigations of the Committee on Interstate and Foreign Commerce in April 1978. At that time several reports of deaths and injury caused by failure of the Firestone tire had come before the subcommittee. After hearing testimony from several witnesses, including representatives of Firestone, and examining material submitted by Firestone at the subcommittee's request, the subcommittee concluded that Firestone 500 steel-belted radial tires presented an unreasonable risk of continuing accidents, injuries, and death to the motoring public and should be immediately recalled. This conclusion was based on the following findings, quoted from the report of the Subcommittee on Oversight and Investigations:

1. Failure of the Firestone 500 steel-belted radials have caused and are continuing to cause an extraordinary number of accidents, injuries, and deaths. Accidents attributable to the 500 number in the thousands, injuries in the hundreds, and known fatalities as of August 1978, 34. . . . Regardless of the mix of product defect and other contributing factors in each case, an overall pattern of Firestone 500 failures associated with human destruction is undeniable.

2. The rate of failure of Firestone 500 steel-belted radial tires, while not precisely known, is exceedingly high. Evidence of a high rate of failure includes:

   a. The high adjustment rate for the Firestone 500 steel-belted radial.

   An "adjustment rate" is the percentage of tires produced by a company which it accepts back from customers because of some problem with tires that occurs before useful tread is worn.

   * * * * *

   b. The significant number of claims settled by Firestone by means of cash payments for damage caused by tire failures.

   * * * * *

   c. The high average number of failures reported per customer.

   In 834 letters received by the subcommittee over the 10-week period following the subcommittee's hearings, users of Firestone 500 steel-belted radials have experienced a total of 3,384 separate tire failures, for an average of 4.06 failures each.

   d. The experience of fleet operators, whose vehicles equipped with Firestone 500 steel-belted radials have experienced large numbers of similar failures.

Firestone's Response

Firestone denied wrongdoing, responding to the congressional investigation and allegations of a defective product, first [by arguing] that radial tire failure is often due to driving with improperly low inflation pressures. Secondly, Firestone cited the considerable body of adverse publicity concerning alleged problems generated by the media, which stirred up concern that, it claimed, would not otherwise have existed.

Firestone also offered additional explanations for the higher-than-ordinary adjustment rate for the 500 as follows:

Firestone's larger production of steel-belted radials when the tire first came into heavy demand for installation on new cars;

The longer life of radials, allowing for greater opportunity for disablement;

The problems owners had in adjusting to the "underinflated look" of a radial; and

The fact that Firestone extended more liberal adjustment policies for the 500s as its top-of-the-line tire.

In the nature of a rebuttal, the subcommittee report on the hearings concluded that Firestone cannot claim to have cornered more than its share of the nation's underinflators as purchasers of the 500. Underinflation might account for some, but not all, of the high adjustment rate for the 500.

Corporate Knowledge of the Problem?

Data provided by Firestone . . . suggests that Firestone may have known as early as 1973 that large numbers of low-mileage tires were being returned to dealers for various reasons. In that year, 5.48 percent of Firestone's 1972 production of over 1 million steel-belted radial 500s were adjusted, including many for failure problems (although the precise number of failures cannot be determined).

Additional evidence that Firestone may have been aware of major failure problems with their 500 steel-belted radial tires as early as November 1972 came from documents released by NHTSA after the Firestone recall decision reached by NHTSA in the fall of 1978. According to a description of these in the *Washington Post,* a memorandum to the then-vice president for tire production, Mario DiFederico, on November 2, 1972, from Firestone's director of tire development, Thomas Robertson, warned that problems with the steel-belted tires were so bad that the company was in danger of losing its business with Chevrolet because of separation failures.

Finally, Firestone confirmed that it had knowledge of tire test results in late 1975, indicating that some of its steel-belted radial tires failed to measure up to acceptable standards after a year or two of storage. This disclosure came in July 1978 after the *Akron Beacon Journal* had obtained computer printouts of the results.

Epilogue

Citing thousands of reported failures, the National Highway Traffic Safety Administration issued an initial determination on July 9, 1978, finding Firestone 500 steel-belted radial tires defective. Subsequently, a recall was ordered on October 20 and a final agreement was signed on November 29, 1978, between Firestone and NHTSA ironing out details of the recall. Under this agreement the company would recall and replace free all five-rib 500 steel-belted radials (including private brands of the same internal construction) manufactured and sold from September 1, 1975, to January 1, 1977, and all seven-rib 500 steel-belted radials made and sold between September 1, 1975, and May 1, 1976. This recall would involve some 7.5 million tires estimated to be still in service. In addition, Firestone agreed to offer an exchange of new tires at half price for some 6 million steel-belted radials sold prior to the three-year legal limitation on free replacements, and not covered by the recall.

[(1) Recall of the Firestone 500 series is estimated to have cost the company something in excess of $100 million. (2) In 1988 Firestone sold its tire factories to a Japanese firm, Bridgestone.—Author.]

Source: Library of Congress Congressional Research Service. Background material for hearings on H.R. 7040. Subcommittee on Crime of the Committee on the Judiciary. House of Representatives, 96th Congress, 2nd session, May 1980.

Questions

1. *Time* magazine Washington Correspondent Jonathan Beaty, who studied hundreds of Firestone documents, reported:

   Internal Firestone corporate records turned over to the NHTSA . . . show that top Firestone managers—including President Mario A. DiFederico, who has just announced his resignation—were deeply enmeshed in the several years' effort to deal with and correct the failure problems of the 500 and were, from the beginning, aware of the tire's flaws. The documents show that while DiFederico and virtually all other top executives at one time or another were receiving detailed reports about tire failure from their own production people and major corporate buyers like General Motors and Atlas Tire Company, they still assured the public that the 500 had no safety defects, and were not telling stockholders of the problems.[98]

    a. What legitimate concerns might have led Firestone to withhold evidence of problems with the 500 series?

    b. Does the duty to stockholders require officers to defend the company with all available, legal tactics? Explain.

    c. Must the officer operate, not in terms of personal ethical standards, but in response to the needs of the company? Explain.

    d. Place yourself in the roles of the Firestone officers. Would you have revealed information regarding these flaws? Explain.

    e. If you would not, are you an unethical person? Explain.

2. According to a Knight-Ridder account, in early 1978 Firestone collected its remaining 500 tires from factories in the Southeast and shipped them to South Florida and Alabama for sale at half price.[99] The sale came a month after the National Highway Traffic Safety Administration announced an investigation of the tires. A Firestone spokesman said the company continued to believe the tires to be safe. Thus the disposal sale was, in the company's eyes, legitimate.

    a. Do you agree that the sale was legitimate? Explain.

    b. Was the sale a wise management strategy? Explain.

3. Would you consider it unethical to continue selling used Firestone 500 radials following the recall? Would the ethical problems, if any, be removed by warning each purchaser of the recall? Explain.

4. According to a *Fortune* account, Firestone's vice president and general counsel, John Floberg, made the following arguments in testifying before a House subcommittee:

> At one point, Floberg stated that the 500 was one of two steel-belted radials that had been rated above all others in a *Consumer Reports* survey. But Lowell Dodge, the subcommittee counsel, pointed out that the ratings, which appeared in the October 1973 issue, had been made according to tread wear, not safety.
>
> A while later, Floberg tried to make the point that the industry encouraged consumers to take proper care of their radial tires. He cited a television ad that Firestone had run on the subject. But, as he conceded, this was not a very potent example, since the advertisement had been forced on Firestone by the Federal Trade Commission, in partial settlement of a lawsuit.[100]

    a. Are "half-truths" of this sort characteristic of the corporate community?

    b. Or is such behavior simply characteristic of human nature? Explain.

5. Are businesspeople unprepared to deal with ethical dilemmas such as those of the Pinto and the Firestone 500? Explain. How might businesspeople become better prepared?

6. How is it that "good" people sometimes do what they know is "bad"?

CHAPTER QUESTIONS

1. According to many published accounts[101] confirmed by National Highway Traffic Safety Administration studies, the Ford Motor Company knew of serious problems in certain of its cars' fan blades and transmissions but declined for several years to acknowledge those problems. Defective fan blades resulting in 1 death and 11 injuries were eventually recalled. According to the NHTSA study, slipping transmissions (Ford cars allegedly slipped into reverse gear after having been left in park) resulted in 98 deaths and 1,710 injuries. Some evidence supports Ford's contention that the problem lies in the driver's failure to shift entirely into park. On the other hand, Ford test track technicians began putting blocks behind the rear wheels of autos after one auto left idling "in park" lurched backward and ran over the foot of Ford engineer Frank Hare.[102] In December 1980 Ford agreed to send a dashboard warning sticker and a letter to each owner, explaining the possible hazard and suggesting precautions. Then, in 1985, the Center for Auto Safety, a consumer lobbying organization, asked NHTSA to reopen its investigation of the transmissions. When NHTSA declined, the center sued. The center claimed at least 400 deaths had been attributed to the allegedly faulty transmissions. The center also estimated that owners had affixed the warning stickers to only 10 percent of the 23 million cars in question and that the stickers were ineffectual in any case. The center has estimated that perhaps 9 million of the transmissions remain in use. The center's lawsuit failed at both the district and appeals court levels, with the latter holding that it did not have jurisdiction to review NHTSA's assessment of "nonsafety" considerations, such as the administration's available resources and priorities and the administration's likelihood of success if it undertook an investigation. Thus at this writing in 1988, the case appears closed without a definitive resolution of the safety issues involved.[103]

   a. Do the Pinto, fan blade, and transmission episodes suggest insensitivity to the public welfare on the part of Ford, or is the complexity of contemporary technology and bureaucracy so extreme that such problems are inevitable?

   b. If the former, how do you account for that insensitivity?

   c. If the latter, what steps may be taken to alleviate the troublesome conditions?

2. Denis Goulet, holder of a chaired professorship at Notre Dame, has argued that we will find no facile resolution to the conflict between the values of a just society and the sharply opposing values of successful corporations.

   a. Do you agree that the values of a just society oppose those of successful corporations? Explain.

   b. Can a solution be found? Explain.

3. In November 1980 a fire in the Las Vegas MGM Grand Hotel resulted in 84 deaths and 500 injuries. Prior to the fire, Las Vegas fire chief Roy Parrish said fire officials and building inspectors had met with hotel officials to urge the expansion of the sprinkler system, even though not required under existing law. The hotel did not undertake the expansion. (At the time of the fire, sprinklers were installed in the basement and the 1st and 26th floors.)

    a. In this case is the legal standard also the proper ethical standard? Explain.

    b. Safety is purchased. Is the failure to make that purchase unethical? Explain.

    c. How can you decide when the cost of doing right is too high?

4. In criticizing General Motors, Ralph Nader is reported to have said:

> Someday we'll have a legal system that will criminally indict the president of General Motors for these outrageous crimes. But not as long as this country is populated by people who fritter away their citizenship by watching TV, playing bridge and Mah-Jongg, and just generally being slobs.[104]

    a. Is the citizenry generally unconcerned about unethical corporate conduct? Explain.

    b. To the extent that corporations engage in misdeeds, does the fault really lie with the corporate community or with society at large? Explain.

5. Michael Kinsley, editor of *New Republic,* expresses some serious reservations about corporate social responsibility:

> In particular, I am not impressed by corporate charity and cultural benefaction, which amount to executives playing Medici with other people's money. You wouldn't know, from the lavish parties corporate officers throw for themselves whenever they fund an art exhibit or a PBS series, that it's not costing them a penny. The shareholders, who aren't invited, pick up the tab.[105]

    Comment on Kinsley's statement.

6. Should corporate chief executive officers submit to press conferences on a regular basis? Explain.

7. Must the corporation adjust to changing societal sentiments (social responsibility), or is the future health of the nation dependent on the corporate community manifesting the strength to adhere to traditional free market principles? Explain.

8. Is the ethical climate of business improving or declining? Explain.

9. Should companies engage in moral judgments? For example, if during the Vietnam War the Dow Chemical Company's leadership had decided that one of its products, napalm (an incendiary gel), was an immoral weapon, should the company have ceased production? Explain.

10. In 1977 actress and social activist Jane Fonda criticized Dow Chemical Company in a speech at Central Michigan University. Dow then notified the university that it would receive no more company financial aid until officials of the two institutions could meet to discuss the use of company grants. Evaluate the wisdom of Dow's position.

11. You are the sole owner of a manufacturing firm employing 500 semi-skilled laborers in the Harlem borough of New York City. Your present profits are sufficient to maintain the firm as a viable enterprise, but insufficient to permit expansion. A study reveals that moving the firm to Phoenix, Arizona, would double your profits to what might be labeled a "reasonable" level when measured by industry norms. Expansion, including the addition of 200 jobs, seems likely in Phoenix. The current unemployment rate in Harlem exceeds 20 percent, while that in Phoenix is below 4 percent (and thus Phoenix is effectively a full-employment economy).

    a. Would the socially responsible businessperson move the firm to Phoenix? Explain.

    b. What would you do?

    c. Would your answers be different were the firm owned by thousands of shareholders? Explain.

12. You are the sole owner of a neighborhood drugstore that stocks brands of toothpaste. Assume that scientific testing has established that one brand is clearly superior to all others in preventing tooth decay.

    a. Would you remove from the shelves all brands except the one judged best in decay prevention? Explain.

    b. What alternative measures could you take?

    c. Should the toothpaste manufacturers be required to reveal all available data regarding the effectiveness of their products? Explain.

13. According to *Business Week,* about 3,000 of the nation's 44,000 major employers were providing some kind of day-care assistance to their employees as of 1987.[106] In your opinion, should all employers provide day-care assistance? Explain. If so, who should pay the bill? Explain.

14. Mark Green argued for federal chartering of corporations:

    > It makes as much sense for states to print money or passports as to issue the legal birth certificates of corporations that market products interstate, if not internationally. The results of this historical anomaly, in the words of a 1969 law, is a kind of "law for sale." States lure companies into their jurisdictions, and thus generate incorporation fees, by adopting corporation codes that are excessively pro-management.[107]

    Comment on Green's statement.

15. Approximately $10 million is expended annually for alcohol ads in college newspapers. Many millions more are expended in other youth-oriented publications like *National Lampoon* and *Rolling Stone.* The

beer industry sponsors many campus athletic contests. And brewers have established promotional relationships with rock bands. Is beer and liquor advertising directed to the youth market unethical? Explain.

16. Many jurisdictions curb alcoholic beverage advertising. Quebec forbids endorsements by famous personalities. Ecuador has banned such ads prior to 9 P.M. Finland forbids all alcohol ads. Even news pictures displaying bottle labels are not allowed. Advertising of hard liquor is forbidden on American TV. Should the United States banish all advertising of alcoholic beverages?[108] Explain.

17. Professor Albert Huebner decries American exports of tobacco to the Third World:

> As efforts to expose and to stop the irresponsible promotion of bottle feeding [of babies] have grown, a new invasion of many of the same countries has begun. Transnational tobacco companies are vigorously stepping up sales efforts in the Third World, which is now seen as the major growth area for their products. These efforts are likely to be more intensive, more successful in achieving their goal, and more disastrous for the health of people in the countries involved than the breast-to-bottle campaign.[109]

   a. Is the promotion and sale of tobacco products in Third World nations socially irresponsible behavior? Explain.

   b. Should the U.S. government attempt to curb such promotion and sales? Explain.

18. Are such episodes as the Beech-Nut apple juice, the Pinto, the Firestone 500, and Buffalo Creek merely regrettable aberrations, not at all characteristic of general corporate conduct and values? Explain.

19. Former General Motors vice president John Z. DeLorean wrote in his book, *On a Clear Day You Can See General Motors:*

> It seemed to me then, and still does now, that the system of American business often produces wrong, immoral, and irresponsible decisions, even though the personal morality of the people running the business is often above reproach. The system has a different morality as a group than the people do as individuals, which permits it willfully to produce ineffective or dangerous products, deal dictatorially and often unfairly with suppliers, pay bribes for business, abrogate the rights of employment, or tamper with the democratic process of government through illegal political contributions.[110]

   a. How can the corporate "group" possess values at odds with those of the individual managers?

   b. Is DeLorean merely offering a convenient rationalization for corporate misdeeds? Explain.

   c. Realistically, can one expect to preserve individual values when employed in a corporate group? Explain.

20. Do you agree or disagree with the following statements? Explain.
    a. "Social responsibility is good business only if it is also good public relations and/or preempts government interference."
    b. "The social responsibility debate is the result of the attempt of liberal intellectuals to make a moral issue of business behavior."
    c. "'Profit' is really a somewhat ineffective measure of business's social effectiveness."
    d. "The social responsibility of business is to 'stick to business.'"[111]
21. How much notice, if any, should an employer give to employees prior to plant closings or layoffs? Explain.

NOTES

1. Burns W. Roper and Thomas A. W. Miller, "Americans Take Stock of Business," *Public Opinion,* August/September 1985, pp. 12–13. Used with permission.
2. Ibid.
3. Adam Clymer, "How Americans Rate Big Business," *The New York Times Magazine,* June 8, 1986, p. 69. Copyright © 1986 by The New York Times Company. Reprinted by permission.
4. Roper and Miller, "Americans Take Stock," p. 15.
5. Clymer, "How Americans Rate," p. 69. Also see, for example, James Stafford and Robert Lehner, *Houston Community Study* (Houston: Hearne Publishing, 1976), p. 34, as reported in James Stafford and Betsy Gelb, "Who's More Critical of Business: Men or Women?" *Business Horizons* 21, no. 1, (February 1978), p. 5.
6. Tracy Timson, M.B.A. candidate, University of Northern Iowa, prepared this paragraph.
7. *Fortune,* April 27, 1987, p. 364.
8. Data drawn from *The World Bank Atlas* (Washington, D.C.: International Bank for Reconstruction and Development/The World Bank, 1987), pp. 6–11; and *Fortune,* April 17, 1987, p. 364.
9. "The World's 100 Largest Companies," *The Wall Street Journal,* September 18, 1987, p. 24D.
10. Peter Asch, *Industrial Organization and Antitrust Policy* (New York: John Wiley & Sons, 1983), p. 162.
11. See, for example, Harold Demsetz, *The Market Concentration Doctrine* (Washington, D.C.: American Enterprise Institute, 1973), pp. 22, 25–26. For related commentary and studies, see, for example, Rogene A. Buchholz, *Business Environment and Public Policy* (Englewood Cliffs, N.J.: Prentice-Hall, 1986), pp. 218–29.
12. Charles Reich, *The Greening of America* (New York: Bantam Books, 1970), pp. 7–8.
13. David Broder, "Wrigley Field, an Anchor in an Insecure World," *Des Moines Register,* June 10, 1987, p. 7A.
14. John J. Fialka, "House Incumbents Increasingly Depend on PAC Campaign Funds, Study Says," *The Wall Street Journal,* April 8, 1987, p. 58. Reprinted

by permission of *The Wall Street Journal,* © Dow Jones & Company, Inc. 1987. ALL RIGHTS RESERVED.

15. Ibid.

16. Robert Samuelson, "The Campaign Reform Fraud," *Newsweek,* July 13, 1987, p. 43.

17. Evan Thomas, "Peddling Influence," *Time,* March 3, 1986, pp. 26–27.

18. Alan Murray, "Lobbyists for Business Are Deeply Divided, Reducing Their Clout," *The Wall Street Journal,* March 25, 1987, p. 1. Reprinted by permission of *The Wall Street Journal,* © Dow Jones & Company, Inc. 1987. ALL RIGHTS RESERVED.

19. Thomas, "Peddling Influence," pp. 26, 33.

20. Richard N. Goodwin, "PACs Gobbling Up Congress," *Waterloo Courier,* December 17, 1985, p. A4.

21. Reich, *Greening of America,* pp. 141–42.

22. Jim Jones, "Prosperity Preachers," *Waterloo Courier,* October 10, 1986, p. 10.

23. Ibid.

24. Debora Silverman, *Selling Culture* (New York: Pantheon Books, 1986).

25. Jonathan Yardley, "New Elite 'Sells Out' Art for 'Culture of Commerce,'" *Des Moines Register,* October 26, 1986, p. 3C.

26. *Business Week,* August 31, 1987, p. 48.

27. Peter F. Drucker, "The Mystery of the Business Leader," *The Wall Street Journal,* September 29, 1987, p. 30. Reprinted by permission of *The Wall Street Journal,* © Dow Jones & Company, Inc. 1987. ALL RIGHTS RESERVED.

28. Betsy Morris, "As a Favored Pastime, Shopping Ranks High with Most Americans," *The Wall Street Journal,* July 30, 1987, pp. 1, 13.

29. From *The Poetry of Robert Frost,* edited by Edward Connery Lathem. Copyright 1916; © 1969 by Holt, Rinehart and Winston. Copyright 1944 by Robert Frost. Reprinted by permission of Holt, Rinehart and Winston, Publishers.

30. Herman Kahn, "Self-Indulgence, Survival, and Space," *The Futurist,* October 1980, pp. 10–11.

31. Thomas Griffith, "Me First," *The Atlantic,* July 1980, p. 20.

32. *University of Iowa Spectator,* March 1980, p. 4.

33. Peter McCabe, "Vanity Fair," *Harper's Magazine,* August 1977, p. 83.

34. Peter Wynn, *Apples, History, Folklore, Horticulture, and Gastronomy,* as reported by Joanee Will for the *Chicago Tribune* and reprinted in the *Lexington Leader,* October 1, 1980, p. D–1.

35. "For What Shall It Profit a Man. . . . ?" *Business Week,* July 6, 1987, p. 104.

36. Myron Magnet, "The Money Society," *Fortune,* July 6, 1987, p. 26.

37. Forum, "Is There Virtue in Profit?" *Harper's Magazine,* December 1986, pp. 37, 42.

38. "The Swing to Practicality in the B-Schools," *Business Week,* July 23, 1979, p. 190.

39. Ronnie Dugger, "The Counting House of Academe," *Harper's Magazine,* March 1974, p. 70.

40. Ted Peters, "The Future of Religion in a Post-Industrial Society," *The Futurist,* October 1980, pp. 20, 22.

41. Tom Uhlenbock for United Press International, "Citizens' Party Attributes America's Problems to Big Corporations," *Lexington Sunday Herald-Leader,* April 6, 1980.

42. Samuel Florman, "Small Is Dubious," *Harper's,* August 1977, pp. 10, 12.

43. "More Leisure in an Increasingly Electronic Society," *Business Week,* September 3, 1979, pp. 208, 212.

44. Steven N. Brenner and Earl A. Molander, "Is the Ethics of Business Changing?" *Harvard Business Review* 55, no. 1 (January–February 1977), pp. 57, 59.

45. Ibid., p. 68.

46. "Mounting Public Pressure for Corporate Social Responsibility," *ORC Public Opinion Index* (Princeton, N.J.: Opinion Research Corporation, January, 1974), as reported in Lyman E. Ostlund, "Attitudes of Managers toward Corporate Social Responsibility," *California Management Review* 19, no. 4 (Summer 1977), p. 35.

47. Clymer, "How Americans Rate," p. 69.

48. Keith Davis and Robert L. Blomstrom, *Business and Society: Environment and Responsibility,* 3rd ed. (New York: McGraw-Hill, 1975), p. 6.

49. Kenneth R. Andrews, *The Concept of Corporate Strategy* (Homewood, Ill.: Dow Jones-Irwin, 1971), p. 120.

50. Milton Friedman, *Capitalism and Freedom* (Chicago: University of Chicago Press, 1962), p. 133.

51. Keith Davis, "The Case for and against Business' Assumption of Social Responsibilities," *Academy of Management Journal* 16, no. 2 (June 1973), p. 312.

52. Henry C. Wallich and John J. McGowan, "Stockholder Interest and the Corporation's Role in Social Policy," in *A New Rationale for Corporate Social Policy,* ed. William J. Baumol, Rensis Likert, Henry C. Wallich, and John J. McGowan, (New York: Committee for Economic Development, 1970), pp. 39–59.

53. Ostlund, "Attitudes of Managers," p. 35.

54. Kamal M. Abouzeid and Charles N. Weaver, "Social Responsibility in the Corporate Goal Hierarchy," *Business Horizons* 21, no. 3 (June 1978), p. 29.

55. Frederick D. Sturdivant and James L. Ginter, "Corporate Social Responsiveness—Management Attitudes and Economic Performance," *California Management Review* 19, no. 3 (Spring 1977), p. 30.

56. Ibid., p. 38.

57. See Phillip I. Cochran and Robert Wood, "Corporate Responsibility and Financial Performance," *Academy of Management Journal* 27, no. 1 (March 1984), p. 42, for an excellent study of the issue and a survey of previous research.

58. For a summary of some of these studies, see Alfred A. Marcus, Philip Bromiley, and Robert Goodman, "Preventing Corporate Crises: Stock Market Losses as a Deterrent to the Production of Hazardous Products," *Columbia Journal of World Business* 22, no. 1 (Spring 1987), p. 33.

59. Gordon J. Alexander and Rogene A. Buchholz, "Corporate Social Responsibility and Stock Market Performance," *Academy of Management Journal* 21, no. 3 (September 1978), p. 479.

60. Marcus et al., "Preventing Corporate Crises," p. 33.

61. S. Prakash Sethi, "Dimensions of Corporate Social Performance: An Analytical Framework," *California Management Review* 17, no. 3 (Spring 1975), p. 58.

62. Edwin M. Epstein, "The Corporate Social Policy Process: Beyond Business Ethics, Corporate Social Responsibility, and Corporate Social Responsiveness," *California Management Review* 29, no. 3 (Spring 1987), p. 99.

63. Ibid., p. 107.

64. Quoted in "Ethical Dilemmas for the Multinational Enterprise," *Business Ethics Report,* Highlights of Bentley College's Sixth National Conference on Business Ethics, October 10–11, 1985, p. 24.

65. *The Nation,* March 29, 1980, pp. 356–57.

66. "Is Pinto a Criminal?" *Regulation,* March–April 1980, p. 21.

67. Andy Pasztor, "Pinto Criminal Trial of Ford Motor Company Opens Up Broad Issues," *The Wall Street Journal,* January 4, 1980, pp. 1, 23.

68. Ibid.

69. Mark Green and John F. Berry, "White-Collar Crime Is Big Business," *The Nation* magazine/The Nation Company, Inc., June 8, 1985, p. 689. © 1985.

70. John E. Conklin, *"Illegal but Not Criminal"—Business Crime in America* (Englewood Cliffs, N.J.: Prentice-Hall, 1977), p. 4.

71. Howard Kurtz, "Hill Focuses on White-Collar Crime," *The Washington Post,* February 28, 1986, p. C10.

72. Charles McCoy, "Financial Fraud: Theories behind Nationwide Surge in Bank Swindles," *The Wall Street Journal,* October 2, 1987, p. 15.

73. Ibid.

74. G. Robert Blakey, "A Vital Hedge against Corporate Fraud," *The New York Times,* January 5, 1986, sect. 3, p. 2.

75. The President's Commission on Law Enforcement and Administration of Justice, *The Challenge of Crime in a Free Society* (Washington, D.C.: U.S. Government Printing Office, 1967), p. 5, as reported in Conklin, "Illegal but Not Criminal," p. 7.

76. Green and Berry, "White-Collar Crime," p. 707.

77. Irwin Ross, "How Lawless Are Big Companies?" *Fortune,* December 1, 1980, p. 56.

78. Orr Kelly, "Corporate Crime—the Untold Story," *U.S. News & World Report*, September 6, 1982, p. 25.

79. Associated Press, "White-Collar Criminals Do Little Time," *Des Moines Register,* November 17, 1986, p. 1A.

80. Ibid.

81. Ibid.

82. Estimates of the number of deaths range from over 2,000 to over 2,800, while injury estimates range from 40,000 to 200,000 or more.

83. Amal Kumar Naj, "India Charges Carbide, Ex-Chairman with Homicide in Bhopal Gas Disaster," *The Wall Street Journal,* December 3, 1987, p. 35.

84. "Union Carbide Fights for Its Life" *Business Week,* December 24, 1984, pp. 52, 56.

85. For additional analysis, see, for example, Fergus Bordewich, "The Lessons of Bhopal," *The Atlantic* 259, no. 3 (March 1987), p. 30.

86. Ibid., "Ethical Dilemmas for the Multinational Enterprises," p. 25.

87. Laird Townsend, reviewing Paul Shrivastava, *India's Saddest Hour* (Cambridge, Mass.: Ballinger, 1987), in *Business and Society Review*, no. 61 (Spring 1987), pp. 74, 76.

88. Ibid.

89. Mark Dowie, "The Corporate Crime of the Century," *Mother Jones,* November 1979, pp. 23, 24.

90. "Employee Voluntarism Spreads," Labor Letter, *The Wall Street Journal,* March 4, 1986, p. 1.

91. Ibid.

92. Milton Moskowitz, "Company Performance Roundup," *Business and Society Review,* Winter 1987, p. 69.

93. Ibid., p. 72; quoted from the *Chicago Reporter,* December 1986.

94. Alice Teffer Martin, Victor Kamber, Jules Bernstein, and Mark Green, "The Case for a Corporate Democracy Act," *Business and Society Review* 34 (Summer 1980), p. 58.

95. "Ex-Officials of Beech–Nut Found Guilty in Juice Case," *The Wall Street Journal,* February 18, 1988, p. 14.

96. *The Washington Post,* "Beech–Nut Execs Imprisoned for Bogus Juice," in *Waterloo Courier,* June 17, 1988, p. C4.

97. Tom Nugent, Bureaucracy of Disasters," *The Nation,* June 18, 1973, pp. 785–86.

98. "Forewarnings of Fatal Flaws," *Time,* June 25, 1979, p. 58.

99. Susan Bitterman, "Tires on Sale after Safety Questioned," *Lexington Leader,* April 13, 1978, p. C–1.

100. Arthur Louis, "Lessons from the Firestone Fracas," *Fortune,* August 28, 1978, p. 44.

101. See, for example, "Firm Knew Hazard, Didn't Recall Cars," *Lexington Leader,* September 1, 1977, p. D–9; and "Record Recall Averted over Ford Transmissions," *Lexington Leader,* December 31, 1980, p. B–5.

102. "Nine Fatalities Linked to Transmissions," *Lexington Leader,* June 2, 1978, p. C–5.

103. Associated Press, "Ford Transmissions Probe Won't Be Reopened," *Waterloo Courier,* May 25, 1988, p. B5.

104. Charles McCarry, *Citizen Nader* (New York: Saturday Review Press, 1972), p. 301.

105. Michael Kinsley, "Companies as Citizens: Should They Have a Conscience?" *The Wall Street Journal,* February 19, 1987, p. 29.

106. Joan O'C. Hamilton, "California Makes Business a Partner in Day Care," *Business Week,* June 8, 1987, p. 100.

107. Mark Green, "The Case for Corporate Democracy," *Regulation,* May–June 1980, p. 20.

108. Michael Jacobson, Robert Atkins, and George Hochers, "Booze Merchants Cheer On Teenage Drinking," *Business and Society Review,* no. 46 (Summer 1983), p. 46.

109. Albert Huebner, "Tobacco's Lucrative Third World Invasion," *Business and Society Review,* no. 35 (Fall 1980), p. 49.

110. John Z. DeLorean with J. Patrick Wright, "Bottom-Line Fever at General Motors," (excerpted from *On a Clear Day You Can See General Motors*), *The Washington Monthly,* January 1980, pp. 26–27.

111. Brenner and Molander, "Ethics of Business," p. 68.

PART II

Introduction to Law

Chapter 4

The American Legal System

Part One—Introduction

Presumably, we can agree that some business practices have unfavorable consequences for society. Thus, the issue becomes: What should be done, if anything, to change those consequences? At least three courses have traditionally been followed: let the market "regulate" the behavior; leave the problem to the individual decision maker's own ethical dictates; or pass a law. Market regulation was discussed in Chapter 1. Self-regulation through ethics was explored in Chapters 2 and 3. This chapter, then, begins the discussion of the legal regulation of business with a brief outline of the American legal system and how it functions.

This chapter will also introduce a fourth alternative for addressing business/society conflicts. This alternative looks at conflict resolution processes other than those resorting to the legal system, such as negotiation, mediation, and arbitration. Although these alternatives are not new, they have been receiving much more attention in recent years.

Part Two—Legal Foundations

LAW DEFINED

Just as this text investigates how business fits into society, it is appropriate to begin our look at the legal system by considering how law fits into our society—from the perspectives of both those intimately associated with the law and outsiders looking at law as a social phenomenon. We begin by asking, what exactly is "law"?

1. Judges' Interpretations.   The great jurists Oliver Wendell Holmes and Benjamin Cardozo held similarly pragmatic visions of the meaning of law. "The prophecies of what the courts will do in fact, and nothing more pretentious, are what I mean by the law," said Holmes.[1] To Cardozo, the law was "a principle or rule of conduct so established as to justify a prediction with reasonable certainty that it will be enforced by the courts if its authority is challenged."[2]

The notion of law as rules of conduct enforced by courts will form our working definition for much of the remainder of the text. These rules, however, are not static; they are changing and changeable by both court and legislative action.

2. Sociologist's Interpretation.   The supremely influential thinker Max Weber emphasized the role of external force in explaining the meaning of law.

> An order will be called law if it is externally guaranteed by the probability that coercion (physical or psychological), to bring about conformity or avenge volition, will be applied by a staff of people holding themselves specially ready for that purpose.[3]

Weber would not require the staff of people employed as enforcers to be part of a political government. In some contexts, for example, it may make sense to the "law of General Motors" to describe internal rules employees are required to follow.

3. Anthropologist's Interpretation.   The respected scholar of primitive law Bronislaw Malinowski seemed to regard the law as the natural product of cooperative, reciprocal human relationships.

> The rules of law stand out from the rest in that they are felt and regarded as the obligations of one person and the rightful claims of another. They are sanctioned not by mere psychological motive, but by a definite social machinery of binding force, based . . . upon mutual dependence, and realized in the equivalent arrangement of reciprocal services.[4]

Thus, under this approach binding social custom is appropriately referred to as law.

4. Philosophers' Interpretations.   To Plato, law was one method of social control, while Cicero found the heart of the law in the distinction between the just and the unjust. Perhaps the most influential legal philosopher, Roscoe Pound, built on the social control theme to argue that the law is a mechanism for ordering private interests for the good of the whole society:

> Looked at functionally, the law is an attempt to satisfy, to reconcile, to harmonize, to adjust these overlapped and often conflicting claims and demands

. . . so as to give effect to the greatest total of interests or to the interests that weigh most in our civilization, with the least sacrifice of the scheme of interests as a whole.[5]

Would Pound agree that legislation that does not promote the interests of society as a whole is therefore not law? Keep this in mind when you read about the history of employment discrimination in the United States in Chapter 12.

5. A Dissenting Opinion.   To the critics of the American legal system, the foregoing explanations fail to capture the reality of the law as an instrument of repression. For example, "radical" sociologist Richard Quinney argues that we should be freed from "the dead hand of the legalistic mentality." To Quinney, our respectful, idealized view of law is a "myth" that fails to recognize the success of Oriental societies—particularly the Chinese—in rejecting the necessity for fixed laws. Quinney asks us to imagine a life without law because, to him, law as practiced in America is the unjust product of the power of special interests.

While law is to protect all citizens, it starts as a tool of the dominant class and ends by maintaining the dominance of that class. Law serves the powerful over the weak. . . . Moreover, law is used by the state (and its elitist government) to promote and protect itself. . . . We are indoctrinated with the ideology that it is our law, to be obeyed because we are all citizens of a single nation. Until law is the law of the people, law can be nothing other than official oppression.[6]

This view is also held by a growing number of legal scholars and practitioners who make up the Critical Legal Studies movement. Keep this definition in mind when you want to criticize particular laws enforced by our legal system or by the legal systems in other countries, such as the apartheid laws in South Africa.

Questions

1. *a.* Under which definitions of law would provisions in a corporate code of employee conduct be considered law?
   b. Under which definitions would a commonly accepted trade practice be considered law?
   c. Under which definitions would the Clean Air Act, for example, be considered law?

2. Terence Cannon, a Marxist "radical activist" and a member of the "Oakland Seven":

If you didn't know anything about how the law works in America, if all you did was read the papers, you would know that American courts and American laws are the enemies of the people. If you're too poor to pay the rent, who puts you out on the street? The law. If workers go out on a wildcat strike, who lays the injunction down on them? The law. . . . Law is the tool that politicians and businessmen use to keep down the people they oppress.

Did you ever hear of a cop busting in the head of a supermarket owner because he charged too much for food? . . . No. Law is the billyclub of the oppressor. He isn't about to use it on himself.[7]

a. What definition(s) of law is Cannon using?
b. Comment on the substance of the statement.

OBJECTIVES OF THE LAW

Law is shaped by social forces. The values, history, ideas, and goals of society are among the forces that determine the nature of a society's legal system. The diverse character of American society leads inevitably to differences of opinion regarding the proper direction for our legal system. However, certain broad goals can be identified.

1. Maintain Order.   The law is instrumental in imposing necessary structure on America's diverse and rapidly changing society. Whether with stop signs, zoning ordinances, marriage licenses, or homicide statutes, the legal system seeks to prevent harm by imposing certain established codes of conduct on the mass of persons. Immediate self-interest is muted in favor of long-term general welfare. The problem then becomes one of how far to go in seeking to preserve a valuable but potentially oppressive commodity. Should the law require all motorcyclists to wear helmets? Or all businesses to close on Sunday? Or all motorists to limit their speed to 55 miles per hour?

2. Resolve Conflict.   Because society cannot and would not wish to successfully regulate all dimensions of human conduct, a system for solving differences is required. An effort is made to substitute enlightened dispute resolution for the barbarism that might otherwise attend inevitable differences of opinion. With the law of contracts, for example, we have developed a sophisticated, generally accepted, and largely successful system for both imposing order and resolving conflict. Nevertheless, enormous problems remain, and new ones always arise.

One test of the vitality and merit of a legal system is its ability to adapt to change. For example, some stars in the entertainment industry have been embroiled in ''palimony'' disputes. If a person functions as a spouse but never lawfully marries, is that person entitled to some form of compensation akin to alimony on dissolution of the living arrangement? In the past, such disputes were resolved among the parties or not at all. Today the legal system is huffing mightily to understand and deal with this notion born of changing societal values.

3. Preserve Dominant Values.   Americans have reached general accord regarding many values and beliefs, and the law has been put to work in preserving those standards. For example, in the Bill of Rights we have set out those fundamental freedoms that must be protected to preserve the character of the nation. Of course, in many instances societal opinion is divided. What happens when no clear consensus emerges about an issue? What if the issue involves a conflict between two values long clutched firmly to the American breast? Freedom of speech is central to a meaningful life, but what if that speech consists of anti-Semitic parades and demonstrations organized by the Ku Klux Klan?

4. Guarantee Freedom.   That Americans are free and wish to remain so is the nation's most revered social value. It is, in a sense, a subset of the third goal in this list; but, because of its preeminence, it properly stands alone. The problem, of course, is that freedom must be limited. Drawing the line often gives rise to severe societal conflict.

In general, you are free to do as you like so long as you do not violate the rights of others; but, what are those rights? Do I have a right to smoke-free air, or do you have a right to smoke wherever you wish? Even if the rights of others are not directly violated, personal freedom is limited. The so-called victimless crimes—vagrancy, gambling, pornography, prostitution—are examples of instances where the law retards freedom in the absence of immediate injury to the rights of others. Should each citizen be free to do as he or she likes so long as harm does not befall others? Or does pornography, for example, inevitably give rise to societal harm?

5. Preserve Justice.   In sum, justice is the goal of the American legal system. In the broadest and best sense, justice is fairness. John Rawls expressed "our intuitive conviction of the primacy of justice":

> Justice is the first virtue of social institutions, as truth is of systems of thought. A theory, however elegant and economical, must be rejected or revised if it is untrue; likewise laws and institutions, no matter how efficient and well arranged, must be reformed or abolished if they are unjust. Each person possesses an inviolability founded on justice that even the welfare of society as a whole cannot override. For this reason justice denies that the loss of freedom for some is made right by a greater good shared by others. It does not allow that the sacrifices imposed on a few are outweighed by the larger sum of advantages enjoyed by many. Therefore in a just society the liberties of equal citizenship are taken as settled; the rights secured by justice are not subject to political bargaining or to the calculus of social interests. The only thing that permits us to acquiesce in an erroneous theory is the lack of a better one; analogously, an injustice is tolerable only when it is necessary to avoid an even greater injustice. Being first virtues of human activities, truth and justice are uncompromising.[8]

Is ours a just legal system? More than any other, that should be the question at the forefront of all legal studies. However, one suspects that justice as a goal sometimes slides a bit to the side in pursuit of more pragmatic goals.

CLASSIFICATIONS OF LAW

Some elementary distinctions will make the role of law clearer.

1. Substantive and Procedural Law.   *Substantive laws* create, define, and regulate legal rights and obligations. Thus, in terms of the topics of this course, the Sherman Act forbids restraints of trade. By judicial interpretation, price-fixing between competitors is a restraint of trade.

Procedural law embraces the systems and methods available to enforce the rights specified in the substantive law. So, procedural law includes the judicial system and the rules by which it operates. Questions of where to hear a case, what evidence to admit, and which decisions can be appealed fall within the procedural domain.

2. Law by Judicial Decision and Law by Enactment.   In general, American rules of law are promulgated by court decisions (*case law*) or via enactments by constitutional assemblies, legislatures, administrative agencies, chief executives, and local government authorities. Enactments include constitutions, statutes, treaties, administrative rules, executive orders, and local ordinances.

a. Case Law (Judicial Decisions).   Our case law has its roots in the early English king's courts where rules of law gradually developed out of a series of individual dispute resolutions. That body of law was imported to America and is known as the *common law*. (This term may be confusing because it is frequently used to designate not just the law imported from England of old but also all judge-made or case law.)

The development of English common law rules and American judicial decisions into a just, ordered package is attributable in large measure to reliance on the doctrine of *stare decisis* (let the decision stand). That is, judges endeavor to follow the precedents established by previous decisions. However, following precedent is not mandatory.

As societal beliefs change, so does the law. For example, a Supreme Court decision approving racially separate but equal education was eventually overruled by a Supreme Court decision mandating integrated schools. However, the principle of stare decisis is generally adhered to because of its beneficial effect. It offers the wisdom of the past and enhances efficiency by eliminating the need for resolving every case as though it were the first of its kind. Stare decisis affords stability and predictability to the law. It promotes justice by, for example, reducing "judge-shopping" and neutralizing judges' personal prejudices.

b. Statutes (Enactments).   As to law by enactment, our primary concern is the category of legislative enactments, that is *statutory law*. Some areas of law, such as torts, continue to be governed primarily by common law rules, but the direction of American law lies largely in the hands of legislators. A significant portion of federal and state legislation has been devoted to clarifying and modifying the common law. Of course, legislators are not free of constraints. Federal legislation cannot conflict with the U.S. Constitution, and state legislation cannot violate either federal law or the constitutions of that state and the nation.

Recognizing the increasing complexity of the law and an increasing general interchange among the states, an effort has been made to achieve uniform laws among the states. Law experts have compiled model statutes that are suggested for adoption by the states. Of special note is the Uniform Commercial Code, which codifies and clarifies the welter of common law rules and statutory enactments that arose over centuries of commercial practice. The Code has been adopted in whole by 49 states and in part by Louisiana.

One of the judiciary's primary tasks is the interpretation of statutory enactments. Much of this text involves an investigation of statutes—the Sherman Act, the Civil Rights Act of 1964, the Federal Trade Commission Act, and so on. Thus, a brief look at statutory interpretation is important.

The first point of examination is the words of the statute. The "plain meaning" rule suggests that jurists' interpretations should be limited to the ordinary and normal meaning commonly attributed to those words. Unfortunately, statutes are rarely drawn with a degree of precision that avoids ambiguity. Indeed, many topics require a deliberate breadth and ambiguity in statutory construction. Therefore, the court will ordinarily also consider other evidence, which typically includes (1) prior relevant judicial decisions, (2) consideration of the issue that provoked the enactment, and (3) examination of the legislative history of the act, such as the debates and committee hearings that preceded its passage.

3. Law and Equity.   Following the Norman conquest of England in 1066, a system of king's courts was established in which the king's representatives settled disputes. Those representatives were empowered to provide remedies of land, money, or personal property. The king's courts became known as *courts of law,* and the remedies were labeled *remedies of law.* However, some litigants sought compensation other than the three provided. They took their plea to the king.

Typically the chancellor, an aide to the king, would hear these petitions and, guided by the standard of fairness, could grant a remedy specifically appropriate to the case. The chancellors' decisions accumulated over time such that a new body of remedies—and with it a new court system, known as *courts of equity*—evolved. Thereafter, a litigant chose her or his court system according to the remedy she or he sought.

Both court systems were adopted in the United States following the American Revolution, but today actions at law and equity are typically heard in the same court. However, two equitable remedies are of special significance today—the injunction and specific performance. An *injunction* is a court order commanding an individual or organization to stop the offending conduct. *Specific performance* is a remedy in which the court compels the defendant to complete the performance he or she had promised. In this situation money is deemed an inadequate remedy. For example, a Picasso painting might not be adequately replaced by a sum of money, however large. Remaining distinctions between actions at law and equity are not important for the purposes of this text.

4. Public Law and Private Law.   *Public law* deals with the relationship between government and the citizens. Constitutional, criminal, and administrative law (relating to such bodies as the Federal Trade Commission) fall in the public law category. *Private law* regulates the legal relationship between individuals. Contracts, agency, and commercial paper are traditional business law topics in the private law category.

5. Civil Law and Criminal Law.   *Civil law* addresses the legal rights and duties arising between individuals. Thus, under the civil law one person can sue another for breach of contract. The *criminal law,* on the other hand, involves wrongs against the general welfare as formulated in specific criminal statutes. Murder and theft are, or course, criminal wrongs because society has forbidden those acts in specific legislative enactments. Hence, wearing one's hat backwards would be a crime if such a statute were enacted and if that statute met constitutional requirements.

Some of our stormiest societal battles have involved conflicts over whether certain classes of conduct are so inimical to the general welfare that they require criminal sanction. The recurrent debate regarding criminal penalties for drug possession illustrates the difficulty in accommodating individual preferences and society's perceived needs. Some actions, such as price-fixing, can carry both civil and criminal penalties.

a. Crimes.   Crimes are of three kinds. In general, *felonies* are more serious crimes, such as murder, rape, and robbery. They are typically punishable by death or by imprisonment in a federal or state penitentiary for more than one year. In general, *misdemeanors* are less serious crimes, such as petty theft, disorderly conduct, and traffic offenses. They are typically punishable by fine or by imprisonment for no more than one year. *Treason* is the special situation in which one levies war against the United States or gives aid and comfort to its enemies.

b. Elements of a Crime.   In a broad sense, crimes consist of two elements: (1) a wrongful act or omission (*actus reus*) and (2) evil intent (*mens rea*). Thus, an individual who pockets a ball-point pen and leaves the store without paying for it may be charged with petty theft. However, the accused may defend by arguing that he or she merely absentmindedly and unintentionally slipped the pen in a pocket after picking it off the shelf to consider its merits. Intent is a state of mind, so the jury or judge must reach a determination from the objective facts as to what the accused's state of mind must have been.

c. Criminal Defenses.   The law recognizes certain defenses to criminal prosecution. Infancy, intoxication, insanity, and self-defense are some of the arguments available to the defendant. Precise standards for each of these and other defenses differ from state to state, depending on the relevant statutory and case law. The federal Constitution and the various state constitutions also afford protections to the accused.

The Fourth Amendment to the federal Constitution prevents unreasonable searches and seizures; the Fifth Amendment requires a grand jury indictment for capital crimes, forbids double jeopardy and self-incrimination, and mandates due process of law; the Sixth Amendment guarantees a speedy and public trial by jury, the right to confront and obtain witnesses, and the right to a competent lawyer; and the Eighth Amendment prohibits excessive bail or fines and cruel and unusual punishment.

d. Criminal Procedure.   In general, criminal law procedure is structured as follows: For more complex, arguably more serious, crimes the process begins with the prosecuting officials bringing their charges before a grand jury or magistrate to determine whether the charges have sufficient merit to justify a trial. If so, an *indictment* or *information* is issued, charging the accused with specific crimes. (Grand juries issue indictments; magistrates issue informations.) In those instances where action by a grand jury or magistrate is not required, cases are initiated by the issuance of a warrant by a judge, based on a showing of probable cause that the individual has committed or will commit a crime. Where necessity demands, arrests may be made without a warrant, but the legality of the arrest will be tested by probable cause standards.

After indictment or arrest, the individual is brought before the court for arraignment, where the charges are read and a plea is entered. If the individual pleads not guilty, he or she will go to trial, where guilt must be established *beyond a reasonable doubt*. (In a civil trial, the plaintiff must meet the lesser standard of *a preponderance of the evidence*.) In a criminal trial, the burden of proof is on the State. The defendant is, of course, assumed innocent. He or she is entitled to a jury trial but may choose to have the case decided by the judge alone. If found guilty the defendant can, among other possibilities, seek a new trial or appeal errors in the prosecution. If found innocent, the defendant may, if necessary, invoke the doctrine of *double jeopardy,* under which a person cannot be prosecuted twice in the same tribunal for the same criminal offense.

Questions

1. Several states and hundreds of communities have enacted legislation designed to ban the display and sale of drug paraphernalia (pipes, spoons, bongs, scales, roach clips, and the like).

     a. Raise the competing arguments regarding such enactments.

     b. Should we rely on the free market to "regulate" commercial enterprise of this nature? That is, should we permit the government to destroy the operations of small businesses designed to meet a need expressed by the market and heretofore considered free of any illegality? Explain.

2. *a.* In Chicago, 48-year-old Bob Koester was arrested for cursing at a transit conductor. "Well, that motherblanker in the last train left a bunch of us stranded!"[9] Koester was convicted and sentenced to 30 days' supervision. Should vulgar language in public be subject to legal regulation? Explain.

     b. Do you believe our legal system places too much emphasis on the establishment and maintenance of order? Explain.

3. Should we remove criminal penalties from the so-called victimless crimes of vagrancy, prostitution, pornography, and gambling? Should we regulate those practices in any way? Explain.

4. What steps would you advocate to reduce crime in America?

Part Three—A Brief Look at the Judicial Process

Excerpts from court cases will periodically be reprinted in the remainder of the text to illustrate particular points being discussed. For example, the first case in the text, *Hresil v. Sears, Roebuck & Co.,* which follows, is intended to illustrate a number of the classification systems previously discussed. A bit of practical guidance at this point may help you better understand these case materials.

The study of law is founded in significant part on the analysis of judicial opinions. Except for the federal level and a few states, trial court decisions are filed locally for public inspection rather than published. Appellate opinions, on the other hand, are generally published in volumes called *reports.* State court opinions are found in the reports of that state, as well as in a regional reporter published by West Publishing that divides the United States into units, such as Southeastern (S.E.) and Pacific (P.). Federal court decisions are found in several reporters, including the *Federal Reporter* (F., F.2d) for decisions of the various circuit courts and the *United States Supreme Court Reports* (U.S.) for decisions of the Supreme Court.

Within each reporter the cases are arranged in a workable fashion and are *cited* by case name, volume, reporter name, and page number. For example, regarding the *Hresil* case, 403 N.E.2d 678 (Ill. App. Ct. 1980) means the opinion will be found in volume 403 of the *Northeastern Reporter,* second series, beginning on page 678. If the identity of the deciding court is not readily apparent from the name of the reporter, the court will be identified in parentheses following the page number. The parenthetical material also includes the year the decision was reached by the court. Thus, the *Hresil* case was decided by the Illinois Appellate Court in 1980.

Most law students find the preparation of *case briefs* (outlines or digests) to be helpful in mastering the complexities of the law. Put simply, briefing is a process of organizing the information presented so that a number of fundamental questions can be answered. A brief should evolve into the form that best suits the individual student's needs. The following approach may be a useful starting point.

1. **Who are the parties?** Identify the plaintiff(s) and the defendant(s).
2. **What is the procedural setting of the case?** What court is hearing the case now? Who brought the appeal? What was the outcome in the lower court(s)?
3. **What are the material facts?** Summarize only those facts critical to the outcome of the case.
4. **What is the legal issue on which the case turns?** This is the central question the court seeks to answer.
5. **What is the holding of the court?** This is the answer the court gives to the central legal issue.
6. **What reasoning did the court use to reach its holding?** Explain the logic, step by step, that supports the court's holding.

LUDMILA HRESIL, PLAINTIFF–APPELLANT, V. SEARS, ROEBUCK & COMPANY, DEFENDANT–APPELLEE
403 N.E.2d 678 (Ill. App. Ct. 1980)

Presiding Justice McGillicuddy

The plaintiff, Ludmila Hresil, brought this action to recover damages for the injuries she suffered when she slipped on a foreign substance in a Sears, Roebuck & Company store. At the conclusion of the plaintiff's evidence on October 6, 1977, the Circuit Court of Cook County directed a verdict in favor of the defendant. The plaintiff appeals this order and the order of January 18, 1978, which denied her motion for a new trial.

On September 14, 1972, the plaintiff and her niece, Geraldine Sandrik, walked to the Sears outlet store located near Cicero and Archer Avenue in Chicago. The time of their visit was approximately 5:30 P.M. and there were few shoppers in the store.

The plaintiff testified that she and her niece first visited the children's department, where they remained approximately half an hour during which her niece purchased some merchandise. As they prepared to leave the department, the niece stopped to make an additional purchase. At this time the plaintiff was observing the women's department where she saw no shoppers for over 10 minutes.

After the niece completed her purchase, the two women walked through the women's department. The plaintiff was pushing a shopping cart and suddenly lost her balance. She began to fall backward and struggled to avoid a fall. Although she managed to keep her balance, her right leg struck the shopping cart and began to swell.

While her niece went for assistance, the plaintiff observed the floor areas upon which she slipped. She saw a ''gob'' on the floor with her heel mark clearly imprinted in it. An employee who came with her niece to assist the plaintiff commented that ''it looked like someone spit on the floor, like it was phlegm.''

The plaintiff went to a hospital emergency room that evening and to her doctor the following day. She testified concerning her treatment and two subsequent operations on her leg. At the time of the trial, the plaintiff still had difficulty walking.

* * * * *

Mrs. Sandrik agreed with her aunt that there were few customers in the store at the time of her accident. She described the outlet as a store in which the customer waits on herself and pays for purchases on the way out. Mrs. Sandrik added that a customer rarely is able to locate a salesperson in the store.

* * * * *

Although a store owner is not the insurer of his customer's safety, he does owe the customer the duty of exercising ordinary care in maintaining the premises in a reasonably safe condition. (*Olinger* v. *Great Atlantic & Pacific Tea Co.* (1961), 21 Ill.2d 469, 173 N.E.2d 443 . . .) If the customer is injured by an accident involving a foreign substance on the premises and there is no evidence explaining the origin of the foreign substance, liability may be imposed on the store owner if the substance was present for a sufficient period of time so that the owner or operator of the premises should have discovered its presence. *Olinger*. . . .

The plaintiff argues that the trial court erred in directing a verdict in favor of the defendant. She states that where evidence exists which tends to show that the defendant should have known of the presence of the foreign substance, the issue of negligence must be submitted to the jury. . . . In the instant case the plaintiff refers to her testimony that for 10 minutes prior to her fall no other customer was present in the women's department. From this evidence she infers that the foreign substance was present in the store at least 10 minutes prior to her fall. She asserts that it is a question of fact for the jury whether 10 minutes is sufficient time to give the defendant constructive notice of the presence of the foreign substance.

A directed verdict should be entered only in those cases in which all the evidence, when viewed most favorably to the opponent, so overwhelmingly favors the movant that no contrary verdict based on that evidence could ever stand. (*Pedrick* v. *Peoria & Eastern R.R. Co.* (1967), 37 Ill.2d 494, 229 N.E.2d 504.) Viewing the evidence most favorably to the plaintiff, we can assume that the foreign substance was present on the floor of the store for at least 10 minutes prior to the plaintiff's fall. However, we conclude, as a matter of law, that 10 minutes was an insufficient period of time to give constructive notice to the operator of this self-service store of the presence of the foreign substance. The accident occurred at a time when few shoppers were present in the store, and the evidence reveals that the salespersons were located at the store exit. To charge the store with constructive notice of the presence of the substance would place upon the store the unfair requirement of the constant patrolling of its aisles. Accordingly, we find that no contrary verdict based on this evidence could ever stand. *Pedrick.*

* * * * *

For the foregoing reasons, the judgment of the Circuit Court of Cook County is hereby affirmed.

    Affirmed.
    McNamara and Simon, JJ. concur.

Questions

1. Brief the *Hresil* case. Be sure your brief answers each of the following questions.
    a. Who are the parties?
    b. What is the procedural setting of the case?
    c. What are the material facts?
    d. What is the legal issue on which the case turns?
    e. What is the holding of the court?
    f. What reasoning did the court use to reach its holding?
2. Do you believe the *Hresil* case represents a just outcome? Explain.
3. Look again at the *Hresil* case. Is the issue facing the appellate court one of substance or of procedure? Is it an issue of public law or private law? Is the court's reasoning based on case law or on statutory interpretation? Is this a criminal case or a civil case? Explain.

Part Four—A Closer Look at the Judicial Process

One of the functions performed by the law, as mentioned above, is the resolution of conflicts. Most disputes are, in fact, settled without resort to litigation; but when agreement cannot be reached, the citizenry can turn to the courts—a highly technical and sophisticated dispute resolution mechanism.

DUE PROCESS OF LAW

Guiding and, in a sense, governing our very complex judicial procedure is the constitutional principle of *due process of law.* The Fifth and Fourteenth Amendments to the federal Constitution prohibit the federal and state governments, respectively, from depriving individuals of life, liberty, and property without due process of law. Hence, it follows that the judicial process, to meet constitutional standards, must be conducted in accordance with fundamental fairness. The process must not be unreasonable, arbitrary, or capricious. The standard is necessarily broad and not readily clarified by definition, but it is our indispensable measure of judicial equity.

STATE COURT SYSTEMS

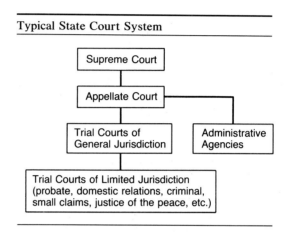

Typical State Court System

Supreme Court

Appellate Court

Trial Courts of General Jurisdiction

Administrative Agencies

Trial Courts of Limited Jurisdiction (probate, domestic relations, criminal, small claims, justice of the peace, etc.)

While state court systems vary substantially, a general pattern can be summarized. At the heart of the court pyramid in most states is a *trial court of general jurisdiction,* commonly labeled a *district court* or a *superior court.* It is here that most trials—both civil and criminal—arising out of state law would be heard, but certain classes of cases are reserved to courts of limited subject matter jurisdiction or to various state administrative agencies (such as the state public utilities commission and the workers' compensation board). Family, small claims, juvenile, and traffic courts are examples of trial courts with limited jurisdiction. At the top of the judicial pyramid in all states is a court of appeals, ordinarily labeled the *supreme court.* Some states also provide for an intermediate court of appeals located in the hierarchy between the trial courts and the highest appeals court.

FEDERAL COURT SYSTEM

District Courts

The district courts provide the foundation of the federal judicial system. The Constitution provides for a Supreme Court and such inferior courts as Congress shall authorize. Pursuant to that authority, Congress has

Federal Court System

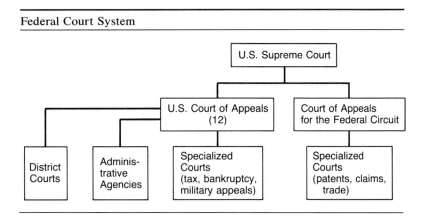

established at least one district court for each state and territory. These are trial courts where witnesses are heard and questions of law and fact are resolved. More populous areas with heavier case loads have additional district courts. As circumstances demand, Congress adds courts at the district level. Most federal cases begin in the district courts or in a federal administrative agency (such as the Interstate Commerce Commission or the Federal Communications Commission). Congress has also provided for several courts of limited jurisdiction, including a tax court, a U.S. Claims Court, a Court of Military Appeals, and a bankruptcy court.

Court of Appeals

Congress has divided the United States geographically into 11 judicial circuits and the District of Columbia and has established a court of appeals for each. Those courts hear appeals from the district courts within their circuit and review decisions and enforce orders of the various federal administrative agencies.

In 1982 Congress created the U.S. Court of Appeals for the Federal Circuit. That court hears all patent appeals and all appeals from the U.S. Claims Court (monetary claims against the United States). Certain district court cases may be appealed directly to the U.S. Supreme Court.

Supreme Court

The Supreme Court consists of nine justices appointed for life by the president and confirmed by the Senate. In limited instances, the Supreme Court serves as an original or trial court, but by far the bulk of its cases rests in appeals and petitions.

Cases reach the Supreme Court under two procedures: by appeal and by petition. Congress has provided that certain classes of cases, if appealed, must be reviewed by the Supreme Court. One example is a decision of a federal court of appeals holding a state statute invalid because it violates the U.S. Constitution or a federal statute. The Court decides whether these appeals are granted a full hearing or are simply affirmed or dismissed after preliminary scrutiny, without filing written briefs or hearing oral arguments. Upon dismissal, the lower court order remains in effect.

Parties whose cases do not fall into one of the appeals categories can petition the Supreme Court to hear their cases by issuing *writs of certiorari* commanding the lower courts to forward the trial records to the Supreme Court. Decisions regarding those petitions are entirely discretionary with the Court. Typically it will hear those cases that will assist in resolving conflicting courts of appeal decisions, as well as those that raise questions of special significance about the Constitution or the national welfare. The Court annually receives more than 5,000 cases but agrees to a full hearing for only about 150 to 200 of those.

JURISDICTION

A plaintiff may not simply take his or her case to any court of his or her preference. The plaintiff must go to a court with *jurisdiction;* that is, with the necessary power and authority to hear the dispute. The court must have jurisdiction over both the subject matter and the persons (or, in some instances, the property) involved in the case. Subject matter jurisdiction imposes bounds on the classes of cases a court may hear. The legislation or constitution creating the court will normally specify that court's jurisdictional authority. For example, state courts of general jurisdiction may hear most types of cases, but a criminal court or probate court is limited as to the subject matter it may hear.

The outer bounds of federal jurisdiction are specified in the Constitution, while Congress has further particularized that issue by statute. Essentially, the federal district courts may hear two types of cases: (1) those involving a federal question and (2) those involving diversity of citizenship and more than $10,000.

Federal question jurisdiction exists in any suit where the plaintiff's claim is based on the U.S. Constitution, a U.S. treaty, or a federal statute. Thus, litigants can bring to the federal courts cases involving, for example, the federal antitrust statutes, federal criminal laws, constitutional issues like freedom of the press, and federal tax questions. Federal question jurisdiction does not require an amount in controversy exceeding $10,000. Further, federal and state courts have *concurrent jurisdiction* for some federal questions. Thus, some federal question cases are decided in state courts applying federal law. Congress has accorded the federal courts exclusive jurisdiction over certain subjects, including federal criminal laws, bankruptcy, and copyrights. Under *diversity jurisdiction,* federal district courts may hear cases involving more than $10,000 where the plaintiff(s) and the defendant(s) are citizens of different states. (Corporations are treated as citizens both of their state of incorporation and the state in which their principal place of business is located.) Diversity cases may also be heard in state courts, but plaintiffs frequently prefer to bring their actions in federal courts. It is generally believed that the quality of the federal judiciary is superior to that of the states and that the federal courts are less likely to be influenced by local bias. Federal court action may also have procedural advantages, such as greater capacity to secure witnesses' testimony.

Judicial authority over the person is known as *in personam jurisdiction.* In general, a state court's powers are limited to the bounds of the state. While the matter is fraught with complexities, it is fair to say that state court jurisdiction can be established in three ways: (1) When the defendant is a resident of the state, a summons may be served at that residence. (2) When the defendant is not a resident, a summons may be personally served should he or she be physically present in the state. (3) All states have legislated "long-arm" statutes that allow a court to secure jurisdiction against an out-of-state party where that defendant has committed a tort in the state or where the defendant is conducting business in the state. Hence, in an auto accident in Iowa involving both an Iowa resident and an Illinois resident, the Iowan may sue in Iowa and achieve service of process over the Illinois defendant as a consequence of the jurisdictional authority afforded by the long-arm statute.

A state court may also acquire jurisdiction via an *in rem action.* In that instance the defendant may be a nonresident, but his or her property, which must be the subject of the suit, must be located within the state.

The following case illustrates some of the jurisdictional issues just discussed.

JOHN PAVOLINI V. BARD–AIR CORP.
645 F.2d 144 (2d Cir. 1981)

Chief Judge Feinberg

---

[1] John Pavolini, a licensed air transport pilot, appeals from an order of the United States District Court for the Northern District of New York, which dismissed his complaint against defendants Bard-Air Corp. and the Barden Robeson Corporation (collectively referred to as "Bard-Air"). Bard-Air is a small charter air carrier certified by the Federal Aviation Administration ("FAA") to transport persons and property for hire over certain designated

air routes. Plaintiff Pavolini, a former employee of Bard-Air, sought some $43 million in compensatory and punitive damages from defendants. The crux of the complaint was that Pavolini had been unlawfully discharged for reporting to the FAA Bard-Air's violations of that agency's air safety regulations promulgated under the Federal Aviation Act of 1958. The main issue on appeal is whether the district court correctly concluded that there is no [proper basis for federal jurisdiction.] We agree with the conclusion of the district court, and we affirm the judgment dismissing the complaint.

I

According to the record before us, the relevant facts are as follows: . . . During June 1979, Pavolini discovered that the aircraft he and four other Bard-Air pilots were assigned to fly were unsafe and did not comply with FAA safety regulations. That same month, Pavolini reported the violations to James Knight, who was Bard-Air's chief pilot and also its Director of Operations and Vice-President. Knight took no action to correct the safety violations and permitted them to continue.

Following Knight's orders, Pavolini piloted air taxi flights on August 14, 20 and 23, 1979, which caused him to exceed flight and/or duty time limitations set by the FAA. Knight also ordered Pavolini to falsify flight records to reflect that the August 14 flight was within the FAA duty time limitations. Pavolini refused to falsify the record and reported this violation to the FAA shortly thereafter. Pavolini requested that the FAA make note of the incident but take no action because he was afraid of losing his job. In late August 1979, a licensed aircraft mechanic informed Pavolini that one of Bard-Air's planes was unsafe and in violation of FAA safety regulations. On the following day, Pavolini reported to the FAA that Bard-Air was flying the unsafe aircraft despite notice of the safety violations. On that same day, the FAA grounded the plane after inspection disclosed numerous safety violations. On September 4, 1979, Knight told Pavolini that what he had done ''was the wrong way to go about it,'' and summarily discharged him.

The FAA's safety investigation of Bard-Air . . . noted that Pavolini was fired for bringing matters to the attention of the FAA and was experiencing considerable difficulty in obtaining employment as a pilot because of his action.

Pavolini sought to recover damages for loss of wages, mental distress and anguish, as well as punitive damages, resulting from his discharge, alleging that it violated the Federal Aviation Act of 1958, the Occupational Safety and Health Act of 1970, the First and Fourteenth Amendments to the United States Constitution, and state law. Bard-Air moved to dismiss the complaint. . . . The district court found that there is no implied cause of action under the Federal Aviation Act for wrongful discharge, that the defendant was not acting as an arm of the government and that the court did not have pendent jurisdiction over any state claim. This appeal followed.

II

[2] In this court, Pavolini first argues that an implied cause of action exists under the Federal Aviation Act in favor of a pilot discharged for reporting violations of safety provisions to the FAA. In pressing this claim, Pavolini offers a detailed analysis of the famous four factors set forth in *Cort* v. *Ash*. However, lengthy discussion of the *Cort* guidelines is not required here, because our first inquiry must be whether the injury complained of

resulted from "disregard of the command of the statute." There must be a duty, the violation of which has caused injury, before we reach the question whether a private remedy exists to redress that injury. Pavolini's claimed injuries were allegedly caused by his discharge, but the Act does not require an air carrier to continue to employ an employee for any reason, nor does the Act prohibit a carrier from discharging an employee for reporting safety violations to the FAA.

It is true that the statute commands the Administrator of the FAA "to promote safety of flight of civil aircraft in air commerce by prescribing" and enforcing standards, rules and regulations, including those governing "inspection, servicing and overhaul of aircraft" and the "maximum hours of periods of service of airmen" and "in such manner as will best tend to reduce or eliminate the possibility of, or recurrence of, accidents in air transportation. . . ." Similarly, an air carrier is required, under pain of civil and criminal penalties, to comply with such regulations and "to perform . . . services with the highest possible degree of safety in the public interest. . . ." And we can assume on this record that Bard-Air has violated the Act in several respects. But nevertheless, this is an action seeking redress for loss of employment and Pavolini's injury does not flow, in a legal sense, from Bard-Air's failure to obey any statutory requirement or from a violation of any statutory prohibition. Under the circumstances, it is not necessary to consider further the issue of implying a right of action.

[3] Pavolini also argues that his termination for reporting the violations deprived him of his constitutional right to freedom of speech under the First and the Fourteenth Amendments. However, before Pavolini can recover for alleged violations of the First and the Fourteenth Amendments, he must establish that his discharge by Bard-Air was "state action." Plaintiff relies principally on extensive governmental regulation of the air transport industry to support his claim that Bard-Air was performing a public function. But regulation, without more, is insufficient to treat the discharge by Bard-Air as action by the state; further, we reject the notion that because the FAA may have in some indirect way approved of plaintiff's reporting a safety violation, the discharge was thereby transformed from private conduct to state action. In the absence of state action, plaintiff's constitutional claims fail.

[4] In light of the above, we reluctantly conclude that there is no proper basis for federal jurisdiction here.[7] Since federal courts are courts of limited jurisdiction, Pavolini's remedy, if any, lies in the state courts, which have traditionally exercised jurisdiction over controversies between employers and employees and where Pavolini still has an action pending. We believe that it is unfortunate that a federal court cannot provide recourse to an employee fired for reporting violations of federal safety regulations. We are well aware that Pavolini was in a difficult situation, facing a loss of his job on the one hand and a potential loss of lives on the other; he should be commended for placing public safety over private concerns. We certainly have no desire to encourage retaliation by employers against their employees who, having failed to obtain voluntary compliance, turn to the appropriate federal agency charged with insuring safety in an effort to prevent injury or death. But we are mindful that we do not sit as a legislature. In view of what has occurred here, Congress may well wish to consider protecting in an appropriate way those who help prevent the loss of life from improper operation or maintenance of aircraft.

The judgment of the district court is affirmed.

---

[7]There is no claim of diversity of citizenship.

Questions

1. The decision in *Pavolini* is the decision of what court? Is this a federal or a state court?
2. The *Pavolini* court asserts that it has no jurisdiction to hear the case. What *kind* of jurisdiction is the court lacking? Explain.
3. Should the defendants be liable to Pavolini? Does this decision mean Pavolini has no further recourse against the defendants? Explain.
4. Why are the states prevented from reaching throughout America to assert jurisdictional authority regardless of "minimal contacts"?
5. The Robinsons filed a product liability suit in an Oklahoma state court to recover for injuries sustained in an automobile accident in Oklahoma. The auto had been purchased in New York from the defendant, World-Wide Volkswagen Corp. Oklahoma's long-arm statute was used in an attempt to secure jurisdiction over the defendant. World-Wide conducted no business in Oklahoma. Nor did it solicit business there.
   a. Build an argument to support the claim of jurisdiction for the Oklahoma court.
   b. Decide. See *World-Wide Volkswagen Corp.* v. *Woodson,* 100 S.Ct. 559 (1980).

STANDING TO SUE

Resorting to the courts is frequently an undesirable method of problem solving. Therefore, all who wish to bring a claim before a court may not be permitted to do so. To receive the court's attention, the litigant must demonstrate that she or he has *standing to sue.* That is, the person must show that her or his interest in the outcome of the controversy is sufficiently direct and substantial to justify the court's consideration. The litigant must show that she or he personally is suffering, or will be suffering, injury. Mere interest in the problem at hand is insufficient to grant standing to sue. Thus, in 1972 the U.S. Supreme Court held that the Sierra Club did not have standing to challenge federal approval of a private skiing development in the Mineral King Valley of the Sequoia National Forest. The membership had a general interest in the issue, but they failed to show a direct, personal stake.[10]

Questions

1. An urban renewal project threatened to result in the destruction of 14 historic buildings in Lexington, Kentucky. A nonprofit corporation, designed to preserve such buildings, filed suit to stop the demolition. The plaintiffs did not own any of the buildings. The defendant government agency argued that the plaintiffs did not have standing to sue. Decide. See *South Hill Neighborhood Association* v. *Romney,* 421 F.2d 454 (1969).
2. Look again at the *Hresil* case. What gave the plaintiff standing to sue?

THE CIVIL TRIAL PROCESS

Civil procedure varies by jurisdiction. The following generalization merely typifies the process.

Pleadings

Pleadings are the documents by which each party sets his or her initial case before the court. A civil action begins when the plaintiff files his or her first pleading, which is labeled a *complaint*. The complaint specifies (1) the parties to the suit, (2) evidence as to the court's jurisdiction in the case, (3) a statement of the facts, and (4) a prayer for relief (a remedy).

The complaint is filed with the clerk of court and a *summons* is issued, directing the defendant to appear in court to answer the claims alleged against him or her. A sheriff or some other official attempts to personally deliver the summons to the defendant. If personal delivery cannot be achieved, the summons may be left with a responsible party at the defendant's residence. Failing that, other modes of delivery are permissible, including a mailing. Publication of a notice in a newspaper will, in some instances, constitute good service of process. Ordinarily a copy of the complaint accompanies the summons so the defendant is apprised of the nature of the claim.

The defendant has several options. He or she may do nothing, but failure to respond may result in a default judgment in favor of the plaintiff. The defendant may choose to respond by filing a *demurrer* or a *motion to dismiss,* the essence of which is to argue that even if the plaintiff's recitation of the facts is accurate, he or she has not stated a claim on which relief can be granted. For example, a student may be offended by a teacher's "bizarre" manner of dress; but, barring unusual circumstances, the student could not, as a matter of law, successfully challenge the teacher's costume.

Alternatively, the defendant may file with the court his or her initial pleading, called an *answer,* wherein the defendant enters a denial by setting out his or her version of the facts and law, or in which the defendant simply concedes the validity of the plaintiff's position. The answer may also contain an *affirmative defense,* which is an allegation of facts that would bar the plaintiff's claim. For example, the defendant might assert the statute of limitations or the statute of frauds. The defendant's answer might include a counterclaim or cross-claim. A *counterclaim* is the defendant's assertion of a claim of action against the plaintiff. A *cross-claim* is the defendant's assertion of a claim of action against a codefendant. In some states these would be labeled *cross-complaints*. In the event of a counterclaim or the assertion of new facts in the answer, the plaintiff will respond with a *reply.* The complaint, answer, reply, and their components are the pleadings that serve to give notice, to clarify the issues, and to limit the dimensions of the litigation.

Motions

As necessary during and after the filing of the pleadings, either party may file motions with the court. For example, a party may move to clarify a pleading or to strike a portion deemed unnecessary. Of special importance is a motion for a judgment on the pleadings or a motion for summary judgment. In a *motion for a judgment on the pleadings,* either party simply asks the judge to reach a decision based on the information in the pleadings. However, the judge will do so only if the defendant's answer constitutes an admission of the accuracy of the plaintiff's claim, or if the plaintiff's claim clearly has no foundation in law.

In a *motion for a summary judgment,* the party filing the motion is claiming that no facts are in dispute. Therefore, the judge may make a ruling about the law without taking the case to trial. In a summary judgment hearing, the court can look beyond the pleadings to hear evidence from affidavits, depositions, and so on. These motions serve to avoid the time and expense of trial. The following case is an example of the use of a summary judgment motion.

WOODRUFF V. GEORGIA STATE UNIVERSITY ET AL.
304 S.E.2d 697 (Ga 1983)

Justice Weltner

Woodruff brought this action against the Board of Regents, Georgia State University and certain Georgia State University professors alleging state and federal constitutional violations, tort, and breach of contract claims. The trial court granted summary judgment and Woodruff appeals.

Woodruff was admitted to a master's degree program in the music department of Georgia State University in 1972. In the fall of 1973, she received an "F" on the basis of plagiarism, and appealed that grade to an appeals committee within the university. The committee changed the grade to an "incomplete." She alleges that thereafter her professors were "hostile and sarcastic" to her, refusing to help her with course work and thesis preparation, changing course requirements prior to graduation, placing damaging information about her in an open file, and giving her undeservedly low grades in an attempt to block her graduation.

In 1979, after seven years in a program which normally takes two or three years to complete, Woodruff was awarded the degree of Master of Arts in Music. She then applied for admittance into a doctoral program at the University of Georgia in Athens, which required recommendations from former professors. Woodruff's former professors either refused or ignored her request for recommendations. In their depositions, several professors testified that Woodruff was an "argumentative and troublesome" student who was erratic in her studies and not academically qualified to proceed to a doctoral program. They offered academic reasons for withholding their recommendations.

Woodruff filed suit in January, 1982, alleging libel and slander, intentional infliction of mental distress, conspiracy in withholding recommendations, negligent supervision of her graduate studies, breach of contract, and constitutional violations. . . .

* * * * *

. . . [T]he central issue is whether or not a dispute concerning academic decisions of a public educational institution is a justiciable controversy.

In the general realm of educational institutions, we have reviewed standards of dismissals and student discipline. We have examined the denial of student eligibility to participate in sports, and we have refused to permit the judiciary to referee high school football games. The Court of Appeals has upheld the authority of a local board of education to impose proficiency requirements as a prerequisite to graduation from high school.

We have not thus far, however, entertained an individual student's complaint seeking money damages for alleged impropriety in academic assessment of her work.

* * * * *

We now decline to review a teacher's academic assessment of a student's work.

This is clearly consistent with the authorities we have mentioned. It is restraint which stems from confidence that school authorities are able to discharge their academic duties in fairness and with competence. It is born alike of the necessity for shielding the courts from an incalculable new potential for lawsuits, testing every Latin grade and every selection for the Safety Patrol.

It protects every teacher from the cost and agony of litigation initiated by pupils and their parents who would rely upon the legal process rather than the learning process.

It protects every school system—all of them laboring under pressures of financing, personnel problems and student discipline, academic performance, taxpayer revolt and patron unrest, and a rising tide of recalls—from an added and unbearable burden of continuous legal turmoil.

Judgment affirmed.

Questions

1. *Woodruff* is the decision of what court?
2. Who were the defendants in *Woodruff* and why did they move for a summary judgment? Was their motion granted by the trial court?
3. What was the legal issue facing the appellate court in *Woodruff?* Do you agree with its decision? Explain.

Discovery

Justice is the goal of the legal system. Information is central to reaching a just result. *Discovery* is the primary information-gathering stage in the trial process. Discovery (1) preserves the testimony of witnesses who may not be available for trial, (2) reduces the likelihood of perjury, (3) aids in defining and narrowing the facts and issues, (4) promotes pretrial settlements, (5) increases the likelihood of concluding the case with a summary judgment, and (6) helps prevent surprises at the trial.

In general, five discovery techniques are provided.

1. **Depositions.** A party or a witness may be required to appear before a court officer to give recorded, sworn testimony in response to questions raised by the attorneys for both sides of the controversy. Testimony is much like that at trial, except it is not limited by the technical rules of evidence. *Depositions* help in trial preparation, in impeaching a witness whose trial testimony differs from her or his deposition, and in securing testimony from witnesses not available at trial due to death or absence from the court's jurisdiction.
2. **Interrogatories.** Written questions calling for written answers signed under oath may be required. Unlike depositions, *interrogatories* may only be directed to parties, and they can call for information outside the party's personal knowledge, requiring the party to peruse her or his records.
3. **Discovery of documents and property.** Either party may request access to documents, as well as real and personal property, for the purpose of inspection relevant to the trial. Where appropriate, copies and photographs may be secured. If cooperation is not forthcoming, a court order may be requested.
4. **Physical and mental examinations.** When the physical and/or mental state of a party is at issue, the court may be asked to enter an order calling for an examination. Good cause must be shown, and the court must be satisfied that the need for information outweighs the party's constitutional right to privacy.
5. **Admissions.** Either party may make written request of the other, seeking an *admission* as to the truth of a specified issue of fact or law. If the receiving party agrees to or fails to deny the truth of the admission, that issue of fact or law is conclusively established for trial purposes. The use of such admissions resolves issues before they reach court, thus enhancing order and reducing trial time. For example, in a suit alleging a defective transmission in a recently purchased automobile, the auto dealer might be asked to agree that the auto was sold under a warranty and that the warranty included the transmission.

Pretrial Conference

Either party may request, and many courts require, a pretrial meeting involving the attorneys, the judge, and occasionally the parties. Usually following discovery, the conference is designed to plan the course of the trial in the interests of efficiency and justice. The participants seek to define and narrow the issues through informal discussion. The parties also attempt to settle the dispute in advance of trial. If no settlement is reached, a trial date is set.

The Judge and Jury

The federal Constitution and most state constitutions provide for the right to a jury trial in a civil case (excepting equity actions). Some states place dollar minimums on that guarantee. At the federal level and in most states, unless one of the parties requests a jury, the judge alone will hear the case and decide all questions of law and fact. If the case is tried before a jury, that body will resolve questions of fact.

Jurors are selected from a jury pool composed of a cross section of the community. A panel is drawn from that pool. The individuals in that panel are questioned by the judge, by the attorneys, or by both to determine if any individual is prejudiced about the case such that he or she could not reach an objective decision on the merits. The questioning process is called *voir dire*.

From an attorney's point of view, jury selection is often not so much a matter of finding jurors without bias as it is a matter of identifying those jurors who are most likely to reach a decision favorable to one's client. To that end, elaborate mechanisms and strategies have been employed— particularly in criminal trials—to identify desirable jurors. For example, sophisticated, computer-assisted surveys of the trial community have been conducted to develop objective evidence by which to identify jurors who would not admit to racial prejudice but whose "profile" suggests the likelihood of such prejudice. A few attorneys have taken the rather exotic tactic of employing body language experts to watch potential jurors during *voir dire* for those mannerisms said to reveal their inner views.

After questioning, the attorneys may *challenge for cause,* arguing to the judge that the individual cannot exercise the necessary objectivity of judgment. Attorneys are also afforded a limited number of *peremptory challenges,* by which the attorney can have a potential juror dismissed without the judge's concurrence and without offering a reason.

Jury selection and the jury system are the subject of considerable debate in the legal community. Are juries necessary to a just system? How small can a jury be and still fulfill its duty? Is the jury process too slow and expensive? Should very long and complex cases, such as those in the antitrust area, be heard only by judges?

The article that follows looks at the jury system from a juror's point of view.

SENTENCED TO THE JURY ROOM

Roger Ricklefs

"OK, everyone," the court officer barked, "line up against the wall."

One might assume we were the criminals. But in fact, we were only the prospective jurors being marched to yet another courtroom in Manhattan. Before a jury could be chosen from our ranks, the defendant pleaded guilty to some less serious form of battering her infant children. And we, the jurors, filed back into Central Casting, to await another audition for productive labor.

For millions of American adults, jury duty is life's most prolonged contact with a government agency. Just as many jurors have come to suspect, this duty really is becoming more of a bureaucratic nightmare. Those who actually serve on juries often walk away with renewed confidence in the system and say their experience was remarkably rewarding. But with the rising use of plea bargaining and peremptory challenges of prospective jurors, fewer and fewer people get chosen. More and more end up as experts on crossword puzzles.

* * * * *

Jurors as Props

On a typical day in New York's borough of Manhattan, about 2,000 people are serving state and local jury duty, but fewer than 10 percent of them ever get on a jury, says Norman Good-

man, the county commissioner of jurors. With the growth in plea bargaining, Los Angeles County officials say fewer than 6 percent of all their proceedings originally designated as jury cases actually go to trial. The prospective juror becomes a prop to nudge the lawyers to a plea bargain.

For a felony trial, Los Angeles courts must now send 40 prospective jurors, up from 25 required 15 years ago, says Ray Arce, a court official. Adds Judge [Benjamin] Aranda [chair of the American Bar Association jury management committee]: "Lawyers are much more sophisticated in using the jury selection process" (to challenge prospective jurors who might not serve their clients' interests).

All this means coast-to-coast frustration. "I just can't go by the courthouse without feeling depression and frustration," says a Los Angeles man. He recently served 10 working days on jury duty without being chosen for a single case. Caught in a frantic period at work, he tried to run his office by using a lap-top computer and a pay telephone.

My own recent court experience in New York started with high hopes. After the dozens of new jurors assembled in the Criminal Court central jury room, a plump, middle-aged jury clerk named Ethel, who liked to run a tight ship, explained the ropes. (The jurors' Coke machine sometimes works and sometimes doesn't, she warned. But in any event, it isn't the jury clerks' responsibility.)

Before you could say *habeas corpus,* the gruff but efficient Ethel had pulled my name out of the hat. I was herded off to court in a group of prospective jurors. But fantasies of usefulness ended quickly as we all stood for a solid hour outside the courtroom. Whatever the defendant's alleged sins were, he pleaded guilty to a lesser version of them as we stood and waited. Apparently, nothing concentrates a lawyer's mind as fast as two dozen prospective jurors breathing outside the courtroom door.

Back to Ethel.

But soon my number came up again, and I was trying out for the child abuse case. As the case involved violence, the judge asked if any of us, our relatives, or close friends had suffered a violent crime. About half the panel members raised their hands. One woman broke into tears, explaining that her mother had been murdered. The judge dismissed her and sent her back to the jury room. Days later, she was still being sent out on panels for violent crimes and being sent back to Ethel.

Next morning, plea bargaining sent us all back to the jury room once again. But now, the pace of trials was slowing. Fewer and fewer people got called. More and more finished their crossword puzzles.

Some knew from the start that their terms of duty would be a total waste. Nobody seriously thought, for instance, that a defense lawyer would let Juan Gonzalez, a prison corrections officer, serve on a criminal trial jury. After being predictably rejected for three juries in three days, he finally persuaded a sympathetic judge to get him transferred to civil court. There, he might have a chance of productive work. When Ethel handed him his transfer, the entire jury room applauded.

Most of us, still collecting our regular salaries, saw the tiny stipend for all this waiting— $12 a day plus $2 carfare—as simply a license

to waste our time. But for some, the low pay caused a real hardship. A free-lance word processor figured the two-week jury duty stint would cost her $1,200; she, too, never got to serve.

Most people recognized their duty to serve on a jury. But as the dream of productive labor faded, talk turned to beating the system. One man said that when he was called for the fifth time in 10 years, he photocopied all of his previous summonses and sent them back to the courthouse with a scrawled note saying, "Enough is enough." The system forgot about him for two more years.

Of course, the best solution is to belong to one of those groups—mostly with strong lobbies—that have gotten themselves permanently excused from jury duty. In New York, embalmers, podiatrists, physicians, lawyers, registered nurses, and people who fit artificial limbs have all been barred from the $12-a-day job.

On the fourth day of our two-week jury stint, a batch of fresh recruits reported for duty. Ethel called them "my new jurors." We hardened jurors were "my reruns." But now, of course, there weren't enough chairs. Even the hard benches that looked like the secondhand pews of a particularly austere denomination were in short supply. Instead of determining guilt or innocence, the object now was finding a seat.

As the hours of crossword puzzles wore on, morale was fading fast. "Who are the real prisoners of the court system?" asked Anne Harrison, a cathedral administrative staff member. "At least the defendants can get bail."

Ethel Becomes a Hero

Of course, jury duty doesn't have to be a bureaucratic waste. According to the Center for Jury Studies in Arlington, Virginia, dozens of court systems from Boston to Phoenix have turned to a one-day, one-trial system. If a juror isn't chosen for a jury on his first day, that's his last day of duty. "One-day, one-trial is the wave of the future," says Judge Aranda. Many courts allow jurors to call in each day; a recorded message tells them if their services are needed that day.

But most courts still use the traditional method. Officials in Los Angeles and New York say one-day, one-trial won't work in their courts because the case loads are too great. If jurors were to cost courts serious wages, one wonders if a way would be found to make it work.

Meanwhile, one depends on Ethel, who turned into a hero on my fifth day. As the horde of loafing jurors swelled, Ethel started dismissing groups of us, selected by lot, a whole week early.

Calling the chosen ones to the back room, she asked us to wait 10 weeks before calling in about that $12 a day the system owed us. When it comes to money, it seems, the computers of justice grind slowly.

Explaining that we couldn't legally be called to jury duty again for 24 months, she gave each of us our canceled jury summons. "Save this for the next two years," she said. "It is your passport to freedom."

Absolutely everyone planned to keep it in a safe place.

The Trial

The trial begins with the opening statement by the attorney having the burden of proof. Then the opposing attorney offers his or her statement. Each is expected to outline what he or she intends to prove. The plaintiff then presents evidence, which may include both testimony and physical evidence, such as documents and photos, called *exhibits*.

The attorney secures testimony from his or her own witness via questioning labeled *direct examination*. After the plaintiff's attorney completes direct examination of the plaintiff's own witness, the defense attorney may question that witness in a process labeled *cross examination*. *Redirect* and *re-cross* may then follow. The plaintiff's attorney then summarizes the testimony and the exhibits and "rests" his or her case.

At this stage the defense may make a motion for a *directed verdict*, arguing, in essence, that the plaintiff has offered insufficient evidence to justify relief, so time and expense may be saved by terminating the trial. Understandably, the judge considers the motion in the light most favorable to the plaintiff. Such motions ordinarily fail, and the trial goes forward with the defendant's presentation of evidence.

At the completion of the defendant's case, both parties may be permitted to offer *rebuttal* evidence, and either party may move for a directed verdict. Barring a directed verdict, the case goes forward with each party making a *closing argument*. When the trial is by jury, the judge must instruct the jurors as to the law to be applied to the case. The attorneys often submit to the judge their view of the proper instructions. Because the law lacks the clarity that lay persons often attribute to it, framing the instructions is a difficult task, frequently resulting in an appeal to a higher court. Finally, the verdict of the jury is rendered and a judgment is entered by the court.

Post-Trial Motions

The losing party may seek a *judgment notwithstanding the verdict (judgment n.o.v.)* on the grounds that in light of the controlling law, insufficient evidence was offered to permit the jury to decide as it did. Such motions are rarely granted. The judge is also empowered to enter a judgment n.o.v. on his or her own initiative.

Either party may also move for a new trial. The winning party might do so on the grounds that the remedy provided was inferior to that warranted by the evidence. The losing party commonly claims an error of law to support a motion for a new trial. Other possible grounds for a new trial include jury misconduct or new evidence.

Appeals

After the judgment is rendered, either party may appeal the decision to a higher court. The winner may do so if he or she feels the remedy is inadequate. Ordinarily, of course, the losing party brings the appeal. The appealing party is the *appellant* or the *petitioner,* while the other party is the *appellee* or *respondent*. The appeals court does not try the case again. In theory at least, its consideration is limited to mistakes of law at the trial level. For example, the appellant will argue that a jury instruction was erroneous or that the judge erred in failing to grant a motion to strike testimony alleged to have been prejudicial. The appeals court does not hear new evidence. It bases its decision on the trial record, materials filed by the opposing attorneys, and oral arguments.

The appellate court announces its judgment and ordinarily explains that decision in an accompanying document labeled an *opinion*. (Most of the cases in this text are appellate court opinions.) If no error is found, the lower court decision is *affirmed*. In finding prejudicial error, the appellate court may simply *reverse* (overrule) the lower court. Or, the judgment may be to *reverse and remand,* wherein the lower court is overruled and the trial court must try the case again in accordance with the law as articulated in the appeals court opinion. After the decision of the intermediate appellate court, a further appeal may be directed to the highest court of the jurisdiction. Most of those petitions are denied.

Question

Look again at the *Hresil* case. What motion was made by the defendant? What motion was made by the plaintiff?

Class Actions

A specialized form of civil proceeding, the class action suit, deserves attention. A *class action* allows a group of individuals to sue or be sued in one judicial proceeding, provided their claim or the claim against them arises out of similar or closely related grievances. For example, if hundreds of people were injured in a hotel fire, a subset of that group might file an action against the hotel on behalf of all the injured parties. The class action thus permits lawsuits that might otherwise be impractical due to the number of people involved or the small amount of each claim. (For example, all purchasers of an elixir guaranteed to stimulate hair growth and sold at $5 a unit join in an action when the potion does not achieve the advertised success.) The class action is also expedient; many potential causes of action can be disposed of in one suit.

Nevertheless, the concept of the class action has received mixed reviews. Some suits are so large and unwieldy that they impose an extreme burden on the judicial process. Others, it is argued, line attorneys' pockets but achieve few substantive legal benefits. Class actions also give rise to considerable problems of procedural fairness. For example, under a recent U.S. Supreme Court decision, all identifiable class members in federal court cases must receive individual notice of the impending action. In some instances, that requirement will prove very weighty, but class actions may be brought more easily under other statutes and rules.[11] Despite its complexities, the class action can be a very effective tool in securing justice, particularly in those instances where the "little guy" must challenge one of America's giant institutions, as is demonstrated by the following case.

IN RE "AGENT ORANGE" PRODUCT LIABILITY LITIGATION
506 F. Supp. 762 (EDNY 1980)

Judge Pratt

Plaintiffs, Vietnam war veterans and members of their families claiming to have suffered damage as a result of the veterans' exposure to herbicides in Vietnam, commenced these actions against the defendant chemical companies. . . . Five motions are now considered: . . . (2) plaintiffs' motion for class action certification; . . .

I. Summary of Claims

There are four groups of plaintiffs: Vietnam veterans, their spouses, their parents, and their children. They assert numerous theories of liability, including strict products liability, negligence, breach of warranty, intentional tort and nuisance. Plaintiff veterans seek to recover for personal injuries caused by their exposure to Agent Orange. The family members seek to recover on various derivative claims; some of the children assert claims in their own right for genetic injury and birth defects caused by their parents' exposure to the Agent Orange; and some of the veterans' wives seek to recover in their own right for miscarriages.

* * * * *

III. The Case Management Plan

There have been pending for some time motions by various parties urging the court to make various orders affecting the overall management of this action, including such matters as class action treatment, . . .

In developing the case management plan described in this section, the court has weighed and considered many problems presented by this litigation. Some of them are:

1. There are a large number of plaintiffs and potential plaintiffs who claim to have been injured by exposure to Agent Orange. There are now approximately 167 suits pending in the Eastern District of New York involving over 3,400 plaintiffs. The court has been informed that there are many thousands more who have, at the court's request and pending decision of the class action motion, refrained from bringing individual actions.
2. There are numerous chemical companies named as defendants. The fact that they may have had differing degrees of involvement in manufacturing and supplying Agent Orange for the government may or may not cause differing levels of responsibility for the effects of Agent Orange on plaintiffs.

* * * * *

4. The causation issues are difficult and complex. Clearly this is not the ''simple'' type of ''disaster'' litigation such as an airplane crash involving a single incident, having a causation picture that is readily grasped through conventional litigation techniques, and presenting comparatively small variations among the claimants as to the effects upon them of the crash. With the Agent Orange litigation, injuries are claimed to have resulted from exposure to a chemical that was disseminated in the air over southeast Asia during a period of several years. Each veteran was exposed differently, although undoubtedly patterns of exposure will emerge. The claimed injuries vary significantly. Moreover, there is a major dispute over whether Agent Orange can cause the injuries in question, and there are separate disputes over whether the exposure claimed in each case did cause the injuries claimed. The picture is further complicated by the use in Vietnam of other chemicals and drugs that also are claimed to be capable of causing many of the injuries attributed to Agent Orange.

* * * * *

6. Many of the people exposed to Agent Orange may not even yet have experienced the harm it may cause.

* * * * *

All of these problems are compounded by the practical realities of having on one side of the litigation plaintiffs who seek damages, but who have limited resources with which to press their claims and whose plight becomes more desperate and depressing as time goes on, and having on the other side defendants who strenuously contest their liability, who have ample resources for counsel and expert witnesses to defend them, and who probably gain significantly, although immeasurably, from every delay that they can produce.

IV. Class Action

Contending that many of the issues here presented are best determined by class action to avoid duplicitous litigation by the individual members of the proposed class, plaintiffs have moved for a conditional order pursuant to [Federal Rule of Civil Procedure] 23 permitting the suit to proceed as a class action on behalf of all persons exposed to Agent Orange and various members of their families.

Before a class action may be maintained under Rule 23, the action must meet the prerequisites of Rule 23(a) and one set of the alternate requirements of Rule 23(b). Defendants oppose class treatment, but continue to advance some outrageous arguments in the name of advocacy; detracting from whatever valid arguments they might otherwise have, they argue that plaintiffs fail to satisfy even one of the elements necessary under Rule 23. Plaintiffs, equally undiscriminating in their advocacy, argue that *every* element of *every* alternative of Rule 23 is met here.

The court has carefully read and considered the voluminous submissions of the parties and has heard and considered oral arguments of counsel on this issue. After due consideration, the court determines that plaintiffs have demonstrated that a class action is appropriate under Rule 23(b)(3). Accordingly, plaintiffs' motion for conditional class action certification is granted as herein provided. Certain specific findings are required.

A. The Prerequisites of Rule 23(a)

1. Numerosity. The members of the plaintiff class here are so numerous that joinder of all members of the class in the same action is impracticable. Rule 23(a)(1). Indeed, if the only members of the class were the plaintiffs in the 167 actions now pending in this court, "numerosity" would be satisfied.

2. Commonality. Rule 23(a)(2) states that a class action may only be maintained if "there are questions of law or fact common to the class." Here, the action raises numerous questions of law *and* fact common to the class. Whatever may be the individual questions relating to the manner and extent of each veteran's exposure to Agent Orange, and relating to the particular effects of Agent Orange on the veteran when considered along with his/her medical history, circumstances, lifestyle and other unique conditions, all of these claims share a common ground when proceeding through the many factual and legal issues relating to the government contract defense, negligence by the defendants, whether Agent Orange was a "defective product," and the many questions embodied in the concept of "general causation." In part, the requirement of commonality is one aimed at determining whether there is a need for combined treatment and a benefit to be derived therefrom. Here the need is compelling, and the benefits are substantial.

3. Typicality. Rule 23(a)(3) requires that in a class action "the claims or defenses of the representative parties [be] typical of the claims or defenses of the class." As already noted, plaintiffs' claims of negligence, products liability and general causation, . . . are not just "typical" of the entire class, they are identical. In a few areas, such as the rules governing liability and the application of various statutes of limitations, the claims may fall into groups that are "typical," but even there the different groups' claims can be efficiently managed either on a subclass basis or directly by way of separately determining the issues. Although the named plaintiffs for purposes of the class action are yet to be designated, the court is satisfied that out of the extremely large pool available representative plaintiffs can be named who will present claims typical of those of the class. As already indicated, the issues of specific causation and damages will, of course, ultimately require individual consideration, but until that point in the litigation is reached, a class action appears to be the only practicable means for managing the lawsuit.

4. Adequacy. Rule 23(a)(4) provides that a class action may only be maintained if "the representative parties will fairly and adequately protect the interests of the class." Adequacy of representation depends on the qualifications and interests of counsel for the class representatives, the absence of antagonism or conflicting interests, and a sharing of interests between class representatives and absentees. Here, the court will select from among the hundreds of plaintiffs representative persons who have a substantial stake in the litigation, who lack conflicts, antagonisms or reasons to be motivated by factors inconsistent with the motives of absentee class members, and who will fairly and adequately protect the interests of the class. Further the class will be represented by experienced, capable counsel, Yannacone and Associates, who have shown themselves willing to undertake the considerable commitment of time, energy and money necessary for the vigorous prosecution of the claims here asserted.

5. Additional Requirements. Courts have implied two additional prerequisites to class action certification that are not specifically mentioned in Rule 23: (1) there must be an identifiable class, and (2) the class representatives must be members of the class. Here, the plaintiff class can be readily identified; they are persons who claim injury from exposure to Agent Orange and their spouses, children and parents who claim direct or derivative injury therefrom. The court has intentionally defined the class in broad terms consistent with the demands of this litigation. If we begin with the broadest possible class, the issues common to all members of that class can be resolved. It may later prove advantageous to create subclasses for various purposes, *e.g.,* for resolving statute of limitations claims, for determining liability in "negligence" as opposed to "product liability" states, and finally, perhaps, for preserving the class action format prior to remand to the transferor judges so as to provide them with the greatest possible flexibility in ultimately determining the issues remaining after multidistrict treatment has ended.

B. The Requirements of Rule 23(b)

Plaintiffs seek certification of a plaintiff class under Rule 23(b)(1)(A), (b)(1)(B), (b)(2) and (b)(3). For the reasons set forth below, however, the court concludes that class certification is appropriate only under Rule 23(b)(3).

* * * * *

3. Rule 23(b)(3). Rule 23(b)(3) authorizes a class action when the court finds "that the questions of law or fact common to the members of the class predominate over any questions affecting only individual members, and that a class action is superior to all other available methods for the fair and efficient adjudication of the controversy." The rule lists four matters pertinent to a consideration of these issues: "(A) the interest of members of the class in individually controlling the prosecution or defense of separate actions; (B) the extent and nature of any litigation concerning the controversy already commenced by or against members of the class; (C) the desirability or un-desirability of concentrating the litigation of the claims in the particular forum; (D) the difficulties likely to be encountered in the management of a class action."

Considering the circumstances of this action, and bearing in mind the manner in which the class action will proceed, the court determines that the interest of class members in individually controlling the prosecution of separate actions is minimal, especially at this early stage of the litigation when the issues under consideration concern the relationship between the defendants and the government, issues that impact equally on every plaintiff's claim. Later stages of this litigation, especially those concerned with individual causation and damages, may require reconsideration of this element and possibly decertification, but at this stage, individual class members have almost no interest in individually controlling the prosecution of separate actions. Indeed, the problems inherent in every one of the individual actions are so great that it is doubtful if a single plaintiff represented by a single attorney pursuing an individual action could ever succeed.

With respect to the extent and nature of currently pending litigation, almost all the Agent Orange litigation currently pending is before this court under the multidistrict litigation procedures. All those cases are advancing simultaneously, and certification of a class action will serve the goals of judicial economy and reduce the possibility of multiple lawsuits. In addition, it will significantly expedite final resolution of this controversy.

With respect to the desirability of concentrating the litigation of the claims in this forum, the actions have already been concentrated before this court. . . . Allowing it to proceed as a class action will minimize the hazards of duplicate efforts and inconsistent results. Moreover, given the location of present counsel and the widely varying citizenships of the interested parties, this court is as appropriate a place to settle the controversy as any.

With respect to the difficulties likely to be encountered in the management of a class action, the court has carefully and humbly considered the management problems presented by an action of this magnitude and complexity, and concluded that great as they are, the difficulties likely to be encountered by managing these actions as a class action are significantly outweighed by the truly overwhelming problems that would attend any other management device chosen. While the burdens on this court might be lessened by denying class certification, those imposed collectively on the transferor courts after remand of the multidistrict cases would be increased many times.

Having carefully considered the above factors and all other circumstances of this action, the court is satisfied that at this time the questions of law and fact common to the members of the class predominate over questions of law or fact affecting only individual members, and that a class action is superior to any other available method for the fair and efficient adjudication of the controversy.

Because over a year ago this court requested plaintiffs not to file actions pending decision on the class action motion, because the facts and issues in all of the pending and future cases are to a great degree identical, or at least parallel, and because this action presents a variety of questions in relatively untested areas of the law, this court sees the . . . interests of justice, best served by determining here, and for all parties, as many legal and factual issues as may properly be decided. To achieve those ends the court will certify this to be a class action. . . .

QUESTIONS

1. What are the purposes and uses of the concept of jurisdiction? Why do we limit the courts to which a claim can be taken?
2. Law cases often read like soap operas while they reveal important truths. A woman and man, each married to others, had engaged in a long-term love affair. The woman's husband died, and she pleaded with her paramour to leave his New York home to visit her in Florida. She affirmed her love for the man. They made arrangements to meet in Miami, but on his arrival at the airport he was served a summons informing him that he was being sued. His Florida "lover" sought $500,000 for money allegedly loaned to him and for seduction inspired by a promise of marriage.
   a. Does the Florida court have proper jurisdiction over him?
   b. What if he had voluntarily come to Florida on vacation? See *Wyman* v. *Newhouse*, 93 F.2d 313 (2d Cir. 1937).
3. The Incompatibility Clause of the Constitution provides that "no person holding any office under the United States, shall be a member of either House during his continuance in the office." An association of Armed Forces reservists, including several U.S. citizens and taxpayers, was opposed to the Vietnam War. The association brought a class action on behalf of all U.S. citizens and taxpayers against the secretary of defense and others. The association argued that several members of Congress violated the Incompatibility Clause by virtue of their Armed Forces Reserve membership.
   Do the plaintiffs have standing to sue? Explain. See *Schlesinger* v. *Reservists Committee to Stop the War*, 418 U.S. 208 (1974).
4. The Fifth and Fourteenth Amendments to the U.S. Constitution guarantee that the citizenry will not be deprived of life, liberty, and property

without due process of law, while the Seventh Amendment guarantees the right to trial by jury. In an unusually complex antitrust case it was argued that the due process clause prohibits trial by jury in instances where the complexity of the case exceeds a jury's ability to reach a reasoned judgment.

  a. Should unusually complex cases be heard by a judge alone? Explain. See *In Re U.S. Financial Securities Litigation,* 609 F.2d 411 (9th Cir. 1979) cert. denied, 446 U.S. 929 (1979). But see *In Re Japanese Electronic Products Antitrust Litigation* (U.S. Court of Appeals for the 3rd Circuit, No. 79-2540) *Antitrust and Trade Regulation Report,* No. 973, July 17, 1980, p. F–1.

  b. Are juries usually successful in reaching fair, impartial verdicts, or do the personal deficiencies and prejudices of the ordinary citizen result in unfair, irrational decisions? Explain.

  c. Should the jury system be abolished? Explain.

5. Scholar Amitai Etzioni has suggested that the advance of science may constitute a threat to the jury system.

> Man has taken a new bite from the apple of knowledge, and it is doubtful whether we will be better for it. This time it is not religion or the family that are being disturbed by the new knowledge but that venerable institution of being judged by a jury of one's peers. The jury's impartiality is threatened because defense attorneys have discovered that by using social science techniques, they can manipulate the composition of juries to significantly increase the likelihood that their clients will be acquitted.[12]

How can the use of the computer, advanced survey techniques, and the like threaten the validity of the trial process?

6. Refer again to the *Agent Orange* case. Who were the members of the proposed class? What six requirements did the court say must be met in all class action suits brought in federal court? Do you think this case is an appropriate one for the certification of a class of plaintiffs? Explain.

7.   [I]n an out-of-court settlement, $218 million in damages was awarded to 30,000 customers of a group of folding-box manufacturers accused of fixing prices. The settlement came after several years of litigation. For the customers, the average award was $6,790, hardly a large sum to them since more than a few were multimillion-dollar businesses. But for the lawyers representing the customers it was a different matter. The 50 law firms involved split $13 million in legal fees, with the most active firms in the case reeling in a cool million each.[13]

On balance, does the class action serve a useful public purpose, or does it merely afford consumer activists the opportunity to harass corporate "villians" while lawyers line their pockets? Explain.

Part Five—Criticisms and Alternatives

CRITICISM

To many Americans our system of justice is neither systematic nor just, and in recent years our court system has come under increasing criticism. For example, the U.S. Supreme Court is routinely accused of upsetting the constitutional balance of power by exercising authority historically vested in the executive and legislative branches. The Court has been accused of "legislating" sweeping changes in American life in such areas as the rights of the criminally accused, discrimination, and abortion. In general, the Court has, according to its critics, failed to maintain the self-discipline and restraint deemed necessary for a carefully deliberative body. The following articles reveal both dangers and virtues in an activist judicial stance.

FEDERAL JUDGE PREACHES GOSPEL OF "THE LITTLE GUY"

Larry Fruhling

Minneapolis, Minn.—The man who delivered the sermon looked like nothing as much as the preacher for the Lutheran flock of a small Minnesota town. And his message seemed suitable for the pulpit.

Balding, graying, his austere features set off by wire-rim glasses, District Judge Miles Lord—the Lord of Federal Court, as he is known—told the three officials of A. H. Robins Co., maker of a contraceptive device called the Dalkon Shield, to "confess to your Maker and beg forgiveness and mend your ways."

The judge said A. H. Robins had sinned grievously by refusing to recall the Dalkon Shield and to make prompt restitution to the women who were injured by it. Rather, Lord said, the company and its lawyers had dragged their feet for 12 years, using every means available to discourage women from gaining compensation for their illnesses.

"You have taken the bottom line as your guiding beacon and the low road as your route," he declared. "Under your direction your company has in fact continued to allow women, tens of thousands of them, to wear this device, a deadly depth charge in their wombs, ready to explode at any time."

Lord said Robins was guilty of corporate greed and irresponsibility. He begged the company to settle its accounts with women who had been made ill and infertile by the device and to appeal to women still using the shields to have them removed at once.

Then the chief federal judge for Minnesota closed his lengthy tirade against the Robins officials on this note: "I just want to say I love you. I am not mad at you."

It was vintage Miles Welton Lord, at either his best as the self-anointed conscience of corporate America and champion of "the little guy," or at his worst as a cannon rumbling loose on the deck of the federal judiciary.

Both views have found many supporters during Lord's 18 turbulent years as one of America's most controversial federal judges, a man whose blunt and frequent rulings and speeches focused attention sharply on the environment, discrimination against women, the abuses by government bureaucracy, corporate misdeeds, and, most recently, the arms race.

In November, the 8th Circuit Court of Appeals, acting on a petition from A. H. Robins, erased Lord's "deadly depth charge" speech from the official record of the proceeding, saying Lord had jumped off the deep end before hearing Robins' side of the case.

* * * * *

Lord has been condemned by *The American Lawyer* magazine as the worst federal judge in the seven midwestern states that answer to the 8th Circuit Court of Appeals.

"Impartiality is a quality that Lord rarely seemed to view as a virtue," the magazine declared in 1980, quoting an unnamed Minnesota lawyer as saying, "Lord loves a good fight, and that's exactly what makes him such a bad judge. He'd rather do the fighting himself than decide the case."

He was praised the following year as the best federal trial judge in the United States by the American Association of Trial Lawyers, which cited his determination to find his way to the heart of a matter by chopping through the labyrinth of delay and obfuscation that corporate lawyers are paid to construct.

A veteran Minnesota lawyer who is no particular fan says Lord probably is no more ar-

bitrary in running his courtroom than some other federal judges secure in their lifetime appointments. What sets Lord apart, the lawyer said, is that "the other judges are on the side of the corporations—they're establishment arbitrary. Miles is little-guy arbitrary." . . .

* * * * *

Lord, who is 65, says he is a devoted fan of the American corporation. Never mind the scalding speeches he has delivered from the bench against Sperry, A. H. Robins, and, in one remarkable case from which he was removed by an appeals court for his biases, Reserve Mining Co. . . .

"If we didn't have corporations I would try to invent them," Lord says. "They're the greatest mechanisms for collecting capital and for production that there is. We have the most powerful, wealthy, productive country in the world, and 85 percent of our gross national product is produced by corporations. There is no way you can help but admire that."

Down Primrose Paths

It's just that corporations occasionally are lured away from the paths of righteousness by pressure to produce profits for their stockholders and by organizational mazes that defy the pinpointing of responsibility for the actions of a big company, he says. . . .

He complains that corporations hire "boosters" to give one-day seminars, at a price of $5,000 or more, on efficiency, productivity, the glories of capitalism. Lord says he is just trying to balance the equation. "These guys don't want to hear that it's a sin to poison a river, to make people sick downstream." . . .

Lord has judged hundreds of cases, ranging from big antitrust suits against drug companies to supermarket mergers, kidnappings, bank robberies, the question of permitting motorboats in the Boundary Waters Canoe Area, and the free-expression rights of naked dancers.

The decision he is proudest of was his ruling in 1972 that two Minnesota high schools had to give girls access to boys' athletic teams or provide equal athletic programs.

"That thing revolutionized the whole country," he says, adding that his daughter's bristling reaction when he wisecracked about girl wrestlers "changed my whole aspect of thinking about the feminist movement."

But the cases that always intrigued him most, he says, are "the ones where you see the av-arice of the human being, individually or collectively."

"Maybe I should have been a preacher and pounded the pulpit every day," Lord says.

[Judge Lord retired from the federal bench in 1985—Author.]

Source: *Des Moines Sunday Register*, February 3, 1985, Section A, pp. 1, 9. Reprinted with permission of the copyright holder, *The Des Moines Register*.

COURTING DISASTER

L. Gordon Crovitz

"The Supreme Court of the United States and the highest courts of the 50 states are like so many loose cannons sliding around the legal deck." The fearsome result is that "every businessperson should always assume that many of the things that he or she is currently doing could result in heavy liability regardless of the current state of the law."

This confirmation of the lesson of *Pennzoil v. Texaco* [See Chapter 9—Author.] is straight from one of the horses' mouths. Richard Neely has been a justice of the West Virginia Supreme Court since 1972, when he was 31 years old. His *Judicial Jeopardy: When Business Collides with the Courts* is a story told with injudicious candor of how he and his robed colleagues have made the American legal system the biggest liability facing U.S. companies.

Justice Neely's thesis is that the once predictable and mostly efficient American rule of law has badly deteriorated in the past 25 years or so. Product liability law is a well-documented example. Absolute liability, lia-bility without fault, has replaced the common law requirement of negligence. The result is the current tort (personal injury law) and insurance crisis.

One reason for the deterioration of law is that judges no longer simply resolve the legal dispute between the parties before them. Instead, courts have become alternative forums for public policy debates. Partly, this is because the kinds of behavior regulated by government have expanded faster than legislators' ability to enact laws. As Justice Neely puts it, "Americans are turning to the courts for political decisions for many of the same reasons that the middle classes in banana republics turn to military juntas." Courts may not be democratic or wise, but they do have the power to resolve issues.

Once a businessperson understands that judges no longer limit themselves to adding incremental changes to the common law—that instead, many consciously make policy—he must figure out how to limit the damage courts do in their new role. Justice Neely offers valuable legal advice.

He asks whether Ford should care more about a $200,000 injury suit based on a defective wheel on a Ford Escort or a $200,000 suit against General Motors based on the theory that the driver was hurt because the Chevy wasn't equipped with inflatable airbags. He says that Ford should devote more resources defending the potentially liability-expanding case against GM. If it's a case against GM today, it will be Ford tomorrow. Courts, unlike legislatures, are under little pressure to worry about cost-benefit analyses. Ford should help the judges see the costs to society if auto makers can be held liable in the airbag case.

Justice Neely's thesis is that one reason judges feel free to create bizarre rules, like expansive product liability, is that they can hide behind a veil of supposed professional disinterest in the likely effects. He gives the example of a ruling by his West Virginia court that nearly throttled the state's economy.

The 1978 case concerned the West Virginia workers' compensation law. Like all such laws, the idea was to immunize employers from tort claims based on work-related injuries in exchange for compensating their workers regardless of who was at fault. An exception is that employers can be sued if they willfully or intentionally harm workers. In the case before the court, managers at a lumber mill ignored the warnings of a saw operator, and had him remove the protective guard. The worker lost several fingers as a result.

The court let the worker sue for damages above the workers' compensation amount. The problem was, as Justice Neely pointed out in dissent at the time, that the court used such broad language favoring the plaintiff that it seemed that the tort exemption for employers "was very close to being abolished in West Virginia by court fiat." Injured workers began suing in droves. Lawyers worried that they could be sued for malpractice if they advised workers that the law prohibited tort claims. By 1982, so much business had fled the state that labor unions lobbied for a statutory retraction. In 1984, the court reversed itself.

Some day, legislatures may limit the jurisdiction of courts so that public policy issues are again decided by the political branches. Until then, Justice Neely suggests treating judges the way many view themselves—as politicians with tenure. He urges businesspersons to lobby judges in much the same way they lobby legislators. He says, for example, that insurance companies should come up with a model set of tort rules for judges to apply. He suggests that since judges aren't very well-paid, they could easily be lured to conferences to hear about such reform proposals if someone else foots the bill.

This book does not paint a pretty picture of the country's judges or the confused state of the law. No one would believe a book that did. The news is that at least one judge is finally willing to talk openly about the problems and offer advice about solving them.

Questions

1. Should judges use the bench as a pulpit of sorts to remind corporate officials of lessons they "don't want to hear"? If judges do not do so, where will those lessons be expressed? Explain.
2. What dangers might result from following the activist posture of Judge Lord?

Cost in Time and Money

The cost in both time and money to parties resorting to courts is well publicized. These costs have implications for the justice achieved by the system. Thus one frequently hears, "Justice delayed is justice denied." One reason for the delays is the often-cited increase in litigation brought to our courts without an equivalent increase in judges to hear the cases. It has been reported that the number of lawsuits filed in our federal courts nearly tripled between 1970 and 1986.[14]

Critics have also claimed that only the rich can afford judicial justice and the poor must do without, either because they cannot get into court in the first place or because they cannot afford to hire the best lawyers to make the court battle a "fair fight."

These and other criticisms are related in the following article.

HAS U.S. TOO MANY LAWS, LAWSUITS, AND LAWYERS?

Stuart Taylor, Jr.

Prominent lawyers, judges, and scholars warn that the justice system is choking on its own complexity and cost as swollen case loads place ever greater demands on it.

Experts as diverse as Chief Justice Warren Burger, Attorney General William French Smith, former Attorney General Griffin Bell, and Derek Bok, president of Harvard University, argue that the country suffers from too many laws, too many lawsuits, too many legal entanglements and—at least in Bok's view— too many lawyers.

* * * * *

Warnings about increased litigiousness alternate with expressions of concern that most citizens cannot afford to hire lawyers to press legitimate claims.

Lloyd Cutler, one of Washington's most prominent corporate lawyers, has written of large law firms like his own: "The rich who pay our fees are less than 1 percent of our fellow citizens, but they get at least 95 percent of our time. The disadvantaged we serve for nothing are perhaps 20 to 25 percent of the population and get at most 5 percent of our time. The remaining 75 percent cannot afford to consult us and get virtually none of our time."

But Bok stresses that "the wealthy and the powerful also chafe under the burden" of regulations, delays, legal uncertainties, and manipulations. Some landlords, for example, complain that federally subsidized legal-aid lawyers use technicalities to help poor tenants avoid eviction while they refuse to pay rent.

Even if the legal system is not too overloaded with lawsuits, examples of the increase in suing abound:

* * * * *

- Many lawsuits nowadays would have been unheard of only a few years ago: high school

school football coaches sued by injured players, psychiatrists sued by victims of their patients' crimes, young people sued by sex partners over herpes infections, universities sued by students, bishops sued by nuns, parents sued by children.

• Complex cases in which opposing lawyers bury one another under thousands of documents and marshal legions of experts and other witnesses have become more common.

Trials are only the top of a pyramid. Most lawyers rarely set foot in court, spending their time drafting memorandums, letters of opinion, interrogatories, motions, and briefs, as well as counseling, lobbying, taking depositions, negotiating deals. The vast majority of lawsuits are settled out of court.

* * * * *

Each year more than 35,000 new law school graduates spill into the market. Big New York corporate law firms offer starting salaries as high as $50,000 to top graduates of elite law schools, but thousands of less fortunate graduates find no jobs in their chosen profession. [This figure has apparently now risen to $90,000[15]—Author.]

* * * * *

Bok says too many of the nation's most talented students are going to law school and then "into legal pursuits that often add little to the growth of the economy or the pursuit of culture or the enhancement of the human spirit."

While Japan trains more engineers to design better products, he said, America trains lawyers whose activities contribute to "a stifling burden of regulations, delays, and legal uncertainties that can inhibit progress and allow unscrupulous parties to misuse the law to harass and manipulate their victims."

* * * * *

A central obstacle to developing any consensus for reforming the civil justice system is that steps to solve one set of problems tend to aggravate others.

The cures for litigiousness proposed by conservatives, business and medical groups, and insurance companies would also raise new barriers to individuals seeking justice at an affordable price.

But proposals from some liberals, consumer groups, and the American Bar Association to subsidize lawyers' fees for the middle class and to increase federal financing of legal aid for the poor would surely spur more lawsuits.

The American tendency to settle issues through formal legal combat that other nations settle by governmental fiat or other means has been remarked on since the birth of the United States.

In 1782 St. John de Crevecoeur, in "Letters from an American Farmer," compared lawyers to weeds and said they "promote litigiousness

---

A Growing Profession

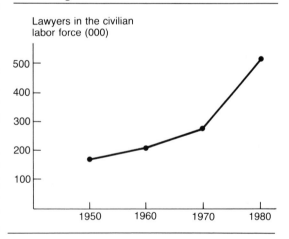

Lawyers in the civilian labor force (000)

Source: Census Bureau.

and amass more wealth than the most opulent farmer with all his toil." In 1835 Alexis de Tocqueville wrote, "There is hardly a political question in the United States which does not sooner or later turn into a judicial one."

The current swollen case loads and other problems of the civil justice system are symptoms of pervasive social problems and reflect the efforts of legislatures and courts in recent decades to adapt to rapid social changes and in some cases to accelerate them.

As the United States became increasingly urbanized, affluent, crowded, socially fragmented, and economically specialized, more dependent on complex machines and chemicals, and more expert at detecting the causes of injuries, disputes that used to be resolved within families, schools, community groups, and churches have spilled over into the courts.

A more direct cause of increased legal activity, especially in federal courts, is an outpouring of new laws, regulations, and judicial decisions expanding the regulation of business, the legal rights of individuals, and access to the courts.

These include the Supreme Court's rulings striking down racial segregation, new civil rights laws and statutes that created new agencies to regulate environmental and consumer protection, workplace safety, and other activities.

* * * * *

Meanwhile, state courts, led by California's, have developed new doctrines that make it easier for people to win lawsuits, especially those seeking compensation for medical malpractice and injuries caused by machines and other products. Many courts have held manufacturers liable for injuries caused by defective products without requiring proof that they were at fault.

Juries, which tend to sympathize with individual plaintiffs injured by corporate or governmental defendants, are increasingly willing to award staggering amounts of damages, including millions of dollars for "pain and suffering" and "punitive damages" on top of measurable losses such as medical expenses.

* * * * *

Most people injured in such accidents could not bring lawsuits or obtain redress if they had to pay their legal fees in advance, as in England. But under the American "contingent fee" approach, lawyer-entrepreneurs agree to represent injured plaintiffs in exchange for a share, typically one third, of any damages they win. The lawyers get nothing if they lose.

According to insurance industry statistics, more of the money that changes hands in product liability suits goes to the opposing lawyers and for other legal costs than to compensate plaintiffs.

* * * * *

Since 1965 the federal government has subsidized local programs around the country providing free legal assistance to poor people, at a rate of $241 million this year. This pays for around 4,800 full-time lawyers in legal aid offices.

Although dwarfed by the $10 billion to $20 billion in federal subsidies for the legal fees of corporations, which deduct them from their taxes, this subsidy has been under attack from President Reagan.

* * * * *

Source: *Des Moines Register*, June 5, 1983, p. 1. Reprinted with permission of the copyright holder, The Associated Press. (Stuart Taylor, Jr., writes for *The New York Times*.)

Win/Lose Nature of Court Decisions

> The nature of the judicial process is normally to declare one party the winner and the other the loser. In many disputes, however, neither party is morally right or wrong; rather, there is just a difference of opinion. In other cases, both parties may be equally in the wrong. In both cases, it is argued that our court system cannot possibly result in justice. The following article points out the problem.

INCIVILITY IN COURT AS LAWYERS STRIVE TO WIN

Elliott M. Abramson

According to [Supreme Court] Chief Justice Warren Burger, [Now retired—Author.] American lawyers are sorely lacking in civility. In a recent talk in London, he stated that "the current generation of lawyers . . . seem[s] to act more like warriors eager to do battle than healers seeking peace."

I believe that the chief justice has definitely put his finger on something—but it may be more than he realizes. Many people who have dealt with attorneys will readily agree that lawyers are hard driving to (perhaps well beyond) the point of incivility. "Ruthlessness" may be the right word.

Not often remarked on is that such attitudes are bred by, integral to, and entirely consistent with the very core and sinews of our legal system and its training grounds—a system in which, first of all, winning and losing are very sharply demarcated and with very little middle ground.

Take a simple example: X has a piece of jewelry she believes to be an imitation diamond. Y wishes to buy it, and they agree on $25. Later, it develops that the object is a real diamond worth perhaps $5,000. X offers Y his $25 back in return for the diamond.

If Y does not comply, and X sues, one party will basically win everything. For, under the fundamental rules of the American legal system, it will be found either that the diamond belongs to Y, with X having no further rights, or Y must return it to X and relinquish all of his rights in it.

The hard rules of the game do not recognize the possibility of coming together in the following way: Neither X nor Y realized the worth of the gem. Since they have now both been rather strongly connected with it, and it suddenly turns out to be worth $5,000, each might be accorded $2,500. Both would thereby gain from a stroke of good fortune for which neither can take credit.

But the contemporary American legal structure mandates that one be a total winner, the other a total loser. Such a state of affairs can induce only frenzy and desperation in its practitioners, certainly not graciousness and civility.

* * * * *

Source: *Des Moines Register,* April 4, 1984, p. 8A. Reprinted with permission of the copyright holder, The Associated Press. (Elliott M. Abramson is a professor in the College of Law at DePaul University.)

ALTERNATIVES

In response to arguments like those identified in the preceding section, many alternatives to court resolution of disputes have received increased attention in recent years.

- In Columbus, Ohio, some 3,000 criminal misdemeanors are referred to mediation each month by intake workers in the prosecutor's office.
- In Maine and California and more than a dozen states in between, courts are recommending, and at times requiring, that divorcing couples attempt to resolve property and custody issues amicably through mediation before contesting these issues in the courts.
- New York and Texas are among at least six states that have legislated the public funding of local dispute resolution programs.
- Massachusetts, New Jersey, Wisconsin, and Alaska are establishing state mediation programs to provide forums for resolving a broad range of multiparty community, environmental, and other public policy disputes.[16]

Alternative dispute resolution mechanisms are quite diverse. There are three main categories and innumerable variations and hybrids. The three categories, described along a continuum from least to most formal, are negotiation, mediation, and arbitration.

Negotiation

Negotiation, which has been defined as communication for the purpose of persuasion,[17] is a process where the parties to the dispute meet and discuss their differences in order to reach a mutually satisfactory resolution; that is, a compromise solution (as opposed to a winner-take-all solution). It is probably the oldest form of dispute resolution other than the use of brute force. In fact, most disputes are probably resolved by negotiation. It is estimated that over 90 percent of the disputes in which a plaintiff actually files a complaint in court are settled out of court before the judge renders a decision in the case.[18]

In general, the initiation and outcome of negotiation are totally controlled by the disputing parties, although statutes may mandate negotiation in certain circumstances, such as collective bargaining. Negotiation has the fewest formal requirements, although the parties themselves can agree on any degree of procedural formality.

Mediation

Mediation introduces a neutral third party into the resolution process. Ideally, the parties devise their own solution, with the mediator as a facilitator, not a decision maker. Even if the mediator does propose a solution, its character will be in the nature of a compromise, not a determination of right and wrong. The bottom line is that only the disputing parties can adopt any particular outcome. The mediator may aid the parties in a number of ways, such as opening up communication between them. Examples are Henry Kissinger's noted "shuttle" diplomacy and President Jimmy Carter's invitations to Prime Minister Begin and President Sadat to meet at Camp David to discuss their differences.

Maine has established a Court Mediation Service in which impartial third parties (professors, businesspeople, retired citizens, and others) devote several hours per week to helping settle arguments out of court. About two thirds of the small claims and contested divorce cases are settled during mediation. State law now requires mediation for all contested divorce cases involving minor children. Mediators now handle about 1,000 such cases annually. Overall about 20 percent of the mediated cases cannot be settled and must be referred to a judge.[19]

Another mediation variant, referred to as a *minitrial,* has been used successfully by a number of corporations to resolve certain conflicts. The minitrial typically follows a format of this nature:

1. The formal court proceedings, if under way, are held in abeyance.
2. The parties develop their own procedural rules and establish deadlines demanding quick resolution.
3. A neutral expert is hired, and the parties submit short statements of their positions.
4. The trial itself is limited to a very brief period, perhaps two days. A critical ingredient is the presence at the trial of top management.
5. After the trial the managers seek to reach an accord. Failing that, the neutral expert issues a nonbinding opinion.[20]
6. Should the minitrial fail, the parties may then turn to the formal judicial process.

Arbitration

Arbitration is a process in which a neutral third party is given the power to determine a binding resolution of the dispute. Depending on the situation, the resolution may be either a compromise solution or a determination of the rights of the parties and a win/lose solution. Even in the latter case, however, it may be quicker and less costly to the parties, and the arbitrator may be an expert in the subject area of the dispute instead of a generalist, as a judge would be. It is procedurally more formal than negotiation or mediation, with the presentation of proofs and arguments by the parties, but less formal than court adjudication.

Frustrated by the time and expense of the trial process, some litigants have developed creative arbitration variations of their own. For example, two resourceful Los Angeles lawyers, representing NBC and Johnny Carson in a contract dispute, relied on an 1872 California statute to implement what is sometimes labeled a "rent-a-judge" system. For approximately $100 per hour, retired judges can be hired to quickly and privately reach binding decisions in civil cases. Both sides simply agree on the judge and on rules for presenting the case.

The first of the articles that follow highlights the argument that America is beset with a "litigation mentality," and the second article tells the story of perhaps the most ambitious alternate dispute resolution effort to date.

LITIGATION MENTALITY: U.S., EUROPE, JAPAN

Robert H. Malott

Differences in liability costs can create a major competitive disadvantage for domestic manufacturers in both local and foreign markets. According to a study by the Commerce Department, the insurance costs that U.S. companies face for product liability coverage are many times higher than those facing manufacturers in Europe and Japan. In fact, some U.S. manufacturers of machine tools and textile machinery must support liability premiums that are 20 to 100 times greater than those paid by their foreign competitors.

FMC's own experience corroborates this. [The author is chairman and chief executive officer of FMC Corporation—Author.] Over the last five years, our total insurance expenses in the United States—including self-insured losses—have cost five times as much as our insurance premiums in international markets.

In considering potential areas for reform, it is instructive to compare our system of liability with that prevailing in Western Europe and Japan, where the incidence of product liability claims is far lower and the average size of awards is much smaller. In my view, there are three critical factors that account for these differences in the frequency and cost of liability litigation:

- Contingent fee arrangements are not allowed in Western Europe or Japan. Instead, plaintiffs must pay their attorneys during the course of litigation and risk paying the legal cost for the defense if they lose.

- Damage awards in Europe and Japan usually only cover actual expenses and loss of income. Punitive damages and awards for pain and suffering are not readily available in Europe, and they are nonexistent in Japan. As a result, plaintiffs must bear a significant financial risk in bringing a case to trial, and generally they have lower expectations for awards. These two factors alone act as a major disincentive to litigation.

- Most importantly, the Europeans and the Japanese have a totally different attitude toward litigation than do Americans. Europeans generally believe that, if a product is made safely, it is up to the consumer to use it safely. The Japanese are even more conservative in their approach to litigation. They rarely use the legal system to resolve disputes and, in fact, tend to consider litigation as a form of harassment.

In contrast, Americans tend to be keenly aware of the availability of legal redress for accidental injury and appear to be willing to pursue such a course without reservation. They rely on the courts not only to settle disputes but also to provide extensive compensation for injuries—often with little regard for who is at fault and with *no* regard for the costs they are imposing on business and society.

In my opinion, this litigation mentality cannot continue. The costs have simply become too great. Our runaway liability system is contributing significantly to higher prices, is reducing choices for consumers, is seriously impacting the availability and cost of insurance, and is impairing the international competitiveness of U.S. industry.

Source: Robert H. Malott, "Litigation Mentality: U.S., Europe, Japan," *Directors & Boards* 10 (Spring 1986), p. 14. Reprinted from the Spring 1986 edition of *Directors & Boards,* published by MLR Publishing Company, Philadelphia.

NOVEL EFFORT TO SETTLE ASBESTOS CLAIMS FAILS AS LAWSUITS MULTIPLY

Cynthia F. Mitchell and Paul M. Barrett

Joseph Kremenic, a strapping six-footer who spent most of his life working in a shipyard, dreamed of a quiet retirement on his farm in East Texas. In 1980, his dreams were shattered by a chilling diagnosis: asbestosis, a respiratory disease that slowly suffocates its victims.

Some sick co-workers were going to court and winning judgments against asbestos concerns. But Mr. Kremenic's claim got stuck in a clogged court. So in 1986, he took his case to a new agency set up by asbestos companies and their insurers that promised victims speedy settlements.

His settlement demands went unanswered for two years. Mr. Kremenic died in March, his claim still unresolved. "I wonder, Will it ever come to an end?" Margaret Kremenic, his widow, says. "I'm inclined to go to a jury, after all this time, all the suffering."

That's precisely what the asbestos and insurance companies had hoped to avoid three years ago when they pledged to lay down their arms and pay victims. The Asbestos Claims Facility was an experiment designed to mix cost savings with compassion. Companies wanted out of the courts, where they were spending huge sums to defend themselves. Victims wanted compensation, without the anguish of fighting for it and, in some cases, dying without it.

The experiment failed.

A Deluge of Claims

Seven of the facility's biggest members have pulled out of the organization in recent months, citing disagreements over settling claims. The departing companies were responsible for providing more than 60 percent of the facility's claims budget. Among them are Eagle-Picher Industries, Inc.; Owens-Illinois, Inc.; and Owens-Corning Fiberglas Corporation. The remaining members have agreed to dissolve the facility, though they say they may form a new, smaller claims agency.

The Asbestos Claims Facility fell apart just as the flood of claims turned into a deluge. Some 63,000 claims, seeking billions in damages, are pending; new ones are pouring in at a rate of 1,300 a month, triple the rate of a few years ago. Asbestos litigation threatens to overwhelm courts in some areas. Nevertheless, asbestos producers and victims now have no choice but to rely on the courts to referee their disputes. And that is likely to mean more delay and bigger legal bills for both sides.

"It puts us back to square one," says Fred Baron, a plaintiff's lawyer in Dallas who represents thousands of asbestos victims. "We're back to the old system of fierce litigation and huge litigation costs."

Bitter History

The history of asbestos litigation is a long and bitter one. The fiber was used widely as insulation for a century, until asbestos exposure was linked to cancer. The first lawsuit against an asbestos producer was filed in the 1950s, but plaintiffs didn't begin to win big until the 1980s. That's when juries, outraged by evidence that indicated the companies knew of the fiber's dangers long before alerting workers, began awarding millions of dollars in damages. Eventually, Manville Corp. and a half-dozen other concerns were forced to seek the protection of Chapter 11 bankruptcy proceedings.

But court was a crapshoot for both sides. Some victims won huge awards or managed to wring sizable settlements from asbestos producers; others got little or nothing. The only ones for whom the dice were always hot were the lawyers. Producers had retained 1,100 law

firms around the United States to defend them by the mid-1980s; thousands more lawyers specialized in representing victims.

Asbestos producers found themselves battling not only victims but also their own insurers as lawsuits multiplied. Some insurance companies reread the fine print in their policies and decided they weren't liable for the billions of dollars the asbestos concerns demanded to cover claims. Those disputes also ended up in court.

Declaring a Truce

As it was first conceived, the Asbestos Claims Facility was supposed to represent a truce among all the combatants. Its founders envisioned a one-stop settlement shop for claims, a system that would offer a faster, less costly, and more orderly way to resolve claims than in court. The facility even had the support of some of the most prominent plaintiffs' lawyers in the United States, who promised their cooperation if the asbestos concerns and the insurers settled their differences.

"What might have been . . . would have been wonderful," says Harry Wellington, who, as then dean of Yale Law School, helped organize the facility. "And it probably would have been advantageous to everybody."

Fifty companies joined, among them some of the biggest names in the asbestos and insurance industries: Aetna Life & Casualty, National Gypsum, Lloyd's of London, and U.S. Gypsum. Under terms, every member agreed to pay a portion of each claim based on the percentage it had historically paid, regardless of whether the claimant had been exposed to its product.

The facility succeeded in meeting some of its goals. Companies' legal bills dropped, in part because the number of law firms representing asbestos concerns was reduced to 55. Since it opened, the facility says, it has settled or tried 21,000 claims, paying out "substantially more" than $500 million to victims.

But ties to the plaintiffs' bar quickly became strained. Then members started to clash. Some wanted to settle claims quickly. Others, especially those that had limited insurance, wanted to delay. Further, some companies chafed at making payments to victims who hadn't been exposed to their products. The arguments got more and more heated as certain members edged closer to insolvency.

"Tyranny of the Minority"

Owens-Illinois, Louisiana-Pacific Corp.'s Fibreboard unit, and Pittsburgh-Corning Corp. led a dissident faction that sought to delay payouts. Though a minority, the group often prevailed, by sheer force of its representatives' personalities, according to other board members and facility executives.

"It was tyranny of the minority," recalls Lawrence Fitzpatrick, the facility's acting chief executive. "They managed to wear everyone down."

Complicating the situation was a sudden surge in new and, in the view of some members, questionable claims. Most of the early victims had worked directly with asbestos, fabricating or installing it. In recent years, thousands who had less exposure to the fiber—steelworkers and rubber workers, to name a few—also have sought compensation.

The claims sparked more dispute. Some members felt that the original formula for splitting the cost of claims among members didn't reflect their liability in the new cases.

Logjam of Claims

The result was a logjam of claims. Victims found themselves waiting months, even years, before their settlement demands were answered. Some never heard from the facility at all before dying of asbestos-related diseases.

R. Bruce Ryan, an industrial electrician from Steubenville, Ohio, was one of them. After years of exposure to asbestos, Mr. Ryan developed mesothelioma, an invariably fatal cancer of the lining of the lung. Thomas White, his lawyer, says the facility never responded to Mr. Ryan's first settlement demand of $750,000, made in June 1986.

A year later, and by then seriously ill, Mr. Ryan made a second settlement demand for $1.5 million. Mr. Ryan died last summer at age 49. "They never responded, even to say yes, no, or maybe," Mr. White says. (The facility concedes it didn't handle the claim in a "timely" way.)

The facility also outraged many by taking a hard line on the types of injuries for which it would offer settlements. It refused to settle cases filed by workers whose lungs had been scarred by asbestos exposure but who weren't yet disabled. Because some victims had won court awards for such injuries, others viewed the ruling as a declaration of war.

Fighting Back

It was as if the facility said, " 'We don't care what the law is. We don't care what the history is,' " says Gene Locks, a plaintiffs' lawyer in Philadelphia. (The facility admits the ruling was "unreasonable." It now allows victims who show early signs of disease to file claims, though they still don't get paid until they are disabled.)

Victims fought back—in court. In some jurisdictions, their plight caught the attention of sympathetic judges. To heighten pressure on the facility to settle claims, some judges scheduled dozens of asbestos lawsuits for trial each month, knowing the facility couldn't risk taking so many cases to trial simultaneously.

The tactic seemed to work, further encouraging lawyers to race to the courthouse. In retrospect, Mr. Fitzpatrick concedes, the facility's tough stance on settling cases undermined its mission to move the asbestos fray out of the courts. "It's a philosophy that shoots you in the foot in the long term," he says.

Bullying Claims Adjusters

Internal strife at the facility further heightened tension. "If I come in with 1,000 cases settled," Mr. Fitzpatrick, the facility's third chief executive, says, "half the board would say, 'Why didn't you settle 2,000?' The other half would say, 'What, are you crazy? You shouldn't settle more than 500.' "

Mr. Fitzpatrick also says some directors tried to bully claims adjusters into disapproving large settlements. In some cases, he says, directors threatened to fire adjusters if they wouldn't comply. The meddling got so disruptive that the board eventually had to pass a resolution ordering directors to leave the staff alone.

Several asbestos producers announced they would drop out of the facility late last year. In February, Eagle-Picher quit, but, unlike the others, it refused to pay on pending claims. It says only about one third of the $63.1 million it paid to settle claims through the facility last year was covered by insurance. The company says it believes it can settle claims for less money by negotiating directly with victims and their lawyers.

The remaining members are trying to form a new settlement organization, but without the support of such big concerns and former members as Eagle-Picher and Owens-Corning Fiberglas, it is unlikely to have a significant impact.

Living Down a Disaster

The facility's collapse is a blow not just to those involved in the asbestos fray. It is also dismaying news for chemical manufacturers and others who face a rising tide of personal injury lawsuits over exposure to toxic substances. Those companies had looked to the facility as a model for resolving mass tort claims.

The failure also is a setback for the alternative dispute resolution movement, which advocates resolving cases out of court. Early on, proponents had hailed the facility as proof that the litigation explosion could be controlled. Eric Green, a Boston University law professor who advises companies on alternative dispute resolution, says: "We're going to be living down this disaster for a long time."

Source: *The Wall Street Journal*, June 7, 1988, pp. 1, 20. Reprinted by permission of *The Wall Street Journal*, © Dow Jones & Company, Inc. 1988. ALL RIGHTS RESERVED.

Questions

1. Robert Malott argues that Americans, more than Europeans and the Japanese, are willing to turn to the courts to resolve disputes. Assuming Malott is correct, what would explain that condition?
2. Based on your reading of the asbestos article, why did the Asbestos Claims Facility fail?

CHAPTER QUESTIONS

1. Are the flaws in our legal system of such magnitude that respect for the law is threatened? Explain.
2. According to Warren Avis, founder of Avis Rent-a-Car:

We've reached a point in this country where, in many instances, power has become more important than justice—not a matter of who is right, but of who has the most money, time, and the largest battery of lawyers to drag a case through the courts.[21]

> *a.* Should the rich be entitled to better legal representation, just as they have access to better food, better medical care, better education, and so on? Explain.
>
> *b.* Should we employ a nationwide legal services program sufficient to guarantee able legal aid to all? Explain.

3. A petitioner, a young, bearded, black male, was convicted in a South Carolina trial court of unlawful possession of marijuana. At trial, the petitioner's attorney had asked the judge to question the prospective jurors regarding their bias due to (1) race, (2) beards, and (3) pretrial publicity relating to the drug problem. The judge asked general questions regarding bias, but the petitioner's specific questions were not raised. The petitioner ultimately appealed his case to the U.S. Supreme Court.

> *a.* What constitutional law violation would you allege on behalf of the petitioner?
>
> *b.* Decide. See *Ham* v. *South Carolina,* 409 U.S. 524 (1973).

4. French correspondent Alain Clement, commenting on the role of lawyers in America:

Truly, American lawyers come as close to being a "ruling class" as is possible in a country too vast and varied to produce one. Since Franklin D. Roosevelt, each president has had around him lawyer-confidants, so that Congress and state legislatures are dominated—even if less so than before—by a majority who come from the bar.[22]

> *a.* Do you agree with Clement? Explain.
>
> *b.* If so, have lawyers earned their influence? Explain.

5. Clement also offered a partial explanation for Americans' increasing reliance on lawsuits to resolve their conflicts:

Diverse causes explain the growth of the contentious mood in America. One could be called the devaluing of the future. In 1911, the Russian political scientist Moise Ostrgorski wrote: "Confident of the future, Americans manifest a remarkable endurance to an unhappy present, a submissive patience that is willing to bargain about not only civic rights, but even the rights of man."[23]

> *a.* What does Clement mean?
>
> *b.* How do you explain our increased reliance on litigation?

6. Maintenance of our adversary system of justice sometimes compels lawyers to engage in practices that some consider unethical. Anne Strick relates one such situation.

Once upon a time, Williston, called by a colleague "Qne of the most distinguished and conscientious lawyers I or any man have ever known," was defending a client in a civil suit. In the course of trial, Williston discovered in his client's letter file material potentially damaging to the man's case. The opposition failed to demand the file; nor did Williston offer it. His client won. But, recounts Williston in his autobiography, the judge in announcing his decision made clear that his ruling was based in part on his belief in one critical fact: a fact Williston, through a letter from the file in his possession, knew to be unfounded.

Did Williston, that "most conscientious lawyer," speak up? Did he correct the Court's unfounded belief, the better to serve both truth and justice? He did not.

"Though," he wrote, "I had in front of me a letter which showed his [Honor's] error," Williston kept silent. Nor did he question the propriety of his behavior. For, said he, the lawyer "is not only not obliged to disclose unfavorable evidence, but it is a violation of his duty to his client if he does so."[24]

    a. Did Williston act properly? Explain.

    b. Should we turn to more cooperative, less combative, approaches to dispute resolution? Explain.

7. On July 5, 1884, four sailors were cast away from their ship in a storm 1,600 miles from the Cape of Good Hope. Their lifeboat contained neither water nor much food. On the 20th day of their ordeal, Dudley and Stevens, without the assistance or agreement of Brooks, cut the throat of the fourth sailor, a 17- or 18-year-old boy. They had not eaten since day 12. Water had been only occasionally available. At the time of the death, the men were probably about 1,000 miles from land. Prior to his death, the boy was lying helplessly in the bottom of the boat. The three surviving sailors ate the boy's remains for four days, at which point they were rescued by a passing boat. They were in a seriously weakened condition.

    a. Were Dudley and Stevens guilty of murder? Explain.

    b. Should Brooks have been charged with a crime for eating the boy's flesh? Explain. See *The Queen* v. *Dudley and Stephens,* 14 Queen's Bench Division 273 (1884).

8. Tompkins is a citizen of Pennsylvania. While walking on a railroad footpath in that state, he was struck by an object protruding from a passing freight train owned by the Erie Railroad Company, a New York corporation. Tompkins, by virtue of diversity of citizenship, filed a negligence suit against Erie in a New York federal court. Erie argued for the application of Pennsylvania common law, in which case Tompkins would have been treated as a trespasser. Tompkins argued that the absence of a Pennsylvania statute addressing the topic meant that federal common law had to be applied to the case. Should the court apply the relevant Pennsylvania state law, or should the federal court be free to exercise its independent judgment about what the common law of the state is or should be? See *Erie Railroad* v. *Tompkins,* 304 U.S. 64 (1938).

9. Burger King conducts a franchise, fast-food operation from its Miami, Florida, headquarters. John Rudzewicz and a partner, both residents of Michigan, secured a Burger King franchise in Michigan. Subsequently, the franchisees allegedly fell behind in payments, and after negotiations failed, Burger King ordered the franchisees to vacate the premises. They declined to do so, and continued to operate the franchise. Burger King brought suit in a federal district court in Florida. The defendant franchisees argued that the Florida court did not have personal jurisdiction over them because they were Michigan residents and because the claim did not arise in Florida. However, the district court found the defendants to be subject to the Florida long-arm statute, which extends jurisdiction to "[a]ny person, whether or not a citizen or resident of this state" who, "[b]reach[es] a contract in this state by failing to perform acts required by the contract to be performed in this state." The franchise contract provided for governance of the relationship by Florida law. Policy was set in Miami, although day-to-day supervision was managed through various district offices. The case ultimately reached the U.S. Supreme Court.

   a. What constitutional argument would you raise on behalf of the defendant franchisees?

   b. Decide. See *Burger King Corp.* v. *Rudzewicz,* 471 U.S. 462 (1985).

10. Refer again to "Incivility in Court as Lawyers Strive to Win." Between X and Y, who *should* win? Why? What dispute resolution procedure would you recommend for determining the outcome? Why?

NOTES

1. Oliver Wendell Holmes, *Collected Legal Papers* (New York: Harcourt Brace Jovanovich, 1920), p. 173.
2. Benjamin Cardozo, *The Growth of Law* (New Haven, Conn.: Yale University Press, 1924), p. 52.
3. Max Weber, *Law in Economy and Society,* ed. Max Rheinstein (Cambridge, Mass.: Harvard University Press, 1954), p. 5.
4. Bronislaw Malinowski, *Crime and Custom in Savage Society* (Patterson, N.J.: Littlefield, 1959), p. 55. Originally published in 1926.
5. Roscoe Pound, "A Survey of Social Interest," *Harvard Law Review* 57 (1943), pp. 1, 39.
6. Richard Quinney, "The Ideology of Law: Notes for a Radical Alternative to Legal Oppression," *Issues in Criminology* 7 (1972), p. 1, as reported in Charles E. Reasons and Robert M. Rich, *The Sociology of Law: A Conflict Perspective* (Toronto: Butterworth, 1978), p. 42.
7. Terence M. Cannon, "Law and Order in America," in *Up against the American Myth,* ed. Tom Christoffel, David Finkelhor, and Dan Gilbarg (New York: Holt, Rinehart & Winston, 1970), pp. 348–49, as quoted in Frederick Sturdivant, *Business and Society—A Managerial Approach,* rev. ed. (Homewood, Ill.: Richard D. Irwin, 1981), p. 52.

8. John Rawls, *A Theory of Justice* (Boston: Belknap Press, 1971), pp. 3–4.

9. Roger Simon, "Don't Say !?*!* in Chicago," *Washington Post,* October 12, 1980, p. F-12.

10. *Sierra Club* v. *Morton,* 405 U.S. 727.

11. The remarks to this point in this section owe much to Mary Kay Kane, *Civil Procedure in a Nutshell* (St. Paul, Minn.: West Publishing, 1979), pp. 226–37.

12. Amitai Etzioni, "Science: Threatening the Jury," *Washington Post,* May 26, 1974, p. C-3.

13. Howard Rudnitsky with Jeff Blyskal, "Getting into Those Deep Pockets," *Forbes,* August 4, 1980, p. 59.

14. "Lawsuits since 1970 Triple in Federal Courts," *The New York Times,* July 16, 1987, p. 11.

15. Patricia B. Gray, "Law Firms' Big Fee Hikes Reflect Higher Pay and Booming Business," *The Wall Street Journal,* March 19, 1987, p. 35.

16. Richard A. Salem, "The Alternative Dispute Resolution Movement: An Overview," *Arbitration Journal* 40, no. 3 (September 1985), p. 3.

17. Stephen B. Goldberg, Eric D. Green, and Frank E. A. Sander, *Dispute Resolution* (Boston: Little, Brown, 1985), p. 19.

18. Marc Galanter, "Reading the Landscape of Disputes: What We Know and Don't Know (and Think We Know) about Our Allegedly Contentious and Litigious Society," *UCLA Law Review* 31 (1983), p. 4.

19. Beverly Watkins, "Unusual Sideline for Maine Academics: Helping People Settle Their Arguments," *The Chronicle of Higher Education* 29, no. 22 (February 13, 1985), p. 41.

20. "Business Saves Big Money with 'Minitrial,'" *Business Week,* October 13, 1980, p. 168.

21. Warren Avis, "Court before Justice," *The New York Times,* July 21, 1978, p. 25.

22. Alain Clement, "Judges, Lawyers Are the Ruling Class in U.S. Society," *Washington Post,* August 22, 1980, p. A-25.

23. Ibid.

24. Anne Strick, *Injustice for All* (New York: Penguin Books, 1978), p. 123.

Chapter 5

Constitutional Law and the Bill of Rights

We the people of the United States, in order to form a more perfect union, establish justice, insure domestic tranquility, provide for the common defense, promote the general welfare, and secure the blessings of liberty to ourselves and our posterity, do ordain and establish this Constitution for the United States of America.

Those words, the Preamble to our Constitution, summarize the lofty goals of America's most central and superior law. It is both inspiring and touching to reflect on the idealism embodied in those words, and one must marvel a bit at the strength that causes us all, 200 years later, to continue to be guided by the vision of the creators of the Constitution. It is a remarkable document. Hence we will dwell on its subtleties for a time.

CREATING A CONSTITUTION

The reader may recall that the Constitution grew out of the Articles of Confederation as enacted by Congress in 1778. The Articles contemplated a "firm league of friendship," but each state was to maintain its "sovereignty, freedom and independence." The Articles soon proved faulty.

Seven years of war had nearly bankrupted the colonies, and both credit and currency were almost worthless. The supposedly united states quarreled fiercely over economic resources, such as oyster-harvesting rights in Chesapeake Bay, and Congress had no real power to keep the peace.[1]

Thus, as described in the following article, the Constitutional Convention began in Philadelphia on May 25, 1787.

HOW THE DEED WAS DONE

Otto Friedrich

Actually the 55 delegates who concocted that remarkable Constitution over the course of a long, hot summer had no real mandate to do what they did. They had gathered only to consider some possible improvements in the Articles of Confederation. . . . Neither Congress nor anyone else had authorized the delegates to invent a whole new political system.

* * * * *

[T]he basic issue was the comparative voting strengths of large states and small. Most of the big states demanded a powerful national government; the small ones feared coercion and insisted on states' rights. And neither side put much trust in the other.

* * * * *

As with many battles that have long since been won, it is hard now to realize how near the delegates came to failure, an event that might have led to the breakdown of the fledgling confederation, even to the reappearance of European forces eager to recapture their lost lands.

* * * * *

It took 60 ballots before the convention could agree on how to pick a president. It voted five times to have the president appointed by Congress and voted once against that. It voted repeatedly on whether a president could be impeached and how long his term should be and whether he must be native born.

The delegates also avoided settling some things, like the future of slavery.

* * * * *

With the coming of September, the framers could finally see the beginning of the end. The Pennsylvania state legislature had reconvened, and it needed the chamber where the Constitutional Convention was meeting. The dwindling collection of delegates, a dozen of whom had already gone home for one reason or another, picked a five-man Committee of Style and Arrangement to undertake the actual writing of the Constitution.

Although they were not supposed to change the substance of what the convention had so far decided, it was hardly accidental that all five were strong-government advocates, and that one of them was [James] Madison [of Virginia].

When the committee presented its constitution on September 12, the delegates eagerly began trying to change things all over again, in ways large and small. [George] Mason of Virginia declared for the first time that summer that there should be a bill of rights. He was voted down by 10 states to none.

The changing continued right up to the scheduled closing day, September 17, but then it was finally time to sign. Three of the delegates present still had objections and refused, among them Virginia's Governor [Edmund] Randolph. The rest, however, generally subscribed to [Benjamin] Franklin's [of Pennsylvania] declaration that although he too still had doubts and reservations, "I consent, sir, to this Constitution because I expect not better."

Still ahead lay nine months of bitter debate before the necessary nine states ratified what had been written that summer in Philadelphia. Ahead lay the creation of the Bill of Rights.

Source: *Time*, July 6, 1987, pp. 58–61. Copyright 1987 Time Inc. All rights reserved. Reprinted by permission from *Time*.

STRUCTURE AND PURPOSE

The Constitution is reprinted for you in Appendix A. We now take some time to review its structure.

The Preamble identifies certain goals for our society, such as unity (among the various states), justice, domestic tranquility (peace), defense from outsiders, an increasing general welfare, and liberty. Article I sets up Congress and enumerates its powers. Article I, Section 8, Clause 3 is particularly important because it gives Congress the power to regulate commerce (the Commerce Clause). Article II sets up the executive branch, headed by the president, while Article III establishes the court system. Articles IV and VI, as well as the Fourteenth Amendment, address the relationship between the federal government and the states. Article VI provides in paragraph 2 (the Supremacy Clause) for the supremacy of federal law over state law. Article V provides for amendments to the Constitution. The first 10 amendments, known as the Bill of Rights, were ratified by the states and put into effect in 1791. The remaining 16 amendments (Eleven through Twenty-six) were adopted at various times from 1798 through 1971.

From this review we can see that the Constitution serves a number of broad roles:

1. "It establishes a national government."
2. "It controls the relationship between the national government and the government of the states."
3. "It defines and preserves personal liberty."
4. "It contains provisions to enable the government to perpetuate itself."[2]

In establishing a national government, the Constitution sets up three branches and provides mechanisms for them to check and balance each other. Even today these checks and balances have a propensity for stirring national debate, as can be seen by President Reagan's repeated attempts in the last year of his presidency to appoint a replacement to the U.S. Supreme Court for the vacancy left by Justice Lewis F. Powell, Jr. Reagan first nominated Judge Robert H. Bork (of the U.S. Court of Appeals for the District of Columbia); but, the Constitution requires the "advise and consent" of the Senate to confirm the president's nominations, and that was not given. Then Reagan nominated Douglas Ginsburg, who withdrew his nomination when the Senate hearings turned rocky. Finally, months after Reagan's first nomination, the Senate confirmed Judge Anthony Kennedy.

Likewise, these checks and balances periodically come up for review before the Supreme Court. For example, in a 1983 decision, which Justice White referred to as "probably the most important case that the Court has handed down in many years," the Court struck down the use of a one-house legislative veto to impose congressional restraint on executive action.[3] The veto was a favorite strategy (used in nearly 200 federal statutes) in forcing the various federal regulatory agencies to comply with the will of Congress, without the necessity of passing new legislation and submitting it to the president for signing. The decision is frequently cited as an enormous boost for presidential authority.

Another role of the Constitution is to balance the central federal authority with dispersed state power. As established by the Constitution, the federal government holds only those powers granted to it by the states. The people via the states hold all of those powers not expressly denied them by the Constitution.

It is also essential to recall that the Constitution was enacted to protect the citizenry from the government. The Constitution does not protect the citizenry from purely private concentrations of power, such as large corporations. In fact, corporations themselves are often entitled to the protections of the Constitution.

Furthermore, the Constitution originally only protected the personal rights in the Bill of Rights from encroachment by the federal government. However, under a process known as the *incorporation doctrine* or *absorption doctrine,* the Supreme Court has interpreted the Due Process Clause of the Fourteenth Amendment, which is directed at the states, to incorporate or absorb those fundamental liberties against intrusion by state government as well.

A DOCUMENT OF CHANGE

The Constitution defines and organizes the government. It is an essential guidepost for the maintenance of order, but the Constitution is much more than the whole of its enormous mechanical functions. It is an expression of the values of the nation. The Constitution embodies our need for strength and certainty in a confused existence, but we recognize the need for change, and we acknowledge the power of the Supreme Court to interpret the Constitution in a manner that fairly accommodates the needs of a constantly changing America. Our constitutional law is under stress from the demands of a complex society, but the system continues to display remarkable adaptability and fortitude that stand as tributes to our legal system and, by extension, to us.

But the debate goes on.

To [former] Attorney General Edwin Meese, the courts strayed too far. The Supreme Court, he complain[ed], made the Constitution ''a draft horse that would pull the American people toward some . . . judicially created concept of the ideal world.'' This ''radical departure,'' he [said], may be corrected only by returning to the Constitution's ''original intention.''

But to many legal experts, Mr. Meese's arguments [were] aimed more at pushing the Reagan administration's social and political agenda than at promoting constitutional purity. The main targets on his hit list [were] the Court's decisions favoring affirmative action and abortion rights and barring prayer in the public schools.[4]

The article that follows captures some of the flavor of the formulation of constitutional policy by the Supreme Court and gives the reader a sense of both the profound impact of the Constitution and the constrained but necessarily evolutionary nature of Supreme Court decision making.

NO WAY TO INTERPRET THE CONSTITUTION

Irving R. Kaufman

We are . . . likely to see a continuation of . . . debate over the proper role of the judiciary in interpreting the Constitution.

Since it appears that judicial review is here to stay, some who remain troubled by it urge that at the very least the enterprise of judges deciding constitutional questions should be limited to discovering the intent of the framers. This approach is advanced to reduce judicial discretion, to increase certainty, and to assure that the dispute at hand will be resolved by reference to the document rather than the judges' personal predilections.

I regard reliance on original intent to be a largely specious mode of interpretation. I often find it instructive to consult the framers when I am called upon to interpret the Constitution, but it is the beginning of my inquiry, not the end. For not only is the quest for "intent" fraught with obstacles of a practical nature—notably that the framers plainly never foresaw most of the problems that bedevil the courts today—it may also be more undemocratic than competing methods of construing the Constitution.

If the search for "intent" sums up the constitutional enterprise, then current generations are bound not merely by general language but by specific conceptions frozen in time by men long dead.

* * * * *

The open-textured nature of most of the vital clauses of the Constitution signifies that the drafters expected future generations to adapt the language to modern circumstances, not to conduct judicial autopsies into the minds of the framers. When the Founding Fathers talked about due process, equal protection, and freedom of speech and religion, they were embracing general principles, not specific solutions.

Another problem of the "original intent" approach is that it fails to deliver on its promise to constrain judicial discretion. In imagining that there is a discrete, discoverable intent behind even the most general constitutional phrases, courts are more apt to be led astray than when they employ less backward-looking approaches.

* * * * *

Even if we could agree that original intent is the true source of constitutional meaning, we would be no better off. No complete and accurate record exists today to tell us what the founders thought. Even [James] Madison's notes, the best record we have of the convention, were far from complete and never intended to serve as an authoritative record.

* * * * *

Yet even if we had a complete transcript of the proceedings, are there any so naive to think that we could harvest definitive answers? As with contemporary Congressional debates, we would encounter unresolved conflict, unexpected omissions and abundant ambiguity.

* * * * *

Another question to which I have never found a satisfactory answer is: Whose "intent" should we be trying to discover? The Constitution and amendments were ratified by state legislatures or conventions, and the ratifiers were more than 1,600 in number. Should we not consult the historian—or more accurately, the oracle—to see what they thought?

More to the point, if the Constitution is truly a document of the people, why not attempt to find out what the electorate thought? Certainly, if "original intent" is a mechanism designed to reconcile judicial review with democratic theory, as its proponents maintain, it makes little sense to preoccupy ourselves with the ideas of the privileged few who had a hand in drafting the Constitution. Searching for the intent of the ratifiers or the people, however, is even more of a wild goose chase—particularly since the Constitution has since been thoroughly transformed as a result of the amendments made after the Civil War.

In short, while judges should make every effort to learn what the framers thought, such a quest cannot be expected to produce definitive answers. The framers' legacy to modern times is the language and spirit of the Constitution, not the conflicting and dated conceptions that may lay beneath that language.

Source: *The New York Times,* January 2, 1987, p. 25. Copyright © 1987 by The New York Times Company. Reprinted by permission.

Questions

1. Refer again to the Friedrich article. In light of what it presents as the circumstances of the Constitutional Convention, which position do you favor in the Meese versus Kaufman controversy over original intent?
2. Referring again to the Constitutional Convention:

> And though they displayed powerful individual differences in both philosophy and temperament, they showed important similarities too. Of the 55 delegates from 12 states (Rhode Island refused to participate), more than half were lawyers and 8 were judges; another quarter were large landowners. All of them had held public office, 42 as congressmen and 7 as governors. And they were young. Madison, for example, was 36; Hamilton was 32. There were no women, of course, not to mention blacks or Indians.[5]

What does this add to the original intent debate?

THE CONSTITUTION AND BUSINESS GENERALLY

The Constitution profoundly shapes the practice of American business. The Constitution embodies and supports America's belief in capitalism.

Indeed, it has been argued that the economic self-interest of the framers had a persuasive impact on the principles embodied in the Constitution. Article 1, Section 8, Clause 3 of the Constitution (the Commerce Clause) affords Congress enormous authority in regulating business. Further discussion of the Commerce Clause will be deferred to Chapter 6. This chapter will look at some of the key intersections between the business community and the Bill of Rights. When we think of the Bill of Rights, corporations ordinarily do not come to mind. However, extensive litigation in recent years serves ample notice that the relationship between the corporate "person" and the fundamental freedoms is both important and murky. We hope the reader will aquire an appreciation for the complex tensions that arise as the government attempts to identify and ensure individual rights while seeking to defend and promote both U.S. commerce and the rights of American business.

THE FIRST AMENDMENT

> Congress shall make no law respecting an establishment of religion, or prohibiting the free exercise thereof; or abridging the freedom of speech, or the press; or the right of the people peaceably to assemble, and to petition the Government for a redress of grievances.

These few words constitute one of the most powerful and noble utterances in recorded history. The freedoms guaranteed in the First Amendment reflect the basic beliefs of American life. Much of the magnificence that we often associate with America is embodied in the protections of the First Amendment. After 200 years it remains a source of wonder that our vast bureaucratic system and our approximately 250 million independent citizens continue to rely on that sentence as a cornerstone of our way of life.

I. Freedom of Religion

The First Amendment clearly forbids the establishment of an official state religion. Government may not give preference to one religion over another. The religion clause is designed to separate church and state. However, the precise boundary of that separation has become one of the more contentious social issues in contemporary life.

Schools. President Reagan made the voluntary school prayer question a centerpiece of his social agenda. Of course, students may pray at their own discretion so long as they avoid disturbing the academic setting. The issue is one of whether government-sponsored, yet voluntary, prayer should be permissible.

In 1962 the Supreme Court struck down as unconstitutional the following nondenominational school prayer: "Almighty God, we acknowledge our dependence upon Thee, and we beg Thy blessings upon us, our parents, our teachers, and our Country."[6] The State Board of Regents of New York had recommended that the prayer be offered aloud at the beginning of each school day. Similarly unconstitutional is the reading of verses from the Bible.[7] The most recent decisions appear to have been significant setbacks for those supporting prayer in the schools. In 1985 the Supreme Court by a 6–3 margin struck down an Alabama statute authorizing a one-minute period of silence in the public schools "for meditation or voluntary prayer." The Court held that the statute violated the First Amendment in that the legislature's motive was the endorsement of religion and that the Establishment Clause protects individual freedom of conscience "to select any religious faith or none at all."[8]

The intersection of the First Amendment, religion, and schools also arises over curricular matters. In 1968 the Supreme Court struck down a state statute forbidding the teaching of evolution in public schools.[9] Then, in 1987, the Court struck down a Louisiana law requiring public school teachers to balance the teaching of evolution with the teaching of "creation science."[10] The Court said the statute violated the First Amendment because it required the teaching of a set of essentially religious beliefs.

Blue Laws.   Freedom of religion as a business issue is less common and ordinarily less volatile than educational issues, but some provocative and important questions have arisen. Statistically most notable are the many and continuing conflicts over the so-called *blue laws,* those statutes and ordinances limiting or prohibiting the conduct of business on Sundays. Blue laws are rather common about the nation. While those laws are often clearly inspired by religious considerations, the courts have rather consistently affirmed their constitutionality. The blue laws cause inconvenience and economic loss to those of religious sects not practicing their Sabbath on Sunday and to those who do not recognize a Sabbath. In the leading case of *McGowan* v. *Maryland*[11] the Supreme Court upheld the constitutionality of a blue law on the grounds that the primary purpose of the law was the furtherance of a legitimate social goal (in this case, provision of a uniform day of rest) rather than a furtherance of religious goals. The Court felt that the practice of treating Sunday as a religious holiday had fallen into disuse.

The Amish.   Minority religious sects often must struggle to maintain their principles in the face of the general will of the masses. Struggles between "Christian schools" and states seeking to apply minimum educational standards regarding such things as teachers' educational credentials and curricular content have been commonplace in recent years. In an important Supreme Court decision, an Amish sect was able to establish the principle that religious belief can, under some circumstances, justify refusal to meet state compulsory education requirements.[12] However, as described in the following article, one Amish citizen has been less successful in his struggle to maintain his business, honor his religious principles, and comply with the law of the land.

IN PENNSYLVANIA: THE AMISH AND THE LAW

Dean Brelis

There are only two kinds of people in northwestern Pennsylvania's Lawrence County—the "English" and the "Dutch." The first category includes nearly everybody—Wasps, Italians, Jews, Irish, blacks. The second category covers only the Amish. To say that the Amish are different is merely to state the obvious. They are followers of a sect that originated in Switzerland back in the 17th century and, in search of religious freedom, fled to England and Holland in the 18th century and moved to America in the 19th. In this day of home computers and space travel, the Amish eschew zippers as decadent, electricity as unnecessary, and flush toilets as wasteful. They forgo the automobile in favor of sleek trotters and canvas-topped carriages of hickory wood. They use fine, sturdy workhorses to spread manure and plow their fields, which is what they are doing these days as spring spreads over their green country.

Ed Lee is one of 5,000 Amish in Lawrence County. He differs from his neighbors for reasons other than the fact that he is not a Byler or a Swatzentrooper or a Hofstader or the bearer of some other traditionally Amish name. Lee is different because he has done something that the Amish rarely do. He has ended up in court. His offense: refusing to pay Social Security taxes for 30 Amish men who worked for

him over an eight-year period as carpenters, building houses. The Internal Revenue Service claimed that he owed the government $27,000. Lee challenged the IRS ruling in federal district court in Pittsburgh. To prove his good intentions, he offered his farm as security in the event he lost. As it turned out, he won, but the IRS then appealed to the Supreme Court.

Lee's refusal to pay Social Security taxes did not stem from any disrespect for the law. He personally had no quarrel with the Social Security system, and believes it is fine—for those who need it. But it is a tenet of their religious belief that the Amish people should take care of their own. They do not collect unemployment or welfare benefits. They do not buy insurance of any kind. By an act of Congress in 1965, self-employed Amish men are exempt from paying Social Security taxes on religious grounds. But the act does not cover Amish men who work for Amish employers. It is this apparent inconsistency that has propelled Lee into the courts.

The Supreme Court, which ruled on Lee's case in February, upheld the IRS. "A comprehensive national Social Security system providing for voluntary participation would be almost a contradiction in terms and difficult, if not impossible, to administer," wrote Chief Justice Warren Burger in the unanimous opinion.

Faced with the loss of his farm, Lee might have bowed to federal *force majeure* at this point. Instead, aided by two non-Amish friends, he is quietly carrying on his fight. Francis X. Caiazza, 46, a local lawyer who had represented Lee before the Supreme Court, was elected a judge the day after arguing the case and is now prevented by law from providing more than moral support. "Amish do not break laws; they are not seen in the courts," Caiazza says. "The Amish care about reason, law, and order, and they are a God-fearing people. This wasn't just another case. It involves a sincere belief in religious freedom and religious rights. We lost the case in the Supreme Court, but I still feel the religious argument should have been the bottom line."

Lee's other friend, Robert Gardner, 43, a high school teacher, is urging another tactic. Aided by hundreds of "English" volunteers, he has collected upwards of 10,000 signatures and hopes to get 10,000 more on petitions urging Congress to enact a law exempting all Amish from paying for Social Security. "The Amish," he says, "are not a fly-by-night religion, just

formed to avoid taxes. Legislation already exists which exempts an Amish individual from paying Social Security taxes when he is self-employed. It should be extended to cover Amish workers on the job for an Amish employer."

Amish customs, Gardner argues, constitute a "built-in form of Social Security." Forcing the Amish to pay Social Security cuts at the heart of their religion, he maintains. . . .

The predicament is something that Lee ponders as he sits by the coal stove in the kitchen of his neat, sturdy farmhouse. His feet are covered with thick blue socks; the Amish remove their shoes before entering the home. His blue eyes are gentle behind sensible, old-fashioned glasses, his beard is appropriately patriarchal, his voice surprisingly soft. "I'm a man who wakes every morning and thanks God for what is," Lee says. "I believe that the government of the United States is fair and just. It is not the Amish habit to be in confrontation; we avoid it. So it was with great difficulty and much prayer that I took this on." . . .

Questions

1. Do you agree with Ed Lee that paying social security taxes for his employees prohibits him from freely exercising his religion? Explain.
2. Should all conscientious objectors be exempt from paying the portion of their taxes used for national defense? Explain.
3. A Seventh Day Adventist was discharged by her employer when she refused to work on Saturday. Those of her faith celebrate the Sabbath on Saturday. She sought unemployment compensation, but the South Carolina Employment Security Commission denied her petition. The commission ruled that she had failed, without good cause, "to accept available work when offered." She carried an appeal to the Supreme Court. How would you rule? Explain. See *Sherbert* v. *Verner*, 374 U.S. 398 (1963).
4. For purposes of applying the First Amendment, how should "religion" be defined? That is, how do we tell the difference between a cult and a religion . . . or do we?

II. Freedom of Speech

None of the remarkable freedoms guaranteed by the Constitution receives greater respect from the judiciary than the right to free expression. And so it should be. Freedom of speech is the primary guarantor of the American approach to life. In particular, Americans believe the free expression of ideas is the most likely path to finding the best of ideas. We believe in a marketplace of ideas just as we believe in a marketplace of goods. So freedom of speech is central to self-respect, to political freedom, and to the maximization of wisdom.

> The freedom of speech and of the press guaranteed by the Constitution embraces at least the liberty to discuss publicly and truthfully all matters of public concern without previous restraint or fear of subsequent punishment . . . . Freedom of discussion, if it would fulfill its historic function in this nation, must embrace all issues about which information is needed or appropriate to enable the members of society to cope with the exigencies of their period.[13]

Freedom of speech is not an absolute. We cannot, for example, utter obscenities at will, yell "fire" in a crowded theatre, or make slanderous statements about another. Interpretation of the very broad bounds of freedom of speech has led to some of the more interesting decisions in judicial history. For example, nonverbal actions expressive of an idea have been protected, such as the wearing of black armbands at school as a protest against the Vietnam War where no evidence of disruption was offered.[14] Similarly, the Court accorded First Amendment protection to a display from an apartment on private property of the American flag flying upside down with peace symbols attached.[15]

Corporations, of course, are not natural persons. Instead, as expressed so eloquently by Chief Justice Marshall in the *Dartmouth College* case of 1819, the corporation is an "artificial being, invisible, intangible, and existing only in contemplation of law." Are the expressions of artificial beings accorded constitutional protection equivalent to that of a person? The question has become increasingly important in recent years as corporations have taken a much more active role in public affairs.

Corporate Political Speech.   Corporations have rapidly established themselves in a critical place in the political process. To some, that development is as it should be. It is argued that corporations should be able to defend their stake in American life, and presumably the marketplace of ideas profits from a fuller dialogue. To others, corporations, with their enormous resources, are a threat to the democratic process. The fear is that the corporate view, supported by extraordinary wealth and power, may drown out other opinions. (See Chapter 3 for a more complete discussion.) Paid corporate expressions on public issues are often labeled *advocacy advertising*. The Johnson & Higgins ad and *Consolidated Edison* case illustrate and analyze the difficult question of the corporation's First Amendment rights.

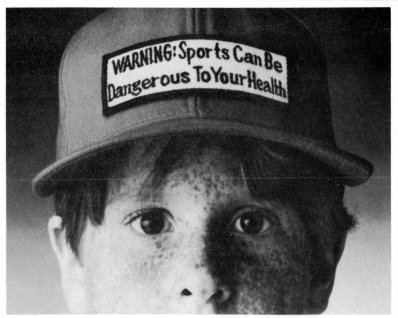

Is It Coming To This?

Once when you took the field you took your chances. Not anymore.

The courts have slipped a third strike past the venerable doctrine of "assumption of risk".

Judgments traditionally reserved for serious injury cases are hemorrhaging into claims from which organized athletics once were virtually immune.

Observes one leading specialist in sports-related law: "Participants have the attitude that someone should be forced to pay. They're suing for the slightest injury, regardless of fault."

One alarming result: at every level of sport, coaches, trainers, athletic directors—even volunteers—are at risk for failure to warn participants in detail of a sport's inherent dangers.

For municipalities and schools, this is an especially tough situation to handle. Court-cultivated expansion of the joint and several liability doctrine makes recreation departments and schools easy targets as "deep pockets" in injury suits.

Regardless of degree of fault, they may (and often do) wind up paying everything.

A return to the concept of genuine fault is clearly necessary. Many states recently have made substantial progress toward this goal by reforming their tort laws. Legislatures that have yet to act should be urged to do so.

The playing field must be level for everyone.

JOHNSON & HIGGINS

Consulting on a lot more than insurance.

RISK AND INSURANCE MANAGEMENT SERVICES: HUMAN RESOURCE AND ACTUARIAL CONSULTING THROUGHOUT THE WORLD.

Source: Used with permission from Johnson & Higgins.

CONSOLIDATED EDISON COMPANY OF NEW YORK, INC. V. PUBLIC SERVICE COMMISSION OF NEW YORK
447 U.S. 530 (1980)

Justice Powell

The question in this case is whether the First Amendment, as incorporated by the Fourteenth Amendment, is violated by an order of the Public Service Commission of the State of New York that prohibits the inclusion in monthly electric bills of inserts discussing controversial issues of public policy.

I

The Consolidated Edison Company of New York, appellant in this case, placed written material entitled "Independence Is Still a Goal, and Nuclear Power Is Needed to Win the Battle" in its January 1976 billing envelope. The bill insert stated Consolidated Edison's views on "the benefits of nuclear power," saying that they "far outweigh any potential risk" and that nuclear power plants are safe, economical, and clean. . . .The utility also contended that increased usage of nuclear energy would further this country's independence from foreign energy sources.

In March 1976, the Natural Resources Defense Council, Inc. (NRDC), requested Consolidated Edison to enclose a rebuttal prepared by NRDC in its next billing envelope. . . .When Consolidated Edison refused, NRDC asked the Public Service Commission of the State of New York to open Consolidated Edison's billing envelopes to contrasting views on controversial issues of public importance. . . .

On February 17, 1977, the Commission, appellee here, denied NRDC's request, but prohibited "utilities from using bill inserts to discuss political matters, including the desirability of future development of nuclear power.". . . The Commission concluded that Consolidated Edison customers who receive bills containing inserts are a captive audience of diverse views who should not be subjected to the utility's beliefs. Accordingly, the Commission barred utility companies from including bill inserts that express "their opinions or viewpoints on controversial issues of public policy." . . .The Commission did not, however, bar utilities from sending bill inserts discussing topics that are not "controversial issues of public policy." The Commission later denied petitions for rehearing filed by Consolidated Edison and other utilities. . . .

Consolidated Edison sought review of the Commission's order in the New York state courts. The State Supreme Court, Special Term, held the order unconstitutional. . . . But the State Supreme Court, Appellate Division, reversed, . . . and the New York Court of Appeals affirmed that judgment. . . .The Court of Appeals held that the order did not violate the Constitution because it was a valid time, place, and manner regulation designed to protect the privacy of Consolidated Edison's customers. . . .We noted probable jurisdiction. . . .We reverse.

II

The restriction on bill inserts cannot be upheld on the ground that Consolidated Edison is not entitled to freedom of speech. In *First National Bank of Boston* v. *Bellotti,* 435 U.S. 765 (1978), we rejected the contention that a State may confine corporate speech to specified issues. That decision recognized that "[t]he inherent worth of the speech in terms of its capacity for informing the public does not depend upon the identity of its source, whether corporation, association, union, or individual.". . . Because the state action limited protected speech, we concluded that the regulation could not stand absent a showing of a compelling state interest. . . .

The First and Fourteenth Amendments guarantee that no State shall "abridg[e] the freedom of speech." . . . Freedom of speech is "indispensable to the discovery and spread of political truth," . . . and "the best test of truth is the power of the thought to get itself accepted in the competition of the market. . . ." The First and Fourteenth Amendments remove "governmental restraints from the arena of public discussion, putting the decision as to what views shall be voiced largely into the hands of each of us, in the hope that use of such freedom will ultimately produce a more capable citizenry and more perfect polity. . . ."

This court has emphasized that the First Amendment "embraces at the least the liberty to discuss publicly and truthfully all matters of public concern. . . ." In the mailing that triggered the regulation at issue, Consolidated Edison advocated the use of nuclear power. The Commission has limited the means by which Consolidated Edison may participate in the public debate on this question and other controversial issues of national interest and importance. Thus, the Commission's prohibition of discussion of controversial issues strikes at the heart of the freedom to speak.

III

The Commission's ban on bill inserts is not, of course, invalid merely because it imposes a limitation upon speech. . . . We must consider whether the State can demonstrate that its regulation is constitutionally permissible. The Commission's arguments require us to consider three theories that might justify the state action. We must determine whether the prohibition is (1) a reasonable time, place, or manner restriction, (2) a permissible subject-matter regulation, or (3) a narrowly tailored means of serving a compelling state interest.

A

This Court has recognized the validity of reasonable time, place, or manner regulations that serve a significant governmental interest and leave ample alternative channels for communication. . . .

A restriction that regulates only the time, place, or manner of speech may be imposed so long as it is reasonable. But when regulation is based on the content of speech, governmental action must be scrutinized more carefully to ensure that communication has not been prohibited "merely because public officials disapprove the speaker's views." . . . As a consequence, we have emphasized that time, place, and manner regulations must be "applicable to all speech irrespective of content.". . .

The Commission does not pretend that its action is unrelated to the content or subject matter of bill inserts. Indeed, it has undertaken to suppress certain bill inserts precisely because they address controversial issues of public policy. The Commission allows inserts that present information to consumers on certain subjects, such as energy conservation measures, but it forbids the use of inserts that discuss public controversies. The Commission, with commendable candor, justifies its ban on the ground that consumers will benefit from receiving "useful" information, but not from the prohibited information. . . . The Commission's own rationale demonstrates that its action cannot be upheld as a content-neutral time, place, or manner regulation.

B

The Commission next argues that its order is acceptable because it applies to all discussion of nuclear power, whether pro or con, in bill inserts. The prohibition, the Commission contends, is related to subject matter rather than to the views of a particular speaker. Because the regulation does not favor either side of a political controversy, the Commission asserts that it does not unconstitutionally suppress freedom of speech.

The First Amendment's hostility to content-based regulation extends not only to restrictions on particular viewpoints, but also to prohibition of public discussion of an entire topic. As a general matter, "the First Amendment means that government has no power to restrict expression because of its message, its ideas, its subject matter, or its content." . . .

Nevertheless, governmental regulation based on subject matter has been approved in narrow circumstances. . . .

* * * * *

The analysis of *Greer* and *Lehman* is not applicable to the Commission's regulation of bill inserts. In both cases, a private party asserted a right of access to public facilities. Consolidated Edison has not asked to use the offices of the Commission as a forum from which to promulgate its views. Rather, it seeks merely to utilize its own billing envelopes to promulgate its views on controversial issues of public policy. . . .

C

Where a government restricts the speech of a private person, the state action may be sustained only if the government can show that the regulation is a precisely drawn means of serving a compelling state interest. . . . The Commission argues finally that its prohibition is necessary (1) to avoid forcing Consolidated Edison's views on a captive audience, (2) to allocate limited resources in the public interest, and (3) to ensure that ratepayers do not subsidize the cost of the bill inserts.

* * * * *

Even if a short exposure to Consolidated Edison's views may offend the sensibilities of some consumers, the ability of government "to shut off discourse solely to protect others from hearing it [is] dependent upon a showing that substantial privacy interests are being invaded in an essentially intolerable manner." . . . Where a single speaker communicates to many listeners, the First Amendment does not permit the government to prohibit speech as intrusive unless the "captive" audience cannot avoid objectionable speech.

. . . The customer of Consolidated Edison may escape exposure to objectionable material simply by transferring the bill insert from envelope to wastebasket. . . .

* * * * *

Finally, the Commission urges that its prohibition would prevent ratepayers from subsidizing the costs of policy-oriented bill inserts. . . . [T]here is no basis on this record to assume that the Commission could not exclude the cost of these bill inserts from the utility's rate base. . . . Mere speculation of harm does not constitute a compelling state interest. . . .

IV

The Commission's suppression of bill inserts that discuss controversial issues of public policy directly infringes the freedom of speech protected by the First and Fourteenth Amendments. . . . Accordingly, the regulation is invalid. . . .

Reversed.

Questions

1. In your opinion, is the Johnson & Higgins ad an effective, useful message? How would you respond to a Johnson & Higgins ad supporting the passage of a balanced-budget amendment?
2. Should Johnson & Higgins be allowed to take a federal income tax deduction for the expenses associated with its ad? Explain.
3. Critics express the fear that the corporate community's vast resources could permit it to dominate political dialogue. Based on the *Consolidated Edison* opinion, do we have reason to believe the Constitution might not afford complete protection for all corporate advocacy? Explain.

Commercial Speech.   On occasion governments seek to regulate communications of a profit-seeking nature (e.g., paid political advertisements or ads for abortion services). In 1942 the Supreme Court held that commercial speech was not entitled to the protection of the First Amendment.[16] However, a series of decisions beginning in 1975 have accorded constitutional protection to commercial speech, and the law has experienced a profound about-face. Governments may yet impose reasonable restrictions on commercial speech where those restrictions are necessary for the public welfare. The case that follows illustrates the current judicial treatment of commercial speech.

BOLGER ET AL. V. YOUNGS DRUG PRODUCTS CORP.
463 U.S. 60 (1983)

Justice Marshall

Title 39 U.S.C. § 3001(e)(2) prohibits the mailing of unsolicited advertisements for contraceptives. The District Court held that, as applied to appellee's mailings, the statute violates the First Amendment. We affirm.

I

Section 3001(e)(2) states that "[a]ny unsolicited advertisement of matter which is designed, adapted, or intended for preventing conception is nonmailable matter, shall not be carried or delivered by mail, and shall be disposed of as the Postal Service directs. . . ."As interpreted by Postal Service regulations, . . . the statutory provision does not apply to unsolicited advertisements in which the mailer has no commercial interest. In addition to the civil consequences . . . 18 U.S.C. § 1461 makes it a crime knowingly to use the mails for anything declared by § 3001(e) to be nonmailable. . . .

Appellee Youngs Drug Products Corp. (Youngs) is engaged in the manufacture, sale, and distribution of contraceptives. Youngs markets its products primarily through sales to chain warehouses and wholesale distributors, who in turn sell contraceptives to retail pharmacists, who then sell those products to individual customers. Appellee publicizes the availability and desirability of its products by various methods. This litigation resulted from Youngs' decision to undertake a campaign of unsolicited mass mailings to members of the public. In conjunction with its wholesalers and retailers, Youngs seeks to mail to the public on an unsolicited basis three types of materials:

- multi-page, multi-item flyers promoting a large variety of products available at a drugstore, including prophylactics;
- flyers exclusively or substantially devoted to promoting prophylactics;
- informational pamphlets discussing the desirability and availability of prophylactics in general or Youngs' products in particular. . . .

In 1979 the Postal Service traced to a wholesaler of Youngs' products an allegation of an unsolicited mailing of contraceptive advertisements. . . . Youngs then brought this action for declaratory and injunctive relief in the United States District Court for the District of Columbia. . . .

The District Court determined that 3001(e)(2), by its plain language, prohibited all three types of proposed mailings. The court then addressed the constitutionality of the statute as applied to these mailings. Finding all three types of materials to be commercial solicitations, the court considered the constitutionality of the statute within the framework established by this Court for analyzing restrictions imposed on commercial speech. The court concluded that the statutory prohibition was more extensive than necessary to the interests asserted by the Government, and it therefore held that the statute's absolute ban on the three types of mailings violated the First Amendment. . . .

Appellants brought this direct appeal pursuant to 28 U.S.C. § 1252. . . .

II

Beginning with *Bigelow* v. *Virginia,* 421 U.S. 809 (1975), this Court extended the protection of the First Amendment to commercial speech. . . . Nonetheless, our decisions have recognized ''the 'common-sense' distinction between speech proposing a commercial transaction, which occurs in an area traditionally subject to government regulation, and other varieties of speech.'' . . . Thus, we have held that the Constitution accords less protection to commercial speech than to other constitutionally safeguarded forms of expression. . . .

. . . In light of the greater potential for deception or confusion in the context of certain advertising messages . . . content-based restrictions on commercial speech may be permissible. . . .

Because the degree of protection afforded by the First Amendment depends on whether the activity sought to be regulated constitutes commercial or noncommercial speech, we must first determine the proper classification of the mailings at issue here. . . .

Most of appellee's mailings fall within the core notion of commercial speech—''speech which does 'no more than propose a commercial transaction.'' . . . Youngs' information pamphlets, however, cannot be characterized merely as proposals to engage in commercial transactions. . . . The mere fact that these pamphlets are conceded to be advertisements clearly does not compel the conclusion that they are commercial speech. . . . Similarly, the reference to a specific product does not by itself render the pamphlets commercial speech. . . . Finally, the fact that Youngs has an economic motivation for mailing the pamphlets would clearly be insufficient by itself to turn the materials into commercial speech. . . .

The combination of *all* these characteristics, however, provides strong support for the District Court's conclusion that the informational pamphlets are properly characterized as commercial speech. . . .The mailings constitute commercial speech notwithstanding the fact that they contain discussions of important public issues . . . such as venereal disease and family planning. We have made clear that advertising which "links a product to a current public debate" is not thereby entitled to the constitutional protection afforded noncommercial speech. . . . A company has the full panoply of protections available to its direct comments on public issues, . . . so there is no reason for providing similar constitutional protection when such statements are made in the context of commercial transactions. . . .

We conclude, therefore, that all of the mailings in this case are entitled to the qualified but nonetheless substantial protection accorded to commercial speech.

III

"The protection available for particular commercial expression turns on the nature both of the expression and of the governmental interests served by its regulation." . . . In *Central Hudson* we adopted a four-part analysis for assessing the validity of restrictions on commercial speech. First, we determine whether the expression is constitutionally protected. For commercial speech to receive such protection, "it at least must concern lawful activity and not be misleading." . . . Second, we ask whether the governmental interest is substantial. If so, we must then determine whether the regulation directly advances the government interest asserted, and whether it is not more extensive than necessary to serve that interest. . . . Applying this analysis, we conclude that § 3001(e)(2) is unconstitutional as applied to appellee's mailings.

* * * * *

We must next determine whether the Government's interest in prohibiting the mailing of unsolicited contraceptive advertisements is a substantial one. . . .

In particular, appellants assert that the statute (1) shields recipients of mail from materials that they are likely to find offensive and (2) aids parents' efforts to control the manner in which their children become informed about sensitive and important subjects such as birth control. . . . The first of these interests carries little weight. . . . At least where obscenity is not involved, we have consistently held that the fact that protected speech may be offensive to some does not justify its suppression.''. . .

. . . We have, of course, recognized the important interest in allowing addressees to give notice to a mailer that they wish no further mailings which, in their sole discretion, they believe to be erotically arousing or sexually provocative. . . . But we have never held that the Government itself can shut off the flow of mailings to protect those recipients who might potentially be offended. The First Amendment "does not permit the government to prohibit speech as intrusive unless the 'captive' audience cannot avoid objectionable speech." *Consolidated Edison Co.* v. *Public Service Comm'n of New York.* . . .

The second interest asserted by appellants—aiding parents' efforts to discuss birth control with their children—is undoubtedly substantial. "[P]arents have an important 'guiding role' to play in the upbringing of their children . . . which presumptively includes counseling them on important decisions." . . . As a *means* of effectuating this interest, however, § 3001(e)(2) fails to withstand scrutiny.

To begin with, § 3001(e)(2) provides only the most limited incremental support for the interest asserted. We can reasonably assume that parents already exercise substantial control over the disposition of mail once it enters their mailboxes. Under 39 U.S.C. § 3008, parents can also exercise control over information that flows into their mailboxes. And parents must already cope with the multitude of external stimuli that color their children's perception of sensitive subjects. . . .

This marginal degree of protection is achieved by purging all mailboxes of unsolicited material that is entirely suitable for adults. We have previously made clear that a restriction of this scope is more extensive than the Constitution permits, for the government may not "reduce the adult population . . . to reading only what is fit for children.". . . In *FCC* v. *Pacifica Foundation,* . . . this Court did recognize that the Government's interest in protecting the young justified special treatment of an afternoon broadcast heard by adults as well as children. . . . At the same time, the majority "emphasize[d] the narrowness of our holding," . . . explaining that broadcasting is "*uniquely* pervasive" and that it is "*uniquely* accessible to children, even those too young to read." . . . The receipt of mail is far less intrusive and uncontrollable. . . .

Section 3001(e)(2) is also defective because it denies to parents truthful information bearing on their ability to discuss birth control and to make informed decisions in this area. . . . Because the proscribed information "may bear on one of the most important decisions" parents have a right to make, the restriction of "the free flow of truthful information" constitutes a "basic" constitutional defect regardless of the strength of the government's interest. . . .

IV

We thus conclude that the justifications offered by appellants are insufficient to warrant the sweeping prohibition on the mailing of unsolicited contraceptive advertisements. As applied to appellee's mailings, § 3001(e)(2) is unconstitutional.
Affirmed.

The Supreme Court had another opportunity to review the First Amendment's protection of commercial speech in 1986. In *Posadas de Puerto Rico Associates* v. *Tourism Company of Puerto Rico,*[17] the Court ruled 5–4 that a certain Puerto Rican statute and related regulations that restricted the advertising of casino gambling aimed to residents of Puerto Rico (as opposed to tourists) by local casinos survived the four-part test (as outlined in *Bolger*) determining what regulation of commercial speech was constitutional. Specifically, the Court found that the Puerto Rican legislature's interest in the health, safety, and welfare of its citizens was a "substantial" government interest and that the statute and regulations, as interpreted by the Superior Court of Puerto Rico, directly advanced the asserted government interest and was no more extensive than necessary to serve that interest. As indicated in the following article, some commentators believe the decision was undesirably conservative.

THE SUPREME COURT SHAKES THE AD BIZ

Michael Brody

It isn't Rehnquist's court—yet. But William Rehnquist, 61, the conservative justice who is President Reagan's nominee to replace retired Warren Burger as Chief Justice of the Supreme Court, chalked up an ideological victory on a controversial issue on which he had long been in the minority—the extent to which the First Amendment's protection of free speech covers advertising. [Rehnquist subsequently won Senate confirmation as Chief Justice—Author.]

The Court was ostensibly dealing with a narrow question: whether the Puerto Rican legislature could bar casinos from advertising to native islanders. Within limits, states may restrict ads, even truthful ones, for the health, safety, and welfare of citizens. Rehnquist, speaking for a 5–4 majority, declared that it is up to state and federal legislatures, not the courts, to decide how best to regulate legal but potentially harmful businesses, such as gambling, liquor, or tobacco. Since the decision could bolster campaigns already under way in the House and Senate to restrict tobacco ads and require warning labels for beer, wine, and liquor, lobbyists for advertisers and ad agencies are girding for a fracas.

The decision gives constitutional support to legislative proposals . . . that would forbid all tobacco advertising—in magazines, newspapers, and on billboards as well. Cigarette ads have been banned from the airwaves since 1971,

and snuff and chewing tobacco join the proscription August 27. In the Senate a bipartisan coalition stretching from conservative Strom Thurmond (R–South Carolina) to liberal Edward Kennedy (D—Massachusetts) is pushing a bill to require that every bottle of beer, wine, and spirits bear a warning label describing the dangers of excessive consumption.

* * * * *

The tobacco wars could provide the next major test of the Court's views on First Amendment coverage of so-called commercial (as opposed to editorial) speech. R. J. Reynolds has challenged a Federal Trade Commission complaint proposing to bar the tobacco company from buying ad space in newspapers and magazines for campaigns attacking the government's conclusions on a study of smoking and heart disease. Is an article by a chief executive protected by the First Amendment if it appears in a single newspaper or magazine as an opinion piece, but not if the same opinion appears all over the country in ad space purchased by his company? The new chief justice and the advertising industry may disagree on the answer.

Questions

1. *a.* Distinguish commercial speech from political speech.
   b. Does commercial speech further the purpose behind the First Amendment right? Explain.
2. Why is commercial speech accorded less protection than other categories of expression?
3. In *Bolger,* which step of the Court's four-part commercial speech test did the Postal Service provision fail?
4. The Township of Willingboro prohibited the posting of real estate "For Sale" or "Sold" signs. The town's purposes were to promote racial integration and to retard the flight of white homeowners. Is the Willingboro action constitutionally permissible? See *Linmark Associates, Inc.* v. *Willingboro,* 431 U.S. 85 (1977).

The Fairness Doctrine. Prior to 1987 the Federal Communications Commission had long had a regulation requiring radio and television broadcasters to provide for discussion of public issues and to allow each side of those issues a fair coverage—the fairness doctrine. Indeed, in 1969 the Supreme Court upheld the doctrine against a First Amendment challenge, stating, "A license permits broadcasting, but the licensee has no constitutional right to be the one who holds the license or to monopolize a radio frequency to the exclusion of his fellow citizens."[18] In 1987 the FCC abolished that requirement, and, as indicated by the following article, both sides are joining battle armed with the First Amendment.

FCC ABOLISHES FAIRNESS DOCTRINE, AROUSING DEBATE

Bob Davis

The Federal Communications Commission abolished the fairness doctrine, igniting a controversy with Congress and a host of consumer groups.

The agency voted 4–0 to eliminate the 38-year-old doctrine—which requires broadcasters airing controversial material to give opponents free air time to respond—because it said the requirement violated the constitutional rights of broadcasters. "Our action should be cause for celebration," said FCC Chairman Dennis Patrick. "By it, we introduce the First Amendment to the 20th century."

But fairness doctrine supporters, who contend the doctrine promotes diverse opinions on television and radio, also wrapped themselves in the Constitution. Consumer advocate Ralph Nader, who helped organize a protest at the FCC meeting, said the decision "erodes the constitutional rights of the audience."

* * * * *

Earlier this year, both houses [of Congress] passed by wide margins a measure to make the fairness doctrine a law. But President Reagan vetoed the legislation in June, and the Senate has been unable to muster the votes to override the veto. Instead, legislators are trying to attach a fairness doctrine provision to a bill that the president would be reluctant to veto.

Supporters of the fairness doctrine say the requirement lies at the heart of a broadcaster's responsibilities to the public under the Communications Act. Unless the requirement is reinstated, Mr. Nader said, he may sue broadcasters over their right to use public airwaves exclusively for their broadcasts. "If the FCC wants diversity," he asked, "why shouldn't four license holders be able to share time" on a particular channel?

Former FCC general counsel Henry Geller, who wrote the fairness doctrine, has said that, absent the obligation, broadcasters should be required to pay for the use of airwaves they now get for free.

* * * * *

Question

Which side of the fairness debate do you believe has the better First Amendment argument? Explain.

III. Freedom of the Press

Although this chapter will not specifically address the First Amendment right of freedom of the press, it should at least be noted in passing because, as the late Supreme Court Justice Potter Stewart once said, the press is "the only organized private business that is given explicit constitutional protection."[19]

THE FOURTH AMENDMENT

In an increasingly complex and interdependent society, the right of the individual to be free of unjustified governmental intrusions has become more important. The Fourth Amendment provides that:

> [T]he right of the people to be secure in their persons, houses, papers, and effects, against unreasonable searches and seizures, shall not be violated, and no Warrants shall issue, but upon probable cause.

It is generally conceded that some constitutional limitations on the police powers of government officials are a necessity. However, the boundaries of freedom from unreasonable search and seizure are the subject of great controversy. For example, the *general* rule is that the scope of a search incident to an arrest is limited to the person being arrested and the physical area within the arrested party's immediate control, but that standard is the target of many challenges.

Certainly the most controversial dimension of Fourth Amendment interpretation is the *exclusionary rule,* which provides that no evidence secured as the product of an illegal search may be admitted as evidence in a court of law. As ultimately applied to all courts by the 1961 U.S. Supreme Court decision in *Mapp* v. *Ohio,*[20] we can see that the exclusionary rule is a very effective device for discouraging illegal searches. In the *Mapp* case, police officers without a search warrant, without permission to search, and without probable cause for arrest broke into a private home. A person was hiding in the home who was wanted for questioning in connection with a bombing. Ms. Mapp was arrested, and, during the search of her home, police discovered certain lewd and lascivious books and pictures. Ms. Mapp was subsequently convicted of a criminal offense of possession of obscene materials, but the U.S. Supreme Court reversed the Ohio Supreme Court's decision upholding the validity of Ms. Mapp's conviction.

The *Mapp* case clearly reveals the competing considerations in typical search and seizure cases. On one hand, the police sometimes abuse the rights of individuals. On the other hand, Chief Justice Burger has lamented the impact of the exclusionary rule: "[Some] clear demonstration of the benefits and effectiveness of [the rule] is required to justify it in view of the high price it extracts from society—the release of countless guilty criminals."[21]

A 1984 Supreme Court decision created a good-faith exception to the exclusionary rule.[22] When judges issue search warrants that are later ruled defective, any illegally gathered evidence may nevertheless ordinarily be used at trial. Justice White noted that the principal justification for the exclusionary rule was to deter police misconduct. Therefore, where police have conducted a search in the good-faith belief that their conduct was lawful, "there is no police illegality and thus nothing to deter." However, evidence would be suppressed in instances where the judge granting the warrant was not impartial or where police lied to secure the warrant.

So we know that the Fourth Amendment has been the subject of dispute in criminal cases, but it may come as a surprise to learn that the contentious issues surrounding search and seizure have also been of importance in civil actions involving the government's efforts to regulate the conduct of business. As stated by the Supreme Court:

> The Warrant Clause of the Fourth Amendment protects commercial buildings as well as private homes. To hold otherwise would belie the origin of that Amendment, and the American colonial experience. . . . "[T]he Fourth Amendment's commands grew in large measure out of the colonists' experience with the writs of assistance . . . [that] granted sweeping power to customs officials and other agents of the king to search at large for smuggled

goods." . . . Against this background, it is untenable that the ban on warrantless searches was not intended to shield places of business as well as of residence.[23]

The case that follows illustrates one application of the Fourth Amendment to commercial property.

DOW CHEMICAL COMPANY V. UNITED STATES
106 S. Ct. 1819 (1986)

Chief Justice Burger

We granted certiorari to review the holding of the Court of Appeals . . . that EPA's aerial photography of petitioner's 2,000-acre plant complex without a warrant was not a search under the Fourth Amendment.

I

Petitioner Dow Chemical Co. operates a 2,000-acre facility manufacturing chemicals at Midland, Michigan. The facility consists of numerous covered buildings, with manufacturing equipment and piping conduits located between the various buildings exposed to visual observation from the air. At all times, Dow has maintained elaborate security around the perimeter of the complex barring ground-level public views of these areas. It also investigates any low-level flights by aircraft over the facility. Dow has not undertaken, however, to conceal all manufacturing equipment within the complex from aerial views. Dow maintains that the cost of covering its exposed equipment would be prohibitive.

In early 1978, enforcement officials of EPA, with Dow's consent, made an on-site inspection of two powerplants in this complex. A subsequent EPA request for a second inspection, however, was denied, and EPA did not thereafter seek an administrative search warrant. Instead, EPA employed a commercial aerial photographer, using a standard floor-mounted, precision aerial mapping camera, to take photographs of the facility from altitudes of 12,000, 3,000, and 1,200 feet. . . .

EPA did not inform Dow of this aerial photography, but when Dow became aware of it, Dow brought suit in the District Court alleging that EPA's action violated the Fourth Amendment. . . . The District Court granted Dow's motion for summary judgment on the ground that EPA had no authority to take aerial photographs and that doing so was a search violating the Fourth Amendment. EPA was permanently enjoined from taking aerial photographs of Dow's premises and from disseminating, releasing or copying the photographs already taken. . . .

* * * * *

The Court of Appeals reversed. . . .

* * * * *

II

The photographs at issue in this case are essentially like those commonly used in map-making. Any person with an airplane and an aerial camera could readily duplicate them. In common with much else, the technology of photography has changed in this century. These developments have enhanced industrial processes, and indeed all areas of life; they have also enhanced law enforcement techniques. . . .

Dow . . . relies heavily on its claim that trade secret laws protect it from any aerial photography of this industrial complex by its competitors, and that this protection is relevant to our analysis of such photography under the Fourth Amendment. That such photography might be barred by state law with regard to competitors, however, is irrelevant to the questions presented here. . . . [E]ven trade secret laws would not bar all forms of photography of this industrial complex; rather, only photography with an intent to use any trade secrets revealed by the photographs may be proscribed. Hence, there is no prohibition of photographs taken by a casual passenger on an airliner, or those taken by a company producing maps for its map-making purposes.

* * * * *

IV

We turn now to Dow's contention that taking aerial photographs constituted a search without a warrant, thereby violating Dow's rights under the Fourth Amendment. In making this contention, however, Dow concedes that a simple flyover with naked-eye observation, or the taking of a photograph from a nearby hillside overlooking such a facility, would give rise to no Fourth Amendment problem.

* * * * *

In the instant case, two additional Fourth Amendment claims are presented: whether the common-law "curtilage" doctrine encompasses a large industrial complex such as Dow's, and whether photography employing an aerial mapping camera is permissible in this context. Dow argues that an industrial plant, even one occupying 2,000 acres, does not fall within the "open fields" doctrine of *Oliver* v. *United States* but rather is an "industrial curtilage" having constitutional protection equivalent to that of the curtilage of a private home. Dow further contends that any aerial photography of this "industrial curtilage" intrudes upon its reasonable expectations of privacy. Plainly a business establishment or an industrial or commercial facility enjoys certain protections under the Fourth Amendment. . . .

* * * * *

As the curtilage doctrine evolved to protect much the same kind of privacy as that covering the interior of a structure, the contrasting "open fields" doctrine evolved as well. . . . In *Oliver,* we held that "an individual may not legitimately demand privacy for activities out of doors in fields, except in the area immediately surrounding the home." . . . To fall within the open fields doctrine the area "need be neither 'open' nor a 'field' as those terms are used in common speech.". . .

Dow plainly has a reasonable, legitimate, and objective expectation of privacy within the interior of its covered buildings, and it is equally clear that expectation is one society is prepared to observe. . . . Moreover, it could hardly be expected that Dow would erect a huge cover over a 2,000-acre tract. . . .

The Court of Appeals held that whatever the limits of an ''industrial curtilage'' barring *ground*-level intrusions into Dow's private areas, the open areas exposed here were more analogous to ''open fields'' than to a curtilage for purposes of aerial observation. . . . In *Oliver,* the Court described the curtilage of a dwelling as ''the areas to which extends the intimate activity associated with the 'sanctity of a man's home and the privacies of life.' '' . . . The intimate activities associated with family privacy and the home and its curtilage simply do not reach the outdoor areas or spaces between structures and buildings of a manufacturing plant.

Admittedly, Dow's enclosed plant complex, like the area in *Oliver,* does not fall precisely within the ''open fields'' doctrine. The area at issue here can perhaps be seen as falling somewhere between ''open fields'' and curtilage, but lacking some of the critical characteristics of both. . . .

* * * * *

Oliver recognized that in the open field context, ''the public and police lawfully may survey lands from the air.'' . . . Here, EPA was not employing some unique sensory device that, for example, could penetrate the walls of buildings and record conversations in Dow's plants, offices or laboratories, but rather a conventional, albeit precise, commercial camera commonly used in map-making. The Government asserts it has not yet enlarged the photographs to any significant degree, but Dow points out that simple magnification permits identification of objects such as wires as small as one-half inch diameter.

It may well be, as the Government concedes, that surveillance of private property by using highly sophisticated surveillance equipment not generally available to the public, such as satellite technology, might be constitutionally proscribed absent a warrant. But the photographs here are not so revealing of intimate details as to raise constitutional concerns. Although they undoubtedly give EPA more detailed information than naked-eye views, they remain limited to an outline of the facility's buildings and equipment. The mere fact that human vision is enhanced somewhat, at least to the degree here, does not give rise to constitutional problems. . . .

We conclude that the open areas of an industrial plant complex with numerous plant structures spread over an area of 2,000 acres are not analogous to the ''curtilage'' of a dwelling for purposes of aerial surveillance; . . . such an industrial complex is more comparable to an open field and as such it is open to the view and observation of persons in aircraft lawfully in the public airspace immediately above or sufficiently near the area for the reach of cameras.

We hold that the taking of aerial photographs of an industrial plant complex from navigable airspace is not a search prohibited by the Fourth Amendment.

Affirmed.

Questions

1. Why is the Dow industrial complex ''more comparable'' to an open field than to the ''curtilage'' of a home for purposes of aerial surveillance?
2. Should businesses be accorded the same constitutional search protections given to homes? Explain.

3. Joseph Burger owned and operated an automobile junkyard where, among other things, he dismantled autos and sold the parts. A New York statute permitted police to conduct warrantless inspections of auto junkyards. Without objection by Burger, police conducted a warrantless inspection of his business. The inspection revealed stolen vehicles and stolen parts. Burger was charged with possession of stolen property. In court, Burger moved to suppress the evidence arising from the search on the grounds that the New York statute under which the search was conducted was unconstitutional.
   a. Does the statute violate the Fourth Amendment's prohibition of unreasonable searches and seizures? Explain.
   b. Why do many states, including New York, explicitly permit the warrantless inspection of automobile junkyards? See *New York* v. *Joseph Burger,* 55 *Law Week* 4890 (1987).

Recently, Fourth Amendment issues have been prominent in cases involving drug testing and searching of employees. As you will recall, the Constitution was enacted to protect the citizenry from the government, rather than from purely private concentrations of power. Hence, in general, a violation of the Fourth Amendment (or other rights in the Bill of Rights) must entail government action that impairs the personal right. Thus, the successful constitutional challenges brought against involuntary drug testing have to this point been brought by government employees, such as public school teachers, U.S. Customs border agents, and prison guards. In a recent case, the Ninth Circuit Court of Appeals struck down mandatory drug and alcohol testing of railroad workers involved in accidents or rule violations governed by the Federal Railroad Administration.[24] The language of the court apparently was broad enough to cover at least some searches by private employers. The decision has been appealed to the Supreme Court.

THE FIFTH AMENDMENT

The Fifth Amendment prohibits the taking of private property for a public purpose without just compensation to the owner. Thus, the Fifth Amendment imposes bounds on the eminent domain processes commonly used by governments to condemn property for such projects as new highways.

One important issue under the Takings Clause is exactly what amounts to a taking. Obviously, if property is transferred to a new owner, a taking has occurred. The harder question is when regulation, such as requiring a developer to set aside land for a park area, amounts to a taking. In spite of recent Supreme Court cases, considerable uncertainty remains.[25] (See Chapter 6.)

COMPETING CONSTITUTIONAL ISSUES

Guaranteed freedoms and protections sometimes appear to be in direct conflict, and the courts must sort through the resulting intellectual rubble. Recently a number of cases, including the one that follows, have highlighted a conflict between speech and private property rights.

PRUNEYARD SHOPPING CENTER V. ROBINS
447 U.S. 74 (1980)

Justice Rehnquist

. . . Appellant PruneYard is a privately owned shopping center in the city of Campbell, Cal. It covers approximately 21 acres—5 devoted to parking and 16 occupied by walkways, plazas, sidewalks, and buildings that contain more than 65 specialty shops, 10 restaurants, and a movie theater. The PruneYard is open to the public for the purpose of encouraging the patronizing of its commercial establishments. It has a policy not to permit any visitor or tenant to engage in any publicly expressive activity, including the circulation of petitions, that is not directly related to its commercial purposes. This policy has been strictly enforced in a nondiscriminatory fashion. The PruneYard is owned by appellant Fred Sahadi.

Appellees are high school students who sought to solicit support for their opposition to a United Nations resolution against "Zionism." On a Saturday afternoon they set up a card table in a corner of PruneYard's central courtyard. They distributed pamphlets and asked passersby to sign petitions, which were to be sent to the President and Members of Congress. Their activity was peaceful and orderly and so far as the record indicates was not objected to by PruneYard's patrons.

Soon after appellees had begun soliciting signatures, a security guard informed them that they would have to leave because their activity violated PruneYard regulations. The guard suggested that they move to the public sidewalk at the PruneYard's perimeter. Appellees immediately left the premises and later filed this lawsuit in the California Superior Court of Santa Clara County. They sought to enjoin appellants from denying them access to the PruneYard for the purpose of circulating their petitions.

The Superior Court held that appellees were not entitled under either the Federal or California Constitution to exercise their asserted rights on the shopping center property. It concluded that there were "adequate, effective channels of communication for [appellees] other than soliciting on the private property of the [PruneYard]." The California Court of Appeal affirmed.

The California Supreme Court reversed, holding that the California Constitution protects "speech and petitioning, reasonably exercised, in shopping centers even when the centers are privately owned.". . .

Appellants first contend that *Lloyd Corp.* v. *Tanner,* prevents the State from requiring a private shopping center owner to provide access to persons exercising their state constitutional rights of free speech and petition when adequate alternative avenues of communication are available. *Lloyd* dealt with the question whether under the Federal Constitution a privately owned shopping center may prohibit the distribution of handbills on its property when the handbilling is unrelated to the shopping center's operations. . . .

We stated that property does not "lose its private character merely because the public is generally invited to use it for designated purposes," and that "[t]he essentially private character of a store and its privately owned abutting property does not change by virtue of being large or clustered with other stores in a modern shopping center."

Our reasoning in *Lloyd,* however, does not limit the authority of the State to exercise its police power or its sovereign right to adopt in its own Constitution individual liberties more expansive than those conferred by the Federal Constitution. In *Lloyd,* there was no state constitutional or statutory provision that had been construed to create rights to the use of private property by strangers, comparable to those found to exist by the California Supreme Court here. It is, of course, well established that a State in the exercise of its police power may adopt reasonable restrictions on private property so long as the restrictions do not amount to a taking without just compensation or contravene any other federal constitutional provision.

Appellants next contend that a right to exclude others underlies the Fifth Amendment guarantee against the taking of property without just compensation and the Fourteenth Amendment guarantee against the deprivation of property without due process of law.

It is true that one of the essential sticks in the bundle of property rights is the right to exclude others. And here there has literally been a "taking" of that right to the extent that the California Supreme Court has interpreted the State Constitution to entitle its citizens to exercise free expression and petition rights on shopping center property. But it is well established that "not every destruction or injury to property by governmental action has been held to be a 'taking' in the constitutional sense." Rather, the determination whether a state law unlawfully infringes a landowner's property in violation of the Taking Clause requires an examination of whether the restriction on private property "forc[es] some people alone to bear public burdens which, in all fairness and justice, should be borne by the public as a whole." This examination entails inquiry into such factors as the character of the governmental action, its economic impact, and its interference with reasonable investment-backed expectations.

Here the requirement that appellants permit appellees to exercise state-protected rights of free expression and petition on shopping center property clearly does not amount to an unconstitutional infringement of appellants' property rights under the Taking Clause. There is nothing to suggest that preventing appellants from prohibiting this sort of activity will unreasonably impair the value of use of their property as a shopping center. The Prune Yard is a large commercial complex that covers several city blocks, contains numerous separate business establishments, and is open to the public at large. The decision of the California Supreme Court makes it clear that the PruneYard may restrict expressive activity by adopting time, place, and manner regulations that will minimize any interference with its commercial functions. Appellees were orderly, and they limited their activity to the common areas of the shopping center. In these circumstances, the fact that they may have "physically invaded" appellants' property cannot be viewed as determinative . . . A State is, of course, bound by the Just Compensation Clause of the Fifth Amendment, but here appellants have failed to demonstrate that the "right to exclude others" is so essential to the use or economic value of their property that the state-authorized limitation of it amounted to a "taking."

There is also little merit to appellants' argument that they have been denied their property without due process of law. . . .

"[N]either property rights nor contract rights are absolute. . . . Equally fundamental with the private right is that of the public to regulate it in the common interest. . . .

" . . . [T]he guaranty of due process, as has often been held, demands only that the law shall not be unreasonable, arbitrary or capricious, and that the means selected shall have a real and substantial relation to the objective sought to be attained."

. . . Appellants have failed to provide sufficient justification for concluding that this test is not satisfied by the State's asserted interest in promoting more expansive rights of free speech and petition than conferred by the Federal Constitution.

Appellants finally contend that a private property owner has a First Amendment right not to be forced by the State to use his property as a forum for the speech of others. They state that in *Wooley* v. *Maynard,* this Court concluded that a State may not constitutionally require an individual to participate in the dissemination of an ideological message by displaying it on his private property in a manner and for the express purpose that it be observed and read by the public. This rationale applies here, they argue, because the message of *Wooley* is that the State may not force an individual to display any message at all.

Wooley, however, was a case in which the government itself prescribed the message, required it to be displayed openly on appellee's personal property that was used "as part of his daily life," and refused to permit him to take any measures to cover up the motto even though the Court found that the display of the motto served no important state interest. Here, by contrast, there are a number of distinguishing factors. Most important, the shopping center by choice of its owner is not limited to the personal use of appellants. It is instead a business establishment that is open to the public to come and go as they please. The views expressed by members of the public in passing out pamphlets or seeking signatures for a petition thus will not likely be identified with those of the owner. Second, no specific message is dictated by the State to be displayed on appellants' property. There consequently is no danger of governmental discrimination for or against a particular message. Finally, as far as appears here appellants can expressly disavow any connection with the message by simply posting signs in the area where the speakers or handbillers stand. Such signs, for example, could disclaim any sponsorship of the message and could explain that the persons are communicating their own messages by virtue of state law. . . .

We conclude that neither appellants' federally recognized property rights nor their First Amendment rights have been infringed by the California Supreme Court's decision recognizing a right of appellees to exercise state-protected rights of expression and petition on appellants' property. The judgment of the Supreme Court of California is therefore affirmed.

Questions

1. Why is the power of eminent domain arguably necessary to the effective operation of government?

2. Explain PruneYard's position that allowing free speech on its property would constitute an infringement of its property rights.
3. Develop the argument in support of the position that free speech (appropriately regulated) in a shopping center is constitutionally required.
4. Might the result in this case have been different had the case arisen in a state other than California? Explain.

AN INSPIRATION FOR ALL

It is fitting that we close this brief inspection of the U.S. Constitution with a reminder of the profound impact of that document on the entire world.

A GIFT TO ALL NATIONS

John Greenwald

In overwhelmingly Catholic Ireland, the constitution outlaws abortion and divorce and proclaims the Holy Trinity the source of all political power. Japan's national charter renounces war. Portugal's forbids private ownership of television stations. Peru reprints its charter in the Lima telephone directory, filling 10 pages of fine print. Yet beneath such diversity, each document can trace its rights and freedoms to U.S. soil. Says Joseph Magnet, a law professor at Canada's University of Ottawa: "America has been and remains the great constitutional laboratory for the entire world."

Of the 170 countries that exist today, more than 160 have written charters modeled directly or indirectly on the U.S. version. Those states range from the giant Soviet Union to the tiny Caribbean island country of Grenada. While Poland and France became the first to follow America's lead when they drafted modern constitutions in 1791, the largest impact has been recent. More than three quarters of today's charters were adopted after World War II. Jawaharlal Nehru, India's first prime minister, could have been speaking for the rest of the Third World when he told the U.S. Congress in 1949, "We have been greatly influenced by your own Constitution."

Some charters are roundly ignored. China's declaration of human rights was powerless to stop the abuses of the 1960s' Cultural Revolution. In Latin America dictators often simply disregard national charters during times of unrest. Many African leaders have stymied democracy by outlawing opposing political parties and turning their countries into one-party states, often without bothering to amend their charters. Yet so strongly have constitutional ideals taken hold worldwide that few countries dare to abandon them completely.

Indeed, constitutions are living documents that are constantly being created and reshaped. Voters in the Philippines went to the polls in January to approve a new charter, the country's fifth, that prohibits human rights violations and retains Corazon Aquino as president until 1992. In Nicaragua this year, the Marxist-influenced Sandinista leadership unveiled that country's 12th constitution in 149 years. Haitians in March approved their 23rd charter since 1804 in the country's first free election in three decades.

As such figures show, many constitutions have managed to survive only until the next upheaval or military coup. Three quarters of the world's constitutions have been completely rewritten since they were first adopted, making America's fidelity to a single charter highly unusual. Some experts contend that frequent constitutional changes can be healthy. Says Albert Blaustein, a Rutgers University law professor who has helped draft six foreign charters: "Jefferson concluded that every 20 years the new generation should have its own constitution to meet current needs. That might not be a good idea for the United States, but it's really not a bad idea for other countries."

Some constitutions are born of disaster. After World War II, Americans played a key role in drafting charters for the defeated nations of Japan and West Germany. The Japanese charter declares that the country will never again make war or maintain an army, navy, or air force. As a result, Japan spends only about 1 percent of its gross national product on defense, freeing the economy for more productive purposes. Ironically, the United States is pressing the Japanese to boost defense outlays.

The West German constitution, written under the watchful eye of U.S. occupation leaders, sought to prevent the rise of another Hitler by limiting the executive branch. Recalls Joachim von Elbe, a Bonn legal expert: "We did not want to make the Germans just imitate the American constitutional model but rely on themselves to reform, rebuild, and overcome the Nazi period." The framers decreed that the

Bundestag, or parliament, could not oust a chancellor without first choosing a successor. That has helped prevent a return of the political chaos that brought the Nazis to power in the 1930s.

Italians, with memories of Mussolini still fresh in their minds, went even further than the Germans in reining in the executive branch. While this has guarded against a new outbreak of tyranny, the inability of any one of Italy's parties to win a majority in parliament has led to frequent political turnover: Italy has had 46 governments since 1945.

The constitutions of Eastern Europe bestow supreme power on the Communist Party. While charters from Bulgaria to Poland ring with declarations of human and civil rights, they all contain loopholes that permit governments to set such rights aside should the party so require. Thus many guarantees—like the widely promised right to complain about government misdeeds without fear of retribution—are honored mainly in the breach, and supposedly independent courts almost never hand down rulings the party does not like.

The same gulf between rhetoric and reality exists in China. The country's current charter, its fifth since 1949, grants "freedom of speech, of the press, of assembly, of association, of procession, and of demonstration." Peking nonetheless responded to widespread student protests last winter by detaining the leaders, firing university officials, and halting demonstrations. Authorities then shut down half a dozen liberal periodicals and banned scores of books, magazines, and films throughout the country.

Among Third World nations, India has often seemed the most faithful to its U.S.-inspired constitutional ideals. The world's largest democracy included a declaration of "fundamental rights" in its 1949 charter and backed them up by borrowing the U.S. system of judicial review. "Thank God they put in the fundamental rights," says Nani Palkhivala, a constitutional expert who was India's ambassador to Washington in the late 1970s. He observes, "Since 1947 we have had more harsh and repressive laws than were ever imposed under British rule." Indian courts, however, overturned most of them.

Leaders in Africa, confronted by tribal rivalries and the constant threat of coups, have taken far greater pains to stay in power than to preserve democratic rights. Troublesome constitutions are usually ignored or tailored to suit. "If anyone speaks to you about a multiparty political system, catch him and hit him hard," declared Gabon President Albert-Bernard (Omar) Bongo in a widely quoted 1983 speech. At least 28 of the continent's 53 states have only one political party, and 27 African nations are under military rule. Countries ranging from Guinea in West Africa to Somalia in the east have gone so far as to declare dissent a treasonable crime that can be punished by death. Notes British historian Lord Blake: "The political tradition in many parts of Africa is authoritarian, and that's what has taken over."

In Latin America, coups and military dictatorships have often been the rule. Chile's 1981 constitution grants dictatorial authority to President Augusto Pinochet, the general who seized power in 1973. In Argentina, the three-year effort at civilian rule under constitutionally mandated human rights principles still sways precariously if the military glowers too hard. Mexico is politically stable and boasts a constitution that provides for separation of powers between branches of government, but the Institutional Revolutionary Party and its forerunner have controlled the presidency— and much of the other branches—since 1929.

Though many U.S.-inspired constitutions have gone their own ways over the years, the seed planted in Philadelphia in 1789 should continue to flower. "The idea that individuals have rights against government is probably the most profound influence of the U.S. Constitution," says Oscar Schachter, professor emeritus of international law and diplomacy at Columbia University. "The whole notion of human rights as a worldwide movement was grounded in part in the Constitution." Those rights may not always be honored, but they have fired the imaginations of individuals, free and otherwise, around the world. After two centuries, the U.S. Constitution remains the standard against which people of all sorts measure their governments, and some governments even measure themselves.

CHAPTER QUESTIONS

1. The Labor Department conducts regular investigations of business records to ensure compliance with the wages and hours provisions (e.g., higher pay for overtime) of the Fair Labor Standards Act. When a compliance officer sought to inspect certain financial records at the Lone Steer restaurant/motel in Steele, North Dakota, the restaurant declined his admittance until the government detailed the scope of the investigation. Not receiving a satisfactory response, the Lone Steer demanded a search warrant prior to inspection. As provided for under the FLSA, the government secured an administrative subpoena, which, unlike a search warrant, does not require judicial approval. Once again,

Lone Steer denied admission. The government then filed suit. Decide. See *Donovan* v. *Lone Steer,* 464 U.S. 408 (1984).

2. A Texas statute forbade the practice of optometry under a trade name. The Texas legislature feared possible deception in optometric practice, such as changes in the staff of optometrists while the trade name remained unchanged or the use of different trade names at shops under common ownership, which practices might create a false impression of competition between the shops. Was the Texas statute a violation of the freedom of speech safeguards of the First Amendment? See *Friedman* v. *Rogers,* 440 U.S. 1 (1979).

3. This chapter noted a number of decisions affording protection to commercial speech. Why are corporations unlikely to begin using their vast resources to speak out on the wide range of public issues from abortion to organized prayer in schools to the death penalty?

4. The California Public Utilities Commission ordered a regulated private utility, Pacific Gas and Electric Company, to include in its billing envelopes the comments of a rate reform group with whose views the company disagreed. The company appealed, claiming its First Amendment rights were violated. Decide. See *Pacific Gas and Electric Company* v. *Public Utilities Commission of California,* 106 S. Ct. 903 (1986).

5. Restaurant-owner Smith reads of studies suggesting that women typically work more diligently than men. He decides therefore to hire only women for his new restaurant. He runs an employment ad in the local newspaper and includes the language, "Only women need apply." Smith is challenged in court on the grounds that the ad violates Title VII of the Civil Rights Act of 1964, which forbids discrimination in employment on the basis of race, religion, color, sex, or national origin. Smith loses the lawsuit, but he appeals the decision on constitutional grounds.
   a. What constitutional law argument might be raised in Smith's behalf?
   b. Decide. See *Pittsburgh Press* v. *Human Relations Commission,* 413 U.S. 376 (1973) for a relevant decision.

6. Members of Local 590 were picketing a grocery store located in Logan Valley's shopping center. The grocery store had hired only nonunion personnel. An injunction was served barring the picketing on the grounds of trespass. The decision was appealed to the U.S. Supreme Court.
   a. What constitutional law argument would you raise on behalf of Local 590?
   b. What argument would you raise on behalf of Logan Valley?
   c. Decide. See *Amalgamated Food Employees Union Local 590 et al.* v. *Logan Valley Plaza, Inc. et. al.,* 391 U.S. 308 (1968).

7. Tanner and others sought to distribute handbills in the interior mall of the Lloyd Corporation shopping center. The literature concerned an anti-Vietnam War meeting. Lloyd Corporation had a strict rule forbidding handbilling. When security guards terminated distributions within

the center, Tanner et al. claimed a violation of their First Amendment rights. Both the district court and the Court of Appeals relied on *Amalgamated Food* (see question 6) in finding a violation of constitutional rights. The decision was appealed to the U.S. Supreme Court. Decide. Explain. See *Lloyd Corporation* v. *Tanner,* 407 U.S. 551 (1972).

8. Philip Zauderer, an Ohio attorney, ran a newspaper ad promising a full refund of legal fees if clients accused of drunk driving were convicted. He later ran an ad soliciting clients who believed themselves to have been harmed by the Dalkon Shield intrauterine contraceptive. That ad included a line drawing of the device as well as a promise that ''[i]f there is no recovery, no legal fees are owed by our clients.'' The Office of Disciplinary Counsel of the Supreme Court of Ohio charged that Zauderer violated several provisions of the Disciplinary Rules of the Ohio Code of Professional Responsibility, including:

   i. The drunk-driving ad was deceptive because it purported to allow a contingent fee arrangement in a criminal case when that payment method was explicitly forbidden by Ohio rules.

   ii. The Dalkon Shield ad failed to disclose the fact that clients might be liable for *litigation costs* (rather than *legal fees*) and, therefore, was deceptive.

   iii. The Dalkon Shield ad violated rules forbidding the use of illustrations in ads.

   iv. The Dalkon Shield ad violated rules forbidding ''soliciting or accepting legal employment through advertisements containing information or advice regarding a specific legal problem.''

   Zauderer was found to have violated the Ohio Disciplinary Rules, and a public reprimand was issued. He took his case to the U.S. Supreme Court.

   a. What constitutional claim should be raised on behalf of Zauderer?

   b. Decide. See *Zauderer* v. *Office of Disciplinary Counsel of the Supreme Court of Ohio,* 471 U.S. 626 (1985).

9. American Bar Association rules seek to discourage lawyers from aggressive pursuit of clients in an ''ambulance-chasing'' fashion. In-person solicitation of clients is entirely forbidden. General mass mailings not directed to individuals known to be in need of legal assistance are permissible under the bar's guidelines. Some attorneys have used targeted mailings to potential clients known to be facing legal difficulties. For example, attorneys have offered their legal assistance via express mail messages to families whose relatives have been killed or injured in crashes or other disasters. ABA rules discourage targeted advertising, and many states have followed the ABA's advice by adopting guidelines restraining that type of advertising by lawyers.

   A Kentucky lawyer sought to mail letters to individuals against whom home foreclosure proceedings had been instituted. He offered ''free information on how you can keep your home.'' Kentucky rules forbade targeted mailings. The attorney claimed a First Amendment violation. How would you rule? Explain. See *Shapero* v. *Kentucky Bar Association*, 56 *Law Week* 4532 (1988).

NOTES

1. Otto Friedrich, "How the Deed Was Done," *Time,* July 6, 1987, p. 59.
2. Jerre Williams, *Constitutional Analysis in a Nutshell* (St. Paul, Minn.: West Publishing, 1979), p. 33.
3. *Immigration and Naturalization Service* v. *Chadha,* 462 U.S. 919.
4. Stephen Wermiel, "Two Centuries Later, There Is Hot Debate over Original Intent," *The Wall Street Journal,* May 20, 1987, p. 1.
5. Supra note 1.
6. *Engel* v. *Vitale,* 370 U.S. 421.
7. *Abington School District* v. *Schempp,* 374 U.S. 203 (1963).
8. *Wallace* v. *Jaffree,* 472 U.S. 38, 52–53.
9. *Epperson* v. *Arkansas,* 393 U.S. 97.
10. *Edwards* v. *Aguillard,* 107 S. Ct. 2573.
11. 366 U.S. 420 (1961).
12. *Wisconsin* v. *Yoder,* 406 U.S. 205 (1972).
13. *First National Bank of Boston* v. *Bellotti,* 435 U.S. 765 (1978).
14. *Tinker* v. *Des Moines School District,* 393 U.S. 503 (1969).
15. *Spence* v. *Washington,* 418 U.S. 405 (1974).
16. *Valentine* v. *Chrestensen,* 316 U.S. 52 (1942).
17. 106 S. Ct. 2968.
18. *Red Lion Broadcasting Co., Inc.* v. *Federal Communications Commission,* 395 U.S. 367, 389.
19. Stephen Wermiel, "Protection of the Press under First Amendment Still Stirs Debate in the Constitution's 200th Year," *The Wall Street Journal,* August 31, 1987, p. 38. Reprinted by permission of the *The Wall Street Journal,* © Dow Jones & Company, Inc. 1987. ALL RIGHTS RESERVED.
20. 367 U.S. 643.
21. Dissenting in *Bivens* v. *Six Unknown Agents,* 403 U.S. 388 (1971), as reported in William B. Lockhart, Yale Kamisar, and Jesse H. Choper, *The American Constitution* (St. Paul, Minn.: West Publishing, 1981), p. 312.
22. *United States* v. *Leon,* 104 S. Ct. 3405.
23. *Marshall* v. *Barlow's, Inc.,* 436 U.S. 307 (1978).
24. Peter Waldman, "Appeals Court Rejects Mandatory Tests of Rail Workers for Drugs and Alcohol," *The Wall Street Journal,* February 12, 1988, p. 4.
25. See, for example, *Keystone Bituminous Coal Association* v. *DeBenedictis,* 107 S. Ct. 1232 (1987); *Nollan* v. *California Coastal Commission,* 107 S. Ct. 3141 (1987).

PART III

Trade Regulation and Antitrust

Government Regulation of Business: An Introduction

INTRODUCTION

Chapter 1 investigated the use of the free market and government dominance (on each end of the economic continuum) as systems by which the role of business in society may be "controlled." Chapter 2 addressed the utility of individual and corporate ethics as self-regulatory mechanisms for governing the behavior of the corporate community. Chapter 3 continued our exploration of the proper role of business in society. Chapters 4 and 5 offered a brief overview of the justice system.

The balance of the text is largely devoted to the government regulation of business. Throughout that investigation the reader is urged to keep in mind the issues of the introductory chapters. What is the proper role of business in society? Has business abused the public trust? If so, is the government the answer to the problem? Or might we rely on self-regulation (ethics and social responsibility) and market "regulation?" What is the proper blend of these "control" devices as well as others left unexplored (e.g., custom)?

The phrase *mixed economy* is commonly applied to the contemporary American system. In an honorable pursuit of the greatest good for the greatest number, America has turned to the government to ameliorate the injustices and discomforts of contemporary life. Market "regulation" and self-regulation have been supplemented by government intervention.

Government regulation pervades our existence. The government directly controls certain dimensions of the economy, such as the public utilities. The government indirectly intervenes across the spectrum of the economy in matters as diverse as child labor and zoning restrictions; and, in the larger sense of national economic policy, the government engages in antitrust activity designed to preserve our conception of a free, efficient marketplace. To the proponents of government intervention, the successes are evident: cleaner air, safer cars, fewer useless drugs, more jobs for minorities, safer workplaces, and so on. To the critics, many government regulatory efforts either did not achieve their purpose or did so at a cost exceeding the benefits. The late 70s and early 80s were marked by increasingly insistent calls from virtually all segments of society to retard the reach of government. Indeed, significant deregulation has been effected. More specifically, freeing business from a portion of its regulatory burden was a key ingredient in former President Reagan's plans to reorder the nation. His intentions for deregulation were broadly applauded, but it stretches credulity to think that the American government will ever play less than a prepossessing role in American business.

WHY REGULATION?

Market Failure

In theory, government intervention in a free enterprise economy would be justified only when the market is unable to maximize the public interest; that is, in instances of market failure.

Market failure is attributed to certain inherent imperfections in the market itself.

1. Inadequate Information. Can the consumer choose the best pain reliever in the absence of complete information about the virtues of the competing products? An efficient free market presumes reasoned decisions about production and consumption. Reasoned decisions require adequate information. Because we cannot have perfect information and often will not have adequate information, the government, it is argued, may impose regulations either to improve the available information or to diminish the unfavorable effect of inadequate information. Hence we have, for example, labeling mandates for consumer goods, licensure requirements for many occupations, and health standards for the processing and sale of goods.

2. Monopoly. Of course, the government intervenes to thwart anticompetitive monopolies and oligopolies throughout the marketplace. (That process is addressed in Chapter 9.) Of immediate interest here is the so-called natural monopoly. Telephone and electrical services are classic examples of a decline in per-unit production costs as the firm becomes larger. Thus, a single large firm is more efficient than several small ones, and a natural monopoly results. In such situations the government has commonly intervened (in the form of public service commissions) to preserve the efficiencies of the large firm while preventing that firm from taking unfair advantage of the consumer.

3. Externalities. When all the costs and/or benefits of a good or service are not fully internalized or absorbed, those costs or benefits fall elsewhere as what economists have labeled *externalities* or *neighborhood effects* or *spillovers*. Pollution is a characteristic example of a negative externality. The environment is used without charge as an ingredient in the production process (commonly as a receptacle for waste). Consequently, the product is underpriced. The consumer does not pay the full social cost of the product, so those remaining costs are thrust on parties external to the transaction. Government regulation is sometimes considered necessary to place the full cost burden on those who generated it, which in turn is expected to result in less wasteful use of resources. Positive externalities are those in which a producer confers benefits not required by the market. An example of such a positive externality is a business firm that, through no direct market compulsion, landscapes its grounds and develops a sculpture garden to contribute to the aesthetic quality of its neighborhood. Positive externalities ordinarily are not the subject of regulation.

4. Public Goods. Some goods and services cannot be provided through the pricing system because we have no method for excluding those who choose not to pay. In such situations, the added cost of benefiting one person is zero or nearly so, and, in any case, no one can effectively be denied the benefits of the activity. National defense, insect eradication, and pollution control are examples of this phenomenon. Presumably most individuals would refuse to voluntarily pay for what others would receive free. Thus, absent government regulations, public goods would not be produced in adequate quantities.

Philosophy and Politics

The correction of market failure could explain the full range of government regulation of business, but an alternative or perhaps supplemental explanation lies in the political process. Three general arguments have emerged.

One view is that regulation is considered necessary for the protection and general welfare of the public. We find the government engaging in regulatory efforts designed to achieve a more equitable distribution of income and wealth. Many believe government intervention in the market is necessary to stabilize the economy, thus curbing the problems of recession, inflation, and unemployment. Affirmative action programs seek to reverse and correct the racism and sexism of the past. We even find the government protecting us from ourselves, both for our benefit and for the well-being of the larger society. For example, cigarette advertising is banned on television, and in some states motorcyclists must wear helmets.

Another view is that regulation is developed at the behest of industry and is operated primarily for the benefit of industry. Here the various subsidies and tax advantages afforded to business might be cited. In numerous instances government regulation has been effective in reducing or entirely eliminating the entry of competitors. Antitrust law has been instrumental in sheltering small businesses. Government regulation has also permitted legalized price-fixing in some industries. Of course, it may be that although regulation is often initiated primarily for the public welfare, industry eventually "captures" the regulatory process and ensures its continuation for the benefit of the industry. As we see in the historical overview that follows, both the public interest and business interests have been very influential in generating government intervention in the marketplace.

Finally, bureaucrats who perform government regulation are themselves a powerful force in maintaining and expanding that regulation.

THE HISTORY OF GOVERNMENT REGULATION OF BUSINESS

Government has always played some role in American commerce. In the early years of the republic, tariffs were imposed to protect manufacturers, subsidies were provided to stimulate commerce, and a few agencies were established (e.g., the Army Corps of Engineers in 1824 and the Patent and Trademark Office in 1836).

Prior to the Civil War the major, if weak, link between government and business was the national bank, which possessed very limited authority. Banking remained a fundamentally private enterprise restrained only by weak state statutes. A meaningful federal banking system simply did not exist. Indeed, it is estimated that by 1860 "some 1,500 banks were issuing about 10,000 different types of bank notes."[1] Then the need for a centralized approach to the Civil War forced Congress to pass the National Banking Act of 1864, which laid the foundation for the dual system of extensive federal and state banking regulation that we know today. However, Americans continued to stoutly resist government intrusion in business affairs. The years following the Civil War were perhaps the zenith of the capitalist era. The "Robber Barons" (Carnegie, Rockefeller, and their colleagues) came to the fore. Philosopher Herbert Spencer adapted Darwin's "survival of the fittest" theory to the world of commerce, thereby giving the business community an intellectual foundation for asserting its leadership. Extraordinary industrial growth followed.

But the public began to feel the impact of big business in the late 1880s, and the feeling often was not pleasant. Anger over the conduct of the rail and industrial trusts manifested itself in the Populist movement, which embodied the struggle of the "common people" against the predatory acts of the moneyed interests. The railroads, then the nation's most powerful private economic force, were bent on growth and seemed unconcerned with the general welfare.

> By discriminating in freight charges between localities, articles, and individuals, the railroads were terrorizing farmers, merchants, and even whole communities until, as a government agency said in 1887, matters "had reached such a pass, that no man dared engage in any business in which transportation largely entered without first obtaining permission of a railway manager."[2]

Rural discontent led to the Grange movement, which became an important lobbying force for agrarian interests. Several states enacted railroad regulatory legislation. By then the confusion and abuse in the rail industry prompted Congress to pass the Interstate Commerce Commission Act of 1887 and ban, among other practices, rate discrimination against short hauls and the practice of keeping rates secret until the day of shipment. In addition to the farmers, small merchants and shippers and the railroads themselves ultimately supported federal intervention. Apparently the railroad owners felt regulation would be meaningless or even advantageous to them. Subsequently the Hepburn Act of 1906 greatly strengthened ICC effectiveness. The Mann-Elkins Act of 1910 extended ICC jurisdiction to interstate telegraph, telephone, cable, and wireless enterprises.

As explained in greater deal in Chapter 9, the development of giant trusts and holding companies (e.g., Standard Oil) led to extraordinary commercial advances but also to widespread abuse in the form of price-fixing, price slashing to drive out competitors, market sharing, and the like. Blacklists and other antilabor tactics were common. At the same time, small merchants and wholesalers were being squeezed by the weight of big manufacturing interests. Around the turn of the century, commercial giants (such as American Tobacco, Quaker Oats, Heinz, Swift, and Anheuser-Busch) made purchases directly from farmers and other suppliers and sold directly to retailers. The result was that wholesalers, who had previously occupied a key economic role in most communities, were increasingly unnecessary. Similarly, retail giants (such as Sears and Woolworth) were applying extreme competitive pressure on smaller businesses. The passage of the Sherman Antitrust Act in 1890 had relatively little immediate impact; however, Presidents Roosevelt, Taft, and Wilson all took up the regulatory cause, and with the passage in 1914 of the Clayton and Federal Trade Commission acts, antitrust law became an important ingredient in American business life. The fever for regulation subsided somewhat during the prosperous 1920s, but the Depression prompted detailed government regulation.

The Depression compelled many arch-conservatives to surrender to the need for government intervention. President Roosevelt took office in 1933, and the first 100 days of his term saw the passage of 15 major pieces of legislation. In all, Roosevelt secured approval of 93 major bills during his first two terms in office. The federal government became the biggest voice in America as the administration sought to correct the tragedy of the Depression. The legislation literally changed the character of American life. Congress established the Civilian Conservation Corps to place the unemployed in public works projects. The Federal Emergency Relief Act funded state-operated welfare programs. The Tennessee Valley Authority established the government as a major participant in producing electrical energy. The Glass-Steagall Act divided investment and commercial banking and provided for insurance on bank deposits. The list went on and on, and the result was a new view of the business—government relationship. Effectively, the government and the citizenry conceded that the old view of an automatically self-correcting economy was invalid. The Depression revealed a fundamental instability in the unregulated market.[3]

Distrust of the market provoked further government regulation in the decades subsequent to the Depression, and that regulation has followed a much broader path. Rather than regulating single industries (transportation, banking, communication), the government interventions of recent years have swept across the entire economy to address such issues as discrimination, pollution, and worker safety. In the 1960s and 1970s, no social problem seemed too daunting for the government's regulatory efforts.[4]

THE CONSTITUTIONAL FOUNDATION OF BUSINESS REGULATION

The Commerce Clause of the U.S. Constitution broadly specifies the power accorded to the federal government to regulate business activity. Article I, Section 8 of the Constitution provides that: "The Congress shall have the power . . . To regulate Commerce with foreign Nations, and among the several States, and with the Indian Tribes. . . ." State authority to regulate commerce resides in the police power reserved to the states by the Constitution. Police power refers to the right of the state governments to promote the public health, safety, morals, and general welfare by regulating persons and property within each state's jurisdiction. The states have, in turn, delegated portions of the police power to local government units.

The Commerce Clause, as interpreted by the judiciary, affords Congress exclusive jurisdiction over foreign commerce. States and localities, nevertheless, sometimes seek in various ways to regulate foreign commerce. For example, a state may seek, directly or indirectly, to impose a tax on foreign goods that compete with those locally grown or manufactured. Such efforts violate both the Commerce Clause and the Supremacy Clause (holding federal law supreme over state law where the two are in conflict) of the U.S. Constitution.

Federal control over interstate commerce was designed to create a free market throughout the United States, wherein goods would move among the states, unencumbered by state and local tariffs and duties. Not surprisingly, that profoundly sensible policy has been the source of extensive conflict and litigation. As with foreign commerce, the states and localities have endeavored in ways subtle and sometimes not so subtle to influence the course of interstate commerce. The judiciary has not been sympathetic with those efforts. Indeed, to the great chagrin of states' rights advocates, judicial decisions have very dramatically expanded the reach of the federal government. Even intrastate activities, having an effect on interstate commerce, are now subject to federal regulation. In *Wickard* v. *Filburn,*[5] the Supreme Court, in interpreting a federal statute regulating the production and sale of wheat, found that 23 acres of homegrown and largely home-consumed wheat affected interstate commerce, and that it was subject to federal regulation. (As a small test of the mind, the student may wish to deduce the economic reasoning that supported the Court's position.) Clearly, the federal lawmakers with the approval of the judiciary have expanded the power of the central government at the expense of states and localities. The argument goes that expansion has been necessary to maximize the general good, which might otherwise be thwarted by narrow self-interest or prejudice in specific states and localities. The following case illustrates both the technical difficulties in determining the constitutional bounds of federal regulation and the conflict between individual rights and the government's view of the general welfare.

HEART OF ATLANTA MOTEL V. UNITED STATES
379 U.S. 241 (1964)

Justice Clark

This is a declaratory judgment action, attacking the constitutionality of Title II of the Civil Rights Act of 1964. . . . [The lower court found for the United States.]

1. The Factual Background and Contentions of the Parties

. . . Appellant owns and operates the Heart of Atlanta Motel, which has 216 rooms available to transient guests. The motel is located on Courtland Street, two blocks from downtown Peachtree Street. It is readily accessible to interstate highways 75 and 85 and state highways 23 and 41. Appellant solicits patronage from outside the State of Georgia through various national advertising media, including magazines of national circulation; it maintains over 50 billboards and highway signs within the State, soliciting patronage for the motel; it accepts convention trade from outside Georgia and approximately 75 percent of its registered guests are from out of State. Prior to passage of the act the motel had followed a practice of refusing to rent rooms to Negroes, and it alleged that it intended to continue to do so. In an effort to perpetuate that policy this suit was filed.

The appellant contends that Congress in passing this act exceeded its power to regulate commerce under [Article I] of the Constitution of the United States; that the act violates the Fifth Amendment because appellant is deprived of the right to choose its customers and operate its business as it wishes, resulting in a taking of its liberty and property without due process of law and a taking of its property without just compensation; and, finally, that by requiring appellant to rent available rooms to Negroes against its will, Congress is subjecting it to involuntary servitude in contravention of the Thirteenth Amendment.

The appellees counter that the unavailability to Negroes of adequate accommodations interferes significantly with interstate travel, and that Congress, under the Commerce Clause, has power to remove such obstructions and restraints; that the Fifth Amendment does not forbid reasonable regulation and that consequently damage does not constitute a "taking" within the meaning of that amendment; that the Thirteenth Amendment claim fails because it is entirely frivolous to say that an amendment directed to the abolition of human bondage and the removal of widespread disabilities associated with slavery places discrimination in public accommodations beyond the reach of both federal and state law. . . .

[A]ppellees proved the refusal of the motel to accept Negro transients after the passage of the act. The district court sustained the constitutionality of the sections of the act under attack and issued a permanent injunction. . . . It restrained the appellant from "[r]efusing to accept Negroes as guests in the motel by reason of their race or color" and from "[m]aking any distinction whatever upon the basis of race or color in the availability of the goods, services, facilities, privileges, advantages, or accommodations offered or made available to the guests of the motel, or to the general public, within or upon any of the premises of the Heart of Atlanta Motel, Inc."

2. The History of the Act

. . . The act as finally adopted was most comprehensive, undertaking to prevent through peaceful and voluntary settlement discrimination in voting, as well as in places of accommodation and public facilities, federally secured programs and in employment. Since Title II is the only portion under attack here, we confine our consideration to those public accommodation provisions.

3. Title II of the Act

This Title is divided into seven sections beginning with § 201(a), which provides that:

"All persons shall be entitled to the full and equal enjoyment of the goods, services, facilities, privileges, advantages, and accommodations of any place of public accommodation, as defined in this section, without discrimination or segregation on the ground of race, color, religion, or national origin."

4. Application of Title II to Heart of Atlanta Motel

It is admitted that the operation of the motel brings it within the provisions of § 201(a) of the act and that appellant refused to provide lodging for transient Negroes because of their race or color and that it intends to continue that policy unless restrained.

The sole question posed is, therefore, the constitutionality of the Civil Rights Act of 1964 as applied to these facts. The legislative history of the act indicates that Congress based the act on §5 and the Equal Protection Clause of the Fourteenth Amendment as well as its power to regulate interstate commerce. . . .

[Part 5 deleted.]

6. The Basis of Congressional Action

While the act as adopted carried no congressional findings the record of its passage through each house is replete with evidence of the burdens that discrimination by race or color places upon interstate commerce. . . . This testimony included the fact that our people have become increasingly mobile with millions of people of all races traveling from state to state; that Negroes in particular have been the subject of discrimination in transient accommodations, having to travel great distances to secure the same; that often they have been unable to obtain accommodations and have had to call upon friends to put them up overnight, and that these conditions have become so acute as to require the listing of available lodging for Negroes in a special guidebook which was itself "dramatic testimony to the difficulties" Negroes encounter in travel. These exclusionary practices were found to be nationwide, the Under Secretary of Commerce testifying that there is "no question that this discrimination in the North still exists to a large degree" and in the West and Midwest as well. This testimony indicated a qualitative as well as quantitative effect on interstate travel by Negroes. The former was the obvious impairment of the Negro traveler's pleasure and convenience that resulted when he continually was uncertain of finding lodging. As for the latter, there was evidence that this uncertainty stemming from racial discrimination had the effect of discouraging travel on the part of a substantial portion of the Negro community. This was the conclusion not only of the Under Secretary of Commerce but also of the Administrator of the Federal Aviation Agency, who wrote the Chairman of the Senate Commerce Committee that it was his "belief that air commerce is adversely affected by the denial to a substantial segment of the traveling public of adequate and desegregated public accommodations." We shall not burden this opinion with further details since the voluminous testimony presents overwhelming evidence that discrimination by hotels and motels impedes interstate travel.

7. The Power of Congress over Interstate Travel

The power of Congress to deal with these obstructions depends on the meaning of the Commerce Clause.

* * * * *

In short, the determinative test of the exercise of power by the Congress under the Commerce Clause is simply whether the activity sought to be regulated is "commerce which concerns more States than one" and has a real and substantial relation to the national interest. Let us now turn to this facet of the problem.

* * * * *

The same interest in protecting interstate commerce which led Congress to deal with segregation in interstate carriers and the white-slave traffic has prompted it to extend the exercise of its power to gambling, to criminal enterprises, to deceptive practices in the sale of products, to fraudulent security transactions, and to racial discrimination by owners and managers of terminal restaurants. . . .

That Congress was legislating against moral wrongs in many of these areas rendered its enactments no less valid. In framing Title II of this act Congress was also dealing with what it considered a moral problem. But that fact does not detract from the overwhelming evidence of the disruptive effect that racial discrimination has had on commercial intercourse. It was this burden which empowered Congress to enact appropriate legislation, and, given this basis for the exercise of its power, Congress was not restricted by the fact that the particular obstruction to interstate commerce with which it was dealing was also deemed a moral and social wrong.

It is said that the operation of the motel here is of a purely local character. But, assuming this to be true, "[i]f it is interstate commerce that feels the pinch, it does not matter how local the operation which applies the squeeze."

* * * * *

Thus the power of Congress to promote interstate commerce also includes the power to regulate the local incidents thereof, including local activities in both the States of origin and destination, which might have a substantial and harmful effect upon that commerce. One need only examine the evidence which we have discussed above to see that Congress may—as it has—prohibit racial discrimination by motels serving travelers, however "local" their operations may appear.

Nor does the act deprive appellant of liberty or property under the Fifth Amendment. The commerce power invoked here by the Congress is a specific and plenary one authorized by the Constitution itself. The only questions are: (1) whether Congress had a rational basis for finding that racial discrimination by motels affected commerce, and (2) if it had such a basis, whether the means it selected to eliminate that evil are reasonable and appropriate. If they are, appellant has no "right" to select its guests as it sees fit, free from governmental regulation.

There is nothing novel about such legislation. Thirty-two states now have it on their books either by statute or executive order and many cities provide such regulation. Some of these acts go back four-score years. It has been repeatedly held by this Court that such laws do not violate the Due Process Clause of the Fourteenth Amendment.

* * * * *

It is doubtful if in the long run appellant will suffer economic loss as a result of the act. Experience is to the contrary where discrimination is completely obliterated as to all public accommodations. But whether this be true or not is of no consequence since this Court has specifically held that the fact that a "member of the class which is regulated may suffer economic losses not shared by others . . . has never been a barrier" to such legislation. . . . Likewise in a long line of cases this Court has rejected the claim that the prohibition of racial discrimination in public accommodations interferes with personal liberty. . . . Neither do we find any merit in the claim that the act is a taking of property without just compensation. The cases are to the contrary. . . .

We find no merit in the remainder of appellant's contentions including that of "involuntary servitude." . . . We could not say that the requirements of the act in this regard are in any way "akin to African slavery." . . .

We, therefore, conclude that the action of the Congress in the adoption of the act as applied here to a motel which concededly serves interstate travelers is within the power granted it by the Commerce Clause of the Constitution, as interpreted by this Court for 140 years. . . .

Affirmed.

Questions

1. In your judgment does the Commerce Clause afford the federal government the authority to regulate a local business like the Heart of Atlanta motel? Explain.
2. Should the federal government regulate local business to further the cause of racial equity? Explain.
3. What arguments were offered by the government to establish that the Heart of Atlanta racial policy affected interstate commerce? Are you persuaded by those arguments? Explain.
4. Explain the Fifth and Thirteenth Amendment arguments raised in *Heart of Atlanta*.
5. What test did the Court articulate to determine when Congress has the power to pass legislation based on the Commerce Clause?
6. Ollie's Barbecue, a neighborhood restaurant in Birmingham, Alabama, discriminated against black customers. McClung brought suit to test the application of the public accommodations section of the Civil Rights Act of 1964 to his restaurant. In the suit the government offered no evidence to show that the restaurant ever had served interstate customers or that it was likely to do so. Decide the case. See *Katzenbach* v. *McClung,* 379 U.S. 294 (1964).
7. May a private club lawfully decline to serve liquor to a black person who is accompanying a white person to the club bar? Build the argument that the club is not "private" as a matter of law. See *Moose Lodge No. 107* v. *Irvis,* 407 U.S. 163 (1972).
8. What economic consequences would you project from a judicial decision permitting Congress to regulate public accommodations clearly interstate in character, while leaving more preponderantly local public accommodations to the regulation of state and local governments?

STATE AND LOCAL REGULATION OF INTERSTATE COMMERCE

As noted, the states via their constitutional police power have the authority to regulate commerce within their jurisdictions for the purpose of maintaining the general welfare. That is, in order to assist in maintaining the public health, safety, and morals, states must be able to control persons and property within their jurisdictional authority. However, we have seen that the Commerce Clause, as interpreted, accords the federal government broad authority over commerce. As explained, the federal government has exclusive authority over foreign commerce. Purely intrastate commerce, having no significant effect on interstate commerce, is within the exclusive regulatory jurisdiction of the states. Of course, commerce purely intrastate in nature is quite rare. The confusion arises in the category of interstate commerce. While federal government regulation of interstate commerce is pervasive, it is not exclusive. In broad terms, states may regulate interstate commerce where:

1. The commerce being regulated does not require uniform, consistent treatment throughout the nation.
2. Congress has not preempted the area by its own complete regulation.
3. The state regulation does not discriminate against interstate commerce in favor of state interests.
4. The state regulation is not an undue burden on commerce.
5. The state regulation is not in conflict with federal law.

In the *Kassel* case that follows, we see how the Supreme Court grappled with a conflict between a state's police power and the Commerce Clause. Before turning to the case, a warning is in order. This introductory treatment of the Commerce Clause has been quite brief. Many subtleties and complexities have not been addressed. Furthermore, several other elements of the Constitution, directly related to government regulation of business, have not been addressed or are treated elsewhere in the text.

KASSEL V. CONSOLIDATED FREIGHTWAYS CORP.
450 U.S. 662 (1980)

Justice Powell

The question is whether an Iowa statute that prohibits the use of certain large trucks within the State unconstitutionally burdens interstate commerce.

I

Appellee Consolidated Freightways Corporation of Delaware (Consolidated) is one of the largest common carriers in the country. It offers service in 48 States under a certificate of public convenience and necessity issued by the Interstate Commerce Commission. Among other routes, Consolidated carries commodities through Iowa on Interstate 80, the principal east–west route linking New York, Chicago, and the west coast, and on Interstate 35, a major north-south route.

Consolidated mainly uses two kinds of trucks. One consists of a three-axle tractor pulling a 40-foot two-axle trailer. This unit, commonly called a single, or "semi," is 55 feet in length overall. Such trucks have long been used on the Nation's highways. Consolidated also uses a two-axle tractor pulling a single-axle trailer which, in turn, pulls a single-axle dolly and a second single-axle trailer. This combination, known as a double, or twin, is 65 feet long overall. Many trucking companies, including Consolidated, increasingly prefer to use doubles to ship certain kinds of commodities. Doubles have larger capacities, and the trailers can be detached and routed separately if necessary. Consolidated would like to use 65-foot doubles on many of its trips through Iowa.

The State of Iowa, however, by statute restricts the length of vehicles that may use its highways. Unlike all other States in the West and Midwest, Iowa generally prohibits the use of 65-foot doubles within its borders. Instead, most truck combinations are restricted to 55 feet in length. Doubles, mobile homes, trucks carrying vehicles such as tractors and other farm equipment, and singles hauling livestock, are permitted to be as long as 60 feet. . . .

Because of Iowa's statutory scheme, Consolidated cannot use its 65-foot doubles to move commodities through the State. Instead, the company must do one of four things: (i) use 55-foot singles; (ii) use 60-foot doubles; (iii) detach the trailers of a 65-foot double and shuttle each through the State separately; or (iv) divert 65-foot doubles around Iowa.

Dissatisfied with these options, Consolidated filed this suit in the District Court averring that Iowa's statutory scheme unconstitutionally burdens interstate commerce. Iowa defended the law as a reasonable safety measure enacted pursuant to its police power. The State asserted that 65-foot doubles are more dangerous than 55-foot singles and, in any event, that the law promotes safety and reduces road wear within the State by diverting much truck traffic to other States.

In a 14-day trial, both sides adduced evidence on safety, and on the burden on interstate commerce imposed by Iowa's law. On the question of safety, the District Court found that the "evidence clearly establishes that the twin is as safe as the semi."

* * * * *

The District Court . . . concluded that the state law impermissibly burdened interstate commerce.

* * * * *

The Court of Appeals for the Eighth Circuit affirmed. . . .

II

It is unnecessary to review in detail the evolution of the principles of Commerce Clause adjudication. . . .

The Commerce Clause does not, of course, invalidate all state restrictions on commerce. It has long been recognized that, "in the absence of conflicting legislation by Congress, there is a residuum of power in the state to make laws governing matters of local concern which nevertheless in some measure affect interstate commerce or even, to some extent, regulate it." . . . For example, regulations that touch upon safety—especially highway safety—are those that "the Court has been most reluctant to invalidate." . . . Indeed, "if safety justifications are not illusory, the Court will not second-guess legislative judgment about their importance in comparison with related burdens on interstate commerce." . . .

But the incantation of a purpose to promote the public health or safety does not insulate a state law from Commerce Clause attack. Regulations designed for that salutary purpose nevertheless may further the purpose so marginally, and interfere with commerce so substantially, as to be invalid under the Commerce Clause. . . .

III

Applying these general principles, we conclude that the Iowa truck-length limitations unconstitutionally burden interstate commerce.

In *Raymond Motor Transportation, Inc. v. Rice,* the Court held that a Wisconsin statute that precluded the use of 65-foot doubles violated the Commerce Clause. This case is *Raymond* revisited. Here, as in *Raymond,* the State failed to present any persuasive evidence that 65-foot doubles are less safe than 55-foot singles. Moreover, Iowa's law is now out of step with the laws of all other Midwestern and Western States. Iowa thus substantially burdens the interstate flow of goods by truck. In the absence of congressional action to set uniform standards, some burdens associated with state safety regulations must be tolerated. But where, as here, the State's safety interest has been found to be illusory, and its regulations impair significantly the federal interest in efficient and safe interstate transportation, the state law cannot be harmonized with the Commerce Clause.

A

Iowa made a more serious effort to support the safety rationale of its law than did Wisconsin in *Raymond,* but its effort was no more persuasive. . . .

The trial focused on a comparison of the performance of the two kinds of trucks in various safety categories. The evidence showed, and the District Court found, that the 65-foot double was at least the equal of the 55-foot single in the ability to brake, turn, and maneuver. The double, because of its axle placement, produces less splash and spray in wet weather. And, because of its articulation in the middle, the double is less susceptible to dangerous ''off-tracking,'' and to wind.

None of these findings is seriously disputed in Iowa. Indeed, the State points to only three ways in which the 55-foot single is even arguably superior: singles take less time to be passed and to clear intersections; they may back up for longer distances; and they are somewhat less likely to jackknife.

The first two of these characteristics are of limited relevance on modern interstate highways. As the District Court found, the negligible difference in the time required to pass, and to cross intersections, is insignificant on four-lane divided highways because passing does not require crossing into oncoming traffic lanes, and interstates have few, if any, intersections. The concern over backing capability also is insignificant because it seldom is necessary to back up on an interstate. In any event, no evidence suggested any difference in backing capability between the 60-foot doubles that Iowa permits and the 65-foot doubles that it bans. Similarly, although doubles tend to jackknife somewhat more than singles, 65-foot doubles actually are less likely to jackknife than 60-foot doubles.

Statistical studies supported the view that 65-foot doubles are at least as safe overall as 55-foot singles and 60-foot doubles. One such study, which the District Court credited, reviewed Consolidated's comparative accident experience in 1978 with its own singles and doubles. Each kind of truck was driven 56 million miles on identical routes. The singles were involved in 100 accidents resulting in 27 injuries and one fatality. The 65-foot doubles were involved in 106 accidents resulting in 17 injuries and one fatality. Iowa's expert statistician admitted that this study provided ''moderately strong evidence'' that singles have a higher injury rate than doubles. Another study, prepared by the Iowa Department of Transportation at the request of the state legislature, concluded that ''[s]ixty-five-foot twin trailer combinations have *not* been shown by experiences in other states to be less safe than 60-foot twin trailer combinations *or* conventional tractor-semitrailers'' (emphasis in original). Numerous insurance company executives, and transportation officials from the Federal Government and various States, testified that 65-foot doubles were at least as safe as 55-foot singles. Iowa concedes that it can produce no study that establishes a statistically significant difference in safety between the 65-foot double and the kinds of vehicles the State permits. . . .

B

Consolidated, meanwhile, demonstrated that Iowa's law substantially burdens interstate commerce. Trucking companies that wish to continue to use 65-foot doubles must route them around Iowa or detach the trailers of the doubles and ship them through separately. Alternatively, trucking companies must use the smaller 55-foot singles or 60-foot doubles permitted under Iowa law. Each of these options engenders inefficiency and added expense. The record shows that Iowa's law added about $12.6 million each year to the costs of trucking companies. Consolidated alone incurred about $2 million per year in increased costs.

In addition to increasing the costs of the trucking companies, . . . Iowa's law may aggravate, rather than ameliorate, the problem of highway accidents. Fifty-five-foot singles carry less freight than 65-foot doubles. Either more small trucks must be used to carry the same quantity of goods through Iowa, or the same number of larger trucks must drive longer distances to bypass Iowa. In either case, as the District Court noted, the restriction requires more highway miles to be driven to transport the same quantity of goods. . . .

Because Iowa has imposed this burden without any significant countervailing safety interest, its statute violates the Commerce Clause. The judgment of the Court of Appeals is affirmed.

Justice Brennan, with whom Justice Marshall joins, concurring in the judgment.

. . . [A]lthough Iowa's lawyers in this litigation have defended the truck-length regulation on the basis of the safety advantages of 55-foot singles and 60-foot doubles over 65-foot doubles, Iowa's actual rationale for maintaining the regulation had nothing to do with these purported differences. Rather, Iowa sought to discourage interstate truck traffic on Iowa's highways. Thus, the safety advantages and disadvantages of the types and lengths of trucks involved in this case are irrelevant to the decision.

Though my Brother Powell recognizes that the State's actual purpose in maintaining the truck-length regulation was ''to limit the use of its highways by deflecting some through traffic,'' he fails to recognize that this purpose, being *protectionist* in nature, is *impermissible* under the Commerce Clause. The Governor admitted that he blocked legislative efforts to raise the length of trucks because the change ''would benefit only a few Iowa-based companies while providing a great advantage for out-of-state trucking firms and competitors at the expense of our Iowa citizens.'' . . .

Questions

1. Based on the *Kassel* decision, are states prohibited from establishing highway safety standards that burden interstate commerce? Explain.
2. How does Justice Brennan's opinion differ with that of Justice Powell?
3. What did Justice Rehnquist mean in his dissenting opinion (not reprinted here) when he said, ''The Commerce Clause is, after all, a grant of authority to Congress, not to the courts.''

4. During the 1973 gasoline shortage, Maryland gasoline stations operated by producers or refiners had received, according to a state government survey, preferential treatment over "independent" dealers in obtaining supplies of gasoline. Thereafter, a statute was enacted providing "a producer or refiner of petroleum products (1) may not operate any retail service station within the state, and (2) must extend all 'voluntary allowances' uniformly to all service stations it supplies." Exxon challenged the statute.
   a. What is the essence of Exxon's claim?
   b. Decide the case. See *Exxon Corp.* v. *Governor of Maryland*, 98 S. Ct. 2207 (1978).

5. In the interest of safety, an Illinois statute required rear fender mudguards of a special contoured design on trucks using Illinois roadways. The required design was not typical of that in use in the industry and possessed no clearly established safety advantage. Was the statute constitutional? See *Bibb* v. *Navajo Freight Lines, Inc.*, 359 U.S. 520 (1959).

6. A New York state statute prohibited the export of milk produced in the state to other states. New York argued that the statute was necessary to avoid milk shortages. Is the statute constitutional? See *H. P. Hood & Sons* v. *DuMond*, 336 U.S. 525 (1949).

The States in "Combat"

The following article illustrates many of the issues in the continuing debate over federal versus state regulation of commerce.

A WAR BETWEEN THE STATES: HOMEGROWN U.S. TRADE BARRIERS COSTLY

David R. Francis

The shooting war between the Union and the Confederacy ended in 1865. But something of an "invisible" trade war between states continues today.

According to two University of Houston–University Park economists [Steven G. Craig and Joel Sailors], the United States of America is not as united a market as many believe. In fact, they calculate that "fantastic numbers" of interstate trade barriers could cost consumers as much as $150 billion a year in higher prices for goods and services.

For instance, one study found more than 1,500 agricultural restrictions on interstate trade in 11 western states alone. . . . Craig admitted that his $150 billion figure is a "rough guesstimate." Since interstate trade is some 15 times as large as international trade, however, the impediments to a unified American trading market are important. Here are some examples:

• State and local governments often give preference to products or services from their own state or town. The usual restriction says local contractors or manufacturers win the bid if their price comes within 5 percent of an out-of-state offer. Since state and local governments purchase around $400 billion of goods and services each year, the preference is costly to taxpayers.

• In the agricultural area, some of the restrictions on interstate trade may be legitimate.

Other restrictions are purely protectionist. For example, since 1967 Texas has not allowed its consumers to eat Florida grapefruit, since Texas maturity standards require that grapefruit must test out at nine parts of sugar to one part acid. Since Florida grapefruit tests out at 7.5 to 1, it is banned from sale in Texas.

Eight states tax imported wine more heavily than wine produced in-state. Or they impose arbitrary licensing, storage, and marketing regulations on imported wine.

• The mobility of professional labor services is sharply restricted through the use of local licensing and certification. One study cited by the two Houston economists found 2,800 state laws affecting more than 7 million workers, including doctors, lawyers, dentists, others in medical professions, and teachers.

Another study calculated that a dentist's income is 12 percent higher than it would be in a free market where professionals could move about without restriction.

• Texas severely restricts insurance sales by out-of-state firms through complicated sets of reserve requirements on firms.

• States have various laws aimed at discouraging competition from out-of-state or foreign banks.

The Supreme Court has stopped some protective measures, invoking the Commerce Clause of the U.S. Constitution. For example, it prevented North Carolina from restricting the import of soft drinks bottled out of state with tax and administrative burdens. It blocked Louisiana from attempting to tax oil-field equipment made out of state.

. . . Craig says the Supreme Court set federal interstate trade policy on a case-by-case basis without a clear legislative mandate from Congress.

State barriers have been upheld by the Supreme Court about 50 percent of the time, Craig notes.

* * * * *

But, Craig concludes, "What may be good for one state industry may be bad for the economy as a whole. Congress needs to look at the problem seriously. If we did not have so many of these trade restrictions, the gross national product would expand, and the nation would be better off."

Summary of State and Local Regulation

The visibility and magnitude of federal regulation of business has obscured our bountiful web of state and local regulations. Indeed, state, rather than federal, government is one of America's true growth industries. From 1970 through 1985, federal civilian employment increased slightly less than 5 percent, while state employment during the same period multiplied by nearly 35 percent.[6] Abundant state and local legislation is designed to regulate business behavior. Those regulations fall into three broad categories: (1) controlling entry into business, (2) regulating competition, and (3) preventing consumer fraud.

The states are primarily responsible for regulating the insurance industry and are heavily involved in regulating banking, securities, and liquor sales. Many businesses and professions—from funeral preparations to barbering to the practice of medicine—require a license from the state. Public utilities (e.g., gas, electricity, and sewage disposal) are the subject of extensive regulation governing entry, rates, customer service, and virtually the fullness of the companies' activities. All states have some form of public service commission charged with regulating utilities in the public interest. Many states seek to directly enhance competition via antitrust legislation. Many states have passed laws forbidding usury, false advertising, stock fraud, and other practices resulting in harm to the consumer.

Local regulation is much less economically significant than state regulation. Local government intervention in business typically involves various licensure requirements. For example, businesses like bars and theatres are often required to obtain a local permit to operate. Certain tradespeople (such as plumbers, electricians, and builders) may be required to gain local (and/or state) occupational licensure to legally engage in their craft. Licensure, it is argued, serves to protect the public from unsafe, unhealthy, and substandard goods and services, but critics contend that the presumed benefits of licensure are exceeded by its costs in increased prices, decreased services, and administrative overhead.

The following article illustrates why Iowa and most other states regulate competition in the home health care and auto dealer industries.

STATE: CARE SERVICES, DEALERSHIP LAWS DON'T HURT CONSUMERS

Leon Lynn

Iowa laws that govern home health care services and car dealerships are being defended against criticism leveled by recently released Federal Trade Commission reports.

The reports contend that laws in Iowa and many other states that limit the establishment of new auto dealers and home health care services cost consumers billions of dollars without any benefits.

* * * * *

Administrators of public home health care agencies have clashed with . . . hospitals that have started similar programs. The administrators have contended the new services duplicate existing programs and inflate health care costs.

The FTC, however, claims open competition in the area would help consumers.

Iowa is among 33 states, plus the District of Columbia and Puerto Rico, where a "certificate of need" must be obtained before a home health care service can be established.

States justify these laws as helping prevent costly duplication of services, the report said. Officials favoring the rules say they promote economic efficiency.

"Certificate of need regulations impose barriers to entry in the home health care field, resulting in reduced competition and increased costs and prices. In addition, there is no evidence that the regulations provide any benefits," noted David Scheffman, acting director of the FTC's economics bureau.

* * * * *

Iowa Assistant Attorney General Richard Cleland said the FTC reports were not produced because of concern for consumers. "It's basically a psychological ploy to reduce government regulation for political reasons," he said.

The FTC report said laws restricting new automobile dealerships cost consumers an estimated $3.2 billion in 1985.

The analyses showed these restrictive state laws "are not in the best interests of the American people," said Terry Calvani, acting chairman of the commission.

* * * * *

The commission reported that laws in Iowa and 35 other states, which create so-called Relevant Market Areas for auto dealers, restrict the establishment of new dealerships in the vicinity of existing dealers selling the same make of car.

Under Relevant Market Area laws, the existing dealer can protest to the state if a new dealer is proposed for his area. If that occurs, the car manufacturer must justify the new dealership, often with the result that the new sales firm does not go into business, the FTC said.

The study looked at 13 states where such laws were in effect, and found prices of new autos averaged 6.14 percent higher than in states without the laws.

Extending that finding to all 36 states with such laws would mean consumers spent an extra $3.2 billion on cars in 1985 because of the dealer restrictions, the study concluded.

* * * * *

But Ted Metier, attorney for the Iowa Department of Transportation's Regulation Authority, said the law is an important one.

A large auto manufacturer, Metier said, "is backed by millions and millions of dollars. The local dealer may have every dollar he has invested in his dealership. Maybe he's making a living and maybe he isn't."

If the franchise law didn't exist, Metier said, "the manufacturer could set up another dealership right across the street if it wanted to." That threat would give the manufacturer unfair leverage over the local dealership, he said.

The law also discourages fly-by-night dealerships that would strand customers when they moved on, Metier said. "It protects peoples' rights to have a reputable dealer in the same place for more than 10 minutes."

Source: *Waterloo Courier,* March 16, 1986, p. B1. Reprinted with permission.

RECENT DEVELOPMENTS

On the other hand, the most interesting legal development in the area of state and local regulation in recent years represents a considerable victory for private enterprise. In *First English Evangelical Church* v. *Los Angeles*[7] and *Nollan* v. *California Coastal Commission,*[8] the Supreme Court, while not rolling back state and local regulation, appears to have imposed oner-ous new compensation burdens on governmental units that restrict prop-erty owners' use of their land. Among other commands, the Fifth Amendment to the U.S. Constitution provides that private property may not be taken for public use without just compensation. State and local governments routinely restrict the use of land via zoning ordinances and other restraints. For example, a local government might require real estate developers to provide some low-income, multifamily housing as part of a middle-income, single-family housing subdivision. Or, on the other side of the coin, a local government might institute zoning laws that would prevent developers from building low-income housing in an economically upper-class neighborhood. Or, a state or local government might impose restrictions on real estate developments in wetlands or open spaces.

In recent decades, land-use law has reflected a steady increase in gov-ernment intervention. Now the *First English* and *Nollan* decisions suggest that the weight of the law has shifted to greater property rights protection under the takings clause of the Fifth Amendment. Previously thought to be largely invulnerable, land-use regulations may now need to be sup-ported with much clearer justifications. However, these decisions did nothing to alter the longstanding rule that property owners do not have a legal right to the *most profitable* use of their land. Indeed, under the reasoning in *Nollan,* property owners ordinarily would receive compen-sation only if they could demonstrate that they had been denied all "eco-nomically viable" use of their property. In the *Nollan* case, Marilyn and James Nollan applied for a permit to replace their beachfront home with a larger structure. The California Coastal Commission agreed on the con-dition that the Nollans grant an easement on their beach that would allow the public to cross that property and thus facilitate movement between the public beaches that lay on both sides of the Nollan beach. The Nollans sued, claiming a violation of the takings clause. The case reached the U.S. Supreme Court, where the Nollans prevailed, with Justice Scalia explaining that "if it [California] wants an easement across the Nollans' property, it must pay for it."

The article that follows summarizes the holding in the *First English* case.

COURT REQUIRES
COMPENSATION FOR LAND LIMITS

Washington, D.C.—In a decision with profound effect on property rights and the regulation of land use, the Supreme Court ruled 6–3 . . . that property owners are entitled to compensation when government restrictions prevent them—even temporarily—from using their land.

Chief Justice William Rehnquist declared for the Court majority that once a zoning or other government regulation amounts to "a taking of all use of property," the government cannot escape being constitutionally required to pay compensation.

The decision was a victory for the building and real estate industries and a serious setback for state and local governments, environmental groups, and conservationists.

The court's main dissenter, Justice John Paul Stevens, called the ruling "a loose cannon" that would set off a "litigation explosion" and make local government officials reluctant to enact zoning, building, and other regulations to protect public health and safety.

Land-Use Limits

Rehnquist acknowledged that the decision "will undoubtedly lessen to some extent the freedom and flexibility of land-use planners and governing bodies of municipal corporations when enacting land-use regulations.

"But such consequences necessarily flow from any decision upholding a claim of constitutional right; many of the provisions of the Constitution are designed to limit the flexibility and freedom of government authorities, and the Just Compensation Clause of the Fifth Amendment is one of them."

The Fifth Amendment provides that private property shall not "be taken for public use, without just compensation."

Gus Bauman, a lawyer for the National Association of Home Builders, called the ruling "the most important land-use decision in over 50 years. For the average home owners and lot owners, this decision means that the right to . . . use their land has been strengthened enormously."

In contrast, Benna Ruth Solomon, chief counsel of the State and Local Legal Center, expressed deep disappointment on behalf of the city, county, and state governments she represents.

"Officials now will be more reluctant to deal with a major public health or safety problem because of fear that a court will second-guess them and find them liable in damages," she said. "They may decide that the risk is not worth it. This will make it more difficult for state and local officials to protect citizens."

Claims of "Taking"

She said that zoning ordinances and other land-use regulations, government restrictions on utility, taxi, or other rates charged to consumers, and rent control laws produce the largest numbers of claims of a government "taking" of property.

The case, *First English Evangelical Lutheran Church of Glendale* v. *County of Los Angeles,* involved a church barred by a 1979 emergency flood control ordinance from reconstructing its buildings in a canyon in the Angeles National Forest.

A fire had denuded nearly 3,900 acres of watershed in 1977 and, less than a year later, a storm flooded the church's campground, known as Lutherglen, and destroyed buildings used as a retreat center and a recreational area for handicapped children.

First English Lutheran filed an "inverse condemnation" suit, contending that even though the county had not formally condemned its property, the flood protection ordinance had had the same effect. Therefore, the church's lawyers argued, payment of compensation was required.

But the California courts, obeying a rule imposed by the state Supreme Court in 1979 to preserve "a degree of freedom" in land-use planning, concluded that the church could seek a court order to invalidate the ordinance, but could not obtain damages.

However, a Supreme Court majority—Rehnquist, William Brennan, Byron White, Thurgood Marshall, Lewis Powell and Antonin Scalia—ruled . . . that the church could obtain damages from the county if a lower court determines that its property had been taken by the land-use regulation.

The case was sent back to the California courts for a decision on whether the flood control ordinance actually deprived the church of all use of its property since 1979. If it did, then the Constitution "requires that the government pay the landowner for the value of the use of the land during this period," Rehnquist wrote.

Critical Issue

The court did not attempt to clarify the critical, but murky, issue of when a government regulation becomes so intrusive that it amounts to a taking of private property.

Stevens, joined in most of his dissent by Harry Blackmun and Sandra Day O'Connor, concluded that the type of regulatory action involved "cannot constitute a taking" because it was a legitimate government effort to preserve life and property.

"In light of the tragic flood and the loss of life that precipitated the safety regulations, it is hard to understand how [the church] ever expected to rebuild on Lutherglen," Stevens wrote.

* * * * *

Source: *Des Moines Register,* June 10, 1987, pp. 1A, 8A.

MORE REGULATION?

Of course, it is easy and intellectually tidy to call for a reduced state and local regulatory presence in the business community and, indeed, throughout life. Certainly that direction is widely applauded currently—and perhaps properly so—but the competing considerations must be carefully weighed. In the article that follows we see a brief evaluation of the success of combined state and federal regulatory efforts to enhance highway safety.

A GOVERNMENT SUCCESS STORY: LIVES SAVED ON NATION'S HIGHWAYS

Joan Claybrook

One of the most rewarding aspects of the effort expended on legislative battles is seeing the payoff from bills successfully enacted. In highway safety, both federal and state legislators can take credit for a number of smashing success stories. And they are important to Americans all over the country whose loved ones are surviving highway crashes rather than suffering fatal or crippling injuries by the tens of thousands each year.

* * * * *

When Congress created NHTSA [the National Highway Traffic Safety Administration] it recognized both the traditional functions of the states in regulating drivers and highway design and the newer precepts that the design and performance of the vehicle are critical in saving lives.

As required by the 1966 law, NHTSA set standards to measure state achievements under newly authorized grant-in-aid programs.

Proven Life-Savers

Over the past 20 years, the efficacy, the cost effectiveness, and the rigor of NHTSA standards and guidelines have been challenged, researched, reviewed, and amended. In some cases, new legislation has been enacted. This process has resulted in a series of programs that are saving thousands of lives and mitigating tens of thousands of injuries per year.

Those with the highest payoff are:

• **55-Mile-per-Hour (MPH) Speed Limit.** Enacted in 1973 to conserve energy, this law saved an estimated 25,000 to 50,000 lives in its first decade. The National Academy of Sciences has estimated that the lower speed limit prevents 2,500 to 4,500 serious, severe, and critical injuries and 34,000 to 61,000 minor and moderate injuries annually. The Academy's Transportation Research Board declared, "Few safety policies can rival the impact of the 55-MPH speed limit in reducing accidental deaths of Americans as they travel about the country. In addition, this law results in the saving of approximately 60 million barrels of petroleum each year, or about 1 percent of the total U.S. consumption." Despite these incredible savings over the past 14 years, these laws continue to be challenged by individuals who argue that saving a few minutes of travel time is more important than saving lives and reducing crippling injuries on the highway. [Speed limits may now be raised to 65 MPH on rural interstates—Author.]

• **Motorcycle Helmets.** Motorcycle crashes account for 10 percent of all motor vehicle fatalities, but only 3.2 percent of the vehicle population. Under pressure from NHTSA, all but three states had enacted helmet-use laws by

1975. The success of this standard in saving lives and reducing injury received a grizzly demonstration in the years after the Congress unexpectedly struck down the federal penalty requirements in 1976. This freed states to repeal their helmet laws without jeopardizing federal aid highway funds. Deaths from motorcycle crashes jumped 48 percent between 1976 and 1980 when 27 states repealed or weakened their helmet laws . . . .

• **Child Restraints.** Nearly 50 percent of all children age four or younger are now protected by special car seats or other safety restraints, compared to less than 5 percent in 1974. The payoff has been significant. Nearly 200 children up to four years old were saved by child restraints (158 lives) or lap belts (34 lives) in 1984. This dramatic change occurred because every state requires use of child restraints by law. Tennessee enacted the first child restraint law in 1977 under pressure from pediatricians . . . promotion of the concept throughout the country by NHTSA culminated in adoption of similar laws in most states by 1983.

• **Age 21 for Drinking.** In 1970, many states dropped their drinking age from 21 to 18, rationalizing that those old enough to be drafted and vote should be able to drink legally. However, extensive research showed that age 21 for drinking would prevent hundreds of teenage highway deaths each year. Driving while alcohol impaired is the leading cause of death for young adults aged 16–24. In 14 states that raised their legal drinking age to 21, nighttime highway fatalities among youths under 21 declined by a total of 380 per year. If the higher drinking age were adopted in all states, an estimated additional 600 young people per year might be saved nationwide.

[All states now must adopt and retain the 21 standard or face the threat of losing federal highway aid—Author.]

Crash Safety—Lap Belts to Air Bags

The more than 50 standards for motor vehicle safety performance issued since the federal government began doing so in 1967 have significantly reduced highway deaths and injury. Vehicle manufacturers routinely oppose new standards as too onerous or costly. When the first safety standards were proposed in 1966, Henry Ford II furiously objected to this government intrusion into the decision-making prerogatives of the manufacturers. He protested, "Many of the temporary standards are unreasonable, arbitrary, and technically unfeasible. . . . If we can't meet them when they are published, we'll have to close down."

Many motor vehicle standards have been delayed, indefinitely postponed, or cut back by industry lobbying. Despite these setbacks to safety protection in cars, very significant improvements have been adopted.

The standards require improved padding and the removal of sharp edges and knobs, installation of lap and shoulder restraints, improved door locks, side-impact protection devices, crashworthy fuel tanks, head restraints, collapsible steering assemblies, and, most recently, automatic restraint systems (air bags or automatic seat belts).

NHTSA estimates that the crash safety standards have saved over 100,000 Americans from being killed on the highway since 1968, a proud record indeed. The number of injuries mitigated are in the many hundreds of thousands.

Under the Department of Transportation standard, automatic restraints are now being installed in 10 percent of all new cars. . . . NHTSA estimates that this standard will save between 6,000 and 9,000 lives and reduce 150,000 injuries per year when the automatic systems are installed in all cars. Other standards are under consideration for pedestrian protection, for side-impact protection, and extension of the car standards to vans and light trucks, which will save hundreds of additional lives per year.

In short, the highway and auto safety programs are something to boast about in an era when the effectiveness of government programs is questioned and ridiculed.

Source: Joan Claybrook, "A Government Success Story: Lives Saved on Nation's Highways," *State Government News* (April 1987), pp. 8–9. Reprinted with permission.

Afterword

Let's remind ourselves of our central inquiries. Should government regulate business? If so, to what extent, and in what manner? Can we safely rely on the market and ethics to ensure the honorable and effective conduct of business? The article that follows offers an opinion and sets the foundation for the balance of the book, where we will review government's extensive regulatory role.

GOVERNMENT OVERSIGHT NEEDED TO KEEP BUSINESS HONEST, RETIRED MANAGERS SAY

Washington, D.C. (AP)—Nearly three out of four recently retired mid-level managers of large corporations say government regulation is necessary because industry cannot police itself entirely, according to a survey released Sunday.

* * * * *

The 117-page study, entitled "Corporate Ethics, Illegal Behavior, and Government Regulation: Views of Middle Management," was conducted by Marshall Clinard, sociology professor emeritus at the University of Wisconsin, for the Justice Department's National Institute of Justice.

Clinard based his findings on lengthy interviews with 64 managers who had retired within the past five years from 51 companies on *Fortune* magazine's listing of the 500 largest companies. The companies included Bendix, Dow Chemical, Firestone Tire & Rubber, General Motors Corp., Lockheed Aircraft Corp., Mobil Oil Corp., RCA Corp., and Westinghouse. The executives had jobs like manager of assembly operations, regional sales manager, or plant manager.

Clinard defined corporate crime as any company action punishable under criminal, civil, or administrative law.

* * * * *

The retired executives were asked, "What do you see as an alternative to government regulations: Can industry police itself?" A majority, 57.2 percent, answered that government is needed and industry cannot police itself. Another 14.1 percent said that, even with industry help, some government regulation is necessary.

When asked whether top management sets the tone for compliance with laws, 92.2 percent said "very much" and 6.3 percent said "some."

The retired managers were asked whether top management knew about legal violations either in advance or afterwards, but before it was detected by the government. Some 71.9 percent said top executives generally did know, 21.9 percent said their superiors knew about some violations, and 6.3 percent said the top executives knew little about them.

Some 69.8 percent said they would report serious unsafe working conditions to the government if the company did nothing about them. But only 23.4 percent said they would report price-fixing, 31.7 percent said they would report illegal rebates and kickbacks, and 35.5 percent said they would report illegal foreign payments.

On the reasons for not reporting price-fixing, Clinard quoted the former manager of a steel company's international division as saying, "Price-fixing is none of middle management's damn business. If there is a general in charge you do not blow the whistle on him."

The former director of business development for a toiletries company was quoted as saying, "Price-fixing involves money, not people's safety or the national interest."

On kickbacks and rebates, a former auto industry general purchasing agent was quoted as saying, "It is not the government's business. I usually got enough gifts from suppliers to fill the bedroom. I gave them away."

A former division manager in the machinery industry said, "We might lose business if we did not give illegal rebates and kickbacks."

Source: *Des Moines Register,* May 16, 1983, p. 3T. Reprinted with permission of the copyright holder, The Associated Press.

CHAPTER QUESTIONS

1. This chapter addressed the issue of increased government involvement in regulating business. How do you explain that trend?
2. What are the definitions given in this chapter for positive and negative externalities? For public goods?

3. If we had not experienced the Depression, would government regulation of business be substantially less pervasive than it is now?

4. As a safety measure, Arizona enacted a statute that limited the length of passenger trains to 14 cars and freight trains to 70 cars. Trains of those lengths and greater were common throughout the United States. The Southern Pacific Railroad challenged the Arizona statute.

   a. What was the legal foundation of the Southern Pacific claim?

   b. Decide the case. See *Southern Pacific Railroad* v. *Arizona,* 325 U.S. 761 (1945).

5. Oregon enacted a "bottle bill" for the purpose of reducing the problems of litter and solid waste. Under the terms of the statute, retailers of beer and carbonated beverages were required to pay consumers a specified refund on all containers. In turn, distributors were required to accept the containers from the retailers and pay the refund value. Pull-top cans were declared unlawful. American Can challenged the constitutionality of the statute, arguing, among other positions, that the impact on interstate commerce outweighed the benefits to the state and that the bill seriously impeded the flow of interstate commerce. Decide. Explain. See *American Can Co.* v. *Oregon Liquor Control Commission,* 517 P.2d 691 (Ore. 1973).

6. Many state dental boards decline to recognize licenses granted in other states. Professor Lawrence Shepard studied the effects of that policy on the price of dental services. He concluded:

   > Empowered by the state legislatures and aligned with the profession they oversee, dental licensing boards inhibit competition through restrictive licensing practices. In the manner of a cartel, most boards have used licensing exams to limit the entry of nonresident practitioners while the number of new dentists trained in their states has also been constrained. This study provides evidence that where regulatory authorities have constructed competitive barriers, dentists systematically raise fees, augmenting their earnings. It is estimated that the price of dental services and mean dentist income are between 12 and 15 percent higher in nonreciprocity jurisdictions when other factors are accounted for. Overall, the annual cost of this form of professional control is approximately $700 million. Pending proposals for licensure reform could eliminate these costs while effecting a more efficient geographical distribution of dentists. These conclusions may have broader applicability, given the large number of occupational groups that control the competitive environment in which they operate through state licensing boards.[9]

   a. Why do many states not adopt a policy of reciprocity as to dental licensure?

   b. Should the dental profession be entirely free of licensure requirements? Should accountants? Explain.

   c. Outline the considerations you believe should be used in deciding which occupations should be licensed.

7. Although the following remarks are not addressed directly to government regulation of business, they do have clear business implications and are a topic of special interest to many.

> Raising the legal age for drivers to 18 would save at least 2,000 lives a year, a public health researcher has concluded. If 16- and 17-year-olds were allowed to drive only during the day, the accident death toll would be cut by more than 1,000 annually, said Dr. Leon S. Robertson of Yale University.
>
> Robertson studied 236,205 fatal automobile crashes in the United States from 1975 to 1977, paying particular attention to the 19,470 crashes involving drivers under 18 years of age.
>
> He said that nearly half of all fatal crashes involving young drivers occurred after 8 P.M. and before 4 A.M. with the peak concentrated in the wee hours of weekends.
>
> "The evidence indicates that if these youngsters weren't driving, at least half of these fatalities, and probably three fourths of them, wouldn't occur," said Robertson, whose study was financed by the Insurance Institute for Highway Safety.
>
> "At least one third of these fatalities involved a single vehicle—a car hitting a tree or a lamp post," Robertson said.
>
> "Studies have found that some measures intended to reduce teen driving accidents actually have produced more accidents," Robertson said.
>
> "The growth in publicly financed high school driver education greatly increased the number of 16- and 17-year-olds licensed without reducing the crashes per licensed driver," he said. "The net result was more crashes.
>
> "In Connecticut, when high school driver education was eliminated from nine school districts in 1976, 75 percent of 16- and 17-year-olds who would have been expected to be licensed if driver education had been continued waited until they were 18 or older to obtain a license.
>
> "As a consequence of there being fewer drivers, there was a commensurate reduction in numbers of crashes involving 16- and 17-year-olds," Robertson said. "If young people didn't have driver's licenses or had licenses that permit daytime driving only, it is likely that few would drive illegally," Robertson said.
>
> In the fatal accidents he studied, very few involved drivers without licenses or with suspended licenses, especially among younger drivers.
>
> "Young people have difficulty obtaining automobiles," he said. "Their parents won't let them have the family car if they were not licensed or if they wanted to drive during hours when it was illegal.
>
> "I suspect many parents would welcome such restrictions."[10]

Should the states tighten their driving regulations for the young in the interests of increased safety? Explain.

8. The following excerpt is from an article criticizing local and state regulations designed to stem growth.

> The growth control and environmental movements have had a very favorable press, stressing the widespread benefits they can achieve by protecting the quality of our common environment against the onslaught of the bulldozer.

A closer look at how the growth control and environmental coalition operates in local controversies shows that its effects are far less benign. It has made a clear and substantial contribution to the escalation of new home prices, yet its success in discouraging home building has failed to produce important environmental benefits for the public at large. Instead, it has protected the environmental, social, and economic advantages of *established* suburban residents who live near land that could be used for new housing.[11]

    a. What are the opposing factors in weighing a no-growth policy?

    b. Should a state or locality be permitted to enact such a policy? Explain.

9. The preponderant government regulatory thrust is currently at the federal level. Should we shift that emphasis to the state and local levels? Explain.

10. In the "Government Oversight" article, a majority of the retired executives surveyed felt that "industry cannot police itself entirely."

    a. In your judgment, which conditions or forces, if any, prevent effective industry self-regulation?

    b. The executives were much less willing to report price-fixing violations than unsafe working conditions. Do you agree that, in general, a manager should not report price-fixing to the government? Explain.

11. A San Francisco law bans smoking in many public places and requires employers to establish smoking and nonsmoking areas satisfactory to employees.

    a. Do you favor the San Francisco law? Explain.

    b. Should the federal government enact similar legislation? Explain.

    c. Why might such laws be to the advantage of much of the business community?

12. The public mass transit authority (SAMTA) in San Antonio, Texas, had been receiving substantial federal aid. In 1979, the Wage and Hour Administration of the Department of Labor took the position that SAMTA, although a local agency, was subject to the federal minimum wage and overtime requirements of the Fair Labor Standards Act (FLSA). In *National League of Cities* v. *Usery,* 426 U.S. 833 (1976), the Supreme Court had held that the Commerce Clause does not accord Congress the power to enforce those requirements against the states "in areas of traditional government functions." The district court in Texas held that municipal ownership and operation of a mass transit system is a "traditional government function," and, therefore, SAMTA was exempt from the FLSA minimum wage and overtime requirements. The case was appealed to the U.S. Supreme Court. Decide. See *Garcia* v. *San Antonio Metropolitan Transit Authority,* 469 U.S. 528 (1985).

13. Alabama's legislature imposed a higher tax on out-of-state insurance companies than on in-state firms. Out-of-state companies could reduce, but not eliminate, the differential by investing in Alabama.
    a. What constitutional objection was raised by the out-of-state firms?
    b. What defense was raised by the state?
    c. Decide. See *Metropolitan Life Ins. Co.* v. *Ward,* 470 U.S. 869 (1985).

14. The Pennsylvania legislature passed legislation requiring all trucks over a specified weight to display an identification marker and pay a $25 annual fee for that marker. Trucks registered in Pennsylvania were exempted from the marker fee on the grounds that the $25 would be treated as a part of the general state vehicle registration fee. Later, the Pennsylvania legislature reduced the $25 fee to $5 and imposed a $36-per-axle fee on all trucks over a specified weight. At the same time, the legislature reduced the fee for registering trucks (of the specified weight class) in Pennsylvania by the amount of the axle tax. The American Trucking Associations challenged the Pennsylvania laws.
    a. Identify the central constitutional issue in this case.
    b. Decide the case. Explain. See *American Trucking Associations, Inc.* v. *Scheiner, 55 Law Week* 4988 (U.S. S. Ct., 1987).

15. Monroe County, which embraces the Florida Keys, is concerned (like so many coastal communities) with the problem of population growth exceeding the county's capacity to produce adequate public services (roads, utilities, schools, and so on). Therefore, in 1987 the county designated 16,000 lots as unsuitable for building. The result, in some instances, was that property owners who held two adjacent lots were told they could build only one structure on the two lots combined.
    a. What constitutional argument would you make on behalf of those lot owners?
    b. Should the government be permitted to restrain growth in this manner, or should we allow the free market to work its will? Explain.

16. Overall, which level of government (local, state, federal) do you consider the most trustworthy? Explain.

NOTES

1. Karl Schriftgiesser, *Business and the American Government* (Washington, D.C.: Robert B. Luce, 1964), p. 14.
2. Ibid., p. 27.
3. The remarks in this paragraph are drawn, in part, from "Interventionist Government Came to Stay," *Business Week,* September 3, 1979, p. 39.

4. Ibid.

5. 317 U.S. 111 (1942).

6. Table no. 467, "Governmental Employment and Payrolls: 1970 to 1985," *Statistical Abstract of the United States* (Washington, D.C.: U.S. Department of Commerce, 1987), p. 280.

7. 55 *Law Week* 4781 (1987).

8. 55 *Law Week* 5145 (1987).

9. Lawrence Shepard, "Licensing Restrictions and the Cost of Dental Care," *The Journal of Law and Economics* 21, no. 1 (April 1978), pp. 187, 200.

10. Jon Van, "Raise Driving Age to 18, Researcher Says," for the *Chicago Tribune* as reprinted in the *Lexington Sunday Herald-Leader,* February 1, 1981, p. A-11.

11. Bernard Frieden, "Regulating the American Dream," *Across the Board,* August 1979, p. 67.

Chapter 7

Administrative Agencies and the Regulatory Process

This chapter is divided into five parts. Parts One through Three discuss the nature and duties of the many federal regulatory agencies. Part Four evaluates the strengths and weaknesses of the federal regulatory process. Part Five explores the business community's methods of dealing with government regulation.

Part One—Introduction to Administrative Agencies

The article that follows raises the central themes in this chapter: (1) our lives suffer from excessive government regulation, but (2) some regulation is necessary in an increasingly complex society; therefore, (3) where do we draw the line? As you proceed through this chapter, these issues should guide your reading.

"REGULATION" ISN'T A DIRTY WORD

Vermont Royster

Every time I leave my house I seem to fall into a web of regulation. If I drive, the township tells me how fast I'm allowed to go, ranging from 25 to 35 miles per hour. If I leave town, the state steps in. . . .

* * * * *

If I go afoot I don't escape. At the intersections there are those signs reading "walk" or "don't walk." Car drivers at the same corner are regulated by red, yellow, and green lights, sometimes with little arrows pointing left or right. . . .

I suppose I should object to all this since the cry of our time is for "deregulation." Deregulate everything. . . .

* * * * *

The theory behind this is that the marketplace will do the regulating. Banks or airlines that don't behave themselves will find their customers going elsewhere. If the customers don't pay attention, caveat emptor.

Much of this cry for deregulation is justified. Much regulation is unnecessary, some actually harmful. The Food and Drug Administration is notorious for its over-caution in protecting us from possibly harmful drugs even at the cost of depriving us of new drugs for many ailments; sometimes it lets a few people have them but prohibits them to the rest of us.

The classic example of too rigid regulation is the Interstate Commerce Commission. In the long-ago days of my youth I once took a train from Raleigh, North Carolina, to Morehead City on the coast. On departure I was the only passenger. On arrival I was the only passenger. Along the way one or two people got on for short trips between towns. The trip took 12 hours. It was gruesome for me and for the railroad. Although the bus, as I learned later, did the trip faster and in more comfort, the railroad had to keep the train running for years because the small towns along the way demanded it and the ICC complied.

If I hesitate to join the hue for deregulation, even when much of the regulation is misguided, it's because I shudder at the thought of a wholly deregulated society. I prefer knowing my pharmacist has to be licensed and that somebody checks on him; so also with the butcher so that I have some assurance his scale registers a true measure.

As a matter of fact, regulation to protect consumers is almost as old as civilization itself. Tourists to the ruins of Pompeii see an early version of the bureau of weights and measures, a place where the townsfolk could go

to be sure they weren't cheated by the local tradesmen. Unfortunately a little larceny is too common in the human species.

So regulation in some form or other is one of the prices we pay for our complex civilization. And the more complicated society becomes, the more need for some watching over its many parts. We shouldn't forget that a great deal of the regulation we encounter today in business or in our personal lives arose from a recognized need in the past.

Take the drug companies. It wasn't so very long ago that the countryside was flooded with snake-oil salesmen hawking cures for every ailment and bamboozling credulous folk with worthless nostrums. The Food and Drug Administration Act in 1906 was the outgrowth of a real need, as was the Meat Inspection Act the same year.

* * * * *

I would be happier today with a little more regulation of the airlines and the air lanes. The deregulation that let more lines into the business and let the marketplace set fares has been a boon to travelers. We have cheaper fares and more choice of carriers. But the result has also been more crowding of the air lanes and, quite possibly, some cutting of the corners on maintenance and pilot training.

* * * * *

As society (our way of life) gets more complicated there will be newer areas calling for some kind of regulation. The whole area of genes research and genetic manipulation, for example. Or the development of surrogate motherhood. Or the growing use of organ transplants, such as the transplant of adrenal glands as a possible treatment for Parkinson's patients. . . .

The hub of the question, of course, will be, as it is now, what kind of regulation? Once government begins to regulate anything there must be some sort of agency to do it, and that inevitably means a bureaucracy that, like the ICC of old, gets stultified. That in turn means regulating the regulators lest they become sovereign unto themselves. The logical place for overseeing this is in Congress, which creates the regulating agency to begin with. But Congress is itself a bureaucracy of 535 members with different constituencies and different ideas.

The last recourse is us, we the people, who must collectively decide not only what should be regulated but how. . . .

THE AGENCIES

That branch of the law governing the administrative operations of government is *administrative law.* The federal Administrative Procedure Act defines an *agency* as any government unit other than the legislature and the courts. Thus administrative law technically addresses the entire executive branch of government. However, our attention will be directed to the prominent regulatory agencies (Interstate Commerce Commission, Federal Communications Commission, Securities and Exchange Commission, etc.) rather than the various executive departments (Agriculture, Defense, etc.) and nonregulatory, welfare agencies (Social Security Administration, Veterans Administration, and the Public Health Service). Although our fundamental concern lies at the federal level, administrative law principles are fully applicable to the conduct of state and local governments. At the local level, planning and zoning boards and property tax assessment appeals boards are examples of administrative agencies. At the state level, one might cite public utility commissions and the various state licensure boards for law, medicine, architecture, and the like.

The authority of the federal regulatory agencies falls broadly into three categories.

1. Control of Supply. Several agencies control entry into various economic activities. Historically, the Civil Aeronautics Board (now defunct) decided which airlines would be granted operating licenses and which routes they could serve. The Interstate Commerce Commission possessed similar authority as to rail, motor, and water carriers and pipelines. The Federal Communications Commission regulates entry to the use of television and radio broadcasting. As will be discussed later in this chapter, the government is in the midst of various deregulation initiatives that have substantially depreciated the agencies' licensing powers. However, much of that authority, such as the Securities and Exchange Commission's regulation of the investment business, will persist and, in the case of the SEC, probably expand in light of the stock market crash of 1987.

2. Control of Rates. Those federal agencies charged with regulating utilities and carriers (Federal Energy Regulatory Commission, ICC, and CAB) have historically set the prices to be charged for the services offered within their jurisdictions. For example, the consumer facing an interstate change of address found little value in comparison shopping for the least expensive furniture mover because the rates, regulated by the Interstate Commerce Commission, were virtually identical. Government regulation of rates remains common, but the deregulation movement has significantly increased the role of the free market in rate setting.

3. Control of Conduct. *(a) Information.* A major element of government regulation is simply requiring information. Agencies commonly compel companies to disclose consumer information that would otherwise remain private. For example, warning labels may be mandated. *(b) Standards.* Where simply requiring information is deemed inadequate to the public need, the government may establish minimum standards that the private sector must meet. For example, a ladder might be required to safely hold at least a specified weight, or workers might lawfully only be exposed to a specified maximum level of radiation. *(c) Product banishments.* In those unusual instances where information alone is deemed inadequate to protect the public, products can be banned from the market. The Consumer Product Safety Commission banned the flame retardant Tris (used in children's sleepwear) from the market because of evidence of the product's cancer-causing properties.

The Environmental Protection Agency has extensive authority to alter business behavior in accord with society's interest in minimizing pollution. The Equal Employment Opportunity Commission, in attacking employment discrimination, has been instrumental in altering personnel policies in American business. These agencies and others like them (e.g., the National Labor Relations Board, the Federal Trade Commission, and the Occupational Safety and Health Administration) were specifically established to regulate particular dimensions of business behavior. Other agencies (e.g., the ICC, the FCC) were established to regulate entire industries, and in doing so they necessarily influence the course of virtually every dimension of those industries' business practices.

In sum, via regulation of supply, rates, and conduct, the grand maze of local, state, and federal regulatory agencies is a significant determinant of the course of American business. The administrative agencies have in some instances largely replaced free market decision making and, in many instances, have acted as supplements to a market taken to be inadequate to the task of fully governing American commerce.

THE AGENCIES AND THE LARGER GOVERNMENT

The various agencies do not fit together comfortably into the larger scheme of the federal government. Some agencies are independent regulatory bodies acting as minigovernments with rather broad executive, legislative, and judicial powers. Other agencies are departments of the executive branch (the Food and Drug Administration and the Social Security Administration are elements of the Department of Health and Human Services) and, as such, are inevitably more subject to pressure from the executive authority. For example, the FTC is fully involved in the traditional executive duties of investigation and prosecution, while at the same time it both enacts rules in the legislative manner and conducts trials (hearings) in the judicial mode. On the other hand, the SEC's duties are largely confined to the executive role of supervising the investment securities industry.

The breadth of duties performed by the agencies has provoked a pair of important policy disputes. It is argued that the agencies are undemocratic centers of extraordinary power, in that they perform all the traditional duties of government but are not subject to public review via elections. And many legal challenges to agency conduct have argued that the agencies are in violation of the constitutional requirement of separation of powers. However, the well-settled judicial view is that the various checks and balances on the administrative agencies are sufficient to meet the constitution framers' goals in providing for the separation of government powers. The formal checks and balances will become apparent in this section. (Perhaps the reader can identify certain informal, but nevertheless persuasive, external influences on agency action.)

The Role of Congress

The agencies are the product of congressional legislation. In creating an agency Congress is, in effect, delegating a portion of its authority to that body. Congress may not simply give away the power vested in it by the people. Constitutional safeguards must be met by providing standards to guide the agency in its rule making. However, numerous judicial decisions have established the position that those standards need not be drawn with great precision. Thus the agencies have rather broad mandates within which to operate. Congressional dissatisfaction can, of course, result in retarding or dissolving agency authority.

The Role of the President

The president, with the advice and consent of the Senate, appoints the administrator or the several commissioners who direct each agency's affairs. Commissioners are appointed in staggered terms, typically of seven years' duration. The appointment of commissioners for most of the agencies must reflect an approximate political balance between the two major parties. Commissioners can be removed from office only for dereliction of duty. Despite these procedural buffers between the agencies and the executive branch, the president can exert considerable political pressure on the agencies' affairs.

The Role of the Courts

Most agency actions are subject to judicial review. Agencies must operate within the bounds of the Constitution and the legislation creating them. In general, courts do not inquire into the wisdom of agency decisions. After all, the agencies are created as specialized centers of expertise. The courts, therefore, defer to that expertise, assuming constitutional and legislative standards have been met.

JUSTIFICATIONS FOR THE ADMINISTRATIVE AGENCY

Administrative agencies are the day-to-day operating arm of a vast array of government programs. The government has sought to attack a range of social problems, including misconduct in the business community. We have looked at the historical roots of business regulation. That some elements of business subjected society to serious abuse is generally acknowledged. That business itself sought certain regulatory measures is likewise widely accepted. So we can fairly conclude that business was instrumental in the growth of government regulation and, hence, the growth of administrative agencies. The point to recognize here is that the agencies that clearly intrude dramatically in all our lives were not born of government's malevolent distaste for business. Rather, with the best of intentions the legislative and executive branches sought to improve the quality of life, and one might powerfully argue that government has been quite successful in that regard.

Congress could have taken more direct control of the various regulatory and administrative programs. It has instead wisely chosen to create what is, in effect, a fourth branch of government. Why did Congress decide to delegate its authority by creating a welter of administrative agencies?

1. As the government gradually assumed a larger regulatory role, it became apparent that Congress could not manage the responsibility on its own. Congress is not in session on a daily basis necessary to attend to regulatory details. Since members of Congress are burdened with heavy workloads, the pragmatics of time dictated the delegation of authority.
2. Similarly, Congress cannot write legislation with the flexibility and breadth necessary to embrace the myriad circumstances altered by changing times. Congress, therefore, delegated to the agencies the task of writing and enforcing the specific rules necessary to fill in and render

operative the broad policy guidelines embodied in congressional legislation.

3. Congress also displayed rare wisdom in acknowledging its own deficiencies as to technical expertise. Life has grown increasingly complex. The duties of agencies like the Nuclear Regulatory Commission, the Environmental Protection Agency, and the Federal Reserve Board require detailed, specialized knowledge. Congress, as a policymaking body, is not well suited to technical fine tuning.

4. The dual constraints of time and expertise likewise prevent the court system from assuming a greater proportion of the regulatory burden. Therefore, many agencies conduct their own "trial-level" hearings.

QUESTIONS

1. The phrase *government regulation* embraces many functions. Define it.

2. For a number of years, the Federal Trade Commission sought to establish rules regulating "children's advertising." Regardless of your personal point of view, make the argument that the issue is more appropriately one for Congress than for the FTC.

3. Is the federal regulatory process limited in its goals to the correction of market failures? Should it be so limited? Explain.

4. Scholar Neil Jacoby, commenting on business' alleged ability to control government:

> There is also abundant evidence that during the 1960s and early 1970s, corporate businesses were generally unable to bend federal administrative agencies to their will—contrary to the popular notion that they have "captured" those agencies.
>
> Today it (business) is relatively less influential than ever. Far from being excessive, it may be too weak to maintain a vibrant market economy over the long run.[1]

   a. Has business "captured" the regulatory process? Explain.
   b. Is business relatively less powerful in relation to the government than was the case during the 19th century? Explain.
   c. Is government regulation a force of such magnitude as to threaten the viability of our market system? Explain.

5. Scholar James Q. Wilson said, "All democratic regimes tend to shift resources from the private to the public sector and to enlarge the size of the administrative component of government."[2] Is this so? Explain.

6. Scholar George Stigler asked, "What benefits can a state provide to an industry?"[3] Answer Stigler's inquiry.

7. Does the real origin of government regulation of business lie in the citizen's fear? That is, do the people consider the market too risky

and, therefore, opt for a system that affords them some protection from economic loss? Explain.

8. Have we reason for concern because the federal agencies have become a fourth branch of government not directly accountable to the public via the electoral process? Explain.

9. Do federal agencies perform executive, legislative, and judicial functions to such an extent that they conflict with the constitutional dictate of separation of powers between the three branches? Explain.

Part Two—Summary of the Administrative Process

Not surprisingly, the administrative process is quite detailed. Administrative law seeks to govern that process in a manner in keeping with the general welfare and constitutional safeguards. The tasks undertaken and the procedures followed differ from agency to agency. Administrative law itself has become a complex, specialized discipline with a vast reservoir of rules and court decisions. What follows is a brief outline of the administrative process and administrative law.[4] Remember that agency duties include the full spectrum of government activities, embracing quasi-legislative (rule-making), quasi-judicial (adjudicatory), and executive functions.

INFORMATION GATHERING

The success of setting rates, managing government property, preventing fraud, protecting the environment, and so on is substantially dependent on the quality of information the agency is able to acquire. For example, in seeking to maintain safe workplaces, the Occupational Safety and Health Administration (OSHA) conducts on-site inspections, along with other information-gathering procedures. Congress has conferred broad investigatory powers on the agencies, but constitutional and statutory safeguards prevent agencies from abusing their authority. In such tasks as developing rules, supervising regulated industries, and prosecuting wrong-doers, information is required for appropriate agency action.

INFORMAL AGENCY ACTION

Procedural flexibility is central to the success of administrative agency conduct. While formal proceedings such as rule making and adjudication achieve greater visibility, a large portion of agency business is conducted on an informal basis of negotiation and day-to-day bureaucratic decision making. For example, each year the Internal Revenue Service engages more than 100 million taxpayers in the process of settling accounts with the government. For most of those taxpayers the procedure remains entirely informal. In a like manner various government agencies process millions of applications and claims each year (e.g., applications for citizen band radio licenses). Another critical, informal role played by many agencies is that of protecting the public with testing and inspection procedures. (The Food and Drug Administration prefers to keep unhealthy products off the market rather than being compelled to take formal, adjudicatory action after the fact.) Likewise most agencies offer informal advice, both in response to requests and on their own initiative, to explain agency policy and positions. For example, each year the FTC receives several hundred inquiries regarding the legal sufficiency of warning labels on various potentially dangerous products. Supervisory duties, including most notably the active and close attention given to the banking industry, are a further illustration of informal agency duties. Finally, the agencies, as required by the Administrative Procedure Act, seek to reach informal, negotiated settlements of cases otherwise bound for administrative adjudication.

RULE MAKING

A major portion of the typical agency's activities are legislative. That is, the agencies adopt rules that often touch the lives of millions and are, in their effect, the equivalent of laws. Acting thus in a quasi-legislative manner, agencies enact three types of rules: (1) *Procedural rules* delineate the agency's internal operating structure and methods. (2) *Interpretive rules* offer the agency's view of the meaning of statutes governing the agency's action. Via both informal policy statements and formal guidelines based on open hearings, the agency seeks to clarify for interested parties the meaning of statutory language that is often very broadly drawn. Interpretive rules do not have the force of law, but they are important expressions of opinion as to what the governing legislation requires. Internal Revenue Service regulations are an example of interpretive rules. (3) *Legislative rules* are policy expressions having the effect of law. The agency is exercising the lawmaking function delegated to it by the legislature. Rate setting is a particularly important agency legislative function. Federal Trade Commission rules providing for a cooling-off period of three business days within which the buyer may cancel door-to-door sales contracts is an example of agency lawmaking that significantly affects business behavior.

A rule can be generated at the agency's own initiative or as a response to public petition. Commonly, as it draws a rule, the agency informally seeks advice from appropriate sources (although it need not do so). After preparing the rule, the agency is typically required by statute to offer public notice and a reasonable opportunity for public comment. A formal hearing is not necessary. To meet the notice requirement, the draft rule is published in the *Federal Register* (a daily publication of all federal rules, regulations, and orders). After evaluation and consultation, the final rule is then published in the *Federal Register* and later codified in the Code of Federal Regulations. As explained in the article that follows, some government agencies are experimenting with a negotiation approach to drafting federal regulations.

EXPERIMENTAL "REG–NEGS" TRY TO HEAD OFF NUMEROUS ATTACKS ON FEDERAL REGULATIONS

Laurie McGinley

Marc Maurer, president of the National Federation of the Blind, is furious that airlines often bar blind passengers from sitting in rows with emergency exits. "These airline people think they can dominate blind people, boss them around," he fumes.

But Walter Coleman of the Air Transport Association, the trade association for the major airlines, insists that airlines merely are trying to ensure the safety of all passengers. "You want to get that evacuation stream moving as quickly as possible," he says. "You don't want a bottleneck at the very beginning of it."

A typical debate in the capital? Hardly. The two sides are having a "reg-neg."

The term, which is short for regulatory negotiation, represents an innovative and still highly experimental way for adversaries to produce draft federal regulations. In this case, the two sides are quarreling over how the Department of Transportation should implement a law prohibiting discrimination against disabled people by airlines. Normally, the DOT would publish proposed rules, take comments

from interested groups, write the final rules— and watch critics possibly attack the rules in court. In this case, however, the interested groups are trying to hash out their differences *before* the rules are proposed.

Difficult Issues

If they do, it's less likely someone will "go running to the courts or Congress to overturn the rule," says Robert Ashby, the Transportation Department lawyer involved in the reg-neg on airlines.

In the past five years, reg-negs have produced agreements on such difficult issues as worker exposure to MDA, an animal carcinogen used in manufacturing; pollution curbs on wood-burning stoves; and the number of hours airline pilots may work—a topic so contentious that the rule hadn't been revised since the 1930s.

* * * * *

Reg-negs draw heavily on the labor–management tradition of face-to-face bargaining between adversaries. The talks are conducted by professional mediators. . . . The agency that will be issuing the rule takes part in the process but doesn't run it. . . . If an agreement is reached, the agency still must publish the draft rule and hear comment, but coming up with a final rule is much quicker and easier.

Still, some question whether reg-negs are the answer. "I'm a skeptic," says Christopher DeMuth, president of the American Enterprise Institute. "Everybody wants to find ways to make the regulatory process less protracted, litigious, and contentious, but whether you can simply do that through a lot of good will and negotiations, I don't know." Mr. DeMuth also worries that sometimes, in the push to get an agreement by the interested parties, the welfare of the general public may be left behind.

* * * * *

A Protracted Process

Other representatives of public-interest groups say one of the biggest drawbacks of reg-negs is the amount of work required—usually several months. "It is extremely labor intensive," says David Doniger, a lawyer for the Natural Resources Defense Council. Pending legislation in Congress would give public-interest groups some compensation for joining reg-negs.

* * * * *

Meanwhile, with a . . . deadline looming for agreement on a draft rule to be issued by the DOT, several difficult issues remain—in addition to the one on where blind passengers may sit. For example, should airlines be required to take extra steps to communicate safety instructions to deaf passengers? And when should airlines be permitted to deny boarding to disabled passengers who are unattended?

"I can play tennis and basketball," says David Capozzi, who uses a wheelchair and is taking part in the talks as national advocacy director for Paralyzed Veterans of America. "But some airlines won't let me fly alone."

ADJUDICATION

Although informal procedures (such as settlements) are preferred, agencies commonly must turn to judicial proceedings to enforce agency duties. Judicial-like administrative hearings touch the breadth of American life. Indeed, administrative hearings are equal in significance and much superior in numbers to all federal court trials each year. Many issues facing agencies could properly be resolved in either the rule-making or the adjudicatory format. The decision lies within the agency's discretion (subject to judicial review) and is based on the nature of the task involved, as well as fairness to the affected parties.

Should an administrative hearing prove necessary, the process is, in general terms, as described in the next paragraphs.

Typically an investigation is conducted, and, if the facts merit, a complaint may be filed. Or the agency may submit the proposed complaint to the respondent first in an effort to reach a settlement via a *consent order,* in which the party being investigated agrees to steps suitable to the agency but under which the respondent makes no admission of guilt (thus retarding the likelihood of subsequent civil liability). If a formal complaint is filed, the respondent may file an answer, and the parties would engage in prehearing discovery proceedings.

After the complaint is filed the agency will, as required by the Administrative Procedure Act, seek to settle the dispute. If evidence of a violation exists, the case may be disposed of via a consent order. If a settlement is not forthcoming, the case goes forward much in the manner of a civil trial. Of course, a settlement is welcomed throughout the proceeding. The case is heard by an administrative law judge. The respondent may be represented by counsel. Parties have the right to present their cases, cross-examine, file motions, raise objections, and so on. However, they do not have the right to a jury trial.

The hearing examiner (judge) decides all questions of law and fact and then issues a decision. In general, that decision is final unless appealed to the agency. Internal agency review may be conducted by intermediate reviewing boards, by the full commission, or by both. After exhausting opportunities for review within the agency, appeal may be taken to the federal court system.

JUDICIAL REVIEW

An individual aggrieved by an act or decision of an agency may bring a challenge in court. Perhaps the major constraint on agency power is the threat of judicial review. However, the sheer bulk of agency activities means only a very small portion of those activities will receive judicial scrutiny. Indeed, many appeals of agency actions may be denied on technical grounds (as when the appealing party does not have standing to sue). However, assuming those procedural hurdles are scaled and review is granted, the question becomes that of the scope of judicial review. Into which issues will the court inquire? Historically the courts have taken a rather narrow approach to judicial review. Two commonsense considerations support that restrained judicial stance. The first is deference to the presumed expertise of the administrative agencies. The jurists, being generalists in the field of law, have been reluctant to overrule the judgment of specialists specifically chosen to regulate within their area of expertise. Second, very crowded judicial calendars act as a natural brake on activist judicial review. For those reasons, judges have traditionally disposed of administrative law cases in an expeditious manner, by readily sustaining the judgment of the agency. Of course, the courts have overruled the agencies when appropriate. Indeed, of late we can see evidence of a firmer judicial role.

Not surprisingly, judicial review of agency decisions raises a variety of technical, esoteric issues of law. The nature of those issues differs in part depending on whether the court is reviewing an agency's rule-making function or its adjudicatory function. Cases turn on questions like these:

1. Does the legislature's delegation of authority meet constitutional requirements?
2. Has the agency exceeded the authority granted by the enabling legislation?
3. Has the appealing party exhausted all the available administrative remedies?
4. Are the agency's findings of fact supported by substantial evidence in the record as a whole?

These issues are close to the heart of the administrative law practitioner, but their exploration is not necessary to the layperson's understanding of the larger regulatory process. The case that follows will be our only consideration of the formalities of judicial review. This appeal from a Federal Communications Commission adjudication sheds some light on the agency regulatory process and judicial review; but, much more important, the case raises fundamental questions regarding freedom of speech in a technologically advanced society.

F.C.C. V. PACIFICA FOUNDATION
98 S. Ct. 3026 (1978)

Justice Stevens

This case requires that we decide whether the Federal Communications Commission has any power to regulate a radio broadcast that is indecent but not obscene.

A satiric humorist named George Carlin recorded a 12-minute monologue entitled "Filthy Words" before a live audience in a California theater. He began by referring to his thoughts about "the words you can't say on the public, ah, airwaves, um, the ones you definitely wouldn't say, ever." He proceeded to list those words and repeat them over and over again in a variety of colloquialisms. The transcript of the recording . . . indicates frequent laughter from the audience.

At about 2 o'clock in the afternoon on Tuesday, October 30, 1973, a New York radio station, owned by respondent Pacifica Foundation, broadcast the "Filthy Words" monologue. A few weeks later a man, who stated that he had heard the broadcast while driving with his young son, wrote a letter complaining to the commission. He stated that, although he could perhaps understand the "record's being sold for private use, I certainly cannot understand the broadcast of same over the air that, supposedly, you control."

The complaint was forwarded to the station for comment. In its response, Pacifica explained that the monologue had been played during a program about contemporary society's attitude toward language and that, immediately before its broadcast, listeners had been advised that it included "sensitive language which might be regarded as offensive to some." Pacifica characterized George Carlin as a "significant social satirist" who "like Twain and Sahl before him, examines the language of ordinary people. . . . Carlin is not mouthing obscenities, he is merely using words to satirize as harmless and essentially silly our attitudes toward those words." Pacifica stated that it was not aware of any other complaints about the broadcast.

On February 21, 1975, the commission issued a declaratory order granting the complaint and holding that Pacifica "could have been the subject of administrative sanctions." . . . The commission did not impose formal sanctions, but it did state that the order would be "associated with the station's license file, and in the event that subsequent complaints are received, the commission will then decide whether it should utilize any of the available sanctions it has been granted by Congress."

* * * * *

[T]he commission concluded that certain words depicted sexual and excretory activities in a patently offensive manner, noted that they "were broadcast at a time when children were undoubtedly in the audiences (i.e., in the early afternoon)" and that the prerecorded language, with these offensive words "repeated over and over," was "deliberately broadcast." . . .

In summary, the commission stated: "We therefore hold that the language as broadcast was indecent and prohibited." . . .

The United States Court of Appeals for the District of Columbia Circuit reversed, with each of the three judges on the panel writing separately. . . .

Judge Tamm concluded that the order represented censorship and was expressly prohibited by ¶ 326 of the Communications Act. Alternatively, Judge Tamm read the commission opinion as the functional equivalent of a rule and concluded that it was "overbroad." . . .

Chief Judge Bazelon's concurrence rested on the Constitution. He was persuaded that ¶ 326's prohibition against censorship is inapplicable to broadcasts forbidden by ¶ 1464 (prohibiting "obscene, indecent, or profane language by means of radio communications"). However, he concluded that ¶ 1464 must be narrowly construed to cover only language that is obscene or otherwise unprotected by the First Amendment. . . .

Judge Leventhal, in dissent, stated that the only issue was whether the commission could regulate the language "as broadcast." . . .

Emphasizing the interest in protecting children, not only from exposure to indecent language, but also from exposure to the idea that such language has official approval, . . . he concluded that the commission had correctly condemned the daytime broadcast as indecent.

Having granted the commission's petition for certiorari, . . . we must decide: (1) whether the scope of judicial review encompasses more than the commission's determination that the monologue was indecent "as broadcast"; (2) whether the commission's order was a form of censorship forbidden by ¶ 326; (3) whether the broadcast was indecent within the meaning of ¶ 1464; and (4) whether the order violates the First Amendment of the United States Constitution.

(I)

The general statements in the commission's memorandum opinion do not change the character of its order. Its action was an adjudication. . . . It did not purport to engage in formal rule making or in the promulgation of any regulations. The order ''was issued in a specific factual context''; questions concerning possible action in other contexts were expressly reserved for the future. The specific holding was carefully confined to the monologue ''as broadcast.'' . . .

(II)

The relevant statutory questions are whether the commission's action is forbidden ''censorship'' within the meaning of ¶ 326 and whether speech that concededly is not obscene may be restricted as ''indecent'' under the authority of ¶ 1464. . . .

* * * * *

The prohibition against censorship unequivocally denies the commission any power to edit proposed broadcasts in advance and to excise material considered inappropriate for the airwaves. The prohibition, however, has never been construed to deny the commission the power to review the content of completed broadcasts in the performance of its regulatory duties.

* * * * *

Entirely apart from the fact that the subsequent review of program content is not the sort of censorship at which the statute was directed, its history makes it perfectly clear that it was not intended to limit the commission's power to regulate the broadcast of obscene, indecent, or profane language. A single section of the [Radio Act of 1927] is the source of both the anticensorship provision and the commission's authority to impose sanctions for the broadcast of indecent or obscene language. Quite plainly, Congress intended to give meaning to both provisions. Respect for that intent requires that the censorship language be read as inapplicable to the prohibition on broadcasting obscene, indecent, or profane language.

We conclude, therefore, that ¶ 326 does not limit the commission's authority to impose sanctions on licensees who engage in obscene, indecent, or profane broadcasting.

(III)

The only other statutory question presented by this case is whether the afternoon broadcast of the ''Filthy Words'' monologue was indecent within the meaning of ¶ 1464. . . .

The commission identified several words that referred to excretory or sexual activities or organs, stated that the repetitive, deliberate use of those words in an afternoon broadcast when children are in the audience was patently offensive and held that the broadcast was indecent. Pacifica takes issue with the commission's definition of indecency, but does not dispute the commission's preliminary determination that each of the components of its definition was present. Specifically, Pacifica does not quarrel with the conclusion that this afternoon broadcast was patently offensive. Pacifica's claim that the broadcast was not indecent within the meaning of the statute rests entirely on the absence of prurient appeal.

The plain language of the statute does not support Pacifica's argument. The words "obscene, indecent, or profane" are written in the disjunctive, implying that each has a separate meaning. Prurient appeal is an element of the obscene, but the normal definition of "indecent" merely refers to nonconformance with accepted standards of morality.

* * * * *

Because neither our prior decisions nor the language or history of ¶ 1464 supports the conclusion that prurient appeal is an essential component of indecent language, we reject Pacifica's construction of the statute. When that construction is put to one side, there is no basis for disagreeing with the commission's conclusion that indecent language was used in this broadcast.

(IV)

Pacifica makes two constitutional attacks on the commission's order. First, it argues that the commission's construction of the statutory language broadly encompasses so much constitutionally protected speech that reversal is required even if Pacifica's broadcast of the "Filthy Words" monologue is not itself protected by the First Amendment. Second, Pacifica argues that inasmuch as the recording is not obscene, the Constitution forbids any abridgement of the right to broadcast it on the radio.

A

The first argument fails because our review is limited to the question of whether the commission has the authority to proscribe this particular broadcast. As the commission itself emphasized, its order was "issued in a specific factual context." . . .

That approach is appropriate for courts as well as the commission when regulation of indecency is at stake, for indecency is largely a function of context—it cannot be adequately judged in the abstract.

* * * * *

It is true that the commission's order may lead some broadcasters to censor themselves. At most, however, the commission's definition of indecency will deter only the broadcasting of patently offensive references to excretory and sexual organs and activities. While some of these references may be protected, they surely lie at the periphery of First Amendment concern. . . .

B

When the issue is narrowed to the facts of this case, the question is whether the First Amendment denies government any power to restrict the public broadcast of indecent language in any circumstances. For if the government has any such power, this was an appropriate occasion for its exercise.

The words of the Carlin monologue are unquestionably "speech" within the meaning of the First Amendment. It is equally clear that the commission's objections to the broadcast were based in part on its content. The order must therefore fall if, as Pacifica argues, the First Amendment prohibits all governmental regulation that depends on the content of speech. Our past cases demonstrate, however, that no such absolute rule is mandated by the Constitution.

The classic exposition of the proposition that both the content and the context of speech are critical elements of First Amendment analysis is Mr. Justice Holmes's statement. . . .

> We admit that in many places and in ordinary times the defendants in saying all that was said in the circular would have been within their constitutional rights. But the character of every act depends upon the circumstances in which it was done. . . . The most stringent protection of free speech would not protect a man in falsely shouting fire in a theatre and causing a panic. It does not even protect a man from an injunction against uttering words that may have all the effect of force. . . . The question in every case is whether the words used are used in such circumstances and are of such a nature as to create a clear and present danger that they will bring about the substantive evils that congress has a right to prevent.

Other distinctions based on content have been approved. . . . The government may forbid speech calculated to provoke a fight. . . . It may pay heed to the "commonsense differences between commercial speech and other varieties." . . . It may treat libels against private citizens more severely than libels against public officials. . . . Obscenity may be wholly prohibited. . . .

The question in this case is whether a broadcast of patently offensive words dealing with sex and excretion may be regulated because of its content. Obscene materials have been denied the protection of the First Amendment because their content is so offensive to contemporary moral standards. . . . But the fact that society may find speech offensive is not a sufficient reason for suppressing it. Indeed, if it is the speaker's opinion that gives offense, that consequence is a reason for according it constitutional protection. For it is a central tenet of the First Amendment that the government must remain neutral in the marketplace of ideas. If there were any reason to believe that the commission's characterization of the Carlin monologue as offensive could be traced to its political content—or even to the fact that it satirized contemporary attitudes about four-letter words—First Amendment protection might be required. But that is simply not this case. These words offend for the same reasons that obscenity offends. . . .

* * * * *

In this case it is undisputed that the content of Pacifica's broadcast was "vulgar," "offensive," and "shocking." Because content of that character is not entitled to absolute constitutional protection under all circumstances, we must consider its context in order to determine whether the commission's action was constitutionally permissible.

C

We have long recognized that each medium of expression presents special First Amendment problems. . . . And of all forms of communication, it is broadcasting that has received the most limited First Amendment protection. . . . The reasons for [that distinction] are complex, but two have relevance to the present case. First, the broadcast media have established a uniquely pervasive presence in the lives of all Americans. Patently offensive, indecent material presented over the airwaves confronts the citizen, not only in public, but also in the privacy of the home, where the individual's right to be left alone plainly outweighs the First Amendment rights of an intruder. . . . Because the broadcast audience is constantly tuning in and out, prior warnings cannot completely protect the listener or viewer from unexpected program content. . . .

Second, broadcasting is uniquely accessible to children, even those too young to read. . . .

It is appropriate, in conclusion, to emphasize the narrowness of our holding. This case does not involve a two-way radio conversation between a cab driver and a dispatcher, or a telecast of an Elizabethan comedy. We have not decided that an occasional expletive in either setting would justify any sanction or, indeed, that this broadcast would justify a criminal prosecution. The commission's decision rested entirely on a nuisance rationale under which context is all-important. The concept requires consideration of a host of variables. The time of day was emphasized by the commission. The content of the program in which the language is used will also affect the composition of the audience, and differences between radio, television, and perhaps closed-circuit transmissions, may also be relevant. . . .

The judgment of the court of appeals is reversed.

[Omitted are the appendix containing a transcript of the "Filthy Words" monologue, as well as the concurring opinions of Justices Powell and Blackmun and the dissenting opinions of Justices Brennan, Marshall, Stewart, and White.]

Afterword

Despite the deregulation movement of recent years, the Federal Communications Commission took steps in 1987–88 to strengthen its control over indecent radio and television programming. Following *Pacifica,* broadcasters had been safe in airing arguably indecent material if that material avoided the seven dirty words, if the broadcast or telecast was transmitted after 10 P.M., and if a warning was issued that explained the program might be inappropriate for children. In April 1987, the commission adopted the following expression of indecency as drawn from the *Pacifica* decision: "Material that depicts or describes, in terms patently offensive as measured by contemporary community standards for the broadcast medium, sexual or excretory activities or organs." After requests for clarification, the commission announced in November 1987 that indecent programs could be safely broadcast only between midnight and 6 A.M. Of course, obscene and pornographic material remained forbidden at all times. (The new rules did not affect cable television.)

Then in June 1988, the FCC levied the maximum $2,000 fine, its first enforcement action under the new standard, for a showing of the movie, "Private Lessons," by a Kansas City television station at the 8 P.M. hour.

The movie, rated R, included nudity in a sexual context according to the FCC. The movie is about a wealthy 15-year-old boy who was seduced by his maid. While denying any violation of the law, the station's ownership indicated that the movie showing violated company policy. The three FCC commissioners agreed that the movie was indecent under FCC standards, but Commissioner Patricia Dennis voted against issuing the fine on the grounds that parents should determine childrens' nighttime television habits.

But in August 1988, a federal appeals court ruled that the 10 P.M. to midnight portion of the FCC's indecency policy was a violation of free speech rights. The issue was returned to the commission, which must either accept 10 P.M. as the permissible hour for beginning indecent broadcasts or build a stronger case in support of its position that substantial numbers of unsupervised children would be exposed to the indecent material if it were broadcast between 10 P.M. and midnight. On the other hand, the court upheld the FCC's definition of indecency and its ban on indecent broadcasts between 6 A.M. and 10 A.M.[5]

Questions

1. Why was the question of whether the Federal Communication Commission's decision constituted adjudication or rule making significant to the subsequent judicial appeals? Explain the Supreme Court's resolution of that issue.
2. What is "prurient appeal"?
3. Are you persuaded by the Court's distinction between "obscene" language and "indecent" language? Explain.
4. Why was the commission's action not considered censorship?
5. Do children of all ages require the same degree of FCC protection?
6. *a.* As you understand them, would the more explicit daytime radio talk shows be forbidden under the FCC's latest indecency standard? Explain.
   b. How would the FCC be expected to rule on a condom ad designed to prevent the spread of AIDS if that ad were aired prior to midnight? Explain.
   c. What indecency standard would you adopt if the power were yours?
7. The *Pacifica* decision is explicitly limited to the facts of the case. But the Court conceded that the decision might lead to some self-censorship. "At most, however, the commission's definition of indecency will deter only the broadcasting of patently offensive references to excretory and sexual organs and activities." Do you agree that the commission's position is casting only a very limited chill over broadcasting? Explain.
8. What is the significance of the distinction the Court draws between the content and the context of the speech in question?
9. Should the Court adopt Pacifica's view that the First Amendment prohibits all government regulation that depends on the content of the speech? Explain.
10. Would a rock tune making occasional reference to sexual and excretory expletives and aired at 5 P.M. on an FM radio station fall within the doctrine suggested in *Pacifica* and the FCC's subsequent interpretations? Explain.

11. Do the *Pacifica* and "Private Lessons" decisions constitute a threat to your conception of freedom of speech? Explain.
12. Is any group, however well qualified, capable of specifying national standards of broadcasting decency? Explain.
13. Develop the argument that rule making is preferable to litigation as a means of settling public policy issues.

Part Three—An Example: The Food and Drug Administration

Having achieved an overview of the administrative process, it should now be helpful to take a closer look at a single agency.

The Food and Drug Administration, a division of the Department of Health and Human Services, is responsible for protecting the public from dangerous food, drugs, and cosmetics and for ensuring the effectiveness of drugs. Our inquiry will be limited largely to those situations in which the FDA governs the entry of new products into the market and in which the agency recalls products from the market that fail to meet government standards (on grounds of mislabeling, subpotency, etc.).

Food and Drug Administration

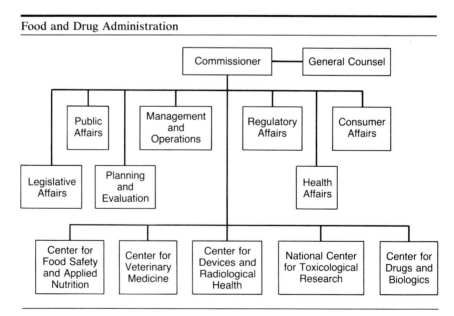

Source: Congressional Quarterly, *Federal Regulatory Directory,* 1985–86, p. 335.

HISTORY OF THE FDA

Today's FDA had its roots in the Bureau of Chemistry in the Department of Agriculture beginning in the 1880s. Consumer abuse of a magnitude that would today generate outrage was commonplace around the turn of the century. For example, adulterated, dangerous, worthless, sometimes habit-forming patent medicines, sold as miracle cures, constituted a significant health hazard. The muckraking literature of the day (e.g., Upton Sinclair's *The Jungle,* an exposé of unsanitary conditions in the meat-packing industry) and the increasing support of the American Medical Association and various industry trade associations led Congress in 1906 to enact the Food and Drug Act. In essence the act prohibited the adulteration and misbranding of foods and drugs under federal jurisdiction. The legislation had been encouraged by the colorful tactics of Dr. Harvey Wiley, head of the Bureau of Chemistry, who formed what he called a "poison squad"—a group of 12 volunteers who ate meals laced with common preservatives of the era (borax, boric acid, formaldehyde, sulfurous acids, and others)—and then submitted the results to Congress.[6]

Weaknesses in the 1906 law generated appeals for further legislation. In 1937 a drug manufacturer released a new sulfa drug without benefit of toxicity tests. The first 40 gallons of "Elixir Sulfanilamide-Massengill" caused more than 100 deaths before its removal from the market.[7] Soon thereafter Congress approved the Food, Drug, and Cosmetics Act of 1938, which, among other requirements, prevented the marketing of new drugs until their safety was established and authorized the new FDA to remove from the market drugs found to be hazardous.

The final major piece of legislation investing the FDA with its current authority was the 1962 Kefauver Drug Amendments Act, which, among other provisions, required the effectiveness of a drug to be established by "substantial evidence" before it could lawfully be marketed. Interestingly, passage of the Kefauver Act was likewise secured by a major scandal. Many pregnant women in Europe and Canada who had used the sedative thalidomide gave birth to children with deformed or missing limbs. The drug had been limited to experimental use in the United States. Although the Kefauver Amendment would have had no impact on the thalidomide product, the publicity surrounding that horror was instrumental in passage of the act.

APPROVAL PROCESS

The administrative process by which drugs are evaluated illustrates the general nature of FDA decision making. After a drug or other sponsor has completed the initial screening and animal testing of a new drug, the

FDA is petitioned for permission to initiate testing on humans. Thereafter, having secured what it takes to be sufficient evidence as to the safety and effectiveness of the drug, the sponsor applies for marketing approval by filing a "New Drug Application (NDA)." The FDA must respond to the NDA within 180 days. The FDA may issue either an "approval" letter (a safe and effective drug), an "approvable" letter (basically sound but with certain issues to be resolved), or a "not approvable" letter (serious deficiencies). Prior to final approval, the FDA and the sponsor negotiate an agreement about the language of the official label that is directed to doctors and pharmacists and describes the uses of the drug, instructions for use, side effects, and so on. In an interesting departure from the old standards, new drugs may now be admitted to the American market based solely on foreign testing data (when the testing meets FDA standards). The FDA believes that the new standard ensures quality while eliminating the need for testing here on products already tested abroad. Following marketing approval, the marketing company must notify the FDA of any problems associated with the drug. The FDA can also receive information from the public, doctors, medical journals, and any other avenues. If warranted, the FDA may take the necessary steps to remove a drug from the market or make adjustments (e.g., a change in labeling) necessary to protect the public interest.

In 1987 the FDA approved the most striking change in drug-approval policy in 25 years. In brief, the FDA has agreed to allow certain classes of "breakthrough" drugs on the market without the extensive testing normally required. Drug companies can now sell drugs designed for serious conditions (such as Alzheimer's disease) if they have preliminary evidence of safety and FDA permission. Drugs being tested for life-threatening conditions (such as AIDS) need meet even less rigorous standards. The companies must show a "reasonable basis for concluding" that the drug "may be effective" and would not expose patients to "significant additional risks."[8] And in 1988, the commission decided to permit Americans to import (for personal use) small amounts of foreign-produced medicine not yet approved for sale in the United States.

The 1985 case of *Heckler* v. *Chaney*[9] offers a novel glimpse of both the drug approval process and plaintiffs' often strikingly imaginative use of the law. In that case a group of prison inmates had been sentenced to death by lethal injection. They petitioned the Food and Drug Administration, alleging that the use of those drugs for that purpose violated the federal Food, Drug, and Cosmetic Act (FDCA). Their claim, among others, was that the drugs had not been approved for use in human executions. The FDA declined to intervene. The inmates filed suit, and, after a court of appeals decision in their favor, the case reached the Supreme Court. The Court held for the government in finding that agency enforcement decisions are presumed to be immune to judicial review under the Administrative Procedure Act in those instances where agency actions are "committed to agency discretion by law." Here the FDCA, as drafted by Congress, revealed no meaningful standard by which to judge the exercise of discretion. Therefore, it may be assumed that Congress intended the decision making to be left exclusively in the hands of the agency. Not without irony, Justice Rehnquist, speaking for the Court, remarked: "We granted certiorari to review the implausible result that the FDA is required to exercise its enforcement power to ensure that states use only drugs that are 'safe and effective' for human execution."[10]

The following articles illustrate a more conventional FDA regulatory problem.

FDA INQUIRY INTO CARTER–GLOGAU IS LATEST OF MANY CONFRONTATIONS

Gregory Stricharchuk

In January 1976, the Food and Drug Administration sent a letter to Carter–Glogau Laboratories, a small Arizona drug manufacturer, rebuking the company for marketing an unapproved drug.

In that instance, the company quickly pulled the drug off the market. But since that time, Carter–Glogau and the FDA have clashed repeatedly.

Now, the agency is investigating E-Ferol, a Carter–Glogau product that grabbed headlines two months ago when it was suspected by the FDA of being linked to the deaths of 39 infants across the country.

The FDA has said that E-Ferol, an injectable vitamin E supplement, was introduced without its approval. Carter–Glogau's parent, Ohio-based Revco D.S. Inc., has replied that the product didn't require such approval because vitamin E is a long-established substance.

But FDA records show that the E-Ferol case is not unique. The disagreements between the agency and Carter–Glogau have focused on the company's marketing of unapproved new drugs

and the quality of its products. The records also allege a string of manufacturing abuses at Carter–Glogau that continued almost until the November 1983 introduction of E-Ferol.

The FDA's records, obtained under the Freedom of Information Act, say that:

- The agency sent 14 warnings concerning 36 unapproved new drugs to the company between 1976 and 1982. In that time, the FDA made several seizures of drugs produced by the company.

- A routine FDA inspection of Carter–Glogau in 1981 found "severe adverse conditions which impact on the quality of finished drug products."

- In June 1983, the agency considered seeking an injunction to stop the company from making any drugs until it corrected manufacturing deficiencies. But the FDA eventually decided that the violations weren't serious enough to support such an action.

Both Carter–Glogau and Revco refused repeated requests to discuss the FDA's findings and the E-Ferol investigation.

Carter–Glogau was founded in 1953 by its president, Ronald Carter, and a partner. The company makes injectible vitamin preparations, hormones, and other drugs under its own label and private labels. Revco bought the concern in 1979.

Still, Mr. Carter runs "virtually all aspects of the firm's operations, in spite of considerable growth" at the company, an FDA inspection report states. The records also appear to show a chief executive at odds with regulators in Washington.

Mr. Carter has repeatedly taken a firm stand against FDA policies on approving new drugs. In May 1981, for example, he wrote the agency: "We don't interpret the [regulations] as requiring premarket approval of generic copies of drugs which have been marketed for dozens of years. (Mr. Carter did not return numerous calls to his office seeking comment on the FDA records.)

In 1979, Carter–Glogau began marketing— without FDA approval—an injectable drug called phenylpropanolamine as an appetite suppressant. The drug had been on the market since the late 1940s to treat nasal congestion. But the FDA said the company hadn't done any scientific studies to show that the drug was safe and effective as a diet aid.

The company, which had marketed the drug with a label that said it could be used for appetite control, discontinued selling the product in May 1980.

At times, the agency has seized new Carter–Glogau drugs that weren't submitted for approval. In June 1981, FDA officials received a federal court's permission to seize 2,379 vials of Carter–Glogau's dalalone, a steroid used to treat swelling, that was distributed by O'Neal Jones & Feldman of St. Louis, the company that later distributed E-Ferol. In the same year, the government made four separate seizures

of steroids and female sex hormones produced by Carter–Glogau because the company hadn't received FDA approval to market the products.

The recurring issue of quality control has presented more serious problems, according to FDA records. In 1981, for example, the FDA said the company made a practice of using data from reference books to show that a drug with a similar formula remains stable, rather than conducting its own tests to back the claim.

A January 1983 inspection report says the company's "sterility testing logbook was discontinued" nine months earlier. According to the report, two Carter–Glogau managers apparently thought the other was keeping the log, which lists results of sterility tests by product name, lot number, and the room where a specific drug was packaged.

Maintaining sterile conditions in drug manufacturing is crucial, says Richard C. Nelson, an FDA compliance officer in Los Angeles. Contaminated drugs may have limited effectiveness and pose a danger to patients. "Injectable drugs are easy to formulate," he says, "but lots of companies don't make them because sterilization has to be perfect."

Mr. Carter did respond to some of the agency's rebukes. In February 1983, the agency's records show, he sent the head of the company's quality-validation department to an FDA-sponsored seminar on proper manufacturing practices.

Still, on August 12, 1983, Mr. Carter was sent a "notice of adverse findings" by Thomas L. Sawyer, head of the FDA's compliance branch in Los Angeles. While noting that the company had corrected some earlier problems, the report stated: "We are concerned that subsequent inspections repeatedly have revealed [manufacturing] deficiencies not previously encountered."

Inspectors wrote that the company didn't have formalized standards for making water for injectable drugs and for washing vials. They also wrote that Carter-Glogau didn't have adequate environmental controls in sterile rooms, including records on the type of organisms and the amount of particles found in the air during drug-filling operations.

Three months later, Carter–Glogau introduced E-Ferol.

The company scored an apparent coup when it became the first drug maker to introduce the intravenous vitamin E solution. Researchers had found that the vitamin helped prevent blindness and other problems that sometimes afflict premature babies as side effects of the extra oxygen they get. Such infants, however, usually don't have enough muscle tissue to withstand repeated injections.

But by January, 11 babies at hospitals in Ohio, Tennessee, and Washington died after treatment with E-Ferol. By April, more deaths suggested a link with the drug, and a recall was started.

FDA officials refuse to answer questions about their investigation of Carter–Glogau, although Mr. Nelson, the FDA compliance officer in Los Angeles, says the company's problems "weren't commonplace." The FDA refuses to compare the frequency of the company's problems with other drug firms.

Meanwhile, four lawsuits totaling almost $100 million have been filed against Carter–Glogau and Revco, claiming that E-Ferol caused the death or illness of four babies. Martin Zeiger, secretary and counsel for Revco, says the company is "vigorously defending" all lawsuits over E-Ferol.

Some physicians now suggest that the drug may have provided infants with too much vitamin E. Dr. Frank Bowen, a director of neonatology at Pennsylvania Hospital in Philadelphia who has studied vitamin E since 1978, says his research shows that babies develop infections at dosage levels one fifth that of E-Ferol's. "There's no question," he says, "that babies could overdose at levels provided by E-Ferol."

The following article brings the E-Ferol story up to late 1987, when criminal indictments were handed down against the drug companies and their officers.

E–FEROL DEATHS CITED IN FED SUIT

St. Louis—The deaths of 10 babies killed several years ago at Santa Rosa Medical Center in San Antonio [Texas] by an untested drug [E-Ferol Aqueous Solution] were cited as evidence a St. Louis drug firm committed fraud, a federal grand jury indictment charges.

The now-defunct company, O'Neal, Jones & Feldman, Inc., two of its top executives, and a second firm were indicted . . . on charges brought by the U.S. Justice Department's Office of Consumer Litigation in Washington, D.C.

* * * * *

O'Neal, Jones & Feldman, Inc., was the sole distributor of the product. The company is now known as O'Neal, Inc., the indictment states.

Also indicted was the manufacturer, Carter–Glogau Laboratories, Inc., of Glendale, Arizona, as well as the company's former president, Ronald M. Carter, Sr. Carter–Glogau is now called Retrac, Inc.

The companies were forced out of business and reorganized following the settlement of civil suits with the infants' families in 1985 and 1986. The exact amount of the settlements is not known, but tens of millions of dollars are known to have gone to the families.

* * * * *

The 32-page indictment says O'Neal, Jones & Feldman, Inc., concealed from medical professionals that such a drug could be fatal to infants. The grand jury also charges that the firm told doctors E-Ferol was safe even though adverse reactions to the drug had been reported to company officials.

In one instance, when one of the defendants was asked by a Santa Rosa pharmacist about dosage levels, the defendant failed to warn the pharmacist that the levels the hospitals were using were too high and potentially dangerous, the indictment states.

That defendant is James B. Madison, former vice president of operations for O'Neal, Jones & Feldman, Inc. Larry K. Hiland, former president and chief executive officer, was also indicted.

The grand jury adds that the company marketed the drug without approval from the Food and Drug Administration. The federal agency would have required that the drug be tested for safety and effectiveness before allowing it on the market.

If convicted of all the charges, Hiland, Madison, and Carter could each be sentenced to 101 years in prison and fined $142,000. The companies face maximum fines of $142,000.

Source: *San Antonio Express-News,* July 11, 1987, p. 2B. Reprinted with permission.

THE FDA REVIEWED

Both the FDA and the pharmaceutical industry are subjects of continuing criticism. Former FDA commissioner Alexander Schmidt admitted that some research laboratories have deliberately falsified test data as to safety.[11] In more general terms, the FDA's own data suggest some deficiencies in protection of the public. In 1982 an FDA examination of 6,410 samples revealed violations of quality or labeling in 1,061 of the drugs.[12] In response to these problems Congress has appropriated additional funds, and the FDA has instituted closer surveillance of drug company testing and reporting. Some drugs have been approved for marketing only on the condition that the drug company agrees to post-approval testing and monitoring. Nevertheless, the criticism has continued. Of particular concern are claims of excessive cooperation between the drug industry and the FDA. For example, Dr. Sidney Wolfe, head of a consumer organization, Health Research Group, accused the FDA of causing many unnecessary deaths and illnesses because of a delay in warning about a link between the use of aspirin and Reye's syndrome, an often fatal children's disease.

"In October 1981 a federal government advisory committee recommended against the use of aspirin for chicken pox or flu because of the increased risk of Reye's syndrome," Dr. Wolfe said, "but, as a result of pressure of the aspirin industry . . . a proposal by the FDA for mandatory warning labels was withdrawn in the fall of 1982. As a result, 150 American children are dead and dozens have brain damage. Most, if not all, would have been avoidable if action had been taken. Now warning labels are mandatory and the problem has practically disappeared, but it is too late for the dead and injured."[13]

The government argues that the voluntary relabeling by the industry and new FDA regulations were effective—perhaps more effective than mandatory standards.

Even as the FDA has been criticized for lax drug regulation, the agency has been criticized for imposing regulatory standards so demanding that they can harm consumers and industry. The time and resources necessary to meet FDA standards necessarily restrict the availability of some valuable new drugs. The average new drug is admitted to the British market approximately nine months more rapidly than to the U.S. market.[14] For example, a cardiovascular drug, practolol, was proven effective in Britain in reducing deaths from heart attacks, but marketing approval in the United States was delayed. William Wardell has estimated that the introduction of the drug in America could have saved 10,000 lives per year with minimal side effects.[15] Similarly persuasive (although disputed) evidence has been offered that regulatory demands have sharply retarded drug innovation in this country. Some estimates suggest that the cost of discovering and introducing new drugs increased 18-fold from 1960 to the mid-70s, with about half of the increase attributed to FDA regulation.[16]

The Reagan administration has succeeded in streamlining the drug-approval process; however, the time actually required for approving drugs (about 24 months) appears not to have declined appreciably, and the number of new drug approvals, while setting a record of 30 in 1985, is not appreciably above historical norms. On the other hand, the aforementioned new regulations for experimental drugs are expected to significantly expedite those products directed to very serious and life-threatening illnesses. The FDA expects those regulations to reduce the total time for approval (from test to final clearance) from nine years to four.[17]

Interestingly, a large and increasing share of the public favors strict drug regulation. A 1983 Roper poll found 73 percent of the respondents favored tight controls and fewer new drugs, while 15 percent preferred less strict regulation with more new drugs on the market.[18]

The question that remains is intriguing—admittedly not so compelling as where to spend one's Spring Break—but interesting, nevertheless. It involves the kind of cost-benefit analysis that goes to the heart of most government regulation. Clearly, drug approval deprives us, at least for a time, of drugs that ultimately prove beneficial. On the other hand, regulation protects us from inferior or even dangerous and useless medicines.

QUESTIONS

1. On May 25, 1979, an American Airlines DC-10 crashed in Chicago, Illinois, with 273 persons aboard.

   > The Federal Aviation Administration [FAA] certified the DC-10 wide-bodied jet without having its own employees check all preproduction tests and design plans, an FAA official says.
   >
   > Douglas Sharman, an FAA aerospace engineer, told a National Transportation Safety Board hearing that only a fraction of the work approved by aircraft manufacturing engineers designated as agents of the FAA actually is checked by the government agency. Thus McDonnell Douglas Corporation, which made the DC-10, "approved" its own work for the government.[19]

   a. Can American corporations be trusted to do their own testing prior to product approval? Explain.

   b. Does the presence of the various regulatory agencies afford the public a false sense of security? Explain.

2. In 1977 a Du Pont official estimated the average cost of bringing a new drug from the laboratory to the pharmacy at $10 million.[20]

   Even if the FDA meets new goals for reduced processing time, average drug approval cases will still require 15 to 17 months, and the total testing process will consume many years.

   a. Would the public be willing to absorb a greater percentage of the cost of drug testing in the interest of greater safety? Explain.

   b. Would a shift of drug-testing responsibility to the government likely result in greater safety? Explain.

   c. Have the costs of drug regulation outweighed the benefits? Explain.

   d. Could we rely to a greater degree on the free market for protection against dangerous products? Explain.

3. In recent years the federal government has been the subject of vigorous criticism for its various decisions regarding the protection of the public from alleged carcinogens (cancer-causing agents), such as tobacco, asbestos, nitrites, and Red Dye No. 2. Should the government (*a*) ban proven carcinogens where practical, (*b*) warn the public of the dangers involved, but leave the substance in the marketplace, or (*c*) remove itself from the business of protecting the public from carcinogens? Explain.

4. The director of the FDA's Bureau of Drugs, in speaking of his agency's regulation of prescription medicines, stated that "We do not pay any attention to the economic consequences of our decisions."[21]

   a. Defend that seemingly arrogant and wasteful attitude.

   b. Should economic considerations be irrelevant to regulations regarding human health and safety? Explain.

5. Oraflex, an arthritis drug manufactured by Eli Lilly & Co., was rejected for the American market in 1980. It was subsequently admitted to the

British market. Later the FDA reversed its position and permitted the sale of Oraflex in the United States. After reports of many illnesses and a number of deaths apparently linked to the drug, it was removed from the market by Lilly. In a subsequent congressional investigation, the acting director of the FDA testified that Lilly had submitted data revealing various side effects from Oraflex, but the FDA did not look at the data, and Lilly failed to bring the data directly to the attention of the FDA.[22]

a. Should all new drug applicants be required to explicitly identify all hazards known to be associated with their products? Explain.

b. Should cigarette manufacturers be required to reveal all the evidence in their possession regarding the health hazards associated with their products? Explain.

c. In either of the cases explored in (a) and (b), should producers be required not merely to reveal known hazards, but to advertise that information broadly? Explain.

Part Four—The Federal Regulatory Process Evaluated

In recent years a variety of forces, including a sometimes sluggish economy, have provoked a zealous inspection of government intervention. In this portion of the chapter we will begin by simply building a list of those criticisms most commonly visited on the federal regulatory process generally and the administrative agencies specifically. That evaluation will be followed by a series of proposed reforms. One of those reforms, deregulation, is so sweeping in its implications and so much at the forefront of contemporary business and government thinking that it will be accorded separate, detailed attention.

The following criticisms, while applying directly to the federal administrative agencies, constitute an evaluation of the total program of federal regulation of business.

CRITICISMS

Excessive Regulation

The complaint is familiar. The government has intruded unnecessarily into the economic life of the nation. The businessperson's freedom of action has been significantly circumscribed. Table 7–1 depicts the dramatic growth of the expense of government regulation in the years prior to the current deregulation effort. The federal budget for the regulatory agencies in 1974 was $2.2 billion. As depicted in the table, that sum

TABLE 7–1   Estimated Cost of Federal Regulation of Business, 1977–1979
(fiscal years, in billions of dollars)

	1977	1978	1979
Administration costs	$ 3.7	$ 4.5	$ 4.8
Compliance costs	75.4	92.2	97.9
Total	$79.1	$96.7	$102.7

expanded by 115 percent to $4.8 billion by 1979. Of course, the more serious financial burden lies in the cost of complying with government regulations. Filling out the required forms, meeting pollution requirements, installing safety devices, declining productivity, and so on are estimated to cost businesses over $100 billion annually. These direct and second-order costs provoke third-order expenses, such as declining innovation and impaired ability to finance growth, which may be severely handicapping the economy.[23]

The Center for the Study of American Business at Washington University of St. Louis reports that the deregulation initiative of recent years was successful in the sense that the striking growth in regulatory expenditures that marked the 1970s was stopped. In President Reagan's first term (1982–86), employment in regulatory agencies fell by about 14 percent, but total spending remained essentially steady (suggesting that internal inflation and outside contracting of work had increased).[24] For fiscal year 1987, an 11 percent real increase in funding was approved, and a 4 percent increase for fiscal 1988 was budgeted. However, most of that money was directed to a strengthening of bank deposit insurance agencies, and thus may not reflect a serious change in direction.[25]

The results of a survey of 300 business executives reveal a general feeling of excessive and costly regulation. Some of the primary complaints:

1. Overlap and conflict among agencies.
2. Overextension of agency authority, not merely in setting goals but in dictating how those goals are to be met.
3. Adversary attitudes toward business.
4. Agency delay in issuing required permits, rules, and standards.
5. Escalating reporting requirements.

A more extended discussion of these concerns is offered in the deregulation section that follows.

Insufficient Regulation

Although it is not currently fashionable, consumer advocates and big-business critics believe that *more,* rather than *less,* regulation is necessary to protect citizen interests. They acknowledge the inefficiencies and excesses of some agency efforts, but they favor correcting these problems and strengthening the regulatory structure. Therefore, they argue that the problem is, in part, one of inadequate funds in those areas where sensible regulation is needed. Wouldn't consumer protection be enhanced if the FDA were able to complete its own testing? And wouldn't antitrust violations be retarded if the FTC were funded such that its lawyers and economists could compete on an equal footing with the resources of the business community? Advocates of increased regulation point to the successes of government intervention: for example, legal equality for blacks; prevention of the sale of dangerous drugs, such as thalidomide; and the Auto Safety Act, which, by some estimates, saves 12,000 lives per year.

The character of this more-versus-less-regulation debate is well illustrated by a pair of recent federal appeals court decisions. In *Action for Children's Television* v. *FCC*[26], a three-judge panel of the District of Columbia federal court of appeals ordered the FCC to reconsider its 1984 decision eliminating federal guidelines that had limited advertising on children's shows to 9½ minutes on weekends and 12 minutes on weekdays. The decision may reopen the question of the wisdom of regulating children's television, or it may simply require a more complete explanation of why the FCC dropped those guidelines in 1984. At this writing Congress is considering legislation to require the advertising guidelines. In *National Association for Better Broadcasting* v. *FCC*[27], a three-judge panel of the same D.C. court of appeals struck down an FCC ruling that had allowed the promotion of toys on cartoon shows without requiring the toymakers to reveal that they had paid for the shows. This case involved the cartoon series, "He-Man and the Masters of the Universe." That show and some 75 others have been produced with the help of toymakers as a way of promoting the sale of their toys.[28] The plaintiff's argument, of course, was that the cartoons amount to program-length commercials. The FCC believes that the forces of the free market (including parental supervision) can protect children from commercial exploitation. The effect of the *Better Broadcasting* decision is to make toy-based cartoons much less desirable for broadcasters. If toymakers are revealed as cartoon sponsors, the television stations will be less able to sell commercial time to those sponsors' competitors.[29]

If you were an FCC commissioner, would you vote in favor of rules limiting advertising and requiring the identification of toy company sponsors on children's television shows?

Excessive Industry Influence

As we have noted, the industries to be regulated were often instrumental in spawning the various federal agencies. Noted economist George Stigler summarizes the argument: "[R]egulation is acquired by the industry and is designed and operated primarily for its benefit."[30] Stigler further contends that, where possible, firms will encourage government regulations restricting entry (licensing), thus limiting competition: "Every industry or occupation that has enough political power to utilize the state will seek to control entry."[31]

As evidence of industry influence in agency affairs, critics argue that agency employees who leave federal service frequently turn to jobs in the industry they were formerly charged with regulating. Similarly, agency recruits are often drawn from the industry being regulated. Certainly industry influence in government generally, and in the agencies specifically, is considerable. However, the public interest is arguably best served by drawing from the private sector's plentiful repository of information and expertise. The many scholarly studies of this topic offer mixed results. For example, one House subcommittee study of top officials in federal regulatory agencies found that about 35 percent of the employees "had prior direct or indirect employment in the regulated industry."[32] But other studies show that a background in law and/or prior government service were common avenues to upper-level agency roles.[33] The House subcommittee study found that one third of the top officials "became directly or indirectly employed in the regulated industry within five years of leaving office."[34] Though specific findings differ, movement from agencies to the regulated industry does appear to be common and a potential source of concern.

Perhaps more alarming are the findings from a study of 25 years of appointments to the Federal Communications Commission and the Federal Trade Commission:

> Partisan political considerations dominate the selection of regulators to an alarming extent. Alarming, in that other factors—such as competence, experience, and even, on occasion, regulatory philosophy—are only secondary considerations. Most commission appointments are the result of well-stoked campaigns conducted at the right time with the right sponsors, and many selections can be explained in terms of powerful political connections and little else: Commission seats are good consolation prizes for defeated Congressmen; useful runner-up awards for persons who ricochet into the appointment as a result of a strong yet unsuccessful campaign for another position; appropriate resting berths for those who have labored long and hard in the party vineyards; and a convenient dumping ground for people who have performed unsatisfactorily in other, more important government posts.[35]

To summarize, industry influence over the regulatory process is considerable. The industry voice should be heard. The question is one of the "volume" of the voice. The allegations of an industry-agency-industry revolving door clearly have some merit and may constitute a threat to the integrity of the regulatory process, but the demands of expertise presumably require some industry-agency ties. In closing, it should be understood that the argument of industry "capture" of an agency is more more persuasive regarding the older, "industrial regulation" agencies (such as the ICC and the FCC) than regarding the newer "social regulation" agencies (such as OSHA, the EPA, and the EEOC). The former are directed primarily at one industry. The latter reach across the face of American commerce. It is difficult to envision an industry capturing the conduct of one of the social regulation agencies.

Underrepresentation of Public Opinion

Another criticism of agencies charges that the diffuse voice of public opinion does not receive the attention accorded the pleas of special interests. For example, a Common Cause (national government reform organization) survey found that commissioners heading federal regulatory agencies meet with industry representatives 10 times more frequently than with spokespersons for consumer or public-interest groups.[36] A former commissioner of the Federal Communications Commission has said that citizen participation in the decision-making process "is 'virtually nonexistent,' with the necessary but unhappy result . . . that the FCC is a 'captive' of the very industry it is purportedly attempting to regulate.' "[37] According to one account, the American Petroleum Institute's budget of $32 million in 1979 was 30 times greater than the combined budgets of all Washington energy-related public-interest organizations.[38] Of course, public opinion is received by many routes, and the final word in the voting booth is preeminently persuasive. Nevertheless, it is generally acknowledged that public sentiment, being largely unorganized, is greatly underrepresented in regulatory matters, while well-financed, skillfully organized special interests carry political weight far beyond the numbers they represent.

These complaints are not meant to represent the full range of criticisms of the federal regulatory process. In particular, the mechanics of agency conduct are frequently assailed. Allegations of inefficiency, incompetence, and arbitrariness are commonplace. The pace of work is said to be slow, and enforcement of policy often appears weak and ineffectual.

DEREGULATION

Dissatisfaction with the federal regulatory process is widespread and reaches across the political spectrum. For example, liberal Senator Edward Kennedy played a leading role in deregulating the airline industry.

Proposals for reform and deregulation have blossomed in staggering abundance.

Regulatory reform deals with efforts to improve the efficiency and equity of the existing regulatory process. The deregulation movement seeks to reduce the quantity of federal regulatory interventions in favor of increased reliance on the free market. Since the two necessarily overlap, we will discuss them as a package.

The Carter administration initiated several reforms, the success of which remains unclear. New legislation required all rules and regulations to be written in plain English. Other legislation eased formidable hurdles against dismissing incompetent federal employees and rewarding those who performed with special distinction.

Proposed reforms are plentiful. The following list captures their flavor.

1. Under sunset legislation, agencies and programs would automatically cease to exist if not periodically (usually every 5 or 10 years) renewed after appropriate review by Congress. Common Cause introduced sunset legislation in Colorado to render agencies more accountable to the legislature. In 1976 Colorado adopted a sunset provision. Other states have followed suit. Whether the desired improvements in efficiency and accountability will come to pass is as yet uncertain. Many states apparently seized on sunset provisions as a deregulation method. However, the sunset notion seems ill suited to the goal of deregulation. Careful legislative review is a very time-consuming process, and virtually all agencies have considerable lobbying support. One state, North Carolina, has actually repealed its sunset legislation.[39]

2. Various mechanisms have been proposed for reducing unnecessary paperwork. For example, regulators might be expected to accept the information they seek, where feasible, in the form it was developed for the company's own purposes.

3. Regulatory burdens might be adjusted according to the size and nature of the firms involved.

4. More of the regulatory burden is thought to be the proper concern of the states.

5. Various suggestions have been offered to afford Congress and the executive branch greater control over the administrative agencies. One proposal is to give either house of Congress the power to review and veto agency rules before they become effective. Another is that personnel appointments to the agencies would be at the pleasure of the president. Thus the agency would presumably be more responsive to the president and hence to the citizenry.

6. Regulatory overlap could be attacked by creating a coordinating board to eliminate conflicting and redundant regulations.

7. Intervenor funding might be provided. That is, government funds could be appropriated to permit public-interest-group witnesses and perhaps small-business witnesses to testify before appropriate agencies.

8. Many, perhaps most, economists support the use of market incentives to achieve regulatory goals. Thus, rather than forbidding undesirable conduct (such as pollution and industrial accidents), the government might impose a tax on those behaviors society wants to discourage. In effect, a business would purchase the right to engage in conduct society considers injurious or inefficient. Similarly, rather than rationing portions of the radio spectrum or the right to land at airports at peak times, the government might auction those rights to the highest bidder. Market incentives would (*a*) encourage companies to use cost-effective compliance means and (*b*) raise the price of dangerous products, thus discouraging their use. However, monitoring difficulties, particularly in the case of pollution, render the taxing or auction methods inexact at best. Some object to the idea of allowing businesses to engage in undesirable conduct or highly prized conduct merely because they have the resources to pay for those privileges.

9. Cost/benefit analysis would be applied to all regulations. Regulations would be imposed only if added benefits equaled or exceeded the added costs. A cost-effectiveness system might be developed for those cases where a dollar value could not be fairly and accurately assigned (e.g., the value of a human life). A goal would be identified, and a cost-effectiveness study would be employed to determine the least expensive way of reaching that goal. The point here is perhaps best illustrated by reference to mandated auto safety standards. For example, seat belts in autos are thought to save approximately 5,000 lives per year at a cost to society of approximately $80,000 per life.[40] On the other hand, the air bag safety device is expected to save as many as 9,000 lives per year, but the cost may reach $2 billion for the first year and an additional $2 billion for each year of their use.[41] (These cost and benefit figures vary substantially depending on the study cited.) President Reagan sought to firmly inject cost/benefit analysis in federal regulation. In 1981 and 1985, the president signed executive orders requiring cost/benefit analyses for a broad spectrum of federal regulations. The 1981 order provided, in part, that: "Regulatory action shall not be undertaken unless the potential benefits to society from the regulation outweigh the potential costs to society."[42] While the momentum now appears to have slowed, Reagan's cost/benefit requirement enjoyed some early success:

> Measured by the criteria of restraining the growth of federal regulation and improving the quality of administrative decisions, this approach has been a clear success. The size of the *Federal Register* has shrunk for three consecutive years since Executive Order 12291 was issued—the first time this has ever happened. Fewer new rules are being issued, and an increasing proportion of rules are aimed at reforming or eliminating existing requirements rather than laying on new ones. New health, safety, and environmental requirements have been substantially more measured and cost-beneficial than in the past.[43]

"Silly" Regulations

Let us immediately dispose of one dimension of the deregulation debate that provides amusement to all—a particularly easy target for James Kilpatrick, Paul Harvey, and other critics of government intervention—but little in the way of grist for useful analysis. That is, we can all agree that some, perhaps many, government regulations are foolish. Bureaucrats, like the rest of us, are imperfect. Pointing to absurd government rules is useful in acquiring publicity, but the practice helps little in reaching a judgment as to the proper balance between freedom and regulation. Noted economist Lester Thurow explains:

> Gleefully finding silly government regulations has almost reached the status of a national parlor game. And nowhere is it easier to play the game than in the domain of OSHA—the Occupational Safety and Health Administration. Whenever silliness arises, it is well to ask why. It could arise because we are chasing after silly ends, or it could arise because we are using inappropriate means to achieve perfectly respectable ends. In the case of OSHA, the latter is clearly true. No one questions the virtues or the seriousness of reducing industrial deaths and injuries. The question is one of means.
>
> Basically the problem is not one of stupid bureaucrats, but one of trying to write universal regulations in an area where it is impossible. A regulation that makes sense in one context may not in another. Take the problem of providing toilet facilities for farm workers. A regulation that may be eminently sensible in a densely populated truck-farming area (a toilet every 40 acres) with hundreds of farm laborers, may not make sense on a Montana ranch where it is miles to the nearest person, and where there are hundreds of thousands of empty acres that seldom, if ever, see an agricultural worker. Yet for a set of regulations to be sensible in every section of a country as large as the United States, it would have to be so lengthy that it would be equally silly. Suppose that someone were to report that it took the government 10,000 pages of regulations to spell out the appropriate toilet facilities for every conceivable condition. Each of those regulations could be sensible, yet the aggregate effect is nonsense. The problem is using an inappropriate means to achieve a respectable objective.
>
> It is also well to remind ourselves that silliness is not limited to public actions or to other individuals. Every example of stupid government could be matched by a private example. The Edsel, for example, has entered our language as the paradigm example of a stupid action that wasted millions of dollars' worth of resources. Boston's John Hancock building, with its falling panes of glass, was a fiasco from the day it was built. What would have happened if some government bureaucrat had built it? The U.S. steel industry misinvested millions on openhearth furnaces, when it should have been building oxygen furnaces. Most of us would have to admit, at least to ourselves, that we have made stupid mistakes in our own budgets.[44]

So we are beset with some foolish regulations. It is generally agreed that some areas are burdened with excessive regulation. But the issue of excessive regulation should be kept in perspective. The United States remains the least regulated of all the industrialized nations. Central planning, direct government investment, and social welfare regulation greatly exceeding our own are represented in varying proportions among all other advanced economies. It is well to note that some of those nations, such as Japan and Germany, currently enjoy economic health in many respects exceeding our own. Thurow reminds us that America's economic performance has improved since the onset of the intensive government intervention of the New Deal.[45] Government regulation does not arise from ideology but from actual problems.[46] America is not committed to government regulation as a matter of political policy—as is the case in many nations. Rather, regulation in this country has, in many instances, resulted from an honorable effort to correct evident wrongs. Much-maligned agencies, such as the EPA, OSHA, and the FDA, were not born of a desire for big government and central planning. Pollution, industrial accidents, and dangerous food and drugs were clearly the impetus for the creation of those agencies.

As a final measure of perspective, note the following excerpts from a *Fortune* magazine interview of prominent management consultant, Jewell Westerman.

LOOK WHO'S COVERED IN RED TAPE

[Ask a businessman if the bureaucracy is getting him down, and he becomes a fountain of indignation about the vexations of dealing with government red tape. Ask him about the bureaucracy in his own company, and you'll likely find he hasn't given the matter much thought. Jewell G. Westerman, 46, a vice president of Hendrick & Co., a management consulting firm in Waltham, Massachusetts, has given the matter quite a bit of thought. At Hendrick and at the Travelers Insurance Companies before that, Westerman developed some provocative views on the productivity of managers, which he set out in an interview with *Fortune* associate editor Jeremy Main.]

Q: How would you compare the penalties imposed on business by government bureaucracy and the penalties imposed by the bureaucracy of business management itself?

A: The latter are far larger. It is very difficult to estimate the cost of the extra requirements imposed by the government, but in a study of a large insurance company we were able to pin it down to something on the order of about $8 million to $10 million a year. Compared with the total salary costs of about $600 million, that was a very small percentage and you're talking mostly about things like filing W-2 forms, making payments to social security, and filing income tax reports. These are standard activities and you probably couldn't eliminate them. I read recently that Goodyear reported it spent 34 employee-years filling out reports required by government regulation. Do you know how many employees Goodyear has? 154,000. So 34 out of 154,000 is not even a measurable percentage.

Q: In the studies done here at Hendrick, how do you go about costing out such activities?

A: When we study a company we create an index of activities, by subfunction and function. We measure the amount of time it takes to perform between 225 and 300 different activities. Several of them result from government regulations. We don't enter any data for an activity that takes less than 5 percent of an employee's time. In many of our studies no labor costs at all show up for complying with government regulations. We have done over 200 such studies at Hendrick and Company, and we cannot recall a single company in which coping with government regulations raised a significant opportunity for lowering labor costs.

Q: And what did you find out about business bureaucracy?

A: The costs are phenomenal. Manager costs are usually No. 1 and secretarial costs No. 2— or vice versa.

Q: Do you mean among white-collar workers?

A: No. Out of all workers.

Q: Even in manufacturing companies?

A: Even in manufacturing companies secretarial costs are higher than the costs of line workers. When you have one manager for every four or five employees and one secretary for every two managers, you're starting to build up a lot of secretaries in an organization. Management, secretaries, data processing, and sometimes budgeting are usually the most costly activities. You usually get down to about the 10th or 12th category of labor expense before you get to line workers. So you have to ask, why are we in business: to manage it and administer it, or to make products?

Source: "A Difference of Opinion," *Fortune,* May 4, 1981, p. 357. Reprinted with permission of the publisher, *Fortune.* Written by Jeremy Main from an interview with Jewell G. Westerman. © 1981 Time Inc. All rights reserved.

The Burdens of Regulation

We turn now to the encompassing inquiry: In what measure and manner, if any, should the American economy be deregulated? Some argue for more regulations. Others would favor exclusive reliance on the free market. Most fall somewhere between. We are now in the midst of a national debate about the proper measure of government regulation of business.

ROLLING BACK REGULATION: A DEBATE RAGES OVER HOW MUCH FREEDOM SHOULD BE GIVEN TO INDUSTRY

Stephen Koepp

"What do you think of deregulation, you ask me?" muses Joe Sixpack as he takes a break from mowing the lawn. "Frankly, I love and I hate it! Take the airlines. I can get a great bargain fare to Miami, but you can be sure my flight will be delayed for two hours because of

air-traffic congestion. As for the bank, it now gives me interest on my checking account, which is nice, but then sticks me with a $5 fee every time I drop below my minimum balance. Our family's long-distance bill has gone down, but somehow the total phone charges have gone way up. And look at the trucking business: the bill was only $500 when I moved a load of furniture from 400 miles away, but I'm scared to be on the same highway with one of those killer rigs!"

Indeed, deregulation has turned industries upside down and whipsawed consumer emotions like no other economic trend in recent history. Airlines, banks, telephone companies, and trucking lines, among others, have all been transformed from placid, tightly regulated industries into volatile hotbeds of competition. Many of the results have been glowing examples of a free market at work: lower prices, greater efficiency, and more choices for consumers. "Across the board, we are much better off with deregulation than without it," says Paul MacAvoy, dean of the graduate school of management of the University of Rochester.

Even so, deregulation has produced plenty of worrisome side effects. One of them is a rising concentration of market share among a few large companies—a shift toward oligopolies that could already be stifling the very competition that deregulation was supposed to stimulate. Another ominous trend is the increased evidence of corporate corner cutting when it comes to safeguarding the health and safety of workers and customers. . . .

Few people want to put back the overgrown regulatory thicket that grew during the 1960s and 1970s. The United States was clearly due for a round of regulatory rollbacks, especially in light of the relatively minimal intervention that the Constitution seemed to contemplate when, for example, it authorized federal regulation of commerce "with foreign nations, and among the several States." At the time, the Constitution's framers championed a free market system with little government interference.

Says W. John Swartz, president of the Santa Fe Railway: "The Founding Fathers would be astonished at the amount of rules we operate under today. Regulators have gone much too far."

Indeed, government involvement grew slowly at first because most trade was carried out within individual states and therefore overseen by local and state officials. But westward expansion and the development of an extensive railroad and canal system spurred interstate markets. In 1887 Congress created the Interstate Commerce Commission, the first major federal business regulatory agency. The commission was established in part to combat price gouging by the railroads.

The first boom time for rule writers came during the Great Depression of the 1930s. . . .

Rule writers mostly took a recess during the wartime and postwar years of the 1940s and 1950s but got back to work during the 1960s and 1970s, when the civil rights movement, consumerism, and environmental consciousness produced the largest flood of business legislation in U.S. history. The *Federal Register,* which publishes all proposed and adopted regulations, ballooned from a yearly total of 14,479 pages in 1960 to 87,012 in 1980.

The deregulation revolution began under Presidents Ford and Carter, but the Reagan administration embraced the idea with energetic zeal. . . . The expense of complying with federal regulations, Reagan claimed, had cost Americans between $50 billion and $150 billion a year. After only 10 days in office, he put a freeze on more than 170 pending regulations. A drastic pullback of government involvement in business followed, especially in federal attempts to control prices and markets. How successful was the correction? Consider four industries that have been deregulated by Congress and administrative action.

Airlines

By decontrolling routes, the Airline Deregulation Act of 1978 enabled dozens of new airlines to enter the business. The number of carriers authorized to fly planes with 60 seats or more increased from 36 in 1978 to a peak of 123 in 1984; there are now 74. The legislation decontrolled prices at the same time, which sparked the fare wars that have saved consumers some $6 billion annually. Today's U.S. airline tickets are estimated to be nearly 40 percent cheaper than they would have been without deregulation. Airline travel has thus become far more popular, rising from 255 million domestic passengers a year in 1978 to 393 million last year.

Yet the ruthless competition that has produced such cheap rides for consumers has inspired a dozen airline mergers in which rabble-rousers like People Express have been swallowed up. The six largest carriers, which controlled 76 percent of the U.S. market in 1978, now have about 81 percent and are expected to get 90 percent by 1990. Large combined airlines command so much market share at some airports that the carriers may be tempted to raise prices with virtual impunity. At least three carriers control more than 80 percent of the business in their main hubs: Northwest Airlines in Minneapolis, TWA in St. Louis, and USAir in Pittsburg.

The most counter-pounding passenger issue is the increasing number of delays. Complaints to the Transportation Department about late flights and poor service reached 4,893 in the first quarter of this year, a 43 percent increase from the same period in 1986. Neither U.S. airports nor the ranks of air-traffic controllers have grown fast enough to keep up with the increase in flights that deregulation has set loose. . . .

Banks

Until deregulation gave them relief in 1980, banks and thrift institutions were rapidly losing business to competitors ranging from Sears to Merrill Lynch, whose money market funds could legally offer much higher yields than the 5¼ percent maximum savings account rate. But the Depository Institutions Deregulation and Monetary Control Act gradually abolished limits on interest, enabling banks and thrifts to offer lucrative accounts like Super NOW checking. The new law was a boon for savers, since it touched off interest-rate wars among financial institutions competing for consumer deposits.

Not all customers, however, have shared in deregulation's bounty. Because banks started paying more to depositors, the institutions felt compelled to start charging higher fees for routine services, usually to customers with puny balances in their accounts. The average fee for a bounced check increased from $5.07 in 1979 to $11.71 last year. . . .

Telephones

The dismantling of Ma Bell in 1984, the result of a government antitrust suit, is probably the most unpopular deregulatory move. According to a *Wall Street Journal*/NBC News poll published in April, 59 percent of consumers think the breakup was a "bad thing." One emerging problem is the perceived decline in the quality of the nation's telephone service since the Bell system was broken up. Customer complaints and confusion are at an all-time high.

No one, however, is seriously proposing to reassemble AT&T. "These are eggs that can't be unscrambled," said Missouri's John Danforth, the ranking Republican on the Senate Commerce Committee. Instead, the administration wants to encourage competition by deregulating the regional phone companies even further to allow diversification into such fields as insurance, real estate, and computer manufacturing.

Since the breakup, telephone users have enjoyed a cut in long-distance rates of about 20 percent, or $4 billion, thanks mainly to deep rate reductions by AT&T that tiny rivals like MCI and US Sprint find difficult to match. But rates for local service, which remains a monopoly business, have jumped nearly 35 percent, or $6 billion. Overall, a typical telephone bill has increased about 25 percent. The increases in local rates appear likely to slow down, but unfortunately so do the long-distance discounts. AT&T so dominates the market, with an 82 percent share, that its competitors may lack the financial clout to survive future rate cuts.

Frustrated consumers can find relief at their local telephone-equipment stores, where they have enjoyed a remarkable bounty. Since the breakup, the number of telephone makers selling to the U.S. market has jumped from 25 to more than 200, which has vastly improved the range of prices, styles, and capabilities. The high-tech scramble has produced phones with such space-age functions as voice-activated dialing and message machines.

Trucking

While most people are probably unaware of it, the Motor Carrier Act of 1980 has saved them a bundle. The law boosted efficiency by dismantling 45 years' worth of interstate hauling rules, including some oddball anomalies like provisions that allowed agricultural haulers to transport milk but not yogurt or ice-cream. All told, trucking deregulation since 1980 has saved consumers $72 billion in lower prices on the goods they buy, according to Citizens for a Sound Economy, a conservative, Washington-based research group.

Deregulation has encouraged new operators to enter the business, but the intense price competition has worn them down like a long, grinding upgrade. About 17,000 new trucking companies have formed since 1980, and more than 6,500 companies have failed during the same period. The newcomers have felt increasing pressure to cut costs by scrimping on safety, which has spawned fleets of so-called killer trucks with bald tires, worn brakes, and bleary-eyed drivers. While most major carriers can afford adequate maintenance programs, struggling trucking companies often put worn-out rigs on the road as a calculated gamble. . . .

The overall winners and losers from deregulation form a mixed gallery, but a few generalizations can be drawn. By and large, consumers who make enough money to take advantage of lowered prices in sufficient quantity, and those canny enough to understand the widening array of choices, will reap the most benefits. Conversely, poor people, who are strained by high minimum-balance requirements at banks and steep local phone rates, may be faring the worst. Says David Schwartzman, economics professor at the New School for Social Research in Manhattan: "Low-income customers have been the real losers in deregulation. They don't use long-distance service, they don't have large deposits at banks, and they don't fly much." Organized labor has also been adversely affected. As airlines and trucking companies have slashed prices, many unions have had to take pay cuts.

In some instances the costs and benefits of government regulation defy meaningful computation. Perhaps we should resist the contemporary tendency to deprecate what cannot be subjected to meaningful quantitative analysis. The following article illustrates just such an occasion.

FORESTS OVERGROWN WITH
RED TAPE

Brooks Jackson

Basswood Lake, Ontario—As our canoes slice through the sparkling black water, I have the feeling I am being watched.

The four of us—a doctor, a lawyer, a computer specialist and myself, a reporter—have come to this birch-and-pine wilderness to escape comfortably civilized routines.

But up ahead, in a log cabin on a remote island, I will soon encounter a stout little man in a square cap with a shiny black bill. On his desk will be a small metal stand holding a half-dozen or so rubber stamps, the tools of his profession.

He is a bureaucrat, the very sort I left Washington, D.C., to elude. I know he may cause us trouble; we are going to ask him for the permits needed to camp and fish in this protected wilderness area on the United States–Canadian border. I have the same feeling I get when I renew my driver's license.

As we paddle along, our soft city muscles are already beginning to complain. We are on a route used 250 years ago by French and later by British and American fur traders. Indian wigwams and wooden forts are long gone. In their places one occasionally sees tents made of red or yellow synthetic fabric. Otherwise, the dense forest and stony shores look as they must have for centuries.

To the left is the Boundary Waters Canoe Area of northern Minnesota, and to the right is the Quetico Provincial Park of Ontario. It seems an odd place to have trouble with a government official. We had in mind an encounter of a different sort: man against nature, survival in the wilderness. But we are discovering that the wilderness survives only by pitting government officials against campers.

Motor boats, for instance, are allowed only along a few routes. Cans and bottles are banned. Trash and garbage must be burned or carried out. Heavy fines await the litterbug.

* * * * *

The ultimate hassle may still be ahead. As we shoved off early this morning, we got word that authorities might decide to close the entire park as a precaution against fires. Our trip would be over.

Apprehensively we glide up to the forest ranger's pier after nearly 2½ hours of paddling. He smiles. We will be allowed in.

We pay customs duty on our freeze-dried foods, fees for camping, and fees for fishing licenses. The ranger issues us a sheaf of permits and papers—white, pink, and green. I notice that one of his rubber stamps reads "Cancelled," and give silent thanks that he isn't issuing it today.

Days later we are catching trout on a lake deep in the park. A small forest fire, perhaps an acre or two in size, has started burning on a hillside a couple of miles downwind. A white, single-engine airplane circles to investigate the fire, then glides down to set its pontoons on the lake, about 200 yards from my canoe.

The government ranger tells us that lightning has started more fires, that the park has been closed, and that campers are being asked to move out. We comply and break camp a day earlier than planned.

On the canoe trip back the thought strikes me that this isn't a real wilderness at all. It is a museum. And it survives in a "natural" state only by unnaturally vigorous human effort.

In a truly wild area, that small fire would have spread by now, whipped by the high wind. But a large orange airplane appeared here and doused the flames by dumping water from aloft.

Moreover, this "wild" area is surprisingly delicate. At our campsite, we wore paths into the forest floor in only a few days. The clear, cold lake water purges itself of waste matter far more slowly than warmer bodies. Without the entry-permit system, this increasingly popular area could be overrun. Before the quota system took effect in the mid-1970s, U.S. rang- ers counted 180 canoe parties going up popular Moose Lake in a single day. The limit now is 40.

The red tape can be maddening. But as our canoes slide past beaver lodges and over lakes filled with fish, it somehow seems a small price to preserve such a treasure.

Source: *The Wall Street Journal,* June 27, 1980, p. 25. Reprinted by permission of *The Wall Street Journal,* © Dow Jones & Company, Inc. 1980. ALL RIGHTS RESERVED.

The Wisdom of Deregulation

Deregulation has largely been limited to the older, industry regulation areas (ICC—transportation, FCC—communications, CAB—airlines) where economic concerns predominate. Deregulation in the new agencies (EPA, EEOC, OSHA) designed to protect health, safety, civil rights, and so on seems unlikely. However, regulatory reform in those areas is well under way. For example, the EPA is adopting more flexible standards that set a goal but allow managers to find the best way of meeting that goal. Illustrative of that flexibility about air pollution is the EPA adoption of the "bubble concept," which treats an industrial plant as though it were a bubble and measures the sum of the pollution rather than that from each pollution source. Thus, the business can reduce pollution from whichever sources best serve its needs and costs, so long as the total reduction meets EPA standards.

Is deregulation desirable? The importance of the issue cannot be discounted. The question is at the heart of this text and of American commerce, and its resolution will significantly shape the nature of American life. Public opinion is a critical ingredient in the deregulation debate. The results are mixed. It is not news that Americans are frustrated with big government. A 1987 *Wall Street Journal*/NBC News poll shows that

> 38 percent of the people still believe there is too much government regulation of the economy, while 32 percent think there is about the right amount, and 23 percent say there isn't enough. But those results represent a major swing toward regulation from polls taken in 1980, when more than two thirds believed Washington was overregulating business and damaging the free market.[47]

Virtually everyone favors reducing paperwork, eliminating red tape, and getting bureaucrats off our backs. However, when applied to specifics, we find remarkably mixed responses depending on the topic. All of the data that follows was gathered from a *Wall Street Journal*/NBC News poll of a cross section of the American public.

1. "43 percent of the public supported more regulation of auto safety, 41 percent wanted about the same amount, and only 13 percent called for less regulation."[48]
2. Because of savings of some $6 billion per year in airline fares, virtually no support was found for re-creating the Civil Aeronautics Board (which had regulated airline routes and fares prior to its elimination).[49]
3. "43 percent said government regulation of the stock market should remain about the same, while 26 percent favored more regulation and 15 percent favored less."[50]
4. "[T]he public, by a wide 59 percent to 31 percent margin, thinks that the 1984 dismantling of American Telephone & Telegraph Co. has been a 'bad thing.' "[51]
5. "Half of those surveyed . . . said there should be more government regulation of on-the-job health and safety, while only 6 percent said there should be less."[52]
6. 61 percent of those surveyed said there should be more government regulation of the environment, while only 6 percent said there should be less."[53]

Interestingly, the business community itself is not wholly committed to deregulation. Indeed, the loudest opposition to, for example, trucking deregulation came from the industry and the Teamsters Union. For some businesspeople, restraints on competition provide a safe harbor. Many simply see some regulation as necessary for the well-being of society and, in turn, for their firms. A Conference Board survey of 300 executives revealed a general acceptance of the need for some regulation, but the executives were also firmly committed to regulatory reform. The comment of a personnel vice president was representative of the survey findings:

> As a company, we cannot argue against sensible safety and health regulations, nor reasonable legislation covering equal opportunity in its broadest aspect. But we are critical of the application and enforcement of these laws by the respective agencies involved. It has been estimated that 40 percent of a personnel department's time currently is spent in dealing with the handling of laws enforced by OSHA, EEOC, and ERISA. This is absolutely ludicrous.[54]

Deregulation Abroad

Now we have at least a superficial picture of the course of deregulation in the United States. Hence the moment is ripe for a lesson that is increasingly vital to the nation's future. We must routinely remind ourselves that we are a part of a global market. All major economic moves in America influence and are influenced by events and policies around the globe. The article that follows introduces us to deregulation initiatives in foreign financial markets. Those markets must respond to our regulatory reforms—and we to theirs.

LONDON CARNAGE: BRITAIN'S SECURITIES FIRMS ARE HIT BY VIRULENT RATE CUTTING IN WAKE OF DEREGULATION

Craig Forman

The British called it Big Bang, October 27, 1986. On that day life in the City was to change dramatically—and, it was hoped, for the better. Financial markets were deregulated, fixed commissions abolished, and barriers between brokers and other financial concerns torn down once and for all. There was culture shock, too. Bowler hats, three-hour lunches, and six-hour days became fond memories.

Today, after slightly less than a year, life may not be that much better after all. Three types of players generally remain in the market here: the bruised, the badly bloodied, and those in a body bag. Lured by visions of huge profits in a rapidly growing market, the Americans, Japanese, and Swiss set off a barroom brawl and a frenzy of mergers among bankers, brokers, and securities firms.

The resulting damage is everywhere. On Monday, Salomon, Inc., as part of a major corporate restructuring, announced plans to slash 150 jobs in London. Chemical Bank also said it would cut its U.K. staff, by 18 percent.

* * * * *

British banks have cut back, too. . . .

Why the carnage?

Trading volume quadrupled amid the biggest bull market here in recent memory, but the competitive free-for-all slashed commission rates, raised overhead, and decimated profits. Some traders do as much as half their business for no commission at all, and when commissions are paid, they run about 200 pounds sterling for a 100,000-pound transaction—50 percent of pre-Big Bang levels. Meanwhile, at many firms, including American houses, overhead quadrupled.

As a result, few firms here are reporting much profits from operations, analysts say. And if you count in the substantial start-up costs, profits disappear at many of them. Even those now making money face a long wait before Big Bang pays off.

* * * * *

However, Big Bang has helped ensure London's prominence as the freest trading center in the European time zone. American and Japanese securities houses have made London their headquarters for the eight hours each day that trading books pass to Europe on their Tokyo-London-New York circuit. That's good for Her Majesty's government, which reckons that the City, as London's financial district is called, now contributes more to gross national product than North Sea oil does.

Deregulation also has benefited investors, who pay lower commissions. It is helping British companies expand their role in the international takeover game by cutting their cost of new capital—a record 19.7 billion pounds has been raised so far this year. It has sparked development of innovative financial instruments that are drawing even more business to London. It has facilitated the government's campaign to turn some state-owned companies private; nearly 9 million Britons now own shares, triple the number in the early 1980s. And in securities firms' trading rooms, some high school dropouts in their 20s have tripled their incomes—to as much as 100,000 pounds ($164,600) a year.

* * * * *

Big Bang has set off a chain of "little bangs" across Europe, as France, Germany, and even Spain try to copy London's success.

But the tougher competition in London has put a premium on finding new business. To get it, some firms have resorted to such financial acrobatics as offering to match any competitor's price, whether the transaction is profitable or not. Such gymnastics raise the financial risks while cutting the potential profits. . . .

The result is the shakeout that many observers think has only begun. "Over the next three to five years, there will be a lot of change. It will make what has happened over the past year seem minor," says Archibald Cox, Jr.,

managing director of Morgan Stanley International in London. . . .

Even so, many observers are surprised by the speed of the shakeout. They say it confirms London's new focus on short-term profits and away from cradle-to-grave relationships. . . .

Moreover, the cutbacks have been occurring during the bull market. What happens when the market turns down? "We are all starting to look over our shoulders a bit," says Peter Meinertzhagen, the head of equities at Hoare Govett, a London stockbrokerage unit of Security Pacific Corporation of Los Angeles. Mr. Brown expects to see a lot of "secondhand Mercedes in the showrooms."

Questions

1. From the reading materials we see that a major complaint about the federal regulatory process is that the regulators share an excessively "cozy" relationship with those being regulated. In Japan, cooperation between government, business, workers, and the public seems to have been instrumental in their remarkable economic success. Indeed, it is commonplace for retiring high-level bureaucrats to be hired as top executives of the companies they once regulated. The practice is labeled *amakudari* (descent from heaven).

   Should the United States emulate the Japanese *amakudari* policy as a step toward a more unified, cooperative industrial policy? Explain.
2. Would the free market succeed in preserving areas such as the Boundary Waters described in "Forests Overgrown with Red Tape"? Explain.
3. Transportation deregulation has resulted in an immediate loss of service to some smaller communities. Some of that loss has been compensated for with the entry of smaller, independent firms.

   a. Has deregulation endangered small-town America? Explain.

   b. Should we apply free market principles to postal service, thus, among other consequences, compelling those in small and remote communities to pay the full cost of service rather than the "subsidized" cost now paid? Explain.
4. The expense of government regulation is not limited to the direct cost of administering the various agencies. Explain and offer examples of the other expenses produced by regulation.

5. To the extent the federal government achieves deregulation, what substitutes will citizens find for protection?

6. Motor carriers have argued that by allowing open entry to new carriers the government has confiscated their property. Explain that argument.

7. From 1976 to 1980, 27 states repealed or weakened laws requiring the use of motorcycle helmets. During that time, new motorcycle registrations increased by less than 1 percent, but fatalities increased by more than 40 percent.[55] Congress has considered reimposing on states the sanctions (e.g., withholding highway safety funds) deemed necessary to encourage states to approve helmet laws.

    a. Build the arguments for and against such federal sanctions.

    b. How would you vote on such legislation? Explain.

8. In complaining about the impact of airline deregulation on less-populous portions of the nation, "Senator Larry Pressler of South Dakota has charged, 'It now costs more to fly 150 miles between two major cities in South Dakota than it does to fly 3,000 miles across the continent.' "[56] Seeming anomalies in airfares like that cited by Senator Pressler are commonplace. Explain why airfares on some short routes are higher than those on some much longer routes.

9. A study by Professor Andrew Chalk of Southern Methodist University concludes, in effect, that the free market is more effective than the rules of the Federal Aviation Administration in ensuring air safety.[57] Assume the role of Professor Chalk. Explain the market mechanisms that have been influential in building our present impressive safety record in air travel.

10. As you know, deregulation of the American airline industry has resulted in a rapid series of consolidations, with fewer, bigger companies emerging from the scramble. In Europe, some 21 national airlines (British Airways, Lufthansa, Air France, etc.) were operational in 1988. The nations of the European Community are debating the wisdom of deregulation of their air system. Assume you are an advisor to the EC. What advice would you offer about European airline deregulation in light of deregulation in America?

Part Five—The Corporate Response to Government Regulation

The weight of government intervention has provoked, in many businesses, an activist stance toward the regulatory process. Traditionally, most companies relied on occasional monitoring, a bit of lobbying, and support of their trade association to achieve their government relations goals. That may well continue to be the dominant mode, but increasingly we find businesspeople seeking to shape government–business relations by anticipating critical issues and endeavoring to cast the outcome in a manner advantageous to the business community. Government relations offices are achieving higher visibility within companies today. The Washington governmental relations office is now less likely to be a place to which soon-to-be retired executives are shipped.

In a Conference Board survey of government relations executives, 29 percent of respondents indicated that their companies have made a "very aggressive commitment" to improved government relations.[58] Trade associations have been strengthened. The Business Roundtable (a group of chief executive officers from America's major corporations) has emerged as perhaps the leading voice of business views in Washington. High-level interaction between business and government is increasing. Business is actively seeking allies among stockholders, competitors, special-interest groups, and so on. Political action committees are a significant new force in the electoral process. As discussed in Chapter 3, some view this new political vigor with alarm. The fear is that business resources will come to dominate political decision making, but the business community takes the position that it is merely exercising its democratic rights in an honorable effort to maximize its interests and the interests of the nation. In any case, dealing with the government is and will remain an important ingredient in corporate success.

So businesspeople are gradually, probably reluctantly, adopting the view that government must be dealt with in an affirmative, even activist, manner. If business must give more attention to that domain, the question then becomes one of tactics. How best may business implement such an effort? Of course, the possibilities are many. The reading that follows sketches one particularly interesting system.

CHASE MANHATTAN'S CORPORATE ISSUES DEPARTMENT

Phyllis S. McGrath

Government relations sometimes can take the form of an issues management program, as is the case at The Chase Manhattan Bank. The government relations unit at the bank actually is called "Corporate Issues."

Utilizing a series of early warning systems, the corporate issues unit identifies legislative matters of potential concern to the bank and its customers. Analyses and summaries of emerging issues are prepared, and as many of Chase's issues contact officers (ICOs) as might be affected are alerted.

Each line department has an ICO, a senior officer named by the department executive, who is responsible for issues interface. Each ICO, and Chase presently has about 20 of them, is charged with bringing departmentwide resources to bear on legislative issues. When corporate issues apprises an ICO, or group of ICOs, of an emerging issue, each of them is asked, in effect, to develop an "impact statement"—setting forth the cost effects and operational constraints implicit in the issue for the department.

It is the responsibility of corporate issues to receive this information from the ICOs, synthesize it, and to develop a corporationwide position on the issue—with the approval of Chase's top management.

Then a strategy to deal with the issue is developed. Chase's Washington office identifies legislators involved in the matter at hand and, with the corporate issues unit, also identifies officers within the bank appropriate to communicate the Chase position to these legislators, or present testimony. Allies in trade associations, and other outside groups are involved, and continuing efforts are made to coordinate activities relative to the issue. Chase's public relations department sometimes is brought in to develop speeches, articles, and other pertinent communications, and some issues have been utilized in advertising campaigns directed to the public.

From time to time, Chase's issues contact officers have a general meeting. At one such recent session, presentations were made on developing societal and legislative trends, as well as on issues expected to emerge in a shorter time frame—which would have specific impact on the business of banking.

Source: *Redefining Corporate-Federal Relations* (New York: The Conference Board, 1979), p. 25. Reprinted with permission of the copyright holder, The Conference Board.

CHAPTER QUESTIONS

1. General Motors executive R. F. Magill argued that business lobbying must be "identified with the public interest."
   a. Has the business community shown itself able to look beyond its self-interest to the larger concerns of society? Explain.
   b. Should the business community seek to do so? Explain.
2. Explain "issue management" in the corporate context.
3. Assume Chase Manhattan learns that a congressional committee staff is preparing a position paper advocating an embargo of all commerce (including loans) with a Middle Eastern nation, Rabatan, on the grounds that Rabatan is encouraging rebellion in Central America. Chase Manhattan would suffer a serious (but not fatal) financial reversal if the policy were effected. Rabatan's Central American involvement has been fully verified. Should Chase Manhattan seek to influence the government's foreign policy decision? Explain.
4. List what you believe are critical ingredients in effectively linking the identification of public affairs issues and the development of corporate plans for dealing with those issues.
5. California Republican Representative Robert F. Dorman: "Corporate managers are whores. They don't care who's in office, what party or what they stand for, they're just out to buy you."[59]
   a. Do you agree? Explain.
   b. If you look forward to a business career, can you envision yourself assuming the apolitical, self-serving, corrupt stance Dorman attributes to businesspeople? Explain.

6. Charles Koch of Koch Industries: "The majority of businessmen today are not supporters of free enterprise capitalism."[60] Does the bulk of the business community favor government intervention? Explain.

7. A major issue facing the Federal Aviation Administration is that of congestion in the airways caused by too many planes seeking to take off or land at peak times at high-demand airports. How might we solve that problem while maintaining reasonable service?

8. Historically, American cities have regulated the taxicab industry by, among other strategies, specifying fares and limiting the number of cab operator permits available to the market. Since 1979, many cities have begun to deregulate the taxi markets by removing controls on fares and by issuing many more medallions.

    a. Build the arguments for and against deregulation of the taxi industry.

    b. What legal challenges are likely to be raised by current permit holders if a city increases the number of available permits?

9. In 1983 Utah passed a law providing that cable television operators may be sued by the government for broadcasting indecent material. Indecency was meant to refer to patently offensive material as determined by community standards and depending on the time of day of the telecast. The attorney general interpreted the law to mean that indecent (but not obscene) material could lawfully be telecast only between midnight and 7 A.M. Utah's position is a response to a problem facing many jurisdictions; that is, how should we regulate cable television to protect children as well as those viewers who simply object to programs displaying themes of sex or violence? Utah's position was challenged in the federal courts as an unconstitutionally broad restraint on freedom of expression. The case reached the U.S. Supreme Court. How would you rule? Explain. See *Jones* v. *Wilkinson,* 800 F2d 989 (1986), aff'd, 55 *Law Week* 3643 (1987). Also see *Wilkinson* v. *Jones, 55 Law Week* 3577 (1987).

10. In 1987, 20 men, frustrated with the quality of radio programming, put together $100,000 to convert a rusty, 200-foot freighter into a radio station. Taking the craft five miles off the Long Island shore, the group began transmission even though they were not licensed by the FCC. Radio Newyork (sic) International, as they called themselves, used a playlist of rock songs from the 60s to today, many with a strong emphasis on antiwar messages. RNI felt that FCC guidelines interfered unfairly with the ability of the disc jockeys to impose their personality and views on the music and other programming. After a few days of broadcasting, agents of the FCC and other federal units boarded the ship, handcuffed the deejays, neutralized the broadcasting equipment, and charged RNI with operating a radio station without a license. Felony charges against the group were subsequently dropped.[61]

   a. Assuming the station's signal was not interfering with the broadcasts of licensed stations, should the FCC intervene? Explain.

   b. RNI argued that they were in international waters and thus not subject to FCC jurisdiction. How would you handle a situation where an unlicensed television station operating well offshore aired sexually explicit material 24 hours per day?

   c. In your view, does American radio programming suffer from blandness provoked by excessive government oversight? Explain.

11. According to a study by Professor Vernon Stone of the University of Missouri, employment in radio news has plummeted since the advent of deregulation. "In major markets, . . . the average full-time news staff dropped from a median of 2.7 in 1985 to 1.4 last year." (1986)[62] He estimates that 2,000 full-time radio news jobs were cut in 1986, while 700 part-time positions were added. Whether that decline in radio news employment is attributable to deregulation or to other factors (such as declining audiences) is unclear. Prior to deregulation at least 8 percent of air time had to be devoted to nonentertainment programming.

   In your judgment, should the government establish rules specifying the length and quality of attention given to news on the radio? Explain.

12. According to a study by economist John Morrall of the federal Office of Management and Budget,[63] the total cost (based on government estimates) of government regulations regarding vehicle collapsible steering column protections is about $100,000 per life saved. Based on government studies, the steering column rules save about 1,300 lives per year. Rules mandating airbags or automatic seat belts cost us about $300,000 for each of the estimated 1,850 lives saved annually. Rules on children's sleepwear flammability cost us about $1.3 million for each of the estimated 106 lives saved annually. At the other end of the scale, an OSHA standard protecting us from arsenic costs about $92.5 million for each of the estimated 11.7 lives saved per year.

   If the power were yours, which of these rules would you banish? Explain, including your standard for assessing the value of a human life.

NOTES

1. Neil H. Jacoby, "The Corporate State: Pure Myth," *Wharton Magazine,* Summer 1977, as quoted in Murray Weidenbaum, *The Future of Business Regulation* (New York: AMACOM, 1979), pp. 168–69.

2. J. Wilson, "The Rise of the Bureaucratic State," *The Public Interest* no. 41 (Fall 1975), as quoted in Robert L. Rabin, *Perspectives on the Administrative Process* (Boston: Little, Brown, 1979), pp. 16, 33.

3. George Stigler, "The Theory of Economic Regulation," *Bell Journal of Economics and Management Science* 2 (Spring 1971), p. 3.

4. For a more detailed discussion of the materials in this section, see Ernest Gellhorn, *Administrative Law and Process in a Nutshell* (St. Paul, Minn.: West Publishing, 1972), pp. 76–237.

5. For a journalistic account of the case see Stuart Taylor, "Court Overturns the FCC Curb on 'Indency' in Evening Shows," *The New York Times*, July 30, 1988, p. 1.

6. Jerry Mashaw, "Regulation, Logic, and Ideology," *Regulation*, November–December 1979, p. 48.

7. Ibid.

8. See Marilyn Chase, "FDA Rule Changes May Rush New Drugs to Very Sick Patients," *The Wall Street Journal*, October 5, 1987, p. 1.

9. 470 U.S. 821 (1985).

10. Ibid., p. 827.

11. "FDA Chief Says Reports Falsified," *Lexington Leader*, November 16, 1976, p. A-6.

12. Judy Grande, "Rules Approving New Drugs Eased by Administration," *Waterloo Courier*, August 7, 1983, p. D-1.

13. Irvin Molotsky, "Critics Say FDA Is Unsafe in Reagan Era," *The New York Times*, January 4, 1987, sec. IV, p. 4. Copyright © 1987 by The New York Times Company. Reprinted by permission.

14. William M. Wardell, "A Close Inspection of the 'Calm Look,'" *Journal of the American Medical Association*, as cited in Paul J. Quirk, "Food and Drug Administration" in *The Politics of Regulation*, ed. James Q. Wilson (New York: Basic Books, 1980), p. 226.

15. Ibid., p. 227.

16. "The Hidden Cost of Drug Safety," *Business Week*, February 21, 1977, p. 80.

17. Joe Davidson, "U.S. Seeks Easing of Experimental Drug Regulations," *The Wall Street Journal*, March 11, 1987, p. 8.

18. "Drug Controls Preferred," *FDA Consumer* 18, no. 4 (May 1984), p. 2.

19. "DC-10 Jet Was 'Certified' but Never Seen by FAA," *Lexington Leader*, August 7, 1979, p. A-4.

20. Mitchell Lynch, "Backing Off Basics," *The Wall Street Journal*, October 18, 1977, pp. 1, 36.

21. J. Richard Crout, in *Drug Development and Marketing*, ed. Robert Helms (Washington, D.C.: American Enterprise Institute, 1975), p. 197, as quoted in Weidenbaum, *Future of Business Regulation*, p. 116.

22. "Congress Wondering How Oraflex Was Approved," *Waterloo Courier*, August 4, 1982, p. B-1.

23. See Weidenbaum, *Future of Business Regulation*, p. 23.

24. "Regulation and the 1986 Budget," *Regulation* 9, no. 2 (March/April 1985), p. 9.

25. George Melloan, "Regulatory Reactionaries Have a Dubious Case," *The Wall Street Journal*, August 11, 1987, p. 27.

26. 56 *Law Week* 2007 (1987).

27. 56 *Law Week* 2211 (1987).

28. Bob Davis, "FCC Ruling that Gave Toy Companies Anonymity on TV Shows Is Overturned," *The Wall Street Journal*, September 30, 1987, p. 27.

29. Ibid.

30. Stigler, "Theory of Economic Regulation," p. 3, as cited in Wilson, ed., *Politics of Regulation*, p. 358.

31. Ibid., p. 5.
32. Barry M. Mitnick, *The Political Economy of Regulation* (New York: Columbia University Press, 1980), p. 219, citing U.S. House of Representatives, Subcommittee on Oversight and Investigations, Committee on Interstate and Foreign Commerce, *Federal Regulation and Regulatory Reform,* 94th Congress, 2nd session (Washington, D.C.: U.S. Government Printing Office, October 1976), pp. 451–52.
33. Mitnick, *Political Economy,* pp. 215–24.
34. Ibid., p. 225, citing U.S. House of Representatives, Subcommittee on Oversight and Investigations, *Federal Regulation and Regulatory Reform.*
35. Mitnick, *Political Economy,* p. 218, citing James M. Graham and Victor H. Kramer, *Appointments to the Regulatory Agencies: The Federal Communications Commission and the Federal Trade Commission (1949–1974).* Committee print, Committee on Commerce, U.S. Senate, 94th Congress, 2nd session (Washington, D.C.: U.S. Government Printing Office, April 1976).
36. "Regulators Too 'Cozy'—Cause," *Lexington Leader,* August 24, 1977, p. A-8.
37. Morton Mintz and Jerry Cohen, *America, Inc.* (New York: Dell Publishing, 1971), p. 296.
38. Frank Greve, "American Petroleum Institute: Gospel according to Big Oil," *Lexington Sunday Herald Leader,* August 5, 1979, p. A-19.
39. Perspectives on Current Developments, "Regulatory Reform in the States: A View from New York," *Regulation* 6, no. 5 (September/October 1982), p. 11.
40. See, for example, James Affleck, "Toward Realistic Risk/Benefit Decisions," *The New York Times,* April 29, 1979, sec. III, p. 16.
41. See, for example, John Tomerlin, "Billion-Dollar Trial Balloon: The Facts behind the Air Bag Mandate," *Road and Track,* May 1979, as reviewed in "Bagfuls of Air?" *Regulation,* January-February 1980, p. 45.
42. *Weekly Compilation of Presidential Documents* 17, no. 8 (February 23, 1981), pp. 124–25.
43. Christopher C. DeMuth, "A Strategy for Regulatory Reform," *Regulation* 8, no. 2 (March/April 1984), pp. 25, 27. DeMuth was administrator for information and regulatory affairs in the Reagan administration's Office of Management and Budget.
44. Lester Thurow, *The Zero-Sum Society* (New York: Penguin Books, 1980), pp. 131–32.
45. Ibid., p. 140.
46. Ibid., p. 136.
47. Laurie McGinley, "Federal Regulation Rises Anew in Matters that Worry the Public," *The Wall Street Journal,* April 21, 1987, p. 1.
48. Ibid., p. 30.
49. Ibid.
50. Bruce Ingersoll, "SEC, despite Its Hands-Off Stance on Takeovers, Pushes Regulation in Inside Trading, Other Areas," *The Wall Street Journal,* April 24, 1987, p. 52.
51. Bob Davis, "Phone Decontrol, despite the Public's Grumblings, Moves Ahead with Boost from New Technology," *The Wall Street Journal,* April 23, 1987, p. 68.

52. Cathy Trost, "Job-Safety Agency Is Firing Buckshot Again, and Industry Runs for Cover as Penalties Fly," *The Wall Street Journal,* April 22, 1987, p. 72.

53. McGinley, "Federal Regulation," pp. 1, 30.

54. James Greene, *Regulatory Problems and Regulatory Reform: The Perceptions of Business* (New York: The Conference Board, 1980), p. 6.

55. "Keep Kentucky's Helmet Law," *Lexington Leader,* November 5, 1980, p. A-20. Also see "Motorcycles, Safety, and Freedom," *Regulation,* July–August 1980, p. 11.

56. Ernest Conine, "Are the Airlines Flying into New Regulations?" *Des Moines Register,* August 11, 1987, p. 7A.

57. Andrew Chalk, "Market Outperforms FAA as Air-Safety Enforcer," *The Wall Street Journal,* September 1, 1987, p. 26.

58. Phyllis S. McGrath, *Redefining Corporate–Federal Relations* (New York: The Conference Board, 1979), p. 3.

59. Quoted in Charles Koch, "Business Can Have Free Enterprise—If It Dares," *Business and Society Review* no. 28 (Winter 1978–79), p. 58.

60. Koch, "Business Can Have Free Enterprise," p. 54.

61. See, for example, Joseph Berger, "Seafaring Protesters Challenge FCC Rules," *The New York Times,* July 27, 1987, p. 1.

62. John Motavelli, "Radio Stations Cutting Out News: Is It Economics or Deregulation?" *Des Moines Register,* November 19, 1987, p. 13A.

63. John F. Morrall III, "A Review of the Record," *Regulation* 10, no. 2 (November/December 1986), p. 25.

Chapter 8

Business Organizations and Securities Regulation

When starting a business, one of the first decisions that must be made by its promoters is which legal format is best for the firm. This decision can be crucial for it will determine many of the rules and requirements governing the operations of the fledgling business. Most large-scale concerns opt for the corporate form, while many smaller ones choose to begin as partnerships or sole proprietorships. Size alone, however, does not determine which form the promoters of a business should prefer. All of the available options—sole proprietorships, partnerships, corporations, Sub S Corporations, and so on—offer various advantages and disadvantages, each of which must be considered, given the circumstances of the particular investment opportunity.

After deciding how the business will be set up, its promoters must determine how and from whom to raise the money needed to establish the business and commence operations. Many small businesses rely solely on their owners for capital, perhaps supplementing their available money with loans from friends or relatives, loans guaranteed by a federal agency (such as the Small Business Administration), or loans collateralized by the owner's house or other assets. Other promoters choose to raise money from banks, insurance companies, or other financial institutions by using the assets of the business or the attractiveness of the investment opportunity to convince the lender that the loan can be repaid. Others rely on risk-taking venture capitalists who are willing to back new companies with impressive expertise, product lines, or ideas in return for a share of ownership in the business, while still other firms opt for issuing stock or securities to small segments of the public, such as friends or acquaintances, or even to the public at large.

The decision of how to raise capital is dictated by market forces. If no bank is willing to extend credit, or no broker is willing to attempt to sell shares in the company, those avenues of money-raising activity must be eliminated from consideration. Of those economically viable possibilities, however, the promoters must choose wisely if they are to raise the needed capital at the lowest possible cost to the business and their ownership of it. As will be seen in the second section of this chapter, major expenses can be avoided if the firm can raise capital without subjecting itself to the requirements of federal securities laws. Many deals are structured in a particular manner solely for the purpose of assuring that the capital raised will not cause the business to fall under the scrutiny of the Securities and Exchange Commission and its mandates.

FORM OF THE ORGANIZATION

When determining which legal form a business will adopt, most thoughtful promoters focus on five factors: cost, continuity, control, liability, and taxes. The order of importance of these considerations will vary from business to business, but all five certainly merit serious analysis before a final decision is made. Cost reflects the initial and subsequent expenses (direct and indirect) associated with a particular form of organization. Continuity refers to the consequences of an owner dying or otherwise withdrawing from participation in the firm, or a new owner joining the business. Control focuses on who will set firm policy and run the business. Liability concerns what assets of the owners may be used to pay firm debts, while tax considerations are based on maximizing the share of corporate resources available to the owner and minimizing those due the government.

Partnerships

Many small businesses start out as sole proprietorships or partnerships. A partnership can be defined as two or more people carrying on as co-owners of a business for profit. A sole proprietorship exists when there is but a single owner of the business. Under either of these arrangements, costs are minimal. There are no legal requirements. A group of people who agree to form a partnership and who act like partners have done just that—created a partnership. No written agreement, filings at the court-house, or other legal notice must be given in advance. While a written partnership agreement is advisable to set forth rights and responsibilities and to limit confusion, it is not necessary. Furthermore, the partners' agreement, whether written or oral, can be changed at any time with their consent.

In the situation where a partnership is created without any thought, either written or oral, being given to how it will operate, the state laws supply the operating conditions for the partnership. Mos† jurisdictions have basically adopted the Uniform Partnership Act (UPA), which provides, for instance, that in the absence of agreements to the contrary:

1. All partners share equally in partnership profits and losses.
2. All partners are expected to devote their full time and energies to partnership business, without compensation.
3. Unanimous consent is necessary to admit a new partner.
4. The partnership can be terminated at any time for any reason by any partner.

A partnership is free to tailor the provisions of its agreement to the particular needs of the partners. Many times, profits and losses are not shared equally, or one partner receives a salary in addition to his or her share of profits, but such variances from the UPA must be spelled out and agreed to. Failure to do so automatically triggers the UPA's provisions and may have costly and perhaps fatal consequences when disputes arise.

Continuity is a problem for partnerships. Every time a partner leaves for any reason (e.g., death, insanity, voluntary or involuntary withdrawal, or personal bankruptcy) or a new partner joins, the partnership must be dissolved and a new one created. Dissolution requires all firm creditors to be notified and appropriate arrangements made. The value of the partnership must be determined, and the withdrawing partner must be given his or her appropriate share or its monetary equivalent of the partnership assets. This process can provoke many disputes and is often time consuming and expensive. Furthermore, from a business point of view, it can be disastrous if partnership assets must be sold quickly to pay off a withdrawing partner. A good partnership agreement can limit the potential problems caused by a partner's withdrawal, but it can never totally eliminate them.

Control in a partnership is relatively simple. Either each partner has an equal say-so in partnership policy, or the partnership agreement sets forth an alternative scheme under which some partners have a greater voice than others. On most issues, unless otherwise agreed to by the partners, a majority vote is necessary to approve a course of action. Thus, if the initial partners are willing, it is easy to set up a system in which one or more partners own less than half the interest of the partnership but have more than half—or effective control—for voting purposes. Other than to benefit or protect individual partners, the most critical issue that must be addressed concerning control is making certain that tie votes among the partners do not occur continually. Many small partnerships have failed because the partners were not able to muster a majority to approve a policy (typically 1–1 or 2–2 votes on a crucial issue) and had not established procedures to prevent the deadlock from becoming a permanent pitfall capable of stifling any partnership action.

Liability is often the issue that forces promoters to choose the corporate form over a partnership. All members of a partnership are personally liable to the full extent of their assets for all partnership debts. If, for instance, the partnership were to lose money and be unable to pay a bank loan on time, or if a partnership truck were to cause the deaths of 10 children in a school bus, the partners might be forced to sell their houses, stock, bonds, and other possessions to meet the demands of various creditors. Because of this uncertainty, many people with substantial assets refuse to invest or participate in partnerships. Clearly, if the business is likely to be sued regularly or face catastrophic losses from accidents or other tort liability, a partnership probably would not be appropriate. On the other hand, if the partners are relatively poor or judgment proof (i.e., have no unencumbered assets), the penalty associated with the unlimited personal liability for partnership debts is largely illusory.

Taxation is the reason many small businesses choose to be partnerships. Partnerships merely serve as conduits for profits flowing from the business directly to the partners. The partners then report partnership profits or losses on their tax returns and pay the appropriate taxes at the ordinary income tax rate. The partnership itself merely reports the amount of income to appropriate taxing agencies and does not actually pay any income tax. Many states also levy a yearly tax against the authorized shares of corporations chartered in their states. Partnerships typically escape such taxes.

Corporations

Partnerships and sole proprietorships make economic sense for people who are essentially selling their own and their partners' labor, expertise, or experience (three doctors, eight attorneys, or five radio repairers). Businesses that utilize many different factors in production, need large amounts of capital, and expect to continue unabated after the founding owners have departed often find partnerships unwieldy and economically unfeasible. For these businesses, a corporate entity is more appropriate. Corporations do business under a charter provided by a state and are an economic entity totally separate and distinct from their owners. Typically, but not always, corporations are chartered in the state where their headquarters are located. Many corporations, however, choose to incorporate in states like Delaware or Texas regardless of where they plan on doing business because the corporate laws and low-taxation policies of these jurisdictions give management more leeway in how it runs the corporation, controls its policies, and benefits itself and the shareholders. Quite often, such state regulations and laws are decisive tools in corporate mergers or takeover attempts.

The cost of setting up a corporation is often substantially higher than that associated with a partnership. Obtaining a charter typically requires an attorney and the completion of numerous forms and procedures dictated by the state. Taxes and license fees often have to be paid. The corporation must also undertake similar obligations in other states in which it plans to do business. After the corporation is chartered, it must file regular reports with the state, pay appropriate taxes and fees, maintain an agent for service of process, and generally comply with the state's corporate laws. This might require election of a board of directors, regular audits, shareholder meetings, and any number of other items thought necessary by the state to ensure the corporation is run fairly for the benefit of all shareholders.

As long as all state requirements are met, a corporation may enjoy a perpetual existence, thus eliminating continuity problems (such as those occurring in a partnership when an important partner decides to withdraw at an inopportune time). Ownership of stock in a corporation does not connote a personal, fiduciary duty like that existing between partners. Shares may be transferred freely to anyone without corporate approval, and the corporation is under no obligation to buy back the shares of a disgruntled or departing shareholder. Likewise, on the death of a shareholder, the shares simply transfer to his or her heirs, and corporate structure remains unchanged.

Control is usually much easier to maintain in a corporation than in a partnership. Shares of stock often are sold to widely diverse groups of people who have no connection with each other, little in common, and no interest in being involved in corporate dealings. Often, large blocks of shares are controlled by banks or insurance companies, which tend to vote for the continuation of current management except in the most unusual situations. The groups that control major corporations often own or control very small percentages of the company's stock but are able to maintain their positions as board members or top corporate officers. Corporations sometimes issue nonvoting as well as voting stock. This nonvoting stock shares in firm profits and dividends but does not vote at shareholder meetings. Through this technique, existing owners can raise additional capital for the firm without risking loss of control.

Shareholder liability is much more limited than partner liability. Because a corporation is a separate entity, it can sue and be sued. Corporate debts are the sole obligations of the corporation and must be paid from corporate assets. In other words, a party aggrieved by an action of a corporation (an unpaid debt or an accident caused by a corporate-owned automobile) but unable to recoup adequate damages from the corporation cannot expect to recover its losses from the personal assets of the individual shareholders. Except in the most egregious or unusual circumstances, shareholders' losses are limited to their original investment in the corporation.

This inability of creditors to use personal shareholder assets to satisfy corporate debts or obligations is referred to as the "corporate veil" and is often a powerful incentive to incorporate. By incorporating, a person starting a small business can rest at night with the assurance that a business reverse will not cause the owner's house, automobiles, jewelry, and so on to be sold to pay corporate debts.

The issue of taxation presents the major drawback for choosing a corporate existence. Because a corporation is a separate economic entity, it is also a separate taxable entity. As such, corporations must pay a corporate income tax to the federal government as well as to most states in which they conduct business. Joint state and federal income taxes can approach 40 percent of profits, although many corporations can substantially lower this figure by using the many provisions of the income tax code. An individual receiving dividends from a corporation must pay income tax on the dividend to state and federal authorities. Thus, corporate profits are said to be subject to "double taxation"—first when the corporation reports a profit, and later when those profits are distributed to owners in the form of dividends. For each dollar of corporate profits it would not be inconceivable to suggest that less than 35 cents would eventually find its way into the shareholders' pockets. Dividends paid to other corporations are partially exempt from taxation, thus minimizing "triple taxation."

Hybrid Organizations

For some investments, a limited partnership may be appropriate. A limited partnership is like a partnership in many respects: it is not a taxable entity, and all losses or gains are passed through to the partners. The principal difference is that there are two classes of partners. One class, typically investors, is referred to as limited partners. They are not allowed to participate in management decision making, but they are also granted limited liability so that their maximum potential exposure to loss is their original investment in the project. The other class, typically the promoters, is referred to as general partners. They manage the business and are personally liable for all losses. A corporation can be the general partner in many instances, thus offering the actual general partners (the owners of the corporation) the equivalent of limited liability. Limited partnerships are particularly suitable for raising capital for single-project alliances among diverse groups of investors (e.g., developing an office building or shopping mall), and when one of the primary motivations for investing in the project is to shelter other income from taxation.

In a limited partnership, the shares or interests of the limited partners may be sold or transferred freely. Death, bankruptcy, insanity, and so on have no effect on the partnership. The general partners, on the other hand, are subject to roughly the same restrictions as in a regular partnership. However, provision is usually made in the limited partnership agreement for an alternate general partner so that the project can continue unabated should a general partner be forced to withdraw. Limited partnerships are as complicated as corporations to form. Failure to comply with all the requirements may subject the limited partners to unlimited liability just as if they were general partners.

Some business projects call for the formation of a Sub S Corporation. This creation of tax law allows, in certain situations, an incorporated business to escape most corporate income tax. The owners of the business then have the best of both worlds—limited liability without double taxation. In order to qualify, a corporation must have fewer than 17 shareholders, over 80 percent of its income must be "earned" income (i.e., not derived from dividends, interest, royalties, and other passive sources), and almost all of its income or losses must be distributed to the owners each year. The shareholders then pay the appropriate personal income tax on their earnings just as a partnership would. Because of these restrictions, Sub S Corporations are suitable only for smaller projects that do not need to retain capital for growth purposes. A suitable situation might be eight individuals who decide to develop 100 acres of land into 200 lots, which will then be sold over a period of years. The early losses generated from building roads, sewers, parks, and so on will be passed through to the individual shareholders to reduce their current income tax, while the taxable gains will be deferred to later years. Furthermore, no additional capital will be needed by the business. When all the lots have been sold, the deal will end and the corporation will simply cease operations.

OPERATING THE ORGANIZATION

While the rules for operating or managing the business organization vary depending on which form is used, one common element is present—the fiduciary duty. Officers, directors, managers, or partners have a particularly strong responsibility to act in the best interest of the business, even if that means putting the needs of the business ahead of personal needs or financial gain. The fiduciary standard is often expressed by such terms as acting in "good faith" or in a "reasonably prudent manner." Obviously, these definitions are not situation specific and leave considerable discretion to the individual involved to decide what is best for the business in a particular circumstance. This lack of specificity, however, does not open up all business decisions to second-guessing by courts or irate shareholders. Protection is offered to managers whose decisions turn out to be in error. The "business judgment" rule says that if a manager acts in a reasonable manner (often defined as "could another manager have rationally made the same decision?"), then the courts will not hold the manager liable for the fact that his or her judgment ultimately turned out to be wrong.

SPECIAL SITUATIONS

Piercing the Corporate Veil

Although shareholders in corporations are said to have limited liability for the debts of the corporation, in certain instances they can be held personally liable when the corporation is unable to pay its obligations. For instance, the corporate veil of limited liability can be pierced if a business is started with so little capital that it is obvious to the courts that the sole purpose of the corporation was for the shareholders to escape liability for their actions.

Suppose a corporation was established with little or no capital to supply propane gas to civic arenas, theaters, and so on. This business kept no insurance, had no assets, and would have nothing to lose should a tank explode, killing or injuring numerous people. Although its owners might think themselves to be insulated from liability and the corporation to be judgment proof, a court might pierce the corporate veil and hold the owners personally liable on the theory that the gross undercapitalization of their business so abused the corporate privileges granted them in their charter that they should be denied limited liability. In other situations, limited liability is denied the owners of a corporation that received a corporate charter but does not comply with all the state requirements that directors be elected, board meetings be held, and so on. Typically, this occurs when one corporation sets up another corporation to perform some activity but the larger corporation does not allow the new one to be run as an independent entity, treating it instead like it was simply another division of the original corporation. If the new corporation suffers large losses, the courts might hold the founding corporation liable for its debts on the grounds that the two were run like a single corporation even though they were issued two charters. One is said to be the alter ego of the other and thus liable.

Reality of Limited Liability

Many businesspeople automatically assume they want to form a corporation because of their concerns about personal liability for business debts. These debts could come from two main sources: tort liability resulting from an accident involving business activities (such as an accident caused by a firm truck) or contract liability occurring because the firm is unable to pay its obligation to a supplier of goods or a lender of money. Concerning tort liability, only the most irresponsible business would fail to have insurance adequate to pay foreseeable losses resulting from accident or death due to negligence. Thus, personal tort liability can be as easily avoided in a partnership as in a corporation. Insurance is not normally obtainable to pay contract liabilities resulting from a firm's inability to meet its debts and other obligations, so the corporate form might appear advantageous as many more businesses fail due to contractual indebtedness than to negligent actions. Banks and other lenders, however, recognize this economic fact of life and want to protect themselves from the limited liability afforded corporate shareholders. The principal way they do this is by refusing to lend money to small or new corporations unless the owners personally guarantee the loans. This usually means the owners must pledge their houses, stocks, bonds, and other assets to the bank. If the business fails, their personal fortunes are just as likely to be lost in a corporation as in a partnership. For a small corporation, limited liability is not always what it seems.

Avoidance of Double Taxation

One of the principal problems for small businesses that choose the corporate form is double taxation. Many corporations that are owned and managed by the same people can take various steps to minimize the bite of corporate taxation. In all instances, the strategy involved revolves around the same simple principle: maximize the benefits received by the owners and minimize the profitability of the corporation. The proper procedure is to use corporate assets in a way that is advantageous to the owners and deductible to the corporation. For instance, the owners can pay themselves large salaries and substantial fringe benefits for running the business. They receive those salaries and benefits directly, much as they would receive dividends if they were passive shareholders, and if they can arrange it so that the corporation earns no profit each year, no corporate income tax will be paid and thus double taxation will be avoided. The IRS recognizes this game, however, and will allow only the deduction of reasonable salaries and benefits. Still, salaries and benefits can be stretched to minimize corporate profitability.

The owner could also choose to lend the firm money and receive interest rather than purchase stock in the corporation and receive dividends in return. As interest is deductible to the corporation while dividends are not, and both are taxable to the recipients at ordinary income tax rates, this strategy also eliminates double taxation. Again, the IRS is not blind to the possibilities of abuse and has the power to disallow interest payments it believes are excessive. Clearly, a business funded 100 percent with debt provided by its owner would not pass IRS muster, but a 50 percent debt/50 percent equity ratio would probably appear reasonable in most circumstances.

Some businesses choose to minimize double taxation by not paying dividends and accumulating earnings. In effect, taxes are deferred until the business is sold or dividends are paid. In the meantime, the money can be used to help the business grow or to invest in other stocks or bonds. The IRS can minimize this ploy by taxing excess accumulated earnings, which it defines as earnings accumulated not for business-related reasons but for tax avoidance purposes. Before the IRS can consider levying the tax, several million dollars of earnings must be accumulated and there must be no valid reason, such as future plans for expansion, for retaining the earnings.

Changing the Form of a Business

Within certain IRS-imposed limitations, businesses are free to change their legal form as they deem advantageous. One simple strategy is to start out as a partnership, because it is cheaper and easier and because any business losses can be deducted immediately from the partners' personal income. If the corporate form were chosen, business losses would not reduce taxes until such time as the corporation itself earned money, which might not occur for years. Later, after profitability is attained and as the needs for continuity and increased capital become more pressing, a transfer to corporate status might be appropriate.

Tax Shelters

The theory of tax shelters is based on taking advantage of provisions in the tax code that allow certain bookkeeping entries (such as depreciation and depletion) to be deducted from the profits of specific investments. If economically viable and properly set up, these projects can have a negative taxable income plus a positive cash flow for a period of years, thus offering shelter from taxation to some part of a wealthy person's income. Suppose, for instance, that a real estate salesperson wants to buy a building but has no money. Doctors have money and tax problems but do not have real estate management skills. This marriage made in heaven results in a limited partnership. Typically, the doctors (limited partners) would invest money to make the down payment on the building, and the real estate salesperson (general partner) would borrow the remaining money, using the building as collateral. The general partner would receive a small percentage of ownership in the building and a fee for managing it, while the limited partner would receive the remaining economic and tax benefits. In sketch form, the benefits might flow as follows:

Building purchase price—including renovation	$20,000,000
Down payment (20 doctors @ $100,000 each)	$ 2,000,000
Amount borrowed	$18,000,000
Annual interest	$ 2,500,000
Depreciation (first year)	2,000,000
Other expenses	500,000
Total expenses	$ 5,000,000
Total income (building is being renovated for much of first year)	3,000,000
Total loss	($ 2,000,000)
Loss per doctor	(100,000)
Tax savings per doctor (assuming 40% personal income tax rate)	40,000
Return on investment (first year)	40%

In other words, the building has not even been totally rented, and the investors have already received a substantial return, with greater earnings expected in future years when the building is fully rented. Should the project fail, the investors will lose nothing but their investment, all of which can be written off against their taxes. Should the project succeed, their return will only increase. This example of a typical tax shelter is based on the general partners' ability to borrow substantial amounts of money with the building as collateral. Similar deals are offered to investors daily. Some promoters actually promise that first-year tax savings will exceed the total investment, which is possible if a very high percentage of borrowed money can be obtained to finance the project.

The IRS has recently begun cracking down on fraudulent tax shelters, and many that appear to offer the greatest tax savings will not pass IRS audit. In addition, the rules on tax shelters are continually being tightened. For instance, in the past much of the desirability of tax shelters was based on the fact that one partner was not personally obligated to pay back the borrowed money if the project failed (nonrecourse financing). Currently nonrecourse financing can yield only in real estate tax shelters. Bulls, movie scripts, and myriad other shelter offerings can no longer use borrowed, nonrecourse money to leverage their expected returns to extremely high levels. Lower personal tax rates have also made tax shelters less attractive to many investors.

Buy/Sell Agreements

Many small businesses fail because one of the principal owner/managers dies. The death causes numerous hardships for the firm. First of all, the deceased's expertise is unexpectedly lost. Second, he or she will have to be replaced, often with more than one person, and the new people must be trained and paid. The time and expense can be substantial. Also, from the deceased's point of view, the spouse and children need to be provided for. Most small businesses are totally illiquid in that no ready purchaser is available to buy the deceased's shares. The remaining owners will probably be unable to purchase the shares because of the increased costs to the business associated with the death and the precarious financial position that the firm is likely to find itself in at this time.

One attractive solution to this dilemma is a buy/sell agreement. This consists of an agreement *negotiated at the formation of the business* concerning the terms under which the business will be valued should an owner die. Once the valuation formula is agreed to, the firm purchases a joint life insurance policy, which pays a specified amount on the first death of an owner. When a death occurs, the firm uses the proceeds of the policy to purchase the shares, and all remaining parties benefit. The spouse and children receive cash to pay estate taxes and living expenses, and the firm receives a cash infusion just when it is needed most. Although the premiums on the policy typically are not deductible, the proceeds normally escape taxation. The only caveat is that these agreements must be negotiated before an owner's health fails. When all parties are healthy, buy/sell agreements are easy to negotiate because all sides want the purchase price to be relatively low. They all expect to be purchasing the stock (i.e., alive), not selling it for the benefit of their heirs. Once it becomes apparent who is likely to survive, the issue of valuation becomes much more difficult.

Questions

1. *a.* In situations like the disaster involving the Buffalo Mining Company (Chapter 3), should the corporate veil be pierced so that the parent corporation can be sued? Explain.
   b. What are the ramifications for business if piercing the corporate veil becomes more common?
2. *a.* Why do you think partnerships are not taxable entities for income tax purposes, yet corporations are taxable? Does this distinction make sense? Explain.
   b. What would be the ramifications of taxing corporations at much lower rates or not taxing them at all?
3. *a.* Why do you think federal law allows Sub S Corporations? Do they serve any useful purpose? What?
   b. Do limited partnerships serve any useful purpose? Explain.

4. *a.* Before tax rates were lowered, the total tax on unearned income in Great Britain exceeded 90 percent. In other words, the government's share of profits derived from rent, interest, and so on exceeded 90 percent, while the investor's share was less than 10 percent. Likewise, the government's share of any losses exceeded 90 percent, if the investor had other income to offset the losses. What are the ramifications of such a policy?

    b. A developer in England built a large office building during this period. Because inflation was so high, the developer decided he could make more money by leaving the building empty, depreciating it, deducting his losses from his other income, and then leasing the building at a higher rate the following year. The following year, inflation was still high, and he made the same decision. This practice continued for several years, until the developer had almost totally depreciated the still-empty building. At that point, the developer demolished the building—and built another. Discuss.

Once the form of organization has been established and the business has started operation and begun to progress, the need for additional funds beyond the financial capacity of the founders and promoters becomes acute. At this time, many firms choose to "go public" or to attempt to raise capital from the general public in a variety of ways to finance their business or personal plans for expansion and growth. To attract this new money, a business not only must offer an attractive investment opportunity but also must comply with numerous state and federal requirements concerning the sale and resale of securities. The following section discusses some of the applicable statutes and regulations.

SECURITIES REGULATION

Condominiums	Stocks
Gold	Annuities
Bonds	Warehouse receipts
Orange groves	Limited partnerships
Bourbon	

Any of the above can be securities and thus subject to many state and federal laws. As these examples suggest, the definition of a security is broad, and care has to be taken so that inadvertent violations of these laws do not occur. State laws, referred to as "blue sky" laws, must be complied with in each state in which the securities are to be sold. Furthermore, one or more federal statutes may be applicable. For instance, the Securities Act of 1933 regulates the public offering of new, nonexempt securities and prohibits their sale until they have been properly registered with the Securities and Exchange Commission (SEC). Fraudulent and deceptive practices are barred by this act. The Securities Exchange Act of 1934 controls the resale of securities and sets up the SEC for the purpose of exercising that responsibility. This act prohibits manipulative or deceptive practices, requires the registration of brokers and dealers, and limits their activities in many respects. Stock exchanges, clearinghouses, and other participants involved in transferring securities also come under its broad umbrella of coverage. The Investment Advisors Act of 1940 is roughly analogous to the 1934 act in the requirements it places on investment counselors.

The Public Utilities Holding Company Act of 1935 corrected problems in the financing of gas and electric holding companies. Very few problems now confront the SEC concerning this area of regulation. The Trust Indenture Act of 1939 set forth standards of independence for trustees involved in large debt issues. Thus, a bond issue might be subject to the provisions of both this act and the 1933 act.

The Investment Company Act of 1940 regulates any publicly owned entities that primarily invest in or buy and sell securities. Insider dealings, capital requirements, sales charges, and so on are covered by this statute. Finally, the Securities Investor Protection Act of 1970 set up the Securities Investor Protection Corporation, which aids customers of bankrupt or illiquid securities companies.

While the SEC is the primary federal agency established to regulate the securities industry, it cannot do the entire job itself. Thus, all regulatory schemes involve a good deal of "self-regulation," in which the regulated entities become participants in their own regulation. The New York Stock Exchange, with SEC approval and oversight, continues to establish many regulations for its members and is active in investigating insider abuses and manipulations by its members. The National Association of Securities Dealers plays a similar role for dealers in over-the-counter securities.

Definition of a Security

The Securities Act of 1933 defines a security as

> any note, stock, treasury stock, bond, debenture, evidence of indebtedness, certificate of interest or participation in any profit-sharing agreement, collateral-trust certificate, preorganizational certificate or subscription, transferable share, investment contract, voting-trust certificate, certificate of deposit for a security, fractional undivided interest in oil, gas, or other mineral rights, or, in general, any interest or instrument commonly known as a "security," or any certificate of interest or participation in, temporary or interim certificate for, receipt for, guarantee of, or warrant or right to subscribe to or purchase, any of the foregoing.

Any instrument called a bond, stock, debenture, share, and so on will almost certainly be considered a security. Most of the disputes involving the applicability of securities laws involve investment contracts or certificates of participation in a profit-sharing agreement. Typically, these involve attempts by promoters to raise money for various schemes in which investors pool their money with the expectation of future returns, but no pieces of paper that look like securities are involved. In *SEC* v. *W. J. Howey Co.,* cited here, orange groves were held to be securities and the following test was put forward: "the person invests his money in a common enterprise and is led to expect profits solely from the efforts of the promoter or a third party."

SECURITIES & EXCHANGE COMMISSION V. W. J. HOWEY CO.
328 U.S. 293 (1946)

Justice Murphy

This case involves the application of § 2(1) of the Securities Act of 1933 to an offering of units of a citrus grove development coupled with a contract for cultivating, marketing and remitting the net proceeds to the investor.

* * * * *

Most of the facts are stipulated. The respondents, W. J. Howey Company and Howey-in-the-Hills Service, Inc., are Florida corporations under direct common control and management. The Howey Company owns large tracts of citrus acreage in Lake County, Florida. During the past several years it has planted about 500 acres annually, keeping half of the groves itself and offering the other half to the public "to help us finance additional development." Howey-in-the-Hills Service, Inc., is a service company engaged in cultivating and developing many of these groves, including the harvesting and marketing of the crops.

Each prospective customer is offered both a land sales contract and a service contract, after having been told that it is not feasible to invest in a grove unless service arrangements are made. While the purchaser is free to make arrangements with other service companies, the superiority of Howey-in-the-Hills Service, Inc., is stressed. Indeed, 85 percent of the acreage sold during the three-year period ending May 31, 1943, was covered by service contracts with Howey-in-the-Hills Service, Inc.

The land sales contract with the Howey Company provides for a uniform purchase price per acre or fraction thereof, varying in amount only in accordance with the number of years the particular plot has been planted with citrus trees. Upon full payment of the purchase price the land is conveyed to the purchaser by warranty deed. Purchases are usually made in narrow strips of land arranged so that an acre consists of a row of 48 trees. During the period between February 1, 1941, and May 31, 1943, 31 of the 42 persons making purchases bought less than five acres each. The average holding of these 31 persons was 1.33 acres and sales of as little as 0.65, 0.7, and 0.73 of an acre were made. These tracts are not separately fenced and the sole indication of several ownership is found in small land marks intelligible only through a plat book record.

The service contract, generally of a 10-year duration without option of cancellation, gives Howey-in-the-Hills Service, Inc., a leasehold interest and "full and complete" possession of the acreage. For a specified fee plus the cost of labor and materials, the company is given full discretion and authority over the cultivation of the groves and the harvest and marketing of the crops. The company is well established in the citrus business and maintains a large force of skilled personnel and a great deal of equipment, including 75 tractors, sprayer wagons, fertilizer trucks and the like. Without the consent of the company, the land owner or purchaser has no right of entry to market the crop; thus there is ordinarily no right to specific fruit. The company is accountable only for an allocation of the net profits based upon a check made at the time of picking. All the produce is pooled by the respondent companies, which do business under their own names.

The purchasers for the most part are nonresidents of Florida. They are predominantly business and professional people who lack the knowledge, skill, and equipment necessary for the care and cultivation of citrus trees. They are attracted by the expectation of substantial profits. It was represented, for example, that profits during the 1943–1944 season amounted to 20 percent and that even greater profits might be expected during the 1944–1945 season, although only a 10 percent annual return was to be expected over a 10-year period. Many of these purchasers are patrons of a resort hotel owned and operated by the Howey Company in a scenic section adjacent to the groves. The hotel's advertising mentions the fine groves in the vicinity and the attention of the patrons is drawn to the groves as they are being escorted about the surrounding countryside. They are told that the groves are for sale; if they indicate an interest in the matter they are then given a sales talk.

It is admitted that the mails and instrumentalities of interstate commerce are used in the sale of the land and service contracts and that no registration statement or letter of notification has ever been filed with the commission in accordance with the Securities Act of 1933 and the rules and regulations thereunder.

Section 2(1) of the act defines the term "security" to include the commonly known documents traded for speculation or investment. This definition also includes "securities" of a more variable character, designated by such descriptive terms as "certificate of interest or participation in any profit-sharing agreement," "investment contract" and "in general, any interest or instrument commonly known as a 'security.'" The legal issue in this case turns upon a determination of whether, under the circumstances, the land sales contract, the warranty deed and the service contract together constitute an "investment contract" within the meaning of § 2(1). An affirmative answer brings into operation the registration requirements of § 5(a), unless the security is granted an exemption under § 3(b). The lower courts, in reaching a negative answer to this problem, treated the contracts and deeds as separate transactions involving no more than an ordinary real estate sale and an agreement by the seller to manage the property for the buyer.

. . . [A]n investment contract for purposes of the Securities Act means a contract, transaction or scheme whereby a person invests his money in a common enterprise and is led to expect profits solely from the efforts of the promoter or a third party, it being immaterial whether the shares in the enterprise are evidenced by formal certificates or by nominal interests in the physical assets employed in the enterprise. Such a definition necessarily underlies this Court's decision in *S.E.C.* v. *Joiner Corp.* and has been enunciated and applied many times by lower federal courts. It permits the fulfillment of the statutory purpose of compelling full and fair disclosure relative to the issuance of "the many types of instruments that in our commercial world fall within the ordinary concept of a security." H. Rep: No. 85, 73d Cong., 1st Sess., p. 11. It embodies a flexible rather than a static principle, one that is capable of adaptation to meet the countless and variable schemes devised by those who seek the use of the money of others on the promise of profits.

The transactions in this case clearly involve investment contracts as so defined. The respondent companies are offering something more than fee simple interests in land, something different from a farm or orchard coupled with management services. They are offering an opportunity to contribute money and to share in the profits of a large citrus fruit enterprise managed and partly owned by respondents. They are offering this opportunity to persons who reside in distant localities and who lack the equipment and experience requisite to the cultivation, harvesting, and marketing of the citrus products. Such persons have no desire to occupy the land or to develop it themselves; they are attracted solely by the prospects of a return on their investment. Indeed, individual development of the plots of land that are offered and sold would seldom be economically feasible due to their small size. Such tracts gain utility as citrus groves only when cultivated and developed as component parts of a larger area. A common enterprise managed by respondents or third parties with adequate personnel and equipment is therefore essential if the investors are to achieve their paramount aim of a return on their investments. Their respective shares in this enterprise are evidenced by land sales contracts and warranty deeds, which serve as a convenient method of determining the investors' allocable shares of the profits. The resulting transfer of rights in land is purely incidental.

Thus all the elements of a profit-seeking business venture are present here. The investors provide the capital and share in the earnings and profits; the promoters manage, control and operate the enterprise. It follows that the arrangements whereby the investors' interests are made manifest involve investment contracts, regardless of the legal terminology in which such contracts are clothed. The investment contracts in this instance take the form of land sales contracts, warranty deeds and service contracts which respondents offer to prospective investors. And respondents' failure to abide by the statutory and administrative rules in making such offerings, even though the failure results from a bona fide mistake as to the law, cannot be sanctioned under the act.

This conclusion is unaffected by the fact that some purchasers choose not to accept the full offer of an investment contract by declining to enter into a service contract with the respondents. The Securities Act prohibits the offer as well as the sale of unregistered, nonexempt securities. Hence it is enough that the respondents merely offer the essential ingredients of an investment contract.

We reject the suggestion of the Circuit Court of Appeals, that an investment contract is necessarily missing where the enterprise is not speculative or promotional in character and where the tangible interest which is sold has intrinsic value independent of the success of the enterprise as a whole. The test is whether the scheme involves an investment of money in a common enterprise with profits to come solely from the efforts of others. If that test be satisfied, it is immaterial whether the enterprise is speculative or nonspeculative or whether there is a sale of property with or without intrinsic value. The statutory policy of affording broad protection to investors is not to be thwarted by unrealistic and irrelevant formulae.

Reversed.

Definition of a Security—Continued

In subsequent cases, various courts have expanded on the *Howey* doctrine of whether the scheme involves an investment of money in a common enterprise with profits to come solely from the efforts of others. For instance, it would be quite easy to avoid this definition and ensuing SEC regulation by structuring the investment so that some effort on the part of investors was required. As the circuit court in *SEC* v. *Koscot Interplanetary, Inc.*[1] and other cases pointed out, however, the critical question is "whether the efforts by those other than the investor are the undeniably significant ones, those essential managerial efforts which affect the failure or success of the enterprise." In *Koscot Interplanetary,* the court discussed a pyramid scheme in which people gave the company money in return for the right to wholesale cosmetics to "beauty advisers" who then sold the cosmetics to the public. For a larger sum, the person could obtain the rights to distribute cosmetics to wholesalers and the beauty advisers and to recruit new participants. These "supervisors" and "distributors" were also allowed to keep a substantial portion of the money that any new prospect they recruited paid to Koscot for the right to participate in the cosmetics scheme. The court held that the involvement of the "supervisors," "distributors," and "beauty advisers" in selling cosmetics was merely incidental to the pyramid scheme of attracting more money from new prospects, and that such payments to Koscot for the right to introduce other prospects to the company, thus receiving a share of *their* initiation payments, was properly an investment subject to SEC jurisdiction.

Given that the courts appear to take an expansive view of what constitutes a security, several other cases yield somewhat surprising results. For instance, in *United Housing Foundation* v. *Forman,*[2] subsidized cooperative nonprofit housing communities were held not to be securities. In a co-op, one buys shares in a corporation that owns or builds an apartment building. Ownership of the shares gives these purchasers the right to occupy certain rooms (an apartment) in the building as long as all fees, rents, expenses, and so on are paid. Typically, there are restrictions on the occupancy of the apartment and the transferability of shares. In this instance, prospective dwellers bought the shares with the expectation that the rent would be around $23 per room. Ten years later, the estimate had escalated to almost $40 per room. Claims by purchasers that this was a securities offering that should have been registered with the SEC were rejected by the Supreme Court on the grounds that the primary motive of the participants was to obtain decent housing. In other words, this "investment" was for personal consumption, not an attempt to receive profits from the efforts of others. The mere inclusion of the word *stock* or *shares* in the deal did not automatically make it a "security" pursuant to federal securities law.

In *International Brotherhood of Teamsters* v. *Daniel*,[3] nonparticipatory retirement plans were held excluded from securities law. Daniel worked as a driver from 1950 to 1973, with the exception of a six-month layoff in 1961. During this period, his employer contributed money on a weekly basis to the Teamsters Union, which invested it for the purpose of paying Daniel and others a pension on retirement. Daniel himself directly contributed no money to the fund. When Daniel retired, he expected a pension of about $500 monthly but was totally denied it because the pension fund rules required 20 years continuous service to qualify for any pension. Despite the compelling facts of this case and the obvious unfairness to Daniel, the court held that a compulsory, noncontributory pension fund was not the type of investment Congress had in mind when it passed the securities acts and that no relief for this unfairness could be had. While securities laws have a broad scope, they do not encompass all investments.

Exemptions

Any securities issued or guaranteed by federal, state, or local governments are exempt from all securities laws, as are those of banks and savings and loans, charitable and religious institutions, and common carriers, such as motor carriers and railroads (for certain types of offerings). The issuance of most insurance and annuity contracts and commercial paper are also exempt from federal securities laws. Reselling these securities may be subject to one or more provisions of the various laws; however, constitutional concerns play a key role in the exemptions of government, religious, and charitable securities. Most of the others are removed from SEC jurisdiction because they are regulated by other state or federal agencies, such as the Federal Reserve System or the Interstate Commerce Commission.

In recent years, major cities like New York and Cleveland have defaulted on some bond issues, and numerous industrial development bonds issued under the auspices of local governments have gone bad (when a corporation goes bankrupt, it may default on its commercial paper). Furthermore, speculation in these securities has proliferated because of their unregulated status. From a stodgy, low-pressure backwater of the securities industry, trading in municipal securities has now become, for many, a very speculative and aggressive arena. By 1985 trades of government securities exceeded by many times (in dollar volume) trades on the New York Stock Exchange and were in excess of $60 billion daily.

TREASURYS ON TRIAL

Daniel Hertzberg and Alan Murray

James Kasch has been rushing around New York City lately, seeing banks and credit-rating agencies and trying to save the financial standing of Toledo, Ohio. He is a man with problems.

Officially, Mr. Kasch is suspended from his job as Toledo's finance director, but he is still at his desk. Toledo faces a possible loss of $19.2 million from its dealings with E.S.M. Government Securities, Inc., of Fort Lauderdale, Florida. E.S.M. owes its customers, including many municipalities, $315 million.

Mr. Kasch's hand shakes as he lights a cigarette and describes "the tragedy." He laments, "There isn't any protection when you deal with government securities dealers." And he insists on the need for a "watchdog" to prevent further disasters.

He is talking about the huge, largely unregulated government securities market, where major dealers trade more than $60 billion daily. For the bold and the skilled, there are rich rewards, but for the unwary or the unlucky, the losses can be swift—and enormous.

Latest Crisis

Right now, the risks, rather than the rewards, are focusing the spotlight on the government securities market. In the latest in a series of scandals to strike the market, the collapse of E.S.M. has sent shock waves through the banking system. E.S.M.'s failure triggered the run by depositors that forced the temporary closing of 71 Ohio thrift institutions.

Pressure for more regulation of this huge market thus is mounting. "If you have a free market, accidents are bound to happen," says Federal Reserve Board Governor Henry Wallich. "But if the accidents get too big and too

frequent, the response cannot be the same." Voices are also being raised in Congress supporting increased regulation.

* * * * *

Role of Federal Debt

The ballooning federal deficits play a big role. They are forcing the Treasury to pump out unprecedented amounts of new government securities. And that is straining major dealers who bid for and then market this new supply of government debt.

Dealings in Treasurys (average daily transactions by primary dealers)

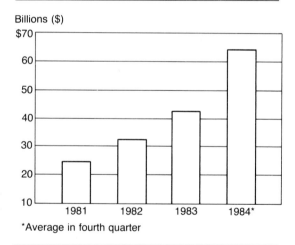

Billions ($)

*Average in fourth quarter

Source: Federal Reserve.

The government debt tripled during the 1970s and hit $1 trillion in 1981, the first year of the Reagan administration. Next year, it will surpass $2 trillion. With federal deficits still running at $200 billion a year, the day-to-day operation of government depends on finding ever more buyers in the United States and abroad for that mountain of debt. Indeed, the federal government is like a hospital patient, sustained by intravenous infusions from the credit markets.

Soon, dealers say, the Treasury may be selling as much as $23 billion in securities at a time during its quarterly refunding operations, when the government rolls over some of its old debt and sells new issues. The most recent one totaled $19 billion.

With the large volumes, any kinks in the market can raise the cost of servicing the federal debt by billions of dollars. As Edward Geng, senior vice president of the New York Fed, told Congress last year, "The U.S. Treasury cannot wait for favorable markets to sell its debt."

To the federal government, the market is a lifeline. But to investors, the government securities market sometimes can be a casino. A look at how the market works is in order.

The market operates largely without regulation. With no centralized marketplace or exchange, the market consists of hundreds of dealers and tens of thousands of customers—mainly portfolio managers at banks, savings and loans, pension funds, and bond funds—watching video-display screens and trading over the telephone.

On the stock exchanges, customers buying securities on credit must put up at least 50 percent in cash, but the government securities market hasn't any such hard-and-fast rules. Dealers are left to decide how much credit to extend to customers. It isn't unusual for a customer to put up only $1 to $3 in cash for every $100 in securities he buys, especially when a dealer believes the customer is creditworthy.

With this huge leverage, both dealers and investors can make huge bets on the direction of interest rates by assembling big securities holdings with borrowed funds. "As a dealer, you can leverage yourself so much, you can take a huge position," says S. Waite Rawls of

New York's Chemical Bank. It isn't uncommon for a dealer to take a $1 billion position, he says, "so your losses can be tremendous." He adds, "Your margin of error is much less" than in other markets.

Even for investors who don't use large amounts of credit, losses can be huge. "Believe me, going home at night, having a beer, and realizing you've lost $100 million is a rude awakening," says William H. Gross, a managing director of Pacific Investment Management Co., which runs an $8.25 billion portfolio of bonds.

The government securities market has been increasingly entwined with the market for Treasury bond futures and futures options. Dealers now routinely use futures to hedge their securities positions and to speculate on the direction of interest rates.

Although the government securities market outwardly appears unstructured, it has its own hierarchy.

The big, privileged players are 36 government securities dealers known as primary dealers. They are the only ones who can trade with the Fed, which buys and sells huge quantities of government securities in its efforts to control the nation's supply of money. In return for that privilege—which dealers use to boost their reputation among customers—they submit to Fed oversight and report to the Fed daily on trading activity and regularly on capital.

The main obligation of a primary dealer is to bid in government auctions of new securities and help sell the national debt. The leading primary dealers include such financial heavyweights as Salomon Brothers, Inc.; First Boston Corp.; Merrill Lynch & Co.; Goldman, Sachs & Co.; Citibank; Bank of America; and Chase Manhattan Bank.

The relationship between the Fed and the 36 is so cozy that the Justice Department has been investigating whether it violates antitrust laws. Justice Department officials say the investigation has been going on for more than a year, but they won't say when it will be completed.

The vast majority of trading in the government market involves those primary dealers. There aren't any good estimates of trading in the secondary market, which includes hundreds of small dealers like E.S.M. But that trading is tiny compared with that of the primary traders, according to Francis Cavanaugh, director of the Treasury's office of government finance.

Although no primary dealer ever has failed, there has been a string of disasters among smaller dealers in recent years. Winters Government Securities in 1977; Drysdale Government Securities, Inc., in 1982; Lombard-Wall, Inc., the same year; Lion Capital Group last year; and now E.S.M.

The Typical Losers

Typically, it isn't the biggest investors who get caught in these collapses. The victims usually have been smaller investors with cash but little experience in judging a dealer's financial soundness. They include thrift institutions, school districts, and city governments.

Frequently, victims have had their money tied up in repurchase agreements, a common type of short-term cash investment. In simple terms, a "repo" is a loan backed by government securities as collateral. A borrower, say, a securities dealer, sells government securities to an investor. The dealer agrees to buy back the securities later at a higher price. Meantime, the dealer uses the cash to trade government securities, and he hopes to reap enough of a profit to offset his "repo" costs.

Repos make the market work. Primary dealers routinely use them to finance their huge securities holdings, including securities bought at government auctions. The procedure "allows a large pool of liquid money to slosh back and forth in the market," says Mr. Rawls of Chemical Bank.

Changes in federal law have eliminated one pitfall for investors. If a borrower, such as a dealer, goes into bankruptcy proceedings, the lender can sell the collateral securities and get all his money quickly. Most other creditors in a bankruptcy have to wait months or years before getting paid and don't have any guarantee that they will get anything back.

Toledo's Trap

But sometimes there's a catch. Toledo, like many losers in the E.S.M. failure, thought it had sole right to the government securities that collateralized its loans. It didn't. Investigators allege that E.S.M. pledged the same securities as collateral for transactions with several customers.

Every time interest rates change, the value of the securities underlying the repo agreement changes. If rates soar, and the bond market nosedives, the value of the collateral can shrink appreciably. The risk increases the longer the repo agreement lasts, especially for long-term bonds. For example, with a 20-year government bond, a one-percentage-point rise in rates (say, to 11 percent from 10 percent) slashes the value of the bond by $7 to $8 for every $100 of its face amount, says Ian Giddy, associate professor of finance at the New York University Graduate School of Business.

As each successive scandal has hit the government securities market, the circle of victims has widened. When Drysdale went bust in 1982, it cost Chase Manhattan Bank more than $135 million and threatened to hobble securities firms.

After Drysdale's collapse, the Fed tentatively tried to expand its influence beyond the primary dealers. It now receives monthly reports on the activities of about 40 secondary dealers, and it will soon publish guidelines on the amount of capital dealers should have in case they suffer large trading losses. But those guidelines will be entirely voluntary, and critics say none of this would have saved E.S.M.

"New Games"

Crafty marketers are constantly inventing new financial instruments to help investors and institutions meet their objectives more effectively. Some of these "new games," such as those involving interest rate swaps, may reduce the cost of capital to large firms, although risks may be associated with the savings. These instruments may also avoid SEC regulation or fall into regulatory gaps. Other financial vehicles appear to be bald-faced attempts to structure highly speculative, and occasionally fraudulent, deals to take advantage of regulatory loopholes.

PLUGGING THE REGULATORY GAPS

Peter Truell

Policing the global financial markets these days is a tough beat.

The big U.S. crackdown on insider trading, for example, swept through Bahamas bank accounts, London trading by arbitrager Ivan Boesky, and other links from Venezuela to Switzerland. And in Britain, authorities have pursued a series of U.S. connections as they study acquisitions by Guinness PLC.

At the same time, though, regulators are questioning the capital adequacy of global banks—those mega-players in the international equity and bond markets—that do much of their business thousands of miles from regulators in their home country. Financial hazards have grown bigger and more complex in recent years, underlining the need for greater international cooperation among regulators.

Says John G. Heimann, a former U.S. comptroller of the currency: "The new global financial-service marketplace, while full of opportunities, brings new types of risks and greater damage potential from old types of risk."

Wide Gaps in Cooperation

To address such worries, financial regulators in London, New York, and other world centers are moving to cooperate more closely. They are trying to agree on common standards of regulation and have begun to exchange more information.

There is "a combination of concern about risks and concern about unfair competition," says Martin Feldstein, president of the National Bureau of Economic Research.

But the gaps in cooperation remain wide, and regulators clearly are worried.

While securities regulators aim primarily to protect investors, bank regulators mostly try to assure the smooth working of the banking system. Many practitioners say this traditional division leaves holes in regulation, especially when banks are increasingly involved in securities markets and securities firms are assuming more credit risks.

In particular, much of the capital markets business by securities houses "slips through the regulatory cracks,'' says Mr. Heimann, currently a vice chairman of Merrill Lynch & Company.

Concern about Swaps

Mr. Feldstein concurs, voicing concern about large hedging positions at major securities firms. He and many financiers say it is important to remember that many of these new hedging techniques have been created in a uniquely favorable environment: booming financial markets, falling interest rates, and smooth economic growth.

What especially worries Mr. Feldstein are risks associated with billions of dollars of currency and interest rate swaps arranged in recent years.

In a swap agreement, two or more borrowers exchange debt-service obligations. "As long as all of the parties [to such agreements] stay solvent, that's fine," Mr. Feldstein says. "But often for savings of as little as [0.1 or 0.15 percentage points], people are engaging in agreements not knowing who their counterparty is."

Haphazard Policing

International cooperation among securities markets regulators is at a much earlier stage than that among banking regulators. And the policing steps that have been taken have been haphazard.

Mr. Boesky's insider trading came to light only because Dennis Levine—another admitted insider trader—gave evidence to U.S. authorities about Mr. Boesky's abuses. And Mr. Levine's illegal trading only came to the attention of the Securities and Exchange Commission because of an anonymous tip from Merrill Lynch's office in Caracas, Venezuela. That postcard from Venezuela helped prompt exchanges of information between the SEC and Britain's Department of Trade and Industry.

The SEC, aware of some of these gaps, signed memorandums of understanding for the exchange of information on insider trading with Switzerland in 1982, the Canadian provinces of Ontario and Quebec in 1985, and Britain in 1986, and also has arranged to share stock-trading information with Japanese regulators. The U.S. Commodity Futures Trading Commission has signed similar agreements with regulatory authorities in Singapore, Canada, Australia, and Britain.

While the agreements are primarily aimed at stopping insider trading, their scope soon could be widened. British securities authorities also hope soon to tie up similar agreements with French and Swiss authorities.

Banking regulators, on the other hand, have a longer history of international coordination. For decades central bankers have been discussing—and sometimes coordinating—monetary policies through meetings at the Bank for International Settlements.

Some of these banking regulators have to monitor securities markets, too. That is because in most major countries—except the United States and Japan—banks are permitted to underwrite and trade securities, and they also own their nations' biggest securities firms.

U.S. and Japanese banks are also active in the investment banking and securities businesses, particularly in London, Frankfurt, and Zurich. Meanwhile, they are breaking down the barriers in their own markets and becoming more involved in New York and Tokyo investment banking.

Because of this shift, central bankers are eager to assume more responsibility for overseeing securities markets, and in European countries they already share responsibility for monitoring commercial banks' securities businesses. Some analysts say that it is likely that any major reform of the U.S. financial system would move in that direction.

More Capital Backing

Recently, the New York Federal Reserve Bank and Britain's central bank, the Bank of England, agreed to require greater capital backing for many newer financial instruments. E. Gerald Corrigan, president of the New York Fed, and senior officials at the Bank of England hope to bring Japan into this agreement, as well as other leading industrialized countries.

While the Bank for International Settlements provides a forum for bank cooperation on regulation and supervision, there is no similar institution for regulators of the world's booming securities markets. Yet credit increasingly flows through the securities markets—much of it beyond the view of central banks, the traditional monitors of most forms of lending.

This makes banking regulators fret. Many of them would like to establish central supervision of securities and banking markets to close such regulatory gaps. But securities markets regulators aren't all convinced this would be easy. "It would be extremely difficult to organize a joint regulation of securities and banking," says a senior official at Britain's Securities and Investments Board Ltd., London's version of the SEC.

Still, securities and banking regulators worry whether they are acting fast enough to safeguard against growing risks in the world's financial markets. Many agree there is little time to waste in the scramble to create better international regulation. As Mr. Feldstein says: "You can't just look at the building and say it hasn't fallen down yet, so we should be safe."

TAX–FREE BOND PROBES BY FEDERAL AGENCIES STIR TALK OF REGULATION

Steve Swartz and John Connor

New York—A federal investigation of Matthews & Wright, Inc., a once-obscure New York municipal bond house, is turning a spotlight on a longstanding problem: The tax-exempt market can be hazardous to some investors' financial health.

The Matthews & Wright Group subsidiary had prospered by specializing in transactions that were too small or too risky for other securities firms and that were arranged on behalf of some unlikely places. These included a $399 million bond offering for the U.S. territory of Palau and a $9 million offering for Lenexa,

Kansas. "I've never heard of a Lenexa, Kansas, bond," says Barnet Sherman, a municipal bond analyst at Smith Barney, Harris Upham & Co. Lenexa "isn't even in our atlas."

Now, Matthews & Wright is at the center of one of the largest federal investigations of the municipal bond business in history. Investigators from several agencies, including the Federal Bureau of Investigation and the Securities and Exchange Commission, are looking into possible fraud, bribery, and tax law violations involving more than $1 billion of tax-exempt bonds underwritten by Matthews &

Wright in 1985 and 1986, people familiar with the investigation say.

Largely Unregulated

The investigation raises questions about the nation's largely unregulated $730 billion municipal bond market. Unlike the market for corporate bonds, municipal bond offerings aren't scrutinized by either the SEC or any other federal agency before the issues are sold. And federal laws give virtually no clues to what must be disclosed to investors beforehand.

Moreover, the industry professionals who are supposed to provide safeguards for bond investors somehow dropped the ball in some recent Matthews & Wright underwritings. The bond attorneys, investment bankers, municipal finance officers, and bank trustees failed to question certain practices now drawing federal scrutiny.

"I think there is a need for more regulation," says Peter A. Cohen, the chairman of Shearson Lehman Brothers Holdings, Inc., a big underwriter of municipals.

Congress Interested

The investigation of Matthews & Wright could ignite a regulatory fire in Congress. Representative John Dingell, the Michigan Democrat who heads the powerful House Energy and Commerce Committee, has already publicly questioned the level of investor protection in the municipal bond market. Senate Banking Committee Chairman William Proxmire, a Wisconsin Democrat, last week raised the possibility of having the SEC scrutinize municipal bond offering documents, and David Ruder, President Reagan's choice to head the SEC, told Congress this week that he favors more regulation of municipals.

Gerald A. Feffer, a Washington-based lawyer representing Matthews & Wright, declines comment on the continuing federal investigation. The firm has denied any wrongdoing and

asserted that all its underwritings were properly handled and legitimately tax exempt. This week it said a preliminary internal investigation hasn't found any evidence of bribery or other improprieties.

Meanwhile, the tax law aspects of the investigation have expanded to include about 100 municipal bond issues valued at some $12 billion and underwritten or sold by several securities firms in addition to Matthews & Wright. The investigation "promises to be the biggest case of its kind," Senator Proxmire says.

* * * * *

Any move toward tougher federal regulation of the municipal bond market would rile states' rights proponents. And many municipals professionals argue that the market is already well policed by state regulators and municipal officials. Michael D. Hernandez, the head of the municipal securities division at First Boston Corp., contends, for example, that municipalities often disclose more information about their offerings than corporate issuers do because cities and towns aren't sure what they have to disclose.

And Robert D. Pope, the president-elect of the National Association of Bond Lawyers, says "the first line of enforcement" is the industry professionals who structure bond sales for local governments. But the investigation of Matthews & Wright and other firms suggests that the self-regulatory mechanisms failed to catch bond-underwriting activities that should have had the professionals raising red flags.

A bond attorney's primary role is to ensure that a bond offering has been validly issued under state law and is tax exempt under state and federal laws. The trustee's job, which varies with the issue, generally is to ensure that the bond proceeds are invested and eventually spent under the terms set out in bond documents. Both professionals normally are hired by the municipality, but the underwriter typically has a strong say over who is selected.

Thus, like accountants doing corporate audits, bond lawyers and trustees can be subject to pressure from underwriters to approve their activities. Industry professionals complain privately of "shopping" by some underwriters, particularly for favorable bond law opinions.

The Matthews & Wright investigation involves a controversial form of bond called an "escrow" or "arbitrage" bond. Municipalities and private developers, who arrange for municipal help in financing projects, liked the bonds because the proceeds could be invested profitably for up to three years while projects got off the ground. Funds borrowed at tax-free interest rates of, say, 6 percent, could be reinvested in Treasury securities at 8 percent. The municipality pocketed the profit.

Investors also liked the bonds because their money wasn't spent but simply reinvested, typically in Treasury securities, in bank certificates of deposit, or with insurance companies. When the developer really wanted funds for his project, anything from an apartment complex to a prison, he usually repaid the arbitrage bond holders and borrowed again at higher long-term rates through another bond sale or from a bank.

But because lawmakers suspected that municipal arbitraging left issuers little incentive to get their projects moving, Congress practically ended the practice. It did so in two steps, touching off a last-minute avalanche of arbitrage offerings in December 1985 and August 1986.

Sales Being Investigated

Now, investigators are probing whether Matthews & Wright constructed sham bond sales in some cases to beat the deadlines and then sold the issues later to the public. For example, the U.S. attorney's office in Philadelphia has requested information on four Matthews & Wright offerings done just before the deadlines, according to officials of Pittsburgh National Bank, the trustee for bondholders in the four issues. The issues are a $335 million financing for a trash-to-steam plant in Chester, Pennsylvania; the $399 million industrial issue for Palau; a $65 million financing for a port authority in Nassau County, Florida; and $29.3 million for sewers and other public improvements in Galt, California.

All four transactions followed a pattern similar to the Galt offering last August, according to Pittsburgh National. Some key participants in the Galt offering now say they aren't sure that there was a legitimate sale. And they don't remember asking any questions about the transaction at that time.

Matthews & Wright said it sold all the city's bonds in a sale completed last August 29. The firm was brought in when the original underwriter, A. R. Altura & Co., of San Ramon, California, was worried that it couldn't place the bonds because of a glutted market. Alan Altura, the firm's president, says he doesn't know to whom Matthews & Wright sold them.

Money Received

Walter E. Gregg, the chief regulatory counsel at Pittsburgh National's parent, PNC Financial Corp., says in an interview that the bank, as trustee, got a check for the Galt bonds from Matthews & Wright drawn on New American Federal Credit Union of Jersey City, New Jersey, which credit union regulators say is controlled by Arthur Abba Goldberg, executive vice president of Matthews & Wright. Mr. Gregg adds that no one at the bank questioned Matthews & Wright's use of the tiny credit union.

Under terms devised by Matthews & Wright, Pittsburgh National immediately endorsed the check over to Commercial Bank of the Americas, which was to invest the proceeds temporarily for Galt, Pittsburgh National says.

Pittsburgh National officials also say the same Commercial Bank was listed as the beneficial owner of the bonds, indicating that the bank bought the bonds itself or held them for private investors. Again, no one at Pittsburgh National questioned the arrangement, Mr. Gregg says. Neither did the bond counsel, Jones Hall Hill & White, of San Francisco, according to Sharon White, a partner in the law firm.

Based on the Pacific island of Saipan, Commercial Bank of the Americas was established by, among others, Frederick Mann, who has worked for Matthews & Wright and was convicted of fraud in Canada in 1984, federal investigators say. A class action lawsuit alleging fraud and filed in federal court in Philadelphia by a disgruntled holder of another Matthews & Wright bond issue alleges that Commercial Bank was simply a "mail drop" controlled "directly or indirectly" by Matthews' Mr. Goldberg and others. In an interview, an investigator for the comptroller of the currency calls the bank "a shell" with "no evidence of any financial capability."

Bank Called "Valid"

George Benoit, Matthews & Wright's chairman, has said it is "absolutely untrue" that Mr. Goldberg controlled Commercial Bank. Mr. Benoit also has called Commercial Bank "a valid corporation."

Mr. Goldberg's attorney, Stanley S. Arkin, says Mr. Goldberg "denies any wrongdoing." Mr. Arkin declines further comment.

If Matthews & Wright wrote a check that was immediately turned over to a bank that it controlled, did anybody really buy Galt's bonds on August 29? "It's a very good question," says Mr. Gregg of Pittsburgh National. Galt's finance director, Roy Mitchell, says he isn't sure who bought the bonds.

And Ms. White, who is the current president of the National Association of Bond Lawyers, says her firm didn't examine the legitimacy of the sale because Pittsburgh National said at the time that it had received the proceeds. The

trustee knows, she says, that "when they sign receipts, that means they've got the money." The law firm concentrated its efforts on ascertaining whether Galt had viable projects to finance with the bonds. "I can see I ought to broaden my focus here," Ms. White comments.

Nevertheless, Ms. White asserts that her firm carried out its responsibilities as bond counsel. "We had no reason to believe there weren't real proceeds," she says. And Mr. Gregg says two outside law firms have examined Pittsburgh National's conduct and concluded that "the actions we took were in compliance with the instructions given" by Galt, Matthews & Wright, and Commercial Bank. Mr. Gregg adds, "In every case, the bondholders have been protected."

Taxes at Issue

Should investigators find there really wasn't a sale before the congressional deadline, interest on the bonds could be declared taxable, and investors could be liable for back taxes. In addition, the municipality could have to refund any profits it made by investing the bond proceeds. Investors already have seen prices of some Matthews & Wright bonds plunge as much as 10 percent because of fears that the bonds' tax-exempt status may be revoked.

The drop in the bond prices is particularly vexing to investors. Many Matthews & Wright issues carry the highest possible ratings from the two leading credit agencies, Moody's Investors Service, Inc., a Dun & Bradstreet Corp. unit, and Standard & Poor's Corp., a McGraw-Hill, Inc., unit. All the underwritings were approved by outside attorneys. And some of the bonds were sold to institutional and individual investors by well-known securities firms such as Smith Barney, a unit of Primerica Corp., and Dean Witter Financial Services Group, a Sears, Roebuck & Co. unit.

"How were we supposed to tell our clients not to buy?" one bond analyst asks. "These were triple-A credits, and Matthews & Wright had never had a problem before."

However, Moody's and Standard & Poor's say the high credit ratings on the issues reflected the safe investments in which the proceeds were placed. Whether the bonds were tax exempt was largely for the outside bond attorney to decide, says Bill De Sante, a Moody's vice-president.

Growth Industry

But in recent years, the number of law firms doing municipal bond work has exploded so fast that monitoring the quality of a bond counsel's opinion is much more difficult, industry professionals concede. "Everyone and their dog thinks they can be a bond counsel these days," a prominent bond lawyer says.

Bond analysts also question how closely municipalities and related issuers have monitored developers, particularly on privately owned projects. "We approved the bonds," says Hop Bailey, the chairman of the Knox County, Tennessee, Health, Education and Housing Facilities Board, which made two bond offerings through Matthews & Wright. "From that point on, I really don't keep up with them."

The question of who should "keep up" with the vast municipals market has long been a contentious issue. The last major regulatory push came in 1975 when Congress, reacting to a series of scandals, created the Municipal Securities Rulemaking Board, a self-regulatory organization that sets standards for municipals underwriters.

The board is barred by law from requesting information from local-government issuers or in any other way regulating them. "The board has been asked to regulate with less than all the tools available to regulate the corporate world," says Christopher Taylor, the board's executive director.

Corporate Requirements

Mr. Taylor notes that corporate bond issuers must, by law, register offerings with the SEC and follow specific guidelines on what information is to be disclosed. Corporations must file quarterly and annual financial statements with the SEC and disclose any material events affecting their financial status.

Although the antifraud provisions of federal securities laws apply to municipals offerings, regulation of the market is largely left to state and local officials. "Some states, like New Jersey, require the filing of financial reports [by municipal issuers] with the secretary of state," Mr. Taylor notes. "Others have little or no supervision of the local units."

The Government Finance Officers Association has published guidelines on disclosure, but they are voluntary and don't apply to private projects, such as apartment complexes built with tax-free funds.

Richard Ciccarone, a vice president of municipals research at Van Kampen Merritt, Inc., in Chicago, scoffs at the notion that any regulators are watching the municipals market effectively. "It's most definitely unregulated," he says.

Questions

1. Investors in certain western states are being offered the opportunity to buy unprocessed gold ore from a company that will extract pure metal from the ore and deliver it to the investor at a future date. The investor is asked to pay the stated price for the unprocessed ore immediately, and the company agrees

to provide any pure gold extracted from the ore at a below-market rate. By some estimates, investors are paying over $150 million per year for unprocessed ore. In effect, if substantial quantities of gold are in the ore, the investor stands to reap a windfall profit after the ore is processed. If no gold is found, the initial investment becomes worthless. Recent court decisions have held that such investments are not securities because investors may profit from future increases in the market price of gold, and thus they are not relying "solely" on the efforts of the promoters to obtain their profits.

Do you agree with this interpretation? What are its drawbacks from the standpoint of a securities regulator? What types of abuses may occur?

2. The SEC is generally considered one of the most effective regulatory bodies, yet problems and potential new abuses keep arising. Can the SEC ever effectively regulate all the new schemes thought up by promoters? Why do investors, often rich, sophisticated individuals or even institutions, continue purchasing these highly speculative, unregulated instruments? Are other methods available for regulators to stamp out abuses? What are the drawbacks to other approaches?

Exemptions—Continued

While some securities are totally exempt from federal securities laws, others are only exempt from certain provisions of the laws. Primarily, Congress has chosen to exempt certain types of securities from registration and disclosure under the 1933 act, although they may still be subject to the antifraud provisions of the law. The issuer of a security attempting to qualify for an exemption has an affirmative duty to demonstrate that it fits under the explicit terms of the particular exemption. In other words, if challenged, the company issuing the security must prove the exemption requirements were satisfied—the SEC does not have to prove they were not complied with. Record-keeping, then, becomes paramount for a company attempting to qualify for an exemption.

Despite the problems of claiming an exemption, the alternatives can be much worse from the point of view of the company promoting the investment. The legal, accounting, and professional fees involved in registering a nonexempt security can be substantial, as are the printing and underwriting costs. Delays in getting approval from regulatory bodies or other costly mistakes can also make prohibitive the expense of obtaining regulatory approval. The costs of floating a $10 million initial public offering could easily exceed $1 million. Thus, for financial reasons, there is quite an incentive to structure a proposed offering so that it is exempt from federal registration requirements.

The three main types of exemptions from compliance with SEC registration requirements are private placements, intrastate offerings, and simplified registrations. *Private placements* are securities sold to a limited number of investors, to "institutional" investors—banks, insurance companies, and pension plans—and to financially sophisticated, wealthy individuals and businesses. The 1933 act exempts these people because they do not need the government to protect them. To qualify for the exemption, all investors must be provided with information similar to that required by the SEC for the sale of new securities, and stringent limitations are placed on the resale of these securities for a period of time. No advertising of these securities is allowed. These prohibitions keep private placements from becoming a tool to avoid SEC registration requirements and immediately market the securities to the general public.

Intrastate offerings are those sold only in a single state to residents of that state. Even if this requirement is met, the issuer must demonstrate that 80 percent of its business (sales, assets, and so on) and 80 percent of the proceeds from the issue are to be used in that state. This exemption is designed to aid purely local businesspeople in obtaining funds without meeting costly SEC registration requirements. To qualify for this exemption, no resale to nonresidents may be made for nine months after the offering is completed.

A company desiring to issue less than about $1.5 million within 12 months to persons other than those involved with the company may file a much-simplified offering circular with the SEC. While not a complete exemption, this *simplified registration* procedure for small placements can lower offering costs substantially and encourage small businesses needing to raise capital to seek it from the public. This partial exemption also helps insulate the company and other people involved in the issuance of the security from liability arising from mistakes in the offering circular. Companies may issue securities worth $500,000 or less to anyone, without providing them with any information. Thus, the SEC has attempted to ensure that small businesses do not face insurmountable transactions costs.

Although an issue may qualify for a total or partial exemption from SEC rules, state blue sky laws in those jurisdictions in which the security is to be sold may not offer the same exemptions. In that case, state laws would still have to be complied with.

Registration Requirements

If no total or partial exemption is available to the issuers, both state and federal laws will have to be considered. State blue sky laws are based on the theory that the state has the duty to protect its citizens from unwise, fraudulent, or excessively speculative investments. Before a security can be sold, most states require the state securities regulator to be convinced that the issue has some investment merit and is not a fraudulent scheme. Normally, securities that qualify under federal laws have no difficulty (just expense) in meeting state blue sky requirements. However, as recently as the 1970s, Massachusetts initially denied its residents the opportunity to buy Apple Computer stock when it was offered because the state felt the risk was too great and the price too high. The clamor was so great and so many residents simply decided to have brokers in other states purchase the stock for them that Massachusetts was finally forced to relent.

The Securities Act of 1933, on the other hand, is not concerned with the value or speculative nature of an issue; rather it focuses on full disclosure of all the material facts. Before an offering can be sold, a detailed registration statement must be submitted to the SEC, which can then scrutinize it to make sure it contains all the data investors need to evaluate the desirability of a security for their investment purposes. A major part of the registration statement is the prospectus, which must be given to all potential investors before they are allowed to purchase the security. The prospectus contains all relevant data, such as the nature of the business and the background of the principals, the uses of the funds, the risks inherent in the enterprise, possible benefits, and various financial statements.

The SEC reviews the prospectus and other data it requires before the security can be sold. It can require additional data or information to be added and risks or other unusual factors to be highlighted. While the SEC cannot reject an offering based on its perception of the likelihood of success, the SEC can lengthen the approval process (and increase the expense) so that offerings it deems undesirable or misleading become practically impossible to market.

The prospectus and any other data on file with the SEC have to be updated if necessary due to changed conditions since the prospectus was originally created. The company issuing the security cannot take any unusual actions, such as advertising on television or exceptional press conferences, that gain favorable publicity for the company. The only advertising it may undertake relating to the sale of new securities is a tombstone ad, which simply sets forth what is being offered, when it is available, and from whom a prospectus may be obtained. The purpose of these restrictions is so that the purchaser can make decisions based on the data in the prospectus, not on some flattering facts put together by the company and contained in a glossy brochure that has not met SEC scrutiny. This is not to imply that all investors read the prospectus and develop informed opinions based on it. Many rely on brokers and other professionals, independent newspaper columns, their own experiences with the product, and so on; but before they buy the stock, they must have received a prospectus. The SEC does not protect foolish investors from folly, rather it ensures that all investors have access to information adequate to reach a reasonable conclusion about the merits of the offering. Whether the potential investor properly evaluates the available data or chooses to ignore the proffered prospectus entirely is totally the investor's business.

Remedies for Violations

In the absence of securities laws, if one has been sold a share of the Brooklyn Bridge, a Ponzi scheme, or a nonexistent South African gold mine, common law fraud theory may be used to recover money from the promoter or the company, assuming that either can be found and is solvent. To recover for fraud, the investor must show all of the following:

1. A material fact was misstated or omitted from the data given the purchaser.
2. The promoter/seller had knowledge of the error—scienter.
3. Reliance on the misstatement by the purchaser.
4. Intent to defraud the purchaser by the seller.
5. Privity of contract between seller and purchaser.
6. The misstatement was the cause of the investor's losses—proximate cause.
7. Damages.

At common law, failure to properly prove any one of these elements of fraud prohibits recovery by the seller. Thus, only in the most egregious cases could an investor recover any money. Typically, the person committing the fraud—the promoter—was unavailable, bankrupt, or in jail and therefore judgment proof, while the other persons the investor had dealt with (such as his broker and financial adviser, the firm's accountants, and attorneys for the firm) had not actively participated in the fraud and could not be liable for the fraud of the promoter.

The 1933 act, however, gave investors much greater potential for recovery when they felt they were defrauded. First of all, criminal liability may be imposed for willful violations of the act. The 1933 act also imposes civil liability for all material misstatements, misleading data, or omissions in the prospectus and other registration material filed with the SEC. Quite simply, anyone who purchases a new security that is subject to registration requirements and contains errors, omissions, or misleading statements or for which no registration material is filed may be able to recover damages in an amount up to the original purchase price for all money lost as a result of the investment. No proof of reliance and causation is necessary. The mere fact that the error was made and that the investor lost money (the price of the security fell) is enough to entitle the investor to a recovery. This means an investor can be perfectly satisfied with a purchase for a long period of time, but if the investment goes bad at a later date, the purchaser can then scan the prospectus for the error, misstatement, or omission. Finding such a problem with the prospectus can lead to the recovery of the total damages resulting from the decline in price of the original purchase.

Furthermore, another section of the act has been used to hold promoters and others liable for material misstatements or omissions regarding the offer or sale of securities not subject to the filing of a registration statement. Under either of these provisions, the company; any officer or director of the company; its accountants, attorneys, real estate appraisers, and other experts who helped develop the offering and registration; the underwriters; and anyone who signed the registration statement are personally liable for damages suffered by purchasers of the security. Thus, an aggrieved purchaser can have a veritable field day in finding the "deepest pockets" from the available, solvent parties and forcing a recovery from them. Once the error or omission has been found, the only significant defense these persons have to a suit by an investor is that they exercised due diligence and the mistake was made by someone else. In other words, the CPA firm cannot be held liable for a mistake by the law firm. However, the issuer of the security is absolutely liable for the mistake regardless of who was at fault.

It should now be readily apparent why the underwriting and registration process is so expensive. Each time an underwriter, accountant, attorney, appraiser, or financial printer becomes involved in a new offer, that person is potentially liable for the total amount of the offering—not only for intentional omissions and misstatements, but also for the most mundane typographical error, skipped line, or misplaced modifier. It is not surprising that Wall Street lawyers often become the world's most expensive proofreaders for many hours before a prospectus is released. An error could translate into hundreds of millions of dollars of liability for their firm and the other involved parties.

Regulation of Publicly Held Companies

The Securities Exchange Act of 1934 regulates many aspects of the financial dealings of publicly held companies. Because of its emphasis on publicly held companies, thousands of smaller businesses that are subject to the 1933 act when they issue securities are not subject to the dictates of the 1934 act. Basically, any company with more than $1 million in assets and 500 shareholders may be subject to some provisions of the act, as are any businesses that have issued a class of securities traded on a national securities exchange. All companies required to register with the SEC must file annual and quarterly reports with the SEC, as well as monthly reports if certain specified occurrences take place. Investment companies, banks, insurance companies, and various other industries are exempt from these disclosure requirements, but over 10,000 firms are required to disclose the specified data to the SEC and the public on a regular basis.

In addition, the 1934 act sets up the SEC and gives markets like the New York Stock Exchange some power of self-regulation, to be exercised with SEC oversight. Furthermore, the SEC is authorized to regulate the extension of credit to buy securities, trading by members of the exchanges, and manipulative practices by members. It may also suspend trading of securities if it becomes necessary. The SEC also requires the regulation of brokers and dealers, municipal securities dealers, clearing and transfer agencies, and entities dealing in securities information.

Besides registration and submission of various reports, publicly held companies are regulated concerning their record-keeping, repurchases of securities, proxy solicitations, director changes, corrupt foreign practices, and many other areas of day-to-day activities. Stockholders who are officers or directors of a company or who own large blocks of the stock are required to report their transactions involving the company's securities to the SEC and are prohibited from engaging in certain stock transactions in which their position could give them an unfair advantage over the uninformed public. It is also a violation for anyone to trade shares on the basis of inside information—information not available to the investing public at the time. An officer of the company might be able to do this frequently, but on occasion so could a low-level employee (such as a field engineer who learns of an oil strike before it is announced to the public). Restrictions also are placed on tender offers (explained below), purchases of substantial blocks of stock, and institutional investment managers. Misleading statements in proxy solicitations or about the purchase or sale of a security, along with other unfair or deceptive practices, can result in criminal or civil liability under the 1934 act.

Short-Swing Profits.   In an attempt to limit the ability of major participants in corporate affairs to gain a short-term economic advantage due to their early access to earnings reports and other inside, nonpublic information that might cause a change in stock prices when made public, the 1934 act prohibits officers, directors, and 10 percent beneficial owners of a corporation from receiving *short-swing profits*. These are any profits made on company stock held for less than six months. Any such profits must be returned to the company, and applicable attorneys' fees may also have to be paid by the person violating the rule. As mentioned previously, the SEC interprets short-swing profits as occurring if any sale price is greater than any purchase price during any six-month period. This interpretation can have some surprising results for someone unaware of how it works, as the following example indicates.

Director:

Buys 500 shares at $35 on June 4.

Sells 300 shares at $30 on September 15.

Buys 1,000 shares at $25 on November 20.

Sells 800 shares at $20 on December 19.

Pursuant to this provision, the director has short-swing profits of $1,500 (300 shares $\times$ $5) because he sold on September 15 at $30 and bought on November 20 at $25. From the example given, either he was not trading on nonpublic information or the information was erroneous, because the stock fell continually during the period. Adding insult to his trading losses is this extra SEC penalty for violating the short-swing profit rule.

Tender Offers.   When one company attempts to take over another, SEC rules can often be crucial. All such *tender offers* must be registered with the SEC. Furthermore, certain disclosure rules are triggered when groups purchase more than 5 percent of a company's outstanding stock. In recent years, as hostile takeover attempts have become more frequent, many strategies have been developed to limit their success. The raiders, however, are sometimes able to use the rules to their advantage. In many such takeovers, both state laws and SEC requirements play a part. Typically, management uses state requirements to slow down or eliminate the possibility of a hostile takeover, while the raiders usually enlist the aid of SEC rules. This is not a hard-and-fast rule, and in this fast-paced, tricky area, the positions can flip-flop regularly.

Bidders for a company can rely on recent amendments to the 1934 act to get more information about the target company and to shorten the period of time during which shareholders can decide whether to accept the offer. These amendments also have placed additional restrictions on a company's ability to use state law to fend off a takeover. For instance, in the Mobil-Marathon takeover battle, the "lockout" defense was rejected by the courts. In this maneuver, the target's board opposed a "totally inadequate" offer by giving another friendly corporation ("white knight") the right to purchase 10 million authorized but unissued shares and a contingent option to purchase a major oil field in the event of a hostile takeover. The purpose of this transaction was to make the takeover candidate more expensive and financially unattractive to the raider. The court held this practice to be "manipulative" in that it set an artificial ceiling on what the shareholders could expect to receive should the company or its assets be sold. In effect, the shareholders were being harmed in order to keep the company from being sold and to keep existing management in power.

On the other hand, such other defenses as questioning whether a takeover violates antitrust law and claiming access to insider information by the bidder or violations of SEC disclosure rules remain important in stopping hostile bids. Another effective technique is to buy a business, such as a radio or television station, railroad, bank, insurance company, or airline, for which state or federal regulatory approval is necessary prior to a change in ownership. Getting necessary regulatory approval may add to the time and expense involved in a takeover and may force a bidder to reconsider. For instance, several attractive takeover candidates have bought Florida-based insurance companies because of that state's rules concerning sales of insurance companies. Other options involve selling large blocks of stock to employees, issuing much new debt, attempting to take over the hostile bidder, requiring that the same sale or exchange terms be offered to all shareholders, mandating that the board or a super-majority of all shareholders must approve takeover bids, selling off the most attractive corporation assets, finding another purchaser, or buying out the bidder at a profit to his group ("greenmail"). Clearly, some of these techniques are more desirable than others from the standpoint of the corporation, and many, such as taking on substantial new debt or selling off attractive corporate assets ("scorched earth" defense), can seriously damage the long-run prospects of the business. One last defense, which has been used frequently but is likely to be curtailed, is "golden parachutes," in which officers are paid large bonuses in the event of a hostile takeover. The shareholder ill will engendered by these bonuses is often substantial, and their legality may be subject to question.

The best way to avoid a takeover remains unchanged, however—run a well-managed company with attractive share prices. Only companies whose assets are thought to be undervalued or whose parts can be spun off at prices greater than current share prices become takeover targets.

HOW T. BOONE PICKENS FINALLY MET HIS MATCH: UNOCAL'S FRED HARTLEY

Frederick Rose, Laurie P. Cohen, and James B. Stewart

Fred Hartley vividly remembers his reaction when he first confirmed that T. Boone Pickens, Jr., was going after Unocal Corp.

The Unocal chairman went home that evening and broke the news to his wife. "I told her that I was born in World War I, survived World War II, and now my management and I were going to have to gird for World War III," the 68-year-old Mr. Hartley recalls.

And a war it was. Immediately at stake was the fate of one of the nation's largest oil companies, with sales of $11 billion a year and some 20,000 employees. For the longer run, it seems likely to be remembered as a landmark in the frenzied takeover struggles of recent years, both for some innovative defensive tactics dreamed up by Unocal and its advisers and for a Delaware Supreme Court decision upholding one of the most crucial maneuvers. Some observers see far-reaching consequences for future takeover battles.

In Messrs. Hartley and Pickens, the fight matched two of the toughest, most determined leaders in American business. Even one of Mr. Hartley's advisers calls him "a pain"—but also someone who clearly called the shots for his side, someone whom "Boone wasn't going to walk around like a chimpanzee." Mr. Pickens, the chairman of Mesa Petroleum Co., had walked around and over several top oil executives in recent years on his way to becoming America's best-known corporate raider.

Each antagonist had his own legion of high-powered, high-priced lawyers, investment bankers, and public relations specialists as well as a war chest running into billions of dollars. The struggle raged in courtrooms from Delaware to California and in executive suites around the country. At times, it took bizarre, even amusing twists.

At one point, during the talks that eventually produced a settlement, the Pickens forces chose to huddle in a hallway of a Los Angeles hotel rather than in a room offered by Unocal, fearing that the room was bugged. At another point, Mr. Hartley lectured Mr. Pickens for taking a limousine to one of their secret meetings, saying it was too conspicuous a way to travel; Mr. Pickens replied that he was paying for the transportation and would travel any way he pleased.

Now, Mr. Pickens undoubtedly isn't happy about where his travels ended. He is generally perceived to have sustained his first defeat after a long string of victories in takeover battles against such oil giants as Gulf Corp., Phillips Petroleum Co., and Cities Service Co. In each of those battles the target company ended up either being acquired by another concern or buying off the Pickens group, which came out ahead in either event and raked in profits totaling several hundred million dollars.

In the Unocal battle, the Pickens group may face losses that some observers estimate could exceed $100 million. Mr. Pickens himself contends that the group will break even or perhaps turn a profit if Unocal's management enhances the value of its remaining shares over the next year. If it does, he says, "we can make $200 million or $300 million here."

In any event, Unocal will remain an independent company. The Pickens group has agreed to sell its 13.6 percent Unocal stake over an extended period and not to make another bid for the company for 25 years.

But although Mr. Hartley "won," Unocal hardly came out of the war unscathed. To buy back stock from the Pickens group and other Unocal shareholders, it will more than quadruple its long-term debt to some $5.3 billion—a move that could pinch its cash flow and its operations for years. "I don't think there is anything to brag about," Mr. Hartley says.

Mr. Hartley had been preparing for such a battle for some time. Besides worrying about his own company, Mr. Hartley sees the wave of takeovers as an attack on the crucial ability of corporations to manage their businesses for long-term goals. "Change can come along, but we don't have to do it in a barbaric manner," he says.

In 1983, Unocal enacted a number of takeover defenses, including staggered terms for directors—so the board couldn't be taken over all at once—and elimination of cumulative voting—so dissidents couldn't concentrate their votes and easily elect their own people to the board. The company also became an active supporter of so-far-unsuccessful efforts in Washington to enact legislation that would curtail takeovers by corporate raiders.

And though Mr. Hartley has almost-legendary disdain for investment bankers, who, he believes, have helped fuel takeover campaigns, Unocal picked two such firms—Dillon, Read & Co. and Goldman, Sachs & Co.—to serve as advisers if needed. Though Mr. Hartley won't say he ruled out investment bankers active in helping raiders in the past, he does say he insisted on firms "spiritually committed to what I consider to be the American economic way." Goldman Sachs, for example, refuses, as a matter of policy, to advise companies making hostile bids.

* * * * *

Purchases Begun

In February, a Pickens-led partnership announced the purchase of 7.9 percent of Unocal's stock but said it was only an investment and not a takeover effort—an assertion that met with widespread skepticism. Unocal played along, at least publicly. Mr. Hartley complimented the Pickens group for choosing a "good investment."

Privately, though, Unocal went on a war footing. "Quite simply," Mr. Hartley says, "we quit working on what we were working on and started working on the immediate problem." Unocal set up a five-executive "strategy" committee headed by Mr. Hartley. Though the professional advisers were frequently called on, all parties on the Unocal side agree that this group, and Mr. Hartley in particular, had the final say on all major decisions. This approach, some observers note, contrasts sharply with the tack taken by some previous managements fighting Mr. Pickens; they tended to give much more power to their investment bankers and lawyers.

As the Pickens group continued to accumulate shares, Unocal started taking more openly hostile steps. It further tightened its rules concerning director nominations and shareholder votes. In March, it also filed suit against its own principal bank, Security Pacific, because the Los Angeles institution was a lender to the Pickens group, too. The Pickens group retaliated with a suit against Unocal, contending that the company was conducting an "intimidation campaign" against the partnership's banks. These suits were only the first of a seemingly endless—and eventually crucial—string of litigation.

Changed Tune

Mr. Pickens still insists that, in February, his group began acquiring Unocal shares for "investment purposes only." He adds that by late March, however, the group had changed its plans because of the company's defensive actions and several remarks by Mr. Hartley.

Unocal amended its bylaws, Mr. Pickens says, "so that management could further entrench itself." In addition, he cites the company's suit against Security Pacific, which later withdrew from the Mesa credit pool. And finally, Mr. Hartley "started calling me an idiot and attacking me verbally," Mr. Pickens says, adding, "He also said he was unwilling to restructure [the company] in any way."

By late March, the Pickens group had accumulated about 23.7 million Unocal shares, some 13.6 percent of those outstanding, and it announced that it was contemplating a takeover or major restructuring of the oil company.

The Pickens group then unveiled a takeover plan similar to ones it has used previously: a $54-a-share cash tender offer that would lift the group's holding to just over 50 percent of Unocal. The bid was several dollars a share over the market price of the stock at the time. The rest of the shares, under the plan, would be bought later for notes valued at $54 a share. The Pickens group put the total value of the offer at $8.1 billion.

Financing Arranged

To show it meant business, the Pickens group, within a week, announced that Drexel Burnham had lined up $3 billion in financing commitments from more than 130 investors. Moreover, Mesa also arranged an additional credit line of $925 million from commercial banks.

"All of us were just shocked," one Unocal adviser says, "when Boone came up with that money. . . . Think of it! That's green for half the company."

However, Unocal unleashed a few maneuvers of its own. It apparently beat back an effort by the Pickens group to postpone Unocal's annual meeting. By delaying the meeting, the Pickens group would have a chance to put together its own slate of directors to run against Unocal's. For a while, the Pickens group—backed by major institutional stockholders, whom Mr. Hartley derides as "absentee landlords"—seemed likely to win that vote.

However, Unocal launched a huge proxy-gathering effort. It was aided by the firm of D. F. King and some 900 Unocal employees, including Mr. Hartley, who boasted on the morning the voting ended of having won over a holder of 600,000 shares. Though an official vote count on the question hasn't been announced, the Pickens camp has already said it believes that it lost.

Probably Unocal's most important move was its offer to repurchase 29 percent of its stock at $72 a share in notes. The company included the crucial and extremely controversial condition that it wouldn't accept any shares from the Pickens group.

The genesis of this idea is murky. Mr. Hartley will say only that it was "the outgrowth of a lot of discussion. I don't think you can pick out any individual genius."

But the amount of talking that went into the plan was nothing compared with the amount it produced. Observers ranging from Wall Street analysts to federal securities regulators said the move seemed to violate the principle of equal treatment of all shareholders.

No one cried foul more loudly than the Pickens group, of course. It stood to make a quick gain in the range of $175 million if it could sell some of its shares back to Unocal. But if it couldn't tender, the group faced the unpleasant prospect that Unocal might simply outbid it for the remaining shares while piling up a mountain of debt. The Pickens group might eventually inherit a company hardly worth having.

The Battle Shifts

So, the main battle shifted to the group's challenge of the exclusion provision in state courts in Delaware, where Unocal is incorporated. And the changing shifting tides of this legal struggle opened the way for settlement talks.

* * * * *

[The first day of talks brought some progress.]

A Setback

On the following day, the atmosphere quickly turned sour when Mr. Pickens and his colleagues read the four-page draft settlement. "It went backwards from where we were the day before. It was the most ridiculous deal you ever saw," a member of the Pickens group says. Mr. Pickens became so incensed he told Unocal, "I've decided to set my watch back to Central Time," and he abruptly left to fly back home to Amarillo, Texas.

Sources say Mr. Hartley and his advisers quickly decided that there wasn't any reason to make major concessions immediately. For one thing, they still hoped the Delaware Supreme Court would overturn a lower court decision ordering Unocal to include the Pickens group in its repurchase offer. And if not, Unocal planned to abandon its exchange offer rather than include the Pickens group—no matter how angry that made its shareholders.

On the court decision, "everybody I knew was praying for me, including the minister of my church," Mr. Hartley says.

Earlier this month, Unocal's prayers were answered when the Delaware Supreme Court, reversing the lower court, upheld the company's exclusion of the Pickens group as a legitimate exercise of business judgment. As a practical matter, Mesa had nowhere to appeal the decision, because "business judgment" is deemed a matter of state law and not appealable to the federal courts. The decision rocked the takeover community and set the stage for the final negotiations on a settlement.

Attorney's Call

About 10 minutes after the court decision was announced on Friday, May 17, Andrew Bogan, an attorney for Unocal, received a call from Robert Stillwell, a partner in the Houston law firm of Baker & Botts and Mesa's general counsel. Mr. Stillwell suggested that the talks resume. "They came running to us like wounded ducks," Mr. Hartley gloats.

Representatives of the two sides talked frequently by telephone over that weekend, trying to whittle down the major hurdles blocking a settlement. Unocal wanted up to $65 million from the Pickens group to cover its costs. Mesa was demanding that Unocal increase its repurchase offer to 75 million shares from 50 million.

Gradually, progress was made. Despite having gained enormous momentum from the Delaware court, Unocal was anxious to end the battle. For one thing, Mr. Hartley admits that he was concerned about what the Pickens group might do next. "He (Mr. Pickens) had 23.7 million shares. Let your imagination run wild," Mr. Hartley says.

Indeed, Mr. Pickens was lining up additional funds to make a cash tender offer for all the shares, though he and his advisers worried that Unocal could continue to outbid them while saddling the company with more debt.

The two sides got down to serious negotiating Sunday and worked through the night at Gibson Dunn's offices without breaking for meals. Breakfast for the Pickens side Monday morning consisted of four cans of warm Coca-Cola.

By 9 A.M. that morning, an agreement had been hammered out. Neither side would pay the other's expenses. Unocal would increase its repurchase offer only enough to include 7.7 million shares from the Pickens group, with the rest to be sold over time under conditions controlled partly by Unocal.

Unocal also agreed to distribute to shareholders over time units in a limited partnership the company is setting up for much of its domestic oil and gas reserves. Pickens sources call this distribution a major victory in the negotiations; Unocal sources contend the company had been thinking about doing something like it for some time.

Though their direct confrontation is over, neither Mr. Hartley nor Mr. Pickens seems to think that the broader struggle over corporate takeovers is finished. Mr. Hartley says the nation still needs "intelligent legislation" to stop the wave of hostile takeovers. And Mr. Pickens says that although "it would be unlikely for us to do another deal for a while," he is still very much interested in future takeover efforts.

The States Respond

To stem hostile takeovers, management has been turning to state legislatures. Takeover candidates are using their political clout to convince legislators of the harmful effects a takeover could have for the state where the business is incorporated or has a major presence. Such economic issues as plant closings, wholesale transfers, or moving the headquarters appear to strike a responsive chord. From the standpoint of investors, regulators, and raiders, such tactics are troublesome.

HOW INDIANA SHIELDED A FIRM
AND CHANGED THE TAKEOVER
BUSINESS

Michael W. Miller

Columbus, Indiana—One day in December 1985, James K. Baker, the chairman of Arvin Industries, Inc., summoned his friend Robert Garton to lunch and let him in on a startling secret. Arvin Industries, an auto-parts giant, had received a letter from Canada's Belzberg family threatening a takeover.

Jim Baker and Bob Garton, the president of the Indiana Senate, went back a long way together in Columbus, a town of tree-lined streets and gingerbread storefronts. They were fellow Rotarians, members of the same gourmet cooking club, and parents of former classmates at Southside Junior High School. Now, Mr. Baker asked his old friend to help stop the takeover and save Arvin Industries and Columbus from wrenching change.

Mr. Garton didn't let him down. Within four weeks, he had steered a tough anti-takeover bill, drafted by Arvin's own lawyers, through the Indiana legislature and onto the governor's desk, where it was promptly signed. The bill, in effect, outlawed most hostile takeovers in the Hoosier state.

Preserving Small Towns

Twenty-one states restrict takeovers, and most of the laws sprang from the same impulse that moved Mr. Baker and Mr. Garton: to preserve small company towns and their ways. For many years, judges across the country deemed those laws touching but unconstitutional. The courts said the states were meddling illegally in the nationwide securities market.

That changed last spring. In a ruling on a second Indiana law—also backed by Arvin—the Supreme Court upheld the right of states to regulate takeovers.

The decision promises to have a sweeping impact on the takeover game, hobbling corporate raiders and giving management a powerful new defensive weapon. It will give state takeover laws unprecedented power and spur states that don't yet have them on their books to consider them.

Last month, two giant companies threatened by hostile bids, Dayton Hudson Corp. of Minneapolis and Gillette Co. of Boston, lobbied for emergency anti-takeover legislation from their state legislatures. (Minnesota passed a bill last week; Massachusetts is expected to act soon.) Delaware, which is home to about half of the Fortune 500 companies, has drafted an anti-takeover law, although the bill has been tabled until autumn. Among other reasons, Delaware wants to see what Congress will do with the various takeover measures it is considering.

The roots of the Supreme Court's landmark decision are here in Indiana, where Arvin, a company listed on the New York Stock Exchange, and the Belzberg family squared off in a corporate drama whose details have been a carefully guarded secret until now.

Arvin's board-room battle and its legislative victory shed light on the origins of a major shift in business law. They also show how economic exigencies, together with human emotions, give birth to state takeover laws.

Fossilizing Industry

At the heart of the saga lie some far-reaching economic issues: How much power should a community have to prevent economic upheavals within its borders? And will towns use this power to preserve harmony and stability or to fossilize aging industrial and social structures?

The assault on Arvin began December 3, 1985, when the Belzberg family wrote the company that it had amassed a 4.9 percent shareholding and was considering buying the remaining shares. The Belzbergs are a powerful Canadian family, immensely wealthy and well-scarred after a decade of tumultuous takeover attempts.

Their rise began when Abraham Belzberg, a Polish fish peddler, migrated to Canada in 1919 and built a successful used-furniture business. His three sons, Samuel, William, and Hyman, moved the family into the real estate, banking, and energy businesses. By the mid-1970s, their flagship company, First City Financial Corp. of Vancouver, oversaw an empire worth billions of dollars.

About eight years ago, the Belzberg sons started showing up on the doorsteps of large U.S. companies, brandishing minority shareholdings in the companies and threatening to take over. They gained a reputation as raiders who could be bought off, and one company after another paid the Belzbergs greenmail—buying back the shares at a juicy premium over the market price.

Grave Misgivings

The Belzbergs confronted a dozen companies, extracting large payments from Ashland Oil, Inc.; USG Corp.; Potlatch Corp.; and others. In 1985, they surprised Wall Street by actually following through on a raid, buying Scovill, Inc. The family likes to work in secret and, through a spokesman, refused to be interviewed for this article.

The Belzbergs are exactly the sort of takeover artists chief executives have in mind when they bemoan the excesses of merger mania. But people in Columbus (population 30,200) weren't only worried about the Belzbergs' brand of corporate raiding. They had grave misgivings about how their town would fare if Arvin was ever taken over.

The fortunes of Columbus have been closely bound to Arvin since 1931, when Q. G. Noblitt moved the company's forerunner, Indianapolis Air Pump Co., into town. Last year, Arvin had sales of nearly $1 billion and a profit of $41 million. It makes mufflers, exhaust pipes, catalytic converters, and scores of other industrial and electronic products; it employs about 2,000 people in Columbus, making it the town's second-largest employer, after Cummins Engine Co.

Arvin is the kind of company that chambers of commerce adore. Hundreds of Columbus children go to a pair of schools that Mr. Noblitt donated to the town in the 1950s. In the summers, they play in a 70-acre wooded youth camp, another Noblitt donation.

When Columbus needed a new superintendent of schools two years ago, Arvin executives helped in the nationwide search. Then the company donated money to help the town lure its top prospect to south-central Indiana. A few years ago, Shirley Lyster, an English teacher at Columbus North High School, called Chairman Baker and told him she wished her class could read Homer in the out-of-print George Herbert Palmer translation. Arvin printed a special edition for her.

Columbus is a town with a social fabric so tight-knit that people joke, "You have to pull the blinds to change your mind in Columbus." When the Belzbergs loomed, the town fathers believed a takeover would shatter the town's long, cozy relationship with Arvin. And it raised the specter of a fate local residents dreaded: Columbus as a mere branch-plant town.

"Had [the Belzbergs] bought Arvin, you'd see that company's personality change overnight," says Brooke Tuttle, an official at the Columbus Chamber of Commerce. "There's a kind of attitude you get from an out-of-town owner—the focus is on the bottom line and the return to shareholders."

Mistrust of Outsiders

"Communities don't become great just being branch-plant towns," declares Robert Stewart, the mayor of Columbus.

But the town's staunch support of Arvin also springs from some emotional biases, including a deep mistrust of outsiders. "The farther away from Columbus you get," says Mr. Baker, "the more we look at them with the suspicion that they're not coming from the same place as us."

It also glosses over a fact that has been painfully clear in Columbus in the 1980s: No matter how hard the town and the state work to keep Arvin, economic necessities are forcing the company to stray far from its beloved hometown. Arvin, the company that doesn't want to become a branch plant, has its own branches in dozens of U.S. cities. In 1970, it opened an electronics factory in Taiwan, which now employs 1,500 people. Meanwhile, unemployment in Bartholomew County, which Columbus

dominates, has been nearly 9 percent in the 1980s, up from about 5 percent in the 70s. Today one out of six Columbus households lives on an income at or below the poverty level.

In short, Indiana and Columbus were fighting to stay wedded to an industry of the past.

Bygone Days

"It used to be that when you got out of high school here, you could always get a job at Cummins or Arvin, no problem," says Mayor Stewart. "Those days are gone."

The Belzbergs' advances threw Arvin's management into turmoil. In December 1985, Marc Belzberg, Samuel's son, was calling the company as often as three times a day, vowing to launch a hostile tender offer for Arvin, company officials say. Arvin managed to extract a promise from the Belzbergs to keep their intentions secret, and Mr. Baker and his top aides jetted back and forth to New York for frantic meetings with their investment banker, Merrill Lynch & Co.

At first, the deep personal tension between the two camps smoldered quietly. But then they erupted: The Belzbergs threatened to mount a tender offer on the day before Christmas.

It was a strategy they had used successfully a year earlier in their bid for Scovill. The days before Christmas are generally the hardest time of the year for a company to line up a takeover defense.

Under the threat, Arvin's executives lost their cool—and their manners. "We said, '*We're* all good gentiles here,'" Mr. Baker recalls. "'*We* like to be with our families on December 24.'"

Too Vulnerable

Christmas passed—the Belzbergs didn't come through on their threat—and a new session was about to get under way in the Indiana legislature. "We decided we'd better bring Brother Garton [the Senate president] into the fold," says Mr. Baker.

As Mr. Baker saw it, the stock market values companies inefficiently, making them vulnerable to raiders. It was, he thought, an inequity so deep that only new laws could remedy it.

A lawyer working for Arvin, James Strain, quickly drafted just such a law and sent it to Senator Garton. Modeled on laws in New York and other states, it banned hostile business combinations for five years after an investor buys 10 percent of a company.

Senator Garton made the anti-takeover bill the state Senate's first bill of the session, a slot reserved for matters of pressing importance. The bill was officially declared "emergency legislation," and it went into effect as soon as the governor signed it. The legislature's haste drew a scolding from the Indianapolis *Star:* "This is not a topic to be whipped through the legislature with a smile and a prayer and no debate."

Two months later, the Indiana legislature passed a second anti-takeover statute as part of a major revision of the state's corporate code. Arvin's lawyer, Mr. Strain, was one of three Indianapolis attorneys who drafted it.

With that law, the trio came up with a novel way to thwart a hostile bidder. The law springs a booby trap on an investor who acquires 20 percent of an Indiana company: He loses his shares' voting rights unless the other shareholders move to reinstate them.

Arvin says the new laws helped repel the Belzbergs' takeover attempt. Shortly after the second law passed, the two sides settled. Arvin agreed to buy for $39 million a Belzberg-owned tire-valve company it had declined to purchase just one year earlier. (Arvin says the Belzbergs lowered the price to a reasonable level.) It also bought for $20.4 million the Belzbergs' Arvin

shares, paying $25.25 each, which was below the market price at the time but still gave the raiders a handsome profit, according to Arvin officials.

Indiana's booby-trap law, formally known as the Control Share Acquisition Chapter, was quickly challenged by Dynamics Corp. of America, a Connecticut electronics firm that bumped up against the law when it tried to buy part of an Indiana company, CTS Corp. Last fall the Supreme Court agreed to consider the law.

Economy "Balkanized"

A slew of lower courts had struck down similar state laws, mostly on the grounds that they blocked interstate commerce. The U.S. Justice Department and the Securities and Exchange Commission filed a brief urging the Supreme Court to do the same. So did Texas takeover artist T. Boone Pickens, who warned that Indiana's law "would lead inexorably to a Balkanization of the nation's corporate economy."

But on April 21, one year after the Belzbergs backed off from Arvin, the Supreme Court rejected the challenge by a 6–3 vote. Four justices who rarely side together joined in retiring Justice Lewis Powell's majority opinion: Justices William Rehnquist, Sandra Day O'Connor, William Brennan, and Thurgood Marshall.

Their opinion dismissed the Indiana law's effect on interstate commerce as "limited." And it declared that the law fell well within states' rights to regulate their corporations and define the kinds of stock they can issue.

The decision came on the heels of Wall Street's insider-trading scandals and amid a national uproar against takeovers. While the justices didn't directly acknowledge that background, their tone indicated that they, too, believed the merger game had gone too far.

The law, according to the court, would allow "shareholders collectively to determine whether the takeover is advantageous to their interests [which] may be especially beneficial where a hostile tender offer may coerce shareholders into tendering their shares."

Justice Antonin Scalia also upheld the law, but he would not sign his name to Justice Pow-ell's broad endorsement of state takeover laws. A law "can be both economic folly and constitutional," he wrote. "The Indiana Control Shares Acquisition Chapter is at least the latter."

Source: *The Wall Street Journal*, July 1, 1987, pp. 1, 14. Reprinted by permission of *The Wall Street Journal*, © Dow Jones & Company, Inc. 1987. ALL RIGHTS RESERVED.

STATE TAKEOVER LAWS: CONSTITUTIONAL BUT DUMB

Roberta Romano

The Supreme Court recently upheld Indiana's state takeover statute. Such legislation may be constitutional, but is it wise? State takeover statutes are controversial because there are serious questions whether these laws benefit shareholders. These new provisions might increase the premium shareholders receive in a takeover bid, but that effect could be swamped by a decrease in the likelihood of an offer being made. The statutes could thus be a lever for preserving management's jobs while reducing shareholder wealth.

In promoting state regulation of takeovers, managers often claim to be furthering shareholders' interests. They also suggest that the interests of workers and local communities are served by these statutes. One way to gauge better who benefits from takeover laws is to examine the politics of the legislation—to investigate, for instance, who initiates the bills and who lobbies for their adoption. If the broad-based constituency to which proponents of the legislation refer were truly benefited, we would expect to see the supposed beneficiaries, who have their own powerful lobbying organiza-tions, at the forefront in the making of takeover statutes. The politics of takeover statutes does not, however, fit such a scenario.

The Connecticut experience provides a case study of who is behind the move for takeover legislation and, correspondingly, who most likely is the beneficiary. In the spring of 1984, Connecticut enacted a fair-price statute, which regulates the second step in a two-tier acquisition, where one price is paid for the shares tendered and another potentially lower price is paid for the rest. In the absence of the statute, as in many states, a merger would be subject to only majority approval. A bidder's successful tender offer for control typically means that it has the votes to approve a second-step merger of the target into a bidder-owned entity, thereby "cashing out" the remaining public shareholders of the target. By requiring instead a super-majority vote, board approval, or a specified minimum price equal to the price in the first step, a fair-price statute can make success more expensive for an acquirer seeking 100 percent control of a target firm.

Connecticut's fair-price statute became law a few months after its introduction. It was drafted and promoted by a prominent local corporation, Aetna Life & Casualty Insurance Corp., aided by the Connecticut Business and Industry Association. Aetna was performing poorly at the time, and presumably feared it might become a takeover target. Having missed—intentionally or not—the expiration of the session's filing date, the proponents of the fair-price statute had their proposal attached as an amendment to an inconsequential bill on reserving corporation names. An additional benefit of this artful-if-intentional maneuver was that the bill's proponents were able to avoid the statutory requirement of a public hearing because the mandated hearing on the bill on corporation names had already been held.

The conventional role of the executive committee of the corporate law section of the state bar association is to suggest revisions to the state corporation code. Yet this group was not even aware of the fair-price bill's existence until a floor vote was scheduled. The committee opposed the bill, but it sailed through both houses anyway and went into effect immediately upon the governor's signing, June 4, rather than on the usual October 1 date. No group besides the corporate bar and the business community expressed an interest in the provision.

The recent experience in other states with takeover tactics closely tracks Connecticut's. The statutes are expeditiously enacted with near unanimous, bipartisan support, most often at the behest of the nervous management of a local firm. Two of the more conspicuous examples occurred in Kentucky and Missouri. The Kentucky legislature amended its takeover statute virtually overnight to enable Ashland Oil to fend off a hostile bid by the Belzbergs. Similarly, Missouri passed emergency legislation extending its takeover statute to out-of-state corporations "that are common

carriers that have benefited from physical facilities financed by Missouri subdivisions and that have over 7,500 employees in Missouri." Trans World Airlines, the only corporation known to meet the statutory requirements, was then contesting Carl Icahn's takeover bid.

The supposed beneficiaries of takeover bills either oppose the legislation or are neutral. The shareholder groups that do lobby, such as T. Boone Pickens' United Shareholders Association, oppose most legislation regulating takeovers. Nor do unions and community-based groups actively initiate or lobby for takeover laws. Unions, for instance, are far more concerned with regulating plant closings, and other matters that directly affect their members, than with takeover statutes that give managers tools with which to impede hostile acquisitions.

Delaware, a consistent leader in corporate law innovations and the incorporation state of about half of the Fortune 500 firms, has been slow to legislate in this area. There are good reasons. Delaware's corporate constituency is far more numerous and diverse than that of other states, which have fewer firms that engage in acquisitions. This appears to create a different political equilibrium in Delaware when it comes to takeover statutes. Delaware's strategy emphasizes self-help, in which shareholders vote for the defensive tactic, rather than mandated statutory solutions. So long as Delaware maintains this policy, the Supreme Court's decision will have a limited effect on the market for corporate control.

What's wrong with anti-takeover statutes? The fair-price component of Connecticut's statute is often endorsed by distinguished legal scholars as protecting shareholders who would otherwise be coerced into tendering their shares at an undesirable price because they fear an even lower price will be paid in a second-step merger. Such a concern appears to motivate the Supreme Court's decision to uphold the constitutionality of Indiana's control share acquisition statute. But firms can, and do, voluntarily adopt changes in their charter provisions affecting possible takeovers. For instance, about one third of the Connecticut firms traded on the New York Stock Exchange had a fair-price charter provision at the time the fair-price statute was enacted. When such provisions are added to a charter, shareholders must vote to approve them.

Given the ready availability of self-help, what need is there for a statute? While a statute certainly saves the cost of a shareholder vote for firms that would otherwise voluntarily adopt such a provision, one cannot help but suspect that managers gripped by fear of losing their jobs lobby for legislation because they worry that a majority of their firm's shareholders would not approve a charter amendment.

Justice Antonin Scalia, in his concurring opinion on state takeover statutes, noted that a law can be both constitutional and foolish. Takeover statutes, while constitutional, are troublesome because they can undermine the shareholder sovereignty on which all of corporate law is premised. For it is most plausible that the principal beneficiaries of this regulation are its prime promoters—managers seeking to circumvent a shareholder vote because they fear the loss of their jobs.

Source: *The Wall Street Journal,* May 14, 1987, p. 22. Reprinted by permission of *The Wall Street Journal,* © Dow Jones & Company, Inc. 1987. ALL RIGHTS RESERVED.

SEC CHIEF URGES CONGRESS TO GIVE AGENCY POWER TO PREEMPT STATE SECURITIES LAWS

Bruce Ingersoll

Washington—Securities and Exchange Commission Chairman David Ruder urged lawmakers to give the SEC sufficient rule-making power to preempt state laws that interfere with the "national market" for securities.

The commission, Mr. Ruder said, needs more statutory authority over tender offers, largely because of the recent Supreme Court ruling on Indiana's takeover law. The ruling upheld for the first time state regulation of corporate takeovers.

The rush by the states to adopt similar or more restrictive legislation "threatens to create a maze of overlapping and conflicting regulation," the former Northwestern University

law professor testified yesterday before the House Energy and Commerce Committee's securities panel.

State attempts to shield their corporations from hostile bids have "presented serious impediments to the free and efficient operation" of the stock markets, Mr. Ruder said. "Drawing the line between appropriate state regulation of internal corporate affairs and improper state regulation of national tender offers is not easy," he added, "but the task is unavoidable."

* * * * *

At yesterday's hearing, Mr. Ruder said the SEC still pursues a policy of neutrality between bidders and target companies, and he assured state regulators that the commission doesn't favor extending federal regulation over such corporate-governance matters as "golden parachutes," which are lucrative severance packages for corporate management, and "greenmail," in which outsiders buy a company's shares and get the company to buy them back in order to avoid a takeover.

Mr. Ruder said that most of the "troublesome" takeover practices can be corrected by strengthening the reporting provisions of the Williams Act, which governs tender offers. He recommended requiring bidders to stop buying stock as soon as they acquire a stake of 5 per-cent or more in a company's stock, and to disclose their stake within 5 business days, rather than the current 10 days. They could resume buying stock as soon as they file a 13-D report with the SEC, he said. Such a standstill requirement would keep raiders from mounting sneak attacks during the so-called 10-day window.

He also asked lawmakers to clarify the definition of an investment "group" for reporting purposes, and to empower the SEC to impose stiff fines for reporting violations.

Source: *The Wall Street Journal*, September 18, 1987, p. 17. Reprinted by permission of *The Wall Street Journal*, © Dow Jones & Company, Inc. 1987. ALL RIGHTS RESERVED.

Questions

1. Who benefits from the anti-takeover provisions in corporate charters or state laws? Who is harmed? How? Do these provisions violate a management's fiduciary duty to its shareholders? Explain.
2. What effect, if any, will these provisions have concerning the efficiency of the U.S. economy?
3. Do managers and workers need greater protection from corporate raiders? Should state governments intervene in takeover battles? Can you think of any unintended consequences of intervention? Explain.

Securities Fraud. The 1934 act and SEC Rule 10b–5 prohibit securities fraud with respect to the sale of registered or unregistered securities. While SEC requirements are greater than those under state common law fraud rules, they are not as burdensome as those of the 1933 act. Reckless behavior, knowledge, or participation in the fraud imposes civil and perhaps criminal liability on all involved persons, but recent cases have established that negligence alone (as is the case with the 1933 act) is not enough to establish an entity as responsible for the losses suffered by investors. These findings have had important implications for professionals like attorneys and accountants. An additional limitation is that under the 1934 act the aggrieved party must demonstrate that it bought or sold the securities and that a relationship exists between the fraud, the transactions, and the losses suffered. Still, the 1934 act can be, and often is, used to hold CPAs and others liable to investors when a company fails.

INVESTORS CALL CPAs TO ACCOUNT

Lee Berton

The accounting profession, which more than a half century ago volunteered to protect the public against financial chicanery, is wondering whether it has put its own head in the lion's mouth.

A recent explosive expansion of liability suits against major accounting firms after their clients reveal financial problems or go bankrupt is beginning to chip away at the financial viability of the biggest CPA firms. Indeed, some partners privately concede that big out-of-court settlements are starting to put reins on their stake in their firm and what they can take out as income each year.

"Our liability insurance is getting expensive enough so that we are seriously considering going bare and covering our own court exposure," says Carl D. Liggio, general counsel for Arthur Young & Co., one of the Big Eight accounting firms.

"Public interest" lawyers filing increasing numbers of class actions against big accounting firms aren't very sympathetic. "When an accountant signs his name to an annual report, a lot of investors, widows, and retirees place trust in that name," says Stuart Savett, a senior partner at a Philadelphia law firm involved in suits against such big CPA firms as Peat, Marwick, Mitchell & Co., and Coopers & Lybrand.

"Professional Standards"

Accounting firms contend that they can only stick to their professional standards but aren't policemen who can unearth fraud. But James E. Treadway, Jr., a Securities and Exchange Commission member who will soon leave the SEC to return to private law practice, recently told an accounting group that it has a way to go before it can claim public confidence. "Public perceptions as to whether a professional is living up to expectations are fragile at best and constantly open to question," he said.

What Mr. Treadway says makes sense. Instead of trying to dodge its responsibilities, the accounting profession should take a harder line with some of its clients; not sticking to the narrow confines of "professional standards," but trying to perceive its job in terms of what the public needs and will take court action to pursue. It should recognize that an intense battle for clients that now includes widespread fee discounts may be eroding its professionalism in the eyes of the public and its critics.

Indeed, Donald Kirk, chairman of the Financial Accounting Standards Board, the rule-making body for accountants, recently told a group of students that "this competitive environment gives rise to a situation in which the [CPA] firms' positions on accounting principles may sometimes be construed as a way of developing new business. This comes about through the giving of accounting opinions on possible financial transactions to investment bankers for their marketing use and the giving of opinions to nonclient corporations for their use in argument with their auditors. . . ."

Critics say this erosion of professionalism is hurting accounting firms in the courts. A decade ago, major accounting firms would carry liability insurance of up to only $50 million total, with deductibles ranging up to $250,000. But with settlements now reaching $50 million for major CPA firms and deductibles ranging as high as $1 million to $5 million per case, accounting firms and their lawyers are beginning to wonder how wide their liability exposure can become. Some insurance rates are due to double this year, and while major CPA firms probably will be able to shoulder this burden, it could lead to more mergers among weaker CPA firms and even stiffer competition for new business.

In the wake of many recent well-publicized examples of "audit failures," the accounting profession feels the public really doesn't understand the limitations of an audit. "The audit may be entirely competent, even though the business later fails," asserts Newton N. Minow, a Chicago lawyer who was a member of the internal quality review board of Arthur Andersen & Co., one of the biggest of the Big Eight, from 1974 through 1983.

* * * * *

For his part, Mr. Savett, the class action lawyer, believes it's more equitable for big CPA firms with millions of dollars in insurance to shoulder or share in the losses of depositors in failed banks or of unsophisticated shareholders in companies that have concealed their problems. "Someone has to pay when a person living on meager retirement income invests in a company that goes sour," he says.

Some critics of the accounting profession wonder whether the big insurance umbrella that major CPA firms carry hasn't made them careless about their duties to the public. Abraham Briloff, an accounting professor at Baruch College in New York and a well-known faultfinder of major accounting firms, says accountants shouldn't carry any insurance: "They only duck behind it after they make mistakes."

State and federal courts increasingly have acted to widen the accountant's responsibilities for protecting the public. But this was a duty the profession sought out when officials began looking for ways to prevent another depression-triggering bank collapse.

Congress in 1933 was told by Arthur H. Carter, president of the New York Society of CPAs, that accountants wouldn't leave their practices to go into government employ and that government expenses for the needed army of 500 to 600 auditors would be prohibitive. Congress bought this argument and gave the job to the private sector.

Toward the end of the 1930s, individuals began suing CPA firms whose clients had business problems or went bankrupt. But until fairly recently, the courts had held that accountants were liable for damages only if they displayed negligence or failed to adhere to their professional standards in certifying their clients' financial reports.

Today, lawyers for accounting firms maintain, the courts are holding accountants more responsible for the business health of their clients and how it may hurt their company's stock performance. In recent years, for example, federal courts have upheld a controversial "fraud-on-the-market" theory that says if financial reports are faulty, even if they aren't relied upon by an investor, third parties such as auditors who helped prepare those reports are liable for damages.

"If a stock goes sour or a business fails, everyone is now looking beyond the distressed or bankrupt company to the outside accountant," frets Harris Amhowitz, the general counsel for Coopers & Lybrand, another large U.S. CPA firm. The accountants, he contends, have become "the deepest of deep pockets" into which claimants want to reach.

Over the past three years, for example, Arthur Andersen has paid out more than $100 million in cases where companies have gone bankrupt or experienced unexpected or questionable losses. In 1982, a jury ordered Arthur Andersen to pay $80.7 million to the Fund of Funds for not properly auditing the mutual fund's books in the late 1960s. A judge subsequently reduced the award, but it's believed to be substantial.

While there's no exact tally of CPA firms' out-of-court settlements with plaintiffs, their increase in recent years has been spectacular. More lawsuits have been filed against accountants in the past 15 years "than in the entire previous history of the profession," says Mr. Minow, the Chicago lawyer. "All that seems necessary to prove now is that the CPA firm has insurance."

A recent decision by the New Jersey Supreme Court, for example, "seems to say that the existence of such insurance justifies pursuing a claim against an accounting firm for false information in financial reports the CPA firms audit," states Mr. Amhowitz.

In a March 1984 decision by the U.S. Supreme Court that forced Arthur Young to give the Internal Revenue Service internal work papers the firm used in auditing a client's tax strategy, Chief Justice Warren Burger broadly extended the outside auditor's role as a "public watchdog."

"By certifying the public reports that collectively depict a corporation's financial status, the independent auditor assumes a *public* responsibility transcending any employment relationship with the client," Justice Burger declared.

Hidden under Gobbledygook

Accounting firms maintain that they battle clients over the information to be included in annual financial statements, often to the point of getting fired, but that these relationships must be kept private or their clients would never reveal all their warts to the outside auditor.

* * * * *

In truth, too many outside auditors would like to enjoy big fees under the guise of protecting the public but plead ignorance when it comes to the client fraud or manipulation of accounting principles.

Accounting firms acting as auditors may not want to don the policeman's hat, but they did ask for the job of certifying annual reports in the 1930s. And they have to agree that there isn't anyone more qualified to keep public companies honest in their disclosure of financial information. The courts obviously aren't going to let them forget that.

Insider Trading. The rule on insider trading appears to be very simple—anyone who has access to nonpublic information of a material nature (such as a recent oil strike, results of a major lawsuit, huge earnings increases, an impending takeover bid) must (1) refrain from trading in the stock and telling friends, relatives, and so on to trade in the stock or (2) release the information to the public, wait a reasonable period of time, and then trade as desired. In recent years, the question of who is an *insider* under Rule 10b–5 and the conditions under which someone can be held liable for dealing in insider information have been in a state of flux. Clearly, corporate officers, directors, and attorneys may have access to inside information; in particular instances, engineers in an oil field also could—but so could brokers, analysts, printers, journalists, and eavesdroppers.

HIGH COURT UPHOLDS CONVICTION OF WINANS, TWO CO–CONSPIRATORS

James B. Stewart and Stephen Wermiel

In a decision that is likely to give new impetus to the government's crackdown on insider trading on Wall Street, the Supreme Court upheld the convictions of former *Wall Street Journal* reporter R. Foster Winans and two co-conspirators.

Government lawyers immediately hailed the ruling as vindication of a campaign that has already produced guilty pleas from such leading Wall Street figures as former arbitrager Ivan F. Boesky and former takeover specialist Martin A. Siegel. "This is tremendous news," says Gary Lynch, the head of enforcement for the Securities and Exchange Commission. "It's an affirmation of our insider-trading program."

The decision "lays out a whole theory of future prosecution for this type of criminal behavior that is very secure," says Rudolph W. Giuliani, the Manhattan U.S. attorney heading the insider-trading investigation. "It gives prosecutors a very clear road map on how to proceed."

Surprising Decision

The Supreme Court's opinion, which surprised many court observers, is as important for what it doesn't do as much as for what it does. In upholding Mr. Winans' conviction for securities, mail, and wire fraud, the Supreme Court didn't reject the so-called misappropriation theory, a doctrine that has been the legal backbone of insider-trading prosecution. And in reinterpreting the law of mail and wire fraud, the Supreme Court handed prosecutors a powerful new weapon, one that could easily eclipse misappropriation as the dominant theory of insider-trading prosecution.

The high court voted 8–0 to uphold the mail- and wire-fraud convictions. It was split, 4–4, on the securities-fraud issue, but the tie has the effect of affirming that count. Although a tie vote has less value as precedent than a majority vote, as a practical matter the split isn't expected to impede the precedent-setting consequences of the decision.

For Mr. Winans, the decision marks the end of a long criminal process that took on unexpected significance when high-profile insider-trading cases proliferated following his 1985 conviction. "We had hoped to prevail," says Don Buchwald, Mr. Winans' lawyer. "We're very disappointed." Mr. Buchwald says that he will move to have Mr. Winans' 18-month prison term reduced but that Mr. Winans probably will be reporting within 30 to 60 days to the federal prison where he will be assigned. Defense lawyers aren't expected to petition for a rehearing.

Reached at his home in Jersey City, New Jersey, Mr. Winans would only say: "I'm not making any comment."

Facts Not in Dispute

From the time criminal charges were first lodged against Mr. Winans in 1984, the facts have never been in serious dispute: Mr. Winans, a former writer of the *Journal*'s "Heard on the Street" stock market column, leaked advance information, usually from pay phones, about the timing and the content of those columns to Peter Brant, a former stock-broker at Kidder Peabody & Co.

Mr. Brant used the information to trade in the stocks mentioned in the columns, later enlisting a Kidder Peabody colleague, Kenneth Felis. Both agreed to give Mr. Winans a stake in the profits. All told, the scheme netted $690,000 in profits, of which $31,000 went to Mr. Winans.

Mr. Brant pleaded guilty to two counts of securities fraud and became the government's star witness against Mr. Winans and the two co-conspirators—Mr. Felis and Mr. Winans' former roommate, David Carpenter, a former *Journal* news clerk, who also shared in the profits from the scheme. The three were convicted after a trial before federal District Judge Charles E. Stewart in New York.

Mr. Felis, who now runs a family-owned labeling company in Bridgeport, Connecticut, didn't return phone calls. Former associates of Mr. Carpenter say he has moved to the Midwest. His lawyers declined to disclose his whereabouts.

Legal Implications

It was the legal theory supporting the criminal charges against Mr. Winans and his co-conspirators that immediately attracted attention. The government alleged that Mr. Winans had misappropriated, or stolen, confidential information entrusted to him about the contents and the timing of columns that potentially could have affected securities prices. This misappropriation constituted fraud, both under the securities laws and under the mail- and wire-fraud statutes, the government argued.

Others have been convicted of insider trading on similar theories, most notably Adrian Antoniu, a former Morgan Stanley & Co. investment banker, whose 1982 case gave rise to the doctrine. But the theory is judge-made law never legislated by Congress, and it had never been explicitly approved by the Supreme Court. In the past, the high court had simply

refused to hear the petitions of those convicted. Nor had the doctrine ever been used to indict a newspaper reporter, someone who wasn't directly involved in the securities industry.

Some lawyers had feared that government prosecutors were risking a reversal of the entire misappropriation doctrine by stretching too far to indict Mr. Winans. And those fears were heightened when, within months of Mr. Winans' conviction and while the case was on appeal, the biggest insider-trading cases in Wall Street's history started breaking. Suddenly it wasn't just the fate of Mr. Winans and his co-conspirators that seemed at stake, but those of a new, far more powerful generation of insider traders: Dennis B. Levine, Mr. Boesky, Mr. Siegel, and those they have implicated.

The pendency of the Winans case cast such a pall over the government crackdown that, just last week, Mr. Giuliani, the Manhattan U.S. attorney, was reported to have said that all insider-trading indictments arising from the government's current huge investigation were being put on hold until the Winans case was decided. Earlier this year, Mr. Lynch said that any reversal of Mr. Winans' conviction that threw out the misappropriation theory would cause "massive problems" for enforcement officials.

Those concerns appear to have vanished with yesterday's decision and the affirmation of the securities law violation, the aspect that most directly threatened the doctrine of misappropriation.

While the effect of the tie vote is to uphold the securities law conviction, the continued uncertainty about that aspect of the case is likely to spur legislative proposals that would incorporate the misappropriation doctrine into an insider-trading statute. It is "essential that the Congress act quickly to clarify and tighten the laws prohibiting insider trading," says Senator Donald Riegle of Michigan, the chairman of the Senate Banking Committee's securities subcommittee. Chairman David Ruder of the

Securities and Exchange Commission last week endorsed a broad definition of insider trading covering not only trading by corporate employees but also trading by other people who misappropriate information for their own benefit.

* * * * *

SEC's Role

Mr. Lynch, the SEC's enforcement chief, discounted speculation that the Court's emphasis on mail and wire fraud rather than securities fraud, the usual basis for SEC jurisdiction, would diminish the SEC's role in insider-trading cases. "It's clear the Court believes misappropriation of information is a fraud," he says. "That's what's important" for SEC jurisdiction. Mr. Lynch says the SEC "will continue to have a very active, aggressive program."

Academic experts were quickly parsing the opinion for future hypothetical cases, but there was widespread agreement that the government's hand has been greatly strengthened for the kinds of cases that have recently dominated the headlines. Noting that the Court didn't overturn the misappropriation theory even when stretched to include a reporter, they say that it is highly unlikely the Court would do so in a case involving stockbrokers, arbitragers, or other Wall Streeters.

Says Harvey Goldschmid, a professor and securities law expert at Columbia University: "If I were an investment banker involved in one of the potential cases, I'd be very worried."

[For the opinion in the *Winans* case, see 56 *Law Week* 4007 (1987)—Author.]

Ivan Boesky.   In addition to the *Foster Winans* case, much larger insider-trading cases have been brought against major Wall Street investors.

FALL OF IVAN F. BOESKY LEADS TO BROADER PROBE OF INSIDER INFORMATION

James B. Stewart and Daniel Hertzberg

In Ivan F. Boesky, government enforcement agents have captured the ultimate font of information about the inner workings of Wall Street. Market professionals now fear that what began as the Dennis B. Levine insider-trading case last May will soon shake Wall Street's very foundations.

"This ranks among the scandals of the century," says Daniel J. Good, a managing director and takeover specialist at Shearson Lehman Brothers, Inc. "Boesky was at the top of the spiral. His relationships go very high with very important people."

Mr. Boesky, America's richest and best-known arbitrager, agreed on Friday to pay $100 million to settle Securities and Exchange Commission charges of insider trading. In addition, he agreed to plead guilty to one felony count that carries a prison term of one to five years. Under the settlement, he will be barred from the securities industry for life.

The announcement by SEC Chairman John Shad and Manhattan U.S. Attorney Rudolph Giuliani, made after the stock market closed Friday, brings to an abrupt end one of the most dazzling careers on Wall Street. The payment, consisting of a $50 million fine and the return of $50 million in illegal profits, is said to strip the 49-year-old Mr. Boesky of most of his fortune and is the largest penalty in the history of the SEC.

Like Mr. Levine before him, Mr. Boesky (pronounced BOE-skee) is cooperating fully with the government's investigation of insider trading. Lawyers familiar with the investigation confirm that, in return for agreeing to plead guilty to only one felony count—a lenient plea bargain given the extent of Mr. Boesky's crime—Mr. Boesky has implicated other major figures on Wall Street, including professionals at some of the country's top securities firms.

The lawyers add that government investigators are closely examining Mr. Boesky's relationships with officials of Drexel Burnham Lambert, Inc., the securities firm that arranged $660 million in financing for Mr. Boesky's most recent limited partnership offering and that owns a stake in Northview Corp., Mr. Boesky's hotel company. [In September 1988, Drexel Burnham Lambert and its junk bond innovator, Michael Milken, were charged by the SEC with various civil violations, including insider trading. Criminal charges were expected to follow.]

* * * * *

Drexel is hardly the only firm with cause for concern. Mr. Boesky is believed to have traded information with many of Wall Street's best-known figures. There is a pervasive fear among market professionals that a government and public backlash will result, leading to lasting changes in the marketplace. For example, Fe-

lix G. Rohatyn, a general partner of Lazard Freres & Co., predicts that there will be "congressional investigations spurred on by a Democratic Congress. It wouldn't be surprising "to see new legislation or regulation."

The SEC's complaint against Mr. Boesky suggests that despite his reputation for having lots of Wall Street sources, it was Mr. Levine who recruited Mr. Boesky into an insider-trading scheme in February 1985, the same month that Mr. Levine moved from Shearson Lehman to Drexel. (Mr. Levine and his lawyers, who have consistently declined comment on the case, couldn't be reached for comment on the SEC's latest allegations.)

The complaint suggests that Mr. Levine baited his hook by passing on some tips, gratis, to Mr. Boesky. Among the deals about which Mr. Levine had inside information at the time were merger negotiations between ITT and Sperry, Coastal's bid for American Natural Resources, and a leveraged buyout of McGraw Edison.

The contacts between Mr. Levine and Mr. Boesky soon turned into a torrent. A Wall Street executive and a lawyer say that Mr. Levine's telephone records, obtained by the SEC, show hundreds of calls to Mr. Boesky, sometimes as many as 20 a day.

Had the relationship stopped there, lawyers say, the government might have had difficulty proving an insider-trading case against Mr. Boesky. The SEC acknowledges that, at least at the outset, Mr. Levine didn't tell Mr. Boesky the sources for his information. Mr. Boesky himself, as an arbitrager, didn't breach any fiduciary relationships with insiders. He might have argued that he didn't know he was receiving inside information that Mr. Levine had stolen from his employer or had obtained from others who had stolen the information. Moreover, stock trades by Mr. Boesky, who routinely speculated in the stocks of rumored and real takeover targets, wouldn't necessarily have corroborated claims by Mr. Levine of trading on inside information.

But according to the SEC's complaint, Mr. Boesky was evidently so impressed by the quality of Mr. Levine's information that he entered into an explicit profit-sharing agreement with Mr. Levine. He promised to pay 5 percent of the profits from information that triggered a purchase of securities and 1 percent of the profits earned on stock positions influenced by information obtained from Mr. Levine. In reaching this agreement, lawyers say, Mr. Levine made explicit what was already obvious: Mr. Boesky was getting inside information.

The two pledged themselves to secrecy, and Mr. Boesky, using his vast capital and Mr. Levine's information, embarked on a highly profitable stock-buying spree. For example, the SEC alleges that Mr. Boesky made $9.2 million in profits from just three stocks—Nabisco, Houston Natural Gas, and FMC—involved in takeovers or restructurings. He also profited from trading Boise Cascade, General Foods, Union Carbide, and others. In all, the SEC says, Mr. Boesky made more than $50 million in unlawful profits. Mr. Boesky's illicit earnings dwarf the unlawful profits earned by others accused of insider trading.

Beginning around September 1985, lawyers familiar with the case say, Mr. Levine knew that he was under investigation by the SEC. He curtailed his own insider trading somewhat, but he apparently thought that his arrangement with Mr. Boesky would continue to reap substantial profits without attracting the attention of the SEC. He accelerated the flow of information and began to press Mr. Boesky for some of the proceeds of the profit-sharing arrangement. Mr. Boesky stalled, quibbling about just how much Mr. Levine was owed. Finally, in April, the two agreed that Mr. Levine would receive $2.4 million as his share of the profits.

But unknown to Mr. Boesky, Mr. Levine had already breached the secrecy pledge. An inveterate name dropper, Mr. Levine had told at least one of his co-conspirators, Robert M. Wilkis, a former investment banker at Lazard

Freres & Co., some details of his arrangement with Mr. Boesky.

For Mr. Boesky, an enormously successful career turned nightmarish on May 12, the day of Mr. Levine's arrest.

Rumors that Mr. Boesky was also involved started almost immediately. Mr. Levine was well known for his contacts among arbitragers, and Mr. Boesky was by far the best known of them. Former prosecutors reasoned at the time that the government was unlikely to strike a plea agreement with Mr. Levine—apparently the ringleader of the largest insider-trading conspiracy in history—unless he had delivered a bigger name to investigators. And sources familiar with the investigation had confirmed to this newspaper that a major arbitrager was a target of the investigation.

But Mr. Boesky was also the least likely of suspects by virtue of his wealth and success. To many on Wall Street, it was inconceivable that a man of Mr. Boesky's stature, with a fortune beyond the reckoning of most, would place his fate in the hands of a Dennis Levine by entering into an illegal insider-trading pact. Despite occasional flurries of rumors, as the summer wore on without any government action, the suspicions about Mr. Boesky faded.

As the rumors subsided, Mr. Boesky's own assessment of his chances of avoiding prosecution and conviction progressively worsened, say lawyers familiar with the case. He assumed that his name had been divulged by Mr. Levine. But he had never actually paid the $2.4 million (Mr. Levine's arrest came before delivery of the funds, leading some to question whether Mr. Boesky would ever have honored the commitment). As a result, the case might have turned on Mr. Levine's word against Mr. Boesky's, a case his lawyers thought Mr. Boesky could win.

However, the government's case proved to be far stronger. Investigators painstakingly compiled telephone and trading records, and they were too consistent with Mr. Levine's disclosures to be coincidental. Moreover, the government had a corroborating witness in Mr. Wilkis, who is cooperating with the government and hasn't yet pleaded guilty to any charges. Mr. Wilkis' testimony, though hearsay, would be admissible in any trial against Mr. Boesky.

Harvey Pitt, Mr. Boesky's principal counsel . . . says settling with the SEC and agreeing to plead guilty was the only feasible option. "Both Mr. Boesky and I are pretty tenacious," Mr. Pitt says, "but you have to assess the situation in a cold and realistic way." He adds that if Mr. Boesky ever considered flight and the life of a fugitive, he isn't aware of it. Mr. Pitt says that widespread reports that Mr. Boesky had a net worth of $200 million are wrong and that Mr. Boesky will keep "very, very little" of his wealth.

* * * * *

A statement Mr. Boesky had read to employees was released . . . to news organizations. The government "justifiably holds me and not my business associates or business entities responsible for my actions. I deeply regret my past mistakes, and know that I alone must bear the consequences of those actions," Mr. Boesky said in the statement. "My life will be forever changed, but I hope that something positive will ultimately come out of this situation. I know that in the wake of today's events, many will call for reform. If my mistakes launch a process of reexamination of the rules and practices of our financial marketplace, then perhaps some good will result."

* * * * *

Charles Carberry, the assistant U.S. attorney prosecuting the Levine case, declined to comment on the specifics of the case or where the Boesky investigation might lead. But he emphasized that while the courts have sometimes wavered on what constitutes insider trading, they have repeatedly affirmed convictions of mail or wire fraud when people profited indirectly from what they knew to be inside information.

In this area, the line between legitimate and criminal conduct may be somewhat blurry. "Everybody talked to Boesky," says a top merger professional. The result is "a lot of sleepless nights for a lot of people," says Joseph Flom, a leading takeover lawyer. . . . That unease is expected to intensify as the government investigation of insider trading reaches what one top Wall Street executive calls the "golden triangle": the relationship between corporate raiders, arbitragers, and the purveyors of junk bonds, most notably Drexel.

Beyond the eventual impact on individuals and their firms, most think that the penalties against Mr. Boesky will ultimately have a positive effect on the markets by countering public skepticism about their integrity. "I don't think the public distinguishes between arbs, Drexel's takeovers," or anything else, says Mr. Flom. "It's all one big mess as far as they are concerned. By and large, the typical attitude is that these Wall Street types are screwing up America."

[Mr. Boesky was sentenced to three years in prison. See Chapter 3—Author.]

Insider Trading Rules Critiqued. As major arbitragers, raiders, and advisors have run afoul of SEC insider-trading rules and interpretations, issues about the appropriateness of insider-trading rules per se have emerged. The following articles look at this debate.

THE SEC'S FIGHT WITH ITSELF

Everyone is worried about where the Securities and Exchange Commission's "insider-trading" cases are headed. We've warned that the vague definition could be used to punish anyone who had more information than someone else, a recipe for market disaster. We're not alone. The people who best know the mindset of the agency's lawyers are the SEC's economists. And they are going public with their horror over the SEC's enforcement strategy.

The Office of the Chief Economist last week presented the lawyers down the hall with a study titled, "Stock Trading before the Announcement of Tender Offers: Insider Trading or Market Anticipation?" The economists warned that busting arbitragers and bankers shouldn't be used to chill the legitimate market for information. Market anticipation of takeovers, reflected in price rises before tenders are announced, is almost entirely based on factors aside from illegal insider trading.

The study was aimed squarely at SEC legal chief Gary Lynch. In the name of "equal information," Mr. Lynch has said he'll go after insider trading until there is no more run-up in share price before the announcement of a tender offer. Gregg Jarrell, who was the SEC's chief economist until he recently left to teach at the University of Rochester, told us he warned Mr. Lynch that run-ups do not necessarily mean insider trading. "When Gary sees the price creep up, he sees evil," Mr. Jarrell says. "I see the ferreting out of valuable information as a sign of the efficient market."

Dormant conflicts within the SEC erupted with this study. The enforcement division managed to block publication of the study's planned appendix titled, "The Law of Insider Trading." Written by Jeffry Netter, a lawyer on the economics staff, the appendix began, "The legal definition of illegal insider trading is somewhat ambiguous." It went on to say that "what

should be remembered at the outset is that most trades involving asymmetric information do not violate insider-trading laws." This was too hot to handle because it showed that the SEC's flat-out attack on "nonpublic" information is legally groundless.

The study the SEC actually allowed to be made public supports the economists' view. The report identified three major causes of pre-bid trading. These are rumors reported on the Dow Jones ticker and in this newspaper, the size of the bidder's "foothold" acquisition, and whether the takeover was hostile or friendly. A study of 172 big takeovers between 1981 and 1985 showed these factors led to a run-up before the formal bid of nearly 40 percent of the premium price.

This was not surprising. Consider the following:

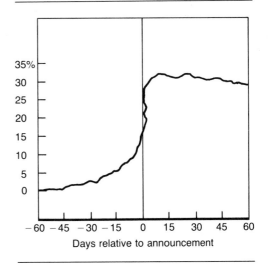

Above-Market Returns on Shares of Target Firms in Tender Offers

Source: James H. Lorie, Peter Dodd, and Mary Hamilton Kimpton, *The Stock Market: Theories and Evidence* (Homewood, Ill.: Dow Jones-Irwin, 1985).

This graph shows the average run-up before the public announcement of tender offers between 1962 and 1978. This ground-breaking study by efficient-market, random-walk economists at the University of Chicago jibes completely with the more recent findings of the SEC economists.

The following graphical bird's-eye view shows the mischief of Mr. Lynch's aggressive stance against information:

The Efficient Market

The price movements of a hypothetical stock shows how depressed share prices rise as traders learn that a family that owns a publicly traded company has begun to bicker, or see heavy trading on the computer tapes. By the time the raider reaches 5 percent and files its 13D with the SEC, the market understands something is going on. The price keeps rising until the bid succeeds or is dropped.

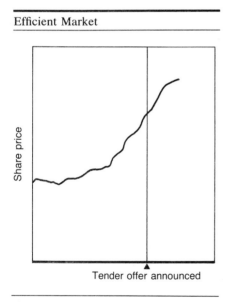

Efficient Market

Gary Lynch's Market

Compare this with the market as Mr. Lynch would apparently have it. Here the enforcers at the SEC have accomplished the goal of take-over bids taking the market completely by surprise. Equal information means no information. No one learns any information before anyone else, even through legitimate research. The share price is flat up to the announcement of the tender offer. The 90-degree angle shows the perfect absence of market forces to point to the true value of shares.

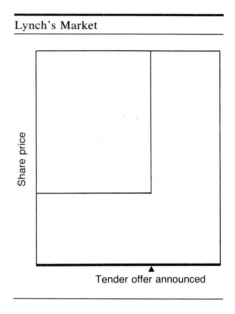

Lynch's Market

Costs of Noninformation

Overlaying the efficient market with Gary Lynch's market shows the costs to market efficiency if the SEC ever managed to end price run-ups. The shaded area measures the misallocated capital. The shares are really worth more, but no one—not arbitragers or pension fund managers—knows it because the SEC makes knowing more than someone else an indictable offense.

The SEC economists concluded that trying to end the price run-up is dangerous. "Legitimate research gives some traders informa-

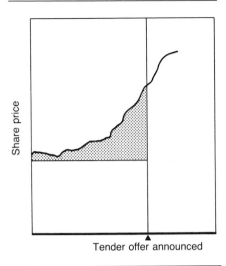

Costs of Noninformation

Share price (vertical axis)

Tender offer announced (horizontal axis)

Mr. Lynch—the downward slope of share prices would be completely vertical except that the information market would by then no longer be efficient enough to funnel even this valuable information very quickly into the market.

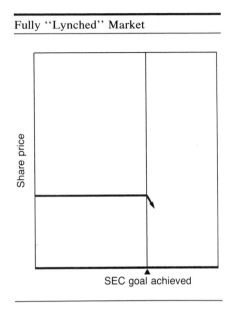

Fully "Lynched" Market

Share price (vertical axis)

SEC goal achieved (horizontal axis)

tional advantages and their earnings serve as compensation for their efforts," the report says. Their trading "aligns actual stock prices with their theoretically correct values, improving the allocation of scarce capital between competing uses."

Fully "Lynched" Market

If Mr. Lynch is serious about equal noninformation, he might be surprised by what he actually would get if the SEC completely chilled information gathering. Investors would flee the markets. We hope one irony won't be lost on

Mr. Lynch can assure the markets that his prosecutions won't go this far by supporting a definition of insider trading that protects all nonstolen information. Until he does, it's clear the SEC's economists have a better understanding of markets than do its lawyers.

Source: *The Wall Street Journal,* March 19, 1987, p. 32. Reprinted by permission of *The Wall Street Journal,* © Dow Jones & Company, Inc. 1987. ALL RIGHTS RESERVED.

REGULATION CLUB WON'T CURB
WALL STREET EXCESSES

Michael Kinsley

> May those who read my book gain some understanding of the opportunity which exists uniquely in this great land.
>
> Traditional stock investing is much closer to gambling than is risk arbitrage.
>
> Ivan Boesky, *Merger Mania* (1985)

I was curled up with a drink and *The Wall Street Journal*'s latest tirade against insider-trading laws last Friday, and was just starting, per instructions, to "ponder whether the securities laws may do more harm than good," when word came that the feds had nailed Ivan Boesky—an event that probably has brought more innocent pleasure to more people than anything the government has done since the Apollo moon landing. Oh, well. We professional opinionists all give hostages to fortune. Just a few months ago I wrote a column on insider trading that used Mr. Boesky as an example of how you can benefit from inside information without troubling to break the law.

The Boesky story is spreading controversy on three levels of generality. First, the question of insider trading itself. How much goes on? Is it bad? Second, the question of corporate raiders and the general Wall Street tumult of recent years. Should the government step in to slow things down? Third, greed and decadence in the Reagan era. Is there too much? Let's take these one at a time.

Insider Trading

Some conservative economists maintain that no one is really hurt by insider trading. It's true that you can get dizzy trying to pinpoint the loss. Those who sold shares to Mr. Boesky would have sold to someone else at about the same price (or a lower one!) if he'd stayed out of the market. Are the losers these sellers? Or the unknown people whom Mr. Boesky edged out of buying? And who are the losers when someone refrains from acting on inside information?

Nevertheless, it's absurd to say there's no loss just because the loss is hard to find. Insider trading doesn't change the price of a stock in the long run. (The value of inside information is knowing where the stock is headed anyway.) Nor does it increase the total value of stocks in the market. Therefore, it's a zero-sum game. If Ivan Boesky is $50 million richer as a result of inside information, others are a total of $50 million poorer, even if exactly who lost exactly how much is unknowable. The conventional wisdom about insider trading—that the loss is to the market in general—isn't just a metaphor. It's a mathematical certainty.

For this reason, the *Journal*'s position that restrictions on the use of inside information should be a matter of private contract between employer and employee, or banker and client, makes no sense. Employers and clients aren't the victims. Dennis Levine might well have been serving his clients' interests by leaking information to Mr. Boesky. *The Wall Street Journal* would have suffered no harm from Foster Winans' dealings if they hadn't become public, and if they weren't illegal they might well not have become public. Even if private organizations had the will to expose themselves, they lack the means. The investigation that uncovered the Levine-Boesky network followed a trail through many organizations, and involved subpoena powers and criminal-charge horse-trading that only the government can use.

On the other hand, the *Journal* is right that any effort to make the stock market an "honest crap game" by putting outsiders and insiders on exactly the same footing would destroy the market's function as an efficient capitalizer of business information. It's an impossible puzzle. The Securities and Exchange Commission's search for a middle ground has led it down several theoretical blind alleys. My own conclusion is that the "loss of public confidence" feared by financial graybeards is perfectly justified. The market is indeed stacked against the typical *Wall Street Journal* reader. Sorry.

Corporate Raiders

There's a distinctly snotty tone to some of the criticism that tars Ivan Boesky with the same brush as Carl Icahn, James Goldsmith, and T. Boone Pickens, as if avarice were unknown on Wall Street until these vulgar *arrivistes* came along. There's no logical connection between Mr. Boesky's outright cheating and the raiders' wheeling and dealing. In general, the *Journal* is right that the raiders' activity is capitalism in action, sending a healthy chilling breeze of market discipline through America's stuffy executive corridors.

On the other hand, the raiders and the arbitragers work closely together in ways that may yet prove scandalous when the Boesky tapes become public. On a broader policy level, the enormous churning of business assets during the past few years has exceeded anything that can be explained as simply the invisible hand at work. The cost in money, in management distraction, in the nation's best young minds burning up their IQ points playing 18-dimension financial chess, has been enormous. At the very least, this is a highly inefficient way to bring about an efficient restructuring of corporate America.

As I argued in this space last year, it's logically inconsistent to maintain that the stock market is efficient and that corporate raiding is efficient, too. That's because the effect of corporate raiding is to overturn the results—share price, management, ownership—achieved by the stock market. If the market price of a company bears little relation to its true value, that's at least odd. If the normal functioning of the stock market doesn't produce well-managed companies, that's disturbing. If (as is sometimes maintained in defense of leveraged buyouts, where management remains in place and ends up owning the show) private ownership is inherently more efficient than publicly traded stock, that is a more damning indictment of American capitalism as currently practiced than most socialists would dare to make.

The truth, as is often asserted but rarely the case, must lie somewhere in between. The raiders and deal makers do some good and also generate an enormous amount of friction and waste. So, new laws? No. The capacity for mischief here is greater than the capacity for benefit. . . .

Reagan-Era Decadence and Greed

Simple answer: Yes, there's too much of it about, although this also does not lend itself to a regulatory solution. Greed is inherent in human nature and essential to capitalism, of course. But the fever of selfishness and value-free wealth-worship that has swept the nation in the past few years is very real and not healthy.

But maybe we've just seen the high tide. An interesting test will be what becomes of Ivan Boesky. Will he become a fashionably risque figure in our culture like Sidney Biddle Barrows (the "Mayflower Madam") and Richard Nixon? Or will he become a period piece, a haunted reminder of yesterday's *Zeitgeist*, the Alger Hiss of the early 1980s?

Questions

1. *a.* Do you support rules against insider trading? Explain.
   b. Should they be general or specific prohibitions? Explain.
   c. Why do you think the SEC would want a general rule against insider trading?
   d. What are the consequences if insiders do not have specific examples or guidance about what they can and cannot do?
2. *a.* Are there degrees of insider trading? Explain.
   b. Is some "good" and some "bad"? Explain.
   c. Can the two be distinguished? Explain.
3. Financial printers are paid large sums of money to prepare documents for tender offers, registration statements, and so on. Advance knowledge of the data contained in these documents could be very valuable, and thus great steps are taken to stop any premature leaks. The printing may be divided up among many printers, or the printers may even be kept incommunicado for a period of time. If a printer were to use information in a document for his or her own benefit, would this constitute insider trading? Explain. See *Chiarella* v. *United States*, 445 U.S. 222 (1980).

CHAPTER QUESTIONS

1. Recent crises in the government securities market have provoked calls for increased government regulation. Do you favor that direction? Explain.
2. Define: (*a*) security, (*b*) private placements, (*c*) blue sky laws, (*d*) fraud, (*e*) short-swing profits, (*f*) tender offers, (*g*) buy/sell agreements, (*h*) partnerships, (*i*) Sub S Corporation, (*j*) registration, (*k*) prospectus.
3. Should accountants be expected to discover and reveal fraud perpetrated by their clients? Explain.
4. Why is insider trading unlawful?
5. X, Y, and Z desire to start a business. X is concerned about liability because he is rich. Y wants to have the right to control all decisions made in running the firm. X and Z do not plan to participate in managing the firm but will contribute money to start it. They expect to lose money for at least three years. How should they structure their organization?
6. Explain the ramifications of abolishing the "business judgment" rule.
7. Should tax shelters be eliminated? How?
8. Discuss the advantages and disadvantages of partnerships and corporations.
9. Discuss the exemptions available for certain types of securities.
10. Explain how federal securities laws attempt to make provisions for small businesses.
11. Ivan Landreth and his sons owned all of the stock in a lumber business they operated in Tonasket, Washington. The owners offered the stock

for sale. During that time a fire severely damaged the business, but the owners made assurances of rebuilding and modernization. The stock was sold to Dennis and Bolten, and a new organization, Landreth Timber Company, was formed with the senior Landreth remaining as a consultant on the side. The new firm was unsuccessful and was sold at a loss. The Landreth Timber Company then filed suit against Ivan Landreth and his sons seeking recession of the first sale, alleging, among other arguments, that Landreth and sons had widely offered and then sold their stock without registering it as required by the Securities Act of 1933. The district court acknowledged that *stocks* fit within the definition of a *security,* and that the stock in question "possessed all of the characteristics of conventional stock." However, it held that the federal securities laws do not apply to the sale of 100 percent of the stock of a closely held corporation. Here the district court found that the purchasers had not entered into the sale with the expectation of earnings secured via the labor of others. Managerial control resided with the purchasers. Thus the sale was a commercial venture rather than a typical investment. The Court of Appeals affirmed, and the case reached the Supreme Court. Decide. See *Landreth Timber Co.* v. *Landreth.* 471 U.S. 681 (1985).

12. For two years, representatives of Basic Incorporated and Combustion Engineering, Inc., had engaged in various meetings and conversations regarding the possibility of a merger. During that time, Basic issued three public statements indicating that no merger talks were in progress. Then, in 1978, the two firms merged. Some Basic shareholders had sold their stock between the first public denial of merger talks and the time when the merger was announced. Those stockholders filed a class action claiming Basic had made false and misleading statements in violation of Section 10(b) of the 1934 Securities Act and SEC Rule 10b–5. The plaintiff stockholders claimed they had suffered injury by selling their stocks at prices artificially depressed by the allegedly false statements. They argued that they would not have sold their stocks had they been truthfully informed of the merger talks. The trial court, in finding for Basic, took the position that preliminary merger discussions are immaterial. But the lower court certified (approved) the stockholders' class action, saying that reliance by the plaintiffs on Basic's statements could be presumed (and thus reliance need not be proved by each plaintiff in turn). In certifying the class action, the lower court embraced the efficient-market theory or the fraud-on-the-market theory. The court of appeals agreed with the lower court's class action certification based on efficient-market reasoning, but the appeals court reversed the immateriality finding regarding preliminary discussions. The case went to the Supreme Court.

    a. Explain the efficient-market theory and its role in this case.

    b. Decide the materiality issue. Explain. See *Basic, Inc.* v. *Max L. Levinson,* 56 *Law Week* 4232 (1988).

13. Christopher Farrell commented in *Business Week* regarding the 1987 stock market crash, which resulted in an immediate 23 percent "devaluation of corporate America":

> Economists will argue for years over what caused the crash of 1987. But it's already clear that the October 19 cataclysm marks the failure of the most pervasive belief in economics today: an unquestioning faith in the wisdom of free markets.

Do you agree? Explain. See "Where Was the Invisible Hand?" *Business Week,* April 18, 1988, p. 65.

14. This chapter addresses insider trading and other suspect practices in the securities markets. Commentator George Will thinks those (and similar) problems, as popularized in the movie *Wall Street,* are "draining capitalism of its legitimacy":

> A moral vulnerability of capitalism today is the belief that too much wealth is allocated capriciously, not only by the randomness of luck but by morally tainted shortcuts around a level playing field for all competitors. The legitimacy of the economic order depends on a consensus that, on balance, rewards are rationally related to the social value of the effort involved.

Do you agree? Explain. See "Capitalist Flaws Should Worry GOP," *Des Moines Register,* December 30, 1987, p. 6A.

NOTES

1. 497 F.2d 473 (5th Cir. 1974).
2. 421 U.S. 837 (1975).
3. 439 U.S. 551 (1979).

Chapter 9

Antitrust Law—Monopolies and Mergers

Preface: A New Direction in Antitrust Policy?

Perhaps more than any other branch of the law, antitrust is a product of political and economic tides. During President Reagan's tenure, a free market mentality prevailed, and reliance on antitrust law declined. In a striking implementation of its philosophical preferences, the Reagan administration in its first six months dropped or settled four of the lengthiest and most complex cases in American history. AT&T, IBM, the three largest cereal companies, and the eight largest oil companies had all been pursued for years (e.g., the IBM case had run for 13 years at a direct government cost of $13.4 million at the time it was dropped) in government actions intended to set new standards in antitrust enforcement. The abrupt settlement of those cases offered convincing evidence of the new disdain for much of antitrust law. While the federal government continued to avidly pursue collusion between competitors and certain other antitrust violations, the prevailing temperament was that the market would function most effectively in the absence of government intervention. That view, so successfully fostered by the so-called "Chicago School" of free market economics, has been dominant through the Reagan years. The following Robert Samuelson editorial argues that antitrust law should continue to fade away. A big portion of the student's responsibility in studying antitrust law is to answer Samuelson's question, "Have the antitrust provisions outlived their usefulness?"

HAVE ANTITRUST PROVISIONS OUTLIVED THEIR USEFULNESS?

Robert Samuelson

The power of antitrust law reached its peak on a day in 1911 when the Supreme Court declared Standard Oil Co. and American Tobacco Co.—industrial titans of their era—illegal restraints of trade.

Ever since, it's been a spasmodic slide into obscurity, if not irrelevance.

* * * * *

. . . Antitrust enforcement is not disappearing. Nor should it. Business executives like high prices and, at times, will try to fix them. In the last five years, the Justice Department has brought hundreds of price-fixing cases against road builders, electrical-construction firms, and government contractors.

Merger restrictions are needed for the same reason. Although standards are looser than 10 years ago, mergers that dramatically concentrate power in specific markets are—and would remain—illegal.

But the importance of antitrust has been doomed by changing economic conditions and, ironically, the triumph of its central political premise: the subordination of private business to public purpose. The major antitrust laws—the 1890 Sherman Act and the 1914 Clayton Act—straddled an era of huge change. Between 1880 and 1920, America's urban population quadrupled, and the industrial empires that this process produced were, in a nation of farmers and small businesses, awesome and alien.

The economic consequences of these vast firms always has been unclear. Monopoly power often was tempered by economies of scale. Although Standard Oil controlled more than 90 percent of all oil refining, it often lowered prices. But these firms also raised political fears they would undermine democratic government. President Wilson said in 1913: "America was created to break every kind of monopoly and to set men free upon a footing of equality."

This debate has now been settled. When the antitrust laws were enacted, Big Business was dominant. Government checks were narrow and weak. Now, the opposite is true. Government regulation is powerful and pervasive, extending from pollution to pensions. Debates rage over whether particular regulations are effective or needed, but "public interest" is the ultimate point of reference.

The economic relevance of antitrust law has diminished. Most important, the rising tide of conglomerate mergers—involving companies in different industries or markets—fall outside the scope of antitrust. The laws were mainly intended to cover mergers of companies with their competitors, suppliers, or customers. . . .

Increased international trade has eroded the power of companies in concentrated industries, such as steel or autos, to exercise pricing power. Finally, the dominant position of firms in some industries reflects superior efficiency, not monopoly power. Breaking up these firms would hurt the economy and, possibly, undermine U.S. international competitiveness. When the Justice Department abandoned its case against IBM, it acknowledged size is not itself illegal.

The result is that less is left for antitrust. Many conglomerate mergers, as economist Dennis Mueller of the University of Maryland argues, are inefficient. But policing them would require a huge—probably self-defeating—extension of government authority. These mergers have not increased the concentration of economic power. In 1958, the top 100 nonfinancial (i.e., nonbank, noninsurance) firms controlled 31.6 percent of nonfinancial assets. In 1982, their share was 28.2 percent.

Even a decade ago, antitrust policy held out much promise to reduce inflation or improve living standards by eliminating pockets of monopolistic power. Now, possible gains seem modest. Increased trade and deregulation have added to competition, while the natural checks of markets seem stronger than they once did.

"Most goods we buy are [luxuries] that could be substituted for other goods," economist Lester Thurow of the Massachusetts Institute of Technology has written. "For those who buy an expensive car, the real trade-off may be with a swimming pool [or] summer home."

The central antitrust idea remains as powerful as in 1890: competition is good politically and economically. But it is less and less fulfilled by antitrust laws. They are not being abandoned so much as they are fading away.

Part One—Introduction: The Roots of Antitrust Law

More than any other, the promise of America is that of personal freedom. The constitutions of the United States and the 50 states are designed to preserve our individual freedom against encroachment by government. As we saw in Chapter 3, Americans likewise fear excessive concentrations of power in private hands. Because the federal and state constitutions afford us no protection from abuse of private power, it has been thought necessary to turn to legislation to curb private concentrations of authority. The primary components of that legislation are the various federal antitrust statutes to which this chapter is addressed.

Anger directed at corporate power came to the fore following the Civil War. Farmers and small businesspersons were particularly incensed by high railroad freight charges and high prices for commodities. Interest groups like "The National Anti-Monopoly Cheap Freight Railway League" called for action to abate the power of the railroads and the so-called trusts in sugar, whiskey, fuel oil, and others.[1] Indeed, by 1914, the upper 2.2 percent of all manufacturing firms employed 35.3 percent of the manufacturing workers and produced 48.7 percent of the manufactured products.[2] A new America was emerging, and many citizens were angry and frightened by what they witnessed.

Public outrage and a growing congressional recognition of free market inadequacies (in company with some elements of the business lobby seeking protection from competition) led in 1887 to the creation of the Interstate Commerce Commission and in 1890 to the passage of the Sherman Antitrust Act as the federal government's first major business regulation measures. The view that market forces must be tempered by government intervention has, of course, resulted in a profound alteration of American life.

ANTITRUST STATUTES

A brief look at the various antitrust statutes will serve to place them in historical context. A further examination will accompany the case materials.

Sherman Antitrust Act, 1890

Section 1 of the act forbids restraints of trade, and Section 2 forbids monopolization, attempts to monopolize, and conspiracies to monopolize. Several enforcement options are available to the federal government:

1. Violation of the Sherman Act subjects participants to criminal penalties. As amended in 1974, the maximum corporate fine is $1 million, while individuals may be fined $100,000 and imprisoned for three years. Sherman Act violations are classified as felonies.
2. Injunctive relief is provided under the civil law. That is, the government or a private party may secure a court order preventing continuing violations of the act and affording appropriate relief (such as dissolution or divestiture).

Perhaps the most important remedy is that available to private parties. An individual or organization harmed by a violation of the act may bring a civil action seeking three times the damages (treble damages) actually sustained. Thus, the victim is compensated, and the wrongdoer is punished. However, the treble-damages remedy is currently being questioned as an excessive penalty.

Clayton and Federal Trade Commission Acts, 1914

After nearly 25 years of experience with the Sherman Act, many members of Congress, along with President Woodrow Wilson, held the view that the federal antitrust law required strengthening. Sherman forbade the continued practice of specified anticompetitive conduct, but it did not forbid conduct that was *likely to lead to* anticompetitive behavior. Furthermore, many felt that judicial interpretations of Sherman had seriously weakened that legislation. The Clayton Act forbids price discrimination, exclusive dealing, tying arrangements, requirements contracts, mergers restraining commerce or tending to create a monopoly, and interlocking directorates.

Civil enforcement of the Clayton Act is similar to the Sherman Act in that the government may sue for injunctive relief, and private parties may seek treble damages. Injunctive relief was also extended to private parties under both the Clayton and Sherman Acts. In general, criminal law remedies are not available under the Clayton Act.

The Federal Trade Commission Act created a powerful, independent agency designed to devote its full attention to the elimination of anticompetitive practices in American commerce. The commission is composed of five members, no more than three of whom may belong to a single political party. The commissioners are appointed by the president and confirmed by the Senate to staggered seven-year terms. As a consequence of the legislation itself and judicial interpretation of that legislation, the FTC is now empowered to proceed under both the Sherman Act (via Section 5 of the FTC Act) and the Clayton Act. Section 5 of the FTC Act declares unlawful "unfair methods of competition" and "unfair or deceptive acts or practices in or affecting commerce." The commission's primary enforcement device is the cease and desist order. The agency's action is subject to judicial review under the principles articulated in Chapter 7. Should the commission's order not be appealed, or if the order is upheld on appeal, the offending party may be fined up to $5,000 per day for each violation until the cease and desist order is obeyed.

In recent years the FTC has instituted actions against many of America's major industries and firms, including soft drink bottlers, the American Medical Association, General Motors, and, as mentioned, the major cereal manufacturers and oil companies. Several of these suits represent rather bold efforts by the commission to strike out at practices not explicitly forbidden by statute but believed to be "unfair methods of competition." However, the current FTC is taking a less interventionist stance. Some commissioners consider the "unfair and deceptive" language overly broad, but the FTC holds in Congress a powerful ally in that the agency affords Congress its "own antitrust arm" corresponding to the executive branch's Justice Department.

FTC authority extends well beyond antitrust matters to touch the fullness of unfair trade practices. That dimension of FTC activity is addressed in Chapter 13.

1915 to the Present

The antitrust zeal that produced the Clayton and FTC Acts was muted by World War I and largely extinguished by a strong free enterprise spirit following the war. The Harding, Coolidge, and Hoover administrations of 1920 to 1932 constituted perhaps the zenith of faith in capitalist principles in America. In time, the suffering of the Depression era brought a search for solutions in the form of renewed government intervention. Among President Roosevelt's many legislative programs to achieve economic recovery, the Robinson-Patman Act of 1936 and the Miller-Tydings Act of 1937 were the only antitrust measures. Robinson-Patman amended the Clayton Act in an effort to achieve firmer controls over price discrimination. Miller-Tydings legalized "fair-trade" pricing where state law allowed such pricing. *Fair-trade pricing* is a policy of resale price maintenance wherein the seller specifies the minimum price at which its product may be resold. The McGuire Act of 1952 sought to strengthen Miller-Tydings, but in 1975 the Consumer Goods Pricing Act repealed both. However, many states still retain fair-trade pricing, and, as will be discussed, resale price maintenance agreements remain a relatively common merchandising strategy.

Since World War II antitrust legislative activity has been relatively sparse. Of particular note, however, was the 1950 passage of the Celler-Kefauver Act, which strengthened the Clayton Act, and the 1976 Hart-Scott-Rodino Antitrust Improvement Act, which requires notice to the FTC and the Justice Department in advance of major mergers.

EXEMPTIONS FROM FEDERAL ANTITRUST LAW

Congress has accorded labor unions partial exemption from antitrust law. One result of the exemption is that unions are able to restrict the supply of labor, thus "artificially" raising prices. The labor exemption has provoked complaints. Robert Tollison observes:

> For a variety of reasons, the most serious cases of monopoly have traditionally been those monopolies sanctioned by the government. . . . It seems clear that without legal sanction, the monopoly power of unions would be quickly eroded by competition in labor markets.[3]

Why have unions been partially shielded from federal antitrust laws? Should unions be fully subject to free market forces? If so, how would all our lives be altered?

Regulated industries (e.g., insurance, utilities, shipping, banking, and securities) have been, in the main, free of the impact of the antitrust laws. Congress and the courts have recognized the government's direct supervisory authority in such critical areas as entry, exit, and pricing and thus have generally declined to apply the antitrust laws. Recent cases, however, suggest an increasing judicial willingness to intervene, particularly in industries where regulation is less intense. State action (laws and regulations) is generally exempt from the Sherman Act when the state has clearly developed a policy of regulating the commerce in question rather than allowing the free market to work its will. A state monopoly over the sale of liquor is an example of state action that inhibits competition but is exempt from the Sherman Act. Two 1985 Supreme Court decisions affirmed the validity of the state action exemption.[4]

Perhaps recalling the innocence of their own sandlot days, the judiciary has seen fit to view baseball as a sport rather than a business, thus removing it from antitrust proscriptions. Curiously, other professional sports are subject to antitrust, and football, in particular, has lately been the subject of extensive litigation. That baseball is considered a sport while football is labeled a business is a reminder that forces other than logic sometimes shape the course of law. The cooperative marketing of agricultural and fish products has been specifically excluded from the sweep of antitrust laws. Associations organized for the purpose of engaging in cooperative export trade are also partially exempt under the terms of the Export Trading Company Act of 1982. Some difficult questions remain about the degree to which professional services (law, medicine, and real estate) should be subject to antitrust. In 1975 the Supreme Court in the *Goldfarb* case[5] held that the Sherman Act applies to at least some anticompetitive conduct by lawyers. Mr. and Mrs. Goldfarb successfully argued that the minimum fee schedule published by the Virginia State Bar constituted a price-fixing scheme in violation of Sherman I. The Goldfarbs' victory has led to a continuing series of challenges to the professions, making it evident that professional services do constitute commerce and that anticompetitive practices may be challenged. However, the judiciary clearly believes regulation of the professions is a matter not best administered at the federal level. In *Goldfarb* the Supreme Court affirmed the limited role of antitrust:

> In holding that certain anticompetitive conduct by lawyers is within the reach of the Sherman Act we intend no diminution of the authority of the State to regulate its professions.[6]

FEDERAL ANTITRUST LAW AND OTHER REGULATORY SYSTEMS

State Law

Most states, through legislation and judicial decisions, have developed their own antitrust laws. However, enforcement at the state level ordinarily receives only passing attention. Indeed, due to the interstate nature of most antitrust problems, states could not effectively pursue the bulk of the cases.

Patents, Copyrights, and Trademarks

Each of these devices constitutes a limited, government-granted monopoly. As such they are in direct conflict with the general thrust of antitrust law. However, each device serves to protect—and thus encourage—commercial creativity and development. The resulting antitrust problem is essentially that of limiting the patent, copyright, or trademark holder to the narrow terms of its privilege.

Law of Other Nations

Refer to the materials addressing international antitrust issues at the end of this chapter.

ANTITRUST: LAW FOR ALL SEASONS

What is it that antitrust law seeks to accomplish? To the reader unacquainted with the national goals embodied in the antitrust laws, the case decisions that follow would seem, at best, confusing, and at worst, irrational. Indeed, even given an understanding of "antitrust philosophy," some of the decisions may agitate the lucid mind.

Many businesses in competition means that none of them may corner economic, political, or social power. It follows that the character and course of American life will reflect the varied inputs of the many rather than the vested interests of the powerful few. Hence, antitrust law seeks to preserve democracy.

Of course, the major, express goal of antitrust legislation has been the preservation of the merits of capitalism. We continue to believe that free and open markets will result in the best product at the lowest price. More specifically, we seek the benefits of competition—efficient allocation of resources, technological innovations, high productivity, price stability, and so on. The development of the law has demonstrated the impossibility of achieving *perfect competition.* Hence, the goal of current antitrust policy is that of *workable competition,* wherein market forces are sufficiently effective to prevent the development of monopolies and other anticompetitive practices.

Furthermore, a charming, but arguably anachronistic, clinging to the American Dream seems to continue to shape our attitude toward "trust-busting." As we will see, most notably in the case of the Robinson-Patman Act, the small-business lobby has been most effective in structuring the law to preserve the opportunity for the "little people" to compete with the giants. However, it has been argued that our protectionist efforts regarding small business have actually resulted in reduced market efficiency. It may be that the national spirit requires the preservation of at least a long-shot opportunity for each of us to start our own business and build our way to the top. Indeed, it could be persuasively argued that the destruction of that key ingredient in the American Dream would ultimately destroy the fabric of the nation. So antitrust legislation is very much more than rules to regulate specific dimensions of business conduct. It is designed to preserve the American way of life.

Finally, the antitrust laws have been, for a segment of society, an expression of a strain of political radicalism. Sentiments against big business are not uncommon in America. For those who feel that business power lies at the heart of American ills, the antitrust laws are taken to be useful tools in reshaping America so that business more nearly meets the needs of the people.

Part Two—Monopoly

Principal legislation: Sherman Act, Section 2.

> Every person who shall monopolize, or attempt to monopolize, or combine or conspire with any other person or persons, to monopolize any part of the trade or commerce among the several States, or with foreign nations, shall be deemed guilty of a felony punishable by a fine not exceeding $1,000,000 if a corporation, or if any other person, $100,000 or by imprisonment not exceeding three years or both.

(Throughout the two antitrust chapters, the "principal legislation" is identified. But it should be understood that most, if not all, antitrust violations are subject to more than one piece of legislation. In particular, Section 5 of the Federal Trade Commission Act is arguably applicable to all antitrust violations.)

From an economic viewpoint, a *monopoly* is a situation in which one firm holds the power to control prices and/or exclude competition in a particular market. By contrast, an *oligopoly* is the situation in which a few firms share monopoly power.

In practice, the courts' analyses of monopoly problems have not adhered particularly rigorously to established economic theory. Jurists have focused their attention on both the structure of the industry in question and on the intent of the alleged monopolist as measured by its conduct. Thus, the critical inquiries are the percentage of the market held by the alleged monopolist and the behavior that produced that market share. The Sherman Act does not, as interpreted, punish efficient companies who legitimately earn and maintain large market shares.

It is important to note that a considerable debate rages in the legal community about whether conduct or structure (or, indeed, several other possibilities) constitutes the best test of anticompetitive conditions. Should we concern ourselves with a firm's behavior, or should we focus on those industries in which a few firms control a large percentage of the market? Is a concentrated market undesirable in and of itself, or should we challenge market concentration only when it has been acquired and/or maintained via abusive conduct? Because current legal and economic reasoning affords us no definitive answer, the student can only be advised to consider the implications of each policy.

Section 2 prohibits combinations, conspiracies, and attempts to monopolize. However, the problems of proof associated with those offenses render them not particularly useful. Hence they will not be addressed here.

Finally, "pure" free market advocates hold a markedly different view of monopoly than that just articulated. Alan Greenspan, noted economist and chairman of the Federal Reserve Board, explains:

> A "coercive monopoly" is a business concern that can set its prices and production policies independent of the market, with immunity from competition, from the law of supply and demand. An economy dominated by such monopolies would be rigid and stagnant.
>
> The necessary precondition of a coercive monopoly is closed entry—the barring of all competing producers from a given field. This can be accomplished only by an act of government intervention, in the form of special regulations, subsidies, or franchises. Without government assistance, it is impossible for a would-be monopolist to set and maintain his prices and production policies independent of the rest of the economy. For if he attempted to set his prices and production at a level that would yield profits to new entrants significantly above those available in other fields, competitors would be sure to invade his industry.[7]

To some laissez-faire advocates the alleged monopolies that, in part, provoked the creation of the Interstate Commerce Commission and the Sherman Act were really the product of government intervention. For example, the railroads, which engendered the farmers' rage over their rate policies in the latter half of the 1800s, were able to secure market dominance in the West only after unusually favorable government treatment, including grants of tens of millions of acres.

MONOPOLIZATION ANALYSIS

While the case law is not a model of clarity, a rather straightforward framework for monopoly analysis has emerged:

1. Define the relevant *product market*.
2. Define the relevant *geographic market*.
3. Compute the defendant's *share of the market* and determine if that share is sufficient to constitute a monopoly. If the share is clearly beneath that necessary for market dominance, the case may be dismissed. As explained later, factors other than market share often strongly influence the court's decision about market power.

4. Assuming the market share is of threatening proportions, the next inquiry is that of *intent*. Do the defendant's acts evidence the necessary deliberateness or purposefulness? If not, the case should be dismissed. If yes, the defendant is, in the absence of further evidence, in violation of the law.

5. The defendant may yet prevail if the evidence demonstrates that the monopoly was *"thrust upon"* the firm, rather than that the firm affirmatively sought its monopoly posture. The thrust-upon defense had its genesis in Judge Learned Hand's opinion in the *Alcoa* case,[8] where that most aptly named jurist suggested the Sherman Act would not be violated if monopoly power were innocently acquired via superior skill, foresight, or industry or by failure of the competition as a consequence of changes in costs or consumer preference. Depending on the circumstances, other defenses (such as possession of a patent, for example) may be persuasive. Recent cases suggest that federal judges increasingly accept the argument that the alleged monopolist earned its market position legitimately and thus should not be punished.

Product Market

Here the court seeks, effectively, to draw a circle that encompasses categories of goods in which the defendant's products or services compete and excludes those not in the same competitive arena. The fundamental test is that of interchangeability as determined primarily by the price, use, and quality of the product in question. An analysis of cross elasticity of demand is a key ingredient in defining the product market.

Geographic Market

Once the product market has been defined, we still must determine where the product can be purchased. The cases offer no definitive explanation of the geographic market concept. A working definition might be "any section of the country where the product is sold in commercially significant quantities." From an economic perspective, the geographic market is defined by elasticity. If prices rise or supplies are reduced within the geographic area in question (e.g., New England) and demand remains steady, will products from other areas enter the market in quantity sufficient to affect price and/or supply? If so, the geographic market must be broadened to embrace those new sources of supply. If not, the geographic market is not larger than the area in question (New England). Perhaps a better approach is to read the cases and recognize that each geographic market must simply be identified in terms of its unique economic properties.

UNITED STATES V. GRINNELL CORP.
384 U.S. 563 (1966)

Justice Douglas

[The United States charged Grinnell with monopolization of the central station protection business in violation of Section 2 of the Sherman Act.]

Grinnell manufactures plumbing supplies and fire sprinkler systems. It also owns 76 percent of the stock of ADT, 89 percent of the stock of AFA, and 100 percent of the stock of Holmes. ADT provides both burglary and fire protection services; Holmes provides burglary services alone; AFA supplies only fire protection service. Each offers a central station service under which hazard-detecting devices installed on the protected premises automatically transmit an electric signal to a central station. The central station is manned 24 hours a day. Upon receipt of a signal, the central station, where appropriate, dispatches guards to the protected premises and notifies the police or fire department direct. There are other forms of protective services. But the record shows that subscribers to accredited central station service (i.e., that approved by the insurance underwriters) receive reductions in their insurance premiums that are substantially greater than the reduction received by the users of other kinds of protection service. . . . ADT, Holmes, and AFA are the three largest companies in the business in terms of revenue: ADT (with 121 central stations in 115 cities) has 73 percent of the business; Holmes (with 12 central stations in three large cities) has 12.5 percent; AFA (with three central stations in three large cities) has 2 percent. Thus the three companies that Grinnell controls have over 87 percent of the business. . . . ADT over the years reduced its minimum basic rates to meet competition and renewed contracts at substantially increased rates in cities where it had a monopoly of accredited central station service. ADT threatened retaliation against firms that contemplated inaugurating central station service. And the record indicates that, in contemplating opening a new central station, ADT officials frequently stressed that such action would deter their competitors from opening a new station in that area.

The district court found that the defendant companies had committed per se violations of [Sherman I and II]. . . .

I

The offense of monopoly under § 2 of the Sherman Act has two elements: (1) the possession of monopoly power in the relevant market and (2) the willful acquisition or maintenance of that power as distinguished from growth or development as a consequence of a superior product, business acumen, or historic accident. We shall see that this second ingredient presents no major problem here, as what was done in building the empire was done plainly and explicitly for a single purpose. . . . In the present case, 87 percent of the accredited central station service business leaves no doubt that the congeries of these defendants have monopoly power—power which, as our discussion of the record indicates, they did not hesitate to wield—if that business is the relevant market. The only remaining question therefore is, what is the relevant market?

[A] product . . . may be of such a character that substitute products must also be considered, as customers may turn to them if there is a slight increase in the price of the main product. That is the teaching of the *Du Pont* case . . . *viz.*, that commodities reasonably interchangeable make up that "part" of trade or commerce which § 2 protects against monopoly power.

The district court treated the entire accredited central station service business as a single market and we think it was justified in so doing. Defendants argue that the different central station services offered are so diverse that they cannot under *Du Pont* be lumped together to make up the relevant market. For example, burglar alarm services are not interchangeable with fire alarm services. They further urge that *Du Pont* requires that protective services other than those of the central station variety be included in the market definition.

But there is here a single use, i.e., the protection of property, through a central station that receives signals. It is that service, accredited, that is unique and that competes with all the other forms of property protection. We see no barrier to combining in a single market a number of different products or services where that combination reflects commercial realities. . . .

. . . First, we deal with services, not with products; and second, we conclude that the accredited central station is a type of service that makes up a relevant market and that domination or control of it makes out a monopoly. . . .

Burglar alarm service is in a sense different from fire alarm service; from waterflow alarms; and so on. But it would be unrealistic on this record to break down the market into the various kinds of central station protective services that are available. Central station companies recognize that to compete effectively, they must offer all or nearly all types of service. . . .

There are, to be sure, substitutes for the accredited central station service. But none of them appears to operate on the same level as the central station service so as to meet the interchangeability test of the *Du Pont* case. Nonautomatic and automatic local alarm systems appear on this record to have marked differences, not the low degree of differentiation required of substitute services as well as substitute articles.

Watchman service is far more costly and less reliable. Systems that set off an audible alarm at the site of a fire or burglary are cheaper but often less reliable. They may be inoperable without anyone's knowing it. Moreover, there is a risk that the local ringing of an alarm will not attract the needed attention and help. Proprietary systems that a customer purchases and operates are available; but they can be used only by a very large business or by government and are not realistic alternatives for most concerns. There are also protective services connected directly to a municipal police or fire department. But most cities with an accredited central station do not permit direct, connected service for private businesses. These alternate services and devices differ, we are told, in utility, efficiency, reliability, responsiveness, and continuity, and the record sustains that position. And, as noted, insurance companies generally allow a greater reduction in premiums for accredited central station service than for other types of protection.

* * * * *

The accredited, as distinguished from nonaccredited, service is a relevant part of commerce. Virtually the only central station companies in the status of the nonaccredited are those that have not yet been able to meet the standards of the rating bureau. The accredited ones are indeed those that have achieved, in the eyes of underwriters, superiorities that other central stations do not have. . . .

We also agree with the district court that the geographic market for the accredited central station service is national. The activities of an individual station are in a sense local as it serves, ordinarily, only that area which is within a radius of 25 miles. But the record amply supports the conclusion that the business of providing such a service is operated on a national level. There is national planning. The agreements we have discussed covered activities in many states. The inspection, certification and rate-making is largely by national insurers. The appellant ADT has a national schedule of prices, rates, and terms, though the rates may be varied to meet local conditions. It deals with multistate businesses on the basis of nationwide contracts. The manufacturing business of ADT is interstate.

* * * * *

We largely agree with the government's views on the relief aspect of the case. We start with ADT, which presently does 73 percent of the business done by accredited central stations throughout the country. It is indeed the keystone of the defendants' monopoly power. The mere dissolution of the combination through the divestiture by Grinnell of its interests in the other companies does not reach the root of the evil. In 92 of the 115 cities in which ADT operates there are no other accredited central stations. Perhaps some cities could not support more than one. Defendants recognized prior to trial that at least 13 cities can; the government urged divestiture in 48 cities. That there should be some divestiture on the part of ADT seems clear; but the details of such divestiture must be determined by the district court as the matter cannot be resolved on this record.

* * * * *

The defendants object to the requirements that Grinnell divest itself of its holdings in the three alarm company defendants, but we think that provision is wholly justified. The defendants object to that portion of the decree that bars them from acquiring interests in firms in the accredited central station business. But since acquisition was one of the methods by which the defendants acquired their market power and was the method by which Grinnell put the combination together, an injunction against the repetition of the practice seems fully warranted. . . .

The judgment below is affirmed except as to the decree. We remand for further hearings on the nature of the relief consistent with the views expressed herein.

* * * * *

Mr. Justice Fortas, with whom Mr. Justice Stewart joins, dissenting.

I agree that the judgment below should be remanded, but I do not agree that the remand should be limited to reshaping the decree. Because I believe that the definition of the relevant market here cannot be sustained, I would reverse and remand for a new determination of this basic issue, subject to proper standards.

* * * * *

In this case, the relevant geographical and product markets have not been defined on the basis of the economic facts of the industry concerned. They have been tailored precisely to fit defendants' business. The government proposed and the trial court concluded that the relevant market is not the business of fire protection, or burglary protection, or protection against waterflow, etc., or all of these together. It is not even the business of furnishing these from a central location. It is the business, viewed nationally, of supplying "insurance accredited central station protection services" . . . that is, fire, burglary and other kinds of protection furnished from a central station which is accredited by insurance companies. The business of defendants fits neatly into the product and geographic market so defined. In fact, it comes close to filling the market so defined. . . .

The geographical market is defined as nationwide. But the need and the service are intensely local. . . .

But because these defendants, the trial court found, are connected by stock ownership, interlocking management and some degree of national corporate direction, and because there is some national participation in selling as well as national financing, advertising, purchasing of equipment, and the like, the court concluded that the competitive area to be considered is national. This Court now affirms that conclusion.

This is a non sequitur. It is not permissible to seize upon the nationwide scope of defendants' operation and to bootstrap a geographical definition of the market from this. The purpose of the search for the relevant geographical market is to find the area or areas to which a potential buyer may rationally look for the goods or services that he seeks. . . .

The central issue is where does a potential buyer look for potential suppliers of the service—what is the geographical area in which the buyer has, or, in the absence of monopoly, would have, a real choice as to price and alternative facilities? This depends upon the facts of the marketplace, taking into account such economic factors as the distance over which supplies and services may be feasibly furnished, consistently with cost and functional efficiency.

The incidental aspects of defendants' business which the court uses cannot control the outcome of this inquiry. They do not measure the market area in which buyer and sellers meet. . . .

Questions

1. Why was the word *accredited* critical in defining the product market in the *Grinnell* case?
2. Explain how the Court could logically place fire and burglary protection in the same market, when the two are clearly not interchangeable.
3. Explain Justice Fortas' objection to the majority's "bootstrapped" geographic market definition. Now build the argument that the majority's geographic market is correct, but not for the reasons Justice Douglas offers.
4. Assume we have historical data showing that when the price of rolled steel has increased, the sales volume of rolled aluminum has remained constant. What, if anything, does that fact tell us about the product market for rolled steel?
5. Define the product market for championship boxing matches. See *United States* v. *International Boxing Club of New York, Inc., 358 U.S. 242 (1959).*

Market Power

We have no firm guidelines as to what percentage of the market must be controlled to give rise to a monopoly. In the *Alcoa* case, Judge Hand found a monopoly where Alcoa had 90 percent of the virgin ingot aluminum market.[9] In *U.S.* v. *United Shoe Machinery Corporation*[10] a 75 percent share of the shoe machinery market was a monopoly share, but a 50 percent share in some supply markets was not large enough to constitute a monopoly. The Fifth Circuit Court of Appeals has indicated that "something more than 50 percent of the market is a prerequisite to a finding of monopoly."[11] In any case, market share is not the only factor of importance in determining the existence of monopoly power. In *ILC Peripherals* v. *IBM*[12] the judge cited a number of factors that were influential in concluding that IBM, regardless of the size of its market share, lacked the power to control prices or exclude competition:

1. The fact that IBM's market share had declined over time.
2. The testimony of both competitors and customers of IBM to the effect that the computer business was "extremely competitive."
3. The fact that IBM was forced to lower its prices on numerous occasions to prevent competitors from "squeezing it out of these markets entirely."
4. The fact that a substantial number of new competitors had entered the market.
5. The fact that the degree of product innovation in the computer industry is high.[13]

Intent

Regrettably, the evidentiary burden necessary to prove purposefulness or deliberateness or general intent is probably even less clear than the market share issue. Certainly overt predatory acts (e.g., deliberately slashing prices below cost to drive a competitor from the market) would be persuasive evidence of intent to monopolize. General intent may be inferred from normal business behavior, depending on the circumstances. In practice, what probably happens in most monopoly cases is a weighing of evils. If the market share is large, the necessary measure of intent is likely to be smaller. On the other hand, if the market share in question is a borderline threat as to size, the court may well expect a higher standard of proof as to intent.

Monopoly Earned

Judge Hand, in the *Alcoa* case, appeared to condemn a monopolist unless it was a "passive beneficiary of a monopoly"; that is, unless the monopoly was "thrust upon" the monopolist. Recent decisions reflect a judicial unease with that view. The 1985 case, *Aspen Skiing Co.* v. *Aspen Highlands Skiing Corp.*[14] demonstrates that monopoly law retains some vigor. In that case the Supreme Court held that a dominant firm, Aspen Skiing, violated the Sherman Act by refusing to cooperate with its smaller competitor, Aspen Highlands. The ski area at Aspen, Colorado, is composed of four mountains. The ski developments on three of those mountains were owned by Aspen Skiing, while Highlands owned the fourth. For years the companies successfully promoted a four-area ski pass that permitted purchasers to ski on any of the mountains. Then Aspen Skiing withdrew from that arrangement and began promoting a pass for its three areas. Highlands' revenues dropped, and its efforts to create its own multipass ticket were frustrated by Aspen Skiing. Highlands filed suit and won a lower court judgment for damages and an injunction reinstituting the four-area pass. That decision was affirmed by the U.S. Supreme Court.

The *Aspen* case is interesting because it demonstrates that monopolists are still a subject of concern to the Supreme Court. But the case also appears to suggest that monopolists who earn and even expand their dominance through superior performance need not fear the antitrust laws:[15]

> [t]he law can usefully attack this form of predation only when there is evidence of specific intent to drive others from the market by means other than superior efficiency.[16]

The article that follows illustrates some of the virtues of the free market, but it also reminds us that monopoly conditions may continue to pose a threat in at least some portions of the economy.

GROWING GIANTS: AN UNEXPECTED RESULT OF AIRLINE DECONTROL IS RETURN TO MONOPOLIES

Scott Kilman

St. Louis—Airline competition here has come full circle.

In the carefree days before deregulation in 1978, five big airlines handled most of the passenger traffic in and out of Lambert-St. Louis International airport. Then came the air wars. After decontrol, nine more airlines invaded the market—all trying to lure a share of the 20 million travelers who use this airport each year.

Now most of the traffic is handled by one carrier: Trans World Airlines. Having driven back or acquired its major rivals, TWA today enjoys a degree of dominance here that any airline would have envied prior to deregulation. Its 317 departures a day dwarf those of its nearest rival, Southwest Airlines, which has 22.

The cycle is occurring at airports across the country—in Minneapolis, Baltimore, Houston, Syracuse, and Denver, to name only several. In fact, at 15 of the nation's top airports, either half the business is already controlled by one carrier, or two share more than 70 percent.

"Fortress Hubs"

Airlines command as many gates as they can—turning airports into so-called fortress hubs—to allow for the maximum number of connections between the cities they serve. And as airlines become increasingly entrenched in these hubs, they are finding new ways of keeping their rivals out. In some cases, carriers have been able to block entry to potential competitors either by tying up gates with exclusive long-term leases or by stalling expansion plans by local airport authorities.

The airline industry is "an oligopoly again," declares Stephen A. George, the director of Greater Pittsburgh International Airport, where USAir carries about 80 percent of the passengers. He adds that "just a surviving handful of major airlines" are left at some airports.

The implications for air travelers seem obvious: higher fares and less service. In St. Louis, the travel department of a major corporation estimates that the average price it paid for airline tickets this past May was 33 percent higher than in May 1986. After it acquired Ozark Airlines last year, TWA discontinued about 40 flights out of St. Louis—reducing service to a number of cities where they both had competed.

Regulatory Backlash?

There also are increasing signs of a regulatory backlash against the industry. In Washington, D.C., several legislators have proposed bills that would subject airlines to new restrictions. Congress also has encouraged a tougher stand on airline mergers.

"Deregulation was supposed to create competition," says Democratic Senator Wendell H.

Ford of Kentucky. Instead, he adds, the traveling public is now "looking down a gun barrel."

* * * * *

Some airline analysts . . . believe that with competition dwindling at airports across the United States, travelers can now expect steady increases in air fares for the next four to five years—particularly because new carriers haven't stepped in to fill the void left by the disappearance of such cut rate carriers as People Express and Frontier Airlines.

* * * * *

Shrinking Competition

Airport	Airline	Percent of Total Passengers Handled*
Denver	Continental and United combined	88%
St. Louis	TWA	82
Pittsburgh	USAir	80
Memphis, Tenn.	Northwest	79
Minneapolis	Northwest	76
Houston	Continental	68
Detroit	Northwest	64

*Latest available figure.

Source: Local airport authorities.

Airlines assert that the dominance of some carriers at certain cities doesn't give a true picture of industry competition, which they say remains intense because of rivalries between hubs for through traffic. Buttressing their argument, airline executives say that fares remain as much as 28 percent lower than they were before deregulation.

Overall, passengers have more options today because the big carriers have expanded "to go almost everywhere," says W. Thomas Lagow, the senior vice president of marketing planning at Northwest Airlines. And in some cases, bigger carriers have the resources to stage bigger wars from which travelers can benefit. Says Philip J. Bakes, the president and chief executive of the Eastern Airlines unit of Texas Air Corp.: "In our industry's case, an even more powerful oligopoly is even more competitive."

But skeptics argue that the trends are nevertheless ominous for bargain hunters. For one thing, it is harder than it was a few years ago for entrepreneurs to raise the money needed to launch the small, upstart carriers that help keep the majors' prices down.

"Our investors got scared off," says Daniel H. Kolber, the former executive vice president of Air Atlanta, which filed in April for protection from creditors under Chapter 11 of the federal bankruptcy laws. New airlines today have to start off much bigger in order to serve enough cities with sufficient frequency to take away business from the entrenched airlines. "Nowadays, you need a hub system to make it," Mr. Kolber says. "We couldn't afford the planes and connections."

Carriers are also getting more ingenious about keeping the upstarts out. Last year, United Airlines dealt a blow to Presidential Airways when United wouldn't allow the smaller airline to connect its gates with the United terminal at Washington's Dulles International Airport.

Local Influence

By dominating a single airport, an airline also can use its local influence to cut back on competition. For instance, local authorities don't have much power to open up gate space because gates are usually leased for long terms.

The airlines that hold these leases have a lot to say about construction inside the airport and who benefits from it. In Denver, United has agreed to pay off bonds valued at about $55 million that were issued for improvements to the B concourse. "I don't intend to let competitors use [the concourse]," says Anthony Chaitin, United senior vice president of corporate services.

A hub airline also can stymie an airport's efforts to build gates for competitors. Pittsburgh wants to erect a $503 million terminal that would double gate space and ease congestion. But USAir, which currently operates 33 of the airport's 52 gates, has dragged its feet on signing the lease agreements needed to finance the new airport.

"Airport construction is a Catch-22," says Lawrence F. Cunningham, a University of Colorado associate professor of transportation marketing. "The airport authority is in the unenviable position of negotiating with the dominant airline to bring in new competition."

Partly as a result, gate space has become tight all over. According to Airport Operators Council International, an industry trade group, 10 to 12 of the nation's 26 largest airports would have "severe difficulty" finding gates for new airlines. "What good is a car if you can't find a parking spot?" asks Mr. Kolber, the former executive vice president of Air Atlanta.

Unused Gates

In Birmingham, Alabama, authorities complain that some gates sit unused because airlines that fly to the city won't let other carriers have them. A new gate would cost $2 million to build, estimates James A. Brough, the executive director of the Birmingham airport authority.

Studies show that the major airlines tend not to expand aggressively at an airport once someone else has established a hub there. For example, Eastern Airlines has let its St. Louis flights dwindle as it puts more planes into its Kansas City hub.

That has left Southwest Airlines as TWA's biggest competition in St. Louis. Southwest's two gates are at the far end of the longest concourse at the airport. Between them and the main terminal is a half-mile stretch of red and gray TWA gates. "That does look dark," says Peter McGlade, the director of Southwest scheduling. "One of the dangers of deregulation is the ability of someone to dominate a market."

And no one seems in a position to make a big run at TWA's monopoly routes. The Justice Department calculates that a carrier would need about 12 contiguous gates at St. Louis in order to build a hub for the cities that Ozark and TWA both used to serve. The gates that TWA doesn't control are scattered among too many carriers to do that easily.

* * * * *

Source: *The Wall Street Journal*, July 20, 1987, pp. 1, 6. Reprinted by permission of *The Wall Street Journal*, © Dow Jones & Company, Inc. 1987. ALL RIGHTS RESERVED.

QUESTIONS, PARTS ONE AND TWO

1. A federal district court found IBM guilty of unlawful monopolization in a portion of the computer industry. IBM manufactured and distributed both central processing units (CPUs) and various peripheral devices (PDs), including magnetic tape drives and printers. Telex manufactured PDs compatible with IBM's CPUs, but not with the CPUs of other manufacturers. It was established at trial that relatively inexpensive interfaces could be used to make Telex PDs compatible with the CPUs of manufacturers other than IBM, and at a relatively modest cost Telex could produce PDs compatible with CPUs other than those of IBM. The district court concluded that the relevant product market was PDs compatible with IBM CPUs and that IBM controlled at least 80 percent of that market. Given IBM's monopoly power, the district court also found IBM guilty of predatory behavior. For example, in response to competition from Telex and others, IBM lowered its leasing fees for PDs and offered more desirable leasing terms. Similarly, IBM reduced the sales prices of its PDs. In setting those prices, IBM considered the ability or inability of its competitors to respond to those prices. At the reduced prices, IBM achieved a 20 percent profit margin and increased its market share.

    Was the district court correct? Explain. See *Telex Corporation* v. *IBM Corporation* (10th Cir. 1975) 510 F.2d 894, cert. denied, 423 U.S. 802 (1975).

2. It is frequently argued that monopolies must be opposed because a lack of competition discourages efficiency and innovation. Argue that monopolies may actually *encourage* innovation.

3. Even if monopolies do not discourage invention, we have firm economic grounds for opposing monopolies. Explain.

4. Historically, perhaps the most important interpretation of the Sherman Act's proscription of monopolization was Judge Learned Hand's opinion in the aforementioned *Alcoa* case. After finding that Alcoa controlled 90 percent of the aluminum ingot market, Hand had to determine whether Alcoa possessed a general intent to monopolize. Hand concluded that Alcoa's market dominance could have resulted only from a "persistent determination" to maintain control [148 F.2d 416, 431 (1945)].

> It was not inevitable that it should always anticipate increases in the demand for ingots and be prepared to supply them. Nothing compelled it to keep doubling and redoubling its capacity before others entered the field. It insists that it never excluded competitors; but we can think of no more effective exclusion than progressively to embrace each new opportunity as it opened, and to face every newcomer with new capacity already geared into a great organization.

Comment on Judge Hand's remarks.

5. Is a monopolist who makes only a "fair" profit in violation of the law? Explain.

6. May a monopolist lawfully increase its market share, assuming it does so without recourse to predatory or exclusionary tactics? Explain. Should it be able to do so? Explain.

7. The U.S. government sued Du Pont, claiming a monopolization of the cellophane market. Du Pont produced almost 75 percent of the cellophane sold in the United States. Cellophane constituted less than 20 percent of the "flexible packaging materials" market. The lower court found "[g]reat sensitivity of customers in the flexible packaging markets to price or quality changes."

What is the relevant product market? Who wins the case? Explain. See *United States* v. *E.I. du Pont de Nemours & Co.*, 351 U.S. 377 (1956).

8. The National Football League was organized in 1920. During the 1960 season it had 14 teams located in 13 cities [Chicago (two teams), Cleveland, New York, Philadelphia, Pittsburgh, Washington, Baltimore, Detroit, Los Angeles, San Francisco, Green Bay, Dallas, and Minneapolis]. The rival American Football League commenced play in 1960 with eight teams in eight cities (Boston, Buffalo, Houston, New York, Dallas, Denver, Los Angeles, and Oakland).

In its first season, the AFL was successful in competing for outstanding players and in acquiring a desirable television contract. "[R]epresentatives of the American League declared that the League's success was unprecedented." Nevertheless, the AFL sued the NFL, claiming monopolization. A central issue in the case was that of the geographic market. The AFL characterized the market as those 17 cities either having an NFL franchise or seriously considered for a franchise. The NFL saw the market as nationwide.

Define the geographic market in this case. Explain. See *American Football League* v. *National Football League,* 323 F.2d 124 (4th Cir. 1963).

9. In the *Aspen* case, the Supreme Court said, "Aspen Skiing Company (Ski Co.) had monopolized the market for downhill skiing services in Aspen, Colorado." That being the case, why doesn't the government challenge Aspen Skiing Company's market dominance?

10. Kodak dominated the American market for provision of amateur photographic films, cameras, and film-processing services. Berkey was a much smaller, but still significant, competitor in that market. In some markets Kodak served as Berkey's supplier. In the "amateur conventional still camera" market (consisting primarily of 110 and 126 instant-loading cameras), Kodak's share of the sales volume between 1954 and 1973 ranged from 64 to 90 percent. Kodak invented both the "126" and "110" cameras. The introduction of the 110 "Pocket Instamatic" and the companion Kodacolor II film in 1972 resulted in a dramatic Kodak camera sales increase of from 6.2 million units in 1971 to 8.2 million in 1972. Rivals were unable to bring competitive units into the market until nearly one year later. Even then, Kodak retained a strong lead. Thereafter, Berkey filed suit, claiming that the introduction of the 110 system was an illegal monopolization of the camera market. The essence of the Berkey argument was as follows:

> Kodak, a film and camera monopolist, was in a position to set industry standards. Rivals could not compete effectively without offering products similar to Kodak's. Moreover, Kodak persistently refused to make film available for most formats other than those in which it made cameras. Since cameras are worthless without film, the policy effectively prevented other manufacturers from introducing cameras in new formats. Because of its dominant position astride two markets, and by use of its film monopoly to distort the camera market, Kodak forfeited its own right to reap profits from such innovations without providing its rivals with sufficient advance information to enable them to enter the market with copies of the new product on the day of Kodak's introduction.

On appeal, the Court noted "little doubt that . . . Kodak had monopoly power in cameras," and the Court observed that Kodak had sometimes "predisclosed" its innovations to its rivals, and sometimes it had not done so.

Was Kodak under a legal duty to predisclose innovations to rivals? What defense would you offer to counter Berkey's monopolization claim? Decide the case, and explain the reasons for your decision. See *Berkey Photo, Inc.* v. *Eastman Kodak Company,* 603 F.2d 263 (2d Cir. 1979). Cert. denied, 444 U.S. 1093 (1980).

Part Three—Mergers

PREFACE: GETTY/PENNZOIL/TEXACO

Texaco's 1984 acquisition of Getty Oil for $10.1 billion was the second-largest and certainly the most notorious U.S. merger in history. The merger earned its notoriety not for its colossal scale but because the Pennzoil Company believed it had acquired Getty Oil a few days prior to the Texaco acquisition.

On January 3, 1984, the board of directors of Getty Oil approved "in principle" a merger with Pennzoil at $112.50 a share. On January 5, while the final papers for the deal were in preparation, Texaco, Inc., met with Gordon Getty, who agreed to sell Getty Oil Company to Texaco for $128 a share. In return, Texaco agreed to insure Getty Oil's board of directors against any damages they might incur as a result of any litigation brought by Pennzoil or others. On February 8,1985, Pennzoil filed a $15 billion breach-of-contract lawsuit against Texaco in a Houston, Texas, state court. The legal dispute between the two companies focused on the question of whether the January 4 agreement in principle between Getty and Pennzoil constituted a contract. Pennzoil claimed unethical tactics were used to persuade Getty to back out of the deal. Texaco, on the other hand, argued that Pennzoil and Getty never had a formal agreement when Texaco made its offer. On November 19, 1985, the Texas jury, all unacquainted with corporate law and finance, decided that Texaco purposely and wrongly interfered in the Pennzoil–Getty merger and ordered Texaco to pay Pennzoil $10.53 billion in damages, the largest award in history. Texaco appealed the decision through the Texas state system to the Texas Supreme Court. Texaco lost at each level, although the award was reduced by some $2 billion.

Meanwhile the case took on even greater complexity and financial immediacy when it became apparent that Texas law required the loser at the trial level, Texaco, to post a $12 billion bond in order to appeal the decision. Texaco, which at the time had a net worth of some $13.5 billion, argued that posting the huge bond would force it into bankruptcy. Therefore, Texaco pursued a series of appeals of the bond issue through the federal courts even as the underlying contracts issue was being appealed in the Texas state courts. Texaco won its bond litigation at the district and court of appeals levels, but on April 6, 1987, the U.S. Supreme Court dissolved the lower court's order protecting Texaco from the bond requirement. Then, on April 12, 1987, Texaco filed for Chapter 11 bankruptcy protection (see Chapter 13).

On December 19, 1987, Texaco and Pennzoil settled their battle when Texaco agreed to pay $3 billion to Pennzoil. Then on March 23, 1988,

Bankruptcy Judge Howard Schwartzberg approved Texaco's reorganization plan which, in turn, permitted the company to emerge from bankruptcy. The heart of the plan was the payment of some $5.5 billion in debts, including the $3 billion to Pennzoil. The plan was approved by 96 percent of the shareholders. However, "corporate raider" Carl Icahn, who held nearly 15 percent of the Texaco stock, was not fully satisfied. Reportedly, Icahn was disturbed that the reorganization plan released Texaco's officers and directors from liability for the Pennzoil episode. Texaco also announced its intention to sell $5 billion worth of assets in an effort to enhance profitability while increasing shareholder value. Texaco was expected to decrease its refining and marketing operations while giving more attention to exploration and production.

During the spring and early summer of 1988, Icahn mounted an attack of sorts on Texaco by attempting to take control of five seats on the Texaco board, with the apparent expectation of selling the company. Texaco resisted, and, as the votes were being tabulated, Icahn conceded that he had lost his proxy fight for the five seats. Icahn had indicated he would sell his Texaco shares if he lost the battle, but other options were open to him. At this writing in mid-1988, the $3 billion settlement has been paid, but the fallout from this titanic struggle is not over.[17]

INTRODUCTION

Principal legislation: Sherman Act, Section 1, and Clayton Act, Section 7:

> That no person engaged in commerce or in any activity affecting commerce, shall acquire, directly or indirectly, the whole or any part of the stock or other share capital and no person subject to the jurisdiction of the Federal Trade Commission shall acquire the whole or any part of the assets of another person engaged also in commerce or in any activity affecting commerce, where in any line of commerce or in any activity affecting commerce in any section of the country, the effect of such acquisition may be substantially to lessen competition, or to tend to create a monopoly.
>
> No person shall acquire, directly or indirectly, the whole or any part of the stock or other share capital and no person subject to the jurisdiction of the Federal Trade Commission shall acquire the whole or any part of the assets of one or more persons engaged in commerce or in any activity affecting commerce, where in any line of commerce or in any activity affecting commerce in any section of the country, the effect of such acquisition, of such stocks or assets, or of the use of such stock by the voting or granting of proxies or otherwise, may be substantially to lessen competition, or to tend to create a monopoly.

Technically, a merger involves the union of two or more enterprises wherein the property of all is transferred to the one remaining firm. However, antitrust law embraces all those situations wherein previously independent business entities are united—whether by acquisition of stock, purchase of physical assets, creation of holding companies, consolidation, or merger.

Of course, the big news in mergers in recent years has been the increasing controversy over a subset of acquisitions labeled *takeovers,* particularly hostile takeovers. To the critics, the economy and the individual welfare of managers, employees, and communities are threatened by takeover attacks from so-called corporate raiders, such as the now-famous T. Boone Pickens. As a result, managers and state governments have mounted all manner of corporate and legislative defensive tactics (shark repellents, greenmail, poison pills, etc.) to protect companies that do not desire acquisition. But the raiders and their admirers see their work as an effort to maximize market efficiency, shake up ineffective management in the acquired firms, and provide the shareholders with the maximum return on their investments. (Takeovers are also discussed in Chapter 8.)

Mergers fall, somewhat awkwardly, into three categories. Horizontal mergers are those where the firms were in direct competition and occupied the same product and geographic markets. A merger of two vodka producers in the same geographic market would clearly fall in the horizontal category. Would the merger of a vodka producer and a gin producer constitute a horizontal merger? Vertical mergers are those involving two or more firms at different levels of the same channel of distribution, such as a furniture manufacturer and a fabric supplier. Conglomerate mergers involve firms dealing in unrelated products. Thus the conglomerate category embraces all mergers that are neither horizontal nor vertical. An example of such a merger would be the acquisition of a pet food manufacturer by a book publisher. Identification of the type of merger being dealt with is essential because, as will be seen, the analysis differs for each.

ENFORCEMENT

Because a challenged merger would allegedly involve either an unlawful monopoly or another restraint of trade, the Sherman Act can be used as the necessary legislative vehicle. However, remember that Sherman requires a showing of the *existence* of anticompetitive conditions, while Clayton requires only a showing of a *reasonable probability* of lessening competition or a *tendency* toward monopoly. However, because Clayton has no criminal provision, the government must rely on Sherman in those cases where a criminal suit is warranted.

Clayton 7 is enforced by the government via the Justice Department and the FTC, as well as by companies and individuals. Those challenging mergers often seek injunctions either to stop the merger or to secure relief after the consumption of a merger. Under the FTC's premerger notification rules, mergers must be reported to the FTC and the Justice Department if the mergers involve purchases of $15 million or more and meet several other criteria. Either agency may then choose to challenge the merger. To provide warning about likely challenges, both the FTC and the Justice Department have issued merger guidelines. The Justice Department guidelines, first issued in 1965, were revised in 1982 and 1984 to improve the technical evaluation of mergers and, presumably, to reflect the Reagan administration's rather sanguine view of the dangers of mergers. Justice Department policy in the 1980s has not regarded most vertical and conglomerate mergers as threatening to competition. Therefore, the guidelines focus on horizontal mergers.

The heart of the guidelines lies in determining market share and in identifying any increase in market concentration arising from the horizontal merger. The degree of market concentration is measured by use of the Herfindahl-Hirschman Index (HHI). Notwithstanding the forbidding title, the index is computed quite easily. The market share of each firm in a market is squared and the results are summed. Thus, if five companies each had 20 percent of a market, the index for that market would be 2,000. The HHI is useful because it measures both concentration and dispersion of market share between big and small firms. If 10 firms each have 10 percent of the market, the resulting HHI is 1,000. The larger the HHI, the more concentrated the market. A merger is unlikely to be challenged if the HHI is 1,000 or less because that market is not considered concentrated. If the HHI is greater than 1,800, the market is considered highly concentrated. If the merger within that market produces an HHI increase of 50 points or more the government will probably challenge the merger. In the 1,000–1,800 range the government will "more likely than not" challenge a merger if it increases the HHI by 100 points or more. To illustrate, consider again a market composed of five companies, each with 20 percent of the market. If two of them merge, the HHI would rise from 2,000 to 2,800, and the merger presumably would be challenged.

While the HHI is perhaps the central component of the guidelines, many other factors will be influential. Among others, ease of entry, foreign competition, the presence of a failing firm, the premerger conduct of the firms, and efficiencies produced by the merger may be considered.

MERGER DATA

Before turning to the more technical dimensions of merger analysis, it is important to acquire some understanding of the business conditions within which merger law operates. As discussed in Chapter 1, the law, to be interesting and understood, must be placed in the context in which it was conceived. The United States has recently been in the midst of what has been labeled, not so charitably, a merger mania. Mergers seem to build in waves of sorts, the most pronounced of which embraced the 1955–69 period. From 1955 to 1959 mergers averaged 1,162 per year, and by the period 1967–69 that annual average reached 3,605. The early and mid-70s witnessed moderated—but still high—merger totals: 1972 (2,839 acquisitions), 1973 (2,359), 1974 (1,474), 1975 (1,047), 1976 (1,171). According to W. T. Grimm & Co. reports, 1981 saw 2,395 mergers with a dollar value of $82.6 billion, which was nearly double the 1980 record total of $44.3 billion (1,889 acquisitions).[18] But those figures pale beside the 1986 total of $176.6 billion (over 3,300 deals).[19] Although these 1986 figures represented a slight decline from 1985 in terms of total dollar volume, a general restructuring of the economy appeared to be under way. That condition—in conjunction with deregulation, a perceived federal reluctance to interfere, and a combination of some undervalued companies with cash-rich companies—seemed to be producing a continuing merger boom. Indeed, in the late 1980s, mergers and acquisitions have become a standard business strategy. International competition, the lure of easy money, and the opportunity to remove arguably ineffective management are likely to propel a continuation of the present takeover trend.

However, the public is not comfortable with these conditions. A 1987 Louis Harris Poll asking whether mergers have been good for America revealed that 16 percent of the 1,250 adults surveyed nationwide approved of the "massive wave of mergers and acquisitions sweeping this country," while 45 percent thought them bad and 34 percent felt they had not made much difference.[20]

At this point the skeptical reader may be politely muttering: "So what?" The fact that we are experiencing another merger boom is not in and of itself threatening, but the further industrial concentration that appears to be accompanying those mergers may, indeed, be cause for concern. For example, of the 500 firms appearing in the 1955 Fortune 500 industrial listing, 185 had been absorbed by merger as of the close of 1979.

The concern is that further concentration will lead to an expansion of the problems outlined in Chapter 3. Political and economic power will reside in fewer hands. Small firms will fail in greater numbers, and barriers to market entry by small firms will increase. Lives will be disrupted by plant closings, changes in management, and relocations. Absentee owners, ignorant of local needs, will alter community lifestyles. Nevertheless, even the most ardent advocate of firmer merger controls will concede the desirability of some mergers. Some of the potential virtues of mergers are:

1. Mergers permit the replacement of inefficient management. Similarly, the threat of replacement disciplines managers to achieve greater efficiency.
2. Mergers may permit stronger competition with formerly larger rivals.

3. Mergers may improve credit access.
4. Mergers may produce efficiencies and economies of scale.
5. Mergers frequently offer a pool of liquid assets for use in expansion.
6. Very often mergers offer tax advantages to at least one of the participants.
7. Growth by merger is often less expensive than internal growth.
8. Mergers help to satisfy the personal ambitions and needs of management.

MERGERS IN PRACTICE

Most of us have great difficulty relating to the machinations of mammoth enterprises and their billion-dollar deals. Several particularly robust mergers in recent years have brought the merger "game" closer to the public eye. In 1984 the federal government approved the largest mergers in U.S. history. Standard Oil of California purchased Gulf Oil for $13.2 billion, and, as explained above, Texaco acquired Getty Oil for $10.1 billion. Between 1981 and 1984, five of America's largest oil firms (Gulf, Getty, Conoco, Marathon, and Cities Service) were gobbled up by mergers. In 1981 the biggest takeover struggle in corporate history to that date ended as Du Pont (15th in the 1980 Fortune 500, according to sales) acquired Conoco (ranked 14th) in a deal valued at $7.4 billion.

The articles that follow put a bit of flesh on the sometimes arid terrain of merger law. The first reveals some of the complexities of engineering a multibillion-dollar transaction, while the second reminds us of the human dimension of corporate high finance.

THE GENERAL ELECTRIC–RCA MERGER: CRAFTING A MEGADEAL

Geraldine Fabrikant

New York—It took just 34 days for the General Electric Co. and the RCA Corp. to forge their multibillion-dollar merger.

Negotiations began late on the pleasant fall afternoon of Friday, November 8, [1985—Author] with a cocktail meeting at the Upper East Side apartment of Felix Rohatyn. Rohatyn, a partner with RCA's investment banking firm, Lazard Freres & Co., had been asked by the chairman of GE, John F. Welch, Jr., to introduce him to the chairman of RCA, Thornton F. Bradshaw.

That introduction was to lead to the deal. . . . With their boards' approval, the two companies disclosed the biggest non-oil merger in U.S. history. GE, the broad-based electronics and defense company, will pay $6.28 billion for RCA, owner of the NBC broadcast network and a leader itself in defense and consumer electronics. The agreement brings stockholders $66.50 a share for the company's 94.4 million shares outstanding.

The news followed six days of frantic, frequently round-the-clock discussions, at GE's law firm, Fried, Frank, Harris, Shriver & Jacobson, right across the street from the South Ferry in the Wall Street area; at GE's headquarters in Fairfield, Connecticut; and at GE's Waldorf Towers apartment, where Welch and Bradshaw met several times.

All weekend, cars ferried documents from Fried, Frank's offices to GE's Connecticut headquarters as lawyers and executives struggled to structure the deal. . . .

The intention was to keep their talks secret. But . . . the word was out that something was up at RCA. . . . Wall Street went wild. RCA's stock rose 10.375 points to reach $63.50 by the close of trading. Volume in RCA totaled a remarkable 5.1 million shares. Late that night, after both boards met, a formal release verified what had been rumored that day.

For Welch, the deal moves GE closer to the structure he has envisioned and that Welch has frequently described to Wall Street bankers and analysts. The tough, aggressive 50-year-old chairman, who took over at GE in 1981, has consistently said he wants to increase GE's investments in the fast-growing services and technology segment of the economy and decrease its exposure to more industrial businesses.

* * * * *

For RCA, the pending merger accomplishes a number of the aims set forth by Bradshaw since he became chairman there, also in 1981. "It gives us enormous amounts of capital, effort, and talent," Bradshaw said Thursday. "It gives us the financial capacity to do what we have to do."

The friendly agreement also protects RCA against the bitter takeover battles that have recently torn apart a host of American companies.

Declaring that "we are safe as a hedgehog," Bradshaw rejected the notion that takeover fears were a motivating factor.

Like most executives, however, he is keenly aware of the forced restructuring that took place at CBS as a result of Ted Turner's bid for that network. And he did say, "We did not want to see the company broken up willy nilly."

One financial expert who has followed RCA for years believes that, "Bradshaw has always been convinced that RCA either had to buy or sell—but that it had to merge big."

* * * * *

As with many deals that come together in the hard-charging Wall Street community, it actually all started at a routine breakfast earlier this fall.

During this particular breakfast Welch mentioned to Rohatyn, with whom he often shares coffee and orange juice, that he wanted to meet Bradshaw.

Rohatyn called Bradshaw, and arranged the November 8 meeting. "The discussions were quite general," Bradshaw said of that first meeting. "It was a very low-key feeling," Bradshaw said.

But GE was galvanized.

Welch immediately put a team of four executives on the case. "We tore the numbers apart," he said. "We knew everything about that company by the time we were through."

By shortly before Thanksgiving, Welch was convinced he wanted the company. Its nationwide network, the National Broadcasting Co., had never been in better health; its television stations were doing very well, and its defense business seemed compatible with GE's.

Welch decided that he and several of his key executives should think the deal over during Thanksgiving weekend. He did his thinking on a brief trip to West Palm Beach with his family.

The following week, he put in a call to Rohatyn, who, in turn, called Bradshaw. A meeting was arranged for Thursday night, December 5.

Bradshaw recalled that Welch came by to see him that night at the Dorset Hotel in midtown Manhattan. . . . "We had a conversation that I could only construe as an offer," Bradshaw said Thursday.

Meanwhile Bradshaw reached Robert Frederick, RCA's president and chief executive, at 6:30 A.M. the next morning in Los Angeles, where he had gone for business meetings. Frederick immediately canceled his plans to stay the weekend and returned to New York to begin a series of meetings with RCA's lawyers and bankers.

Bradshaw also began contacting board members to plan a Sunday afternoon meeting at the law office of Wachtel, Lipton, Rosen & Katz. Martin Lipton, the firm's senior partner, has been advising RCA on takeover issues. "There was the usual concern that RCA was losing its independence," said one source familiar with RCA. "But the board was very thorough and very fair." Ultimately both boards voted unanimously for the deal.

Meanwhile talks among Welch, Frederick, and Bradshaw continued on Monday and Tuesday at GE's Waldorf Towers apartment.

According to sources familiar with the negotiations, there was some wrangling over price. Initially, GE offered about $61 a share, but RCA held out for more.

Another key issue was how GE would protect itself, and its offer, if a second bidder surfaced with a higher offer.

The sources said GE wanted to protect itself with what is known in the takeover game as the "Crown Jewel" arrangement involving two of RCA's five television stations—those in New York and Los Angeles. Guaranteeing their sale to GE would destroy much of the value of RCA to another bidder. However, RCA argued that such an agreement would seriously affect the value of the television network.

"It would have been imprudent to lock up the stations, because they are an integral part of a network system," Robert Frederick, president of RCA recalled. . . . Instead the companies agreed on what is known as a "stock lock up." That is: GE has an option to buy 28 million shares of RCA stock at $53 a share.

These issues were resolved during meetings Monday and Tuesday at the Waldorf Towers apartment, as well as at various lawyers' offices.

Lawyers at Fried, Frank, including Arthur Fleisher, a leading takeover lawyer, worked all Tuesday night on the final papers. About 2 A.M., Lipton, the takeover specialist and partner at Wachtel, Lipton joined the Fried, Frank contingent and discussions continued for another several hours. Finally the papers were complete and the lawyers went home to shower and change.

By Wednesday night the boards had approved the deal. At GE, there was euphoria. "We've looked at 3,000 companies in the past five years," said Larry Bossidy, a top executive at GE. "But this one is a blockbuster."

Source: Reprinted in the *Des Moines Register,* December 15, 1985, p. 11F, from "The General Electric—RCA Merger: Forging a Megadeal," *The New York Times,* December 13, 1985. Copyright © 1985 by The New York Times Company. Reprinted by permission.

THE TRAUMA IN A TAKEOVER

Robert E. Tomasson

Stamford, Conn., January 8—As the United States Steel Corporation went about completing its acquisition of the Marathon Oil Company, Marathon's 16,000 employees today began receiving assurances that they need not fear any changes that the new order might bring.

"Marathon will continue to operate and manage the corporate assets utilizing all of the personnel and facilities now in place around the world" was the message sent out from Marathon's headquarters in Findlay, Ohio.

It is in the nature of corporate takeovers, however, that all such guarantees of the status quo tend to be short-lived. Indeed, the recent experiences of three other major corporate acquisitions—Conoco, Kennecott, and Texasgulf—show how profoundly the changes that follow takeovers can affect the lives of thousands of employees, from board chairmen to receptionists and laborers.

Some may be dismissed, others transferred; some careers will be cut short while others will climb. Some will find excitement in being taken over by a stronger corporate entity. For others, there will be despair as their business world is turned upside down.

The acquisitions of Conoco, Kennecott, and Texasgulf, all with headquarters in Stamford, offer some striking contrasts in the nature of takeovers of . . . giant natural resource corporations.

At all three companies, the first reaction was apprehension if not dread, employees said. . . .

"I know that this situation is difficult for employees and their families," said Thomas D. Barrow, the chairman of Kennecott who has since been named a vice chairman of the parent Sohio.

"They walk out that door without even saying goodbye," said a receptionist outside the 15th-floor executive offices, referring to the exodus of headquarters staff over the past several weeks. . . .

Major Staff Changes

Of the 50 employees of the 200-member headquarters staff who have left thus far, 46 have been dismissed, have quit, or have retired. Four others have been taken by Sohio.

About 100 of the remaining staff personnel will be dismissed, will retire, or will resign, according to Eric Nielsen, vice president in charge of personnel. If Kennecott had not been purchased, Mr. Barrow said, "we'd be in very serious financial shape today."

"Yes, it's hard on the headquarters staff, but there are the 38,000 other Kennecott workers out there and for them it has been a very sound move," he added.

What Mr. Barrow called the "fairly tough-minded" position affecting the Kennecott headquarters staff was in distinct contrast to the corporate paternalism at Texasgulf, which was taken over by the French government-controlled oil giant, Société Nationale Elf Aquitaine last June.

For Texasgulf's chairman, Richard D. Mollison, the takeover was the second stunning event within months of what was to have been the last year of his career.

Expecting to retire as vice chairman of the company he had been with since 1947, Mr. Mollison was named to replace Charles F. Fogerty, the company's chairman, who was killed with five other top Texasgulf officers in a Westchester County plane crash in February 1981.

Agreeing to stay on until his 65th birthday last June, Mr. Mollison was presented with the fait accompli of the French takeover. He said he had neither participated in nor been informed about the takeover.

For Texasgulf officials, however, initial apprehension gave way to reassurances as the French company moved to maintain the existing corporate leadership. Mr. Mollison and 22 other top executives were all offered five-year contracts and not one of the more than 200 persons on the office staff has been shifted because of the takeover.

Other Employees Shifted

But while the Texasgulf headquarters staff remained intact, the number of workers in company mines and plants throughout North America has dropped to 3,850 from the pre-takeover force of 6,480. Most were shifted to the Canada Development Corporation, which had been Texasgulf's largest shareholder and which had engineered the sale of the company in secret to Elf Aquitaine.

One jarring element that confronted employees at Texasgulf was the requirement to cash in their stock in the company as it could not be exchanged for stock of the new parent.

Since Elf Aquitaine is not traded in this country, many executives of Texasgulf found they were at a noticeable tax disadvantage as the stock was cashed in all at once.

A hundred yards or so from the fortress-like Texasgulf building, complete with moat, stands the corporate headquarters of Conoco, object of the largest corporate takeover ever in this country, where the 200-member headquarters staff oversees 41,000 employees worldwide.

"Business as Usual"

While there have been distinct changes at Kennecott, which sought merger, and at Texasgulf, which did not, the atmosphere at Conoco, after an initial wave of anxiety following its acquisition by Du Pont last August, has returned to what some employees call "business as usual."

"For a corporation with combined 1980 sales of over $30 billion, there is little overlap in either operations or business lines" with the new parent, said C. S. Nicandros, a Conoco group executive vice president.

To Ralph E. Bailey, Conoco's chairman and chief executive officer, "the merger creates a synergistic partnership, a company that is even stronger than the sum of its parts."

Source: *The New York Times,* January 9, 1982, pp. 21 and 31. Copyright © 1982 by The New York Times Company, Reprinted by permission.

HORIZONTAL AND VERTICAL MERGERS

Horizontal

The government's concern with horizontal mergers rests on the presumed decline in competition and increase in market concentration that accompanies the acquisition by one firm of another firm in the same market. The resulting firm raises concerns similar to those in a monopoly situation, and, indeed, the market analysis to be applied to horizontal mergers is very similar to that previously discussed in the monopoly section. Essentially, we must define the product and geographic markets and then apply the Clayton Act, Section 7 test; that is, some unspecified probability of substantially lessening competition or tending to create a monopoly.

Vertical

A *vertical merger* involves an alliance between a supplier and a purchaser. The primary threat thus arising is that of market foreclosure. As illustrated in the accompanying diagram, a vertical merger may deny a source of supply to a purchaser or an outlet for sale to a seller, which might then threaten competition so as to violate the Clayton Act.

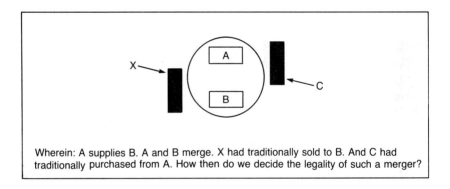

Wherein: A supplies B. A and B merge. X had traditionally sold to B. And C had traditionally purchased from A. How then do we decide the legality of such a merger?

Some other economic considerations may influence the legality of a vertical merger.

1. *Deep pockets.* The merger may provide the merged firm with financial advantages that smaller rivals could not match.
2. *Price squeeze.* In the diagram, the newly merged AB may be able to arbitrarily raise prices of raw materials to C while temporarily depressing the price of its finished goods. The result may, of course, severely pinch C.
3. *Barriers to entry.* A market composed of integrated—and thus often larger—firms would pose a more formidable hurdle in terms of capital requirements and courage than one of many small suppliers and purchasers.

The *Brown Shoe* case illustrates the Court's early efforts to interpret Congress' intent in passing the amended Clayton Act. Note that *Brown* embraces both horizontal and vertical dimensions.

BROWN SHOE CO. V. UNITED STATES
370 U.S. 294 (1961)

Chief Justice Warren

This suit was initiated in November 1955 when the Government filed a civil action in the United States District Court for the Eastern District of Missouri alleging that a contemplated merger between the G. R. Kinney Company, Inc. (Kinney), and the Brown Shoe Company, Inc. (Brown), through an exchange of Kinney for Brown stock, would violate Sec. 7 of the Clayton Act. . . .

* * * * *

In the District Court, the Government contended that the effect of the merger of Brown—the third largest seller of shoes by dollar volume in the United States, a leading manufacturer of men's, women's, and children's shoes, and a retailer with over 1,230 owned, operated or controlled retail outlets—and Kinney—the eighth largest company, by dollar volume, among those primarily engaged in selling shoes, itself a large manufacturer of shoes, and a retailer with over 350 retail outlets—"may be substantially to lessen competition or to tend to create a monopoly."

* * * * *

The Industry

The District Court found that although domestic shoe production was scattered among a large number of manufacturers, a small number of large companies occupied a commanding position. Thus, while the 24 largest manufacturers produced about 35 percent of the Nation's shoes, the top 4—International, Endicott-Johnson, Brown (including Kinney), and General Shoe—alone produced approximately 23 percent of the Nation's shoes or 65 percent of the production of the top 24.

In 1955, domestic production of nonrubber shoes was 509.2 million pairs, of which about 103.6 million pairs were men's shoes, about 271 million pairs were women's shoes, and about 134.6 million pairs were children's shoes. The District Court found that men's, women's, and children's shoes are normally produced in separate factories.

The public buys these shoes through about 70,000 retail outlets, only 22,000 of which, however, derive 50 percent or more of their gross receipts from the sale of shoes and are classified as "shoe stores" by the Census Bureau. These 22,000 shoe stores were found generally to sell (1) men's shoes only, (2) women's shoes only, (3) women's and children's shoes, or (4) men's, women's, and children's shoes.

The District Court found a "definite trend" among shoe manufacturers to acquire retail outlets. For example, International Shoe Company had no retail outlets in 1945, but by 1956 had acquired 130; General Shoe Company had only 80 retail outlets in 1945 but had 526 by 1956. . . . Brown, itself, with no retail outlets of its own prior to 1951, had acquired 845 such outlets by 1956. Moreover, between 1950 and 1956 nine independent shoe store chains, operating 1,114 retail shoe stores, were found to have become subsidiaries of these large firms and to have ceased their independent operations.

And once the manufacturers acquired retail outlets, the District Court found there was a "definite trend" for the parent-manufacturers to supply an ever increasing percentage of the retail outlets' needs, thereby foreclosing other manufacturers from effectively competing for the retail accounts. Manufacturer-dominated stores were found to be "drying up" the available outlets for independent producers.

Another "definite trend" found to exist in the shoe industry was a decrease in the number of plants manufacturing shoes. And there appears to have been a concomitant decrease in the number of firms manufacturing shoes. In 1947, there were 1,077 independent manufacturers of shoes, but by 1954 their number had decreased about 10 percent to 970.

Brown Shoe

Brown Shoe was found not only to have been a participant, but also a moving factor, in these industry trends. Although Brown had experimented several times with operating its own retail outlets, by 1945 it had disposed of them all. However, in 1951, Brown again began to seek retail outlets by acquiring the Nation's largest operator of leased shoe departments, Wohl Shoe Company (Wohl), which operated 250 shoe departments in department stores throughout the United States. Between 1952 and 1955 Brown made a number of smaller acquisitions. . . .

The acquisition of these corporations was found to lead to increased sales by Brown to the acquired companies. . . .

During the same period of time, Brown also acquired the stock or assets of seven companies engaged solely in shoe manufacturing. As a result, in 1955, Brown was the fourth largest shoe manufacturer in the country, producing about 25.6 million pairs of shoes or about 4 percent of the Nation's total footwear production.

Kinney

Kinney is principally engaged in operating the largest family-style shoe store chain in the United States. At the time of trial, Kinney was found to be operating over 400 such stores in more than 270 cities. These stores were found to make about 1.2 percent of all national retail shoe sales by dollar volume. . . .

In addition to this extensive retail activity, Kinney owned and operated four plants which manufactured men's, women's, and children's shoes and whose combined output was 0.5 percent of the national shoe production in 1955, making Kinney the 12th largest shoe manufacturer in the United States.

Kinney stores were found to obtain about 20 percent of their shoes from Kinney's own manufacturing plants. At the time of the merger, Kinney bought no shoes from Brown; however, in line with Brown's conceded reasons for acquiring Kinney, Brown had, by 1957, become the largest outside supplier of Kinney's shoes, supplying 7.9 percent of all Kinney's needs.

It is in this setting that the merger was considered and held to violate § 7 of the Clayton Act. The District Court ordered Brown to divest itself completely of all stock, share capital, assets or other interests it held in Kinney. . . .

Legislative History

The dominant theme pervading congressional consideration of the 1950 amendments [to the Clayton Act, Section 7] was a fear of what was considered to be a rising tide of economic concentration in the American economy. . . .

Other considerations cited in support of the bill were the desirability of retaining "local control" over industry and the protection of small businesses. Throughout the recorded discussion may be found examples of Congress' fear not only of accelerated concentration of economic power on economic grounds, but also of the threat to other values a trend toward concentration was thought to pose.

The Vertical Aspects of the Merger

. . . The primary vice of a vertical merger or other arrangement tying a customer to a supplier is that, by foreclosing the competitors of either party from a segment of the market otherwise open to them, the arrangement may act as a "clog on competition." . . .

The Product Market

The outer boundaries of a product market are determined by the reasonable interchangeability of use or the cross-elasticity of demand between the product itself and substitutes for it. However, within this broad market, well-defined submarkets may exist which, in themselves, constitute product markets for antitrust purposes. . . . The boundaries of such a submarket may be determined by examining such practical indicia as industry or public recognition of the submarket as a separate economic entity, the product's peculiar characteristics and uses, unique production facilities, distinct customers, distinct prices, sensitivity to price changes, and specialized vendors. . . .

Applying these considerations to the present case, we conclude that the record supports the District Court's finding that the relevant lines of commerce are men's, women's, and children's shoes. These product lines are recognized by the public; each line is manufactured in separate plants; each has characteristics peculiar to itself rendering it generally noncompetitive with the others; and each is, of course, directed toward a distinct class of customers. . . .

The Geographic Market

We agree with the parties and the District Court that insofar as the vertical aspect of this merger is concerned, the relevant geographic market is the entire Nation. The relationships of product value, bulk, weight and consumer demand enable manufacturers to distribute their shoes on a nationwide basis, as Brown and Kinney, in fact, do. . . .

The Probable Effect of the Merger

Once the area of effective competition affected by a vertical arrangement has been defined, an analysis must be made to determine if the effect of the arrangement "may be substantially to lessen competition, or to tend to create a monopoly" in this market.

Since the diminution of the vigor of competition which may stem from a vertical arrangement results primarily from a foreclosure of a share of the market otherwise open to competitors, an important consideration in determining whether the effect of a vertical arrangement "may be substantially to lessen competition, or to tend to create a monopoly" is the size of the share of the market foreclosed. However, this factor will seldom be determinative.

* * * * *

[I]t is apparent both from past behavior of Brown and from the testimony of Brown's President, that Brown would use its ownership of Kinney to force Brown shoes into Kinney stores. . . .

Another important factor to consider is the trend toward concentration in the industry. . . .

The existence of a trend toward vertical integration, which the District Court found, is well substantiated by the record. Moreover, the court found a tendency of the acquiring manufacturers to become increasingly important sources of supply for their acquired outlets. The necessary corollary of these trends is the foreclosure of independent manufacturers from markets otherwise open to them. . . .

Brown argues, however, that the shoe industry is at present composed of a large number of manufacturers and retailers, and that the industry is dynamically competitive. But remaining vigor cannot immunize a merger if the trend in that industry is toward oligopoly. It is the probable effect of the merger upon the future as well as the present which the Clayton Act commands the courts and the commission to examine.

Moreover, as we have remarked above, not only must we consider the probable effects of the merger upon the economics of the particular markets affected but also we must consider its probable effects upon the economic way of life sought to be preserved by Congress. Congress was desirous of preventing the formation of further oligopolies with their attendant adverse effects upon local control of industry and upon small business. Where an industry was composed of numerous independent units, Congress appeared anxious to preserve this structure. . . .

The Horizontal Aspects of the Merger

. . . The acquisition of Kinney by Brown resulted in a horizontal combination at both the manufacturing and retailing levels of their businesses. Although the District Court found that the merger of Brown's and Kinney's *manufacturing* facilities was economically too insignificant to come within the prohibitions of the Clayton Act, the Government has not appealed from this portion of the lower court's decision. Therefore, we have no occasion to express our views with respect to that finding. On the other hand, appellant does contest the District Court's finding that the merger of the companies' *retail* outlets may tend substantially to lessen competition.

The Product Market

. . . In . . . this opinion we hold that the District Court correctly defined men's, women's, and children's shoes as the relevant lines of commerce in which to analyze the vertical aspects of the merger. For the reasons there stated we also hold that the same lines of commerce are appropriate for considering the horizontal aspects of the merger.

The Geographic Market

The criteria to be used in determining the appropriate geographic market are essentially similar to those used to determine the relevant product market. Moreover, just as a product submarket may have § 7 significance as the proper "line of commerce," so may a geographic submarket be considered the appropriate "section of the country." Congress prescribed a pragmatic, factual approach to the definition of the relevant market and not a formal, legalistic one. The geographic market selected must, therefore, both "correspond to the commercial realities" of the industry and be economically significant. Thus, although the geographic market in some instances may encompass the entire nation, under other circumstances it may be as small as a single metropolitan area. The fact that two merging firms have competed directly on the horizontal level in but a fraction of the geographic markets in which either has operated, does not, in itself, place their merger outside the scope of § 7. That section speaks of "any . . . section of the country," and if anticompetitive effects of a merger are probable in "any" significant market, the merger—at least to that extent—is proscribed.

The parties do not dispute the findings of the District Court that the nation as a whole is the relevant geographic market for measuring the anticompetitive effects of the merger viewed vertically or of the horizontal merger of Brown's and Kinney's manufacturing facilities. As to the retail level, however, they disagree.

* * * * *

We agree that the District Court properly defined the relevant geographic markets in which to analyze this merger as those cities with a population exceeding 10,000 and their environs in which both Brown and Kinney retailed shoes through their own outlets. Such markets are large enough to include the downtown shops and suburban shopping centers in areas contiguous to the city, which are the important competitive factors, and yet are small enough to exclude stores beyond the immediate environs of the city, which are of little competitive significance.

The Probable Effect of the Merger

. . . The market share which companies may control by merging is one of the most important factors to be considered when determining the probable effects of the combination on effective competition in the relevant market. In an industry as fragmented as shoe retailing, the control of substantial shares of the trade in a city may have important effects on competition. If a merger achieving 5 percent control were now approved, we might be required to approve future merger efforts by Brown's competitors seeking similar market shares.

* * * * *

At the same time appellant has presented no mitigating factors, such as the business failure or the inadequate resources of one of the parties that may have prevented it from maintaining its competitive position, nor a demonstrated need for combination to enable small companies to enter into a more meaningful competition with those dominating the relevant markets. . . .

The judgment is affirmed.

Questions

1. As to the vertical element of *Brown Shoe*, what potential harm did the Court identify?
2. In *Brown Shoe* why did the Supreme Court settle on different geographic markets for the horizontal and vertical elements of the merger?

3. In *Brown Shoe* the Court followed the mandate of Congress that tendencies toward concentration are to be curbed in their incipiency. Why must the Court bow to the will of Congress in this matter?

4. How did the Supreme Court justify its prohibition of the merger in light of the rather small market shares involved (e.g., Brown produced 4 percent of the nation's shoes, while Kinney sold about 1.2 percent of the nation's total)?

5. In 1958 Pabst Brewing Company acquired Blatz Brewing Company. Pabst was America's 10th-largest brewer, while Blatz was the 18th largest. After the merger Pabst had 4.49 percent of the nationwide beer market and was the fifth-largest brewer. In the regional market of Wisconsin, Michigan, and Illinois the merger gave Pabst 11.32 percent of the sales. After the merger, Pabst led beer sales in Wisconsin with 23.95% of that statewide market. The beer market was becoming increasingly concentrated, with the total number of brewers declining from 206 to 162 during the years 1957 to 1961. In *United States* v. *Pabst Brewing Co.*, 384 U.S. 546 (1966), the Supreme Court found the merger violated the Clayton Act, Section 7. The Court did not choose among the three geographic market configurations, saying that the crucial inquiry is whether a merger may substantially lessen competition *anywhere* in the United States. Thus the Court held that, under these facts, a 4.49 percent share of the market was too large.

   Respected scholar and jurist Richard Posner labeled the *Pabst* decision an "atrocity" and the product of a "fit of nonsense" on the part of the Supreme Court.[21] What economic arguments would support Posner's colorful complaint?

6. In the period 1917–19 Du Pont acquired 23 percent of the stock in the then-fledgling General Motors Corporation. By 1947 Du Pont supplied 68 percent of GM's automotive finish needs and 38 percent of its fabric needs. In 1955 General Motors ranked first in sales and second in assets among all U.S. industrial corporations, while accounting for approximately two fifths of the nation's annual automobile sales. In 1949 the Justice Department challenged Du Pont's 1917–19 acquisitions of GM stock.

   a. Why did the government challenge Du Pont's acquisition?

   b. May an acquisition be properly challenged 30 years after the fact, as in *Du Pont?*

   c. Given your general understanding of finishes and fabrics, how would you defend Du Pont?

   d. Decide. Explain. See *United States* v. *E. I. du Pont de Nemours & Co.,* 353 U.S. 586 (1957).

7. In 1961 Ford Motor Company acquired the trade name and other assets of the Electric Autolite Company, a producer and distributor of spark plugs and other automotive parts. At the time of the acquisition three firms controlled 95 percent of the spark plug market: Champion (50 percent), General Motors-AC (30 percent), and Autolite (15 percent). Spark plug producers traditionally sold them to automakers at a price below cost. The profit came in the replacement market where mechanics ordinarily replaced the original plug with the same brand of aftermarket plug. Ford, in seeking entry to the profitable aftermarket, concluded that it would require five to eight years to successfully create its own spark plug division, and the cost involved would be greater than that of buying Autolite. Ford accounted for approximately 9.6 percent of all the spark plugs sold in America. After the acquisition Autolite began a new spark plug business, which garnered 1.6 percent of the market by 1964. The government challenged the acquisition.

   a. What category—or categories—of merger are we dealing with here?

   b. What harm did the government fear with the acquisition of Electric Autolite?

   c. Argue that the Ford–Electric Autolite merger strengthened competition.

   d. Decide. Explain. See *Ford Motor Company* v. *United States,* 405 U.S. 562 (1972).

CONGLOMERATE MERGERS

In essence, conglomerate mergers fall into four categories of analysis:

1. Potential Entrant.   When a firm might have entered a market on its own but chose instead to acquire an existing firm, the government may raise a challenge under Clayton § 7. Potential entrant mergers are of two types: product extension and market extension.

Product extension involves two products that are not competitors but are closely related in their production or distribution. The merger of Procter & Gamble, a soap manufacturer, and Clorox, a bleach manufacturer, exemplifies the product extension conglomerate merger.

Market extension involves two companies that produce the same product but sell it in different geographic markets. The merger of Narragansett Brewing, marketing its products in New England, and Falstaff Brewing, marketing in 32 states but not in New England, is an example of the market extension conglomerate.[22]

2. Market Power Entrenchment.   The government may challenge those conglomerate mergers involving a large firm acquiring a leading firm in a concentrated market, in cases when the acquisition may solidify or entrench the acquired firm's already strong market posture. For example, where the acquiring and acquired firms deal in related products, the size of the acquiring firm may convince distributors to accord the acquired firm favored treatment. The government is concerned that some conglomerate mergers will enhance the ability of the merged firm to increase product differentiation. That is, the acquiring firm can use its superior resources in the acquired firm's market, via advertising and the like, with the result that competition is reduced and barriers to entry are increased. The general area of market entrenchment is sometimes referred to by the terms *deep pockets* or *rich parent*. Consideration of the merger guidelines and the *Procter & Gamble* case that follow will clarify this line of analysis.

3. Reciprocity.   Essentially, reciprocity involves a "you scratch my back, and I'll scratch yours" sales arrangement in which two parties agree to both buy from and sell to each other. For example, A buys chemicals from B on the condition that B agrees to buy soap from A. Reciprocity takes two forms:

1. *Coercive reciprocity* is the situation in which one of the parties uses its purchasing power to force the other to enter a reciprocal buying arrangement. A says to B, in effect, I buy plenty of chemicals from you. You need my business. To keep my business, you must agree to purchase soap from me. Coercive reciprocity bears the characteristics of tying arrangements (see Chapter 10) where a seller with market

power forces a buyer to take unwanted product X in order to be supplied with desired product Y.

2. *Mutual patronage reciprocity* involves the same mutual purchase, but no force is involved. Both parties merely believe themselves to be advantaged by buying from each other. The argument is frequently made that mutual patronage reciprocity is harmless in that it involves no abuse and presumably results in maximum consumer welfare and efficiency. However, the historically dominant view in this modestly litigated area is as expressed in a 1966 *General Dynamics* case: "Reciprocity, whether mutual or coercive, serves to exclude competitors by the exercise of large-scale purchasing power."[23]

Conglomerate mergers sometimes exacerbate reciprocity. The accompanying diagram illustrates the problem.

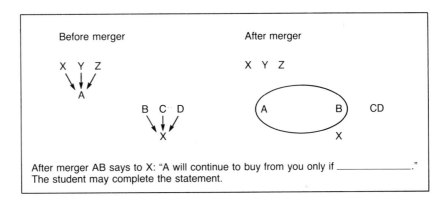

After merger AB says to X: "A will continue to buy from you only if _____."
The student may complete the statement.

4. Aggregate Concentration. In several cases the Justice Department has secured consent decrees on the grounds that the mergers in question would have resulted in unacceptable increases in overall commercial concentration. The argument is that commerce is already substantially concentrated, therefore, further significant concentration should be challenged on that ground alone. Despite the Justice Department's occasional success with this line of analysis, no recorded judicial opinion has explicitly supported it.

DEFENSES

At least in theory, certain conditions seem to justify otherwise illegal mergers. However, of the defenses that follow only the fourth has received judicial approval. The defenses are:

1. Economies born of efficiencies unrelated to advertising or promotion.
2. The market in question retains substantial ease of entry.

3. The merger may enhance competition. How might a merger improve competition in, for example, the computer industry?
4. A company or division is failing.

The government's 1984 merger guidelines explicitly approved the failing company defense.

Case

A careful reading of the *Procter & Gamble* case should provide a reasonably clear picture of the main lines of conglomerate analysis.

FTC V. PROCTER & GAMBLE CO.
386 U.S. 568 (1967)

Justice Douglas

This is a proceeding initiated by the Federal Trade Commission charging that respondent, Procter & Gamble Co., had acquired the assets of Clorox Chemical Co. in violation of § 7 of the Clayton Act. . . . The charge was that Procter's acquisition of Clorox might substantially lessen competition or tend to create a monopoly in the production and sale of household liquid bleaches.

[The FTC found the merger unlawful and ordered divestiture.] The Court of Appeals for the Sixth Circuit reversed and directed that the Commission's complaint be dismissed. . . . We find that the Commission's findings were amply supported by the evidence, and that the Court of Appeals erred.

. . . This merger may most appropriately be described as a "product-extension merger," as the Commission stated. . . .

At the time of the merger, in 1957, Clorox was the leading manufacturer in the heavily concentrated household liquid bleach industry. It is agreed that household liquid bleach is the relevant line of commerce. . . . It is a distinctive product with no close substitutes.

. . . The relevant geographical market is the nation and a series of regional markets. Because of high shipping costs and low sales price, it is not feasible to ship the product more than 300 miles from its point of manufacture. Most manufacturers are limited to competition within a single region since they have but one plant. Clorox is the only firm selling nationally; it has 13 plants distributed throughout the nation. Purex, Clorox's closest competitor in size, does not distribute its bleach in the northeast or mid-Atlantic States; in 1957, Purex's bleach was available in less than 50 percent of the national market.

At the time of the acquisition, Clorox was the leading manufacturer of household liquid bleach, with 48.8 percent of the national sales—annual sales of slightly less than $40 million. Its market share had been steadily increasing for the five years prior to the merger. Its nearest rival was Purex, which accounted for 15.7 percent of the household liquid bleach market. The industry is highly concentrated; in 1957, Clorox and Purex accounted for almost 65 percent of the nation's household liquid bleach sales, and, together with four other firms, for almost 80 percent. The remaining 20 percent was divided among over 200 small producers. Clorox had total assets of $12 million; only eight producers had assets in excess of $1 million, and very few had assets of more than $75,000.

* * * * *

Since all liquid bleach is chemically identical, advertising and sales promotion are vital. In 1957 Clorox spent almost $3.7 million on advertising, imprinting the value of its bleach in the mind of the consumer. In addition, it spent $1.7 million for other promotional activities. The Commission found that these heavy expenditures went far to explain why Clorox maintained so high a market share despite the fact that its brand, though chemically indistinguishable from rival brands, retailed for a price equal to or, in many instances, higher than its competitors.

Procter is a large, diversified manufacturer of low-price, high-turnover household products sold through grocery, drug, and department stores. Prior to its acquisition of Clorox, it did not produce household liquid bleach. Its 1957 sales were in excess of $1.1 billion, from which it realized profits of more than $67 million; its assets were over $500 million. Procter has been marked by rapid growth and diversification. . . .

In the marketing of soaps, detergents, and cleansers, as in the marketing of household liquid bleach, advertising and sales promotion are vital. In 1957, Procter was the nation's largest advertiser, spending more than $80 million on advertising and an additional $47 million on sales promotion. Due to its tremendous volume, Procter receives substantial discounts from the media. As a multiproduct producer Procter enjoys substantial advantages in advertising and sales promotion. Thus, it can and does feature several products in its promotions, reducing the printing, mailing, and other costs for each product. It also purchases network programs on behalf of several products, enabling it to give each product network exposure at a fraction of the cost per product that a firm with only one product to advertise would incur.

Prior to the acquisition, Procter was in the course of diversifying into product lines related to its basic detergent-soap-cleanser business. Liquid bleach was a distinct possibility since packaged detergents—Procter's primary product line—and liquid bleach are used complementarily in washing clothes and fabrics, and in general household cleaning.

* * * * *

The anticompetitive effects with which this product-extension merger is fraught can easily be seen: (1) the substitution of the powerful acquiring firm for the smaller, but already dominant, firm may substantially reduce the competitive structure of the industry by raising entry barriers and by dissuading the smaller firms from aggressively competing; (2) the acquisition eliminates the potential competition of the acquiring firm.

The liquid bleach industry was already oligopolistic before the acquisition, and price competition was certainly not as vigorous as it would have been if the industry were competitive. Clorox enjoyed a dominant position nationally, and its position approached monopoly proportions in certain areas. The existence of some 200 fringe firms certainly does not belie that fact. Nor does the fact, relied upon by the court below, that, after the merger, producers other than Clorox "were selling more bleach for more money than ever before."

. . . In the same period, Clorox increased its share from 48.8 percent to 52 percent. The interjection of Procter into the market considerably changed the situation. There is every reason to assume that the smaller firms would become more cautious in competing due to their fear of retaliation by Procter. It is probable that Procter would become the price leader and that oligopoly would become more rigid.

The acquisition may also have the tendency of raising the barriers to new entry. The major competitive weapon in the successful marketing of bleach is advertising. Clorox was limited in this area by its relatively small budget and its inability to obtain substantial discounts. By contrast, Procter's budget was much larger; and, although it would not devote its entire budget to advertising Clorox, it could divert a large portion to meet the short-term threat of a new entrant. Procter would be able to use its volume discounts to advantage in advertising Clorox. Thus, a new entrant would be much more reluctant to face the giant Procter than it would have been to face the smaller Clorox.

Possible economies cannot be used as a defense to illegality. Congress was aware that some mergers which lessen competition may also result in economies but it struck the balance in favor of protecting competition. . . .

The Commission also found that the acquisition of Clorox by Procter eliminated Procter as a potential competitor. . . . The evidence . . . clearly shows that Procter was the most likely entrant. . . . Procter was engaged in a vigorous program of diversifying into product lines closely related to its basic products. Liquid bleach was a natural avenue of diversification since it is complementary to Procter's products, is sold to the same customers through the same channels, and is advertised and merchandized in the same manner. . . . It is clear that the existence of Procter at the edge of the industry exerted considerable influence on the market. First, the market behavior of the liquid bleach industry was influenced by each firm's predictions of the market behavior of its competitors, actual and potential. Second, the barriers to entry by a firm of Procter's size and with its advantages were not significant. There is no indication that the barriers were so high that the price Procter would have to charge would be above the price that would maximize the profits of the existing firms. Third, the number of potential entrants was not so large that the elimination of one would be insignificant. Few firms would have the temerity to challenge a firm as solidly entrenched as Clorox. Fourth, Procter was found by the Commission to be the most likely entrant. . . .

The judgment of the Court of Appeals is reversed and remanded with instructions to affirm and enforce the Commission's order.

Questions

1. Make the argument that Procter & Gamble beneficially influenced and disciplined the bleach market, even though it had not actually entered that market.
2. Argue that Procter & Gamble was not a likely potential entrant into the bleach market.
3. Could General Motors lawfully acquire Clorox? Explain.
4. Could Procter & Gamble lawfully acquire Purex, at that time the number two liquid bleach producer with 15.7 percent of the market? Explain.
5. Would the outcome of the *Procter & Gamble* case be altered if bleaches were of differing chemical composition and quality? Explain.

Part Four—American Antitrust Laws and the International Market

America's commercial market now very clearly embraces the entire globe. Multinational corporations dominate international business. Antitrust questions can become extremely complex in transactions involving multiple companies, in multiple nations, where those transactions are potentially governed by U.S. and foreign antitrust laws. U.S. antitrust laws are, of course, applicable to foreign firms doing business here. The Sherman, Clayton, and FTC acts, among others, are all potentially applicable to American business abroad. In the aforementioned *Alcoa* case, the U.S. Court of Appeals held that the U.S. courts have authority over antitrust activity abroad if that activity affected and was intended to affect commerce in the United States.[24]

Sherman Act

The Sherman Act applies to the conduct of American business abroad when that business has a direct effect on domestic commerce. That the business was conducted entirely abroad or that the agreement was entered in another nation does not excuse an American firm from the reach of the Sherman Act (assuming American courts can achieve the necessary jurisdiction).

Clayton Act

Section 7 of the Clayton Act is clearly applicable to acquisitions combining domestic and foreign firms and is potentially applicable to acquisitions not involving American firms if the effect would be harmful to competition in the American market. For example, in 1975 Gillette was prevented from acquiring Braun, a leading European manufacturer of electric razors. Braun had not entered the American market, but it did have the potential to do so. Thus, under the potential entrant reasoning illustrated in the *Procter & Gamble* case, the merger was disallowed. Braun, as a potential entrant, could "police" the conduct of Gillette and the others in the oligopolistic American razor market.

Federal Trade Commission Act

As noted earlier, the FTC shares antitrust enforcement authority with the Justice Department, and Section 5 of the act strengthens Clayton 7.

Enforcement

The complexity and uncertainty of the antitrust laws can be particularly daunting in the international arena. However, the Justice Department has provided a mechanism for achieving greater clarity. Under its Business Review Procedure, the Justice Department will prepare a statement of its likely response to a proposed ''transaction so that the parties will have advance notice of the government's antitrust stance.''

Notwithstanding our ample statutory framework and a history of some antitrust oversight of international business, the clear tone of American antitrust law in the late 1980s is to relax oversight to encourage American commercial competitiveness in the global market. During the 1980s Congress passed legislation giving U.S. companies greater latitude to enter joint research agreements abroad and to create export cartels. And Justice Department practice during the Reagan years effectively shielded most U.S.–foreign joint ventures and most foreign investors from the effects of American antitrust laws where that business was carried out overseas. Similarly, the department adopted a more permissive stance toward foreign companies doing business in the United States.

Furthermore, foreign governments have grown increasingly antagonistic toward the application of U.S. antitrust laws within their boundaries. England, France, Canada, and Australia (among others) have adopted so-called blocking legislation that seeks to stop or render difficult the application of U.S. antitrust laws on business in those countries. These blocking statutes either simply render foreign court orders unenforceable or seek to interfere in providing the documents or information requested by foreign states.[25]

FOREIGN ANTITRUST LAWS

The United States historically has taken a much more aggressive attitude toward antitrust policy and enforcement than have the nations of Western Europe and Japan. Indeed, those nations generally regard cooperative economic arrangements and concentrations of industrial power as necessary and desirable components of economic success. Of course, Japan and the European Community also practice economic policies of involving government quite directly in regulating and ''managing'' commercial practice for the general good.

At this writing in mid-1988, European merger activity appears to be increasing rapidly and the Common Market nations are attempting to work out a new policy to deal with the increasingly volatile market. European Community regulators hope to install a common merger policy for the 12 EC nations to replace the national laws governing European acquisitions. A draft of the proposed policy sets no specific market share limits but rather calls for EC review of every merger involving companies with combined annual sales exceeding $1.25 billion. Were that guideline approved, EC regulators would expect to review perhaps 150 mergers annually while actually intervening in only two or three of that number. The new rules, if adopted, would be substantially more liberal than existing legislation in some European nations. For example, Great Britain's Monopolies and Mergers Commission has blocked mergers involving a 25 percent share of the market. The new policy, which is not expected before 1989, would almost certainly encourage U.S. interest in European acquisitions.[26]

As discussed in the next article, Japanese antitrust laws are very similar to those in the United States, but enforcement has been quite mild.

IS BIGNESS BAD?

In spite of our rather extensive investigation of antitrust law, we do not yet have an answer to the question that is, at least emotionally, at the heart of much antitrust analysis: Is bigness bad? The question calls for an assessment of one's economic and political philosophies. Can the free market operate effectively? Even if it can, are we satisfied with the resulting distribution of benefits? Is some government intervention necessary? If so, how do we know when enough is enough? Is market concentration a threat to political freedom? The article that follows addresses some of these issues and raises the possibility of taking the Japanese approach to solving them. The article consists of a debate between an advocate of stern antitrust enforcement and an advocate of relaxed antitrust policies that permit the growth of the Japanese model of global cooperation between corporate giants and between those giants and their governments.

COOPERATION, COMPETITION, AND ANTITRUST: TWO VIEWS

Irvin Grossack and David A. Heenan

Irvin Grossack: "The Japanese Model and American Antitrust Laws: Comments on an Article by David Heenan"

In "Building Industrial Cooperation through Japanese Strategies" (*Business Horizons,* No-vember–December 1985), David Heenan attempts to explain the failure of American firms to compete effectively in international markets. His basic thesis can be summarized as follows:

1. Japan has demonstrated that "cooperation" among its firms, largely under the leadership of governmental and quasi-governmental agencies, has led to extraordinary export success, which in turn has brought about a high level of economic growth in that country.

2. Other countries are increasingly emulating Japan in their "industrial policies."

3. American firms are unable to get on the Japanese bandwagon because of the American antitrust laws.

4. By implication, these laws should be radically changed in light of the new international realities.

Although his arguments are by no means novel, Heenan is commendably more forthright than others as to where an adoption of the Japanese model will lead us. I propose here to (1) defend the antitrust laws from the charge that they are responsible for American international failures; (2) suggest more plausible reasons that account for America's shortcomings in international trade; and (3) indicate what might happen were the Japanese model to be adopted.

The Case for Antitrust Laws
All the "cooperation" in Japan that Heenan refers to is among large firms. Indeed, obtaining cooperation among large numbers of small firms would be unwieldy, if not impossible. Of special importance is the pooling of resources of such firms to develop new products and technologies. Another form of cooperation is joint ventures, which are becoming increasingly important among firms of different countries. Heenan does not mention cooperation on pricing and output, although one can reasonably infer that it is part of the cooperation package. These types of cooperation are not only permitted but encouraged and in some cases made mandatory by governmental power. Heenan points out that such cooperation has

become nothing less than collectivism: "Taken together, these efforts reflect the collectivism undergirding Japan's industrial policies" (p. 10).

Have the American antitrust laws inhibited the international competitiveness of American firms? These laws, of course, are designed to maintain free competitive markets by opposing collusive practices, monopolization, and mergers that reduce competition. Yet it is one of the interesting paradoxes of our times that the antitrust laws are being attacked by many of the same "conservative" groups who loudly proclaim themselves ardent defenders of the competitive free market system. And, perhaps more understandably, these laws are also under attack by "liberals" who advocate a much more active role for the government in the economy. The failure of American firms on the international level has provided grist for these attacks. But are they really justified?

"Large" Doesn't Equal "Competitive"
Heenan and others argue that large firms are needed in international competition and that the antimerger provisions of the antitrust laws inhibit their development. But what is the record of large American firms in this regard?

The greatest import competition in the United States is now in autos, steel, and a wide range of electronic goods. The firms that have been unable to compete with these imports in the *American* market are such corporations as General Motors, U.S. Steel, G.E., and IBM. Are we to conclude that this failure has come about because these firms are too small? Although some assert that large firms are more innovative, one would be hard put to defend the innovative record of the American auto and steel firms over the last four decades.

Antitrust "Jitters" Don't Hit a Nerve
Heenan writes that fear of antitrust prosecution inhibits American firms from growing through merger, from cartelizing, from joint

research activities (and so forth). If we omit outright price-fixing cartels, it is hard to see what these firms have to fear.

For the last 10 years or so there has been virtually no antitrust prosecution by either the Justice Department or the FTC. Indeed, the Reagan administration has had assistant attorney generals who made it clear that they oppose much in the very antitrust laws that they are supposed to enforce.

There certainly seems to be no opposition to the huge current merger wave. Even such large horizontal mergers as G.E./RCA, and Chevron/Gulf, which would have been unthinkable 20 years ago, are now virtually unchallenged. The most important of the successful antitrust cases in recent times—the breakup of AT&T—was instigated mainly on behalf of the large electronic firms, who argued that AT&T's monopoly of telephone utilities was being used to monopolize the manufacture of the whole range of communication equipment. Indeed, we pretty much now depend upon private suits to enforce the antitrust laws, but there are proposals to limit such suits.

* * * * *

Cartels Can Backfire

Heenan seems to imply that the cartelization of its firms gives a nation a competitive advantage in international competition. But it is just the reverse. When a cartel sets a high price (which is the aim of cartels), then of course it is easy (and profitable) for noncartel members to increase their sales. Indeed, it was largely because of tacit collusion in the American steel and auto industries that firms from other countries were so successful in penetrating the American market for such items.

On the basis of these points, there seems to be no reason why the American antitrust laws should be blamed for American foreign trade problems. Indeed, one can argue rather persuasively that lax enforcement of the antitrust

laws and reduced American international competitiveness went hand in hand.

Plausible Reasons for the Imbalance of Trade

There are much more plausible explanations than antitrust for the poor performance of the United States in international trade. Above all, there has been the emergence of the Asian nations as tough new competitors. Although it has created major problems for the United States, this new state of affairs also has conferred benefits and, moreover, reflects a success for American political foreign policy. Many of the exports to the United States are from American firms that have located production facilities abroad, lured mainly by lower wages and governmental incentives. American capital, technology, and management are now available to foreign firms on the same terms offered to American firms, thereby emasculating these traditional sources of American comparative advantages in international trade.

Then there are the "industrial policies" of our overseas competitors. Government-owned firms and government subsidies to privately owned firms have given our competitors advantages of a sort that are manifestly inconsistent with a free market, free trade, international economic system.

These developments do indeed create very real problems for U.S. competitiveness in international markets. But the solutions to them lie in American foreign economic policy, not in doing away with the antitrust laws.

The High Price of Imitation

An emulation of the Japanese system by the United States would surely result in a completely different economic (and probably political) system in this country. Although Heenan gives it the nice name of "cooperation," this system almost certainly would evolve into an oligarchy. A small number of large firms would be allied with a small number of large banks, guided and protected by a powerful government. There is little reason to believe that the mass of Americans would benefit from such a system.

It is no surprise that many liberal "planners" favor such a system. They see it as the avenue to governmental control of the economy—although the results may turn out quite differently from what they expect. What *is* surprising is that a conservative administration preaching the virtues of Adam Smith, laissez-faire, and an entrepreneurial spirit can consider seriously policies that would bring about such a system.

David A. Heenan: "Cooperate We Must: A Rejoinder"

Professor Grossack's comments raise interesting questions on the societal costs and benefits of greater corporate collaboration. In so doing, they sharpen the level of public discussion of a phenomenon which, I believe, will dominate the balance of this century.

My thesis is this: to be globally *competitive,* multinational corporations must be globally *cooperative.* This notion is not easily accepted by most Americans, weaned on an ideology of the traditional competitive model of the firm, where cooperation is viewed with skepticism and suspicion. Yet increasing numbers of U.S. businesses are witnessing the benefits of joining forces: large-scale economies, technology and resource pooling, and improved access to foreign markets. In today's high-performance aircraft industry, for instance, no manufacturer can afford to go it alone. Development costs for a prototype aircraft can run anywhere from $1.5 to $2 billion—hence, the need for well-heeled partners.

Global Strategic Partnerships: Something New under the Sun

Accordingly, we are seeing a rise in what the Wharton School's Howard Perlmutter and I call *global strategic partnerships* (GSPs). These pacts are not mere extensions of the traditional, international joint ventures—localized partnerships that focus on one or two national markets. Rather, GSPs are those alliances in which:

1. Two or more companies develop a common, long-term strategy aimed at world leadership as low-cost suppliers, differentiated marketers, or both, in an international arena.

2. The relationship is reciprocal. The partners possess specific strengths that they are prepared to share with their colleagues.

3. The partners' efforts are global, extending beyond a few developed countries to include nations of the newly industrializing, less developed, and socialist world.

4. The participating companies retain their national and ideological identities while competing in those markets excluded from the partnership.

5. The relationship is organized along horizontal, not vertical lines. Technology exchanges, resource pooling, and other "soft" forms of combination are the rule.

GSPs represent a systematic effort by companies to link the principles of competitive advantage with global strategy. What emerges are compacts in which multinational corporations join forces in some markets while retaining autonomy in others.

Size, contrary to Professor Grossack's comments, is not a deterrent to strategic partnering. For smaller companies, GSPs with both peers and giants often represent the most profitable route to future opportunities. Large companies will frequently combine with smaller ones to exploit their entrepreneurial capabilities and market niches. This was the case when IBM teamed up with Microsoft to exploit the latter's growing expertise in software for desktop computers. Smaller companies, like Microsoft, benefit by gaining access to global markets and the resource strength of their bigger partners.

* * * * *

Partnership Is Hard Work: Antitrust Laws Make It Even Harder

Make no mistake, strategic partnering for firms large or small is anything but easy. Witness, for instance, the splitup of Dunlop-Pirelli, Volvo-Saab, and the London-based consortium banks. Cultural differences, poor communications, and political infighting contributed to their demise. But for U.S. companies, restrictive antitrust laws represent an added concern.

To its credit, the White House is attempting to create a more positive antitrust environment for GSPs. The administration accepts the University of Chicago's view that many practices long considered anticompetitive are actually good for the economy, either because they increase economic efficiency or because they promote rather than destroy competition. To the Reaganites, bigness is no longer equated with badness, particularly where global markets are at stake.

But how enduring will be the administration's sentiments? Gordon B. Spivak, a leading Wall Street specialist on antitrust, believes that the Chicago doctrine and the recent reforms discussed by Professor Grossack won't last beyond the decade. . . . Beyond these uncertainties at the federal level, individual states, the courts, and private litigants are keeping the flame of antitrust very much alive. Last December, 50 state attorneys general unanimously supported a hard line against vertical restraints. Similarly, last year Congress passed a resolution asking the Justice Department to withdraw its permissive guidelines on these restraints.

States are also intervening in the merger area. For example, the 1983 Texas Free Enterprise and Antitrust Act outlaws mergers that affect competition.

* * * * *

Therefore, America's antitrust environment remains clouded and confused, and U.S. multinationals are exercising great care in forging GSPs. . . .

* * * * *

Nevertheless, it would be inaccurate as well as naive to suggest that antitrust practices have been the major cause of America's declining competitiveness in world markets. At worst, they have been a minor irritant for U.S. multinationals. On this point, Professor Grossack and I agree.

While our antiquated antitrust system is a component of the "tilted playing field" that hinders U.S. business, its reform is no panacea. If America's global competitiveness is to be restored, far more important is the need to internalize top management, revitalize the civil service, restore the work ethic—and a good deal more.

* * * * *

Note: Irvin Grossack is professor of business economics and public policy at the Indiana University School of Business. David A. Heenan is chairman and CEO of Theo. H. Davies & Co., Ltd., Honolulu. He served as dean of the business school and vice president for academic affairs at the University of Hawaii.
Source: *Business Horizons* 29, no. 5 (September–October 1986), pp. 24–28. Copyright, 1986, by the Foundation for the School of Business at Indiana University. Reprinted by permission.

Questions

1. Should the United States adopt the Japanese model, as suggested by Heenan, or should we opt for firm antitrust enforcement, as Grossack contends? Explain.
2. William G. Shepherd, University of Michigan economist and economic advisor to the Justice Department's Antitrust Division during the administration of President Lyndon Johnson:

   > It may not be too late to turn back from this road to serfdom by reviving the case for antitrust, but the odds aren't favorable. More probably, antitrust will continue to sink.[27]

   a. As you see it, what is the future of antitrust law in the United States?
   b. Is bigness bad? Explain.

QUESTIONS, PARTS THREE AND FOUR

1. Is the influence of big business so persuasive that it nullifies the effective enforcement of the antitrust laws? Explain.
2. On the average, would firms pursuing expansion via an active merger policy be more or less profitable than those firms not involved in frequent acquisitions? See Linda Hayes, "Twenty-Five Years of Change in the Fortune 500," *Fortune,* May 5, 1980, p. 88.
3. Consolidated, a large food processor and distributor, acquired Gentry, a producer of dehydrated onion and garlic. Consolidated made substantial purchases from various food processors who, in turn, used dehydrated onion and garlic in preparing and packaging their foods. Prior to the merger, Gentry had 32 percent of its market while its chief competitor, Basic, held about 58 percent, with two other firms splitting the balance. Eight years after the merger, Gentry's share rose to 35 percent, while Basic's fell to 55 percent. Basic's products were considered, even by Gentry's president, to be superior to Gentry's products. The Federal Trade Commission challenged the merger as a violation of Section 7 of the Clayton Act. See *Federal Trade Commission* v. *Consolidated Foods Corp.,* 380 U.S. 592 (1965).
   a. What anticompetitive practice did the FTC allege?
   b. Decide the case. Explain.
4. The Justice Department has traditionally been reluctant to accept economies of scale as a defense to an otherwise unlawful merger. Why?
5. How can a merger benefit society?
6. Which economic considerations support the view that unilateral growth is preferable to growth by merger?
7. In 1968 Heublein, Inc., was America's 16th largest seller of wine. In 1969 Heublein acquired United Vintners, Inc., which, as the producer of Italian Swiss Colony, Petri, and Inglenook, was the nation's second-ranking wine seller. In 1979 an administrative law judge found the

acquisition in violation of the Clayton Act, Section 7, and the Federal Trade Commission Act, Section 5. Heublein appealed to the full commission.

Horizontal Theory. The commission concluded that the appropriate market was all wines, with Heublein having .79 percent of that market and United, 17.9 percent. The commission further found that the market was not highly concentrated nor was it moving in that direction. The four-firm concentration ratio was 47.9 percent, with the top two firms holding 41.9 percent of the wine market.

Potential Competition. The commission found that Heublein had the capacity, interest, and economic incentive to expand and thus strengthen competition, but the commission also found 21 other firms similarly prepared to enter or expand. In addition, the commission noted that the wine market was rapidly expanding.

Entrenchment. The administrative law judge found that the acquisition conferred three significant competitive benefits on United: (1) the ability to obtain desirable financing; (2) the ability to share in a large advertising budget, and (3) possible leverage from Heublein's Smirnoff vodka and other liquor products, but commission studies suggested that those advantages were unlikely to have a significant competitive effect.

Decide the case. See In re *Heublein, Inc.,* 1980 *Trade Regulation Reporter* ¶21763 (FTC).

8. Excel, a division of Cargill, was the second-largest firm in the beef-packing market. It sought to acquire Spencer Pack, a division of Land-O-Lakes, and the third-largest beef packer. After the acquisition, Excel would have remained second ranked in the business, but its market share would have been only slightly smaller than that of the leader, IBP. Monfort, the nation's fifth-largest beef packer, sought an injunction to block the acquisition, claiming a violation of Clayton 7. In effect, Monfort claimed the merger would result in a dangerous concentration of economic power in the beef-packing market, with the result that Excel would pay more for cattle and charge less for its processed beef, thus placing its competitors in a destructive and illegal price-cost squeeze. Monfort claimed Excel's initial losses in this arrangement would be covered by its wealthy parent, Cargill. Then, when the competition was driven from the market, Monfort claimed, Excel would raise its processed beef prices to supracompetitive levels. Among other arguments, Excel averred that Monfort was alleging heavy losses based on intense competition, a condition that would not constitute a violation of the antitrust laws. The district court found for Monfort and the appeals court, considering the cost-price squeeze a form of predatory pricing, affirmed. Excel appealed to the Supreme Court. Decide. Explain. See *Cargill, Inc.* v. *Monfort of Colorado, Inc.,* 93 L. Ed. 2d 427, 479 U.S. _____ (1986).

NOTES

1. See A. D. Neale, *The Antitrust Laws of the U.S.A.,* 2nd ed. (Cambridge: Cambridge University Press, 1970), p. 190.
2. Solomon Fabricant, *The Output of Manufacturing Industries, 1899–1937* (New York: National Bureau of Economic Research, 1940), pp. 84–85, as reported in Martin C. Schnitzer, *Contemporary Government and Business Relations* (Skokie, Ill.: Rand McNally, 1978), p. 114.
3. Robert Tollison, "Labor Monopoly and Antitrust Policy," *Policy Report.* April 1979.
4. *Town of Hallie* v. *City of Eau Claire,* 471 U.S. 34 (1985); and *Southern Carriers Rate Conference, Inc.* v. *U.S.,* 471 U.S. 48 (1985).
5. *Goldfarb* v. *Virginia State Bar et al.,* 95 S. Ct. 2004 (1975).
6. Ibid., p. 2016.
7. Alan Greenspan, "Antitrust" in Ayn Rand, *Capitalism: The Unknown Ideal* (New York: Signet, 1967), p. 68.
8. *U.S.* v. *Aluminum Company of America,* 148 F.2d 416 (2d Cir. 1945).
9. Ibid.
10. 110 F. Supp. 295 (Mass. 1953), aff'd per curium, 347 U.S. 521 (1954).
11. *Cliff Food Stores, Inc.* v. *Kroger Co.,* 417 F.2d 203, 207 n.2 (5th Cir. 1969).
12. 458 F. Supp. 423 (Cal. 1978).
13. Wesley J. Liebeler, 1980 Cumulative Supplement, *Antitrust Adviser,* 2nd ed. (Colorado Springs: Shepard's McGraw-Hill, 1978), pp. 26–27, citing *ILC Peripherals* v. *IBM,* 458 F. Supp. 423 (Cal. 1978).
14. 105 S. Ct. 2847 (1985).
15. For an analysis supporting this interpretation of the *Aspen* case, see Daniel W. Ladd, "The Efficiency Defense: Section 2 Limits on Monopolist Conduct after *Aspen,*" *Columbia Law Review* 86, December 1986, p. 1712.
16. *Aspen,* 105 S. Ct. at 2860, n. 39 (quoting R. Bork, *The Antitrust Paradox* at 157).
17. Ms. Tracy Timson, graduate assistant, University of Northern Iowa School of Business, prepared portions of the materials in this section.
18. Reported in *Antitrust and Trade Regulation Report* 42, no. 1048 (January 21, 1982), p. 154.
19. Staff Reporter, "Corporate Mergers Climbed 12% for 1986, Grimm Says," *The Wall Street Journal,* February 12, 1987, p. 15.
20. *Business Week*/Harris Poll, "Is Antitrust Backlash Building?" *Business Week,* July 20, 1987, p. 71.
21. Richard Posner, *Antitrust Law* (Chicago: The University of Chicago Press, 1976), p. 130.
22. *U.S.* v. *Falstaff Brewing Corp.,* 410 U.S. 526 (1973).
23. *United States* v. *General Dynamics Corp.,* 258 F. Supp. 36, 66 (S.D.N.Y. 1966).
24. 148 F.2d 416 (2d Cir.) as reported in Note, "Reassessment of International Application of Antitrust Laws: Blocking Statutes, Balancing Tests, and Treble Damages," *Law & Contemporary Problems* 50, no. 3 (Summer 1987), p. 197.

25. Ibid.
26. The remarks in this paragraph are drawn from Jonathan Kapstein, ''Loosening the Restraints on Europe's Merger Mania,'' *Business Week*, June 13, 1988, p. 44.
27. William G. Shepherd, ''Bust the Reagan Trustbusters,'' *Fortune,* August 4, 1986, pp. 225, 227.

Chapter 10

Antitrust Law—Restraints of Trade

INTRODUCTION

The past 20 years or so have produced a revolution of sorts in our view of antitrust law. The Chicago School, with its reliance on free market economics, has been successful in reshaping antitrust analysis. Efficiency has become the goal and cornerstone of the new view of antitrust. And businesses, the Chicago School argues, should be free to pursue whatever arrangements best serve their needs so long as those arrangements are not designed to exclude a competitor on some basis other than efficiency (e.g., horizontal price-fixing). Long-standing governmental and public fear of bigness has been muted. But even so, dramatic Supreme Court reversals of "old" antitrust law have been the exception. Mistrust of big business and doubts about the free market as a complete cure for our problems will continue to compete with the undeniable intellectual power of efficient markets thinking. So, antitrust law of the 1990s is an item of speculation. But the declining antitrust activism of recent years should not be interpreted as an open door to business abuse. As illustrated by the following article, restraint of trade remains a problem in American commerce, and antitrust law is our primary tool for addressing that problem. The balance of the chapter will describe the antitrust law that has evolved to deal with allegations like these against portions of the soft-drink industry.

COLA SELLERS MAY HAVE BOTTLED UP THEIR COMPETITORS

Andy Pasztor and Larry Reibstein

When four executives of local Coca-Cola and Pepsi-Cola bottling companies gathered at a popular, late-night restaurant in Norfolk, Virginia, four years ago, they did more than share a meal.

By the end of the meeting, the executives allegedly established a single wholesale price—$5.50 a case—for cans of Coke and Pepsi sold in much of Virginia, according to sworn testimony, government filings, and other federal court documents in Norfolk. The participants also agreed on the size and timing of future price increases for both cans and bottles, Justice Department prosecutors and government witnesses allege.

Over the next year and a half, executives of the two area bottlers conspired to share confidential price and marketing information at meetings in such places as hotel bathrooms and lounges, parking lots, fast-food outlets, and an airport coffee shop, according to prosecutors and the testimony, filings, and other court documents.

The result, prosecutors charge, was to inflate soft-drink prices paid by consumers while effectively blocking smaller competitors from expanding their share of the market.

Like Wrestling

The activities in Virginia and elsewhere are at odds with the public perception that Coke and Pepsi, which account for 70 percent of the $30-billion-a-year soft-drink market, are locked in a no-holds-barred struggle for America's taste buds. David McFarland, a University of North Carolina economics professor who has studied soft-drink marketing, likens the competition to televised wrestling. "They make a lot of sounds and groans and bounce on the mat, but they know who is going to win." Both Coke and Pepsi stand to benefit from this arrangement, he argues, but many smaller companies can't even enter the ring to compete.

In some markets, for instance, Atlanta-based Coca-Cola Co. and PepsiCo Inc., Purchase, New York, have each agreed with bottlers to make large payments to grocery chains in return for crucial advertising and store displays. This practice tends to lock out rivals such as Seven Up, RC Cola, and regional brands, from similar promotional advantages, and the Federal Trade Commission staff is looking into the matter. In some cases, pricing and promotional moves for Coke and Pepsi have been worked out ahead of time in a way that avoids direct competition.

Coca-Cola Co. and PepsiCo Inc., haven't been accused of any criminal violations. Coke and Pepsi directly control a sizable share of their bottling network, but they also rely on independently owned bottlers to mix, bottle, and market their drinks. The companies' spokesmen maintain that local bottling executives violated companywide policies and acted on their own. Still, units of both companies are subjects of some of the criminal inquiries, according to attorneys familiar with the matter.

Spate of Prosecutions

Inquiries into such practices are expected to spread. Already, a total of 13 bottling companies and individuals have been convicted or charged in a spate of recent federal price-fixing prosecutions—stretching from Virginia's Tidewater region to rural Georgia and Baltimore's inner city. The criminal investigations are accelerating, with at least 13 federal grand juries continuing to delve into the industry.

And, in a civil suit in Charlotte, North Carolina, last year, a federal jury found that a local Coke bottling company conspired with a Pepsi bottler to control prices and advertising promotions. The Pepsi bottler settled out of court for an undisclosed amount while the Coke affiliate was ordered to pay a total of $2.7 million to four smaller rivals. The case was later settled for an undisclosed amount.

A Coca-Cola Co. spokesman said in a statement that its marketing programs "encourage competition" and benefit consumers by "increasing the number of soft-drink promotions and reducing prices to consumers." The company declined to answer questions.

A PepsiCo spokesman maintains that the soft-drink industry is intensely competitive and that "isolated instances" of price-fixing are local aberrations. The wide variety of brands available and the relatively slow rise in prices since 1981 have benefited consumers, he asserts, adding that grocers routinely use marketing agreements to govern promotions and displays for many other products.

Charles Rule, head of the Justice Department's antitrust division, won't comment on whether the two leading soft-drink companies are targets of the grand jury investigations. "At this time, the focus is on the bottlers," he says, noting that "it doesn't appear that these are isolated instances."

The inquiries so far are zeroing in on two major areas, alleged price-fixing schemes and marketing agreements.

Price-Fixing

Here is how court records, prosecutors, and other sources say the price-fixing scheme in Norfolk evolved:

In late 1982 or 1983, Morton Lapides, chairman of then Allegheny Pepsi-Cola Bottling Co., of Baltimore, gathered his top aides to talk about the problem of shrinking profits, according to attorneys and others familiar with the investigations. His primary competitor, Mid-Atlantic Coca-Cola Bottling Co., of Silver Spring, Maryland, was aggressively discounting wholesale prices to customers in Norfolk; Richmond, Virginia; and other markets.

So, prosecutors and witnesses have told the courts, Mr. Lapides directed an assistant to contact James Harford, then president of Mid-Atlantic Coke, to try to halt such practices. Mr. Harford allegedly was receptive to the notion and, according to the government, over the months an elaborate price-fixing scheme was hatched.

The two bottlers—after years of civil charges and countercharges over unfair pricing—agreed to jointly set and stick to the prices listed in so-called promotional letters sent to wholesale customers, according to felony charges filed in federal court in Norfolk against the two bottling companies and Messrs. Harford and Lapides.

By mid-1983, senior executives policed *each other's* wholesale prices through a system of anonymous, unsigned letters. And they talked surreptitiously on the phone every few weeks—using aliases such as "The Birdie"—about discounts offered to such customers, according to testimony in a recent criminal trial in federal court in Norfolk.

When Pepsi introduced a new, less-expensive plastic package for its six-pack sodas in the fall of 1983, Mid-Atlantic Coke's executives feared the competition might lower prices, according to sworn testimony and attorneys familiar with the investigation. But when executives of the two companies got together, Pepsi bottling officials promised that they wouldn't reduce prices to reflect the lower packaging cost, prosecutors contend.

Mr. Lapides is contesting the conspiracy charges against him. His lawyers, among other things, have filed court papers arguing that a lie-detector test shows their client wasn't involved in any illegal price-fixing. Mr. Harford and the Allegheny bottling operation—which is now a unit of PepsiCo—also deny violating any laws.

Marketing Agreements

Over the years, bottlers also used a variety of less obvious—but equally controversial—methods to reduce competition.

Some bottlers pay grocers, convenience stores, drug stores, and others huge sums of money in return for coveted in-store display cases. The payments also guarantee the Coke and Pepsi bottlers featured newspaper advertising and preferential pricing arrangements. Weaker competitors are denied or can't afford such advantages, yet they are the lifeblood of soda sales. Prominent displays and advertising can boost soda sales sixfold or more during some periods.

In many markets, Coke and Pepsi have, in effect, divided up the year between themselves for these special pricing and promotion programs. Using so-called calendar marketing agreements, retailers agree to promote Coke and sell it at a low price one week, and Pepsi the next week, and so on for the entire year.

Consider the similar, but separate agreements that Southland Corp.'s 7-Eleven stores signed with Coke and Pepsi bottlers, according to testimony at the Charlotte trial. The convenience store chain agreed to price Coke's two-liter bottles at around $1.59, and to give its products exclusive promotional displays. In return for this and other pricing arrangements, Coke gave each 7-Eleven store in the chain's Charlotte-based division 108 free cases of 16-ounce cans of soda during six months of 1985. Those free cases amounted to more than $500,000 for the division. Meanwhile, Pepsi also agreed to pay 7-Eleven as much as $400,000 for its own pricing and promotional advantages, covering the rest of the year.

For consumers, the result of such agreements was to deter price competition among rival brands that were excluded, according to testimony.

For instance, Coke or Pepsi's wholesale price to grocers—which tend to sell soda for a lower price than convenience stores—for a two-liter bottle was about 98 cents, and the grocer would mark it up only to 99 cents. Meanwhile, RC Cola, for example, charged a supermarket about 80 cents for a two-liter bottle in some instances, but the grocer would sell it for about $1 retail.

Using Retailers

At the trial, witnesses contended that while the bottlers probably didn't meet face to face, they coordinated their policies indirectly, using retailers as intermediaries.

Henry James, Jr., general counsel for Pepsi-Cola Bottling Co. of Charlotte, responds that "absolutely, positively" no evidence of a conspiracy exists between Coke and Pepsi bottlers. "It happens that Pepsi asked for 26 weeks of promotional advertising and display, and bought it," he says. "That's all we were involved with."

In a statement, Pepsi says that its agreements help retailers to "more effectively organize and manage promotional activities" in their stores, and are pro-competitive.

A spokesman for Coca-Cola Bottling Co. Consolidated, of Charlotte, which is 20 percent owned by Coca Cola Co., asserts that the marketing and advertising agreements under attack by critics are, in fact, intended to foster competition, and retailers are free to set whatever price they want "on our products, or anybody else's."

Neither Coca-Cola nor PepsiCo were defendants in the civil lawsuit.

Nevertheless, the Charlotte trial disclosed that the two major soft-drink companies were intimately involved in the preparation and enforcement of the earlier agreements.

One 1982 memo from a Coke USA executive, which was introduced as evidence at the

Charlotte trial, bluntly urged Coke bottlers to refrain from aggressively promoting products when they knew special Pepsi promotional programs were under way, and the memo noted that Pepsi bottlers "will also refrain from this activity when Coke bottlers are featuring."

Questions

1. *a.* If you were in charge of the U.S. Justice Department, would you challenge Coke and Pepsi's practice of making "large payments to grocery chains in return for crucial advertising and store displays"? Explain.

   b. Assume you are an attorney for Coke and Pepsi. Defend those payments.

2. In your opinion, could any product gain the market dominance of Coke and Pepsi if that product were not the best of its kind? Explain.

Part One—Horizontal Restraints

RULE OF REASON

Not surprisingly, our legal system casts a particularly unyielding eye on horizontal restraints of trade. After all, cooperation among putative competitors nullifies much of the virtue of the market system. The various horizontal restraints are governed by Section 1 of the Sherman Act which forbids contracts, combinations, or conspiracies in restraint of trade. The statute was, of course, broadly drawn to embrace the many possibilities that arise in American commerce. Therefore, the courts were left to determine what Congress meant by the phrase *restraint of trade.* In the *Standard Oil*[1] decision of 1911, the U.S. Supreme Court articulated what has come to be known as the Rule of Reason. In essence the Court said that the Sherman Act forbids only *unreasonable* restraints of trade. Standard Oil was charged in 1904 with controlling approximately 90 percent of all the refined oil produced in the United States. It was accused of intentionally seeking that monopoly posture through the use of espionage, bribery, secret rebates, and other predatory practices. In ordering the dissolution of the company, the Court found that Standard Oil had abused its power and subverted commerce, thus *unreasonably* restraining trade.

The Rule of Reason has remained a source of considerable controversy because it recognized the possibility of lawful restraints of trade and "good" as well as "bad" trusts. However, that 1911 interpretation, as applied to both Sections 1 and 2, remains the law today.

PER SE VIOLATIONS

Some antitrust violations are perceived to be so injurious to competition that their mere existence constitutes unlawful conduct. That is, the plaintiff must prove that the violation in question occurred, but he or she need not prove that the violation caused, or is likely to cause, harm. Such violations are simply unreasonable on their face. The per se rule has been applied by the courts to a number of offenses, including, for example, horizontal price-fixing.

However, in recent years the use of the per se doctrine has declined. The economics-based notions of efficiency and consumer welfare are increasingly causing jurists to insist on a showing of the defendant's economic power before finding an antitrust violation. Hence, in areas like group boycotts and market divisions (discussed later) per se decisions are less likely (and Rule-of-Reason decisions more likely) than was the case even 10 years ago.[2]

HORIZONTAL PRICE–FIXING

Principal legislation: Sherman Act, Section 1.

> Every contract, combination in the form of trust or otherwise, or conspiracy, in restraint of trade or commerce, among the several States, or with foreign nations, is hereby declared to be illegal.

A contract, combination or conspiracy among competitors that dampens price competition is an unreasonable restraint of trade and is per se unlawful. We need not inquire into the reasonableness of the price, nor need we offer proof of its harmful effect. It is simply illegal. We must give attention to the major dilemma in price-fixing and all other Sherman 1 violations; that is, what measure of proof satisfies the requirement of a contract, combination, or conspiracy. We need not worry over the precise meaning of the three critical words. Rather, a general showing of cooperative action must be offered. That action in concert may, of course, be proved by evidence of an explicit accord, but it may also be inferred from a collection of circumstantial evidence. Law professor Lawrence Sullivan offers this very useful summary:

> All considered, there is a wide range of possible ways to show conspiracy; anything logically indicative will likely be admissible and will warrant a jury

making the damning inference. Thus, evidence of meetings or correspondence or memoranda or opportunities for communication may be admissible as foundation evidence of concerted agreement and, given such a foundation, acts of one or more conspirators consistent with the alleged conspiracy may be admitted against all. For example, evidence that a series of meetings among competitors occurred shortly before each change of price in the industry is enough to warrant the inference that price changes were agreed upon. Alternatively, evidence of the entire course of dealings by major firms in an industry, including various acts that seem explicable only on the assumption of concerted goals, may be used to establish a conspiracy.[3]

An unlawful conspiracy is to be distinguished from independent but parallel business behavior by competitors. So-called *Conscious Parallelism* is fully lawful because the competitors have not agreed either explicitly or by implication to follow the same course of action. Rather their business judgment has led each to independently follow parallel courses of action. In a variation on the general conspiracy theme, the Supreme Court in 1984 firmly rejected the "intra-enterprise conspiracy" doctrine in holding that a parent corporation and its wholly owned subsidiary are incapable, as a matter of law, of conspiracy in violation of Sherman 1.[4]

The evidence suggests price-fixing is not an unusual commercial practice. For example, in recent years the Justice Department has vigorously pursued the problem of bid-rigging in the highway construction business. From 1979 to 1982, the Justice Department initiated 230 criminal prosecutions involving 208 corporations and 221 individuals in 15 states. The conviction rate was about 90 percent with 154 companies and 167 individuals actually pleading guilty. The result is savings of at least $750 million annually, based on a General Accounting Office estimate that bid rigging inflates contract prices by about 10 percent.[5]

That at least some elements of the business community do not take the price-fixing laws entirely seriously is suggested by the following February 1982 conversation between Robert L. Crandall, chief executive officer of American Airlines, and Howard Putnam, then president of Braniff. The conversation became a matter of public record after it was submitted to a federal court.

Mr. Crandall

I think it's dumb as hell for Christ's sake, all right, to sit here and pound the [expletive] out of each other and neither one of us making a [expletive] dime.

Mr. Putnam

Well. . . .

Mr. Crandall

I mean, you know, goddamn, what the [expletive] is the point of it?

Mr. Putnam

Do you have a suggestion for me?

Mr. Crandall

> Yes I have a suggestion for you. Raise your goddamn fares 20 percent. I'll raise mine the next morning.

Mr. Putnam

> Robert, we . . .

Mr. Crandall

> You'll make more money and I will too.

Mr. Putnam

> We can't talk about pricing.

Mr. Crandall

> O [expletive], Howard. We can talk about any goddamn thing we want to talk about.[6]

The *NCAA* case that follows illustrates the Court's reasoning in a price-fixing and output restriction situation. This case is unusual in that it represents one of those rare instances where horizontal price-fixing was analyzed under the Rule of Reason rather than the per se standard.

NATIONAL COLLEGIATE ATHLETIC ASSOCIATION, PETITIONER V. BOARD OF REGENTS OF THE UNIVERSITY OF OKLAHOMA AND UNIVERSITY OF GEORGIA ATHLETIC ASSOCIATION
468 U.S. 85 (1984)

Justice Stevens

The University of Oklahoma and the University of Georgia contend that the National Collegiate Athletic Association has unreasonably restrained trade in the televising of college football games. After an extended trial, the District Court found that the NCAA had violated § 1 of the Sherman Act. . . . The Court of Appeals agreed that the statute had been violated but modified the remedy in some respects. . . . We granted certiorari . . . and now affirm.

I: The NCAA

Since its inception in 1905, the NCAA has played an important role in the regulation of amateur collegiate sports. It has adopted and promulgated playing rules, standards of amateurism, standards for academic eligibility, regulations concerning recruitment of athletes, and rules governing the size of athletic squads and coaching staffs. In some sports, such as baseball, swimming, basketball, wrestling and track, it has sponsored and conducted national tournaments. It has not done so in the sport of football, however. With the exception of football, the NCAA has not undertaken any regulation of the televising of athletic events.

The NCAA has approximately 850 voting members. The regular members are classified into separate divisions to reflect differences in size and scope of their athletic programs. Division I includes 276 colleges with major athletic programs; in this group only 187 play intercollegiate football. Divisions II and III include approximately 500 colleges with less extensive athletic programs. Division I has been subdivided into Divisions I–A and I–AA for football.

Some years ago, five major conferences together with major football-playing independent institutions organized the College Football Association (CFA). The original purpose of the CFA was to promote the interests of major football-playing schools within the NCAA structure. The Universities of Oklahoma and Georgia, respondents in this Court, are members of the CFA. . . .

The Current [Television] Plan

The plan adopted in 1981 for the 1982–1985 seasons is at issue in this case. This plan, like each of its predecessors, recites that it is intended to reduce, insofar as possible, the adverse effects of live television upon football game attendance. It provides that ''all forms of television of the football games of NCAA member institutions during the Plan control periods shall be in accordance with this Plan.'' . . .

The plan recites that the television committee has awarded rights to negotiate and contract for the telecasting of college football games of members of the NCAA to two ''carrying networks.''

* * * * *

The plan also contains ''appearance requirements'' and ''appearance limitations'' which pertain to each of the two-year periods that the plan is in effect. The basic requirement imposed on each of the two networks is that it must schedule appearances for at least 82 different member institutions during each two-year period. Under the appearance limitations no member institution is eligible to appear on television more than a total of six times and more than four times nationally, with the appearances to be divided equally between the two carrying networks. . . .

Thus, although the current plan is more elaborate than any of its predecessors, it retains the essential features of each of them. It limits the total amount of televised intercollegiate football and the number of games that any one team may televise. No member is permitted to make any sale of television rights except in accordance with the basic plan.

Background of This Controversy

Beginning in 1979 CFA members began to advocate that colleges with major football programs should have a greater voice in the formulation of football television policy than they had in the NCAA. CFA therefore investigated the possibility of negotiating a television agreement of its own, developed an independent plan, and obtained a contract offer from the National Broadcasting Co. (NBC). This contract, which it signed in August 1981, would have allowed a more liberal number of appearances for each institution, and would have increased the overall revenues realized by CFA members. . . .

In response the NCAA publicly announced that it would take disciplinary action against any CFA member that complied with the CFA–NBC contract. . . . On September 8, 1981, respondents commenced this action in the United States District Court . . . and obtained a preliminary injunction preventing the NCAA from initiating disciplinary proceedings or otherwise interfering with CFA's efforts to perform its agreement with NBC. . . .

Decision of the District Court

After a full trial, the District Court held that the controls exercised by the NCAA over the televising of college football games violated the Sherman Act. The District Court defined the relevant market as "live college football television" because it found that alternative programming has a significantly different and lesser audience appeal. . . . The District Court then concluded that the NCAA controls over college football are those of a "classic cartel" with an

> almost absolute control over the supply of college football which is made available to the networks, to television advertisers, and ultimately to the viewing public. Like all other cartels, NCAA members have sought and achieved a price for their product which is, in most instances, artificially high. The NCAA cartel imposes production limits on its members and maintains mechanisms for punishing cartel members who seek to stray from these production quotas. The cartel has established a uniform price for the products of each of the member producers, with no regard for the differing quality of these products or the consumer demand for these various products.

The District Court found that competition in the relevant market had been restrained in three ways: (1) NCAA fixed the price for particular telecasts; (2) its exclusive network contracts were tantamount to a group boycott of all other potential broadcasters and its threat of sanctions against its own members constituted a threatened boycott of potential competitors; and (3) its plan placed an artificial limit on the production of televised college football. . . .

In the District Court the NCAA offered two principal justifications for its television policies: that they protected the gate attendance of its members and that they tended to preserve a competitive balance among the football programs of the various schools. The District Court rejected the first justification because the evidence did not support the claim that college football television adversely affected gate attendance. With respect to the "competitive balance" argument, the District Court found that the evidence failed to show that the NCAA regulations on matters such as recruitment and the standards for preserving amateurism were not sufficient to maintain an appropriate balance. . . .

Decision of the Court of Appeals

The Court of Appeals held that the NCAA television plan constituted illegal per se price-fixing.

* * * * *

II

There can be no doubt that the challenged practices of the NCAA constitute a "restraint of trade" in the sense that they limit members' freedom to negotiate and enter into their own television contracts. In that sense, however, every contract is a restraint of trade, and as we have repeatedly recognized, the Sherman Act was intended to prohibit only unreasonable restraints of trade.

It is also undeniable that these practices share characteristics of restraints we have previously held unreasonable. The NCAA is an association of schools which compete against each other to attract television revenues, not to mention fans and athletes. As the District Court found, the policies of the NCAA with respect to television rights are ultimately controlled by the vote of member institutions. By participating in an association which prevents member institutions from competing against each other on the basis of price or kind of television rights that can be offered to broadcasters, the NCAA member institutions have created a horizontal restraint—an agreement among competitors on the way in which they will compete with one another. A restraint of this type has often been held to be unreasonable as a matter of law. Because it places a ceiling on the number of games member institutions may televise, the horizontal agreement places an artificial limit on the quantity of televised football that is available to broadcasters and consumers. By restraining the quantity of television rights available for sale, the challenged practices create a limitation on output; our cases have held that such limitations are unreasonable restraints of trade. Moreover, the District Court found that the minimum aggregate price in fact operates to preclude any price negotiation between broadcasters and institutions, thereby constituting horizontal price-fixing, perhaps the paradigm of an unreasonable restraint of trade.

Horizontal price-fixing and output limitation are ordinarily condemned as a matter of law under an "illegal per se" approach because the probability that these practices are anticompetitive is so high; a per se rule is applied when "the practice facially appears to be one that would always or almost always tend to restrict competition and decrease output." *Broadcast Music, Inc.* v. *CBS*, 441 U.S. 1, 19–20 (1979). In such circumstances a restraint is presumed unreasonable without inquiry into the particular market context in which it is found. Nevertheless, we have decided that it would be inappropriate to apply a per se rule to this case. This decision is not based on a lack of judicial experience with this type of arrangement, on the fact that the NCAA is organized as a nonprofit entity, or on our respect for the NCAA's historic role in the preservation and encouragement of intercollegiate amateur athletics. Rather, what is critical is that this case involves an industry in which horizontal restraints on competition are essential if the product is to be available at all.

As Judge Bork has noted: "[S]ome activities can only be carried out jointly. Perhaps the leading example is league sports. When a league of professional lacrosse teams is formed, it would be pointless to declare their cooperation illegal on the ground that there are no other professional lacrosse teams." . . . What the NCAA and its member institutions market in this case is competition itself—contests between competing institutions. Of course, this would be completely ineffective if there were no rules on which the competitors agreed to create and define the competition to be marketed. A myriad of rules affecting such matters as the size of the field, the number of players on a team, and the extent to which physical violence is to be encouraged or proscribed, all must be agreed upon, and all restrain the manner in which institutions compete.

. . . Thus, the NCAA plays a vital role in enabling college football to preserve its character, and as a result enables a product to be marketed which might otherwise be unavailable. In performing this role, its actions widen consumer choice—not only the choices available to sports fans but also those available to athletes—and hence can be viewed as procompetitive.

III

Because it restrains price and output, the NCAA's television plan has a significant potential for anticompetitive effects. The findings of the District Court indicate that this potential has been realized. The District Court found that if member institutions were free to sell television rights, many more games would be shown on television, and that the NCAA's output restriction has the effect of raising the price the networks pay for television rights. Moreover, the court found that by fixing a price for television rights to all games, the NCAA creates a price structure that is unresponsive to viewer demand and unrelated to the prices that would prevail in a competitive market. And, of course, since as a practical matter all member institutions need NCAA approval, members have no real choice but to adhere to the NCAA's television controls.

* * * * *

Petitioner argues, however, that its television plan can have no significant anticompetitive effect since the record indicates that it has no market power—no ability to alter the interaction of supply and demand in the market. We must reject this argument for two reasons, one legal, one factual.

As a matter of law, the absence of proof of market power does not justify a naked restriction on price or output. To the contrary, when there is an agreement not to compete in terms of price or output, "no elaborate industry analysis is required to demonstrate the anticompetitive character of such an agreement." . . .

As a factual matter, it is evident that petitioner does possess market power. The District Court employed the correct test for determining whether college football broadcasts constitute a separate market—whether there are other products that are reasonably substitutable for televised NCAA football games. . . . It found that intercollegiate football telecasts generate an audience uniquely attractive to advertisers and that competitors are unable to offer programming that can attract a similar audience. These findings amply support its conclusion that the NCAA possesses market power. . . .

IV

Relying on *Broadcast Music,* petitioner argues that its television plan constitutes a co-operative "joint venture" which assists in the marketing of broadcast rights and hence is procompetitive. . . .

The District Court did not find that the NCAA's television plan produced any procompetitive efficiences which enhanced the competitiveness of college football television rights; to the contrary it concluded that NCAA football could be marketed just as effectively without the television plan. There is therefore no predicate in the findings for petitioner's efficiency justification. Indeed, petitioner's argument is refuted by the District Court's finding concerning price and output. If the NCAA's television plan produced procompetitive efficiencies, the plan would increase output and reduce the price of televised games. The District Court's contrary findings accordingly undermine petitioner's position. . . .

V

Throughout the history of its regulation of intercollegiate football telecasts, the NCAA has indicated its concern with protecting live attendance.

* * * * *

There is, however, a . . . fundamental reason for rejecting this defense. The NCAA's argument that its television plan is necessary to protect live attendance is not based on a desire to maintain the integrity of college football as a distinct and attractive product, but rather on a fear that the product will not prove sufficiently attractive to draw live attendance when faced with competition from televised games. At bottom the NCAA's position is that ticket sales for most college games are unable to compete in a free market. The television plan protects ticket sales by limiting output—just as any monopolist increases revenues by reducing output.

VI

Petitioner argues that the interest in maintaining a competitive balance among amateur athletic teams is legitimate and important and that it justifies the regulations challenged in this case. We agree with the first part of the argument but not the second.

* * * * *

The NCAA does not claim that its television plan has equalized or is intended to equalize competition within any one league. The plan is nationwide in scope and there is no single league or tournament in which all college football teams compete. . . .

The television plan is not even arguably tailored to serve such an interest. It does not regulate the amount of money that any college may spend on its football program, nor the way in which the colleges may use the revenues that are generated by their football programs, whether derived from the sale of television rights, the sale of tickets, or the sale of concessions or program advertising. The plan simply imposes a restriction on one source of revenue that is more important to some colleges than to others. There is no evidence that this restriction produces any greater measure of equality throughout the NCAA than would a restriction on alumni donations, tuition rates, or any other revenue-producing activity. At the same time, as the District Court found, the NCAA imposes a variety of other restrictions designed to preserve amateurism which are much better tailored to the goal of competitive balance than is the television plan, and which are "clearly sufficient" to preserve competitive balance to the extent it is within the NCAA's power to do so. Affirmed.

Questions

1. Why was the NCAA's challenged television arrangement analyzed under the Rule of Reason rather than the per se rule?
2. What defenses were offered by the NCAA?
3. Does the *NCAA* ruling mean colleges and universities may not lawfully join together in groups to arrange mutually agreeable television football packages? Explain.
4. Assume two drugstores, located across the street from each other and each involved in interstate commerce, agree to exchange, on a monthly basis, a list of prices charged for all nonprescription medications. Is that arrangement lawful in the absence of any further cooperation? Explain.
5. As common sense and the cases reveal, sharing of price information among competitors can facilitate anticompetitive collusion, but how might that sharing facilitate competition?
6. Justify the use of per se rulings.
7. The gasoline dealers association in a community reaches an agreement providing: (1) both major brands and independents will not give trading stamps or other premiums and (2) majors agree not to advertise their prices except on the pumps.

a. What is the purpose of the arrangement?

b. What violation of law might be alleged? Decide the case. Explain. See *U.S.* v. *Gasoline Retailers Association*, 285 F.2d 688 (1961).

8. Assume 10 real estate firms operate in the city of Gotham. Further assume each charges a 7 percent commission on all residential sales.

a. Does that uniformity of prices in and of itself constitute price-fixing? Explain.

b. Assume we have evidence that the firms agreed to set the 7 percent level. What defense would be raised against a price-fixing charge?

c. Would that defense succeed? Explain. See *McLain* v. *Real Estate Board of New Orleans, Inc.*, 444 U.S. 232 (1980).

9. Assume the bar owners in a college community are concerned about serving liquor to patrons younger than the legal drinking age (18, in this case). The owners reach an agreement to reject admission to anyone under 19 years of age. Is that agreement lawful? Explain.

Afterword

To date, the victory by Oklahoma and Georgia in the *NCAA* case appears to have been harmful to the financial interests of the bulk of the NCAA football schools. The smaller, less-prominent schools argue that their home attendance has been harmed because of competition from the expanded number of telecasts of games involving well-known schools. But the large schools as a group also appear to have been hurt.

> With so many more games on the tube, it's only natural that ratings have declined as the audience is split. And when ratings drop, it's only natural that advertising dollars will sink accordingly.
>
> The full impact of unlimited TV has started to show up this season. Average revenues are down a staggering 50 percent—from an average $1.5 million per game under the NCAA plan ruled invalid in 1984 to about $800,000 per game in the wide-open market.
>
> NCAA research figures show that rights fees have tumbled 37.9 percent, the average number of TV games has increased 28.1 percent, money paid per exposure has decreased 50.4 percent, and commercial availability has jumped 88.8 percent. In other words, there is more time than advertisers.[7]

Of course, some schools and conferences (e.g., Notre Dame and the Big Ten) have prospered under the new arrangements because they are located in very large television market areas.

HORIZONTAL DIVISION OF MARKETS

Principal legislation: Sherman Act, Section 1.

The issue here is whether competitors can lawfully agree (1) to divide their market geographically and/or (2) to allocate customers among themselves. In simplest terms, could Company X lawfully agree to sell only on the east side of the Mississippi River if Company Y (X's competitor) agrees to sell only on the west side? Why would they wish to do so? Under what conditions might such an arrangement enhance competition? Similarly, could Manufacturers X and Y lawfully agree to sell only to retailers rather than to wholesalers? The *Topco* case answers these questions.

UNITED STATES V. TOPCO ASSOCIATES, INC.
405 U.S. 596 (1972)

Justice Marshall

I

Topco is a cooperative association of approximately 25 small and medium-sized regional supermarket chains that operate stores in some 33 states. Each of the member chains operates independently; there is no pooling of earnings, profits, capital, management, or advertising resources. No grocery business is conducted under the Topco name. Its basic function is to serve as a purchasing agent for its members. In this capacity, it procures and distributes to the members more than 1,000 different food and related nonfood items, most of which are distributed under brand names owned by Topco. The association does not itself own any manufacturing, processing, or warehousing facilities, and the items that it procures for members are usually shipped directly from the packer or manufacturer to the members. Payment is made either to Topco or directly to the manufacturer at a cost that is virtually the same for the members as for Topco itself. . . .

Topco was founded in the 1940s by a group of small, local grocery chains, independently owned and operated, that desired to cooperate to obtain high-quality merchandise under private labels in order to compete more effectively with larger national and regional chains. . . . By 1964, Topco's members had combined retail sales of more than $2 billion; by 1967, their sales totaled more than $2.3 billion, a figure exceeded by only three national grocery chains.

Members of the association vary in the degree of market share that they possess in their respective areas. The range is from 1.5 percent to 16 percent, with the average being approximately 6 percent. While it is difficult to compare these figures with the market shares of larger regional and national chains because of the absence in the record of accurate statistics for these chains, there is much evidence in the record that Topco members are frequently in as strong a competitive position in their respective areas as any other chain. The strength of this competitive position is due, in some measure, to the success of Topco-brand products. Although only 10 percent of the total goods sold by Topco members bear the association's brand names, the profit on these goods is substantial and their very existence has improved the competitive potential of Topco members with respect to other large and powerful chains.

II

. . . The United States charged that, beginning at least as early as 1960 and continuing up to the time that the complaint was filed, Topco had combined and conspired with its members to violate § 1 . . . in two respects. First, the government alleged that there existed:

> a continuing agreement, understanding and concert of action among the co-conspirator member firms acting through Topco, the substantial terms of which have been and are that each co-conspirator member firm will sell Topco-controlled brands only within the marketing territory allocated to it, and will refrain from selling Topco-controlled brands outside such marketing territory.

Following approval, each new member signs an agreement with Topco designating the territory in which that member may sell Topco-brand products. No member may sell these products outside the territory in which it is licensed. Most licenses are exclusive, and even those denominated "coextensive" or "non-exclusive" prove to be *de facto* exclusive. . . . When combined with each member's veto power over new members, provisions for exclusivity work effectively to insulate members from competition in Topco-brand goods. Should a member violate its license agreement and sell in areas other than those in which it is licensed, its membership can be terminated. . . .

From the inception of this lawsuit, Topco accepted as true most of the government's allegations regarding territorial divisions and restrictions on wholesaling, although it differed greatly with the government on the conclusions, both factual and legal, to be drawn from these facts. . . .

Topco essentially maintains that it needs territorial divisions to compete with larger chains; that the association could not exist if the territorial divisions were anything but exclusive; and that by restricting competition in the sale of Topco-brand goods, the association actually increases competition by enabling its members to compete successfully with larger regional and national chains.

* * * * *

While the Court has utilized the "rule of reason" in evaluating the legality of most restraints alleged to be violative of the Sherman Act, it has also developed the doctrine that certain business relationships are per se violations of the act without regard to a consideration of their reasonableness. . . .

. . . One of the classic examples of a per se violation of § 1 is an agreement between competitors at the same level of the market structure to allocate territories in order to minimize competition. Such concerted action is usually termed a "horizontal" restraint, in contradistinction to combinations of persons at different levels of the market structure, e.g., manufacturers and distributors, which are termed "vertical" restraints. This Court has reiterated time and time again that "[h]orizontal territorial limitations . . . are naked restraints of trade with no purpose except stifling of competition." . . .

Such limitations are per se violations of the Sherman Act. . . .

* * * * *

In applying these rigid rules, the Court has consistently rejected the notion that naked restraints of trade are to be tolerated because they are well intended or because they are allegedly developed to increase competition.

* * * * *

The District Court determined that by limiting the freedom of its individual members to compete with each other, Topco was doing a greater good by fostering competition between members and other large supermarket chains. But, the fallacy in this is that Topco has no authority under the Sherman Act to determine the respective values of competition in various sectors of the economy. On the contrary, the Sherman Act gives to each Topco member and to each prospective member the right to ascertain for itself whether or not competition with other supermarket chains is more desirable than competition in the sale of Topco-brand products. . . .

There have been tremendous departures from the notion of a free-enterprise system as it was originally conceived in this country. These departures have been the product of congressional action and the will of the people. If a decision is to be made to sacrifice competition in one portion of the economy for greater competition in another portion, this too is a decision that must be made by Congress and not by private forces or by the courts. Private forces are too keenly aware of their own interests in making such decisions and courts are ill-equipped and ill-situated for such decision-making. To analyze, interpret, and evaluate the myriad of competing interests and the endless data that would surely be brought to bear on such decisions, and to make the delicate judgment on the relative values to society of competitive areas of the economy, the judgment of the elected representatives of the people is required.

* * * * *

We reverse the judgment of the District Court and remand the case. . . .

Chief Justice Burger, dissenting.

This case does not involve restraints on interbrand competition or an allocation of markets by an association with monopoly or near-monopoly control of the sources of supply of one or more varieties of staple goods. Rather, we have here an agreement among several small grocery chains to join in a cooperative endeavor that, in my view, has an unquestionably lawful principal purpose; in pursuit of that purpose they have mutually agreed to certain minimal ancillary restraints that are fully reasonable in view of the principal purpose and that have never before today been held by this Court to be per se violations of the Sherman Act.

In joining in this cooperative endeavor, these small chains did not agree to the restraints here at issue in order to make it possible for them to exploit an already established line of products through noncompetitive pricing. There was no such thing as a Topco line of products until this cooperative was formed. The restraints to which the cooperative's members have agreed deal only with the marketing of the products in the Topco line, and the only function of those restraints is to permit each member chain to establish, within its own geographical area and through its own local advertising and marketing efforts, a local consumer awareness of the trademarked family of products as that member's "private-label" line. The goal sought was the enhancement of the individual members' abilities to compete, albeit to a modest degree, with the large national chains which had been successfully marketing private-label lines for several years. The sole reason for a cooperative endeavor was to make economically feasible such things as quality control, large-quantity purchases at bulk prices, the development of attractively printed labels, and the ability to offer a number of different lines of trademarked products. All these things, of course, are feasible for the large national chains operating individually, but they are beyond the reach of the small operators proceeding alone.

After a careful review of the economic considerations bearing upon this case, the District Court determined that "the relief which the government here seeks would not increase competition in Topco private label brands"; on the contrary, such relief "would substantially diminish competition in the supermarket field." . . . This Court has not today determined, on the basis of an examination of the underlying economic realities, that the District Court's conclusions are incorrect. . . .

Questions

1. In *Topco* how does the defendant association seek to justify its division of the market? How do you evaluate that defense?
2. In exchange for royalties, Sealy allocated mutually exclusive sales territories among the various firms it licensed to construct and sell mattresses bearing the Sealy label. Sealy's agreement with each licensee provided that Sealy would not license others to manufacture or sell in the designated area, and the licensee agreed not to manufacture or sell Sealy products outside its designated area. Sealy's licensees numbered approximately 30. Those licensees owned substantially all of Sealy's stock. Sealy's business was managed by its board of directors. Each director had to be a stockholder or his nominee. Sealy contended that its primary purpose in its licensing arrangement was to exploit the Sealy name and trademark. The government filed suit against Sealy, alleging price-fixing and horizontal territorial limitations. At the trial level, Sealy was found guilty of price-fixing but innocent as to territorial restraint. The government appealed the latter, while Sealy chose not to contest the former.
   a. Defend Sealy.
   b. Decide the case. See *United States* v. *Sealy, Incorporated,* 388 U.S. 350 (1967).
   c. Would your decision in *Sealy* be changed if the U.S. Supreme Court were to embrace Judge Bork's reasoning in *Rothery* (see below)? Explain.
3. In analyzing horizontal territorial restraints, Professor Wesley Liebeler argues:

   > But it does not appear that collusion between dealers who handle the product of only one manufacturer—White truck dealers, Chevrolet dealers, or Sylvania television dealers, for example—will result in higher prices and restricted output.[8]

   What economic logic supports his position?

Afterword

The most interesting and provocative antitrust decision in recent years casts some doubt on the *Topco* reasoning. In *Rothery Storage & Van Co.* v. *Atlas Van Lines, Inc.*[9] the District of Columbia Federal Circuit Court of Appeals reasoned that recent U.S. Supreme Court decisions, including the *NCAA* price-fixing case had, in effect, overruled *Topco* "as to the per se illegality of all horizontal restraints."[10] Interest in the opinion is perhaps now more intense than at the time of its issuance because it was authored by then Judge Robert Bork, who, in 1987, was the subject of intense public and political scrutiny as President Reagan's (rejected) choice to fill a Supreme Court vacancy. Notwithstanding his Supreme Court rejection, Bork's influence, particularly in antitrust law, has been immense. In *Rothery* he adhered to his view of market efficiency as the primary determinant of antitrust standards.

The *Rothery* facts were not in dispute. Rothery and other independent moving companies operated under contracts with Atlas Van Lines in which the independents would act as agents of Atlas, moving furniture and other goods as instructed. The advent of deregulation permitted the independents to move furniture on their own in interstate commerce, a power that prior to deregulation had largely been beyond their grasp. The result was that Atlas was then in competition with its own agents. Therefore, Atlas announced it would terminate the contract of any agent that persisted in handling interstate business on its own as well as for Atlas. Rothery and other Atlas agents sued, claiming (among other possibilities) that Atlas was guilty of a per se illegality (in this case, horizontal price maintenance because the agents were required to adhere to the shipping rates established by Atlas). The district court upheld the Atlas policy based on a balancing of the benefits and harms from the arrangement (a Rule of Reason analysis). The circuit court affirmed, but in so doing the panel reasoned that a balancing of good and bad was unnecessary in the case because Atlas' less-than-6-percent share of the market could not create any harm. To the circuit court, the Atlas arrangement was an efficient method of providing nationwide moving services that also prevented the Atlas agents from free riding on the Atlas name when those agents moved goods on their own. The effect of Bork's reasoning was to treat market share as perhaps the only measure of anticompetitive impact in Rule of Reason cases. Whether Bork's reasoning will ultimately carry the day remains to be seen. In her concurring opinion in *Rothery,* Judge Patricia Wald declined to adopt market power as an exclusive measure in all such cases:

> Until the Supreme Court indicates that the *only* goal of antitrust law is to promote efficiency, as the panel uses that term, I think it is more prudent to proceed with a . . . Rule of Reason analysis, than to adopt a market power test as the exclusive filtering-out device for all potential violaters who do not command a significant market share. Under any analysis, market power is an important consideration; I am not yet willing to say it is the only one.[11]

REFUSALS TO DEAL

Principal legislation: Sherman Act, Section 1.

A *group boycott* is yet another instance of concerted action in which a collectivity of traders jointly refuses to deal with another trader or traders. Typically, the purpose of such an arrangement is to remove or "police" a competitor. Depending on the facts, group boycotts may be analyzed under the Rule of Reason or they may be treated as per se violations. What boycott might arise from the facts diagrammed here?

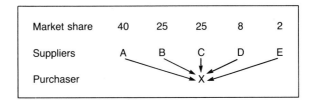

The following case summarizes current boycott law.

NORTHWEST WHOLESALE STATIONERS, INC. V. PACIFIC STATIONERY & PRINTING CO.
472 U.S. 284 (1984)

Justice Brennan

This case requires that we decide whether a *per se* violation of § 1 of the Sherman Act occurs when a cooperative buying agency comprising various retailers expels a member without providing any procedural means for challenging the expulsion. The case also raises broader questions as to when *per se* antitrust analysis is appropriately applied to joint activity that is susceptible of being characterized as a concerted refusal to deal.

I

Because the District Court ruled on cross-motions for summary judgment after only limited discovery, this case comes to us on a sparse record. Certain background facts are undisputed. Petitioner Northwest Wholesale Stationers is a purchasing cooperative made up of approximately 100 office supply retailers in the Pacific Northwest States. The cooperative acts as the primary wholesaler for the retailers. Retailers that are not members of the cooperative can purchase wholesale supplies from Northwest at the same price as members. At the end of each year, however, Northwest distributes its profits to members in the form of a percentage rebate on purchases. Members therefore effectively purchase supplies at a price significantly lower than do nonmembers. Northwest also provides certain warehousing facilities. The cooperative arrangement thus permits the participating retailers to achieve economies of scale in purchasing and warehousing that would otherwise be unavailable to them. In fiscal 1978 Northwest had $5.8 million in sales.

Respondent Pacific Stationery & Printing Co. sells office supplies at both the retail and wholesale levels. Its total sales in fiscal 1978 were approximately $7.6 million; the record does not indicate what percentage of revenue is attributable to retail and what percentage is attributable to wholesale. Pacific became a member of Northwest in 1958. In 1974 Northwest amended its bylaws to prohibit members from engaging in both retail and wholesale operations. A grandfather clause preserved Pacific's membership rights. In 1977 ownership of a controlling share of the stock of Pacific changed hands at 70, and the new owners did not officially bring this change to the attention of the directors of Northwest. This failure to notify apparently violated another of Northwest's bylaws.

In 1978 the membership of Northwest voted to expel Pacific. Most factual matters relevant to the expulsion are in dispute. No explanation for the expulsion was advanced at the time, and Pacific was given neither notice, a hearing, nor any other opportunity to challenge the decision. Pacific argues that the expulsion resulted from Pacific's decision to maintain a wholesale operation. Northwest contends that the expulsion resulted from Pacific's failure to notify the cooperative members of the change in stock ownership. The minutes of the meeting of Northwest's directors do not definitively indicate the motive for the expulsion. It is undisputed that Pacific received approximately $10,000 in rebates from Northwest in 1978, Pacific's last year of membership. Beyond a possible inference of loss from this fact, however, the record is devoid of allegations indicating the nature and extent of competitive injury the expulsion caused Pacific to suffer.

Pacific brought suit in 1980 in the United States District Court. . . . The gravamen of the action was that Northwest's expulsion of Pacific from the cooperative without procedural protections was a group boycott that limited Pacific's ability to compete and should be considered *per se* violative of § 1. . . . [T]he District Court rejected application of the *per se* rule and held instead that rule-of-reason analysis should govern the case. Finding no anticompetitive effect on the basis of the record as presented, the court granted summary judgment for Northwest.

The Court of Appeals for the Ninth Circuit reversed, holding "that the uncontroverted facts of this case support a finding of *per se* liability." . . .

II

The decision of the cooperative members to expel Pacific was certainly a restraint of trade in the sense that every commercial agreement restrains trade. Whether this action violates § 1 of the Sherman Act depends on whether it is adjudged an *unreasonable* restraint. Rule-of-reason analysis guides the inquiry unless the challenged action falls into the category of "agreements or practices which because of their pernicious effect on competition and lack of any redeeming virtue are conclusively presumed to be unreasonable and therefore illegal without elaborate inquiry as to the precise harm they have caused or the business excuse for their use."

This *per se* approach permits categorical judgments with respect to certain business practices that have proved to be predominantly anticompetitive. Courts can thereby avoid the "significant costs" in "business certainty and litigation efficiency" that a full-fledged rule-of-reason inquiry entails. The decision to apply the *per se* rule turns on "whether the practice facially appears to be one that would always or almost always tend to restrict competition and decrease output . . . or instead one designed to 'increase economic efficiency and render markets more, rather than less, competitive.' " . . .

This Court has long held that certain concerted refusals to deal or group boycotts are so likely to restrict competition without any offsetting efficiency gains that they should be condemned as *per se* violations of § 1 of the Sherman Act. The question presented in this case is whether Northwest's decision to expel Pacific should fall within this category of activity that is conclusively presumed to be anticompetitive. . . .

Cases to which this Court has applied the *per se* approach have generally involved joint efforts by a firm or firms to disadvantage competitors by "either directly denying or persuading or coercing suppliers or customers to deny relationships the competitors need in the competitive struggle." In these cases, the boycott often cut off access to a supply, facility, or market necessary to enable the boycotted firm to compete, and frequently the boycotting firms possessed a dominant position in the relevant market. In addition, the practices were generally not justified by plausible arguments that they were intended to enhance overall efficiency and make markets more competitive. . . .

* * * * *

Wholesale purchasing cooperatives such as Northwest are not a form of concerted activity characteristically likely to result in predominantly anticompetitive effects. Rather, such cooperative arrangements would seem to be "designed to increase economic efficiency and render markets more, rather than less, competitive." The arrangement permits the participating retailers to achieve economies of scale in both the purchase and warehousing of wholesale supplies, and also ensures ready access to a stock of goods that might otherwise be unavailable on short notice. The cost savings and order-filling guarantees enable smaller retailers to reduce prices and maintain their retail stock so as to compete more effectively with larger retailers.

Pacific, of course, does not object to the existence of the cooperative arrangement, but rather raises an antitrust challenge to Northwest's decision to bar Pacific from continued membership. It is therefore the action of expulsion that must be evaluated to determine whether *per se* treatment is appropriate. The act of expulsion from a wholesale cooperative does not necessarily imply anticompetitive animus and thereby raise a probability of anticompetitive effect. Wholesale purchasing cooperatives must establish and enforce reasonable rules in order to function effectively. Disclosure rules, such as the one on which Northwest relies, may well provide the cooperative with a needed means for monitoring the creditworthiness of its members. Nor would the expulsion characteristically be likely to result in predominantly anticompetitive effects, at least in the type of situation this case presents. Unless the cooperative possesses market power or exclusive access to an element essential to effective competition, the conclusion that expulsion is virtually always likely to have an anticompetitive effect is not warranted. . . . Absent such a showing with respect to a cooperative buying arrangement, courts should apply a rule-of-reason analysis. At no time has Pacific made a threshold showing that these structural characteristics are present in this case.

* * * * *

Reversed.

Unilateral Refusals to Deal

While *Northwest* clearly involved group action, completely unilateral refusals to deal have been found unlawful where the refusal to deal serves to further an unlawful arrangement, such as tying, price-fixing, or market allocation. Further, any refusal to deal entered for predatory purposes (e.g., to drive a party out of business) rather than as a normal business judgment would be suspect.

Questions

1. Klor's, Inc., operated a retail store on Mission Street, San Francisco, California. Broadway-Hale Stores, Inc., a chain of department stores, operated one of its stores next door. The two stores competed in the sale of radios, television sets, refrigerators, and other household appliances.

   Klor's made the following allegations: George Klor started an appliance store some years before 1952. Klor's was as well equipped as Broadway-Hale to handle all brands of appliances. Nevertheless, manufacturers and distributors of such well-known brands as General Electric, RCA, Admiral, Zenith, Emerson, and others conspired among themselves and with Broadway-Hale either not to sell to Klor's or to sell to it only at discriminatory prices and highly unfavorable terms. Broadway-Hale used its "monopolistic" buying power to bring about this situation.

   Broadway-Hale submitted unchallenged affidavits showing there were hundreds of other household appliance retailers, some within a few blocks of Klor's, who sold many competing brands of appliances, including those the defendants refused to sell to Klor's.

   Klor's filed suit, claiming a violation of the Sherman Act.

   Decide. Explain. See *Klor's, Inc.* v. *Broadway-Hale Stores, Inc.*, 359 U.S. 207 (1959).

2. Boycotts often serve what might generally be regarded as "good" purposes. Give some examples of those boycotts. As a matter of law, are "good" boycotts treated differently than anticompetitive boycotts? Explain.

3. In 1977 the board of directors of the National Organization for Women (NOW) approved the use of economic boycotts, where appropriate, as a means of securing passage of the Equal Rights Amendment to the Constitution. NOW was successful in discouraging other organizations (e.g., the American Association of University Women) from holding meetings or conventions in states where the ERA had not been adopted. Was NOW's boycott program unlawful? Explain. See *Missouri* v. *National Organization for Women*, 620 F.2d 1301 (8th Cir. 1980), cert. den. No. 79–2037, October 6, 1980.

4. Each year the member teams of the National Football League conduct a draft of college seniors. The draft is conducted in inverse order of the teams' records in the previous season. By giving the weaker teams the earlier choices the hope is that the competitive balance of the league will be enhanced. Yazoo Smith was drafted by the Washington Redskins, and under league rules he was compelled to sign with them if he wanted to play in the NFL that season. He did so, but he was injured in preseason play. The injury ended his career. He brought an antitrust action to recover his economic losses.

    a. What violation did he allege?

    b. Is it a per se violation? Explain.

    c. Decide the case. See *Smith* v. *Pro Football, Inc.,* 593 F.2d 1173 (D.C. Cir. 1978).

5. Jane Blalock, a member of the Ladies Professional Golf Association, was accused of cheating by moving her ball without permission and without recording an additional stroke. The LPGA Executive Committee voted to suspend Blalock from play for one year. Blalock filed suit to contest the suspension. Decision? *Blalock* v. *Ladies Professional Golf Ass'n,* 359 F. Supp. 1260 (N.D. Ga. 1973).

INTERLOCKING DIRECTORATES

Principal legislation: Clayton Act, Section 8:

> [N]o person at the same time shall be a director in any two or more corporations, any one of which has capital, surplus, and undivided profits aggregating more than $1 million engaged in whole or in part in commerce . . . if such corporations are or shall have been . . . competitors, so that the elimination of competition by agreement between them would constitute a violation of any of the provisions of any of the antitrust laws.

Federal Trade Commission Act, Section 5:

> Unfair methods of competition in or affecting commerce, and unfair or deceptive acts or practices in or affecting commerce are hereby declared unlawful.

Congress was concerned that companies appearing to be competitors might actually behave cooperatively by the simple expedient of having the same set of persons control each company through their roles as directors. The possibilities for information sharing and other potentially anticompetitive conduct are considerable. The government has successfully broken certain important interlocks, but Section 8 is replete with loopholes. As a consequence, the government has of late turned more frequently to Section 5 of the Federal Trade Commission Act to intercede against interlocks. Interlocks remain somewhat common, the government having given them only modest attention.

A 1983 Supreme Court decision did clarify a continuing dispute in interpreting Section 8. We have known that interlocks involving two or more banks are, with exceptions, forbidden by the Clayton Act. However, the *BankAmerica* decision makes it clear that interlocks involving banks and competing nonbank institutions are exempt from the act. Therefore, individuals can continue to lawfully serve as directors of both banks and competing nonbank financial institutions (e.g., insurance companies).[12]

Part Two—Vertical Restraints

RESALE PRICE MAINTENANCE / VERTICAL TERRITORIAL AND CUSTOMER RESTRAINTS

Principal legislation: Sherman Act, Section 1; Federal Trade Commission Act, Section 5.

Manufacturers and distributors often seek to specify the price at which their customers may resell their products. Having sold its product, why should a manufacturer or distributor seek to influence the price at which the product is resold? The primary reasons are twofold: (1) by establishing a minimum price, the product's reputation for quality may be enhanced and (2) resale price maintenance policy seeks to prevent discount stores from undercutting regular retail outlets. (Why does the manufacturer or distributor prefer its products to be sold in traditional retail stores rather than in discount enterprises?)

An *agreement* between a seller and its buyer, fixing the price at which the buyer may resell the product, is a per se violation. However, sellers may lawfully engage in resale price maintenance if they do nothing more than specify prices at which their products are to be sold and unilaterally refuse to deal with anyone who does not adhere to those prices. [This is the so-called *Colgate* doctrine announced in *United States* v. *Colgate & Co.*, 250 U.S. 300 (1919).]

The Justice Department filed a brief in the 1984 *Monsanto* case,[13] asking the Supreme Court to reevaluate the per se standard. The Court declined to do so, noting that such actions "have been per se illegal since the early years of antitrust enforcement." Furthermore, at this writing in 1988, Congress is expected to approve legislation expressly affirming the resale price maintenance prohibition despite the Justice Department's preference for a Rule-of-Reason approach.

In addition to price restraints, manufacturers commonly wish to impose restrictions on where and to whom their products may be resold. Those restrictions typically afford an exclusive sales territory to a distributor. Similarly, manufacturers may prevent distributors from selling to some classes of customers (e.g., a distributor might be forbidden to sell to an unfranchised retailer). Of course, such arrangements necessarily retard or eliminate intrabrand competition. Because price and service competition among dealers in the same brand ordinarily is of benefit to the consumer, the courts have frequently struck down such arrangements. Indeed, until the *GTE* case (noted in the *B.E.C.* case below), the leading Supreme Court case of *United States* v. *Arnold, Schwinn & Co.*[14] held such restraints to be per se unlawful. Still, it is generally agreed that territorial and customer allocations also have merits. The *GTE Sylvania* case[15] enunciated those virtues and established the position that vertical restrictions are to be judged on a case-by-case basis, balancing interbrand and intrabrand competitive effects. Thus the Rule of Reason is now to be applied to vertical territorial and customer restraints.

At this point, the student will want to understand the critical distinction between horizontal and vertical territorial and customer allocations. The former is per se unlawful. The latter is to be resolved under the Rule of Reason unless it involves an agreement on prices. *Horizontal* restrictions are those arising from an agreement among the *competitors* themselves, while *vertical* restrictions are those imposed on buyers by their *suppliers*. The *B.E.C.* case offers a useful and up-to-date summary of the Supreme Court's analyses of both vertical price and nonprice restraints.

BUSINESS ELECTRONICS CORPORATION, PETITIONER V. SHARP ELECTRONICS CORPORATION
56 U.S.L.W. 4387–4392 (1988)

Justice Scalia

Petitioner Business Electronics Corporation seeks review of a decision of the United States Court of Appeals for the Fifth Circuit holding that a vertical restraint is *per se* illegal under § 1 of the Sherman Act, only if there is an express or implied agreement to set resale prices at some level. We granted certiorari to resolve a conflict in the Courts of Appeals regarding the proper dividing line between the rule that vertical price restraints are illegal *per se* and the rule that vertical nonprice restraints are to be judged under the rule of reason.

I

In 1968, petitioner became the exclusive retailer in the Houston, Texas area of electronic calculators manufactured by respondent Sharp Electronics Corporation. In 1972, respondent appointed Gilbert Hartwell as a second retailer in the Houston area. During the relevant period, electronic calculators were primarily sold to business customers for prices up to $1,000. While much of the evidence in this case was conflicting—in particular, concerning whether petitioner was "free riding" on Hartwell's provision of presale educational and promotional services by providing inadequate services itself—a few facts are undisputed. Respondent published a list of suggested minimum retail prices, but its written dealership agreements with petitioner and Hartwell did not obligate either to observe them, or to charge any other specific price. Petitioner's retail prices were often below respondent's suggested retail prices and generally below Hartwell's retail prices, even though Hartwell too sometimes priced below respondent's suggested retail prices. Hartwell complained to respondent on a number of occasions about petitioner's prices. In June 1973, Hartwell gave respondent the ultimatum that Hartwell would terminate his dealership unless respondent ended its relationship with petitioner within 30 days. Respondent terminated petitioner's dealership in July 1973.

Petitioner brought suit in the United States District Court for the Southern District of Texas, alleging that respondent and Hartwell had conspired to terminate petitioner and that such conspiracy was illegal *per se* under § 1 of the Sherman Act. The case was tried to a jury. The District Court submitted a liability interrogatory to the jury that asked whether ''there was an agreement or understanding between Sharp Electronics Corporation and Hartwell to terminate Business Electronics as a Sharp dealer because of Business Electronics' price cutting.'' The District Court instructed the jury at length about this question:

> The Sherman Act is violated when a seller enters into an agreement or understanding with one of its dealers to terminate another dealer because of the other dealer's price cutting. Plaintiff contends that Sharp terminated Business Electronics in furtherance of Hartwell's desire to eliminate Business Electronics as a price-cutting rival.
>
> If you find that there was an agreement between Sharp and Hartwell to terminate Business Electronics because of Business Electronics' price cutting, you should answer yes to Question Number 1.

* * * * *

> A combination, agreement or understanding to terminate a dealer because of his price cutting unreasonably restrains trade and cannot be justified for any reason. Therefore, even though the combination, agreement or understanding may have been formed or engaged in . . . to eliminate any alleged evils of price cutting, it is still unlawful.
>
> If a dealer demands that a manufacturer terminate a price-cutting dealer, and the manufacturer agrees to do so, the agreement is illegal if the manufacturer's purpose is to eliminate the price cutting.

The jury answered Question 1 affirmatively and awarded $600,000 in damages. . . .

* * * * *

The Fifth Circuit reversed. . . .

II
A

Section 1 of the Sherman Act provides that ''[e]very contract, combination in the form of trust or otherwise, or conspiracy, in restraint of trade or commerce among the several States, or with foreign nations, is declared to be illegal.'' Since the earliest decisions of this Court interpreting this provision, we have recognized that it was intended to prohibit only unreasonable restraints of trade. Ordinarily, whether particular concerted action violates § 1 of the Sherman Act is determined through case-by-case application of the so-called rule of reason. . . . Certain categories of agreements, however, have been held to be *per se* illegal, dispensing with the need for case-by-case evaluation. . . .

* * * * *

Although vertical agreements on resale prices have been illegal *per se* since *Dr. Miles Medical Co.* v. *John D. Park & Sons Co.*, we have recognized that the scope of *per se* illegality should be narrow in the context of vertical restraints. In *Continental T.V., Inc.* v. *GTE Sylvania Inc.* we refused to extend *per se* illegality to vertical nonprice restraints, specifically to a manufacturer's termination of one dealer pursuant to an exclusive territory agreement with another. We noted that especially in the vertical restraint context "departure from the rule-of-reason standard must be based on demonstrable economic effect rather than . . . upon formalistic line drawing." We concluded that vertical nonprice restraints had not been shown to have such a " 'pernicious effect on competition' " and to be so " 'lack[ing] [in] . . . redeeming value' " as to justify *per se* illegality. Rather, we found, they had real potential to stimulate interbrand competition, "the primary concern of antitrust law":

> [N]ew manufacturers and manufacturers entering new markets can use the restrictions in order to induce competent and aggressive retailers to make the kind of investment of capital and labor that is often required in the distribution of products unknown to the consumer. Established manufacturers can use them to induce retailers to engage in promotional activities or to provide service and repair facilities necessary to the efficient marketing of their products. Service and repair are vital for many products. . . . The availability and quality of such services affect a manufacturer's goodwill and the competitiveness of his product. Because of market imperfections such as the so-called free-rider effect, these services might not be provided by retailers in a purely competitive situation, despite the fact that each retailer's benefit would be greater if all provided the services than if none did.

Moreover, we observed that a rule of *per se* illegality for vertical nonprice restraints was not needed or effective to protect *intra*brand competition. First, so long as interbrand competition existed, that would provide a "significant check" on any attempt to exploit intrabrand market power. In fact, in order to meet that interbrand competition, a manufacturer's dominant incentive is to lower resale prices. Second, the *per se* illegality of vertical restraints would create a perverse incentive for manufacturers to integrate vertically into distribution, an outcome hardly conducive to fostering the creation and maintenance of small businesses.

* * * * *

Our approach to the question presented in the present case is guided by the premises of *GTE Sylvania:* that there is a presumption in favor of a rule-of-reason standard; that departure from that standard must be justified by demonstrable economic effect, such as the facilitation of cartelizing, rather than formalistic distinctions; that interbrand competition is the primary concern of the antitrust laws; and that rules in this area should be formulated with a view towards protecting the doctrine of *GTE Sylvania.* These premises lead us to conclude that the line drawn by the Fifth Circuit is the most appropriate one.

There has been no showing here that an agreement between a manufacturer and a dealer to terminate a "price cutter," without a further agreement on the price or price levels to be charged by the remaining dealer, almost always tends to restrict competition and reduce output. Any assistance to cartelizing that such an agreement might provide cannot be distinguished from the sort of minimal assistance that might be provided by vertical nonprice agreements like the exclusive territory agreement in *GTE Sylvania,* and is insufficient to justify a *per se* rule. Cartels are neither easy to form nor easy to maintain. . . .

The District Court's rule on the scope of *per se* illegality for vertical restraints would threaten to dismantle the doctrine of *GTE Sylvania.* Any agreement between a manufacturer and a dealer to terminate another dealer who happens to have charged lower prices can be alleged to have been directed against the terminated dealer's "price cutting." In the vast majority of cases, it will be extremely difficult for the manufacturer to convince a jury that its motivation was to ensure adequate services, since price cutting and some measure of service cutting usually go hand in hand. Accordingly, a manufacturer that agrees to give one dealer an exclusive territory and terminates another dealer pursuant to that agreement, or even a manufacturer that agrees with one dealer to terminate another for failure to provide contractually obligated services, exposes itself to the highly plausible claim that its real motivation was to terminate a price cutter. Moreover, even vertical restraints that do not result in dealer termination, such as the initial granting of an exclusive territory or the requirement that certain services be provided, can be attacked as designed to allow existing dealers to charge higher prices. Manufacturers would be likely to forgo legitimate and competitively useful conduct rather than risk treble damages and perhaps even criminal penalties.

We cannot avoid this difficulty by invalidating as illegal *per se* only those agreements imposing vertical restraints that contain the word "price," or that affect the "prices" charged by dealers. Such formalism was explicitly rejected in *GTE Sylvania*. As the above discussion indicates, all vertical restraints, including the exclusive territory agreement held not to be *per se* illegal in *GTE Sylvania,* have the potential to allow dealers to increase "prices" and can be characterized as intended to achieve just that. In fact, vertical nonprice restraints only accomplish the benefits identified in *GTE Sylvania* because they reduce intrabrand price competition to the point where the dealer's profit margin permits provision of the desired services. As we described it in *Monsanto:* "The manufacturer often will want to ensure that its distributors earn sufficient profit to pay for programs such as hiring and training additional salesmen or demonstrating the technical features of the product, and will want to see that 'free-riders' do not interfere."

* * * * *

. . . Petitioner has provided no support for the proposition that vertical price agreements generally underlie agreements to terminate a price cutter. That proposition is simply incompatible with the conclusion of *GTE Sylvania* and *Monsanto* that manufacturers are often motivated by a legitimate desire to have dealers provide services, combined with the reality that price cutting is frequently made possible by "free riding" on the services provided by other dealers. The District Court's *per se* rule would therefore discourage conduct recognized by *GTE Sylvania* and *Monsanto* as beneficial to consumers.

* * * * *

Affirmed.

Justice Stevens, with whom Justice White joins, dissenting.

In its opinion the majority assumes, without analysis, that the question presented by this case concerns the legality of a "vertical nonprice restraint." As I shall demonstrate, the restraint that results when one or more dealers threatens to boycott a manufacturer unless it terminates its relationship with a price-cutting retailer is more properly viewed as a "horizontal restraint." Moreover, an agreement to terminate a dealer because of its price cutting is most certainly not a "nonprice restraint." The distinction between "vertical nonprice restraints'' and ''vertical price restraints,'' on which the majority focuses its attention, is therefore quite irrelevant to the outcome of this case.

* * * * *

Reprinted with permission of the Bureau of National Affairs, Inc.

Questions

1. Summarize the essence of the *B.E.C.* holding.
2. What practical effects would you expect the *B.E.C.* decision to have on the behavior of (*a*) manufacturers and (*b*) discounters?
3. *a.* What is the *Colgate* doctrine?
   b. Is the *Colgate* doctrine a practical, workable standard of conduct? Explain.
4. Assume a manufacturer communicates to its distributors a ''suggested retail price'' for its product. Further assume the distributors individually decide to follow that suggestion.
   a. Does that conduct violate the law? Explain.
   b. Would it matter whether the product is heavily advertised? Explain.
   c. What is fair-trade pricing?
   d. What is its current status?
5. In *Albrecht* v. *Herald Co.*, 390 U.S. 145 (1968), a newspaper distributor, Albrecht, lost his distributorship because he charged a retail price in excess of that specified by the *Herald.*
   a. Is the setting of a maximum resale price illegal? Explain.
   b. Argue the case both for and against Albrecht.
6. In *Continental T.V., Inc.,* v. *GTE Sylvania Inc.*, 433 U.S. 36 (1977), the Supreme Court took the position that interbrand, rather than intrabrand, agreements must be the primary concern of antitrust law.
   a. Why does the Court take that view?
   b. Is the Court correct? Explain.
7. The *GTE* decision distinguished vertical ''nonprice'' restrictions (such as location clauses) from vertical price restrictions (resale price maintenance). Make the argument that the Court's distinction was not meaningful.
8. What is the ''free-rider'' problem that frequently concerns the courts in cases involving vertical territorial restraints?
9. Assume a manufacturer assigns an ''area of primary responsibility'' to a distributor. The distributor's sales are not confined to that area, but he/she must devote his/her best efforts to that area, and failure to do so may result in termination of the distributorship. Is that arrangement lawful? Explain.
10. In 1977 Michelin failed to renew its dealership agreement with the Donald B. Rice Tire Company of Frederick, Maryland. After seven years with Michelin, approximately 80 percent of Rice's business was derived from wholesaling the tires to smaller authorized and unauthorized dealers. Other authorized dealers complained to Michelin of Rice's wholesale business. In an effort to assume primary wholesaling responsibility, Michelin chose not to renew its relationship with Rice. Rice contended that the nonrenewal was

a consequence of its refusal to comply with Michelin's customer and territorial restraints, and Rice filed an antitrust action on that basis. Michelin argued that it was a new entrant into a concentrated market, and as such, restraints on intrabrand competition were necessary to induce retailers to carry Michelin tires. However, the court found frequent shortages of Michelin tires. Michelin also argued that nonrenewal was "necessary to prevent free riding by retailers on the services provided by other dealers."

Rice had not advertised in a quantity commensurate with his sales volume. He sold to unauthorized dealers who were not bound to do any advertising and could thus reap the benefits of advertising by authorized dealers. Michelin wanted to encourage point-of-sales services and the offering of specialized services but feared authorized dealers would not invest the necessary expenditures because of their fear of being underpriced by unauthorized dealers. Decide the case. See *Donald B. Rice Tire Company Inc.* v. *Michelin Corporation,* 483 F. Supp. 750 (D.Md., 1980), 638 F.2d 15 (1981), cert. den. 454 U.S. 864 (1981).

TYING ARRANGEMENTS

Principal legislation: Clayton Act, Section 3; Sherman Act, Sections 1 and 2; Federal Trade Commission Act, Section 5.

Clayton Act, section 3. That it shall be unlawful for any person engaged in commerce, in the course of such commerce, to lease or make a sale or contract for sale of goods . . . or other commodities . . . or fix a price charged therefor, or discount from or rebate upon, such price, on the condition, agreement or understanding that the lessee or purchaser thereof shall not use or deal in the goods . . . or other commodities of a competitor or competitors of the lessor or seller, where the effect of such lease, sale, or contract for sale or such condition, agreement, or understanding may be to substantially lessen competition or tend to create a monopoly in any line of commerce.

The typical tying arrangement permits a customer to lease or buy a desired product (the tying product) only if she or he also leases or buys another product (the tied product). Of course, such an arrangement harms the consumer, but the primary antitrust concerns are twofold: (1) A party who already enjoys market power over the tying product is able to extend that power into the tied product market. (2) Competitors in the tied product market are foreclosed from equal access to that market.

In brief, a violation requires:

1. Proof of a tying arrangement (that is, two products bound together, not merely one product consisting of two or more components bound together, or two entirely separate products that happen to be a part of a single transaction).
2. Market power in the tying product.

3. That a substantial amount of commerce in the tied product is adversely affected. Where those conditions are established, the arrangement constitutes a per se violation.

Under guidelines announced in 1985, the Justice Department has refined its view of the tying standards. Justice will challenge a tying arrangement only if the party imposing the tie (the seller) controls more than 30 percent of the market for the tying product.

While the courts have clearly looked with disfavor on tying agreements, certain conditions do justify such arrangements. For example, a tying agreement is more likely to be acceptable when employed by a new competitor seeking entry against established sellers. What argument would the reader offer in defense of a computer lessor who required its lessee to use only the tabulating cards supplied by the lessor? [See *IBM* v. *U.S.*, 298 U.S. 131 (1936)].

The *Principe* case that follows in the Franchises and Price Discrimination section of this chapter is an excellent illustration of the judiciary's treatment of tying cases.

EXCLUSIVE DEALING AND REQUIREMENTS CONTRACTS

Principal legislation: Clayton Act, Section 3; Sherman Act, Section 1.

An *exclusive dealing* contract is an agreement in which a buyer commits itself to deal only with a specific seller, thus cutting competing sellers out of that share of the market. A *requirements* contract is one in which a seller agrees to supply all of a buyer's needs, or a buyer agrees to purchase all of a seller's output, or both. These arrangements have the disadvantage of closing markets to potential competitors. After defining the relevant product and geographic markets, the test is essentially that applied to vertical mergers; that is, what percentage of the relevant market is foreclosed by the agreement? Does the agreement foreclose a source of supply of sufficient magnitude as to substantially lessen competition? Does the agreement foreclose a market for sales of sufficient magnitude to substantially lessen competition?

Exclusive dealing and requirements contracts do not constitute per se violations of the law. Indeed, it is important to recognize some of the merits of such arrangements, as once articulated by Justice Frankfurter of the U.S. Supreme Court.[16] For the buyer, these merits are:

1. Assuring supply.
2. Protecting against price rises.
3. Enabling long-term planning on the basis of known costs.
4. Reducing the risk and expense of storing products with fluctuating demand.

For the seller, the merits are:

1. Reducing selling expenses.
2. Protecting against price fluctuation.
3. Offering a predictable market.

Afterword—Justice Department Vertical Restraint Guidelines

In January 1985 the Justice Department released guidelines addressing vertical restraints. Of course, the guidelines only express the opinion of the Justice Department. However, they are accorded great respect by the courts, and they do clearly confirm the federal government's reluctance to challenge most vertical marketing restrictions. The Justice Department believes most *nonprice* marketing arrangements between manufacturers and wholesalers or distributors (e.g., territorial restrictions and exclusive dealing arrangements) should not be unlawful. For example, the guidelines declare the Justice Department will not challenge vertical marketing arrangements when the manufacturer controls less than 10 percent of the market in question or when the distributors or dealers involved control 60 percent or less of the relevant market.

Vertical *price-fixing* arrangements will not be challenged merely because they raise consumer prices. Rather, the Justice Department will insist on "direct or circumstantial evidence" showing a conspiracy about "specific prices at which goods or services would be sold."

The Justice Department has not been aggressively pursuing nonprice vertical restraint cases, at least since the inception of the Reagan administration. Whether the Justice Department's position remains persuasive over the years depends on analyses of the actual effects in the marketplace of the new leniency, as well as the outcome of future presidential and congressional elections. For now, the law of vertical restraints remains as expressed in this section.

Part Three—Franchises and Price Discrimination

A *franchise* is a contractual arrangement wherein a parent firm grants a person or group of persons the right to conduct business in a specified manner and place and for a specified time. The rights accompanying the franchise may include selling the parent's products, using its name, using its business techniques, or copying its symbols, trademark, or architecture.[17] Franchises, exemplified perhaps most visibly by McDonald's and Kentucky Fried Chicken, are a powerful force in the American economy, accounting for more than one third of all retail sales and employing more than 7 million persons.

The economic significance of franchising and evidence of abuse in franchising arrangements led the Federal Trade Commission to establish a rule regulating the offering of franchises. In sum, the rule requires franchise sellers to provide purchasers with a document embodying a series of disclosures. (A number of franchises, including those for oil, gas, and autos and those not requiring a payment of $500 or more to the franchisor within the first six months, are exempt from the rule.)

The required document must disclose, among other details:

1. The franchisor's name and address and the names of its officers and directors.
2. The business experience, relevant felony convictions, relevant civil or administrative agency litigation, and bankruptcy proceedings of the officers and directors.
3. A description of the franchise (e.g., trademarks, expected competition, expected market) and the requirements imposed on the franchisee (e.g., payments; training program; territorial, site, or customer restrictions).
4. Rules for franchise termination or nonrenewal, data regarding the frequency of terminations, as well as balance sheets and income statements for the three previous years.
5. The reasonable basis for any projections regarding sales, income, or profit for the franchisee. The existing franchisees' success in meeting those projections must also be recorded.
6. Finally, a series of caveats warning the potential franchisee of the hazards of income projection and advising the potential franchisee to proceed cautiously.

Violators of the FTC rule may be fined in a civil suit up to a maximum of $10,000. The FTC may bring actions on behalf of individual franchisees to secure damages or appropriate injunctive relief.

Given the nature of the franchise relationship, it is not surprising that lawsuits alleging tying arrangements, exclusive dealing, vertical territorial restrictions, and the like are not uncommon. Resolution of these allegations is significantly complicated by some rather well-balanced competing considerations. The franchisor's interest in maintaining its product image may cause it to impose restrictions that may impinge on the franchisee's independence and efforts at profit maximization. In holding a government-approved trademark, under the terms of the Lanham Act (the federal trademark act) as interpreted by the judiciary, the franchisor must maintain control over the use of the mark so that the source of the goods is not misrepresented. The act is designed, in part, to prevent the passing or "palming off" of one party's goods as those of a competitor.

On the other hand, the government's antitrust policy is designed to curb some of the very practices most useful in protecting the trademark. The *Principe* case addresses the trademark issue and goes on to explore the franchise as an entire business method reaching well beyond the limits of the mark itself. The case also indicates the arrangements, financial and otherwise, involved in franchise ownership. The reader is cautioned that the law in this area remains unsettled, although the *GTE Sylvania* decision certainly suggests a greater willingness to consider the merits, if any, of vertical trade restraints imposed by a franchisor.

PRINCIPE V. McDONALD'S CORP.
631 F.2d 303 (4th Cir., 1980)

Senior Circuit Judge Phillips

This appeal presents the question of whether a fast food franchisor that requires its licensees to operate their franchises in premises leased from the franchisor is guilty of an illegal tying arrangement in violation of § 1 of the Sherman Act. . . . On the facts of this case we hold it does not and affirm the directed verdict for the defendants.

I

The appellants, Frank A. Principe, Ann Principe, and Frankie, Inc., a family owned corporation, are franchisees of McDonald's System, Inc. The Principes acquired their first franchise, a McDonald's hamburger restaurant in Hopewell, Virginia, in 1970. At that time, they executed a 20-year franchise license agreement and a store lease of like duration. In consideration for their rights under these agreements, the Principes paid a $10,000 license fee and a $15,000 security deposit, and agreed to remit 2.2 percent of their gross receipts as royalties under the franchise agreement and 8.0 percent as rent under the lease. In 1974, Frank Principe and his son, Raymond, acquired a second franchise in Colonial Heights, Virginia, on similar terms. The Colonial Heights franchise subsequently was transferred to Frankie, Inc., a corporation owned jointly by Frank and Raymond Principe.

The Principes sought to purchase a third franchise in 1976 in Petersburg, Virginia. Robert Beavers, McDonald's regional manager, concluded the plaintiffs lacked sufficient management depth and capabilities to take on a third store without impairing the quality of their existing operations. During the next 20 months, the Principes obtained corporate review and reconsideration of the decision to deny them the franchise. They were notified in May 1978 that the Petersburg franchise was being offered to a new franchisee.

They filed this action a few days later alleging violations of federal and state antitrust and securities laws and state franchising laws. Counts I and II alleged McDonald's violated federal antitrust laws by tying store leases and $15,000 security deposit notes to the franchise rights at the Hopewell and Colonial Heights stores. Count XII alleged McDonald's denied the Principes a third franchise in retaliation for their refusal to follow McDonald's pricing guidelines. . . .

Following discovery the district court granted summary judgment for McDonald's on the security deposit note tie in claims. District Judge D. Dortch Warriner found the notes represented deposits against loss and do not constitute a product separate from the store leases to which they pertain.

The court directed a verdict for McDonald's on the store lease tie in counts at the close of all the evidence. . . . Judge Warriner held the Principes had failed to introduce any evidence of McDonald's power in the tying product market, which he held is the food retailing market. The court held, however, McDonald's sells only one product: the license contract and store lease are component parts of the overall package McDonald's offers its prospective franchisees. Accordingly, Judge Warriner held as a matter of law there was no illegal tie in.

The remaining issue, whether McDonald's denied the Principes a third franchise in retaliation for their pricing independence, went to the jury which held for the defendants. The jury returned an unsolicited note stating they felt the Principes had been wronged, although price-fixing was not the reason, and should be awarded the Petersburg franchise. The court disregarded the jury's note and entered judgment on the verdict for McDonald's.

The Principes appeal. . . . We affirm.

II

. . . McDonald's is not primarily a fast food retailer. While it does operate over a thousand stores itself, the vast majority of the stores in this system are operated by franchisees. Nor does McDonald's sell equipment or supplies to its licensees. Instead its primary business is developing and collecting royalties from limited menu fast food restaurants operated by independent business people.

McDonald's uses demographic data generated by the most recent census and its own research in evaluating potential sites. McDonald's attempts to analyze and predict demographic trends in the geographic area. This process serves a twofold purpose: (1) by analyzing the demographic profile of a given market area, McDonald's hopes to determine whether the residents are likely to buy fast food in sufficient quantities to justify locating a restaurant there; (2) by anticipating future growth, McDonald's seeks to plan its expansion to maximize the number of viable McDonald's restaurants within a given geographic area. Based on a comparison of data for various available sites, the regional staffs select what they believe is the best site in each geographic area.

* * * * *

After the specifics of each proposed new restaurant are approved, McDonald's decides whether the store will be company operated or franchised. If the decision is to franchise the store McDonald's begins the process of locating a franchisee. This involves offering the store either to an existing franchisee or to an applicant on the franchise waiting list. Applicants need not live near the store in order to be offered the franchise, and they need not accept the first franchise they are offered. The Principes lived in Kenosha, Wisconsin, and rejected 11 separate McDonald's restaurants before accepting their first franchise in Hopewell, Virginia. McDonald's often does not know who will operate a franchised store until it is nearly completed because a new restaurant may be offered to and rejected by several different applicants.

Meanwhile, Franchise Realty acquires the land, either by purchase or long-term lease and constructs the store. Acquisiton and development costs averaged over $450,000 per store in 1978. . . .

As constructed, McDonald's restaurants are finished shells; they contain no kitchen or dining room equipment. Furnishing store equipment is the responsibility of the operator, whether a franchisee or McOpCo. McDonald's does provide specifications such equipment must meet, but does not sell the equipment itself.

Having acquired the land, begun construction of the store and selected an operator, McDonald's enters into two contracts with the franchisee. Under the first, the franchise agreement, McDonald's grants the franchisee the rights to use McDonald's food preparation system and to sell food products under the McDonald's name. The franchise pays a $12,500 franchise fee and agrees to remit 3 percent of his gross sales as a royalty in return. Under the second contract, the lease, McDonald's grants the franchisee the right to use the particular store premises to which his franchise pertains. In return, the franchisee pays a $15,000 refundable security deposit (as evidence of which he receives a 20-year nonnegotiable noninterest-bearing note) and agrees to pay 8.5 percent of his gross sales as rent. These payments under the franchise and lease agreements are McDonald's only sources of income from its franchised restaurants. The franchisee also assumes responsibility under the lease for building maintenance, improvements, property taxes and other costs associated with the premises. Both the franchise agreement and the lease generally have 20-year durations, both provide that termination of one terminates the other, and neither is available separately.

III

The Principes argue McDonald's is selling not one but three distinct products, the franchise, the lease, and the security deposit note. The alleged antitrust violation stems from the fact that a prospective franchisee must buy all three in order to obtain the franchise.

As evidence that this is an illegal tying arrangement, the Principes point to the unfavorable terms on which franchisees are required to lease their stores. Not only are franchisees denied the opportunity to build equity and depreciate their property, but they must maintain the building, pay for improvements and taxes, and remit 8.5 percent of their gross sales as rents. In 1978 the gross sales of the Hopewell store generated about $52,000 in rent. That figure nearly equalled Franchise Realty's original cost for the site and corresponds to more than a fourth of the original cost of the entire Hopewell restaurant complex. At that rate of return, the Principes argue, Franchise Realty will have recouped its entire investment in four years and the remainder of the lease payments will be pure profit. The Principes contend that the fact the store rents are so high proves that McDonald's cannot sell the leaseholds on their own merits.

Nor has McDonald's shown any need to forbid its licensees to own their own stores, the Principes say. . . . Before 1959 McDonald's itself permitted franchisees to own their own stores. McDonald's could maintain its desired level of uniformity by requiring franchisees to locate and construct stores according to company specifications. The company could even provide planning and design assistance as it apparently does in connection with food purchasing and restaurant management. The Principes argue McDonald's has not shown that the success of its business or the integrity of its trademarks depends on company ownership of all store premises.

A separate tied product is the note that evidences the lessee's $15,000 security deposit, according to the appellants. The Principes argue the security deposit really is a mandatory contribution to McDonald's working capital, not security against damage to the store or breach of the lease contract. By tying the purchase of these $15,000 20-year nonnegotiable noninterest-bearing notes to that of the franchise, McDonald's allegedly has generated a capital fund that totalled over $45 million in 1978. It is argued that no one would purchase such notes on their own merits. The Principes assert that only by requiring franchisees to purchase the notes as a condition of obtaining a franchise has McDonald's been able to sell them at all.

McDonald's responds that it is not in the business of licensing use of its name, improving real estate for lease, or selling long-term notes. Its only business is developing a system of hamburger restaurants and collecting royalties from their sales. The allegedly tied products are but parts of the overall bundle of franchise benefits and obligations. . . .

IV

"There is, at the outset of every tie-in case, including the familiar cases involving physical goods, the problem of determining whether two separate products are in fact involved." . . . Because we agree with McDonald's that the lease, note, and license are not separate products but component parts of the overall franchise package, we hold on the facts of this case there was no illegal tie in. . . .

As support, for their position, the Principes rely primarily on the decision of the Ninth Circuit in *Siegel v. Chicken Delight, Inc.*, 448 F.2d 43 (9th Cir. 1971), cert. denied, 405 U.S. 955 (1972), one of the first cases to address the problem of franchise tie-ins. Chicken Delight was what McDonald's characterizes as a "rent a name" franchisor: it licensed franchisees to sell chicken under the Chicken Delight name but did not own store premises or fixtures. The company did not even charge franchise fees or royalties. Instead, it required its franchisees to purchase a specified number of cookers and fryers and to purchase certain packaging supplies and mixes exclusively from Chicken Delight. These supplies were priced higher than comparable goods of competing sellers. . . .

. . . Viewing the essence of a Chicken Delight franchise as the franchisor's trademark, the court sought to determine whether requiring franchisees to purchase common supplies from Chicken Delight was necessary to ensure that their operations lived up to the quality standards the trademark represented. Judged by this standard, the aggregation was found to consist of separate products:

> This being so, it is apparent that the goodwill of the Chicken Delight trademark does not attach to the multitude of separate articles used in the operation of the licensed system or in the production of its end product. It is not what is used, but how it is used and what results that have given the system and its end product their entitlement to trademark protection. It is to the system and the end product that the public looks with the confidence that established goodwill has created.

* * * * *

The Principes urge this court to apply the *Chicken Delight* reasoning to invalidate the McDonald's franchise lease note aggregation. They urge that McDonald's can protect the integrity of its trademarks by specifying how its franchisees shall operate, where they may locate their restaurants and what types of buildings they may erect. Customers do not and have no reason to connect the building's owner with the McDonald's operation conducted therein. Since company ownership of store premises is not an essential element of the trademark's goodwill, the Principes argue, the franchise, lease, and note are separable products tied together in violation of the antitrust laws.

* * * * *

Without disagreeing with the result in *Chicken Delight,* we conclude that the court's emphasis in that case upon the trademark as the essence of a franchise is too restrictive. Far from merely licensing franchisees to sell products under its trade name, a modern franchisor such as McDonald's offers its franchisees a complete method of doing business. It takes people from all walks of life, sends them to its management school, and teaches them a variety of skills ranging from hamburger grilling to financial planning. It installs them in stores whose market has been researched and whose location has been selected by experts to maximize sales potential. It inspects every facet of every store several times a year and consults with each franchisee about his operation's strengths and weaknesses. Its regime pervades all facets of the business. . . .

Given the realities of modern franchising, we think the proper inquiry is not whether the allegedly tied products are associated in the public mind with the franchisor's trademark, but whether they are integral components of the business method being franchised. Where the challenged aggregation is an essential ingredient of the franchised system's formula for success, there is but a single product and no tie in exists as a matter of law.

Applying this standard to the present case, we hold the lease is not separable from the McDonald's franchise to which it pertains. McDonald's practice of developing a system of company owned restaurants operated by franchisees has substantial advantages, both for the company and for franchisees. It is part of what makes a McDonald's franchise uniquely attractive to franchisees.

First, because it approaches the problem of restaurant site selection systematically, McDonald's is able to obtain better sites than franchisees could select. Armed with its demographic information, guided by its staff of experts and unencumbered by preferences of individual franchisees, McDonald's can wield its economic might to acquire sites where new restaurants will prosper without undercutting existing franchisees' business or limiting future expansion. . . .

Second, McDonald's policy of owning all of its own restaurants assures that the stores remain part of the McDonald's system. McDonald's franchise arrangements are not static: franchisees retire or die; occasionally they do not live up to their franchise obligations and must be replaced; even if no such contingency intervenes, the agreements normally expire by their own terms after 20 years. If franchisees owned their own stores, any of these events could disrupt McDonald's business and have a negative effect on the system's goodwill. . . .

Third, because McDonald's acquires the sites and builds the stores itself, it can select franchisees based on their management potential rather than their real estate expertise or wealth. Ability to emphasize management skills is important to McDonald's because it has built its reputation largely on the consistent quality of its operations rather than on the merits of its hamburgers. A store's quality is largely a function of its management. McDonald's policy of owning its own stores reduces a franchisee's initial investment, thereby broadening the applicant base and opening the door to persons who otherwise could not afford a McDonald's franchise. . . . Their ability to begin operating a McDonald's restaurant without having to search for a site, negotiate for the land, borrow hundreds of thousands of dollars and construct a store building is of substantial value to franchisees.

Finally, because both McDonald's and the franchisee have a substantial financial stake in the success of the restaurant, their relationship becomes a sort of partnership that might be impossible under other circumstances. McDonald's spends close to half a million dollars on each new store it establishes. Each franchisee invests over $100,000 to make the store operational. Neither can afford to ignore the other's problems, complaints, or ideas. . . .

All of these factors contribute significantly to the overall success of the McDonald's system. The formula that produced systemwide success, the formula that promises to make each new McDonald's store successful, that formula is what McDonald's sells its franchisees. To characterize the franchise as an unnecessary aggregation of separate products tied to the McDonald's name is to miss the point entirely. Among would-be franchisees, the McDonald's name has come to stand for the formula, including all that it entails. We decline to find that it is an illegal tie in. . . .

We have examined the Principes' other contentions and do not believe they warrant extended discussion. The security deposit note was just that: evidence of a security deposit on a lease which we have held was a legitimate part of the franchise package. . . . The jury's unsolicited comment that the Principes had been wronged was expressly qualified by their statement that price-fixing was not the reason. The district court correctly determined that the note did not affect the integrity of the jury verdict.

Affirmed.

Questions

1. *a.* Do you agree with the court's view that McDonald's franchises an entire business system rather than an aggregation of separate products? Explain.
   b. Does the court's decision benefit or harm the consumer? Explain.
2. Can Fotomat lawfully require its franchisees to lease kiosks (small, drive-in, photo service buildings) from the franchisor? See *Photovest Corporation* v. *Fotomat Corporation*, 606 F.2d 704 (7th Cir. 1979), cert. den. 100 S. Ct. 1278 (1980).
3. For approximately a decade, Alpha Distributing Company of California had held the exclusive distribution rights for Jack Daniel's liquor in northern California. Alpha had built the distributorship to some 3,500 customers when Jack Daniel's turned the distributorship over to Rathjen Bros. and encouraged Rathjen to assume Alpha's customers.
   a. What violation of antitrust law should Alpha allege?
   b. Decide the case. See *Alpha Distrib. Co. of Cal., Inc.* v. *Jack Daniel Distillery*, 454 F.2d 442 (9th Cir. 1972), cert. den. 419 U.S. 842 (1974).
4. The cases suggest that one who holds market power in the tying product would naturally wish to achieve market power in the tied product. That is precisely the evil the government seeks to prevent.
   a. However, at least as to complementary products (computers and disks, mimeograph machines and ink, or stereos and records), make the argument that possession of market power in the tying product would not, of itself, permit that producer to seek monopoly power and charge monopoly prices for the tied product.
   b. Put another way, how can a seller force a buyer to accept an undesired tied product?
5. Is a tying arrangement the economic equivalent of predatory pricing? If so, is the law regarding tying arrangements essentially the same as the law regarding predatory pricing? Explain.
6. Audio manufactures a stereo receiver that is technically superior to all others on the market. Audio will sell its receiver only in conjunction with its own turntable and speakers. Is Audio in violation of the law? Explain.
7. Assume Shoes Unlimited has market power in the retail sale of cowboy boots. James buys a pair of boots at Shoes Unlimited and inadvertently loses one in a peculiar affair of the night. James now seeks to replace the lost boot by purchasing one identical to

it, but the store policy requires the purchase of both boots or none at all. Could James successfully challenge Shoes Unlimited on tying grounds? Explain.

8. In *Belliston v. Texaco, Inc.*, 455 F.2d 175 (1972), cert. den. 408 U.S. 928 (1972), certain Texaco dealers claimed damages because of Texaco's policy of requesting that they buy only those brands of tires, batteries, and accessories specified by Texaco. Texaco received a 10 percent commission from the manufacturers of those items. Texaco did nothing to coerce its dealers into compliance with that request.

   a. What phrase describes this rather commonplace marketing tactic?
   b. What violation of law was alleged?
   c. Decide. Explain.

PRICE DISCRIMINATION

Principal legislation: Clayton Act, Section 2, as amended by the Robinson-Patman Act:

That it shall be unlawful for any person engaged in commerce . . . to discriminate in price between different purchasers of commodities of like grade and quality, where either or any of the purchases involved in such discrimination are in commerce . . . and where the effect of such discrimination may be substantially to lessen competition or tend to create a monopoly in any line of commerce, or to injure, destroy, or prevent competition with any person who either grants or knowingly receives the benefit of such discrimination, or with customers of either of them. . . . Provided that nothing herein contained shall prevent differentials which make only due allowance for differences in the cost of manufacture, sale, or delivery resulting from the differing methods or quantities in which such commodities are to such purchasers sold or delivered. . . . And, provided further, that nothing herein contained shall prevent price changes from time to time where in response to changing conditions affecting the market for or the marketability of the goods concerned, such as but not limited to actual or imminent deterioration of perishable goods, obsolescence of seasonal goods, distress sales under court process, or sales in good faith in discontinuance of business in the goods concerned. . . . Provided, however, that nothing herein contained shall prevent a seller rebutting the prima facie case thus made by showing that his lower price or the furnishing of services or facilities to any purchaser or purchasers was made in good faith to meet an equally low price of a competitor, or the services or facilities furnished by a competitor.

Having persevered to this point in exploring antitrust law, the reader cannot be unacquainted with at least a measure of intellectual frustration. If so, what follows may produce a paroxysm of despair. Price discrimination may be the most confused dimension of antitrust law.

In brief, *price discrimination* involves selling substantially identical goods (not services) at reasonably contemporaneous times to different purchasers at different prices, where the effect may be to substantially lessen competition or to tend to create a monopoly. A seller may prevail against such a charge by establishing one of the following defenses: (1) The price differential is attributable to cost savings associated with the least expensive sale. However, in practice the difficulties in proving cost savings have made successful defenses on that ground quite uncommon. (2) The price differential is attributable to a good faith effort to meet the equally low price of a competitor. (3) Certain transactions are exempt from the act. Of special note is a price change made in response to a changing market. Thus, prices might lawfully be altered for seasonal goods or perishables. Price discrimination is perhaps best understood by reference to a series of diagrams.[18]

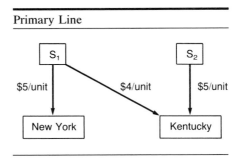

The harm here falls at the seller's level, the primary line, in that S_1's pricing policy may harm S_2. The specific fear is that S_1 will use its income from sales in New York to subsidize its lower price in Kentucky. S_1 may then be able to drive S_2 from the market. This is precisely the harm that Congress feared would be generated by the advance of chain stores across the nation. Of course, S_1 may be able to offer a defense to explain the pricing differential. For example, the price differential might be permissible if designed to allow S_1 to get a foothold in a new market. Remember that a price discrimination violation requires a showing of competitive injury. At the risk of oversimplification, competitive harm will probably be found where this is proof of (*a*) predatory intent or (*b*) a general decline in the strength of the seller's competitors. The *Utah Pie* case both explores the competitive injury issue and reveals much of the philosophical confusion surrounding Robinson-Patman. The case offers the reader a particularly useful vehicle for assessing the relative merits of government regulation versus a free market approach. This case and Robinson-Patman generally have been criticized for promoting inefficiency and actually harming competition. However, the economic history of the 1920s and 30s reveals the increasing power of chain stores and the decline of smaller businesses prior to the enactment of Robinson-Patman. Specifically, volume buyers were able to extract various price concessions from suppliers.

It does not seem exaggerated to say that an understanding of America requires an understanding of the competing economic ideologies illustrated by the facts of *Utah Pie*.

UTAH PIE CO. V. CONTINENTAL BAKING CO.
386 U.S. 685 (1967)

Justice White

[This suit for treble damages was brought by Petitioner, Utah Pie Company, against respondents, Continental Baking Company, Carnation Company, and Pet Milk Company. The complaint charged violations by each respondent of 2(a) of the Clayton Act as amended by the Robinson-Patman Act. The jury found for petitioner on the price discrimination charge.]

The Court of Appeals reversed, addressing itself to the single issue of whether the evidence against each of the respondents was sufficient to support a finding of probable injury to competition within the meaning of § 2(a) and holding that it was not. . . .

We granted certiorari. . . . We reverse.

The product involved is frozen dessert pies. . . . Petitioner is a Utah corporation which for 30 years has been baking pies in its plant in Salt Lake City and selling them in Utah and surrounding states. It entered the frozen pie business in late 1957. It was immediately successful with its new line and built a new plant in Salt Lake City in 1958. The frozen pie market was a rapidly expanding one; 57,060 dozen frozen pies were sold in the Salt Lake City market in 1958; 111,729 dozen in 1959; 184,569 dozen in 1960; and 266,908 dozen in 1961. Utah Pie's share of this market in those years was 66.5 percent, 34.3 percent, 45.5 percent, and 45.3 percent, respectively, its sales volume steadily increasing over the four years. Its financial position also improved. Petitioner is not, however, a large company. At the time of the trial, petitioner operated with only 18 employees, 9 of whom were members of the Rigby family, which controlled the business. . . .

Each of the respondents is a large company and each of them is a major factor in the frozen pie market in one or more regions of the country. Each entered the Salt Lake City frozen pie market before petitioner began freezing dessert pies. None of them had a plant in Utah. . . .

The major competitive weapon in the Utah market was price. . . . For most of the period involved here [petitioner's] prices were the lowest in the Sale Lake City market. It was, however, challenged by each of the respondents at one time or another and for varying periods. There was ample evidence to show that each of the respondents contributed to what proved to be a deteriorating price structure over the period covered by this suit, and each of the respondents in the course of the ongoing price competition sold frozen pies in the Salt Lake market at prices lower than it sold pies of like grade and quality in other markets considerably closer to its plants. Utah Pie, which entered the market at a price of $4.15 per dozen at the beginning of the relevant period, was selling "Utah" and "Frost 'N' Flame" pies for $2.75 per dozen when the instant suit was filed some 44 months later. Pet, which was offering pies at $4.92 per dozen in February 1958, was offering "Pet-Ritz" and "Bel-air" pies at $3.56 and $3.46 per dozen, respectively, in March and April 1961. Carnation's price in early 1958 was $4.82 per dozen but it was selling at $3.46 per dozen at the conclusion of the period, meanwhile having been down as low as $3.30 per dozen. The price range experienced by Continental during the period covered by this suit ran from a 1958 high of over $5 per dozen to a 1961 low of $2.85 per dozen.

I

We deal first with petitioner's case against the Pet Milk Company.

First, Pet successfully concluded an arrangement with Safeway, which is one of the three largest customers for frozen pies in the Salt Lake market, whereby it would sell frozen pies to Safeway under the latter's own "Bel-air" label at a price significantly lower than it was selling its comparable "Pet-Ritz" brand in the same Salt Lake market and elsewhere. . . .

Second, it introduced a 20-ounce economy pie under the "Swiss Miss" label and began selling the new pie in the Salt Lake market in August 1960 at prices ranging from $3.25 to $3.30 for the remainder of the period. This pie was at times sold at a lower price in the Salt Lake City market than it was sold in other markets.

Third, Pet became more competitive with respect to the prices for its "Pet-Ritz" proprietary label. . . . According to the Court of Appeals, in 7 of the 44 months Pet's prices in Salt Lake were lower than prices charged in the California markets. This was true although selling in Salt Lake involved a 30- to 35-cent freight cost.

* * * * *

[T]he Court of Appeals almost entirely ignored . . . evidence which provides material support for the jury's conclusion that Pet's behavior satisfied the statutory test regarding competitive injury. This evidence bore on the issue of Pet's predatory intent to injure Utah Pie. . . . [T]he jury could have concluded that Pet's discriminatory pricing was aimed at Utah Pie. . . . Moreover, Pet candidly admitted that during the period when it was establishing its relationship with Safeway, it sent into Utah Pie's plant an industrial spy to seek information that would be of use to Pet in convincing Safeway that Utah Pie was not worthy of its custom. Pet denied that it ever in fact used what it had learned against Utah Pie in competing for Safeway's business. The parties, however, are not the ultimate judges of credibility. . . .

Finally, Pet does not deny that the evidence showed it suffered substantial losses on its frozen pie sales during the greater part of the time involved in this suit. . . .

It seems clear to us that the jury heard adequate evidence from which it could have concluded that Pet had engaged in predatory tactics in waging competitive warfare in the Salt Lake City market. Coupled with the incidence of price discrimination attributable to Pet, the evidence as a whole established, rather than negated, the reasonable possibility that Pet's behavior produced a lessening of competition proscribed by the act.

II

Petitioner's case against Continental is not complicated. . . . Effective for the last two weeks of June it offered its 22-ounce frozen apple pies in the Utah area at $2.85 per dozen. It was then selling the same pies at substantially higher prices in other markets. The Salt Lake City price was less than its direct cost plus an allocation for overhead. . . . The Court of Appeals concluded that Continental's conduct had had only minimal effect, that it had not injured·or weakened Utah Pie as a competitor, that it had not substantially lessened competition and that there was no reasonable possibility that it would do so in the future.

* * * * *

We again differ with the Court of Appeals. Its opinion that Utah was not damaged as a competitive force apparently rested on the fact that Utah's sales volume continued to climb in 1961 and on the court's own factual conclusion that Utah was not deprived of any pie business which it otherwise might have had. But this retrospective assessment fails to note that Continental's discriminatory below-cost pie price caused Utah Pie to reduce its price to $2.75. . . .

. . . [The jury] could have reasonably concluded that a competitor who is forced to reduce his price to a new all-time low in a market of declining prices will in time feel the financial pinch and will be a less effective competitive force. . . .

III

We need not dwell long upon the case against Carnation, which in some respects is similar to that against Continental and in others more nearly resembles the case against Pet. After [a] temporary setback in 1959 [Carnation] instituted a new pricing policy to regain business in the Salt Lake City market. The new policy involved a slash in price of 60 cents per dozen pies, which brought Carnation's price to a level admittedly well below its costs, and well below the other prices prevailing in the market. The impact of the move was felt immediately, and the two other major sellers in the market reduced their prices. Carnation's banner year, 1960, in the end involved eight months during which the prices in Salt Lake City were lower than prices charged in other markets. The trend continued during the eight months in 1961 that preceded the filing of the complaint in this case. In each of those months the Salt Lake City prices charged by Carnation were well below prices charged in other markets, and in all but August 1961 the Salt Lake City delivered price was 20 cents to 50 cents lower than the prices charged in distant San Francisco. . . .

IV

Section 2(a) does not forbid price competition which will probably injure or lessen competition by eliminating competitors, discouraging entry into the market or enhancing the market shares of the dominant sellers. But Congress has established some ground rules for the game. Sellers may not sell like goods to different purchasers at different prices if the result may be to injure competition in either the sellers' or the buyers' market unless such discriminations are justified as permitted by the act. In this context, the Court of Appeals placed heavy emphasis on the fact that Utah Pie constantly increased its sales volume and continued to make a profit. But we disagree with its apparent view that there is no reasonably possible injury to competition as long as the volume of sales in a particular market is expanding and at least some of the competitors in the market continue to operate at a profit. Nor do we think that the act only comes into play to regulate the conduct of price discriminators when their discriminatory prices consistently undercut other competitors. . . . Courts and commentators alike have noted that the existence of predatory intent might bear on the likelihood of injury to competition. In this case there was some evidence of predatory intent with respect to each of these respondents. . . . We believe that the act reaches price discrimination that erodes competition as much as it does price discrimination that is intended to have immediate destructive impact. In this case, the evidence shows a drastically declining price structure which the jury could rationally attribute to continued or sporadic price discrimination. . . .

[Reversed and remanded.]

Questions

1. Why is *Utah Pie* a case of primary line price discrimination?
2. What is predatory intent?
3. Make the argument that the *Utah Pie* decision is unsound as a matter of economic reasoning.
4. Is it always unlawful to sell one's products below cost (as Continental did)? Explain.

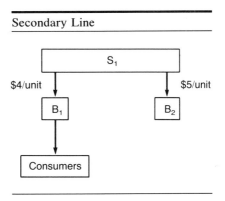

B$_1$ and B$_2$ are direct competitors. Absent a defense, S$_1$ is clearly engaging in price discrimination. Here the harm falls at the buyers' level (secondary line). Again these facts illustrate the concerns that caused Congress to approve Robinson-Patman. That is, the fear was that the economic power of the large chain stores would permit them to extract price concessions from sellers. Small stores would then be unable to compete, and the American Dream would be threatened. Additional facts alter the situation and remind the student of the importance of doing the proper product and geographic market analysis. Assume the product involved is plywood. If S$_1$ is a lumber mill, B$_1$ is a lumberyard, and B$_2$ is a building contractor, no violation is likely to result because B$_1$ and B$_2$ are not competitors. They operate in different product markets and, therefore, could not harm competition. Similarly, if B$_1$ is located in Oregon and B$_2$ in Florida, no competitive harm is likely to result because they would ordinarily be in separate geographic markets.

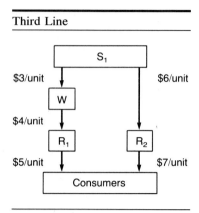

Here the injury falls at the third line; that is, customers of customers. Assume lumber mill S_1 sells plywood to favored purchaser W (a wholesaler) at $3 beneath the price charged to R_2. W and R_2 are not competitors, and one might, therefore, argue the price differential could not cause harm. However, if the lower price to W leads to a lower price to R_1—who does compete with R_2—thus permitting R_1 to undersell R_2, a court might well find a violation of Robinson-Patman (absent a sound defense). This reasoning may appear a bit awkward and at odds with normal marketing practices. However, a decision to the contrary would seriously limit the effectiveness of Robinson-Patman. If S_1 wished to sell to R_1 at a lesser price than to R_2 or perhaps was forced to do so by pressure from R_2, how might a skeptic explain the presence of W in the chain of distribution?

BUYER DISCRIMINATION

Robinson-Patman also forbids price discrimination on the part of buyers. That is, a buyer may not knowingly induce or receive a discriminatory price. This prohibition resulted from the legislators' concern that large purchasers (e.g., supermarket chains and discount stores) would take advantage of their buying power to compel suppliers to sell to them at much lower prices than would be accorded to smaller purchasers (e.g., the corner grocery store). The result would be to give a competitive advantage to the larger purchasers. In such situations, buyers may assert the Robinson-Patman defenses in the manner we have described for sellers.

CHAPTER QUESTIONS

1. After reading this entire chapter, what is your judgment about the antitrust system?

a. Does it work? Explain.

b. How might it be altered?

c. Could we place more reliance on the market? Explain.

d. Do the statutes and case law, as a body, seem to form a rational package? Explain.

2. Scholar and jurist Richard Posner argues:

> [T]he protection of small business whatever its intrinsic merit cannot be attained within the framework of antitrust principles and procedures. The small businessman is, in general, helped rather than hurt by monopoly, so unless the antitrust laws are stood completely on their head they are an inapt vehicle (compared, say, to tax preferences) for assisting small business.[19]

a. Is antitrust law an inappropriate vehicle for protecting small business? Explain.

b. Should we protect small business? Explain.

c. How does the presence of monopolies benefit small business?

d. If it is not the proper vehicle for protecting small business, what role should antitrust law properly serve? For example, should "social considerations" (such as the maintenance of full employment and the dispersal of political power) assume greater importance? Or should antitrust policy hew as closely as possible to economic goals? Explain.

3. Falls City, formerly a brewer in Evansville, Indiana, raised prices to its wholesale distributor in Kentucky, just across the state line from Evansville. At the same time, Falls City raised its prices to its distributor in Indiana, Vanco Beverages, by a greater margin than that to the Kentucky distributor. The resulting price differential caused higher retail beer prices in the Indiana market than in Kentucky. (Indiana law prohibits wholesalers from selling out of state and prohibits retailers from going out of state to make purchases. Further, brewers must maintain a uniform price throughout Indiana.) The higher Indiana price was, at least in part, a product of Falls City's policy of following the pricing patterns of other Indiana brewers. Vanco sued, claiming a violation of the Robinson-Patman Act.

a. Are the facts sufficient to support a prima facie case of price discrimination? Explain.

b. What defense would you raise on behalf of Falls City?

c. Decide the case. Explain. See *Falls City Industries, Inc.* v. *Vanco Beverage, Inc.,* 103 S. Ct. 1282 (1983).

4. A California statute required wine producers and wholesalers to file a fair-trade pricing schedule or fair-trade contracts with the state. If a producer had not established prices via a fair-trade contract, wholesalers were required to post a price schedule and adhere to it in sales to retailers. A California wine wholesaler challenged the state statute.

    a. What violation was alleged?

    b. Decide the case. See *California Retail Liquor Dealers Ass'n* v. *Midcal Alum.,* 100 S. Ct. 937 (1980).

5. A utility charged home building contractors up to $200 as the fee for completing underground connections, but no charge for connection was assessed where the builder agreed to make the home "all electric." The plaintiff alleged a violation of the antitrust laws.

    a. What was the alleged violation?

    b. Decide the case. Explain. See *Washington Gas Light Co.* v. *Virginia Elec. and Power Co.,* 438 F.2d 248 (4th Cir. 1971).

6. Could Amana, the appliance manufacturer, lawfully refuse to deal with any purchaser who sells the products of a competitor, such as Maytag? Explain.

7. Assume you seek to build and operate a clothing store. You hire a contractor, who purchases cement blocks from a manufacturer. After the building is complete, you discover evidence suggesting that your contractor was overcharged for the blocks because of a price-fixing scheme to which the block manufacturer was a party. Does the law permit you as an indirect purchaser to file an antitrust suit to recover the damages you sustained as a consequence of the conspiracy? Explain. See *Illinois Brick Co.* v. *Illinois,* 431 U.S. 720 (1977), for a similar situation.

8. SIDA, the State Independent Drivers Association, Inc., is the largest taxi company on Oahu, Hawaii. SIDA's membership is limited to independent taxis. Fleet operators are not admitted. Hawaii's Department of Transportation awarded SIDA the exclusive right to provide taxi service from Honolulu Airport. No restrictions were placed on taxi service to the airport. Charley's Taxi Radio Dispatch Corporation, the largest fleet service on the island, filed suit, challenging, among other things, SIDA's refusal to grant membership to Charley's. At trial, the facts demonstrated that taxi competition was strong on the island of Oahu.

    a. What violation was alleged by Charley's?

    b. Decide. Explain. See *Charley's Taxi Radio Dispatch* v. *SIDA of Hawaii,* 810 F.2 869 (9th Cir. 1987).

9. Assume two fertilizer dealerships, Grow Quick and Fertile Fields, respectively, hold 70 percent and 30 percent of the fertilizer business in the farm community of What Cheer, Iowa. Assume the owner of Fertile Fields learns via inquiry, hearsay, and the like of Grow Quick's price quotes. Then, each growing season the Fertile Fields owner sets her prices exactly equal to those of her competitor. Is that practice unlawful? Explain.

10. Given identical competing products, why is identical pricing virtually inevitable—at least over the long run?

11. The FTC found the Boise Cascade Corporation in violation of Section 5 of the Federal Trade Commission Act (forbidding unfair methods of competition) for using a delivered pricing system for southern plywood, the price for which was based in part on a rail freight charge computed as though the shipping point of origin was the Pacific Northwest. Historically, plywood had originated largely in the Northwest, but technological developments spurred southeastern production. However, southeastern producers continued to quote plywood prices as though the material had been shipped from the West Coast. The commission contended that the practice inhibited price competition. Boise Cascade argued that the freight factor eased price comparisons between southeastern and northwestern plywood. No agreement among southern plywood producers as to West Coast-delivered pricing was proved. In the absence of an agreement, is this practice unlawful? Explain. *Boise Cascade Corp.* v. *FTC,* 637 F.2d 573 (9th Cir. 1980).

12. Assume firms A, B, C, D, E are charged with price-fixing under Sherman 1 because they have a program of exchanging pricing information among themselves.
    a. What element of Robinson-Patman might be used as a defense in that Sherman 1 action?
    b. Would the court find that defense persuasive? Explain.

13. The A. E. Staley Manufacturing Company, located in Decatur, Illinois, sold its glucose products at a delivered price computed as though Chicago was the shipping point, when in fact shipments originated some distance from Chicago in Decatur. The Federal Trade Commission challenged this policy.
    a. What was the basis of that challenge?
    b. What name is applied to such pricing systems? What predatory purposes might be achieved by those pricing systems?
    c. Decide the case. Explain. See *Federal Trade Commission* v. *A. E. Staley Manufacturing Co.,* 324 U.S. 746 (1945).

14. In *Bruce's Juices, Inc.* v. *American Can Co.,* 87 F. Supp. 985 (S.D. Fla. 1949), aff'd 187 F.2d 919 (5th Cir.), modified 190 F.2d 73 (5th Cir.), cert. dismissed 342 U.S. 875 (1951), American Can defended itself against a price discrimination charge by arguing that the cans in question were not of "like grade and quality." The cans sold to Bruce's Juices were 3.14 inches in height, while those sold at a reduced price to Bruce's competitors (but refused to Bruce's) were 3.12 inches in height. Otherwise the cans were functionally identical.
    a. Is American Can's defense persuasive? Explain.
    b. Why is the presence of price discrimination good evidence of the presence of a monopoly?
    c. In what sense does the Robinson-Patman Act conflict with the Sherman Act?

NOTES

1. *Standard Oil Co. of New Jersey* v. *United States*, 221 U.S. 1 (1911).
2. See, for example, John DeQ. Briggs and Stephen Calkins, "Antitrust 1986–87: Power and Access (Part I)," *The Antitrust Bulletin* 32, no. 2 (Summer 1987), p. 275.
3. See L. Sullivan, *Handbook of the Law of Antitrust* (St. Paul, Minn.: West Publishing, 1977), p. 315.
4. *Copperweld Corporation* v. *Independence Tube Corp.*, 467 U.S. 752 (1984).
5. The materials in this paragraph are drawn from "How the Justice Dept. Is Bagging Highway Bid-Riggers," *Business Week,* July 4, 1983, p. 89; and Albert Karr and Robert Taylor, "Building Costs on Highways Are Declining," *The Wall Street Journal,* March 25, 1983, p. 17.
6. Russell Mokhiber, "Bigness Isn't Better," *Sloan Management Review* 28, no. 3 (Spring 1987), p. 63 reviewing Walter Adams and James W. Brock, *The Bigness Complex: Industry, Labor, and Government in the American Economy* (New York: Pantheon Books, 1986).
7. Buck Turnbull, "Most Schools Drowning in Flood of Television Games," *Des Moines Register,* November 3, 1987, p. 35. Reprinted with permission.
8. Wesley J. Liebeler, 1980 Cumulative Supplement to *Antitrust Advisor, 2nd ed.* (Colorado Springs: Shepard's/McGraw-Hill, 1978).
9. *Rothery Storage & Van Co.* v. *Atlas Van Lines, Inc.*, 792 F.2d 210 (D.C. Circuit 1986).
10. Ibid., p. 229.
11. Ibid., p. 231–32.
12. *BankAmerica Corporation, et al.* v. *United States,* 462 U.S. 122 (1983).
13. *Monsanto Co.* v. *Spray-Rite Service Corp.,* 465 U.S. 752 (1984).
14. 388 U.S. 365 (1967).
15. *Continental T.V., Inc.* v. *GTE Sylvania Inc.,* 433 U.S. 36 (1977).
16. *Standard Oil of Cal.* v. *United States,* 337 U.S. 293 (1949).
17. See Charles L. Vaughn, *Franchising* (Lexington, Mass.: Lexington Books, 1979), p. 2, for a detailed discussion.
18. See Earl Kintner, *A Robinson-Patman Primer* (New York: MacMillan, 1970), p. 93.
19. Richard Posner, *Antitrust Law* (Chicago: University of Chicago Press, 1976), p. 4.

Employer–Employee Relations

Chapter 11

Labor and General Employment Law

Part One—Introduction

To understand contemporary labor relations and labor law, one must first know something about the history of labor conflict in this country and the causes of that conflict. The Industrial Revolution brought about vast changes—not only in terms of means and methods of production in the United States and throughout the world, but also in terms of the effects those changes had on the social order and the distribution of wealth.[1]

During a relatively short period of time, the United States moved from an agrarian to an industrial society. Goods formerly produced in the home or in small shops by a craftsman and a few apprentices suddenly became the products of factories employing hundreds of people. Then, because of the large number of workers, intermediaries were necessary to supervise and manage the operation of the workplace. The personal relationship that had once existed between workers and their employer disappeared.[2]

Competition among these developing firms in the late 1800s was fierce. Increases in demand often caused firms throughout an industry to expand their operations to keep pace with the growing market. However, since the firms within a given industry all increased output at the same time, production often exceeded the demand for goods.[3] To stay in business, companies had to cut production costs to sell their goods at lower prices than their competitors and reap a greater profit from their sales. Faced with fixed costs for raw materials and overhead expenses, companies found that one production cost that could be reduced: the cost of labor. By paying workers as little as possible and making them work 14- or 18-hour days, employers could lower their total production costs. Thus, employers had an economic incentive for ignoring the human needs of the workers. The presence of an economic incentive to abuse workers, combined with the absence of the personal relationship between employer and worker, led to a severe deterioration of working conditions.[4]

At the same time, two other situations had a significant influence on the development of labor conflict. The first was that workers often left the farms and moved to cities to be near their jobs. Unfortunately, that movement destroyed an important safety net. That is, if wages did not provide the full measure of living expenses, farm families still had their gardens and chickens and cows to use for food. Once these families moved to the cities, all expenses had to be covered by whatever wages were paid, no matter how meager an amount that might be.[5]

A second major factor generating labor conflict was foreign immigrants' influx into northern and midwestern industrial centers. The availability of people anxious to work meant competition for jobs was fierce and employers could fill jobs easily, regardless of low wages and deplorable working conditions.[6] In addition, some highly educated immigrants were escaping political and religious persecution in their homelands. These people brought to the United States ideas, philosophies, and experiences in class struggle and labor conflict, which presumably exacerbated a struggle that was coming to a head in any case.[7]

> The immigrant is usually accustomed to some form of social organization. He is not as individualistic as is the typical American. He can be organized with others into labor unions; and when the unskilled immigrants from a variety of birthplaces are thus associated, the resulting union is usually strong, coherent, and easily directed by capable and enthusiastic leaders.[8]

To say that working conditions for many people at this time were unpleasant or even dismal would be a vast understatement. The term *desperate* better describes the problem. Children were impressed into service as soon as they were big enough to do a job and then made to work 12- and 14-hour days.[9] Textile companies would send men called "slavers" to New England and southern farm communities to gather young women to work in the mills.[10] Employers built factory and mining towns where workers would be forced to rent company-owned tenements and buy provisions from company stores at exorbitant rates.[11] Reports like the following about labor and living conditions in the forepart of the 20th century reveal the grim picture:

> When I moved from the North to the South in my search for work, I entered a mill village to work in a cotton mill as a spinner. There I worked 11 hours a day, five and a half days a week, for $7 a week. In a northern mill I had done the same kind of work for $22 a week, and less hours. I worked terribly hard. My boss was a farmer who knew nothing about regulating the machines. I had not been there long when he was fired and an overseer from the North with his speed-up and efficiency system was hired in his place. I do not know which was worse: to work under a man who did not know how to make the work run

well but who was pleasant to work with, or to have well-regulated machines which ran better but a driving boss.

The sanitary conditions were ghastly. When I desired a drink of water, I had to dip my cup into a pail of water that had been brought into the mill from a spring in the fields. It tasted horrible to me. Often I saw lint from the cotton in the room floating on top of the lukewarm water. All of the men chewed tobacco, and most of the women used snuff. Little imagination is needed to judge the condition of the water which I had to drink, for working in that close, hot spinning room made me thirsty. Toilet facilities were provided three stories down in the basement of the mill in a room without any ventilation. Nowhere was there any running water; even in the houses provided by the company there was no running water.

The married women of the South work extremely hard. The majority of them work in the mill besides having large families to care for. They arise about five to take the cow out to the pasture, to do some weeding in the garden, and to have hot cakes ready for their husbands' breakfasts when they arise. Then they prepare their children for school and finally start their work in the mills at 6:30, where they work for 11 hours. Upon their return to their homes, they have housework to do. They have no conveniences. Instead of a sink they have a board stretched across one corner of a room. When the washing on the dishes is done, the refuse is thrown out of the back door. When a woman desires meat for her family, she orders it at the company store. When the manager has enough orders of meat he kills a cow.

Everything in the village is company owned. The houses look like barns on stilts, and appear to have been thrown together. When I would go inside one of them, I could see outside through the cracks in the walls. The workers do all of their trading at the company store and bank, and use the company school and library for they have no means of leaving the village. The money is kept circulating from the employer to the employees, employees to company store, store to company bank, and from the bank to the company again. The result is old torn bills in the pay envelope each week.

I worked in the South for nine months, and during that time I could not reconcile myself to the conditions of the mills and village. Therefore, I left the South and returned to the North—back to the clock punching, speed-up and efficiency system of the northern mills.

Five years have passed since then, and I have learned through experience that I may go North, South, East, or West in my search for work, and find miserable working conditions for miserable wages. I know that the workers in any industry are in a most deplorable condition, but the workers of the South are in virtual slavery.[12]

Compare these working-class conditions with those of the more famous American entrepreneurs of the same era:

[Frederick Allen] describes the homes of the wealthy.

Frederick W. Vanderbilt's great house at Hyde Park, in which the dining room was approximately 50 feet long; . . . William K. Vanderbilt's Idle Hour at Oakdale—with 110 rooms, 45 bathrooms, and a garage ready to hold 100 automobiles. But the champion of all the turn-of-the-century chateaux was

George W. Vanderbilt's ducal palace at Asheville, North Carolina, which he called Biltmore. . . .

It had 40 master bedrooms, a Court of Palms, an Oak Drawing Room, a Banqueting Hall, a Print Room, a Tapestry Gallery, and a Library with 250,000 volumes. It was surrounded by an estate which . . . covered 203 square miles.

The secretary of agriculture noted that George W. employed more men and spent more money on his hobby of landscape gardening and wildlife management at Biltmore than did the entire Department of Agriculture on the needs of all the farmers in the United States.

Historians have depicted John D. Rockefeller as a man of notoriously frugal habits—his standard tip for any service was a dime. Allen describes his estate at Pocantico Hills as containing

more than 75 buildings. . . . Within his estate were 75 miles of private roads on which he could take his afternoon drive; a private golf links on which he could play his morning game; and anywhere from 1,000 to 1,500 employees, depending on the season.

. . . Rockefeller also owned an estate at Lakewood, which he occupied in the spring; an estate at Ormond Beach in Florida for his winter use; a townhouse . . . in New York; an estate at Forest Hill, Cleveland, which he did not visit; and a house on Euclid Avenue in Cleveland, likewise unused by him.

Concludes Allen, "Never, perhaps, did any man live a more frugal life on a more colossal scale."[13]

Contrasting these conditions with those of the workers enables us to better understand the sense of injustice felt by many workers and the belief of many that a redistribution of the wealth might provide the only solution to the class conflict. Because these fortunes were built in part through the exploitation of workers, it is not surprising that the characterization of these men and women of the leisure class as American heroes is distasteful to many.

ORGANIZING LABOR

The Knights of Labor, initially a secret society, was the first major labor organization in the United States. The Knights of Labor, led first by Uriah Stephens and then by Terence V. Powderly, had a large following during the 1870s and 1880s.[14] The order admitted any workers to its ranks, regardless of occupation, race, sex, or nationality; in fact, the only people excluded from the group were gamblers, bankers, stockbrokers, and liquor dealers.[15] The Knights of Labor dedicated itself to principles of social reform. For example, the group sought the protection of wage and hour laws, improved health care systems, and mandatory education.[16] The goals of the Knights of Labor were perhaps too broad and far reaching to bring workers any relief from their immediate problems. Thus, despite Powderly's insistence that workers should strike only as a last resort, dissidents within the organization instigated strikes under the name of the order.[17] Great philosophical divisions within the Knights brought about its rapid decline.[18]

Samuel Gompers, who built and developed the American Federation of Labor (AFL), had more practical, attainable goals in mind for his organization. Gompers, a worker in the cigar industry, saw the need to organize workers along craft lines so that each craft group could seek gains for its own workers, all of whom had the same type of skills and, presumably, all of whom shared the same occupational goals.[19] The efforts of the craft groups were directed toward getting higher wages and better working conditions for laborers.[20] This approach proved to be much more effective than that of the Knights of Labor.

The Congress of Industrial Organizations (CIO) was organized in response to the need of an entire segment of the working population to which the AFL was virtually unresponsive.[21] The AFL consisted of unions of craft labor. By the 1930s, however, millions of workers were employed in highly compartmentalized jobs requiring very little skill. Assembly-line production fostered jobs that required repetitive tasks capable of being performed by untrained workers.[22] The interests of these unskilled workers differed greatly from those of skilled workers, and ordinarily the unskilled workers did not qualify for membership in most craft unions. Therefore, funneling these workers into the craft unions was not a particularly practical solution to their need for organization. Further, the members of the AFL were not willing to accept the idea of unions set up along industry, rather than craft, lines. John L. Lewis, Sidney Hillman, David Dubinsky, and a number of others saw the need for industrywide unionization in mass production industries. When their suggestions were rejected out of hand at the 1935 international meeting of the AFL, these people started the CIO.[23]

A great deal of competition existed between the AFL and the CIO through the 1930s and 40s. Each organization had its own approach to improving the lot of workers.The AFL remained attached to traditional notions of labor–management struggle; that is, trying to achieve gains through intrafirm improvements. The CIO was less conventional (in its day) in its approach. It strove for industrywide improvements coupled with political solutions, such as price control, public health, low-cost housing, better educational opportunities, and foreign trade policies that would minimize competition from low-cost foreign labor.[24]

Eventually, the two labor federations decided to combine forces against their common "foe"—management. In 1952 the organizations agreed to stop raiding one another for members. Three years later the two groups united forces, and they function together today as the AFL–CIO.[25]

It should be noted that the AFL and the CIO were not the only organizations seeking to unite workers in the 1800s and 1900s. These included, for example, the National Labor Union and the National Colored Labor Union (created in response to the exclusionary policies of the white labor organizations).[26] Groups representing the political left enjoyed a large measure of success, as well. Perhaps the most notable of these was the Industrial Workers of the World, known popularly as the IWW or the Wobblies, led by Eugene V. Debs, Daniel DeLeon, and Mother Mary Jones.[27] The IWW believed that an inherent conflict would always exist between the "capitalist class and the workers it employed." Thus, the Wobblies ultimately sought to achieve a socialist society.[28] In addition, the IWW recognized the special needs and problems of black people and women. This approach should be contrasted with the highly exclusionary and racist attitudes adopted by large segments of the AFL and the CIO.

Question

1. *a.* Do you agree with the IWW that an inherent conflict exists between the interests of the capitalist and working classes? Why?
   b. If such an inherent conflict exists, do you believe there is any way to resolve that conflict?
   c. How would you approach the problem?
   d. If you do not believe such a conflict exists, is there any reason you would prefer being a member of one class rather than the other? Why?

UNIONIZATION AND THE LAW

Attempts to unionize have traditionally met with a great deal of resistance from employers. Not only did companies have economic power to wield over the workers but, until the passage of protective legislation in 1935, employers had the backing of the legal system as well.

Two devices used by employers to block or discourage unionization were "yellow dog" contracts and blacklists. A *yellow dog contract* was an employment agreement under which the employee was bound by the contract's terms not to become a member of a union. *Blacklists* were simply lists of union organizers or sometimes even participants in labor activities circulated among all the companies in an industry or geographic locale telling employers not to hire the people named on the lists because they were union instigators.[29]

The most effective legal means to halt unionization in its incipiency was the court injunction. If a group of workers began picketing a factory, for example, an employer could easily obtain from the state or federal court an order forbidding the workers to continue such activities. Although picketing itself was not actually considered illegal, judicial doctrine developed that tied the act of picketing inextricably to violence. Thus, striking employees could be stopped for taking part in criminal conspir-acies. Eventually, the idea that union activities constituted criminal ac-tions was rejected and replaced by the notion that such actions involved civil tort liability. In either event, once an injunction had been issued, any workers who continued picketing were in contempt of court, subject to imprisonment and dismissal by their employer.[30]

Passage of the Sherman Antitrust Act in 1890 added a new legal weapon to the employers' arsenal against employees. In 1908 the U.S. Supreme Court used the Sherman Act prohibition on activities that were in "re-straint of trade" to find workers involved in a boycott liable for treble damages under the provisions of that act. The Court's opinion indicated that virtually any concerted activity that employees engaged in could be construed as a restraint of trade and that federal courts could issue in-junctions to prevent such activities under the authority vested in them by the Sherman Act.[31]

By 1932 public pressure had mounted so that Congress, in passing the Norris-LaGuardia Act (designed primarily to prevent antitrust problems), withdrew from the federal courts the right to issue injunctions against labor activities and clarified its legislative intent that the terminology "restraint of trade" was not meant to include the organization or activities of labor. The Norris-LaGuardia Act also specifically outlawed the use of yellow dog contracts. Even the Norris-LaGuardia Act proved ineffectual, however, because employers were still able to go into state courts to obtain injunctive relief.[32]

From 1932 to 1935, labor tensions continued to mount. The nation was still caught in the Great Depression. Believing that one element essential to economic recovery was stability in the work force, Congress addressed the labor "question" with comprehensive legislation.[33] Congress had tried its hand at drafting labor legislation once before when it enacted the Railway Labor Act of 1926, an act designed to protect workers in the railroad industry who chose to organize. Although the Railway Labor Act affected workers *only* in the railroad industry, the 1926 legislation laid a good foundation from which Congress could work in developing a stat-utory scheme to apply to workers in other segments of industry and the work force.[34]

Congress passed the Wagner Act in 1935. This legislation, patterned after the Railway Labor Act, gave workers for the first time the unequiv-ocal right to organize and to engage in concerted activities for their mutual aid and benefit. To protect this right, Congress identified a number of "unfair labor practices" and made them illegal. These unfair labor prac-tices were all activities that Congress feared employers might use to thwart workers' attempts to unionize and to undermine the economic power that would come from workers' newfound rights.[35] Through the Wagner Act, Congress also established the National Labor Relations Board (NLRB), an administrative agency charged with the responsibility of overseeing and ensuring fair union representation elections and investigating, prosecuting, and trying employers accused of committing unfair labor practices.[36]

Armed with these legislative protections and a governmental bias in favor of unionization, labor organized rapidly. In 1935 only 3 million workers were members of labor organizations; 12 years later, the ranks had swelled to 15 million.[37] By 1947, Congress decided labor no longer needed such a protective watchdog and, in fact, thought management might need a little help in coping with ever-growing labor organizations.[38] Thus, Congress decided to "neutralize" its position vis-à-vis labor organizations by imposing some responsibilities on these organizations where before there had been none. Congress did so by enacting the Taft-Hartley Act, a series of amendments to the Wagner Act that identified as unfair labor practices certain activities unions used to hamper, rather than help, the collective bargaining process. The Taft-Hartley Act also added a provision to the existing labor legislation that ensured employers' right to speak out in opposition to unionization—in effect, protecting their First Amendment right to freedom of speech. Thus, the Taft-Hartley Act signaled a move by the government away from unconditional support for labor, toward a balance of rights between labor and management.[39]

Congressional hearings in the 1950s uncovered a new source of concern in the area of labor relations. This time the problems were not between labor and management, although certainly friction between the two continued to exist. Attention now was focused on union leaders who were abusing their power. Once in power, some union leaders had prevented others from challenging their power by not holding meetings of the union's rank and file, not scheduling elections, and using union funds to promote their own election campaigns. Stories came to light accusing some union officials of accepting collective bargaining agreements with terms that were against the interest of their constituencies, in exchange for bribes paid to them by corporate management. These agreements were aptly called "sweetheart" deals. Evidence indicated certain union officials had looted their unions' treasuries.[40]

In response to the growing evidence that union leaders were benefiting at the expense of the membership, Congress in 1959 enacted the Landrum-Griffin Act, also known as the Labor–Management Reporting and Disclosure Act (LMRDA). This act contains provisions requiring unions to keep records of their funds, including statements of their assets, liabilities, salaries paid, and all other expenditures. It also prohibits unions from loaning money except under specified circumstances and in conformity with certain procedural rules. These financial statements and transactions must all be reported annually to the government.

The Landrum-Griffin Act also contains a set of provisions often referred to as the "Bill of Rights" for the individual laborer. These provisions are designed to protect union members by requiring that union meetings be held, that members be permitted to speak and vote at these meetings, that every employee covered by a collective bargaining agreement have the right to see a copy of that agreement, and that a union member be informed of the reasons and given a chance for a hearing if the union wishes to suspend or take disciplinary action against that member, unless he or she is being suspended for nonpayment of dues.[41] Although these provisions had the potential for eliminating the internal union problems, recent court decisions have done much to emasculate the protections provided in Landrum-Griffin. These court decisions will be discussed later in this chapter.

This historical progression—from labor's helplessness to active unionization following passage of the Wagner Act in 1935, to restoration of balance between labor and management in 1947, and, finally, to a recognition of the powerlessness of the individual within the union—sounds very smooth and logical. The entire process has been likened by many to the swinging of a pendulum. One should not forget, however, that labor conflicts in the United States have often been attended by severe violence; have driven apart towns, factories, even families; and have raised emotions to higher pitches than perhaps any other social or political issue. Labor disputes have the potential, as with nationwide strikes, for bringing industry and production to a grinding halt. Any exposition of the law on this subject must be understood within this context.

Part Two—Labor Legislation Today

THE STATUTORY SCHEME AND ITS GOALS

Today labor–management relations are governed by the National Labor Relations Act (NLRA).[42] This act includes the Wagner Act, the Taft-Hartley Act, and portions of the Landrum-Griffin Act. The remaining provisions of the Landrum-Griffin Act make up the aforementioned Labor–Management Reporting and Disclosure Act and the "Bill of Rights of Members of Labor Organizations." These provisions deal with the internal operations of labor organizations and the relationship between the individual union member and the union itself rather than with the relationship between the union and the employer.

The National Labor Relations Act sets out the following policy statement:

It is declared to be the policy of the United States to eliminate the causes of certain substantial obstructions to the free flow of commerce and to mitigate and eliminate these obstructions when they have occurred by encouraging the practice and procedure of collective bargaining and by protecting the exercise by workers of full freedom of association, self-organization, and designation of representatives of their own choosing, for the purpose of negotiating the terms and conditions of their employment or other mutual aid or protection.

Note that Congress couches its findings and declarations of policy in terms of maintaining the free flow of commerce or, conversely, eliminating the obstructions to freely flowing commerce caused by labor conflicts. Note, too, that Congress identifies labor conflict to be due, in large part, to lack of bargaining power on the part of individual employees and, thus, sets out to correct the problem by promoting concerted activity by employees and collective bargaining between labor organizations and management.

It is important to keep these ideas in mind as one examines the choices made by Congress in regulating labor–management relations and the decisions made by the NLRB and the courts in interpreting and applying these statutory mandates. First, the NLRA gives employees the right to engage in concerted activity. Section 7 of the NLRA states:

> Employees shall have the right to self-organization, to form, join or assist labor organizations, to bargain collectively through representatives of their own choosing, and to engage in other concerted activities for the purpose of collective bargaining or other mutual aid or protection, and shall also have the right to refrain from any or all of such activities except to the extent that such right may be affected by an agreement requiring membership in a labor organization as a condition of employment.

Second, as previously mentioned, the act describes and outlaws certain activities by employers that would hamper or discourage employees from exercising the rights granted to them in Section 7. Thus, Section 8(a) of the act makes it an unfair labor practice for an employer to:

1. Interfere with employees in the exercise of the rights given to them by Section 7.
2. Dominate, interfere, or assist with the formation of any labor organization (including contributing financial support to it).
3. Encourage or discourage membership in any labor organization by discrimination in regard to hire, tenure of employment, promotion, salary, or any other term of employment.
4. Discharge or take any other action against an employee because he or she has filed charges or given testimony under the act.
5. Refuse to bargain collectively with a duly certified representative of the employees.

These five provisions are designed to allow employees to organize in an atmosphere free from intimidation by the employer, with minds clear of the fear that the employer might be able to affect their jobs adversely because of their choice to participate in a labor organization. The provisions also ensure that the employer, through his or her position of authority, will not be able to interfere with union activities by either seizing control of the union or rendering it impotent by refusing to bargain collectively.

Section 8(b) lists activities constituting unfair labor practices by a labor organization. Some of these provisions mirror some of the activities prohibited to employers. That is, at least since the enactment of the Taft-Hartley Act, the law is not sympathetic to labor organizations that try to use coercive tactics, threats of the loss of livelihood, or any other strong-arm methods to recruit members. Reasoned persuasion is the order of the day. Thus, a labor organization is not permitted to:

1. Restrain or coerce any employee in the exercise of his or her rights as granted by Section 7.
2. Cause or attempt to cause an employer to discriminate against an employee who has chosen not to join a particular labor organization or has been denied membership in such an organization.
3. Refuse to bargain collectively with an employer on behalf of the bargaining unit it is certified to represent.
4. Induce or attempt to induce an employer to engage in secondary boycott activities.
5. Require employees to become union members and then charge them excessive or discriminatory dues.
6. Try to make an employer compensate workers for services not performed.
7. Picket or threaten to picket an employer where the object of the picketing is to force the employer to recognize or bargain with a labor organization that is not the duly certified representative of a bargaining unit.

The remaining subparts of Section 8 cover a variety of problems: Section 8(c) protects the First Amendment rights of people involved in labor disputes while spelling out limitations on those rights. Section 8(d) describes and defines the duties of employers and labor organizations to bargain collectively over certain mandatory subjects. This section also sets up a "cooling-off" process under which a party who wishes to renegotiate a collective bargaining agreement must serve notice of its desire to do so 60 days in advance of the agreement's expiration date. Sections 8(e) and (f) describe situations in which it is impermissible for both employers and labor organizations to pursue their disputes in ways that extend those disputes beyond the confines of their own internal conflict.

NATIONAL LABOR RELATIONS BOARD (NLRB)

The NLRB is an administrative agency instrumental in regulating labor–management relations. Its primary tasks are designating appropriate bargaining units of workers (that is, deciding which workers have a sufficient "community of interest" to afford them unity when bargaining); conducting elections for union representation within the chosen bargaining unit; certifying the results of such elections; and investigating, prosecuting, and adjudicating charges of unfair labor practices.[43]

Although the congressional mandate by which the NLRB was formed gives the agency jurisdiction theoretically to the full extent of the interstate commerce powers vested in Congress, the agency has neither the funding nor the staff to administer its duties to all of American industry. Thus, some limitations have been placed on the board by both statute and the agency's own decisions.

These restrictions on jurisdiction take two basic forms. First, the board itself requires the portion of an employer's business involved in interstate commerce to exceed certain dollar amounts. These amounts differ depending on the nature of the industry. Second, entire groups of employees are excluded from coverage. For example, public employees, agricultural workers, and supervisors and other managerial employees are not protected by the board.[44]

Questions

1. Why do you think these groups have been excluded from coverage? Do these groups share any common characteristics? Do you agree that they ought to be excluded? Explain.
2. Assume a union seeks a bargaining unit that would include all full-time and regular part-time employees at a supermarket, including head cashiers, produce managers, stock managers, and baggers. The unit would exclude meat department employees, salespeople, security guards, store managers, and assistant managers.
   a. Do you think a "community of interest" exists among these workers such that the board should approve this unit?
   b. If not, how should the group be changed?
   c. Do you need any additional facts before making your decision? See *Daylight Grocery Co., Inc.* v. *NLRB,* 678 F.2d 905 (11th Cir. 1982).

CHOOSING A BARGAINING REPRESENTATIVE—ELECTIONS

A bargaining representative is chosen by an election held within the bargaining unit that has been certified appropriate by the NLRB. The board oversees the election to ensure the process is carried on under "laboratory conditions."[45] In other words, the elections must be held under circumstances that, to the extent possible, are free from undue or unfair influence by either the employer or by unions vying for the position of representative of the bargaining unit.

Unfair labor practices are frequently committed at this juncture by employers anxious to prevent their plants from becoming unionized. This is not meant to suggest that overzealous unions never commit unfair labor practices or that employers always do. However, employers who are resistant to unionization have a great many natural advantages in the struggle against it. For example, employers have at their disposal lists of names and addresses for all their employees; the union does not. The employer could distribute written arguments and objections to unionization along with paychecks and thereby ensure that every employee sees the document. (Such an action, by itself, is *not* an unfair labor practice.)[46] The employer effectively has a captive audience. The employer generally is in better financial shape to stage a battle than the union is. Finally, and perhaps most important, the employer is the one who, in the final analysis, doles out or withholds benefits to the employees and provides them with jobs in the first place. It is not always terribly difficult for an employer to cross the line from using this position of natural authority to abusing the position and committing an unfair labor practice.

Before Congress passed the Taft-Hartley Act, board decisions reflected its belief that any attempts by an employer to influence the voting of his or her employees (including, for example, the distribution of antiunion pamphlets, speeches, or circulars) was an unfair labor practice. These decisions, however, raised First Amendment questions in the minds of many who thought the employers' constitutional right to free speech was being abridged by these rulings.[47] Congress determined to remedy this problem with a provision of the Taft-Hartley Act by adding Section 8(c), designed to ensure employers' and labor organizations' traditional First Amendment rights so long as they do not overstep certain bounds. The section states the following:

> The expressing of any views, argument or opinion, or the dissemination thereof, whether in written, printed, graphic, or visual form, shall not constitute or be evidence of an unfair labor practice . . . if such expression contains no threat of reprisal or force or promise of benefit.

Even with the inclusion of Section 8(c) in the NLRB, the board and the courts have continued in a struggle to define the parameters of protected and unprotected speech. The following decision of the NLRB provides an example of an employer's preelection tactics that contained no threats of force or reprisal but for which the board was nonetheless willing to set aside an election.

SEWELL MFG. CO. AND AMALGAMATED CLOTHING WORKERS OF AMERICA, AFL–CIO
138 NLRB No. 12, Case No. 10-RC-5016, August 9, 1962

Before McCulloch, Leedom, Fanning, and Brown

[A]n election by secret ballot was conducted . . . to determine whether the employees therein desired to be represented by the petitioner for purposes of collective bargaining. Upon the conclusion of the balloting the parties were furnished with a tally which showed that of approximately 1,339 eligible voters, 1,322 cast ballots of which 331 were for, and 985 against, the petitioner, 5 ballots were challenged, and 1 ballot was void. The number of challenged ballots was insufficient to affect the election results. Thereafter the petitioner filed timely objections to conduct affecting the results of the election.

* * * * *

The petitioner objected to the election upon the ground . . . that the employer, by various propaganda means, had resorted to appeals to racial prejudice to prevent a free election.

The elections were held on July 21, 1961, at Bremen and Temple, Georgia, where the employer's plants are located. Bremen has a population of less than 3,000; Temple a population of under 1,000. Both are located in Haralson County, on the Alabama border, in northwest Georgia, approximately 50 miles west of Atlanta.

On July 7, 1961, two weeks before the scheduled election, the employer mailed to its employees a large picture showing a close-up of an unidentified Negro man dancing with an unidentified white lady. Underneath was a caption in large, bold letters reading: "The CIO Strongly Pushes and Endorses the FEPC." On the same day the employer also sent the employees a reproduction of the June 4, 1957, front page of the *Jackson Daily News,* a newspaper published in Jackson, Mississippi, which contains a picture, four columns wide, of a white man dancing with a Negro lady. The caption beneath the picture reads:

UNION LEADER JAMES B. CAREY
DANCES WITH A LADY FRIEND
He is president of the IUE
Which Seeks to Unionize
Vickers Plant here.

Underneath the picture is a story headed: "Race Mixing Is An Issue As Vickers Workers Ballot."

On July 19, 1961, the president of the employer sent a letter to employees setting forth reasons why the president would vote against the petitioner if he were permitted to vote. Among these reasons is the following: "I would object to paying assessments so the union can promote its political objectives such as the National Association for the Advancement of Colored People, and the Congress of Racial Equality."

* * * * *

During the four months preceding the election, the employer distributed to employees copies of *Militant Truth,* a four-page monthly paper published in Greenville, South Carolina.

In its columns are a number of statements dealing with racial matters. In a two-page article entitled "Militant Truth and the Labor Unions," there is this statement:

> It isn't in the interest of our wage earners to tie themselves to organizations that demand racial integration, socialistic legislation, and free range of communist conspirators.

In a two-column article listing plants in which unions had lost elections, there is the statement:

> Another factor that merits consideration is the large percentage of union victories in plants that employ all, or nearly all, Negro labor. Because the communists always operate under the guise of being "the great uplifters" of "the underprivileged," and promise social equality to the Negro, it is easy to understand why many Negroes are more easily influenced and misled by the radical labor union organizers.

In an article on integration (not on labor matters), there is a reference to the Garland Fund as having made a contribution to the NAACP, and reference to "Sidney Hillman, the Russian-born Founder of the Amalgamated Clothing Workers," as one of its directors. The same issue contains a reprint of an article from "The Worker," dealing with "freedom riders." According to *Militant Truth,* the "Worker" article takes time out "to praise the various AFL–CIO unions for their part in demanding total integration and promoting both class and race warfare." Another article dealing with the Negro's progress in America refers to "The Communist Party, the NAACP, the labor unions, the National Council of Churches, the Kennedy Administration and their ilk" as those who "would have us believe that the Negro race in America is a poor, starving, down-trodden people."

The Regional Director ruled that the foregoing literature did not justify setting aside the election upon the ground that, "while the Board has consistently held that appeals to religious and racial prejudices are not condoned, such literature does not exceed the permissible bounds of preelection propaganda." For this conclusion, the Regional Director cited the *Sharnay* case, in which a union objected to an election because the employer, in a letter to employees, had discussed the union's position on the issue of racial integration. The letter had stated that the union was strongly prointegration, had submitted a prointegration brief to the Supreme Court, was striving to eliminate segregation from every walk of life, and was a member of the AFL–CIO which had made a monetary contribution to the NAACP. In refusing to set aside the election because of this letter, the Board said:

> The petitioner concedes that there were no threats or promises, and it is not suggested that the employer misrepresented the petitioner's position. We are asked, rather, to hold that the mere mention of the racial issue, in an election campaign, is per se improper and grounds for setting aside any and all elections where such might occur. . . . We note that there is no misrepresentation, fraud, violence, or coercion and that the statements here were temperate and factually correct. They therefore afford no basis for setting aside the results of the election.

We do not agree with the Regional Director that the rationale of the *Sharnay* case requires overruling of the objections in the present case.

A Board election is not identical with a political election. In the latter, public officials conducting the election have no responsibility beyond the mechanics of the election. Aside from such things as libel restrictions and legal requirements to identify the source of campaign literature and advertising, the law permits wide latitude in the way of propaganda—truth and untruth, promises, threats, appeals to prejudice. It is only the sense of decency of the candidates and their supporters and the maturity of the electorate which places a restraint upon the kind of propaganda used.

By way of contrast, the Board not only conducts elections, but it also oversees the propaganda activities of the participants in the election to insure that the voters have the opportunity of exercising a reasoned, untrammeled choice for or against labor organizations seeking representation rights. The Board has said that in election proceedings it seeks "to provide a laboratory in which an experiment may be conducted, under conditions as nearly ideal as possible, to determine the uninhibited desires of the employees." Where for any reason the standard falls too low the Board will set aside the election and direct a new one. Unsatisfactory conditions for holding elections may be created by promises of benefits, threats of economic reprisals, deliberate misrepresentations of material facts by an employer or a union, deceptive campaign tactics by a union, or by a general atmosphere of fear and confusion caused by a participant or by members of the general public. Standards, particularly those of permissive propaganda, are not fixed and immutable. They have been changed and refined, generally in the direction of higher standards.

Our function, as we see it, is to conduct elections in which the employees have the opportunity to cast their ballots for or against a labor organization in an atmosphere conducive to the sober and informed exercise of the franchise, free not only from interference, restraint, or coercion violative of the act, but also from other elements which prevent or impede a reasoned choice.

We are faced in this case with a claim that by a deliberate sustained appeal to racial prejudice the employer created conditions which made impossible a reasoned choice of a bargaining representative and therefore that the election should be set aside.

Some appeal to prejudice of one kind or another is an inevitable part of electoral campaigning, whether in the political or labor field. Standards must be high, but they cannot be so high that for practical purposes elections could not effectively be conducted. There are propaganda appeals used in elections which we do not approve or condone, but which we tolerate, leaving the proper weighing of such appeals to the good sense and judgment of the electorate. Such tolerated propaganda has been characterized as "prattle rather than precision." The Board has stated its practice as follows:

The Board normally will not censor or police preelection propaganda by parties to elections, absent threats or acts of violence. . . . Exaggerations, inaccuracies, partial truths, name-calling, and falsehoods, while not condoned, may be excused as legitimate propaganda, provided they are not so misleading as to prevent the exercise of a free choice by employees in the election of their bargaining representative. The ultimate consideration is whether the challenged propaganda has lowered the standards of campaigning to the point where it may be said that the uninhibited desires of the employees cannot be determined in an election.

The Board has considered as propaganda a single-sentence reference to the religious background of the employer. But the appeals made to racial prejudice in this case are different both in kind and intensity from the single, casual religious reference made in the *Paula Shoe* case.

We take this as datum that prejudice based on color is a powerful emotional force. We think it also indisputable that a deliberate appeal to such prejudice is not intended or calculated to encourage the reasoning faculty.

What we have said indicates our belief that appeals to racial prejudice on matters unrelated to the election issues or to the union's activities are not mere "prattle" or puffing. They have no place in Board electoral campaigns. They inject an element which is destructive of the very purpose of an election. They create conditions which make impossible a sober, informed exercise of the franchise. The Board does not intend to tolerate as "electoral propaganda" appeals or arguments which can have no purpose except to inflame the racial feelings of voters in the election.

This is not to say that a relevant campaign statement is to be condemned because it may have racial overtones. In *Sharnay,* supra, the employer in a letter to employees made a temperate, factually correct statement of the petitioning union's position on integration. In the *Allen-Morrison Sign* case . . . the employer also informed the employees about the petitioning union's position on segregation as well as on union monetary contributions towards eliminating segregation. In the view of Chairman McCulloch, and Members Leedom and Fanning again the statement was temperate in tone, germane and correct factually.

We would be less than realistic if we did not recognize that such statements, even when moderate and truthful, do in fact cater to racial prejudice. Yet we believe that they must be tolerated because they are true and because they pertain to a subject concerning which employees are entitled to have knowledge—the union's position on racial matters. As Professor Sovern has pointed out: no one would suggest that Negro employees were not entitled to know that the union which seeks to represent them practices racial discrimination.

So long, therefore, as a party limits itself to *truthfully* setting forth another party's position on matters of racial interest and does not deliberately seek to overstress and exacerbate racial feelings by irrelevant, inflammatory appeals, we shall not set aside an election on this ground. However, the burden will be on the party making use of a racial message to establish that it was truthful and germane, and where there is doubt as to whether the total conduct of such party is within the described bounds, the doubt will be resolved against him.

Viewed against the test set forth above, we find that the employer's propaganda directed to race exceeded permissible limits and so inflamed and tainted the atmosphere in which the election was held that a reasoned basis for choosing or rejecting a bargaining representative was an impossibility. It seems obvious from the kind and extent of propaganda material distributed that the employer calculatedly embarked on a campaign so to inflame racial prejudice of its employees that they would reject the petitioner out of hand on racial grounds alone. This is most readily apparent from the distribution of photographs showing a Negro man dancing with a white woman, and a white man, identified in the photograph as James B. Carey, president of the IUE (which is not the petitioner in this case), dancing with a Negro woman, to the latter of which was appended a news story headed: "Race Mixing Is An Issue As Vickers Workers Ballot." These photographs and the news articles were not germane to any legitimate issue involved in the election and reinforce our conclusion that their purpose was to exacerbate racial prejudice and to create an emotional atmosphere of hostility to the petitioner.

Accordingly, we shall set aside the election and direct that a second election be held.

Questions

1. Does it surprise you to learn that a company would use tactics like those described above to try to discredit unions and their leadership? Explain.

2. If you were called on, as a manager or officer in a company, to participate in such tactics, what would you do?

3. If you were instructed by your superiors at the company to develop a program designed to discourage unionization, what would be your plan of action?

4. Suppose the employees of Steno Office Supply, Inc., a large manufacturing firm, have petitioned the NLRB for an election. Company management personnel begin inviting workers to lunch to discuss the upcoming election and the likely "consequences" of unionization. These lunches are held at the local country club. During these discussions, at which employee comments are encouraged, although not forced, managers make allusions to the union organizer's sexual orientation. The comments, made in the form of jokes, suggest that homosexual favors may be required in lieu of dues.

   a. If the union loses the election, should the NLRB set the election aside because of the tactics used? Explain.

   b. Which, if any, of these tactics seem problematic?

   c. Would any one of the tactics by itself be enough to set aside the election? Explain.

   d. What standard should the board use in making its determination?

   e. What additional information might you want to have before making a decision in this particular case? See *General Knit of California,* 239 NLRB 619 (1978) 99 LRRM 1687, for a discussion of the general standard.

Threats of Reprisal or Force

Even within the confines of Section 8(c)'s language, problems often arise in determining whether "antiunion" arguments put forth by an employer are legitimate or whether they contain veiled threats. Suppose, for instance, that a company owner warns her employees that if she has to pay higher wages (a demand that a union would be likely to make), she will be forced to go out of business and the employees will all lose their jobs. Such statements of economic "forecast" by employers have been the subject of a great deal of litigation. The following case explains the issues involved.

NLRB V. GISSEL PACKING CO.
395 U.S. 575 (1969)

[The president of Sinclair Company, one of four companies whose actions were being examined in this case, tried to dissuade his employees from joining a union. To that end, he informed them that, if the union won the election, it was bound to call a strike because the Teamsters were a "strike-happy" outfit. He told the employees on more than one occasion that the company's financial position was precarious and that a strike would likely force the plant to close. He suggested that the out-of-work employees would have a difficult time finding new jobs because of their age and lack of education. The union lost the election by a vote of 7 to 6 and filed objections to the election with the NLRB.

Both the NLRB and later the Court of Appeals agreed that the election should be set aside, despite the company's claim that it had merely been exercising its First Amendment rights to express its views to employees. The Supreme Court affirmed the Court of Appeals decision.]

Chief Justice Warren

We note that an employer's free speech right to communicate his views to his employees is firmly established and cannot be infringed by a union or the Board. Thus, § 8(c) [29 U.S.C. § 158(c)] merely implements the First Amendment by requiring that the expression of "any views, arguments, or opinion" shall not be "evidence of an unfair labor practice," so long as such expression contains "no threat of reprisal or force or promise of benefit" in violation of § 8(a)(1). Section 8(a)(1), in turn, prohibits interference, restraint, or coercion of employees in the exercise of their right to self-organization.

Any assessment of the precise scope of employer expression, of course, must be made in the context of its labor relations setting. Thus, an employer's rights cannot outweigh the equal rights of the employees to associate freely, as those rights are embodied in § 7 and protected by § 8(a)(1) and the proviso to § 8(c). And any balancing of those rights must take into account the economic dependence of the employees on their employers, and the necessary tendency of the former, because of that relationship, to pick up intended implications of the latter that might be more readily dismissed by a more disinterested ear. Stating these obvious principles is but another way of recognizing that what is basically at stake is the establishment of a nonpermanent, limited relationship between the employer, his economically dependent employee, and his union agent, not the election of legislators or the enactment of legislation whereby that relationship is ultimately defined and where the independent voter may be freer to listen more objectively and employers as a class freer to talk.

Within this framework, we must reject the company's challenge to the decision below and the findings of the Board on which it was based. The standards used below for evaluating the impact of an employer's statements are not seriously questioned by petitioner and we see no need to tamper with them here. Thus, an employer is free to communicate to his employees any of his general views about unionism or any of his specific views about a particular union, so long as the communications do not contain a "threat of reprisal or force or promise of benefit." He may even make a prediction as to the precise effects he believes unionization will have on his company. In such a case, however, the prediction must be carefully phrased on the basis of objective fact to convey an employer's belief as to demonstrably probable consequences beyond his control or to convey a management decision already arrived at to close the plant in case of unionization. If there is any implication that an employer may or may not take action solely on his own initiative for reasons unrelated to economic necessities and known only to him, the statement is no longer a reasonable prediction based on available facts but a threat of retaliation based on misrepresentation and coercion, and as such without the protection of the First Amendment. We therefore agree with the court below that "[c]onveyance of the employer's belief, even though sincere, that unionization will or may result in the closing of the plant is not a statement of fact unless, which is most improbable, the eventuality of closing is capable of proof.'' As stated elsewhere, an employer is free only to tell ''what he reasonably believes will be the likely economic consequences of unionization that are outside his control,'' and not ''threats of economic reprisal to be taken solely on his own volition.''

Equally valid was the finding by the court and the Board that petitioner's statements and communications were not cast as a prediction of ''demonstrable 'economic consequences,' '' but rather as a threat of retaliatory action. The Board found that petitioner's speeches, pamphlets, leaflets, and letters conveyed the following message: that the company was in a precarious financial condition; that the ''strike-happy'' union would in all likelihood have to obtain its potentially unreasonable demands by striking, the probable result of which would be a plant shutdown, as the past history of labor relations in the area indicated; and that the employees in such a case would have great difficulty finding employment elsewhere. In carrying out its duty to focus on the question ''[W]hat did the speaker intend and the listener understand?'' the Board could reasonably conclude that the intended and understood import of that message was not to predict that unionization would inevitably cause the plant to close but to threaten to throw employees out of work regardless of the economic realities. In this connection, we need go no further than to point out (1) that petitioner had no support for its basic assumption that the union, which had not yet even presented any demands, would have to strike to be heard, and that it admitted at the hearing that it had no basis for attributing other plant closings in the area to unionism; and (2) that the Board has often found that employees, who are particularly sensitive to rumors of plant closings, take such hints as coercive threats rather than honest forecasts.

Affirmed.

Question

1. *a.* Why does the Court suggest the NLRB has a duty to determine what the speaker intended and what the listener understood?
   b. How does that differ from merely looking at what the employer actually said?
   c. Why is that difference important?

Promise of Benefit

While threats of force or reprisal are considered objectionable elements in union campaigns, the rationale behind the prohibition against promises of benefit is not as intuitively obvious. In the case of *NLRB* v. *Exchange Parts Co.* 375 U.S. 409 (1964), Exchange Parts sent its employees a letter shortly before a representation election, which spoke of ''the *Empty Promises* of the Union'' and ''the *fact* that *it is the Company that puts things in your envelope . . .*'' After mentioning a number of benefits, the letter said: ''The Union can't put any of those things in your envelope— *only the Company can do that.''* Further on, the letter stated: ''[I]t didn't take a Union to get any of those things and . . . it won't take a Union to get additional improvements in the future." Accompanying the letter was a detailed statement of the benefits granted by the company since 1949 and an estimate of the monetary value of such benefits to the employees.

In addition, the letter outlined further benefits, such as additional vacation days and overtime pay, that the company had recently decided to institute. In the representation election held two weeks later, the union lost. The Court of Appeals did not think the employer's action constituted an unfair labor practice. The Supreme Court disagreed. Justice Harlan stated:

> We think the Court of Appeals was mistaken in concluding that the conferral of employee benefits while a representation election is pending, for the purpose of inducing employees to vote against the union, does not "interfere with" the protected right to organize.
>
> The broad purpose of § 8(a)(1) is to establish "the right of employees to organize for mutual aid without employer interference." We have no doubt that it prohibits not only intrusive threats and promises but also conduct immediately favorable to employees which is undertaken with the express purpose of impinging upon their freedom of choice for or against unionization and is reasonably calculated to have that effect. In *Medo Photo Supply Corp.* v. *N.L.R.B.,* this Court said: "The action of employees with respect to the choice of their bargaining agents may be induced by favors bestowed by the employer as well as by his threats or domination." Although in that case there was already a designated bargaining agent and the offer of "favors" was in response to a suggestion of the employees that they would leave the union if favors were bestowed, the principles which dictated the result there are fully applicable here. The danger inherent in well-timed increases in benefits is the suggestion of a *fist inside the velvet glove.* [Emphasis added.] Employees are not likely to miss the inference that the source of benefits now conferred is also the source from which future benefits must flow and which may dry up if it is not obliged. The danger may be diminished if, as in this case, the benefits are conferred permanently and unconditionally. But the absence of conditions or threats pertaining to the particular benefits conferred would be of controlling significance only if it could be presumed that no question of additional benefits or renegotiation of existing benefits would arise in the future; and, of course, no such presumption is tenable.

* * * * *

Reversed.

Union Persuasion

Employers, of course, are not the only parties affected by Section 8(c). Unions are also restricted in the type of preelection persuasion they employ. In cases involving promises of benefits made by the union, the board has been more reluctant to set aside elections than it has when such promises have been made by management. The board's reasoning is that employees realize that union preelection promises are merely expressions of a union platform, so to speak. Employees recognize that these are benefits for which the union intends to fight. Employers, on the other hand, really do hold within their power the ability to confer or withdraw benefits—the so-called fist inside the velvet glove. Nonetheless, occasionally a union does promise a benefit in a manner that violates Section 8(c).

Questions

1. *a.* What is the Court in *Exchange Parts Co.* talking about when it refers to the "fist inside the velvet glove"?
   b. Do you think the Court is justified in thinking that workers would be fooled or cowed by a sudden move by management to grant benefits? Explain.
   c. Do you think the efforts to unionize or negotiate would be undermined? Explain.
2. Suppose a union seeking to organize employees tells those employees that any employee who voices support for the union before the election will not have to pay union dues for a full year if the union is voted in.
   a. Do you see any difference between this and the *Gissel* case? Explain.
   b. Who do you think workers feel more threatened by—their employers or their peers? Explain.
   c. Should the Court's reasoning in this case be the same as it was in *Gissel?* Why? See *NLRB* v. *Savair Manufacturing Co.,* 414 U.S. 274 (1973).

Collective Bargaining

Section 8(a)(5) of the NLRA requires an employer to engage in collective bargaining with a representative of the employees. Section 8(b)(3) imposes the same duty on labor organizations; that is, if the organization is the representative of the employees, that organization has an obligation to bargain collectively with the employer. Failure to bargain by either an employer or representative of the employees constitutes an unfair labor practice.

What is collective bargaining? What must one do to discharge the duty imposed? According to Section 8(d) of the National Labor Relations Act:

> [T]o bargain collectively is the performance of the mutual obligation of the employer and the representatives of the employees to meet at reasonable times and confer in good faith with respect to wages, hours, and other terms and conditions of employment . . . but such obligation does not compel either party to agree to a proposal or require the making of a concession.

Three distinct questions are raised by Sections 8(a)(5), 8(b)(3), and 8(d). First, what duties are imposed on employers and employees' representatives by the requirement that they confer "in good faith"? Second, about which subjects must the parties bargain? Finally, what are the implications of the union's recognition as the *exclusive* bargaining agent for a bargaining unit?

Bargaining in Good Faith.   The concept that collective bargaining requires the parties to bargain in good faith is one of the controversial legal issues arising from the NLRA. Attempts to define the term *good faith* generally result in some notion that good faith is related to the intent of the parties. Trying to determine the state of mind of the participants in a negotiation session is a tricky proposition at best, especially if the determination has to be made on the basis of evidence presented by the parties to that negotiation.[48]

Because of the difficulties involved in trying to determine whether an employer or bargaining agent has the appropriate frame of mind, the board and the courts tend to apply tests that look at objective rather than subjective factors. The act itself specifies that a mere inability to reach an agreement or the failure to make a concession does not mean the parties have abrogated their duties to bargain collectively. However, would that duty be abrogated by the unwillingness of one party to agree to *anything?* Although cases of this sort continue to be decided on the basis of the peculiar facts of each incident, the Circuit Courts of Appeal diverge greatly on the issue of whether they should consider the final terms of the agreement or the bargaining posture of one of the parties to be relevant in demonstrating lack of good faith.[49]

The board and the courts have struggled with the question of whether there are any actions that, if taken by one of the bargaining parties, would constitute a per se breach of the duty to bargain in good faith; that is, whether there are actions so detrimental to the bargaining process that use of them is enough to justify a finding of bad faith.

Suppose a union was in the midst of bargaining with management over terms of a new collective bargaining agreement and began using economic weapons against the employer while negotiations were proceeding. In the case of *NLRB* v. *Insurance Agents' International Union,*[50] Insurance Agents' International Union was negotiating a collective bargaining agreement with Prudential Insurance Company of America. The union decided to use its economic power to harass the company during these negotiations. The union's tactics included:

> [R]efusal for a time to solicit new business, and refusal (after the writing of new business was resumed) to comply with the company's reporting procedures; refusal to participate in the company's "May Policyholders' Month Campaign"; reporting late at district offices the days the agents were scheduled

to attend them, and refusing to perform customary duties at the offices, instead engaging there in "sit-in-mornings," "doing what comes naturally," and leaving at noon as a group; absenting themselves from special business conferences arranged by the company; picketing and distributing leaflets outside the various offices of the company on specified days and hours as directed by the union; distributing leaflets each day to policyholders and others and soliciting policyholders' signatures on petitions directed to the company; and presenting the signed policyholders' petitions to the company at its home office while simultaneously engaging in mass demonstrations there.[51]

The NLRB thought the union's use of economic weapons against the company during a time when negotiations were not at an impasse showed bad faith on the part of the union, even though no evidence had been presented indicating the union had refused to cooperate at the bargaining table. The board's reasoning was that:

[T]he respondent's [union's] reliance upon harassing tactics during the course of negotiations for the avowed purpose of compelling the company to capitulate to its terms is the antithesis of reasoned discussion it was duty-bound to follow. Indeed, it clearly revealed an unwillingness to submit its demands to the consideration of the bargaining table where argument, persuasion, and the free interchange of views could take place. In such circumstances, the fact that the respondent continued to confer with the company and was desirous of concluding an agreement does not *alone* establish that it fulfilled its obligation to bargain in good faith.[52]

Justice Brennan, writing the opinion for the Supreme Court, disagreed with the board, saying that:

It is apparent from the legislative history of the whole Act that the policy of Congress is to impose a mutual duty upon the parties to confer in good faith with a desire to reach agreement, in the belief that such an approach from both sides of the table promotes the over-all design of achieving industrial peace. Discussion conducted under that standard of good faith may narrow the issues, making the real demands of the parties clearer to each other, and perhaps to themselves, and may encourage an attitude of settlement through give and take. The mainstream of cases before the Board and in the courts reviewing its orders, under the provisions fixing the duty to bargain collectively, is concerned with insuring that the parties approach the bargaining table with this attitude. But apart from this essential standard of conduct, Congress intended that the parties should have wide latitude in their negotiations, unrestricted by any governmental power to regulate the substantive solution of their differences.

We believe that the Board's approach in this case—unless it can be defended, in terms of § 8(b)(3), as resting on some unique character of the union tactics involved here—must be taken as proceeding from an erroneous view of collective bargaining. It must be realized that collective bargaining, under a system where the government does not attempt to control the results of negotiations, cannot be equated with an academic collective search for truth—or even with what might be thought to be the ideal of one. The parties—even granting the modification of views that may come from a realization of economic interdependence—still proceed from contrary and to an extent antagonistic viewpoints and concepts of self-interest. The system has not reached the ideal of the philosophic notion that perfect understanding among people would lead to perfect agreement among them on values. The presence of economic weapons in reserve, and their actual exercise on occasion by the parties, is part and parcel of the system that the Wagner and Taft-Hartley Acts have recognized. Abstract logical analysis might find inconsistency between the command of the statute to negotiate toward an agreement in good faith and the legitimacy of the use of economic weapons, frequently having the most serious effect upon individual workers and productive enterprises, to induce one party to come to the terms desired by the other. But the truth of the matter is that at the present statutory stage of our national labor relations policy, the two factors—necessity for good-faith bargaining between parties, and the availability of economic pressure devices to each to make the other party incline to agree on one's terms—exist side by side. One writer recognizes this by describing economic force as "a prime motive power for agreements in free collective bargaining." Doubtless one factor influences the other; there may be less need to apply economic pressure if the areas of controversy have been defined through discussion; and at the same time, negotiation positions are apt to be weak or strong in accordance with the degree of economic power the parties possess. A close student of our national labor relations laws writes: "Collective bargaining is curiously ambivalent even today. In one aspect collective bargaining is a brute contest of economic power somewhat masked by polite manners and voluminous statistics. As the relation matures, Lilliputian bonds control the opposing concentrations of economic power; they lack legal sanctions but are nonetheless effective to contain the use of power. Initially it may be only fear of the economic consequences of disagreement that turns the parties to facts, reason, a sense of responsibility, a responsiveness to government and public opinion, and moral principle; but in time these forces generate their own compulsions, and negotiating a contract approaches the ideal of informed persuasion." Cox, The Duty to Bargain in Good Faith, 71 *Harv. L. Rev.* 1401, 1409.

For similar reasons, we think the Board's approach involves an intrusion into the substantive aspects of the bargaining process—again, unless there is some specific warrant for its condemnation of the precise tactics involved here. The scope of § 8(b)(3) and the limitations on Board power which were the design of § 8(d) are exceeded, we hold, by inferring a lack of good faith not from any deficiencies of the union's performance at the bargaining table by reason of its attempted use of economic pressure, but solely and simply because tactics designed to exert economic pressure were employed during the course of the good-faith negotiations. Thus the Board in the guise of determining good or bad faith in negotiations could regulate what economic weapons a party might summon to its aid. And if the Board could regulate the choice of economic weapons that may be used as part of collective bargaining, it would be in a position to exercise considerable influence upon the substantive terms on which the parties contract. As the parties' own devices became more limited, the government might have to enter even more directly into the negotiation of collective agreements. Our labor policy is not presently erected on a foundation of government control of the results of negotiations. Nor does it contain a charter for the National Labor Relations Board to act at large in equalizing disparities of bargaining power between employer and union.

The use of economic pressure, as we have indicated, is of itself not at all inconsistent with the duty of bargaining in good faith.[53]

Bargaining in Good Faith—Continued.   If using economic weapons during the negotiating process is not an exercise of bad faith and if the NLRB must close the door of the bargaining room, so to speak, and not judge what goes on behind it, can you think of any activities short of a complete refusal to bargain that would constitute lack of good faith?

Two practices have provided the major source of "bad-faith" findings by the Supreme Court. The first arises when a company, during negotiations, announces that it cannot accede to higher wage demands, for example, without sending the company into bankruptcy. The union is willing to accept that limitation because, after all, it will do the employees no good to have high wages if they then lose their jobs as a result. The union, however, asks to see the company's books to verify that the company is, indeed, in the financial straits that it claims. If the company refuses to disclose such information to the union, this is a refusal to bargain in good faith.[54]

The second set of circumstances involves a situation in which the company institutes a change unilaterally during the bargaining period that affects one of the subjects of collective bargaining or offers better terms directly to the employees than the company has ever proposed to the union. For example, at the bargaining table, the company has only been willing to offer one week's paid vacation to employees of two years or less. Company officials then announce (not at the bargaining table but directly to the employees themselves) that effective immediately, all employees who have worked for six months or more are entitled to two weeks' paid vacation. According to the Supreme Court, such an action taken by the company would be strong evidence of bad faith.[55]

Subjects of Bargaining.   While employers and labor representatives are free to discuss whatever they mutually choose to discuss, Section 8(d) of the NLRA clearly sets out some mandatory subjects over which the parties must bargain. These are wages, hours, and "other terms and conditions of employment." Although these topics for mandatory bargaining seem simple enough, questions still arise frequently. For example, suppose the union and employer bargain over wages and agree to institute merit increases for employees. Must the employer also bargain over which employees are entitled to receive these increases or who will make the decision at the time the increases are to be given? Does the question of bringing in subcontractors to perform certain jobs fall within the scope of "wages, hours, and terms and conditions of employment," since the use of subcontractors may reduce the amount of work available to regular employees? Or does that subject belong more directly to the management of the firm? What about a decision to close a plant?

Generally, the board and the courts will balance three factors. First, they look to the effect of a particular decision on the workers—how direct is it and to what extent is the effect felt? Second, they consider the degree to which bargaining would constitute an intrusion into entrepreneurial interests or, from the opposite side, the degree of intrusion into union affairs. Third, they examine the practice historically in the industry or the company itself.[56]

Another question that sometimes arises is whether it is unfair for one of the negotiating parties to refuse to consider any of the mandatory bargaining subjects until the other party agrees to a demand that does not fall within the range of mandatory bargaining subjects. In the case of *NLRB* v. *Wooster Division of Borg-Warner*,[57] the Supreme Court was called on to answer that question. Borg-Warner insisted the union agree to a "ballot" clause calling for a prestrike secret vote of all employees regarding the company's most recent offer. Borg-Warner also insisted the collective bargaining agreement was to be signed by the uncertified local affiliate of the certified international union rather than by the international union itself. Borg-Warner took the position that it would offer the employees an economic package only if the union agreed to these two "noneconomic" clauses. The Supreme Court found this to be an unfair labor practice.

Question

1. *a.* Is there anything about the two particular demands made by Borg-Warner that made the Court's decision easier to reach than it otherwise might have been?
   b. Can you think of a nonmandatory bargaining point about which the Court might have had greater sympathy?

The Union as Exclusive Bargaining Agent.   Once a union has been elected and certified as the representative of a bargaining unit, it becomes the exclusive agent for employees within that bargaining unit, whether they voted for the union or not. The exclusivity of the union's authority has a number of implications, but one is particularly relevant in determining whether an employer has failed to demonstrate good faith at the bargaining table. Specifically, the employer must deal with the certified representative. The employer commits an unfair labor practice if he or she attempts to deal directly with the employees or recognizes someone other than the workers' chosen representative. In both instances the issue is fairly straightforward. The employer is undermining the position of the representative by ignoring him or her.

Somewhat less obvious than this direct violation, but based on the same reasoning, is the problem of an employer who, during the course of negotiations, institutes a unilateral change in employee benefits. For example, in the 1962 Supreme Court case of *NLRB* v. *Katz*,[58] an employer made three unilateral changes. He granted merit increases, changed the sick leave policy, and instituted a new system of automatic wage increases. This strategy was considered a failure to bargain in good faith because it effectively denied the union the right to joint participation in the decision making, and because the employer's actions tended to obstruct the process and make the negotiations more difficult. If negotiations had come to a complete impasse before the employer instituted these changes, the Court might have decided differently. However, the employer clearly demonstrated a lack of good faith when it unilaterally granted better benefits than any offered at the bargaining table.

Can you imagine any instance in which the unilateral granting of benefits might be permissible? If raises are always given in December and labor negotiations are in progress during December in a given year, should the employer be permitted to grant pay increases without negotiating them? Is your answer conditional in any way?

SHOP AGREEMENTS AND RIGHT–TO–WORK LAWS

Unions must keep their forces strong if they wish to wield economic power. Thus, in order to maintain their membership, unions typically seek a collective bargaining clause requiring all employees to become union members after they have been employed for some period of time—generally, 30 days—("open-shop agreements") or, at the least, requiring them to pay union dues and fees (union security clause). These clauses are called "union shop agreements" and are allowed by most states. The courts have upheld these practices.

Some states have enacted so-called *right-to-work* laws, which prohibit union security arrangements in collective bargaining agreements. In these states nonmembers receive all the benefits of having union representation. Needless to say, unionized plants are far less common in right-to-work states than in states without those laws.

Finally, at one time, unions with a great deal of bargaining leverage would insist on clauses in collective bargaining agreements that restricted employers from hiring anyone not already a union member. These "closed-shop agreements" are now prohibited by the NLRA.

STRIKES

For many, the initial image of labor conflict is one of employees on strike, picketing a store or factory. Striking is, however, an extremely drastic measure under which employees must bear an immediate loss of wages while, in many instances, risking job loss.

Strikes fall into two basic categories: (1) those used purely as economic weapons to persuade an employer to provide more favorable employee benefits or better working conditions and (2) those instituted by workers in response to the employer's commission of an unfair labor practice. Both types of strikes are considered "concerted activities" for the mutual aid or benefit of the workers. Thus, as long as workers are not striking in violation of a collective bargaining agreement provision, their actions are protected under Section 7 of the NLRA.[59]

A strike that begins as an economic strike may be converted into a strike in protest of an unfair labor practice if an employer, during the course of the strike, violates one of the provisions of NLRA Section 8(a). The permissibility of replacing striking workers depends on the type of strike being waged. The following case states the rules the courts have applied and illustrates the problems involved in classifying a strike as economic or as an unfair labor practice protest.

**NATIONAL LABOR RELATIONS BOARD V. INTERNATIONAL VAN LINES
409 U.S. 48 (1972)**

[Four employees of International Van Lines refused to cross a picket line in front of the company's premises. The following day each received a telegram informing him that he was being permanently replaced for having failed to report to work. At the time of the discharge, the company (respondent) had not yet hired any permanent replacements. The employees brought an action against the company, claiming that they had been engaged in protected activity when they refused to cross the picket line and that the company had, therefore, committed an unfair labor practice in discharging them. The NLRB agreed with the employees. The Court of Appeals reversed in part, deciding that the employees were economic strikers, rather than unfair labor practice strikers. The latter, according to the Court of Appeals, were entitled to unconditional reinstatement, while the former could be discharged if the employer had substantial business justification for letting them go. The Supreme Court granted certiorari to examine the question.]

Justice Stewart

It is settled that an employer may refuse to reinstate economic strikers if in the interim he has taken on permanent replacements. . . . It is equally settled that employees striking in protest of an employer's unfair labor practices are entitled, absent some contractual or statutory provision to the contrary, to unconditional reinstatement with back pay, "even if replacements for them have been made." . . . Since the strike in the instant case continued after the unfair labor practices had been committed by the employer, the Board reasoned that the original economic strike became an unfair labor practice strike on October 5, when the telegrams were sent.

* * * * *

Both the Board and the Court of Appeals have agreed that the labor picketing was a lawful economic strike, and the validity of that conclusion is not before us. Given that hypothesis, the Board and the Court of Appeals were clearly correct in concluding that the respondent committed unfair labor practices when it fired its striking employees. "[T]he discharge of economic strikers prior . . . to the time their places are filled constitutes an unfair labor practice." . . .

We need not decide, however, whether the Board was correct in determining that the discharged employees assumed the status of unfair labor practice strikers on October 5, 1967, to reach the conclusion that the Court of Appeals erred in refusing to enforce the Board's order of reinstatement with back pay.

Unconditional reinstatement of the discharged employees was proper for the simple reason that they were the victims of a plain unfair labor practice by their employer. Quite apart from any characterization of the strike that continued after the wrongful discharges occurred, the discharges *themselves* were a sufficient ground for the Board's reinstatement order. "Reinstatement is the conventional correction for discriminatory discharges," . . . and was clearly within the Board's authority.

It would undercut the remedial powers of the Board with respect to § 8 violations, and subvert the protection of § 7 of the Act, to hold that the employees' rights to reinstatement arising from the discriminatory discharges were somehow forfeited merely because they continued for a time to engage in their lawful strike after the unfair labor practices had been committed.

The judgment of the Court of Appeals is reversed insofar as it refused to enforce the Board's order that the discharged employees be reinstated with back pay.

Questions

1. Can you envision any problems that are likely to arise as a result of the distinction drawn between economic strikers and unfair labor practice strikers?
2. What do you think the policy justifications are for distinguishing between these two types of strikers?
3. Assume Mary Wills, a bottle inspector for Pop Soda Inc. and a member of a certified bargaining unit, struck along with other bottle inspectors to protest an allegedly unfair labor practice committed by the employer. The bottle inspectors offered to return to work after a one-week strike, and, although their positions were not filled, Pop Soda offered them entirely different positions as bottle sorters, telling the employees that they would shortly thereafter be returned to their regular inspector jobs. Wills was the only one who accepted this offer; the other employees insisted that they were legally entitled to their former jobs. Wills made subsequent inquiries, attempting to get her inspecting job back, but the company at no time made a proper offer for that position. After three and a half months of working as a bottle sorter, Wills resigned because of physical problems with her hand. She then made a claim to the NLRB that Pop Soda had committed an unfair labor practice by not reinstating her to her inspecting position. She asked for reinstatement and back pay.

   Do you think she is entitled to either or both of these remedies? See *The Coca-Cola Bottling Company of Memphis and International Brotherhood of Teamsters, et. al.,* 269 NLRB No. 160 (1983–84 CCH NLRB ¶ 16,259), decided April 23, 1984.

Notification of the Intent to Strike

Congressional desire to maintain industrial peace is manifested, in part, through the conditions imposed by Section 8(d) of the NLRA. These provisions are designed to prevent ill-conceived strikes by requiring that any party desiring to terminate or renegotiate a collective bargaining agreement must serve written notice on the other party at least 60 days prior to the expiration of the agreement then in force. Within 30 days of notifying the other party of its desires, the moving party must also notify the Federal Mediation and Conciliation Service and any state or local conciliation boards set up for the purpose of resolving that type of dispute. Failure to give this notice is considered a refusal to bargain in good faith. Moreover, any worker who goes on strike during this "cooling off" period loses his or her status as an employee for purposes of being protected by the NLRA. Such an employee may be discharged by the employer without any repercussions from the act. The strike itself is called a "wildcat" strike.

The 60-day notification period allows both parties some leeway during which they can discuss and hopefully resolve their contract disputes before the old contract terminates. The notification provision ensures that neither employers nor employees are left in the lurch, unprepared for or unaware of the other party's dissatisfaction with the present bargaining agreement. Perhaps more important, the public is protected to a great extent. A strike in any sector of industry tends to have a ripple effect, creating disturbances throughout the economy.

EMPLOYEES' RIGHTS WITHIN OR AGAINST THE UNION

The Union's Duty of Fair Representation

As you have seen in previous sections of this chapter, the union is given statutory authority to be the *exclusive* bargaining agent for the employees in the designated bargaining unit. This means that even if an individual employee in the bargaining unit does not agree with union policies or is not a member of the union, he or she cannot bargain individually with the employer. Such an employee will still be bound by the terms of the collective bargaining agreement.

No express statutory provision in the federal labor laws requires a union to represent employees fairly, be they union members or not. The Supreme Court, however, has announced that a duty of fair representation is implicit in § 9(a) of the NLRA.

A union, despite its duty to fairly represent all members of a bargaining unit, may have serious difficulty doing so because of divergent interests within that unit. (That is one reason the choice of an appropriate bargaining unit is such an important part of unionization.) For example, if a company is in difficult financial straits, it may tell union negotiators that the company must do one of two things to stay viable: lay off workers or give all employees a cut in salary. The workers who have seniority and would not lose their jobs in a layoff are likely to push for the former; workers with less seniority, who would normally be let go during a layoff, will prefer in most instances to retain their jobs even if they are forced to take a cut in wages. In such a situation, the union could not possibly represent both groups' interests to the fullest.

This type of situation, however, is a far cry from those in which a union has arbitrarily or with purposeful intent discriminated against some segment of its rank-and-file membership. In addition to the racial discrimination found in many unions, sex discrimination was also rampant. Unions were notorious for negotiating contracts in which women were excluded from certain jobs and paid lower wages for performing work identical to their male counterparts. In recognition of the discrimination being practiced by many unions, Congress built special provisions into the Equal Pay Act of 1963 and the Civil Rights Act of 1964, making it illegal for unions to discriminate on the basis of race, color, creed, national origin, or sex.

The "Bill of Rights" of Labor Organization Members

The "Bill of Rights" for members of labor organizations is contained in Title I, Section 101 of the Labor–Management Reporting and Disclosure Act (LMRDA or Landrum-Griffin Act). The Bill of Rights was designed to ensure equal voting rights, the right to sue the union, and the rights of free speech and assembly, as embodied in the U.S. Constitution's Bill of Rights. These rights of union members are tempered by the union's right to enact and enforce "reasonable rules governing the responsibilities of its members."[60]

People generally, and judges specifically, hold widely divergent views of the honesty and trustworthiness of union officials and also differ in the amount of faith they place in the machinery of union democracy. Many people are extremely skeptical about the union leaders' ability and/or desire to be responsive to the interests of the membership rather than to their own needs for power or money. This skepticism is due, at least in part, to the information brought to light in congressional hearings in the late 1950s.

Prior to the enactment of the LMRDA in 1959, the Select Senate Committee discovered widespread corruption, dictatorship, and racketeering in a number of large international unions. The committee found that the president of the Bakery and Confectionary Workers' International Union of America had "railroaded through changes in the union constitution which destroyed any vestigial pretenses of union democracy . . ." it reported that Dave Beck, general president of the International Brotherhood of Teamsters, "shamefully enriched himself at [the] expense [of the union members] and that in the final instance he capitulated to the forces within the union who promoted the interests of racketeers and hoodlums." The committee likewise found Teamster officials joining with others to take over illegal gambling operations with an "underworld combine," . . . and the top officers of the United Textile Workers of America avariciously misappropriating union funds. "Democracy [was] virtually nonexistent" in the International Union of Operating Engineers because the union was ruthlessly dominated through "violence, intimidation, and other dictatorial practices." Practices in the Teamsters "advanced the cause of union dictatorship." The committee cited other similar instances of widespread abuses in its 462-page report.[61]

Even though union members are guaranteed the rights of free speech and assembly, federal court cases at both the district and circuit court levels have made clear that unions are not obligated to provide space in union newspapers for articles containing viewpoints opposed to those of union leadership, nor is the union obligated to hold meetings at the behest of their membership even when the union constitution provides a procedural means for calling such a meeting. Moreover, the union meeting agenda can be set by the union leadership in such a way as to preclude discussion of particular issues. The union is permitted to establish "reasonable" rules to govern such situations. In the 1967 circuit court case of *Yanity* v. *Benware*,[62] the Court of Appeals found that the protections for freedom of speech and assembly included in the employee Bill of Rights were only designed to safeguard union members who met with each other outside of regular union meetings. Supposedly the reason Congress adopted the clause was to enable workers to meet with other workers without union approval and without fear that the union would, in some way, retaliate against the union members.

Other federal court decisions have come down equally firmly in interpreting other "rights" guaranteed by the workers' Bill of Rights. Thus, although union members are entitled to vote in union elections, they do not have the right to demand a vote on a decision of whether to strike. Likewise, the union is not required to submit a proposed collective bargaining agreement to the membership for ratification or approval, although the Bill of Rights gives members the right to see a copy of the agreement under which they are working.[63]

As a result of these court rulings, one could make a tenable argument that employees are now caught in a double-bind. Not only is the employer a potential source of trouble for the employee, but so may be the very union that was supposed to be his or her vehicle for relief. These conditions should raise concerns for the psychological well-being of workers made to feel alienated because they cannot effectuate any meaningful change in the work environment to which they are captive 40 hours a week. The consequences of a labor force experiencing widespread despair and powerlessness might be worth considering.

POLITICS AND NLRB DECISIONS

One problem that has plagued the student of labor law is the inconsistency in NLRB decisions over time. While you may have the impression, after reading the bulk of this chapter, that the development of labor law has progressed along a straight and rational line, that has not been the case at all. The NLRB has been (and continues to be) affected by political winds. Consider, for example, the following article.

LABOR LAW BALANCE SHIFTING

James J. Kilpatrick

Washington—The purpose of elections, a political philosopher once observed, is not only to throw the old rascals out. It is also to throw new rascals in.

A splendid manifestation of that enduring truth is taking shape at the National Labor Relations Board, where three Reagan appointees are putting some balance back in labor law.

Members of the NLRB serve for five-year terms, staggered so that one member's term expires every year. In 1981 Ronald Reagan inherited a board dominated by Jimmy Carter's guys. The president systematically has eliminated every one of them, and now has a board of three true believers. Two seats are vacant.

Under the leadership of Chairman Donald L. Dotson, the reconstituted board is doing exactly what the president hoped it would do. For a recent example of what elections are all about, consider what is known as the case of Rossmore House.

The case arose in 1982 in Los Angeles, when Shyr-Jim Tsay bought a residential retirement hotel. He then hired Ronald Tvenstrup as manager. Tvenstrup promptly moved to cut operating costs by changing the hotel's food service from table service to buffet. Six waiters were laid off in midsummer. The hotel's cook, War-

ren Harvey, who had been hired in 1981, was about to be fired in late July for insubordination and "dreadful" cooking.

On August 1, Tvenstrup received a mailgram from Local 11 of the Hotel and Restaurant Employees Union, AFL–CIO, advising him that Warren Harvey and others had formed an organizing committee. The record discloses two versions of what happened next, but this much was clear: Tvenstrup went to the kitchen with the mailgram in his hand and asked Harvey a question. "What's this about a union? Is this true?" A week later Tsay also put a question to Harvey: "Why are you trying to get a union in here?" In both conversations Harvey readily acknowledged his leading role in seeking to organize the staff.

So much for the essential facts. The union charged the hotel with an unfair labor practice under Section 8(a)(1) of the National Labor Relations Act. In March 1983 an administrative law judge agreed with the union's charge that the two brief conversations between Harvey and his employers amounted to coercive interrogation.

The judge recommended to the board that Rossmore House be found guilty and ordered to post remedial notices.

Before the Carter board took control, a string of decisions in similar cases had established a rule of "all of the circumstances." That is, the mere act of an employer's asking a union-related question of an employee openly identified with union activity was not deemed to be coercive in and of itself. This reasonable standard was laid down in such cases as B. F. Goodrich Footwear in 1973 and Stumpf Motor Co. in 1974.

Along came the Carter appointees. In 1980, in a case known as PPG Industries, the Carter members swept aside the Stumpf and Goodrich precedents and for all practical purposes created a new per se rule forbidding any such questions whatever. A rule that had been neutral now had tilted wholly to the unions' side.

But in March 1983, when the administrative law judge made his recommendation in Rossmore House, the Reagan appointees were in control. They rejected the judge's recommendation; they overruled the precedent of the PPG case; they restored the interpretation of Section 8(a)(1) to the "totality of circumstances;" they concluded that "the reality of the marketplace" should be given its old weight; they

found no violation in the conversations with Harvey; and they dismissed the union's complaint altogether.

The union appealed to the 9th U.S. Circuit Court of Appeals. Last month the court held, without dissent, that the board's action was consistent with the act. "A large body of case law upholds the all-the-circumstances test." Findings of coercive interrogation are to be made "on a case-by-case basis."

In 1984, you will recall, organized labor fought the reelection of Ronald Reagan with all the resources it could throw behind Walter Mondale's campaign.

If Mondale had won, he never would have nominated Dotson (or Robert Hunter or Patricia Diaz Dennis) to the NLRB. Mondale would have nominated his own kind of folks, and Rossmore House would have been differently decided. Once more, let me say for the record: This is what elections are all about.

Source: Reprinted in the *Waterloo Courier,* July 1, 1985, p. A4, from "A Conservative View" by James J. Kilpatrick. Copyright 1988 Universal Press Syndicate. Reprinted with permission. All rights reserved.

Questions

1. Why is the inconsistency in the board's decisions a problem?
2. Do you think such inconsistency creates problems equally for labor and management? Explain.
3. Do you think that the board's "political" nature is a positive force in any way? Explain.

Part Three—General Employment Law

The focus of the chapter thus far has been labor law—that is, laws regulating union relationships. But today, unions represent less than 20 percent of the workers in the United States.[64] So who or what provides protection for the remaining 80+ percent of the work force, or are those workers simply left to the whims of their employers? The answer: these workers are increasingly protected by a vast array of federal and state laws and by a growing body of court decisions. The variety of existing protections is prodigious: wage and hour laws, worker safety laws, unemployment compensation laws, workers' compensation laws, and social security provisions, to name a few. The following sections will briefly describe a number of the more important protections and will more thoroughly cover a few select topics currently in the news. Complete coverage of employment law is beyond the scope of this text.

TERMS OF EMPLOYMENT

Most terms of employment and employee benefits are not mandated programs. The primary exceptions are wage and hour provisions, unemployment compensation, and social security. The latter two will be discussed in later sections.

The primary wage and hour legislation is contained in the federal Fair Labor Standards Act of 1938 (FLSA). It requires covered employees to be paid a specified minimum wage and to be paid "time and a half" for any work in excess of 40 hours per week. Generally speaking, covered employees are those employed by businesses engaged in interstate commerce or manufacturing goods for interstate commerce. However, a number of significant exceptions exist: professional, administrative, and executive employees are not covered. State wage and hour laws also exist in every state that, among other things, cover some employees not covered by the FLSA.

Many employee benefits are voluntarily provided by employers, and the total cost of both voluntary and mandated programs is substantial. "In 1986, employee benefits reached the highest percentage of payroll costs—39.3 percent—in the past 40 years."[65] And many businesses are becoming quite creative in the types of benefits offered.

> Several employers try to make like easier for workers with children. The Iowa Methodist Medical Center in Des Moines plans a summer program including field trips and swimming lessons. . . . When doctors and nurses are delayed in the operating room, the child care center at St. Thomas Hospital in Nashville, Tennessee, stays open.
>
> Wilmer, Cutler & Pickering, a Washington, D.C., law firm, runs an emergency day care facility that is available when employees' regular care arrangements fall through.[66]
>
> After Tenneco, the Houston-based oil company, opened its own fitness facility in 1982, an internal study found that annual medical bills for male employees who exercised regularly averaged $442 less than the bills for nonexercisers. Among female employees, the difference was $896.[67]

But the tenor of the times may be changing—toward more mandated benefits—as argued in the following article.

MANDATED UNCOMPETITIVENESS

After listening to them say it over and over the past three months, we're convinced that all 535 members of Congress can speak five syllables at once—"competitiveness." It might help, though, if some of them gave it more than lip service, because on the evidence of recent congressional actions, especially among Democrats, Congress is more interested in raising business costs than lowering them.

There's even an official buzzword for this congressional assault on U.S. competitiveness—"mandated benefits." Mandated benefits are an old cost-shifting game dating back at least to the Clean Air Act of 1970. Congress dreams up some social good no reasonable person can be against, the social good's up-front costs are laid off on the private sector, which then redistributes the mandated costs among higher prices, reduced wage increases, lower dividends, and delayed capital investment. In a global economy, this is a formula for reducing your country's competitiveness.

Evidence of this revival of off-budget legislating abounds:

Health Insurance

Senator Edward Kennedy (D., Massachusetts) is preparing legislation that would require employers to provide health insurance for all employees working more than 17½ hours a week. This "minimum health" plan would require almost all firms to pick up 80 percent of the premium costs.

Parental Leave

Representatives Bill Clay (D., Missouri) and Pat Schroeder (D., Colorado) want to require employers with more than 15 workers to provide up to 18 consecutive weeks of unpaid leave in the event of a birth, adoption, or serious illness of a child or parent. Employees would keep all health benefits during their absence and upon returning would be guaranteed their old job. The bill calls for a study on the feasibility of requiring *paid* leave in the future.

Immigration

The new immigration bill requires employers to bear the costs of making certain they do not hire illegal aliens. [The Immigration Control and Reform Act of 1986 forbids employing unauthorized aliens. However, seasonal agricultural workers may be given temporary residence.—Author.] Some Sun Belt businesses already say they are hiring additional workers just to check job-applicant documents.

* * * * *

Pensions

Last year Congress required that companies continue pension contributions for employees over 65. At the same time Congress outlawed mandatory retirement policies.

* * * * *

Talking tough about "competitiveness" is the easiest thing in the world. Mandating benefits, however, are just one more way for Congress to slip out from under the hard decision of saying no to higher spending. It simply imposes more costs on someone else.

Questions

1. *a.* Would you recommend the creation of additional mandated benefits? Why?
   b. What benefits would you add?
   c. Would you disband any presently mandated benefits?
2. Are our various employment laws anticompetitive? Explain.

INCOME SECURITY

As mentioned previously, two of the major mandated employee benefit programs are unemployment compensation and social security. Both programs are funded, at least in part, by employer contributions. Individual employees are also required to contribute to social security. Today unemployment compensation is primarily a state program, while social security is a federal program under the Federal Insurance Contributions Act (FICA). Unemployment compensation typically provides income security to covered employees who are fired or laid off for a specified period of time. FICA primarily provides old-age benefits and payments to disabled workers, as well as survivors' benefits to certain family members of covered deceased workers.

Recently a few state legislatures have provided a more unique form of income security—laws requiring employers to give employees a specified amount of notice before shutting down a plant and obligating such employers to pay severance pay to workers affected by the plant closures. And in 1988 Congress approved the Worker Adjustment and Retraining Notification Act that requires all firms of 100 or more employees to provide 60-day advance notification to workers and communities of plant closings and layoffs involving 50 or more full-time workers. President Reagan allowed the bill to become law without his signature. Such provisions are highly controversial, in part because they reduce the ability of employers to respond quickly to changing economic conditions.

PROTECTION FROM ON–THE–JOB INJURY

Abuse of employees is nothing new, as shown by the historical material at the beginning of this chapter. Abuse of employees has also not vanished.

They call it the odor patrol. Four times a day, every day, a Union Carbide truck tours Institute, West Virginia, to check for deadly gas leaks from the company's local plant. The workers' technique for locating leaks is simple: they sniff the air for unusual odors. Ten times during a round they do a more detailed analysis: they stop the truck and take a deep breath.

This practice is anything but harmless. And Union Carbide's odor patrol is not an isolated example. Chemical workers throughout the country are expected to use their senses to identify toxic chemicals—chemicals that can kill. Not only do workers use their noses to detect leaks, but in some cases they must taste chemicals to evaluate them. And this is happening daily.[68]

On the flip side of the coin, employers have also lost—and lost big—by taking an ethical stance to protect their employees.

Concerned that toxic chemicals in its plants might harm fetuses, American Cyanamid announced in 1978 that all women capable of becoming pregnant would be removed from jobs exposing them to any of 29 substances. As a result, five women at a West Virginia plant underwent surgical sterilization to avoid losing their jobs, and the company transferred two others to lower-paying positions. These seven and others filed a lawsuit, claiming Cyanamid's fetal protection policy constituted illegal sex discrimination. After nearly four years of pretrial proceedings and unfavorable publicity, Cyanamid continued to deny wrongdoing but paid an out-of-court cash settlement.[69]

Three major ways workers are protected with regard to on-the-job injuries are the Occupational Safety and Health Act (OSHA), right-to-know laws, and workers' compensation laws.

OSHA

To carry out the broad policy of OSHA—to ensure relatively danger-free workplaces—Congress created a federal agency, the Occupational Safety and Health Administration (also known as OSHA). The statute contains some very broad grants of power to the agency, allowing it to regulate virtually any aspect of the workplace that could have an effect on worker health and safety. During its first years in existence, the agency was sharply criticized for promulgating volumes of regulations, most of which addressed comparatively insignificant matters in a very detailed manner while ignoring wide-ranging and serious threats to worker health.

OSHA has subsequently taken steps to correct its past "sins." The agency has eliminated some of the many rules it had originally adopted and has simplified many of those it kept. In addition, OSHA has begun tackling some of the serious problems of worker safety. For example, in May 1988 the Labor Department proposed new regulations requiring employers to put warning tags or safety locks on machinery while it is being serviced or cleaned. The point of the proposed regulations was to prevent workers from starting machines while others are cleaning or servicing them. OSHA believes about 7 percent of all occupational deaths and 2 percent of accident-caused injuries are attributable to re-starts while machinery is being serviced or cleaned. The regulations were expected to save about 122 lives annually and prevent some 60,000 injuries. Final approval was anticipated in the late summer or fall of 1988.[70]

But even as new regulations are being implemented, OSHA, with approximately 1,125 inspectors, is able to reach only about 2 percent of the

3.4 million work forces covered by federal law.[71] And new health and safety hazards are expected as technology advances. For example, a study found an unusually high number of miscarriages among women working at semiconductor plants, and some preliminary concerns have been raised regarding health hazards associated with video-display terminals.[72]

OSHA has frequently been in the news in recent years for the sizable fines it has been issuing to some very prominent American businesses. For example, in July 1987 OSHA fined Chrysler Corporation $1.5 million for 811 job health and safety violations, including willfully exposing workers to such chemicals as lead and arsenic.[73] Later that same month, OSHA proposed a $2.59 million fine against IBP, Inc., the largest meat-packing company in the United States, for failing to report more than a thousand job-related injuries and illnesses over a two-year period.[74] In October 1987, General Motors agreed to a settlement of $500,000 with OSHA over various recordkeeping violations.[75] As the following article demonstrates, however, OSHA still has critics.

WORKPLACE SAFETY UNIT
ASSAILED FOR LAX EFFORTS

Philip Shabecoff

Washington, June 25—The Occupational Safety and Health Administration's program to protect workers from on-the-job hazards is beset by "systematic weaknesses," according to a draft report by the inspector general's office at the Labor Department.

The report, which has not been officially released, focuses on what it says are failings at the New York and Philadelphia offices of the occupational safety agency. But the report says that many of the problems arise from poor management at the agency's national headquarters and that the same weaknesses are likely to be found at other regional offices.

The report said efforts to safeguard workers from hazards are compromised by inadequate and untimely inspections, a failure to make sure that dangers are eliminated after they are found by the agency, and a failure to impose strict penalties on employers who willfully and repeatedly break the law.

Labor unions, public health organizations, and other critics have frequently assailed the agency under the Reagan administration for what they said was its failure to carry out adequately the law to protect occupational health and safety.

* * * * *

In general, the report said a lack of effective management control meant that the "agency cannot insure the safety and health of the workplace—its primary enforcement goal."

Although the health and safety law is explicit with regard to the penalties that must be imposed on employers who violate the law, the agency policy on such penalties is "unclear," the report said. It also complained that agency officials had made sizable reductions in penalties imposed for "willful and repeated violations" of the law after the officials held "informal" meetings with the guilty employers.

For example, the report described the case of a construction company that had been cited repeatedly for violations of a rule requiring workers on suspended scaffolds to wear safety belts. After a worker died as a result of not wearing a safety belt, the employer was fined $1,400, much lower than the maximum for repeated violations.

Then after a "conference" between agency officials and the employer, at which the employer presented no evidence to justify any changes in the charges against him, the report said, the fine was cut to $700.

Another failing identified by the inspector general was that the regional offices, after discovering a violation of the law that endangered workers, often accepted the assurances of the employer involved that the problem would be corrected and did not check to see if it had been. Sometimes, the regional offices accepted the employer's claim that there was no remedy available to correct the problem.

* * * * *

The report found that a "lack of a sufficient number of health inspectors causes a major deficiency in targeting and scheduling inspections."

* * * * *

Despite criticism of the agency under the Reagan administration, its budget has risen modestly in recent years. In 1980, the last year of the Carter administration, its budget was $186 million. In 1986 its budget was $209 million, and this year is expected to be $226 million.

Right-to-Know Laws

Perhaps the most far-reaching of OSHA's regulations to date is the Hazard Communication Rule.[76] About half of the states have similar rules, commonly referred to as right-to-know laws, which require certain employers to divulge information to employees on hazardous substances used in the workplace.[77]

OSHA's rule requires all employers classified as manufacturers to develop rather elaborate programs to inform workers about the hazards of chemicals used in the workplace. All hazardous substances must be identified and labeled, and the employer must keep on hand, in readily accessible form, detailed information sheets about each chemical. In addition, employees must each be given a written manual and an in-person training session in the proper and safe use of each chemical they might encounter in the workplace, both in normal use and due to an accident, spill, or leak.

Compliance is a costly process.

OSHA estimates it is costing manufacturers about $43 per employee to provide that training and meet the other requirements. Just keeping up with new products and new workers is expected to add a cost of $160 million annually, or about $11 per employee.[78]

Workers' Compensation

In spite of the laws just discussed, as well as a variety of others, injuries at work still occur. In 1987 the National Institute for Occupational Safety and Health made public its first compilation of occupational deaths in the United States: The report stated that between 1980 and 1984, 32,342 workers died at work in this country.[79] Of course, on-the-job injuries not resulting in death far exceed that number.

How does a worker injured on the job obtain compensation for his or her losses? The primary source of compensation is under state workers' compensation laws. These laws are typically administered by a state agency that adjudicates all claims under the law and is funded by employers. In general, a worker injured in a work-related accident may receive compensation for medical expenses and certain preset payments for the loss of certain body parts, as well as disability payments or death benefit payments. To obtain this recovery, the worker must establish that the injury arose out of his or her employment and happened in the course of that employment. The worker need not, however, prove any fault on the part of his or her employer or fellow workers. The following case illustrates a common understanding of the requirement that the injury occur "in the course of employment."

SANTA ROSA JUNIOR COLLEGE V. WORKERS' COMPENSATION APPEALS BOARD AND JOANNE SMYTH
708 P.2d 673 (Cal. 1985)

Justice Kaus

The Workers' Compensation Act establishes the liability of an employer "for any injury sustained by his or her employees arising out of and in the course of the employment." Almost 70 years ago, we adopted the "going and coming rule" as an aid in determining whether an injury occurred in the course of the employment. Generally prohibiting compensation for injuries suffered by an employee while commuting to and from work, the going and coming rule has been criticized by courts and commentators alike as being arbitrary and harsh. It has generated a multitude of exceptions which threaten, at times, to defeat the rule entirely. This appeal confronts us with the question of whether one such exception should be dramatically expanded to create, in effect, a "white-collar" nullification of the rule.

Santa Rosa Junior College (college) challenges a decision of the Workers' Compensation Appeals Board (board) awarding death benefits to JoAnne Smyth, widow of a community college instructor who was killed in an automobile accident on his way home from the campus. At issue is the applicability of the going and coming rule to school teachers who regularly take work home. If, in such cases, the home may be fairly regarded as a "second jobsite," the rule does not apply and injuries sustained en route are compensable. If the fact that the employee regularly takes work home does not establish the home as a second jobsite, compensation is barred.

We conclude that—unless the employer requires the employee to labor at home as a condition of the employment—the fact that an employee regularly works there does not transform the home into a second jobsite for purposes of the going and coming rule.

Facts

Joseph Smyth was a mathematics instructor and head of the mathematics department at the college. At about 6 P.M. on March 16, 1982, he was killed in an accident while driving his personal automobile home from work. His home was located in Ukiah, about 60 miles from the Santa Rosa campus. The family had moved to Ukiah six years earlier for their own convenience. . . .

It is undisputed that at the time of the accident Smyth had with him some student papers he intended to grade that evening. Indeed, Smyth regularly worked at home in the evenings. For several years before the accident, he stayed overnight in Santa Rosa once every two or three weeks and worked at home on some week nights. In 1981–1982, he assumed additional responsibilities as department head. In that school year, he worked late on campus once or twice per week, stayed overnight in Santa Rosa once or twice per week, and brought home one or two hours of work "about every night." At home, he worked in a section of the living room reserved for that purpose, where he kept duplicate copies of necessary books. The work usually consisted of grading papers or exams; occasionally, he would also prepare lesson plans or future class schedules at home. Mrs. Smyth testified that her husband worked at home rather than on campus because on campus, he was subject to interruption by students or other business, and, in addition, he wished to spend time with his family.

Smyth's habit of working at home in the evenings was not unusual for members of the college's faculty; . . . Patrick Boyle, one of Smyth's colleagues and a former department head, testified that . . . in his opinion, the work could not be completed during normal working hours because teachers were subject to interruption in their offices by students (both during the day and at night) and no suitable alternatives for uninterrupted work existed on campus.

* * * * *

Edmund Buckley, associate dean of instruction at the college, testified that the administration neither encouraged nor discouraged working at home. . . . He had never received any complaints from instructors to the effect that their working facilities on campus were inadequate.

William Wilbur, dean of business services . . . stated that neither Smyth nor any other staff member received financial or other consideration to account for the distance and time of their commutes. He knew of no benefit to the employer by reason of the work being done at home rather than on campus.

An office was provided for each instructor at the college. Undisputed evidence shows that Smyth could have eliminated or reduced student interruptions by posting office hours. Moreover, the record shows—not surprisingly—that Smyth was also subject to interruption while working at home.

The workers' compensation judge concluded that Smyth's death did not occur in the course of employment. He found that Smyth had adequate facilities and sufficient time to complete his work on campus and that it was Smyth's choice to work at home.

Acting on a petition for reconsideration, a three-member board panel, by a two-to-one vote, held that the death arose out of and occurred during the course of employment. The board concluded that because of the nature of the work and the frequent interruptions from students and phone calls, Smyth was "essentially required to maintain a second worksite in his home." It reasoned that in this case "[t]he work at home was more a matter of business necessity than of personal convenience." Accordingly, the board awarded death benefits to Mrs. Smyth.

The college seeks review of the board's decision.

Discussion

As the employer, the college is liable for the death benefits provided under the act only if Smyth's accident arose "out of and in the course of the employment" and if certain "conditions of compensation" were present. We note at the outset that where, as here, there is no real dispute as to the facts, "the question of whether an injury was suffered in the course of employment is one of law and a purported finding of fact on that question is not binding on an appellate court."

We originally adopted the going and coming rule as one means of determining when an accident should be treated as an "accident arising out of and in the course of the employment."

Of course, we recognized that in the broadest sense an injury occurring on the way to one's place of employment is an injury "growing out of and incident to his employment," since "a necessary part of the employment is that the employee shall go to and return from his place of labor." However, the right to an award is founded not "upon the fact that the injury grows out of and is incidental to his employment" but, rather, "upon the fact that the *service* he is rendering at the time of the injury grows out of and is incidental to the employment." Therefore, we reasoned, "an employee going to and from his place of employment is not rendering any service, and begins to render such service only when [arriving at the place of employment]." . . .

The going and coming rule resulted from the type of judicial line-drawing frequently required when construing and applying vague or open-ended statutory provisions. With its genesis in the practical need of drawing a "line" delineating an employee's "scope of employment," the rule was necessarily arbitrary, later explanations of its underlying rationale notwithstanding. California courts—manifesting much unease both in applying as well as in refusing to apply the rule—have recognized this essential arbitrariness and its potential harshness.

* * * * *

The trouble is that the facts in this case do not fit convincingly into any of the established limitations or exceptions. . . .

* * * * *

. . . [W]e have recognized a "home as a second jobsite" exception to the going and coming rule. It is this exception—or an extension of it—which the board used in concluding that the rule does not preclude compensation in this case. Generally, "[w]ork done at home may exempt an injury occurring during a regular commute from the going and coming rule if circumstances of the employment—and not mere dictates of convenience to the employee—make the home a second jobsite. If the home becomes a second business situs, the familiar rule applies that injury sustained while traveling between jobsites is compensable." We noted that the commute does not constitute a business trip if the employees work at home for their own convenience: "serving the employee's own convenience in selecting an off-premise place to work is a personal and not a business purpose."

The facts underlying Smyth's claim to a "home as a second jobsite" exception closely resemble those advanced by the applicant in *Wilson*. Like Smyth, Wilson was a teacher. She was injured in an automobile accident while driving to her school. . . .

In *Wilson,* we affirmed the board's determination that the applicant's home did *not* constitute a second jobsite warranting exemption from the going and coming rule. Her explicit job requirements demanded only that she report to the school premises, and "[h]er employer's implicit requirement to work beyond classroom hours did not require labor at home."

Applicant in the present case contends that the board properly concluded that it was an implied term or condition of Smyth's employment contract that he take work home in the evenings—that it was "more a matter of business necessity than of personal convenience." On this basis, the board distinguished *Wilson,* wherein there was no claim that school facilities were not sufficient to allow completion of the required work.

* * * * *

. . . *Wilson* makes quite clear that a home does not become a second jobsite simply because one's employment requires long working hours and the employer knows that the employee frequently brings work home. As we observed in *Wilson,* "[t]he contemporary professional frequently takes work home. There, the draftsman designs on a napkin, the businessman plans at breakfast, the lawyer labors in the evening. But this hearthside activity—while commendable—does not create a white-collar exception to the going and coming rule." Thus, to the extent that the board's "implicit requirement" determination amounts to a legal conclusion, it cannot be reconciled with *Wilson*.

Furthermore, we find little to commend the white-collar exception which we refused to establish in *Wilson*. It would, a fortiori, extend workers' compensation benefits to workers injured in the homes themselves, as well as en route to and from their regular work places. . . .

On the other hand, insofar as the board's determination that the employee was "implicitly required" to maintain his home as a second jobsite was intended as a finding of fact, it is simply not supported by substantial evidence in the record. Although the evidence shows that most faculty members took work home and that the employer was well aware of this practice, there is nothing in the record which indicates that faculty members were *required*—implicitly or otherwise—to work at home rather than on campus. Rather, the evidence reveals that professors worked at home by choice, not because of the dictates of their employer. On this record, there is no room for a factual finding that working at home was a condition of Smyth's employment.

Therefore, applying established "going and coming rule" principles and precedents, we conclude that the board erred in awarding compensation. . . .

* * * * *

The decision of the board is annulled. Mosk, Broussard, Grodin and Lucas, JJ., concur. Reynoso, Justice, dissenting.

Questions

1. What are some of the societal costs of work-related injury and disease?
2. *a.* Is a cost-benefit analysis of regulations proposed by OSHA an appropriate factor for the agency to consider when deciding whether to adopt certain rules?
   b. Or should worker safety transcend all questions of cost?
   c. What ethical dilemmas could arise when trying to balance worker safety and health against other societal costs? Explain.
3. *a.* Do you think the Hazard Communication Rule goes far enough, or do you think it is overly intrusive? Explain.
   b. What would you think of a law that required companies to notify former workers, going as far back as 30 years, who had been exposed to dangerous substances in the workplace?[80] Explain.
4. Refer to the *Santa Rosa Junior College* case.
   a. Do you think Smyth's widow *should* have received death benefits under the workers' compensation statute? Explain.
   b. If Smyth was covered, what other employees or what other injuries might also be covered by the statute?
   c. Do you agree with the court that such coverage would essentially create a "white-collar exception" to the going and coming rule? Explain.

PROTECTION OF WORKERS' PRIVACY

In recent years employers have starting testing and monitoring employees by more numerous methods: drug testing through urinalysis, drug-sniffing dogs brought into the workplace, polygraph tests for job applicants, blood tests for AIDS antibodies, and computer monitoring of employee output. Needless to say, such testing is receiving a lot of publicity. Employer testing of job applicants and employees, however, is not new.

[T]he 1950s may have marked an earlier zenith of testing, as companies gathered reams of information on their prospective workers through psychological profiles, employment histories, criminal records, and personal data. The shifting values and mores of the 1960s and 1970s changed all that. . . . Federal equal-employment-opportunity guidelines put the onus on employers to ensure that testing was a scientifically valid selection tool and that it didn't discriminate against specific racial or social groups.[81]

Common complaints about such practices are that they are an invasion of the applicant's or employee's privacy and amount to an unreasonable search of the individual. Both complaints are based on concepts in the U.S. Constitution. The difficulty of using these arguments in court to prohibit testing, however, is that the U.S. Constitution typically protects private individuals only from *government* invasion of personal rights. This means government employees can succeed in having such practices outlawed in court, but, employees of private companies usually cannot. It has been pointed out that private employees can be protected only by federal or state statutes or by union contracts.[82] And indeed many states have stepped in to legislate against the use of various procedures, such as testing for AIDS as a condition of employment,[83] using polygraphs on job applicants, and restricting the use of arrest records in hiring.[84]

Indeed, in 1988, President Reagan approved legislation banning most uses of polygraph tests by private employers. The law forbids the use of lie detector tests in screening job applicants and in random testing of employees, but it does permit the test in special security situations involving, for example, pharmaceutical companies or where the employer has sound evidence tying an employee to theft or other wrongdoing. About two million employees annually had taken polygraph tests.[85]

According to a 1988 Gallup survey of 1,118 U.S. companies, 28 percent of those with 5,000 or more employees (for example, AT&T and GM) are using drug tests to screen applicants.[86] Estimates of the annual cost to business and society of employee drug abuse range from $33.3 billion[87] to $70 billion.[88] A national study of 180 companies listed on the Fortune 500 revealed that the most common reasons for instituting drug tests were "a belief that drugs were being used by employees at work" and "concern for employee safety."[89] The following article points out some of the perceived benefits and problems with drug testing in the workplace.

DRUG TESTING IN THE WORKPLACE: WHOSE RIGHTS TAKE PRECEDENCE?

Michael Waldholz

Amid growing national concern over substance abuse, drug testing in the workplace has become an explosive issue.

To those who support it, testing, which is commonly done through urinalysis, is often a question of protecting business interests. "For us, it is the financial security of billions of dollars entrusted to us by clients," says Edwin A. Weihenmayer, vice president and director of the human resources group at Kidder, Peabody & Co. The New York-based investment bank began drug testing this summer as part of a comprehensive drug-prevention program.

Critics, for their part, tend to view such measures as unnecessarily or even unconstitutionally invasive. "For us, it just doesn't make good business sense to police our employees' private lives," says Lewis L. Maltby, vice president of Drexelbrook Engineering Co. The small instrumentation company in Horsham, Pennsylvania, has decided against drug tests.

What follows is a debate organized by *The Wall Street Journal* between the two executives.

Mr. Maltby

We've considered testing and totally rejected it. One reason is the accuracy problem. In an often-cited study, the U.S. Centers for Disease Control got false positive results of up to 66 percent from 13 randomly chosen private labs. The CDC said none of the labs were reliable. That isn't a very strong base to build a program on.

Mr. Weihenmayer

You've hit on the one controversial aspect of drug-prevention programs. Our program consists of policy statements and a lot of communication: manager-awareness training, employee-assistance programs. And, yes, testing–of new hires, and just recently we began unannounced testing of current employees too.

We want to create a workplace mentality where people say, "If I work at Kidder, I don't do drugs." I see our workers accepting that objective, and I believe it's due to an umbrella of programs. . . .

Testing can be inaccurate if you use lousy labs, fail to monitor movement of the urine specimens, don't do reconfirmation tests. But we've addressed those problems. When an employee provides a sample, it is sealed and signed. Prescription-drug use is noted. Everywhere the sample moves, it's signed. If a test is positive for drugs, we feel we have an obligation to reconfirm. And if that's positive, we go back and give the employee a chance to explain any extenuating circumstance before we act.

Mr. Maltby

. . . But the state-of-the-art test for reconfirmation costs from $75 to $100, which will multiply your costs an order of magnitude or so. Spending that much money isn't cost-justified for most companies. But unless you do, you're going to be firing people who shouldn't be fired.

Mr. Weihenmayer

If it's an important business issue, you'll spend the money. We'll spend over $100,000 this year on our drug program. And that's just direct costs. . . . But I don't think you can put a price tag on the comfort that our clients have with the way we're processing and managing their money.

Mr. Maltby

I think we disagree on the relevance of the information you get from testing. Kidder tests, at least in part, to assure its customers. Our only concern is job performance. But drug testing isn't a job-performance test. For instance, traces of drugs can remain in the system for days. I can't tell, if an employee takes a drug test on Monday, whether he is impaired now, whether he is sober as a judge, or whether he had a couple of puffs on a joint Saturday night.

Mr. Weihenmayer

We're concerned about performance. We're concerned about the effects of alcohol, but I can tell from someone's behavior if they come to work drunk. Not so with drugs. About 80 percent of performance problems from drugs are invisible. I equate our concern with that of the airline industry. When you walk on a plane, you don't want pilots to just appear drug free. You want to be absolutely sure they are.

We're also concerned about the potential pressures that result from drug use, whether it's done at work or not. Drug use can be expensive, and can exert financial demands—temptations—we don't want on employees who are dealing with transactions worth millions of dollars.

Mr. Maltby

I challenge the idea that you can't detect drug-related deterioration in job performance. In my experience, a really good supervisor who's paying attention is the best way to detect a problem. . . .

Mr. Weihenmayer

I can tell you there are situations where supervisors were paying attention, where performance seemed fine, but that until an account problem surfaced through computer controls we didn't know we had a drug-related problem. We just aren't prepared to tolerate a problem until it arises, just as the airline industry can't tolerate drug use until a collision makes it visible.

Our program isn't designed to get rid of people. We invest a lot of money to find people and train them. And what we want to do is influence them toward working in our way, which is drug free. . . .

Mr. Maltby

We just don't think you need to test to keep the workplace drug free. After all, drugs are just a symptom of something else. What you really want is a committed, dedicated work force, people who like their jobs and care enough not to come to work stoned. What we do is select and nurture employees that are going to do a good job. We think if we do that, the drug problem takes care of itself.

We're incredibly careful about the people we hire. We do multiple reference checks, even for floor sweepers. And then we take a lot of time and trouble to really know our people. Our supervisors know their people's families; they work to build trust and rapport. If they have problems, financial or otherwise, (the supervisors) want to know about it, and we have programs to provide them help. We've found

that with that kind of trust people will confide in you when a problem arises, before they feel they must use drugs in a dangerous way. I think the proof is that we believe drug problems affect only about 1 percent of our work force.

Mr. Weihenmayer

The relationship and concern expressed here is commendable, and everyone should strive for that. But the point is you think your drug incidence is 1 percent, but you don't know. . . .

Mr. Maltby

. . . If we had drug problems at work, it would affect our product and cause life-threatening problems, and we'd be up to our eyeballs in lawsuits.

Mr. Weihenmayer

Our belief, put simply, is that certain industries require this type of assured security—pilots, air-traffic controllers, for instance. I think protecting a person's savings is crucial too. We want people to feel Kidder is doing everything possible to protect their savings. At the same time, we are trying to be very sensitive to the needs of our employees.

Mr. Maltby

You're saying you can have a testing program *and* the kind of employee relations I'm talking about. I say you can't. The two are inimical. . . . When you say to an employee, "You're doing a great job; just the same, I want you to pee in this jar and I'm sending someone to watch you," you've undermined that trust.

Mr. Weihenmayer

I'll grant you it makes it more difficult. It bothers us if they're bothered. That's why we spend so much time explaining our objectives. Also, when we test a department, everyone from top to bottom is tested. For most employees who test positive, we reexplain our policy, ask them to commit themselves to be drug free and to undergo periodic testing. The company makes available, at its expense, help if they feel they need it. But if they test positive again, they are subject to immediate termination.

We've had employees who say in good conscience they can't take the test. We treat that person with respect, but we explain that on this matter we have to call the shots. You may anguish a bit over the damage which is done, but it's extremely important for the program's integrity that everyone take the test.

We don't have watchers. It would make the program more accurate, but we have drawn the line because it would be too embarrassing.

Mr. Maltby

But that's the kind of swamp you get into with testing. . . . [A]s people learn how to beat the system, the only way you're going to keep people from monkeying around is to watch them.

Mr. Weihenmayer

I don't think it will be a problem. Who is going to carry a urine sample around 365 days of the year?

Questions

1. Who do you think has the better side of the argument, Edwin A. Meihenmayer or Lewis Maltby? Why?
2. *a.* Would you favor state legislation to prevent drug testing of all employees?
   b. Of employees in only security or sensitive positions?
   c. Of some other class of employees? Explain.
3. *a.* Would you favor state legislation to prevent AIDS testing of all employees?
   b. Or allowing testing only of teachers?
   c. Only of individuals employed in food-preparation industries? Explain.
4. [N]early a third of the corporations in the Fortune 500 also screen employees for abuse or even casual intake of such substances as marijuana and cocaine. Countless other firms monitor workers' honesty with lie detectors or written exams or probe their psyches with an array of personality tests. Some corporations have begun monitoring employees for diseases such as AIDS. And in quest of the perfect employee, many firms may one day be able to screen out workers with hundreds of genetic traits that could predispose them to serious and costly illnesses.[90]

Is this going too far? Explain.

PROTECTIONS FROM DISCHARGE

Probably the vast majority of jobs in this country are based on employment contracts for an indefinite term. Traditionally such contracts have been subject to the *employment-at-will doctrine*, developed in the

19th century, which allows either the employee or the employer to terminate the contract at any time for any reason. Baldly stated, this allows an employer to fire an employee for good reasons, bad reasons, or no reason at all. As previously described, however, the working world has changed considerably since the Industrial Revolution, and the employment-at-will doctrine has been eroded by various statutes, such as the employment discrimination laws, which will be discussed in the following chapter.

Beyond those extended statutory protections, state courts have been aggressive in recent years in muting the sometimes harsh consequences of the employer's historical right to fire at-will employees for any reason or for no reason at all. Those judicial decisions were provoked by a variety of transparently unjust dismissals including, for example, whistle blowers who exposed misdeeds by their employers, employees who declined to commit perjury on behalf of their employers, and employees who declined their superiors' romantic/sexual advances.

At present, the law varies dramatically across the nation, with some states retaining the traditional at-will position while others have afforded new protections to the unjustly dismissed. The bulk of the decisions expanding employee protection have fallen under a public policy rationale. That is, many state courts have ruled that the dismissal of at-will employees under some conditions may be in violation of public policy (the general preferences of the citizenry) as expressed in state constitutions and laws and in professional codes of ethics, or as broadly interpreted by the courts.

The list of principles eroding the doctrine of employment at will continues to expand. For example, some discharged employees, instead of bring suit for wrongful discharge, are suing their former employers for defamation.

> Say you've been laid off—fired, sacked, let go. What do you do? In the old days you went looking for a new job and prayed that the next company you interviewed with didn't call your former employer for a reference. But these days there's another approach: warn your ex-boss that he'd *better not* give you a bad reference or you'll hit him with a libel and slander suit.[91]

The basic requirements for a winning defamation suit are the employee's proof that his or her past employer knowingly made a false statement in writing (libel) or speech (slander) to a third party, such as the employee's prospective employer or the employee's former co-workers.

The following case exemplifies a growing body of case law permitting wrongful discharge suits where an employer does not follow the discharge procedures identified in a personnel manual supplied to all employees.

RICHARD M. WOOLLEY V. HOFFMANN–LA ROCHE, INC.
491 A.2d 1257 (N.J. 1985)

Chief Justice Wilentz

I

The issue before us is whether certain terms in a company's employment manual may contractually bind the company. We hold that absent a clear and prominent disclaimer, an implied promise contained in an employment manual that an employee will be fired only for cause may be enforceable against an employer even when the employment is for an indefinite term and would otherwise be terminable at will.

II

Plaintiff, Richard Woolley, was hired by defendant, Hoffmann-La Roche, Inc., in October 1969, as an Engineering Section Head in defendant's Central Engineering Department at Nutley. There was no written employment contract between plaintiff and defendant. Plaintiff began work in mid-November 1969. Sometime in December, plaintiff received and read the personnel manual on which his claims are based.

In 1976, plaintiff was promoted and in January 1977 he was promoted again . . . In March 1978, plaintiff was directed to write a report to his supervisors about piping problems in one of defendant's buildings in Nutley. This report was written and submitted to plaintiff's immediate supervisor on April 5, 1978. On May 3, 1978, stating that the General Manager of defendant's Corporate Engineering Department had lost confidence in him, plaintiff's supervisors requested his resignation. Following this, by letter dated May 22, 1978, plaintiff was formally asked for his resignation, to be effective July 15, 1978.

Plaintiff refused to resign. Two weeks later defendant again requested plaintiff's resignation, and told him he would be fired if he did not resign. Plaintiff again declined, and he was fired in July.

Plaintiff filed a complaint alleging breach of contract, intentional infliction of emotional distress, and defamation, but subsequently consented to the dismissal of the latter two claims. The gist of plaintiff's breach of contract claim is that the express and implied promises in defendant's employment manual created a contract under which he could not be fired at will, but rather only for cause, and then only after the procedures outlined in the manual were followed. Plaintiff contends that he was not dismissed for good cause, and that his firing was a breach of contract.

Defendant's motion for summary judgment was granted by the trial court, which held that the employment manual was not contractually binding on defendant, thus allowing defendant to terminate plaintiff's employment at will. The Appellate Division affirmed. We granted certification.

III

. . . [t]he question is whether Hoffmann-La Roche retained the right to fire with or without cause or whether, as Woolley claims, his employment could be terminated only for cause.

We believe another question, not explicitly treated below, is involved: should the legal effect of the dissemination of a personnel policy manual by a company with a substantial number of employees be determined solely and strictly by traditional contract doctrine? Is that analysis adequate for the realities of such a workplace?

IV

As originally conceived in the late 1800s, the law was that an employment contract for an indefinite term was presumed to be terminable at will; an employee with an at-will contract could be fired for any reason (or no reason) whatsoever, be it good cause, no cause, or even morally wrong cause. Pursuant to that rule, in New Jersey employers were free to terminate an at-will employment relationship with or without cause.

The at-will rule has come under severe criticism from commentators who argue that the economic justifications for the development of the rule have changed dramatically and no longer support its harshness. The Legislature here, as in most states, has limited the at-will rule to the extent that it conflicts with the policies of our various civil rights laws so that, for instance, a firing cannot be sustained in New Jersey if it is based on the employee's race, color, religion, sex, national origin, or age.

This Court has clearly announced its unwillingness to continue to adhere to rules regularly leading to the conclusion that an employer can fire an employee at-will, with or without cause, for any reason whatsoever. Our holding in *Pierce* v. *Ortho Pharmaceutical Corp.*, while necessarily limited to the specific issue of that case (whether employer can fire employee at-will when discharge is contrary to a clear mandate of public policy), implied a significant questioning of that rule in general.

* * * * *

This Court has long recognized the capacity of the common law to develop and adapt to current needs. . . . The interests of employees, employers, and the public lead to the conclusion that the common law of New Jersey should limit the right of an employer to fire an employee at will.

* * * * *

In recognizing a cause of action to provide a remedy for employees who are wrongfully discharged, we must balance the interests of the employee, the employer, and the public. Employees have an interest in knowing they will not be discharged for exercising their legal rights. Employers have an interest in knowing that they can run their businesses as they see fit as long as their conduct is consistent with public policy. The public has an interest in employment stability and in discouraging frivolous lawsuits by dissatisfied employees.

The spirit of this language foreshadows a different approach to these questions. No longer is there the unquestioned deference to the interests of the employer and the almost invariable dismissal of the contentions of the employee. Instead, as Justice Pollock so effectively demonstrated, this Court was no longer willing to decide these questions without examining the underlying interests involved, both the employer's and the employees', as well as the public interest, and the extent to which our deference to one or the other served or disserved the needs of society as presently understood.

In the last century, the common law developed in a laissez-faire climate that encouraged industrial growth and approved the right of an employer to control his own business, including the right to fire without cause an employee at will. . . . The twentieth century has witnessed significant changes in socioeconomic values that have led to reassessment of the common law rule. Businesses have evolved from small and medium size firms to gigantic corporations in which ownership is separate from management. Formerly there was a clear delineation between employers, who frequently were owners of their own businesses, and employees. The employer in the old sense has been replaced by a superior in the corporate hierarchy who is himself an employee. We are a nation of employees. Growth in the number of employees has been accompanied by increasing recognition of the need for stability in labor relations.

The thrust of the thought is unmistakable. There is an interest to be served in addition to "freedom" of contract, an interest shared by practically all. And while "stability in labor relations" is the only specifically identified public policy objective, the reference to the "laissez-faire climate" and "the right to fire without cause an employee at will" as part of the "last century" suggests that any application of the employee-at-will rule . . . must be tested by its legitimacy today and not by its acceptance yesterday.

Given this approach, the issue is not whether the rules applicable to individual lifetime or indefinite long-term employment contracts should be changed, but rather whether a correct understanding of the "underlying interests involved" in the relationship between the employer and its workforce calls for compliance by the employer with certain rudimentary agreements voluntarily extended to the employees.

V

* * * * *

What is before us in this case is not a special contract with a particular employee, but a general agreement covering all employees. There is no reason to treat such a document with hostility.

The trial court viewed the manual as an attempt by Hoffmann-La Roche to avoid a collective bargaining agreement. Implicit is the thought that while the employer viewed a collective bargaining agreement as an intrusion on management prerogatives, it recognized, in addition to the advantages of an employment manual to both sides, that unless this kind of company manual were given to the workforce, collective bargaining, and the agreements that result from collective bargaining, would more likely take place.

A policy manual that provides for job security grants an important, fundamental protection for workers. If such a commitment is indeed made, obviously an employer should be required to honor it. When such a document, purporting to give job security, is distributed by the employer to a workforce, substantial injustice may result if that promise is broken.

We do not believe that Hoffmann-La Roche was attempting to renege on its promise when it fired Woolley. On the contrary, the record strongly suggests that even though it believed its manual did not create any contractually binding agreements, Hoffmann-La Roche nevertheless almost invariably honored it. In effect, it gave employees more than it believed the law required. Its position taken before us is one of principle: while contending it treated Woolley fairly, it maintains it had no legal obligation to do so.

VI

Given the facts before us and the common law of contracts interpreted in the light of sound policy applicable to this modern setting, we conclude that the termination clauses of this company's Personnel Policy Manual, including the procedure required before termination occurs, could be found to be contractually enforceable. Furthermore, we conclude that when an employer of a substantial number of employees circulates a manual that, when fairly read, provides that certain benefits are an incident of the employment (including, especially, job security provisions), the judiciary, instead of "grudgingly" conceding the enforceability of those provisions, should construe them in accordance with the reasonable expectations of the employees.

* * * * *

XI

Our opinion need not make employers reluctant to prepare and distribute company policy manuals. Such manuals can be very helpful tools in labor relations, helpful both to employer and employees, and we would regret it if the consequence of this decision were that the constructive aspects of these manuals were in any way diminished. We do not believe that they will, or at least we certainly do not believe that that constructive aspect *should* be diminished as a result of this opinion.

All that this opinion requires of an employer is that it be fair. It would be unfair to allow an employer to distribute a policy manual that makes the workforce believe that certain promises have been made and then to allow the employer to renege on those promises. What is sought here is basic honesty: if the employer, for whatever reason, does not want the manual to be capable of being construed by the court as a binding contract, there are simple ways to attain that goal. All that need be done is the inclusion in a very prominent position of an appropriate statement that there is no promise of any kind by the employer contained in the manual; that regardless of what the manual says or provides, the employer promises nothing and remains free to change wages and all other working conditions without having to consult anyone and without anyone's agreement; and that the employer continues to have the absolute power to fire anyone with or without good cause.

Reversed and remanded for trial.

Questions

1. Regarding defamation suits based on information given by former employers to prospective employers, is society better off encouraging or discouraging these suits?
2. Was the decision in *Woolley* v. *Hoffmann-La Roche, Inc.*, just? Explain.

Part Four—Labor and Employment Law Abroad

Labor unrest and dissatisfaction is, of course, not a phenomenon exclusive to the United States. Other countries have labor difficulties as diverse as their cultures. The following excerpts are intended only as a brief look at a variety of problems faced by other nations. Some of the problems will be reminiscent of problems previously discussed in this chapter; others will be quite unique to the country involved.

Mexico

The minimum wage in Tijuana and other border cities went up 32 percent in January [1986–Author.], increasing to 11,550 pesos for a 48-hour week, or 1,650 pesos per day based on seven days a week.

That comes to about 241 pesos an hour, or about $4 for an eight-hour day.[92]

Some U.S. corporations are exporting health and safety hazards as well as jobs when they move operations to Mexico, according to Dr. Monica Jasis, one of a handful of academics who have studied health problems among Mexican workers in the U.S.-owned plants.

However, the companies that operate the export-oriented factories known as maquiladoras disagree with Jasis, saying safety and health standards in their Mexican facilities are no different from those in the United States, even though Mexican laws aren't as stringent.[93]

South Africa

Late in the evening of August 9 [1987—Author.], black mine workers in the Transvaal began laying down their tools and walking off night shifts. Only a few thousand miners left their jobs that night, but by the end of the next day, the total had passed a quarter of a million.

What would become the biggest and longest strike in South African history had begun.

Now in its 13th day, the strike is more than a wage dispute. It is a direct challenge to a government that has snuffed out all other forms of black protest.

By disrupting a system in which black laborers help produce enormous wealth for South Africa at minuscule wages, the miners are at the forefront of the antiapartheid struggle.[94]

Japan

TRAUMA OF JOB UNCERTAINTY
CONFRONTS WORKERS AS
JAPAN'S MANUFACTURERS ARE
FORCED TO RETRENCH

Karl Schoenberger

Muroran, Japan—Until three weeks ago, Katsuro Yamada's life was making steel. Today he is taking a disorienting crash course in computer programming, writing software instead of casting molten metal into steel bars.

His employer, Nippon Steel Corp., has promised to try to return him to the plant floor in five months. But his old job will be gone. Indeed, it won't be long before the last furnace in Muroran is cold after eight decades of steel-making in this industrial port on Hokkaido, the northernmost island in Japan.

The 34-year-old steelworker isn't counting anymore on the company's tacit guarantee of lifetime employment. Mastering computer skills may be his only hope.

Mr. Yamada's dilemma tells the story of a structural upheaval in Japanese industry. Hurt by the yen's sharp appreciation, manufacturers are scrambling to retrench. They are investing in plants overseas and diversifying into "soft" industries at home to protect profits—and jobs.

Some economists and labor leaders fear that Japan might repeat the mistakes of U.S. industry. Others see deindustrialization as a painful but necessary way to curb Japan's reliance on exports and fit more harmoniously into the global economy.

Scratch the surface of the debate, however, and there is deep anxiety about economic stability. There is a stubborn belief that exports are synonymous with jobs. Despite the nation's fabulous wealth, a sense of vulnerability makes the coming changes in economic structure confusing and traumatic. Japan's ethos of austerity, urgent national purpose, and full employment is dying hard.

Mr. Yamada, the steelworker, says it is Japan's destiny to export goods. "We bring in raw materials, process them and export products, and we have to eat on that margin," says the wiry retrainee, who joined Nippon Steel out of high school 16 years ago. "Japan isn't big enough to survive on its own resources."

Nippon Steel, the world's largest steel-maker, says it doesn't want to cast off surplus workers like Mr. Yamada. But the company said Friday that it incurred an unconsolidated net loss of 13.08 billion yen ($90.8 million) in the year ended March 31 on a 19 percent decline in sales and a 29 percent fall in exports. With the yen having risen 70 percent against the dollar since September 1985, labor costs in Japan's steel industry are now seven times those in South Korea, which has become a major steel exporter.

To cope, Nippon Steel plans to slash capacity over four years and "rationalize" 19,000 jobs, nearly one third of its work force. By 1995, less than half the company's annual sales target of 4 trillion yen ($27.8 billion) is to be derived from steelmaking. New businesses in such areas as computer systems, urban development, and language schools would account for 40 percent of sales.

About half the job cuts are to be achieved through early retirement, says Shigeaki Sugita, a senior manager in the corporate planning division. . . . The rest of the redundant workers will be transferred to subsidiaries and new business ventures, or will simply join the *adog-iwa-zoku*—literally, the "window-seat tribe"—which Mr. Sugita defines as "unemployed people within the company." In some cases, Nippon Steel will bankroll small enterprises to lure employees out the door.

The Japanese corporate commitment to full employment is legendary. During the oil crisis of the late 1970s, about 2 million idled workers were kept on company payrolls. They resumed work when exports picked up.

But now, the social contract is cracking. Superfluous labor in industries such as coal and shipbuilding is getting cut. Even Nippon Steel hints it may actually dismiss workers outright.

Estimates of the number of expendable workers range from 500,000 to 1.2 million, as profits decline and the nation skids into a deflationary period. At the same time, Japan's wide trade surplus, which totaled $89.77 billion in the year ended March 31, has become intolerable to its trading partners.

* * * * *

. . . Unemployment already has reached 3 percent of the labor force; although low by the standards of many other industrialized countries, the rate is a record for Japan.

Moreover, the job security of big corporations doesn't extend to many subcontractors and suppliers, so certain regional manufacturing centers are hard hit. In the steelmaking town of Muroran, for instance, unemployment is approaching 7 percent.

Source: *The Wall Street Journal,* June 1, 1987, p. 12. Reprinted by permission of *The Wall Street Journal,* © Dow Jones & Company, Inc. 1987. ALL RIGHTS RESERVED.

Australia

AUSSIE WORKPLACE: THEATER OF THE ABSURD

Geraldine Brooks

Sydney—Last December [1986—Author.], workers on this city's ferries won a special pay raise. The reason: The ferry terminal is being rebuilt and commuters had abused ferry staff about the inconvenience.

The raise, equivalent to $15.50 per week until completion of renovations this year, is to compensate for the unpleasantness.

Australia's industrial disputes frequently border on the bizarre.

Last year, for instance, male flight attendants threatened to disrupt Ansett Transport Industries, one of the country's two major domestic airlines, during the Easter holiday period because they wanted to wear short-sleeved shirts. The attendants won the right to bare arms, even though Ansett's management felt short sleeves didn't fit the carrier's image.

Attendants Bugged

At around the same time, Qantas Airways passengers found themselves stranded in Sydney overnight because flight attendants walked off the job over the issue of germs in the international carrier's hot towels.

"This kind of self-inflicted stupidity is a product of a 1950s and 1960s we've-never-had-it-so-good syndrome," says David Abba, executive director of the Chamber of Commerce in New South Wales. . . .

But with falling world prices for most of Australia's exports, a sagging domestic dollar and soaring interest rates, it isn't like that any more. In September, the government met with unions and employers' representatives to find ways of changing some of the work practices that are damaging Australia's competitiveness.

"Now that we're out-banana-ing the banana republics with the size of our national debt, we have to do something very quickly to change our attitude," Mr. Abba says.

With most wage increases decided by a national tribunal, Australia's 57 percent-unionized labor force has turned to winning improvements at the workplace. Safety standards have been a particular focus of industrial action, and a study of the construction industry, for example, shows that fatal accidents on Australian building sites are four times fewer than on U.S. projects.

Laughable Demands

But in some cases, a combination of strong unionism and weak management has led to demands that are more laughable than laudable.

In 1981, workers building an entertainment center adjacent to Sydney's Chinatown demanded daily "tea money" from their employer. They complained that appetizing aromas wafting from the nearby restaurants were "creating hardship in the gastronomical expectations of the employees." (The claim was later dropped.)

Even organized labor acknowledges the silliness of some practices—like the "one on, all on" rule at some construction sites that everyone must be offered overtime even if only one worker is needed.

. . . Wayne Gilbert, general manager of the South East Queensland Electricity Board, . . . blames the proliferation of costly work practices largely on "weak and remote management," especially in large companies and mature industries. "Abuse of union power isn't the main cause," he says.

Until 1983, Mr. Gilbert worked for a beer-making concern that had allowed unusual work practices to creep into its breweries. When he took the job as chief executive officer of Tooth & Co.'s two Sydney breweries in 1978, Mr. Gilbert says he was surprised to find a "pat man" on his staff. The pat man's job was to sweep up the droppings left by cart horses—even though the breweries hadn't used horses to cart beer for more than 20 years.

A rule that only electricians could start electric motors had become so rigidly interpreted at the breweries that in some instances an electrician was required to turn on a light. "In summer, on Sundays, we had to have an electrician come in to turn on the lights so a laborer could hose down the kegs to prevent the wood drying out and springing leaks," Mr. Gilbert recalls. But in fact, wooden kegs had been replaced by metal casks a decade earlier.

Another brewery tradition was that if a wooden keg sprang a leak the workers were allowed to consume its contents. When metal casks were introduced the workers insisted that some kegs be designated "leakers" so they wouldn't forgo any free beer.

South Korea

> Corporate profits soared in South Korea in the first half [of 1987—Author.], adding fuel to the nation's labor unrest.
>
> The government reported scores of new strikes Friday, but it appeared to tilt further toward support for the workers' demands.
>
> Securities analysts said that the combined earnings of 250 companies listed on the Korean Stock Exchange increased 69 percent in the first half from a year earlier, to 541.9 billion won ($677.4 million). . . .
>
> Among companies posting sizable gains were many that have been dogged by strikes and sit-ins since the labor unrest erupted three weeks ago. . . . Reacting to higher earnings, a spokesman for striking . . . workers said there wasn't any excuse for why the workers "are still so underpaid."[95]

Questions

1. Do U.S. employment and labor laws make us uncompetitive?
2. Should U.S. companies be required to adhere to U.S. health and safety standards in their foreign subsidiaries? Should an international body establish labor standards for foreign companies in any country? Explain.
3. Is it appropriate for labor groups to strike for political purposes? Under what conditions?
4. In the ongoing saga of labor–management relations, what are labor's moral and ethical duties?

CHAPTER QUESTIONS

1. In your opinion, what are the average blue-collar worker's biggest sources of job dissatisfaction? Can they be eliminated through collective bargaining? Explain.
2. In your opinion, what are the average white-collar worker's biggest sources of job dissatisfaction? What means do such workers have for eliminating those sources of dissatisfaction?
3. If chimpanzees could be trained to perform unskilled, repetitious jobs, should they be allowed to do so? If chimpanzees could be trained to perform hazardous jobs like mining coal, should they be allowed to do so? Explain.
4. Many workers in the United States are very disturbed by the practices of some American companies that set up factories in other countries.
   a. What is the basis for the U.S. workers' hostility to such practices?
   b. Why do American companies choose to move their operations to other countries?
   c. Do you think there should be some attempt by the federal government to regulate these practices? Explain.
   d. If so, what form should the legislation take?

5. Imagine what the world will be like 100 years from now. In what ways do you picture the worklife of the average American to have changed?

6. Imagine the ideal work world. How close does that picture come to the one you conjured up in response to question 5? What types, if any, of labor or other legislation would bring society closer to that ideal?

7. What societal changes over the past 30 years have affected the workplace the most, in your estimation? Has labor law kept pace with workplace changes? If not, what new legislation is necessary?

8. A union representing a bargaining unit comprising both men and women and different racial and ethnic groups demands to see detailed information that the employer keeps on wages paid to women and minorities, as well as hiring statistics about these members of the work force.

   a. Should the employer be required to let the union see this data?

   b. What circumstances might affect your decision? See *Westinghouse Electric Corp.,* 239 NLRB No. 18 (1978).

   c. Suppose that, instead of asking for wage information, the union asked to see the questions, answers, and individual scores achieved by employees on psychological aptitude tests that the employer requires employees to take. If the employer refuses to turn these scores over, has it committed an unfair labor practice? Explain.

   d. Does this situation differ significantly from the previous situation? See *Detroit Edison Co.* v. *NLRB,* 440 U.S. 301 (1979).

9. Aavco Hardware Company learns that union organizers (not Aavco employees) have been passing out literature to Aavco employees in the Aavco parking lot, which is surrounded by a chainlink fence but does not have a closed gate or guardhouse. Aavco officials want to throw these ''union instigators'' off the property.

   a. Will the officials be committing an unfair labor practice if they do?

   b. Would it matter if Aavco had a general ''no-solicitation'' rule?

   c. What if Aavco adopted a no-solicitation rule only after the first union organizers started handing out literature? See *Central Hardware Co.* v. *NLRB,* 407 U.S. 539 (1972).

10. United Plant Guard Workers of America (UPGWA) sought union certification at Arbitron Security Services, Inc. The union and the company stipulated certain election procedures to be followed, including, among other things, the hours, date, and location at which balloting would be held and the posting of notices of the election. Several days before the election, the company posted notices of the election in several conspicuous locations. Two days before the election, the union mailed notices to employees listed on sheets supplied to the union by the company. The election was held on a regular payday. Out of 314 employees eligible to vote, a total of only 64 valid votes (26 of them for the union) were cast. The UPGWA petitioned the NLRB following

the union's defeat, claiming that the low voter turnout led to the inference that notice of the election to the employees had been inadequate and that the election results should be set aside. What do you think the NLRB's response is likely to be? See *Iowa Security Services, Inc. and National Union, United Plant Guard Workers of America,* 269 NLRB No. 53 (1983–84 CCH NLRB ¶16,145), March 21, 1984.

11. A bargaining unit, consisting of 56 employees at the time of a union representation election, voted in favor of unionization by a vote of 29 to 23. The employer sought to have the election results nullified, alleging that six days prior to the election, a union official meeting with 20 employees had referred to a company vice president as a "stingy Jew." The company had witnesses to substantiate this claim, and the union did not deny it.

    a. Do you think the election results should be set aside? Explain. See *NLRB* v. *Silverman's Men's Wear, Inc.,* 656 F.2d 53 (3d Cir. 1981).

    b. Suppose, instead, union officers came to campaign meetings for a Japanese-owned company wearing T-shirts that said, "Remember Pearl Harbor" and "Japs speak with forked tongue and slant eyes." Do you think the result would be any different? Explain. See *YKK (U.S.A.) Inc. and Sandra M. Collins et al.,* 296 NLRB No. 8 (1983–84 CCH NLRB ¶16,158), March 8, 1984.

12. The government provides food stamps for those in need. As a savings measure, Congress passed an amendment to the Food Stamp Act providing that neither workers on strike nor their families could collect food stamps. The amendment was challenged on constitutional grounds.

    a. What constitutional objections might legitimately be raised?

    b. Decide. Explain. See *Lyng* v. *Auto Workers,* 56 *Law Week* 4268 (1988).

13. The Clayton Act (see Chapters 9 and 10) exempts union wage negotiations from the antitrust laws; that is, workers in many different and competing companies may (and have) lawfully join together to form a single bargaining unit (for example, the Teamsters Union). Of course, the antitrust laws forbid competing companies from joining together in the manner workers are allowed to do. Economist Gary Becker of the University of Chicago argues that the time has come to treat union conspiracies in the same manner as those of management. Becker argues for replacing traditional trade unions with company unions (unions limited in membership to a single company), such as those used in Japan. He says union shop laws and other protections could be strengthened so management could not dominate the union. He notes the general decline of union membership in the United States: "In 1955 one of every

three members of the U.S. labor force belonged to a union, compared with 17 percent in 1987." He believes those declines are largely due to the growth of such protections as unemployment compensation, social security, medicare, and new barriers against unfair dismissals. Should labor unions be fully subject to the antitrust laws? Explain. See Gary Becker, "It's Time to Scrap a Few Outmoded Labor Laws," *Business Week,* March 7, 1988, p. 18.

14. Consider the following account of a contrast in labor/management relations in the United States and Japan.

> By 1989 Nippon Steel planned to reduce jobs in steel by 19,000 (41 percent of the work force). However, Nippon did not intend to dismiss "surplus personnel" or to offer voluntary retirement. Those workers were to be reemployed elsewhere in the steel division, or they were to be retrained for new jobs in other divisions. On the other hand, USX (the American leader in steel) released some 87,000 workers from 1980 to 1987. Of course, those workers received many benefits, such as jobless pay, insurance, and early retirements. Nonetheless, USX officials explained that company health took priority over worker welfare. Executive Vice President Bruce Johnson remarked that "it would have been futile to devise a human relations strategy ahead of a business strategy" during the massive cutbacks in steel.

Do you support the Nippon approach or that at USX, or are the situations simply not comparable? Explain. See Associated Press, "Japanese Job Traditions under Attack," *Des Moines Register,* October 8, 1987, p. 9S.

15. Under the National Labor Relations Act, labor unions may not "threaten, coerce, or restrain any person" to "cease doing business with any other person." The Edward J. DeBartolo construction company was building a department store at the East Lake Square Mall in Tampa, Florida. A building trades union peacefully distributed handbills at the mall's entrances (but did not otherwise picket), asking consumers not to shop at the mall because, in the union's view, DeBartolo was paying substandard wages and fringe benefits. Does the union handbilling constitute a secondary boycott in violation of the act? Explain. See *Edward J. DeBartolo Corp.* v. *Florida Gulf Coast Building and Construction Trades Council and National Labor Relations Board,* 56 *Law Week* 4328 (1988).

16. As discussed in this chapter, many recent judicial decisions have afforded at-will employees much improved protection against unfair dismissals. A special area of concern is whether at-will employees can be dismissed for off-duty conduct. The decisions are split, but the trend seems to be toward greater respect and protection for employee privacy. Nonetheless, companies still retain broad latitude to dismiss. For example, an employee convicted of selling drugs would most likely not be protected by the courts from a company dismissal.

    a. Ms. Virginia Rulon-Miller, an IBM salesperson, had been dating another IBM employee, Matt Blum, for several years. Her superiors were aware of the relationship. Blum left IBM to join a competitor, QYX, and he moved from San Francisco to Philadelphia. He was transferred back to San Francisco, and he and Rulon-Miller resumed dating. Again her superiors were aware of the relationship, and one mentioned that he didn't "have any problem" with her romance. Rulon-Miller did well in her sales role and was promoted to a management position, where she continued to do well as evidenced by a $4,000 raise. Nonetheless, one week after receiving notice of the raise, Rulon-Miller was either dismissed (her version) or "transferred" (the company's version). IBM felt her romance and her concern for the success of Blum created a conflict of interest. Despite being an at-will employee, Rulon-Miller argued that she was protected by IBM's written policies that detail those circumstances under which an employee's private life can become a company issue. She filed suit, claiming wrongful discharge. Decide. Explain. See *Rulon-Miller* v. *IBM,* 1 IER Cases 405 [162 Cal App 3d 241 (1984)].

    b. An Arizona nurse, employed in an at-will arrangement, claimed she was fired because she refused to join in a skit that required "mooning" the audience while singing "Moon River." The alleged incident was part of an off-duty raft trip with her supervisor and other nurses. She sued for wrongful dismissal. The Arizona courts had generally not supported constraints on an employer's right to dismiss at-will employees. Decide. Explain. See *Wagenseller* v. *Scottsdale Memorial Hospital,* 1 IER Cases 526 (Arizona S. Ct., 1985).

17. Illinois state law forbids the retaliatory discharge of employees who file workers' compensation claims. The law provides that the employee must show she/he was discharged and the employer's motive for doing so was to deter the employee's exercise of workers' compensation rights.

    Assembly line worker Jonna Lingle, a union member, filed a workers' compensation claim for a wrist injury suffered on her job making washing machine parts for the Norge Division of Magic Chef, Inc. She was fired. The company said her claim was fraudulent. The union filed a grievance on her behalf, claiming a violation of their collective bargaining agreement protecting employees from discharge in the absence of "just cause." While that action was proceeding, Lingle sued Norge, claiming an unlawful retaliatory discharge. The lower court dismissed her case, saying it was preempted by the Labor–Management Relations Act of 1947 because her claim was "inextricably intertwined" with the union/management agreement prohibiting discharge without just cause. And the court found that allowing the state law case to proceed would undermine the arbitration proceedings provided for under the collective bargaining agreement. The federal court of appeals affirmed, finding that the disposition of the retaliatory discharge claim would require an interpretation of the collective bargaining agreement and that any such interpretation was to employ federal labor law principles, thus assuring uniformity across the country and effectively preempting the application of state laws.

Lingle appealed to the U.S. Supreme Court. (A victory for her would significantly expand potential protections for those filing workers' compensation claims, whistle blowers, victims of discrimination, and others who are parties to contracts but seek the shelter of state statutes providing protection greater than the contracts. The key to the case is whether the resolution of her state law retaliatory discharge claim requires an interpretation of the meaning of the collective bargaining agreement to which she was a party.) Decide. Explain. See *Jonna R. Lingle* v. *Norge Division of Magic Chef, Inc.,* 56 *Law Week* 4512 (1988).

18. In 1987 the Bureau of National Affairs issued a report indicating that the U.S. employment market "is facing a new and potentially devastating financial burden—employees who feel stressed out by the workplace increasingly are seeking monetary recovery either in the form of workers' compensation claims or high-damages personal-injury lawsuits."[96] BNA reported that four stress-related cases were filed in 1976, while 14 were filed just in the first half of 1987.

   a. In general, how should our legal system respond to problems of job-related stress?

   b. More specifically, how would you have voted had you been a juror dealing with the following cases: "An asbestos worker who feared he would contract an asbestos-related disease filed suit under the Federal Employers Liability Act (in 1987), or a San Francisco nurse who suffered a stress-related ulcer and claimed it was linked to her fear of contracting AIDS infection?"[97]

NOTES

1. The historical and political background information used in this chapter was drawn from a number of sources and amalgamated in such a way that precise footnoting was difficult. Many of the sociological trends described, for example, are discussed in three or four sources. The author would, therefore, like to acknowledge the works of the following people, whose research and insights proved to be invaluable resources on which to draw: Richard S. Belous, Hyman Berman, Angela Y. Davis, Richard Edwards, John J. Flagler, Eli Ginzberg, J. David Greenstone, Isaac A. Hourwich, and Sar A. Levitan.

The author of this chapter would like especially to acknowledge and thank Professor Archibald Cox, from whom she took a course in labor law in 1978, and whose textbook and class lectures provided the cornerstone of her understanding of the subject. The author hopes that her own good fortune at having had the opportunity to study labor law under Professor Cox will translate into a richer educational experience for students using this textbook.

2. Archibald Cox, with Derek Bok and Robert A. Gorman, *Cases and Materials on Labor Law,* 8th ed. (Mineola, N.Y.: Foundation Press, 1977), pp. 7–8.

3. Richard Edwards, *Contested Terrain: The Transformation of the Workplace in the Twentieth Century* (New York: Basic Books, 1979), pp. 40–41.

4. John J. Flagler, *The Labor Movement in the United States* (Minneapolis: Lerner Publications, 1972), pp. 26–33.

5. Cox, *Labor Law,* p. 8.

6. Isaac A. Hourwich, *Immigration and Labor* (New York: Arno Press, 1969), pp. 125–45.

7. Cox, *Labor Law,* p. 9.

8. Hourwich, *Immigration and Labor,* p. 349, quoting Frank Tracy Carlton, *The History and Problems of Organized Labor,* pp. 346–47.

9. Flagler, *Labor Movement,* pp. 26–28.

10. Ibid.

11. Hourwich, *Immigration and Labor,* pp. 232–49.

12. Eli Ginzberg and Hyman Berman, *The American Worker in the Twentieth Century: A History through Autobiographies* (New York: Free Press, 1963), pp. 193–95, taken from Andria Taylor Hourwich and Gladys L. Palmer, eds., *I Am a Woman Worker,* Affiliated Schools for Workers, 1936, pp. 17 ff.

13. Flagler, *Labor Movement,* pp. 33 and 36, quoting Frederick Lewis Allen, *The Big Change . . . 1900–1950.*

14. Ibid., p. 47.

15. J. David Greenstone, *Labor in American Politics* (New York: Alfred A. Knopf, 1969), p. 21.

16. Cox, *Labor Law,* p. 11.

17. Flagler, *Labor Movement,* p. 47.

18. Greenstone, *Labor in American Politics,* p. 22.

19. Ibid., p. 23.

20. Cox, *Labor Law,* pp. 11–12.

21. Flagler, *Labor Movement,* pp. 81–83.

22. Greenstone, *Labor in American Politics,* pp. 41–42.

23. Cox, *Labor Law,* pp. 86–87.

24. Ibid., pp. 87–88.

25. Ibid., p. 88.

26. Angela Y. Davis, *Women, Race and Class* (New York: Random House, 1981), p. 138.

27. Flagler, *Labor Movement,* p. 60.

28. Davis, *Women, Race, and Class,* p. 150.

29. Flagler, *Labor Movement,* pp. 54–56.

30. Cox, *Labor Law,* pp. 18–35.

31. Ibid., pp. 35–40; see *Loewe* v. *Lawlor,* 208 U.S. 274 (1908).

32. Cox, *Labor Law,* pp. 60–66.

33. Greenstone, *Labor in American Politics,* p. 47.

34. Cox, *Labor Law,* p. 75.
35. Ibid., p. 83.
36. Greenstone, *Labor in American Politics,* p. 47.
37. Cox, *Labor Law,* p. 89.
38. Ibid., p. 91.
39. Ibid., p. 94.
40. Ibid., pp. 1107–08.
41. Ibid., p. 1108.
42. The National Labor Relations Act is found in Title 29 U.S.C. § 151 et seq.
43. Cox, *Labor Law,* pp. 113–22.
44. Ibid., pp. 99–101.
45. See, for example, *Dal-Tex Optical Co.,* 137 NLRB 1782, in which repeated references are made to the departure in the election process from "laboratory conditions."
46. Section 8(c) of the NLRA specifically states that "[t]he expressing of any views, arguments, or opinion, or the dissemination thereof . . . shall not constitute or be evidence of an unfair practice . . . if such expression contains no threat of reprisal or force or promise of benefit."
47. See discussion, for example, in *NLRB* v. *Golub Corp.,* 388 F.2d 921 (2d Cir. 1967).
48. See, for example, *NLRB* v. *General Electric Co.,* 418 F.2d 736 (2d Cir. 1970). See also Section 8(c) of the NLRA, which indicates that the mere expression of a viewpoint cannot constitute, in and of itself, an unfair labor practice. This is true at the bargaining table as it is elsewhere.
49. See, for example, *NLRB* v. *Fitzgerald Mills Corp.,* 313 F.2d 260 (2d Cir.), cert. denied 375 U.S. 834 (1963); *NLRB* v. *Herman Sausage Co.,* 275 F.2d 229 (5th Cir. 1960). Contra *NLRB* v. *Reed & Prince Mfg. Co.,* 205 F.2d 131 (1st Cir.), cert. denied 346 U.S. 887 (1953).
50. *NLRB* v. *Insurance Agents' International Union,* 361 U.S. 477 (1960).
51. 361 U.S. at 480–481.
52. 361 U.S. at 482, citing 119 NLRB 769–771.
53. 361 U.S. at 488.
54. *NLRB* v. *Truitt Mfg. Co.,* 351 U.S. 149 (1956).
55. *NLRB* v. *Katz,* 369 U.S. 736 (1962).
56. See, for example, *First National Maintenance Corporation* v. *NLRB,* 101 S. Ct. 2573 (1981).
57. *NLRB* v. *Wooster Division of Borg-Warner,* 356 U.S. 342 (1958).
58. *NLRB* v. *Katz,* 369 U.S. 736 (1962).
59. See, for example, *NLRB* v. *Mackay Radio and Telegraph Co.,* 304 U.S. 333 (1938); and *NLRB* v. *Erie Resistor Co.,* 373 U.S. 221 (1963).
60. *United Steelworkers of America* v. *Sadlowski,* 457 U.S. 102 (1982).
61. *Sadlowksi* v. *United Steelworkers of America,* 645 F.2d 1114, 1124 (D.C. Cir. 1981).
62. 376 F.2d 197 (2d Cir.), cert. denied 389 U.S. 874 (1967).
63. Zech and Kuhn, "National Labor Policy: Is It Truly Designed to Protect the Worker?" Selected Papers of the American Business Law Association: *National Proceedings,* 1982, 433, at 442–43.
64. "Beyond Unions, a Revolution in Employee Rights Is in the Making," *Business Week,* July 8, 1985, p. 72.

65. "Big Benefits," *The Wall Street Journal,* January 26, 1988, p. 1.
66. "Child-Care Aid," *The Wall Street Journal,* January 26, 1988, p. 1.
67. "Fizzling Fitness?" *The Wall Street Journal,* May 14, 1987, p. 31.
68. Mark D. Grossman, "Workers' Noses Sniff Out Chemical Leaks," *Business and Society Review* 59, Fall 1986, p. 62.
69. Lisa J. Raines and Stephen P. Push, "Protecting Pregnant Workers," *Harvard Business Review* 86, no. 3 (May–June 1986), p. 26.
70. Associated Press, "Key Industry Safety Rule Finally Unveiled," *Des Moines Register,* April 30, 1988, p. 4A.
71. Cathy Trost, "Occupational Hazard," *The Wall Street Journal,* April 22, 1988, p. 25R.
72. Ibid.
73. John Holusha, "U.S. Fines Chrysler $1.5 Million, Citing Workers' Exposure to Peril," *The Wall Street Journal,* July 7, 1987, p. 1.
74. Philip Shabecoff, "Record Fine Urged on Injury Reports," *The New York Times,* July 22, 1987, p. 1.
75. Albert R. Karr, "GM Agrees to Pay Fine of $500,000 on OSHA Charges," *The Wall Street Journal,* October 6, 1987, p. 8.
76. 29 C.F.R. 1910. 1200 (Revised July 1, 1984).
77. "Beyond Unions," p. 73.
78. "Workplace Right-to-Know Regulations in Effect," *Waterloo Courier,* May 27, 1986, p. D6.
79. "Miners and Construction Workers Are Found to Hold Riskiest Jobs," *The New York Times,* July 27, 1987, p. 9.
80. "Debating a Bill on Job Hazards," *The New York Times,* July 13, 1987, p. 22.
81. "Can You Pass the Job Test?" *Newsweek,* May 5, 1986, p. 47.
82. "Drug Testing in the Workplace," *Civil Liberties,* Spring 1986, p. 6.
83. "Can You Pass the Job Test?" p. 46.
84. "Beyond Unions," p. 73.
85. "Ban on Most Uses of Polygraph Tests Clears Congress," *The Wall Street Journal,* June 10, 1988, p. 40.
86. *Washington Post,* "28 Percent of Biggest U.S. Firms Screen Their Job Applicants for Drug Use," as reprinted in the *Waterloo Courier,* June 12, 1988, p. C2.
87. Mei-Mei Chan and Mireille Grangenois Gates, "Worker Drug Testing Gains Momentum," *USA Today,* August 14, 1986, p. 2A.
88. William Scobie, "Controversy on Drug Testing Heating Up," *Waterloo Courier,* May 11, 1986, p. F5.
89. David Elbert, "Drug Tests Embraced by Employers," *Des Moines Sunday Register,* March 16, 1986, p. 1F.
90. "Can You Pass the Job Test?" p. 46.
91. "The Revenge of the Fired," *Newsweek,* February 16, 1987, p. 46.
92. Gene Erb, "U.S. Plants in Mexico: Better Life at Low Wages," *Des Moines Register,* March 17, 1986, p. 1A.
93. Gene Erb, "Mexican Plants' Health Dangers Alleged," *Des Moines Register,* March 22, 1986, p. 1A.

94. David Zucchino, "Mine Strike in South Africa More than a Labor Fight," *Philadelphia Inquirer,* August 21, 1987, p. 1A.

95. Joseph P. Manguno, "South Korean Corporate Profits Surge, Adding Fuel to Country's Labor Unrest," *The Wall Street Journal,* August 17, 1987, p. 11. Reprinted by permission of *The Wall Street Journal,* © Dow Jones & Company, Inc. 1987. ALL RIGHTS RESERVED.

96. Karen-Lee Ryan, "More Workers Are Suing Their Employers," *Waterloo Courier,* August 18, 1987, p. B6.

97. Ibid.

Chapter 12

Employment Discrimination

Part One—Introduction

The study of discrimination, perhaps more than any other topic in this text, reflects both the base spirit and the grandeur of American values. We have affirmed our belief that all men and women are created equal. We have undertaken what has been, in retrospect, a profoundly complex and burdensome effort to eliminate and even make up for the wrongs of the past. The abolition of slavery, voting rights, school integration, open accommodations, equal pay, protection of the handicapped, broadened religious safeguards—we have sought and achieved a remarkable reformation in human conduct, and we have achieved those results in a comparatively short time. However, the problem of discrimination remains far from resolution.

DISCRIMINATION DEFINED

University students sometimes think themselves the victims of discrimination. May landlords lawfully decline to rent to students? May a publicly supported university fund, for example, a men's swim team while declining to do the same for women? May an insurance company lawfully impose higher premiums on younger drivers? May a bar owner offer free admission to women while imposing a cover charge for men? May a state university lawfully impose higher tuition charges for out-of-state students? Each issue involves a distinction in treatment among identifiable classes of citizens. Of course, life is replete with such distinctions. How are we to identify those that constitute unlawful discrimination? In the broadest sense, such distinctions become unlawful when not grounded in reason.

That is, the distinction must be based on objective criteria such that the difference in treatment is rational rather than the product of whim, caprice, or bias. In practice, the measure of discrimination lies in the constitutional provisions, laws, regulations, executive orders, and judicial opinions that address discrimination. For example, one court elegantly identified discrimination in these words:

> In constitutional law, the effect of a statute which confers particular privileges on a class arbitrarily selected from a large number of persons, all of whom stand in the same relation to the privileges granted and between whom and those not favored no reasonable distinction can be found.[1]

More directly pertinent to this chapter is one scholar's view of discrimination in job selection:

> Unfair discrimination or bias is said to exist when members of a minority group have lower probabilities of being selected for a job when, in fact, if they had been selected, their probabilities of performing successfully in a job would have been equal to those of nonminority group members.[2]

EMPLOYMENT DISCRIMINATION: THE FOUNDATION IN LAW

History

In 1941 A. Philip Randolph, president of the predominantly black Brotherhood of Sleeping Car Porters, organized black leaders who threatened a massive protest march in Washington, D.C. In response, President Franklin Roosevelt issued Executive Order 8802 (such orders have the force and effect of law), which created a Fair Employment Practice Committee. Congress was hostile to the order and limited the committee's budget, but Roosevelt's action was a striking first step for the federal government in addressing racial discrimination. Likewise, during the 1940s several states enacted their own fair employment laws.

While civil rights lawyers actively pursued litigation during the 1930s and 1940s and several significant decisions were handed down, the next firm impetus for racial equality was the landmark *Brown* v. *Board of Education*[3] decision in 1954 in which the Supreme Court forbade "separate but equal" schools. *Brown* repudiated the doctrine enunciated in an 1896 Supreme Court case, *Plessy* v. *Ferguson,*[4] in which the Court held that a Louisiana statute requiring equal but separate accommodations for whites and blacks on trains was not unconstitutional. (The history of *Plessy* and *Brown* is a particularly apt illustration of the living, changing character of the law. While stability and hence predictability in the law are important, they must not stand in the way of achieving justice in a changing society.) A period of intense activism followed *Brown* as citizens engaged in sit-ins, freedom rides, boycotts, and the like to press claims for racial equality in housing, public transportation, employment, and so on. It was a turbulent, sometimes violent era, but those activities were critical ingredients in subsequent advances for the black population. Then, in 1964, the National Labor Relations Board asserted its jurisdiction over racial discrimination where it constitutes an unfair labor practice. With the passage of the 1964 Civil Rights Act the campaign against discrimination solidified as one of the most energetic and successful social movements in American history.[5]

In 1988 Congress rather dramatically affirmed its commitment to civil rights by enacting, over President Reagan's veto, the Civil Rights Restoration Act. The new law protects women, minorities, the elderly, and the handicapped from discrimination in all parts of a public institution (government agencies, schools, colleges, etc.) if any one part of that institution receives federal money. Private organizations, including corporations, are subject to the act although, in some circumstances, only the unit actually receiving federal money, rather than the entire organization, may be reached by the act. And small "mom-and-pop" businesses are given greater flexibility in meeting the access requirements of federal handicap legislation. The act is an interesting lesson in the constitutional balance of powers and in politics in that it overrides a 1984 U.S. Supreme Court case, *Grove City College,*[6] in which the Court ruled that federal antidiscrimination laws applied only to specific programs receiving federal aid, but not to the entire institution. Now, with the passage of the Restoration Act, if a college receives federal money to help support its library, for example, that college must be free of discrimination in all of its units, including the men's and women's athletic programs.

Constitutional Provisions

The Fourteenth Amendment to the federal Constitution provides that no state shall deny to any person life, liberty, or property without *due process of law* or deny him or her the *equal protection of the laws.* Thus, citizens are protected from discrimination at the instigation of a state government. Then, by Supreme Court decision in 1954, the due process clause of the Fifth Amendment ("nor shall any person . . . be deprived of life, liberty, or property, without due process of law") was interpreted to forbid invidious discrimination by the federal government. Thus the Fifth and Fourteenth Amendments have been useful tools against government discrimination. Problems arise when a government body passes a law or takes some other action that results in treating one class of people differently than another. For example, an Oklahoma statute provided that females could lawfully purchase 3.2 percent beer at age 18 but males could not do so until age 21. The equal protection clause does not require all persons to be treated equally. Rather, the test is that of whether the classification (women may drink at 18, but men must wait until 21) is substantially related to the achievement of an important government goal. In general the courts have deferred to the lawmakers unless the classification is clearly arbitrary. How would you rule in the Oklahoma case [*Craig* v. *Boren,* 97 S. Ct. 451 (1976)]?

Civil Rights Act of 1866

Of course, the constitutional provisions are broadly drawn and thus open to variation in interpretation. The Constitution protects the citizenry from the government but not from private-sector abuse. Therefore, statutes and executive orders were necessary to attack discrimination more explicitly and to reach private-sector problems. A civil rights provision dating from the Reconstruction period (subsequently codified as section 1981 of Title 42 of the United States Code) has become particularly important in discrimination cases involving questions of race, color, or alienage. Section 1981 provides that all persons within the jurisdiction of the United States shall have the same right in every state or territory to make and enforce contracts as is enjoyed by white citizens. Employment relationships are, of course, founded in contract. Thus, when a black person is discriminated against by a private employer or by a labor union, Section 1981 has been violated. In 1982 the Supreme Court held that a violation of Section 1981 requires proof of *intentional* racial discrimination.[7]

In *Runyon* v. *McCrary,* the Supreme Court found a violation of Section 1981 when a private school denied admission to black applicants.[8] [At this writing in mid-1988, the Supreme Court has voted to use a pending civil rights case (*Patterson* v. *McLean Credit Union*) to decide whether to overrule the *Runyon* holding that section 1981 applies to private contracts. The *Patterson* decision is expected in 1989.]

Executive Orders

Although a number of executive orders (EO) address discrimination issues, one is of special importance here. EO 11246 requires each government agency to include an "equal opportunity" clause in its agreements with federal contractors. Thus all firms doing business in excess of $10,000 with the federal government must agree, in a broad sense, not to discriminate because of race, color, religion, sex, or national origin and to take affirmative action to avoid and correct underutilization of minorities and women.

Civil Rights Act of 1964

Relying on its authority to regulate interstate commerce, Congress forbade (in Title VII of the act) discrimination in employment because of race, color, religion, sex, or national origin. The act applies to private-sector employers with 15 or more employees, employment agencies procuring employees for a firm already employing 15 or more individuals, and labor unions operating a hiring hall. The Equal Employment Opportunity Act of 1972 amended the 1964 act to extend coverage to all state and local governments. The Civil Rights Act forbids employment discrimination in most units of the federal government, but Congress itself and those judicial and legislative positions not subject to competitive civil service standards are exempt. Private clubs are exempt from the act, and religious organizations may discriminate in employment on the basis of religion.

The act, as interpreted, prohibits discrimination in hiring, discharge, and general conditions of employment. While the act forbids employment discrimination against the specified protected classes (race, color, religion, sex, national origin), a number of exceptions are recognized. The more important exceptions are those regarding seniority, employee testing, bona fide occupational qualifications, and veterans' preferences.

Many statutes accord preference to veterans in such matters as employment selection. For example, the veteran applying for a public-sector job might automatically be elevated to the top of the hiring list if he or she simply passes the required examination. Title VII explicitly provides that it is not to be interpreted to repeal or modify laws affording veterans' preferences. However, in *Personnel Administrator of Massachusetts* v. *Feeney*[9], a woman attacked (on sex discrimination grounds) a Massachusetts statute giving veterans absolute preference in state employment. The U.S. Supreme Court sustained the statute because it found *no discriminatory purpose* in the legislature's action. The law was not enacted to *exclude* women. Rather it was designed to *prefer* veterans. (The other Civil Rights Act defenses are discussed later in the chapter.)

Other Federal Statutes

A number of federal statutes in addition to the Civil Rights Act of 1964 offer protection against various forms of employment discrimination. Among those are the Equal Pay Act, the Age Discrimination in Employment Act of 1967, and the Rehabilitation Act of 1973. Discussion of those statutes and their judicial interpretations is deferred until later in the chapter.

ENFORCEMENT

The Equal Employment Opportunity Commission (EEOC), a federal agency created under the terms of the Civil Rights Act of 1964, is primarily responsible for enforcing the provisions of the act. The commission is composed of five members appointed by the president with the advice and consent of the Senate for terms of five years. No more than three appointees may be members of the same political party. The commission has broad authority to hold hearings, seek documents, question witnesses under oath, and the like.

In essence, Title VII established two methods of enforcement: individual actions and "pattern or practice" suits.

Individual Actions

The private party seeking redress under Title VII faces some formidable administrative hurdles. Before bringing a private suit, an individual ordinarily must file a charge with the EEOC or wait 180 days until the commission's exclusive jurisdiction expires, at which point a private action may be filed.

Going forward with EEOC action is often frustrating because the agency is always burdened with a backlog of cases. Furthermore, in states or localities having agencies to deal with employment discrimination, the statute requires deferral of filing with the EEOC until those state/local agencies have exercised their authority. When a charge is filed, the commission must investigate the charge and attempt to conciliate the claim. That failing, the commission may file a civil suit in a federal district court and may represent the aggrieved party.[10] Thus several years may pass before the administrative process and any subsequent lawsuits have run their course.

Pattern or Practice Suits

In brief, the commission has the authority to investigate and take action on charges of a pattern or practice of discrimination. Pattern or practice claims seek to prove a general policy of discrimination rather than a specific instance of bias. Pattern or practice suits are based primarily on a statistically significant "deficiency" in the percentage of minority employees in the employer's work force as compared with the percentage of minority employees in the relevant labor pool. The employer may be able to rebut the discriminatory inference in a variety of ways. For example, it might be demonstrated that the relevant labor market was improperly drawn or that the statistical disparity is the result of nondiscriminatory conditions.

Remedies under Title VII include granting back pay, affording seniority relief, issuing injunctions, imposing reporting requirements, and so on. Injunctive relief might take the form of ordering the employment of an individual or requiring a promotion.

Department of Labor

Under its authority to enforce Executive Order 11246, the Office of Federal Contract Compliance Programs (OFCCP) of the Department of Labor has broad power to combat employment discrimination in firms performing federal contracts. Using its enormous leverage as a purchaser, the government requires contractors to agree not to discriminate in hiring or during employment because of race, color, religion, sex, or national origin. Furthermore, OFCCP regulations require "affirmative action" on the part of covered employer-contractors to ensure an end to discrimination. In general terms, the contractor must determine whether minorities and women are being "underutilized." If so, the contractor must develop a plan to achieve a work force representation appropriate to the minority and women's representation in the relevant labor market.

The chief enforcement mechanism for noncompliance is the power of the OFCCP to terminate contracts and, where appropriate, render such firms ineligible for future federal business.

Part Two—Discrimination on the Basis of Race, Color, or National Origin

Title VII places race, color, and national origin among those "protected classes" against which discrimination is forbidden. The act was directed primarily to improving the employment opportunities of blacks, but it applies to all races and colors (including whites and native Americans). The national origin proviso forbids discrimination based on one's nation of birth, ancestry, or heritage. Therefore, an employment office sign reading "Vietnamese need not apply" or "Mexicans need not apply" might reflect some of the recent tension regarding the assimilation of new immigrants, but such policies would clearly be unlawful.

To make some sense of the study of the law of equal opportunity, it must be understood that discrimination remains a serious problem. For example, the public opinion polls set out here suggest generally declining but persistent strains of racism.

Blacks

Question: How strongly would you object if a member of your family wanted to bring a (Negro/black) friend home to dinner? Would you object strongly, mildly, or not at all?

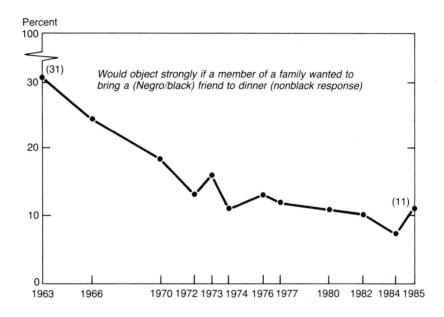

Percent

Would object strongly if a member of a family wanted to bring a (Negro/black) friend to dinner (nonblack response)

	Object Strongly	
By education: (nonblack response)	**1963**	**1985**
Less than high school graduate	40%	19%
High school graduate	25	12
Some college	22	8
College graduate	13	2

Blacks (*continued*)

Question: Do you think there should be laws against marriage between (Negroes/blacks) and whites?

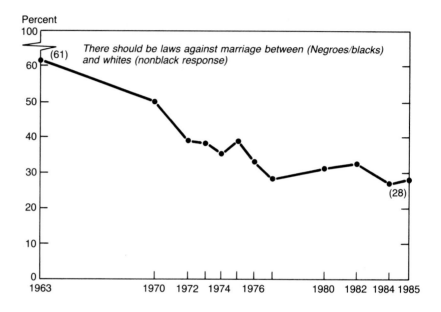

Percent

There should be laws against marriage between (Negroes/blacks) and whites (nonblack response)

(61)

(28)

1963   1970   1972   1974   1976   1980   1982   1984 1985

By education: (nonblack response)	Should Be Laws	
	1963	**1985**
Less than high school graduate	76%	52%
High school graduate	57	29
Some college	41	16
College graduate	27	9

Blacks (*concluded*)

Question: Which statement on the card comes closest to how you, yourself, feel? . . . (Negroes/blacks) shouldn't push themselves where they're not wanted.

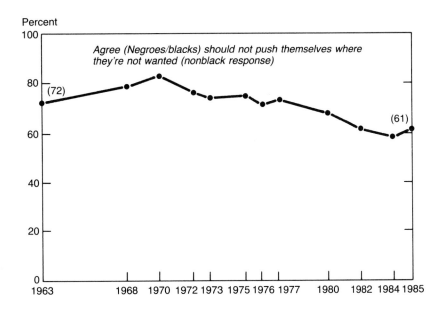

Percent

Agree (Negroes/blacks) should not push themselves where they're not wanted (nonblack response)

(72)

(61)

1963   1968   1970 1972 1973 1975 1976 1977   1980   1982 1984 1985

	Agree Strongly/Slightly	
By education: (nonblack response)	**1963**	**1985**
Less than high school graduate	78%	78%
High school graduate	71	66
Some college	61	59
College graduate	57	36

Source: Surveys by the National Opinion Research Center, 1963–1970; and National Opinion Research Center, General Social Surveys, 1972–1985. *Public Opinion* 10, no. 2 (July/August 1987), p. 24. Reprinted by permission.

PROGRESS?

The black community has enjoyed significant progress in recent years. For example, the percentage of black families that might be classified as poor (beneath the government poverty line) has fallen from 71 in 1940 to 30 in 1980, while the percentage of affluent (based on the annual income of the top 25 percent of white families in 1960 adjusted annually for inflation) black families has risen from 3 to 11 during that same period. Hence, by 1980, 70 percent of all American black families were either middle class or affluent in terms of income.[11] And for individual black male and female wage earners, economic conditions, on the average, have improved very significantly:

> In the late 1960s, black males earned 59 percent of what whites earned; today it is 75 percent, and the disparity is even narrower among young and hence better-educated blacks. The comparable figures for black females are 58 percent and 91 percent, with black females with at least two years of college pulling in slightly higher incomes than their white counterparts.[12]

However, enormous problems remain. The unemployment rate for blacks in 1986 was 14.5 percent, as compared with 6 percent for whites.[13] Nearly one in three (31.1 percent) blacks were living with an income beneath the government's poverty line in 1986 ($11,203 for a family of four), while 11 percent of whites fell into that category.[14] Black family income as compared with that of white families remains a source of special concern. Most white families now include two wage earners, while most black families do not. As documented in the table, the income gap between white and black families in the mid-80s was approximately equal to that same gap in the mid-60s.

Median Income of U.S. Families			
	Black	*White*	*Ratio*
1959	$ 3,047	$ 5,893	0.52
1964	3,724	6,858	0.54
1968	5,360	8,937	0.60
1970	6,279	10,236	0.61
1973	7,269	12,595	0.58
1983	13,598	24,593	0.55
1985	16,786	29,152	0.56

Source: Census Bureau and Urban League, *The State of Black America* (1987).

All Americans bear the costs of discrimination. While the direct cost is most painful for the victims of bias, the total bill is not restricted by color or sex. Employment discrimination significantly lowers total societal productivity. While the economic impact of discrimination is broadly understood, many much more subtle problems tend to remain largely unnoticed. For example, a number of studies show that blacks are disadvantaged in our justice system. One study of the decisions of criminal justice prosecutors in South Carolina found that requests for the death penalty "were made in 49 percent of the cases of capital murder in which a black killed a white but in only 11 percent of the cases in which a black killed a black."[15] And data from another study shows that nonwhites (not limited exclusively to blacks) among kidney transplant patients in the 21-to-45 age group "had only half the chance of receiving transplants as white patients of the same age and sex."[16]

The article that follows explores both the progress achieved and the distance remaining in the case of black professionals.

FOR THE BLACK PROFESSIONAL, THE OBSTACLES REMAIN

Lena Williams

More than two decades after civil rights victories made equal opportunity in the workplace a matter of law, many black professionals say they still face formidable obstacles to success.

In interviews around the country, dozens of blacks in government and private industry who were among the early beneficiaries of the civil rights gains said these obstacles had caused them to be bypassed or pushed aside. At a time when they should be advancing to the highest levels of their professions, they said, their careers have stalled because they are black.

Some, such as James Lowry and Eunice Jackson, have left the large concerns that recruited them after college and have started their own ventures. Others, such as Rodney Cran-dall, say they have resigned themselves to making the best of the jobs they have.

"I was receiving excellent performance ratings for years," recalled Mr. Crandall, who was chosen over several other qualified applicants for a promising position at a federal agency in Washington and three years later was promoted to a mid-management supervisory post. "Then a young white male was hired for a position similar to mine. From then on, nothing I seemed to do pleased my supervisor."

For Ms. Jackson, the end came when she sensed that she would be permanently cast as an anonymous "lawyer's lawyer" at the Exxon Corporation's Houston office, researching cases rather than dealing with clients or judges.

For Mr. Lowry, a management consultant at the Chicago office of McKinsey & Company, frustration was compounded by a feeling that white executives showed no interest in helping him along.

What the Numbers Are Showing

Whites hit career dead ends too, of course, since there are only so many places at the very top. But the record on blacks in management positions is striking.

Department of Labor statistics show that blacks in management areas of the labor market increased nationally from 2.4 percent of the total in 1958 to 6.0 percent in 1986. But even the higher figure is barely half [of] 11.8 percent, the proportion of all Americans who are black. This despite ambitious efforts by some major corporations and countless court decisions that gave further strength to the Civil Rights Act of 1964 and to the other federal laws and presidential orders on affirmative action of the same decade.

Further, no Fortune 500 company is headed by a black, according to a recent survey by Heidrick and Struggles, an executive research company with headquarters in Chicago.

The number of blacks holding policymaking and managerial positions in the federal government has also dropped dramatically since before President Reagan took office, from 44 in 1980 to 20 in 1986, according to the Equal Employment Opportunity Commission. At the same time, the commission says, the number of racial discrimination complaints filed by federal workers is on the rise.

* * * * *

White Employers Insist They're Trying

In their defense, many white employers say it is difficult to find blacks with the necessary prerequisites for top-level positions because they have not, as a group, been in the management work force long enough.

* * * * *

Spokesmen for many corporations say there is no limit to how far a qualified black can rise. While conceding that there are no pure meritocracies, many white employers view their companies as color-blind societies where good workers are rewarded.

Earl G. Graves, publisher and editor of *Black Enterprise* magazine, notes that the Xerox Corporation began minority training programs more than five years ago and now has 12 black vice presidents in various subsidiaries and divisions and a nationwide black employee organization that sponsors career counseling sessions.

One black professional who has succeeded is A. Barry Rand of Xerox. Earlier this year he was appointed head of the company's U.S. marketing operation, which has sales of nearly $5 billion and a 33,000-member work force.

Mr. Graves said Xerox ranked first among 25 corporations surveyed by his magazine on such issues as fairness, salary, and promotional opportunity for minorities. International Business Machines, Avon Products, and the American Telephone and Telegraph Company were also highly rated, he said.

The Obstacles and the Pressure

Black employees frequently say there is a "glass ceiling"—invisible but very real—that keeps them from the top. Those interviewed said they faced obstacles peculiar to black people in predominantly white institutions. Besides plain prejudice, which often manifests itself in the implication that blacks "are not intelligent enough," according to those interviewed, there are factors more subtle.

These include, black executives said, the predilection of some managers to promote peo-

---

Blacks in the Professions (percentage of jobs filled by blacks in 1986)

Managerial and professional specialty	**6.0%**
Officials and administrators, public administration	8.4
Financial managers	3.0
Personnel and labor relations managers	5.5
Purchasing managers	4.1
Managers: marketing, advertising, and public relations	2.5
Administrators: education and related fields	8.9
Managers: medicine and health	8.1
Managers: properties and real estate	5.2
Accountants and auditors	5.6
Underwriters and other financial officers	6.0
Personnel, training, and labor relations specialists	11.9
Buyers, wholesale and retail trade (except farm products)	3.2
Construction inspectors	4.5
Professional specialties	**6.7%**
Architects	3.2
Engineers	3.7
Mathematical and computer scientists	7.2
Natural scientists	2.5
Physicians and dentists	3.3
Nurses	6.7
Pharmacists	4.0
Dieticians	17.7
Therapists	7.8
Teachers: college and university	4.0
Other teachers	9.5
Counselors: educational and vocational	12.9
Librarians, archivists, and curators	7.4
Social scientists and urban planners	5.5
Social, recreation, and religious workers	12.5
Lawyers and judges	3.0
Writers, artists, entertainers, and athletes	5.2

Source: Bureau of Labor Statistics.

ple similar to themselves, and the social and professional estrangement that many blacks say they feel among white colleagues, especially in the absence of a black mentor.

"You always feel like you're being watched or judged," said a black investment banker with a big Wall Street firm, who asked not to be identified.

"No matter what they do, it won't necessarily mean they'll be rewarded," said Glegg Watson, co-author, with George Davis of *Black Life in Corporate America,* a book written in 1982 that looks at the professional and personal lives of blacks in predominantly white corporations. "We're not in those elite circles in corporate America where the decisions are made."

A black who does break through finds himself at times being one of only a few blacks among hundreds of people at his job level, and thus faced with severe pressure to prove himself.

When a sense of estrangement is added to a competitive environment, such as that at a law firm or an investment banking house, a black employee can feel devastating tension.

A black associate at a New York law firm, who like most other blacks interviewed did not want to be identified, asked a reporter to take notes in his office on a legal pad rather than in a reporter's notebook.

"That way," he explained, "they'll think you're a client. I have too much at stake here. I'm one year removed from being considered as a partner. I don't want to say or do anything that could jeopardize my standing."

The associate went on to say that he felt blacks were held to higher standards than their white counterparts and that the slightest irregularity in their work or personality would be used to exclude them from the reward of partnership.

Integrated Offices, Segregated Lives

Dissimilarity in background, which can produce awkwardness even among people of the same race, is a widely acknowledged cause of uneasiness between blacks and whites.

Specialists in black advancement say that more than 50 percent of black executives are graduates of predominantly black universities, and black executives are frequently the first from their families and neighborhoods to move into the upper echelon of American society. While they may work in integrated offices, the lives they lead outside the office are in many ways segregated.

"No One Ever Told Me"

On the job, a common complaint of black professionals is that white managers give them too little training, guidance, and informal moral support.

* * * * *

Legal Profession Is No Haven

By all accounts, the law is one of the most difficult professions for blacks. A study issued last year by a task force of the American Bar Association reported that the relatively few minority group people who became lawyers found their opportunities "largely circumscribed."

"Discrimination still persists in some parts of the legal profession," the study said. "Minorities sometimes leave law firms and corporate legal departments before the opportunity for promotion and advancement arises, because of feelings of alienation and isolation."

Eunice Jackson, who graduated from Columbia Law School in 1977, worked for Exxon as a tax attorney before deciding to go into private practice. The future she envisioned at Exxon was different from what the company had in mind, Ms. Jackson said, adding that she felt she would not have reached her full potential.

"My options were getting smaller," she recalled. "Had I stayed, I would have been doing a lot of 'lawyer's lawyering' because that's what the company saw as my strength. But it wasn't what I wanted to do."

Decisions on Partnerships

Partners and others involved in management of firms say they are eager to hire and promote black lawyers. But the task, they add, is easier said than done.

A white senior partner at a major Philadelphia law firm said the criteria used in partnership decisions were often not related strictly to performance and operated against minority members. As noted by the bar association's study, many firms, in deciding on new partners, consider an associate's record in bringing in clients, and a minority member's ability to attract clients is limited by segregation in the larger society.

* * * * *

How One Firm Has Responded

In an effort to draw more minority lawyers to New York law firms and keep them there, Milbank, Tweed, Hadley & McCoy, a Wall Street firm, has undertaken a program that pairs black law students at Columbia and New York universities with practicing black lawyers who act as mentors. The program was informally begun two years ago by Patricia L. Irvin, one of three black associates at Milbank, Tweed.

"Minority students were having problems getting jobs at the major firms, particularly in New York," Ms. Irvin said. "Many felt intimidated by the whole aura of Wall Street, so they didn't even bother to sign up to interview with some of the major firms. Another problem was that the firms themselves weren't actively recruiting blacks."

Milbank, Tweed provides financing and the staff for administering the program, which now has 167 lawyers, black and Hispanic, advising 83 students. The firm recently hired one of the students who participated in the program and says there are other promising prospects.

Help or Stigma?
While some people say such recruitment programs help bring in blacks who might otherwise find doors closed to them, many believe they stigmatize blacks as people who need special assistance.

* * * * *

Source: *The New York Times,* July 14, 1987, p. A16. Copyright © 1987 by The New York Times Company. Reprinted by permission.

Questions

1. Joe DiMaggio, Hall of Fame centerfielder for the New York Yankees, once husband of Marilyn Monroe, and immensely admired American, was the subject in 1939 of a photo-article in *Life* magazine. Contemporary sports columnist Bill Conlin recounted segments of that 1939 article:

   > Italians, bad at war, are well suited for milder competitions. . . . Although he learned Italian first, Joe, now 24, speaks English without an accent, and is otherwise well adopted [sic] to most U.S. mores. Instead of olive oil or smelly bear grease he keeps his hair slick with water. He never reeks of garlic and prefers chicken chow mein to spaghetti. . . . Joe DiMaggio's rise in baseball is a testimonial to the value of general shiftlessness. . . . His inertia caused him to give up school after one year in high school. . . . He is lazy, rebellious and endowed with a bad stomach.[17]

   As Mr. Conlin demonstrates, 50 years ago Italians were the subject of offensive stereotypes. Today we find those views foolish.
   a. Are blacks in contemporary America the subjects of stereotypes? Explain.
   b. If so, will those stereotypes become absurd historical artifacts 50 years hence? Explain.

2. Hong Kong-based Hawley and Hazel Chemical Company produces one of the most popular tooth cleansers in Asia, Darkie Toothpaste. The package is adorned

with the face of a black man displaying a "toothy smile." The logo was based on popular singer Al Jolson, a white American man who performed as a minstrel in black face in the early 1900s. The product has been popular in Asia for more than 60 years.[18]

a. Would you label the name or the logo "racist"? Explain.

b. Should Americans or the American government apply pressure to change the name and logo? Explain.

c. In 1985 Colgate-Palmolive bought a 50 percent interest in Hawley and Hazel. Is that company obliged to apply American values to the marketing of Darkie Toothpaste? Explain.

EMPLOYMENT DISCRIMINATION ANALYSIS

The Civil Rights Act of 1964 is the primary vehicle for pursuing employment discrimination claims. However, the reader is reminded of the other constitutional, statutory, and executive order protections mentioned above. Title VII provides two primary theories of liability—disparate treatment and disparate impact. (A third theory of liability, perpetuation of past intentional discrimination, will not be discussed here.)

Disparate Treatment[19]

The basic elements of disparate treatment exist where an employer purposefully treats some people less favorably than others because of their race, color, religion, sex, or national origin. Purposeful conduct or intent ordinarily is established by circumstantial evidence. In a simplified form a claim under disparate treatment analysis would proceed as follows:

1. Plaintiff's (Employee's) Prima Facie Case (sufficient to be presumed true unless proved otherwise). Optimally the plaintiff would present direct, explicit evidence of intentional disparate treatment. For example, that evidence might take the form of a letter from an employer to an employment agency indicating that "women would not be welcome as applicants for this physically taxing job." Because direct evidence of that nature is ordinarily unavailable, the plaintiff must build the following prima facie case from which intent and, hence, disparate treatment may be inferred:

a. Plaintiff belongs to a protected class.

b. Plaintiff applied for a job for which the defendant was seeking applicants.

c. Plaintiff was qualified for the job.

d. Plaintiff was denied the job.

e. The position remained open, and the employer continued to seek applications.

2. Defendant's (Employer's) Case.   If the plaintiff builds a successful prima facie case, the burden shifts to the defendant, who may either concede the discrimination but argue that the conduct was lawful based on a good defense, such as a bona fide occupational qualification (see below), or may "articulate some legitimate, nondiscriminatory reason for the employee's rejection" (for example, greater work experience). However, the defendant need not prove its decision not to hire the plaintiff was, in fact, based on that legitimate, nondiscriminatory reason. The defendant simply must raise a legitimate issue of fact disputing the plaintiff's discrimination claim. Further, and perhaps most important, the defendant is not required to prove that it is *not* guilty of discrimination.

3. Plaintiff's Response.   Assuming the defendant met the standard set forth for the defendant's case, the burden of proof then shifts back to the plaintiff to prove that the "legitimate, nondiscriminatory reason" offered by the defendant was, in fact, merely a pretext for discrimination. That is, the plaintiff must show that although the defendant's reason may be superficially plausible, it does not square with the facts based on the employer's hiring patterns or other evidence.

Disparate Impact

Disparate impact analysis arose out of situations in which employers used legitimate employment standards that, despite their apparent neutrality, worked a heavier burden on a protected class than on other employees. For example, a preemployment test, offered with the best of intentions and constructed to be a fair measurement device, may disproportionately exclude members of a protected class and thus be unacceptable (barring an effective defense). Alternatively, an employer surreptitiously seeking to discriminate may establish an apparently neutral, superficially valid employment test that has the effect of achieving the employer's discrimination goal. For example, a tavern might require its "bouncer" to be at least 6 feet 2 inches tall and weigh at least 180 pounds. Such a standard disproportionately excludes women, Orientals, and Hispanics from consideration and is impermissible (barring an effective defense). Disparate impact analysis is similar to that of disparate treatment, but critical distinctions mark the two approaches. In particular, note that disparate treatment requires proof of intent, while disparate impact does not. The disparate impact test is as follows:

1. The plaintiff must show that the challenged employment practice burdens a protected class more heavily than others.
2. Assuming the plaintiff establishes a prima facie case under step 1, the defendant then must show that, notwithstanding the disparate impact,

the challenged practices were either (*a*) a business necessity or (*b*) job related. Some judicial opinions seem to treat ''business necessity'' and ''job-relatedness'' as interchangeable tests. The circumspect view is to await clarification to firmly establish the relationships and distinctions between the tests. Certainly business necessity appears to be a broader standard in that it would permit reference to considerations beyond the circumstances of an employee's particular job.

3. Even if the defendant establishes a job-relatedness or business necessity defense, the plaintiff can still prevail by demonstrating that the employer's legitimate goals can be met using an alternative employment practice that is free of the prejudicial effect. In doing so, the plaintiff would then have established that the questioned employment practice was merely a ''pretext for discrimination.''

The *Griggs* case remains the signal judicial expression of employment discrimination law. Steps 1 and 2 in the disparate impact test are developed in *Griggs.* (Step 3, a refinement of *Griggs,* was articulated in *Albemarle Paper Company* v. *Moody.*[20])

GRIGGS V. DUKE POWER CO.
401 U.S. 424 (1971)

Chief Justice Burger

We granted the writ in this case to resolve the question whether an employer is prohibited by the Civil Rights Act of 1964, Title VII, from requiring a high school education or passing of a standardized general intelligence test as a condition of employment in or transfer to jobs when (a) neither standard is shown to be significantly related to successful job performance, (b) both requirements operate to disqualify Negroes at a substantially higher rate than white applicants, and (c) the jobs in question formerly had been filled only by white employees as part of a longstanding practice of giving preference to whites.

Congress provided, in Title VII of the Civil Rights Act of 1964, for class actions for enforcement of provisions of the Act and this proceeding was brought by a group of incumbent Negro employees against Duke Power Company. . . .

The district court found that prior to July 2, 1965, the effective date of the Civil Rights Act of 1964, the company openly discriminated on the basis of race in the hiring and assigning of employees at its Dan River plant. The plant was organized into five operating departments: (1) Labor, (2) Coal Handling, (3) Operations, (4) Maintenance, and (5) Laboratory and Test. Negroes were employed only in the Labor Department where the highest-paying jobs paid less than the lowest-paying jobs in the other four ''operating'' departments in which only whites were employed. Promotions were normally made within each department on the basis of job seniority. Transferees into a department usually began in the lowest position.

In 1955 the company instituted a policy of requiring a high school education for initial assignment to any department except Labor, and for transfer from the Coal Handling to any "inside" department (Operations, Maintenance, or Laboratory). When the company abandoned its policy of restricting Negroes to the Labor Department in 1965, completion of high school also was made a prerequisite to transfer from Labor to any other department. From the time the high school requirement was instituted to the time of trial, however, white employees hired before the time of the high school education requirement continued to perform satisfactorily and achieve promotions in the "operating" departments. Findings on this score are not challenged.

The company added a further requirement for new employees on July 2, 1965, the date on which Title VII became effective. To qualify for placement in any but the Labor Department it became necessary to register satisfactory scores on two professionally prepared aptitude tests, as well as to have a high school education. Completion of high school alone continued to render employees eligible for transfer to the four desirable departments from which Negroes had been excluded if the incumbent had been employed prior to the time of the new requirement. In September 1965 the company began to permit incumbent employees who lacked a high school education to qualify for transfer from Labor or Coal Handling to an "inside" job by passing two tests—the Wonderlic Personnel Test, which purports to measure general intelligence, and the Bennett Mechanical Comprehension Test. Neither was directed or intended to measure the ability to learn to perform a particular job or category of jobs. The requisite scores used for both initial hiring and transfer approximated the national median for high school graduates.

The District Court had found that while the company previously followed a policy of overt racial discrimination in a period prior to the Act, such conduct had ceased. The District Court also concluded that Title VII was intended to be prospective only and, consequently, the impact of prior inequities was beyond the reach of corrective action authorized by the Act.

. . . The Court of Appeals concluded there was no violation of the Act.

* * * * *

The objective of Congress in the enactment of Title VII is plain from the language of the statute. It was to achieve equality of employment opportunities and remove barriers that have operated in the past to favor an identifiable group of white employees over other employees. Under the Act, practices, procedures, or tests neutral on their face, and even neutral in terms of intent, cannot be maintained if they operate to "freeze" the status quo of prior discriminatory employment practices.

The Court of Appeals' opinion, and the partial dissent, agreed that, on the record in the present case, "whites register far better on the company's alternative requirements" than Negroes. This consequence would appear to be directly traceable to race. Basic intelligence must have the means of articulation to manifest itself fairly in a testing process. Because they are Negroes, petitioners have long received inferior education in segregated schools.

. . . Congress did not intend by Title VII, however, to guarantee a job to every person regardless of qualifications. In short, the Act does not command that any person be hired simply because he was formerly the subject of discrimination, or because he is a member of a minority group. Discriminatory preference for any group, minority or majority, is precisely and only what Congress has proscribed. . . .

. . . The Act proscribes not only overt discrimination but also practices that are fair in form, but discriminatory in operation. The touchstone is business necessity. If an employment practice which operates to exclude Negroes cannot be shown to be related to job performance, the practice is prohibited.

On the record before us, neither the high school completion requirement nor the general intelligence test is shown to bear a demonstrable relationship to successful performance of the jobs for which it was used. Both were adopted, as the Court of Appeals noted, without meaningful study of their relationship to job-performance ability. Rather, a vice president of the company testified, the requirements were instituted on the company's judgment that they generally would improve the overall quality of the work force.

The evidence, however, shows that employees who have not completed high school or taken the tests have continued to perform satisfactorily and make progress in departments for which the high school and test criteria are not used. . . .

The Court of Appeals held that the company had adopted the diploma and test requirements without any "intention to discriminate against Negro employees." We do not suggest that either the District Court or the Court of Appeals erred in examining the employer's intent; but good intent or absence of discriminatory intent does not redeem employment procedures or testing mechanisms that operate as "built-in headwinds" for minority groups and are unrelated to measuring job capability.

* * * * *

The facts of this case demonstrate the inadequacy of broad and general testing devices as well as the infirmity of using diplomas or degrees as fixed measures of capability. . . .

The company contends that its general intelligence tests are specifically permitted by § 703(h) of the Act. That section authorizes the use of "any professionally developed ability test" that is not "designed, intended *or used* to discriminate because of race. . . ." (Emphasis added.)

The Equal Employment Opportunity Commission, having enforcement responsibility, has issued guidelines interpreting § 703(h) to permit only the use of job-related tests. The administrative interpretation of the Act by the enforcing agency is entitled to great deference. Since the Act and its legislative history support the commission's construction, this affords good reason to treat the guidelines as expressing the will of Congress.

. . . From the sum of the legislative history relevant in this case, the conclusion is inescapable that the EEOC's construction of § 703(h) to require that employment tests be job related comports with congressional intent.

Nothing in the Act precludes the use of testing or measuring procedures; obviously they are useful. What Congress has forbidden is giving these devices and mechanisms controlling force unless they are demonstrably a reasonable measure of job performance. Congress has not commanded that the less qualified be preferred over the better qualified simply because of minority origins. Far from disparaging job qualifications as such, Congress has made such qualifications the controlling factor, so that race, religion, nationality, and sex become irrelevant. What Congress has commanded is that any tests used must measure the person for the job and not the person in the abstract.

The judgment of the Court of Appeals is . . . reversed.

Questions

1. According to the Supreme Court, what was Congress' objective in enacting Title VII?

2. Had Duke Power been able to establish that its reasons for adopting the diploma and test standards were entirely without discriminatory intent, would the Supreme Court have ruled differently? Explain.

3. What is the central issue in this case?

4. Why was North Carolina's social and educational history relevant to the outcome of the case?

5. Gregory, a black male, was offered employment by Litton Systems as a sheet metal worker. As part of a standard procedure he completed a form listing a total of 14 nontraffic arrests but no convictions. Thereupon the employment offer was withdrawn. Gregory then brought suit claiming he was a victim of racial discrimination.

   a. Explain the foundation of his argument.

   b. Decide the case. See *Gregory* v. *Litton,* 472 F.2d 631 (9th Cir. 1972).

6. In 1970 Lane pleaded guilty to the offense of smuggling marijuana into the United States. In 1971 he secured an Atlanta taxi operator's permit. In 1973 a dispute with a passenger and a subsequent review of his file revealed the prior smuggling conviction (which he had disclosed at the time of application). His permit was revoked. Lane, a black man, felt he had been discriminated against.

   a. Decide the validity of Lane's claim.

   b. Would the result be different had he been dismissed from his job as a truck driver for the city? Explain. See *Lane* v. *Inman,* 509 F.2d 184 (5th Cir. 1975).

7. As explained previously, in *Personnel Administrator of Massachusetts* v. *Feeney,* 442 U.S. 256 (1979), a state policy of absolute hiring preference for veterans was upheld against a charge of gender-based discrimination in that few veterans are women. The disparate impact on women was clear, and Massachusetts governing authorities can be assumed to have been aware of the "natural and probable consequence" of this preference. The Supreme Court found an absence of discriminatory purpose. Explain and justify that decision.

8. In many Title VII cases, a critical ingredient is that of identifying the relevant labor market. How would you counter Justice Stevens' argument in dissent in *Hazelwood School District* v. *United States,* 433 U.S. 299 (1976), that as a starting point the relevant labor pool should encompass the geographic area from which incumbent employees come?

9. As demonstrated in *Griggs,* when disparate impact analysis is applied to *objective* employment selection and promotion methods (such as standardized tests), intent need not be established to build a successful case. Now consider the situation where the employment selection or promotion method in question is *subjective* in character (for example, letters of reference or interviews). Are those situations to be analyzed only under the disparate treatment standard including its proof of intent requirement, or may the disparate impact analysis be employed, thus eliminating the intent issue? Explain. See *Clara Watson* v. *Fort Worth Bank and Trust,* 56 *Law Week* 4922 (1988).

Statutory Defenses

In a broad sense, business necessity, as explained above, is the principle defense to discrimination charges. However, as mentioned previously, Title VII affords four specific exemptions or defenses of particular note: seniority, employee testing, bona fide occupational qualification, and veterans' preferences. Discussion of veterans' preferences appears above. Bona fide occupational qualifications are addressed in the next section as a part of the sex discrimination materials. Seniority issues and employee testing standards are explored here.

Seniority. Section 703(h) of the Civil Rights Act provides that an employer may lawfully apply different standards of compensation or different conditions of employment pursuant to a bona fide (good faith) seniority system, provided such differences are not the product of an intent to discriminate. That is, the seniority system must not have been created for a discriminatory or other illegal purpose, and the seniority provisions must apply equally to all.

Seniority systems are either the product of the employer's initiative or of a collective bargaining agreement. Seniority is important because (1) those with less seniority are ordinarily the first to be laid off in the event of a work force reduction and (2) benefits—including vacations and such working conditions as a choice of shifts—often depend on seniority.

Many complicated issues have arisen out of Congress' effort to abolish employment discrimination while preserving legitimate seniority plans. In sum, the dilemma is that a seniority system, otherwise entirely legitimate, sometimes has the effect of perpetuating past discriminatory practices. Employees once discriminated against in hiring or promotion suffer the further loss of reduced seniority. However, as established in the *Teamsters*[21] and *American Tobacco*[22] cases, the result of a bona fide seniority system may be to perpetuate discrimination, but such a result is illegal only if discriminatory intent is proved.

In 1984 the U.S. Supreme Court addressed the difficult issue of whether, in times of employment reductions, employers may lay off workers according to seniority (thereby ordinarily reaching white males after women and minorities) or whether affirmative action requires retaining those low-seniority, protected-class employees while laying off white males of greater seniority. The *Firefighters* case answered the question when the Supreme Court, in effect, held that when layoffs are necessary the legal system may not protect newly hired workers by interfering with legitimate seniority systems.[23] In the *Firefighters* case, a federal district court had approved two affirmative action plans in Memphis, Tennessee, for increasing the number of blacks in the fire department. Soon thereafter, budgetary problems required Memphis to lay off 40 firefighters. The city faced the problem of whether to maintain its affirmative action program by laying off firefighters with greater seniority than the recently hired protected-class employees or to honor the provisions of the collectively bargained agreement on seniority, which, in effect, required laying off those most recently hired. The city decided to follow the collective bargaining agreement, and black firefighters filed suit. In the end, the Supreme Court upheld the seniority system despite its impact on affirmative action. That is, the pursuit of affirmative action goals cannot upset legitimate seniority rights where layoffs are necessary. Thus affirmative action plans may not "re-allocate jobs currently held."[24] However, as articulated in the *Cleveland Firefighters* case,[25] *forward-looking* affirmative action (such as special training programs and special selection procedures for promotion, apprenticeships, and so on) is fully permissible. In the Supreme Court's view, those *forward-looking* programs do not unnecessarily interfere with the rights of white employees.

Employee Testing.   Testing is, of course, central to professional personnel practice and to maximizing employee productivity, but testing has often been, both intentionally and unintentionally, a primary vehicle in perpetuating discrimination. Recall that the Supreme Court in the *Griggs* case reasoned that tests having a disparate impact on a protected class could be used lawfully only if the tests were proven to be job related. Then in *Albemarle* the Court made it clear that such tests would be acceptable only if supported by detailed, statistical evidence as to the tests' scientific validity.

Under the Uniform Guidelines on Employee Selection Procedures, the Department of Justice and Labor, the EEOC, and the Civil Service Commission have agreed on standards specifying acceptable hiring practices for covered business and government employers. (The guidelines reflect the EEOC's interpretation of the act and, as such, are not binding on the courts. However, the judiciary accords great deference to the guidelines.) In essence the guidelines embrace the standards that professional industrial psychologists have established for determining test validity. The guidelines are rather specific as to the meaning of disparate or adverse impact. An employer will generally be presumed in noncompliance with the guidelines if the selection rate (such as the percentage passing a test, being hired, or being promoted) for any protected class is less than 80 percent of the selection rate for the group with the highest rate. The employer falling below that standard must prove the job relatedness of the employment practice in question and demonstrate that a good faith effort was made to find a selection procedure that lessened the disparate impact on protected classes.

A 1982 Supreme Court decision in *Connecticut* v. *Teal*[26] resolved a very important variation on the issues raised in *Griggs* and *Albemarle*. In *Teal*, 54 percent of the black candidates and 79 percent of the white candidates passed an exam to become permanent supervisors in a Connecticut state agency. Some of those black employees who failed the test filed suit, claiming a violation of Title VII. Prior to the trial the defendants in the suit promoted 22.9 percent of the blacks and 13.5 percent of the whites on the eligibility list (those passing the test). At trial, the defendants raised a "bottom-line" defense, arguing that the pass rate on the examination was, in effect, irrelevant because the overall selection policy (the bottom line) resulted in hiring proportionately more black than white applicants. The district court agreed with the bottom-line defense. The federal Court of Appeals reversed. The Supreme Court affirmed, thus rejecting the bottom line as a defense in these Title VII cases. The Court concluded that disparate impact is not to be measured only at the bottom line. Title VII guarantees all employees "the *opportunity* to compete equally with white workers on the basis of job-related criteria."

Part Three—Sex Discrimination

INTRODUCTION

The dramatic shift in the role of women in American life in the past two decades has amounted to a social revolution. The Civil Rights Act of 1964 had not originally included a provision regarding sex. Congressman Smith of Virginia, apparently seeking to block passage of the act, introduced an amendment to include sex among the protected classes. The passage of that amendment and the act afforded the legislative tool necessary to legitimize and effectuate women's civil rights claims. Sex discrimination refers to unequal treatment on the basis of gender. By judicial interpretation, sexual practices and sexual orientation (such as homosexuality) are not governed by Title VII.

Historically, a major ingredient in employment discrimination on the basis of sex was the paternalistic governmental and employer view that women require protection. In 1908 the U.S. Supreme Court upheld the constitutionality of state protective legislation as a valid exercise of the police power. Women were limited to 10 hours per day in a factory because:

> it would still be true that she is so constituted that she will rest upon and look to him (the man) for protection; that her physical structure and a proper discharge of her maternal functions . . . having in view not merely her own health but the well-being of the race . . . justify legislation to protect her from the greed as well as the passion of man.[27]

That protective legislation now has largely been abolished, and remaining invidious or irrational distinctions based on gender are being litigated. For example, the following practices have all been found discriminatory: a law forbidding women to tend bar, a law providing premium overtime pay for women only, a policy of hiring only women to serve as flight attendants, a policy refusing to hire women for jobs requiring night work, and a company policy requiring airline stewardesses but not stewards to wear contact lenses rather than eyeglasses.

Gender-based protective legislation may be one of the few areas in which social welfare law in the United States appears to be more "progressive" than that in Europe. In 1987 the European Community Commission argued that protective laws for women should either be banished or applied equally to men. In most European Community nations, women cannot "work in mines or at night in factories." "They're banned from 'dangerous or unhealthy' work in Belgium and Ireland. Some laws limit women's hours or give more leave."[28]

The feminist movement and sex discrimination issues have been the focus of considerable societal conflict in recent years. Several of those issues are of particular significance to this discussion.

Pregnancy and Childbirth

In 1976 the U.S. Supreme Court held in *General Electric Co.* v. *Gilbert*[29] that a fringe benefit plan paying a wage substitute to employees for disabilities not arising from employment but excluding pregnancy disability from coverage was not an instance of sex discrimination. Then, in an excellent illustration of the balance-of-powers concept, Congress in 1978 amended Title VII to require the treatment of pregnancy discrimination as sex discrimination. The Pregnancy Discrimination Act forbids an employer from making adverse employment decisions (hiring, promotion, etc.) because of a woman's pregnancy, childbirth, or related conditions. Pregnant women, married or not, must be treated the same as other employees. Mandatory time limits for pregnancy leave are proscribed, and an employer may not compel a pregnant woman, able to continue her duties, to leave work before the child's birth. Finally, the 1978 amendments explicitly reverse the *Gilbert* result by providing that pregnancy-related conditions cannot be excluded from disability coverage.

In 1983 the Court interpreted the act to apply to employees' pregnant spouses. By a 7-to-2 vote the Court ruled that pregnancy-related expense benefits for the spouses of male employees must be equal to the pregnancy-related expense benefits accorded to married female employees.[30] Then, in 1987, the Court upheld a California law giving pregnant women a four-month leave from work and guaranteeing them their job back after the leave.[31] The California law had been challenged, in part, on the grounds that it discriminated in favor of women and thus violated the federal Pregnancy Discrimination Act. But the Court found that Congress intended the PDA to be a floor beneath which benefits could not drop rather than a ceiling beyond which benefits could not rise. Although most feminist groups supported the decision, some had opposed the California law because they feared approval of special benefits for women would undermine women's claims for freedom from discrimination throughout life. In a related ruling the Supreme Court held that states may lawfully deny unemployment compensation to women who voluntarily leave their jobs because of pregnancy.[32] The unanimous Court found that federal unemployment laws do not require pregnant women to be treated *better* than other employees.

These developments in pregnancy discrimination law have provoked considerable national discussion about the related issue of maternity leave or, more broadly, parental leave. Despite opposition from many employers, mandatory maternal leave policies are now (in 1988) required by at least 15 states. In 1987 Minnesota became the first state to require leaves for both fathers and mothers. The Ladies Garment Workers Union won six months' leave for new parents. Many companies now voluntarily provide parental leave. They argue that the leaves make good business sense as a means of retaining trained employees in an increasingly competitive labor market. A survey of small New York firms found that 15 percent gave eight or more weeks' leave to mothers, while 8 percent did so for fathers.[33] The terms of the leave policies vary widely. A law now under consideration in Congress would provide for unpaid leave to both parents for both newborn and adoptive children for up to 10 weeks. The federal government's General Accounting Office has estimated the annual cost to employers of unpaid leaves for both parents for up to 10 weeks at $340 million. A Chamber of Commerce study arrived at a "very conservative" estimate of $2.6 billion.[34]

Now emerging, and yet unanswered, is the difficult question of how to treat women in workplaces that may prove hazardous (because of chemicals, etc.) to their unborn young or to their capacity to have children. If women are removed from those dangerous settings, as some companies have done, are those companies guilty of sex discrimination?[35]

Equal Rights Amendment (ERA)

> Equality of rights under the law shall not be denied or abridged by the United States or by any state on account of sex.

This proposed ERA to the Constitution was approved by Congress and 35 states. However, approval by the three additional legislatures necessary for adoption was not forthcoming, and the amendment expired in June 1982. It will likely be resurrected by Congress. Ironically, women have led the well-organized opposition to ERA, fearing perhaps the loss of such rights as alimony. It is interesting to note that the public has consistently supported ERA, and men have given the amendment greater support than women. An April 1982 Louis Harris poll showed 63 percent of the public approved passage of the amendment.[36]

Insurance and Pensions

In 1987 Massachusetts became the second state (after Montana) to require insurance companies to charge men and women equal insurance fees for equal coverage. In all other states premiums differ dramatically by sex. Critics attribute the differences at least partially to sex discrimination, while the insurance companies say differences in risks and subsequent claim patterns account for the distinction in premiums. For example, women pay smaller premiums for life insurance because "at almost every age, a woman's chances of dying within the next year are about 40 percent less than a man's."[37] On the other hand, at most ages women's health insurance rates substantially exceed those of men. For example, "Aetna charges a 35-year-old woman between 30 percent and 50 percent more than the male rate."[38] The table below illustrates the effect of the Montana law on premiums in that state.

Changing Rates—Average Changes in Insurance Premiums in Montana since Passage of Unisex Law

	Percent Change	
	Women	*Men*
Life insurance		
Whole-life policy, $50,000		
Age 30	+15%	−3%
Health insurance		
Individually purchased		
major-medical policy		
Age 40	−13	+28
Auto insurance		
$25,000 policy with $100		
deductible on mid-size auto		
Age 20	+49	−16

Source: Data from the *Montana Insurance Department* in John R. Dorfman, "Proposals for Equal Insurance Fees for Men and Women Spark Battle," *The Wall Street Journal,* August 27, 1987, p. 23.

In 1983 the Supreme Court, by a 5-to-4 vote, ruled that employers must not provide pension plans offering unequal benefits for men and women.[39] The case was brought by Natalie Norris, an Arizona state employee, who was making $199 monthly contributions to a pension plan but was scheduled to receive $34 less per month in benefits than male employees making identical contributions. Because of the use of sex-based mortality tables, women (who, as a group, live longer than men) received lower monthly pension payments than did men who made identical contributions to the pension funds. The Court concluded that such pension plans constituted sex discrimination in violation of Title VII. The ruling applies only to employer-sponsored annuities and is expected to affect about 16 million pensions. The decision was not imposed retroactively. Therefore, past discrimination need not be rectified, but for the future all affected pension plans must be free of sex discrimination.

"Private" Organizations

We Americans want to preserve our right to, in general, freely associate with whomever we wish. However, that principal constitutional value must be carefully balanced against our wish to banish discrimination. In the *Jaycees* case (*Kathryn R. Roberts* v. *United States Jaycees*[40]), the Supreme Court was required to resolve the conflict between Minnesota's efforts to eliminate sex discrimination and the First Amendment freedom of association claimed by the Jaycees, a "private" service organization that declined to admit women as full voting members. Two local Minnesota chapters had been violating the national bylaws by admitting women as regular members. When notified that the national Jaycees were contemplating revocation of their charter, the Minnesota chapters filed discrimination charges with the Minnesota Department of Human Rights. They claimed a violation of the Minnesota Human Rights Act, which makes it discriminatory conduct to deny any person the full and equal enjoyment of public accommodations because of race, color, creed, religion, disability, national origin, or sex. The human rights hearing examiner concluded that the Jaycees were a "place" of "public accommodation" and that their membership policy was discriminatory. He ordered the Jaycees to desist from that discrimination.

On appeal, the U.S. Supreme Court held that compelling the Jaycees to accept women as regular members did not deny the male members' freedom of association. The essence of the Supreme Court's position was that the Jaycees were not a fundamentally private organization entitled to freedom from unjustified state interference. Jaycees chapters were not selective as to membership. They were large organizations. Their activities regularly involved strangers as well as other nonmembers of both sexes. Therefore, the Jaycees are now required to admit women as full members.

The Court added emphasis to the *Jaycees* decision with a 1987 ruling that had the effect of opening the all-male Rotary clubs to women.[41] Then, in 1988, the Court upheld the constitutionality of a New York City law that forbids discrimination in public accommodations but exempts "distinctly private" places.[42] The law provides that clubs are not private if they have more than 400 members, are used for business by both members and nonmembers, and provide regular meal service. Of course, these decisions do not forbid discrimination in those "distinctly private" organizations.

Must your local country club now admit all otherwise qualified applicants regardless of race, religion, sex, and so on?

EQUALITY FOR WOMEN?

Is the women's rights movement on the wane? Have we "gone too far" in striving for equality of the sexes? Is such equality possible or even desirable? Can legal equality, if secured, produce economic and social equality? Despite general acceptance of a new role for women, despite striking legal victories, despite a fervor that has altered American life, women continue by perhaps the most important barometers to remain in a distinctly secondary status.

In 1986 women working full time earned, according to the Census Bureau, about 64 percent of what men earned.[43] (Note that we refer here to median incomes by sex across all full-time jobs rather than to comparisons of men and women holding "identical" jobs.) Census Bureau figures also demonstrate that in 1984 the average female college graduate earned $20,257, while the average male high school dropout earned $19,120 and the average male college graduate earned $31,487.[44] In the same vein, recent survey evidence reveals that female corporate officers suffer, in many ways, when compared with their male counterparts:

> Separate surveys of corporate officers by executive search firms . . . underscore sharp disparities in the routes, rewards, and penalties of getting to the top. The male officers tend to be older, 51 against 44, and have been at their companies longer. Though they put in the same 55-hour weeks, the men earn $215,000 a year, compared to $116,810 for the women.
>
> To advance their careers, 82 percent of the women say they have paid with personal sacrifices. One in five never married; among males, only 0.7 percent have never wed. One fifth of the women are separated or divorced, five times the male rate. More than half are childless; 95 percent of the men had children, and the average had three.[45]

These discouraging figures are rendered all the more lamentable when contrasted with comparable data from Europe: "In Sweden, for example, women now average 81 percent of male annual earnings, up from 71 percent in 1970. In France, women's wages are 78 percent of men's, and in Italy, the figure is 86 percent."[46]

Of course, the news is not altogether grim. Women have made striking gains in recent years. For example, we can find at least some encouragement in the 64 percent ratio of women's to men's wages in that it represents a significant increase from the 1960–80 period when the ratio ranged from .57 to .60.[47] And we can see bigger changes in the offing. "For people age 18 to 24, the ratio of female to male income was 88 percent in 1984, up from 76 percent in 1980."[48] A study from the Rand Corporation, a conservative "think tank," projects women's wages, on the average, to reach 74 percent of average male wages by the year 2000.[49] Women have also made significant inroads in traditionally male occupations. For example, in 1976, 9 percent of our scientists and engineers were female, but by 1984 that figure had jumped to 13 percent.[50] And while 17 percent of our physicians are women, medical school first-year classes now average more than one-third female. In 1970, 33.9 percent of our managerial and professional specialty jobs (administrators, financial managers, buyers) were women; in 1986 that figure had risen to 43.4 percent.[51]

On the other hand, the historical record suggests the movement of women into traditionally male occupations often signals the economic and social decline of those occupations. For example, pre–World War II bank tellers, usually men, earned good wages. Now tellers, usually women, are poorly paid. The pattern (seen from cigar makers to typesetters to pharmacists) seems to be that once some factor, such as automation, depreciates the pay and prestige in an occupation, men leave and women assume those roles.[52]

American women continue to be disadvantaged in employment. As noted, women in many western democracies are several strides ahead of their American counterparts. However, to add some perspective to this topic and to achieve a sense of the cultural variables that influence sex discrimination, consider the following account of the role of women in Japan.

WHAT IT'S LIKE TO BE A WOMAN IN JAPAN

Carol Rose

Kanagasaki, Japan—It is just past lunchtime at the Oki agricultural collective. Women dressed in bright blue and yellow bonnets are loaded into pickup trucks for the drive to the cucumber fields, where they will toil beneath the blazing summer sun all afternoon.

But just before the trucks pull away, the man who heads the collective motions for one of the women to come to the central office where I am to interview a group of men.

She is needed to serve tea.

It is a scene repeated time and again throughout my travels in Japan. Whether at a remote farmhouse or a modern office complex in downtown Tokyo, it is always women who serve the tea and then vanish without a word.

To most Americans, the relationship between the sexes in Japan is a constant source of indignation and bewilderment. . . .

* * * * *

. . . Japanese women appear long-suffering, hiding shyly behind screens of simpering or giggling. They rarely participate in conversations with men, even when Western women are present. In most Japanese homes, the wife appears only long enough to serve tea and sweets, before shuffling back into the kitchen.

Despite lingering signs of discrimination, the status of Japanese women in the postwar era has improved dramatically. Today, virtually all women finish high school and attend the same courses given men. Around 23 percent of Japanese university students are women.

But equality in education has not yet translated into equality in jobs. Japanese law prohibits discrimination based on gender. But common practice is summed up in a recent Japanese popular magazine: "Because of marriage or childbirth, it is understandable that companies, for the sake of their long-term interests, entrust highly paid positions to men."

Want-ads in the newspaper are filled with job openings for women under 22 years of age. Older and more educated women have a difficult time getting a job, since employers fear they might demand retirement benefits. Women are discouraged from staying at a job beyond the age of 25, which is considered the proper time for marriage.

Once a woman quits her job, however, it is virtually impossible for her to ever again work full time. . . .

Women who do stay on the job earn only 50 cents for every dollar earned by men in the same job. . . .

But nowhere is the gender imbalance more striking than in rural Japan. Staying with a farm family near Esashi City, 400 miles north of Tokyo, it is easy to see why young Japanese women are leaving the farm in search of greater opportunity in the cities.

Kinichi Oikawa, a farm wife, gets up more than one hour before the rest of the family and is out in the barn shoveling manure while her husband and 26-year-old son sleep. She then prepares breakfast while they read the morning paper. At night, she is the last person to bathe, following the traditional Japanese custom that men in the family bathe first (women have traditionally been considered dirty in Japan and thus are believed to soil the waters of the communal family bath).

Asked if she resented the hardships of farm life, Oikawa giggles and hides her face.

* * * * *

On the surface, the outlook for Japanese women appears bleak. But there is a subculture in which women have enormous power.

Wives control the purse strings in nearly every family; husbands get an allowance. While the house belongs to the husband, the furnishings belong to the wife. Divorce in Japan is uncommon, about one-quarter the U.S. rate. When it does occur, women are entitled to half of the family possessions.

Child-rearing is also a source of power. Since most men work long hours, six days a week, they rarely participate in family activities. Education of the children is strictly controlled by the mothers, as are marriage arrangements.

The result is not always pleasant. Denied opportunities to better themselves, Japanese women often seek success through their sons. As a result, many are called "Kyoiku Mama" or "education mothers" because they constantly push their children to excel in school.

But few Japanese women expressed envy of my position as an American woman. One farm wife asked if I was forced into a career because I could not find a husband. "A woman's happiness is in home and marriage," she said. A young male government worker, who has traveled extensively in the United States, said he thought Japanese women were less lonely than those in America.

He may be right. At birth, Japanese women have a clear position in the family and in society, while American women are breaking out of traditional roles. Freedom presents American women with difficult choices. But they are choices rarely available in Japan.

Source: *Des Moines Register*, August 30, 1987, p. 3C. © *Des Moines Register*. Reprinted by permission.

ANALYSIS OF SEX DISCRIMINATION

Under Title VII of the 1964 Civil Rights Act, sex discrimination analysis proceeds in essentially the manner outlined earlier in the chapter; that is, disparate treatment and disparate impact are the key tests. An important variation of disparate treatment analysis is sex plus discrimination. *Sex plus* is the term applied to those situations where an employer has attempted to distinguish between male and female workers by imposing a second employment criterion (in addition to sex) on one gender but not on the other. For example, in *Phillips* v. *Martin Marietta*[53] the employer refused to hire women with preschool-age children but welcomed men with preschool-age children. For the assembly trainee position for which Phillips applied, 75 to 80 percent of those hired had been women. The Supreme Court struck down the sex-plus classification. What consequences might have been anticipated from a contrary ruling?

Bona Fide Occupational Qualification

As explained earlier, Title VII permits discrimination under limited circumstances. Among those exemptions or defenses is the bona fide occupational qualification (BFOQ). That is, discrimination is lawful where sex, religion, or national origin is a BFOQ reasonably necessary to the normal operation of that business. The exclusion of race and color from the list suggests Congress thought those categories always unacceptable as bona fide occupational qualifications. The judicially created defense of business necessity is applicable to racial classifications. The BFOQ was meant to be a very limited exception applicable to situations where specific inherent characteristics are necessary to the job (e.g., wet nurse) and where authenticity is required (e.g., actors).

The BFOQ defense is lawful only if the following conditions are met:

1. Proof of a *nexus* between the classification and job performance,
2. *"necessity"* of the classification for successful performance, and,
3. that the job performance affected by the classification is the *"essence"* of the employer's business operation.[54]

Nexus.   Will the classification affect job performance? For example, will "maleness" depreciate performance in a job requiring manual dexterity, or will "femaleness" depreciate performance in a laboring job requiring night work and long hours? The courts have thoroughly rejected distinctions based on such stereotypes.

Necessity.   Mere customer preference or, in general, higher costs will not justify an otherwise discriminatory employment practice. Thus, that restaurant customers prefer to be served by women or that hiring women will require the addition of another washroom or that hiring blacks, for example, will anger customers and cause a decline in income are not justifications for discrimination.

Essence.   An employer can lawfully insist on a woman to fill a woman's modeling role because being female goes to the essence of the job. However, airlines, for example, cannot hire only women as flight attendants even if females are shown to perform the "nonmechanical" portions of the job better than most men. Those duties "are tangential to the essence of the business involved."[55]

Many employers have simply assumed that women could not perform certain tasks. Women were thought to be insufficiently aggressive for sales roles, and women were denied employment because they were assumed to have a higher turnover rate due to the desire to marry and have children. Those stereotypes are at the heart of sex discrimination litigation generally and sex as a BFOQ particularly. The following case illustrates a difficult sex discrimination issue and the appropriate mode of analysis, including the BFOQ defense.

DOTHARD V. RAWLINSON
97 S. Ct. 2720 (1977)

Justice Stewart

Appellee Dianne Rawlinson sought employment with the Alabama Board of Corrections as a prison guard, called in Alabama a "correctional counselor." After her application was rejected, she brought this class suit under Title VII of the Civil Rights Act of 1964, . . .

alleging that she had been denied employment because of her sex in violation of federal law. A three-judge Federal District Court for the Middle District of Alabama decided in her favor. . . .

At the time she applied for a position as correctional counselor trainee, Rawlinson was a 22-year-old college graduate whose major course of study had been correctional psychology. She was refused employment because she failed to meet the minimum 120-pound weight requirement established by an Alabama statute. The statute also establishes a height minimum of 5 feet 2 inches.

After her application was rejected because of her weight, Rawlinson filed a charge with the Equal Employment Opportunity Commission, and ultimately received a right-to-sue letter. She then filed a complaint in the District Court on behalf of herself and other similarly situated women, challenging the statutory height and weight minima as violative of Title VII and the Equal Protection Clause of the 14th Amendment. A three-judge court was convened. While the suit was pending, the Alabama Board of Corrections adopted Administrative Regulation 204, establishing gender criteria for assigning correctional counselors to maximum-security institutions for "contact positions," that is, positions requiring continual close physical proximity to inmates of the institution. Rawlinson amended her class-action complaint by adding a challenge to Regulation 204 as also violative of Title VII and the 14th Amendment.

Like most correctional facilities in the United States, Alabama's prisons are segregated on the basis of sex. Currently the Alabama Board of Corrections operates four major all-male penitentiaries. . . . [These] are maximum-security institutions. Their inmate living quarters are for the most part large dormitories, with communal showers and toilets that are open to the dormitories and hallways. The Draper and Fountain penitentiaries carry on extensive farming operations, making necessary a large number of strip searches for contraband when prisoners re-enter the prison buildings.

* * * * *

The gist of the claim that the statutory height and weight requirements discriminate against women does not involve an assertion of purposeful discriminatory motive. It is asserted, rather, that these facially neutral qualification standards work in fact disproportionately to exclude women from eligibility for employment by the Alabama Board of Corrections.

* * * * *

Although women 14 years of age or older compose 52.75 percent of the Alabama population and 36.89 percent of its total labor force, they hold only 12.9 percent of its correctional counselor positions. In considering the effect of the minimum height and weight standards on this disparity in rate of hiring between the sexes, the District Court found that the 5 feet 2 inches requirement would operate to exclude 33.29 percent of the women in the United States between the ages of 18–79, while excluding only 1.28 percent of men between the same ages. The 120-pound weight restriction would exclude 22.29 percent of the women and 2.35 percent of the men in this age group. When the height and weight restrictions are combined, Alabama's statutory standards would exclude 41.13 percent of the female population while excluding less than 1 percent of the male population. Accordingly, the District Court found that Rawlinson had made out a prima facie case of unlawful sex discrimination.

The appellants argue that a showing of disproportionate impact on women based on generalized national statistics should not suffice to establish a prima facie case. They point in particular to Rawlinson's failure to adduce comparative statistics concerning actual applicants for correctional counselor positions in Alabama. There is no requirement, however, that a statistical showing of disproportionate impact must always be based on analysis of the characteristics of actual applicants.

* * * * *

For these reasons, we cannot say that the District Court was wrong in holding that the statutory height and weight standards had a discriminatory impact on women applicants. . . .

We turn, therefore, to the appellants' argument that they have rebutted the prima facie case of discrimination by showing that the height and weight requirements are job related. These requirements, they say, have a relationship to strength, a sufficient but unspecified amount of which is essential to effective job performance as a correctional counselor. In the District Court, however, the appellants produced no evidence correlating the height and weight requirements with the requisite amount of strength thought essential to good job performance. Indeed, they failed to offer evidence of any kind in specific justification of the statutory standards.

If the job-related quality that the appellants identify is bona fide, their purpose could be achieved by adopting and validating a test for applicants that measures strength directly. Such a test, fairly administered, would fully satisfy the standards of Title VII because it would be one that "measure[s] the person for the job and not the person in the abstract." . . . But nothing in the present record even approaches such a measurement.

For the reasons we have discussed, the District Court was not in error in holding that Title VII of the Civil Rights Act of 1964, as amended, prohibits application of the statutory height and weight requirements to Rawlinson and the class she represents.

* * * * *

Unlike the statutory height and weight requirements, Regulation 204 explicitly discriminates against women on the basis of their sex. In defense of this overt discrimination, the appellants rely on § 703 (e) of Title VII, which permits sex-based discrimination "in those certain instances where . . . sex . . . is a bona fide occupational qualification reasonably necessary to the normal operation of that particular business or enterprise."

The District Court rejected the bona fide occupational qualification (BFOQ) defense, relying on the virtually uniform view of the federal courts that § 703 (e) provides only the narrowest of exceptions to the general rule requiring equality of employment opportunities. . . . [T]he federal courts have agreed that it is impermissible under Title VII to refuse to hire an individual woman or man on the basis of stereotyped characterizations of the sexes, and the District Court in the present case held in effect that Regulation 204 is based on just such stereotypical assumptions.

We are persuaded—by the restrictive language of § 703 (e), the relevant legislative history, and the consistent interpretation of the Equal Employment Opportunity Commission—that the BFOQ exception was in fact meant to be an extremely narrow exception to the general prohibition of discrimination on the basis of sex. In the particular factual circumstances of this case, however, we conclude that the District Court erred in rejecting the State's contention that Regulation 204 falls within the narrow ambit of the BFOQ exception.

The environment in Alabama's penitentiaries is a peculiarly inhospitable one for human beings of whatever sex. Indeed, a federal district court has held that the conditions of confinement in the prisons of the State, characterized by "rampant violence" and a "jungle atmosphere," are constitutionally intolerable. The record in the present case shows that because of inadequate staff and facilities, no attempt is made in the four maximum-security male penitentiaries to classify or segregate inmates according to their offense or level of dangerousness—a procedure that, according to expert testimony, is essential to effective penological administration. Consequently, the estimated 20 percent of the male prisoners who are sex offenders are scattered throughout the penitentiaries' dormitory facilities.

In this environment of violence and disorganization, it would be an oversimplification to characterize Regulation 204 as an exercise in "romantic paternalism." In the usual case, the argument that a particular job is too dangerous for women may appropriately be met by the rejoinder that it is the purpose of Title VII to allow the individual woman to make that choice for herself. More is at stake in this case, however, than an individual woman's decision to weigh and accept the risks of employment in a "contact" position in a maximum-security male prison.

The essence of a correctional counselor's job is to maintain prison security. A woman's relative ability to maintain order in a male, maximum-security, unclassified penitentiary of the type Alabama now runs could be directly reduced by her womanhood. There is a basis in fact for expecting that sex offenders who have criminally assaulted women in the past would be moved to do so again if access to women were established within the prison. There would also be a real risk that other inmates, deprived of a normal heterosexual environment, would assault women guards because they were women. In a prison system where violence is the order of the day, where inmate access to guards is facilitated by dormitory living arrangements, where every institution is understaffed, and where a substantial portion of the inmate population is composed of sex offenders mixed at random with other prisoners, there are few visible deterrents to inmate assaults on women custodians.

* * * * *

There was substantial testimony from experts on both sides of this litigation that the use of women as guards in "contact" positions under the existing conditions in Alabama maximum-security male penitentiaries would pose a substantial security problem directly linked to the sex of the prison guard. On the basis of that evidence, we conclude that the District Court was in error in ruling that being male is not a bona fide occupational qualification for the job of correctional counselor in a "contact" position in an Alabama male maximum-security penitentiary.

The judgment is accordingly affirmed in part and reversed in part, and the case is remanded to the District Court. . . .

Questions

1. What evidence supported the Court's conclusion that Alabama's height requirements for prison guards constituted sex discrimination?

2. How might Alabama have strengthened its case for height and weight requirements?
3. What evidence supported the Court's view that being male was a BFOQ in this instance?
4. Would you vote with the majority or the dissent? Explain.
5. Is the majority opinion *sexist* according to your understanding of the term? Explain.
6. Can a hospital lawfully agree to patients' demands for intimate care only by those of the same sex? Explain. See *Carey* v. *New York State Human Rights App. Bd.*, 61 A.D. 2d 804, 402 N.Y.S. 2d 207 (1978).
7. How might an airline justify a policy forbidding the assignment of pregnant flight attendants to flight duty? Is such a policy lawful? Explain. See *Condit* v. *United Airlines, Inc.*, 558 F.2d 1176 (4th Cir. 1977), cert. denied 435 U.S. 934 (1978). Compare *Burwell* v. *Eastern Air Lines, Inc.*, CA4, 1980, 23 FEP Cases 949.
8. The Southern Pacific railroad denied employment as an agent-telegrapher to Rosenfeld, a woman. The railroad cited hard work (some 80-hour weeks and some lifting of 50 pounds or more) and California labor laws restricting hours of work and weights to be lifted by women.
   a. Is sex a BFOQ under these facts? Explain.
   b. Does the California statute govern this situation? Explain.
   c. The *Rosenfeld* court articulated the following very narrow test of those circumstances under which sex is a legitimate BFOQ: "sexual characteristics, rather than characteristics that might, to one degree or another, correlate with a particular sex, must be the basis for the application of the BFOQ exception." Explain the court's test and offer an example of a job wherein sex would clearly constitute a BFOQ. See *Rosenfeld* v. *Southern Pacific Co.*, 444 F.2d 1219 (1971).

SEXUAL HARASSMENT

Sexual harassment has been the subject of extensive publicity and litigation in recent years. In 1980 the EEOC issued guidelines on sexual harassment providing that:

> Unwelcome sexual advances, requests for sexual favors, and other verbal or physical conduct of a sexual nature constitute sexual harassment when (1) submission to such conduct is made either explicitly or implicitly a term or condition of an individual's employment, (2) submission to or rejection of such conduct by an individual is used as the basis for employment decisions affecting such individual, or (3) such conduct has the purpose or effect of unreasonably interfering with an individual's work performance or creating an intimidating, hostile, or offensive working environment.

Recall that the guidelines do not have the force of law, but the courts tend to accord them considerable respect. Court decisions to this point are generally consistent with the guidelines.

Sexual harassment claims under Title VII may be supplemented by various civil and criminal actions. For example, assault, battery, breach of contract, and criminal assault are all possibilities, depending on the circumstances.

Apparently many businesspeople are extremely skeptical regarding the seriousness and magnitude of the sexual harassment problem:

> "This entire subject is a perfect example of a minor special interest group's ability to blow up any 'issue' to a level of importance which in no way relates to the reality of the world in which we live and work"—A 38-year-old plant manager (male) for a large manufacturer of industrial goods.[56]

A *Redbook–Harvard Business Review* survey of *HBR* subscribers found that nearly two thirds of the men and about half of the women agreed (or partially agreed) with the statement that "The amount of sexual harassment at work is greatly exaggerated."[57] However, survey evidence suggests that behavior taken to be sexual harassment is common. For example, in a 1988 survey of federal employees, 42 percent of the women surveyed said they had experienced such harassment during the previous two years; this is the same percentage as was reported in a similar survey in 1981.[58] And 49 percent of the United Nations' female employees surveyed felt sexual pressure on the job,[59] while a 1985 study of working adults found over half of them believed they had been harassed.[60] In another survey, 6 out of 10 responding companies reported that the most common form of harassment is comments, innuendoes, and jokes of a sexual nature.[61]

In less than a decade feminists, civil rights activists, and lawyers in particular (and the changing nature of the work force in general) have been successful in attaching credibility and legal sanction to a problem previously unrecognized, scorned, or ridiculed. The movement is interesting testimony to America's vices and virtues, as well as to the power of commitment. The citizenry is taking this rather striking metamorphosis in stride and, indeed, with admirable wit. Some "unforgettable quotes" from the *Redbook–HBR survey:*

> "My department is financial, rather staid. The creative side of the business might well be rife with cases of sexual harassment." (female)
>
> "I married a subordinate. I believe there was no coercion involved." (male)
>
> "Have not had any experience in this area. Too busy working." (male)
>
> "I have never been harassed but I would welcome the opportunity." (anonymous)[62]

The following Supreme Court case reveals firm judicial approval of sexual harassment as sex discrimination but leaves important questions unresolved.

MERITOR SAVINGS BANK V. VINSON
91 L Ed 2d 49 (1986)

Justice Rehnquist

I

In 1974, respondent Mechelle Vinson met Sidney Taylor, a vice president of what is now petitioner Meritor Savings Bank (the bank) and manager of one of its branch offices. When respondent asked whether she might obtain employment at the bank, Taylor gave her an application, which she completed and returned the next day; later that same day Taylor called her to say that she had been hired. With Taylor as her supervisor, respondent started as a teller-trainee, and thereafter was promoted to teller, head teller, and assistant branch manager. She worked at the same branch for four years, and it is undisputed that her advancement there was based on merit alone. In September 1978, respondent notified Taylor that she was taking sick leave for an indefinite period. On November 1, 1978, the bank discharged her for excessive use of that leave.

Respondent brought this action against Taylor and the bank, claiming that during her four years at the bank she had "constantly been subjected to sexual harassment" by Taylor in violation of Title VII. She sought injunctive relief, compensatory and punitive damages against Taylor and the bank, and attorney's fees.

At the 11-day bench trial, the parties presented conflicting testimony about Taylor's behavior during respondent's employment. Respondent testified that during her probationary period as a teller-trainee, Taylor treated her in a fatherly way and made no sexual advances. Shortly thereafter, however, he invited her out to dinner and, during the course of the meal, suggested that they go to a motel to have sexual relations. At first she refused, but out of what she described as fear of losing her job she eventually agreed. According to respondent, Taylor thereafter made repeated demands upon her for sexual favors, usually at the branch, both during and after business hours; she estimated that over the next several years she had intercourse with him some 40 or 50 times. In addition, respondent testified that Taylor fondled her in front of other employees, followed her into the women's restroom when she went there alone, exposed himself to her, and even forcibly raped her on several occasions. These activities ceased after 1977, respondent stated, when she started going with a steady boyfriend.

Respondent also testified that Taylor touched and fondled other women employees of the bank, and she attempted to call witnesses to support this charge. But while some supporting testimony apparently was admitted without objection, the District Court did not allow her "to present wholesale evidence of a pattern and practice relating to sexual advances to other female employees in her case in chief, but advised her that she might well be able to present such evidence in rebuttal to the defendants' cases." Respondent did not offer such evidence in rebuttal. Finally, respondent testified that because she was afraid of Taylor she never reported his harassment to any of his supervisors and never attempted to use the bank's complaint procedure.

Taylor denied respondent's allegations of sexual activity, testifying that he never fondled her, never made suggestive remarks to her, never engaged in sexual intercourse with her and never asked her to do so. He contended instead that respondent made her accusations in response to a business-related dispute. The bank also denied respondent's allegations and asserted that any sexual harassment by Taylor was unknown to the bank and engaged in without its consent or approval.

The District Court denied relief, but did not resolve the conflicting testimony about the existence of a sexual relationship between respondent and Taylor. It found instead that

If [respondent] and Taylor did engage in an intimate or sexual relationship during the time of [respondent's] employment with [the bank], that relationship was a voluntary one having nothing to do with her continued employment at [the bank] or her advancement or promotions at that institution.

The court ultimately found that respondent "was not the victim of sexual harassment and was not the victim of sexual discrimination" while employed at the bank.

Although it concluded that respondent had not proved a violation of Title VII, the District Court nevertheless went on to address the bank's liability. After noting the bank's express policy against discrimination, and finding that neither respondent nor any other employee had ever lodged a complaint about sexual harassment by Taylor, the court ultimately concluded that "the bank was without notice and cannot be held liable for the alleged actions of Taylor."

The Court of Appeals for the District of Columbia Circuit reversed. . . .

Respondent argues, and the Court of Appeals held, that unwelcome sexual advances that create an offensive or hostile working environment violate Title VII. Without question, when a supervisor sexually harasses a subordinate because of the subordinate's sex, that supervisor "discriminate[s]" on the basis of sex. Petitioner apparently does not challenge this proposition. It contends instead that in prohibiting discrimination with respect to "compensation, terms, conditions, or privileges" of employment, Congress was concerned with what petitioner describes as "tangible loss" of "an economic character," not "purely psychological aspects of the workplace environment." . . .

We reject petitioner's view. First, the language of Title VII is not limited to "economic" or "tangible" discrimination. The phrase "terms, conditions, or privileges of employment" evinces a congressional intent " 'to strike at the entire spectrum of disparate treatment of men and women' " in employment.

Second, . . . the EEOC guidelines fully support the view that harassment leading to noneconomic injury can violate Title VII.

In defining "sexual harassment," the guidelines first describe the kinds of workplace conduct that may be actionable under Title VII. These include "[u]nwelcome sexual advances, requests for sexual favors, and other verbal or physical conduct of a sexual nature." Relevant to the charges at issue in this case, the guidelines provide that such sexual misconduct constitutes prohibited "sexual harassment," whether or not it is directly linked to the grant or denial of an economic quid pro quo, where "such conduct has the purpose or effect of unreasonably interfering with an individual's work performance or creating an intimidating, hostile, or offensive working environment."

* * * * *

Since the guidelines were issued, courts have uniformly held, and we agree, that a plaintiff may establish a violation of Title VII by proving that discrimination based on sex has created a hostile or abusive work environment.

* * * * *

Of course, not all workplace conduct that may be described as "harassment" affects a "term, condition, or privilege" of employment within the meaning of Title VII. . . . For sexual harassment to be actionable, it must be sufficiently severe or pervasive "to alter the conditions of [the victim's] employment and create an abusive working environment." Respondent's allegations in this case—which include not only pervasive harassment but also criminal conduct of the most serious nature—are plainly sufficient to state a claim for "hostile environment" sexual harassment.

The question remains, however, whether the District Court's ultimate finding that respondent "was not the victim of sexual harassment" effectively disposed of respondent's claim. The Court of Appeals recognized, we think correctly, that this ultimate finding was likely based on one or both of two erroneous views of the law. First, the District Court apparently believed that a claim for sexual harassment will not lie absent an *economic* effect on the complainant's employment. . . . Since it appears that the District Court made its findings without ever considering the "hostile environment" theory of sexual harassment, the Court of Appeals' decision to remand was correct.

Second, the District Court's conclusion that no actionable harassment occurred might have rested on its earlier "finding" that "[i]f [respondent] and Taylor did engage in an intimate or sexual relationship . . . , that relationship was a voluntary one." But the fact that sex-related conduct was "voluntary," in the sense that the complainant was not forced to participate against her will, is not a defense to a sexual harassment suit brought under Title VII. The gravamen of any sexual harassment claim is that the alleged sexual advances were "unwelcome." While the question whether particular conduct was indeed unwelcome presents difficult problems of proof and turns largely on credibility determinations committed to the trier of fact, the District Court in this case erroneously focused on the "voluntariness" of respondent's participation in the claimed sexual episodes. The correct inquiry is whether respondent by her conduct indicated that the alleged sexual advances were unwelcome, not whether her actual participation in sexual intercourse was voluntary.

Petitioner contends that even if this case must be remanded to the District Court, the Court of Appeals erred in one of the terms of its remand. Specifically, the Court of Appeals stated that testimony about respondent's "dress and personal fantasies," which the District Court apparently admitted into evidence, "had no place in this litigation." The apparent ground for this conclusion was that respondent's voluntariness vel non in submitting to Taylor's advances was immaterial to her sexual harassment claim. While "voluntariness" in the sense of consent is not a defense to such a claim, it does not follow that a complainant's sexually provocative speech or dress is irrelevant as a matter of law in determining whether he or she found particular sexual advances unwelcome. To the contrary, such evidence is obviously relevant. The EEOC guidelines emphasize that the trier of fact must determine the existence of sexual harassment in light of "the record as a whole" and "the totality of circumstances, such as the nature of the sexual advances and the context in which the alleged incidents occurred." . . .

III

Although the District Court concluded that respondent had not proved a violation of Title VII, it nevertheless went on to consider the question of the bank's liability. Finding that "the bank was without notice" of Taylor's alleged conduct, and that notice to Taylor was not the equivalent of notice to the bank, the court concluded that the bank therefore could not be held liable for Taylor's alleged actions. The Court of Appeals took the opposite view, holding that an employer is strictly liable for a hostile environment created by a supervisor's sexual advances, even though the employer neither knew nor reasonably could have known of the alleged misconduct. The court held that a supervisor, whether or not he possesses the authority to hire, fire, or promote, is necessarily an "agent" of his employer for all Title VII purposes, since "even the appearance" of such authority may enable him to impose himself on his subordinates.

The parties and amici suggest several different standards for employer liability. Respondent, not surprisingly, defends the position of the Court of Appeals. Noting that Title VII's definition of "employer" includes any "agent" of the employer, she also argues that "so long as the circumstance is work-related, the supervisor is the employer and the employer is the supervisor." Notice to Taylor that the advances were unwelcome, therefore, was notice to the bank.

Petitioner argues that respondent's failure to use its established grievance procedure, or to otherwise put it on notice of the alleged misconduct, insulates petitioner from liability for Taylor's wrongdoing. A contrary rule would be unfair, petitioner argues, since in a hostile environment harassment case the employer often will have no reason to know about, or opportunity to cure, the alleged wrongdoing.

The EEOC . . . contends that courts formulating employer liability rules should draw from traditional agency principles. Examination of those principles has led the EEOC to the view that where a supervisor exercises the authority actually delegated to him by his employer, by making or threatening to make decisions affecting the employment status of his subordinates, such actions are properly imputed to the employer whose delegation of authority empowered the supervisor to undertake them. Thus, the courts have consistently held employers liable for the discriminatory discharges of employees by supervisory personnel, whether or not the employer knew, should have known, or approved of the supervisor's actions.

* * * * *

This debate over the appropriate standard for employer liability has a rather abstract quality about it given the state of the record in this case. We do not know at this stage whether Taylor made any sexual advances toward respondent at all, let alone whether those advances were unwelcome, whether they were sufficiently pervasive to constitute a condition of employment, or whether they were "so pervasive and so long continuing . . . that the employer must have become conscious of [them]," . . .

We therefore decline the parties' invitation to issue a definitive rule on employer liability, but we do agree with the EEOC that Congress wanted courts to look to agency principles for guidance in this area. While such common-law principles may not be transferable in all their particulars to Title VII, Congress' decision to define "employer" to include any "agent" of an employer surely evinces an intent to place some limits on the acts of employees for which employers under Title VII are to be held responsible. For this reason, we hold that the Court of Appeals erred in concluding that employers are always automatically liable for sexual harassment by their supervisors. For the same reason, absence of notice to an employer does not necessarily insulate that employer from liability.

Finally, we reject petitioner's view that the mere existence of a grievance procedure and a policy against discrimination, coupled with respondent's failure to invoke that procedure, must insulate petitioner from liability. While those facts are plainly relevant, the situation before us demonstrates why they are not necessarily dispositive. Petitioner's general non-discrimination policy did not address sexual harassment in particular, and thus did not alert employees to their employer's interest in correcting that form of discrimination. Moreover, the bank's grievance procedure apparently required an employee to complain first to her supervisor, in this case Taylor. Since Taylor was the alleged perpetrator, it is not altogether surprising that respondent failed to invoke the procedure and report her grievance to him. Petitioner's contention that respondent's failure should insulate it from liability might be substantially stronger if its procedures were better calculated to encourage victims of harassment to come forward.

IV

In sum, we hold that a claim of "hostile environment" sex discrimination is actionable under Title VII, that the District Court's findings were insufficient to dispose of respondent's hostile environment claim, and that the District Court did not err in admitting testimony about respondent's sexually provocative speech and dress. As to employer liability, we conclude that the Court of Appeals was wrong to entirely disregard agency principles and impose absolute liability on employers for the acts of their supervisors, regardless of the circumstances of a particular case.

Affirmed.

Questions

1. Distinguish between "quid pro quo" sexual harassment and "environmental" sexual harassment.
2. Explain the *Meritor* court's reasoning in rejecting voluntariness as an issue in the case and concluding that the proper inquiry was whether the employee regarded the sexual advance as "welcome or unwelcome."
3. Based on the *Meritor* decision, is an employer liable for sexual harassment on the part of its supervisors? Explain.
4. Could an employer successfully defend against a female employee's claim of a hostile work environment (e.g., male supervisors regularly questioning female subordinates about their sexual activities and preferences) by offering testimony from other female employees that they are untroubled by the conduct? See *Morgan* v. *Hertz Corp.*, 27 FEP 990 (W.D. Tenn. 1981) as reported in Vern E. Hauck and Thomas G. Pearce, "*Vinson:* Sexual Harassment and Employer Response," *Labor Law Journal* 38, no. 12 (December 1987), pp. 770, 772.
5. Soon after her employment in the federal Environmental Protection Agency, a black woman, Paulette Barnes, was allegedly the subject of social and sexual advances from her supervisor (not the defendant and appellee in the case). Despite firm refusals, the supervisor is alleged to have repeatedly sought her company after working hours and

suggested on numerous occasions that her employment status would be enhanced were she to engage in a sexual relationship with him. She had made clear her insistence on a purely professional relationship. Then, according to Barnes, her supervisor and other administrators began a program of harassment, including taking many duties from her. Ultimately her job was abolished in apparent retaliation for her resistance to the unwanted advances. She then filed a complaint with the EEOC.

Decide. Explain. See *Barnes* v. *Costle,* 561 F.2d 983 (D.C. Cir. 1977). (Costle was an administrator of the Environmental Protection Agency and was a litigant in this case solely by reason of his official position.)

EQUAL PAY

Title VII affords broad protection from discrimination in pay because of sex. The Equal Pay Act of 1963 directly forbids discrimination on the basis of sex by paying wages to employees of one sex at a rate less than the rate paid to employees of the opposite sex for equal work on jobs requiring equal skill, effort, and responsibility and performed under similar working conditions (*equal* has been interpreted to mean "substantially equal").[63] The act provides for certain exceptions. Unequal wage payments are lawful if paid pursuant to (*a*) a seniority system; (*b*) a merit system; (*c*) a system that measures earnings by quantity or quality of production; or (*d*) a differential based on "any other factor other than sex."[64] Thus if the plaintiff builds a prima facie case based on the statute's prohibitions, the defendant must then assume the burden of asserting and proving one or more of the specified defenses. Typically, those discriminated against can recover "back wages" in a sum equal to the amount of pay discrimination. The employee may also secure "liquidated damages" to penalize the employer.[65] The employer seeking to avoid a violation of the Equal Pay Act can adjust its wage structure by raising the pay of the disfavored sex. Lowering the pay of the favored sex violates the act.

Paying women and men the same amount for the same work is simple enough in principle, but the legal issues have proved slippery, indeed. For example:

1. Is travel reimbursement a "wage"? Maternity payments?[66]
2. Must the plaintiff establish a *pattern* of sex-based wage discrimination?[67]
3. Are jobs unequal in effort and thus "unequal work" when a part of one job includes tasks that females are physically unable to perform?[68]

In the leading case of *Corning Glass Works* v. *Brennan*[69] the Supreme Court was faced with the question of whether different shifts constituted differing "working conditions." Women had been engaged in glass inspection on the day shift. Corning added a night shift of inspectors, which, due to state "protective" laws, was composed entirely of males. The night shift demanded and received higher wages than the female day inspectors. The Supreme Court held that the time of day in and of itself is not a *working condition*. That term, the Court said, refers to "surroundings" and "hazards." However, shift differentials could lawfully constitute a "factor other than sex" if established by the employer.

COMPARABLE WORTH

Equal pay for equal work is hardly a radical notion, but equal pay for work of comparable value will, if fully realized, dramatically alter the nature of the American labor market. *Comparable worth* calls for determining the compensation to be paid for a position based on the job's intrinsic value in comparison to wages being paid for other jobs requiring comparable skills, effort, and responsibility and having comparable worth to the organization.

The argument is that the dollar value assigned to jobs held predominantly by men is higher than the value assigned to jobs held predominantly by women. To proponents of comparable worth, such disparities cannot be explained by market forces. They argue that women are the continuing victims of sex discrimination in violation of Title VII of the Civil Rights Act of 1964.

A variety of studies have contrasted pay scales in traditionally female jobs with those in traditionally male jobs where the jobs are judged to be of "comparable worth." For example, licensed practical nurses in Illinois in 1983 earned an average of $1,298 per month, while electricians earned an average of $2,826.[70] Typing pool supervisors in Minnesota earned an average of $1,373 per month, while painters averaged $1,707.[71] A Child Welfare League study of 50 occupations found those who care for children rank near the bottom of salary scales. The 1987 league study fixed the median salary of garbage collectors at $14,872 annually, as compared with $12,800 for child care workers.[72] The same study found social workers with master's degrees earned about $21,800 per year, while auto salespeople averaged $22,048.[73]

Women have been the victims of discrimination in the employment market. Is comparable worth a just and workable remedy? According to the National Committee on Pay Equity, 20 states have appropriated money specifically to address pay imbalances attributed to sex or race.[74] The cost of doing so has averaged from 2 to 5 percent of the states' payroll budgets.[75] And *Business Week* reports that a number of major American firms (including AT&T, BankAmerica, and IBM) have "very quietly" begun to experiment with comparable worth.[76] However, opponents believe the market remains the best and fairest method of determining worth.

They argue that we cannot accurately compare fundamentally dissimilar jobs to reach an objective determination of the skills required and the worth of each job. Furthermore, those opponents question the wisdom of establishing the bureaucracy necessary to administer comparable worth programs. Of course, to comparable worth advocates, government intervention is the only possible tactic for combating males' continuing domination of the market.

The U.S. Supreme Court has yet to directly explore the substance of the comparable worth debate. In the *Gunther*[77] case the Court held, in effect, that Title VII does not forbid the comparable worth theory. However, the leading cases (*Spaulding* v. *The University of Washington*[78] and *American Federation of State, County, and Municipal Employees* v. *Washington*[79]) squarely addressing the total question resulted in considerable setbacks for comparable worth supporters. In *Spaulding,* nursing faculty members at the University of Washington filed suit, claiming the university engaged in discriminatory compensation practices in violation of the Equal Pay Act and Title VII. The equal pay claim was based on data showing that faculty salaries in nursing (positions primarily occupied by women) were lower than faculty salaries in "comparable" departments (health services, social work, architecture, speech and hearing, and pharmacy practice) where the faculty members were primarily male. The Ninth Circuit Court of Appeals rejected that equal pay claim by finding that the plaintiffs failed to show that they performed work substantially equal to that performed by males in other departments. The court noted that attention to research, training, and community service varied widely from department to department.

Turning to the heart of the comparable worth claim, the court addressed the question of "whether the disparate impact model is available to plaintiffs who . . . make a broad-ranging sex-based claim of wage discrimination based upon comparable worth." The nurses sought to demonstrate a disparate impact by showing a wage disparity between comparable jobs. Then, following the reasoning of *Griggs* and other cases, the plaintiffs sought to demonstrate that the disparate impact was a product of the "facially neutral policy or practice" of the university in setting wages according to market prices. That is, the plaintiffs claimed that following market prices was a nonjob-related pretext to hide discrimination (just as height, weight, intelligence tests, and the like had served as a pretext to hide discrimination in other cases). The court rejected that reasoning in finding that reliance on market prices is not a "facially neutral policy or practice." In so doing, the court clearly recognized the market's role in setting wages.

> Every employer constrained by market forces must consider market values in setting his labor costs. Naturally, market prices are inherently job related, although the market may embody social judgments as to the worth of some jobs. Employers relying on the market are, to that extent, "price-takers." They deal

with the market as a given and do not meaningfully have a "policy" about it in the relevant Title VII sense.[80]

In sum, the court rejected the comparable worth theory as raised by the nursing faculty in the context of Title VII. The U.S. Supreme Court later declined to review the *Spaulding* decision. Nonetheless, the state of Washington has voluntarily agreed to a comparable worth plan for its employees that promises to eliminate pay disparities based on race or sex by 1992 by providing salary increases of at least 2.5 percent for the disadvantaged employees at a reported total cost of $482 million.[81]

In your opinion, is male dominance of many job markets a product of discrimination? If so, should the comparable worth theory be employed to correct the resulting wage disparities?

Sexual Stereotypes

Ann B. Hopkins, a Price Waterhouse manager, was hoping in 1982 to be promoted to partner. She had earned at least $34 million in consulting contracts for the firm, a record exceeding that of the 87 other candidates for partner—all of whom were male. Despite her success, Hopkins was denied partnership. She left the firm and filed a sex discrimination claim. The firm says she was an "overbearing, arrogant, and abrasive manager."[82] She argued that her occasional cursing and her sometimes brusque manner would have been overlooked had she been a male. At trial, she introduced the partners' written evaluations, which included such words and phrases as "macho," "lady partner," and "charm school." One mentioned that "she may have overcompensated for being a woman." Hopkins testified that a chief partner suggested she wear makeup, have her hair styled, walk more femininely, talk more femininely, and so on. Based on that evidence and expert testimony, Hopkins claimed she was a victim of sexual stereotyping. The firm offered evidence in support of its contention that Hopkins' personality and interpersonal skills were the issue in the case. One consultant said he left the firm in part because of what he perceived to be the difficulty in working with Hopkins, whom he accused of once "screaming obscenities over the phone at him for 'up to' 45 minutes."[83]

Hopkins won at the district court level, where the court found that Price Waterhouse was guilty of sex discrimination by "filtering her partnership candidacy through a system that gave great weight to negative comments and recommendations, despite evidence that those comments reflected unconscious sexual stereotyping by male evaluators based on outmoded attitudes toward women."[84] The court noted that interpersonal problems can constitute a legitimate reason for denying partnership, but the court felt the "evident sexism" in the Price Waterhouse evaluation system had "tainted" the decision making. The District of Columbia Court of Appeals affirmed, finding "ample support for the district court's finding that the partnership selection process was impermissibly infected by stereotypical attitudes toward women."[85] The court went on to hold that Price Waterhouse had to show that bias as a consequence of sexual stereotyping was not the decisive factor in the decision to deny promotion.

At this writing in 1988, the case is at the U.S. Supreme Court, which is expected to hand down its decision in 1989. How would you rule on this claim of sexual stereotyping as sex discrimination?

Part Four—Religious Discrimination

In general terms, discrimination on the basis of religion is to be analyzed in the manner of the other protected classes specified by Title VII. "Religion" is not limited to orthodox faiths, but it does exclude mere shams designed to legitimize otherwise impermissible conduct. The Supreme Court has defined the necessary faith as a "sincere and meaningful belief occupying in the life of its possessor a place parallel to that filled by the God of those admittedly qualified."[86]

Absent an appropriate defense (for example, BFOQ), an employer, of course, cannot decline to hire or otherwise discriminate against an individual or group on the grounds of religion. The plaintiff's problem in such cases is to offer proof that religious bias was the motivation for the disputed employment practice. Discrimination on the grounds of religion is permissible if "an employer demonstrates that he is unable to reasonably accommodate an employee's or prospective employee's religious observance or practice without undue hardship on the conduct of the employer's business." Thus the primary issue in the area of religious discrimination has come to be that of determining "reasonable accommodation" in varying factual settings.

The leading case is *Trans World Airlines, Inc.* v. *Hardison*[87], in which the sabbitarian plaintiff worked in a parts warehouse that operated around the clock, seven days a week. Because of a transfer Hardison was at the bottom of the departmental seniority list and was unable to take his Sabbath off. The company conferred with Hardison and permitted the union to seek a swap of shifts or a change in jobs, but the efforts were unsuccessful. A seniority modification could not be agreed on, and the company rejected Hardison's request for a four-day week because the solution would have required the use of another employee at premium pay. The Supreme Court's opinion in the case reduced the employer's duty to a very modest standard: "To require TWA to bear more than a de minimis cost in order to give Hardison Saturdays off is an undue hardship." Saturdays off for Hardison would have imposed extra costs on TWA and would have constituted religious discrimination against other employees who would have sought Saturday off for reasons not grounded in religion. The *Hardison* court also took the position that the collective bargaining agreement's seniority provisions need not give way to accommodate religious observance. The Court found sufficient accommodation in TWA's reducing weekend shift sizes and allowing the voluntary trading of shifts.

Court decisions subsequent to *Hardison* are adding insight to that ruling. For example, in *Ansonia Board of Education* v. *Philbrook*,[88] the Supreme Court made it clear that an employer is not compelled to accept an employee's preferred arrangement among a range of reasonable accommodations. That is, any reasonable accommodation, even if it is not the employee's first choice, is sufficient to meet the employer's responsibility.

Part Five—Affirmative Action

Affirmative action is a policy under which employers take positive steps to increase female and minority employment in an effort to overcome the effects of past discrimination. Title VII and other measures discussed in this chapter, while meeting with initial resistance, have enjoyed marked success as vehicles for preventing future employment discrimination. However, the mere abandonment of discriminatory policies would not eradicate the lingering penalties of two centuries of bias. In consequence, a series of federal policies and judicial decisions have combined to create an affirmative action standard for the nation's employers.

Employers who are government contractors must meet the affirmative action expectations of the Office of Federal Contract Compliance Programs. As discussed above, those expectations consist essentially of established goals and timetables for strengthening the representation of "underutilized" minorities and women.

A heavy preponderance of judicial decisions to date have supported the general policy of affirmative action, but the specific details of some programs have been struck down. For example, in the famous *Bakke*[89] case (where the medical school at the University of California at Davis had reserved a minimum number of places in each entering class for racial minorities), the U.S. Supreme Court upheld the claim of the petitioner, a white male. Bakke argued that he had been the victim of "reverse discrimination" in that he had better "paper" credentials than a number of students admitted under the "quota" system. The ruling appeared to forbid quotas while permitting consideration of race as a factor in affirmative action plans designed to redress past discrimination. (But see *Paradise*, p. 645.)

United Steelworkers of America v. *Weber*, 99 S. Ct. 2721 (1979), is the Supreme Court's definitive statement to date in this sensitive and contentious area. Weber, a white male, challenged the legality of an affirmative action plan that set aside for black employees 50 percent of the openings in a training program until the percentage of black craft workers in the plant equaled the percentage of blacks in the local labor market. The plan was the product of a collective bargaining agreement between the Steelworkers and Kaiser Aluminum and Chemical. In Kaiser's Grammercy, Louisiana, plant only 5 of 273 skilled craft workers were black, while the local work force was approximately 39 percent black. In the first year of the affirmative action plan, seven blacks and six whites were admitted to the craft training program. The most junior black employee accepted for the program had less seniority than several white employees who were not accepted. Weber was among the white males denied entry to the training program.

Weber filed suit, claiming Title VII forbade an affirmative action plan that granted a racial preference to blacks when there was no proof of discrimination but when whites dramatically exceeded blacks in skilled craft positions. The federal district court and the federal court of appeals held for Weber, but the U.S. Supreme Court reversed. Therefore, under *Weber,* race-conscious affirmative action remedies may be permissible. The Court was careful to not precisely detail those characteristics that would describe a lawful affirmative action plan. However, several qualities of the Steelworkers' plan were instrumental in the Court's favorable ruling:

1. The affirmative action was part of a *plan*.
2. The plan was designed to "open employment opportunities for Negroes in occupations which have been traditionally closed to them."
3. The plan was temporary.
4. The plan did not unnecessarily harm the rights of white employees. That is—
   a. The plan did not require the discharge of white employees.
   b. The plan did not create an absolute bar to the advancement of white employees.

Therefore, affirmative action in situations like that in *Weber* does not constitute unlawful reverse discrimination.

The Supreme Court clarified the law's affirmative action commands a bit further in the *Burdine* case, in which the Court asserted that Title VII does not require the employer to hire a minority or female applicant whenever that person's objective qualifications were equal to those of a white male applicant. Therefore, "the employer has discretion to choose among equally qualified candidates, provided the decision is not based upon unlawful criteria."[90]

In sum, we now have a substantial degree of clarity in the affirmative action area. As a result of recent decisions, we know that employers and labor unions have little fear of reverse discrimination lawsuits where they voluntarily seek to erase discrimination by undertaking properly drawn affirmative action strategies. And we know that those strategies, if properly and narrowly defined to achieve a lawful purpose (see the *Weber* standards), are enforceable even though the individuals who benefit were not themselves actual victims of discrimination. However, the Supreme Court decisions have been badly split, and the Reagan administration, at this writing in 1988, continues to take the position that racial preferences and numerical goals are impermissible and race-conscious remedies must be directed only to identified victims of discrimination. Nonetheless, affirmative action in principle is clearly the law of the land. Decisions to come will fill in more details about when affirmative action is appropriate and what remedies are permissible. The case that follows explores the application of affirmative action to sex discrimination.

JOHNSON V. TRANSPORTATION AGENCY
94 L Ed 2d 615 (1987)

Justice Brennan

Respondent, Transportation Agency of Santa Clara County, California, unilaterally promulgated an Affirmative Action Plan applicable, inter alia, to promotions of employees. In selecting applicants for the promotional position of road dispatcher, the Agency, pursuant to the Plan, passed over petitioner Paul Johnson, a male employee, and promoted a female employee applicant, Diane Joyce. The question for decision is whether in making the promotion the Agency impermissibly took into account the sex of the applicants in violation of Title VII of the Civil Rights Act of 1964. The District Court for the Northern District of California . . . held that respondent had violated Title VII. The Court of Appeals for the Ninth Circuit reversed. We granted certiorari.

I

A

In December 1978, the Santa Clara County Transit District Board of Supervisors adopted an Affirmative Action Plan (Plan) for the County Transportation Agency. The Plan implemented a County Affirmative Action Plan, which had been adopted, declared the County, because ''mere prohibition of discriminatory practices is not enough to remedy the effects of past practices and to permit attainment of an equitable representation of minorities, women and handicapped persons.'' Relevant to this case, the Agency Plan provides that, in making promotions to positions within a traditionally segregated job classification in which women have been significantly underrepresented, the Agency is authorized to consider as one factor the sex of a qualified applicant.

* * * * *

The Agency stated that its Plan was intended to achieve "a statistically measurable yearly improvement in hiring, training and promotion of minorities and women throughout the Agency in all major job classifications where they are underrepresented." As a benchmark by which to evaluate progress, the Agency stated that its long-term goal was to attain a work force whose composition reflected the proportion of minorities and women in the area labor force. Thus, for the Skilled Craft category in which the road dispatcher position at issue here was classified, the Agency's aspiration was that eventually about 36 percent of the jobs would be occupied by women.

The Plan acknowledged that a number of factors might make it unrealistic to rely on the Agency's long-term goals in evaluating the Agency's progress in expanding job opportunities for minorities and women. Among the factors identified were low turnover rates in some classifications, the fact that some jobs involved heavy labor, the small number of positions within some job categories, the limited number of entry positions leading to the Technical and Skilled Craft classifications, and the limited number of minorities and women qualified for positions requiring specialized training and experience. . . .

The Agency's Plan . . . set aside no specific number of positions for minorities or women, but authorized the consideration of ethnicity or sex as a factor when evaluating qualified candidates for jobs in which members of such groups were poorly represented. One such job was the road dispatcher position that is the subject of the dispute in this case.

B

On December 12, 1979, the Agency announced a vacancy for the promotional position of road dispatcher in the Agency's Roads Division. Dispatchers assign road crews, equipment, and materials, and maintain records pertaining to road maintenance jobs. The position requires at minimum four years of dispatch or road maintenance work experience for Santa Clara County. The EEOC job classification scheme designates a road dispatcher as a Skilled Craft worker.

Twelve County employees applied for the promotion, including Joyce and Johnson. Joyce had worked for the County since 1970, serving as an account clerk until 1975. She had applied for a road dispatcher position in 1974, but was deemed ineligible because she had not served as a road maintenance worker. In 1975, Joyce transferred from a senior account clerk position to a road maintenance worker position, becoming the first woman to fill such a job. During her four years in that position, she occasionally worked out of class as a road dispatcher.

Petitioner Johnson began with the county in 1967 as a road yard clerk, after private employment that included working as a supervisor and dispatcher. He had also unsuccessfully applied for the road dispatcher opening in 1974. In 1977, his clerical position was downgraded, and he sought and received a transfer to the position of road maintenance worker. He also occasionally worked out of class as a dispatcher while performing that job.

Nine of the applicants, including Joyce and Johnson, were deemed qualified for the job, and were interviewed by a two-person board. Seven of the applicants scored above 70 on this interview, which meant that they were certified as eligible for selection by the appointing authority. The scores awarded ranged from 70 to 80. Johnson was tied for second with a score of 75, while Joyce ranked next with a score of 73. A second interview was conducted by three Agency supervisors, who ultimately recommended that Johnson be promoted. Prior to the second interview, Joyce had contacted the County's Affirmative

Action Office because she feared that her application might not receive disinterested review. The Office in turn contacted the Agency's Affirmative Action Coordinator, whom the Agency's Plan makes responsible for keeping the Director informed of opportunities for the Agency to accomplish its objectives under the Plan. At the time, the Agency employed no women in any Skilled Craft position, and had never employed a woman as a road dispatcher. The Coordinator recommended to the Director of the Agency, James Graebner, that Joyce be promoted.

Graebner, authorized to choose any of the seven persons deemed eligible, thus had the benefit of suggestions by the second interview panel and by the Agency Coordinator in arriving at his decision. After deliberation, Graebner concluded that the promotion should be given to Joyce. As he testified: "I tried to look at the whole picture, the combination of her qualifications and Mr. Johnson's qualifications, their test scores, their expertise, their background, affirmative action matters, things like that . . . I believe it was a combination of all those."

The certification form naming Joyce as the person promoted to the dispatcher position stated that both she and Johnson were rated as well-qualified for the job. The evaluation of Joyce read: "Well qualified by virtue of 18 years of past clerical experience including 3½ years at West Yard plus almost 5 years as a [road maintenance worker]." The evaluation of Johnson was as follows: "Well qualified applicant; two years of [road maintenance worker] experience plus 11 years of Road Yard Clerk. Has had previous outside Dispatch experience but was 13 years ago." Graebner testified that he did not regard as significant the fact that Johnson scored 75 and Joyce 73 when interviewed by the two-person board.

Petitioner Johnson filed a complaint with the EEOC alleging that he had been denied promotion on the basis of sex in violation of Title VII. He received a right-to-sue letter from the agency on March 10, 1981, and on March 20, 1981, filed suit in the United States District Court for the Northern District of California. The District Court found that Johnson was more qualified for the dispatcher position than Joyce, and that the sex of Joyce was the *"determining factor* in her selection." The court acknowledged that, since the Agency justified its decision on the basis of its Affirmative Action Plan, the criteria announced in *Steelworkers* v. *Weber* should be applied in evaluating the validity of the plan. It then found the Agency's Plan invalid on the ground that the evidence did not satisfy *Weber's* criterion that the Plan be temporary. The Court of Appeals for the Ninth Circuit reversed, holding that the absence of an express termination date in the Plan was not dispositive, since the Plan repeatedly expressed its objective as the attainment, rather than the maintenance, of a work force mirroring the labor force in the county. The Court of Appeals added that the fact that the Plan established no fixed percentage of positions for minorities or women made it less essential that the Plan contain a relatively explicit deadline. The court held further that the Agency's consideration of Joyce's sex in filling the road dispatcher position was lawful. The Agency Plan had been adopted, the court said, to address a conspicuous imbalance in the Agency's work force, and neither unnecessarily trammeled the rights of other employees, nor created an absolute bar to their advancement.

II

* * * * *

In reviewing the employment decision at issue in this case, we must first examine whether that decision was made pursuant to a plan prompted by concerns similar to those of the employer in *Weber*. Next, we must determine whether the effect of the plan on males and non-minorities is comparable to the effect of the plan in that case.

The first issue is therefore whether consideration of the sex of applicants for skilled craft jobs was justified by the existence of a "manifest imbalance" that reflected underrepresentation of women in "traditionally segregated job categories." In determining whether an imbalance exists that would justify taking sex or race into account, a comparison of the percentage of minorities or women in the employer's work force with the percentage in the area labor market or general population is appropriate in analyzing jobs that require no special expertise, . . . or training programs designed to provide expertise. . . . Where a job requires special training, however, the comparison should be with those in the labor force who possess the relevant qualifications. . . .

* * * * *

. . . [W]omen were concentrated in traditionally female jobs in the Agency, and represented a lower percentage in other job classifications than would be expected if such traditional segregation had not occurred. Specifically, 9 of the 10 Para-Professionals and 110 of the 145 Office and Clerical Workers were women. By contrast, women were only 2 of the 28 Officials and Administrators, 5 of the 58 Professionals, 12 of the 124 Technicians, none of the Skilled Craft Workers, and 1—who was Joyce—of the 110 Road Maintenance Workers.

* * * * *

As the Agency Plan recognized, women were most egregiously underrepresented in the Skilled Craft job category, since *none* of the 238 positions was occupied by a woman. In mid-1980, when Joyce was selected for the road dispatcher position, the Agency was still in the process of refining its short-term goals for Skilled Craft Workers in accordance with the directive of the Plan. This process did not reach fruition until 1982, when the Agency established a short-term goal for that year of three women for the 55 expected openings in that job category—a modest goal of about 6 percent for that category.

* * * * *

. . . Given the obvious imbalance in the Skilled Craft category, and given the Agency's commitment to eliminating such imbalances, it was plainly not unreasonable for the Agency to determine that it was appropriate to consider as one factor the sex of Ms. Joyce in making its decision. The promotion of Joyce thus satisfies the first requirement enunciated in *Weber*, since it was undertaken to further an affirmative action plan designed to eliminate Agency work force imbalances in traditionally segregated job categories.

We next consider whether the Agency Plan unnecessarily trammeled the rights of male employees or created an absolute bar to their advancement. In contrast to the plan in *Weber*, which provided that 50 percent of the positions in the craft training program were exclusively for blacks, and to the consent decree upheld last term in *Firefighters* v. *Cleveland*, which required the promotion of specific numbers of minorities, the Plan sets aside no positions for women. The Plan expressly states that "[t]he 'goals' established for each Division should not be construed as 'quotas' that must be met." Rather, the Plan merely authorizes that consideration be given to affirmative action concerns when evaluating qualified applicants. As the Agency Director testified, the sex of Joyce was but one of numerous factors he took into account in arriving at his decision. . . . No persons are automatically excluded from consideration; *all* are able to have their qualifications weighed against those of other applicants.

In addition, petitioner had no absolute entitlement to the road dispatcher position. Seven of the applicants were classified as qualified and eligible, and the Agency Director was authorized to promote any of the seven. Thus, denial of the promotion unsettled no legitimate, firmly rooted expectation on the part of the petitioner. Furthermore, while the petitioner in this case was denied a promotion, he retained his employment with the Agency, at the same salary and with the same seniority, and remained eligible for other promotions.

Finally, the Agency's Plan was intended to *attain* a balanced work force, not to maintain one. . . .

The Agency acknowledged the difficulties that it would confront in remedying the imbalance in its work force, and it anticipated only gradual increases in the representation of minorities and women. It is thus unsurprising that the Plan contains no explicit end date, for the Agency's flexible, case-by-case approach was not expected to yield success in a brief period of time. . . . In this case, substantial evidence shows that the Agency has sought to take a moderate, gradual approach to eliminating the imbalance in its work force, one which establishes realistic guidance for employment decisions, and which visits minimal intrusion on the legitimate expectations of other employees. Given this fact, as well as the Agency's express commitment to "attain" a balanced work force, there is ample assurance that the Agency does not seek to use its Plan to maintain a permanent racial and sexual balance.

III

* * * * *

The Agency earmarks no positions for anyone; sex is but one of several factors that may be taken into account in evaluating qualified applicants for a position. As both the Plan's language and its manner of operation attest, the Agency has no intention of establishing a work force whose permanent composition is dictated by rigid numerical standards.

We therefore hold that the Agency appropriately took into account as one factor the sex of Diane Joyce in determining that she should be promoted to the road dispatcher position. The decision to do so was made pursuant to an affirmative action plan that represents a moderate, flexible, case-by-case approach to effecting a gradual improvement in the representation of minorities and women in the Agency's work force. Such a plan is fully consistent with Title VII, for it embodies the contribution that voluntary employer action can make in eliminating the vestiges of discrimination in the workplace.

Affirmed.

Justice **O'Connor,** concurring in the judgment.

* * * * *

In my view, the proper initial inquiry in evaluating the legality of an affirmative action plan by a public employer under Title VII is no different from that required by the Equal Protection Clause. In either case, consistent with the congressional intent to provide some measure of protection to the interests of the employer's nonminority employees, the employer must have had a firm basis for believing that remedial action was required. An employer would have such a firm basis if it can point to a statistical disparity sufficient to support a prima facie claim under Title VII by the employee beneficiaries of the affirmative action plan of a pattern or practice claim of discrimination.

* * * * *

In this case, I am . . . satisfied that the respondent had a firm basis for adopting an affirmative action program. Although the district Court found no discrimination against women in fact, at the time the affirmative action plan was adopted, there were *no* women in its skilled craft positions. The petitioner concedes that women constituted approximately 5 percent of the local labor pool of skilled craft workers in 1970. Thus, when compared to the percentage of women in the qualified work force, the statistical disparity would have been sufficient for a prima facie Title VII case brought by unsuccessful women job applicants.

Justice **White,** dissenting.

. . . My understanding of *Weber* was, and is, that the employer's plan did not violate Title VII because it was designed to remedy intentional and systematic exclusion of blacks by the employer and the unions from certain job categories. That is how I understood the phrase "traditionally segregated jobs" we used in that case. The Court now interprets it to mean nothing more than a manifest imbalance between one identifiable group and another in an employer's labor force. As so interpreted, that case, as well as today's decision, as Justice Scalia so well demonstrates, is a perversion of Title VII. I would overrule *Weber* and reverse the judgment below.

Justice **Scalia,** with whom The **Chief Justice** joins, and with whom Justice **White** joins in Parts I and II, dissenting.

* * * * *

Several salient features of the plan should be noted. Most importantly, the plan's purpose was assuredly not to remedy prior sex discrimination by the Agency. It could not have been, because there was no prior sex discrimination to remedy. The majority, in cataloguing the Agency's alleged misdeeds, neglects to mention the District Court's finding that the Agency "has not discriminated in the past, and does not discriminate in the present against women in regard to employment opportunities in general and promotions in particular." This finding was not disturbed by the Ninth Circuit.

* * * * *

The most significant proposition of law established by today's decision is that racial or sexual discrimination is permitted under Title VII when it is intended to overcome the effect, not of the employer's own discrimination, but of societal attitudes that have limited the entry of certain races, or of a particular sex, into certain jobs.

* * * * *

The Agency here was not seeking to remedy discrimination—much less "unusual" or "egregious" discrimination. . . .

In fact, however, today's decision goes well beyond merely allowing racial or sexual discrimination in order to eliminate the effects of prior societal *discrimination*. The majority opinion often uses the phrase "traditionally segregated job category" to describe the evil against which the plan is legitimately (according to the majority) directed. As originally used in *Steelworkers* v. *Weber* that phrase described skilled jobs from which employers and unions had systematically and intentionally excluded black workers. . . . But that is assuredly not the sense in which the phrase is used here. It is absurd to think that the nationwide failure of road maintenance crews, for example, to achieve the Agency's ambition of 36.4 percent female representation is attributable primarily, if even substantially, to systematic exclusion of women eager to shoulder pick and shovel. It is a "traditionally segregated job category" *not* in the *Weber* sense, but in the sense that, because of long-standing social attitudes, it has not been regarded *by women themselves* as desirable work. . . . There are, of course, those who believe that the social attitudes which cause women themselves to avoid certain jobs and to favor others are as nefarious as conscious, exclusionary discrimination. Whether or not that is so (and there is assuredly no consensus on the point equivalent to our national consensus against intentional discrimination), the two phenomena are certainly distinct. And it is the alteration of social attitudes, rather than the elimination of discrimination, which today's decision approves as justification for state-enforced discrimination. This is an enormous expansion, undertaken without the slightest justification or analysis.

Questions

1. Explain the majority's reasoning in upholding the promotion of a female over a marginally better-qualified male.
2. How does Justice O'Connor's concurring opinion differ from that of the majority?
3. Why does Justice White call for overruling the *Weber* decision?
4. Justice Scalia in a portion of his dissent not reproduced above:
   A statute [Title VII of the Civil Rights Act of 1964] designed to establish a color-blind and gender-blind workplace has thus been converted into a powerful engine of racism and sexism, not merely *permitting* intentional race- and sex-based discrimination, but often making it, through operation of the legal system, compelled.
   Do you agree? Explain.
5. In 1972 a federal district court found that Alabama's public safety department had violated the equal protection clause of the Fourteenth Amendment by systematically excluding blacks from employment as state troopers. The court ordered the department to hire one black for every white hired until blacks held 25 percent of the trooper positions. In 1974 the court found that the department had employed strategies and policies that frustrated full relief. Then, in 1981, black troopers sought an order requiring a one-for-one policy in promotions pending departmental implementation of a valid promotion policy of its own. A federal district court then ordered the department to initiate that one-for-one promotion policy, assuming sufficient qualified black candidates, until the 25 percent standard was reached. In the mid-1980s about 27 percent of the arresting officers were black, but none held a position higher than sergeant. The promotion decision was appealed to the U.S. Supreme Court. Decide. Explain. See *United States* v. *Phillip Paradise,* 94 L.Ed. 2d 203 (1987).
6. The Equal Employment Opportunity Commission engaged in a lawsuit to prevent a labor union and its apprenticeship program from engaging in discrimination against black and Hispanic individuals. The district court found evidence of discrimination and, among

other things, set a 29 percent nonwhite membership goal based on the percentage of nonwhites in the labor pool in New York City. The union was twice found in contempt for failure to comply, and the membership goal was raised to 29.23 percent. The U.S. Supreme Court upheld the plan, finding that Title VII does not prohibit race-conscious relief as a remedy where such circumstances as persistent or particularly egregious discrimination obtain.

Write a dissenting opinion. See *Sheet Metal Workers* v. *Equal Employment Opportunity Commission,* 92 L.Ed. 2d 344 (1986).

Part Six—Additional Discrimination Topics

AGE DISCRIMINATION

The Age Discrimination in Employment Act (ADEA), as amended, forbids employers (including state and local governments), employment agencies, and labor organizations from discriminating because of age against employees 40 years of age or older, thus eliminating mandatory retirement for most occupations. The ADEA permits both private lawsuits and action by the EEOC. Among other possibilities, the remedies available under ADEA include back pay, liquidated damages, and injunctive relief.

Like racial and sexual discrimination, age discrimination is established via disparate treatment, disparate impact, and pattern or practice analysis. Under ADEA a plaintiff-employee must show that he or she: "(1) belongs to the protected class (age 40 or older); (2) was qualified for his or her position; (3) was terminated; and (4) was replaced by a younger person."[91] If the plaintiff establishes that prima facie case, the burden of proof shifts to the defendant-employer to show that the discharge was for "some legitimate, nondiscriminatory reason." If the defendant succeeds, the burden then shifts back to the plaintiff to prove that the employer's reasons for discharge were merely a pretext for discrimination.

The chief defense available to the employer-defendant is the bona fide occupational qualification. In essence, an employer must demonstrate that only employees of a certain age can safely and/or efficiently complete the work in question. Thus, in *Hodgson* v. *Greyhound Lines*[92], the bus company defended its policy of hiring intercity drivers 34 years of age or younger. Greyhound demonstrated that its safest drivers were those 50–55 years of age with 16–20 years of driving experience with Greyhound— two qualifications that those 40 years of age or older (the protected class) could not attain. Given that evidence, the company was able to lawfully maintain its policy.

Of course, employers can lawfully dismiss employees aged 40 or older for reasons other than age.

The case law in the area of age discrimination is somewhat undeveloped. A tight job market, the likelihood of declining social security benefits, an increasingly elderly population, and the elimination or elevation of mandatory retirement ages suggests intense conflict in the future. For example, can employers lawfully replace older, higher-paid employees with younger, equally qualified, lower-paid employees when employees' salaries are closely related to seniority and thus to age? The article that follows illustrates the major age discrimination themes.

FORCED EXITS? COMPANIES CONFRONT WAVE OF AGE–DISCRIMINATION SUITS

Sydney P. Freedberg

A jury in Dade City, Florida, found Lykes Pasco, Inc., a juice processor, guilty of age discrimination when it fired Malcolm Anderson, a 59-year-old worker with 30 years of service. The jurors awarded Mr. Anderson $196,940—about 10 times his final annual salary.

Whatever the merits of Mr. Anderson's case (the company is appealing), the outcome was typical in one respect: When juries hear age-discrimination lawsuits, the odds favor the worker.

"It's very hard to convince a jury that a nice, white-haired man who lost his job after 20 years doesn't deserve something against the big, bad corporation," says Larry Besnoff, a management lawyer in Philadelphia.

Age discrimination is the fastest-growing type of bias charge in the workplace. Last year, almost 27,000 complaints were lodged with federal and state agencies—more than twice the number filed in 1980. . . .

* * * * *

Who Sues?

The typical age-bias litigant is a white male supervisor in his 50s who was discharged in a corporate belt-tightening. A recent study by Syracuse University School of Management, which reviewed more than 10,000 age-discrimination claims, says the average litigant sees a lawsuit as his only refuge; he has no union to represent him and can't qualify for racial or sexual discrimination.

A majority of the complaints, the study says, originate in right-to-work states outside the Northeast, where employers "may be more aggressive in discharging or forcing the retirement of older workers."

* * * * *

In Court

Only about one age-discrimination case in five makes it to a jury. "A lot of these complaints ought not to be in court," says Christopher S.

Miller, an Atlanta lawyer who co-authored the Syracuse study. "They're straight grievance claims by older workers who were the unfortunate victims of companies that were forced to cut back."

The Syracuse study says judges rule for companies about two thirds of the time, not including those cases decided on procedural issues. Conversely, Mr. Miller says, juries side with older workers about two thirds of the time. Says San Francisco management lawyer Victor Schachter, "Juries are inherently biased in favor of long-term employees who work for deep-pocket companies."

Rave Reviews

To avoid age-bias lawsuits, management specialists caution companies to avoid inflating performance appraisals and to ensure a thorough, accurate paper trail for each employee.

Such reviews played a role in the recent judgment against Miles, Inc., which merged with Cutter Laboratories, Inc., in 1983 and inherited age-bias charges. At the trial in August, Miles argued that $60 million in losses prompted Cutter to lay off 1,200 workers in 1982 and that it picked the least productive employees with the worst sales records. But the nine workers who sued claimed that the company's standards were biased against workers over 40, and their lawyer produced records showing that they had received glowing performance evaluations over the years.

The six-member district court jury—all but one over 40 years old—believed the salespeople. What's more, the jury found the discrimination "willful" and awarded double damages—$1.63 million.

What To Do?

Any hiring or firing decision in which age has crept into the process is suspect under the law.

A company can be held liable, for instance, if an age-neutral layoff policy ends up having a disproportionate effect on older workers. An employer could also have trouble in court for involuntarily transferring an older worker who performs at a minimally acceptable level. And a company can lose a lawsuit simply on the basis of a seemingly harmless aside. In the case of Lykes Pasco, a subsidiary of Tampa, Florida-based Lykes Bros., Inc., two secretaries testified that two executives called Mr. Anderson "the old man" and "too darned old." (The executives denied it.) In the Miles-Cutter case, a manager allegedly commented that he preferred salespeople in their 20s. (The manager denied it.)

"Remarks like, 'We need new blood,' can be the kiss of death for a company defending against an age-bias claim," says Mr. Miller, the Atlanta lawyer.

Even a company's manuals and forms can cause trouble if they reflect any age bias. Some businesses, for example, have decided to remove the "Date of Birth" box from their job-application forms and have stopped asking what year an applicant graduated from high school or college.

Golden Handcuffs

To thwart lawsuits, some companies are starting to ask retiring employees to sign notorized releases waiving all age-discrimination claims. Some lawyers, however, debate the validity of such releases. Last year in Cincinnati, a federal appeals court overturned a decision that had declared such a release illegal. The employee who had signed the release was a lawyer for NCR Corp.

Coming Attractions

The current interest in age discrimination, lawyers say, may be nothing compared to what lies ahead. By the year 2010, people age 40 or over—those protected by the law—are expected to make up half the work force. More older people with medical handicaps are likely to file suit, alleging both age and handicap bias. ''More older women and more older blacks will be contending for the same jobs held by older white men,'' says Mr. Miller.

As more companies seek ways to streamline aging work forces, new age-discrimination issues are likely to crop up in court: When does a ''voluntary'' early-retirement plan become subtly coercive? Can a company fire an older, higher-salaried worker to save money? And is the fast-track method of management—in which younger ''bright stars'' are transferred from department to department to broaden their experience—legal?

Questions

1. Metz alleges that he was fired in violation of the ADEA. He had been a plant manager for a company that was experiencing financial problems. His employer notified him that the plant would be closed and he would be laid off. The company then sent the assistant manager of another plant, Burzloff, to Metz's plant to inspect it and make repairs. Burzloff requested that he be allowed to manage Metz's plant; the employer approved this request and discharged Metz. At the time of his layoff, the 54-year-old Metz had a salary of $15.75 an hour; when the 43-year-old Burzloff replaced Metz, his salary was $8.05 per hour.[93]

   Metz had worked for Transit for 27 years. He had received raises each year, even though the company was not profitable during some of those years. The company decided its poor financial performance did not justify retaining Metz, whose salary was comparatively high. Metz was not asked to take a pay cut before he was dismissed. The court framed the issue in the case in this manner:

   > The sole issue on appeal is whether the salary savings that can be realized by replacing a single employee in the ADEA age-protected range with a younger, lower-salaried employee constitutes a permissible, nondiscriminatory justification for the replacement.[94]

   Resolve that issue. Explain. See *Metz* v. *Transit Mix, Inc.,* 828 F.2d 1202 (7th Cir. 1987).

2. Assume you own a clothing store designed to appeal primarily to the ''young adult'' market. In your opinion, should the law permit you to hire only ''young adults'' as salespersons? Explain.

3. Under its collective bargaining agreement, Trans World Airlines maintained a policy of automatically transferring flight captains to positions as flight engineers when they were disqualified from their pilot's role for reasons other than age (for example, medical disability or a labor force reduction). Under the agreement, the captains were entitled to ''bump'' any less-senior flight engineer. However, pilots who were retired on reaching age 60 were not automatically entitled to move into a flight engineer position. Rather, they were allowed to remain with TWA only if they had secured a flight engineer position prior to their 60th birthday. They could do so only by submitting a bid in the hope that

a vacancy would arise prior to their 60th birthday. Three pilots, forced to retire by TWA, filed suit, claiming a violation of the Age Discrimination in Employment Act, which forbids differential treatment of older workers "with respect to a privilege of employment." Does the ADEA *require* TWA to grant transfer privileges to disqualified pilots? Explain. See *Trans World Airlines, Inc.* v. *Thurston,* 469 U.S. 111 (1985).

DISCRIMINATION AGAINST THE HANDICAPPED

The Rehabilitation Act of 1973 and the Vietnam Era Veterans Readjustment Assistance Act are federal statutes designed to both afford equal opportunity and expand employment prospects for the handicapped.

The primary provisions of the Rehabilitation Act provide that:

1. Federal agencies must take an affirmative action approach toward hiring the handicapped.
2. Federal contractors having contracts that exceed $2,500 must include in those contracts affirmative action clauses providing for hiring and promoting the handicapped.
3. Federal agencies and programs receiving federal financial assistance are prohibited from discrimination on the basis of handicaps.

Those holding contracts of $10,000 or more with the federal government must include in those contracts clauses providing for affirmative action in hiring and promoting handicapped veterans of the Vietnam era.

Under the terms of the Rehabilitation Act, a *handicapped individual* is "any person who (*a*) has a physical or mental impairment, which substantially limits one or more of such person's major life activities; (*b*) has a record of such an impairment; or (*c*) is regarded as having such an impairment."[95] Amputation, cancer, blindness, and mental retardation are clearly covered. Alcohol or drug abuse rising to the level of a disease or defect is covered. In 1988 the Supreme Court ruled that alcoholic veterans may be denied benefits on the grounds that their condition is one of "willful misconduct" rather than disease. The Court held by a 4–3 vote that the Veterans Administration had not violated federal laws by treating alcoholism as misconduct, thus denying benefits to the veterans who argued that alcoholism is a handicap. Justice White, writing for the majority, said Section 504 of the Rehabilitation Act did not require treating alcoholism as a disease. However, White said the VA is not barred from treating alcoholism as a disease. The Court itself simply decided against resolving "this medical issue on which the authorities remain sharply divided."[96]

An example of the breadth of handicap coverage as well as the cost of allegedly discriminatory practices is a 1980 conciliation agreement involving a Dallas electronics firm. Varo Semiconductor Company agreed to pay $225,000 to 85 applicants allegedly denied jobs because of "disabilities" that included obesity, color blindness, arthritis, hypertension, allergies, and varicose veins. The firm also agreed to establish a preferential hiring list for 32 of the alleged discrimination victims who still desired jobs with the firm.

The employer is, of course, under no duty to hire a handicapped individual who, because of the handicap, cannot fulfill the requirements of the job. Affirmative action requirements do not include underutilization analysis and the establishment of numerical goals and timetables. However, those covered by the act must make special efforts to reach and hire the handicapped. "Reasonable accommodation" must be made to the handicapped employee's needs.

AIDS

At this writing in early 1988, the most pressing unsettled question in discrimination law concerns the applicability of the Rehabilitation Act of 1973 to Acquired Immune Deficiency Syndrome (AIDS). Is AIDS a handicap? At this time at least 21 states and several cities have legislation or court orders treating AIDS as a handicap.[97] On the other hand, in 1987 the U.S. Justice Department issued an opinion (advisory and nonbinding) that an employer may fire a carrier of the AIDS virus without violating the Rehabilitation Act if the dismissal reflects the employer's legitimate conclusion that retaining the employee would lead to the spread of the disease in the workplace.

A 1987 Gallup Poll revealed broad public sympathy for AIDS sufferers. Sixty-four percent objected to the "right of employers to dismiss victims," 65 percent said they would not object to working with someone afflicted with AIDS, and 71 percent do not want someone with AIDS to be "isolated from society."[98] But that public sympathy may not translate to legal protection. An *American Bar Association Journal* nationwide poll of 578 lawyers found only 28 percent believed "victims of contagious diseases should be entitled to federal protection from discrimination." Fifty-two percent said no.[99] That poll was conducted prior to the *Arline* decision set out below. Advocates of treating AIDS as a handicap point to the *Arline* decision as a victory for their cause, even though that case deals with tuberculosis. But even if *Arline* is read as an indication of the Supreme Court's future stance toward AIDS as a handicap, other questions remain. In particular, would those who carry the AIDS virus but are not actually afflicted with AIDS fall under the protection of the act? And, in any case, remember that *Arline* and the Rehabilitation Act apply only to those businesses dealing with the government to the extent described above. These issues are immensely important because the Centers for Disease Control estimate that by 1991 nearly 100,000 Americans will be suffering from AIDS and perhaps 10 million more may be carrying the virus.[100] As you read *Arline,* contemplate the far-reaching implications of federal handicap protection on the business community.

SCHOOL BOARD OF NASSAU COUNTY V. ARLINE
94 L Ed 2d 307 (1987)

Justice Brennan

Section 504 of the Rehabilitation Act of 1973 prohibits a federally funded state program from discriminating against a handicapped individual solely by reason of his or her handicap. This case presents the questions whether a person afflicted with tuberculosis, a contagious disease, may be considered a "handicapped individual" within the meaning of § 504 of the Act, and, if so, whether such an individual is "otherwise qualified" to teach elementary school.

I

From 1966 until 1979, respondent Gene Arline taught elementary school in Nassau County, Florida. She was discharged in 1979 after suffering a third relapse of tuberculosis within two years. After she was denied relief in state administrative proceedings, she brought suit in federal court, alleging that the School Board's decision to dismiss her because of her tuberculosis violated § 504 of the Act.

. . . Arline was hospitalized for tuberculosis in 1957. For the next 20 years, Arline's disease was in remission. Then, in 1977, a culture revealed that tuberculosis was again active in her system; cultures taken in March 1978 and in November 1978 were also positive.

The superintendent of schools for Nassau County, Craig Marsh, then testified as to the School Board's response to Arline's medical reports. After both her second relapse, in the Spring of 1978 and her third relapse in November 1978, the School Board suspended Arline with pay for the remainder of the school year. At the end of the 1978–1979 school year, the School Board held a hearing, after which it discharged Arline, "not because she had done anything wrong," but because of the "continued reoccurrence [sic] of tuberculosis."

In her trial memorandum, Arline argued that it was "not disputed that the [School Board dismissed her] solely on the basis of her illness. Since the illness in this case qualifies the Plaintiff as a 'handicapped person' it is clear that she was dismissed solely as a result of her handicap in violation of Section 504." The District Court held, however, that although there was "[n]o question that she suffers a handicap," Arline was nevertheless not "a handicapped person under the terms of that statute." The court found it "difficult . . . to conceive that Congress intended contagious diseases to be included within the definition of a handicapped person." The court then went on to state that, "even assuming" that a person with a contagious disease could be deemed a handicapped person, Arline was not "qualified" to teach elementary school.

The Court of Appeals reversed, holding that "persons with contagious diseases are within the coverage of section 504." . . . The court remanded the case "for further findings as to whether the risks of infection precluded Mrs. Arline from being 'otherwise qualified' for her job and, if so, whether it was possible to make some reasonable accommodation for her in that teaching position'' or in some other position. We granted certiorari.

II

In enacting and amending the Act, Congress enlisted all programs receiving federal funds in an effort "to share with handicapped Americans the opportunities for an education, transportation, housing, health care, and jobs that other Americans take for granted." To that end, Congress not only increased federal support for vocational rehabilitation, but also addressed the broader problem of discrimination against the handicapped by including § 504, an antidiscrimination provision patterned after Title VI of the Civil Rights Act of 1964. Section 504 of the Rehabilitation Act reads in pertinent part:

> No otherwise qualified handicapped individual in the United States, as defined in section 706(7) of this title, shall, solely by reason of his handicap, be excluded from participation in, be denied the benefits of, or be subjected to discrimination under any program or activity receiving Federal financial assistance.

In 1974 Congress expanded the definition of "handicapped individual" for use in § 504 to read as follows:

> [A]ny person who (i) has a physical or mental impairment which substantially limits one or more of such person's major life activities, (ii) has a record of such an impairment, or (iii) is regarded as having such an impairment.

* * * * *

III

. . . [W]e must consider whether Arline can be considered a handicapped individual. According to . . . testimony . . . Arline suffered tuberculosis "in an acute form in such a degree that it affected her respiratory system," and was hospitalized for this condition. Arline thus had a physical impairment as that term is defined by the regulations, since she had a "physiological disorder or condition . . . affecting [her] . . . respiratory [system]." This impairment was serious enough to require hospitalization, a fact more than sufficient to establish that one or more of her major life activities were substantially limited by her impairment. Thus, Arline's hospitalization for tuberculosis in 1957 suffices to establish that she has a "record of . . . impairment" and is therefore a handicapped individual.

Petitioners concede that a contagious disease may constitute a handicapping condition to the extent that it leaves a person with "diminished physical or mental capabilities," and concede that Arline's hospitalization for tuberculosis in 1957 demonstrates that she has a record of a physical impairment. Petitioners maintain, however, Arline's record of impairment is irrelevant in this case, since the School Board dismissed Arline not because of her diminished physical capabilities, but because of the threat that her relapses of tuberculosis posed to the health of others.

We do not agree with petitioners that, in defining a handicapped individual under § 504, the contagious effects of a disease can be meaningfully distinguished from the disease's physical effects on a claimant in a case such as this. Arline's contagiousness and her physical impairment each resulted from the same underlying condition, tuberculosis. It would be unfair to allow an employer to seize upon the distinction between the effects of a disease on others and the effects of a disease on a patient and use that distinction to justify discriminatory treatment.[7]

Nothing in the legislative history of § 504 suggests that Congress intended such a result. That history demonstrates that Congress was as concerned about the effect of an impairment on others as it was about its effect on the individual. . . .

Allowing discrimination based on the contagious effects of a physical impairment would be inconsistent with the basic purpose of § 504, which is to ensure that handicapped individuals are not denied jobs or other benefits because of the prejudiced attitudes or the ignorance of others. By amending the definition of "handicapped individual" to include not only those who are actually physically impaired, but also those who are regarded as impaired and who, as a result, are substantially limited in a major life activity, Congress acknowledged that society's accumulated myths and fears about disability and disease are as handicapping as are the physical limitations that flow from actual impairment. Few aspects of a handicap give rise to the same level of public fear and misapprehension as contagiousness. . . . The fact that *some* persons who have contagious diseases may pose a serious health threat to others under certain circumstances does not justify excluding from the coverage of the Act *all* persons with actual or perceived contagious diseases. . . . We conclude that the fact that a person with a record of a physical impairment is also contagious does not suffice to remove that person from coverage under § 504.

IV

The remaining question is whether Arline is otherwise qualified for the job of elementary school teacher. To answer this question in most cases, the District Court will need to conduct an individualized inquiry and make appropriate findings of fact. Such an inquiry is essential if § 504 is to achieve its goal of protecting handicapped individuals from deprivations based on prejudice, stereotypes, or unfounded fear, while giving appropriate weight to such legitimate concerns of grantees as avoiding exposing others to significant health and safety risks. The basic factors to be considered in conducting this inquiry are well established. In the context of the employment of a person handicapped with a contagious disease, we agree with amicus American Medical Association that this inquiry should include:

> [findings of] facts, based on reasonable medical judgments given the state of medical knowledge, about (a) the nature of the risk (how the disease is transmitted), (b) the duration of the risk (how long is the carrier infectious), (c) the severity of the risk (what is the potential harm to third parties), and (d) the probabilities the disease will be transmitted and will cause varying degrees of harm.

In making these findings, courts normally should defer to the reasonable medical judgments of public health officials. The next step in the "otherwise-qualified" inquiry is for the court to evaluate, in light of these medical findings, whether the employer could reasonably accommodate the employee under the established standards for that inquiry.

Because of the paucity of factual findings by the District Court, we, like the Court of Appeals, are unable at this stage of the proceedings to resolve whether Arline is "otherwise qualified" for her job. The District Court made no findings as to the duration and severity of Arline's condition, nor as to the probability that she would transmit the disease. Nor did the court determine whether Arline was contagious at the time she was discharged, or whether the School Board could have reasonably accommodated her. Accordingly, the resolution of whether Arline was otherwise qualified requires further findings of fact.

V

We hold that a person suffering from the contagious disease of tuberculosis can be a handicapped person within the meaning of § 504 of the Rehabilitation Act of 1973, and that respondent Arline is such a person. We remand the case to the District Court to determine whether Arline is otherwise qualified for her position.

Affirmed.

---

[7]The United States argues that it is possible for a person to be simply a carrier of a disease, that is, to be capable of spreading a disease without having a "physical impairment" or suffering from any other symptoms associated with the disease. The United States contends that this is true in the case of some carriers of the Acquired Immune Deficiency Syndrome (AIDS) virus. From this premise the United States concludes that discrimination solely on the basis of contagiousness is never discrimination on the basis of a handicap. The argument is misplaced in this case, because the handicap here, tuberculosis, gave rise both to a physical impairment *and* to contagiousness. This case does not present, and we therefore do not reach, the questions whether a carrier of a contagious disease such as AIDS could be considered to have a physical impairment, or whether such a person could be considered, solely on the basis of contagiousness, a handicapped person as defined by the Act.

Questions

1. Explain the reasoning supporting Justice Brennan's conclusion that tuberculosis, a contagious disease, constitutes a handicap within the meaning of the Rehabilitation Act of 1973.
2. Does the *Arline* decision preclude employers from dismissing handicapped persons who cannot perform their duties? Explain.
3. Define *reasonable accommodation* in the context of the Rehabilitation Act of 1973.
4. *a.* How did the Court handle the question of the application of the Rehabilitation Act of 1973 to AIDS?
   b. Based on *Arline,* explain the reasoning that would be employed in deciding whether AIDS is to be treated as a handicap.

SEXUAL PREFERENCE

The Title VII prohibition against sex discrimination refers to gender-based distinctions and, therefore, in general does not reach discrimination based on sexual practice and preference. Therefore, homosexuals, transsexuals, and those wronged due to effeminacy or masculinity must look to local and state statutes and to constitutions for legal relief. A number of major corporations have established equal opportunity policies as to homosexuals. Homosexuality is not a bar to most federal employment. Some states and cities have enacted legislation offering varying measures of protection to homosexuals. The due process and equal protection provisions of the Fifth and Fourteenth Amendments offer protection to homosexuals and transsexuals employed in the public sector. Some cases have also raised First Amendment and right-to-privacy constitutional claims.

The decisions have been mixed. For example, in *Norton* v. *Macy*[101] a federal employee was dismissed as a consequence of an alleged off-the-job homosexual advance. The employee argued that the government had to show a relationship between his sexual preference and his job performance. A federal appeals court ruled that the government's judgment as to the immorality of the conduct involved was inadequate to establish its case. The Florida Supreme Court held that a homosexual could not be denied admission to the state bar merely because of sexual preference; however, many decisions have found homosexuals unfit for jobs. The U.S. Supreme Court declined to hear an appeal of a lower court decision affirming the legality of dismissing a homosexual school teacher when no evidence was offered showing that the teacher's sexual preference interfered with his job performance.[102] On the other hand, in 1985 a divided court (four to four) struck down an Oklahoma statute barring public school teachers from advocating homosexual conduct. The statute was invalidated on freedom of speech grounds.[103]

But a striking February 1988 decision by a three-member panel of the 9th U.S. Circuit Court of Appeals suggested a greater willingness to afford protection to homosexuals. The panel held that an army regulation requiring the dismissal of homosexuals was a violation of plaintiff Perry Watkins' constitutional right to equal protection under the law.[104] At the time of his original enlistment in the army, Watkins had admitted his homosexual inclinations. After 14 years of exemplary service, which earned him promotions to the rank of sergeant, he was denied reenlistment. In effect, the court applied racial discrimination reasoning to the *Watkins* case, finding that the army's argument that homosexuals hurt discipline is analogous to the now thoroughly discredited arguments used to justify racial discrimination. Note that the decision addresses sexual orientation rather than homosexual conduct. Then, in June 1988, in response to a Justice Department request, the court agreed to rehear the case before an 11-member panel of judges. At this writing in mid-1988, that rehearing is pending. But in any event, the case almost certainly will be taken to the U.S. Supreme Court. Previous Supreme Court and appeals court decisions in the general areas of homosexual conduct and homosexuality in the service are not supportive of the original *Watkins* conclusion. Of course, Watkins' equal protection claim would not be directly available in purely private-sector cases, because constitutional protection is limited to governmental action. But a victory for Watkins would doubtless be useful to homosexuals who believe they are victims of discrimination in housing and employment.

STATE LAW

Employees who believe they are victims of discrimination often must exhaust available state remedies before proceeding to litigation at the federal level. Some 40 states have statutes roughly paralleling the protections of Title VII and the Age Discrimination in Employment Act. Protections vary widely from state to state, and states may provide greater or lesser protections than does the federal government. For example, some states prohibit discrimination on the basis of marital status, and some explicitly offer protection against discrimination on the basis of appearance.

Most state antidiscrimination legislation provides for an administrative agency, such as a Human Rights Commission or a Fair Employment Practices Commission. Such bodies ordinarily have the power to issue rules to carry out the terms of the legislation, conciliate disputes, hold hearings, and, if the charges warrant, issue orders necessary to stop the offensive practice and correct its effects.

THE RESULTS

We have erected a comprehensive web of laws, orders, and opinions to combat wrongful discrimination. As suggested in the readings, the overall results for the protected classes are encouraging, but a vast gap remains. What of the individual cases? After studying the complexities of the various statutes and their judicial interpretations, examining the pragmatics of some settlements will be helpful. The following cases illustrate the results in wage adjustments, back pay, hiring policies, and so on.

1. In 1983 General Motors agreed to a $42.5 million settlement of discrimination charges raised by the EEOC and the United Auto Workers. The settlement, a product of 10 years of negotiations, was the largest in the history of the EEOC. GM promised to spend $15 million of the total over a five-year period for college scholarships for minority members and women. Twenty-one million dollars is to be spent for other training programs designed to enhance the ability of protected class members to reach apprenticeship and managerial roles.[105] As of 1986 GM had directed payments to 32 colleges and universities, including checks of $200,000 each to four historically black institutions: Fisk, Wilberforce, Xavier of New Orleans, and Savannah State.[106]

2. In 1988 State Farm Insurance settled a California sex discrimination case by promising money to those victimized and guaranteeing affirmative action to women. Two female plaintiffs who claimed State Farm refused to recruit women in the same manner as men for lucrative agent positions were awarded $420,822 each. About 80 percent of State Farm employees in California were women, but 98 percent of the agents were men. As part of the settlement, State Farm agreed that at least half of its agent jobs in California during the next decade would go to women. Other women who can prove they were the subjects of sex discrimination can also recover damages. The dollar settlements were based on a study of what those discriminated against would probably have earned had they been hired at the time they applied.[107]

3. In 1985 the Equitable Life Assurance Society agreed to pay $12.5 million to 300 former employees who claimed to be victims of age discrimination. Equitable did not admit wrongdoing, nor did it agree to rehire any of the employees. The dismissals resulted from what Equitable labeled a cost-cutting drive.[108]

4. Motorola, Inc., agreed in 1980 to settle five discrimination suits involving its Illinois plants. Motorola negotiated a settlement with the EEOC providing back pay totaling an estimated $8 million to $10 million for an estimated 10,000 blacks who had been denied semiskilled factory jobs. The company also agreed to fill 20 percent of its semiskilled job vacancies and 6.7 percent of its craft jobs with blacks, 11.2 percent of its sales positions with women, and 3.5 percent of its sales positions with Hispanics over the next five years. The cost of the expanded affirmative action program was expected to be $5 million.[109]

5. Individuals have often used discrimination prohibitions to rectify grievances. For example, a black man alleged that he had been denied employment with a tool and die firm due to his race. The firm then agreed to hire him. Subsequently, a conciliation hearing resulted in an award of $1,000 in partial back pay based on the employer's initial act of discrimination. Also, the employee's seniority date was applied retroactively to the date on which he was initially refused employment.[110]

CHAPTER QUESTIONS

1. Can an employer lawfully request information as to age on employment applications? Explain.
2. Can a private organization lawfully dismiss an employee on the grounds of homosexuality when that sexual preference does not interfere with job performance? Explain.
3. A union was composed entirely of white people. The union imposed a nepotism rule providing that new members would be either relatives of or recommended by current members. Did that membership policy violate the law? Explain. See *Local 53, Asbestos Workers* v. *Vogler*, 407 F.2d 1047 (5th Cir. 1969).
4. Title VII disparate impact cases do not require a showing of purposefulness or intent to establish unlawful discrimination. A finding of discrimination under the Fifth and Fourteenth Amendments does require such a showing. Would you favor amending Title VII to require direct explicit proof of actual discriminatory purpose? Explain.

5. Pan American Airways, Inc., maintained a policy of excluding men from positions as flight attendants. The policy was challenged on sex discrimination grounds. Pan American defended its policy with a survey showing that 79 percent of all passengers preferred being served by females. Then Pan Am offered expert testimony to show that the passenger preference was attributable to "feminine" qualities possessed by few males. The district court ruled for Pan Am on the grounds that "all or substantially all" [the test articulated in *Weeks* v. *Southern Bell Telephone,* 408 F.2d 228 (5th Cir. 1969)] men were unable to successfully fulfill the duties of flight attendants. The decision was appealed. Decide. Explain. See *Diaz* v. *Pan American Airways, Inc.,* 311 F. Supp. 559 (S.D. Fla. 1970), 442 F.2d 385 (5th Cir.), cert. denied 404 U.S. 950 (1971).

6. Can a Polynesian restaurant lawfully limit employment to "brown-skinned persons" in those jobs visible to the public? Explain.

7. Would a readily visible office wall display of nude and seminude female figures located in a common work area (for example, one poster, on display for eight years, depicted a "prone woman with a golf ball on her breasts and a man standing over her, golf club in hand, yelling "fore.") in combination with obscene comments about women on a routine basis (for example, "whores," "All that bitch needs is a good lay.") give rise to an intimidating, hostile, or offensive working environment within the meaning of the sexual harassment law? Explain. See *Rabidue* v. *Osceola Refining Co.,* 805 F.2d 611 (6th Cir. 1986); but also see *Barbetta* v. *Chemlawn Services Corp.,* 56 *Law Week* 2203 (1987).

8. The teachers union and the Jackson, Michigan, school board included a clause in their collectively bargained contract calling for protecting members of certain minority groups from layoffs. The clause provided that the percentage of minority teachers laid off would not exceed the percentage of minority teachers employed by the school district at the time of the layoffs. The clause was justified on the basis of general racial tension and discrimination in the community and society rather than on an explicit judicial determination of job discrimination. The clause resulted in the layoff of "nonminority" teachers, while minority teachers with less seniority were retained. The displaced teachers filed suit, claiming a violation of their rights under Title VII and the equal protection clause of the U.S. Constitution. Decide. Explain. See *Wygant* v. *Jackson Board of Education,* 106 S. Ct. 1842 (1986).

9. Assume a private country club excludes blacks and women from employment. Does that practice violate Title VII? Explain.

10. Define *affirmative action.*

11. A flight attendant was discharged in 1968 in accordance with her employer's "no marriage" rule. The rule was later abolished. She was rehired in 1972 and sought to have her seniority based on her

original date of hire rather than the time at which she was rehired. She argued that the seniority system operated to perpetuate past discrimination. She brought suit against the airline. Decide. Explain. See *United Airlines, Inc.* v. *Evans*, 431 U.S. 553 (1977).

12. Blacks employed at the Georgia Power Company were concentrated in the four lowest job classifications, which were maintained as separate seniority units under a collective bargaining agreement. Workers moving to higher classifications were required to forfeit all accumulated seniority. All other classifications were overwhelmingly composed of whites. Movement from those classifications did not require seniority forfeiture. A consent decree in 1979 settled a Title VII lawsuit. The company agreed to count blacks' total time for seniority. Then, with the Supreme Court's *Teamsters* decision, the union that was a party to the consent decree argued that the law had been altered and the old seniority system was bona fide. Thus the union sought to have the consent decree rescinded. Decide. Explain. See *U.S.* v. *Georgia Power Co.*, 634 F. 2d 929 (1981).

13. Thornton worked as a manager at a Connecticut retail store. In accordance with his religious beliefs, Thornton notified his manager that he could no longer work on Sundays as required by company (Caldor, Inc.) policy. A Connecticut statute provided that "No person who states that a particular day of the week is observed as his Sabbath may be required by his employer to work on such day. An employee's refusal to work on his Sabbath shall not constitute grounds for his dismissal." Management offered Thornton the options of transferring to a Massachusetts store where Sunday work was not required or transferring to a lower-paying supervisory job in the Connecticut store. Thornton refused both, and he was transferred to a lower-paying clerical job in the Connecticut store. Thornton claimed a violation of the Connecticut statute. The store argued that the statute violated the Establishment Clause (see Chapter 5) of the First Amendment, which forbids establishing an official state religion and giving preference to one religion over another or over none at all. Ultimately the case reached the U.S. Supreme Court.

    a. Decide. Explain.

    b. Do the religious accommodation provisions of Title VII of the Civil Rights Act violate the Establishment Clause? See *Estate of Thornton* v. *Caldor, Inc.*, 472 U.S. 703 (1985).

14. A male employee of a private social service organization was dismissed after three years of employment. The employee filed suit, contending he was a victim of sex discrimination forbidden under Title VII. The employee contended his discharge was in retaliation for his resistance to his male supervisor's sexual advances. The employer argued that Title VII does not reach such claims. Decide. See *Wright* v. *Methodist Youth Services, Inc.*, 511 F. Supp. 307 (DC NIll. 1981).

15. A woman sought a freightyard job. Her application was denied because she failed to meet the company's requirement of two years' truck-driving experience or truck-driving training. The woman believed she was a victim of sex discrimination.
    a. Build a case on her behalf.
    b. Build a case for the trucking company.
    c. Decide the case. Explain. See *Chrisner* v. *Complete Auto Transit, Inc.*, 645 F.2d 1251 (1981).

16. The National Teachers Examination measured substantive knowledge, but it did not measure teaching ability per se. The test had a disparate impact on a protected class, but the Court found no evidence of intent to discriminate. The test was used for the certification of teachers. Is the test lawful? Explain. See *United States* v. *South Carolina*, 434 U.S. 1026 (1978).

17. In 1972 a trucking firm hired one black worker and one white worker as temporary employees. The white worker had more experience, but when a full-time position became available the black employee was selected. The hiring manager acknowledged that the decision was made to meet the "attainment levels" of the employer's informal affirmative action plan. The affirmative action plan was not "organized," and the manager was allegedly only "vaguely aware" of the employer's minority hiring expectations. The white worker filed suit, claiming Title VII violations. In particular he alleged that the company's racial preference amounted to an impermissible quota system. Decide. Explain. See *Lehman* v. *Yellow Freight System*, 651 F.2d 520 (1981).

18. A new Texas airline, flying out of Dallas' Love Field, was in a precarious financial posture. Thus a campaign was mounted to sell itself as "the airline personification of feminine youth and vitality." In commercials its customers, who were primarily businessmen, were promised "in-flight love," including "love potions" (cocktails), "love bites" (toasted almonds), and a ticketing process (labeled a "quickie machine") that delivered "instant gratification." A male was denied a job with the airline because of his sex. He filed a Title VII action. The airline argued that attractive females were necessary to maintain its public image under the "love campaign," a marketing approach that the company claimed had been responsible for its improved financial condition. Decide. Explain. See *Wilson* v. *Southwest Airlines Co.*, USDC N Tex., CA-3-80-0689-G, June 12, 1981.

19. An employer assigned customers to employees based on the race or national origin of the customer. For example, Hispanic customers were assigned to Hispanic employees. Otherwise, employees were treated equally as to pay and working conditions. Is the employer guilty of employment discrimination? Explain. See *Rogers* v. *EEOC*, 454 F.2d 234 (5th Cir. 1971).

20. A bus company fired a black employee for violating the employer's rule forbidding beards. The beard had been grown on a doctor's advice in response to a skin condition known as pseudo folliculitis barbae. The condition affects people with curved hair follicles. After shaving, the facial hair sometimes curled back into the skin, causing inflammation and abscesses. The employee claimed a Title VII violation.
    a. Is the race of the employee critical to the resolution of this case?
    b. Build the plaintiff's argument.
    c. Build the defendant's argument.
    d. Decide. Explain. See *EEOC* v. *Greyhound Lines, Inc.* 22 EPD II 30, 604 (DC ED Pa. 1979).
21. Is sexual harassment a problem that should properly be addressed via federal intervention (EEOC)? Explain.
22. On balance, has the feminist movement and accompanying legal victories improved the quality of life for American women? For American men? Explain.
23. Nearly equal numbers of blacks and whites applied for jobs, but only 24 percent of those hired were black. The area population was 26 percent black. Was the employer guilty of discrimination? Explain. See *Robinson* v. *Union Carbide Co.*, 538 F.2d 652 (5th Cir. 1976).
24. Plaintiffs challenged a rule prohibiting the employment of drug users, including former heroin addicts who had engaged in methadone maintenance for over a year. Plaintiffs offered proof that 63 percent of all persons in public methadone programs were black or Hispanic, while the area population was 36 percent black and Hispanic. Are those facts sufficient to make out a prima facie case of employment discrimination? Explain. See *New York City Transit Authority* v. *Beazer,* 440 U.S. 568 (1979).
25. Elizabeth Hishon, an attorney employed by the Atlanta law firm of King and Spaulding, alleged that the firm had engaged in sex discrimination in failing to elevate her to the rank of partner. King and Spaulding argued that Title VII should not apply to partnership decisions because those "promotions" change the individual's status from "employee" to "employer." They further contended that the freedom of association guarantees of the Constitution permit them to choose whomever they wish as partners. Is Hishon's claim governed by Title VII? Explain. See *Hishon* v. *King and Spaulding,* 467 U.S. 69 (1984).
26. An EEOC guideline defines sexual harassment as "unwelcome sexual advances, requests for sexual favors, and other verbal or physical conduct of a sexual nature" when submission to the conduct affects employment decisions and/or the conduct interferes with work performance or creates a hostile work environment. In your opinion, is the guideline fair and workable? Explain.

27. The author of a *Harvard Law Review* article argues for discrimination claims based on appearance:

> The most physically unattractive members of our society face severe discrimination. . . . The unattractive ("those individuals who depart so significantly from the most commonly held notions of beauty that they incur employment discrimination") are poorly treated in such diverse contexts as employment decisions, criminal sentencing, and apartment renting. Although appearance discrimination can have a devastating economic, psychological, and social impact on individuals, its victims have not yet found a legal recourse.

Should we treat some aspects of appearance (for example, shortness, obesity, and unattractive facial characteristics) as handicaps within the meaning of the Rehabilitation Act of 1973, thus forbidding discrimination based on those characteristics? Explain. See Note, "Facial Discrimination: Extending Handicap Law to Employment Discrimination on the Basis of Physical Appearance," *Harvard Law Review* 100, no. 8 (June 1987), p. 2035.

28. The following ad appeared in the December 11, 1987, issue (p. 22) of *The Nation,* an English-language newspaper published in Bangkok, Thailand.

An American Bank
invites applications for
CORPORATE FOREIGN EXCHANGE DEALERS
for its Bangkok branch

Qualifications:
- Thai national
- Age 23–30 years, preferably male
- University graduate in Finance, Economics or related field
- 1–2 years dealing experience
- Good command of both spoken and written English

Salary is negotiable and attractive benefits will be provided for the successful candidates. The bank offers excellent opportunities for career advancement.

Send application stating details of qualifications and experience, present salary and a recent photo to

The Nation
Class 1191
GPO Box 594
Bangkok 10501

    a. Analyze the legality of the ad based on American law.

    b. Should American firms abroad adhere to American antidiscrimination policies even if those policies might put the American firms at a competitive disadvantage or offend the values and mores of the host country? Explain.

29. Philosopher Hugh Lehman applies equal pay and comparable worth principles to the practice of transnational corporations establishing manufacturing operations in Third World nations where labor costs are reduced:

> If the principle of equal pay for work of equal value is valid as a principle of justice, then it appears that the practice of paying workers in Third World countries at a lower rate than workers doing the same jobs in industrialized nations is unjust.[111]

Comment.

30. Richard Burr, a research analyst at the Center for the Study of American Business at Washington University in St. Louis, conducted a study of the process of assigning points to jobs for the purpose of comparable worth evaluations. Burr concluded that the process was highly judgmental, with, for example, a Minnesota librarian being worth 30 percent more than a Vermont librarian, who is, in turn worth 20 percent more than a librarian in Iowa (figures based on professional job evaluations undertaken to develop comparable worth plans). Burr concludes:

> Work does not correspond to a particular dollar figure. Typing letters or building houses has no intrinsic monetary worth; its value is determined by what people are willing to pay. In other words, the market is the proper mechanism for determining wages—not whimsical committees of lawyers and aggrieved feminists.[112]

Comment.

31. As discussed in this chapter, American law forbids a variety of forms of discrimination. At the same time, we revere personal freedom. For example, we protect the First Amendment rights of neo-Nazi groups and the Ku Klux Klan, notwithstanding their racist goals. Should we pass legislation banning racist remarks? That is, should we pass laws forbidding "group defamation"—malicious and degrading remarks directed to a racial or ethnic group? Explain. See Tamar Jacoby, "Time to Outlaw Racial Slurs?" *Time,* June 6, 1988, p. 59.

NOTES

1. *Franchise Motor Freightway Ass'n* v. *Leavey,* 196 Cal. 77, 235 P. 1000, 1002.
2. Richard Arvey, *Fairness in Selecting Employees* (Reading, Mass.: Addison-Wesley Publishing, 1979), p. 7.
3. 347 U.S. 483 (1954).

4. 163 U.S. 537 (1896).
5. A portion of the material in this paragraph is drawn from William P. Murphy, Julius G. Getman, and James E. Jones, Jr., *Discrimination in Employment,* 4th ed. (Washington: Bureau of National Affairs, 1979), pp. 1–4.
6. *Grove City College* v. *Bell,* 465 U.S. 555 (1984).
7. *General Building Contractors Association, Inc.* v. *Pennsylvania,* 458 U.S. 375 (1982).
8. 427 U.S. 160 (1976).
9. 442 U.S. 256 (1979).
10. The materials in this paragraph draw heavily from Charles A. Sullivan, Michael J. Zimmer, and Richard F. Richards, *Federal Statutory Law of Employment Discrimination* (Charlottesville, Va.: Bobbs-Merrill, 1980), pp. 266–69.
11. *The State of Black America 1987* (New York: National Urban League, 1987), p. 108, citing a study by James P. Smith.
12. Stephan Thernstrom, Winthrop Professor of History, Harvard University, "Black Progress Is Difficult to Measure," Letter to the Editor, *The Wall Street Journal,* March 28, 1988, p. 15.
13. U.S. Bureau of the Census, *Statistical Abstract of the United States: 1988,* 108th ed. (Washington, D.C., U.S. Government Printing Office, 1987), p. 365.
14. Ibid., p. 435.
15. Christopher Muldor, "Do Black Crime Victims Matter?" *The Wall Street Journal,* May 9, 1988, p. 16.
16. "Study Indicates Bias in Organ Transplants," *Des Moines Register,* June 3, 1988, p. 1T.
17. Bill Conlin, "How *Life* Magazine Stereotyped Joe DiMaggio," *Des Moines Register,* January 24, 1988, p. 11D.
18. William Kazer, " 'Darkie' Manufacturers Fail to Brush Off Charges of Racism," *The Nation,* (Bangkok, Thailand), December 11, 1987, p. 30.
19. Sullivan et al., *Federal Statutory Law,* pp. 16–33.
20. 422 U.S. 405 (1975).
21. *International Brotherhood of Teamsters* v. *United States,* 97 S. Ct. 1843 (1977).
22. *American Tobacco* v. *Patterson,* 456 U.S. 63 (1982).
23. *Firefighters Local Union No. 1784* v. *Stotts,* 467 U.S. 561 (1984).
24. See Malcolm H. Liggett, "Recent Supreme Court Affirmative Action Decisions and a Reexamination of the *Weber* Case," *Labor Law Journal* 38, no. 7 (July 1987), p. 415.
25. *Local No. 93, International Association of Firefighters* v. *City of Cleveland,* 92 L.Ed. 2d 344 (1986).
26. 457 U.S. 440 (1982).
27. *Muller* v. *Oregon,* 208 U.S. 412 (1908), as quoted in *Discrimination in Employment—A Study of Six Countries by the Comparative Labor Law Group,* ed. Folke Schmidt (Stockholm: Almqvist & Wiksell International, 1978), p. 130.
28. "Protective Law for Women," Labor Letter, *The Wall Street Journal,* August 11, 1987, p. 1.
29. 429 U.S. 125 (1976).
30. *Newport News Shipbuilding & Dry Dock Co.* v. *EEOC,* 462 U.S. 669 (1983).
31. *California Federal Savings and Loan Association* v. *Mark Guerra, Director, Department of Fair Employment and Housing,* 55 *Law Week* 4077 (1987).

32. *Linda Wimberly* v. *Labor and Industrial Relations Commission of Missouri,* 55 *Law Week* 4146 (1987).

33. "Six Months' Leave," Labor Letter, *The Wall Street Journal,* August 18, 1987, p. 1.

34. Albert R. Karr, "Unpaid Parental-Leave Bill to Cost Firms at Most $340 Million a Year, GAO Says," *The Wall Street Journal,* October 30, 1987, p. 7.

35. For a discussion of this topic see, for example, Lisa J. Raines and Stephen P. Push, "Protecting Pregnant Workers," *Harvard Business Review* 86, no. 3 (May–June 1986), p. 26.

36. Cited in *"Business Week*/Harris Poll," *Business Week,* August 1, 1983, p. 92.

37. John R. Dorfman, "Proposals for Equal Insurance Fees for Men and Women Spark Battle," *The Wall Street Journal,* August 27, 1987, p. 23.

38. Ibid.

39. *Arizona Governing Committee for Tax-Deferred Annuity and Deferred Compensation Plans* v. *Norris,* 463 U.S. 1073 (1983).

40. 468 U.S. 609 (1984).

41. *Board of Directors of Rotary International* v. *Rotary Club of Duarte,* 55 *Law Week* 4606 (1987).

42. *New York State Club Association Inc.* v. *New York City,* 56 *Law Week* 4653 (1988).

43. A more recent study, "The American Woman 1987–1988," by the Women's Research and Education Institute, the research arm of the Congressional Caucus for Women's Issues, reported a 68 percent ratio of women's to men's wages. See Barbara Gamarekian, "Status of Women Rises, but Pay Is Found to Lag," *The New York Times,* July 22, 1987, p. 14.

44. Ibid.

45. "Male versus Female," Labor Letter, *The Wall Street Journal,* December 9, 1986, p. 1. Reprinted by permission of *The Wall Street Journal,* © Dow Jones & Company, Inc. 1986. ALL RIGHTS RESERVED.

46. John Leo, "Motherhood versus Sisterhood." *Time,* March 31, 1986, p. 62, citing Sylvia Ann Hewlett, *A Lesser Life: The Myth of Women's Liberation in America* (New York: William Morrow, 1986).

47. James D. Gwartney, "Reasons behind the Male–Female Pay Gap," *The Wall Street Journal,* March 20, 1987, p. 10.

48. Randolph E. Schmid, "Analysts Say Women Remain in Lower-Paying Jobs," *Waterloo Courier,* March 4, 1987, p. B7.

49. "Study: Wages of Women Gain on Men's," *Des Moines Register,* October 31, 1984, p. 4A.

50. Boyce Rensberger, "Technical Jobs Lack Women, Blacks," *Washington Post,* February 23, 1986, p. A5.

51. Lydia Chavez, "Women's Movement, Its Ideals Accepted, Faces Subtler Issues," *The New York Times,* July 17, 1987, p. 8.

52. Aaron Bernstein, "So You Think You've Come a Long Way, Baby?" *Business Week,* February 29, 1988, p. 48.

53. 400 U.S. 542 (1979).

54. Mack A. Player, *Federal Law of Employment Discrimination in a Nutshell,* 2nd ed. (St. Paul, Minn.: West Publishing, 1981), p. 202.

55. See generally *Diaz* v. *Pan American World Airways, Inc.,* 442 F.2d 385 (5th Cir.), cert. denied 404 U.S. 950 (1971).

56. Eliza G. C. Collins and Timothy Blodgett, "Sexual Harassment . . . Some See It . . . Some Won't," *Harvard Business Review* 59, no. 2 (March–April 1981), p. 77.

57. Ibid., p. 78.

58. Joseph Verrengia, "Sexual Harassment: Criminal vs. Crude," *Waterloo Courier*, July 10, 1988, p. C2.

59. *New York University Law Review* 51, April 1976, pp. 148–49, as reported in Terry L. Leap and Edmund R. Gray, "Corporate Responsibility in Cases of Sexual Harassment," *Business Horizons* 23, no. 5 (October 1980), p. 58.

60. Sharon Warren Walsh, "Confronting Sexual Harassment at Work," *Washington Post,* July 21, 1986, p. 1.

61. The Bureau of National Affairs, *Sexual Harassment and Labor Relations—A BNA Special Report* (426), Part II (July 30, 1981), p. 24.

62. Collins and Blodgett, "Sexual Harassment," p. 92.

63. 29 USC Section 206(d) (1).

64. Ibid.

65. Player, *Federal Law,* p. 107.

66. No, according to the Department of Labor's Interpretive Bulletin, as reported in Sullivan et al., *Federal Statutory Law,* p. 596.

67. No. Ibid., pp. 598–601.

68. No, if those tasks do not constitute a substantial part of the job. Ibid., p. 608, reporting *Shultz* v. *American Can Co.—Dixie Prods., 424 F.2d 356 (8th Cir. 1970).

69. 417 U.S. 188 (1974).

70. Council on the Economic Status of Women, State of Minnesota, "Men's, Women's Comparable Jobs," *Des Moines Sunday Register,* January 8, 1984, p. 3C.

71. Ibid.

72. "Child Care Workers Near Pay Bottom," *Waterloo Courier,* January 3, 1988, p. A8.

73. Ibid.

74. Michel McQueen, "States Set Pace on Innovative Laws for Child Care, Parental Leaves, Women's Pay-Equity Standards," *The Wall Street Journal,* October 1, 1987, p. 60.

75. "Comparable Pay for Comparable Work Gains Acceptance, If Slowly," Labor Letter, *The Wall Street Journal,* July 15, 1986, p. 1.

76. Aaron Bernstein, "Comparable Worth: It's Already Happening," *Business Week,* April 28, 1986, p. 52.

77. *County of Washington* v. *Gunther,* 452 U.S. 161 (1981).

78. *Spaulding* v. *The University of Washington*, 740 F.2d 686 (1984).

79. 54 *Law Week* 2144 (9th Cir. 1985).

80. *Spaulding* v. *The University of Washington*, p. 708.

81. Associated Press, "Comparable Worth OK'd; 35,000 to Get Raises," *Des Moines Register,* April 12, 1986, p. 4A.

82. Michael J. McCarthy, "Supreme Court to Rule on Sex-Bias Case," *The Wall Street Journal,* June 14, 1988, p. 33.

83. Ibid.

84. *Hopkins* v. *Price Waterhouse,* 56 *Law Week* 2088 (1987).

85. Ibid.

86. *United States* v. *Seeger,* 380 U.S. 163 (1965).
87. 432 U.S. 63 (1977).
88. 55 *Law Week* 4019 (1987).
89. *University of California Regents* v. *Bakke,* 438 U.S. 265 (1978).
90. *Texas Department of Community Affairs* v. *Burdine,* 450 U.S. 248 (1981).
91. *Metz* v. *Transit Mix, Inc.,* 828 F.2d 1202, 1204 (7th Cir. 1987).
92. 499 F.2d 859 (7th Cir. 1974).
93. "Age Discrimination," 56 *Law Week* 2155 (1987), summarizing *Metz* v. *Transit Mix, Inc.*
94. *Metz* v. *Transit Mix, Inc.,* p. 1205.
95. 29 U.S.C.A. § 706(6).
96. *Traynor* v. *Turnage,* 56 *Law Week* 4319 (1988).
97. Joan O'C. Hamilton, "The AIDS Epidemic and Business," *Business Week,* March 23, 1987, p. 122.
98. George Gallup, Jr., AIDS Poll: More Compassion for Its Victims," *Des Moines Register,* November 22, 1987, p. 9A.
99. Cited in Roger Ricklefs, "AIDS Cases Prompt a Host of Lawsuits," *The Wall Street Journal,* October 7, 1987, p. 31.
100. Hamilton, "AIDS Epidemic."
101. 417 F.2d 1161 (D.C. Cir. 1969).
102. *Gaylord* v. *Tacoma School Dist. No. 10,* 88 Wash. 2d 286, 559 P. 2d 1340, cert. denied 434 U.S. 879 (1977).
103. *Board of Education of the City of Oklahoma City* v. *National Gay Task Force,* 470 U.S. 903 (1985).
104. For a news account, see Carrie Dolan, "Appeals Court Rules that Army's Policy against Homosexuals Is Unconstitutional," *The Wall Street Journal,* February 11, 1988, p. 3.
105. "GM Pact on Bias Offers Millions in Scholarships," *Chronicle of Higher Education,* October 26, 1983, p. 1.
106. Associated Press, "GM Gives Checks in Bias Settlement," *Des Moines Register,* October 28, 1986, p. 8A.
107. *Chicago Tribune,* "State Farm Settles Suit on Female Agents," *Des Moines Register,* January 20, 1988, p. 4A.
108. "Equitable Age Bias Case Settled," *Waterloo Courier,* January 20, 1985, p. C-12.
109. *The Bureau of National Affairs, Fair Employment Practices—Summary of Latest Developments,* no. 415, October 9, 1980, p. 6.
110. Francis Kornegay, *Equal Employment* (New York: Vantage Press, 1979), p. 103.
111. Hugh Lehman, "Equal Pay for Equal Work in the Third World," *Journal of Business Ethics* 4, no. 6 (December 1985), p. 487.
112. Richard Burr, "Job Values Are Unmeasurable," *Des Moines Register,* December 31, 1986, p. 7A.

PART V

Business and Selected Social Problems

Chapter 13

Consumer Protection

INTRODUCTION

Consumer abuse episodes like Chrysler Corporation's odometer fraud, described below, enrage the consuming public and, in many instances, exact a heavy price in personal injuries and dollars. Consumer protection organizations argue that wrongs against the buyer pervade American commercial practice.

CHRYSLER PLEADS NO CONTEST TO CHARGES IN ODOMETER CASE, TO PAY $16.4 MILLION

Joseph B. White

Chrysler Corp., which admitted it had been "dumb" to disconnect the odometers of certain test vehicles, pleaded no contest to charges that its odometer tampering was criminal.

Chrysler also formally agreed to pay at least $16.4 million to settle most, but not all, of the civil litigation filed by states and individuals in the wake of revelations that some executives of the company would disconnect the odometers of new Chrysler cars, drive them as much as 400 miles, then sell the cars as brand new.

. . . [T]he $16.4 million settlement represents the total amount Chrysler has agreed to pay to owners of at least 32,750 cars, which had been driven with disconnected odometers prior to sale. The figure doesn't include any fines arising from the criminal case, or the cost of the extended warranties Chrysler has offered on affected vehicles.

* * * * *

A federal grand jury in St. Louis indicted the number three auto maker and two execu-

671

tives . . . on 16 counts of odometer fraud, wire fraud, and conspiracy to commit mail fraud. The criminal charges provoked a rush of civil claims from states, charging that Chrysler violated their odometer fraud laws, and from customers who were angry at having paid new car prices for used cars.

In July, Chrysler Chairman Lee A. Iacocca called the odometer tampering "dumb" and offered aggrieved customers extended warranties and, in some cases, replacement vehicles.

Having done that, "it makes no sense to go to trial to defend that practice" of off-the-odometer test drives, a company spokesman said. When the judge agreed to drop all charges against the two executives, the company agreed to the no-contest plea, according to Lewis Goldfarb, assistant general counsel to Chrysler Motors. . . .

Under the separate civil settlement, Chrysler will pay at least $500 to current owners of every vehicle that can be identified as having been involved in what Chrysler called its "Overnight Evaluation Program." The company's records, which go back only to 1984, show that at least 32,750 vehicles were driven with the odometers disconnected before being sold as new, said Missouri Attorney General William L. Webster.

* * * * *

But Chrysler's troubles aren't over. Judge [John] Nangle has scheduled a sentencing hearing . . . and could impose additional criminal penalties, including fines up to $120 million.

In addition, Kentucky Attorney General David L. Armstrong said . . . he will pursue his litigation against Chrysler in Kentucky courts despite the settlement. The Kentucky action charges at least 351 violations and seeks civil penalties of as much as $7,000 per vehicle.

Source: *The Wall Street Journal,* December 15, 1987, p. 50. Reprinted by permission of *The Wall Street Journal,* © Dow Jones & Company, Inc. 1987. ALL RIGHTS RESERVED.

Whether conduct like Chrysler's is commonplace in the business community is the subject of dispute. But we do know that many companies not only obey the law as a matter of course but voluntarily impose on themselves standards in excess of the legal minima. For example, the Calderon Company of Locust Valley, New York, recalled one of its products, a child's mobile, when a 15-month-old boy was strangled by the mobile's 26-inch nylon cord. The mobile, which featured large stuffed animals, came with a warning label indicating it should not be used for children under age three. The warning label had been removed.[1] Similarly, Artsana of America of New York recalled its "Spinning Windmill Rattle" out of fear that the toy might be a choking hazard for children. The company had received no reports of actual choking incidents involving the toy.[2] The companies initiated these recalls in cooperation with the federal Consumer Product Safety Commission.

CONSUMERISM: PAST AND FUTURE

To the surprise of most, concern for the consumer is an ancient policy:

Until the Age of Reason in England, nothing resembling the doctrine of caveat emptor [buyer beware] existed in the custom and usage of the trade. Throughout the Middle Ages, church manuals laid down strict standards for market conduct, including requirements for warranties of quality. In the marketplace, merchants who dealt with their neighbors on a face-to-face basis took care to safeguard the quality of their products.[3]

However, the market changed from the craftsperson, face-to-face approach of that era to the complexities of mass production. At the same time, the influence of the church in commercial matters receded profoundly. In America scandals in foods and drugs and a general feeling of abuse by corporate giants led to what might be labeled the first wave of consumer protection pleas and subsequent legislation. In 1906 Congress passed the Pure Food and Drug Act. Drugs had been largely unregulated. In particular, the public was regularly victimized by patent medicines, often either valueless, addictive, or both. And Upton Sinclair's book, *The Jungle,* brought the filthy conditions in the meatpacking industry vividly to the public eye. Then, in 1914, Congress created the Federal Trade Commission to stem "unfair methods of competition."

Consumer concerns were muted during World War I and the prosperous 1920s, but the Depression of the 30s provoked a second wave of protection. In the private sector, Consumers Union and its magazine, *Consumer Reports,* was founded. President Roosevelt appointed a Consumers Advisory Board, and during his administration Congress passed the Food, Drug and Cosmetic Act of 1938, which provided for the seizure of food, drugs, cosmetics, and therapeutic devices that were adulterated or misbranded. Likewise, in 1938 Congress passed the Wheeler-Lea Amendment to the Federal Trade Commission Act, which extended FTC jurisdiction to "unfair and deceptive acts or practices in commerce."

The third major wave of consumer protection activity was felt in the mid-1960s, largely through the efforts of the quintessential consumer activist, Ralph Nader. Nader's bestselling book, *Unsafe at Any Speed,* led to the demise of General Motors' Corvair. Nader has been an enormously influential voice in the passage of many pieces of legislation. He has attacked virtually every segment of American commerce. In concert with his "Nader's Raiders" (student aides) and other allies, he has marshalled untiring research, the law, and public opinion to reshape consumer protection law. He became such an aggravation to General Motors that the company hired a law firm that then hired private detectives to investigate Nader in the hope of discrediting him. The head of the detective agency allegedly encouraged his subordinates to find out what they could about Nader's "women, boys, etc." Nader learned of the scheme and sued GM. The suit was settled out of court, and GM President James Roche publicly apologized to Nader.[4]

For a variety of reasons, the consumer movement cooled in the late 1970s and the conservative flavor of the 80s has dampened the ardor for further government intervention. However, the public's strong appreciation for consumer protection is well documented. As commentator Robert Samuelson reminds us, America has changed.

Twenty years ago, the vague concepts of "social responsibility" and "consumerism" barely existed; now (diluted, to be sure) they are the conventional wisdom, even in business. . . . And, Reagan notwithstanding, Nader's social regulation—of everything from auto safety to pollution—has triumphed. . . .[5]

COMMON LAW CONSUMER PROTECTION

Later in this chapter we will explore government efforts to protect us from misleading advertising, unfair lending practices, and the like. Before turning to that legislation we need to appreciate the common law (judge-made law) that preceded and, in some respects, provided the foundation for the striking federal, state, and local initiatives of recent years. In addition to the products liability protection (negligence, warranties, and strict liability) discussed in Chapter 14, the injured consumer can look to several common law "protections," including actions for fraud, misrepresentation, and unconscionability.

Fraud and Innocent Misrepresentation

If the market is to operate efficiently, the buyer must be able to rely on the truth of the seller's affirmations regarding a product. Regrettably, willful untruths appear common in American commerce. The victim of fraud is entitled to rescind the contract in question and to seek damages, including, in cases of malice, a punitive recovery. While fraud arises in countless situations and thus is difficult to define, the legal community has generally adopted the following elements, each of which must be proved:

1. A misrepresentation of a material fact with knowledge of the falsehood.
2. Intent to deceive.
3. Justifiable reliance on the falsehood by the injured party.
4. Damages resulting from reliance on the falsehood.

Fraud can involve false conduct as well as false expressions (of course, fraud should not be confused with mere puffing), and fraud sometimes arises from silence. If a serious problem or potential problem is known to the seller and the problem is of the sort that the buyer would not be likely to discover even after reasonable inspection (for example, a cracked automobile engine block where the cracks were filled with a sealer and covered with a compound),[6] a claim of fraud may well prevail. However, the general rule is that the parties to a contract have no duty to disclose the facts at their command.

A variation on the general theme of fraud is *innocent misrepresentation,* which differs from fraud only in that the falsehood was unintentional. The wrongdoer believed the statement or conduct in question to be true, but he or she was mistaken. In such cases the wronged party may secure rescission of the contract, but ordinarily damages are not awarded.

Before plunging into the famous fraud case that follows, take a moment to reflect on the extreme complexity in reaching a societal judgment about conduct that constitutes a wrong. The law of fraud illustrates the notion most excellently. Is the use of an unmarked patrol car a fraud against the public? Is a party to a marriage contract guilty of fraud in failing to disclose his or her propensity to snoring? Should a seller be expected to disclose all that is known about his or her product? Is a university guilty of fraud where it purports in its catalogs, inscriptions, and so on to purvey wisdom, when a student does not believe wisdom has been delivered?[7] The excerpt and the case that follow should be read for fun and for a sense of the ubiquity of "fraud," as well as for an appreciation of the difficulty in deciding how far society should intervene to correct all arguable wrongs.

Fraud in Nature

In his book *The Social Contract,* Robert Ardrey illustrates nature's propensity for fraud.

> Since we are inspecting man as a portion of nature, the capacity for lying should not be skipped. A few students of human language have implied that only through the complexity of our communication has the telling of lies become possible. I seize on the happy opportunity to announce that lying is a natural process. Man has enough to answer for; he need not answer for this.
>
> Some of the most outrageous liars in the natural world are found among species of orchid. To gain perspective on what might be called natural square deals as opposed to natural larceny, we may recall that plants evolved before birds and flying insects, and depended on wind or water to scatter their pollen. It was an inefficient system, and a colorless one, too, in this time before flowers. But then came the insects and sensuality became possible. The scents we enjoy, the colors we delight in, evolved as signals to attract this insect, that bird. Partnerships were established—what zoologists call symbiosis—so that the fuchsia, for example, offered the hummingbird nectar in exchange for hauling fuchsia pollen around. Everyone got a fair shake. But there must always be liars.
>
> There are species of orchids that have puzzled naturalists since the days of Darwin. They seemed to offer no inducement as their part of the deal, yet still insects did their job. At last, in 1928, a woman named Edith Coleman solved the problem in her study of an Australian orchid named *Cryptosylia.* The scent, a perfect imitation of the smell of the female of a species of fly, acted as an

aphrodisiac on the male. He was drawn to the flower. There he encountered as part of the orchid's structure a perfect imitation of the female's abdomen. It was all too much for him, and in his efforts to copulate with the orchid he got himself nicely dusted with pollen. I am aware of no more immoderate fraud in the natural world.

Fraud, however, is normal in nature. There are deep-sea fish prowling dark depths with lanterns on their snouts. Smaller fish are attracted by the light and promptly eaten. . . . A Madagascar snake called *Langaha nasuta* has a weird structure on its head resembling a finger, which it slowly moves as it approaches its victim. The victim normally stares too long. . . .

Not all the wonders of natural fraud are the property of villains, however. Many a lie is told on behalf of the potential victim. The tropical fish called *Chactodon*, for example, has spots resembling eyes on either side of its tail. It swims slowly backwards, apparently head-on. But if a predator strikes at it, the fish is off at high speed in the proper direction. All camouflage, indeed, is deception. That both fish and seabirds tend to have white undersides to provide camouflage against the sky from an underwater point of view has been long assumed. The proposition was demonstrated during World War II when British planes on antisubmarine patrol improved their records by painting the planes' undersides white. It is further confirmed by a mixed-up creature, the Nile catfish, who through some unhappy mutation got his white on top and the dark beneath. He compensates successfully by swimming upside down. . . .

In the Ceylon shrike one finds a perfect evolutionary union of body, culture, and behavior. The parents are black and white. The young are a mottled color blending precisely with the appearance of the lichen-plastered nest. But it is the behavior of the young that leaves the observer in awe. There are usually three, and when the parents leave the nest the young sit facing the center, immobile, their beaks raised at a sharp angle and almost touching in the center. The tableau presents the most exquisite imitation of old splinters at a break in the branch, and the young will not stir until the parents return. What the family has achieved, and what must puzzle the evolutionist, is a social lie in which each member plays its part.

The natural history of prevarication is, indeed, without end. Human communication, like most of our capacities, has merely provided superb elaboration on an old, old theme. Through our use of words we delude each other with grave conviction; we have our way, as the Ceylon shrike has his. In one sense only is our capacity unique and entirely our own. Man, so far as I know, is the only animal capable of lying to himself.

That we lie successfully to each other is natural; that we successfully lie to ourselves is a natural wonder.[8]

Question

Is "fraud" inherent in human nature? Explain.

VOKES V. ARTHUR MURRAY, INC.
212 So.2d 906 (Florida, 1968)

Justice Pierce

This is an appeal by Audrey E. Vokes, plaintiff below.

Defendant Arthur Murray, Inc., a corporation, authorizes the operation throughout the nation of dancing schools under the name of ''Arthur Murray School of Dancing'' through local franchised operators, one of whom was defendant J. P. Davenport whose dancing establishment was in Clearwater.

Plaintiff Mrs. Audrey E. Vokes, a widow of 51 years and without family, had a yen to be ''an accomplished dancer'' with the hopes of finding ''new interest in life.'' So, on February 10, 1961, a dubious fate, with the assist of a motivated acquaintance, procured her to attend a ''dance party'' at Davenport's ''School of Dancing'' where she whiled away the pleasant hours, sometimes in a private room, absorbing his accomplished sales technique, during which her grace and poise were elaborated upon and her rosy future as ''an excellent dancer'' was painted for her in vivid and glowing colors. As an incident to this interlude, he sold her eight one-half-hour dance lessons to be utilized within one calendar month therefrom for the sum of $14.50 cash in hand paid, obviously a baited ''come-on.''

Thus she embarked upon an almost endless pursuit of the terpsichorean art during which, over a period of less than 16 months, she was sold 14 ''dance courses'' totaling in the aggregate 2,302 hours of dancing lessons for a total cash outlay of $31,090.45, all at Davenport's dance emporium. All of these 14 courses were evidenced by execution of a written ''Enrollment Agreement—Arthur Murray's School of Dancing'' with the addendum in heavy black print, ''No one will be informed that you are taking dancing lessons. Your relations with us are held in strict confidence,'' setting forth the number of ''dancing lessons'' and the ''lessons in rhythm sessions'' currently sold to her from time to time, and always of course accompanied by payment of cash of the realm.

These dance lesson contracts and the monetary consideration therefor of over $31,000 were procured from her by means and methods of Davenport and his associates which went beyond the unsavory, yet legally permissible, perimeter of ''sales puffing'' and intruded well into the forbidden area of undue influence, the suggestion of falsehood, the suppression of truth, and the free exercise of rational judgment, if what plaintiff alleged in her complaint was true. From the time of her first contact with the dancing school in February 1961, she was influenced unwittingly by a constant and continuous barrage of flattery, false praise, excessive compliments, and panegyric encomiums, to such extent that it would be not only inequitable, but unconscionable, for a court exercising inherent chancery power to allow such contracts to stand.

She was incessantly subjected to overreaching blandishment and cajolery. She was assured she had ''grace and poise''; that she was ''rapidly improving and developing in her dancing skill''; that the additional lessons would ''make her a beautiful dancer, capable of dancing with the most accomplished dancers''; that she was ''rapidly progressing in the development of her dancing skill and gracefulness'', etc., etc. She was given ''dance aptitude tests'' for the ostensible purpose of ''determining'' the number of remaining hours [of] instructions needed by her from time to time.

At one point she was sold 545 additional hours of dancing lessons to be entitled to award of the ''Bronze Medal'' signifying that she had reached ''the Bronze Standard,'' a supposed designation of dance achievement by students of Arthur Murray, Inc.

Later she was sold an additional 926 hours in order to gain the ''Silver Medal,'' indicating she had reached ''the Silver Standard,'' at a cost of $12,501.35.

At one point, while she still had to her credit about 900 unused hours of instruction, she was induced to purchase an additional 24 hours of lessons to participate in a trip to Miami at her own expense, where she would be ''given the opportunity to dance with members of the Miami Studio.''

She was induced at another point to purchase an additional 126 hours of lessons in order to be not only eligible for the Miami trip but also to become ''a life member of the Arthur Murray Studio,'' carrying with it certain dubious emoluments, at a further cost of $1,752.30.

At another point, while she still had over 1,000 unused hours of instruction, she was induced to buy 151 additional hours at a cost of $2,049 to be eligible for a ''Student Trip to Trinidad,'' at her own expense as she later learned.

Also, when she still had 1,100 unused hours to her credit, she was prevailed upon to purchase an additional 347 hours at a cost of $4,235.74, to qualify her to receive a ''Gold Medal'' for achievement, indicating she had advanced to ''the Gold Standard.''

On another occasion, while she still had over 1,200 unused hours, she was induced to buy an additional 175 hours of instruction at a cost of $2,472.75 to be eligible ''to take a trip to Mexico.''

Finally, sandwiched in between other lesser sales promotions, she was influenced to buy an additional 481 hours of instruction at a cost of $6,523.81 in order to ''be classified as a Gold Bar Member, the ultimate achievement of the dancing studio.''

All the foregoing sales promotions, illustrative of the entire 14 separate contracts, were procured by defendant Davenport and Arthur Murray, Inc., by false representations to her that she was improving in her dancing ability, that she had excellent potential, that she was responding to instructions in dancing grace, and that they were developing her into a beautiful dancer, whereas in truth and in fact she did not develop in her dancing ability, she had no ''dance aptitude,'' and in fact had difficulty in ''hearing the musical beat.'' The complaint alleged that such representations to her ''were in fact false and known by the defendant to be false and contrary to the plaintiff's true ability, the truth of plaintiff's ability being fully known to the defendants, but withheld from the plaintiff for the sole and specific intent to deceive and defraud the plaintiff and to induce her in the purchasing of additional hours of dance lessons.'' It was averred that the lessons were sold to her ''in total disregard to the true physical, rhythm, and mental ability of the plaintiff.'' In other words, while she first exulted that she was entering the ''spring of her life,'' she finally was awakened to the fact there was ''spring'' neither in her life nor in her feet.

* * * * *

. . . Defendants contend that contracts can only be rescinded for fraud or misrepresentation when the alleged misrepresentation is as to a material fact, rather than an opinion, prediction or expectation, and that the statements and representations set forth at length in the complaint were in the category of ''trade puffing,'' within its legal orbit.

It is true that "generally a misrepresentation, to be actionable, must be one of fact rather than of opinion." . . . But this rule has significant qualifications, applicable here. It does not apply where there is a fiduciary relationship between the parties, or where there has been some artifice or trick employed by the representor, or where the parties do not in general deal at "arm's length" as we understand the phrase, or where the representee does not have equal opportunity to become apprised of the truth or falsity of the fact represented. . . . As stated by Judge Allen of this Court in *Ramel* v. *Chasebrook Construction Company:* "A statement of a party having . . . superior knowledge may be regarded as a statement of fact although it would be considered as opinion if the parties were dealing on equal terms."

It could be reasonably supposed here that defendants had "superior knowledge" as to whether plaintiff had "dance potential" and as to whether she was noticeably improving in the art of terpsichore. And it would be a reasonable inference from the undenied averments of the complaint that the flowery eulogiums heaped upon her by defendants as a prelude to her contracting for 1,944 additional hours of instruction in order to attain the rank of the Bronze Standard, thence to the bracket of the Silver Standard, thence to the class of the Gold Bar Standard, and finally to the crowning plateau of a Life Member of the Studio, proceeded as much or more from the urge to "ring the cash register" as from any honest or realistic appraisal of her dancing prowess or a factual representation of her progress.

Even in contractual situations where a party to a transaction owes no duty to disclose facts within his knowledge or to answer inquiries respecting such facts, the law is if he undertakes to do so he must disclose the *whole truth*. . . . From the face of the complaint, it should have been reasonably apparent to defendants that her vast outlay of cash for the many hundreds of additional hours of instruction was not justified by her slow and awkward progress, which she would have been made well aware of if they had spoken the "whole truth." . . .

[The Court below held the complaint not to state a cause of action. We reverse.]

Questions

1. In *Vokes,* defendant Arthur Murray, Inc., was not found to have misrepresented *facts.* How then did the Court find in favor of the plaintiff?
2. Build a case for Arthur Murray.
3. How would you have decided the case? Explain.
4. The plaintiff, a home buyer, purchased a home from a builder. Prior to the sale no water had entered the cellar. The builder had described the house as having "a good concrete floor, good foundation walls." A month after the sale, water appeared in the cellar, but the builder told the buyer not to be concerned: "Any new house will have water in the cellar [but] it will disappear when the earth around the foundation becomes firm." The builder assured the buyer that he would stand behind the house if anything went wrong. The cellar continued to leak, and the buyer brought suit for deceit. Decide the case. See *Fagerty* v. *Van Loan,* 183 N.E.2d 111 (Mass. 1962). But also see *Berryman* v. *Riegert,* 175 N.W.2d (Minn. 1970).

5. The plaintiff, Herbert Williams, bought an auto in March 1968, in Milwaukee, Wisconsin. Williams had sought an air-conditioned car. A salesman for the defendant, Rank & Son Buick, Inc., said the car was air conditioned, and Williams noted a knob on the dash labeled "Air." Williams drove the car for one and a half hours prior to purchase, and he otherwise had ample opportunity for inspection. Several days after the purchase Williams discovered that "Air" referred only to ventilation. The car was not air conditioned. Williams sued. Decide the case. See *Williams* v. *Rank & Son Buick, Inc.*, 44 Wis.2d 239, 170 N.W.2d 807 (1969).

UNCONSCIONABLE CONTRACTS

The efficiency and success of the American economy depends, in no small part, on the reliability of contractual relationships. The buyer must know that the goods will be delivered, and the seller must know that the bill will be paid. It is, therefore, only with the greatest reluctance that the legal system intervenes in freely bargained arrangements. Jurists adopted the concept of unconscionability to nullify or reform contracts that are so unfair or oppressive as to demand societal intervention. Mere foolishness or a want of knowledge do not constitute grounds for unconscionability, nor is a contract unconscionable and hence unenforceable merely because one party is spectacularly clever and the other is not.

Unconscionability is a concept not easily pinned down, and so it should be. The Uniform Commercial Code (UCC 2-302) governs unconscionability. As the following case illustrates, some situations are so patently unfair that justice requires intervention, but we wish to do so only in rare instances when *(a)* the bargaining power of the parties was so unbalanced that the agreement was not truly freely entered or *(b)* the clause or contract in question is so unfair as to violate societal values.

WILLIAMS V. WALKER–THOMAS FURNITURE COMPANY
350 F.2d 445 (C.A.D.C., 1965)

Chief Justice Wright

Appellee, Walker-Thomas Furniture Company, operates a retail furniture store in the District of Columbia. During the period from 1957 to 1962 each appellant in these cases purchased a number of household items from Walker-Thomas, for which payment was to be made in installments. The terms of each purchase were contained in a printed form contract which set forth the value of the purchased item and purported to lease the item to appellant for a stipulated monthly rent payment. The contract then provided, in substance, that title would remain in Walker-Thomas until the total of all the monthly payments made equaled the stated value of the item, at which time appellants could take title. In the event of a default in the payment of any monthly installment, Walker-Thomas could repossess the item.

The contract further provided that ''the amount of each periodical installment payment to be made by [purchaser] to the company under this present lease shall be inclusive of and not in addition to the amount of each installment payment to be made by [purchaser] under such prior leases, bills or accounts; *and all payments now and hereafter made by [purchaser] shall be credited pro rata on all outstanding leases, bills, and accounts* due the company by [purchaser] at the time each such payment is made.'' (Emphasis added.) The effect of this rather obscure provision was to keep a balance due on every item purchased until the balance due on all items, whenever purchased, was liquidated. As a result, the debt incurred at the time of purchase of each item was secured by the right to repossess all the items previously purchased by the same purchaser, and each new item purchased automatically became subject to a security interest arising out of the previous dealings.

On May 12, 1962, appellant Thorne purchased an item described as a Daveno, three tables, and two lamps, having total stated value of $391.10. Shortly thereafter, he defaulted on his monthly payments and appellee sought to replevy all the items purchased since the first transaction in 1958. Similarly, on April 17, 1962, appellant Williams bought a stereo set of stated value of $514.95. She too defaulted shortly thereafter, and appellee sought to replevy all the items purchased since December 1957. The court of general sessions granted judgment for appellee. The District of Columbia Court of Appeals affirmed, and we granted appellants' motion for leave to appeal to this court.

Appellants' principal contention, rejected by both the trial and the appellate courts below, is that these contracts, or at least some of them, are unconscionable and, hence, not enforceable.

* * * * *

. . . [T]he Uniform Commercial Code . . . specifically provides that the court may refuse to enforce a contract which it finds to be unconscionable at the time it was made. . . . [W]e hold that where the element of unconscionability is present at the time a contract is made, the contract should not be enforced.

Unconscionability has generally been recognized to include an absence of meaningful choice on the part of one of the parties together with contract terms which are unreasonably favorable to the other party. Whether a meaningful choice is present in a particular case can only be determined by consideration of all the circumstances surrounding the transaction. In many cases the meaningfulness of the choice is negated by a gross inequality of bargaining power. The manner in which the contract was entered is also relevant to this consideration. Did each party to the contract, considering his obvious education or lack or it, have a reasonable opportunity to understand the terms of the contract, or were the important terms hidden in a maze of fine print and minimized by deceptive sales practices? Ordinarily, one who signs an agreement without full knowledge of its terms might be held to assume the risk that he has entered a one-sided bargain. But when a party of little bargaining power, and hence little real choice, signs a commercially unreasonable contract with little or no knowledge of its terms, it is hardly likely that his consent, or even an objective manifestation of his consent, was ever given to all the terms. In such a case the usual rule that the terms of the agreement are not to be questioned should be abandoned and the court should consider whether the terms of the contract are so unfair that enforcement should be withheld.

In determining reasonableness or fairness, the primary concern must be with the terms of the contract considered in light of the circumstances existing when the contract was made. The test is not simple, nor can it be mechanically applied. The terms are to be considered "in the light of the general commercial background and the commercial needs of the particular trade or case." *Corbin* suggests the test as being whether the terms are "so extreme as to appear unconscionable according to the mores and business practices of the time and place." We think this formulation correctly states the test to be applied in those cases where no meaningful choice was exercised upon entering the contract.

. . . Since the record is not sufficient for our deciding the issue as a matter of law, the cases must be remanded to the trial court for further proceedings.

Questions

1. Explain the court's reasoning in *Williams*.
2. Plaintiff Willie had listed his business in the Wichita, Kansas, Yellow Pages for 13 years. Plaintiff was expanding his business, and he entered into an agreement with the defendant phone company to include additional telephone numbers in the directory. Defendant inadvertently failed to include one of the numbers in the directory. The contract signed by the parties included a conspicuous exculpatory clause limiting the phone company's liability for errors and omissions to an amount equal to the cost of the ad. On discovering the omission, plaintiff had begun advertising the number on television at a cost of approximately $5,000. Plaintiff contends the exculpatory clause is unconscionable and, therefore, unenforceable. Decide. Explain. See *Willie* v. *Southwestern Bell Telephone Company*, 549 P.2d 903 (Kan. 1976).
3. A door-to-door salesman representing Your Shop at Home Services, Inc., called on Clifton and Cora Jones, who were welfare recipients. The Jones couple decided to buy a freezer from the salesman for $900. Credit charges, insurance, etc. were added to that $900 base so that the total purchase price was $1439.69. Mr. and Mrs. Jones signed a sales agreement that accurately stipulated the price and its ingredients. The Joneses sued to reform the contract on unconscionability grounds. They had paid $619.88 toward the total purchase price. At trial, the retail value of the new freezer at the time of purchase was set at approximately $300.
   a. What is the issue in this case?
   b. Decide. Explain. See *Jones* v. *Star Credit Corp.*, 298 N.Y.S. 2d 264 (1969).

OTHER COMMON LAW PROTECTIONS

Although we will not be addressing them in detail here, the reader should understand that the law provides a number of other consumer protections arising out of judge-made contract law. For example, some bargains are void because an element of the bargain is illegal. Gambling contracts are a familiar example (in those states where gambling is illegal), but more to the point for the "typical" consumer is a contract rendered illegal because it provides for the payment of interest at a usurious rate (a rate beyond the maximum permitted under state law). A contract can also be rescinded because it was entered as a result of duress ("Buy my house or I will reveal all the sordid details of your recent trip to Los Angeles") or undue influence ("All right, son, I know your dear departed parents left that $500,000 to you, but as your loving uncle and guardian I must expect and demand that you turn the money over to me for safekeeping").

THE CONSUMER AND GOVERNMENT REGULATION OF BUSINESS

Having established the common law foundation for consumer protection, we now turn to some of the many governmental measures that provide shelter in the often unforgiving marketplace. States and localities have adopted a wealth of protective measures, but those cannot be meaningfully summarized here. Rather, we will look exclusively at a sample of federal activity. The reader is urged to repeatedly confront the question of proper balance, if such exists, between the free market and government intervention.

The Federal Trade Commission—Rule Making

The Federal Trade Commission was created in 1914 to prevent "unfair methods of competition and unfair or deceptive acts or practices in and affecting commerce." In conducting its business the FTC performs as a miniature government with extensive and powerful quasi-legislative and quasi-judicial roles. The primary legislative direction is in issuing trade regulation rules to enforce the specific intent of broadly drawn congressional legislation. That is, the rules define with particularity those acts or practices that the commission deems unfair or deceptive. Violations of trade regulation rules are punished by civil penalties, injunctions, and other appropriate redress.

In the same vein the FTC issues industry guides, which are the commission's interpretations of laws it enforces. The guides provide direction to the public, and although they do not have the force of law, a failure to observe the guides might result in adjudication.

The FTC's quasi-legislative role is well illustrated by its long and vigorously contested investigation of various funeral industry practices. After 10 years of inquiry, the FTC voted to require funeral directors to both itemize prices and quote them over the phone. Furthermore,

> [T]he rule requires funeral directors to "unbundle" funeral packages and allow customers to choose the services they want. It also prohibits embalming without a relative's permission, and forbids undertakers from misrepresenting the law to customers, such as saying embalming is required by a state when it is not.[9]

Critics of the rule argued that it was based more on anecdotes than on solid evidence. Supporters pointed to the great expense associated with funerals and the likelihood that consumers would not engage in careful shopping when dealing with the stress of a death.

As explained in the following article, the FTC recently declined to draw a new trade rule regulating the often-criticized health club industry.

FISCAL FITNESS: EFFORTS TO REGULATE HEALTH CLUBS FAIL TO END ABUSES

Richard B. Schmitt

Two years ago the Beverly Hills Workout, a Santa Monica, California, health club, drew a fast crowd when it began selling $49 annual memberships.

But within weeks after the promotional drive began, the four-year-old club was gone and the owners of its parent company, On the Move, Inc., were moving on to bankruptcy court. Several hundred people lost a total of $65,000, and the building was converted into a dry-cleaning business.

Scores of similar failures, along with a wide array of operating problems, have focused growing regulatory attention on the health club industry. And the crackdown seems to be helping—somewhat.

In many cases, for instance, legislation is proving ineffectual because the clubs are easy to open and their sheer number makes them hard to police. Prosecution for abuses also is often difficult. . . .

Fewer Frauds?

Not everyone agrees that the industry's problems are so widespread, and certainly many clubs are legitimate. Even some health club critics concede that there are now fewer ex-amples of outright fraud than there were several years ago.

Moreover, in 1985, the Federal Trade Commission decided against issuing federal rules for health spas, questioning the pervasiveness of fraud and other abuses. Terry Calvani, acting chairman of the commission at the time, was also concerned that a law enabling consumers to get refunds more easily would "make the spa business less attractive to investors."

The states, though, have taken action. Some 27 of them currently have health club laws, compared with 17 in 1983. Increasingly, they are requiring clubs to post bonds to cover potential losses and to stop selling "lifetime" memberships, because members have often proved more enduring than the clubs themselves. Connecticut collects a registration fee from the clubs that is used to reimburse victims in fraud cases. Last year, Maryland named a health spa commissioner to enforce the state's regulations.

* * * * *

Hand-to-mouth financing also creates intense pressure on salesmen, which they sometimes turn on potential members. For example, Washington State's Family Fitness Centers, operated by Traveler's Financial Services, Inc., used "coercion, intimidation, or severe embarrassment" to get people to join, the state charged in a 1983 lawsuit filed in the state superior court for King County. The clubs allegedly tried to break down stubborn customers by subjecting them to hour-long sales pitches in crowded offices, posing such questions as "Do you really want to look like that for the rest of your life?"

The clubs also tricked people into signing binding membership contracts, according to the suit, giving them the impression that they were merely filling out applications. The contracts were then allegedly turned over to collection agencies.

Family Fitness, without admitting or denying guilt, settled the charges by refunding about $500,000 to disgruntled members. Last May the state sued again in the same court, citing the same practices, and the club agreed to give back $600,000 more. But not all the money has been paid, and a full recovery appears remote because the club has gone out of business. Club officials couldn't be reached for comment.

* * * * *

Another common complaint is that clubs pressure customers into making quick decisions about discounts that, in reality, aren't discounts at all.

Special Deals

Pacific West Sport and Racquet Club, which succeeded Family Fitness as Washington's biggest club chain, advertised discounts of up to 45 percent to first-time visitors, who were also told that enrollments would be limited, according to a suit brought by the state last fall in the King County Superior Court charging unfair and deceptive business practices. However, the suit alleged, hardly anyone ever paid more than the discounted prices, and the membership limits were a fiction.

Neither admitting nor denying guilt, Pacific West agreed to refund up to $750,000. The club asserts that the complaints were isolated and that it has taken steps to resolve any problems.

Although regulation of the industry has increased, prosecution of operators is rare because intent to commit fraud must be proved in court, and intent is notoriously hard to establish. If nothing else, owners can argue that they were simply bad or unlucky managers.

* * * * *

Questions

1. Why should the funeral industry be required to meet standards (for example, itemizing prices) not required in other industries?
2. How would you vote on the funeral industry rule? Explain.
3. As noted in the health club article, more than half of the states have taken action to regulate health clubs. Would a uniform federal rule applying to all states be preferable to the existing situation where state rules differ and many states decline to interpose any regulations? Explain.

The Federal Trade Commission—Adjudication

On its own initiative or as a result of a citizen complaint, the FTC may conduct investigations into suspect trade practices. At that point the commission may drop the proceeding, settle the matter informally, or issue a formal complaint. An informal settlement normally takes the form of a consent agreement in which the party under investigation voluntarily discontinues the practice in question but is not required to admit guilt. If agreement cannot be reached, the commission may proceed with a formal complaint. In that case, the matter proceeds essentially as a trial conducted before an administrative law judge. Both the government and the "accused" party may be represented by counsel, and the proceeding is conducted in accordance with due process of law. If the government prevails, the judge may issue a cease and desist order forbidding further wrongful conduct. That order may be appealed to the full commission and to the federal Court of Appeals (assuming the existence of proper grounds for appeal).

The FTC is designed to prevent wrongdoing. Hence it has no authority to impose criminal sanctions. Although it can impose civil penalties of up to $10,000 per violation per day, the commission often engages in more creative remedies, for example, ordering corrective advertising to counteract previous, misleading ads or requiring contracts to be altered. In the case of "high-pressure sales," the commission has allowed the consumer a cooling-off period in which to cancel a contract.

The Federal Trade Commission—Deceptive Practices

FTC regulatory efforts range across the spectrum of consumer activity. For example, the FTC issued a rule specifying that mail-order sellers are in violation of the Federal Trade Commission Act if they solicit orders through the mail without a reasonable expectation that the goods can be shipped in 30 days or less. The FTC has pursued broad-scale regulatory initiatives against a number of industries, including insurance, used autos, and credit cards; but perhaps the best examples of FTC rule-making and adjudicatory actions lie in the area of advertising.

Unfair and deceptive trade practices, including those in advertising, are forbidden under Section 5 of the Federal Trade Commission Act. The term *unfair* has been only loosely defined. And "unfairness" in the absence of "deception" is uncommon. Nonetheless, from time to time the FTC has pursued unfairness cases that do not have their roots in either deception or anticompetitive activity. But we will focus our inquiry on deception, particularly deception in advertising. Historically, the commission has pursued a variety of deceptions in advertising. For example, bait-and-switch tactics are forbidden. In those cases the seller ordinarily advertises a product at very low prices to attract customers. Then the customer's attention is deliberately switched to another more expensive product. Another commonplace deceptive tactic involves advertising price reductions. When the price is indeed reduced but from a highly inflated original price established merely to facilitate a reduction, the ad is deceptive.

The courts have traditionally found unlawful deception in those acts or practices having "a tendency or capacity to deceive." However, in 1983 the FTC adopted a narrower interpretation requiring (1) a representation, omission, or practice likely to mislead, (2) that those misled were acting reasonably, and (3) that the deception was material. Some elaboration here may be helpful. Proof of actual deception is not necessary; rather a showing of some probability of deception is sufficient. The words in an ad must be examined in their total context, and the commission will consider evidence regarding consumers' actual interpretation of those words. For example, a breakfast cereal ad suggesting that its consumers might readily leap tall buildings would not be taken literally. Reasonable consumers are something like "ordinary people." However, ads directed to a specific subset of the population, are measured by the reasonableness standards of that subset. *Materiality* refers to those situations where the ad is likely to affect what consumers actually do when buying products. The materiality requirement limits deception claims because deception is "common and often inoffensive."[10] Apparently, the materiality standard means that neither a showing of consumer injury nor of likely consumer injury is necessary to a successful deception claim.[11] However, opinion differs on that topic. Finally, where an advertiser omits information that might be considered germane to the claim, the FTC will employ the materiality standard to determine whether the ad is deceptive as a consequence of the omission. That is, did the omission affect consumer choice?[12]

When an advertiser makes a claim for the quality of its product, the FTC requires the advertiser to have a reasonable basis for asserting that claim. For example, the FTC charged Sunbeam and Norelco with engaging in false and deceptive advertising when they claimed their air cleaners were effective in eliminating indoor air pollution. According to the commission, the air cleaners were not useful in significantly reducing pollution. In 1985 the two companies signed consent orders agreeing not to misrepresent their products. Those consent orders did not constitute admissions of guilt, but both companies were required to be able to support all advertising claims made for their air cleaners.[13]

Future commissions may or may not follow the 1983 standard. The courts give great weight to the commission's stance, but whether the new standard will be generally embraced remains to be seen. The article that follows tells the story of a high-stakes battle over dubious advertising practices.

A JUDGE PRESCRIBES A DOSE OF
TRUTH TO EASE THE PAIN OF
ANALGESIC ADS

William Power

New York—Extra-Strength Tylenol's claim that "You can't buy a more potent pain reliever without a prescription" was one of the most heavily promoted, and by some accounts one of the more successful, slogans in the history of Madison Avenue.

Trouble is, it was "not true."

That was the conclusion of federal Judge William C. Conner in a fiercely contested civil suit over Tylenol's ads brought against the brand's maker, Johnson & Johnson, by rival American Home Products Corp. Judge Conner ruled that Johnson & Johnson was guilty of making "false and misleading" advertising claims about its prized Tylenol product. He also said the company "misleadingly exaggerated" Tylenol's superiority over such competing pain-relief products as Anacin-3 and Advil, both marketed by American Home.

But the judge, who sits in U.S. District Court in Manhattan, also gave American Home a dose of the same medicine: some long-running Anacin-3 ads also weren't true, he said in his decision.

The judge decided to bar both companies from further offensive advertising. In an attempt to avoid appeals, he left it up to the companies' lawyers to agree on wording an injunction; so far they have failed to do that. As is common in civil cases, the first trial determined the facts but didn't award damages. There may be a second trial on damages, even though the judge said neither side would win enough to justify its trial costs.

The judge's 65-page ruling, issued after two years of filings and counterfilings and four weeks of testimony, is jarring to the $1.8 billion-a-year nonprescription analgesic market. Over-the-counter drugs are so similar that they rely almost totally on marketing for success. That's why drug companies have for years sued each other silly, hoping to put a dent in each other's niches.

"Small nations have fought for their very survival with less resources and resourcefulness than these antagonists have brought to their epic struggle for commercial primacy in the over-the-counter analgesic field," Judge Conner said.

The case led Judge Conner to make some cutting observations on what happens when medicine and advertising mix.

Lesson 1

Don't be Fooled by Headlines and Pictures
Tylenol's "rotten apple" ad appeared in medical journals in 1985 before the company yanked it after doctors complained that it was in bad taste. It featured a large color picture of an apple infected by a rotted worm hole. The ad was an attempt by Tylenol to lump aspirin's renowned problems—such as causing stomach upset—with ibuprofen, the active ingredient in Advil and in Nuprin, made by Upjohn Co.

Below the headline, "Aspirin and Ibuprofen—The Closer You Look . . . ," are listed four nasty side effects: gastric ulcers, "ulcer craters,'' gastrointestinal irritation, and allergic reaction.

A closer look at the ad, though, reveals that of the four items, only allergic reaction is actually ascribed to ibuprofen.

Judge Conner ruled that the ad was indeed misleading enough to break the law, "particularly when accompanied by dramatic and distasteful analogies, such as rotten fruit."

Johnson & Johnson says the judge merely had a problem with how the ad—aimed at medical professionals—was "laid out," not with the medical claims. "Professionals would understand what we're saying there," says Jim Murray, a company spokesman. Adds Roger Fine, Johnson & Johnson's associate general counsel, "It goes to format rather than content."

Lesson 2

Beware of Every Word, Even the Smallest Ones

One part of a series of Johnson & Johnson print and television ads really caused a headache for the judge. The ad claimed that Tylenol provides relief "without the stomach irritation you can get" from aspirin or Advil.

The judge said that kind of phrasing is a clever way to mislead consumers. Saying "the stomach irritation" makes Advil and aspirin seem equally irritating, which isn't true, he said. Studies show that Advil is less irritating than aspirin.

Johnson & Johnson now has found another way to lump ibuprofen (meaning Advil) with aspirin—as in "Tylenol doesn't irritate your stomach the way aspirin or even ibuprofen can." Similar effect, but legal.

Mr. Fine emphasizes that the Tylenol ads found misleading had been accurate when used and had been withdrawn voluntarily before the trial. "We're continually reevaluating our ad

claims in light of new medical evidence that might be helpful to consumers," he says. American Home declined comment on any details of the case, on grounds it isn't over.

Lesson 3

Numbers Don't Mean Much, Even the Big Ones

The judge said American Home was guilty of some "commercial puffery," too. He noted the "McDonald's-fashion" ads for Advil that use such phrases as "recommended over 5 million times for headaches and other kinds of pain"—even though only 2.4 percent of the doctors' recommendations were specifically for headache.

And the judge tweaked the contorted calculations behind an American Home slogan that "70,000 doctors and dentists" recommend Anacin-3. The company had sent free samples of Anacin-3 to 250,000 doctors, half of whom mailed in a postcard that entitled them to more free samples. The company then surveyed 404 of that group, 65 percent of whom said they recommended Anacin-3. Multiplying 65 percent by the total who mailed in postcards, the company proudly claimed that 70,000 doctors had recommended Anacin-3.

Besides, the judge said, most of the doctors "recommending" the product probably didn't do anything more than "pass on to patients free samples which AHP had furnished them." Such action "is certainly not a recommendation," he added.

Still, the AHP ad isn't technically false, added the judge. Similarly, Johnson & Johnson is able to claim in its ads that "hospitals trust Tylenol" because it makes sure hospitals consistently get the product more cheaply than competing products, which is why they use more of it, the judge said. And the judge concluded: "What [American Home] has done is to carry [Tylenol's] scheme to its logical extreme and cut the price of Anacin-3 to doctors all the way to zero."

Lesson 4

Know the Ingredients behind the Brand

More misleading on American Home's part, according to the judge, is its slogan that hospitals recommend "acetaminophen, the aspirin-free pain reliever in Anacin-3, more than any other pain reliever."

What most consumers might not know, though, is that Tylenol is the acetaminophen product that those hospitals recommend—or at least pass along—because of that favorable price they get on Tylenol.

Here's a more accurate, though less catchy, version of the slogan, courtesy of the judge: "Hospitals have recommended a product containing acetaminophen more than all other types of pain-reliever combined. Anacin-3 contains acetaminophen."

Lesson 5

Repeating a Slogan Doesn't Make It True

Here's how Johnson & Johnson tried to justify that famous Tylenol slogan (a slogan that the judge noted has been "repeated with wearying persistence"):

At the trial, company attorneys conceded that Extra-Strength Tylenol isn't "more" effective than Advil, but they insisted it is "as" effective, supposedly making the slogan true.

The judge plowed through a mountain of medical evidence on this one, finally declaring that for mild to moderate pain of a headache, there's no big difference between a two-tablet, 1,000-milligram dose of Extra-Strength Tylenol and a two-tablet, 400-milligram dose of Advil. The same dose of Advil, though, is more potent for severe pain, although that added potency (with added risk of side effects) isn't necessarily needed for a simple headache.

Thus, another of the judge's stabs at an honest slogan: "For mild to moderate pain, you can't buy a more effective pain reliever without a prescription."

Spruce that up and you get Tylenol's current slogan: "Nothing you can take without a prescription is more effective for headache than Extra-Strength Tylenol."

Johnson & Johnson doesn't give credit to the judge, though. It says it stopped using the famous slogan in January 1986 to get away from the "more potent" phrasing in favor of the "more effective" phrasing. Anyway, it adds, potency to fight severe pain is irrelevant in the "over-the-counter pain" market for which Tylenol is intended.

Source: *The Wall Street Journal,* May 13, 1987, p. 33. Reprinted by permission of *The Wall Street Journal,* © Dow Jones & Company, Inc. 1987. ALL RIGHTS RESERVED.

Afterword

At this writing in 1988, the "endless war" between American Home Products and Johnson & Johnson continues unabated. According to published accounts, the two firms have engaged in at least six lawsuits in recent years.[14] For example, in October 1987 Judge Conner declined to dismiss an American Home Products suit challenging a new Johnson & Johnson claim that Extra-Strength Tylenol is "unbeatable for headache." The judge indicated that the claim exceeded the bounds of the order explained in the article above. (Note that the judge's preliminary ruling is not a decision on the merits. He merely indicated that American Home's claim justifies complete litigation.)[15]

Questions

1. *a.* On balance, would American society be better off if we abolished laws forbidding unfair and deceptive advertising and instead allowed the free market to work its will in this area? Explain.

   b. How would the free market operate to protect the consumer in situations like that described in the American Home Products/Johnson & Johnson article?

2. For years American Home Products had claimed via advertising that its product, Anacin (a painkiller), had a unique formula that was superior in effectiveness to all other nonprescription painkillers. In fact, the only active painkilling ingredient in Anacin was aspirin. The Federal Trade Commission found that American Home Products was engaging in deceptive advertising. The commission ordered AHP to stop its deceptive advertising and required AHP to support any future claims about the superiority of its product as a painkiller with two scientifically valid studies. AHP appealed the commission's decision. Decide. Explain. See *American Home Products* v. *F.T.C.,* 695 F.2d 681 (3d Cir. 1982).

3. Listerine mouthwash has been marketed since 1879 with no change in its formula. Beginning in 1921 Listerine was advertised as being effective in preventing, curing, and alleviating colds and sore throats. The Federal Trade Commission found those claims to be untrue and ordered Listerine's producer, Warner-Lambert, to desist from those claims and to include the following words in its Listerine ads for a period of time expected to extend for approximately one year: "Contrary to prior advertising, Listerine will not prevent colds or sore throats or lessen their severity." Warner-Lambert appealed. Decide. Explain. See *Warner-Lambert* v. *Federal Trade Commission,* 562 F.2d 749 (D.C. Cir. 1977).

4. Mary Carter Paint Company manufactured and sold paint and related products. Carter Paint ads stated that for every can of Carter paint purchased, Carter would give the buyer a free can of equal quality and quantity. The price specified in these ads from the early 1960s was $6.98 per can. The FTC challenged the ads as deceptions in violation of Section 5 of the Federal Trade Commission Act.

   a. In what sense were the ads considered deceptive?

   b. Decide the case. Explain. See *Federal Trade Commission* v. *Mary Carter Paint Co.,* 382 U.S. 46 (1965).

The Consumer Product Safety Commission

Commonplace consumer products, such as toys, lawn mowers, power saws, bicycles, and portable heaters, are often instruments of harm in

American life. In 1970 the congressionally created National Commission on Product Safety completed two and a half years of study by recommending the creation of a federal agency to regulate product safety. The commission cited the heavy personal and financial costs of consumer product accidents.

Given those burdens and the belief that federal supervision was dispersed and inadequate, Congress created the Consumer Product Safety Commission (CPSC) in 1972. In its 1985 report the commission estimated that the use of consumer products leads to 29,000 deaths and 33 million injuries annually. Costs of $10 billion annually are attributed to emergency room treatments alone.[16]

The commission's authority extends over the full range of consumer products (glass, toys, ladders, saws, stoves, and so on). Its duties are many, but the heart of its activities may be summarized as follows:

1. Data Collection. The commission conducts research and collects information as a foundation for regulating product safety. The commission's National Electronic Injury Surveillance System (NEISS) collects data from many hospital emergency rooms across the country. The hospitals report all injuries involving consumer products. Analysis of that data base then suggests directions for more intensive investigations.

2. Rule Making. The commission, via its rule-making authority, promulgates mandatory consumer product safety standards. The commission invites any person or group to submit a safety standard for the product in question. Industry trade associations have been more active in submitting "offers" to set standards, but consumers and consumer groups (such as the Consumers Union) have been encouraged to participate. Safety standards essentially are technical specifications requiring certain minimums in strength, design, flammability, corrosiveness, labeling, and so on. The commission issues *performance standards,* which specify the minimum level of service expected from a product. For example, a ladder may be required to hold a specified amount of weight. Similarly, the commission issues *labeling standards,* which may require the attachment of a warning label to certain products. For example, the CPSC has provided that children's sleepwear must meet certain flame-resistance standards, must be labeled to show that they meet those standards, must be labeled with care instructions to preserve flame retardants (where used), and production and distribution records must be maintained so that the product's history can be traced. Because safety is not free, proposed product standards must include a statement of the anticipated economic and environmental impact.

Standards are processed under traditional due process requirements, including publication in the *Federal Register,* notice to affected parties, and hearings. Affected parties may petition a federal Court of Appeals to reverse CPSC rules.

3. Compliance. The CPSC is empowered to use a variety of strategies in securing compliance with safety standards. Manufacturers must certify before distribution that products meet federal safety standards. Agents of the commission may inspect manufacturing sites. The commission can mandate specific product safety testing procedures, and businesses other than retailers are required to keep records sufficient for the commission to see that they are in compliance with safety standards.

4. Enforcement. In cases of severe and imminent hazards, the commission may seek an immediate court order to remove a product from the market. In less urgent circumstances the commission may proceed with its own administrative remedy. Because it prefers to secure voluntary compliance, the commission may urge the company to issue public and/ or private notices of a defect, or it may seek the repair or replacement of defective parts. Where voluntary negotiations fail, the commission may proceed with an adjudicative hearing, conducted in the manner of a trial, before an administrative law judge or members of the commission. The decision may be appealed to the full commission and thereafter to the appropriate U.S. Court of Appeals. In its first six years, the CPSC issued approximately 1,200 product recalls.

Only a few products have actually been banned from the market. For example, at this writing in mid-1988, the CPSC has voted preliminary approval for a ban on most lawn darts. The play items have resulted in three deaths in recent years and several thousand injuries. Most lawn dart injuries are suffered by children. In recent years the CPSC has been hotly criticized for regulatory footdragging—particularly in the area of child safety. From 1981 to 1988 the commission's budget was cut by nearly one quarter. Critics point to slow attention to such problems as toys with small parts. In 1985 12,000 injuries and 18 deaths were linked to those toys, with most of the problems occurring when children swallowed the small parts.[17] But regulation in this area is treacherous. Should we ban the bicycle, which accounts for perhaps 800 children's deaths annually?[18] Failure to comply with safety provisions may result in civil fines up to $500,000. Criminal penalties for knowing and willful violations may total $50,000 and up to one year in jail.

The materials that follow illustrate the actual practice and impact of the Consumer Product Safety Commission in a particularly controversial product line—all-terrain vehicles.

ACCIDENTS SPUR DEBATE OVER SAFETY OF ALL–TERRAIN VEHICLES

William Petroski

Rollin Schmeder, a farm safety specialist at the University of Nebraska, says if all-terrain vehicles "were used properly, there would be no problem. . . . But most people just buy them and take off and don't get any training."

The squat-looking riding machines with fat tires have soared in popularity in recent years. About 450,000 of them are sold each year in the United States, and about 2.5 million of them are in use, say industry spokesmen. The cost generally runs from $800 to $4,000, depending on the model, including some machines with peak speeds of about 40 MPH. Most are manufactured in Japan.

Destructive Trail

All-terrain vehicles are used for off-road joyriding, hauling hay, checking cattle, and other farm work. Some construction companies use them at work sites.

* * * * *

Young People Hurt

. . . Nina Moroz, a spokeswoman for the National Safety Council in Chicago, says nearly half of all-terrain vehicle casualties are under age 21, and about one in five are under age 12.

Some of the victims are barely old enough to steer. In a March 1986 accident in Poweshiek County [Iowa], a five-year-old boy was killed when he rode an all-terrain vehicle from his parents' driveway into the path of a car on Highway 21, state records show.

In response to complaints about all-terrain vehicle accidents, industry representatives say there are no inherent problems with the design or engineering of the machines, and safety problems can be solved through better public education and increased state regulatory action. They also point out that the industry generates $1.5 billion in economic activity annually, and 38,000 American jobs are linked to all-terrain vehicle dealers and distributors.

The vehicles are being unfairly singled out for criticism, primarily by people who lack knowledge about the machines, says Wayne Jugenheimer, a longtime dealer. . . . They entail some risk, he says, just as "everything we do carries risk." But, he adds, the risk is "not more than a bicycle or skateboard."

* * * * *

Alan Isley, president of the Specialty Vehicle Institute of America, says his California trade organization has distributed safety material to dealers and individuals across the nation and has certified 1,000 instructors to teach proper driving techniques. The group also is asking states to adopt model laws to encourage safety.

More than 7 million people regularly ride all-terrain vehicles, and only about 1 percent of them are injured each year, Isley says. Furthermore, about 9 of 10 people hurt in accidents are treated and released from hospital emergency rooms, he adds.

Source: *Des Moines Sunday Register,* July 5, 1987, pp. 1B, 4B. © *Des Moines Register.* Reprinted by permission.

DEADLY THREE–WHEELERS

Editorial

After 900 Americans had been killed and 300,000 injured in accidents involving motorized tricycles, the U.S. Consumer Product Safety Commission finally announced [a preliminary agreement banning—Author] future sales. That won't make life any safer for the hundreds of thousands still riding some of the 1.6 million all-terrain vehicles, known as ATVs, already sold.

Meanwhile, newer four-wheeled ATVs are still on the market and are beginning to pile up their own grim statistics.

. . . Dr. Richard M. Narkewicz, president of the American Academy of Pediatrics, . . . supports legislation requiring manufacturers to offer refunds to owners of the three-wheelers. The compromise reached between manufacturers and the CPSC—which took effect just after the 1987 Christmas buying rush—calls only for a shift to four-wheelers and an education program aimed at owners of the three-wheelers ["hands-on" training of new owners and warnings—Author].

Education won't give youngsters the reflexes and coordination needed to handle ATVs. Moreover, the compromise gives the false impression that some significant step has been taken toward safety, when it has not.

Besides action to curtail the danger the ATVs pose, some steps should be taken to mitigate the damage they cause—or make manufacturers and users financially responsible for it.

The off-road machines tear up urban turf and rural pastures, dig dusty ruts through erosion-prone hills, and leave trails of wasteland in pristine areas formerly protected only by their inaccessibility to motorized vandals.

Yet manufacturers are allowed to build them, and riders to use them, with little or no regard for where they are used, whose property they destroy, how the damage will be undone—if it can be, at all.

Source: *Des Moines Register,* February 24, 1988, p. 6A.
© *Des Moines Register*. Reprinted by permission.

Afterword

In March 1988 the CPSC announced a new settlement to replace the preliminary understanding explained above. The final settlement, if approved in a later federal district court hearing, will continue the ban on the sale of three-wheeled ATVs and require the expenditure of $8 million in corrective advertising.

Questions

1. *a.* Should the CPSC recall all three-wheeled ATVs? Explain.
   b. Should children be banned from driving three-wheeled ATVs? Explain.

2. Representative Jim Florio (D–New Jersey), chair of the U.S. House of Representatives subcommittee on consumer protection, responded to the preliminary ATV agreement by saying, "This isn't so much a settlement as a sellout. It simply doesn't address the crucial issue of protection for people who have already purchased ATVs that they mistakenly believed to be safe."[19] Comment.

3. The *Des Moines Register* editorial refers to the environmental damage caused by ATVs. How significant a role should that damage play in the decision regarding a ban on three-wheeled ATVs?

4. Should product recalls and bans be publicized with advertising equal to that used to sell the product in the first place? Explain.

CONSUMER FINANCE LAW

For a considerable portion of American history, frugality was a virtue of the first rank. Saving was esteemed. Borrowing for consumer goods was, to many, foolish and a sign of weakness or decay. Today we live in quite another world. We are encouraged to experience the good life by spending lavishly. To do so we may well need to borrow. Now purchases on credit are not only tolerated, they are encouraged. American consumer debt now approaches $2 trillion (including home mortgages). Our shift to a commercial world predicated on the extension of credit opened seductive new windows of pleasure for the consumer, but the spread of indebtedness as a way of life led to new problems and, in some instances, abuses for both the debtor-consumer and the creditor-business. Predictably, and perhaps necessarily, we turned to the law for relief.

Credit Regulations

Congress has extended a variety of protections to the consumer seeking and securing credit. We will take an abbreviated look at five particularly important pieces of creditor protection legislation:

1. Truth in Lending Act.
2. Equal Credit Opportunity Act.
3. Fair Credit Reporting Act.
4. Fair Credit Billing Act.
5. State Usury laws.

Truth in Lending Act (TILA).[20] As we increasingly turned to credit financing, consumers often did not understand the full cost of buying on credit. In 1968 Congress passed and President Lyndon Johnson approved the Consumer Credit Protection Act, of which TILA was Title I. TILA was designed for consumer protection; hence, it does not cover all loans. The following standards determine TILA's applicability:

1. The debtor must be a "natural person" rather than an organization.
2. The creditor must be regularly engaged in extending credit or arranging for the extension of credit.
3. The purpose of the credit must be "primarily for personal, family, or household purposes" not in excess of $25,000. However, "consumer real property transactions" are covered by the act. Hence, home purchases fall within TILA provisions.
4. The credit must be subject to a finance charge or payable in more than four installments.

Following the enactment of TILA, the Federal Reserve Board developed regulations (labeled Regulation Z) detailing the specific requirements of the act. TILA was designed both to protect consumers from credit abuse and to assist consumers in becoming more informed regarding credit terms and costs so they could engage in comparison shopping. Congress presumed the increased information would stimulate competition in the finance industry. The act contains many provisions, but its heart is the required conspicuous disclosure of the finance charge (the actual dollar sum to be paid for credit) and the annual percentage rate (APR) (that is, the total cost of the credit expressed at an annual rate). The finance charge includes not just interest but service charges, points, loan fees, carrying charges, and others. TILA disclosure requirements apply to both *open-end* (for example, VISA and MasterCard) and *closed-end* (loans of a fixed amount for a definite time) transactions.

TILA provisions are enforceable both by several government agencies, including the Federal Trade Commission, and by private parties. Government enforcement is ordinarily accomplished through negotiation, but the agency may turn to a variety of mechanisms, including cease and desist orders. Criminal liability arises only in instances of knowing and willful violations. In such instances the U.S. Attorney General's Office may seek penalties up to $5,000 and/or one year in prison. Private parties may bring civil actions alleging damages resulting from TILA violations. Liability is limited to twice the amount of the finance charge for the transaction in question. However, the recovery cannot be less than $100 or more than $1,000. Attorney's fees may be secured under appropriate circumstances.

Under the terms of the Simplification and Reform Act of 1980, Congress approved some significant adjustments in TILA. For example, the elements of the finance charges and the APR need not be itemized in the disclosure form unless requested by the consumer in writing, and civil liability for unintentional mechanical errors (for example, inaccurate calculations) was eliminated.

The interesting and important dimension of the TILA reform is the change in philosophy it reflects. Congress moved away from a clear consumer protection stance and appeared to seek a balance between consumer and business interests. Critics had argued that TILA requirements were so complex that small businesses, in particular, encountered great difficulty and expense in complying. The Federal Reserve Board felt that the many disclosure standards increased the cost of credit and thus reduced consumer access to financing. Of course, consumer advocates argue that the simplifications reduce available information and afford the creditor more opportunities to willfully or carelessly abuse the credit seeker.

While TILA is directed largely to financial disclosure, it embraces some other issues of importance to the consumer. Of particular note is a series of rules governing credit cards. Cards cannot be issued unless requested, and cardholder liability for unauthorized use (lost or stolen card) cannot exceed $50. At this writing in 1988, Congress is considering a variety of bills designed to (1) place limits on credit card interest rates and (2) expand disclosure requirements for credit cards. Discussion of an interest rate cap has been stirred by a rise in credit card rates from 17.6 percent in 1981 to 18.1 percent in 1988 while the prime interest rate actually fell from 19.5 percent to 7.5 percent during that time. Under one interest rate formula (based on one-year Treasury bill rates) being considered, the cap at this writing in 1988 would be at 13.8 percent. Disclosure requirements under one of the bills was summarized by *The Wall Street Journal:*

> The bill . . . would require all credit card applications, direct-mail solicitations, and print advertisements to disclose a card's interest rate, its annual fee, and the grace period within which any credit extended may be repaid without incurring a finance charge.[21]

The case that follows is an excellent description, of both the goals of TILA and the actual details of required financial disclosure.

WISE FURNITURE V. DEHNING
343 N.W.2d 26 (Minn. 1984)

Chief Justice Amdahl

This case addresses the question of whether Wise Furniture (Wise) violated the Truth in Lending Act (TILA), and regulations promulgated thereunder by failing to disclose properly the finance charge and the retained security interest in its contracts with Marjorie Dehning. The trial court found that Wise violated TILA. . . .

The facts in this case are relatively simple. The critical factual dispute concerns Wise's compliance with Regulation Z. Dehning purchased consumer goods on credit from Wise on four separate occasions between February 9, 1979, and October 22, 1979. On February 9, 1979, she purchased a carpet and two lamps with a cash price of $250 and a finance charge of $28.61. Sometime after February 9, 1979, she also purchased a vacuum cleaner that was added to the February 9, 1979, contract. A separate agreement with cash price and financing charge does not appear to exist; the addition of the vacuum cleaner is only apparent because of reference to the vacuum cleaner as part of the "old contract" in the April 2 contract.

On April 2, 1979, Dehning purchased four chairs with a cash price of $300.00 and an added finance charge of $113.90.

On October 22, 1979, she purchased a sofa and two tables. The cash price was $729.95 and a finance charge of $277.78 was added.

Each contract refinanced the previous contract. For example, the April 2 contract totaled $634.00 plus the finance charge. The $634.00 was composed of the $300.00 cash price for the chairs, plus $11.05 tax, plus a $322.95 balance on the April 2 contract. The credit agreement recites "the old contract" and is unclear whether the $322.95 balance of "the old contract" includes the old finance charge, nor is it clear whether the new finance charge is computed on a total figure which includes the old finance charge. Furthermore, the newly computed finance charge is added in twice in arriving at the deferred payment price of the new contract. The October 22, 1979, agreement also appears to refinance the balance due and owing, including the finance charge, on the April 2 contract.

The April 2 and October 22 agreements seem to attempt to retain a security interest in all of the goods purchased by respondent.

On March 4, 1981, Dehning defaulted on the last contract with an outstanding balance of $811.23 due. Dehning made payments totaling $947.55 prior to default.

The express purpose of TILA is:

> [T]o assure a meaningful disclosure of credit terms so that the consumer will be able to compare more readily the various credit terms available to him and avoid the uninformed use of credit, and to protect the consumer against inaccurate and unfair credit billing and credit card practices.

. . . TILA and its regulations create a comprehensive scheme governing consumer credit transactions and impose a system of strict liability in favor of consumers. Protection of unsophisticated consumers is the overriding purpose of TILA and consequently creditors are required to comply with both the letter and spirit of the law.

Under TILA an "open-end credit plan" is defined as a credit arrangement "prescribing the terms of credit transactions which may be made thereunder from time to time and under the terms of which a finance charge may be computed on the outstanding unpaid balance from time to time thereunder." Although the transactions between Dehning and Wise appear to be closed-end credit transactions, *i.e.*, the amount of debt being fixed at the time of purchase, the transactions also have open-end characteristics. The carrying forward of the balance due on each previous contract resembles a revolving charge. The disclosures required for open-end credit transactions are more stringent than those for closed-end transactions. Notwithstanding the hybrid nature of the transaction, the intent of the parties appears to have been to create a closed-end consumer credit transaction.

. . . This is consistent with the trial court's conclusion. The parties' intent to create closed-end transactions will govern our characterization of these contracts.

* * * * *

. . . Marjorie Dehning was the archetype of the unsophisticated consumer TILA was designed to protect.

Section 1638 of Title 15 requires that the finance charge be accurately and fairly disclosed. When there is a refinancing transaction, Regulation Z requires that new disclosures be made to the consumer. . . . The April 2, 1979, contract clearly does not disclose whether the balance forward from February 9, 1979, was refinanced; whether the finance charge was subtracted from that contract so that a new finance charge could be computed; or whether the February 9, 1979, balance (including the finance charge) was included in the computation of the new finance charge that, in effect, resulted in a charging of interest twice for part of the items purchased on February 9, 1979. If the financing charges of the first two agreements were in fact incorporated into the final agreement, then this, alone, constitutes a violation of TILA.

Security interests retained by a seller of goods, even though unenforceable under state law, are required to be disclosed "on the same side as and above or adjacent to the place for the customer's signature." TILA and its regulations mandate that the description of the security interest retained by the seller be clear and unequivocal. In the instant case, the security interest retained by Wise is vague and ambiguous. Whether Wise continued to intend to hold a security interest in goods purchased under the February 9 and April 2 agreements by referring to the "old contract" even though Dehning had paid a total of $946.55 is uncertain. The descriptions of the security interests held by Wise are not clear and unequivocal. The trial court's conclusion that Wise violated TILA and Regulation Z is not clearly erroneous.

* * * * *

Affirmed.

Questions

1. Why was the consumer's want of "sophistication" an issue in this case?
2. Why did the Court treat this arrangement as a closed-end transaction?
3. Exactly how was Wise Furniture Company in violation of TILA and Regulation Z?
4. A health spa sells some memberships for cash and some on an installment basis. The price is the same whether the buyer pays cash or buys on the installment plan. The spa has an arrangement with a financing agency to sell the installment contracts to the agency at a discount (that is, at a price lower than the face value of the contract).
   a. How would you argue that the installment contract sales are in violation of TILA and Regulation Z?
   b. How would you rule on such a case? See *Joseph* v. *Norman's Health Club, Inc.*, 532 F.2d 86 (8th Cir. 1976).[22]

Equal Credit Opportunity Act (ECOA). In a society historically beset with discrimination, it is hardly surprising that credit was often denied on the basis of prejudices and stereotypes. In 1974 Congress enacted the Equal Credit Opportunity Act to combat bias in lending. Credit must be extended to all creditworthy applicants regardless of sex, marital status, age, race, color, religion, national origin, good faith exercise of rights under the Consumer Credit Protection Act, and receipt of public assistance. ECOA was in large part a response to anger over differing treatment of women and men in the financial marketplace. Creditors often would not loan money to married women under the woman's own name. Single, divorced, and widowed women were at a great disadvantage, vis-à-vis their male counterparts, in securing credit; and frequently women who married had to reapply for credit under their husband's name.

In addition to forbidding explicit discrimination in granting credit, ECOA includes a variety of provisions limiting the information that a creditor can require in processing an application. In general the creditor cannot seek information that could be used to engage in discrimination. Hence, among others, inquiries as to marital status, income from alimony, child support, maintenance payments, birth control practices, and child-bearing plans are either forbidden or limited.

Those discriminated against in violation of the act may recover actual damages, punitive damages up to $10,000, and other appropriate equitable and declaratory relief. Various agencies, including the Federal Trade Commission, enforce the act.

MILLER V. AMERICAN EXP. CO.
688 F.2d 1235 (1982)

Circuit Judge Boochever

Facts

Maurice Miller, plaintiff's late husband, applied for and received an American Express credit card in 1966. His account was denominated a Basic Card Account. Later in 1966, plaintiff Virginia Miller applied for and was granted a supplementary card. Her application was signed by her husband as the basic cardholder and by her. Mrs. Miller agreed to be personally liable for all charges made on her supplementary card. Her card bore a different account number from her husband's card, was issued in her own name, required a separate annual fee, and bore a different expiration date from Mr. Miller's card. The Millers used their American Express cards until Mr. Miller passed away in May, 1979. Two months after her husband's death, Mrs. Miller attempted to use her card during a shopping trip and was informed by the store clerk that her account had been cancelled. This was the first notice she received of the cancellation. Subsequently, Amex informed her that her account had been cancelled pursuant to a policy of automatically terminating the account of a supplementary cardholder upon the death of a basic cardholder. Amex invited her to apply for a basic account. Her application for a new account consisted merely of filling out a short form, entitled "Request to Change Membership status from Supplementary to Basic Card Member," which did not require any financial or credit history data. Amex issued Mrs. Miller a new card, apparently on the basis of her 13-year credit history in the use of the card it had just cancelled. Mrs. Miller brought suit against Amex for violation of the ECOA.

In the district court, the parties made cross motions for summary judgment on the issue of liability. Mrs. Miller argued that because her supplementary card had been cancelled after a change in her marital status, 12 C.F.R. § 202.7(c) had been violated, giving rise to a cause of action under the ECOA. Amex argued that Mrs. Miller was not within the terms of the regulation, and that she had not raised an issue of fact as to whether its allegedly uniform cancellation policy was discriminatory in motive or effect. The court awarded summary judgment to Amex without specifying its reasons.

Analysis

The issues on this appeal are whether Amex's policy of cancelling a spouse's supplementary account upon the death of the basic cardholder violates the ECOA and whether a plaintiff must always show discriminatory intent or effect to establish an ECOA violation. The facts are undisputed, therefore, we must decide whether the substantive law was correctly applied. . . .

The ECOA makes it unlawful for any creditor to discriminate with respect to any credit transaction on the basis of marital status. . . .

In order to carry out the purposes of the ECOA, the Board promulgated the regulations codified at 12.C.F.R. §§ 201.1 *et seq.* Section 202.7(c)(1) provides that a creditor shall not terminate the account of a person who is contractually liable on an existing open-end account on the basis of a change in marital status in the absence of evidence of inability or unwillingness to repay. Under certain circumstances, a creditor may require a reapplication after a change in the applicant's marital status.

Mrs. Miller's Amex card was cancelled after her marital status changed from married to widowed. Under § 202.7(c)(2), Amex could have asked her to reapply for credit, but instead it first terminated her card and then invited reapplication. There was no contention or evidence that her widowhood rendered Mrs. Miller unable or unwilling to pay, indeed, Amex's prompt issuance of a new card to her indicates that she was considered creditworthy.

* * * * *

Termination on the Basis of Marital Status: Proof of Credit Discrimination

The ECOA outlaws credit discrimination on the basis of marital status. The regulations proscribe particular adverse actions, including account terminations, which violate the Act if performed on the basis of marital status. Amex argues that it was entitled to summary judgment because Mrs. Miller did not attempt to show that Amex's policy of cancelling all supplementary cardholders on the death of the basic cardholder either was adopted with discriminatory intent or had an adverse impact on widows as a class. In light of the purposes of the ECOA, we do not think such a restrictive interpretation of the regulation is warranted.

The ECOA was meant to protect women, among others, from arbitrary denial or termination of credit. It establishes "as clear national policy that no credit applicant shall be denied . . . on the basis of characteristics that have nothing to do with his or her creditworthiness."

. . . As another court has noted, not requiring proof of discriminatory intent is especially appropriate in analysis of ECOA violations because "discrimination in credit transactions is more likely to be of the unintentional, rather than the intentional, variety."

* * * * *

The conduct here was squarely within that prohibited by § 202.7(c). Mrs. Miller's account was terminated in response to her husband's death and without reference to or even inquiry regarding her creditworthiness. It is undisputed that the death of her husband was the sole reason for Amex's termination of Mrs. Miller's credit. Amex contends that its automatic cancellation policy was necessary to protect it from noncreditworthy supplementary card-holders. The regulations, however, prohibit termination based on a spouse's death in the absence of evidence of inability or unwillingness to repay. Amex has never contended in this action that the death of her husband rendered Mrs. Miller unable or unwilling to pay charges made on her card. The fact that the cancellation policy could also result in the termination of a supplemental cardholder who was not protected by the ECOA, such as a sibling or friend of the basic cardholder, does not change the essential fact that Mrs. Miller's account was terminated solely because of her husband's death. The interruption of Mrs. Miller's credit on the basis of the change in her marital status is precisely the type of occurrence that the ECOA and regulations thereunder are designed to prevent.

We hold that the undisputed facts show, as a mattter of law, that Amex violated the ECOA and regulations thereunder in its termination of Mrs. Miller's supplementary card. For this reason, we reverse. . . .

Circuit Judge Poole, dissenting.

The majority today holds in effect that a credit practice need not be discriminatory to violate the Equal Credit Opportunity Act (the Act). Because this holding is contrary to the clear language and purpose of the Act, I respectfully dissent.

* * * * *

Violation of § 202.7(c)

It is a fact that American Express cancelled appellant's supplementary card after the death of her husband. Section 202.7(c), however, does not prohibit the termination of an account after a change in an applicant's marital status; it prohibits only the termination of an account "on the basis of" such a change. Since the change in appellant's marital status was not the basis for American Express's decision to cancel her supplementary card, there has been no violation of § 202.7(c).

Under the terms of the agreement by which it issues both basic and supplementary cards, American Express reserves the right to cancel a supplementary card if the basic cardholder is unable or unwilling to meet all the obligations relating either to the supplementary card or to the basic card account. It was undisputed that American Express uniformly cancels both the basic card account and all supplementary cards issued thereon upon the death of the basic cardholder, since the basic cardholder's death renders him or her unable to meet these obligations. This is a neutral policy, evenhandedly applied whatever the relationship between the basic and supplementary cardholders, i.e., whether they are brother and sister, mother and son, father and daughter, or husband and wife. The fact that in a particular case the death of the basic cardholder also changes the marital status of the supplementary cardholder is thus entirely incidental and immaterial to the basis for the cancellation of the supplementary card.

* * * * *

American Express's practice is not discriminatory since cancellation of supplementary cards is an evenhanded and uniform consequence suffered by all supplementary cardholders and is not at all operative because of a change in a cardholder's marital status. The majority's holding thus does not contribute to the eradication of credit discrimination. Rather, it prevents American Express from treating all supplementary cardholders alike and instead forces it to give preferential treatment to those supplementary cardholders who happen to have been married to the basic cardholder. Such a result stands the Act on its head.

* * * * *

Questions

1. Explain the majority's reasoning.
2. Do you agree with the majority opinion or that of the dissenting judge? Explain.
3. Does ECOA increase or decrease the cost of credit? Explain.
4. Mrs. John P. Harbaugh applied for a Master Charge credit card. Her application included information regarding her employment as a teacher, her salary, etc. She forwarded the application to Continental National Bank and Trust Company. In response Continental issued two credit cards in the name of John P. Harbaugh. Mrs. Harbaugh understood that she could use the cards, and that she could sign them Mrs. John P. Harbaugh or Mrs. Helen D. Harbaugh. However, she was unsatisfied with that arrangement and filed suit, claiming discriminatory denial of credit based on the sex or marital status of the applicant in violation of the ECOA. Although she could use the card issued in her husband's name, Mrs. Harbaugh indicated she wanted to have her own account and her own credit rating "in case something should happen to her husband." In fact, the bank did establish Mrs. Harbaugh's own account but under the name John P. Harbaugh because the bank's computer system deleted courtesy titles like Mrs. The bank argued that the deletion of courtesy titles was consistent with the legal requirements of a credit-granting policy "neutral as to sex." Testimony at trial indicated that Mrs. Harbaugh's account under the name John P. Harbaugh would not establish a separate credit history in her own name. But under federal law, creditors are required to send notice that married women can have credit information for joint accounts reported in both the husband's and the wife's names. Mrs. Harbaugh was so notified, and she understood she could use that mechanism to establish her own credit history. Given these conditions, Mrs. Harbaugh made two alternative claims: "(1) the bank was under an affirmative duty to use the courtesy title 'Mrs.' in opening her account or (2) if the courtesy title of 'Mrs.' was deleted, the bank was under a duty to insure that she receive a separate credit history in her own name."

   How would you rule on Mrs. Harbaugh's claims? Explain. See *Harbaugh* v. *Continental Ill. Nat. Bank*, 615 F.2d 1169 (1980).

Fair Credit Reporting Act (FCRA). For most of us a favorable credit rating is necessary to the full enjoyment of the material fruits of American life. We seek credit so commonly that credit bureaus process upwards of 100 million credit reports annually. Given these conditions, it is essential that credit information be accurate, that the information be used only for proper purposes, and that credit inquiries not unnecessarily disturb the consumer's privacy. Congress passed the FCRA in 1970, in recognition of both the potential for abuse in gathering and reporting credit information and the necessity for accurate, fair credit reports.

Rather than conduct their own credit investigations, businesses commonly turn to firms that specialize in gathering, storing, and reporting that information. Those credit bureaus (or, in the language of the act, "consumer reporting agencies" that regularly engage in the business of gathering and reporting consumer credit data to third parties) are covered by the terms of the act. The key requirements of the FCRA are as follows.

1. Consumer Rights. If requested, consumer reporting agencies must—with certain exceptions—provide each consumer with the information in his or her file. However, the consumer does not have the right to see the file itself. Inaccurate, obsolete, and unverifiable information must be removed. If the contents of the file remain in dispute, the consumer has the right to include in the file a brief statement of her or his version of the issues in question. If a consumer should be denied employment, credit, or insurance because of an agency report, the user of the report must so inform the consumer, and the consumer must be advised as to the origin of the credit report.

2. Reporting Agency Responsibilities. In brief, agencies are required to follow reasonable procedures to ensure that information is both accurate and up to date. Consumer credit reports can be furnished only for the following purposes, absent the consumer's permission or a court order: *(a)* credit, *(b)* insurance, *(c)* employment, *(d)* obtaining a government benefit, or *(e)* other legitimate business purpose involving a consumer. Inasmuch as protection of privacy is one of the stated purposes of the act, it is interesting that Congress imposed no limitation on the kinds of information that may be included in a file. Hence, sexual practices, political preferences, hair length, friendships, organizational memberships, and the like can lawfully be reported.

3. User Responsibilities. Those who purchase a consumer credit investigation must inform the consumer in advance of the pending inquiry.

When a consumer is denied credit, employment, or insurance, or where financial charges are increased because of an adverse credit report, the consumer must be apprised of the name and address of the consumer reporting agency that provided the information.

4. Penalties. Wronged consumers may secure actual damages in cases of negligent noncompliance with the FCRA. Punitive damages may also be secured in cases of willful noncompliance. In the criminal venue, fines of up to $5,000 and jail terms of up to one year may be assessed against those who knowingly and willfully secure information under false pretenses, and those credit agency employees who provide information to unauthorized persons are likewise subject to those criminal punishments. A number of federal agencies have statutory authority to enforce the act, but the primary burden lies with the Federal Trade Commission. The FTC can issue cease and desist orders against credit reporting agencies because violations of the FCRA are treated as unfair and deceptive trade practices.

Fair Credit Billing Act (FCBA). The FCBA, passed in 1974, provides a mechanism to deal with the billing errors that inevitably attend credit card transactions. The credit card holder who receives an erroneous bill must complain in writing to the creditor within 60 days of the receipt of the bill. If so, the creditor must acknowledge receipt of the complaint within 30 days. Then, within two billing cycles but not more than 90 days, the creditor must issue a response either acknowledging or denying the error. If the former, appropriate adjustments must be made. If the latter, the creditor must explain why the bill is correct. After filing its response, the creditor must wait 10 days before reporting the account as delinquent. If the consumer continues to dispute the accuracy of the bill, the creditor must file notice of the continuing dispute with any third party to whom notice of the delinquency is directed. Penalties for a creditor in violation of the act are quite modest. The consumer can collect the amount in question and any accompanying finance charges, but those finance charges cannot exceed $50 for each charge in dispute.

Predictably, the miracle of the credit card has led to an abundance of new headaches. Notwithstanding the FCBA, consumers remain the frequent victim of billing errors. As demonstrated in the following article, the consequences of those errors can be calamitous, and the pursuit of justice can be exhausting.

BEATING THE BANK: HOW ONE WOMAN FOUGHT A CREDIT CARD ERROR—AND WON

Jose De Cordoba

Lauderhill, Florida—"Settle," Lottye Carlin's friends would tell her at their weekly canasta game. "Settle for $50 and save yourself all that aggravation."

Sitting on a sofa in her South Florida home, Mrs. Carlin, a 69-year-old widow from Great Neck, New York, tells why she ignored her friends' well-meant advice: "If you tell me I owe you $50, I better owe it to you, or I'll fight it."

Last month, after an eight-year battle over erroneous credit card charges totaling $2,064.35, Southeast Banking Corp. agreed to pay Mrs. Carlin $150,000 in damages, write a letter of apology, and correct her credit records. The Miami-based bank holding company declines to comment on details of the suit, but a spokesman says the settlement was "in the best interests of both the individual and the bank."

Fighting Back

Credit card specialists say that errors in billings aren't unusual. In a consumer-credit system so gigantic and byzantine, foul-ups are bound to occur. What set Mrs. Carlin's story apart was the bank's persistence and her tenacious response.

* * * * *

It was a sweet victory for someone unaccustomed to fighting corporate Goliaths. Mrs. Carlin, a retiree, came to Florida 18 years ago after a life of selling clothes with her husband at their Long Island shop. Southeast, with $12.6 billion in assets, is Florida's second-biggest banking concern.

* * * * *

It all started innocently enough. In January 1979, says Mrs. Carlin's attorney, David Baron, Southeast issued a MasterCard to a "Lothye" Carlin, apparently after misreading Mrs. Carlin's response to the bank's offer of a credit card to her late husband. Mrs. Carlin says she neither requested nor received the MasterCard.

* * * * *

By late 1979, whoever was using the MasterCard had piled up more than $2,000 in unpaid charges. Mrs. Carlin says she soon began to receive phone calls from Southeast's collection department. For two years, at all hours of the day and once late at night, Mrs. Carlin says, she would get calls telling her to pay.

She says she usually answered the calls— more than 50 in all—the same way: Show me an itemized statement with my signature on it and I'll gladly pay. She says her callers refused, and one told her it would cost too much to produce an itemized statement. At any rate, she never received a bill for the MasterCard charges.

During the late-night call, she says, a woman told her she had "better pay the $2,000 or never get credit again." In 1981, after Mrs. Carlin put down a $9,000 deposit on a new $90,000 condominium, she found the threat hadn't been idle: She applied for a mortgage and was refused. Her credit, the lender said, was bad.

"At this point, all hell broke loose," she says. Punctilious in her bill paying, Mrs. Carlin couldn't fathom the reason for her fall from credit grace. An inquiry to a credit-reporting agency produced the answer: She owed MasterCard $2,064.35.

Upset and worried, Mrs. Carlin drove to Miami to meet with a representative from Southeast's collection department. At the meeting, the bank official told her it would wipe the slate clean if she paid $50, the fee for closing the account. "I called up the bank and said nuts to that," she says. "I wasn't going to pay 50 cents because I didn't owe them a nickel."

In the meantime, Mrs. Carlin's plans to buy a condominium had been dashed and her down payment forfeited by her failure to get financing. She eventually was able to recoup about half the down payment through a settlement with the developer.

But her troubles were just beginning. Eight months after offering to settle for $50, Southeast sued in state court to collect the $2,064.35.

Mrs. Carlin girded for battle. She hired a lawyer on an hourly basis, and for 15 months prepared for trial. But on the morning the trial was to begin, Southeast dropped the suit.

She then demanded that Southeast pay her legal expenses. A judge awarded her $3,500 in legal fees, but Southeast appealed, and in 1985 the award was overturned. By this time Mrs.

Carlin had lost more than $8,000 and was feeling the strain of the six-year battle, her lawyer says.

In February 1985, she turned the tables and hauled Southeast into state court, alleging malicious prosecution. The trial was set to begin last month on June 23. On June 22, Southeast agreed to pay $150,000 to settle the suit. But to Mrs. Carlin it was more important that the bank promise to apologize in writing.

"For no amount of money would my client agree to settle without the letter of apology," Mr. Baron says. The bank confirmed that it agreed to write a letter that could be characterized as an apology.

Public Vindication

The bank, he adds, wanted a confidentiality clause included in the settlement to prohibit Mrs. Carlin from disclosing the terms. Mrs. Carlin refused. She wanted her friends to see that "she was right and the bank was wrong," Mr. Baron says.

Thus informed, Mrs. Carlin's canasta group toasted her at the Woodlands Country Club, where she goes twice a week. As she sipped her Bloody Mary, club members congratulated her.

Source: *The Wall Street Journal*, July 9, 1987, p. 29. Reprinted by permission of *The Wall Street Journal*, © Dow Jones & Company, Inc. 1987. ALL RIGHTS RESERVED.

Question

If you were in such a situation, would you settle by paying $50? Explain.

Usury Statutes.   Fearing that consumers of limited bargaining power will be victimized by lenders, all states have passed usury laws imposing a limit on the amount of interest that can lawfully be charged for borrowed money. Usury laws have their roots in the church's historical opposition to the harshness of the "money changers" and in a well-intended solicitude for the financially unsophisticated and those forced to borrow under troubled circumstances. In general, contracts for loans at interest rates in excess of that permitted by law are illegal, and criminal penalties are often imposed. Depending on state law, the creditor may be able to collect none or only the lawful portion of the interest in question. In practice, the vitality of state usury laws is often sapped by exceptions that have the effect of lifting the allowable maximum rate. For example, the lender may be permitted to add a "carrying charge" to the terms of the loan. In most states the usury laws offer little protection, and many critics believe those laws to be of more harm than good to the consumer.

Is, for example, a 20 percent interest rate a *moral* wrong? A 30 percent rate?

DEBTOR PROTECTION

Generosity of spirit and deed is one of the more noble dimensions of the American character. However legitimately one may criticize our foreign policy in Vietnam, our tardiness in attacking discrimination, our devotion to sometimes crass materialism, it cannot legitimately be denied that Americans struggle sincerely to help those in need. Hence, for charitable reasons as well as for some "hard-nosed" economic considerations, the American legal system has enacted careful protections for those who find themselves indebted.

Debt Collection

The Fair Debt Collection Practices Act (FDCPA) of 1977 (amended in 1986) is designed to shield debtors from unfair debt collection tactics by debt collection agencies and attorneys who routinely operate as debt collectors. The act does not extend to creditors who are themselves trying to recover money owed to them. Some 5,000 debt collection agencies nationwide pursue those who are delinquent in their debts. The agencies are normally paid on a commission basis and are often exceedingly aggressive and imaginative in their efforts.

The FDCPA forbids, among others, the following practices:

1. Use of obscene language.
2. Contact with third parties other than for the purpose of locating the debtor. (That provision is an attempt to prevent harm to the debtor's reputation.)
3. Use of or threats to use physical force.
4. Contact with the debtor during "inconvenient" hours. For debtors who are employed during "normal" working hours, the period from 9 P.M. to 8 A.M. would probably be considered inconvenient.
5. Repeated phone calls with the intent to harass.
6. Contacting the debtor in an unfair, abusive, or deceptive manner.

The Federal Trade Commission is responsible for administering the FDCPA, and violations of the act are treated as unfair or deceptive trade practices under the Federal Trade Commission Act. A wronged debtor may also file a civil action to recover all actual damages (for example, payment for job loss occasioned by wrongful debt collection practices as well as damages for associated embarrassment and suffering). A civil penalty up to $1,000 as well as attorneys' fees and court costs may also be collected.

Bankruptcy

Our culture encourages indebtedness. For various reasons some debtors become encumbered beyond reasonable hope of recovery. Those individuals and organizations may, under appropriate circumstances, seek relief under the terms of our bankruptcy laws. Bankruptcy has become common in American life. We wish to afford a fresh beginning to the debtor and to avoid rendering the debtor an unproductive, helpless burden on society. We also want the involved creditors to recover as much of their losses as possible. So, although the reasons for our bankruptcy provisions are in large part quite pragmatic, it is nevertheless touching that we retain the humane recognition that some of us occasionally need a lift to overcome our ill fortune or foolishness.

> The word *bankruptcy* originally meant broken bench. In common-law England, when a merchant or craftsman was unable to pay his debts, the custom in the community was to break his work bench. This publicly established that the craftsman was no longer in business. Quite often, the creditors at that time would seek to perform the ceremony across the head of the impecunious debtor.[23]

Debtors are able to seek relief through both state and federal legislation. Our attention will be limited to federal law. The federal Bankruptcy Reform Act of 1978 repealed all previous bankruptcy law. It was, in turn, amended by the Bankruptcy Amendments and Federal Judgeship Act of 1984. In 1986 Congress passed the "Bankruptcy Judges, United States Trustees, and Family Farmer Bankruptcy Act." The act authorizes additional bankruptcy judges, makes some technical adjustments in existing law, and adds a new Chapter 12, which provides special bankruptcy arrangements for farmers. Those arrangements roughly parallel the Chapter 13 pattern briefly addressed below.

Bankruptcy is an adjudication relieving a debtor of all or part of the liabilities incurred to date. Under the terms of the Constitution, Congress is empowered to enact uniform bankruptcy legislation. Any person, partnership, or corporation may seek debtor relief. The three forms of bankruptcy action that are important to us are:

1. *Liquidation* (Chapter 7 of the Reform Act), in which all assets except exemptions are distributed to creditors.
2. *Reorganization* (Chapter 11), in which creditors are kept from the debtor's assets while the debtor negotiates a settlement.
3. *Adjustment of debts of an individual with regular income* (Chapter 13), in which individuals may achieve an arrangement similar to a Chapter 11 reorganization.

"Straight" Bankruptcy.   A Chapter 7 liquidation petition can be *voluntarily* filed in federal court by the debtor (individual, partnership, or corporation), or creditors can seek an *involuntary* bankruptcy judgment.

In a voluntary action the debtor files a petition with the appropriate federal court. The court then has jurisdiction to proceed with the liquidation, and the petition becomes the *order for relief*. The debtor need not be insolvent to seek bankruptcy.

An involuntary bankruptcy can be compelled only if the creditors have an individual or aggregate claim of at least $5,000. The debtor may challenge the bankruptcy action. The court will enter an order for relief if it finds the debtor has not been paying his or her debts when due or if most of the debtor's property is under the control of a custodian for the purpose of enforcing a lien against that property.

After the order for relief is granted, voluntary and involuntary actions proceed in a similar manner. Creditors are restrained from reaching the debtor's assets. An interim bankruptcy trustee is appointed by the court. The creditors then hold a meeting, and a permanent trustee is elected. The trustee collects the debtor's property and converts it to money, protects the interests of the debtor and creditors, may manage the debtor's business, and ultimately distributes the estate proceeds to the creditors. Both federal and state laws permit the debtor to exempt certain property (for example, household goods and clothing not to exceed $4,000, and equity in a vehicle not to exceed $1,200). The debtor's nonexempt property is then divided among the creditors according to the priorities prescribed by statute. Secured creditors are paid first. If funds remain, "priority" creditors, such as those responsible for administering the debtor's estate, are paid. Then, funds permitting, general creditors are paid. Each class must be paid in full before a class of lower priority will be compensated. Any remaining funds will return to the debtor.

When distribution is complete, the bankruptcy judge may issue an order *discharging* the debtor of any remaining debts except for certain statutorily specified claims. Those include, for example, alimony, child support, taxes, and educational loans. The debtor might fail to receive a discharge if the debtor had received a discharge in the previous six years, if property was concealed from the court, or if good faith in the bankruptcy process was lacking in other respects.

Reorganization.   Our primary concern in Chapter 11 of the act is with debtor protection for consumers, but recently an important and novel confluence of products liability theory (see Chapter 14) and bankruptcy law has brought corporate reorganization to the consumer (and worker) protection arena. Many workers and consumers are bringing products liability suits claiming personal injury from "toxic" products like asbestos, formaldehyde, benzene, and Agent Orange. Chapter 11 of the Bankruptcy Reform Act is being used by some companies in an attempt to "manage" those claims. Chapter 11 is the bankruptcy proceeding most commonly employed by corporations, but its provisions also apply to other debtors, including partnerships and individuals. Under Chapter 11 the debtor keeps existing property but establishes with the court a schedule under which creditors will be paid. The debtor is permitted to continue business activities. The court prevents creditors from reaching the debtor's assets other than through the agreed payment plan. The plan may provide for payment of all or only a portion of the debt. The court will hold a hearing, at which creditors and other "interested parties" may file objections. The court will confirm the plan if certain conditions are met. If the payments provided for in the plan are completed, the debtor will ultimately receive a discharge. And under certain hardship circumstances a debtor may receive a discharge even if the plan was not completed in full.

The discussion of the Texaco, Pennzoil, Getty case at the beginning of the merger materials in Chapter 9 illustrated an oil giant's use of Chapter 11 to avoid a financial collapse.

Adjustment of Debts.   Under Chapter 13 of the Bankruptcy Reform Act, individuals (not partnerships or corporations) can seek the protection of the court to arrange a debt adjustment plan. Chapter 13 permits only voluntary bankruptcies. After the necessary petition is filed, creditors are restrained from reaching the debtor's assets. A trustee is appointed, and the debtor files a plan for repayment.

Contrast our capitalist view of bankruptcy with the Chinese position depicted in the following article.

AS FACTORY'S FORCED BANKRUPTCY SHOWS, CHINA WON'T EASILY ACCEPT INSOLVENCIES

Adi Ignatius

Shenyang, China—After hemming and hawing for years, China's rubber-stamp parliament approved legislation at its just-ended annual session that institutionalized one of the country's most controversial economic reforms: bankruptcy.

In the capitalist world, bankruptcy is an accepted matter of course for companies in financial trouble. But in communist countries like China, where the state controls production and guarantees every citizen a job, bankruptcies, which often put people out of work, go against the grain.

Even the new law won't make Chinese leaders any less uneasy about the concept of bankruptcy, as evidenced by a trial bankruptcy in Shenyang, a bleak, polluted industrial city about 380 miles northeast of Beijing. In 1985, Shenyang adopted the nation's first trial insolvency law. Since then, city officials have declared only one enterprise bankrupt: the Shenyang Explosion-Proof Equipment Factory.

Big Losses

The small factory makes equipment that is built to withstand high-pressure operations. Located on the city's outskirts, it started operations in 1965 to make pumps for trucks. For 10 years it was profitable. But demand plummeted and, between 1976 and 1978, the factory incurred wide losses. Desperate, its state-owned parent organization offered the directorship to anyone who could devise a rescue plan.

Shi Yongjie, a veteran laborer at the plant, tried his hand. Working without pay for more than a year, he and several colleagues developed a new product line: strong aluminum equipment for use in hazardous manufacturing processes. Borrowing money from parts suppliers, Mr. Shi reopened the factory. He was named director in mid-1983.

The factory quickly met its wage and pension commitments, though it couldn't repay debts, which had increased to about $115,000. Mr. Shi believed he could gradually pay off the borrowings but says his attempt to manage the factory was thwarted by interference from government officials. He complains, for example, that officials constantly transferred personnel, including his top managers.

As Mr. Shi struggled to gain more than nominal control, the rug was pulled out from under him. In early 1985 he was dismissed. A new director took over, and a few months later received government notice that the factory would be declared bankrupt and closed if it didn't drastically improve within a year. The Chinese refer to this warning procedure as "giving the yellow card," a reference to the soccer practice in which referees caution players once for flagrant violations and remove them for a second infraction.

Example Was Needed

During its 12-month probation, the factory did nothing to improve its situation—apparently because the government had selected it as a test case for the country's first factory liquidation since the Communists took power in 1949. Says Han Yaoxian, a government spokesman: "Shenyang needed an example while it was testing its trial bankruptcy law."

After the enterprise was declared insolvent in August 1986, the city auctioned it off to a gas-supply company. The factory's 72 workers received unemployment benefits for six months. Most have applied for new jobs through the local labor bureau.

The government, having decided to enforce the liquidation, had to determine if any directors were responsible for the collapse. Assess-

ing personal culpability is crucial to China's bankruptcy law, because its major goal is to warn other managers to improve efficiency at their enterprises. Directors can be fined and even sentenced to prison for "dereliction of duty."

Publicly Humiliated

In this instance, former factory director Shi shouldered the blame, even though he had devised the plan to salvage the ailing factory and had been removed from his post before the factory was warned that it might be liquidated. He was barred from taking a new job and publicly humiliated. He forfeited $270 in welfare benefits, a significant amount compared with his former wage of $25 a month. Today, the 56-year-old Mr. Shi passes the time helping his wife run her tiny private business.

"I still don't understand why I was dismissed," says the former director, seated in a Shenyang hotel room dressed in blue padded clothes and a snap-brim cap. "If the government had given me more time, I think I could have turned the factory around."

To date, China has officially liquidated only one other enterprise, a small department store in the southern city of Nanchang. But more cases are on the way. The National People's Congress on Wednesday passed an "industrial enterprise law" that will give directors greater responsibility to run their factories without interference from government and party officials. That law will bring into force a national bankruptcy code next year.

To be sure, the regulations aren't likely to lead to a rash of failures. China's goal is to use the threat of bankruptcy to spur lumbering state-owned enterprises to become less of a drain on state coffers. Subsidies to cover losses at state enterprises this year are expected to total $10.97 billion, or 13 percent of budget expenditures.

As Shenyang's experience indicates, officials view bankruptcy as a last resort. Six other money-losing enterprises in the city have been yellow-carded. All but the explosion-proof equipment factory have returned to profitability, thanks largely to the government, which provided cut-rate loans and tax breaks and helped recruit technicians to develop new products.

"If we overemphasize bankruptcy, we will just create unemployment," says Zheng Silin, assistant to the governor in Shenyang's province of Liaoning. "That could cause chaos."

Source: *The Wall Street Journal*, April 15, 1988, p. 22. Reprinted by permission of *The Wall Street Journal*, © Dow Jones & Company, Inc. 1988. ALL RIGHTS RESERVED.

Bankruptcy Critique.   As explained in the following article, the business community has welcomed the reforms in U.S. bankruptcy law.

A BETTER BALANCE IN BANKRUPTCY LAW

Mary-Margaret Wantuck

Meet Charlie, a computer executive making $75,000 a year in 1979. He owned a beautifully furnished $175,000 country home with a $150,000 mortgage and commuted daily into New York City. He and his wife, Sylvia, enjoyed Broadway shows and exclusive Manhattan restaurants.

Charlie loved credit and lived on it—a stockpile of charge cards, a credit union revolving loan, and overdraft checking. In early 1980 he reached his credit limit and had to start paying cash for entertainment. But with so much of his monthly income committed to debt service, there was just not that much cash left over to play with, and that annoyed Charlie and Sylvia.

Enter the Bankruptcy Reform Act of 1978, which went into effect in October 1979.

It was an answer to the couple's prayer. They declared bankruptcy under Chapter 7, which erased all their debts. They were able to keep their house and continue to enjoy all of Charlie's $75,000 salary. They resumed their lives without any obligation to repay any of their creditors.

Charlie and Sylvia are not a particularly extreme example of the new kind of debtor encouraged by the looseness of the 1978 law. During the law's first full year of operation, between October 1979 and October 1980, U.S. bankruptcy cases rose 59 percent. The next year personal bankruptcies climbed another 43 percent, to 515,355.

Sears, Roebuck & Company, for example, found that its bankruptcy losses jumped more than 120 percent from 1979 to 1980.

Lenders discovered there were many Charlies and Sylvias—people who were current on their required monthly payments, had little or no previous history of delinquency, and many have even had additional credit available at the time their creditors received the bankruptcy notice—but who decided to cash in on the bonanza, get rid of all their unsecured debts, and keep their real estate and personal property.

A study conducted by Purdue University's Credit Research Center in 1981 found that 4 out of 10 people who filed for Chapter 7 bankruptcy relief could have paid 50 percent or more of their nonmortgage obligations over the following five years; 29 percent could have repaid all of them.

* * * * *

Creditor uproar over bankruptcy losses finally hit home on Capitol Hill. Last June, Congress passed the Bankruptcy Amendments Act of 1984. Among many changes are tighter consumer provisions, which took effect in October. . . .

Most lenders call the new law better balanced between creditors and debtors. "What it represents is a livable compromise," says Laurence P. King, who was a member of a group at New York University that studied bankruptcy law problems. "The old law was a farce."

Bankruptcy judges can now consider a debtor's current income and expenditures in determining whether his financial situation dictates a Chapter 7 filing or a plan for debt repayment under Chapter 13. Under the old law, only assets and liabilities could be weighed.

Chapter 13 filings have also been modified. An unsecured creditor can object to a Chapter 13 repayment plan that does not include repayment of the entire debt and use all of the debtor's projected disposable income (beyond the basic necessities) over a three-year period for repayment. Before, a nominal payback was acceptable as long as the debtor's plan showed an effort to pay back something to the creditors.

Consumers may no longer "load up" just before declaring bankruptcy. Any debts of $500 or more for "luxury goods and services," owed to a single creditor and incurred within 40 days of filing, must be paid. So must cash advances of more than $1,000 that are extended under an open-ended credit plan obtained by the debtor within 20 days before filing.

Federal exemptions have also undergone a facelift. In a Chapter 7 bankruptcy, a debtor's personal assets are converted to cash to reimburse creditors as much as possible. However, before a liquidation occurs, the debtor can exempt specified personal items.

Under the law, a debtor can no longer exempt $200 of value on each item of household goods and clothes. There is now a flat $4,000 maximum amount. In addition, a debtor can exempt only $3,750 of equity in real property used as a residence plus $400 in value of other property. The old amount was $7,500 of equity plus $400 in other property.

An added bonus for creditors is that now couples can take either a federal or state exemption—not both, as was permitted before. . . .

Lenders like Jimmie Bearden, president of the Aero Engineering Development Center Federal Credit Union in Memphis, are especially happy about more restrictive collateral provisions.

"Debtors can't hang onto collateral like a car for months now, running it into the ground and having its value depreciate measurably as each day goes by," she says. Debtors have 30 days from the time of the bankruptcy petition to file a statement of intent as to whether they will redeem the collateral, voluntarily surrender the collateral, claim the property as exempt, or reaffirm the underlying debt. They have another 45 days in which they can change that decision.

If a debtor elects to reaffirm his debt, no court approval is required.

Bankruptcy judges now have the authority to dismiss a Chapter 7 bankruptcy petition if the judge determines that granting the request would constitute "substantial abuse" of the bankruptcy code.

* * * * *

Lawyers' responsibilities have increased. A debtor's attorney must now inform his client of relief other than Chapter 7 that is available for resolving his financial problems.

In the past, "in courts where not too many Chapter 13s were filed, the debtor may not have known there was another recourse," says Lawrence Young, a Houston attorney with expertise in the consumer bankruptcy area. "Much of the preparatory work was handled by paralegals; it was a fill-out-the-forms-and-file atmosphere. Now, instead of running an assembly line in court, lawyers are back in the business of lawyering again.''

* * * * *

Creditors say the law still has weaknesses. Too much potential for abuse exists, according to Alexander Cole, senior vice president of credit administration for Industrial Valley National Bank & Trust Company in Philadelphia.

''As long as consumers have the right to retain some equity in their homes and on other assets under federal exemptions, notwithstanding state overrides,'' he notes, ''they may find ways of abusing that right.''

Determining whether there is substantial abuse in a Chapter 7 filing may take so much time that a busy judge may leave review of a debtor's financial status to a court trustee. The trustee would then have a major say in whether a case should remain Chapter 7 or be switched to Chapter 13.

''Many bankruptcy courts are very, very busy,'' Young says. ''In the southern district of Texas, for example, there are 17,000 bankruptcy cases pending, and only two judges; the third position is vacant. But even three judges are not going to make much difference.''

* * * * *

Many creditors argue that bankruptcy write-offs would decrease dramatically if the new law ordered bankruptcy courts to take a debtor's future earnings into account.

In the specialized publication *Credit World,* Harry Wolpoff and Ronald Canter, lawyers

specializing in consumer credit law, have described what can happen when future income is not taken into account.

A doctor is serving a one-year residency at a hospital where he receives a weekly salary of $150 plus living accommodations. Shortly, he will fill a $40,000 teaching post at a medical school. His debts total $15,000. Two months before starting his new job, he files for Chapter 7 bankruptcy. The income statement disclosed to the court reflects only his present $150 salary. Disposable income left after paying necessary expenses is minimal. The authors say his filing probably would not be challenged.

* * * * *

Credit counselors are decrying the law's omission of a requirement that all petitioners go through counseling.

''There are people who go through the bankruptcy process, are adjudicated as debtors, and released by the courts without having learned anything,'' says Robert E. Gibson, president of the National Foundation for Consumer Credit, whose members are credit counseling services. ''They are subject to continuing money mismanagement and financial catastrophes.''

* * * * *

But creditors say most of the changes in bankruptcy laws are good, and they do not expect to see any more revisions soon. After struggling for years over changing the law, ''the last thing Congress wants to see on its agenda is bankruptcy,'' Young says.

Source: Reprinted by permission, *Nation's Business,* April 1985, pp. 50–53. Copyright 1985, U.S. Chamber of Commerce.

Questions

1. Why do we permit debtors to reduce or escape their indebtedness via bankruptcy?
2. Does our bankruptcy law make it too easy for people and businesses to ''walk away'' from their debts? Explain.

3. Representative Billy Evans of Georgia has argued that America's moral attitude toward bankruptcy is changing. That is, he says, the stigma once attaching to bankruptcy is gone, and "payment of one's debt is no longer important." Is he correct? Explain.
4. Should those filing for bankruptcy under Chapter 7 not be allowed to exempt equity in their homes and automobiles? Explain.

ELECTRONIC FUND TRANSFERS

"Electronic money" is rapidly encroaching on paper as the preferred means of commercial exchange. The computer, the telephone, and the coded plastic card are among the instruments that may, in the future, substantially replace checks and cash as value exchange mechanisms. For example, bank customers may withdraw or deposit funds at any time by using their encoded card in an unattended teller machine. The growth of electronic fund transfers caused Congress in 1978 to pass the Electronic Fund Transfer Act as Title IX of the Consumer Credit Protection Act. Congress was concerned that established legal principles were not adequate to the task of resolving the many new legal problems arising from electronic transfers. The act defines electronic fund transfers (and hence the act's coverage) as "any transfer of funds other than a transaction originated by check, draft, or similar paper instrument, which is initiated through an electronic terminal, telephonic instrument, computer, or magnetic tape so to order, instruct, or authorize a financial institution to debit or credit an account."

Electronic fund transfer systems include:

1. Point-of-sale transfers where a computer is used to immediately transfer funds from a consumer's bank account to that of the merchant from whom the consumer is making a purchase.
2. Automated tellers.
3. Direct bank deposit and withdrawal systems for automatic deposit of checks or automatic payment of a regularly recurring bill.
4. Transfers initiated by phone, where consumers call their bank to order payments or transfer funds between accounts.

The act provides remedies for an extended series of problems that may confront the EFT consumer. For example:

1. A resolution system is provided when the consumer believes an error has been made in an EFT billing.
2. In general, if a consumer's EFT card is lost or stolen, the consumer's liability for unauthorized use is limited to $50, but liability may exceed $50 if the financial institution is not notified of the loss within two days.
3. With certain exceptions, the bank is liable for all actual damages sustained by the consumer in situations when the bank failed to transfer funds in a timely manner, following a proper order by the consumer.

4. Civil and criminal penalties ranging from $100 (as well as court costs and attorneys' fees) to $5,000 fines and up to one year in prison may be imposed on financial institutions failing to comply with the act.

The reader is cautioned to understand that EFT law is only now emerging, and the brief glimpse offered here merely suggests what may become a murky area of legal inquiry.

CHAPTER QUESTIONS

1. What are electronic fund transfers? Why did the development of electronic fund transfers provoke a need for new legislation (the Electronic Fund Transfer Act)?
2. In sum, would the consumer's lot be improved if we sharply reduced or eliminated the many consumer protection efforts outlined in this chapter? Explain.
3. Once the government decided to intervene in the free market on behalf of consumers, two broad options presented themselves: (a) the government could have limited its effort to generating and distributing information to consumers or (b) the government could have set safety standards for all products. Assuming the government were forced to choose one or the other but not elements of both, which option should it choose? Explain.
4. In recent years the government has struck down professional and state regulations forbidding advertising by doctors and advertisements for some products (for example, contact lenses). Why did the government open the door to advertising in those areas?
5. The Consumer Federation of America (CFA) argues that state and federal lawmakers should pass legislation ensuring affordable checking service for the poor. The CFA cites the following Federal Reserve Board data in support of its position:

   > Sixty-five percent of the poorest half of the surveyed households had checking accounts in 1983, down from 71 percent in a 1977 survey. And the proportion of households with checking accounts in the poorest 10 percent of the survey dropped to 44 percent from 56 percent in 1977.[24]

   Is a checking account so central to a successful, comfortable contemporary life that Congress should pass legislation requiring banks to adopt special standards that would give the less affluent more ready access to checking privileges? Explain.
6. In recent years Congress has considered legislation banning tobacco advertising. Leaving health and legal issues aside, international marketing professor J. J. Boddewyn of the City University of New York argues that an advertising ban would be ill advised. Boddewyn ex-

plains that tobacco advertising is banned in five free market countries (Italy, Iceland, Singapore, Norway, and Finland). Per capita tobacco consumption did not decline in those countries following the advertising prohibitions; indeed, it increased by margins ranging from 3 percent in Finland to 68 percent in Italy. A study in five nations found only 1 percent of the 7- to 15-year-old children interviewed pointed to advertising as the most important reason for their decisions to begin smoking. The influence of parents, siblings, and friends was easily the dominant factor as they understood their decisions. And the results of the survey were the same across the five nations, even though one nation actually banned tobacco advertising (Norway), two significantly restricted it (Australia and the United Kingdom), and two employed modest restrictions (Spain and Hong Kong).[25]

a. What arguments would you raise in favor of a ban on tobacco advertising?

b. How would you vote on such a bill? Explain.

7. Cite some examples of consumers abusing businesspeople.

8. Some have argued for consumer protection, not merely from fraud and the like but from bad taste as well:

> To introduce Maxwell House coffee's new vacuum-packed bags, General Foods Corporation is sponsoring a 27-city tour through the South featuring country singers Waylon Jennings and Jerry Reed. (About 70 percent of southern customers buy their coffee in bags instead of cans.) "We needed an event to build awareness of our new package," Michael W. Jardon, a Maxwell House promotion manager, says of the sponsorship. "Everybody else does it; we ought to compete in that arena."
>
> The Waylon Jennings tour was conceived and scheduled entirely by Maxwell House. "We picked the venues, the time of year, everything," says Mr. Jardon. But the tour isn't "grossly commercial," he adds. "We'll be there, and fans will know it, but Waylon is *not* going to wear a blue coffee can with his guitar."[26]

a. Is the concert-going public harmed by Jennings' arrangement with General Foods? Explain.

b. Is Jennings and/or his music debased by the commercial support for his tour? Explain.

9. According to a recent survey, consumers in six industrialized nations overwhelmingly favor the creation of "National Departments of Consumer Protection." A consumer protection agency was favored by 65 percent or more of those surveyed: in Australia (80 percent), Canada (82 percent), England (74 percent), Israel (86 percent), Norway (65 percent), and the United States (74 percent).[27] Would you favor the creation of such a body? Explain.

10. The Consumer Product Safety Commission, relying on hospital statistics, reported that in 1980, 75 persons were killed and 63,293 injured

while using chain saws. According to the CPSC, chain saw accidents ordinarily occur when the tip of the chain saw strikes resistance, causing the operator to lose control.[28] Based on these figures, should chain saw sales be banned until a safer product is produced? If enacted, would such a ban be effective? Explain.

11. Swedish law requires safety messages to be included in ads to children. ("Always wear a helmet when skateboarding.") In the Netherlands ads for candy must include a picture of a toothbrush.[29] Should those policies be adopted in the United States? Explain.

12. Professor and advertising scholar J. J. Boddewyn argues that *(a)* "There are more lies in personal ads than by all business combined—from 'apartment with river view [from the bathroom,]' to 'attractive woman wants to meet man.' " *(b)* "Some government ads are downright misleading"; "armed forces recruitment posters . . . promise you will 'see the world' but do not include a warning [from the Surgeon General?] that you could be shot at and die."[30] Comment.

13. The plaintiff, a wholesaler, reached an agreement with Philco, a manufacturer, to distribute Philco appliances to retailers. The plaintiff agreed to carry an adequate inventory of Philco parts. The agreement provided that either party could terminate the contract with 90 days' written notice. In the event of termination the wholesaler agreed on demand to resell and deliver its remaining Philco stock to Philco. The resale price was to be agreed. The agreement was terminated, but Philco declined to exercise its option to repurchase. The wholesaler was unable to sell most of the remaining Philco inventory and demanded that Philco repurchase, but Philco declined. The plaintiff brought suit, claiming the contract was unconscionable. Decide. Explain. See *W. L. May Co., Inc.* v. *Philco-Ford Corporation,* 543 P.2d 283 (Or. 1975).

14. Townsend, a retailer, purchased a cash register from Stronach, a salesperson for National Cash Register. Townsend had relied on Stronach's assertions that the cash register would save Townsend the cost of a bookkeeper and perhaps half the cost of a sales clerk. Stronach had sold a number of cash registers to various retailers over a period of years. Several months subsequent to the purchase, Townsend recognized that the cash register had not produced the savings projected by Stronach. Is Stronach guilty of fraud? Explain. See *National Cash Register Co.* v. *Townsend Grocery Store,* 50 S.E. 306 (N.C. 1905).

15. Roseman resigned from the John Hancock Insurance Company following allegations of misuse of his expense account. He reimbursed the account. Subsequently he was denied employment by another insurance firm after that firm read a Retail Credit Company credit report on him. The credit report included accurate information regarding Roseman's resignation. Was Retail Credit in violation of the Fair Credit Reporting Act in circulating information regarding the

resignation? Explain. See *Roseman* v. *Retail Credit Co., Inc.*, 428 F. Supp. 643 (Pa., 1977).

16. Parker Pen Company issued ads for a fountain pen containing the words "Guaranteed for Life." The same ads included the following language in smaller print and in a less prominent location: "Pens marked with the Blue Diamond are guaranteed for the life of the owner against everything except loss or intentional damage, subject only to a charge of 35 cents for postage, insurance, and handling, provided complete pen is returned for service." Was the ad deceptive? Explain. See *Parker Pen Co.* v. *FTC,* 159 F.2d 509 (9th Cir. 1946).

17. Dun & Bradstreet, Inc., a credit reporting agency, erroneously reported to five subscribers that Greenmoss Builders had filed for voluntary bankruptcy. A correction was subsequently issued. Greenmoss, remaining dissatisfied, filed suit for defamation. The Supreme Court has held [see *New York Times* v. *Sullivan,* 376 U.S. 254 (1964)] that a public official cannot recover damages for defamation in the absence of a showing that the statement was made with "actual malice," that is, with knowledge that it was false or with reckless disregard for whether it was false. Here the credit report in question was not a matter of public importance. Must the plaintiff, Greenmoss, show "actual malice" by Dun & Bradstreet? Explain. See *Dun & Bradstreet, Inc.* v. *Greenmoss Builders, Inc.,* 472 U.S. 749 (1985).

18. The Ogilvy & Mather ad agency found in a recent survey that only 59 percent of people today "like advertising a lot or a little," compared with 68 percent in a similar 1985 study. What's more, half of the consumers surveyed consider most ads to be in poor taste, while just 43 percent felt that way two years ago. Even the number of people who believe ads provide useful information has slipped: 71 percent versus 76 percent in 1985.[31]

   a. Is advertising doomed to a continuing decline in respect and influence? Explain.

   However, Ogilvy found that consumers around the world are generally less cynical than Americans about advertising:

   People in Hong Kong, Colombia, Brazil, and Britain are much bigger fans of advertising, according to a multinational study conducted by Ogilvy. Consumers in Hong Kong and Colombia praise advertising as a way to obtain valuable information about products, while most Brazilians consider ads entertaining and enjoyable. In the six countries Ogilvy studied, only West Germans dislike ads more than Americans.[32]

   b. How do you account for Americans' greater skepticism regarding advertising?

19. In early 1988 the Consumer Product Safety Commission announced the initiation of an effort to make cigarette lighters child resistant. According to a commission study the lighters caused "an estimated 7,800 fires leading to 120 deaths, 860 injuries, and $60.5 million in

property damage in 1985."[33] The nature of the necessary changes and the cost associated with those changes are not clear at this writing. However, you might acquire some modest cost/benefit insight by thinking about your latest effort to open a child-resistant medical bottle.

Should the government stay out of the cigarette lighter safety business and simply expect adults to keep lighters out of the hands of children? Explain.

NOTES

1. "State Announces Recall of Toys, *Des Moines Register,* November 11, 1987, p. T1.
2. Ibid.
3. D. Rothschild, "The Magnuson-Moss Warranty Act: Does It Balance Warrantor and Consumer Interests?" *George Washington University Law Review* 44 (1976), pp. 335 and 337, as reported in Donald Rothschild and David Carroll, *Consumer Protection Reporting Service* (Owings Mills, Md.: National Law Publishing Corporation, 1983), vol. I, p. Intro–2.
4. See, for example, "The U.S.'s Toughest Customer," *Time,* December 12, 1969, pp. 89–98.
5. Robert J. Samuelson, "The Aging of Ralph Nader," *Newsweek,* December 12, 1985, p. 57.
6. *Lindberg Cadillac Co.* v. *Aron,* 371 S.W.2d 651 (1963).
7. See *Trustees of Columbia University* v. *Jacobsen,* 53 N.J. Super. 574, 148 A.2d 63 (1959).
8. Robert Ardrey, *The Social Contract* (New York: Dell Publishing, 1974), pp. 9–12.
9. Daniel Mintz, "FTC Votes Funeral Rate Disclosures," *Des Moines Register,* July 29, 1982, p. B5.
10. Gary T. Ford and John E. Calfee, "Recent Developments in FTC Policy on Deception," *Journal of Marketing* 50, July 1986, pp. 82, 89.
11. Ibid., p. 94.
12. Ibid., p. 98.
13. Associated Press, "FTC, Firms Agree on Air Cleaners," *Waterloo Courier,* November 26, 1985, p. C4.
14. "Johnson & Johnson's Bid to Dismiss Suit by Rival Is Rejected," *The Wall Street Journal,* October 20, 1987, p. 6.
15. Ibid.
16. Consumer Product Safety Commission, *Product Safety, It's No Accident,* Fiscal Year 1985 Annual Report, vol. 1, p. 15.
17. Steven Waldman, "Kids in Harm's Way," *Newsweek,* April 18, 1988, pp. 47–48.
18. George Will, "What Should the Government Do about Dangerous Toys?" *Des Moines Sunday Register,* May 8, 1988, p. 6C.
19. Associated Press, "Doctors' Group, Others Rap ATV Agreement," *Waterloo Courier,* December 31, 1987, p. A3.

20. The materials in this section are drawn, in part, from Rothschild and Carroll, *Consumer Protection Reporting Service.*

21. John E. Yang, "Congress Faces Array of Proposals to Cap Credit Card Rates and Increase Disclosure," *The Wall Street Journal,* March 26, 1987, p. 37.

22. This question is drawn from David Epstein and Steve Nickles, *Consumer Law in a Nutshell* (St. Paul, Minn.: West Publishing, 1980), p. 106.

23. Jeff A. Schnepper, *The New Bankruptcy Law—A Professional's Handbook* (Reading, Mass.: Addison-Wesley Publishing, 1981), p. 1.

24. "Are Checking Charges Choking Poor?" *Des Moines Register,* November 11, 1987, p. T1.

25. J. J. Boddewyn, "Smoking Ads Don't Get People Hooked," *The Wall Street Journal,* November 21, 1986, p. 24.

26. "Advertisers Use Music Groups to Reach Young Consumers," *The Wall Street Journal,* July 28, 1983, sect. 2, p. 19.

27. Hiram Barksdale et al., "A Cross-National Survey of Consumer Attitude towards Marketing Practices, Consumerism, and Government Regulations," *Columbia Journal of World Business* 17, no. 2 (Summer 1982), pp. 71, 83.

28. Michael Hinds, "Business Says Products Recall Makes Sense," *The New York Times,* October 17, 1981, p. L-9.

29. J. J. Boddewyn, "The Global Spread of Advertising Regulation," *MSU Business Topics,* Spring 1981, pp. 5, 9.

30. Ibid., p. 12.

31. Ronald Alsop, "Advertisers Find the Climate Less Hostile outside the United States," *The Wall Street Journal,* December 10, 1987, p. 25.

32. Ibid.

33. Associated Press, "Safety Agency Calls for Child-Resistant Lighters," *Waterloo Courier,* January 8, 1988, p. C6.

Chapter 14

Products Liability

INTRODUCTION

Products liability is that branch of the law governing litigation for injuries resulting from defective products. As recently as the early 1960s products liability was little more than an obscure corner of the law. Strict liability, today's primary weapon for the plaintiff in a defective product action, did not exist. Today, through a steady accumulation of judicial decisions and legislative enactments, products liability litigation is so common and often so successful that it has changed the business community's manufacturing and distribution practices. Perhaps 100,000 products liability suits are filed annually. Business argues that the system now unfairly favors the consumer. Consumer lawyers argue that the business community is, at last, being compelled to pay the full cost of producing unfit goods. That cost can be staggering. About $254 million in products liability insurance claims were paid in 1980.[1] In 1986 the Ford Motor Company revealed that it was facing lawsuits from accident victims with claims totaling $1.1 billion for the company's failure to provide airbags and other kinds of restraint systems. Indeed, in 1988 one of the first lap belt cases to go to trial resulted in a $3.3 million judgment against Ford. In that case a 13-year-old boy was paralyzed from the waist down following an accident in a Ford Escort. He was riding in the rear seat. The jury cited both the lack of a rear shoulder belt and a defect in design of the rear lap belt. At this writing Ford is contemplating an appeal.[2] For other companies the threat of truly immense claims has become quite real. Manville Corporation, an asbestos products producer, entered bankruptcy in 1982 when it was facing some 16,500 suits claiming over $12 billion in damages from exposure to asbestos. Asbestos is now acknowledged to contribute to lung cancer and other health problems. Although the Manville case is not fully resolved, we know the company and its insurers will be providing at least $2.5

billion for a 30-year trust fund to compensate present and future victims.[3]

We will explore both the technical dimensions of products liability actions and the policy dispute regarding the fairness and wisdom of contemporary products liability law. The three major causes of action are negligence, breach of warranty, and strict liability.

NEGLIGENCE

In dangerously simplified terms, *negligence* is a breach of the duty of due care. To paraphrase *Black's Law Dictionary,* a negligent act is the failure to do what a reasonable person, guided by those considerations that ordinarily regulate human affairs, would do or doing what a reasonable person would not do. Thus, a producer or distributor has a duty to exercise reasonable care in the entire stream of events associated with the development and sale of a product. In designing, manufacturing, testing, repairing, and warning of potential dangers, those in the chain of production and distribution must meet the standard of the reasonably prudent person. Failure to do so constitutes negligence. Furthermore, rather recent decisions extend potential liability to those situations in which a product is being put to an unintended but reasonably foreseeable misuse.

Historically, product producers were ordinarily protected from negligence liability under the combined effects of the doctrines of privity and caveat emptor (let the buyer beware). *Privity* is the label applied to the legal relationship arising when parties enter a contract. As a consequence of the privity requirement, wronged consumers could reach only those in the chain of distribution with whom a contractual relationship (privity) had been established. Therefore, consumers ordinarily could not recover against a remote manufacturer. Under the caveat emptor principle the vendor was liable for defects only to the extent that an agreement was reached to provide for that liability. In previous centuries consumers might have expected to deal face-to-face with the product producer. Therefore, the privity and caveat emptor notions held at least the superficial legitimacy of a buyer and seller, presumed to be of equal bargaining power, protecting their own interests in an equitable contract. However, the development of elaborate, multilayered systems of production and distribution prompted a revision of legal standards. In a famous 1916 New York state decision (*MacPherson* v. *Buick Motor Co.*),[4] brilliant jurist Benjamin Cardozo held that an action could be maintained against a remote manufacturer of an automobile with a defective wheel that broke and caused injury. In so doing Cardozo put aside the view that the plaintiff's right to recovery grew only out of a contractual relationship. Cardozo's view has since been uniformly adopted, thus permitting victims of negligence to bring actions against all wrongdoers in the chain of production and distribution.

To establish a successful negligence claim the plaintiff must meet each of the following requirements:

1. *Duty*. The plaintiff must establish that the defendant owed a duty of due care to the plaintiff. In general, the standard applied is that of the fictitious reasonable man or woman. That "reasonable person" acts prudently, sensibly, and responsibly. The standard of reasonableness depends, of course, on the circumstances of the situation.

2. *Breach of duty*. The plaintiff must demonstrate that the defendant breached the duty of due care by engaging in conduct that did not conform to the reasonable person standard. Breach of the duty of due care may result from either the commission of a careless act or the omission of a reasonable, prudent act. Would a reasonable man or woman discharge a firearm in a public park? Would a reasonable person foresee that failure to illuminate one's front entry steps might lead to a broken limb?

3. *Causation*.
   a. *Cause in fact*. Did the defendant's breach of the duty of due care actually cause the harm in question? Commonly, the "but for" test is applied to determine cause in fact. That is, but for the defendant's failure to stop at the red light, the plaintiff pedestrian would not have been struck down in the crosswalk.
   b. *Proximate cause*. The plaintiff must establish that the defendant's actions were the proximate cause of the injury. As a matter of policy, is the defendant's conduct sufficiently connected to the plaintiff's injury as to justify imposing liability? Many injuries arise from a series of events—some of them wildly improbable. Did the defendant's negligence lead directly to the plaintiff's harm, or did some intervening act break the causal link between the defendant's negligence and the harm? For example, the community's allegedly negligent maintenance resulted in a blocked road, forcing the plaintiff to detour. While on the detour route, the plaintiff's vehicle was struck by a plane attempting to land at a nearby airport. Was the defendant's negligence the proximate cause of the plaintiff's injury?[5]

4. *Injury*. The plaintiff must have sustained injury, and, due to problems of proof, that injury must be physical.

Proximate cause may be the most inscrutable ingredient in the test for negligence. Establishing proximate cause often requires addressing the slippery notion of foreseeability and its relation to duty. The following case illustrates the difficulty in anticipating the consequences of one's actions.

WEIRUM V. RKO GENERAL, INC.
539 P.2d 36 (CA. S. Ct. 1975)

Justice Mosk

A rock radio station with an extensive teenage audience conducted a contest which rewarded the first contestant to locate a peripatetic disc jockey. Two minors driving in separate automobiles attempted to follow the disc jockey's automobile to its next stop. In the course of their pursuit, one of the minors negligently forced a car off the highway, killing its sole occupant. In a suit filed by the surviving wife and children of the decedent, the jury rendered a verdict against the radio station. We now must determine whether the station owed decedent a duty of due care.

The facts are not disputed. Radio station KHJ is a successful Los Angeles broadcaster with a large teenage following. At the time of the accident, KHJ commanded a 48 percent plurality of the teenage audience in the Los Angeles area. In contrast, its nearest rival during the same period was able to capture only 13 percent of the teenage listeners. In order to attract an even larger portion of the available audience and thus increase advertising revenue, KHJ inaugurated in July of 1970 a promotion entitled "The Super Summer Spectacular." The "spectacular," with a budget of approximately $40,000 for the month, was specifically designed to make the radio station "more exciting." Among the programs included in the "spectacular" was a contest broadcast on July 16, 1970, the date of the accident.

On that day, Donald Steele Revert, known professionally as "The Real Don Steele," a KHJ disc jockey and television personality, traveled in a conspicuous red automobile to a number of locations in the Los Angeles metropolitan area. Periodically, he apprised KHJ of his whereabouts and his intended destination, and the station broadcast the information to its listeners. The first person to physically locate Steele and fulfill a specified condition received a cash prize. In addition, the winning contestant participated in a brief interview on the air with "The Real Don Steele." The following excerpts from the July 16 broadcast illustrate the tenor of the contest announcements:

> 9:30 and The Real Don Steele is back on his feet again with some money and he is headed for the Valley. Thought I would give you a warning so that you can get your kids out of the street.
>
> The Real Don Steele is out driving on—could be in your neighborhood at any time and he's got bread to spread, so be on the lookout for him.
>
> The Real Don Steele is moving into Canoga Park—so be on the lookout for him. I'll tell you what will happen if you get to The Real Don Steele. He's got 25 dollars to give away if you can get it . . . and baby, all signed and sealed and delivered and wrapped up.
>
> 10:54—The Real Don Steele is in the Valley near the intersection of Topanga and Roscoe Boulevard, right by the Loew's Holiday Theater—you know where that is at, and he's standing there with a little money he would like to give away to the first person to arrive and tell him what type car I helped Robert W. Morgan give away yesterday

morning at KHJ. What was the make of the car. If you know that, split. Intersection of Topanga and Roscoe Boulevard—right nearby the Loew's Holiday Theater—you will find The Real Don Steele. Tell him and pick up the bread.

In Van Nuys, 17-year-old Robert Sentner was listening to KHJ in his car while searching for "The Real Don Steele." Upon hearing that "The Real Don Steele" was proceeding to Canoga Park, he immediately drove to that vicinity. Meanwhile in Northridge, 19-year-old Marsha Baime heard and responded to the same information. Both of them arrived at the Holiday Theater in Canoga Park to find that someone had already claimed the prize. Without knowledge of the other, each decided to follow the Steele vehicle to its next stop and thus be the first to arrive when the next contest question or condition was announced.

For the next few miles the Sentner and Baime cars jockeyed for position closest to the Steele vehicle, reaching speeds up to 80 miles an hour.[1] About a mile and a half from the Westlake offramp the two teenagers heard the following broadcast:

11:13—The Real Don Steele with bread is heading for Thousand Oaks to give it away. Keep listening to KHJ. . . . The Real Don Steele out on the highway with bread to give away—be on the lookout, he may stop in Thousand Oaks and may stop along the way. . . . Looks like it may be a good stop Steele—drop some bread to those folks."

The Steele vehicle left the freeway at the Westlake offramp. Either Baime or Sentner, in attempting to follow, forced decedent's car onto the center divider, where it overturned. Baime stopped to report the accident. Sentner, after pausing momentarily to relate the tragedy to a passing peace officer, continued to pursue Steele, successfully located him and collected a cash prize.

Decedent's wife and children brought an action for wrongful death against Sentner, Baime, RKO General, Inc., as owner of KHJ, and the maker of decedent's car. Sentner settled prior to the commencement of trial for the limits of his insurance policy. The jury returned a verdict against Baime and KHJ in the amount of $300,000 and found in favor of the manufacturer of decedent's car. KHJ appeals. . . .

The primary question for our determination is whether defendant owed a duty to decedent arising out of its broadcast of the giveaway contest. . . . Any number of considerations may justify the imposition of duty in particular circumstances, including the guidance of history, our continually refined concepts of morals and justice, the convenience of the rule, and social judgment as to where the loss should fall. While the question whether one owes a duty to another must be decided on a case-by-case basis, every case is governed by the rule of general application that all persons are required to use ordinary care to prevent others from being injured as the result of their conduct. However, foreseeability of the risk is a primary consideration in establishing the element of duty. Defendant asserts that the record here does not support a conclusion that a risk of harm to decedent was foreseeable.

While duty is a question of law, foreseeability is a question of fact for the jury. . . .

We conclude that the record amply supports the finding of foreseeability. These tragic events unfolded in the middle of a Los Angeles summer, a time when young people were free from the constraints of school and responsive to relief from vacation tedium. Seeking to attract new listeners, KHJ devised an "exciting" promotion. Money and a small measure of momentary notoriety awaited the swiftest response. It was foreseeable that defendant's youthful listeners, finding the prize had eluded them at one location, would race to arrive first at the next site and in their haste would disregard the demands of highway safety.

Indeed, "The Real Don Steele" testified that he had in the past noticed vehicles following him from location to location. He was further aware that the same contestants sometimes appeared at consecutive stops. This knowledge is not rendered irrelevant, as defendant suggests, by the absence of any prior injury. Such an argument confuses foreseeability with hindsight, and amounts to a contention that the injuries of the first victim are not compensable. "The mere fact that a particular kind of an accident has not happened before does not . . . show that such accident is one which might not reasonably have been anticipated." Thus, the fortuitous absence of prior injury does not justify relieving defendant from responsibility for the foreseeable consequences of its acts.

It is of no consequence that the harm to decedent was inflicted by third parties acting negligently. Defendant invokes the maxim that an actor is entitled to assume that others will not act negligently. This concept is valid, however, only to the extent the intervening conduct was not to be anticipated. If the likelihood that a third person may react in a particular manner is a hazard which makes the actor negligent, such reaction whether innocent or negligent does not prevent the actor from being liable for the harm caused thereby. Here, reckless conduct by youthful contestants, stimulated by defendant's broadcast, constituted the hazard to which decedent was exposed.

It is true, of course, that virtually every act involves some conceivable danger. Liability is imposed only if the risk of harm resulting from the act is deemed unreasonable—i.e., if the gravity and likelihood of the danger outweigh the utility of the conduct involved.

* * * * *

We are not persuaded that the imposition of a duty here will lead to unwarranted extensions of liability. Defendant is fearful that entrepreneurs will henceforth be burdened with an avalanche of obligations: an athletic department will owe a duty to an ardent sports fan injured while hastening to purchase one of a limited number of tickets; a department store will be liable to injuries incurred in response to a "while-they-last" sale. This argument, however, suffers from a myopic view of the facts presented here. The giveaway contest was no commonplace invitation to an attraction available on a limited basis. It was a competitive scramble in which the thrill of the chase to be the one-and-only victor was intensified by the live broadcasts which accompanied the pursuit. In the assertedly analogous situations described by defendant, any haste involved in the purchase of the commodity is an incidental and unavoidable result of the scarcity of the commodity itself. In such situations there is no attempt, as here, to generate a competitive pursuit on public streets, accelerated by repeated importuning by radio to be the very first to arrive at a particular destination. Manifestly the "spectacular" bears little resemblance to daily commercial activities.

Affirmed.

[1] It is not contended that the Steele vehicle at any time exceeded the speed limit.

Questions

1. What was the central issue in this case?
2. What test does the court employ in determining whether the radio station owed a duty to the deceased?
3. Plaintiff was seven months' pregnant and the mother of 17-month-old James. She was standing on the sidewalk, and James was in the street. A truck being negligently driven

bore down on the boy, running him over. The shock caused the mother to miscarry and suffer actual physical and emotional injury. She brought suit against the driver for harm to herself and the infant child.

    a. What is the issue in this case?

    b. Decide the case. Explain. See *Amaya* v. *Home Ice, Fuel & Supply Co.*, 379 P.2d 513 (CA. S. Ct., 1963). But also see *Dillon* v. *Legg*, 441 P.2d 912 (CA. S. Ct., 1968).

  4. Is a fireworks manufacturer liable for harm to children who ignited an explosive that had failed to detonate in the town's public display the previous day? Explain.

Classes of Negligence Claims

Personal injuries resulting from negligence are commonplace, but certain classes of problems deserve particular mention.

Improper manufacturing, handling, and/or inspection of products often give rise to negligence claims. However, the extremely complex process of producing, distributing, and using a product sometimes so obscures the root of the injury in question that proof of fault is nearly impossible to establish. This class of negligence actions and the difficulties associated with them are illustrated by a case in which a child passenger was paralyzed when a nearly new Corvair driven by a friend went out of control and landed in a culvert. The child-plaintiff sued the manufacturer, General Motors, alleging negligence in the failure "to properly tighten and inspect a nut on a bolt in the left rear suspension system," but experts differed as to whether the bolt was lost before or during the accident. The appeals judge affirmed the verdict for the plaintiff, saying that in a "battle of experts" determination of the facts must rest with the jury.[6]

Defective design of a product may provoke a negligence action. In general a manufacturer holds a duty to design the product so that it is safe for any reasonably foreseeable use. For example, in the leading case of *Larsen* v. *General Motors Corporation*,[7] a U.S. Court of Appeals found GMC guilty of negligence in the design of the steering assembly of a 1963 Chevrolet Corvair, even though the steering assembly had no causal relationship with the accident that led to the lawsuit. In that case the plaintiff received severe injuries from a head-on collision in which the steering mechanism of the Corvair was shoved back into his head as he was driving the car. The court explained that auto accidents, as a class, are foreseeable:

> While automobiles are not made for the purpose of colliding with each other, a frequent and inevitable contingency of normal use will result in collisions and injury-producing impacts. No rational basis exists for limiting recovery to situations where the defect in design or manufacture was the causative factor of the accident, as the accident and the resulting injury, . . . all are foreseeable.[8]

A negligence claim may arise from a supplier's *failure to warn* of a danger associated with the product. According to the Restatement of Torts, liability attaches if the supplier "knows or has reason to know that the chattel is or is likely to be dangerous for the use for which it is supplied" and "has no reason to believe" that the user "will realize its dangerous condition." Judicial decisions in duty to warn cases are influenced by such factors as the feasibility of an effective warning and the probable seriousness of the injury. The case that follows offers a poignant example of the hazards accompanying inadequate warnings.

WELLS V. ORTHO PHARMACEUTICAL CORP.
788 F.2d 741 (11th Cir. 1986)

Circuit Judge Vance

Defendant Ortho Pharmaceutical Corporation ("Ortho") appeals a $5.1 million judgment in favor of plaintiffs Katie Laurel Wells, an infant, Mary Maihafer, her mother, and Gary Wells, her father, under [the theory] of negligent failure to warn. . . . The case concerns a spermicide [Ortho-Gynol] manufactured by Ortho that allegedly caused Katie Wells to be born with birth defects. . . .

Factual Background

Katie Laurel Wells was born on July 1, 1981, with birth defects including deformity of her right hand, the complete lack of a left arm with only partial development of her left clavicle and shoulder, a cleft lip, and nostril deformity. A later diagnosis showed that she also has an optic nerve defect in her right eye. The plaintiffs alleged that these birth defects were caused by a spermicidal jelly used by the mother for approximately four weeks after conception until she discovered that she was pregnant. The spermicidal jelly used by Mary Maihafer, in conjunction with a diaphragm, was manufactured and marketed without a prescription by Ortho. . . . The Ortho-Gynol label and package insert in 1980 contained only this warning—the spermicide might cause irritation to the female or male genitalia, is not 100 percent effective, and should be kept out of the reach of children.

Plaintiffs brought suit against Ortho alleging that Ortho-Gynol caused Katie Wells' birth defects, that Ortho negligently failed to warn that its spermicide could cause serious birth defects, and that Ortho's failure to warn proximately caused the birth defects. . . . The district court found that plaintiffs had proven to a reasonable degree of medical certainty that the birth defects of Katie Wells' left arm and shoulder and her right hand were proximately caused by Ortho's product, but found otherwise with respect to her cleft lip, nostril deformity and right optic nerve defect. The district court also found that Ortho knew or should have known that its product might cause birth defects. Damages were awarded exceeding $5.1 million. . . .

* * * * *

A. Causation

Defendant Ortho argues that plaintiffs failed to prove causation to a reasonable degree of medical certainty. . . . Ortho complains that despite the inconclusive nature of the scientific and medical studies introduced, the district court erroneously held that plaintiffs carried their burden of proof regarding causation. . . . In Ortho's estimation plaintiffs failed to focus sufficiently on epidemiology—the field of science dealing with the relationships of the various factors which determine the frequencies and distributions of certain conditions and diseases in human populations. . . .

After reviewing the record we reject Ortho's arguments and conclude that the district court's finding of causation is not clearly erroneous. We note that plaintiffs presented well-qualified experts who testified at length concerning causation. . . . Plaintiffs presented several epidemiological studies that indicated an association between spermicide use and deleterious effects on the fetus. . . . The court stated that it "found the studies to be inconclusive on the ultimate issue of whether the Product caused Katie Wells' birth defects." In facing this "battle of the experts," the district court was thus forced to make credibility determinations to "decide the victor."

* * * * *

The district court properly noted that "its ultimate focus was *the birth defects suffered by Katie Wells.* Plaintiffs' burden of proving that Katie Wells' defects were caused by the Product did not necessarily require them to produce scientific studies showing a statistically significant association between spermicides and congenital malformations in a large population." As the D.C. circuit noted in *Ferebee,* a distinction exists between legal sufficiency and scientific certainty. If the factfinder here is convinced that plaintiffs have proven to a reasonable degree of medical certainty, which is the legal standard employed in this case, that Ortho-Gynol caused Katie Wells' arm, shoulder and hand defects, it does not matter in terms of deciding the case that the medical community might require more research and evidence before conclusively resolving the question. . . .

B. Failure to Warn

Ortho next argues that the district court's liability finding based on Ortho's negligent failure to warn is clearly erroneous. . . . We reject Ortho's arguments and conclude that the district court's finding concerning Ortho's negligent failure to warn is not clearly erroneous.

Georgia law states that a manufacturer has a duty to warn of non-obvious foreseeable dangers from the normal use of its product. If a manufacturer has actual or constructive knowledge of potential dangers of a product, the manufacturer must warn purchasers at the time of sale and delivery. Properly applying Georgia law, the district court found that prior to July 1980 when Mary Maihafer purchased Ortho-Gynol, Ortho had actual or constructive knowledge that Ortho-Gynol might cause birth defects and thus was under a duty to warn purchasers, including Ms. Maihafer, of this risk. We conclude that this finding is not clearly erroneous in light of the evidence present in the record. Several studies existed prior to 1980 indicating that the use of spermicides might cause an increased risk of birth defects. The district court found, and we agree, that these studies were available to Ortho. Plaintiffs' experts presented credible testimony that a warning was necessary, that the duty to warn arose prior to Mary Maihafer's purchase of the product, and that the failure to warn proximately caused Katie Wells' birth defects. The warning present on the Ortho-Gynol label and package insert at the time Mary Maihafer bought the product clearly did not mention the risk of birth defects.

* * * * *

We affirm the district court's findings concerning Ortho's negligent failure to warn. [Damages were reduced to $4.7 million—Author.]

Questions

1. The lower court "found the studies to be inconclusive on the ultimate issue of whether the product caused Katie Wells' birth defects."
   a. How was the appeals court able to sustain the judgment for the plaintiff, given the admittedly inconclusive character of the evidence?
   b. Given the uncertainty of the evidence, what decision would you have reached had you been a judge in this case? Explain.
2. In your judgment, is this decision an example of excessive protection for the consumer? Explain.
3. A minor operating a power lawn mower slipped, thrusting his hand through an unguarded hole in the mower. An effective guard for the hole was available at a cost of less than $1. The hole was visible on casual inspection. The minor sued to recover for the injury to his hand. See *Luque* v. *McLean*, 501 P.2d 1163 (Cal. 1972).
   a. Build an argument for the defendant.
   b. Decide the case. Explain.
   c. If you found for the plaintiff in the lawn mower case, how would you rule if all the facts were the same but the instrument causing the injury was a sharp, pointed rake? Explain.

Res Ipsa Loquitur

As alluded to previously, problems of proof are sometimes so daunting as to render negligence law an ineffectual tool in serving the injured consumer. In part because of that condition, the courts have adopted the doctrine of *res ipsa loquitur* (the thing speaks for itself). The doctrine permits the court to infer the defendant's negligence even though that negligence cannot be proved. That is, the facts suggest that the plaintiff's injury must have resulted from negligence on the part of the defendant, but the circumstances are such that the plaintiff is unable to prove both negligence and causation. The case that follows sets out the test for applying *res ipsa loquitur*.

ESCOLA V. COCA–COLA BOTTLING CO. OF FRESNO
Supreme Court of California, 24 Cal.2d 453, 150 P.2d 436 (1944)

Chief Justice Gibson

Plaintiff, a waitress in a restaurant, was injured when a bottle of Coca-Cola broke in her hand. She alleged that defendant company, which had bottled and delivered the alleged defective bottle to her employer, was negligent in selling "bottles containing said beverage which on account of excessive pressure of gas or by reason of some defect in the bottle was dangerous . . . and likely to explode." This appeal is from a judgment upon a jury verdict in favor of plaintiff.

Defendant's driver delivered several cases of Coca-Cola to the restaurant, placing them on the floor, one on top of the other, under and behind the counter, where they remained at least 36 hours. Immediately before the accident, plaintiff picked up the top case and set it upon a nearby ice-cream cabinet in front of and about three feet from the refrigerator. She then proceeded to take the bottles from the case with her right hand, one at a time, and put them into the refrigerator. Plaintiff testified that after she had placed three bottles in the refrigerator and had moved the fourth bottle about 18 inches from the case "it exploded in my hand." The bottle broke into two jagged pieces and inflicted a deep five-inch cut, severing blood vessels, nerves and muscles of the thumb and palm of the hand. Plaintiff further testified that when the bottle exploded, "It made a sound similar to an electric light bulb that would have dropped. It made a loud pop." . . . A fellow employee . . . testified that plaintiff . . . didn't bang either the case or the door or another bottle . . . when it popped. . . .

Plaintiff . . . rested her case, having announced to the court that being unable to show any specific acts of negligence she relied completely on the doctrine of *res ipsa loquitur.*

Defendant contends that the doctrine of *res ipsa loquitur* does not apply in this case, and that the evidence is insufficient to support the judgment.

* * * * *

Res ipsa loquitur does not apply unless (1) defendant had exclusive control of the thing causing the injury and (2) the accident is of such a nature that it ordinarily would not occur in the absence of negligence by the defendant.

Many authorities state that the happening of the accident does not speak for itself where it took place some time after defendant had relinquished control of the instrumentality causing the injury. Under the more logical view, however, the doctrine may be applied upon the theory that defendant had control at the time of the alleged negligent act, although not at the time of the accident, *provided* plaintiff first proves that the condition of the instrumentality had not been changed after it left the defendant's possession.

. . . Plaintiff must also prove that she handled the bottle carefully. . . . It is not necessary, of course, that plaintiff eliminate every remote possibility of injury to the bottle after defendant lost control, and the requirement is satisfied if there is evidence permitting a reasonable inference that it was not accessible to extraneous harmful forces and that it was carefully handled by plaintiff or any third person who may have moved or touched it. If such evidence is presented, the question becomes one for the trier of fact. . . .

Upon an examination of the record, the evidence appears sufficient to support a reasonable inference that the bottle here involved was not damaged by any extraneous force after delivery to the restaurant by defendant. It follows, therefore, that the bottle was in some manner defective at the time defendant relinquished control, because sound and properly prepared bottles of carbonated liquids do not ordinarily explode when carefully handled.

The next question, then, is whether plaintiff may rely upon the doctrine of *res ipsa loquitur* to supply an inference that defendant's negligence was responsible for the defective condition of the bottle at the time it was delivered to the restaurant. Under the general rules pertaining to the doctrine, as set forth above, it must appear that bottles of carbonated liquid are not ordinarily defective without negligence by the bottling company.

* * * * *

Although it is not clear in this case whether the explosion was caused by an excessive charge or a defect in the glass there is a sufficient showing that neither cause would ordinarily have been present if due care had been used. Further, defendant had exclusive control over both the charging and inspection of the bottles. Accordingly, all the requirements necessary to entitle plaintiff to rely on the doctrine of *res ipsa loquitur* to supply an inference of negligence are present.

* * * * *

The judgment is affirmed.

Questions

1. In *Escola* the plaintiff was unable to prove fault on the part of Coca-Cola. That being the case, why was Coca-Cola held liable for plaintiff's injuries?
2. Do you agree with the court's decision? Explain.
3. Judge Traynor's concurring opinion in *Escola* (not reproduced in this text) noted the dramatic alteration of the buyer-seller relationship in the era of mass production. He then argued that the consumer could no longer protect herself or himself. Hence, extended legal protection was required. Regardless of your point of view, build the argument that Judge Traynor was wrong, both about the consumer's helplessness and as to the appropriateness of legal intervention.
4. A bartender, Parrillo, was opening a bottle of grenadine when it exploded, causing injury. Parrillo sued Giroux Company, the producer of the liquor. Giroux packaged the liquor itself after buying bottles from a manufacturer. Giroux visually inspected the bottles and ordinarily found defects in 1 of every 400 to 500 bottles. The evidence showed that Parrillo did not mishandle the bottle. Decide the case. Explain. See *Parrillo v. Giroux Co.*, 426 A.2d 1313 (R.I. 1981).

Defenses against Negligence

Even if the plaintiff has proven all of the necessary elements of a negligence claim, the defendant may still prevail by establishing a good defense. Two of those defenses and some variations are of special importance: contributory negligence and assumption of risk.

Contributory Negligence. The law is designed to encourage us to conduct ourselves with care. Hence, I may file suit if injured by the negligence of another, but what if I contribute to my harm by virtue of my own negligence? I am then said to be guilty of contributory negligence. Historically, contributory negligence operated as a complete bar to recovery. That is, if the defendant can show that I, as the plaintiff, contributed to my own injury because of my own negligence, I cannot recover from that defendant. That has been the case even if the plaintiff's contribution to his or her own harm was miniscule.

The harshness of the contributory negligence standard has led most states to adopt a variation labeled *comparative negligence*. This standard requires a weighing of the relative negligence of the parties. Though the formula may vary from state to state, typically the plaintiff's recovery is reduced by a percentage equal to the percentage of the plaintiff's fault in the case. Assume a plaintiff sustained $10,000 in injuries in an accident. If the plaintiff's negligence is found to be 20 percent responsible for the injuries, then the plaintiff's recovery will total $8,000. When the plaintiff's fault actually exceeds that of the defendant, the plaintiff may be barred from recovery.

Another muting of the absolutist character of contributory negligence is the doctrine of *last clear chance*. Assume the plaintiff is found to be contributorily negligent. The plaintiff may yet recover in full if she or he can show that the defendant had the last clear chance to avoid the accident and that the defendant did not take advantage of that opportunity. For example, assume that A, while intoxicated, removes his children's video games and record players from his home and meticulously places them in a line spanning the street. B approaches in a car, sees the machines in ample time to stop, but instead thinks it amusing to plow into them. Notwithstanding his own negligence, A now sues and may recover for the loss of the items, arguing that B had the last clear chance to avoid the collision.

Assumption of Risk. A plaintiff who willingly enters a dangerous situation and is injured will not be permitted to recover. For example, if a driver sees that the road ahead is flooded, he will not be compensated for the injuries sustained when he loses control as he attempts to drive through the water. His recovery is barred even though the road was flooded due to operator error in opening a floodgate. The requirements for use of the assumption of risk defense are (1) knowledge of the risk and (2) voluntary assumption of the risk.

The case that follows illustrates the application of the contributory/comparative negligence defense.

INSURANCE CO. OF NORTH AMERICA V. PASAKARNIS
451 So.2d 447 (Fla. 1984)

Chief Justice Alderman

The facts of this case are simple and straightforward. While driving a jeep, without having fastened the available and fully operational seat belt contained therein, Richard Pasakarnis was injured in an accident caused entirely by John Menninger who had run a stop sign and struck Pasakarnis's jeep broadside. Pasakarnis was thrown from the jeep and landed on his posterior. As a result, he sustained a compression-type injury to his lower back. His treating physician testified that his injury was caused by his flying through the air and impacting on the pavement.

In their answer to the complaint, defendants, petitioners here, alleged as an affirmative defense that at the time of the accident, Pasakarnis had available for his use a seat belt which, had it been utilized, would have substantially reduced or prevented any bodily injuries to him; that Pasakarnis was negligent in failing to use this safety device; and that his damages should be reduced in proportion to his negligence. Pasakarnis moved to strike this affirmative defense, contending that, because he had no duty to wear a seat belt, the fact that he was not wearing his seat belt when this accident occurred does not establish a legal basis to reduce the amount of his damage award. The trial court granted the motion to strike, holding that expert testimony pertaining to the nonuse of seat belts and the causal relationship between nonuse and Pasakarnis's injuries would not be admissible at trial. . . .

The defendants proffered the deposition of an engineer-accident analyst who stated that had Pasakarnis properly utilized his seat belt, it would have restrained him in the seat of the jeep and he would not have been ejected. . . . Further, in response to the question of whether Pasakarnis would have been likely to suffer any injury inside the jeep itself if he had been restrained by his seat belt and shoulder harness at the time of impact, the expert opined that within a high degree of probability, Pasakarnis would not have sustained any injury.

The jury found that Menninger was 100 percent responsible for the accident and that the total amount of Pasakarnis's damages was $100,000. . . .

Upon appeal, the District Court of Appeal, Fourth District, affirmed the judgment of the trial court holding the seat belt evidence inadmissible. The Fourth District . . . elected to follow a line of authority which disallows evidence of failure to use an available operational seat belt. It found that the effectiveness of seat belts in preventing or limiting injury is still questionable and concluded that their nonuse should not be deemed prima facie unreasonable. It asserted judicial restraint as a compelling reason to answer the certified question in the negative and . . . decided that it was not within the province of the courts to legislate on the use of seat belts.

* * * * *

We disagree and find this issue particularly appropriate for judicial decision. In the past, this Court has not abdicated its continuing responsibility to the citizens of this state to ensure that the law remains both fair and realistic as society and technology change. In fact, the law of torts in Florida has been modernized, for the most part, through the courts.

* * * * *

To abstain from acting responsibly in the present case on the basis of legislative deference would be to consciously ignore a limited area where decisions by the lower courts of this state have created an illogical exception to the doctrine of comparative negligence . . . and the underlying philosophy of individual responsibility upon which the decisions of this Court . . . have been predicated. In addition to our emphasis on individual responsibility, the other common thread running through our decisions has been that the law will step in to protect people against risks which they cannot adequately guard against themselves.

In *Hoffman* v. *Jones,* we decided that contributory negligence as a complete bar to a plaintiff's action was unjust. We reasoned that contemporary conditions must be met with contemporary standards which are realistic and better calculated to obtain justice among all parties involved, based upon the circumstances, and stated that it was inequitable to vest an entire accidental loss on one of the parties whose negligent conduct combined with the negligence of another to produce the loss. The best argument in favor of comparative negligence we found was that it simply provided a more equitable system of determining liability. We stated that in the field of tort law, the most equitable result to be achieved is to equate liability with fault. In adopting the doctrine of comparative negligence, we explained that under this theory a plaintiff is prevented from recovering *"only that proportion of his damages for which he is responsible."*

* * * * *

. . . [W]e hold that the "seat belt defense" is viable in Florida. The seat belt has been proven to afford the occupant of an automobile a means whereby he or she may minimize his or her personal damages prior to occurrence of the accident.

. . .[A]utomobile collisions are foreseeable as are the so-called "second collisions" with the interior of the automobile. The seat belt has been a safety device required by the federal government for nearly 20 years. In a 1982 study by the United States Department of Transportation, . . . it is reported that the evidence for the effectiveness of safety belts in reducing deaths and injury severity is substantial and unequivocal. In view of the importance of the seat belt as a safety precaution available for a plaintiff's protection, failure to wear it under certain circumstances may be a pertinent factor for the jury to consider in deciding whether plaintiff exercised due care for his or her own safety. . . .

* * * * *

Those jurisdictions adopting the "seat belt defense" have considered three different approaches: (1) plaintiff's nonuse is negligent per se; (2) in failing to make use of an available seat belt, plaintiff has not complied with a standard of conduct which a reasonable prudent man would have pursued under similar circumstances, and therefore he may be found contributorily negligent; and (3) by not fastening his seat belt, plaintiff may, under the circumstances of a particular case, be found to have acted unreasonably and in disregard of his or her best interests and, therefore, should not be able to recover those damages which would not have occurred if his or her seat belt had been fastened.

Because Florida does not by statute require the use of available seat belts, we reject the rule that failure to wear a seat belt is negligence per se as have the majority of jurisdictions. We also reject the second approach because contributory negligence is applicable only if plaintiff's failure to exercise due care causes in whole or in part the accident rather than enhancing the severity of the injuries. Rather, we adopt the third approach. . . . Nonuse of the seat belt may or may not amount to a failure to use reasonable care on the part of the plaintiff. Whether it does depends on the particular circumstances of the case. Defendant has the burden of pleading and proving that the plaintiff did not use an available and operational seat belt, that the plaintiff's failure to use the seat belt was unreasonable under the circumstances, and that there was a causal relationship between the injuries sustained by the plaintiff and plaintiff's failure to buckle up. If there is competent evidence to prove that the failure to use an available and operational seat belt produced or contributed substantially to producing at least a portion of plaintiff's damages, then the jury should be permitted to consider this factor, along with all other facts in evidence, in deciding whether the damages for which defendant may otherwise be liable should be reduced. Nonuse of an available seat belt, however, should not be considered by the triers of fact in resolving the issue of liability unless it has been alleged and proved that such nonuse was a proximate cause of the accident.

[District Court decision quashed. Case remanded.]

Questions

1. Why did the court treat the failure to wear a seat belt as a comparative negligence issue rather than negligence per se or contributory negligence?
2. Does this decision mean citizens of Florida who fail to wear a seat belt will be denied recovery for any injuries they might suffer in a motor vehicle accident? Explain.
3. Justice Shaw in dissent in *Pasakarnis:*

   Despite statistics determining that seat belts can be effective in reducing the number of serious injuries and deaths caused by automobile accidents, a vast majority of the motoring public declines to use them. If one accepts the proposition that there is no common law or statutory duty to wear seat belts, and that the wearing of such belts has been rejected by a majority of the public despite the urging of industry and the federal government, then the duty this decision places upon the Florida motorist is at the very least based upon a debatable public policy determination best left to the legislature.[9]

   a. Should the seat belt issue have been left to the legislature? Explain.
   b. In your judgment have America's courts, as a whole, assumed an undesirably aggressive, activist role that amounts to an intrusion on the legislative function? Explain.
4. Should the federal government pass a law requiring the use of seat belts at all times in automobiles? Explain.
5. Giles, a guest at the Pick Hotel, leaned across his car to remove his briefcase from the passenger side of the front seat. In doing so, he placed his hand for support on the metal pillar between the front and rear doors. As he did so, a bellboy closed the rear door on Giles' hand. Giles sued Pick. Decide the case. Explain. *Giles* v. *Pick Hotels Corp.*, 232 F.2d 887 (1956).

6. Distinguish contributory negligence and assumption of risk.
7. David Clapham lost an eye when he was hit by a foul ball at Yankee Stadium in New York City. He sued the Yankees and the city, which owns the stadium, contending they were negligent in failing to extend the protective screen to reach the box seat he was occupying behind the Yankee dugout.
   a. What defense would you raise on behalf of the Yankees?
   b. Decide the case. Explain.
   c. What if Mr. Clapham had left the game early and was struck by a foul ball while walking through the city-owned parking lot?

WARRANTIES

As explained previously, negligence claims are often difficult to prove. For that reason and others, the wronged consumer may wish to raise a breach of warranty claim in addition to or in place of a negligence action. A *warranty* is simply a guarantee arising out of a contract. If the product does not conform to the standards of the warranty, the contract is violated (breached), and the wronged party is entitled to recovery. Note that a negligence claim arises from breach of the duty of due care, while a warranty claim arises from a breach of contract. The following sections describe how express and implied warranties are created. (Discussion of the warranty of good title is omitted. See UCC 2–312.)

Express Warranties

The seller of goods affirms a fact or makes a promise regarding the character or quality of the goods. Warranties are governed primarily by the terms of the Uniform Commercial Code. The UCC is designed to codify and standardize the law of commercial practice throughout the United States. Forty-nine states have adopted all or the bulk of the UCC. Louisiana has adopted only portions.

UCC 2–313. Express Warranties by Affirmation, Promise, Description, Sample

(1) Express warranties by the seller are created as follows:
  (a) Any affirmation of fact or promise made by the seller to the buyer which relates to the goods and becomes part of the basis of the bargain creates an express warranty that the goods shall conform to the affirmation or promise.
  (b) Any description of the goods which is made part of the basis of the bargain creates an express warranty that the goods shall conform to the description.
  (c) Any sample or model which is made part of the basis of the bargain creates an express warranty that the whole of the goods shall conform to the sample or model.

The philosophy undergirding UCC 2–313 is straightforward. The seller who seeks to enhance the attractiveness of his or her product by offering representations as to the nature and/or quality of the product must fulfill those representations or fall in breach of contract and be subject to the payment of damages.

Perhaps the area of greatest confusion in determining the existence and coverage of an express warranty is distinguishing a seller's promise from a mere expression of opinion. The latter, often referred to as sales talk or puffing, does not create an express warranty. The UCC requires an affirmation of fact or promise. Hence, a statement of opinion is not covered by the code. For example, the sales clerk who says, "This is the best TV around," would not be guaranteeing that the television in question is the best available. The salesperson is expressing a view. We, as consumers, seem to be quite patient with sellers' exaggerations. If, on the other hand, the clerk said, "This TV has a solid walnut cabinet," when in fact it was a pine veneer stained to a walnut tone, a breach of warranty action might ultimately be in order. The test to be applied in such situations is one of reasonable expectations. An expression of opinion coming from an expert may well rise to the level of an affirmation of fact or promise because the buyer should reasonably expect to be able to rely on the expert's affirmations. For example, if a handwriting expert seeking to sell a purportedly rare historical document says, "This handwriting is clearly that of Adolph Hitler," that statement might well be treated as an affirmation of a fact.

Implied Warranties

A seller enters into a contract for the sale of goods and, as a consequence, an implied warranty arises by operation of law. That is, an implied warranty automatically attaches to the sale of goods unless the warranty is disclaimed (disavowed) by the seller.

Two types of implied warranties are provided for:

UCC 2–314. Implied Warranty: Merchantability; Usage of Trade

(1) Unless excluded or modified (Section 2–316), a warranty that the goods shall be merchantable is implied in a contract for their sale if the seller is a merchant with respect to goods of that kind. Under this section the serving for value of food or drink to be consumed either on the premises or elsewhere is a sale.

UCC 2–315. Implied Warranty: Fitness for Particular Purpose

Where the seller at the time of contracting has reason to know any particular purpose for which the goods are required and that the buyer is relying on the seller's skill or judgment to select or furnish suitable goods, there is unless excluded or modified under the next section an implied warranty that the goods shall be fit for such purpose.

The implied warranty of merchantability is a powerful tool for the wronged consumer in that the warranty arises automatically by operation of law. If the seller is a merchant regularly selling goods of the kind in question, the warranty of merchantability simply accompanies the sale unless the warranty is excluded via a disclaimer (explained below). The warranty arises even if the seller made no certification as to the nature or quality of the goods. UCC 2–314 enshrines the consumer's reasonable expectation that only safe goods of at least ordinary quality will appear on the market.

The implied warranty of fitness for a particular purpose likewise arises by operation of law, but only when the seller (merchant or not) knows (or has reason to know) that the goods are to be used for a specific purpose, and the seller further knows that the buyer is relying on the seller's judgment. If those conditions obtain, the warranty exists automatically unless disclaimed. For example, Chris Snapp engages an audio products clerk in a discussion regarding the proper stereo system for Chris's Austin Healey sports car. Chris explains the joy he expects to receive in driving his car along the winding Kentucky roads with the convertible top down and the stereo booming. Alas, the stereo selected on the clerk's advice proves insufficiently powerful to be heard clearly above the rushing wind. Should Chris recover for breach of the implied warranty of fitness for a particular purpose? Merchantability?

Disclaimers

Express warranties may be disclaimed (excluded) or modified only with great difficulty. In any contract displaying both an express warranty and language disclaiming that warranty (for example, sold "as is" or "with all faults"), the warranty will remain effective unless the warranty and the disclaimer can reasonably be read as consistent.

Implied warranties may be excluded or modified by following either of the two patterns explained in UCC sections 2–316(2) and (3)(a).

    (2) Subject to subsection (3), to exclude or modify the implied warranty of merchantability or any part of it the language must mention merchantability and in case of a writing must be conspicuous, and to exclude or modify any implied warranty of fitness the exclusion must be by a writing and conspicuous . . .

    (3) Notwithstanding subsection (2)
        (a) unless the circumstances indicate otherwise, all implied warranties are excluded by expressions like "as is," "with all faults" or other language which in common understanding calls the buyer's attention to the exclusion of warranties and makes plain that there is no implied warranty . . .

Finally, when a buyer, before entering a contract, inspects the goods (or a sample thereof), or declines to inspect, no implied warranty exists with regard to defects that should have been apparent on inspection [UCC 2–316(3)(b)].

The following case illustrates the evolution of warranty law in an increasingly complex commercial society.

HENNINGSEN V. BLOOMFIELD MOTORS, INC.
Supreme Court of New Jersey, 161 A. 2d 69 (1960)

Justice Francis

Plaintiff Claus H. Henningsen purchased a Plymouth automobile, manufactured by defendant Chrysler Corporation, from defendant Bloomfield Motors, Inc. His wife, plaintiff Helen Henningsen, was injured while driving it and instituted suit against both defendants to recover damages on account of her injuries. Her husband joined in the action, seeking compensation for his consequential losses. The complaint was predicated upon breach of express and implied warranties and upon negligence. At the trial the negligence counts were dismissed by the court and the cause was submitted to the jury for determination solely on the issues of implied warranty of merchantability. Verdicts were returned against both defendants and in favor of the plaintiffs. Defendants appealed and plaintiffs cross-appealed from the dismissal of their negligence claim. . . .

On May 7, 1955, Mr. and Mrs. Henningsen visited the place of business of Bloomfield Motors, Inc., an authorized De Soto and Plymouth dealer, to look at a Plymouth. . . . They were shown a Plymouth which appealed to them and the purchase followed. The record indicates that Mr. Henningsen intended the car as a Mother's Day gift to his wife. When the purchase order or contract was prepared and presented, the husband executed it alone. The purchase order was a printed form of one page. . . .

The testimony of Claus Henningsen justifies the conclusion that he did not read the two fine print paragraphs referring to the back of the purchase contract. And it is uncontradicted that no one made any reference to them, or called them to his attention. With respect to the matter appearing on the back, it is likewise uncontradicted that he did not read it and that no one called it to his attention.

The reverse side of the contract contains 8½ inches of fine print. . . .

In the seventh paragraph, about two-thirds of the way down the page, the warranty, which is the focal point of the case, is set forth.

7. It is expressly agreed that there are no warranties, express or implied, *made* by either the dealer or the manufacturer on the motor vehicle, chassis, or parts furnished hereunder except as follows. . . .

The new Plymouth was turned over to the Henningsens on May 9, 1955. . . . That day, Mrs. Henningsen drove to Asbury Park. On the way down and in returning the car performed in normal fashion until the accident occurred. She was proceeding north on Route 36 in Highlands, New Jersey, at 20 to 22 miles per hour. The highway was paved and smooth, and contained two lanes for northbound travel. She was riding in the righthand lane. Suddenly she heard a loud noise "from the bottom, by the hood." It "felt as if something cracked." The steering wheel spun in her hands; the car veered sharply to the right and crashed into a highway sign and a brick wall. . . .

The insurance carrier's inspector and appraiser of damaged cars, with 11 years of experience, advanced the opinion, based on the history and his examination, that something definitely went "wrong from the steering wheel down to the front wheels" and that the untoward happening must have been due to mechanical defect or failure; "something down there had to drop off or break loose to cause the car" to act in the manner described. . . .

The Claim of Implied Warranty against the Manufacturer

. . . [W]e come to a study of the express warranty on the reverse side of the purchase order signed by Claus Henningsen. At the outset we take notice that it was made only by the manufacturer and that by its terms it runs directly to Claus Henningsen. . . .

The terms of the warranty are a sad commentary upon the automobile manufacturers' marketing practices. Warranties developed in the law in the interest of and to protect the ordinary consumer who cannot be expected to have the knowledge or capacity or even the opportunity to make adequate inspection of mechanical instrumentalities, like automobiles, and to decide for himself whether they are reasonably fit for the designed purpose. But the ingenuity of the Automobile Manufacturers Association, by means of its standardized form, has metamorphosed the warranty into a device to limit the maker's liability. . . .

The manufacturer agrees to replace defective parts for 90 days after the sale or until the car has been driven 4,000 miles, whichever is first to occur, *if the part is sent to the factory, transportation charges prepaid, and if examination discloses to its satisfaction that the part is defective.* It is difficult to imagine a greater burden on the consumer, or less satisfactory remedy. . . .

Moreover, the guaranty is against defective workmanship. That condition may arise from good parts improperly assembled. There being no defective parts to return to the maker, is all remedy to be denied? . . .

The matters referred to represent only a small part of the illusory character of the security presented by the warranty. Thus far the analysis has dealt only with the remedy provided in the case of a defective part. What relief is provided when the breach of the warranty results in personal injury to the buyer? . . . But in this instance, after reciting that defective parts will be replaced at the factory, the alleged agreement relied upon by Chrysler provides that the manufacturer's "obligation under this warranty" is limited to that undertaking: further, that such remedy is "in lieu of all other warranties, express or implied, and all other obligations or liabilities on its part." The contention has been raised that such language bars any claim for personal injuries which may emanate from a breach of the warranty. . . .

Putting aside for the time being the problem of the efficacy of the disclaimer provisions contained in the express warranty, a question of first importance to be decided is whether an implied warranty of merchantability by Chrysler Corporation accompanied the sale of the automobile to Claus Henningsen.

* * * * *

Chrysler points out that an implied warranty of merchantability is an incident of a contract of sale. It concedes, of course, the making of the original sale to Bloomfield Motors, Inc., but maintains that this transaction marked the terminal point of its contractual connection with the car. Then Chrysler urges that since it was not a party to the sale by the dealer to

Henningsen, there is no privity of contract between it and the plaintiffs, and the absence of this privity eliminates any such implied warranty.

* * * * *

Under modern conditions the ordinary layman, on responding to the importuning of colorful advertising, has neither the opportunity nor the capacity to inspect or to determine the fitness of an automobile for use; he must rely on the manufacturer who has control of its construction, and to some degree on the dealer who, to the limited extent called for by the manufacturer's instructions, inspects and services it before delivery. In such a marketing milieu his remedies and those of persons who properly claim through him should not depend "upon the intricacies of the law of sales. The obligation of the manufacturer should not be based alone on privity of contract. It should rest, as was once said, upon 'the demands of social justice.' "

Accordingly, we hold that under modern marketing conditions, when a manufacturer puts a new automobile in the stream of trade and promotes its purchase by the public, an implied warranty that it is reasonably suitable for use as such accompanies it into the hands of the ultimate purchaser. Absence of agency between the manufacturer and the dealer who makes the ultimate sale is immaterial.

The Effect of the Disclaimer and Limitation of Liability Clauses on the Implied Warranty of Merchantability

. . . [W]hat effect should be given to the express warranty in question which seeks to limit the manufacturer's liability to replacement of defective parts, and which disclaims all other warranties, express or implied? In assessing its significance we must keep in mind the general principle that, in the absence of fraud, one who does not choose to read a contract before signing it, cannot later relieve himself of its burdens.

But in the framework of modern commercial life and business practices, such rules cannot be applied on a strict, doctrinal basis. The conflicting interests of the buyer and seller must be evaluated realistically and justly, giving due weight to the social policy evinced by the Uniform Sales Act, the progressive decisions of the courts engaged in administering it, the mass production methods of manufacture and distribution to the public, and the bargaining position occupied by the ordinary consumer in such an economy. This history of the law shows that legal doctrines, as first expounded, often prove to be inadequate under the impact of later experience. In such case, the need for justice has stimulated the necessary qualifications or adjustments.

In these times, an automobile is almost as much a servant of convenience for the ordinary person as a household utensil. For a multitude of other persons it is a necessity. . . .

The traditional contract is the result of free bargaining of parties who are brought together by the play of the market, and who meet each other on a footing of approximate economic equality. In such a society there is no danger that freedom of contract will be a threat to the social order as a whole. But in present-day commercial life the standardized mass contract has appeared. It is used primarily by enterprises with strong bargaining power and position. Such standardized contracts have been described as those in which one predominant party will dictate its law to an undetermined multiple rather than to an individual. They are said to resemble a law rather than a meeting of the minds. . . .

The warranty before us is a standardized form designed for mass use. It is imposed upon the automobile consumer. He takes it or leaves it, and he must take it to buy an automobile. No bargaining is engaged in with respect to it. In fact, the dealer through whom it comes to the buyer is without authority to alter it; his function is ministerial—simply to deliver it. . . .

The gross inequality of bargaining position occupied by the consumer in the automobile industry is thus apparent. There is no competition among the car makers in the area of the express warranty.

* * * * *

Assuming that a jury might find that the fine print referred to reasonably served the objective of directing a buyer's attention to the warranty on the reverse side, and, therefore, that he should be charged with awareness of its language, can it be said that an ordinary layman would realize what he was relinquishing in return for what he was being granted? . . . *In the context* of this warranty, only the abandonment of all sense of justice would permit us to hold that, as a matter of law, the phrase "its obligation under this warranty being limited to making good at its factory any part or parts thereof" signifies to an ordinary reasonable person that he is relinquishing any personal injury claim that might flow from the use of a defective automobile. . . .

The Dealer's Implied Warranty

The principles that have been expounded as to the obligation of the manufacturer apply with equal force to the separate express warranty of the dealer.

* * * * *

. . . [W]e conclude that the disclaimer of an implied warranty of merchantability by the dealer, as well as the attempted elimination of all obligations other than replacement of defective parts, are violative of public policy and void. . . .

The Defense of Lack of Privity against Mrs. Henningsen

Both defendants contend that since there was no privity of contract between them and Mrs. Henningsen, she cannot recover for breach of any warranty made by either of them. On the facts, as they were developed, we agree that she was not a party to the purchase agreement. Her right to maintain the action, therefore, depends upon whether she occupies such legal status thereunder as to permit her to take advantage of a breach of defendants' implied warranties. . . . We are convinced that the cause of justice in this area of the law can be served only by recognizing that she is such a person who, in the reasonable contemplation of the parties to the warranty, might be expected to become a user of the automobile. . . .

It is important to express the right of Mrs. Henningsen to maintain her action in terms of a general principle. To what extent may lack of privity be disregarded in suits on such warranties? . . . [I]t is our opinion that an implied warranty of merchantability chargeable to either an automobile manufacturer or a dealer extends to the purchaser of the car, members of his family, and to other persons occupying or using it with his consent. It would be wholly opposed to reality to say that use by such persons is not within the anticipation of parties to such a warranty of reasonable suitability of an automobile for ordinary highway operation. Those persons must be considered within the distributive chain. . . .

Affirmed.

Questions

1. Define the doctrine of privity of contract.
2. List those considerations that permitted the *Henningsen* court to disavow the privity requirement under the facts of that case.
3. Why was the Chrysler disclaimer ruled invalid?
4. A father asks his 11-year-old son to go to the kitchen, open a bottle of beer, and return with it. In opening the beer, the son's hand is cut when the bottle breaks. The father sues the bottler on behalf of his son. The father raises both negligence and breach of warranty claims. At trial it is established that the son was not negligent. The bottler defends by establishing that the beer was purchased by the father. Decide. Explain.

Magnuson-Moss Warranty Act

While the Uniform Commercial Code embodies our primary expression of warranty rules, Congress has extended and clarified those rules by passing the Magnuson-Moss Warranty Act. Congress approved the act following a study that found widespread abuse of consumers. Warranties were often vague, deceptive, or simply incomprehensible to the average purchaser. The act, administered by the FTC, applies only to consumer products and only to written warranties. The act does not require offering an express written warranty, but where such a warranty is offered and the cost of the goods is more than $10, the warranty must be labeled *full* or *limited*. A full warranty requires free repair of any defect. If repair is not achieved within a reasonable time, the buyer may elect either a refund or replacement without charge. If a limited warranty is offered, the limitation must be conspicuously displayed.

If a warranty is offered on goods costing more than $15, the warrantor must "fully and conspicuously disclose in simple and readily understandable language the terms and conditions of the warranty." The FTC has developed various rules to implement the intent of the disclosure requirement. For example, if the warrantor requires return of the completed warranty registration card in order to "activate" the warranty, that return requirement must be clearly disclosed in the warranty.

The effect of the Magnuson-Moss Act has not been entirely consistent with Congress' hopes. In practice, many sellers may have either offered limited warranties or eliminated them entirely.

STRICT LIABILITY

Negligence and warranty actions are helpful to the harmed consumer. However, rapid changes in the nature of commercial practice, as well as an increasing societal concern for consumer protection, led the legal community to gradually embrace yet another cause of action. *Strict liability in tort* offers the prospect of holding all of those in the chain of distribution liable for damages from a defective product, rather than imposing the entire burden on the injured consumer. Manufacturers and sellers are best positioned to prevent the distribution of defective products, and they are best able to bear the cost of injury by spreading the loss via pricing policies and insurance coverage.

Strict liability as an independent tort emerged in 1963 in the famous California case of *Greenman* v. *Yuba Products, Inc.*[10] In the ensuing two decades, most states, via either their judiciary or their legislature, have adopted strict liability in concept. The essence of the strict liability notion is expressed in Section 402A of the Restatement of Torts. (Note that the Restatement of Torts does not constitute law. Rather it is a summary of the law of torts as interpreted by a group of legal scholars.) In sum, 402A imposes liability where a product is sold in a *defective condition, unreasonably dangerous*[11] to the user:

1. One who sells any product in a defective condition, unreasonably dangerous to the user or consumer or to his property, is subject to liability for physical harm thereby caused to the ultimate user or consumer, or to his property, if
   a. the seller is engaged in the business of selling such a product, and,
   b. it is expected to and does reach the user or consumer without substantial change in the condition in which it is sold.
2. The rule stated in Subsection (1) applies although
   a. the seller has exercised all possible care in the preparation and sale of his product, and
   b. the user or consumer has not bought the product from or entered into any contractual relation with the seller.

Coverage

All of those engaged in the preparation and distribution of a defective product may be liable for any harm caused by the defect, regardless of proof of actual fault. Furthermore, although not addressed in Section 402A, the courts have extended strict liability coverage to reach injured bystanders. Coverage generally extends to both personal injuries and property damage, but in some states the latter is excluded. Some states limit strict liability recovery to new goods, and some have limited liability to a designated period (for example, 15 years) after the manufacture or sale of the product.

Defenses

Assumption of risk and *misuse of the product* are both good defenses and, if factually supported, can act as a complete bar to strict liability recovery. In theory, strict liability is a no-fault concept. Hence *contributory negligence* should not constitute a useful defense. The South Dakota Supreme Court summarized the law in this area in 1979:

> Many courts have considered the question of what defenses are available in strict liability cases. Classifying them is difficult because all of the courts do not mean the same thing when they use the terms *contributory negligence* and *assumption of risk*. A reading of the cases from other jurisdictions satisfies us that regardless of the nomenclature used, they can be divided into four classifications:
>
> 1. The classical negligence defenses are all available.
> 2. A restricted species of contributory negligence is a defense.
> 3. Most jurisdictions hold that contributory negligence—whether classical or restricted—is not a defense.
> 4. Finally, California and Alaska hold that contributory negligence is not a defense, but plaintiff's recovery may be reduced on a theory of "comparative fault" which balances the user's negligence against the defectiveness of the product.[12]

Since then we appear to be witnessing an increasing willingness to accept the comparative fault position attributed to California and Alaska.

The *Leichtamer* case, which follows, offers a good overview of strict liability reasoning. The *Daniel* case then serves as a summary of product liability action in general.

LEICHTAMER V. AMERICAN MOTORS CORP.
424 N.E.2d 568 (Oh. 1981)

Justice Brown

This litigation arises out of a motor vehicle accident which occurred on April 18, 1976. On that date, Paul Vance and his wife, Cynthia, invited Carl and Jeanne Leichtamer, brother and sister, to go for a ride in the Vance's Jeep Model CJ–7. The Vances and the Leichtamers drove together to the Hall of Fame Four-Wheel Club, of which the Vances were members. The Vances were seated in the front of the vehicle and the Leichtamers rode in the back. The club, located near Dundee, Ohio, was an "off-the-road" recreation facility. The course there consisted of hills and trails about an abandoned strip mine.

While the Vance vehicle was negotiating a double-terraced hill [proceeding *down* the hill], an accident occurred. The hill consisted of a 33-degree slope followed by a 70-foot-long terrace and then a 30-degree slope. Paul Vance drove over the brow of the first of these two slopes and over the first flat terrace without incident. As he drove over the brow of the second hill, the rear of the vehicle raised up relative to the front and passed through the air in an arc of approximately 180 degrees. The vehicle landed upside down with its front pointing back up the hill. This movement of the vehicle is described as a pitch-over.

The speed that the Vance vehicle was travelling at the time of the pitch-over was an issue of dispute. The Leichtamers, who are the only surviving eyewitnesses to the accident, described the vehicle as travelling at a slow speed. Carl Leichtamer described the accident as occurring in this fashion:

> Well, we turned there and went down this trail and got to the top of this first hill. . . . And Paul looked back and make sure that everybody had their seat belt fastened. That it was fastened down; and he pulled the automatic lever down in low and he put it in low wheel, four wheel, too. . . . And then he just let it coast like over the top of this hill and was using the brake on the way down, too. We came to the level-off part. He just coasted up to the top of the second hill, and then the next thing I remember is the back end of the Jeep going over. . . . When we got to the top of the second hill, the front end went down like this (demonstrating) and the back end just started raising up like that (demonstrating).

John L. Habberstad, an expert witness for American Motors Corporation, testified that the vehicle had to be travelling between 15 and 20 miles per hour. This conclusion was based on evidence adduced by American Motors that the vehicle landed approximately 10 feet from the bottom of the second slope, having traversed about 47 feet in the air and having fallen approximately 23.5 feet.

The pitch-over of the Jeep CJ–7, on April 18, 1976, killed the driver, Paul Vance, and his wife, Cynthia. Carl Leichtamer sustained a depressed skull fracture. The tail gate of the vehicle presumably struck Jeanne Leichtamer. Jeanne was trapped in the vehicle after the accident and her position was described by her brother as follows: "She was like laying on her stomach although her head was sticking out of the jeep and the—she was laying on her stomach like and the tailgate of the jeep like, was laying lower, just a little bit lower or right almost on her shoulders and then the back seat of the jeep was laying on her lower part of her back. . . . [H]er legs were twisted through the front seat." Jeanne Leichtamer is a paraplegic as a result of the injury.

Carl and Jeanne Leichtamer, appellees, subsequently sued American Motors Corporation, American Motors Sales Corporation and Jeep Corporation, appellants, for "enhanced" injuries they sustained in the accident of April 18, 1976. The amended complaint averred that the permanent trauma to the body of Jeanne Leichtamer and the other injuries to her brother, Carl, were causally related to the displacement of the "roll bar" on the vehicle. Appellees claimed that Paul Vance's negligence caused the accident, but alleged that their injuries were "substantially enhanced, intensified, aggravated, and prolonged" by the roll bar displacement.

Paul Vance purchased his Jeep CJ–7 four-wheel-drive motor vehicle from a duly licensed, factory-authorized dealer, Petty's Jeep & Marine, Inc., owned and operated by Norman Petty. Vance purchased the vehicle on March 9, 1976. The vehicle came with a factory-installed roll bar. The entire vehicle was designed and manufactured by Jeep Corporation, a wholly owned subsidiary of American Motors. American Motors Sales Corporation is the selling agent for the manufacturer. Appellees did not claim that there was any defect in the way the vehicle was manufactured in the sense of departure by the manufacturer from design specifications. The vehicle was manufactured precisely in the manner in which it was designed to be manufactured. It reached Paul Vance in that condition and was not changed.

The focus of appellees' case was that the weakness of the sheet metal housing upon which the roll bar had been attached was causally related to the trauma to their bodies. Specifically, when the vehicle landed upside down, the flat sheet metal housing of the rear wheels upon which the roll bar tubing was attached by bolts gave way so that the single, side-to-side bar across the top of the vehicle was displaced to a position 12 inches forward of and 14½ inches lower than its original configuration relative to the chassis. The movement of the position of the intact roll bar resulting from the collapse of the sheet metal housing upon which it was bolted was, therefore, downward and forward. The roll bar tubing did not punch through the sheet metal housing, rather the housing collapsed, taking the intact tubing with it. That this displacement or movement of the intact roll bar is permitted by the thin nature of the sheet metal wheel housing to which it is attached and the propensity of the bar to do so when the vehicle lands upside down is central to appellees' case.

The appellants' position concerning the roll bar is that, from an engineering point of view, the roll bar was an optional device provided solely as protection for a side-roll.

* * * * *

The other principal element of appellees' case was that the advertised use of the vehicle involves great risk of forward pitch-overs. The accident occurred at the Hall of Fame Four-Wheel Club, which had been organized, among others, by Norman Petty, the vendor of the Vance vehicle. Petty allowed the club to meet at his Jeep dealership. He showed club members movies of the performance of the Jeep in hilly country. This activity was coupled with a national advertising program of American Motors Sales Corporation, which included a multimillion-dollar television campaign. The television advertising campaign was aimed at encouraging people to buy a Jeep, as follows: "Ever discover the rough, exciting world of mountains, forest, rugged terrain? The original Jeep can get you there, and Jeep guts will bring you back."

The campaign also stressed the ability of the Jeep to drive up and down steep hills. One Jeep CJ–7 television advertisement, for example, challenges a young man, accompanied by his girlfriend: "[Y]ou guys aren't yellow, are you? Is it a steep hill? Yeah, little lady, you could say it is a steep hill. Let's try it. The King of the Hill, is about to discover the new Jeep CJ–7." Moreover, the owner's manual for the Jeep CJ–5/CJ–7 provided instructions as to how "[a] four-wheel-drive vehicle can proceed in safety down a grade which could not be negotiated safely by a conventional two-wheel-drive vehicle." Both appellees testified that they had seen the commercials and that they thought the roll bar would protect them if the vehicle landed on its top.

Appellees offered the expert testimony of Dr. Gene H. Samuelson that all of the physical trauma to the body of Jeanne Leichtamer were causally related to the collapse of the roll bar support. These injuries—fractures of both arms, some ribs, fracture of the dorsal spine, and a relative dislocation of the cervical spine and injury to the spinal cord—were described by Samuelson as permanent. He also testified that the physical trauma to the body of Carl Leichtamer was causally related to the collapse of the roll bar.

Appellants' principal argument was that the roll bar was provided solely for a side-roll. Appellants' only testing of the roll bar was done on a 1969 Jeep CJ–5, a model with a wheel base 10 inches shorter than the Jeep CJ–7. Evidence of the test was offered in evidence and refused. With regard to tests for either side-rolls or pitch-overs on the Jeep CJ–7, appellants responded to interrogatories that no "proving ground," "vibration or shock," or "crash" tests were conducted.

The jury returned a verdict for both appellees. Damages were assessed for Carl Leichtamer at $100,000 compensatory and $100,000 punitive. Damages were assessed for Jeanne Leichtamer at $1 million compensatory and $1 million punitive. . . .

I(A)

Appellants' first three propositions of law raise essentially the same issue: that only negligence principles should be applied in a design defect case involving a so-called "second collision." In this case, appellees seek to hold appellants liable for injuries "enhanced" by a design defect of the vehicle in which appellees were riding when an accident occurred. This cause of action is to be contrasted with that where the alleged defect causes the accident itself. Here, the "second collision" is that between appellees and the vehicle in which they were riding.

Appellants assert that the instructions of law given to the jury by the trial court improperly submitted the doctrine of strict liability in tort as a basis for liability. The scope of this review is limited to the question of whether an instruction on strict liability in tort should have been given. For the reasons explained herein, we answer the question in the affirmative.

I(B)

The appropriate starting point in this analysis is our decision in *Temple* v. *Wean United, Inc.* (1977). In *Temple,* this court adopted Section 402A of the Restatement of Torts 2d, thus providing a cause of action in strict liability for injury from a product in Ohio.

* * * * *

. . . [T]he vast weight of authority is in support of allowing an action in strict liability in tort, as well as negligence, for design defects. We see no difficulty in also applying Section 402A to design defects. As pointed out by the California Supreme Court, "[a] defect may emerge from the mind of the designer as well as from the hand of the workman." A distinction between defects resulting from manufacturing processes and those resulting from design, and a resultant difference in the burden of proof on the injured party, would only provoke needless questions of defect classification, which would add little to the resolution of the underlying claims. A consumer injured by an unreasonably dangerous design should have the same benefit of freedom from proving fault provided by Section 402A as the consumer injured by a defectively manufactured product which proves unreasonably dangerous.

* * * * *

Strict liability in tort has been applied to design defect "second collision" cases. While a manufacturer is under no obligation to design a "crash-proof" vehicle, an instruction may be given on the issue of strict liability in tort if the plaintiff adduces sufficient evidence that an unreasonably dangerous product design proximately caused or enhanced plaintiff's injuries in the course of a foreseeable use. Here, appellants produced a vehicle which was capable of off-the-road use. It was advertised for such a use. The only protection provided the user in the case of roll-overs or pitch-overs proved wholly inadequate. A roll bar should be more than mere ornamentation. The interest of our society in product safety would best be served by allowing a cause in strict liability for such a roll bar device when it proves to be unreasonably dangerous and, as a result, enhances the injuries of the user.

I(C)

We turn to the question of what constitutes an unreasonably dangerous defective product.

Section 402A subjects to liability one who sells a product in a "defective condition, unreasonably dangerous" which causes physical harm to the ultimate user. Comment *g* defines defective condition as "a condition not contemplated by the ultimate consumer which will be unreasonably dangerous to him." Comment *i* states that for a product to be unreasonably dangerous, "[t]he article sold must be dangerous to an extent beyond that which would be contemplated by the ordinary consumer who purchases it, with the ordinary knowledge common to the community as to its characteristics."

With regard to design defects, the product is considered defective only because it causes or enhances an injury. "In such a case, the defect and the injury cannot be separated, yet clearly a product cannot be considered defective simply because it is capable of producing injury." Rather, in such a case the concept of "unreasonable danger" is essential to establish liability under strict liability in tort principles.

The concept of "unreasonable danger," as found in Section 402A, provides implicitly that a product may be found defective in design if it is more dangerous in use than the ordinary consumer would expect. Another way of phrasing this proposition is that "a product may be found defective in design if the plaintiff demonstrates that the product failed to perform as safely as an ordinary consumer would expect when used in an intended or reasonably foreseeable manner."

* * * * *

Thus, we hold a cause of action for damages for injuries "enhanced" by a design defect will lie in strict liability in tort. In order to recover, the plaintiff must prove by a preponderance of the evidence that the "enhancement" of the injuries was proximately caused by a defective product unreasonably dangerous to the plaintiff.

* * * * *

[Part II omitted—Author.]

III

Appellants . . . contend that it was error for the trial court to have admitted in evidence television commercials which advertised the Jeep CJ–7 as a vehicle to "discover the rough, exciting world of mountains, forests, rugged terrain." Appellants further contend that "a jury may not base its verdict upon such television commercials in the absence of a specific representation contained in the commercials as to the quality or merit of the product in question and in the absence from the plaintiff that the use of the product was in reliance upon such representations." [sic]

We held that a product is unreasonably dangerous if it is dangerous to an extent beyond the expectations of an ordinary consumer when used in an intended or reasonably foreseeable manner. The commercial advertising of a product will be the guiding force upon the expectations of consumers with regard to the safety of a product, and is highly relevant to a formulation of what those expectations might be. The particular manner in which a product is advertised as being used is also relevant to a determination of the intended and reasonably foreseeable uses of the product. Therefore, it was not error to admit the commercial advertising in evidence to establish consumer expectation of safety and intended use.

Affirmed.

Justice Holmes, dissenting:
The majority reaches its decision by virtue of the application in a second collision case of the doctrine of strict liability as contained in Section 402A of the Restatement of Torts 2d.

I am unable to join in this analysis. In a products liability action based upon an alleged design defect of the product, which allegedly has enhanced the plaintiff's injuries, I feel that the manufacturer should be held liable only when the plaintiff is able to prove that the manufacturer was negligent in adopting his chosen design.

It is my view that the proper rule to be applied in crashworthiness cases is set forth in *Larsen* v. *General Motors Corp.* as follows:

> The manfacturers are not insurers but should be held to a standard of reasonable care in design to provide a reasonably safe vehicle in which to travel.
>
> This duty of reasonable care in design rests on common law negligence that a manufacturer of an article should use reasonable care in the design and manufacture of his product to eliminate any unreasonable risk of foreseeable injury.

> There should be no requirements in the law that manufacturers must design their automotive products to withstand extraordinary accidents of unusual circumstance or severity. . . .

* * * * *

My belief that these enhanced injury cases should be determined upon negligence principles rather than upon strict liability, or implied warranty principles, is based upon a number of reasons. I do not feel that the standards for imposition of liability under Section 402A provide sufficient guidance to the jury. . . .

Additionally, courts have seemingly had a difficult time defining what Section 402A means. . . .

* * * * *

Applying the appropriate standard to the facts in this case, the plaintiff, in addition to proof of specific knowledge of, and reliance upon, any claims of protective security offered by the roll bars in instances of Jeep pitch-overs, would have to prove that the accident was one reasonably foreseeable and not an extraordinary accident, or of unusual circumstance or severity. Also, the plaintiff would have to prove that there was a safer alternative design available, practicable under the circumstances.

As stated, there was a significant absence of specific proof as to any reliance by these plaintiffs upon the capability of the roll bar in a pitch-over situation or otherwise. Additionally, there was an insufficiency of proof that this type of an accident, involving a pitch-over of a Jeep, was a common accident and one reasonably foreseeable. In fact, the evidence would tend to controvert such a finding in that there was testimony from both plaintiffs and defense witnesses that pitch-overs are rare events which occur infrequently and only if the specific conditions necessary to bring it about exist.

American Motors presented testimony that the roll bars were installed on these Jeeps to aid in the protection of occupants in roll-over situations, not pitch-over accidents as was occasioned here.

* * * * *

There also was a failure of proof here as to any alternate safer design practicable under the circumstances of a pitch-over rather than a roll-over, and absence of any proof of any lessened or differential injuries that might have been sustained had an alternate design been installed in this jeep.

As stated, in the application of the proper standards here, the manufacturer's duty is to exercise reasonable care in the design of its product to eliminate any reasonable risk of foreseeable injury, but it need not be designed to make the vehicle accident proof. The liability of this defendant under the facts should have been submitted to the jury, not on the strict liability theory, but upon the theory of negligence with applicable standards of ordinary care and foreseeability.

Questions

1. Many courts now employ what is known as the risk/utility test in deciding design defect cases like *Leichtamer* under a strict liability analysis. The risk/utility test holds that "a product is defective if the utility of particular features of its design is outweighed by risks attendant to those features."[13] In *Leichtamer* the court relied on the consumer expectations test.
   a. Explain that test.
   b. Criticize it.
2. The dissent in *Leichtamer* argued for the application of a negligence standard in this case. Had the court adopted that view, rather than relying on strict liability reasoning, would the decision have been different? Explain.
3. *a.* Why did the *Leichtamer* court apply strict liability to this case?
   b. Are you persuaded by the court's reasoning? Explain.
4. Does this decision have the effect of requiring the Jeep to be "accident proof" (as argued by the dissent) to avoid liability? Explain.
5. Had Jeep designed the vehicle without a roll bar of any kind, who would have won this case? Explain.
6. The deceased had rented an auto from the Hertz Corporation. A tire blew out, and a fatal crash resulted. The tire was manufactured by Firestone. The estate of the deceased filed suit against Hertz and Firestone. Evidence presented at trial caused the jury to believe that the dangerous condition of the tire arose after its manufacture.
   a. Can the plaintiff successfully raise a strict liability claim against Hertz? Explain.
   b. Against Firestone? Explain. See *Stang* v. *Hertz Corp.*, 83 N.M. 730, 497 P.2d 732 (1972).
7. The plaintiff received a blood transfusion at St. Joseph's Hospital. Shortly thereafter, the plaintiff was discovered to have contracted serum hepatitis (a disease sometimes transmitted via transfusions). The blood was purchased from Blood Services, Inc. Can the plaintiff recover on strict liability grounds from either St. Joseph's or Blood Services? See *Hines* v. *St. Joseph's Hospital*, 86 N.M. 763, 527 P.2d 1075 (1974).

Afterword

So-called utility vehicles (Jeeps, Isuzu Troopers, Suzuki Samurai, and so on), which have rather high centers of gravity and somewhat narrow wheel bases, have been heavily criticized because of their allegedly greater-than-normal propensity to rollover under some conditions. In June 1988 Consumers Union, publisher of *Consumer Reports,* argued for a recall of all Suzuki Samurai vehicles and urged the automaker to buy back all of the vehicles currently in use. Based on its testing, Consumers Union found a "hazardous propensity" to rollover in those instances where drivers must take abrupt measures to avoid an accident. The nonprofit testing organization gave the Samurai a "not acceptable" rating, the first such vehicle judgment in 10 years.[14] Consumers Union also petitioned the federal government to set vehicle stability standards measured by testing.

The Samurai was introduced in 1985. Prior to mid-1988, the federal government had "received 44 reports of rollover accidents involving Samurais, which reportedly caused 16 deaths and 53 injuries."[15] Suzuki officials have indicated that their vehicles are fully safe and that the Consumers Union tests were flawed. However, federal government data suggests utility vehicles generally have rather high rollover risks:

> A recent National Highway Traffic Safety Administration study estimates that such vehicles are involved in rollover accidents two to three times more frequently than passenger cars. Moreover, while 24 percent of all deaths in cars occur in rollovers, the rate is 66 percent in utility vehicles. This represented more than 600 fatalities in 1986, with thousands more injured.[16]

No matter what the vehicles' quality may be, they have become quite popular, with sales in the late 1980s of about 6 percent of the market, up from 2 percent in the late 1970s.[17]

DANIELL V. FORD MOTOR CO., INC.
581 F.Supp. 728 (N. M. 1984)

District Judge Baldock

In 1980, the plaintiff became locked inside the trunk of a 1973 Ford LTD automobile, where she remained for some nine days. Plaintiff now seeks to recover for psychological and physical injuries arising from that occurrence. She contends that the automobile had a design defect in that the trunk lock or latch did not have an internal release or opening mechanism. She also maintains that the manufacturer is liable based on a failure to warn of this condition. Plaintiff advances several theories for recovery: (1) strict products liability under § 402A of the Restatement 2d of Torts (1965), (2) negligence, and (3) breach of express warranty and implied warranties of merchantability and fitness for a particular purpose.

Three uncontroverted facts bar recovery under any of these theories. First, the plaintiff ended up in the trunk compartment of the automobile because she felt "overburdened" and was attempting to commit suicide. Second, the purposes of an automobile trunk are to transport, stow and secure the automobile spare tire, luggage and other goods and to protect those items from elements of the weather. Third, the plaintiff never considered the possibility of exit from the inside of the trunk when the automobile was purchased.

The overriding factor barring plaintiff's recovery is that she intentionally sought to end her life by crawling into an automobile trunk from which she could not escape. This is not a case where a person inadvertently became trapped inside an automobile trunk. The plaintiff was aware of the natural and probable consequences of her perilous conduct. Not only that, the plaintiff, at least initially, sought those dreadful consequences. Plaintiff, not the manufacturer of the vehicle, is responsible for this unfortunate occurrence.

Recovery under strict products liability and negligence will be discussed first because the concept of duty owed by the manufacturer to the consumer or user is the same under both theories in this case. As a general principle, a design defect is actionable only where the condition of the product is unreasonably dangerous to the user or consumer. Restatement 2d of Torts, § 402A (1965). Under strict products liability or negligence, a manufacturer has a duty to consider only those risks of injury which are foreseeable. A risk is not foreseeable by a manufacturer where a product is used in a manner which could not reasonably be anticipated by the manufacturer and that use is the cause of the plaintiff's injury. The plaintiff's injury would not be foreseeable by the manufacturer.

. . . The design features of an automobile trunk make it well near impossible that an adult intentionally would enter the trunk and close the lid. The dimensions of a trunk, the height of its sill and its load floor and the efforts to first lower the trunk lid and then to engage its latch, are among the design features which encourage closing and latching the trunk lid while standing outside the vehicle. The court holds that the plaintiff's use of the trunk compartment as a means to attempt suicide was an unforeseeable use as a matter of law. Therefore, the manufacturer had no duty to design an internal release or opening mechanism that might have prevented this occurrence.

Nor did the manufacturer have a duty to warn the plaintiff of the danger of her conduct, given the plaintiff's unforeseeable use of the product. Another reason why the manufacturer had no duty to warn the plaintiff of the risk inherent in crawling into an automobile trunk and closing the trunk lid is because such a risk is obvious. There is no duty to warn of known dangers in strict products liability or tort. Moreover, the potential efficacy of any warning, given the plaintiff's use of the automobile trunk compartment for a deliberate suicide attempt, is questionable.

The court notes that the automobile trunk was not defective under these circumstances. The automobile trunk was not unreasonably dangerous within the contemplation of the ordinary consumer or user of such a trunk when used in the ordinary ways and for the ordinary purposes for which such a trunk is used.

* * * * *

Having considered the products liability and negligence claims, plaintiff's contract claims for breach of warranty are now analyzed. Plaintiff has come forward with no evidence of any express warranty regarding exit from the inside of the trunk. . . .

Any implied warranty of merchantability in this case requires that the product must be fit for the ordinary purposes for which such goods are used. . . . Plaintiff's use of the trunk was highly extraordinary, and there is no evidence that that trunk was not fit for the ordinary purpose for which it was intended.

Lastly, plaintiff's claim for a breach of implied warranty of fitness for a particular purpose cannot withstand summary judgment because the plaintiff has admitted that, at the time she purchased the automobile, neither she nor her husband gave any particular thought to the trunk mechanism. Plaintiff has admitted that she did not even think about getting out from inside of the trunk when purchasing the vehicle. Plaintiff did not rely on the seller's skill or judgment to select or furnish an automobile suitable for the unfortunate purpose for which the plaintiff used it.

Defendant's Motion for Summary Judgment is granted.

Questions

1. To most readers, Daniell's claim may seem preposterous, even outrageous. Nonetheless, build the general case, not limited to the facts in *Daniell,* that auto manufacturers should be liable for damages suffered by those entrapped in trunks.
2. The court cited the fact that the plaintiff "never considered the possibility of exit from the inside of the trunk when the automobile was purchased." Why was that fact important to the outcome of the case?
3. With the widespread adoption of the comparative negligence approach, many courts are struggling with the question of applying comparative negligence to strict liability actions. A recent California case addressed the issue. A car struck a metal divider fence, causing a door to open. The driver was ejected and killed. Plaintiff argued that the ejection was the result of a defective door lock. Defendant argued that the driver was negligent in failing to lock the door, in failing to use a seat belt, and in driving while intoxicated. Should the court compare the negligence, if any, of the plaintiff with the strict liability of the defendant? See *Daly* v. *General Motors Corp., 575 P.2d 1162* (Cal. 1978).
4. Damages resulted from the defective braking system in a used car. At trial no evidence was offered to show that the used-car dealer was responsible for the defect. A strict liability claim was raised against the used-car dealer. Decide. Explain. See *Peterson* v. *Low Bachrodt Chevrolet Co., 329 N.E.2d 785* (Ill. 1975), but also see *Realmuto* v. *Straub Motor, Inc., 322 A.2d 440* (N.J. 1974).

THE LIMITS OF STRICT LIABILITY

The *Sindell* case and the Liggett/Cipollone reading that follow represent potentially striking departures in products liability law. *Sindell* has already had a marked impact on legal thinking. Liggett/Cipollone is merely a trial court decision. Although its significance remains to be seen, the case is striking in its own right because it represents the first time a tobacco company has been found in any way legally responsible for a smoker's death. Both cases explore the frontiers of products liability while illustrating the judiciary's continuing search for the most equitable and sensible means of allocating risk.

SINDELL V. ABBOTT LABORATORIES
163 Cal. Rptr. 132, 607 P.2d 924 (1980), cert. denied 449 U.S. 912 (1980)

Justice Mosk

This case involves a complex problem both timely and significant: may a plaintiff, injured as the result of a drug administered to her mother during pregnancy, who knows the type of drug involved but cannot identify the manufacturer of the precise product, hold liable for her injuries a maker of a drug produced from an identical formula?

Plaintiff Judith Sindell brought an action against 11 drug companies . . . on behalf of herself and other women similarly situated. The complaint alleges as follows:

Between 1941 and 1971, defendants were engaged in the business of manufacturing, promoting, and marketing diethylstilbesterol (DES), a drug which is a synthetic compound of the female hormone estrogen. The drug was administered to plaintiff's mother and the mothers of the class she represents, for the purpose of preventing miscarriage. In 1947, the Food and Drug Administration authorized the marketing of DES as a miscarriage preventative, but only on an experimental basis, with a requirement that the drug contain a warning label to that effect.

DES may cause cancerous vaginal and cervical growths in the daughters exposed to it before birth, because their mothers took the drug during pregnancy. The form of cancer from which these daughters suffer is known as adenocarcinoma, and it manifests itself after a minimum latent period of 10 or 12 years. It is a fast-spreading and deadly disease, and radical surgery is required to prevent it from spreading. DES also causes adenosis, precancerous vaginal and cervical growths which may spread to other areas of the body. The treatment for adenosis is cauterization, surgery, or cryosurgery. Women who suffer from this condition must be monitored by biopsy or colposcopic examination twice a year, a painful and expensive procedure. Thousands of women whose mothers received DES during pregnancy are unaware of the effects of the drug.

In 1971, the Food and Drug Administration ordered defendants to cease marketing and promoting DES for the purpose of preventing miscarriages, and to warn physicians and the public that the drug should not be used by pregnant women because of the danger to their unborn children.

During the period defendants marketed DES, they knew or should have known that it was a carcinogenic substance, that there was a grave danger after varying periods of latency it would cause cancerous and precancerous growths in the daughters of the mothers who took it, and that it was ineffective to prevent miscarriage. Nevertheless, defendants continued to advertise and market the drug as a miscarriage preventative. They failed to test

DES for efficacy and safety; the tests performed by others, upon which they relied, indicated that it was not safe or effective. In violation of the authorization of the Food and Drug Administration, defendants marketed DES on an unlimited basis rather than as an experimental drug, and they failed to warn of its potential danger.

Because of defendants' advertised assurances that DES was safe and effective to prevent miscarriage, plaintiff was exposed to the drug prior to her birth. She became aware of the danger from such exposure within one year of the time she filed her complaint. As a result of the DES ingested by her mother, plaintiff developed a malignant bladder tumor which was removed by surgery. She suffers from adenosis and must constantly be monitored by biopsy or colposcopy to insure early warning of further malignancy.

The first cause of action alleges that defendants were jointly and individually negligent in that they manufactured, marketed, and promoted DES as a safe and efficacious drug to prevent miscarriage, without adequate testing or warning, and without monitoring or reporting its effects.

A separate cause of action alleges that defendants are jointly liable regardless of which particular brand of DES was ingested by plaintiff's mother because defendants collaborated in marketing, promoting and testing the drug, relied upon each other's tests, and adhered to an industrywide safety standard. DES was produced from a common and mutually agreed upon formula as a fungible drug interchangeable with other brands of the same product; defendants knew or should have known that it was customary for doctors to prescribe the drug by its generic rather than its brand name and that pharmacists filled prescriptions from whatever brand of the drug happened to be in stock.

Other causes of action are based upon theories of strict liability, violation of express and implied warranties, false and fraudulent representations, misbranding of drugs in violation of federal law, conspiracy, and "lack of consent."

Each cause of action alleges that defendants are jointly liable because they acted in concert, on the basis of express and implied agreements, and in reliance upon and ratification and exploitation of each other's testing and marketing methods.

Plaintiff seeks compensatory damages of $1 million and punitive damages of $10 million for herself. For the members of her class, she prays for equitable relief in the form of an order that defendants warn physicians and others of the danger of DES and the necessity of performing certain tests to determine the presence of disease caused by the drug, and that they establish free clinics in California to perform such tests.

Defendants demurred to the complaint. . . . [T]he court dismissed the action.

* * * * *

This case is but one of a number filed throughout the country seeking to hold drug manufacturers liable for injuries allegedly resulting from DES prescribed to the plaintiffs' mothers since 1947. . . . [E]stimates of the number of women who took the drug during pregnancy range from 1.5 million to 3 million. Hundreds, perhaps thousands of the daughters of these women suffer from adenocarcinoma, and the incidence of vaginal adenosis among them is 30 to 90 percent. . . . Most of the cases are still pending. With two exceptions, those that have been decided resulted in judgments in favor of the drug company defendants because of the failure of the plaintiffs to identify the manufacturer of the DES prescribed to their mothers. . . . The present action is another attempt to overcome this obstacle to recovery.

We begin with the proposition that, as a general rule, the imposition of liability depends upon a showing by the plaintiff that his or her injuries were caused by the act of the defendant or by an instrumentality under the defendant's control. . . .

There are, however, exceptions to this rule. . . .

Plaintiff places primary reliance upon cases which hold that if a party cannot identify which of two or more defendants caused an injury, the burden of proof may shift to the defendants to show that they were not responsible for the harm. This principle is sometimes referred to as the "alternative liability" theory.

The celebrated case of *Summers* v. *Tice,* a unanimous opinion of this court, best exemplifies the rule. In *Summers,* the plaintiff was injured when two hunters negligently shot in his direction. It could not be determined which of them had fired the shot which actually caused the injury to the plaintiff's eye, but both defendants were nevertheless held jointly and severally liable for the whole of the damages. We reasoned that both were wrongdoers, both were negligent toward the plaintiff, and that it would be unfair to require plaintiff to isolate the defendant responsible, because if the one pointed out were to escape liability, the other might also, and the plaintiff-victim would be shorn of any remedy. In these circumstances, we held, the burden of proof shifted to the defendants, "each to absolve himself if he can." . . . We stated that under these or similar circumstances a defendant is ordinarily in a "far better position" to offer evidence to determine whether he or another defendant caused the injury.

* * * * *

There is an important difference between the situation involved in *Summers* and the present case. There, all the parties who were or could have been responsible for the harm to the plaintiff were joined as defendants. Here, by contrast, there are approximately 200 drug companies which made DES, any of which might have manufactured the injury-producing drug.

* * * * *

In our contemporary complex industrialized society, advances in science and technology create fungible goods which may harm consumers and which cannot be traced to any specific producer. The response of the courts can be either to adhere rigidly to prior doctrine, denying recovery to those injured by such products, or to fashion remedies to meet these changing needs. . . .

The most persuasive reason for finding plaintiff states a cause of action is that advanced in *Summers:* as between an innocent plaintiff and negligent defendants, the latter should bear the cost of the injury. Here, as in *Summers,* plaintiff is not at fault in failing to provide evidence of causation, and although the absence of such evidence is not attributable to the defendants either, their conduct in marketing a drug the effects of which are delayed for many years played a significant role in creating the unavailability of proof.

From a broader policy standpoint, defendants are better able to bear the cost of injury resulting from the manufacture of a defective product. As was said by Justice Traynor in *Escola,* "[t]he cost of an injury and the loss of time or health may be an overwhelming misfortune to the person injured, and a needless one, for the risk of injury can be insured by the manufacturer and distributed among the public as a cost of doing business." . . . The manufacturer is in the best position to discover and guard against defects in its products and to warn of harmful effects; thus, holding it liable for defects and failure to warn of harmful effects will provide an incentive to product safety. . . .

Where, as here, all defendants produced a drug from an identical formula and the manufacturer of the DES which caused plaintiff's injuries cannot be identified through no fault of plaintiff, a modification of the rule of *Summers* is warranted. . . . [A]n undiluted *Summers* rationale is inappropriate to shift the burden of proof of causation to defendants because if we measure the chance that any particular manufacturer supplied the injury-causing product by the number of producers of DES, there is a possibility that none of the five defendants in this case produced the offending substance and that the responsible manufacturer, not named in the action, will escape liability.

But we approach the issue of causation from a different perspective: we hold it to be reasonable in the present context to measure the likelihood that any of the defendants supplied the product which allegedly injured plaintiff by the percentage which the DES sold by each of them for the purpose of preventing miscarriage bears to the entire production of the drug sold by all for that purpose. Plaintiff asserts in her briefs that Eli Lilly and Company and five or six other companies produced 90 percent of the DES marketed. If at trial this is established to be the fact, then there is a corresponding likelihood that this comparative handful of producers manufactured the DES which caused plaintiff's injuries, and only a 10 percent likelihood that the offending producer would escape liability.

If plaintiff joins in the action the manufacturers of a substantial share of the DES which her mother might have taken, the injustice of shifting the burden of proof to defendants to demonstrate that they could not have made the substance which injured plaintiff is significantly diminished. . . .

The presence in the action of a substantial share of the appropriate market also provides a ready means to apportion damages among the defendants. Each defendant will be held liable for the proportion of the judgment represented by its share of that market unless it demonstrates that it could not have made the product which caused plaintiff's injuries.

* * * * *

We are not unmindful of the practical problems involved in defining the market and determining market share. . . . But under the rule we adopt, each manufacturer's liability for an injury would be approximately equivalent to the damages caused by the DES it manufactured.

The judgments are reversed.

Questions

1. Explain the alternative liability theory.
2. Explain how *Sindell* extends the *Summers* approach to alternative liability.
3. How can a defendant avoid liability under the *Sindell* decision?
4. How does the *Sindell* court justify its decision?
5. The dissent in *Sindell* (not reproduced in this text) argued that although "the majority purports to change only the required burden of proof by shifting it from plaintiffs to defendants, the effect of the holding is to guarantee that the plaintiffs will prevail on the causation issue because defendants are no more capable of disproving factual causation than plaintiffs are of proving it. 'Market share' liability thus represents a new high-water mark in tort law." Comment.
6. A victim of asbestosis could not identify all of the manufacturers of the asbestos to which he was exposed. Should the court apply the "market share" theory of liability to his case? Explain. See *Copeland* v. *Celotex Corp.*, 447 So.2d 908 (Fla. App. 3 Dist. 1984).

LIGGETT ORDERED TO PAY $400,000 IN DAMAGES FOR SMOKER'S DEATH

**Alix M. Freedman,
Timothy K. Smith,
and John Helyar**

A federal jury found that Liggett Group, Inc., wrongly implied that cigarettes were safe in its advertising before 1966 and awarded $400,000 in damages to the widower of a smoker who died of lung cancer.

It was the first defeat for the tobacco industry in three decades of court battles over liability for smokers' deaths.

The six-person jury in Newark, New Jersey, also held that Durham, North Carolina-based Liggett was aware of the dangers of smoking and should have warned Rose Cipollone and other customers before 1966, when Congress started requiring tobacco companies to put warnings on cigarette packages. Mrs. Cipollone, a lifelong smoker, died in 1984.

However, in one of the most crucial parts of the closely watched case, the jury found that Liggett and the other defendants—the Philip Morris, Inc., unit of Philip Morris Cos. and the Lorillard, Inc., unit of Loews Corp., both based in New York—didn't conspire to mislead the public about the dangers of smoking before 1966.

Attorneys for the tobacco companies called the jury's findings a victory. But others said the outcome was at the least a major symbolic blow to the industry. Tobacco companies have never before had even a partial defeat in the more than 300 tobacco liability cases that have been tried, nor have they ever settled a case out of court.

"It's certainly a 'shot heard 'round the world,'" said David A. Goldman, an analyst at Fahnestock & Co., New York.

* * * * *

Partly to Blame

According to Cynthia Walters, an attorney for plaintiff Antonio Cipollone, the case marks the first time a jury has found that a smoker's death was at least partly due to smoking. In previous cases, tobacco companies have typically won by arguing that there's no proof cigarettes cause lung cancer and that even if they do, they didn't cause the particular death at issue in the trial.

* * * * *

The direct financial impact on the industry isn't expected to be large. Even a flood of new lawsuits—which Ms. Walters doesn't expect—and damage awards would add only a few cents to the price of a pack of cigarettes, analysts estimate. That's partly because the industry generally is considered vulnerable only to claims involving its conduct before 1966.

Moreover, future damage awards aren't expected to be large. Marc Cohen, an analyst at Sanford C. Bernstein & Co., New York, says that in contrast to claims involving asbestos exposure—where the dangers generally weren't known by the victims—even persons who smoked before 1966 will have a hard time convincing juries they didn't know smoking was dangerous.

But the Cipollone decision "certainly will have an impact on the [tobacco] industry's political base of support," said Calvert Crary, a liability specialist at Martin Simpson & Co., a

New York brokerage concern. The case, he said, could lead to more stringent regulation of cigarette distribution and consumption. "That is the big consequence of this case," Mr. Crary said.

* * * * *

The jury awarded the $400,000 to Mr. Cipollone after finding that Liggett breached an "express warranty" in its pre-1966 advertising that its cigarettes were safe. For example, in the 1950s, it promoted its L&M brand, which Mrs. Cipollone smoked, as "just what the doctor ordered."

Although trial testimony indicated that Mrs. Cipollone knew smoking was dangerous, Marc Edell, the lead plaintiff's attorney, argued that such advertising gave her a conflicting message.

The jurors also held that Liggett failed to warn Mrs. Cipollone of the dangers of smoking before 1966. But they found she bore 80 percent of the blame for her death, despite Mr. Edell's efforts to persuade them that she was addicted to smoking and couldn't quit.

As a result, Liggett wasn't found liable for damages on the failure-to-warn claim. The damage award on the warranty issue didn't involve an assessment of Mrs. Cipollone's conduct.

Defense attorneys argued that Mrs. Cipollone was a well-informed, intelligent woman who was aware of the risks and smoked because she enjoyed it.

The fraud and conspiracy charges were unique to the Cipollone case and were what made the four-month trial the subject of national attention. For the first time, cigarette makers were forced to disclose thousands of pages of confidential documents that suggested, according to the plaintiff's attorneys, that the companies knew smoking is linked to cancer and other diseases.

The evidence suggested, they said, that manufacturers sought to suppress research data on smoking and health and to undercut scientific findings by generating controversy in the press and the medical community over the causes of lung cancer.

The jury's finding that there was no conspiracy was hailed by defense attorneys as the key decision in the case.

"We think it's a victory," said Alan Naar, an attorney for Liggett. "The major claims—fraud, misrepresentation, and conspiracy—that were presented to the jury . . . were completely rejected by the jury." Mr. Naar said Liggett will appeal the "express warranty" ruling and is confident it will be overturned.

* * * * *

Source: *The Wall Street Journal*, June 14, 1988, pp. 3, 18. Reprinted by permission of *The Wall Street Journal*, © Dow Jones & Company, Inc. 1988. ALL RIGHTS RESERVED.

Questions

1. As you understand the facts of the *Cipollone* case, what vote would you have cast had you been a member of the jury? Explain.
2. Why have smokers been unable to recover, in cases like *Cipollone*, on strict liability and breach of the warranty of merchantability? See, for example, *Green v. American Tobacco Co.,* 391 F.2d 97 (1968), cert. denied 397 U.S. 911 (1970).
3. Would you favor legislation banning cigarette advertisements and promotions? Explain.

CORPORATION PROTECTION?

We have seen that products liability law—particularly that of strict liability—has wrought a revolution in the degree of protection afforded to the consumer. It is clear that the courts and legislatures believed consumers had been relatively powerless in the face of defective products, and that powerlessness had become particularly pronounced as commercial practice left behind straightforward, face-to-face bargaining and entered an era of multiple and complex layers of parts suppliers, manufacturers, distributors, retailers, and so on. That imbalance of power was addressed in part by expanded products liability theories. In keeping with the generally egalitarian tone of the past two decades (for example, the civil rights movement, the feminist cause), the law of consumer protection seemed to move toward the presumed ideal of righting every wrong. Now, predictably enough, those in the business community and others believe the balance of power has swung too profoundly in favor of the consumer. They see business laboring under an excessive burden, born of an unjust effort to shift losses to those with the deepest pockets.

To combat some of the perceived unfairness in product liability law and to lend some uniformity to the law from state to state, the Department of Commerce has offered to the states a Uniform Product Liability Act (UPLA). As yet few states have adopted the act in significant part. It supports some of the concerns of the business community in, for example, approving contributory negligence, assumption of risk, product misuse, and product alteration defenses. Another provision shields sellers from liability "in circumstances where they do not have a reasonable opportunity to inspect the product in a manner which would, or should, in the exercise of reasonable care, reveal the existence of the defective condition." Although the UPLA proposes these and other provisions generally favorable to the business community's point of view, strict liability is unquestionably here to stay. Indeed, the UPLA generally imposes liability for injury resulting from any defectively designed or defectively produced product or from any dangerous product not displaying adequate warnings.

The business community's concerns regarding the growth of product liability recoveries caused Congress to adopt the Risk Retention Act of 1981 (RRA). In brief summary, the act facilitates the creation of "captive" insurance companies. In effect, a group of sellers join together to insure themselves against products liability losses. In so doing, the self-insurers hope to keep their own premiums at manageable levels and at the same time encourage moderation in insurance industry premiums.

For several years Congress has been considering a federal products liability law. However, passage does not appear to be imminent. Whether the UPLA, the RRA, and the other proposals to regulate the product liability area are necessary or will prove effective remains to be seen.

The two articles that follow give us a glimpse of some major themes in the debate. FMC Corporation Chief Executive Officer Robert Malott argues for reforms to counter what he believes is our excessive reliance on litigation. But in the next article we see that, as of the summer of 1988, the English government was planning an overhaul of its personal injury approach that would lead to a system much more like ours.

AMERICA'S LIABILITY
EXPLOSION: DEFUSING THE BOMB

Robert H. Malott

The destructive and rapidly escalating trend toward liability litigation in this country is costing the American public billions of dollars each year, is undermining the competitiveness of U.S. industry, and is threatening the very existence of some businesses in this country. Yet it is a trend that the vast majority of the American people have either failed to understand or have persistently chosen to ignore.

The disturbing truth is that America has become the most litigious society in the world. In 1984, 1 out of 15 Americans filed a private civil lawsuit of some kind. In all, over 13 million private civil lawsuits were filed in state and federal courts.

To halt their red ink, insurance companies have resorted to a host of defensive measures—hiking rates, cancelling coverage, narrowing the conditions of their policies, and, in some cases, simply closing up shop. As a result, businesses nationwide are facing a precipitous decline in liability coverage—if they can get coverage at all—at costs that range anywhere from 25 to 500 percent over their previous premiums. FMC, as an example, had its premium increased 350 percent last year for

less than one half the coverage we enjoyed in 1984—and this was after an extensive search of all alternatives in the worldwide insurance market.

Liability Chaos

It would seem that insurance companies are trying to tell this country that something is seriously wrong with our system of liability. Indeed, Lloyd's of London, the single largest insurance market in the world, has indicated it may withdraw from its U.S. activities if it does not see some action on tort law reform.

What is causing the chaos in liability? I attribute the current situation to the following three factors.

First is *the ambiguity of current liability laws.* Since the early 1960s, the concept of liability for product-related injuries has been relentlessly expanded by both state and federal courts.

The courts first created a new legal theory, strict liability, to enable claimants to recover damages for injuries caused by defectively manufactured products. This happened because the courts believed that business—rather than the injured party—should bear the cost of manufacturing errors, regardless of fault. Then the concept of strict liability was extended from defects in manufacturing to defects in a particular product's design, in its operating instructions, or in its safety warnings. In essence, the focus of product liability was shifted from the conduct of manufacturers to the condition of the product itself.

However, unlike the test for manufacturing defects, there are no clear-cut standards to guide judicial decisions on the adequacy of a product's design or its safety warnings. Although some 30 states have now enacted product liability statutes, no two are alike. Consequently, cases based on similar facts, but tried in different states, can produce strikingly different and often contradictory judgments.

Obvious Hazards

In an FMC case concerning a construction worker who had driven a crane into high-voltage lines, an Illinois court ruled *against* FMC for not providing adequate safety warnings and for not installing automatic warning devices, even though the devices available at the time the crane was manufactured were not reliable. Yet courts in two other states—in similar cases—ruled that the crane manufacturers were *not* liable, because the hazard of driving a steel boom into electrical lines was obvious. Any resulting injury was therefore the responsibility of the crane operator.

Such inconsistency in product liability judgments has produced enormous confusion among manufacturers and consumers alike, with neither side knowing what rights or responsibilities they have and what limits, if any, there are on liability.

The second factor contributing to the chaos in liability law is the growing *attitude of entitlement in compensating injury victims,* even in those cases where it is obvious that the man-

ufacturer cannot be charged with responsibility or, at a minimum, responsibility is shared between the manufacturer and the injured party.

A decade ago, injured persons whose own carelessness was responsible for injury could not successfully prosecute. However, since the mid-1970s, 10 states have adopted comparative fault standards that allow plaintiffs to recover damages even if they share responsibility for their injuries. By adopting the concept of comparative fault, these states have precipitated a whole new generation of lawsuits and are encouraging increasing numbers of people to seek compensation through suit or the threat of litigation.

Underlying this attitude toward victims' compensation is the assumption that the insurance industry—fed by corporate premiums—has a bottomless pool of funds to compensate the injured, no matter how tenuous their claims. Indeed, in some cases, courts and juries have seemed far more concerned with compensating the plaintiffs than in establishing the liability of the manufacturer. Witness the recent litigation over Agent Orange: The judge pressured the seven corporate defendants to pay $180 million in death and disability compensation to Vietnam veterans and their families even though, as he said later, he did not believe there was any medical evidence to support their claims.

The third factor contributing to the number and cost of liability claims is *the contingency system for determining legal fees.* Because plaintiffs do not incur liability by initiating action, they are encouraged to pursue injury suits even if the evidence for their claims may be relatively weak. Similarly, with liability awards now reaching a million dollars or more, lawyers have a powerful incentive to keep filing liability cases, even if the prospect of winning any one case is highly uncertain. In short, by eliminating the financial risk of bringing a case to trial, contingency fees are encouraging both plaintiffs and trial lawyers to clog the courts with suits.

Preserving the Status Quo

In addition, contingency fees tend to increase the size of injury awards, as juries factor in the cost of legal counsel when determining the total size of damages for the plaintiff. This cost is far from insignificant. Indeed, if one considers the legal fees for both plaintiff and defendant, it becomes clear that more money is being paid today to adjudicate a claim than is being paid to victims. According to a study by the Rand Institute for civil justice, only 37 percent of the amounts paid for compensation and legal fees typically goes to the claimant. The balance—or 63 percent of the assessed damages—goes to pay the legal fees of the litigants. Because of high contingency fees and the potential for lucrative awards, liability lawyers have an enormous stake in preserving the status quo. The plaintiff's bar is well aware of this and is well organized to resist change.

Enormous Costs

The growing tide of liability litigation is imposing enormous costs on consumers, on business, and on society as a whole. As consumers, we are paying not only through higher product prices, but also through the reduced availability of many products and services. Already, astronomical legal settlements and escalating insurance premiums have forced more than a few companies to drop product lines or, in some cases, to go out of business. This trend is cutting across all segments of U.S. industry, as the following examples illustrate:

- In the past decade, 10 of the 13 U.S. firms making football helmets have had to stop production, due to runaway jury awards.

- In 1983, Merrell Dow was forced to discontinue production of the drug bendectin, although the Food and Drug Administration approved the drug for treating women who suffered nausea during pregnancy. The reason? The cost of liability insurance for making bendectin had reached $10 million a year—or over 80 percent of the company's annual sales from the drug.

- The continued production of small aircraft in this country is being seriously threatened by burgeoning liability costs. Those costs to general aviation airframe manufacturers will amount to $100 million, requiring an average increase of $80,000—or as much as 50 percent—to the cost of the average plane. Such cost increases have already led one manufacturer, Piper Aircraft Corporation, to temporarily suspend production of 9 of its 15 aircraft models.

Arrest the Trend

The challenge before us is to arrest the dangerous trend toward excessive litigation and ever-rising damage awards. Although this trend will not be reversed overnight, I propose that we begin with federal reform of our nation's product liability laws.

It is imperative that the United States have uniform, nationwide standards of product liability. A federal bill should include:

* * * * *

- A fault-based standard for judging the adequacy of product design and the appropriateness of safety warnings.

- A clear presumption that a product conforming to mandatory government safety requirements is reasonably safe.

- A statute of limitation on the time period during which manufacturers can be held liable for a defective product.

- A standard limiting the number and size of punitive damage awards for injuries from a particular product defect.
- A standard requiring that damages reflect the extent to which plaintiffs contributed to their injuries.

These are the central goals that the business community has sought to achieve in nearly a decade of effort to reform product liability law.

* * * * *

Source: Reprinted from the Spring 1986 edition of *Directors & Boards,* published by MLR Publishing Company, Philadelphia. Reprinted by permission.

ENGLAND BRACES FOR JOLT IN COURT AWARDS

Joann S. Lublin

London—In 1983, an 11-year-old English girl died from an allergic reaction to a shot. Her parents sued the physician, alleging negligence. They settled for damages of £3,500 ($6,300)—less than their legal costs but the maximum court award.

"My barrister says in the United States, I would have gotten $1 million for the same damages," observes Paul Hayter, the child's father and a Hampshire surveyor. "To get a pittance . . . is inhuman." English justice, he adds, "just isn't fair."

But hefty awards for victims of medical mishaps, defective products, and disasters soon may become more common in England. Its antiquated civil justice system is heading for a shake-up. In a report out tomorrow, a government judicial panel probably will decry the system's sluggishness and propose ways to make civil justice swifter and fairer.

The overhaul, perhaps the most far-reaching since Charles Dickens satirized the system in the 1850s, largely results from growing public clamor for a U.S.-style approach to personal injury cases.

For the first time, England could have class action suits and a form of contingency fees as well as significantly higher damages. . . .

The likely upshot: more litigation and legal expenses for major corporations, British and foreign alike. "This is bound to have a bottom-line impact on manufacturers and their insurers," warns David McIntosh. He was chief outside counsel for Eli Lilly & Co. in a string of recent suits here over Oraflex, the arthritis medicine that the big U.S. drug maker withdrew from the market.

The Lilly suits, settled in January, aroused much of the present furor. About 500 plaintiffs appeared ready to drop their cases until a British property tycoon offered to help foot their legal bills. The company's nearly £3 million settlement of the 1,300 health-damage claims also outraged some of the Oraflex plaintiffs. At less than £2,400 a claimant, the offer represented far less than the $6 million a U.S. jury awarded one Georgia man whose mother died after she took the drug. (Lilly later settled for a confidential sum in return for dropping its appeal of the 1983 jury award.)

Greater compensation awards here could encourage similar moves by other countries and slow American drug manufacturers' practice of marketing new products overseas first. "As more of the world starts granting greater worth to human lives, the ante is going to go up for drug companies," predicts Sidney Wolfe, director of the Public Citizen Health Research Group, a Washington, D.C.-based advocacy group. "There will be more caution before dumping [new] drugs on the market."

In England, larger awards could arise from the introduction of class action suits. A class action bill sponsored by the Conservative government would allow even middle-class consumers involved in such litigation to receive government legal aid, which is usually limited to the less affluent. . . .

* * * * *

[T]he campaigners' push for limited contingency fees, now outlawed in England, will stir a fierce fight. Many personal injury victims either don't bring suits or quickly accept bargain settlements because protracted, failed litigation can ruin them financially. Losers must pay their lawyers' charges as well as the other side's. Contingency fees "could well work in the interests of getting justice for people who don't have deep pockets," says Michael Grylls, an influential Tory member of Parliament.

Doctors disagree. "We know it [contingency fees] leads to ambulance chasing and inflated damages," asserts John Havard, a barrister and secretary of the politically powerful British Medical Association. "You'll get more of a United States-type situation, with huge sums for pain and suffering."

* * * * *

Whatever reforms do emerge, the English civil justice system will remain a different breed from its American cousin. Lawyers usually don't seek damages for medical care here because of the essentially free National Health Service. And the lack of juries in personal injury suits means even higher damage awards probably won't match the multimillion-dollar ones in the United States.

The Confederation of British Industry, Britain's leading employer group, plans a . . . conference on how businesses should grapple with the coming overhaul of personal injury litigation. Industry nevertheless "shouldn't be fearful of people bringing [additional] actions when mistakes are few and far between," argues Norman Rose, the confederation's senior attorney.

Mr. McIntosh, Lilly's outside counsel, is aghast. He thinks the employer group should join the fray now because "the changes are inevitable and consequential." He vows he will single-handedly fight "emotionally motivated consumerists. They will do more harm than good."

Questions

1. Regardless of your personal opinion, build a brief argument opposing the central elements of Robert Malott's position.
2. Much of the legal cost associated with product liability law is, of course, generated in attempting to prove or disprove fault. Strict liability, at least in theory, is a no-fault concept. Should we recast products liability law entirely in a no-fault mode? In so doing we would recognize the inevitability of defective products and careless consumers. Costs would be borne by all. Comment.

3. How do you account for the British interest in moving toward the U.S. system of personal injury litigation even as we are having a stormy national debate about how we can reform our system?

CHAPTER QUESTIONS

1. Plaintiff suffered a spider bite while trying on slacks in the dressing room of the defendant's Mode O'Day store. Plaintiff sued both the local retailer and the parent firm. She based her claim on negligence, breach of the implied warranty of fitness for a particular purpose, and strict liability.
   a. Defend Mode O'Day and the local retailer.
   b. Decide. Explain. See *Flippo* v. *Mode O'Day Frock Shops of Hollywood,* 248 Ark. 1, 449 S.W.2d 692 (1970).
2. A passenger ran after a train as it was leaving a station. Two railroad employees boosted the passenger aboard, but in doing so a package carried by the passenger fell beneath the wheels of the train and exploded. The package, unbeknownst to the employees, contained fireworks. The force of that explosion caused a scale many feet away to topple over, injuring the plaintiff, Mrs. Palsgraf. Mrs. Palsgraf sued the railroad on negligence grounds.
   a. Defend the railroad.
   b. Decide. Explain. See *Palsgraf* v. *Long Island R.R.,* 162 N.E. 99 (N.Y. 1928).
3. Plaintiff was riding as a passenger in an auto that was struck in the rear by a 1960 Chevrolet Impala driven by Michael Bigham (not a party to the suit) at a speed of approximately 115 miles per hour. Plaintiff sustained personal injuries and filed suit against General Motors Corporation, the manufacturer of the Chevrolet. Plaintiff argued that defendant was negligent in truthfully advertising the speed at which the auto could be driven, thus encouraging its reckless use.
   a. What further argument(s) would you make on plaintiff's behalf?
   b. Decide. Explain. See *Schemely* v. *General Motors Corporation,* 384 F.2d 802 (1967), cert. denied 390 U.S. 945 (1968).
4. The plaintiff, born and raised in New England, was eating fish chowder at a restaurant when a fish bone lodged in her throat. The bone was removed and plaintiff sued the restaurant, claiming breach of implied warranty under the UCC. Evidence was offered at trial to show that fish chowder recipes commonly did not provide for removal of bones. Decide. Explain. See *Webster* v. *Blue Ship Tea Room, Inc.,* 347 Mass. 421, 198 N.E.2d 309 (1964).
5. The plaintiff, a farmer, argued that the defendant's insecticide, Ortho Bux Ten Granular, failed to control rootworms, resulting in damage to his crops. Corn grown in another section of the field and protected

by another insecticide, Thimet, matured normally. One side of the bag containing the Ortho insecticide displayed the following language: "Chevron Ortho Bux Ten Granular for control of corn rootworm larvae (insecticide)." The opposite side of the bag displayed language offering an express warranty limited to the guarantee that the insecticide conformed to its chemical description. All other warranties were explicitly excluded. The plaintiff claimed a breach of express warranty. Decide. Explain. See *Swenson* v. *Chevron Chem. Co.,* 234 N.W.2d 38 (1975).

6. Embs, the plaintiff, was shopping in a self-serve grocery store. A carton of 7UP was on the floor about one foot from where she was standing. She was unaware of the carton. Several of the bottles exploded, severely injuring Embs's leg. Embs brought a strict liability action against the bottler.
   a. Raise a defense against the strict liability claim.
   b. Decide. Explain. See *Embs* v. *Pepsi-Cola Bottling Co. of Lexington, Kentucky, Inc.,* 528 S.W.2d 703 (1975).

7. Plaintiff suffered injury from ingesting a defective prescription drug, MER/29. Plaintiff sued the druggist from whom the product was purchased in its original, unbroken package. The druggist issued the drugs under a doctor's instructions.
   a. Which causes of action might the plaintiff plausibly bring?
   b. Decide. Explain. See *McLeod* v. *W. S. Merrell Co., Div. of Richardson-Merrell,* 174 So.2d 736 (Fla. 1965).

8. Plaintiffs Dr. Arthur Weisz and David and Irene Schwartz bought two paintings at auctions conducted by the defendant, Parke-Bernet Galleries, Inc. The paintings were listed in the auction catalogue as those of Raoul Dufy. It was later discovered that the paintings were forgeries. The plaintiffs took legal action to recover their losses. Parke-Bernet defended itself by, among other arguments, asserting that the "Conditions of Sale" included a disclaimer providing that all properties were sold "as is." The conditions of sale were 15 numbered paragraphs embracing several pages in the auction catalogue. The bulk of the auction catalogue was devoted to descriptions of the works of art to be sold, including artists' names, dates of birth and death, and, in some instances, black-and-white reproductions of the paintings. It was established at trial that plaintiff Weisz had not previously entered bids at Parke-Bernet, and he had no awareness of the conditions of sale. Plaintiffs David and Irene Schwartz, however, were generally aware of the conditions of sale. Is the Parke-Bernet disclaimer legally binding on the plaintiffs? Explain. See *Weisz* v. *Parke-Bernet,* 325 N.Y.S. 2d 576 (Civ. Ct. N.Y.C. 1971).

9. An earth-moving machine being driven in reverse struck and killed a worker who was clothed in a luminous jacket. The machine operator could not see the worker because a large engine box at the rear of

the earth-mover created a blind spot. The earth-mover had no rear-view mirror, a fact immediately observable to the operator. In the lawsuit that followed, what principal argument would you raise on behalf of the defendant machine manufacturer? Decide. Explain. See *Pike* v. *Frank G. Hough Co.,* 467 P.2d 229 (Cal. 1970).

10. Plaintiff's decedent had worked in asbestos plants at various times from 1936 to 1969. He subsequently died of two forms of cancer. Plaintiff sued 11 asbestos manufacturers for their failure to warn of the dangerous linkage between asbestos and cancer, which was alluded to in the scientific literature "at least as early as the 1930s." The court noted that asbestos might be the kind of product that is unavoidably unsafe, but whose benefits outweigh the risks. Rule on the plaintiff's strict liability claim. Explain. See *Borel* v. *Fibreboard Paper Products Corp.,* 493 F.2d 1076 (5th Cir. 1973), cert. denied 419 U.S. 869 (1974).

11. Plaintiff-employee was operating a machine designed to flatten and then curve metal sheets. The metal was shaped by three long rollers. Plaintiff turned off the rollers to remove a piece of slag. He left the power on. In trying to remove the slag he accidentally brushed a gear lever, which activated the rollers. His hand was drawn into the rollers, and injury resulted. At the time of the machine's manufacture, two safety mechanisms were available to prevent such accidents. What defense would you offer on behalf of the defendant machine manufacturer? Decide. Explain. See *Suter* v. *San Angelo Foundry and Machine Co.,* 406 A.2d 140 (N.J. 1979).

12. In June 1983 a San Diego, California, jury awarded $2.5 million to the family of a man killed while riding, as a passenger, in a Porsche Turbo 930. The plaintiff had argued, among other things, that the car was too powerful and too unstable for the average driver and that the manufacturer should have provided a warning regarding the power of the car. During the trial the plaintiff's attorney received an internal anonymous memo from Porsche headquarters in West Germany that described the car's handling as "poisonous" and argued that the car had a tendency to oversteer. At the time of the accident the car was traveling at 60 MPH in a 25-MPH zone. The jury voted 10 to 2 in finding the car unsafe for street driving.[18] Comment.

13. Because few states have taken any meaningful, consistent action in adopting the Commerce Department's suggested Uniform Product Liability Act, Congress has considered a variety of federal laws. Among others, such a law might include the following provisions. Comment on the wisdom of such legislation.

    a. Lawsuits would be limited to 25 years from when the product was first sold.

    b. Plaintiff would be required to name a specific defendant, thus nullifying market share decisions like *Sindell.*

    c. Design defects and improper warnings would be grounds for liability only when negligence could be demonstrated.

14. Plaintiff James L. Maguire was seriously injured when the motor vehicle in which he was a passenger was struck by another motor vehicle. Plaintiff alleges that Vikki Paulson, the driver of the other vehicle, was intoxicated at the time of the accident. Following the accident Paulson entered guilty pleas to (1) operating a motor vehicle while under the influence of alcohol, (2) involuntary manslaughter as a consequence of the death of another passenger riding with Maguire, and (3) failure to stop at a stop sign. During the time in question in the case, Pabst Brewing Company had engaged in an advertising campaign promoting the sale of its products. Plaintiff claims the defendant Pabst was liable for his injuries because (among other claims) its advertising promoting the consumption of alcohol by those who drove to taverns constituted a danger to highway safety and because the brewer had failed to warn consumers of the dangers of alcohol consumption. Decide. Explain. See *Maguire* v. *Pabst Brewing Company,* 387 N.W.2d 565 (Iowa 1986).

15. The plaintiff, a mother, claimed she went to the defendant physician to seek a therapeutic abortion. She further claimed the abortion was negligently performed, resulting in the "wrongful birth" of a healthy child. Plaintiff sought to recover, in a negligence action, for the costs of rearing the child. Decide. Explain. See *Nanke* v. *Napier,* 346 N.W.2d 520 (Iowa 1984). But see *Jones* v. *Malinowski,* 473 A.2d 429 (Md. 1984).

16. John W. Hinckley, Jr., used a small, .22-caliber pistol to shoot President Ronald Reagan, press secretary James Brady, and others in his 1981 attempt to assassinate the president. The shooting resulted in serious injuries and suffering for Brady, who remains confined to a wheelchair. Brady continues to litigate claims against Roehm, a German company whose subsidiary, R. G. Industries of Miami, makes so-called Saturday Night Specials.

    a. As a matter of law, are gun manufacturers liable for deaths and injuries caused by cheap handguns? Explain. For a similar case, see *Kelley* v. *R. G. Industries,* 497 A.2d 1143 (1985).

    b. As a matter of social policy, should those gun manufacturers bear liability for deaths and injuries caused by their cheap handguns? Explain.

17. Suppose that you are the fourth purchaser of a 10-year-old home. After completion of the sale, you discover various defects in the home.

    a. Could you successfully sue the builder of the home? Explain.

    b. What claims of law would you raise?

    c. Would the outcome be influenced by whether the defects were latent (hidden) or patent (readily observable)? Explain. See, e.g., *Cosmopolitan Homes, Inc.* v. *Weller,* 663 P.2d 1041 (Colo. 1983).

But see *Crowder* v. *Vandendeale,* 564 S.W.2d 879 (Mo. 1978) and *Redarowicz* v. *Ohlendorf,* 92 Ill.2d 171, 441 N.E.2d 324 (1982).

NOTES

1. Clemens P. Work, ''Product Safety: A New Hot Potato for Congress,'' *U.S. News & World Report,* June 14, 1982, p. 62.
2. John R. Emshwiller, ''Car Makers Face Lawsuits Alleging Rear Seat Belts Aren't Safe Enough,'' *The Wall Street Journal,* January 6, 1988, p. 19.
3. Cynthia F. Mitchell, ''Manville, Its Bankruptcy Plan in Hand, Girds for the Long Haul to Pay Its Debts,'' *The Wall Street Journal,* December 18, 1986, p. 8.
4. 111 N.E. 1050 (N.Y. 1916).
5. *Doss* v. *Town of Big Stone Gap,* 134 S.E. 563 (1926).
6. *Jenkins* v. *General Motors Corp.,* 446 F.2d 377 (5th Cir. 1971), as cited in Dix Noel and Jerry Phillips, *Products Liability in a Nutshell* (St. Paul, Minn.: West Publishing, 1980), p. 137.
7. *Larsen* v. *General Motors Corporation,* 391 F.2d 495 (8th Cir. 1968).
8. Ibid., p. 502.
9. *Insurance Co. of North America* v. *Pasakarnis,* 451 So.2d 447 (Fla. 1984) at 455-6.
10. 27 Cal.Rptr. 697, 377 P.2d 897 (1962).
11. Some states have eliminated the ''unreasonably dangerous'' standard from their strict liability tests.
12. 278 N.W.2d 155 (S.D. 1979).
13. ''Handguns and Products Liability,'' Note, *Harvard Law Review* 97, June 1984, pp. 1912–13.
14. Robert Daniels, ''Suzuki Urged to Recall Samurai Vehicles as Consumer Group Calls Them Unsafe,'' *The Wall Street Journal,* June 3, 1988, p. 9.
15. *Los Angeles Times,* ''Suzuki Challenges Samurai Charges,'' *Waterloo Courier,* June 9, 1988, p. B1.
16. John Emshwiller, ''Rollover Worry Plagues Utility Vehicles,'' *The Wall Street Journal,* May 23, 1988, p. 17.
17. Ibid.
18. ''Jury Finds Porsche Turbo Dangerous on Streets,'' *Des Moines Register,* June 30, 1983, p. 4A.

Chapter 15

Environmental Protection

This natural inequality of the two powers of population, and of production in the earth, and that great law of our nature which most constantly keep their effects equal, form the great difficulty that to me appears insurmountable in the way to the perfectibility of society. . . . No fancied equality, no agrarian regulations in their utmost extent, could remove the pressure of it even for a single century. And it appears, therefore, to be decisive against the possible existence of a society all the members of which should live in ease, happiness and comparative leisure. . . .

Thomas Malthus, *An Essay on the Principle of Population, 1798*

Part One—Introduction[1]

Although the earth is a natural recycler of wastes—a very effective garbage dump—its ability to successfully neutralize the cumulative refuse of modern society is finite. Some concerns about pollution are centuries old, but the upsurge in population and increased industrialization and urbanization in the last hundred years have concentrated ever-increasing amounts of waste matter in small areas and put much greater pressure on the assimilative capabilities of the planet. Further, an improved understanding of the effects of various waste materials on the environment has generated widespread interest and public awareness of pollution problems. This awareness has greatly increased with the extensive publicity received by various threats to the health of the natural world.

Business certainly is not the sole contributor to the environmental pollution we face—for example, individual citizens are primarily responsible for particulate matter discharged by wood-burning stoves, for indoor pollution from cigarette smoking, and for air pollution caused by our national one-worker-per-car commuting habits. Most forms of pollution, however, probably do have some business connection—whether direct or indirect. Thus, the subject matter of this chapter provides a superb opportunity to review the ethical considerations of business decision making and the overall social responsibility of business.

Environmental protection is also a good capstone subject for investigating the interrelationships of law, business, and society because of the growing number of international environmental problems. Part Two of this chapter focuses on that topic.

QUESTIONS

Make a list of what you believe are the most serious environmental hazards we face today.

   a. To which of these hazards has business contributed?
   b. Without discussing whether it should, *can* business contribute solutions to any of these hazards? Explain.

Part Two—A Global Concern

1. Pending Treaty Worries Chlorofluorocarbon Industry

About 40 nations are working this week to complete a treaty designed to protect the earth's ozone layer by limiting the emission of some of the chemicals known as chlorofluorocarbons into the atmosphere.

The prospect has the five U.S. makers of the chemicals and thousands of users in a wide range of industries wondering what to do until substitutes reach the market in 5 to 10 years.

* * * * *

U.S. manufacturers sell about $750 million of the compounds annually to about 5,000 customers in the refrigeration, air-conditioning, automotive, plastic-foam, and electronics industries.

Those industries in turn produce each year $27 billion in goods and services directly dependent on chlorofluorocarbons.

* * * * *

The problem occurs when chlorofluorocarbons escape or are released into the atmosphere. Scientists believe the compounds travel to the ozone layer that protects the earth from ultraviolet rays and decompose, releasing chlorine that attacks the ozone.

If trends in use of the compounds continue, scientists theorize that people would be exposed to increased ultraviolet radiation, which could lead to more skin cancers and other environmental damage.

* * * * *

Despite their reservations, [Alliance for Responsible CFC Policy] officials [a group of some 500 makers and customers of chlorofluorocarbons] say the treaty is better than any potential unilateral U.S. action, which, they argue, would harm the United States's competitiveness abroad. . . .[2]

Ozone depletion also contributes to the "greenhouse effect"—global warming that could substantially alter temperature and precipitation patterns, which in turn could raise sea levels that would flood lower land areas, such as Charleston, South Carolina, and Galveston, Texas.

2. Jump in 1986 Death Rate Sparks Dispute: Did Chernobyl Cause Surge in U.S. Mortality?

A mysterious surge in U.S. mortality in the summer of 1986 has confounded and disturbed some statisticians.

While no one yet claims to know the cause of the surge, a hypothesis suggested by Jay M. Gould, a fellow of the Institute for Policy Studies in Washington, is getting wide attention. He thinks the April 1986 accident at the nuclear reactor at Chernobyl, in the Ukraine, could have hastened the deaths of many Americans.

* * * * *

In the May-through-August period immediately following the disaster, between 20,000 and 40,000 more Americans than usual died.

* * * * *

By Mr. Gould's calculation, the probability that so many extra deaths could have occurred by chance is less than one in a million.

The radioactive cloud emanating from the Soviet reactor arrived in the United States in early May 1986. The fallout varied widely, depending on the cloud's path and the levels of rainfall in different regions. Nowhere did the low levels of radiation exceed levels deemed tolerable by the government.

When Mr. Gould looked at mortality data by geographic region, he turned up a correlation between deaths and radioactive fallout.

In states like Arizona and Texas, where iodine-131 levels were the lowest, the summer mortality rates were about normal. But California and Washington, where concentrations of iodine-131 were the highest, recorded the sharpest increases in mortality.[3]

3. Taking His Acid Rain Fight on the Road

Canada's Environment Minister Tom McMillan . . . [is] a committed environmental spokesman who will soon become a more familiar figure in the United States as he leads a new Canadian government offensive against acid rain. Acid rain has been a source of friction between the two countries for years, and Mr. McMillan—advocating a "massive effort to influence U.S. public opinion"— has embarked on a series of trips speaking to U.S. groups and universities.

Canada asserts that much of its acid rain—precipitation with a high concentration of acids—is the by-product of pollution that spews from tall smokestacks of coal-burning power plants in the Ohio Valley. Carried by prevailing winds into the northeastern United States and Canada, it is blamed for damage to fish, wildlife, forests, buildings, and even human health. Canada itself has already moved to curb acid rain from smelters and factories within its borders.

For years, Prime Minister Brian Mulroney's Conservative government tried to coax the Reagan administration to do something to solve the problem, and the usually outspoken Mr. McMillan kept silent. Now, frustrated with what it sees as U.S. foot-dragging, the Mulroney government is taking a harder line.

* * * * *

Mr. McMillan, who hands out red-and-white umbrellas emblazoned with "Stop Acid Rain," is now planning a U.S. advertising campaign, aimed at, among others, U.S. tourists who vacation on Canadian lakes. He has doubled his acid rain communications budget to 850,000 Canadian dollars [$650,000] and is seeking more funding.[4]

4. Dumping Trash on Third World

Regarding the news item, "Radioactive Milk Dilemma for Germans": According to the report, there is a large quantity of radioactively contaminated milk waiting at the milk-processing plants to be converted to powder to make animal feed for delivery to Third World countries. And the Germans are concerned about it—not because of their thoughts for the lesser mortals living in those third-rate countries but because of the fear that some of this feed might eventually find its way back into their own food chain.

As a third-class, subhuman being from a hunger-, disease-, ignorance-, and poverty-ridden Third World country, I am extremely pleased with the thought that my first-class brothers in the developed world are taking such good care of us by letting us have such products like animal feed for a nominal price so that the demons of hunger can be fought and killed.

* * * * *

You have often given us precious gifts of grains which you couldn't sell or even give away free to your other first-class brothers!

Isn't it strange that we place our trust and faith in you and this is what we get in return? That is why, when my brothers in Lebanon and the Philippines get frustrated by our inability to repay this overwhelming generosity of our more fortunate friends, we have to resort to "barbarian" techniques like hijacking planes, kidnapping civilians and all that, because there is absolutely no other way of paying you back in the same rotten coin.[5]

Each of the foregoing examples demonstrates that pollution problems do not respect national boundaries. So how can solutions for these problems be found? This is a good time to review the resolution mechanisms discussed throughout this text. For example, it is understood that most people want a cleaner environment, yet the "invisible hand" envisioned by Adam Smith apparently is not of sufficient strength to guide the economy in that direction. The problem is not a failure in the theory behind the pricing system, but rather that the pricing system works to perfection, albeit in the wrong directions. This inconvenience can be traced to what economists call the externality, free good, or commons problem. Simply stated, the environment has been treated as a *free good,* meaning that using the environment for waste disposal is costless to producers. In effect, producers can pollute a river and pass the costs (in the form of dirty water, dead fish, disease, and so forth) on to society as a whole. If a good can be obtained at no cost, an economist or a businessperson would be inclined to use as much of the free good as possible, and producers have done just that. There is no pricing incentive to minimize pollution if pollution has no direct cost to the company; in fact, the incentive is to maximize pollution. In effect, a pricing system that allocates no cost to an industry dirtying the environment encourages additional work, regardless of the common need of society for a clean environment. In this instance the welfare of individuals acting in their own private interests does not coincide with the general good.

Another way in which an economist might examine the problem is as a *collective good.* If the citizens want a clean environment, the market would presumably reflect that desire by paying nonpolluting companies higher prices for their goods. Unfortunately, the benefits of clean air and water are not restricted to those paying for them through higher prices, because equal benefits are bestowed on those persons still trading (at lower prices) with polluting companies. Thus a clean environment benefits everyone equally, regardless of each individual's contribution toward it. A rational utility-maximizing strategy for each person, then, is to patronize cheaper, polluting firms to the exclusion of the more expensive nonpolluters, despite the desire of society for a clean environment. Therefore industries have no incentive not to pollute. Externalities and public goods are instances of "market failure." (See Chapter 6.)

Another solution mechanism for conflicts between business and society, which was discussed in Chapters 2 and 3, is letting the individual ethics of decision makers determine which course of action to take. However, some Canadians believe U.S. businesspeople have made the wrong choice vis-à-vis discharging their ethical duties with regard to acid rain.

Such international problems cannot be cured by, for example, passing laws in the United States regulating the offending business or setting "acceptable" levels of various forms of pollution. Such global problems would require an *international law* to even begin resolving the issues. However, no international government at present can enact and then enforce such provisions. Perhaps the most binding international law existing today is that found in various treaties among nations, some of which do touch on environmental concerns. Give some thought, however, to what enforcement mechanisms presently exist with respect to *any* treaty agreement.

The mechanisms presently used in the international arena as conflict resolution devices principally resemble the processes discussed in Part Five of Chapter 4 under the heading "Criticisms and Alternatives." In fact, treaties are probably best described as the outcome of a negotiation (or sometimes, mediation) procedure.

QUESTIONS

1. Does each American or the American business community or our whole society have responsibility for the impacts of our pollution (for example, acid rain in Canada, ocean dumping, oil spills in international waters, and American industry located in foreign countries and polluting locally) felt outside the United States? Explain.
2. *a.* Should Germany be allowed to sell radioactive powdered milk to Third World countries? Explain.
   b. How can such activities be stopped?

Part Three—Environmental Protection in the United States

Despite the existence of global concerns in the environmental area, many environmental problems are primarily felt close to their source. Where this is true, the United States has developed a wide variety of environmental protection laws and remedies, some of which are discussed in this part.

Throughout this discussion, keep in mind a particular problem in the area of environmental law—what remedy or remedies are appropriate for that particular problem? This is not an easy question to answer. For one thing, cost/benefit issues are pervasive, and their resolution is anything but simple. For example, as a society, do we want clean air at any cost? How do we value human life so we can decide how much to spend to reduce the statistical incidence of a particular hazard, thereby saving some estimated number of lives annually?

THE FEDERAL PRESENCE

The federal government has long maintained a role in the protection of the environment. For example, an 1899 congressional enactment required a permit to discharge refuse into navigable waters. As it became apparent that private, state, and local environmental protection efforts were not adequate to the burgeoning problem, Congress began in the early 1970s to take a number of legislative initiatives.

National Environmental Policy Act

In 1970 President Nixon signed the National Environmental Policy Act (NEPA), which established a strong federal presence in the promotion of a clean and healthy environment. NEPA represents a general commitment by the federal government to "use all practicable means" to conduct federal affairs in a fashion that both promotes "the general welfare" and operates in "harmony" with the environment. A portion reads:

Public Law 91–190 (1969), 42 U.S.C. § 4331 *et seq.*
PURPOSE

Sec. 2. The purposes of this Act are: To declare a national policy which will encourage productive and enjoyable harmony between man and his environment; to promote efforts which will prevent or eliminate damage to the environment and biosphere and stimulate the health and welfare of man; to enrich the understanding of the ecological systems and natural resources important to the Nation; and to establish a Council on Environmental Quality.

The Council on Environmental Quality serves as an advisor to the president. Specifically, the CEQ must "assist and advise the president in the preparation of the [annual] Environmental Quality Report." The CEQ is a watchdog of sorts. It is required to conduct studies and collect information regarding the state of the environment. The council then develops policy and legislative proposals for the president and Congress.

But NEPA's primary influence results from its environmental impact statement (EIS) requirements. With few exceptions, "proposals for legislation and other major federal action significantly affecting the quality of the human environment" must be accompanied by an EIS explaining the impact on the environment and detailing reasonable alternatives. Major federal construction projects (highways, dams, and nuclear reactors) would normally require an EIS; but less-visible federal programs (ongoing timber management or authorizing the abandonment of a lengthy railway) may also require EIS treatment. A major private-sector action supported by federal funding or by one of several varieties of federal permission may also require an EIS. Hence private companies receiving federal contracts, funding, licenses, and the like may be parties to the completion of an EIS.

Environmental Protection Agency

In 1970 Congress created the Environmental Protection Agency (EPA) to oversee the public regulation of environmental issues. EPA duties include, among others: *(a)* information gathering, particularly in surveying pollution problems, *(b)* research regarding pollution problems, and *(c)* assisting state and local pollution control efforts.

A major EPA responsibility is administering many of the federal laws directed to environmental concerns. Several of those laws are discussed hereafter in some depth, but the reader should be aware of a number of additional statutes that might have been included: the Safe Drinking Water Act; the Marine Protection, Research, and Sanctuaries Act of 1972; the Federal Insecticide, Fungicide, and Rodenticide Act; and the Federal Environmental Pesticide Control Act of 1972.

AIR POLLUTION

We depend on (indeed, we emotionally embrace) the automobile. In doing so we have opened vistas of opportunity not previously imagined, but we may also have eliminated clean air forever. Motor vehicles discharge carbon monoxide, nitrogen oxide, and hydrocarbons as by-products of the combustion of fuel. Motor vehicles are the major source of air pollution, but industrial production and the combustion of fossil fuels in homes and industry are also significant contributors to the dilemma of dirty air. For most Americans, air pollution is simply an unpleasant fact of life. To the average Los Angeles resident, smog is more central to daily activity than the area's beaches and mountains. That air pollution may contribute to the deaths of 8,000 citizens annually in the Ohio River basin[6] is simply the regrettable consequence of progress.

"Seventeen years after passage of the Clean Air Act there are still 80 million people living in areas that have unhealthy air," complains David Doniger, a lawyer for the Natural Resources Defense Council, an environmental group.

The picture isn't entirely bleak. Despite industrial and population growth, Americans breathe generally cleaner air today than they did a decade or two ago; common air pollutants are within healthy levels in most areas. The gains stem largely from pollution controls on new cars and trucks, factories, and power plants.

But achieving clean air is proving more difficult than anyone anticipated. Federal law requires states and localities to purge certain pollutants to healthy levels or risk sanctions: curbs on new plants, highways, and sewer construction. Yet the Environmental Protection Agency is loathe to enforce the sanctions, even though most states are moving at a snail's pace in the face of growing opposition.[7]

As the polls clearly reveal, Americans abhor pollution. But, having seldom experienced the satisfactions of pure air, most Americans have not raised a clamor for decisive action to correct the problem. We should perhaps take a moment now to be reminded of what we have lost and what we are yet losing.

KEEPING THE BIG SKY PURE

Michael Parfit

In the village of Lame Deer, under the broad skies of eastern Montana, the Northern Cheyenne tribe gathered solemnly in the tribal gym. On the floor there were chairs, tables, microphones, a row of tribal council members, a television camera, and an interpreter with a booming voice. As the meeting began, a small crowd of high school students filed slowly into the room and up into the bleachers, the younger generation brought to witness the making of history. Outside, sleet splattered on the dirt roads and on the small homes of the reservation town, and wind tossed the dark pine trees on the hills. As the day continued, the wind grew colder, the sleet turned to bitter snow and, in the gym, a succession of speakers marched past the microphone, each pleading in English or Cheyenne for the thing that concerned this tribe most: clear air.

To a city resident who occasionally regrets the stinging, beige sky that envelops him while he pursues matters that seem more important than atmosphere, clean air as a cause doesn't have much urgency—it seems a bit like worrying about litter in the street after a parade. But to the Northern Cheyenne Indians, the word for air is the same as the word for breath—

"Omotome"—and they cherish being able to breath clean air. Why else would this small tribe on a remote reservation have spent several years and thousands of dollars struggling to preserve the quality of their air—air which is now threatened by industrial pollution?

The Northern Cheyenne live on 446,784 acres of low hills and prairie that lie a few dozen miles east of the meadow on the Little Big Horn where General George Armstrong Custer earned fame for foolishness in the summer of 1876. The reservation's towns, Ashland, Busby, Birney, and Lame Deer, are dusty little villages in which a total population of about 3,000 lives a collective life of struggle against common reservation evils: poverty, disease, alcoholism, unemployment, and despair. Two matters of geography, however, make this reservation and its people unique. The land, which lies on and among some of the richest coal fields of the West, is a tribute to the historical persistence of the Northern Cheyennes. Today, the unusual degree of unity and the morale of the tribe are based on that determination.

The federal government did not plan to have Cheyennes in Montana at all. After the Custer fight all Cheyennes were rounded up and lumped together in a reservation in Oklahoma, but in 1878 about 300 members of the Northern Cheyenne tribe broke out and began to walk home as described in Mari Sandoz's *Cheyenne Autumn*. Most were captured and then killed in a sordid episode of starvation and murder at an Army fort in Nebraska, but a remnant survived. In response to this tenacity, the federal government eventually gave the Northern Cheyennes their present reservation. But the walk itself gave them something almost as lasting. Today when you talk to members of this tribe about their history, their culture, or their present struggles, one phrase recurs: "the long walk back." In the past few years the memory of that time has been repeatedly evoked to support the Northern Cheyennes' struggle for clean air.

The situation which has brought Cheyenne history to bear upon such an unlikely issue is deceptively simple. Since 1974, a group of five utilities has been planning to build a 1,400-megawatt power plant adjacent to coal mines about 15 miles north of the reservation at a place called Colstrip. Two plants, Colstrip I and Colstrip II, have already been built. In 1977, efforts to build Colstrip III and Colstrip IV met opposition when the Northern Cheyennes, using an opportunity offered all Indian tribes by federal clean air laws, asked the U.S. Environmental Protection Agency (EPA) to cover their land with the legal umbrella of designation as a Class I air quality area. A Class I area, in EPA terms, is a refuge for the cleanest air in the country, purity undefiled. The request was granted. The reservation joined national parks and wilderness areas under this ultimate protection, and the Northern Cheyennes celebrated.

In 1978 and through part of 1979 the EPA backed up its promise by repeatedly telling the power consortium that its plant would unduly soil the atmosphere of the reservation and thus could not be built as designed. Later, in 1979, however, despite negative data from a smaller power plant already running nearby, EPA reopened the issue. The agency agreed to hear renewed requests from pro-power plant interests because of improvements in plant design and pressure generated by the national energy crisis. Finally, it approved construction of the plant.

The hypothetical city resident, whose skies are murky all day, would consider this action to be positive—a useful compromise. Although it is probable that the reservation will on occasion be polluted beyond the limits of the Class I definition, how much, he or she would ask, does that matter? Isn't this more a case of sacrificing a group's marginal interests in the name of national need, rather than an infringement of rights? Or the promise—if not fact—of job opportunities in a depressed economy as opposed to some esoteric value tenaciously held?

The trouble is that these initial impressions have roots in America's system of economic and social priorities in which clean air obviously does not rate highly. In times of recession or energy need, pollution laws are usually the first to be swept off the tables. Clean air is labeled an environmental issue, and in the prevailing system, environmentalism, in all its varied glory, is considered a game of affluence, like golf. Who cares about air quality if your landlord sells your home or your job is threatened due to an energy shortage?

But to the Northern Cheyennes the landlord has already sold most of the place to outsiders. And for Indians, there just isn't much work—winter unemployment on the Northern Cheyenne reservation runs from 50 to 70 percent. And still they fight for clean air. Their priorities are simply not the same.

"Our ancestors regarded the ground as sacred," said Joe Bear, trying to explain. Bear is a tribal vice chairman who ranches on the eastern side of the reservation. "A Cheyenne is right next to the earth. All we're asking is just to keep our air clear. That's what it takes to grow things. Land, water, air."

* * * * *

There is, of course, more than one way to read this rhetoric. Those who favor the power plant argue that the Cheyenne are manipulating an emotion-laden issue for reasons that are remote from actual air quality—political power, tribal cohesion, revenge, and financial gain. The extensive Cheyenne coal reserves might well feed the Colstrip furnaces under different circumstances.

The Cheyenne themselves point out that the drive for clean air is partly based on a fear of the social problems that the polluting power plant would bring, and not just the smoke. However, since oil development would be significantly cleaner and less disruptive than the power plant and strip mining, a recent tribal referendum gave overwhelming support to oil exploration on the reservation.

A Cheyenne report which was prepared in order to support the request for Class I status said:

> You can see we are concerned about the direct results of a deterioration in the quality of our air. We are [also] worried about any large influx of outsiders associated with the construction and operation of power plants. Partly we fear the overcrowding, crime, and inflation as more affluent people compete with us for limited housing and services. But our fear is even more basic. Nearly all Indians have personally experienced prejudice and discrimination, and we worry about becoming a minority on our own reservation, in our own towns.

The Cheyennes express their philosophy of relationships in life with a design called the Cheyenne Circle, which is cut into wedges like a pie graph showing the allocation of a tax dollar. In the Cheyenne Circle, however, the four wedges are equal in size (and hence importance), and the slice which represents air is as large as that for living things. . . .

Twice in the past decade the tribe has chosen to put long-term environmental concerns ahead of immediate financial gain: once in the early 70s, when it quashed an attempt by the Bureau of Indian Affairs to lease over half the reservation for strip mining; and once with the request for Class I air. Both actions cost the Cheyenne thousands of dollars in legal fees and millions in lost revenues and jobs.

So it is probably fair to say that the scale of values other Americans might place on matters such as those raised by the construction of a power plant—giving more weight, for instance, to social concerns than to what we would call environmental ones—would misrepresent the Cheyennes' own priorities. It is more likely that the Northern Cheyennes—as driven by self-interest as any other group—see the air, the land, and their health as webbed together by the forces of life; an assault on one damages all the rest. If there is truth anywhere in the words of Joe Bear . . . it is that the Northern Cheyennes, reacting to the industrial world from the point of view of a culture in which respect for the land has played a central role for centuries, consider the quality of their air to be a fundamental right, as necessary as work and respect to human vitality.

From this perspective, the construction of the power plant close to the reservation becomes less a matter of sacrificing niceties to need and more a matter of oppression. And, unfortunately, this incident is not unique. The pattern of energy development in the West—in which rural areas are being dug up, polluted, and subjected to devastating social turmoil, while the coal and electricity produced are carried away to fuel cities—can only be described as avaricious and Native Americans are among the people most badly used. The Navajo and

Hopi tribes in Arizona, for instance, have been so roundly exploited for their coal, oil, natural gas, and uranium that the terrible phrase "national sacrifice area," a concept that should have been abandoned with the burning of witches, has recently been resurrected to describe their homelands.

* * * * *

If the Northern Cheyenne experience is any indication, company executives may find themselves dealing with a new set of priorities. While measured development is appreciated, the list of priorities does not begin and end with the word *profit*. On that basis, at least, the Northern Cheyennes may have something to offer to the value systems of all Americans.

Source: *Perspectives* 13, no. 1 (Spring 1981), pp. 40–44. Reprinted with permission of the copyright holder, *New Perspectives*.

Questions

1. Is clean air more important to the Cheyenne than to most Americans? Why?
2. In the face of wintertime unemployment in the 50–70 percent range, the Cheyenne nevertheless argue for clean air rather than development. Should the entire nation adopt the Cheyenne priorities? Explain.
3. Regardless of your beliefs, build the argument that other Americans are paying for the Cheyenne's clean air luxury.

Government Policy

Despite continuing unsatisfactory air quality in many locations, the federal and state governments have, in 20 years of effort, significantly reduced U.S. air pollution. After the limited success of clean air legislation in 1963 and 1965, it became apparent to Congress that drastic adjustments were necessary. The Clean Air Act Amendments of 1970 and 1977 gave the federal Environmental Protection Agency the authority to set air quality standards and to assure that those standards were achieved, according to a timetable prescribed by the EPA. Among the standards established were the following:

1. *National Ambient Air Quality Standards (NAAQS).* National standards have been established for carbon monoxide, hydrocarbons, lead, nitrogen oxide, ozone, particulates, and sulfur dioxide. A primary standard sets a ceiling on air pollution that is safe for humans. A secondary standard sets a ceiling for the balance of the environment, including soil, visibility, animals, and vegetation.

2. *Emergency Standards.* When air pollution reaches a level that poses an imminent and substantial danger to health, emergency action, such as stopping production by a polluting industry, may be taken.
3. *Motor Vehicle Emission and Fuel Standards.* New and imported cars and engines must meet EPA emission standards, and the EPA can control or prohibit substances that significantly retard the performance of motor vehicle emission control systems.

With the establishment of NAAQS, each state was required to develop a state implementation plan (SIP) to achieve a level of pollution beneath the federal ceiling. The EPA is empowered to impose appropriate regulations should a state fail to do so. Standards for each industrial plant were to be established, and those standards were to be achieved by a specified date.

New industrial construction is subject to special requirements. The nature of the standards to be applied depends on the air quality where the plant is to be located. Locales with relatively clean air that meets national standards are labeled "Prevention of Significant Deterioration" areas (PSD). Locales with relatively dirty air that does not meet the standards are labeled "nonattainment areas." In PSD areas new plants are permissible only if total emissions do not exceed specific standards as established by the Clean Air Act. The owners would be required to show that their proposed industry would not exceed the limitations. The owners would also be required to install the "best available control technology" (BACT) to ensure compliance.

Those seeking to build in nonattainment areas must meet three standards to receive a government permit:

1. All other pollution sources owned or operated by the applicant in the state must meet all applicable limits and compliance standards.
2. The new source must be controlled at the "lowest achievable emission rate" (LAER). LAER means either the lowest emission level achieved by any source in the same category or the most demanding emission standard in any SIP (unless it proves unachievable).
3. New plants in nonattainment areas are permissible only if the added air pollution is offset on a "more than one-for-one" basis by reductions in pollutants of the same character from plants in that geographical area.

Clean Air Act violations unaccompanied by criminal intent may result in a civil fine of $25,000 per day, along with injunctive action. "Knowing" violations, as defined by the act, may result in a criminal fine of not more than $25,000 per day and/or imprisonment for a term of not more than one year. Those penalties may be doubled for a second offense. Congress was concerned that the aforementioned penalties were such that it might be cheaper for a firm to fail to comply than to undertake the cost of necessary corrections. Therefore, the 1977 amendments impose a penalty equivalent to the "savings" achieved by noncompliance from the time of receipt from the EPA of a notice of noncompliance. Citizen suits are provided for under the Clean Air Act.

The business community and others have been distressed by the inhibitions in industrial development that the Clean Air Act has imposed. Years may be required to secure the necessary environmental permits to build a new factory or generator. In the early 1980s Congress considered, but failed to approve, a number of amendments to the act. Those included (1) easing auto emissions standards, (2) allowing the use of low-sulfur coal rather than antipollution "scrubbers" in new coal-burning plants, and (3) eliminating deadlines for installing pollution control devices where SIPs provide for continuing improvement in air quality. However, a 1984 Supreme Court decision affirming the "bubble concept" represented an important victory for advocates of more relaxed pollution standards. In nonattainment areas, states must develop a permit program regulating "new or modified major stationary sources" of air pollution. The EPA issued regulations in 1981 allowing states to adopt a plantwide definition of the term *stationary source*. Under that standard a firm can replace or modify old equipment or add new equipment even if those individual pieces of machinery fail to meet the standards of the permit program so long as the total emissions from the plant are not increased. All pollution-producing devices within an industrial grouping are treated as a unit—as though they are under a bubble. The Natural Resources Defense Council challenged the bubble concept, but the Supreme Court held that the EPA's plantwide definition of the term *stationary source* is lawful.[8]

In 1985 the EPA announced a new policy that would shift some federal air quality responsibilities to state and local governments.[9] The new direction was partly based on a study suggesting that 75 percent of the "routine" air pollution in America comes from "area sources" (such as gasoline stations and dry cleaners) rather than from "point sources" (such as steel mills). Further, the EPA notes that air quality problems are highly dependent on specific local conditions, such as weather and geography. Environmentalists criticized the new approach. David Doninger, senior attorney for the National Resources Defense Council, said that the EPA was turning its "longstanding failure to protect public health from passive neglect into deliberate policy."[10] However, the EPA contends that the new policy will actually broaden the federal role by reaching previously unregulated emission sources.

The following case illustrates the process followed by the EPA in setting a particular standard and the review of that process by a federal court.

**NATURAL RESOURCES DEFENSE COUNCIL, INC. V. U.S. ENVIRONMENTAL
PROTECTION AGENCY
824 F.2d 1146 (D.C. Cir. 1987)**

Judge Bork

Current scientific knowledge does not permit a finding that there is a completely safe level
of human exposure to carcinogenic agents. The Administrator of the Environmental Protection Agency, however, is charged with regulating hazardous pollutants, including carcinogens, under section 112 of the Clean Air Act by setting emission standards "at the
level which in his judgment provides an ample margin of safety to protect the public health."
We address here the question of the extent of the Administrator's authority under this
delegation in setting emission standards for carcinogenic pollutants.

Petitioner Natural Resources Defense Council ("NRDC") contends that the Administrator must base a decision under section 112 exclusively on health-related factors and,
therefore, that the uncertainty about the effects of carcinogenic agents requires the
Administrator to prohibit all emissions. The Administrator argues that in the face of this
uncertainty he is authorized to set standards that require emission reduction to the lowest
level attainable by best available control technology whenever that level is below that
at which harm to humans has been demonstrated. We find no support for either position
in the language or legislative history of the Clean Air Act. We therefore grant the petition
for review and remand to the Administrator for reconsideration in light of this opinion.

I

Section 112 of the Clean Air Act provides for regulation of hazardous air pollutants, which
the statute defines as "air pollutant[s] to which no ambient air quality standard is applicable
and which in the judgment of the Administrator cause[s], or contribute[s] to, air pollution
which may reasonably be anticipated to result in an increase in mortality or an increase
in serious irreversible, or incapacitating reversible, illness." The statute requires the Administrator to publish a list containing each hazardous pollutant for which he intends to
adopt an emission standard, to publish proposed regulations and a notice of public hearing
for each such pollutant, and then, within a specified period, either to promulgate an emission
standard or to make a finding that the particular agent is not a hazardous air pollutant.
The statute directs the Administrator to set an emission standard promulgated under section
112 "at the level which in his judgment provides an ample margin of safety to protect the
public health."

This case concerns vinyl chloride regulations. Vinyl chloride is a gaseous synthetic
chemical used in the manufacture of plastics and is a strong carcinogen. In late 1975, the
Administrator issued a notice of proposed rulemaking to establish an emission standard
for vinyl chloride. In the notice, the EPA asserted that available data linked vinyl chloride
to carcinogenic, as well as some noncarcinogenic, disorders and that "[r]easonable ex-
trapolations" from this data suggested "that present ambient levels of vinyl chloride may
cause or contribute to [such] disorders." The EPA also noted that vinyl chloride is "an
apparent non-threshold pollutant," which means that it appears to create a risk to health

at all non-zero levels of emission. Scientific uncertainty, due to the unavailability of dose-response data and the 20-year latency period between initial exposure to vinyl chloride and the occurrence of disease, makes it impossible to establish any definite threshold level below which there are no adverse effects to human health. The notice also stated the "EPA's position that for a carcinogen it should be assumed, in the absence of strong evidence to the contrary, that there is no atmospheric concentration that poses absolutely no public health risk."

Because of this assumption, the EPA concluded that it was faced with two alternative interpretations of its duty under section 112. First, the EPA determined that section 112 might require a complete prohibition of emissions of non-threshold pollutants because a "zero emission limitation would be the only emission standard which would offer absolute safety from ambient exposure." The EPA found this alternative "neither desirable nor necessary" because "[c]omplete prohibition of all emissions could require closure of an entire industry," a cost the EPA found "extremely high for elimination of a risk to health that is of unknown dimensions."

The EPA stated the second alternative as follows:

> An alternative interpretation of section 112 is that it authorizes setting emission standards that require emission reduction to the lowest level achievable by use of the best available control technology in cases involving apparent non-threshold pollutants, where complete emission prohibition would result in widespread industry closure and EPA has determined that the cost of such closure would be grossly disproportionate to the benefits of removing the risk that would remain after imposition of the best available control technology.

The EPA adopted this alternative on the belief that it would "produce the most stringent regulation of hazardous air pollutants short of requiring a complete prohibition in all cases."

On October 21, 1976, the EPA promulgated final emission standards for vinyl chloride which were based solely on the level attainable by the best available control technology. The EPA determined that this standard would reduce unregulated emissions by 95 percent. With respect to the effect of the standard on health, the EPA stated that it had assessed the risk to health at ambient levels of exposure by extrapolating from dose-response data at higher levels of exposure and then made the following findings:

> EPA found that the rate of initiation of liver angiosarcoma among [the 4.6 million] people living around uncontrolled plants is expected to range from less than 1 to 10 cases of liver angiosarcoma per year of exposure to vinyl chloride. . . . Vinyl chloride is also estimated to produce an equal number of primary cancers at other sites, for a total of somewhere between less than 1 and 20 cases of cancer per year of exposure among residents around plants. The number of these effects is expected to be reduced at least in proportion to the reduction in the ambient annual average vinyl chloride concentration, which is expected to be 5 percent of the uncontrolled levels after the standard is implemented.

The EPA did not state whether this risk to health is significant or not. Nor did the EPA explain the relationship between this risk to health and its duty to set an emission standard which will provide an "ample margin of safety."

The Environmental Defense Fund ("EDF") filed suit challenging the standard on the ground that section 112 requires the Administrator to rely exclusively on health and prohibits consideration of cost and technology. . . .

* * * * *

III

The NRDC's challenge to the EPA's withdrawal of the 1977 amendments is simple: because the statute adopts an exclusive focus on considerations of health, the Administrator must set a zero level of emissions when he cannot determine that there is a level below which no harm will occur.

We must determine whether the EPA's actions are arbitrary, capricious, an abuse of discretion, or otherwise not in accordance with law. Review begins with the question of whether "Congress has directly spoken to the precise question at issue" and has expressed a clear intent as to its resolution. If so, "that intention is the law and must be given effect." "[I]f the statute is silent or ambiguous with respect to the specific issue," we must accept an agency interpretation if it is reasonable in light of the language, legislative history, and underlying policies of the statute. We find no support in the text or legislative history for the proposition that Congress intended to require a complete prohibition of emissions whenever the EPA cannot determine a threshold level for a hazardous pollutant. Instead, there is strong evidence that Congress considered such a requirement and rejected it.

Section 112 commands the Administrator to set an "emission standard" for a particular "hazardous air pollutant" which in his "judgment" will provide an "ample margin of safety." Congress' use of the term "ample margin of safety" is inconsistent with the NRDC's position that the Administrator has no discretion in the face of uncertainty. The statute nowhere defines "ample margin of safety." . . .

And while Congress used the modifier "ample" to exhort the Administrator not to allow "the public [or] the environment. . . . to be exposed to anything resembling the maximum risk" and, therefore, to set a margin "greater than 'normal' or 'adequate,' " Congress still left the EPA "great latitude in meeting its responsibility."

Congress' use of the word "safety," moreover, is significant evidence that it did not intend to require the Administrator to prohibit all emissions of non-threshold pollutants. As the Supreme Court has recently held, "safe" does not mean "risk-free." Instead, something is "unsafe" only when it threatens humans with "a significant risk of harm."

Thus, the terms of section 112 provide little support for the NRDC's position [which] would eliminate any discretion and would render the standard "ample margin of safety" meaningless as applied to carcinogenic pollutants. Whenever *any* scientific uncertainty existed about the ill effects of a nonzero level of hazardous air pollutants—and we think it unlikely that science will ever yield *absolute* certainty of safety in an area so complicated and rife with problems of measurement, modeling, long latency, and the like—the Administrator would have no discretion but would be required to prohibit all emissions. Had Congress intended that result, it could very easily have said so by writing a statute that states that no level of emissions shall be allowed as to which there is any uncertainty. But Congress chose instead to deal with the pervasive nature of scientific uncertainty and the inherent limitations of scientific knowledge by vesting in the Administrator the discretion to deal with uncertainty in each case.

* * * * *

IV

We turn now to the question whether the Administrator's chosen method for setting emission levels above zero is consistent with congressional intent. The Administrator's position is that he may set an emission level for non-threshold pollutants at the lowest level achievable by best available control technology when that level is anywhere below the level of demonstrated harm and the cost of setting a lower level is grossly disproportionate to the benefits of removing the remaining risk. The NRDC argues that this standard is arbitrary and capricious because the EPA is never permitted to consider cost and technological feasibility under section 112 but instead is limited to consideration of health-based factors. Thus, before addressing the Administrator's method of using cost and technological feasibility in this case, we must determine whether he may consider cost and technological feasibility at all.

A

On its face, section 112 does not indicate that Congress intended to preclude consideration of any factor. Though the phrase "to protect the public health" evinces an intent to make health the primary consideration, there is no indication of the factors the Administrator may or may not consider in determining, in his "judgment," what level of emissions will provide "an ample margin of safety." Instead, the language used, and the absence of any specific limitation, gives the clear impression that the Administrator has some discretion in determining what, if any, additional factors he will consider in setting an emission standard.

* * * * *

V

Since we cannot discern clear congressional intent to preclude consideration of cost and technological feasibility in setting emission standards under section 112, we necessarily find that the Administrator may consider these factors. We must next determine whether the Administrator's use of these factors in this case is "based on a permissible construction of the statute." We must uphold the Administrator's construction if it represents "a reasonable policy choice for the agency to make." We cannot, however, affirm an agency interpretation found to be "arbitrary, capricious, or manifestly contrary to the statute." Nor can we affirm if "it appears from the statute or its legislative history that the accommodation [chosen] is not one that Congress would have sanctioned."

Our role on review of an action taken pursuant to section 112 is generally a limited one. Because the regulation of carcinogenic agents raises questions "on the frontiers of scientific knowledge," we have recognized that the Administrator's decision in this area "will depend to a greater extent upon policy judgments" to which we must accord considerable deference. We have also acknowledged that "EPA, not the court, has the technical expertise to decide what inferences may be drawn from the characteristics of . . . substances and to formulate policy with respect to what risks are acceptable," and we will not second-guess a determination based on that expertise.

Our only role is to determine whether " 'the agency has exercised a reasonable discretion, with reasons that do not deviate from or ignore the ascertainable legislative intent.' " Despite this deferential standard, we find that the Administrator has ventured into a zone of impermissible action. The Administrator has not exercised his expertise to determine an acceptable risk to health. To the contrary, in the face of uncertainty about risks to health, he has simply substituted technological feasibility for health as the primary consideration under Section 112. Because this action is contrary to clearly discernible congressional intent, we grant the petition for review.

Given the foregoing analysis of the language and legislative history of section 112, it seems to us beyond dispute that Congress was primarily concerned with health in promulgating section 112. Every action by the Administrator in setting an emission standard is to be taken "to protect the public health." In setting an emission standard for vinyl chloride, however, the Administrator has made no finding with respect to the effect of the chosen level of emissions on health. Nor has the Administrator stated that a certain level of emissions is "safe" or that the chosen level will provide an "ample margin of safety." Instead, the Administrator has substituted "best available technology" for a finding of the risk to health.

* * * * *

The absence of any finding regarding the relationship between the risk to health at a certain level of emissions and the "ample margin of safety" standard is . . . evident in the Administrator's decision adopting the 1976 standards. . . . [T]he Administrator mentioned the risks to health before and after regulation, but did not provide any explanation as to whether the risk was significant, or whether the chosen standard provided an "ample margin of safety."

* * * * *

Thus, in setting emission standards for carcinogenic pollutants, the Administrator has decided to determine first the level of emissions attainable by best available control technology. He will then determine the costs of setting the standard below that level and balance those costs against the risk to health below the level of feasibility. If the costs are greater than the reduction in risk, then he will set the standard at the level of feasibility. This exercise, in the Administrator's view, will always produce an "ample margin of safety."

If there was any doubt that the Administrator has substituted technological feasibility for health as the primary consideration in setting emission standards under section 112, that doubt was dispelled by counsel for the EPA at oral argument. In response to a question from the court regarding a carcinogenic pollutant known to cause certain harm at 100 ppm, counsel stated that the Administrator could set an emission level at 99 ppm if that was the lowest feasible level and the costs of reducing the level below 99 ppm would be grossly disproportionate to the reduction in risk to health. Given the strong inference that harm would also certainly result at 99 ppm, the Administrator appears to have concluded that the "ample margin of safety" standard does not require any finding that a level of emissions is "safe." Instead, the Administrator need only find that the costs of control are greater than the reduction in risk to health. We disagree.

We find that the congressional mandate to provide "an ample margin of safety" "to protect the public health" requires the Administrator to make an initial determination of what is "safe." This determination must be based exclusively upon the Administrator's determination of the risk to health at a particular emission level. Because the Administrator in this case did not make any finding of the risk to health, the question of how that determination is to be made is not before us. We do wish to note, however, that the Administrator's decision does not require a finding that "safe" means "risk-free," or a finding that the determination is free from uncertainty. Instead, we find only that the Administrator's decision must be based upon an expert judgment with regard to the level of emission that will result in an "acceptable" risk to health. In this regard, the Administrator must determine what inferences should be drawn from available scientific data and decide what risks are acceptable in the world in which we live. . . . This determination must be based solely upon the risk to health. The Administrator cannot under any circumstances consider cost and technological feasibility at this stage of the analysis. The latter factors have no relevance to the preliminary determination of what is safe. Of course, if the Administrator cannot find that there is an acceptable risk at any level, then the Administrator must set the level at zero.

Congress, however, recognized in section 112 that the determination of what is "safe" will always be marked by scientific uncertainty and thus exhorted the Administrator to set emission standards that will provide an "ample margin" of safety. This language permits the Administrator to take into account scientific uncertainty and to use expert discretion to determine what action should be taken in light of that uncertainty. . . . In determining what is an "ample margin" the Administrator may, and perhaps must, take into account the inherent limitations of risk assessment and the limited scientific knowledge of the effects of exposure to carcinogens at various levels, and may therefore decide to set the level below that previously determined to be "safe." This is especially true when a straight line extrapolation from known risks is used to estimate risks to health at levels of exposure for which no data is available. This method, which is based upon the results of exposure at fairly high levels of the hazardous pollutants, will show some risk at every level because of the rules of arithmetic rather than because of any knowledge. In fact the risk at a certain point on the extrapolated line may have no relationship to reality; there is no particular reason to think that the actual line of the incidence of harm is represented by a straight line. Thus, by its nature the finding of risk is uncertain and the Administrator must use his discretion to meet the statutory mandate. It is only at this point of the regulatory process that the Administrator may set the emission standard at the lowest level that is technologically feasible. In fact, this is, we believe, precisely the type of policy choice that Congress envisioned when it directed the Administrator to provide an "ample margin of safety." Once "safety" is assured, the Administrator should be free to diminish as much of the statistically determined risk as possible by setting the standard at the lowest feasible level. Because consideration of these factors at this stage is clearly intended "to protect the public health," it is fully consistent with the Administrator's mandate under section 112.

We wish to reiterate the limited nature of our holding in this case because it is not the court's intention to bind the Administrator to any specific method of determining what is "safe" or what constitutes an "ample margin." We hold only that the Administrator cannot consider cost and technological feasibility in determining what is "safe." This determination must be based solely upon the risk to health. The issues of whether the Administrator can proceed on a case-by-case basis, what support the Administrator must provide for the determination of what is "safe," or what other factors may be considered, are issues that must be resolved after the Administrator has reached a decision upon reconsideration of the decision withdrawing the proposed 1977 amendments.

For the foregoing reasons, the petition for review is granted, the decision withdrawing the 1977 proposed rule is vacated, and this case is hereby remanded for timely reconsideration of the 1977 proposed rule consistent with this opinion.

It is so ordered.

Questions

1. *a.* Which position do you prefer—the EPA's, the NRDC's, or the court's? Why?
   b. If you were Congress, which would you make law? Explain.
2. Following the court's remand to the EPA, could the EPA ultimately set the same standard for vinyl chloride as it set in 1975? Explain.

WATER POLLUTION

As with the air, we have displayed a tendency to treat our water resources as free goods. Rather than paying the full cost of producing goods and services, we have simply piped a portion of that cost into the nearest body of water. That is, the waste from production—indeed, from the totality of our life experience—has commonly been disposed of in the water at a cost beneath that required to dispose of the waste in an ecologically sound fashion.

The corruption of our water system arose in a variety of ways. It is important to recognize that we have not always realized what we now know about the danger of wastes and the cleansing limits of our lakes and streams. Raw sewage and industrial waste reduced Lake Erie, in the judgment of many, to an open sewer. Ohio's Cuyahoga River, the victim of chemical and oil waste disposal, actually was in flames twice. Approximately 10 percent of the freshwater runoff in the United States is used for industrial cooling. The result is often water that is inhospitable to aquatic life. Herbicides, pesticides, acid runoff from strip mining, and oil spills are more examples of our assault on the waterways. It is also becoming clear that airborne pollutants are severely damaging our water resources as well.

Federal Policy

The Clean Water Act (CWA), designed to "restore and maintain the chemical, physical and biological integrity of the nation's waters," establishes two national goals: (1) achieving water quality sufficient for the protection and propagation of fish, shellfish, and wildlife and for recreation in and on the water; and (2) eliminating the discharge of pollutants into navigable waters. The states have primary responsibility for enforcing the Clean Water Act; but the federal government, via the Environmental Protection Agency, is empowered to assume enforcement authority if necessary.

The goals of the Clean Water Act are to be implemented primarily by imposing limits on the amount of pollutants that may lawfully enter the water of the United States from any "point source" (typically a pipe). The law provides for a permit program specifying the obligations of all pollutant dischargers (private and public). Each discharger must receive an EPA permit; comply with the effluent maximums specified by the permit; monitor its own performance; and report on that performance to the state or the EPA, as appropriate.

In brief, industrial pollution sources are required to progressively improve the quality of the nation's water via the following standards: All plants were required by 1977 to have installed pollution control devices that constituted the "best practicable pollution control technology" (BPT). Then, by 1984, plants discharging "conventional pollutants" (oil, grease, etc.) were required to use the "best conventional pollutant control technology" (BCT), while "toxic pollutants" were to be controlled by the "best available technology economically achievable" (BAT). Finally, by 1987, nonconventional pollutants (those neither conventional nor toxic) were likewise subject to the BAT.

The Water Quality Act of 1987 attempts to close a gap in the Clean Water Act by regulating so-called nonpoint pollution. Water runoff from the land commonly carries with it pollutants including silt, fertilizers, and pesticides. Virtually the entire U.S. coastline, as well as many bays and other waterways, are affected by these nonpoint pollutants. The problems are multiple—for example, fertilizer runoff from agricultural land feeds algae which spreads to the point that it consumes the oxygen in some inlets and coves thus eliminating other plant and animal life. The act provides authority for the federal government to join states and localities in attacking pollution problems in a number of vital American waterways including the Great Lakes, San Francisco Bay, and the Chesapeake Bay.

Penalties

Noncompliance with an order issued under the Clean Water Act or violation of the act may result in a civil penalty of $10,000 per day and an injunction. Criminal penalties reach a maximum of $25,000 and/or one year in prison for the first offense. Those penalties may be doubled in the event of a second conviction. Criminal penalties are authorized in instances of "willful and negligent" violations. The Clean Water Act does not include a noncompliance penalty equivalent to accrued "savings," as was the case with the Clean Air Act. Citizen suits are provided for under the CWA.

The case that follows addresses the somewhat murky Clean Water Act standards.

CHEMICAL MANUFACTURERS ASSN. V. NRDC
470 U.S. 116 (1985)

[The Supreme Court answers the question of whether the Environmental Protection Agency may grant variances (exceptions) from Clean Water Act limitations upon toxic discharges into public water treatment plants. Those limitations are set by reference to BPT and BAT levels.]

Justice White

I

[R]espondent National Resources Defense Counsel (NRDC) sought a declaration that § 301(*l*) of the Clean Water Act prohibited EPA from issuing "fundamentally different factor" (FDF) variances for pollutants listed as toxic under the Act. Petitioners EPA and Chemical Manufacturers Association (CMA) argued otherwise. . . .

* * * * *

EPA has developed its FDF variance as a mechanism for ensuring that its necessarily rough-hewn categories do not unfairly burden atypical plants. Any interested party may seek an FDF variance to make effluent limitations either more or less stringent if the standards applied to a given source, because of factors fundamentally different from those considered by EPA in setting the limitation, are either too lenient or too strict.

The 1977 amendments to the Clean Water Act reflected Congress' increased concern with the dangers of toxic pollutants. The Act, as then amended, allows specific statutory modifications of effluent limitations for economic and water quality reasons in § 301(c) and (g). Section 301(*l*), however, added by the 1977 amendments, provides:

The administrator may not modify any requirement of this section as it applies to any specific pollutant which is on the toxic pollutant list under section 1317(a)(1) of this title.

In the aftermath of the 1977 amendments, EPA continued its practice of occasionally granting FDF variances for BPT requirements . . . and BAT requirements. . . .

. . . NRDC sought a declaration that § 301(*l*) barred any FDF variance with respect to toxic pollutants. In an earlier case, the Fourth Circuit had rejected a similar argument, finding that § 301(*l*) was ambiguous on the issue of whether it applied to FDF variances and therefore deferring to the administrative agency's interpretation that such variances were permitted. . . . Contrariwise, the Third Circuit here ruled in favor of NRDC, and against petitioners EPA and CMA, holding that § 301(*l*) forbids the issuance of FDF variances for toxic pollutants. We granted certiorari to resolve this conflict between the Courts of Appeals and to decide this important question of environmental law. . . . We reverse.

II

Section 301(*l*) states that EPA may not "modify" any requirements of § 301 insofar as toxic materials are concerned. EPA insists that § 301(*l*) prohibits only those modifications expressly permitted by other provisions of § 301, namely, those that § 301(c) and § 301(g) would allow on economic or water-quality grounds. Section 301(*l*), it is urged, does not address the very different issue of FDF variances. This view of the agency charged with administering the statute is entitled to considerable deference; and to sustain it, we need not find that it is the only permissible construction that EPA might have adopted but only that EPA's understanding of this very "complex statute" is a sufficiently rational one to preclude a court from substituting its judgment for that of EPA. . . .

A

NRDC insists that the language of § 301(*l*) is itself enough to require affirmance of the Court of Appeals, since on its face it forbids any modifications of the effluent limitations that EPA must promulgate for toxic pollutants. If the word "modify" in § 301(*l*) is read in its broadest sense, that is, to encompass any change or alteration in the standards, NRDC is correct. But it makes little sense to construe the section to forbid EPA to amend its own standards, even to correct an error or to impose stricter requirements. Furthermore, reading § 301(*l*) in this manner would forbid what § 307(b)(2) expressly directs: EPA is there required to "revise" its pretreatment standards "from time to time, as control technology, processes, operating methods, or other alternatives change." As NRDC does and must concede . . . § 301(*l*) cannot be read to forbid every change in the toxic waste standards. The word "modify" thus has no plain meaning as used in § 301(*l*) and is the proper subject of construction by EPA and the courts. . . . Since EPA asserts that the FDF variance is more like a revision permitted by § 307 than it is like a § 301(c) or (g) modification, and since, as will become evident, we think there is a reasonable basis for such a position, we conclude that the statutory language does not foreclose the agency's view of the statute. We should defer to that view unless the legislative history or the purpose and structure of the statute clearly reveal a contrary intent on the part of Congress. NRDC submits that the legislative materials evince such a contrary intent. We disagree.

B

. . . While the Conference Committee Report did not explain the reason for proposing § 301(*l*), Representative Roberts, the House floor manager, stated:

Due to the nature of toxic pollutants, those identified for regulation will not be subject to waivers from or modification of the requirements prescribed under this section, *spe-*

cifically, neither section 301(c) waivers based on the economic capability of the discharger nor 301(g) waivers based on water quality considerations shall be available.

Another indication that Congress did not intend to forbid FDF waivers as well as § 301(c) and (g) modifications is its silence on the issue. Under NRDC's theory, the Conference Committee did not merely tinker with the wording of the Senate bill, but boldly moved to eliminate FDF variances. But if that was the Committee's intention, it is odd that the Committee did not communicate it to either House, for only a few months before we had construed the Act to permit the very FDF variance NRDC insists the Conference Committee was silently proposing to abolish. In *E. I. du Pont de Nemours & Co.* v. *Train,* 430 U.S. 112 (1977), we upheld EPA's class and category effluent limitations, relying on the availability of FDF waivers. Congress was undoubtedly aware of *Du Pont,* and absent an expression of legislative will, we are reluctant to infer an intent to amend the Act so as to ignore the thrust of an important decision.

* * * * *

After examining the wording and legislative history of the statute, we agree with EPA and CMA that the legislative history itself does not evince an unambiguous congressional intention to forbid all FDF waivers with respect to toxic materials.

C

Neither are we convinced that FDF variances threaten to frustrate the goals and operation of the statutory scheme set up by Congress. The nature of FDF variances has been spelled out both by this Court and by the agency itself. The regulation explains that its purpose is to remedy categories which were not accurately drawn because information was either not available to or not considered by the administrator in setting the original categories and limitations. An FDF variance does not excuse compliance with a correct requirement, but instead represents an acknowledgement that not all relevant factors were taken sufficiently into account in framing that requirement originally, and that those relevant factors, properly considered, would have justified—indeed, required—the creation of a subcategory for the discharger in question. . . . It is essentially, not an exception to the standard-setting process, but rather a more fine-tuned application of it.

We are not persuaded by NRDC's argument that granting FDF variances is inconsistent with the goal of uniform effluent limitations under the Act. Congress did intend uniformity among sources in the same category, demanding that "similar point sources with similar characteristics . . . meet similar effluent limitations," . . . EPA, however, was admonished to take into account the diversity within each industry by establishing appropriate subcategories.

* * * * *

NRDC argues, echoing the concern of the Court of Appeals below, that allowing FDF variances will render meaningless the § 301(*l*) prohibition against modifications on the basis of economic and water quality factors. That argument ignores the clear difference between the purpose of FDF waivers and that of § 301(c) and (g) modifications. . . . FDF variances are specifically unavailable for the grounds that would justify the statutory modifications. . . . Both a source's inability to pay the foreseen costs, grounds for a § 301(c) modification, and the lack of a significant impact on water quality, grounds for a § 301(g) modification, are irrelevant under FDF variance procedures. . . .

EPA and CMA point out that the availability of FDF variances makes bearable the enormous burden faced by EPA in promulgating categories of sources and setting effluent limitations. Acting under stringent timetables, EPA must collect and analyze large amounts of technical information concerning complex industrial categories. Understandably, EPA may not be apprised of and will fail to consider unique factors applicable to atypical plants during the categorical rulemaking process, and it is thus important that EPA's nationally binding categorical pretreatment standards for indirect dischargers be tempered with the flexibility that the FDF variance mechanism offers, a mechanism repugnant to neither the goals nor the operation of the Act.

III

Viewed in its entirety, neither the language nor the legislative history of the Act demonstrates a clear congressional intent to forbid EPA's sensible variance mechanism for tailoring the categories it promulgates. In the absence of congressional directive to the contrary, we accept EPA's conclusion that § 301(*l*) does not prohibit FDF variances. That interpretation gives the term "modify" a consistent meaning in § 301(c), (g), and (*l*), and draws support from the legislative evolution of § 301(*l*) and from congressional silence on whether it intended to forbid FDF variances altogether and thus to obviate our decision in *Du Pont*.

* * * * *

The judgment of the Court of Appeals is reversed.

Justice Marshall, with whom Justice Blackmun and Justice Stevens join, and with whom Justice O'Connor joins as to Parts I, II, and II, dissenting.

In this case, the Environmental Protection Agency (EPA) maintains that it may issue, on a case-by-case basis, individualized variances from the national standards that limit the discharge of toxic water pollutants. EPA asserts this power in the face of a provision of the Clean Water Act that expressly withdraws from the agency the authority to "modify" the national standards for such pollutants. The Court today defers to EPA's interpretation of the Clean Water Act even though that interpretation is inconsistent with the clear intent of Congress. . . .

* * * * *

. . . Congress pointedly determined that water pollution control standards should take the form of general rules, to apply uniformly to categories of dischargers. As a result, the Court validates outcomes substantially less protective of the environment than those mandated by Congress. The only view of FDF variances consistent with the scheme of the Clean Water Act is that they are individual exceptions that soften the hardship of general rules. As such, they are undoubtedly disallowed by § 301(*l*).

This case is not about whether exceptions are useful adjuncts to regulatory schemes of general applicability. That is a policy choice on which courts should defer to Congress in the first instance, and to the administrative agency in the absence of a clear congressional mandate. Here, Congress has made the policy choice. It has weighed competing goals and determined that, whatever the general merits of exceptions schemes, they are simply inappropriate in the context of the control of toxic water pollution. As a result, an exceptions scheme such as the one challenged here simply cannot stand.

Questions

1. Explain the difference between BPT and BAT.
2. What is meant by "fundamentally different factor" variances?
3. To prevail in this case of statutory interpretation, was the EPA required to prove that its reading of the Clean Water Act was the "only permissible construction" that might be put on that language? Explain.
4. Do you regard the Court's decision as a sensible accommodation to the realities of commercial needs, or as a dramatic hole in the nation's antipollution armor, or as neither? Explain.

LAND POLLUTION

Pollution does not fit tidily into the three compartments (air, water, land) used for convenience in this text. Acid rain, as discussed above, debases air and water as well as the fruits of the water and land (fish and trees). Similarly, the problems of land pollution addressed in this section often do damage to the fullness of the natural world. For most of recorded history we felt safe and comfortable in using the Earth as a garbage dump. When we did begin to recognize emerging dangers, our initial concern was simply the problem of disposing of the enormous bulk of our solid wastes.

The problem is real in that we annually produce approximately 20 to 30 tons of such waste for every American. Each year the city of Philadelphia incinerates 360,000 tons of waste, but that leaves 540,000 tons that must be piled in landfills. The city generates over 60,000 tons of sludge annually. At one time the sludge was handled comfortably merely by dumping it in the Atlantic Ocean. Since 1980 that approach has been illegal, so the city has turned to more ingenious disposal techniques. Sixty percent of the sludge is used in strip mine reclamation. Some 15 to 20 percent is given away or sold (as fertilizer), and the remainder is applied to Philadelphia land (for example, golf courses). Now the city is experimenting with a combination of sludge and incinerator residue to be used as highway aggregate for bituminous paving.[11]

Of course, many cities and counties have established recycling centers and plants to convert waste to energy. In 1972 Oregon became the first state to approve a "bottle bill." That law forbade cans with pull-tab openers and provided that all beer and soft-drink containers sold in the state were to have a refund value of 2 or 5 cents. Since then a number of states have enacted similar legislation, and the federal government has considered many such bills.

Solid Waste Disposal Act

To attack the massive garbage problem, Congress approved the Solid Waste Disposal Act of 1965. The act, in brief, leaves solid waste problems to states and localities, while the federal government offers research and financial support. In 1970 the act was reauthorized, and Congress required a report on hazardous wastes.

Toxic Substances Control Act

In 1976 Congress approved the Toxic Substances Control Act (TSCA) to identify toxic chemicals, assess their risks, and control dangerous chemicals. Under the terms of the TSCA, the Environmental Protection Agency requires the chemical industry to report any information it may have suggesting that a chemical poses a "substantial risk." The EPA is empowered to review and limit or stop the introduction of new chemicals.

As illustrated in this section, we have displayed a good deal of zeal and ingenuity in addressing pollution problems. However, we are beginning to recognize that the clever solutions of today often become tomorrow's problems. For example, the incineration of waste rids us of bulk but creates air pollution. The interdependence of all elements of the global environment magnifies the difficulties of pollution control.

Resource Conservation and Recovery Act

By 1976 the dangers of hazardous substances were becoming apparent to all, and Congress complemented the TSCA with the Resource Conservation and Recovery Act (RCRA). The act addresses both solid and hazardous wastes. Its solid waste provisions are more supportive than punitive in tone and approach. The federal government is authorized, among other strategies, to provide technical and financial assistance to states and localities; to prohibit future open dumping; and to establish cooperative federal, state, local, and private-enterprise programs to recover energy and valuable materials from solid wastes.

Subtitle C of the RCRA is designed to ensure the safe movement and disposal of hazardous wastes. The generator of the waste must determine if that waste is hazardous under EPA guidelines and, if so, report the waste site and waste activities to the government. The waste generator must then create a manifest to be used in tracking the waste from its creation to its disposal. Along the "cradle-to-grave" path of the waste, all those with responsibility for it must sign the manifest and safely store and transport it. Once at a licensed disposal facility, the owner signs for the waste and returns a copy to the generator.

In 1984 Congress strengthened the RCRA by extending its provisions to generators of small quantities of hazardous wastes and by banning land disposal of hazardous wastes by approximately 1990 unless (1) those wastes had been determined by the EPA to be safe for land disposal or (2) the waste was treated with the best available technology which "substantially diminishes" toxicity or "substantially reduces the likelihood of migration of the hazardous constituents in the waste."[12]

Failure to comply with the hazardous waste provisions may result in civil penalties of up to $25,000 per day and criminal penalties up to $50,000 per day and/or one year in prison. In cases of "knowing endangerment" of human life, individuals may be fined up to $250,000 and/or imprisoned for not more than five years, while businesses may be fined not more than $1 million.

Comprehensive Environmental Response, Compensation, and Liability Act of 1980

According to *The Wall Street Journal:*

> U.S. companies each year produce more than 200 pounds of hazardous waste for every man, woman, and child in the country, and the government contends the bulk of that material has been disposed of improperly for decades. When landfills and other facilities are close to underground water supplies or wetlands, the chemical wastes seep out and frequently contaminate wells, irrigation water, and even the soil around some homes and other buildings. It isn't unusual to have cleanup efforts costing tens of millions of dollars, with millions more required for annual maintenance.[13]

The RCRA was essentially prospective in direction and, as such, did not address the problem of cleaning up thousands of existing, abandoned hazardous waste sites. CERCLA, known as the "Superfund," established a $1.6 billion fund to begin the cleanup process. The bulk of the fund is drawn from taxes on chemicals and petroleum. The act empowers the government to order the cleanup of hazardous waste released into the environment. All parties responsible for any illegal hazardous waste discharge are strictly liable (with certain limitations) for all costs associated with the necessary cleanup. However, it is doubtless unrealistic to expect all, or nearly all, of the money to be recovered. Private citizens suffering injury from hazardous wastes do not receive relief under the terms of CERCLA. Rather they must pursue their claims through the judicial system.

Spurred by the Bhopal, India, chemical plant disaster (See Chapter 3), Congress passed the Emergency Planning and Community Right-to-Know Act of 1986 as an amendment to the Superfund law. The act, which became effective in the summer of 1988, requires companies to notify the government if they release any extremely hazardous chemicals into the environment, and they must submit an inventory of their hazardous chemicals to the government. Each state must establish emergency response commissions, local emergency planning committees, and emergency plans to deal with chemical discharges. In general, information regarding dangerous chemicals must be released to the public upon request. Beyond preparing for chemical release emergencies, the hope behind the law is that its disclosure requirements will enhance community awareness of chemical hazards thus provoking sufficient community pressure to cause companies to voluntarily reduce their emissions.

It is important to understand that liability for hazardous waste remains with the producer of the waste "to the grave" and beyond. For example, those who generate hazardous waste and dispose of it at a dump site may be liable for damages should waste leak from the dump site. Court decisions imposing this burden on hazardous waste producers have had the effect of compelling more careful dump site selection as well as more rigorous efforts to reduce hazardous waste production and waste toxicity. The legal complexity of the hazardous waste problem is illustrated by a moment's reflection on the difficulty of assigning fault for waste leaking from a dump used by many waste generators who deposit materials varying widely in toxicity. How can we determine which "dumper" caused the harm? To what extent is the dump site ownership and management liable? What if one company's waste combines with that of another at the dump site, resulting in the creation of a still more hazardous chemical?[14]

By 1985 the Superfund had resulted in cleaning up only 11 of the 679 sites on the national priority list and 435 emergency cleanups (for example, tank car spills). The original Superfund taxing authority expired in October 1985 but was kept alive, although in a very slow state, through emergency funding provided by Congress. Then, on October 17, 1986, President Reagan signed a bill providing an additional $9 billion for toxic waste clean up.

The legislation, which took Congress nearly two years to mold, calls for the government to begin cleaning up 375 of the nation's toxic waste sites over the five-year life of the law, and it imposes strict environmental standards to assure that those sites are rendered safe.[15]

The federal Office of Technology Assessment has estimated that as much as $100 billion may be required to clean waste sites over the next 50 years.[16]

The magnitude and complexity of the hazardous waste problem is illustrated by the following article.

WIDESPREAD FEAR OF HAZARDOUS-WASTE SITES THWARTS STATE AND INDUSTRY DISPOSAL PLANS

Ronald Alsop

Perth Amboy, New Jersey—This dingy little industrial town endured a chemical fire in 1980 that flared for 110 hours. Its sewers are tainted with toxic polychlorinated biphenyls (PCBs). Now comes a proposal to build a hazardous-waste disposal facility along the waterfront.

Locally and nationally, the timing couldn't be worse. Perth Amboy officials and businessmen have been trying to polish the town's image by attracting condominium and office-building developers. "Nobody will want to buy a $120,000 condominium if there are drums of toxic waste piled up down the block," says Marianthe Patras, a local restauranteur.

* * * * *

Such are the frustrations that companies and state environmental officials face these days as they try to open disposal sites in a country terrified of hazardous waste. Waste-management firms want to build landfills, incinerators, and other facilities to dispose of the millions of tons of toxic waste generated each year by industry, as well as old waste that must be removed from leaking, abandoned dumps.

Many existing landfills are expected to close rather than try to meet stringent new government regulations, and chemical industry officials believe that without new sites, there could be a shortage of disposal space in a few years.

Although the new regulations require higher-quality disposal facilities and closer monitoring of the sites, the waste-management industry is struggling against what it has dubbed "the NIMBY (Not in My Backyard) syndrome."

At a rally in Perth Amboy . . . , speakers warned of carcinogens, birth defects, and liver damage. Civic boosters peddled baby-blue T-shirts that call the town "New Jersey's best-kept secret, not New Jersey's Love Canal." . . .

Hazardous-waste facilities fit the same category as prisons and airports. Nobody wants to live near them, but they are essential to this country's way of life. A 1980 public opinion survey showed that a majority of people will accept hazardous-waste facilities only if the sites are at least 100 miles away from their homes. And in a study last year for the Chemical Manufacturers Association, half of the "politically active" individuals interviewed said they don't believe it's possible to dispose of hazardous waste safely.

* * * * *

But industry officials believe the public is inviting trouble if it blindly opposes any project involving toxic substances. They claim that refusal to permit well-regulated facilities will result in a capacity crisis that could disrupt manufacturing operations. "We could see plants closing in two to five years because there's nowhere to put the waste they generate," says William Moore, an environmental specialist at Rohm & Haas Co., a chemical manufacturer. "That certainly is a fear coming closer to reality for us."

The scarcity of landfills already is costing companies. Rohm & Haas plants in Pennsylvania now ship waste to Alabama at a cost of about $75 a drum. But in Texas, where there are several disposal sites to choose from, the cost is only $35 to $40 a drum.

For irresponsible companies, the capacity problem could mean continued illegal dumping and contamination of the environment. "The question the public should ask itself is: Do I want to know where the wastes are going, or do I want to play Russian roulette and have them mysteriously turn up in my backyard in a few years," says Joan Berkowitz, a vice president at Arthur D. Little Inc., the consulting firm.

What troubles most people are the unknown environmental and health risks. "I worry that if they dump anything and everything from our state, Ohio, New Jersey, and who knows where

else, there could be a leak and a terrible chemical reaction," says Ted Lingham, a cattle rancher and the mayor of Lowndesboro, Alabama, population 204. He and his constituents, who are battling a proposed landfill in Lowndesboro, support a new state law that calls for legislative approval of commercial hazardous-waste disposal sites in Alabama.

"In my humble opinion, we've pretty much eliminated any more sites in Alabama with that law," says Alfred Chipley, an official in the state environmental-management department. "The only criterion the legislators have is what the electorate says, and I don't know anyone welcoming a dump." For now, Browning-Ferris Industries Inc. says it has postponed its Lowndesboro landfill project.

Even when local residents believe a hazardous waste facility can be operated safely, many homeowners and businessmen claim they can't afford the stigma. They fear it will weaken property values and drive away customers.

* * * * *

In Tennessee, legislators have introduced a bill that would reward a town with $500,000 this year and more in future years for accepting a waste-disposal site. Massachusetts offers its municipalities technical-assistance grants to study a project, so that they don't have to settle for the developer's claims about its safety.

* * * * *

Some states believe waste companies should provide money for additional emergency equipment and training of firemen and policemen, as well as compensation for any drop in property values. Other incentives might be a new park or school.

Aware of their image problem, some waste-management companies are trying to ingratiate themselves with the community. Rollins Environmental Services Inc. holds open houses regularly for the people living near its landfills and incinerators, and it encourages its officials to join the Rotary and other civic clubs. "We do everything we can to maintain good relations with the local citizenry," explains Barney Wander, a spokesman for the commercial waste-disposal company. "There's nothing to stop citizens from filing suit against us on nuisance grounds."

Questions

1. Presumably most of us bear some responsibility for the hazardous waste problem because our consumption preferences lead to the creation of waste. Because market preferences created the problem, should we let the market resolve it by permitting hazardous waste disposal in the most profitable fashion? Explain.
2. Hazardous waste sites are necessary, but few communities will accept them. Assume government intervention is necessary to manage the hazardous waste problem. Should the federal government pass legislation requiring all states and localities to accept all hazardous waste sites that comply with the federal government's disposal standards? Explain.

THE FREE MARKET REVISITED

The government's significant success in pollution abatement is acknowledged by all, but many economists, businesspeople, and others believe government environmental policy should take a decided shift toward free market principles. To them, pollution control is not so much a matter of law as of economics. If the proper incentives are offered, they believe the market will be effective in further improving our ecological health. For example, the Clean Air Act has been conspicuously successful in reducing emissions from large, centralized sources like power plants. However, the free market proponents argue that complex bureaucratic regulations that govern large sources will, if applied to the many remaining small sources, prove so expensive that we will experience rapidly diminishing returns on the dollars invested in pollution control. Therefore, the EPA has adopted an emissions trading policy founded on market incentives. According to the Council on Environmental Quality:

> EPA's emissions trading policy incorporates four innovative regulatory mechanisms, all of which take advantage of market incentives to reduce air emissions at the lowest possible cost. First, EPA's bubble policy allows existing plants, or groups of plants, to be excused from imposing controls on one or more emissions sources in exchange for compensating controls on other, less costly to control, sources. Second, the netting policy excuses plants from new source

review requirements usually required when they expand or modernize, if any increase in plantwide emissions is insignificant. Third, under EPA's emissions offset policy new or modified sources in nonattainment areas may be required to secure surplus emissions restrictions which more than offset increased emissions, thus allowing indust ial growth while improving air quality. Fourth, the emissions banking policy lets firms store up emissions reductions for later use in bubble, netting, or offset transactions, or for sale to other firms that cannot achieve the same level of reductions as cheaply. All in all, these four innovative approaches mark this nation's first comprehensive attempt to apply free market cost-minimizing principles to pollution control.[17]

Not surprisingly, the business community has found in the EPA trading policy an opportunity to both meet the government's expectations at reduced costs and, in some instances, make a few dollars.

MARKET BOOMS FOR "RIGHTS" TO POLLUTE

Andy Pasztor

Stuart Rupp of Richmond, California, proudly calls himself a "broker." But he doesn't sell stocks, bonds, or futures.

Instead, Mr. Rupp, a partner in an environmental consulting firm, helps companies trade the "right" to spew additional pollutants into the atmosphere.

Such transactions are part of a new approach to reducing air pollution that relies on the marketplace rather than on federal regulations. A company that closes a plant or installs improved pollution-control equipment can receive "emission credits" for its cleanup efforts. These credits, in turn, may be purchased by another firm to offset increased air pollution caused by construction or expansion. The idea is to allow industry to negotiate the price and details of the trade-offs as long as the overall level of air pollution in an area isn't increased.

Hydrocarbons at $50,000

Times Mirror Co. was able to complete the $120 million expansion of a paper-making plant near Portland, Oregon, after purchasing the right to emit about 150 tons of extra hydrocarbons into the air annually. A local dry cleaning firm and the owners of a wood coating plant that had gone out of business sold the necessary credits for about $50,000. Without the credits, Times Mirror couldn't have persuaded state and federal regulators to permit the expansion, says Rod Schmall, manager of environmental and energy services for the subsidiary that runs the plant.

Companies are "just beginning to realize in large numbers that they actually can turn a profit by reducing pollution by a certain amount" and then striking a deal to sell off the resulting credits at handsome prices, says Bob

Fuller of First Wisconsin Corp., a Milwaukee bank holding company that started experimenting with pollution credits for its clients three years ago.

The Carter administration promoted the notion first, but President Reagan's environmental advisers have endorsed it, too, as a way to simplify and loosen clean-air regulations. The General Accounting Office estimates that a "viable market in air pollution rights" could cut pollution-control costs at least 40 percent and perhaps as much as 90 percent for many businesses. After nearly two years of study, the GAO concluded that trading credits substantially increases industry flexibility in complying with clean-air laws and encourages the use of innovative technologies. . . .

VW's Approach

When Volkswagen of America built its first car and truck assembly plant in Pennsylvania several years ago, the company needed a lot of credits. It received some from Jones & Laughlin Steel Co., apparently on the promise that the plant would buy some of its steel from the company each year in return. Volkswagen also persuaded the state transportation department to sharply curtail the use of certain road asphalts that give off hydrocarbon fumes when they dry. That estimated reduction in pollution also was credited to VW's account.

* * * * *

Many environmental groups support the offset trading concept but are concerned about how the Environmental Protection Agency intends to monitor and enforce private deals to ensure that air quality is improved in the long run. Jack McKenzie, an environmental official with Pacific Gas & Electric Co., complains that a few environmentalists "appear absolutely paranoid that someone will make money from cleaning up a facility."

Source: *The Wall Street Journal,* June 18, 1981, p. 25. Reprinted by permission of *The Wall Street Journal,* © Dow Jones & Company, Inc. 1981. ALL RIGHTS RESERVED.

Questions

1. The emissions-trading policy often results in shifting pollution from one site to another without actually reducing the overall level of pollution. Is that policy defensible? Explain.
2. According to the article, how can firms make a profit by reducing pollution?
3. According to a study completed for the government, the cost of controlling hydrocarbons ranged from $16,550 per ton in an auto-painting operation to $41 per ton for a gas terminal in the same area. Explain how emissions trading or sale between those firms might protect the environment while reducing costs.

STATE AND LOCAL REGULATION

Under the "police powers" granted by the Constitution as previously discussed in Chapter 6, state and local governments have the right to impose various controls on citizens to protect and maintain the public health and safety and its general welfare. State and local governments are increasingly acting in the area of environmental protection to do just that. The purity of drinking water continues to be of primary importance for state health officials. Many states also regulate air quality in a variety of ways, including limiting the amount of particulate matter that an industrial plant can emit into adjacent areas. A growing number of local governments are prohibiting smoking in public buildings and other public areas, such as restaurants. A greater understanding of hazards has contributed to state activism, resulting in such various actions as the passage of "bottle bills" and electric utility siting laws. A citizen-sponsored initiative in California now requires prominent warnings if people are being exposed to certain toxic substances.

New signs will be sprouting all over California this week as wary businesses get ready for partial implementation of one of the most controversial environmental laws ever passed in the nation.

Gasoline stations to supermarkets will post notices something like: "Proposition 65 requires that California consumers be warned about products containing chemicals known to the state to cause cancer or other reproductive harm or birth defects." A toll-free number will be provided for further information.

* * * * *

The state issued regulations last week laying out warning levels for 29 substances ranging from benzene and lead to asbestos and arsenic. Others will be added to the state's list in the months ahead.

The levels were set so that a daily dose of the substance over a lifetime would be expected to produce no more than 1 excess cancer per 100,000 people, says Steven Book, science adviser to the state agency carrying out Proposition 65.

A company that fails to issue warnings faces fines of as much as $2,500 a day for each violation. Businessmen worry that fines could quickly multiply into millions of dollars as courts may decide that every individual exposure is a separate violation.[18]

Some states have their own environmental policy acts that require impact statements to be prepared before such decisions as granting a building permit or changing a zoning ordinance can be made, while other state and local governments are putting absolute caps on growth.

In last November's election, Los Angeles residents overwhelmingly approved a measure halving the maximum permissible density on 85 percent of Los Angeles' commercial and industrial land. After decades of real estate boosterism, Los Angeles has joined the no-growth/slow-growth movement, as have dozens of other towns and cities across America recently.

Business can no longer overlook this movement. Corporations that want to construct new office buildings and industrial facilities will find their choice of location severely narrowed. Notwithstanding frequent reports of high vacancy rates in major U.S. cities, many office and retail tenants will face a shortage of space and, hence, higher rents in desirable but restricted areas.

Why has the long-simmering no-growth/slow-growth movement suddenly become a powerful nationwide force for business to contend with? It is primarily because millions of jobs are now being created at the outskirts of our metropolitan areas, and politically savvy middle-class suburbanites don't want office buildings and business parks rising near their neighborhoods and attracting traffic to their once-tranquil streets.

* * * * *

Or consider Boston. In 1982, downtown and Back Bay accounted for just under 75 percent of the metropolitan area's office space. By 1986, the Boston office market was very different, with 58 percent of the metropolitan area's total office space located in the suburbs. Metropolitan Boston has increased its total office space by more than one and one-half times in just four years, and nearly 80 percent of that growth has occurred in the suburbs.[19]

In addition to the usual land use restrictions concerning location (building on flood plains, earthquake fault areas, or sites that fail percolation tests) and zoning (height restriction; minimum lot sizes; and single family, multifamily, commercial, or industrial zones), some communities are adopting new and novel ordinances to protect the character of their areas. For example, the Long Island village of Bell Terre approved an ordinance prohibiting more than two unmarried people from living together within the community. The ordinance was challenged by six students who had rented a house. Justice Douglas, speaking for the U.S. Supreme Court, affirmed the village's authority, under its police power, to control environmental quality, in the broadest sense:

> The regimes of boarding houses, fraternity houses, and the like present urban problems. More people occupy a given space; more cars rather continuously pass by; more cars are parked; noise travels with crowds.
>
> A quiet place where yards are wide, people few, and motor vehicles restricted are legitimate guidelines in a land use project addressed to family needs. This goal is a permissible one. . . . The police power is not confined to the elimination of filth, stench, and unhealthy places. It is ample to lay out zones where family values, youth values, and the blessings of quiet seclusion and clean air make the area a sanctuary for people.[20]

QUESTIONS

1. Should states get into the business of regulating toxic wastes as California has done? Explain.
2. As one writer has asked, "What can be done to permit growth that balances the needs of business with the very real concerns of citizens about the quality of life in their communities?"[21]

3. Imagine what life would be like if all of the federal, state, and local laws previously discussed were repealed. Describe both short- and long-run impacts.

Part Four—Remedies Revisited

THE COMMON LAW

Long before the federal government became actively involved in environmental issues, courts were grappling with the problem. As early as the 1500s city officials were ordered by a court to keep the streets clean of dung deposited by swine allowed to run loose; the air was said to be "corrupted and infected" by this practice. Legal arguments have typically revolved around the right of a person to use and enjoy private or public property if such usage caused harm to a neighbor's property.

The doctrines of nuisance and trespass are paramount in common law environmental litigation. A private nuisance is a substantial and unreasonable invasion of the private use and enjoyment of one's land, while a public nuisance is an unreasonable interference with a right common to the public. Harmful conduct may be both a public and private nuisance simultaneously; the case law distinctions between the two are often blurred. A trespass occurs and liability is imposed with *any* intentional invasion of the right to one's exclusive use of one's own property.

The distinction between trespass and nuisance is fine, and the two may be coextensive. Nuisance and trespass causes of action have been entered for such offenses as fouling a neighbor's water, flooding another's land, or causing excessive noise, smell, or particulate matter on another's property. The remedies available to a successful plaintiff are monetary damages for the harm suffered and/or an injunction to prevent similar conduct by the defendant in the future. An injunction is a much more serious remedy and often requires a balancing of the hardships faced by each party if the injunction is granted and an analysis of whether the public interest is served by a continuation of the practice that led to the nuisance.

Negligence and strict liability claims may also arise from pollution cases. For example, a company might well be guilty of negligence if it failed to correct a pollution problem where the technology and necessary resources were available to do so, and that failure caused harm to someone to whom the company owed a duty. In addition, certain activities, such as the use of toxic chemicals, might be so abnormally dangerous as to provoke a strict liability claim. (See Chapter 14 for a discussion of negligence and strict liability.)

The following case illustrates a common law approach to a pollution problem.

BOOMER V. ATLANTIC CEMENT CO.
26 N.Y.2d 219, 257 N.E.2d 870 (1970)

Judge Bergan

Defendant operates a large cement plant near Albany. These are actions for injunction and damages by neighboring land owners alleging injury to property from dirt, smoke and vibration emanating from the plant. A nuisance has been found after trial, temporary damages have been allowed but an injunction has been denied.

* * * * *

. . . The threshold question raised by the division of view on this appeal is whether the court should resolve the litigation between the parties now before it as equitably as seems possible; or whether, seeking promotion of the general public welfare, it should channel private litigation into broad public objectives.

A court performs its essential function when it decides the rights of parties before it. Its decision of private controversies may sometimes greatly affect public issues. Large questions of law are often resolved by the manner in which private litigation is decided. But this is normally an incident to the court's main function to settle controversy. It is a rare exercise of judicial power to use a decision in private litigation as a purposeful mechanism to achieve direct public objectives greatly beyond the rights and interests before the court.

* * * * *

It seems apparent that the amelioration of air pollution will depend on technical research in great depth; on a carefully balanced consideration of the economic impact of close regulation; and of the actual effect on public health. It is likely to require massive public expenditure and to demand more than any local community can accomplish and to depend on regional and interstate controls.

A court should not try to do this on its own as a by-product of private litigation and it seems manifest that the judicial establishment is neither equipped in the limited nature of any judgment it can pronounce nor prepared to lay down and implement an effective policy for the elimination of air pollution. This is an area beyond the circumference of one private lawsuit. It is a direct responsibility for government and should not thus be undertaken as an incident to solving a dispute between property owners and a single cement plant—one of many—in the Hudson River Valley.

The cement-making operations of defendant have been found by the court at Special Term to have damaged the nearby properties of plaintiffs in these two actions. That court, as it has been noted, accordingly found defendant maintained a nuisance and this has been affirmed at the Appellate Division. The total damage to plaintiffs' properties is, however, relatively small in comparison with the value of defendant's operation and with the consequences of the injunction which plaintiffs seek.

The ground for the denial of injunction, notwithstanding the finding both that there is a nuisance and that plaintiffs have been damaged substantially, is the large disparity in economic consequences of the nuisance and of the injunction. This theory cannot, however, be sustained without overruling a doctrine which has been consistently reaffirmed in several leading cases in this court and which has never been disavowed here, namely that where a nuisance has been found and where there has been any substantial damage shown by the party complaining an injunction will be granted.

The rule in New York has been that such a nuisance will be enjoined although marked disparity be shown in economic consequence between the effect of the injunction and the effect of the nuisance.

* * * * *

. . . [T]o follow the rule literally in these cases would be to close down the plant at once. This court is fully agreed to avoid that immediately drastic remedy; the difference in view is how best to avoid it.

One alternative is to grant the injunction but postpone its effect to a specified future date to give opportunity for technical advances to permit defendant to eliminate the nuisance; another is to grant the injunction conditioned on the payment of permanent damages to plaintiffs which would compensate them for the total economic loss to their property present and future caused by defendant's operations. For reasons which will be developed the court chooses the latter alternative.

If the injunction were to be granted unless within a short period—e.g., 18 months—the nuisance be abated by improved methods, there would be no assurance that any significant technical improvement would occur.

* * * * *

Moreover, techniques to eliminate dust and other annoying by-products of cement making are unlikely to be developed by any research the defendant can undertake within any short period, but will depend on the total resources of the cement industry nationwide and throughout the world. The problem is universal wherever cement is made.

For obvious reasons the rate of the research is beyond control of defendant. If at the end of 18 months the whole industry has not found a technical solution a court would be hard put to close down this one cement plant if due regard be given to equitable principles.

On the other hand, to grant the injunction unless defendant pays plaintiffs such permanent damages as may be fixed by the court seems to do justice between the contending parties. All of the attributions of economic loss to the properties on which plaintiffs' complaints are based will have been redressed.

The nuisance complained of by these plaintiffs may have other public or private consequences, but these particular parties are the only ones who have sought remedies and the judgment proposed will fully redress them. The limitation of relief granted is a limitation only within the four corners of these actions and does not foreclose public health or other public agencies from seeking proper relief in a proper court.

It seems reasonable to think that the risk of being required to pay permanent damages to injured property owners by cement plant owners would itself be a reasonably effective spur to research for improved techniques to minimize nuisance.

* * * * *

Judge Jasen (dissenting).

It has long been the rule in this State, as the majority acknowledges, that a nuisance which results in substantial continuing damage to neighbors must be enjoined. . . . To now change the rule to permit the cement company to continue polluting the air indefinitely upon the payment of permanent damages is, in my opinion, compounding the magnitude of a very serious problem in our State and Nation today.

In recognition of this problem, the Legislature of this State has enacted the Air Pollution Control Act . . . declaring that it is the State policy to require the use of all available and reasonable methods to prevent and control air pollution.

* * * * *

. . . It is interesting to note that cement production has recently been identified as a significant source of particulate contamination in the Hudson Valley. This type of pollution, wherein very small particles escape and stay in the atmosphere, has been denominated as the type of air pollution which produces the greatest hazard to human health. We have thus a nuisance which not only is damaging to the plaintiffs, but also is decidedly harmful to the general public.

I see grave dangers in overruling our long-established rule of granting an injunction where a nuisance results in substantial continuing damage. In permitting the injunction to become inoperative upon the payment of permanent damages, the majority is, in effect, licensing a continuing wrong. It is the same as saying to the cement company, you may continue to do harm to your neighbors so long as you pay a fee for it. Furthermore, once such permanent damages are assessed and paid, the incentive to alleviate the wrong would be eliminated, thereby continuing air pollution of an area without abatement.

* * * * *

I would enjoin the defendant cement company from continuing the discharge of dust particles upon its neighbors' properties unless, within 18 months, the cement company abated this nuisance.

* * * * *

I am aware that the trial court found that the most modern dust control devices available have been installed in defendant's plant, but, I submit, this does not mean that *better* and more effective dust control devices could not be developed within the time allowed to abate the pollution.

Moreover, I believe it is incumbent upon the defendant to develop such devices, since the cement company, at the time the plant commenced production (1962), was well aware of the plaintiffs' presence in the area, as well as the probable consequences of its contemplated operation. Yet, it still chose to build and operate the plant at this site.

Questions

1. What remedy was mandated by the *Boomer* court?
2. The defendant was required to pay a ''tax'' for the right to continue to pollute. In your opinion was the court correct in imposing that ''tax'' rather than requiring further pollution abatement? Explain.
3. In a portion of the opinion not reprinted here, the dissenting Judge Jasen argues that the use of permanent money damages in place of an injunction has been limited to cases where ''the use to which the property was intended to be put was primarily for the public benefit.'' Why might the denial of the injunction be acceptable in public benefit cases but not in cases of private benefit?
4. In a portion of the opinion not reprinted here, the dissenting Judge Jasen argues: ''The promotion of the polluting cement company has, in my opinion, no public use or benefit.'' Do you agree? Explain.
5. Plaintiff Webb developed Sun City, a retirement village near Phoenix, Arizona. At the time, a distance of two and one half to three miles separated plaintiff's development from defendant Spur Industries' cattle-feeding operation. The feed lot was well managed and clean for a business of that character. Prior to the Sun City project the area around the feed lot had been largely undeveloped. Sun City and related growth brought large numbers of people in proximity to the cattle lot. As time passed, the two businesses expanded, until at the initiation of the suit, only 500 feet separated the two. Plaintiff filed suit to enjoin defendant's operation as a nuisance. Decide. Explain. See *Spur Industries, Inc.* v. *Del E. Webb Development Co.*, 494 P.2d 700 (1972).

CITIZEN SUITS

Many of the statutes previously discussed provide for citizen suits to be brought against violators. The next two articles take a closer look at such suits—and raise some questions about their desirability and efficacy.

"CITIZEN SUITS" BECOME A POPULAR WEAPON IN THE FIGHT AGAINST INDUSTRIAL POLLUTERS

Barry Meier

A new mobile laboratory tests for chemical pollutants in Connecticut soil, courtesy of General Electric Co. Olin Corp. is underwriting environmental-law enforcement in Louisiana. Bethlehem Steel Corp. is helping to clean up Chesapeake Bay.

This corporate largess wasn't volunteered. The contributions stem from "citizen suits," an increasingly common type of environmental lawsuit in which activists sue polluters on their own behalf and then help to decide how any settlement funds will be spent. Over the past four years, an estimated 600 citizen suits have been filed against scores of companies by individuals and such environmentalist groups as the Natural Resources Defense Council and the Sierra Club.

Not surprisingly, the suits have ignited controversy. Some corporate officials argue that many of the actions are frivolous. Others charge that the suits are being used to coerce contributions for pet projects.

Despite such contentions, the number of citizen suits is expected to continue rising, along with the stakes involved. Congress recently approved amendments to the Clean Water Act—the federal statute under which most of the suits are filed—that increase daily fines for each violation to $25,000 from $10,000. And a new round of citizen actions is anticipated. "Three years from now I expect to have a couple hundred of these cases going," says James Thornton, a lawyer with the New York-based NRDC, which has brought more than 100 citizen suits.

Targeting the Companies

Citizen suits began in the 1970s as a result of provisions in federal environmental legislation. Typically, they were directed against the federal and state governments, with the aim of compelling them to enforce the laws. In the early 1980s, the focus of the suits started to shift toward the polluters themselves.

Nearly all U.S. environmental laws empower citizens to sue companies for pollution and recover legal fees in addition to damage or settlement awards if successful. But most citizen suits are brought under the Clean Water Act because it requires companies to file public reports listing pollutant discharges into public sewerage systems. . . .

* * * * *

Moreover, lawyers note that because of the size of the fines involved, nearly all citizen suits are quickly settled. "These are no-risk lawsuits," says John Proctor, a Washington-based attorney who has defended companies in citizen actions. "It's like going to the bank."

Some of the settlements have been substantial. For example, Bethlehem Steel's participation in the Chesapeake Bay cleanup arose from a recent $1.5 million settlement of a citizen suit brought against it by the NRDC and the Chesapeake Bay Foundation, another activist group. As part of the plan, the company also agreed to pay an additional $500,000 to cover the groups' legal expenses.

While companies can pay settlement awards to the federal or state governments, most agree to give the money to an environmental group or specific project. "If you make a contribution, it's tax deductible," says John Frawley, a top environmental official with Hercules, Inc., a Wilmington, Delaware-based chemical producer. . . .

* * * * *

As citizen suits mount, corporate frustration with them is increasing. Mr. Frawley, for example, maintains that some permit violations are inevitable because of equipment malfunctions or regulatory delays in approving new pollution-control programs. He contends, too, that companies are frequently sued over minor infractions that don't pose a serious threat.

Corporate officials have also charged that citizen suits are often merely fund-raising schemes. . . .

* * * * *

Activists such as Mr. Thornton contend that environmental donations are a fitting way to resolve citizen actions. They also note that companies are free to donate settlement proceeds to government agencies, but don't because they would lose tax benefits.

Not all citizen suits end in acrimony. Two years ago, in the face of a citizen suit brought by the NRDC, officials at a Texas Instruments, Inc., metal-finishing plant in Attleboro, Massachusetts, convinced the activists that the facility's violations weren't serious. The NRDC dropped the action, and plant officials in turn funded a one-day seminar on pollution controls for several hundred local metal-finishing companies. . . .

Source: *The Wall Street Journal,* April 17, 1987, p. 11. Reprinted by permission of *The Wall Street Journal,* © Dow Jones & Company, Inc. 1987. ALL RIGHTS RESERVED.

ENDLESS TRIAL: DIOXIN DAMAGE SUIT TIES UP COURTHOUSE AND ANGERS JUDICIARY

Patricia Bellew Gray

Belleville, Illinois—The 488th day of trial resumes with a discussion of shinsplints, which follows three years of testimony on such ailments as diaper rash, halitosis, and leukemia. By the time the doctor on the stand painstakingly picks his way through a scholarly discourse on the shin's location, a delicate snore whistles through the courtroom.

Four jurors are sound asleep, including one elderly man who has donned sunglasses to block the light. One man trims his nails with a pocketknife and a woman examines the contents of her purse. . . .

Kemner versus Monsanto is breaking other records, too. The longest jury trial in the nation's history, it has held 14 jurors hostage to this sort of mind-numbing tedium since early 1984. At issue is whether 65 residents of Sturgeon, Missouri, were harmed when 22,000 gallons of wood-preserving chemicals spilled from a rail car in the center of their town eight years ago. The chemicals contained minute traces of dioxin—about a thimbleful in all.

Catalog of Ailments

The plaintiffs complain that their exposure to the dioxin caused a catalog of ailments, such as headaches, insomnia, and depression, and heightened their risk of developing more serious ailments. They seek millions of dollars in damages from Monsanto Co., the St. Louis manufacturer of the chemicals.

Both sides are spending millions of dollars to present their cases to the jury, whose members get $5 a day for dutifully enduring it all. So far, 130 witnesses have testified and more than 5,000 exhibits have been displayed. And no one seems to know when this desperate battle will end.

. . . The trial began with 12 jurors and six alternates. So far, four jurors have been excused for ill health. Only two alternates remain. The loss of three more jurors will mean a mistrial.

. . . [A]fter Kemner versus Monsanto marked its second year in trial, lawyers and judges complained that the case was delaying other cases in one of the state's busiest courts. Advocates of court reform point to the case as an example of litigants' abuse of the courts—and of a judiciary too timid to stop it. Kemner versus Monsanto, they say, is litigation out of control.

* * * * *

Toxic-tort cases can be difficult to try because the link between plaintiffs' injuries and their exposure to a toxic substance is hard to prove. Dioxin cases are even tougher because there is little research on the long-term health effects of exposure. Thus, trials often turn into battles of expert witnesses.

* * * * *

The January 1979 spill forced a two-day evacuation of Sturgeon, a hard-scrabble farm town of 900 in mid-Missouri. When residents returned, they complained of watery eyes, nausea, and difficulty breathing. A powerful stench hung over the town. Then in February, Monsanto disclosed that the rail car had contained traces of dioxin. Panic swept the town.

By mid-summer 1979, 57 lawsuits had been filed. . . .

* * * * *

Monsanto had sought a mistrial last year on the grounds that no jury could make sense of the marathon trial. But the plaintiffs' lawyers assert that the company is taking a classic defense tactic—delay—to new extremes. Judge Goldenhersh apparently agrees. The company's tedious cross-examinations are often of "questionable relevance," the judge wrote in an order denying the mistrial request. . . .

* * * * *

Courtroom observers say that by establishing a reputation as a fierce adversary with an apparently unlimited budget for battle, Monsanto may discourage similar cases in the future. . . .

* * * * *

Questions

1. *a.* Should environmental pollution cases based on statutes be allowed to be brought by injured parties?
   b. By environmental groups? Develop the best arguments you can on both sides of these questions.
2. *a.* Are environmental pollution cases appropriate for resolution by juries? Why?
   b. Will judges be too pro-business? Explain.
3. How should claims like that made in *Kemner* v. *Monsanto* be resolved?
4. Dow Chemical was a major producer of the herbicide 2,4,5–T, a part of the Agent Orange defoliant used in Vietnam. Dioxin is an unwanted by-product of the manufacture of herbicides. Dioxin was present in the Agent Orange used in Vietnam. Twenty thousand veterans and their families filed suit against Dow and other manufacturers, alleging severe injuries from use of the dioxin-contaminated Agent Orange. Their lawsuit alleged that Dow documents reveal the company's knowledge of dioxin hazards as early as the mid-1960s. According

to documents gathered for the lawsuit, Dow's toxicology director wrote in 1965 to another Dow official that dioxin "is exceptionally toxic; it has tremendous potential for producing chloracne [an ugly skin disease] and systemic injury."[22] The suit was settled out of court with $180 million plus interest to be divided among the plaintiffs over the expected 25-year life of the fund. The chemical companies acknowledged no wrongdoing. (It should be understood that definitive proof of a link between Agent Orange and afflictions other than chloracne has not yet been established to the satisfaction of the government or industry.)

a. Must we simply accept hazards like dioxin as an inevitable by-product of our society's heavy reliance on exotic chemicals? Explain.

b. Or should we erect even firmer civil and criminal law mechanisms for attacking firms that produce contaminants? Explain.

EFFECTIVENESS OF THE ENVIRONMENTAL PROTECTION SYSTEM

We are committing enormous resources to environmental protection and improvement. Are we receiving our money's worth? Public opinion may or may not constitute an accurate assessment of the value of our environmental policy. However, that opinion most assuredly offers evidence of likely directions in government programs. We have ample polling evidence to confirm the view that the public supports governmental pollution control efforts. A 1981 Harris poll found 42 percent of the public feeling that federal air pollution standards are "not protective enough," 40 percent thought the standards "just about right," and 19 percent thought the government "overly protective of people's health."[23] A 1983 ABC News/*Washington Post* poll found similar results:

> Most Americans don't think air pollution, unsafe drinking water, or toxic wastes are serious problems in the area where they live, but most don't want the government to relax antipollution laws, either. On the contrary, even though the large majority of Americans believe compliance with antipollution laws costs business firms at least a fair amount of money, more than three out of four say those laws are worth the cost. . . .[24]

And in a 1985 Common Cause survey, 86 percent of the respondents wanted more extensive government regulation of the environment even if that effort would result in higher taxes and higher deficits.[25] In the late 1980s, public support for environmental regulation is firm. Other issues such as drug use, crime, and the federal deficit may be more compelling, but any sharp governmental retreat on environmental questions would not be well received. Perhaps the highly publicized problems of the greenhouse effect, acid rain, depletion of the ozone layer, and numerous chemical/oil spills have convinced the populace that the problem is real and that the government is a necessary ingredient in resolving the problem. And the fact that the air is visibly cleaner and the water now purer than prior to the government's environmental intervention presumably has not been lost on the public.

At the same time, we have paid a heavy price for the cleanup. According to the EPA, the total bill for complying with air and water pollution standards for the 1980s is expected to reach about $525 billion.[26] One percent of our GNP is devoted to air and water cleanup.[27] And additional money is spent on managing hazardous wastes. Whether the benefits of pollution regulation exceed the costs cannot be definitively established. In addition to the various direct costs of environmental regulation, we can see that those regulations often have a profound ripple impact on the successful practice of business. For example, plant closings causing the loss of thousands of jobs have been attributed entirely or partially to environmental requirements.

> Phelps Dodge Co., in closing its New Cornelia smelter in Ajo, Ariz., . . .said that, under present circumstances in the world copper market, it could not justify spending $5 million to install air pollution control equipment needed to meet EPA standards on particulate emissions. The closure idled 235 workers in the small desert town for an indefinite period.[28]

A 1983 study by economist B. Peter Pashigian concludes that one of the results of environmental regulation is that it is now more difficult for small plants to compete with large ones. Environmental regulation, he demonstrates, has reduced the number of plants in industries with emission problems, and it has raised average plant size. Via a sophisticated statistical analysis he shows that "compliance with environmental regulation was the major reason for the decline in the small plants' market share in high-pollution industries after 1972."[29]

Thus, while the gains have been striking, the bill is enormous. Whether the benefits of pollution regulation exceed the costs defies accurate quantification. However, we do know with certainty that the public is convinced that the investment is wise and, indeed, necessary.

Part Five—The Business Response

Pollution control is a pressing and difficult problem. The business community's role in resolving the dilemma has been one of ambivalence. Certainly the business community has invested heavily in corrective measures, both voluntarily and at government insistence, but business has also lobbied extensively for adjustments in governmental expectations (such as relaxed clean air standards and increased off-shore oil and gas drilling). Identifying the correct course for business is largely a matter of philosophy. The two articles that follow illustrate a number of ways business has responded to environmental considerations.

A FLORIDA UTILITY WINS NATURALISTS' PRAISE FOR GUARDING WILDLIFE

Eric Morgenthaler

Turkey Point, Florida—As a great blue heron glides off from the bank ahead, two Florida Power & Light Co. airboats rip down a cooling canal near the company's nuclear plant here and ease to a stop on a muddy bank. Ross Wilcox climbs out of the first of the boats, walks up the bank, and pauses to examine a small indentation in the mud.

It is a crocodile nest.

Before FPL built its plant here in the early 1970s, crocodiles didn't nest at Turkey Point, a finger of land on the southeast edge of the Florida peninsula. But as a condition for approving the plant, regulators required FPL to dig a huge grid of cooling canals to prevent the plant's warm-water discharges from harming the marine life in adjacent Biscayne Bay. The canals soon began attracting crocodiles. Today, there seems to be a population of 25 or 30 adults, making the nuclear plant one of only three places in the United States known to have breeding populations of the . . . species. . . .

Extra Effort

Mr. Wilcox, as FPL's chief ecologist, is the utility's point man for the big reptiles. This morning, he is lobbying plant managers, who have joined him on the inspection tour, to create buffer zones around any crocodile nests they find. By afternoon, the managers agree.

"What we're trying to show is that with a little extra effort on our part or understanding of the species, our activities can be compatible with the needs of wildlife," . . . says Mr. Wilcox, who has a doctorate in oceanography.

In addition to his crocodile responsibilities, Mr. Wilcox is also the point man for manatees, sea turtles, wood storks, bald eagles, indigo snakes, and the many other endangered or threatened species that live on FPL property. His job is a sign of how the environmental movement of the 1970s continues to affect business in the 1980s, as environmental management becomes an increasingly mainstream corporate specialty. It is also part of an effort that has made FPL, Florida's largest electric utility and a unit of FPL Group, Inc., a company that even environmentalists praise for its efforts to fit in with the natural world.

Corporate Award

"There's a certain amount of public relations behind it, which is expectable in any sort of business venture," says Charles Lee, a long-time environmental activist and senior vice president of the Florida Audubon Society. "But our experience with FPL in its environmental programs has been very good."

He says people such as Mr. Wilcox "are environmental professionals" who "have a real and genuine feeling for these issues and want to do the right thing." He adds that their sensitivity "sort of permeates up through the company," though it "perhaps gets diluted a little bit along the way." . . .

* * * * *

. . . "We feel it's wiser to work with them than against them," says Edward Colson, a senior biologist with Pacific Gas & Electric Co., California's biggest utility, who adds that his company gets along "extremely well" with environmentalists these days. "That has evolved since the 70s, when confrontations were common and frequent," he says.

Attitudes vary, of course. Companies that, unlike utilities, aren't subject to close regulatory review still sometimes tear up the land with impunity. And many environmentalists remain skeptical of corporate claims of sensitivity. . . .

Even companies with well-regarded environmental programs are often faulted for other aspects of their operations. Nuclear power itself remains very controversial, and FPL has been fined on several occasions for operating problems at its plants. . . .

* * * * *

FPL formed its environmental affairs department in 1972, after it was burned badly in a battle over construction of the Turkey Point plant. The company originally planned to discharge the plant's cooling water directly into Biscayne Bay; but environmentalists and others persuaded regulators to require FPL to dig some 168 miles of cooling canals (the same ones that later attracted crocodiles). The changes in plans, as well as delays, pushed the project millions of dollars over budget.

Like many companies in those days, FPL was caught completely off guard by the ferocity of the environmental attack. "They had no concept that warm-water pollution might be a problem," says Audubon's Mr. Lee. But, he adds: "They got smart and realized that if they brought some good environmental scientists on board, they would be in a much better position to watch their own operations."

Today, the environmental affairs department comprises 35 people, including a toxicologist, a meteorologist and a geohydrologist. . . .

* * * * *

This is all driven by good business," says Mr. Wilcox, who has worked for FPL since 1975. "When I call up an agency and say I need a permit to do something, I don't walk in with two strikes against me." The environmental monitoring also provides a strong data base to back up company proposals. "All you need is for a major project not to be tied up in litigation for a couple of months, with interest charges and so on, and the crocodile program has paid for itself," Mr. Wilcox says.

It is difficult to separate out the cost of such programs, but in the overall scheme of things—FPL Group last year had sales of $4.09 billion—it clearly isn't much. "They're not terribly expensive," Mr. Tucker says of the endangered species efforts. "Not expensive at all in terms of the benefits derived."

* * * * *

REQUIRED ENVIRONMENTAL INSPECTIONS BECOME COMMON

Bill Paul

Jersey City, New Jersey—The environmental inspection is becoming to industrial and commercial property sales what the termite inspection is to home sales.

Some states are imposing regulations requiring sellers to notify buyers that hazardous waste has been disposed of or stored on a given parcel. . . .

* * * * *

The courts, too, are spurring environmental inspections. Lending institutions increasingly require inspections in the wake of recent rulings that found them potentially liable for contamination on property on which they foreclosed.

Toughest in New Jersey

"This issue is becoming pervasive," says Leo Motiuk, chairman of the environmental law committee of the American Bar Association's real property section. Adds Steven A. Tasher, coauthor of a handbook on environmental laws and real estate: "You have to be an idiot not to look at the [environmental] risks before buying a piece of property."

* * * * *

Business is booming for the hundreds of independent consultants who perform most environmental inspections, which typically cost a few thousand dollars and can take from a day to several weeks. . . .

* * * * *

Source: *The Wall Street Journal*, October 13, 1987, p. 6. Reprinted by permission of *The Wall Street Journal*, © Dow Jones & Company, Inc. 1987. ALL RIGHTS RESERVED.

Part Six—Environmental Protection Abroad

As suggested earlier in this chapter, the United States is not the only country facing environmental pollution at home.

THIRD WORLD NATIONS START FACING UP TO SEVERE POLLUTION PROBLEMS

Peter Grier

In Chile, the government last year set aside the first National Chinchilla Reserve to protect the endangered Long-Tailed Chinchilla. . . .

India, where about 2 million acres of forest are stripped down for fuelwood each year, in 1981 launched a $125 million "social forestry" program.

The environmental ethic is not limited to rich, developed nations. In 1972, only 11 Third World countries had environmental agencies. Today 110 have arms of the government whose sole purpose is to protect land, water, and air. . . .

But these fledgling Environmental Protection Agencies face daunting problems. Some of the nastiest pollution in the world occurs in small, poor nations. And "even those countries with established environmental regulations often do not have the resources—technical, human, and financial—to monitor and enforce them," concludes the United Nations World Environment Handbook.

Take Kenya, one of the most environmentally advanced countries in Africa, according to the UN. Kenya's Ministry of Environment and Natural Resources, now five years old, has 30 scientists to deal with the pollution caused by the fastest-growing population in the world.

The demand for fuelwood in Kenya is so great that there will be little forest left in a decade, unless depletion slows. Coastal factories often pollute with impunity. Dairy-processing waste and slaughterhouse refuse is dumped directly into the waterways surrounding Mombasa and into Lake Victoria. . . .

A sampling of environmental actions in other nations, as detailed in the UN handbook, includes:

* * * * *

Cuba
Cuba's Center for the Protection of the Environment and Rational Use of National Resources was established in 1980, along with bylaws protecting soil, forests, air, and water.

The cleanup of Havana Harbor is listed as a national priority in the country's latest five-year plan; a reforestation program has already begun. Ironically, one area of the country that is endangered by population expansion is the Sierra Maestra Range—the pine woodlands that sheltered President Fidel Castro's guerrillas before the revolution.

* * * * *

Philippines
The Philippines, an archipelago of some 7,000 islands, has much coastline, and much coastline pollution. Half the coral reefs surrounding the islands are dead or dying, according to UN estimates. The country's national Pollution Control Commission was created in 1964 but has come under criticism from other government agencies for lax enforcement.

Mexico
The rapid urbanization of Mexico has created some of the most acute pollution problems in the world. Mexico City's smog is legendary; the Panuco River basin, on the Gulf coast, receives untreated waste from 15 million people and 35,000 industries. A Secretariat of Urban Development and Ecology was recently established, but "environmental degradation, caused in large part by poverty, is worsening," the UN warns.

Source: *The Christian Science Monitor,* October 11, 1984, p. 3. Reprinted by permission from *The Christian Science Monitor.* © 1984 The Christian Science Publishing Society. All rights reserved.

Question

What advice would you give a developing country on an appropriate stance on environmental protection? Be realistic in terms of recognizing probable budget and technology constraints.

CHAPTER QUESTIONS

1. Why might the cost of environmental compliance affect small plants and large plants differently?
2. Economist B. Peter Pashigian: "It is widely thought that environmental controls are guided by the public-spirited ideal of correcting for 'negative externalities'—the pollution costs that spill over from private operations. This view is not wrong by any means. But it is

suspiciously incomplete. After all, there are numerous studies of regulatory programs in other fields that show how private interests have used public powers for their own enrichment.''[30] What forces in addition to correcting for negative externalities might be influencing the course of federal pollution control?

3. William Tucker argues that environmentalism is ''essentially aristocratic in its roots and derives from the land- and nature-based ethic that has been championed by upper classes throughout history. Large landowners and titled aristocracies . . . have usually held a set of ideals that stresses 'stewardship' and the husbanding of existing resources over exploration and discovery. This view favors handicrafts over mass production and the inheritance ethic over the business ethic.''[31]

   Tucker goes on to argue that environmentalism favors the economic and social interests of the well-off. He says people of the upper middle class see their future in universities and the government bureaucracy. They have little economic stake in industrial expansion. Indeed, such expansion might threaten their suburban property values. Comment.

4. Culprits in indoor pollution include cigarette smoke, asbestos, carbon monoxide from heaters, and radon. The problem has been exacerbated in recent years by our success in ''tightening'' buildings as an energy conservation measure. The EPA is beginning to explore the question of indoor pollution. Assume the EPA finds a problem roughly as threatening to our welfare as that of external air pollution. Should the government intervene? Explain.

5. The Fifth Amendment to the Constitution provides that private property cannot be taken for public use without just compensation. Four oil companies had entered a lease arrangement with the federal government for oil and gas rights in the Santa Barbara Channel, off the California coast. Two productive platforms had been erected, and a third was requested. The request was granted, but before the platform was constructed one of the earlier wells experienced a ''blowout,'' causing enormous ecological damage in the Santa Barbara Channel. The secretary of the interior then suspended all operations in the channel pending congressional cancellation of the leases. The oil companies then brought suit. Does the indefinite suspension of oil-drilling rights constitute a ''taking'' in violation of the Fifth Amendment? See *Union Oil Co.* v. *Morton,* 512 F.2d 743 (1975).

6. From its inception in 1981, the administration of President Ronald Reagan made clear its intention to significantly ease environmental controls. By 1983 little reform had been achieved, and Congress was considering tighter regulation in certain areas. Scandals involving EPA chief Anne Gorsuch and administrator Rita Lavelle diverted the administration's efforts. Consequently, the business community began expressing disillusionment with the Reagan approach:

The bruising congressional battles and resulting delay have prompted many businesspeople to argue that the administration must be prepared to compromise. Public interest in environmental protection "is alive and well . . .," says S. Bruce Smart, the chairman of Continental Group, Inc. Corporate executives, he maintains, are beginning to realize that "business as usual must give way to environmental realities."[32]

Do you favor former President Reagan's firmer position or the more conciliatory approach suggested by Smart? Explain.

7. It is argued that so-called frost belt states will be particularly insistent on maintaining strict air quality standards for new emission sources.
   a. Other than general concern for air quality, why would the frost belt states have a particular interest in maintaining those standards?
   b. Might the frost belt states be expected to modify that stand over time? Explain.

8. In reviewing the first year of the Reagan administration's environmental reform efforts, Robert Crandall argues:

   I agree, however, that our best chances for regulatory reform in certain environmental areas, particularly in air pollution policy, come from the states. Probably, responsibility for environmental regulation belongs with the states anyway, and most of it ought to be returned there.[33]

   a. What reasoning supports Crandall's notion that responsibility for environmental regulation belongs with the states?
   b. How might one reason to the contrary?
   c. If the power were yours, would environmental regulation rest primarily at the state or the federal level? Explain.

9. Why do plaintiffs typically experience great difficulty in prevailing in negligence actions alleging injury from toxic substances?

10. The doctrine of strict liability—originally applied to extra-hazardous activities and more recently to defective products—may be extended to the area of toxic waste. Jeremy Main commented on that possibility in *Fortune* magazine:

    If strict liability were now extended to toxic wastes, then it would do a company no good to plead that it had obeyed the laws and followed approved procedures when it disposed of its wastes. It would still be liable, even if the hazards are seen only in retrospect.[34]

    Should the strict liability doctrine routinely be extended to toxic waste cases? Explain.

11. The Pennsylvania Coal Company owned coal land in the drainage basin of the Meadow Brook. The company's mining operation released water into the brook, thus polluting it. Sanderson owned land near the stream, and she had been securing water from it. However, the mining operation rendered the stream useless for Sanderson's purposes. Sanderson filed suit against the coal company. In 1886 a

final verdict was rendered in the case. Should Sanderson prevail? See *Pennsylvania Coal Co.* v. *Sanderson and Wife,* 6 A. 453 (1886).

12. In a realignment of resources, the U.S. Army decided to close the Lexington-Blue Grass Army Depot. The expected loss of over 2,600 jobs caused various parties to file suit in an effort to stop the closing. The plaintiffs contended that the Army and the Department of Defense violated the National Environmental Policy Act by failing to file an environmental impact statement. NEPA requires an EIS in all cases of "major federal actions significantly affecting the quality of the human environment." Decide. Explain. See *Breckinridge* v. *Rumsfeld,* 537 F.2d 864 (1976), cert. denied 429 U.S. 1061 (1977).

13. A number of groups and individuals filed suit to block Duke Power's planned construction of nuclear power plants in North and South Carolina. The plaintiffs challenged the federal Price-Anderson Act, which provided that damages resulting from nuclear incidents would be limited to $560 million. In the event of damages exceeding $560 million, the act provided that Congress would review the situation and take appropriate action. The district court had ruled that there was a "substantial likelihood" that Duke would not be able to complete the plant unless protected by the act. The district court ruled that the $560 million limit in the act violated the constitutional requirement that neither life nor property may be taken by the government without due process of law. The case was appealed to the U.S. Supreme Court. Decide. Explain. See *Duke Power Co.* v. *Carolina Environmental Study Group, Inc.,* 438 U.S. 59 (1978).

14. Environmental protection has become a "religion," of sorts, to many Americans. (See William Tucker, "Of Mites and Men," *Harpers,* August 1978, p. 43.) Have we devoted too much of our attention and resources to the environmental cause? Explain.

NOTES

1. The author owes a debt to Professor James Freeman of the University of Kentucky for his significant contributions to this chapter.

2. Elliot D. Lee, "Pending Treaty Worries Chlorofluorocarbon Industry," *The Wall Street Journal,* September 15, 1987, p. 6. Reprinted by permission of *The Wall Street Journal,* © Dow Jones & Company, Inc. 1988. ALL RIGHTS RESERVED.

3. Ellen Graham, "Jump in 1986 Death Rate Sparks Dispute," *The Wall Street Journal,* February 8, 1988, p. 6. Reprinted by permission of *The Wall Street Journal,* © Dow Jones & Company, Inc. 1988. ALL RIGHTS RESERVED.

4. John Urquhart, "Taking His Acid Rain Fight on the Road," *The Wall Street Journal,* October 16, 1987, p. 28. Reprinted by permission of *The Wall Street Journal,* © Dow Jones & Company, Inc. 1987. ALL RIGHTS RESERVED.

5. R. M. Srivastava, "Dumping Trash on Third World," *Des Moines Register,* February 13, 1987, p. 9A.

6. 1981 Ohio River Basin Energy Study, as reported in Guy Molinari, "Why We Need a Strong Clean Air Act," *Sierra,* May–June 1982, p. 86.

7. Robert E. Taylor, "Despite Nearly Two Decades of Federal Efforts, Many in the United States Still Breathe Unhealthy Air," *The Wall Street Journal,* April 6, 1987, p. 52. Reprinted by permission of *The Wall Street Journal,* © Dow Jones & Company, Inc. 1987. ALL RIGHTS RESERVED.

8. *Chevron U.S.A., Inc.* v. *Natural Resources Defense Council, Inc.,* 467 U.S. 837 (1984).

9. "Current Developments," *Environment Reporter* 16, no. 6 (June 7, 1985), p. 235.

10. Ibid.

11. See The Council on Environmental Quality, *Environmental Quality 1982* (Washington, D.C.: U.S. Government Printing Office, 1983), pp. 206–7.

12. "Current Developments," *Environment Reporter* 16, no. 4 (May 24, 1985), pp. 166–67.

13. Andy Pasztor, "Dump-Cleanup Effort Gets Mired in Politics, High Costs, Red Tape," *The Wall Street Journal,* March 11, 1983, p. 1.

14. The remarks in this paragraph are entirely the product of advice from co-author Amy Gershenfeld Donnella.

15. Matthew Purdy, "Superfund Bill Is Signed by President," *Des Moines Register,* October 18, 1986, p. 1A.

16. "Current Developments," *Environment Reporter* 16, no. 1 (May 3, 1985), p. 7.

17. Council on Environmental Quality, *Environmental Quality 1982,* p. 8.

18. John R. Emshwiller, "California Ushers in Environmental Law Placing Warning Levels on 29 Substances," *The Wall Street Journal,* February 23, 1988, p. 62. Reprinted by permission of *The Wall Street Journal,* © Dow Jones & Company, Inc. 1988. ALL RIGHTS RESERVED.

19. Christopher B. Leinberger, "Curbing Growth Controls," *The Wall Street Journal,* January 22, 1987, p. 28. Reprinted by permission of *The Wall Street Journal,* © Dow Jones & Company, Inc. 1987. ALL RIGHTS RESERVED.

20. *Village of Belle Terre* v. *Boraas,* 416 U.S. 1, 10 (1974).

21. Leinberger, "Curbing Growth Controls."

22. "No Longer So Secret an Agent," *Time,* July 18, 1983, p. 17.

23. Survey by Louis Harris and Associates, May 6–10, 1981, as reported in *Public Opinion,* February/March 1982, p. 32.

24. Paul Cramer, "Reagan Gets Bad Marks on the Environment: Public Does Not Want Pollution Laws Relaxed," ABC News/*Washington Post* Poll, April 1983, p. 4. Reported by Robert Cameron Mitchell, "Public Opinion and Environmental Politics in the 1970s and 1980s," In Norman J. Vig and Michael E. Kraft, *Environmental Policy in the 1980s: Reagan's New Agenda* (Washington, D.C.: Congressional Quarterly Press, 1984), p. 56.

25. "Issues Poll Results—1985," *Common Cause Magazine*, May/June 1985, as reported in George A. Steiner and John F. Steiner, *Business, Government, and Society*, 5th Edition (New York: Random House, 1988), p. 407.

26. "15 Years of Pollution Control Laws Reflect Intensive Period of Institutionalization, Cleanup, Litigation, Investment, Public Awareness," *Current Developments, Environment Reporter*, May 3, 1985, p. 12.

27. Ibid.

28. Ibid.

29. B. Peter Pashigian, "How Large and Small Plants Fare under Environmental Regulation," *Regulation*, September/October 1983, pp. 19, 23.

30. Ibid., p. 19.

31. "Tucker contra Sierra," *Regulation,* March/April 1983, pp. 48–49.

32. Andy Pasztor, "Reagan Goal of Easing Environmental Laws Is Largely Unattained," *The Wall Street Journal,* February 18, 1983, pp. 1, 16.

33. Robert Crandall, "The Environment," in "Regulation—The First Year," *Regulation,* January/February 1982, pp. 19, 29, 31.

34. Jeremy Main, "The Hazards of Helping Toxic Waste Victims," *Fortune,* October 31, 1983, pp. 158, 166.

The Constitution of the United States of America

Preamble

We the People of the United States, in Order to form a more perfect Union, establish Justice, insure domestic Tranquility, provide for the common defence, promote the general Welfare, and secure the Blessings of Liberty to ourselves and our Posterity, do ordain and establish this Constitution for the United States of America.

Article I

Section 1. All legislative Powers herein granted shall be vested in a Congress of the United States, which shall consist of a Senate and House of Representatives.

Section 2. (1) The House of Representatives shall be composed of Members chosen every second Year by the People of the several States, and the Electors in each State shall have the Qualifications requisite for Electors of the most numerous Branch of the State Legislature.

(2) No Person shall be a Representative who shall not have attained to the Age of twenty-five Years, and been seven Years a Citizen of the United States, and who shall not, when elected, be an Inhabitant of that State in which he shall be chosen.

(3) Representatives and direct Taxes shall be apportioned among the several States which may be included within this Union, according to their respective Numbers, which shall be determined by adding to the whole Number of free Persons, including those bound to Service for a Term of Years, and excluding Indians not taxed, three fifths of all other Persons.[1] The actual Enumeration shall be made within three Years after the first Meeting of the Congress of the United States, and within every subsequent Term of ten Years, in such Manner as they shall by Law direct. The Number of Representatives shall not exceed one for

---

[1]Refer to the Fourteenth Amendment.

every thirty Thousand, but each State shall have at Least one Representative; and until such enumeration shall be made, the State of New Hampshire shall be entitled to chuse three, Massachusetts eight, Rhode Island and Providence Plantations one, Connecticut five, New York six, New Jersey four, Pennsylvania eight, Delaware one, Maryland six, Virginia ten, North Carolina five, South Carolina five, and Georgia three.

(4) When vacancies happen in the Representation from any State, the Executive Authority thereof shall issue Writs of Election to fill such Vacancies.

(5) The House of Representation shall chuse their Speaker and other Officers; and shall have the sole Power of Impeachment.

Section 3. (1) The Senate of the United States shall be composed of two Senators from each State, chosen by the Legislature thereof,[2] for six Years; and each Senator shall have one Vote.

(2) Immediately after they shall be assembled in Consequence of the first Election, they shall be divided as equally as may be into three Classes. The Seats of the Senators of the first Class shall be vacated at the Expiration of the Second Year, of the second Class at the Expiration of the fourth Year, and of the third Class at the Expiration of the sixth Year, so that one third may be chosen every second Year; and if Vacancies happen by Resignation, or otherwise, during the Recess of the Legislature of any State, the Executive thereof may make temporary Appointments until the next Meeting of the Legislature, which shall then fill such Vacancies.[3]

(3) No Person shall be a Senator who shall not have attained to the Age of thirty Years, and been nine Years a Citizen of the United States, and who shall not, when elected, be an Inhabitant of that State for which he shall be chosen.

(4) The Vice President of the United States shall be President of the Senate, but shall have no Vote, unless they be equally divided.

(5) The Senate shall chuse their other Officers, and also a President pro tempore, in the Absence of the Vice President, or when he shall exercise the Office of President of the United States.

(6) The Senate shall have the sole Power to try all Impeachments. When sitting for that Purpose, they shall be on Oath or Affirmation. When the President of the United States is tried, the Chief Justice shall preside: And no Person shall be convicted without the Concurrence of two thirds of the Members present.

(7) Judgment in Cases of Impeachment shall not extend further than to removal from Office, and disqualification to hold and enjoy any Office of honor, Trust, or Profit under the United States: but the Party convicted shall nevertheless be liable and subject to Indictment, Trial, Judgment, and Punishment, according to Law.

Section 4. (1) The Times, Places and Manner of holding Elections for Senators and Representatives, shall be prescribed in each State by the Legislature thereof; but the Congress may at any time by Law make or alter such Regulations, except as to the Places of chusing Senators.

(2) The Congress shall assemble at least once in every Year, and such Meeting shall be on the first Monday in December, unless they shall by Law appoint a different Day.[4]

---

[2]Refer to the Seventeenth Amendment.
[3]Ibid.
[4]Refer to the Twentieth Amendment.

Section 5. (1) Each House shall be the Judge of the Elections, Returns, and Qualifications of its own Members, and a Majority of each shall constitute a Quorum to do Business; but a smaller Number may adjourn from day to day, and may be authorized to compel the Attendance of absent Members, in such Manner, and under such Penalties as each House may provide.

(2) Each House may determine the Rules of its Proceedings, punish its Members for disorderly Behavior, and, with the Concurrence of two thirds, expel a Member.

(3) Each House shall keep a Journal of its Proceedings, and from time to time publish the same, excepting such Parts as may in their Judgment require Secrecy; and the Yeas and Nays of the Members of either House on any question shall, at the Desire of one fifth of those Present, be entered on the Journal.

(4) Neither House, during the Session of Congress, shall, without the Consent of the other, adjourn for more than three days, nor to any other Place than that in which the two Houses shall be sitting.

Section 6. (1) The Senators and Representatives shall receive a Compensation for their Services, to be ascertained by Law, and paid out of the Treasury of the United States. They shall in all Cases, except Treason, Felony and Breach of the Peace, be privileged from Arrest during their Attendance at the Session of their respective Houses, and in going to and returning from the same; and for any Speech or Debate in either House, they shall not be questioned in any other Place.

(2) No Senator or Representative shall, during the Time for which he was elected, be appointed to any civil Office under the Authority of the United States, which shall have been created, or the Emoluments whereof shall have been encreased during such time; and no Person holding any Office under the United States, shall be a Member of either House during his Continuance in Office.

Section 7. (1) All Bills for raising Revenue shall originate in the House of Representatives; but the Senate may propose or concur with Amendments as on other Bills.

(2) Every Bill which shall have passed the House of Representatives and the Senate, shall, before it becomes a Law, be presented to the President of the United States; If he approve he shall sign it, but if not he shall return it, with his Objections to the House in which it shall have originated, who shall enter the Objections at large on their Journal, and proceed to reconsider it. If after such Reconsideration two thirds of that House shall agree to pass the Bill, it shall be sent together with the Objections, to the other House, by which it shall likewise be reconsidered, and if approved by two thirds of that House, it shall become a Law. But in all such Cases the Votes of both Houses shall be determined by yeas and Nays, and the Names of the Persons voting for and against the Bill shall be entered on the Journal of each House respectively. If any Bill shall not be returned by the President within ten Days (Sundays excepted) after it shall have been presented to him, the Same shall be a Law, in like Manner as if he had signed it, unless the Congress by their Adjournment prevent its Return in which Case it shall not be a Law.

(3) Every Order, Resolution, or Vote, to Which the Concurrence of the Senate and House of Representatives may be necessary (except on a question of Adjournment) shall be presented to the President of the United States; and before the Same shall take Effect, shall be approved by him, or being disapproved by him, shall be repassed by two thirds of the Senate and House of Representatives, according to the Rules and Limitations prescribed in the Case of a Bill.

Section 8. (1) The Congress shall have Power To lay and collect Taxes, Duties, Imposts and Excises, to pay the Debts and provide for the common Defence and general Welfare of the United States; but all Duties, Imposts and Excises shall be uniform throughout the United States;

(2) To borrow money on the credit of the United States;

(3) To regulate Commerce with foreign Nations, and among the several States, and with the Indian Tribes;

(4) To establish an uniform Rule of Naturalization, and uniform Laws on the subject of Bankruptcies throughout the United States;

(5) To coin Money, regulate the Value thereof, and of foreign Coin, and fix the Standard of Weights and Measures;

(6) To provide for the Punishment of counterfeiting the Securities and current Coin of the United States;

(7) To Establish Post Offices and Post Roads;

(8) To promote the Progress of Science and useful Arts, by securing for limited Times to Authors and Inventors the exclusive Right to their respective Writings and Discoveries;

(9) To constitute Tribunals inferior to the supreme Court;

(10) To define and punish Piracies and Felonies committed on the high Seas, and Offenses against the Law of Nations:

(11) To declare War, grant Letters of Marque and Reprisal, and make Rules concerning Captures on Land and Water;

(12) To raise and support Armies, but no Appropriation of Money to that Use shall be for a longer Term than two Years;

(13) To provide and maintain a Navy;

(14) To make Rules for the Government and Regulation of the land and naval Forces;

(15) To provide for calling forth the Militia to execute the Laws of the Union, suppress Insurrections and repel Invasions;

(16) To provide for organizing, arming, and disciplining, the Militia, and for governing such Part of them as may be employed in the Service of the United States, reserving to the States respectively, the Appointment of the Officers, and the Authority of training the Militia according to the discipline prescribed by Congress;

(17) To exercise exclusive Legislation in all Cases whatsoever, over such District (not exceeding ten Miles square) as may, by Cession of particular States, and the Acceptance of Congress, become the Seat of the Government of the United States, and to exercise like Authority over all Places purchased by the Consent of the Legislature of the State in which the Same shall be, for the Election of Forts, Magazines, Arsenals, dock-Yards, and other needful Buildings;—And

(18) To make all Laws which shall be necessary and proper for carrying into Execution for the foregoing Powers, and all other Powers vested by this Constitution in the Government of the United States, or in any Department or Officer thereof.

Section 9. (1) The Migration or Importation of Such Persons as any of the States now existing shall think proper to admit, shall not be prohibited by the Congress prior to the Year one thousand eight hundred and eight, but a Tax or duty may be imposed on such Importation, not exceeding ten dollars for each Person.

(2) The privilege of the Writ of Habeas Corpus shall not be suspended, unless when in Cases of Rebellion or Invasion the public Safety may require it.

(3) No Bill of Attainder or ex post facto Law shall be passed.

(4) No Capitation, or other direct, Tax shall be laid, unless in proportion to the Census or Enumeration herein before directed to be taken.[5]

(5) No Tax or Duty shall be laid on Articles exported from any State.

(6) No Preference shall be given by any Regulation of Commerce or Revenue to the Ports of one State over those of another: nor shall Vessels bound to, or from, one State be obliged to enter, clear, or pay Duties in another.

(7) No money shall be drawn from the Treasury, but in Consequence of Appropriations made by Law; and a regular Statement and Account of the Receipts and Expenditures of all public Money shall be published from time to time.

(8) No Title of Nobility shall be granted by the United States: And no Person holding any Office of Profit or Trust under them, shall, without the Consent of the Congress, accept of any present, Emolument, Office or Title, of any kind whatever, from any King, Prince, or foreign State.

Section 10. (1) No State shall enter into any Treaty, Alliance, or Confederation; grant Letters of Marque and Reprisal; coin Money; emit Bills of Credit; make any Thing but gold and silver Coin a Tender in Payment of Debts; pass any Bill of Attainder, ex post facto Law, or Law impairing the Obligation of Contracts, or grant any Title of Nobility.

(2) No State shall, without the Consent of the Congress, lay any Imposts or Duties on Imports or Exports, except what may be absolutely necessary for executing its inspection Laws: and the net Produce of all Duties and Imposts, laid by any State on Imports or Exports, shall be for the Use of the Treasury of the United States; and all such Laws shall be subject to the Revision and Controul of the Congress.

(3) No State shall, without the Consent of Congress, lay any Duty of Tonnage, keep Troops, or Ships of War in time of Peace, enter into any Agreement or Compact with another State, or with a foreign Power, or engage in War, unless actually invaded, or in such imminent Danger as will not admit of delay.

Article II

Section 1. (1) The executive Power shall be vested in a President of the United States of America. He shall hold his Office during the Term of four Years, and, together with the Vice President, chosen for the same Term, be elected, as follows:

(2) Each State shall appoint, in such Manner as the Legislature thereof may direct, a Number of Electors, equal to the whole Number of Senators and Representatives to which the State may be entitled in the Congress; but no Senator or Representative, or Person holding an Office of Trust or Profit under the United States, shall be appointed an Elector.

(3) The Electors shall meet in their respective States, and vote by Ballot for two Persons, of whom one at least shall not be an Inhabitant of the same State with themselves. And they shall make a List of all the Persons voted for, and of the Number of Votes for each; which List they shall sign and certify, and transmit sealed to the Seat of the Government of the United States, directed to the President

---

[5]Refer to the Sixteenth Amendment.

of the Senate. The President of the Senate shall, in the Presence of the Senate and House of Representatives, open all the Certificates, and the Votes shall then be counted. The Person having the greatest Number of Votes shall be the President, if such Number be a Majority of the whole Number of Electors appointed; and if there be more than one who have such Majority, and have an equal Number of Votes, then the House of Representatives shall immediately chuse by Ballot one of them for President; and if no Person have a Majority, then from the five highest on the List the said House shall in like Manner chuse the President. But in chusing the President, the Votes shall be taken by States, the Representation from each State have one Vote; A quorum for this Purpose shall consist of a Member or Members from two thirds of the States, and a Majority of all the States shall be necessary to a Choice. In every Case, after the Choice of the President, the Person having the greater Number of Votes of the Electors shall be the Vice President. But if there should remain two or more who have equal Votes, the Senate shall chuse from them by Ballot the Vice President.[6]

(4) The Congress may determine the Time of chusing the Electors, and the Day on which they shall give their Votes; which Day shall be the same throughout the United States.

(5) No person except a natural born Citizen, or a Citizen of the United States, at the time of the Adoption of this Constitution, shall be eligible to the Office of President; neither shall any Person be eligible to that Office who shall not have attained to the Age of thirty-five Years, and been fourteen Years a Resident within the United States.

(6) In case of the removal of the President from Office, or of his Death, Resignation or Inability to discharge the Powers and Duties of the said Office, the Same shall devolve on the Vice President, and the Congress may by Law provide for the Case of Removal, Death, Resignation or Inability, both of the President and Vice President, declaring what Officer shall then act as President, and such Officer shall act accordingly, until the Disability be removed, or a President shall be elected.[7]

(7) The President shall, at stated Times, receive for his Services, a Compensation, which shall neither be encreased nor diminished during the Period for which he shall have been elected, and he shall not receive within that Period any other Emolument from the United States, or any of them.

(8) Before he enter on the Execution of his Office, he shall take the following Oath or Affirmation: "I do solemnly swear (or affirm) that I will faithfully execute the Office of President of the United States, and will to the best of my Ability, preserve, protect and defend the Constitution of the United States."

Section 2. (1) The President shall be Commander in Chief of the Army and Navy of the United States, and of the militia of the several States, when called into the actual Service of the United States; he may require the Opinion, in writing, of the principal Officer in each of the executive Departments, upon any Subject relating to the Duties of their respective Offices, and he shall have Power to grant Reprieves and Pardons for Offenses against the United States, except in Cases of Impeachment.

---

[6]Refer to the Twelfth Amendment.
[7]Refer to the Twenty-fifth Amendment.

(2) He shall have Power, by and with the Advice and Consent of the Senate, to make Treaties, provided two thirds of the Senators present concur; and he shall nominate, and by and with the Advice and Consent of the Senate, shall appoint Ambassadors, other public Ministers and Consuls, Judges of the supreme Court, and all other Officers of the United States, whose Appointments are not herein otherwise provided for, and which shall be established by Law; but the Congress may by Law vest the Appointment of such inferior Officers, as they think proper, in the President alone, in the Courts of Law, or in the Heads of Departments.

(3) The President shall have Power to fill up all Vacancies that may happen during the Recess of the Senate, by granting Commissions which shall expire at the End of their next Session.

Section 3. He shall from time to time give to the Congress Information of the State of the Union, and recommend to their Consideration such Measures as he shall judge necessary and expedient; he may, on extraordinary Occasions, convene both Houses, or either of them, and in Case of Disagreement between them, with Respect to the Time of Adjournment, he may adjourn them to such Time as he shall think proper; he shall receive Ambassadors and other public Ministers; he shall take Care that the Laws be faithfully executed, and shall Commission all the Officers of the United States.

Section 4. The President, Vice President and all civil Officers of the United States, shall be removed from Office on Impeachment for, and Conviction of, Treason, Bribery, or other high Crimes and Misdemeanors.

Article III

Section 1. The judicial Power of the United States, shall be vested in one supreme Court, and in such inferior Courts as the Congress may from time to time ordain and establish. The Judges, both of the supreme and inferior Courts, shall hold their Offices during good Behaviour, and shall, at stated Times, receive for their Services a Compensation, which shall not be diminished during their Continuance in Office.

Section 2. (1) The judicial Power shall extend to all Cases, in Law and Equity, arising under this Constitution, the Laws of the United States, and Treaties made, or which shall be made, under their Authority;—to all Cases affecting Ambassadors, other public Ministers and Consuls;—to all Cases of admiralty and maritime Jurisdiction,—to Controversies to which the United States shall be a Party;—to Controversies between two or more States;—between a State and Citizens of another State,[8]—between Citizens of different States;—between Citizens of the same State claiming Lands under the Grants of different States, and between a State, or the Citizens thereof, and foreign States, Citizens or Subjects.

(2) In all Cases affecting Ambassadors, other public Ministers and Consuls, and those in which a State shall be a Party, the supreme Court shall have original Jurisdiction. In all the other Cases before mentioned, the supreme Court shall have appellate Jurisdiction, both as to Law and Fact, with such Exceptions, and under such Regulations as the Congress shall make.

---

[8]Refer to the Eleventh Amendment.

(3) The trial of all Crimes, except in Cases of Impeachment, shall be by Jury; and such Trial shall be held in the State where the said Crimes shall have been committed; but when not committed within any State, the Trial shall be at such Place or Places as the Congress may by Law have directed.

Section 3. (1) Treason against the United States, shall consist only in levying War against them, or, in adhering to their enemies, giving them Aid and Comfort. No Person shall be convicted of Treason unless on the Testimony of two Witnesses to the same overt Act, or on Confession in open Court.

(2) The Congress shall have Power to declare the Punishment of Treason, but no Attainder of Treason shall work Corruption of Blood, or Forfeiture except during the Life of the Person attainted.

Article IV

Section 1. Full Faith and Credit shall be given in each State to the public Acts, Records, and judicial Proceedings of every other State. And the Congress may by general Laws prescribe the Manner in which such Acts, Records and Proceedings shall be proved, and the Effect thereof.

Section 2. (1) The Citizens of each State shall be entitled to all Privileges and Immunities of Citizens in the several States.

(2) A Person charged in any State with Treason, Felony, or other Crime, who shall flee from Justice, and be found in another State, shall on demand of the executive Authority of the State from which he fled, be delivered up, to be removed to the State having Jurisdiction of the Crime.

(3) No Person held to Service or Labour in one State, under the Laws thereof, escaping into another, shall, in Consequence of any Law or Regulation therein, be discharged from such Service or Labour, but shall be delivered up on Claim of the Party to whom such Service or Labour may be due.[9]

Section 3. (1) New States may be admitted by the Congress into this Union; but no new State shall be formed or erected within the Jurisdiction of any other State; nor any State be formed by the Junction of two or more States, or Parts of States without the Consent of the Legislatures of the States concerned as well as of the Congress.

(2) The Congress shall have Power to dispose of and make all needful Rules and Regulations respecting the Territory or other Property belonging to the United States; and nothing in this Constitution shall be so construed as to Prejudice any Claims of the United States, or of any particular State.

Section 4. The United States shall guarantee to every State in this Union a Republican Form of Government, and shall protect each of them against Invasion; and on Application of the Legislature, or of the Executive (when the Legislature cannot be convened) against domestic Violence.

Article V

The Congress, whenever two thirds of both Houses shall deem it necessary, shall propose Amendments to this Constitution, or, on the Application of the Legis-

---

[9]Refer to the Thirteenth Amendment.

latures of two thirds of the several States, shall call a Convention for proposing Amendments, which, in either Case, shall be valid to all Intents and Purposes, as part of this Constitution, when ratified by the Legislatures of three fourths of the several States, or by Conventions in three fourths thereof, as the one or the other Mode of Ratification may be proposed by the Congress; Provided that no Amendment which may be made prior to the Year One thousand eight hundred and eight shall in any Manner affect the first and fourth Clauses in the Ninth Section of the first Article; and that no State, without its Consent, shall be deprived of its equal Suffrage in the Senate.

Article VI

(1) All Debts contracted and Engagements entered into, before the Adoption of this Constitution shall be as valid against the United States under this Constitution, as under the Confederation.

(2) This Constitution, and the Laws of the United States which shall be made in Pursuance thereof; and all Treaties made, or which shall be made, under the Authority of the United States, shall be the supreme Law of the Land; and the Judges in every State shall be bound thereby, any Thing in the Constitution or Laws of any State to the Contrary notwithstanding.

(3) The Senators and Representatives before mentioned, and the Members of the several State Legislatures, and all executive and judicial Officers, both of the United States and of the several States, shall be bound by Oath or Affirmation, to support this Constitution; but no religious Test shall ever be required as a Qualification to any Office or public Trust under the United States.

Article VII

The Ratification of the Conventions of nine States shall be sufficient for the Establishment of this Constitution between the States so ratifying the Same.

[Amendments 1–10, the Bill of Rights, were ratified in 1791.]

Amendment I

Congress shall make no law respecting an establishment of religion, or prohibiting the free exercise thereof; or abridging the freedom of speech, or of the press; or the right of the people peaceably to assemble, and to petition the Government for a redress of grievances.

Amendment II

A well regulated Militia, being necessary to the security of a free State, the right of the people to keep and bear Arms, shall not be infringed.

Amendment III

No Soldier shall, in time of peace be quartered in any house, without the consent of the Owner, nor in time of war, but in a manner to be prescribed by law.

Amendment IV

The right of the people to be secure in their persons, houses, papers, and effects, against unreasonable searches and seizures, shall not be violated, and no Warrants shall issue, but upon probable cause, supported by Oath or affirmation, and particularly describing the place to be searched, and the persons or things to be seized.

Amendment V

No person shall be held to answer for a capital, or otherwise infamous crime, unless on a presentment or indictment of a Grand Jury, except in cases arising in the land or naval forces, or in the Militia, when in actual service in time of War or public danger; nor shall any person be subject for the same offence to be twice put in jeopardy of life or limb; nor shall be compelled in any criminal case to be a witness against himself, nor be deprived of life, liberty, or property, without due process of law; nor shall private property be taken for public use, without just compensation.

Amendment VI

In all criminal prosecutions, the accused shall enjoy the right to a speedy and public trial, by an impartial jury of the State and district wherein the crime shall have been committed, which district shall have been previously ascertained by law, and to be informed of the nature and cause of the accusation; to be confronted with the witnesses against him; to have compulsory process for obtaining witnesses in his favor, and to have the Assistance of Counsel for his defence.

Amendment VII

In Suits at common law, where the value in controversy shall exceed twenty dollars, the right of trial by jury shall be preserved, and no fact tried by jury, shall be otherwise re-examined in any Court of the United States, than according to the rules of the common law.

Amendment VIII

Excessive bail shall not be required, nor excessive fines imposed, nor cruel and unusual punishments inflicted.

Amendment IX

The enumeration in the Constitution, of certain rights, shall not be construed to deny or disparage others retained by the people.

Amendment X

The powers not delegated to the United States by the Constitution, nor prohibited by it to the States, are reserved to the States respectively, or to the people.

Amendment XI [1798]

The Judicial power of the United States shall not be construed to extend to any suit in law or equity, commenced or prosecuted against one of the United States by Citizens of another State, or by Citizens or Subjects of any Foreign State.

Amendment XII [1804]

The Electors shall meet in their respective states and vote by ballot for President and Vice-President, one of whom, at least, shall not be an inhabitant of the same state with themselves; they shall name in their ballots the person voted for as President, and in distinct ballots the person voted for as Vice-President, and they shall make distinct lists of all persons voted for as President, and of all persons voted for as Vice-President, and of the number of votes for each, which lists they shall sign and certify, and transmit sealed to the seat of the government of the United States, directed to the President of the Senate;—The President of the Senate shall, in the presence of the Senate and House of Representatives, open all the certificates and the votes shall then be counted;—The person having the greatest number of votes for President, shall be the President, if such number be a majority of the whole number of Electors appointed; and if no person have such majority, then from the persons having the highest numbers not exceeding three on the list of those voted for as President, the House of Representatives shall choose immediately, by ballot, the President. But in choosing the President, the votes shall be taken by states, the representation from each state having one vote; a quorum for this purpose shall consist of a member or members from two-thirds of the states, and a majority of all the states shall be necessary to a choice. And if the House of Representatives shall not choose a President whenever the right of choice shall devolve upon them before the fourth day of March next following, then the Vice-President shall act as President, as in the case of the death or other constitutional disability of the President.[10]—The person having the greatest number of votes as Vice-President, shall be the Vice-President, if such number be a majority of the whole number of Electors appointed, and if no person have a majority, then from the two highest numbers on the list, the Senate shall choose the Vice-President; a quorum for the purpose shall consist of two-thirds of the whole number of Senators, and a majority of the whole number shall be necessary to a choice. But no person constitutionally ineligible to the office of President shall be eligible to that of Vice-President of the United States.

Amendment XIII [1865]

Section 1. Neither slavery nor involuntary servitude, except as a punishment for crime whereof the party shall have been duly convicted, shall exist within the United States, or any place subject to their jurisdiction.

    Section 2. Congress shall have power to enforce this article by appropriate legislation.

---

[10]Refer to the Twentieth Amendment.

Amendment XIV [1868]

Section 1. All persons born or naturalized in the United States, and subject to the jurisdiction thereof, are citizens of the United States and of the State wherein they reside. No State shall make or enforce any law which shall abridge the privileges or immunities of citizens of the United States; nor shall any State deprive any person of life, liberty, or property, without due process of law; nor deny to any person within its jurisdiction the equal protection of the laws.

Section 2. Representatives shall be apportioned among the several States according to their respective numbers, counting the whole number of persons in each State, excluding Indians not taxed. But when the right to vote at any election for the choice of electors for President and Vice President of the United States, Representatives in Congress, the Executive and Judicial officers of a State, or the members of the Legislature thereof, is denied to any of the male inhabitants of such State, being twenty-one years of age,[11] and citizens of the United States, or in any way abridged, except for participation in rebellion, or other crime, the basis of representation therein shall be reduced in the proportion which the number of such male citizens shall bear to the whole number of male citizens twenty-one years of age in such State.

Section 3. No person shall be a Senator or Representative in Congress, or elector of President and Vice President, or hold any office, civil or military, under the United States, or under any State, who having previously taken an oath, as a member of Congress, or as an officer of the United States, or as a member of any State legislature, or as an executive or judicial officer of any State, to support the Constitution of the United States, shall have engaged in insurrection or rebellion against the same, or given aid or comfort to the enemies thereof. But Congress may by a vote of two thirds of each House, remove such disability.

Section 4. The validity of the public debt of the United States, authorized by law, including debts incurred for payment of pensions and bounties for services in suppressing insurrection or rebellion, shall not be questioned. But neither the United States nor any State shall assume or pay any debt or obligation incurred in aid of insurrection or rebellion against the United States, or any claim for the loss or emancipation of any slave; but all such debts, obligations and claims shall be held illegal and void.

Section 5. The Congress shall have power to enforce, by appropriate legislation, the provisions of this article.

Amendment XV [1870]

Section 1. The right of citizens of the United States to vote shall not be denied or abridged by the United States or by any State on account of race, color, or previous condition of servitude.

Section 2. The Congress shall have power to enforce this article by appropriate legislation.

---

[11]Refer to the Twenty-sixth Amendment.

Amendment XVI [1913]

The Congress shall have power to lay and collect taxes on incomes, from whatever source derived, without apportionment among the several States, and without regard to any census or enumeration.

Amendment XVII [1913]

(1) The Senate of the United States shall be composed of two Senators from each State, elected by the people thereof, for six years; and each Senator shall have one vote. The electors in each State shall have the qualifications requisite for electors of the most numerous branch of the State legislatures.

(2) When vacancies happen in the representation of any State in the Senate, the executive authority of such State shall issue writs of election to fill such vacancies: *Provided,* That the legislature of any State may empower the executive thereof to make temporary appointments until the people fill the vacancies by election as the legislature may direct.

(3) This amendment shall not be so construed as to affect the election or term of any Senator chosen before it becomes valid as part of the Constitution.

Amendment XVIII [1919]

Section 1. After one year from the ratification of this article the manufacture, sale, or transportation of intoxicating liquors within, the importation thereof into, or the exportation thereof from the United States and all territory subject to the jurisdiction thereof for beverage purposes is hereby prohibited.

Section 2. The Congress and the several States shall have concurrent power to enforce this article by appropriate legislation.

Section 3. This article shall be inoperative unless it shall have been ratified as an amendment to the Constitution by the legislatures of the several States, as provided in the Constitution, within seven years from the date of the submission hereof to the States by the Congress.[12]

Amendment XIX [1920]

(1) The right of citizens of the United States to vote shall not be denied or abridged by the United States or by any State on account of sex.

(2) Congress shall have power to enforce this article by appropriate legislation.

Amendment XX [1933]

Section 1. The terms of the President and Vice President shall end at noon on the 20th day of January, and the terms of Senators and Representatives at noon on the 3rd day of January, of the years in which such terms would have ended if this article had not been ratified; and the terms of their successors shall then begin.

---

[12]Refer to the Twenty-first Amendment.

Section 2. The Congress shall assemble at least once in every year, and such meeting shall begin at noon on the 3rd day of January, unless they shall by law appoint a different day.

Section 3. If, at the time fixed for the beginning of the term of the President, the President elect shall have died, the Vice President elect shall become President. If the President shall not have been chosen before the time fixed for the beginning of his term or if the President elect shall have failed to qualify, then the Vice President elect shall act as President until a President shall have qualified; and the Congress may by law provide for the case wherein neither a President elect nor a Vice President elect shall have qualified, declaring who shall then act as President, or the manner in which one is to act shall be selected, and such person shall act accordingly until a President or Vice President shall have qualified.

Section 4. The Congress may by law provide for the case of the death of any of the persons from whom the House of Representatives may choose a President whenever the right of choice shall have devolved upon them, and for the case of the death of any of the persons from whom the Senate may choose a Vice President whenever the right of choice shall have devolved upon them.

Section 5. Sections 1 and 2 shall take effect on the 15th day of October following the ratification of this article.

Section 6. This article shall be inoperative unless it shall have been ratified as an amendment to the Constitution by the legislatures of three-fourths of the several States within seven years from the date of its submission.

Amendment XXI [1933]

Section 1. The eighteenth article of amendment to the Constitution of the United States is hereby repealed.

Section 2. The transportation or importation into any State, Territory, or possession of the United States for delivery or use therein of intoxicating liquors, in violation of the laws thereof, is hereby prohibited.

Section 3. This article shall be inoperative unless it shall have been ratified as an amendment to the Constitution by conventions in the several States, as provided in the Constitution, within seven years from the date of the submission hereof to the States by the Congress.

Amendment XXII [1951]

Section 1. No person shall be elected to the office of the President more than twice, and no person who has held the office of President, or acted as President, for more than two years of a term to which some other person was elected President shall be elected to the office of President more than once. But this Article shall not apply to any person holding the office of President when this Article was proposed by the Congress, and shall not prevent any person who may be holding the office of President, or acting as President, during the term within which this Article becomes operative from holding the office of President or acting as president during the remainder of such term.

Section 2. This article shall be inoperative unless it shall have been ratified as an amendment to the Constitution by the legislatures of three-fourths of the several States within seven years from the date of its submission to the States by the Congress.

Amendment XXIII [1961]

Section 1. The District constituting the seat of Government of the United States shall appoint in such manner as the Congress may direct:

A number of electors of President and Vice President equal to the whole number of Senators and Representatives in Congress to which the District would be entitled if it were a State, but in no event more than the least populous state; they shall be in addition to those appointed by the states, but they shall be considered, for the purposes of the election of President and Vice President, to be electors appointed by a state; and they shall meet in the District and perform such duties as provided by the twelfth article of amendment.

Section 2. The Congress shall have power to enforce this article by appropriate legislation.

Amendment XXIV [1964]

Section 1. The right of citizens of the United States to vote in any primary or other election for President or Vice President, for electors for President or Vice President, or for Senator or Representative in Congress, shall not be denied or abridged by the United States or any State by reason of failure to pay any poll tax or other tax.

Section 2. The Congress shall have power to enforce this article by appropriate legislation.

Amendment XXV [1967]

Section 1. In case of the removal of the President from office or of his death or resignation, the Vice President shall become President.

Section 2. Whenever there is a vacancy in the office of the Vice President, the President shall nominate a Vice President who shall take office upon confirmation by a majority vote of both Houses of Congress.

Section 3. Whenever the President transmits to the President pro tempore of the Senate and the Speaker of the House of Representatives his written declaration that he is unable to discharge the powers and duties of his office, and until he transmits to them a written declaration to the contrary, such powers and duties shall be discharged by the Vice President as Acting President.

Section 4. Whenever the Vice President and a majority of either the principal officers of the executive departments or of such other body as Congress may by law provide, transmit to the President pro tempore of the Senate and the Speaker of the House of Representatives their written declaration that the President is unable to discharge the powers and duties of his office, the Vice President shall immediately assume the powers and duties of the office as Acting President.

Thereafter, when the President transmits to the President pro tempore of the Senate and the Speaker of the House of Representatives his written declaration that no inability exists, he shall resume the powers and duties of his office unless the Vice President and a majority of either the principal officers of the executive departments or of such other body as Congress may by law provide, transmit within four days to the President pro tempore of the Senate and the Speaker of the House of Representatives their written declaration that the President is unable to discharge the powers and duties of his office. Thereupon Congress shall decide the issue, assembling within forty-eight hours for that purpose if not in session. If the Congress, within twenty-one days after receipt of the latter written declaration, or, if Congress is not in session, within twenty-one days after Congress is required to assemble, determines by two-thirds vote of both Houses that the President is unable to discharge the powers and duties of his office, the Vice President shall continue to discharge the same as Acting President; otherwise, the President shall resume the powers and duties of his office.

Amendment XXVI [1971]

Section 1. The right of citizens of the United States, who are eighteen years of age or older, to vote shall not be denied or abridged by the United States or by any State on account of age.

    Section 2. The Congress shall have power to enforce this article by appropriate legislation.

The Securities Act of 1933 (excerpts)

Definitions

Section 2. When used in this title, unless the context otherwise requires—(1) The term "security" means any note, stock, treasury stock, bond, debenture, evidence of indebtedness, certificate of interest or participation in any profit-sharing agreement, collateral-trust certificate, preorganization certificate or subscription, transferable share, investment contract, voting-trust certificate, certificate of deposit for a security, fractional undivided interest in oil, gas, or other mineral rights, any put, call, straddle, option, or privilege on any security, certificate of deposit, or group or index of securities (including any interest therein or based on the value thereof), or any put, call, straddle, option, or privilege entered into on a national securities exchange relating to foreign currency, or, in general, any interest or instrument commonly known as a "security," or any certificate of interest or participation in, temporary or interim certificate for, receipt for, guarantee of, or warrant or right to subscribe to or purchase, any of the foregoing.

Exempted Securities

Section 3. (a) Except as hereinafter expressly provided the provisions of this title shall not apply to any of the following classes of securities:

* * * * *

(2) Any security issued or guaranteed by the United States or any territory thereof, or by the District of Columbia, or by any State of the United States, or by any political subdivision of a State or Territory, or by any public instrumentality of one or more States or Territories, or by any person controlled or supervised by and acting as an instrumentality of the Government of the United States pursuant to authority granted by the Congress of the United States; or any certificate of deposit for any of the foregoing; or any security issued or guaranteed by any bank; or any security issued by or representing an interest in or a direct obligation of a Federal Reserve bank. . . .

(3) Any note, draft, bill of exchange, or banker's acceptance which arises out of a current transaction or the proceeds of which have been or are to be used for current transactions, and which has a maturity at the time of issuance of not exceeding nine months, exclusive of days of grace, or any renewal thereof the maturity of which is likewise limited;

(4) Any security issued by a person organized and operated exclusively for religious, educational, benevolent, fraternal, charitable, or reformatory purposes and not for pecuniary profit, and no part of the net earnings of which inures to the benefit of any person, private stockholder, or individual;

* * * * *

(11) Any security which is a part of an issue offered and sold only to persons resident within a single State or Territory, where the issuer of such security is a person resident and doing business within, or, if a corporation, incorporated by and doing business within, such State or Territory.

(b) The Commission may from time to time by its rules and regulations and subject to such terms and conditions as may be described therein, add any class of securities to the securities exempted as provided in this section, if it finds that the enforcement of this title with respect to such securities is not necessary in the public interest and for the protection of investors by reason of the small amount involved or the limited character of the public offering; but no issue of securities shall be exempted under this subsection where the aggregate amount at which such issue is offered to the public exceeds $5,000,000.

Exempted Transactions

Section 4. The provisions of section 5 shall not apply to—
(1) transactions by any person other than an issue, underwriter, or dealer.
(2) transactions by an issuer not involving any public offering.

* * * * *

(4) brokers' transactions executed upon customers' orders on any exchange or in the over-the-counter market but not the solicitation of such orders.

Prohibitions Relating to Interstate Commerce and the Mails

Section 5. (a) Unless a registration statement is in effect as to a security, it shall be unlawful for any person, directly or indirectly—
(1) to make use of any means or instruments of transportation or communications in interstate commerce or of the mails to sell such security through the use or medium of any prospectus or otherwise; or
(2) to carry or cause to be carried through the mails or in interstate commerce, by any means of instruments of transportation, any such security for the purpose of sale or for delivery after sale.

(b) It shall be unlawful for any person, directly or indirectly—
(1) to make use of any means or instruments of transportation or communication in interstate commerce or of the mails to carry or transmit any prospectus relating to any security with respect to which a registration statement has been filed under this title, unless such prospectus meets the requirements of section 10; or

(2) to carry or cause to be carried through the mails or in interstate commerce any such security for the purpose of sale or for delivery after sale, unless accompanied or preceded by a prospectus that meets the requirements of subsection (a) of section 10.

(c)It shall be unlawful for any person, directly or indirectly to make use of any means or instruments of transportation or communication in interstate commerce or the mails to offer to sell or offer to buy through the use or medium of any prospectus or otherwise any security, unless a registration statement has been filed as to such security, or while the registration statement is the subject of the refusal order or stop order. . . .

Registration of Securities and Signing of Registration Statement

Section 6. (a) Any security may be registered with the Commission under the terms and conditions hereinafter provided, by filing a registration statement in triplicate, at least one of which shall be signed by each issuer, its principal executive officer or officers, its principal financial officer, its comptroller or principal accounting officer, and the majority of its board of directors or persons performing similar functions. . . .

* * * * *

The Securities Exchange Act of 1934 (excerpts)

Definitions

Section 3. (a) When used in this title, unless the context requires—

* * * * *

(4) The term ''broker'' means any person engaged in the business of effecting transactions in securities for the account of others, but does not include a bank.

(5) The term ''dealer'' means any person engaged in the business of buying and selling securities for his own account, through a broker or otherwise, but does not include a bank, or any person insofar as he buys or sells securities for his own account, either individually or in some fiduciary capacity, but not as part of a regular business.

* * * * *

(7) The term ''director'' means any director of a corporation or any person performing similar functions with respect to any organization, whether incorporated or unincorporated.

(8) The term ''issuer'' means any person who issues or proposes to issue any security; except that with respect to certificates of deposit for securities, voting-trust certificates, or collateral-trust certificates, or with respect to certificates of interest or shares in an unincorporated investment trust not having a board of directors of the fixed, restricted management, or unit type, the term ''issuer'' means the person or persons performing the acts and assuming the duties of depositor or manager pursuant to the provisions of the trust or other agreement or instrument under which such securities are issued; and except that with respect to equipment-trust certificates or like securities, the term ''issuer''' means the person by whom the equipment or property is, or is to be, used.

(9) The term ''person'' means a natural person, company, government, or political subdivision, agency, or instrumentality of a government.

Securities and Exchange Commission

Section 4. (a) There is hereby established a Securities and Exchange Commission (hereinafter referred to as the "Commission") to be composed of five commissioners to be appointed by the President by and with the advice and consent of the Senate. Not more than three of such commissioners shall be members of the same political party, and in making appointments members of different political parties shall be appointed alternately as nearly as may be practicable.

Transactions on Unregistered Exchanges

Section 5. It shall be unlawful for any broker, dealer, or exchange, directly or indirectly, to make use of the mails or any means or instrumentality of interstate commerce for the purpose of using any facility of an exchange within or subject to the jurisdiction of the United States to effect any transaction in a security, or to report any such transaction, unless such exchange (1) is registered as a national securities exchange under . . . this title, or (2) is exempted from such registration upon application by the exchange because, in the opinion of the Commission, by reason of the limited volume of transactions effected on such exchange, it is not practicable and not necessary or appropriate in the public interest or for the protection of investors to require such registration.

Regulation of the Use of Manipulative and Deceptive Devices

Section 10. It shall be unlawful for any person, directly or indirectly, by the use of any means or instrumentality of interstate commerce or of the mails, or of any facility of any national securities exchange—

(a) To effect a short sale, or to use or employ any stop-loss order in connection with the purchase or sale, of any security registered on a national securities exchange, in contravention of such rules and regulations as the Commission may prescribe as necessary or appropriate in the public interest or for the protection of investors.

(b) To use or employ, in connection with the purchase or sale of any security registered on a national securities exchange or any security not so registered, any manipulative or deceptive device or contrivance in contravention of such rules and regulations as the Commission may prescribe as necessary or appropriate in the public interest or for the protection of investors.

Registration Requirements for Securities

Section 12. (a) It shall be unlawful for any member, broker, or dealer to effect any transaction in any security (other than an exempted security) on a national securities exchange unless a registration is effective as to such security for such exchange in accordance with the provisions of this title and the rules and regulations thereunder.

Appendix D

The National Labor Relations Act (excerpts)

Rights of Employees

Section 7. Employees shall have the right to self-organization, to form, join, or assist labor organizations, to bargain collectively through representatives of their own choosing, and to engage in other concerted activities for the purpose of collective bargaining or other mutual aid or protection, and shall also have the right to refrain from any or all of such activities except to the extent that such right may be affected by an agreement requiring membership in a labor organization as a condition of employment as authorized in section 8(a)(3).

Unfair Labor Practices

Section 8. (a) It shall be an unfair labor practice for an employer—

(1) to interfere with, restrain, or coerce employees in the exercise of the rights guaranteed in section 7;

(2) to dominate or interfere with the formation or administration of any labor organization or contribute financial or other support to it: *Provided,* That subject to rules and regulations made and published by the Board pursuant to section 6, an employer shall not be prohibited from permitting employees to confer with him during working hours without loss of time or pay;

(3) by discrimination in regard to hire or tenure of employment or any term or condition of employment to encourage or discourage membership in any labor organization: *Provided,* That nothing in this Act, or in any other statute of the United States, shall preclude an employer from making an agreement with a labor organization (not established, maintained, or assisted by any action defined in section 8(a) of this Act as an unfair labor practice) to require as a condition of employment membership therein on or after the thirtieth day following the beginning of such employment or the effective date of such agreement, whichever is the later, (i) if such labor organization is the representative of the employees as provided in section 9(a), in the appropriate collective-bargaining unit covered by such agreement when made, and (ii) unless following an election held as

provided in section 9(e) within one year preceding the effective date of such agreement, the Board shall have certified that at least a majority of the employees eligible to vote in such election have voted to rescind the authority of such labor organization to make such an agreement: *Provided further,* That no employer shall justify any discrimination against an employee for nonmembership in a labor organization (A) if he has reasonable grounds for believing that such membership was not available to the employee on the same terms and conditions generally applicable to other members, or (B) if he had reasonable grounds for believing that membership was denied or terminated for reasons other than the failure of the employee to tender the periodic dues and the initiation fees uniformly required as a condition of acquiring or retaining membership;

(4) to discharge or otherwise discriminate against an employee because he has filed charges or given testimony under this Act;

(5) to refuse to bargain collectively with the representatives of his employees, subject to the provisions of section 9(a).

(b) It shall be an unfair labor practice for a labor organization or its agents—

(1) to restrain or coerce (A) employees in the exercise of the rights guaranteed in section 7: *Provided,* That this paragraph shall not impair the right of a labor organization to prescribe its own rules with respect to the acquisition or retention of membership therein; or (B) an employer in the selection of his representatives for the purposes of collective bargaining or the adjustment of grievances;

(2) to cause or attempt to cause an employer to discriminate against an employee in violation of subsection (a)(3) or to discriminate against an employee with respect to whom membership in such organization has been denied or terminated on some ground other than his failure to tender the periodic dues and the initiation fees uniformly required as a condition of acquiring or retaining membership;

(3) to refuse to bargain collectively with an employer, provided it is the representative of his employees subject to the provisions of section 9(a);

(4) (i) to engage in, or to induce or encourage any individual employed by any person engaged in commerce or in an industry affecting commerce to engage in, a strike or a refusal in the course of his employment to use, manufacture, process, transport, or otherwise handle or work on any goods, articles, materials, or commodities or to perform any services; or (ii) to threaten, coerce, or restrain any person engaged in commerce or in an industry affecting commerce, where in either case an object thereof is—

(A) forcing or requiring any employer or self-employed person to join any labor or employer organization or to enter into any agreement which is prohibited by section 8(e);
(B) forcing or requiring any person to cease using, selling, handling, transporting, or otherwise dealing in the products of any other producer, processor, or manufacturer, or to cease doing business with any other person, or forcing or requiring any other employer to recognize or bargain with a labor organization as the representative of his employees unless such labor organization has been certified as the representative of such employees under the provisions of section 9: *Provided,* That nothing contained in this clause (B) shall be construed to make unlawful, where not otherwise unlawful, any primary strike or primary picketing;

(C) forcing or requiring any employer to recognize or bargain with a particular labor organization as the representative of his employees if another labor organization has been certified as the representative of such employees under the provisions of section 9;

(D) forcing or requiring any employer to assign particular work to employees in a particular labor organization or in a particular trade, craft, or class rather than to employees in another labor organization or in another trade, craft, or class, unless such employer is failing to conform to an order or certification of the Board determining the bargaining representative for employees performing such work:

Provided, That nothing contained in this subsection (b) shall be construed to make unlawful a refusal by any person to enter upon the premises of any employer (other than his own employer), if the employees of such employer are engaged in a strike ratified or approved by a representative of such employees whom such employer is required to recognize under this Act: *Provided further,* That for the purposes of this paragraph (4) only, nothing contained in such paragraph shall be construed to prohibit publicity, other than picketing, for the purpose of truthfully advising the public, including consumers and members of a labor organization, that a product or products are produced by an employer with whom the labor organization has a primary dispute and are distributed by another employer, as long as such publicity does not have an effect of inducing any individual employed by any person other than the primary employer in the course of his employment to refuse to pick up, deliver, or transport any goods, or not to perform any services, at the establishment of the employer engaged in such distribution:

(5) to require of employees covered by an agreement authorized under subsection (a)(3) the payment, as a condition precedent to becoming a member of such organization, of a fee in an amount which the Board finds excessive or discriminatory under all the circumstances. In making such a finding, the Board shall consider, among other relevant factors, the practices and customs of labor organizations in the particular industry, and the wages currently paid to the employees affected;

(6) to cause or attempt to cause an employer to pay or deliver or agree to pay or deliver any money or other thing of value, in the nature of an exaction, for services which are not performed or not to be performed; and

(7) To picket or cause to be picketed, or threatened to picket or cause to be picketed, any employer where an object thereof is forcing or requiring an employer to recognize or bargain with a labor organization as the representative of his employees, or forcing or requiring the employees of an employer to accept or select such labor organization as their collective bargaining representative, unless such labor organization is currently certified as the representative of such employees:

(A) where the employer has lawfully recognized in accordance with this Act any other labor organization and a question concerning representation may not appropriately be raised under section 9(c) of this Act,

(B) where within the preceding twelve months a valid election under section 9(c) of this Act has been conducted, or

(C) where such picketing has been conducted without a petition under section 9(c) being filed within a reasonable period of time not to exceed thirty days from the commencement of such picketing; *Provided,* That when such a petition has been filed the Board shall forthwith, without regard to the provisions of section 9(c)(1) or the absence of a showing of a substantial interest on the part of the labor organization, direct an election in such unit as the Board finds to be appropriate and shall certify the results thereof: *Provided further,* That nothing in this subparagraph (C) shall be construed to prohibit any picketing or other publicity for the purpose of truthfully advising the public (including consumers) that an employer does not employ members of, or have a contract with, a labor organization, unless an effect of such picketing is to induce any individual employed by any other person in the course of his employment, not to pick up, deliver or transport any goods or not to perform any services.

Nothing in this paragraph (7) shall be construed to permit any act which would otherwise be an unfair labor practice under this section 8(b).

(c) The expressing of any views, argument, or opinion, or the dissemination thereof, whether in written, printed, graphic, or visual form, shall not constitute or be evidence of an unfair labor practice under any of the provisions of this Act, if such expression contains no threat of reprisal or force or promise of benefit.

(d) For the purposes of this section, to bargain collectively is the performance of the mutual obligation of the employer and the representative of the employees to meet at reasonable times and confer in good faith with respect to wages, hours, and other terms and conditions of employment, or the negotiation of an agreement, or any question arising thereunder, and the execution of a written contract incorporating any agreement reached if requested by either party, but such obligation does not compel either party to agree to a proposal or require the making of a concession. . . .

* * * * *

Representatives and Elections

Section 9. (a) Representatives designated or selected for the purposes of collective bargaining by the majority of the employees in a unit appropriate for such purposes, shall be the exclusive representatives of all the employees in such unit for the purposes of collective bargaining in respect to rates of pay, wages, hours of employment, or other conditions of employment: *Provided,* That any individual employee or a group of employees shall have the right at any time to present grievances to their employer and to have such grievances adjusted, without the intervention of the bargaining representative, as long as the adjustment is not inconsistent with the terms of a collective-bargaining contract or agreement then in effect: *Provided further,* That the bargaining representative has been given opportunity to be present at such adjustment.

(b) The Board shall decide in each case whether, in order to assure to employees the fullest freedom in exercising the rights guaranteed by this Act, the unit appropriate for the purposes of collective bargaining shall be the employer unit, craft unit, plant unit, or subdivision thereof: *Provided,* That the Board shall not (1) decide that any unit is appropriate for such purposes if such unit included both professional employees and employees who are not professional employees unless a majority of such professional employees vote for inclusion in such unit;

or (2) decide that any craft unit is inappropriate for such purposes on the ground that a different unit has been established by a prior Board determination, unless a majority of the employees in the proposed craft unit vote against separate representation or (3) decide that any unit is appropriate for such purposes if it includes, together with other employees, any individual employed as a guard to enforce against employees and other persons rules to protect property of the employer or to protect the safety of persons on the employer's premises; but no later organization shall be certified as the representative of employees in a bargaining unit of guards if such organization admits to membership, or is affiliated directly or indirectly with an organization which admits to membership, employees other than guards.

(c)(1) Whenever a petition shall have been filed, in accordance with such regulations as may be prescribed by the Board—

(A) by an employee or group of employees or an individual or labor organization acting in their behalf alleging that a substantial number of employees (i) wish to be represented for collective bargaining and that their employer declines to recognize their representative as the representative defined in section 9(a), or (ii) assert that the individual or labor organization, which has been certified or is being currently recognized by their employer as the bargaining representative, is no longer a representative as defined in section 9(a); or

(B) by an employer, alleging that one or more individuals or labor organizations have presented to him a claim to be recognized as the representative defined in section 9(a); the Board shall investigate such petition and if it has reasonable cause to believe that a question of representation affecting commerce exists shall provide for an appropriate hearing upon due notice. Such hearing may be conducted by an officer or employee of the regional office, who shall not make any recommendations with respect thereto. If the Board finds upon the record of such hearing that such a question of representation exists, it shall direct an election by secret ballot and shall certify the results thereof.

* * * * *

(3) No election shall be directed in any bargaining unit or any subdivision within which, in the preceding twelve-month period, a valid election shall have been held. Employees engaged in an economic strike who are not entitled to reinstatement shall be eligible to vote under such regulations as the Board shall find are consistent with the purposes and provisions of this Act in any election conducted within twelve months after the commencement of the strike. In any election where none of the choices on the ballot receives a majority, a run-off shall be conducted, the ballot providing for a selection between the two choices receiving the largest and second largest number of valid votes cast in the election.

* * * * *

The Civil Rights Act of 1964, Title VII (excerpts)

Definitions

Section 701.

* * * * *

(j) The term "religion" includes all aspects of religious observance and practice, as well as belief, unless an employer demonstrates that he is unable to reasonably accommodate to an employee's or prospective employee's religious observance or practice without undue hardship on the conduct of the employer's business.

(k) The terms "because of sex" or "on the basis of sex" include, but are not limited to, because of or on the basis of pregnancy, childbirth or related medical conditions; and women affected by pregnancy, childbirth, or related medical conditions shall be treated the same for all employment-related purposes, including receipt of benefits under fringe benefit programs, as other persons not so affected but similar in their ability or inability to work, and nothing in Section 703(h) of this title shall not be interpreted to permit otherwise. This subsection shall not require an employer to pay for health insurance benefits for abortion, except where the life of the mother would be endangered if the fetus were carried to term, or except where medical complications have arisen from an abortion: *Provided,* That nothing herein shall preclude an employer from providing abortion benefits or otherwise effect bargaining agreements in regard to abortion.

Unlawful Employment Practices

Section 703. (a) It shall be an unlawful employment practice for an employer—

(1) to fail or refuse to hire or to discharge any individual, or otherwise to discriminate against any individual with respect to his compensation, terms, conditions, or privileges of employment, because of such individual's race, color, religion, sex, or national origin; or

(2) limit, segregate, or classify his employees or applicants for employment in any way which would deprive or tend to deprive any individual of employment opportunities or otherwise adversely affect his status as an employee, because of such individual's race, color, religion, sex, or national origin.

(b) It shall be an unlawful employment practice for an employment agency to fail or refuse to refer for employment, or otherwise to discriminate against, an individual because of his race, color, religion, sex, or national origin, or to classify or refer for employment any individual on the basis of his race, color, religion, sex, or national origin.

(c) It shall be an unlawful employment practice for a labor organization—

(1) to exclude or to expel from its membership, or otherwise to discriminate against, any individual because of his race, color, religion, sex, or national origin;

(2) to limit, segregate, or classify its membership or applicants for membership or to classify or fail or refuse to refer for employment any individual, in any way which would deprive or tend to deprive any individual of employment opportunities, or would limit such employment opportunities or otherwise adversely affect his status as an employee or as an applicant for employment, because of such individual's race, color, religion, sex, or national origin; or

(3) to cause or attempt to cause an employer to discriminate against an individual in violation of this section.

(d) It shall be an unlawful employment practice for any employer, labor organization, or joint labor management committee controlling apprenticeship or other training or retraining, including on-the-job training programs to discriminate against any individual because of his race, color, religion, sex, or national origin in admission to, or employment in, any program established to provide apprenticeship or other training.

(e) Notwithstanding any other provision of this title, (1) it shall not be an unlawful employment practice for an employer to hire and employ employees, for an employment agency to classify, or refer for employment any individual, or for any employer, labor organization, or joint labor management committee controlling apprenticeship or other training or retraining programs to admit or employ any individual in any such program, on the basis of his religion, sex, or national origin in those certain instances where religion, sex, or national origin is a bona fide occupational qualification reasonably necessary to the normal operation of that particular business or enterprise, and (2) it shall not be an unlawful employment practice for a school, college, university, or other educational institution or institution of learning to hire and employ employees of a particular religion if such school, college, university, or other educational institution or institution of learning is, in whole or in substantial part, owned, supported, controlled, or managed by a particular religion or by a particular religious corporation, association, or society, or if the curriculum of such school, college, university, or other educational institution or institution of learning is directed toward the propagation of a particular religion.

* * * * *

(h) Notwithstanding any other provision of this title, it shall not be an unlawful employment practice for an employer to apply different standards of compensation, or different terms, conditions, or privileges of employment pursuant to a bona fide seniority or merit system, or a system which measures earnings by quantity or quality of production or to employees who work in different locations, provided that such differences are not the result of an intention to discriminate because of race, color, religion, sex, or national origin; nor shall it be an unlawful employment practice for an employer to give and to act upon the results of any professionally developed ability test provided that such test, its administration or action upon the results is not designed, intended, or used to discriminate because of race, color, religion, sex, or national origin. It shall not be an unlawful employment practice under this title for any employer to differentiate upon the basis of sex in determining the amount of wages or compensation paid or to be paid to employees of such employer if such differentiation is authorized by the provision of Section 6(d) of the Fair Labor Standards Act of 1938 as amended (29 U.S.C. 206(d)).

* * * * *

(j) Nothing contained in this title shall be interpreted to require any employer, employment agency, labor organization, or joint labor-management committee subject to this title to grant preferential treatment to any individual or to any group because of the race, color, religion, sex, or national origin of such individual or group on account of an imbalance which may exist with respect to the total number or percentage of persons of any race, color, religion, sex, or national origin employed by any employer, referred or classified for employment by any employment agency or labor organization, admitted to membership or classified by any labor organization, or admitted to, or employed in, any apprenticeship or other training program, in comparison with the total number or percentage of persons of such race, color, religion, sex, or national origin in any community, State, section, or other area, or in the available work force in any community, State, section, or other area.

Other Unlawful Employment Practices

Section 704. (a) It shall be an unlawful employment practice for an employer to discriminate against any of his employees or applicants for employment, for an employment agency, or joint labor-management committee controlling apprenticeship or other training or retraining, including on-the-job training programs, to discriminate against any individual, or for a labor organization to discriminate against any member thereof or applicant for membership, because he has opposed any practice, made an unlawful employment practice by this title, or because he has made a charge, testified, assisted, or participated in any manner in an investigation, proceeding, or hearing under this title.

(b) It shall be an unlawful employment practice for an employer, labor organization, employment agency, or joint labor-management committee controlling apprenticeship or other training or retraining, including on-the-job training programs, to print or cause to be printed or published any notice or advertisement relating to employment by such an employer or membership in or any classification or referral for employment by such a labor organization, or relating to any classification or referral for employment by such an employment agency, or relating to admission to, or employment in, any program established to provide apprenticeship or other training by such a joint labor-management committee indicating any preference, limitation, specification, or discrimination, based on race, color, religion, sex or national origin, except that such a notice or advertisement may indicate a preference, limitation, specification, or discrimination based on religion, sex or national origin when religion, sex, or national origin is a bona fide occupational qualification for employment.

Glossary of Legal Terms

A

adjudication The formal pronouncement of a judgment in a legal proceeding.

administrative law That branch of public law addressing the operation of the government's various agencies and commissions. Also the rules and regulations established by those agencies and commissions.

Administrative Procedure Act A federal statute specifying the procedural rules under which the government's agencies and commissions conduct their business.

affidavit A written statement sworn to by a person officially empowered to administer an oath.

affirmative action A government program, springing from the civil rights movement, designed to *actively promote* the employment and educational opportunities of protected classes rather than merely forbidding discrimination.

affirmative defense A portion of defendant's answer to a complaint in which the defendant presents contentions which, if proved true, will relieve the defendant of liability even if the assertions in the complaint are correct.

alternate dispute resolution The growing practice of employing strategies other than conventional litigation to solve conflicts. Those strategies include negotiation, arbitration, and mediation with variations like "minitrials" and "rent-a-judge" arrangements.

amicus curiae A "friend of the court" who, though not a party to the case, files a brief because of a strong interest in the litigation.

answer The defendant's first pleading in a lawsuit, in which the defendant responds to the allegations raised in the plaintiff's complaint.

apartheid Literally, the government-imposed economic, political, and social separation of the four major population groups in South Africa—black Africans, whites, "coloreds," and Asians. The policy, imposed in 1948 by the white Nationalist Party, was designed for the purpose of "preserving and safeguarding the racial identity of the white population of the country."

appeal The judicial process by which a party petitions a higher court to review the decision of a lower court or agency in order to correct errors.

appellant The party filing an appeal.

appellee The party against whom an appeal is filed.

arbitration An extrajudicial process in which a dispute is submitted to a mutually agreeable third party for a binding decision.

arraignment A criminal law proceeding in which a defendant is brought before a judge to be informed of the charges and to file a plea.

assumption of the risk An affirmative defense in a negligence case in which the defendant seeks to bar recovery by the plaintiff by showing that the plaintiff knowingly exposed himself or herself to the danger that resulted in injury.

at-will employee An individual not under contract for a specified term and therefore, under the general rule, subject to discharge by the employer at any time and for any reason.

B

bait-and-switch advertising An unlawful sales tactic in which the seller attracts buyer interest by insincerely advertising a product at a dramatically reduced price while holding no genuine intent to sell the product at that price. The seller then disparages the "bait" and diverts the buyer's attention to a higher-priced product (the switch), which was the sales goal from the first.

"blue sky" laws Statutes regulating the sale of stocks and other securities to prevent consumer fraud.

bona fide In good faith; honestly.

boycott A confederation or conspiracy involving a refusal to do business with another or an attempt by the confederation to stop others from doing business with the target person or organization.

C

cause of action Facts sufficient to support a valid civil lawsuit.

caveat emptor Let the buyer beware.

cease and desist order An instruction from an agency instructing a party to refrain from a specified act.

certiorari A legal procedure affording an appellate court the opportunity to review a lower court decision. Also a writ asking the lower court for the record of the case.

civil law The branch of law dealing with private rights. Contrast with criminal law.

class action A legal action brought by one on behalf of himself or herself and all others similarly situated.

common law   Judge-made law. To be distinguished from statutory law as created by legislative bodies.

comparable worth   The legal theory that all employees should be paid the same wages for work requiring comparable skills, effort, and responsibility and having comparable worth to the employer.

comparative negligence   A rule of law in which the plaintiff's recovery in a negligence suit is reduced by a percentage equal to the percentage of the plaintiff's contribution to his or her own harm. Contrast with contributory negligence.

complaint   The first pleading filed by the plaintiff in a civil lawsuit.

conglomerate merger   A merger between firms operating in separate markets and having neither a buyer-seller nor competitive relationships with each other.

consent decree   A settlement of a lawsuit arrived at by agreement of the parties. Effectively, an admission by the parties that the decree is a just determination of their rights.

conspiracy   An agreement between two or more persons to commit an unlawful act.

contingent fee   An arrangement wherein an attorney is compensated for her or his services by receiving a percentage of the award in a lawsuit rather than receiving an hourly wage or specified fee.

contributory negligence   A defense in a negligence action wherein the defendant attempts to demonstrate that the plaintiff contributed to the harm on which the litigation was based. Contributory negligence acts as a complete bar to the plaintiff's recovery. Contrast with comparative negligence.

counterclaim   A cause of action filed by the defendant in a lawsuit against the plaintiff in the same suit.

criminal law   Wrongs against society that the state has seen fit to label crimes and that may result in penalties against the perpetrator(s). Contrast with civil law.

D

deceptive advertising   Advertising practices likely to mislead the reasonable consumer where the practice in question is material in that it affected consumer choice.

declaratory judgment   A judicial action expressing the opinion of the court or articulating the rights of the parties without actually ordering that anything be done.

defamation   A false and intentional verbal or written expression that damages the reputation of another.

defendant   The party in a civil suit against whom the cause of action was brought and, in a criminal case, the party against whom charges have been filed.

deposition   A discovery procedure wherein a witness' sworn testimony is taken out of court, prior to trial, for subsequent use at trial.

dicta   Statements in a judicial opinion that are merely views of the judge(s) and are not necessary for the resolution of the case.

discovery   Legal procedures by which one party to a litigation may obtain information from the other party. Depositions and interrogatories are examples of discovery procedures.

divestiture   In antitrust law, a remedy wherein the court orders a defendant to dispose of specified assets.

dividend   A shareholder's earnings from his or her stock in a corporation.

due process   A constitutional principle requiring fairness in judicial proceedings and that government laws and conduct be free of arbitrariness and capriciousness.

E

eminent domain   The state's power to take private property for public use.

equity   A body of law based on fairness wherein monetary damages will not afford complete relief.

exclusive dealing contract   An agreement under which a buyer agrees to purchase all of its needs from a single seller or under which a seller agrees to dispose of all of its production to a single purchaser.

F

federalism   The division of authority between the federal government and the states to maintain workable cooperation while diffusing political power.

fraud   An intentional misrepresentation of a material fact with intent to deceive where the misrepresentation is justifiably relied on by another and damages result.

G

good faith   Honesty; an absence of intent to take advantage of another.

H

horizontal merger   Acquisition by one company of another company competing in the same product and geographic markets.

I

in personam jurisdiction   The power of the court over a person.

indictment   A grand jury's formal accusation of a crime.

information   A prosecutor's formal accusation of a crime.

injunction   A court order commanding a person or organization to do or not do a specified action.

interrogatories   An ingredient in the discovery process wherein one party in a lawsuit directs written questions to another party in the lawsuit.

J

judgment notwithstanding the verdict (judgment n.o.v.)   A judge's decision overruling the verdict of the jury.

judicial review   A court's authority to review statutes and, if appropriate, declare them unconstitutional. Also refers to appeals from administrative agencies.

jurisdiction   The power of a judicial body to adjudicate a dispute. Also the geographical area within which that judicial body has authority to operate.

jurisprudence   The philosophy and science of law.

L

long-arm statute   A state enactment that accords the courts of that state the authority to claim jurisdiction over people and property beyond the borders of the state so long as certain "minimum contacts" exist between the state and the people or property.

M

mediation   An extrajudicial proceeding in which a third party (the mediator) attempts to assist disputing parties to reach an agreeable, voluntary resolution of their differences.

merger   The union of two or more business organizations wherein all of the assets, rights, and liabilities of one are blended into the other with only one firm remaining.

monopoly   Market power permitting the holder to fix prices and/or exclude competition.

moot   An issue no longer requiring attention or resolution because it has ceased to be in dispute.

motion   A request to a court seeking an order or action in favor of the party entering the motion.

motion for a directed verdict   A request by a party to a lawsuit arguing that the other party has failed to prove facts sufficient to establish a claim and that the judge must, therefore, enter a verdict in favor of the moving party.

N

negligence   The omission to do something that a reasonable person, guided by those ordinary considerations that ordinarily regulate human affairs, would do, or an action that a reasonable and prudent person would not take.

nolo contendere   A no-contest plea in a criminal case in which the defendant does not admit guilt but does submit to such punishment as the court may accord.

nuisance   A class of wrongs that arises from the unreasonable, unwarrantable, or unlawful use by a person of his or her property that produces material annoyance, inconvenience, discomfort, or hurt.

O

oligopoly   An economic condition in which the market for a particular good or service is controlled by a small number of producers or distributors.

ordinance   A law, rule, or regulation enacted by a local unit of government (e.g., a town or city).

over-the-counter securities   Those stocks, bonds, and like instruments sold directly from broker to customer rather than passing through a stock exchange.

P

per curiam   "By the court." Refers to legal opinions offered by the court as a whole rather than those instances where an individual judge authors the opinion.

per se   By itself; inherently.

peremptory challenge   At trial, an attorney's authority to dismiss prospective members of the jury without offering any justification for that dismissal.

plaintiff   One who initiates a lawsuit.

pleadings   The formal entry of written statements by which the parties to a lawsuit set out their contentions and thereby formulate the issues on which the litigation will be based.

police power The government's inherent authority to enact rules to provide for the health, safety, and general welfare of the citizenry.

precedent A decision in a previously decided lawsuit that may be looked to as an authoritative statement for resolving current lawsuits involving similar questions of law.

prima facie case A litigating party may be presumed to have built a prima facie case when the evidence is such that it is legally sufficient unless contradicted or overcome by other evidence.

"privatization" A word (of sorts) popularized in recent years to embrace the many strategies for shifting public-sector activities back to private enterprise. Those strategies include contracting out government work to private parties, raising the user fees charged for public services, selling state-owned property and enterprises, and returning government services, such as garbage collection, to the private sector.

privity of contract The legal connection that arises when two or more parties enter a contract.

proximate cause Occurrences that in a natural sequence, unbroken by potent intervening forces, produce an injury that would not have resulted absent those occurrences.

proxy Written permission from a shareholder to others to vote his or her share at a stockholders' meeting.

R

remand To send back. For example, a higher court sends a case back to the lower court from which it came.

res ipsa loquitur "The thing speaks for itself." Negligence doctrine under which the defendant's guilt is not directly proved but rather is inferred from the circumstances that establish the reasonable belief that the injury in question could not have happened in the absence of the defendant's negligence.

res judicata "A thing decided." A doctrine of legal procedure preventing the retrial of issues already conclusively adjudicated.

restraints of trade Contracts, combinations, or conspiracies resulting in obstructions of the marketplace, including monopoly, artificially inflated prices, artificially reduced supplies, or other impediments to the natural flow of commerce.

reverse Overturn the decision of a court.

right-to-know laws Federal and state laws and regulations requiring employers to assume the affirmative responsibility of acquainting employees with hazardous substances and conditions in the workplace.

right-to-work laws State legislation forbidding or restricting labor contracts that permit employment only for those who belong to unions.

S

secondary boycott   Typically, a union strategy that places pressure not on the employer with whom the union has a dispute but rather with a supplier or customer of that employer in the hope that the object of the boycott will persuade the employer to meet the union's expectations.

security   A stock, bond, note, or other investment interest in an enterprise designed for profit and operated by one other than the investor.

separation of powers   The strategy of dividing government into separate and independent executive, legislative, and judicial branches, each of which acts as a check on the power of the others.

sexual harassment   Unwelcome sexual advances, requests for sexual favors, and other unwanted physical or verbal conduct of a sexual nature.

shareholder   One holding stock in a corporation.

standing   A stake in a dispute sufficient to afford a party the legal right to bring or join a litigation exploring the subject of the dispute.

stare decisis   "Let the decision stand." A doctrine of judicial procedure expecting a court to follow precedent in all cases involving substantially similar issues unless extremely compelling circumstances dictate a change in judicial direction.

statute   A legislative enactment.

strict liability   The imposition of legal liability in a civil case as a matter of policy even though the defendant has exercised due care and has not been proved negligent.

subpoena   An order from a court or administrative agency commanding that an individual appear to give testimony or produce specified documents.

summary judgment   A judicial determination prior to trial holding that no factual dispute exists between the parties and that, as a matter of law, one of the parties is entitled to a favorable judgment.

summons   A document originating in a court and delivered to a party or organization indicating that a lawsuit has been commenced against him, her, or it. The summons constitutes notice that the defendant is expected to appear in court to answer the plaintiff's allegations.

sunset legislation   A statute providing that a particular government agency will automatically cease to exist as of a specified date unless the legislative body affirmatively acts to extend the life of the agency.

supremacy clause   An element of the U.S. Constitution providing that all constitutionally valid federal laws are the paramount law of the land and, as such, are superior to any conflicting state and local laws.

T

takeover bid   A tender offer designed to assume control of a corporation.

tort   A civil wrong not arising from a contract.

treble damages   An award of damages totaling three times the amount of the actual damages, authorized by some statutes in an effort to discourage further wrongful conduct.

tying contract   A sales or leasing arrangement in which one product or service may be bought or leased only if accompanied by the purchase or lease of another product or service as specified by the seller/lessor.

U

unconscionability   A contract so one-sided and oppressive as to be unfair.

usury   Charging an interest rate exceeding the legally permissible maximum.

V

venue   The specific geographic location in which a court holding jurisdiction should properly hear a case given the convenience of the parties and other relevant considerations.

verdict   The jury's decision as to who wins the litigation.

vertical merger   A union between two firms holding a buyer-seller relationship with each other.

voir dire   The portion of a trial in which prospective jurors are questioned to determine their qualifications, including absence of bias, to sit in judgment in the case.

W

warranty   Any promise, express or implied, that the facts are true as specified. For example, in consumer law, the warranty of merchantability is a guarantee that the product is reasonably fit for the general purpose for which it was sold.

workers' compensation laws   State statutes providing fixed recoveries for injuries and illnesses sustained in the course of employment. Under those statutes, workers need not establish fault on the part of the employer.

Table of Cases

Note: Cases in capital letters are discussion cases within the chapters; the other cases listed here are referred to in the text, in newspaper or magazine articles, or in questions.

Index

A